P9-CMF-802

CYCLOPEDIA

OF

MORAL AND RELIGIOUS

ANECDOTES:

A COLLECTION OF NEARLY THREE THOUSAND FACTS, INCIDENTS, NARRATIVES, EXAMPLES AND TESTIMONIES, CONTAINING THE BEST OF THE KIND IN MOST FORMER COLLECTIONS AND SOME HUNDREDS IN ADDITION, ORIGINAL AND SELECTED, THE WHOLE CRITICALLY ARRANGED AND CLASSIFIED ON A NEW PLAN, WITH COPIOUS TOPICAL AND SCRIPTURAL INDEXES.

BY REV. KAZLITT ARVINE, A.M.

AND

AN INTRODUCTION BY REV. GEORGE B. CHEEVER, D.D.

FUNK & WAGNALLS.

NEW YORK: 18 & 20 ASTOR PLACE.

1890.

LONDON: 44 FLEET STREET.

PRINTED IN THE UNITED STATES.

INTRODUCTION.

THE importance of illustration for the purpose of enforcing truth is so obvious, that it seems a work of supererogation to say one word concerning it. Much *has* been said in books of rhetoric in regard to the use of figures, tropes, metaphors, and so forth, to add animation to style, and vigor and beauty to eloquence. But the best rhetorical rules will be insensibly discovered and adopted by the mind itself, in familiarity with the most thoughtful, suggestive, and illustrative writers.

Principal Campbell, in his Philosophy of Rhetoric, observes, that the senator and the lawyer, in the matter of eloquence, have the advantage of the preacher, because, *their* subject is generally *persons*, while *his* is mainly *things*. A preacher ought, therefore, to endeavor to *personify*, as far as possible, the *things* of his argument, the truths he is called to announce; putting them in the shape of persons, and showing them in action. Interesting relations of fact, will sometimes accomplish this object with great power and success.

In the selection and use of such facts, there is need of judgment. A greater benefit can hardly be bestowed upon the cause of truth, than a good collection of authentic and interesting points in the current of man's life and God's providence. Such an encyclopedia may be a book of reference, in which a man may often find materials to enliven and render attractive a discourse which might otherwise have proved very dull, or to fasten on the conscience a truth or a warning, which otherwise would have fallen on the ear unnoticed, and glided past the mind unfelt. It is not enough that truth be pointed, like a straight, smooth piece of steel; it needs side points, as a dart, that it may not draw out, when it effects an entrance. Sometimes, a discourse may be so smooth, so polished, and pointed so *finely*, that it may go quite through the understanding and the heart, *without stopping in it*, or leaving any trace of its passage. It is a great mistake to have truth go *through* its mark, and fall out and be lost on the other side.

Barbed arrows are good, not for the purpose of inflicting unnecessary pain, but of compelling notice; they may be barbed with anecdote and illustration, in such a way, that it shall be hardly possible for them to fail. But barbs *alone* are useless. An archer would be poorly off, if he had nothing in his quiver but arrow-heads or feathers. For an illustration to be useful or successful, there must be something to be illustrated. A sermon made up of anecdotes and flowers, is quite as deficient as a sermon of the driest abstractions.

Anecdotes and illustrations, may not only illustrate a point, and make an audience see and feel the argument, but they may themselves add to the argument; they may be at once a part of the reasoning, and an elucidation of it. Indeed a just figure always adds power to a chain of logic, and increases the amount of truth conveyed. It is also of great use in relieving the attention; as a stopping place where the mind is rested, and prepared to resume the reasoning without fatigue, without loss. Almost any expedient, which decorum permits, may be justified in order to prevent drowsiness, keep the mind awake, and fix the attention of an audience. Nevertheless, such attention, however it may be gained by extraordinary expedients, cannot be *kept* but by truth worth illustrating.

We have heard of an eccentric preacher, who had a church member named Mark, in the habit of sleeping under the discourses of his pastor. One day, in the midst of his sermon, the preacher, being about to enunciate an important text, raised his voice, exclaiming, "Mark! Mark! Mark!" The unfortunate church dreamer, taken suddenly in the depths of a profound nap, started bolt upright, in the midst of the congregation, at the call, when the preacher continued "*Mark* the perfect man, and behold the *upright*, for the end of that man is peace!"

Now a forcible illustration, a vivid, or pathetic, or exciting apologue, or incident, or fact, answers all the purpose of such eccentricities, in waking the mind from its slumbers. The hearer feels as if he were addressed by name, when the preacher sends the truth, thus clothed, thus armed, home upon him. Dr. Abercrombie speaks of the importance of illustrations and analogies, for assisting and training the memory of children. The same discipline is equally necessary for the hearers of sermons. Although they may have forgotten the text, the subject, and almost the whole design of the preacher; they will not unfrequently carry away the illustrations, and every thing in the train of thought lying immediately in their neighborhood. And, indeed, a single illustration will sometimes flash the meaning of a whole sermon upon minds that otherwise would have departed scarcely knowing the application of a sentence.

Unfortunately, some men are so habitually destitute of any thing approximating to the nature of illustration, so neglectful of it, so monotonous in the abstract mould of their discourses, that the unexpected introduction of a story or even a pointed comparison or incident, would rouse the congregation, almost as thoroughly, as if the preacher were to carry a loaded pistol into the pulpit, and fire it off at the third head of his discourse. How is it possible for an audience to be interested or stirred, even by the most important truth, if presented so monotonously, and in mere generalities?

The hearers of the gospel, are like poor men coming to be clothed from a public charity. If you give them cloth in the piece, they will dispose of it as they can, and keep their own rags. But if you have it made up, and give them plain, well-fitting garments, they will be likely to put them on and wear them. The truths of the gospel should, as much as possible, come saying, *thou art the man*. It is not necessary for this purpose to add, thou David, or thou Mark, unless it be by private expostulation, where this is needed. An authentic incident, a forcible illustration, a striking analogy, a recorded case, will often so point the moral, that the consciences of all may apply it, without being afraid lest others should see them putting on the coat.

Illustrations from Divine Providence, especially in Christian biography, but also in history, in particular interpositions, and in marked steps in all men's lives, are a great help in fastening Divine truth. If a preacher merely say, I will tell you what such or such a person said to me, even *that* may fasten a sermon. It is like driving a nail into the mind, and hanging up the lesson upon it. "The words of the wise are as goads, and as nails fastened by the masters of assemblies." Cecil records the effect of a few such words driven unexpectedly into his own mind, by a plain man from the country, who said to him one day, as he was coming out of the church, that men might cheer themselves in the morning, and they might pass on tolerably well, perhaps, without God at noon; *but the cool of the day was coming, when God would come down to talk with them.* Cecil says that he had himself been some time in a dry, fruitless frame, but persuading himself that all was going on well, when it pleased God to shoot an arrow, by the hand of this simple but weak minister, into his heart. It was a message from God; he felt as though God had descended into the church, and was about to call him to his account.

Now this was a goad, a nail, unconsciously driven by one of his hearers, into the conscience of the master of the assembly himself. The hearer gave the preacher an illustration that fastened his own sermon. And how much good Cecil himself may have afterwards accomplished, simply by repeating that same message, none can tell. Sometimes, when we come upon such landing places, in the midst of a sermon, it is like anchoring at a verdant island, after a somewhat tiresome sail. You remember the lake itself more by the island in the midst of it, and by what happened there, than by the smooth expanse of water. We once heard the preaching of Rev. Christopher Anderson of Edinburgh, author of of the Annals of the English Bible, and other works. Although the whole sermon was deeply interesting, we cannot now recall but one thing in it, and that was a striking saying of the eminent and excellent Andrew Fuller, which Mr. Anderson gave, as spoken by Mr. Fuller to himself. Ah, dear brother, said that man of God, there was never but one being in this world, who could say, when he died, *It is finished!* *We* have to leave all our works unfinished. But we must work on, and do what we can, while the day lasts, and then we shall know all.

Every one must have observed the effect of the introduction of such lights and illustrations, upon an audience. The whole assembly may have appeared up to that point uninterested, listless, even oppressed with stupor. But the moment the preacher says, I will illustrate this point, by a relation of what took place in the life of such or such a person, an entire change comes on the whole congregation. Every countenance is lighted up with expectation, every mind is on the alert, every ear is open and attentive. Even if the preacher simply says, We will suppose a case, for the purpose of illustration; we will suppose a man placed in such or such a position, involved in such or such an emergency, or having committed such or such a crime. Even then, the attention of the hearers is at once aroused. The presentation of actual facts, or cases of interest in point, is so attractive, that if real incidents are not at hand, it were better to suppose them, than leave the subject without such illustration, in instances where it admits of it. Accordingly, in the Scriptures, and in the discourses of our blessed Lord, it is evident that suppositions are made, and fables are related, to illustrate and enforce truth, to give it life and action.

This constituted a powerful charm in our Savior's preaching, even for those who cared nothing for the spiritual lessons he was enforcing. The beauty and exceeding aptness of his cases and illustrations, may have caught many a careless soul, when the bare, dry truth, would have failed to touch the heart. The truth that a man is miserable, who layeth up treasure for himself, and is not rich towards God, might have been stated in ever so forcible language, without reaching the conscience of the hearers. But when our Lord proceeded to say, The ground of a certain rich man brought forth plentifully; with the solemn close of the apologue, Thou fool! this night thy soul shall be required of thee! what conscience could remain unmoved? It may have been under some such application, that Joseph of Arimathea himself was arrested and brought to repentance.

The hearers of our blessed Lord were so deeply interested and absorbed in such narratives, that sometimes they seem to have forgotten that they were merely illustrative relations; and interrupted him, carried away by their feelings, or desiring the thread of the narrative to unwind differently; as in the case when they broke in upon one of his parables with the declaration, Lord, he hath ten pounds already! One can see the company, their interest, their eagerness, the truth taking hold upon them; we can hear their exclamations, as if a drama of real life were enacting before them. And it *was* life, taken out of the form of abstract truth, and dramatized for *their* life, their instruction.

Much depends, we might almost say *every thing* depends, upon the manner, the feeling, the purpose, with which the parable, or illustration, or incident, is introduced and told. If it grows out of the subject and heart together, it makes a powerful impression. To use a familiar phrase, *it tells.* If well told it tells, and it *is* well told when it comes warm from the heart; and in that way, although gained from abroad, becomes like the mind's own creation, like an original part of the argument or persuasion of a mind glowing under the excitement of truth, and intent on fastening it upon others. Illustrations, incidents, experiences, which have deeply impressed ourselves, will make a deep impression upon others, if related in the simplicity and solemnity of the same feeling with which the Spirit and the providence of God invested them in our own consciousness. Old things become new; tame and common things become inexplicably and unexpectedly charged with life and interest; truisms become mighty discoveries, issuing from the mint of personal and deep feeling. And the feeling, in such a case, is the best guide of the manner and the judgment.

One of the most remarkable preachers ever heard in England, was old Hugh Latimer, the venerable martyr of the early Reformation. No man, with such a fund of native humor and satire, ever went so deep and so familiarly into men's consciences. He owed not a little of his power to the use he made of anecdote and incident. He was like a master, converting the Scriptures themselves into a pictorial story-book for his children, and studying it with them. Sometimes his preaching consisted very much in personal recollections and experiences, with accounts of the dealings of God with individual consciences; so that some of the most interesting notices of the English Reformation, are now to be derived from his sermons. He knew how to seize hold of occurrences that were exciting interest among the people, and to turn them to their profit in the gospel.

John Bradford, Latimer's interesting convert, a child of God by some years after him, but a martyr by some months before him, was another remarkable preacher, of great power in dealing with the conscience and the heart. He was full of penitence and prayer; and as it was Latimer's searching and personal appeals to the conscience, that were blest of God for his conversion, the mantle of his spiritual father seemed to have descended on the son; and in a still loftier style, but with much of Latimer's power of illustration, especially from the Scriptures, he poured the truth burning upon men's minds. One of his contemporaries tells us, that "he used to make unto himself a journal, in which he used to write all such notable things as either he did see or hear each day that passed; but whatever he did hear or see, he did so pen it, that a man might see in that book the signs of his smitten heart; for if he did see or hear any good in any man, by that sight he found and noted the want thereof in himself, and added a short prayer, craving mercy and grace to amend. If he did hear or see any plague or misery, he noted it as a thing procured by his own sins, and still added, Lord have mercy upon me." Now, in this habit of close dealing with himself, and noting and applying the ways of God's providence and man's guilt, we see the secret of his power over others, and of his happy faculty in apt and quick Christian reproof, which, says one who knew him, he used with such Divine grace and Christian majesty, that ever he stopped the mouths of gainsayers; speaking with such power, and yet so sweetly, that they might see their evil to be evil, and his good to be good.

In modern times, one of the most eminent examples of power in the use of incident, in illustrating and enforcing Divine truth, is that of Whitefield. He drew thousands upon thousands to hear him, who probably never would have come to listen, or never stayed a sermon through, but for his wonderful fertility and quickness in the dramatic applications of his subject. He was master of such pathos and naturalness, in describing events illustrative of the grace of God, the solemnity of Divine Providence, the power of conscience, and the nearness of eternal realities, that his facts seemed to come flaming from the fire of his feelings, by which he burnt them in upon the soul, and the truths of his subject along with them. An old fact put on a startling aspect in his hands; he *galvanized* every incident, and then threw it, in an electric stream, upon the conscience.

He had a most inimitable ease and happiness in the introduction of occurrences into his sermon, that had fallen under his own observation, or had been related to him by others. He brought out the meaning of them, and traced their application, with such natural art, and spontaneous deep feeling, that they seemed a new revelation of truth, even to the original narrator of them. A clergyman of this country states, that he once told an affecting occurrence to Mr. Whitefield, relating it, however, with but the ordinary feeling and brevity of a passing conversation; when afterwards, on hearing Mr. Whitefield preach, up came his own story, narrated by the preacher in the pulpit, with such nature, pathos, and power, that the clergyman himself, who had furnished Whitefield with the dry bones of the illustration, found himself weeping like a child. The tones of the soul possess an intensity and penetrating depth of feeling to subdue the soul; and Whitefield, amidst all the thunder of a voice that could be heard to an incredible distance, spake with the *tones of the soul;* and his gestures were impelled by the same spontaneous, magic influence, that made *them*, as well as his words, seem *part* of the soul. According to the common saying, so common that we forget the depth of meaning it covers up, he *threw his soul into them.*

And yet it is said that Whitefield, when a boy, had been taught to ridicule this way of preaching in others. There was an excellent, familiar, plain minister named Cole, whose manner would seem to have been in some way so original as to excite notice, but whose method of story-telling drew young Whitefield's contempt. One of the congregation, asked the lad one day, what business he intended to pursue? He said he meant to be a minister; but he would take care never to tell stories in the pulpit, like old Cole. About twelve years afterwards, when Whitefield had begun his career of flame, this old gentleman heard him preach, illustrating, in his own powerful way, the application of his subject by some interesting narrative. "I find," said he, "that young Whitefield can now tell stories, as well as old Cole." Some of young Whitefield's stories may have been, indeed, the very same as old Cole's; but they had a new power, because they came from the young man's soul, and not from the mere lumber-room of the memory.

This alchemy of fervent love to Christ and to souls, this power of intense religious feeling, turns all things into gold, creates out of all knowledges, arts, stories in the memory, all scenes of observation, all experiences, inward and external, the means and materials of a vivid eloquence. But there must be discipline of mind, to save even religious feeling from being wasted, and the stores of the memory wantoned away. There may be an idle habit of profuse story-telling, that, as we have hinted, is almost worse than no illustration at all. It is a poor resort to drag in stories merely to help out a sermon, or to conceal the want of thought. It is like our city milkmen stopping at the last pump, and filling their cans with water, when the milk threatens to give out. There must be *thought;* and true religious feeling, in a well disciplined mind, *produces* thought, more than all things else together; and then illustrations will be used, not for mere amusement, but to convey thought, and make it suggestive and productive. Habits of close attention, Cowper says:

> Habits of close attention, thinking heads,
> Become more rare, as dissipation spreads,
> Till authors hear at length one general cry,
> Tickle and entertain us, or we die.

The desire to be *tickled* is not confined to the dissipated readers of a trifling literature. Sometimes, the preacher becomes to the congregation "as a very lovely song of one that hath a pleasant voice, and can play well upon an instrument;" and they go to church mainly to hear the music, and be amused. Instead of going to *muse* upon the things of God, they go to be *a-mused*, and drawn away from them. In this case, if the fault be in the preacher, there is, as John Randolph once said, both a *lyre* and a *liar* in the pulpit; and the preacher is a *liar*, because he is *merely* a *lyre*, to play them a pleasant tune.

A man must have the magnificent anatomy of the doctrines of the gospel, to be clothed upon with his illustrations and feelings, or else he might as well be constructing a balloon. When those great doctrines occupy and absorb the soul, being doctrines of life, and not speculation merely, illustration and intense feeling will grow out of them, and grow upon them, and that is the perfection of eloquence. The trite old rhetorical maxim, *Ars est celare artem*, is only a piece of rhetorical foolery or hypocrisy, having no place, where there is real, deep heavenly interest in the subject, where the mind is kindled upon it. And illustration, to quote again a few lines from our sweet English Christian Poet, with the change of a word:

> For illustration, choose what theme we may,
> And chiefly when religion leads the way,
> Should flow like waters after summer showers,
> Not as if raised by mere mechanic powers.

This is the secret of familiar, life-giving instruction with children. To attract them, we must, in a measure, be their playmates, and draw them on, and draw out their minds in companionship with our own, in illustrations that shall seem to delight us as much as them.

And here we come upon another great use of the excellent and important volume, to which these thoughts are introductory, that of interest and instruction in Sabbath schools. A fund of authentic stories and anecdotes, moral, providential, religious, is to Sabbath school teachers invaluable. And such should know how to apply them. They should be at pains to gather and select them for their purpose. One or two little stories happily told, or the simplest anecdotes or incidents dwelt upon with interest, and bringing the lesson home to the heart, may make each exercise an enjoyment instead of a task, a delight instead of a mere duty. The teacher may present apples of gold in baskets of silver, and every youthful mind will take home a part of the fruit, and keep it. The truth so presented, the lesson so inculcated, will stay in the memory, will circulate in the understanding, as the air does in a room, instead of knocking at the door in vain for admittance. A child receives truth into the mind, presented in lively and interesting incident, as a quiet unruffled lake receives into its bosom the reflection of the sky and the clouds above it, or the trees and flowers upon its margin. There is nothing so susceptible of impression as a child's mind to Divine truth, when it comes in the shape of a story or a life, told in a winning, familiar, affectionate manner.

Here it is that teachers are often extremely deficient; and here is the reason why the pupils of one class will sometimes be charmed with their Sabbath exercises, so that the Sabbath shall be the day to which, perhaps, they look forward with more pleasure than to any other in the week; while those of another find the same lessons tiresome, and the Sabbath without delight. One teacher enlivens the exercise with anecdote, drawing from the Scriptures and from real life, a variety of beautiful proof and illustration; the other merely presents the truth in the abstract, dry form of question and answer, without life, without incident. A teacher had better, every Sabbath, tell *something* to awaken an interest, even if disconnected from the lesson, than leave his little class without such attraction. A volume which provides the materials of such interest, is a great and important gift, to the Sabbath school, the social circle, and the family fireside.

The use of *the pictorial*, whether in words or engravings, is an element of indispensable importance and incalculable power. The enemies of God, of the truth, and of the soul, employ it with dreadful art and energy for the destruction of men in sin, for awakening and depraving the passions, and then supplying them with pernicious gratifications and fiery stimulants. Let good men take the art of illustration, and use it for God, for heaven, for the salvation of the soul.

GEORGE B. CHEEVER.

PREFACE.

Origin and Design of the Work.—One of the best means which I have found to fasten moral and religious truths on the popular mind, is to present them clothed in tangible forms, as in anecdotes, historical sketches, and kindred illustrations. They do much, when *rightly used*, to enlist attention, convince the judgment, and persuade the heart. I have often seen the truth of the proverb, "One fact is worth a ship-load of arguments." As we might naturally suppose, an example of virtue is more forcible than a precept, because men are more ready to imitate than they are to obey. And citing an instance of the effects of sin, often tells more loudly than a lecture against it; because men more readily imagine fallacy in our logic than falsehood in our statements, and give more deference to the doings of God than to the sayings of man. Besides, in most men, the perceptive predominate over the reflective faculties; hence, fact and incident which strike the former, are more easily remembered than trains of reasoning which appeal to the latter.

The great moral uses of such illustrations in the family and social circle, in the Sabbath school and the pulpit, have not only been proved in my own experience, but I find that the experience of many others is similar to mine. To supply, therefore, their wants and my own, I have devoted much time and pains for two or three years past, to the preparation of the present work.

Character of the Work.—The anecdotes, incidents, and historical sketches, here assembled, are moral and religious; a wider range of subjects would have made the work too costly and cumbersome. A large and interesting class of materials, embracing anecdotes used in the way of simile or comparison, striking analogies, parables, and the like, have been omitted on the same account: I intend before long to publish them in a separate volume.

Many of the anecdotes here presented, are, of course, adapted rather to the fireside, the Sabbath school, and the platform, than to the pulpit: what are adapted to the latter, and what are not, the preacher qualified for his office, is qualified to decide.

A large portion of the anecdotes of this volume have been more or less abridged, and many partly or wholly re-written; thus, the number embraced in such a volume is far more extensive, and the truths they prove or exemplify, are, I trust, rendered more clear and distinct to the mind. All strictly sectarian anecdotes have been avoided. The writer has introduced no anecdotes which he considered of doubtful or apocryphal character. But in most cases he has not deemed it important to give the original authorities. As a general thing, anecdotes rather secure credence by being true to nature, than by being vouched for by this or that witness, unless he be a person whom we greatly confide in.

Sources and Extent of the Work.—In preparing this volume, I have gone over nearly all former collections published in this country and Great Britain, (amounting to scores of volumes,) and have taken from them all the moral and religious portions of much interest or value. To the twelve volumes published by the London Religious Tract Society, I am, however, as much indebted as to all the rest. This excellent series was edited by the Rev. Dr. Belcher, now pastor of a church in Philadelphia; and I may gratefully add that I have received from him some valuable suggestions and friendly encouragement in the preparation of this work.

In addition to the above collections, I have examined the files of the religious journals of our more prominent evangelical denominations; such as the New-York Observer, New-York Evangelist, Christian Advocate and Journal, Churchman, Protestant Churchman, Christian Intelligencer, Boston Recorder, Christian Watchman, Christian Reflector, Millennial Harbinger, and others which it is needless to mention. Magazines, biographies, and similar works have likewise been consulted. New anecdotes have also been furnished by clergymen and others.

This work, therefore, contains nearly all the best anecdotes of the kind to be found in previous collections, and several hundred others, original and selected.

Arrangement, Classification, and Indexes.—All anecdotal works which I have met with, two or three excepted, are of a very miscellaneous and jumbled character and very deficient in their indexes. Thus they are of very little use as *books of reference.* Unless a person has a very tenacious memory, and has read them carefully, it often costs more time to find some half-forgotten anecdote than it is worth. One great effort of the writer in this work has been to obviate these difficulties; to prepare a book which could be referred to with the greatest possible facility, in the illustration and pointing of truth.

Accordingly, the main topics or subjects follow each other in alphabetical order; and when the subject is extensive, and the facts numerous, they are placed under those analytical divisions and subdivisions of the subject which they illustrate. In addition to this, copious topical and Scriptural indexes will be found at the end of the work. Each division of anecdotes is numbered, 1, 2, 3, &c.; and each anecdote is marked by the letters of the alphabet, (*a*), (*b*), (*c*), &c. In the Index, anecdotes are referred to in whole classes, by the above-mentioned figures, or a *particular* anecdote is referred to by joining both figure and letter; thus, 20a, 30b, 40d, &c. With a little practice, therefore, it will be easy for one but partially acquainted with the contents of the book, to find facts in a moment on any topic or Scripture, which the facts can illustrate.

In closing, I would very gratefully acknowledge my obligations to the Rev. Francis Smith, of Providence, R. I., and the Rev. O. B. Judd, of this city, for the valuable assistance which I have received from them in the prosecution of my labors.

K. ARVINE.

CYCLOPEDIA

OF

MORAL AND RELIGIOUS ANECDOTES.

ABSTINENCE, TOTAL, FROM INTOXICATING DRINKS.

1. The Pecuniary Advantage of Total Abstinence.

(*a*) "THERE GOES A TEETOTALER!"—A drunkard assailed a Washingtonian, but could only say, "There goes a teetotaler!" The gentleman waited until the crowd had collected, and then, turning upon the drunkard, said, "There stands a drunkard!—Three years ago he had a sum of $800, now he cannot produce a penny. I know he cannot. I challenge him to do it, for if he had a penny he would be at a public house. There stands a drunkard, and here stands a teetotaler, with a purse full of money, honestly earned and carefully kept. There stands a drunkard!—Three years ago he had a watch, a coat, shoes, and decent clothes; now he has nothing but rags upon him, his watch is gone, and his shoes afford free passage to the water. There stands a drunkard; and here stands a teetotaler, with a good hat, good shoes, good clothes, and a good watch, all paid for. Yes, here stands a teetotaler! And now, my friends, which has the best of it?" The bystanders testified their approval of the teetotaler by loud shouts, while the crestfallen drunkard slunk away, happy to escape further castigation.

(*b*) A SAVING OF FIVEPENCE A DAY.—At a meeting, in Birmingham, of a total abstinence society, the following statement was made by a working coach painter, who was called on in his turn to speak on the subject of temperance. He said he had made a few calculations which he wished to communicate, with the view of showing the pecuniary benefit he had derived during the four years he had been a teetotal member. Previous to that time he had been in the practice of spending, on an average, in intoxicating drink, fivepence per day, or £7 12s. 1d. per annum, and which in four years would amount to £30 8s. 4d. He would now show how this sum had been expended during the four years he had abstained from all intoxicating drinks. First, it had enabled him to allow an aged father £3 5s. per annum towards rent, or in four years, £13. Secondly, he had entered a benefit society, and paid one shilling and sevenpence per week, or £4 2s. 4d. per annum, or £16 9s. 4d. for the four years. For this payment he secured the following advantages: in case of his being disabled from doing his accustomed work by illness or accident, the society will pay him eighteen shillings per week, until restored to health: in case of death, his widow or rightful heir is entitled to a bonus of £9, besides half the amount paid into the society by the deceased up to the time of his death, with the inter est due thereon. Thirdly, it left him four shillings and ninepence per annum, or nineteen shillings for the four years, to be expended in temperance periodicals. It might further be added, that when the sum of £54 had been paid into the society's funds, no further payment would be required, and the contributor would be entitled to all the benefits before enumerated; medicine and medical attendance were included in the arrangement. Reader, how much may be done with fivepence a day!

(*c*) THE BAD LUMP.—The following incident we relate on the authority of the old sailor, who delivered a temperance lecture on board a steamboat running between New York and New Haven.

Having found a man who was divested of all decent clothing, and in a wretched state of health in consequence of drinking, he induced him, amidst the discouragements of the tavern-keeper, at whose house he had found him, to sign the temperance pledge for one year. The landlord prophesied that he would not keep the pledge a year, or that if he did he would never renew it. As the year was coming to a close, the old sailor called upon the man, and secured his signature again. He signed it for 999 years, with the privilege of a life lease afterward! When the day arrived upon which his first pledge expired, he roguishly went to visit his old friend the tavern-keeper. "There he comes," (said the eager rum-seller,) "he will have a great spree now to pay for his long abstinence." When he arrived at the tavern, he complained of a bad feeling at his stomach, and of various evils, among which was a bad lump on one side, which had been growing for a number of months. "Ah," said the landlord, "did I not tell you it would kill you to break off drinking so suddenly? I wonder you have lived as long as you have.—Come, what will you take?" and suiting the action to the word, he placed a decanter before him.

"But," said the visitor, "I have signed the pledge again for 999 years, with the privilege of a life lease after it!"

"What a fool!" said the landlord; "if you go on as you have done, you will not live another year."

"Do you really think so, landlord?"

"Certainly. Come, what will you take?"

"Oh no, landlord; I have signed the pledge again, and then this terrible lump on my side. I do not believe that drinking will make it any better."

"It is all," said the landlord, "because you left off drinking. You will have a bigger lump than that on the other side before long, if you continue another year as the last."

"Do you think I will? Well, then so be it. I will not violate my pledge, for look here, landlord, (pulling out a great purse, with a hundred dollars in silver shining through the interstices,) that is my lump which has been growing for so many months, and, as you say, is all in consequence of signing the pledge. This is what you would have had, if I had not signed it; and if I have a bigger one than that for 999 years, I will not go to drinking again!"

(*d*) THE WAY TO PAY RENT.—A blacksmith in the city of Philadelphia, was complaining to his iron merchant that such was the scarcity of money that he could not pay his rent. The merchant then asked him how much rum he used in his family, in the course of the day. Upon his answering this question, the merchant made a calculation, and showed him that his rum amounted to more money in the year than his house-rent. The calculation so astonished the mechanic, that he determined from that day to buy and drink no spirits of any kind. In the course of the ensuing year he paid his rent and bought a new suit of clothes out of the savings of his temperance. He persisted in it through the course of his life, and the consequence was competence and respectability.

2. Total Abstinence the only Safe Ground

(*a*) THE LAST OF THE MOHEGANS.—The Mohegans were an excellent tribe of Indians, who lived about Norwich, Ct. They had a long line of kings in the family of Uncas. One of the last was Zachary; but he was a great drunkard. But a sense of the dignity of his office came over him, and he resolved he would drink no more. Just before the annual election, he was accustomed to go every year to Lebanon, and dine with his brother Governor, the first Gov. Trumbull. One of the Governor's boys had heard old Zachary's story, and thought he would try him, and see if he would stick to his cold water. So at table he said to the old chief:—"Zachary, this beer is excellent; will you taste it?"

The old man dropped his knife, leaned forward with stern intensity of expression, his black eye sparkling with indignation, was fixed on him: "John," said he, "you do not know what you are doing. You are serving the devil, boy! I tell you that I am an Indian! I tell you that I am; and that if I should but taste your beer, I could not stop until I got to ruin, and become again the drunken, contemptible wretch your father remembers me to have been. John, while you live, never tempt a man to break a good resolution."

This story the venerable Col. Trumbull tells of himself. Let all our readers remember it, and never tempt a man to break a good resolution.

(*b*) THE FATAL TEMPTATION.—An intemperate man, and one of the most brilliant gems of the age, made a desperate effort to reform. For three months, he promised and confined himself to drinks no more stimulating than tea and coffee. The hopes of his friends and his country were much excited; but in an evil hour he was induced to take a little beer and water. The slight intoxicating quality contained in this liquor, lighted up the latent fires within him. Desire was again renewed; resolution weakened; he relapsed, and went from beer to wine, from wine to brandy, until reason was dethroned, and he became a madman.

(*c*) DRINKING MODERATELY.—A gentleman, of the most amiable dispositions, had contracted confirmed habits of intemperance. His friends persuaded him to come under a written engagement, that he would not drink, except *moderately*, in his own house, or the house of a friend. In a few days he was brought home in a state of bestial intoxication. His apology to a gentleman, a short time after, was, that had the engagement allowed no intoxicating liquor whatever, he was safe; "but if," said he, "I take the half-full of a thimble, I have no power over myself at all." He practised entire abstinence afterwards, and was strong and well.

(*d*) ORIGIN OF MAHOMET'S PROHIBITION OF WINE.—"Mahomet is said to have been led to put the prohibition against the use of wine, in the Koran, by an incident which occurred to himself. Passing through a village one day, he was delighted at the merriment of a crowd of persons enjoying themselves with drinking at a wedding party—but being obliged to return by the same way next morning, he was shocked to see tbe ground, where they had been, drenched with blood, and, asking the cause, he was told that the company had drunk to excess, and, getting into a brawl, fell to slaughtering each other. From that day his mind was made up,—the mandate went forth from Allah, that no child of the faithful should touch wine, on pain of being shut out from the joys of Paradise. The simple truth we suppose to be, that Mahomet foresaw there would be no stability to the religion and empire he was building up, if the use of arden spirits was permitted to his followers."

(*e*) A CHANGE AND CONTRAST.—On an extreme cold night, shivering by the stove in a grog-shop in Cincinnati, sat a young man about twenty-five years of age, (although he appeared much older,) who was evidently the victim of a depraved appetite. His eye, though swollen and bloodshot, had not entirely lost the power of its expression, and a careful observer could discover that he once possessed a bright intellect and a commanding genius. He gazed on vacancy, reflecting perhaps upon the misery he had brought upon himself and relatives, in consequence of his dissipation. He was thinly clad, and seemed to be laboring under some horrible sensation.

Those who came and went, looked with disgust upon him, and then passed on. At length, one entered who was acquainted with him, and after looking at him for a moment, turned upon his heel and said to the bar-tender:

"Brown, why do you let such loafers as that sit here, to the annoyance of respectable people?" This last speaker, whom we will call Somers, was also a young man, respectably clad, and belonged to the same mechanical business, as did the one whom he was pleased to term "*loafer*." *He* was a *moderate drinker*, the other a *drunkard!* The bar-tender replied:

"I have told him a number of times to keep away from the place, and am determined that if he comes here again drunk, I will send him, head and heels, into the street."

This rebuke cut poor William H—, (for that was his name,) to the very quick. He was not so drunk but that he could see and understand—nor had rum entirely obliterated that manly pride which once burned brightly within his bosom. Although he was degraded,

'——he had one virtue left;
That true shoot which precept doth inculcate,
And keep the root and trunk alive,—
One virtue—Manhood!"

He rose and left the place to go—he knew not whither. * * * *

Two years passed away, and William H— had become a Washingtonian, and a highly respectable member of society—surrounded by innumerable friends, who placed the most implicit confidence in his integrity as a man and a citizen, and was doing a prosperous business. One morning, as he took up the daily paper, his eye fell upon that department devoted to "Coroner's inquests"—and, to his utter astonishment and grief, he read that George Somers had died on the previous day at the Alms House from the effects of intemperance!

(*f*) WESLEY AND THE DYSPEPTIC CLERGYMAN.—When stationed in the city of Bath, says Rev. Mr. Towle, I was introduced into the company of an aged man, whom I understood to have been intimate with Mr. Wesley, and once a useful local preacher. We entered into conversation about Mr. Wesley's times, when among other things he observed,—"On one occasion, when Mr. Wesley dined with me, after dinner, as usual, I prepared a *little* brandy and water. On perceiving this, with an air of surprise he cried, —'What! my brother, what's that?' 'It's brandy,' said I; 'my digestion is so bad, I am obliged to take a little after dinner.' 'How much do you take?' said he, 'let me see.' 'Only about a table-spoonful.' 'Truly,' said he, 'that is not much; but one table-spoonful will soon lose its effect, and then you will take two; from two you will get to a full glass; and that, in like manner, by habituating yourself to it, will lose its effect, and then you will take two glasses, and so on, till in the end, perhaps you will become a drunkard. O my brother, take care what you do!'"

Happy had it been for that man, if he had taken the timely warning of his good friend Wesley. But alas! he trifled with his *little drops*, until he actually did become a drunkard, ruined his reputation, and at the very time I had an interview with him, he was a poor, old, miserable backslider, apparently within a few steps of the grave.

3. Only those who totally abstain exert a good influence over the Intemperate, or command respect as Christians.

(*a*) A DISTILLER HOOKED.—A Washingtonian in Pennsylvania says, "I went to see a distiller and offered him the pledge to sign. 'No, sir,' said he, 'I manufacture the article, and do you suppose I would sign? I'll tell you what I'll do,' said he; 'I have a son, and I should be right glad if you could get him to sign; and you may tell him if he will, there are five hundred dollars in the hands of Mr. Taylor, and the home farm, and he shall have them both if he signs it.' Like many a father he was willing to give any thing but the influence of example. So off I went in search of the son. I told him what his father said. 'Well now,' said he, 'how can you expect me to trot, when daddy and mammy both paces!' I turned round, and went right off after the old man—now, said I, what do you say to that? "Well, sir," said he, "I pledge you my word I never saw it in that light before; and I never will drink or manufacture another drop as long as I live;" and he put down his name upon the spot. I took the pledge to the young man with his father's name to it, and he signed it directly.

(*b*) WILLIAM LADD AND HIS WINE.—William Ladd was a man always ready for every good work. He early enlisted in the cause of Temperance. He had seen so much of the awful effects of the vice against which we contend, that he gladly heard and obeyed the call to be up and doing what he could to suppress it. But, as he told me, he for a long while opposed only the use of distilled spirits, and continued himself to drink wine daily and freely. To be consistent, however, he took pains to send all the way to New-York to procure wine that was not infused with brandy. And you know, sir, that article can be readily obtained in that city or our own; for there are kind, accommodating merchants, who wish to suit their purchasers so much, that they can draw you wine with alcohol, or wine without alcohol, from the same cask. Well, sir, Mr. Ladd obtained his pure wine at a considerable additional expense, had it conveyed down to Minot, and carefully bestowed in his cellar, and continued to regale himself as he saw fit with his unadulterated juice of the grape, even while he was going about preaching the doctrine of total abstinence. Of this he made no secret, for he was too good a man to do that in private which he was ashamed to acknowledge before all men. Indeed he did not perceive, he did not suspect his inconsistency. But, on a great occasion, at a large county meeting, he exerted himself more than ever, and, as he told me, with great success. "I never," said he, with his wonted frankness, "I never made so good a temperance speech in my life. I used up the objections of the opposers of our cause. I thought nobody could get away from my arguments. I sat down," said he, "thinking that he who could withstand the appeal that I had made must be a hard one indeed, when a little crusty-looking man got up in a distant part of the house, and merely said, 'Ha, if the squire 'll give us some of his good wine, we won't drink the nasty rum no more.'" This was too much for Mr. Ladd. It revealed to him, as with a flash, to what little purpose he had labored. He rose at once before the assembly, acknowledged his inconsistency, renounced from that moment the use of any and every kind of intoxicating drink, resolving, in the spirit of the apostle, that he would not drink wine nor any other thing whereby his fellow man might be led to offend. This, sir, is the true spirit of our great reform. For the sake of ourselves, and for the sake of others, we must abstain wholly from the use of intoxicating drinks of every sort. We must show our faith by our practice.

(*c*) TIMING IT.—A minister in the Highlands of Scotland, found one of his parishioners intoxicated. The next day he called to reprove him for it.

"It is very wrong to get drunk," said the parson.

"I ken that," said the guilty person, "but then I dinna drink as meikle as you do!"

"What, sir! How is that?"

"Why, gin it please ye, dinna ye aye take a glass o' whisky and water after dinner?"

"Why yes, Jemmy, surely I take a little whisky after dinner merely to aid digestion."

"An dinna ye take a glass o' whisky toddy every night before ye gang to bed?"

"Yes, to be sure, I just take a little toddy at night to help me sleep!"

"Weel," continued the parishioner, "that's jist fourteen glasses a week, an about sixty every month. I only get paid off once a month, an then if I'd take sixty glasses, it wad make me dead drunk for a week;—now ye see the only difference is, ye *time it* better than I do!"

This is pretty much the view most people take of this matter; a moderate drinking clergyman may talk to his drunken parishioner till doomsday, but he will never make him a sober man so long as he drinks himself.

(*d*) A CONVERT CHARGED WITH HYPOCRISY.—It is a fact, of

which I have been but recently convinced, (says a writer in the N. Y. Evangelist,) that the world in general, those who have no religion, and even opposers, consider the conversion of those persons to religion as spurious and hypocritical, who do not approve of and practice total abstinence from ardent spirits.

In a town where there has been a revival the past winter, there is a person who has been from a child in the habit of drinking ardent spirit freely, perhaps almost to excess; and who, until recently, seldom attended a religious meeting. This individual became a hopeful subject of renewing grace, and professed his faith in Christ. So changed, so exemplary was his walk and conversation, that even the enemies of religion could have nothing to say against him. After a while, this person had occasion to purchase some whisky for medicinal purposes, and then the cry was raised against him by opposers, that he had no religion, and that the purchase of the whisky proved his hypocrisy!

(*e*) DEACON BARNES AND THE DRUNKARD.—A man once addicted to intemperance, but who for some months had entirely abstained, though he had not joined the Temperance Society, took occasion not long since to relate, in a temperance meeting, his experience in regard to the influence of temperate drinkers of respectable standing in society, upon the habits of the drunkard. "Many a time," said he, "have I gone to Captain Johnson's tavern and waited for half an hour, or an hour, for some respectable man to come in and go to the bar and call for liquor. After a while, Deacon Barnes would come in and call for some spirit and water. Then I could get up to the bar and do as he did."

Deacon Barnes hearing of this, asked him if it was so.

"It is," said the man.

"Well," rejoined the deacon, "you shall hang on me no longer. I joined the Temperance Society yesterday."

"Did you?"

"Yes."

"Well, then I will join to-day, for I can do without liquor as long as Deacon Barnes can."

He did join, and remained a consistent temperance man afterwards.

4. Illustrious Examples of Total Abstinence.

(*a*) REFUSING TO DRINK WINE WITH WASHINGTON.—Towards the close of the revolutionary war, says Dr. Cox, an officer in the army had occasion to transact some business with General Washington, and repaired to Philadelphia for that purpose. Before leaving, he received an invitation to dine with the General, which was accepted, and upon entering the room he found himself in the company of a large number of ladies and gentlemen. As they were mostly strangers to him, and he was of a naturally modest and unassuming disposition, he took a seat near the foot of the table, and refrained from taking an active part in the conversation. Just before the dinner was concluded, General Washington called him by name and requested him to drink a glass of wine with him.

"You will have the goodness to excuse me, General," was the reply, "as I have made it a rule not to take wine."

All eyes were instantly turned upon the young officer, and a murmur of surprise and horror ran around the room. That a person should be so unsocial and so *mean* as to never drink wine, was really too bad; but that he should abstain from it on an occasion like that, and even when offered to him by Washington himself, was perfectly intolerable! Washington saw at once the feelings of his guests, and promptly addressed them:—"Gentlemen," said he, "Mr. —— is right. I do not wish any of my guests to partake of any thing against their inclination, and I certainly do not wish them to violate any established *principle* in their social intercourse with me. I honor Mr. —— for his frankness, for his consistency in thus adhering to an established rule which can never do him harm, and for the adoption of which, I have no doubt, he has good and sufficient reasons."

(*b*) REV. JOSEPH WOLF AND THE RECHABITES.—The Rev. Joseph Wolf says:—On my arrival in

Mesopotamia, some Jews that I saw there, pointed me to one of the ancient Rechabites. He stood before me, wild, like an Arab—holding the bridle of his horse in his hand. I showed him the Bible in Hebrew and Arabic, which he was much rejoiced to see, as he could read both languages, but had no knowledge of the New Testament. After having proclaimed to him the tidings of salvation, and made him a present of the Hebrew and Arabic Bibles and Testaments, I asked him,—"Whose descendant are you?"

"Mousa," said he, boisterously, "is my name, and I will show you who were my ancestors;" on which he immediately began to read from the fifth to the eleventh verse of Jeremiah xxxv.

"Where do you reside?" said I.

Turning to Genesis x. 27, he replied, "At Hadoram, now called Simar by the Arabs: at Uzal, now called Sanan by the Arabs;" and again referring to the same chapter, verse 30th, he continued, "At Mesha, now called Mecca, in the deserts around those places. We drink no wine, and plant no vineyard, and sow no seed; and live in tents, as Jonadab, our father, commanded us: Hobab was our father too. Come to us, and you will find us sixty thousand in number; and you see thus the prophecy has been fulfilled, 'Therefore, thus saith the Lord of Hosts, the God of Israel, Jonadab, the son of Rechab, shall not want a man to stand before me forever;'" and saying this, Mousa, the Rechabite, mounted his horse and fled away, and left behind a host of evidence in favor of sacred writ.

(*c*) GOOD EXAMPLE OF A KING.—A heathen king, who had been for years confirmed in the sin of drunkenness, by the evil practices of white men on the Sandwich Islands, had been led to forsake the dreadful habit. He said lately to a missionary, "Suppose you put four thousand dollars in one hand, and a glass of rum in the other, you say you drink this rum I give you four thousand dollars, I no drink it; you say you kill me, I no drink it."

(*d*) AN EXAMPLE FOR YOUTH.—A little boy in destitute circumstances was put out as an apprentice to a mechanic. For some time he was the youngest apprentice, and of course had to go upon errands for the apprentices, and not unfrequently to procure for them ardent spirits, of which all, except himself, partook, because, as they said, it did them good. He however used none; and, in consequence of it, was often the object of severe ridicule from the older apprentices, because, as they said, he had not sufficient manhood to drink rum. And as they were reveling over their poison, he, under their insults and cruelty, often retired and vented his grief in tears. But now every one of the older apprentices, we are informed, is a drunkard, or in the drunkard's grave; and this youngest apprentice, at whom they used to scoff, is sober and respectable, and worth a hundred thousand dollars. In his employment are about one hundred men, who do not use ardent spirits; and he is exerting upon many thousands an influence in the highest degree salutary, which may be transmitted by them to future generations, and be the means, through grace, of preparing multitudes not only for usefulness and respectability on earth, but for an exceeding and eternal weight of glory.

(*e*) A PATRIOT'S RESOLVE.—An old man of more than fourscore years, afflicted with a bodily infirmity, for which he had been advised by a physician to use ardent spirit as a medicine, was presented with the total abstinence pledge. After reading it he said,

"That is the thing that will save our country—I will sign it!"

"No," said one, "you must not sign it, because ardent spirit is necessary for you as a medicine."

"I know," said he, "I have used it, but if something is not done, our country will be ruined, and I will not be accessory to its ruin. I will sign it!"

"Then," says another, "you will die."

"Well," said the old man, in the true spirit of '76, "for my country I *can* die"—and he signed the pledge, gave up his medicine, and his disease fled away.

It was the remedy that kept up the disease, and when he had renounced the one, he was relieved of the other. So it probably would be in nine cases out of ten where this poison is used as a medicine.

(*f*) NOT OLD ENOUGH TO NEED IT.—When the subject of forming a Temperance Society began to be agitated in the town of W——, it met with strong opposition from a class of *temperate drinkers*. The number, however, who were ready to join a Society, was considerable, and their character and standing in the community, respectable. Among this number was a gentleman who had attained the great age of *ninety-one years*. When it became known that this hoary veteran of other days was thinking of becoming a member of the Temperance Society, some of his drinking and *compassionate* neighbors expostulated with him in this manner:—"You have occasionally drank a little spirit during your whole life, and it has not injured you; surely it would be folly for you to deny yourself of this beverage for the little remnant of your days. Besides, old people, as their corporeal powers decay, need a little ardent spirit to sustain them." The old man, whose head was whitened with the frosts of 91 winters, replied—"I do not know but old people need ardent spirit; *but I am not old enough yet* to need it."

5. Lessons from the Brutes.

(*a*) THE MONKEY AND THE DRUNKARD.—Mr. Pollard states that in his drinking days he was the companion of a man in Arundel Co., Maryland, who had a monkey which he valued at a thousand dollars. "We always took him out on our chesnut parties. He shook off all our chesnuts for us, and when he could not shake them off, he would go to the very end of the limb and knock them off with his fist. One day, we stopped at a tavern and drank freely. About half a glass of whisky was left, and Jack took the glass, and drank it all up. Soon he was merry, skipped, hopped, and danced, and set us all in a roar of laughter. Jack was drunk.

"We all agreed, six of us, that we would come to the tavern next day, and get Jack drunk again, and have sport all day. I called at my friend's house next morning, and we went out for Jack. Instead of being as usual on his box, he was not to be seen. We looked inside, and he was crouched up in a heap. 'Come out here,' said his master. Jack came out on three legs; his fore-paw was upon his head. Jack had the head-ache; I knew what was the matter with him. He felt just as I felt, many a morning. Jack was sick and couldn't go. So we waited three days. We then went, and while drinking, a glass was provided for Jack. But where was he? Skulking behind the chairs. 'Come here Jack, and drink,' said his master, holding out the glass to him. Jack retreated, and as the door was opened, slipped out and in a moment was on top of the house. His master went out to call him down, but he would not come. He got a cow-skin and shook it at him. Jack sat on the ridge-pole and refused to obey. His master got a gun and pointed it at him. A monkey is much afraid of a gun. Jack slipped over the backside of the house. His master then got two guns, and had one pointed each side of the house, when the monkey seeing his bad predicament, at once whipped up on the chimney and got down in one of the flues, holding on by his fore-paws! The master was beaten. The man kept that monkey twelve years, but could never persuade him to taste another drop of whisky. The beast had more sense than a man who has an immortal soul, and thinks himself the first and best of God's creatures on earth."

(*b*) AS DRUNK AS A BEAST.—While Dr. Patton was dining in London with a number of the clergy, one of them remarked, after turning off his glass of wine, "I do not think I am called upon to give up my glass of wine because some men, by using it to excess, make beasts of themselves." The Doctor replied, he thought great injustice was done to the beasts by the comparison—that quadrupeds might be taken in *once* by strong drink, but very rarely the second time. It was left to intelligent man to follow up the habit until overtaken by destruction. He instanced the case of a goat, whose habit was to follow his master to a beer shop, where he would sleep under the table while his master was drinking; on one occasion, either by fair or foul means, one of the waiters made the poor goat drunk on vile beer—but from that time he would, as usual, follow his master to his drinking haunts, but could never again be tempted to enter, but would wait the movement of his master outside the door.

(*c*) "DOTH NOT EVEN NATURE HERSELF TEACH?"—A clergyman in one of the towns in the State of New-York, at the time when the protests against the use of liquors became somewhat earnest from the pulpit, one Sabbath delivered to his congregation a thorough discourse on the subject. On their way home, some of his hearers inquired of each other, "What does all this mean?" One gentleman, who professed some shrewdness of guessing, said, "I will tell you, gentlemen, what is the difficulty; we have none of us sent Mr. —— any thing to replenish his decanter lately. And my advice is that we attend to the matter." Accordingly, on Monday, a full-sized demijohn of "old spirits," or "cogniac," was sent to Rev. Mr. ——, accompanied with a very polite note requesting his acceptance of it, from a few friends, as a testimony of their regard.

Our worthy clergyman felt himself at first in somewhat of a dilemma. But wit, invention, and a good conscience, are sometimes found in close companionship; and they met in the present instance to help our good minister to "back out" of the difficulty. He took the demijohn to the watering trough of his stable, and poured some of the liquor in, and brought his horse to it. Pony expanded his nostrils and snorted and blowed at it, as though he thought it rather too hot, and seemed to say, "What's this?" Next he drove his cow to the trough, to see if she liked it any better. The cow snuffed at it, and shook her horns, and went her way, with no fondness for such a "villanous potation." Mr. —— then carried his demijohn to the pig-stye, and called his pig out of his bed-room, to taste. Piggy grunted and snuffed, dipped his nose in and coughed, and went back again to finish his nap in his straw.

Mr. —— then returned to his study, and penned, in substance, the following note to the present-makers, with which he returned the demijohn and its contents:

"Gentlemen—With due acknowledgments for your present, received this morning, permit me to say, that I have offered some of it to my horse, my cow, and my swine, and neither of them will drink it. That which neither horses, cattle, nor hogs will drink, I cannot think to be either useful or safe for man to drink. I beg you to excuse me therefore for returning the demijohn and its contents; and believe me, gentlemen, your most obedient, &c."

(*d*) THE REFORMED CROWS.—Colonel B. had one of the best farms on the Illinois river. About one hundred acres of it were covered with waving corn. When it came up in the spring, the crows seemed determined on its entire destruction. When one was killed, it seemed as though a dozen came to its funeral; and though the sharp crack of the rifle often drove them away, they always returned with its echo. The Colonel at length became weary of throwing grass, and resolved on trying the virtue of stones. He sent to the druggist's for a gallon of alcohol, in which he soaked a few quarts of corn, and scattered it over his field. The blacklegs came and partook with their usual relish, and, as usual, they were pretty well "corned;" and such a cooing and cackling—such strutting and swaggering! When the boys attempted to catch them, they were not a little amused at their staggering gait and their zigzag way through the air. At length they gained the edge of the woods, and there being joined by a new recruit which happened to be sober, they united at the top of their voices in haw-haw-hawking, and shouting either praises or curses of alcohol, it was difficult to tell which, as they rattled away without rhyme or reason. But the Colonel saved his corn. As soon as they became sober, they set their faces steadfastly against alcohol. Not another kernel would they touch in his field.

6. ACTORS.

(*a*) WORKING LIKE A FOOL TO PLEASE FOOLS.—The late Rev. Samuel Lowell, of Bristol, being once at Brighton, expressed a wish to walk on the Steyne, and to have the public characters pointed out to him. Amongst the rest, a celebrated comedian was noticed. "Ah," said Mr. L., "is that ——, my old school-fellow? I'll speak to him." He accosted him, and the following conversation took place.

Lowell. Sir, I believe I have the pleasure of addressing Mr. ——.

Player. Yes, sir, my name is ——; but I have not the pleasure of being acquainted with you.

L. What! not know your old school-fellow, Samuel Lowell?

P. What! are you Samuel Lowell?

L. Yes, I am.

P. Well, I am very glad to see you; now tell me your history in five minutes.

L. First, my name is Samuel Lowell; I am a dissenting minister at Bristol, where I have lived upwards of twenty years; I have a large family.

P. So, you are a dissenting minister; well, you are a happy man, for you go to your work with pleasure, and perform it with pleasure: you are a happy man. *I go to my work like a fool, to please fools:* I am not a happy man.

(*b*) CARLINI AND HIS PHYSICIAN.—A French physician was once consulted by a person who was subject to the most gloomy fits of melancholy. He advised his patient to mix in scenes of gayety, and particularly to frequent the Italian theatre; and added, "If Carlini does not dispel your gloomy complaint, your case must be desperate indeed." The reply of the patient is worthy the attention of those who frequent such places in search of happiness, as it shows the emptiness and insufficiency of these amusements. "Alas, sir, I am Carlini; and while I divert all Paris with mirth, and make them almost die with laughter, I myself am dying with melancholy and chagrin.—A similar anecdote is related of a well-known English buffoon, who consulted an English physician, celebrated for eccentric advice.

(*c*) DEATH OF PETERSON.—The death of Joseph Peterson, an actor long attached to the Norwich company, (Eng.,) was somewhat remarkable. In October, 1758, he was performing the Duke, in "Measure for Measure." Mr. Moody was the Claudio, and in the third act, where, as the friar, he was preparing Claudio for execution next morning, at these words:—

> "——— Reason thus with life:
> If I do lose thee, I do lose a thing
> That none but fools would keep: a breath
> Thou art."

Here he dropped into Mr. Moody's arms, and never spake more.

(*d*) THE ACTOR STABBING HIMSELF.—A number of young men were once engaged in acting the tragedy of "Bertram, or the Castle of St. Aldobrand," at Nashville. Mr. J. J. McLaughlin, formerly of Hopkinsville, Ky., was engaged to act the part of Bertram, whose part it was during the progress of the play to feign to stab himself. For this purpose he had provided himself with a Spanish knife. "As the tragedy wore to its denouement his excitement increased, and the gloomy spirit of the play was upon him with a power that made a strong impression of reality upon the hearers, and made them shudder as he pronounced the following, accompanied by the plunge of the dagger that brought him to his death:—

> 'Bertram hath but one fatal foe on earth,
> *And he is here.*' [*Stabs himself.*]

It was at this moment that he plunged the weapon to his heart. It was doubtless the result of the excited feelings of the actor, who had too absorbingly entered into the dreadful spirit of his hero. We charitably suppose that he had no premeditated design of ending his life with the play; but his complete identification of feeling with the part he acted, led him to suicide as a natural consequence.

"The hallucination, if such we may call it, did not end with the plunge of the dagger. His feelings bore him along yet further. There was still, after some exclamations of surprise from the tragic monks, a dying sentence for him to repeat. He went through it with a startling effect:—

[*With a burst of exultation,*]

'I died no felon's death—
A warrior's weapon freed a warrior's soul.'

While he was pronouncing these, the last words of the tragedy, his eye and manner were fearfully wild; the blood was falling from his bosom upon the young gentleman who had personated the then lifeless lady *Imogene!* As soon as the last words were pronounced, he fell—to rise no more."

AFFECTION.

7. Affection, Conjugal.

(*a*) MAGNANIMOUS HUSBAND. —Philip, surnamed the Good, the founder of that greatness to which the House of Burgundy latterly attained, was, at an early age, married to the Princess Michelea, sister to Charles the Dauphin. The father of Philip was afterwards slain through the villany and perfidiousness of Charles; and on the news being brought to Philip, full of grief and anger, he rushed into the chamber of his wife: "Alas!" said he, "my Michelea, thy brother has murdered my father." The Princess, who loved her husband most tenderly, broke out into the most affecting cries and lamentations; and fearful lest this accident should lose her the affections of her spouse, refused all comfort. Philip, the *good* Philip, however, assured her that she should not be the less dear to him on that account; that the deed was her brother's and none of hers. "Take courage, my life," said he, "and seek comfort in a husband that will be faithful and constant to thee forever." Michelea was revived by these tender assurances; nor during the three years longer which she lived, had she occasion to suspect the smallest diminution of Philip's affection and respect.

(*b*) A WIFE ON THE BATTLE FIELD.—The following heroic conduct of a Hindoo woman was attested by one of the Baptist missionaries in India:—

Our friend Mrs. W., who invited our missionaries to preach at her house, made us a visit yesterday with some others, for the first time. I was much gratified by the zealous spirit which she evinced, as well as by her anxiety to join the church. She had hitherto waited to see if the Lord would bless her endeavors to draw her husband into the right way. See what a blessing this native woman aims to be to her European husband. She was a Hindoo, before he took her as a slave, of the vilest description. This man was sergeant of artillery in the late war, under Lord Lake, and had an active part in most of the bloody conflicts of the time. This woman's attachment to her partner was so strong, that she accompanied him in the heat of every battle, and often lent him a hand when exhausted, and supplied his place at the guns. In one of these scenes Mr. W. received a musket-ball above the temples, which penetrated nearly through his skull, carrying a part of the brass hoop of his hat along with it, and instantly dropped down, to all appearance dead. She however neither lost her fortitude nor her affection: even in this trying moment, when, in addition to the situation of her partner, the shots were falling like hailstones about her own head, she took him upon her back, with the intent of performing the last friendly office of burying him, and carried him out of the scene of action!

(*c*) THE MOTTO ON THE BRIDAL RING.—A young gentleman of fine intellect, of a noble heart, and one well known to many of our readers, (says the Hartford Courant,) was suddenly snatched by the hand of death from all the endearments of life. Surrounded by every thing that could make existence pleasant and happy—a wife that idolized him—children that loved him as they only can love, and friends devoted to him; the summons came, and he lay upon the bed of death. But a few short years ago, she to whom he was wedded, placed a bridal ring upon his finger, upon the inside of which he had a few words privately engraven. The husband would never permit the giver to read them, telling her that the day would come when her wish should be gratified, and she should know the secret. Seven years glided away, and a day or two since, when conscious that he must soon leave his wife forever, he called her to his bedside, and with his dying accents told her that the hour had at last come when she should see the words upon the ring she had given him. The young mother took it from his cold finger, and though heart-stricken with grief, eagerly read the words: "I HAVE LOVED THEE ON EARTH—I WILL MEET THEE IN HEAVEN."

(*d*) THE COUNTESS' JOURNEY.—I cannot refrain, says Sir Wm. Jones, from giving one beautiful illustration of devoted duty and affection in the instance of the Countess Confalonieri. The moment she heard that the count was condemned to death, she flew to Vienna, but the courier had already set out with the fatal mandate. It was midnight, but her agonies of mind pleaded for instant admission to the empress. The same passionate despair which won the attendants, wrought its effect on their royal mistress. She hastened that moment to the emperor, and having succeeded, returned to the unhappy lady with a commutation of the sentence: her husband's life was spared. But the death-warrant was on its way;—could she overtake the courier? Throwing herself into a conveyance, and paying four times the amount for relays of horses, she never, it is stated, stopped or tasted food till she reached the city of Milan. The count was preparing to be led to the scaffold: but she was in time—she had saved him. During her painful journey, she had rested her throbbing brow upon a small pillow, which she bathed with her tears; in the conflict of mingled terror and hope, lest all might be over. This interesting memorial of conjugal tenderness and truth in so fearful a moment, was sent by his judges to the count, to show their sense of his wife's admirable conduct.

(*e*) THE LOST HUSBAND FOUND.—During a very heavy fall of snow in the winter of 1784, two gentlemen rode on horseback from Berwick to Kelso, regardless of the remonstrances of many, who insisted that the roads were impassable: and, in truth, it was an act of hardihood and folly, as the congealed flakes were drifted by the blast, and beat violently against their eyes and teeth. At every step the jaded animals were more than knee-deep, and may be rather said to have plunged onward than otherwise. When they arrived, with much difficulty, at a lonely ale-house, near Tweezie, on the river Till, they found an inhabitant of Kelso, who had been detained in this thatched hovel two days by the inclement season: he sat in a contracted state, inclining over the embers on the hearth, like the personification of the ague. When he recognised them, his features assumed their wonted firmness, and, gathering intrepidity from example, he resolved to accompany them, although the roads and ditches were so filled up that the vast face of the country seemed an unbroken white expanse. On their arrival in the middle of a heath, which they did not accomplish until the approaches of night, they faintly discovered a female form wading and floundering irregularly towards them, in the trackless snow. her attire was so loose, and involved so much of the simplicity of a villager, that she appeared as if habited merely to pass from one neighbor's house to another. Viewing her through the misty atmosphere, they hesitated to pronounce her as human; the contour of her body was so softened by the intermediate vapors, that she seemed aerial. On their coming nearer, they ascertained her, with extreme astonishment, to be the wife of their companion: she had been wandering in a spirit of desperation, thirteen miles from her home and her infants, in that bleak day, to find the remains of her beloved Willy; believing him, from his unusual and alarming absence, to have perished in the hard weather. Upon the instantaneous assurance that she beheld her husband once more, she issued a loud and piercing shriek, and sank motionless in the snow. When they had chafed her temples, and imperfectly recovered her, she clasped her hands, in all the fervor of piety, and raising her eyes to heaven, blessed her God for her deliverance from trouble. At the conclusion of her prayer, they placed the shivering amiable woman on the ablest horse, and conveyed her to Coldstream, overpowered by the sensations of an excessive joy, succeeding the conflicts of severe duty and agonizing woe! What an inspiring instance of conjugal tenderness!—Could Cornelia or Portia have done more?

(*f*) THE INDIAN AND HIS FAMISHING WIFE.—In the year 1762, (says the Rev. Mr. Heckwelder,) I was witness to a remarkable instance of the disposition of the Indians to indulge their wives. There was a famine in the land, and a sick Indian woman expressed a great desire for a mess of Indian corn. Her husband having heard that a trader at lower Sandusky had a little, set off on horseback for that place, one hundred miles distant, and returned with as much corn as filled the crown of his hat, for which he gave his horse in exchange, and came home on foot, bringing his saddle back with him.

(*g*) THE SHAWNEE'S LOVE TO HER HUSBAND.—A married woman of the Shawnee Indians, made this beautiful reply to a man whom she met in the woods, and who implored her to love and look on him. "Oulman, my husband," said she, "*who is forever before my eyes*, hinders me from seeing you or any other person."

(*h*) A GOOD WIFE.—The Rev. William Jay, of Bath (Eng.), on the fiftieth anniversary of his ordination, gave his wife the following noble compliment. Being presented by the ladies of his congregation with a purse containing £650, after a few remarks he turned to Mrs. Jay, and said: "I take this purse, and present it to you, madam —to you, madam, who have always kept my purse, and therefore it is that it has been so well kept. Consider it entirely sacred—for your pleasure, your use, your service, your comfort. I feel this to be unexpected by you, but it is perfectly deserved. Mr. Chairman, and Christian friends, I am sure there is not one here but would acquiesce in this, if he knew the value of this female, as a wife, for more than fifty years. I must mention the obligation the public are under to her (if I have been enabled to serve my generation), and how much she has raised her sex in my estimation; how much my church and congregation owe to her watchings over their pastor's health, whom she has cheered under all his trials, and reminded of his duties, while she animated him in their performance; how often has she wiped the evening dews from his forehead, and freed him from interruptions and embarrassments, that he might be free for his work. How much, also, do my family owe to her; and what reason have they to call her blessed! She is, too, the mother of another mother in America, who has reared thirteen children, all of whom are walking with her in the way everlasting."

8. Affection, Filial—Exemplified.

(*a*) ALEXANDER AND HIS MOTHER.—Olympias, the mother of Alexander, was of so very unhappy and morose a disposition, that he could not employ her in any of the affairs of government. She, however, narrowly inspected the conduct of others, and made many complaints to her son, which he always bore with patience. Antipater, Alexander's deputy in Europe, once wrote a long letter to him, complaining of her conduct; to whom Alexander returned this answer: "Knowest thou not that one tear of my mother's will blot out a thousand such letters?"

(*b*) QUINTUS AND HIS SON.—Among the multitude of persons who were proscribed under the second triumvirate of Rome, were the celebrated orator Cicero and his brother Quintus. The latter took means to conceal himself so effectually at home, that the soldiers could not find him. Enraged at their disappointment, they put his son to the torture, in order to make him discover the place of his father's concealment; but filial affection was proof against the most exquisite torments. An involuntary sigh, and sometimes a deep groan, were all that could be extorted from the youth. His agonies were increased; but, with amazing fortitude, he still persisted in his resolution of not betraying his father. Quintus was not far off; and it may be imagined, better than can be expressed, how his heart must have been affected with the sighs and groans of a son expiring in torture to save his life. He could bear it no longer; but, quitting the place of his concealment, he presented himself to the assassins, begging of them to put him to death, and dismiss the innocent youth. But the inhuman monsters, without being the least affected with the tears either of the father or the son, answered that they must both die; the father because he was proscribed, and the son because he had concealed the father. Then a new contest of tenderness arose who should die first; but this the assassins soon decided, by beheading them both at the same time.

(*c*) AFFECTION'S CHOICE TREASURES.—Ancient history records, that a certain city was besieged, and at length obliged to surrender. In the city there were two brothers, who had, in some way, obliged the conquering general; and in consequence of this, received permission to leave the city before it was set on fire, taking with them as much of their property as each could carry about his person. Accordingly the two generous youths appeared at the gates of the city, one of them carrying their father, and the other their mother.

(*d*) PRISONER RESCUED BY HIS DAUGHTER.—M. Delleglaie being ordered from a dungeon at Lyons, to the Conciergerie, departed thither. His daughter, who had not quitted him, asked to be admitted into the same vehicle, but was refused. The heart, however, knows no obstacles; though she was of a very delicate constitution, she performed the journey on foot; and followed for more than a hundred leagues the carriage in which her father was drawn, and only left it to go into some town and prepare his food; and in the evening, to procure some covering to facilitate his repose in the different dungeons which received him. She ceased not for a moment to accompany him, and watch over his wants, till the Conciergerie separated them. Accustomed to encounter jailers, she did not despair of disarming oppressors. During three months, she every morning implored the most influential members of the committee of public safety, and finished, by overcoming their refusals. She reconducted her father to Lyons, happy in having rescued him. She fell ill on the road, overcome by the excess of fatigue she had undergone, and, while she had preserved her beloved parent's life, she lost her own.

(*e*) HENRY HOCK AND HIS FATHER.—A few years ago, five Dutch gentlemen set out from Rotterdam, to travel on skates to Amsterdam. They had passed over about twelve miles of the waste of inland waters which extends between the two cities, and were, with the exception of one of the party, who kept apart, skating with great velocity, in close files, and hands linked, in the Dutch manner, and were striking out far from the shore, when at once, the whole file was precipitated through the ice, and two out of the four were hardly seen to rise again. The other two were father and son, both remarkably fine men, and the father an expert swimmer, which enabled him to support himself, and his son too, for a considerable time, during which he was so collected as to give directions to the only one of the party who had not fallen in, how he should conduct himself to afford assistance; but at length he gave utterance to the thought, that his son's continuing to hold him would be the death of both. The son immediately kissed the father and, with the familiar and endearing expression he was accustomed to, bade him "good night," loosed his hold, and deliberately resigned himself to death. The father lived; and the name, at least, of Henry Hock, the son, must live also.

(*f*) THE BEST PRESENT.—The three sons of an eastern lady were invited to furnish her with an expression of their love, before she went a long journey. One brought a marble tablet, with the inscription of her name; another presented her with a rich garland of fragrant flowers; the third entered her presence and thus accosted her: "Mother, I have neither marble tablet nor fragrant nosegay, but I have a heart: here your name is engraved, here your memory is precious, and this heart full of affection will follow you wherever you travel, and remain with you wherever you repose."

(*g*) ARCHBISHOP TILLOTSON'S AFFECTION.—There are some children who are almost ashamed to own their parents, because they are poor, or in a low situation of life. We will, therefore, give an example of the contrary, as displayed by the Dean of Canterbury, afterwards Archbishop Tillotson. His father, who was a plain Yorkshireman, perhaps something like those we now call "Friends," approached the house where his son resided, and inquired whether "John Tillotson was at home." The servant, indignant at what he thought his insolence, drove him from the door: but the dean, who was within, hearing the voice of his father, instead of embracing the opportunity afforded him, of going out and bringing in his father in a more private manner, came running out, exclaiming, in the presence of his astonished servants, "It is my beloved father;" and falling down on his knees, asked for his blessing.

(*h*) THE HAPPY MEETING.—Some years ago, a pious widow in America, who was reduced to great poverty, had just placed the last smoked herring on her table, to supply her hunger and that of her children, when a rap was heard at the door, and a stranger solicited a lodging and a morsel of food, saying, that he had not tasted bread for twenty-four hours. The widow did not hesitate, but offered a share to the stranger, saying, "We shall not be forsaken, or suffer deeper for an act of charity."

The traveller drew near to the table; but when he saw the scanty fare, filled with astonishment, he said, "And is this all your store? And do you offer a share to one you do not know? Then I never saw charity before! But, madam, do you not wrong your children, by giving a part of your last morsel to a stranger?" "Ah," said the widow, weeping, "I have a boy, a darling son, somewhere on the face of the wide world, unless Heaven has taken him away; and I only act towards you as I would that others should act towards him. God, who sent manna from heaven, can provide for us as he did for Israel; and how should I this night offend him, if my son should be a wanderer, destitute as you, and he should have provided for him a home, even as poor as this, were I to turn you unrelieved away!"

The widow stopped, and the stranger, springing from his seat, clasped her in his arms; "God, indeed, has provided just such a home for your wandering son, and has given him wealth to reward the goodness of his benefactress. My mother! O my mother!"

It was indeed her long lost son, returned from India. He had chosen this way to surprise his family, and certainly not very wisely; but never was surprise more complete, or more joyful. He was able to make the family comfortable, which he immediately did: the mother living for some years longer, in the enjoyment of plenty.

9. Affection, Filial—Rewarded.

(*a*) THE PRISONER AND HER DAUGHTER.—Valerius Maximus relates, that a woman of distinction having been condemned to be strangled, was delivered to the triumvir, who caused her to be carried to prison in order to be put to death. The gaoler who was ordered to execute her was struck with compunction, and could not resolve to kill her. He chose, however, to let her die with hunger; but meanwhile suffering her daughter to visit her in prison, taking care that she brought her nothing to eat. Many days passed over in this manner, when the gaoler at length, surprised that the prisoner lived so long without food, took means of secretly observing their interviews. He then discovered that the affectionate daughter had all the while been nourishing her mother with her own milk. Amazed at so tender, and at the same time so ingenious an artifice, he related it to the triumvir, and the triumvir to the praetor, who thought the fact merited stating in the assembly of the people. This produced the happiest effects; the criminal was pardoned, and a decree passed that the mother and daughter should be maintained for the remainder of their lives, at the expense of the public; and that a temple, sacred to filial piety, should be erected near the prison.

(*b*) TITUS MANLIUS AND HIS FATHER.—A certain Roman, in the days of paganism, called Titus Manlius, was treated extremely ill by his father, for no other reason than a defect in his speech. A tribune of the people brought an accusation against his father before the people, who hated him for his imperious conduct, and were determined to punish him with severity. The young man hearing this, went one morning very early from his father's country farm, where he was forced to live like a slave, and finding out the house of the tribune who had impeached his father, entreated that he would immediately drop the prosecution. The tribune declared before the people that he withdrew his charge against old Manlius, because his son Titus had obliged him to promise upon oath that he would carry it no farther. The people, charmed with the filial piety of Titus, shown to so unnatural a father, not only forgave the old man, but the next year advanced his generous son to the supreme honors of the state.

(*c*) THE JUDGE OFFERING TO DIE WITH THE CRIMINAL.—While Octavius was at Samos, after the battle of Actium, which made him master of the universe, he held a council to examine the prisoners who had been engaged in Antony's party. Among the rest, there was brought before him an old man, Metellus, oppressed with years and infirmities, disfigured with a long beard, a neglected head of hair, and tattered clothes. The son of this Metellus was one of the judges; but it was with great difficulty he knew his father in the deplorable condition in which he saw him. At last, however, having recollected his features, instead of being ashamed to own him, he ran to embrace him. Then turning towards the tribunal, he said: "Cæsar, my father has been your enemy, and I your officer; he deserves to be punished, and I to be rewarded. One favor I desire of you; it is, either to save him on my account, or order me to be put to death with him." All the judges were touched with compassion at this affecting scene; Octavius himself relented, and granted to old Metellus his life and liberty.

(*d*) EFFORT TO RANSOM A FATHER.—Montesquieu, being at Marseilles, hired a boat, with an intention of sailing for pleasure. He entered into conversation with the two young boatmen, and learned, to his surprise, that they were silversmiths by trade, and had agreed to employ themselves thus as watermen, only that they might increase their earnings. On expressing his surprise, and his fears, that this must arise only from an avaricious disposition, "Oh, sir," said one of them, "if you knew our reasons, you would not think so. Our father, anxious to assist his family, scraped together all he was worth, and purchased a vessel, for the purpose of trading to the coast of Barbary; but was unfortunately taken by a pirate, carried to Tripoli, and sold for a slave. He writes that he has happily fallen into the hands of a master who uses him well, but that the sum demanded for his ransom is so exorbitant, that it will be impossible for him ever to raise it, and says we must therefore relinquish all hope of ever seeing him, and be contented. With the hope of restoring to his family a beloved father, we are striving, by every means in our power, to collect the sum necessary for his ransom; and for such a purpose, we are not ashamed to employ ourselves in this occupation of watermen."

Montesquieu was struck with this account, and on his departure made them a handsome present. Some months afterwards, the two brothers, being at work in their shop, were greatly surprised at seeing their father enter: he threw himself into their arms, exclaiming, that he was fearful they had taken some unjust method to raise the money that procured his ransom. They professed their ignorance of the whole affair, and could only attribute their father's release to that stranger, to whose generosity they had been before so much indebted.

(*e*) A COURAGEOUS SON.—At the siege of Knaresborough, by the Parliament's army, under the command of Colonel Lilburn, a young man who resided in the town, and whose father was one of the garrison, had, several times, at the hazard of his life, conveyed provisions to him, which he effected in the night by getting into the moat, which was dry, climbing up the glacis, and putting the provisions into a hole, where his father was ready to receive them. Being at last discovered by the guard belonging to the besiegers, they fired but missed him. He was, however, taken prisoner, and, having made a full confession of his conduct, was sentenced to be hanged the next day, in the sight of the besieged, to deter others from giving them the least assistance. The sentence was about to be carried into execution, when a lady, whose name was Wincup, with several others, petitioned the commander to pardon the unhappy youth. They succeeded so far as to have him respited; and when the troops left the place, he was set at liberty.

(*f*) FREDERIC AND HIS PAGE. —Frederic, King of Prussia, day one rung his bell, and nobody answering, he opened his door, and found his page fast asleep in an elbow-chair. He advanced towards him, and was going to awaken him, when he perceived part of a letter hanging out of his pocket. His curiosity prompting him to know what it was, he took it out and read it. It was a letter from this young man's mother, in which she thanked him for having sent her a part of his wages to relieve her misery; and finished with telling him, that God would reward him for his dutiful affection. The king, after reading it, went back softly into his chamber, took a bag full of ducats, and slipped it with the letter into the page's pocket. Returning to the chamber, he rang the bell so loudly, that it awakened the page, who instantly made his appearance. "You have had a sound sleep," said the king. The page was at a loss how to excuse himself; and putting his hand into his pocket by chance, to his utter astonishment, he there found a purse of ducats. He took it out, turned pale, and looking at the king, shed a torrent of tears without being able to utter a single word. "What is that?" said the king. "What is the matter?" "Ah! sire," said the young man, throwing himself on his knees, "somebody seeks my ruin! I know nothing of this money which I have just found in my pocket!" "My young friend," replied Frederic, "God often does great things for us, even in our sleep. Send that to your mother; salute her on my part, and assure her that I will take care of both her and you."

(*g*) THE SWEDISH PRISONER'S SON—A gentleman of Sweden was condemned to suffer death, as a punishment for certain offences committed by him in the discharge of an important public office, which he had filled for a number of years with an integrity that had never before undergone either suspicion or impeachment. His son, a youth about eighteen years of age, was no sooner apprised of the affecting situation to which his father was reduced, than he flew to the judge who had pronounced the fatal decree, and, throwing himself at his feet, prayed that he might be allowed to suffer in the room of a father whom he loved, and whose loss he thought it was impossible for him to survive. The magistrate was amazed at this extraordinary procedure in the son, and would hardly be persuaded that he was sincere in it. Being at length satisfied, however, that the young man actually wished to save his father's life at the expense of his own, he wrote an account of the whole affair to the king; and his majesty immediately sent orders to grant a free pardon to the father, and to confer a title of honor on his son. The last mark of royal favor, however, the youth begged leave with all humility to decline; and the motive for the refusal of it was not less noble than the conduct by which he had deserved it was generous and disinterested. "Of what avail," exclaimed he, "could the most exalted title be to me, humbled as my family already is in the dust? Alas! would it not serve but as a monument to perpetuate in the minds of my countrymen the remembrance of an unhappy father's shame!" His majesty, the king of Sweden, actually shed tears when this magnanimous speech was reported to him; and, sending for the heroic youth to court, he appointed him to a confidential office.

(*h*) FREDERIC AND HIS POMERANIAN SERVANT.—Frederic the Great, of Prussia, during his last illness, endured many restless nights, which he endeavored to soothe by conversing with the servant who sat up with him. On one of these occasions, he inquired of a young Pomeranian from whence he came. "From a little village in Pomerania." "Are your parents living?" "An aged mother." "How does she maintain herself?" "By spinning." "How much does she gain daily by it?" "Sixpence." "But she cannot live well on that?" "In Pomerania it is cheap living." "Did you never send her any thing?" "O yes, I have sent her, at different times, a few dollars." "That was bravely done; you are a good boy. You have a deal of trouble with me. Have patience: I shall endeavor to lay something by for you, if you behave well." The monarch kept his word; for, a few nights after, the Pomeranian, being again in attendance, received several pieces of gold; and heard, to his great joy and surprise, that one hundred rix dollars had been settled on his mother during her life.

(*i*) THE HAUGHTY CREDITOR AND HIS POOR DEBTOR'S SON.—A shopkeeper, who resided two or three days' journey from Paris, preserved his good conduct and integrity for many years. At last, by some persons taking undue credit, and keeping him too long out of his money, he was obliged to take a journey to Paris, to desire two things of his creditors: the one was a lengthening out their forbearance; and the other was, to be furnished with a fresh assortment of goods, that he might keep open his shop with credit. They were so pleased with the honesty and frankness of the man, that they all agreed to grant his request, except one; this was his chief creditor, a proud and haughty merchant, who had never felt any adversity, and knew not how to sympathize with the afflicted. "So," said he, "I find, by your asking for a prolongation of credit, and a further indulgence of goods, that you are going down hill; and therefore I am resolved to have my money." Accordingly, he sent immediately for an officer, who arrested the poor man and carried him to jail. In this distressing situation, he wrote home to his wife, who communicated the news to her six children: they were all overwhelmed in sorrow. What could be done? To sit still in despair, was the ready way to ruin. After a deliberate conversation with her eldest son, a young man of fine sense and excellent virtue, about nineteen years of age, he resolved to fly to Paris, with a view to soften this cruel creditor. After a short interview with his father, he went to the house of the merchant, sent in his name, and desired an audience. The cruel and haughty man, thinking he had come to pay him, admitted him into his presence; but he soon found that his first request was, that he should release his father from jail, to go home and comfort his mother, and keep up the credit of the shop. The merchant, being disappointed in his expectation, flew into a violent passion, and declared he would have the money or the bones of his father. The young man, finding him inexorable, fell down on his knees, and with uplifted hands and tears rolling down his cheeks, he addressed himself to the merchant in this manner:—"Sir," said he, "if I go home without my father, I shall see my mother die with a broken heart, the credit of the shop will be entirely ruined, and we, the poor children, must be turned as vagabonds and beggars into the open street. I have this one, this last request to make—let me be sent to jail in the room of my father, and keep me there until all demands are satisfied." The merchant walked backwards and forwards in the room with great emotion. The young man continued his cries and entreaties on his knees. At last the merchant flew to him with great tenderness and took hold of his hand. "Rise, young man," said he: "I have but one daughter in the world, for whose happiness I am concerned; I'll give thee my daughter—she must be happy with a fellow of thy virtue; I'll settle upon you all my fortune; I'll release your father out of prison, and make you all happy together." And he was as good as his word.

(*j*) LOVE FOR AN UNNATURAL MOTHER.—The Rev. James Churchill relates, in his "Analecta," that a widowed mother lived to see her youngest son, who was a babe at her husband's death, grow up to manhood in the esteem of all but herself. His temper was mild, and his manners affable; yet it is said that when he had attained the age of twenty, he had never known what the affection of a mother was towards him; nay, nor had ever received a single kind word from her. Blessed, however, by Providence, he flourished greatly in conducting his late father's business, employing a number of men. He took his mother under his own roof, settled upon her a liberal annuity, and studied to make her happy. It was all in vain. She murmured, reproached him, and, on one occasion, rushed into the manufactory and abused him violently before all the men. The people were shocked at her conduct; and the son withdrew, overwhelmed with grief. But worse events were yet in reserve for him. She immediately commenced legal proceedings against him for an assault! The men offered readily to appear on their master's behalf. Their master thanked them, but chose rather to be accounted guilty, and suffer judgment to go by default, than to appear against his own mother: and though he had a fine to pay, this made no alteration in his conduct towards her. About three months after this, she was found dead in her bed, with marks of violence about her body. The coroner's verdict was, wilful murder, against her son. The poor youth was confined some months in prison, among the vilest of characters, to await his trial. His mind was at times distressed to a very great degree; reflecting that his character was ruined, his business nearly lost, and his prospect that of ending his days at a gallows but what harrowed his heart most was, that all this was brought about by his own mother! Still his confidence in that Providence which watches over all, did not entirely fail him. He could exercise hope; and that hope was sustained not in vain. For as the time for his trial drew near, two of the men who had worked in his manufactory were taken up, on the charge of having committed some petty depredations; and, feeling the torments of a conscience burdened with guilt, these wretched creatures voluntarily confessed to a magistrate, that they could no longer endure the thought that so innocent and so worthy a master should lie under the vile imputation; that they were the murderers of Mrs. ——; and that the idea of getting her money and jewels had induced them to strangle her one night while in her sleep! The prison doors were soon thrown open to the suffering young man; joy was diffused through the town; his character shone out with a greater lustre; God prospered his reviving business; his family increased; and his children and grandchildren treated him with the respect and tenderness which he always manifested to his mother.

(*k*) GUSTAVUS AND THE PEASANT GIRL.—Gustavus III., King of Sweden, passing one morning on horseback through a village in the neighborhood of his capital, observed a young peasant girl, of interesting appearance, drawing water at a fountain by the wayside. He went up to her and asked her for a draught. Without delay she lifted up her pitcher, and with artless simplicity put it to the lips of the monarch. Having satisfied his thirst, and courteously thanked his benefactress, he said, "My girl, if you would accompany me to Stockholm, I would endeavor to fix you in a more agreeable situation."

"Ah, sir," replied the girl, "I cannot accept your proposal. I am not anxious to rise above the state of life in which the providence of God has placed me·

but, even if I were, I could not for an instant hesitate."

"And why?" rejoined the king, somewhat surprised.

"Because," answered the girl, coloring, "my mother is poor and sickly, and has no one but me to assist or comfort her under her many afflictions: and no earthly bribe could induce me to leave her, or to neglect the duties which affection requires from me."

"Where is your mother?" asked the monarch.

"In that little cabin," replied the girl, pointing to a wretched hovel beside her.

The king, whose feelings were interested in favor of his companion, went in, and beheld stretched on a bedstead, whose only covering was a little straw, an aged female, weighed down with years, and sinking under infirmities. Moved at the sight, the monarch addressed her: "I am sorry, my poor woman, to find you in so destitute and afflicted a condition."

"Alas, sir," answered the venerable sufferer, "I should be indeed to be pitied, had I not that kind and attentive girl, who labors to support me, and omits nothing she thinks can afford me relief. May a gracious God remember it to her for good," she added, wiping away a tear.

Never, perhaps, was Gustavus more sensible than at that moment, of the pleasure of occupying an exalted station. The gratification arising from the consciousness of having it in his power to assist a suffering fellow-creature, almost overpowered him; and putting a purse into the hand of the young villager, he could only say, "Continue to take care of your mother; I shall soon enable you to do so more effectually. Good-bye, my amiable girl, you may depend on the promise of your king."

On his return to Stockholm, Gustavus settled a pension for life on the mother, with the reversion to her daughter at her death.

(*l*) THE CLERK'S DYING REGRET.—A young man, who was clerk to Mr. Cuthbert, a merchant in the East Indies, being taken very ill, became unusually thoughtful and melancholy. Mr. Cuthbert inquired the cause of his uneasiness. The young man replied, that he was not afraid to die; but he had a mother, and two sisters, in England, to whom he had been accustomed to send £100 every year; and his only regret at dying, was, that they would be left destitute. Mr. Cuthbert begged him to make his mind perfectly easy on that account, as he would take care of his mother and sisters. He was as good as his word, for he instantly went to his attorney, and executed a deed, granting an annuity of £100 a year, in favor of the mother and her two daughters, during their joint lives; and with the benefit of survivorship. He then sent the bond to his clerk, who, clasping it in his hands, exclaimed, "Now I can die in peace; my mother and sisters are saved;" and almost instantly expired.

(*m*) THE INSOLVENT NEGRO.—A negro of one of the kingdoms on the African coast, who had become insolvent, surrendered himself to his creditor, who, according to the established custom of the country, sold him to the Danes. This affected his son so much that he came and reproached his father for not selling his children to pay his debts; and after much entreaty, he prevailed on the captain to accept him, and liberate his father. The son was put in chains, and on the point of sailing to the West Indies; when the circumstance coming to the knowledge of the governor, through the means of Mr. Isert, he sent for the owner of the slaves, paid the money that he had given for the old man, and restored the son to his father.

(*n*) THE INVALID AND HIS DAUGHTERS.—In the year 1773, Peter Burrell, Esq. of Beckenham, in Kent, whose health was rapidly declining, was advised by his physicians to go to Spa for the recovery of his health. His daughters feared that those who had only motives entirely mercenary, would not pay him that attention which he might expect from those who, from duty and affection united, would feel the greatest pleasure in ministering to his ease and comfort; they, therefore, resolved to accompany him. They proved that it was not a spirit of dissipation and gayety that led them to Spa, for they were not to be seen in any of the gay and fashionable circles; they were never out of their father's company, and never stirred from home except to attend him, either to take the air or drink the waters; in a word, they lived a most recluse life in the midst of a town then the resort of the most illustrious and fashionable personages of Europe.

This exemplary attention to their father procured these three amiable sisters the admiration of all the English at Spa, and was the cause of their elevation to that rank in life, to which their merits gave them so just a title. They all were married to noblemen: one to the Earl of Beverly; another to the Duke of Hamilton, and afterwards to the Marquess of Exeter; and a third to the Duke of Northumberland. And it is justice to them to say, that they reflected honor on their rank, rather than derived any from it.

(*o*) THE POOR SERVANT AND HER AFFLICTED PARENTS.—A female servant, who was past the prime of life, in an inferior station, but much respected for her piety and integrity, had saved a little money from her wages, which, as her health was evidently on the decline, would probably soon be required for her own relief. Hearing that her aged parents were, by unavoidable calamity, reduced to extreme indigence, and having reason to fear they were strangers to the comforts of religion, she obtained leave to visit them; shared with them the little she had, and used her utmost endeavors to make them acquainted with the consolations and supports of the gospel, apparently not without success. Being reminded by an acquaintance that, in all probability, she would soon stand in need of what she had saved, she replied, "that she could not think it her duty to see her aged parents pining in want, while she had more than was needful for her present use, and that she trusted God would find her some friend, if he saw good to disable her for service." Having continued to assist her parents till their death, she was soon after deprived of health, so as to become incapable of labor. God, in a wonderful manner, however, raised her up friends where she least expected them. For years she was comfortably supported, and circumstances were at length so ordered, that her maintenance to the end of life was almost as much insured, as any thing can be in this uncertain world.

(*p*) WASHINGTON'S REGARD FOR HIS MOTHER.—General George Washington, when quite young, was about to go to sea as a midshipman; every thing was arranged, the vessel lay opposite his father's house, the little boat had come on shore to take him off, and his whole heart was bent on going. After his trunk had been carried down to the boat, he went to bid his mother farewell, and saw the tears bursting from her eyes. However, he said nothing to her; but he saw that his mother would be distressed if he went, and perhaps never be happy again. He just turned round to the servant and said, "Go and tell them to fetch my trunk back. I will not go away to break my mother's heart." His mother was struck with his decision, and she said to him, "George, God has promised to bless the children that honor their parents, and I believe he will bless you."

10. Affection, Fraternal.

(*a*) TIMOLEON AND HIS WOUNDED BROTHER.—Timoleon, the Corinthian, was a noble pattern of fraternal love. Being in battle with the Argives, and seeing his brother fall by the wounds he had received, he instantly leaped over his dead body, and with his shield protected it from insult and plunder; and though severely wounded in the generous enterprise, he would not on any account retreat to a place of safety, till he had seen the corpse carried off the field by his friends.

(*b*) THE WATER-BEARER AND HIS BROTHER.—As one of the water-bearers at the fountain of the Fauxbourg St. Germain, in Paris, was at his usual labors, in August, 1766, he was taken away by a gentleman in a splendid coach, who proved to be his own brother and who, at the age of three years, had been carried to India, where he made a considerable fortune. On his return to France, he made inquiry respecting his family; and hearing that he had only one brother alive, and that he was in the humble condition of a water-bearer, he sought him out, embraced him with great affection, and brought him to his house, where he gave him bills for upwards of a thousand crowns per annum.

(*c*) THE BROTHERS AND THE SNOW-STORM.—In the year 1804, some young men of the Morayshire and Inverness-shire militia, being quartered at Edinburgh, obtained a short furlough. They were seven in number, two of them being brothers, named Forsythe. They had to walk, in the very depth of winter, one hundred and thirty miles. As they proceeded, they were overtaken by one of those sudden snow-storms which are usual in the mountains. And now the night began to close in around them, while the snow and the wind still grew thicker and stronger. At last, being bewildered by the shade of the evening, which was rendered yet more dismal by the incessant snow-drift, they strayed, as might be expected, from the right path, and exhausted their strength. They could just see one another; but the storm was so violent, they could not converse. Thus struggling onward, and scarcely knowing where they went, one of them sank in a hollow in the rock, and was buried. The others passed on, unconscious of his loss. Soon after, the younger Forsythe also dropped down, being quite spent. His body lay in the pathway of the rest, but being much weakened themselves, they, without helping him, stepped on; all did so but one. This one was the elder Forsythe, who, knowing that he had a brother amongst the party, stooped when he came up to him, and felt his features. Having in this manner assured himself that it was his own brother, he, without hesitation, took him up, and placed him on his back. And now the number rapidly diminished; one after another perished, being frozen to death. Forsythe yet went on, bearing his burden, which neither his fatigue, nor the difficulties of the way, could induce him to cast off As long as he had any strength, he persevered, holding his brother on his back, until at length, his powers giving way before his affection, he sank beneath the weight, and immediately expired. Before, however, he thus died, it appeared that he had succeeded in saving his brother, though he lost himself: for the younger Forsythe had been gradually reanimated by the warmth of his brother's body; and, when he dropped, was so thoroughly aroused, that he was enabled to reach his home, having escaped death by his brother's generous sacrifice of himself, and had the melancholy duty imposed upon him of attending his kind brother's funeral.

11. Affection, Maternal.

(*a*) A MOTHER'S SACRIFICE.—Joanna Martin, the wife of a day-laborer at Huntspill, in the northern part of Somersetshire, England, was left a widow with six young children, and not a shilling in the world to feed them with. The parish officers had no objection to receive the children into the poor-house; but the good mother would not part with them, determining to depend, under Providence, on her activity for their support.

"For many a long month," said she, "have I risen daily at two o'clock in the morning, done what was needful for the children; gone eight or ten miles on foot, to a market, with a large load of pottery-ware on my head, sold it, and returned with the profits before noon."

By this hard labor, in the course of a year, she saved a guinea and a half; when, being under the necessity of leaving her cottage, she determined to erect one for herself. She did much of the labor with her own hands; and told some gentlemen, some years afterwards, "Well, with the assistance of a gracious God, I was able to finish my cottage; which, though I say it myself, is a very tight little place."

She afterwards bought a cart and pony, travelled still to market, brought up her family, and, without either begging, or seeking relief from the parish, obtained a living.

To what labor and privation will pa

ental affection animate the heart! How much may be done by a person under the influence of industry, temperance, and piety!

(*b*) THE FISHERMAN'S WIFE.—One of the small islands in Boston Bay was inhabited by a single poor family. The father was taken suddenly ill. There was no physician. The wife, on whom every labor for the household devolved, was sleepless in care and tenderness by the bedside of her suffering husband. Every remedy in her power to procure was administered, but the disease was acute, and he died. Seven young children mourned around the lifeless corpse. They were the sole beings upon that desolate spot. Did the mother indulge the grief of her spirit, and sit down in despair? No: she entered upon the arduous and sacred duties of her station. She felt that there was no hand to assist her in burying her dead. Providing, as far as possible, for the comfort of her little ones, she put her babe into the arms of the oldest, and charged the two next in age to watch the corpse of their father. She unmoored her husband's fishing boat, which, but two days before he had guided over the seas, to obtain food for his family. She dared not yield to those tender recollections, which might have unnerved her arm. The nearest island was at the distance of three miles. Strong winds lashed the waters to foam. Over the loud billows, that wearied and sorrowful woman rowed, and was preserved. She reached the next island, and obtained necessary aid. With such energy did her duty to her desolate babes inspire her, that the voyage, which depended on her individual effort, was performed in a shorter time than the returning one, when the oars were managed by two men, who went to assist in the last offices to the dead.

(*c*) THESE ARE MY JEWELS.—A Campanian lady, who was very rich, and fond of pomp and show, being on a visit to Cornelia, the illustrious mother of the Gracchi, displayed the diamonds and jewels she possessed, with some ostentation, and then requested Cornelia to permit her to see *her* jewels. This eminent woman dextrously contrived to turn the conversation to another subject, till her sons returned from one of the public schools; when she introduced them, saying, "These are my jewels."

(*d*) THE SLAVE MOTHER CROSSING THE OHIO.—We remember, says a writer in the True American, the story of a cruel master, who, without cause, had determined to sever a slave mother, and her only child. She had been faithful under the very worst usage, and she determined to remain so, until he told her, that on the morrow, her child must be borne to New Orleans to be sold there in the slave mart. It was mid-winter. The earth was frosted with a hard crust, yet at midnight she started for the Ohio, determined, if she could, to live and die with her child. She reached its banks as the pursuers rose on the hill beyond—no boat was near—masses of broken ice were sluggishly drifting along—what was she to do? Trusting to heaven, she put her feet on the treacherous element, and with it bending and breaking beneath her, (spectators on either side expecting to see her and her child sink at every moment,) she boldly pushed on from cake to cake, until she landed safely on the Ohio shore. Five minutes sooner and she must have perished—two minutes later and she would have met with a watery grave, for before she had proceeded twenty steps the ice behind her, close on the Kentucky side, had broken and was scattered ere she reached the mid river. "Thank God you and your child are safe," exclaimed the hard-hearted master, as he saw her land, rejoiced that he had escaped the responsibility of their death. "Brave woman," said a Kentuckian who had wittnessed her escape and met her at the landing, "you have won your freedom and shall have it." The mother and the child were kept together, and liberty and love is now their lot in their humble but happy home. Was there not true heroism here, and is not the scene worthy the sweetest song of poetry or the holiest praise of man?

(*e*) "THE MOTHER'S ROCK."—Humboldt, in his celebrated travels. tells us, that after he had left the abodes of civilization far behind, in the wilds of South America, he found, near the confluence of the Atabapo and Rio Ternie rivers, a high rock—called the "MOTHER'S ROCK." The circumstances which gave this remarkable name to the rock, were these:

In 1799, a Roman Catholic Missionary led his half-civilized Indians out on one of those hostile excursions, which they often made to kidnap slaves for the Christians. They found a Guahiba woman in a solitary hut, with three children—two of whom were infants. The father, with the older children, had gone out to fish, and the mother in vain tried to fly with her babes. She was seized by these man-hunters, hurried into a boat, and carried away to a missionary station at San Fernando.

She was now far from her home; but she had left children there who had gone with their father. She repeatedly took her three babes and tried to escape, but was as often seized, brought back, and most unmercifully beaten with whips. At length the missionary determined to separate this mother from her three children; and for this purpose, sent her in a boat up the Atabapo River, to the missions of the Rio Negro, at a station called *Javita*. Seated in the bow of the boat, the mother knew not where she was going, or what fate awaited her. She was bound solitary and alone in the bow of the long-boat; but she judged from the direction of the sun, that she was going away from her children. By a sudden effort she broke her bonds, plunged into the river, swam to the left bank of the Atabapo, and landed upon a *Rock*.

She was pursued, and at evening retaken, and brought back to the rock, where she was scourged till her blood reddened the rock,—calling for her children! and the rock has ever since been called, "THE MOTHER'S ROCK!" Her hands were then tied upon her back, still bleeding from the manatee thongs of leather. She was then dragged to the mission at Javita, and thrown into a kind of stable. The night was profoundly dark, and it was in the midst of the rainy season. She was now full seventy-five miles from her three children in a straight line. Between her and them lay forests never penetrated by human footsteps; swamps and morasses, and rivers, never crossed by man. But her children are at San Fernando;—and what can quench a mother's love! Though her arms were wounded, she succeeded in biting her bonds with her teeth, and in the morning she was not to be found! At the fourth rising sun she had passed through the forests, swam the rivers, and all bleeding and worn out, was seen hovering round the little cottage in which her babes were sleeping!

She was seized once more; and before her wounds were healed, she was torn again from her children, and sent away to the missions on the upper Oroonoko River, where she drooped, and shortly died, refusing all kinds of nourishment—died of a broken heart at being torn from her children! Such is the history of the "MOTHER'S ROCK!"

This fact might be employed to show the pernicious tendency of slavery, even when engaged in by those who profess Christianity; but it is cited here to show the strength of maternal affection. Wherever you find woman, whether exalted to her place by the Gospel, reduced to a mere animal by Mohammedanism, or sunk still lower by Paganism, you find this same unquenchable love for her children!

12. Affection, Paternal.

(*a*) THE WARRIOR PLAYING WITH HIS CHILDREN.—The warlike Agesilaus was, within the walls of his own house, one of the most tender and playful of men. He used to join with his children in all their innocent gambols, and was once discovered by a friend showing them how to ride upon a hobby-horse. When his friend expressed some surprise at beholding the great Agesilaus so employed, Wait," said the hero, "till you are yourself a father, and if you then blame me, I give you liberty to proclaim this act of mine to all the world."

(*b*) SOCRATES' REPLY TO ALCIBIADES.—Socrates was once

surprised by Alcibiades, playing with his children. The gay patrician rather scoffed at him for joining in such sports, to which the philosopher replied, "You have not such reason as you imagine to laugh so at a father playing with his child. You know nothing of that affection which parents have to their children; restrain your mirth till you have children of your own, when you will, perhaps, be found as ridiculous as I now seem to you to be."

(*c*) THE FATHER'S DILEMMA.—History informs us, that a father went to the agents of a tyrant to endeavor to redeem his two sons, military men, who, with some other captives of war, were appointed to die. He offered as a ransom to surrender his own life and a large sum of money. The soldiers who had it in charge to put them to death, informed him that this equivalent would be accepted for one of his sons, and for one only, because they should be accountable for the execution of two persons: he might therefore choose which he would redeem. Anxious to save even one of them, thus, at the expense of his own life, he yet was utterly unable to decide which should die, and remained in the agony of his dilemma so long, that his sons were both slain.

(*d*) FATHER, WHIP ME BUT DON'T CRY.—A pious father had devoted very great attention to the moral and religious education of his son, who had maintained an unblemished reputation for veracity until the age of fourteen, when he was detected in a deliberate falsehood. The father's grief was great, and he determined to punish the offender severely. He made the subject one of prayer; for it was too important, in his esteem, to be passed over as a common occurrence of the day. He then called his son, and prepared to inflict the punishment. But the fountain of the father's heart was broken up. He wept aloud. For a moment the lad seemed confused. He saw the struggle between love and justice in his parent's bosom, and broke out with all his usual ingenuousness, "Father, father, whip me as much as you please; but don't cry." The point was gained. The father saw that the lad's character was sensibly affected by this incident. He grew up, and became one of the most distinguished Christians of America.

AFFLICTION.

13. Benefits of Affliction.

(*a*) CECIL AND THE BOOKSELLER.—Many years ago, a pious and devoted clergyman entered the shop of a prosperous London bookseller, with whom he was on terms of intimate and Christian friendship. He inquired for his friend, and when told that he was at home, but particularly engaged, sent a messenger to him to the effect that he wanted an interview with him, if but for a few minutes. This message being delivered, the clergyman was invited to walk up stairs, into the bookseller's sitting room. He entered the room, and found his friend sitting by his child's cot. The child was dying, but, with affection strong in death, it had clasped its father's hand, and was holding it with a convulsive grasp.

"You are a father," said the afflicted parent, "or I should not have allowed you to witness such a scene."

"Thank God, thank God," fervently exclaimed the minister, as he instinctively comprehended at a glance the situation of his friend: "thank God. He has not forgotten you! I have been much troubled on your account, my dear sir. I have thought much about you lately. I have been much afraid for you. Things have gone on so well with you for so long a time, you have been so prosperous, that I have been almost afraid that God had forgotten you. But I said to myself, surely God will not forsake such a man as this; will not suffer him to go on in prosperity, without some check, some reverse! And I see he has not. No; God has not forgotten you."

These were the sentiments of Richard Cecil on the design of affliction; and his friend, Thomas Williams, thankfully and joyfully responded to them. Within three weeks of his death, he related the incident, as it is related here, and the feeling of his heart was, "He hath done all things well."

(*b*) MR. DOD AND HIS PERSECUTIONS.—While the eminent Puritan minister, Mr. Dod, resided at Hanwell, (Eng.) he was the subject of much persecution and sorrow. Going once to see his relative, the Rev. Mr. Greenham, of Dry-Drayton, and lamenting the state of his mind to him, the worthy minister replied, "Son, son, when affliction lieth heavy, sin lieth light." This saying conveyed great comfort to Mr. Dod, who rejoiced that God could make affliction the means of his sanctification; and used afterwards to say, that, "sanctified afflictions are spiritual promotions."

(*c*) NOW HAVE I KEPT THY WORD.—Sarah Howard, a poor old widow who had been bedridden fourteen years, when visited by her minister, thus spoke of her afflictions:—"I can set to my seal, that 'the Lord has chastened me sore, but he hath not given me over unto death,' Psalm cxviii. 19. I have been chastened in my person, and am quite helpless, by long and severe illness; I have been chastened in my circumstances ever since I was left a widow; yes, I know what oppressing a widow, what bad debts, and hard creditors are: I have been chastened in my family, by a son, whom I was dotingly fond of, running away and going to sea. Besides all these, I have been chastened in mind, 'walking in darkness and having no light:' yet after all, I trust I can say with David, 'Before I was afflicted I went astray, but now have I kept thy word.' And I hope I can say that I am now returned to the Shepherd and Bishop of souls," 1 Pet. ii. 25.

(*d*) SAVED BY A DISEASED LIMB.—A young man, who had been long confined with a diseased limb, and was near his dissolution, was attended by a friend, who requested that the wound might be uncovered. When this was done, "There," said the young man, 'there it is, and a precious treasure it has beer to me; it saved me from the folly and vanity of youth; it made me cleave to God as my only portion, and to eternal glory as my only hope: and I think it has now brought me very near to my Father's house."

(*e*) THE SICK CHRISTIAN USEFUL.—Ann Meiglo, a poor distressed woman in the parish of Portmoak, when visited by Mr. Ebenezer Erskine, said to him, "O, sir, I am just lying here a poor useless creature." "Think you?" said he. "I think, sir, what is true, if I were away to heaven, I would be of some use to glorify God without sin."—"Indeed, Annie," said Mr. Erskine, "I think you are glorifying God by your resignation and submission to his will, and that in the face of many difficulties and under many distresses. In heaven the saints have no burdens to groan under; your praises, burdened as you are, are more wonderful to me, and I trust acceptable to God."

(*f*) OWEN ON FORGIVENESS.—The orign of Dr. Owen's great practical work on the Forgiveness of Sin, or Psalm 130, was related by the doctor in the following circumstances:

A young man, who afterwards became a minister, being under serious impressions, came to him for counsel. In the course of conversation the doctor asked, "Pray, in what manner do you think to go to God?" "Through the Mediator, sir," said the young man. To which Dr. Owen replied, "That is easily said; but it is another thing to go to God through the Mediator than what many who use the expression are aware of. I myself preached some years when I had but very little if any experimental acquaintance with access to God through Christ, until the Lord was pleased to visit me with sore affliction, by which I was brought to the mouth of the grave, and under which my soul was oppressed with horror and darkness. But God graciously relieved my spirit by a powerful application of Psalm cxxx. 4, 'There is forgiveness with thee that thou mayest be feared;' from whence I received special instruction, peace and comfort in drawing near to God through the Mediator, and I preached thereupon after my recovery."

None who seriously and prayerfully read this treatise will fail to discover the grounds and the appropriateness of the above appeal to an inquiring youth, the rich sources from which the author has drawn divine instruction, and its adaptation to the wants of every perishing soul.

(*g*) THE STUDENT'S SICKNESS.—A New England divine, who was preaching on the benefit derived from affliction, said: I once knew a young man, who was a student in one of our universities, who, by reading Dr. Combe's works and others, had become very skeptical on some important points—the doctrine of prayer, total depravity, regeneration, and the special influences of the Holy Spirit. Though he professed religion and was studying for the ministry, he had lost all religious enjoyment, and was fast going down an inclined plane into the abyss of infidelity. During a vacation in midwinter, he was travelling on business among the Germans in the interior of Pennsylvania, when he was prostrated on his bed with a dangerous disease—hundreds of miles from home, "a stranger in a strange land." When he began to think of dying, he found himself all unprepared. His new sentiments hovered like dismal clouds around his sick-bed, that not a star of hope shone through. There was little time for logic then: but one species of short-hand logic swept away his skeptical notions like chaff. He reasoned from effect to cause. "Embracing these new sentiments has evidently brought my mind into this wretched condition; and as the fruit is bad, the tree must be bad also. 'He that followeth me,' says Christ, 'shall not walk in darkness;' therefore, as I am walking in darkness, it must be because I have been led astray from him. These new opinions must, therefore, be erroneous, and I will renounce them forever, embrace, in all humility and simplicity, the truths of the Gospel, as I embraced them at the first." Right speedily did he put his resolve into action; and he soon found his way back to the fold of Christ, to the Shepherd and Bishop of souls. He recovered from his sickness and returned home, rejoicing to tell his friends what God had done for his soul. And that young man, my hearers, is preaching to you to-day! I have many blessings for which to thank God, for He has strown my way with the gifts of His providence; but for the blessing of that afflicting illness, I sometimes feel as if I ought to praise and thank Him most. And if I am ever so happy as to get home to heaven, I know I shall remember that affliction with gratitude still! It will be a theme on which I shall love to linger, one which shall prompt many anthems of my rejoicing there.

(*h*) THE BACKSLIDER BEREAVED AND RESTORED.—A young lady, who belonged to a church in the city of New-York, married a young man who was not a Christian. He was a merchant, engaged in a lucrative business, and the golden stream of wealth flowed in upon him till he had amassed a large fortune. He accordingly retired from business and went into the country. He purchased a splendid residence; fine trees waved their luxuriant foliage around it; here was a lake filled with fish, and there a garden full of rare shrubbery and flowers. Their house was fashionably and expensively furnished; and they seemed to possess all of earth that mortal could desire. Thus prospered, and plied with an interchange of civilities among her gay and fashionable neighbors, the piety of the lady declined, and her heart became wedded to the world. And it is not to be wondered at, that her three children, as they grew up, imbibed her spirit and copied her example.

"A severe disease," it is said, "demands a severe remedy," and that God soon applied. One morning intelligence came that her little son had fallen into the fish-lake and was drowned. The mother's heart was pierced with the affliction, and she wept and murmured against the providence of God. Soon after, her only daughter, a blooming girl of sixteen, was taken sick of a fever and died. It seemed then as if the mother's heart would have broken. But this new stroke of the rod of a chastening Father seemed but to increase her displeasure against his will.

The only remaining child, her oldest son, who had come home from college to attend his sister's funeral, went out into the fields soon after, for the purpose of hunting. In getting over a fence, he put his gun over first to assist himself in springing to the ground, when it accidentally discharged itself and killed him! What then were that mother's feelings? In the extravagance of her grief, she fell down, tore her hair, and raved like a maniac against the providence of God. The father, whose grief was already almost insupportable, when he looked upon the shocking spectacle and heard her frenzied ravings, could endure his misery no longer. The iron entered into his soul, and he fell a speedy victim to his accumulated afflictions. From the wife and mother her husband and all her children were now taken away. Reason returned, and she was led to reflection. She saw her dreadful backslidings, her pride, her rebellion; and she wept with the tears of a deep repentance. Peace was restored to her soul. Then would she lift her hands to heaven, exclaiming, "I thank thee, O Father! The Lord hath given, the Lord hath taken away, and blessed be the name of the Lord." Thus did her afflictions yield the peaceable fruit of righteousness, and her heavenly Father chasten her, "not for His pleasure, but for her profit, that she might become partaker of His holiness."

(*i*) SAVED FROM A ROBBER BY RAIN.—A merchant was one day returning from market. He was on horseback, and behind him was a valise filled with money. The rain fell with violence, and the good old man was wet to his skin. At this he was vexed, and murmured because God had given him such bad weather for his journey.

He soon reached the borders of a thick forest. What was his terror on beholding on one side of the road a robber, with levelled gun, aiming at him and attempting to fire! But the powder being wet by the rain, the gun did not go off, and the merchant, giving spurs to his horse, fortunately had time to escape.

As soon as he found himself safe, he said to himself: "How wrong was I, not to endure the rain patiently as sent by Providence. If the weather had been dry and fair, I should not, probably, have been alive at this hour, and my little children would have expected my return in vain. The rain which caused me to murmur, came at a fortunate moment, to save my life and preserve my property." And thus it is with a multitude of our afflictions; by causing us slight and short sufferings, they preserve us from others far greater, and of longer duration.

(*j*) A CHAIN OF CALAMITIES.—A Christian whom God had prospered in his outward estate, and who lived in ease and plenty on his farm, suffered the world to encroach so much upon his affections, as sensibly to diminish the ardor of his piety. The disease was dangerous, and the Lord adopted severe measures for its cure. First, his wife was removed by death; but he still remained worldly-minded. Then a beloved son; but, although the remedy operated favorably, it did not effect a cure. Then his crops failed and his cattle died; still his grasp on the world was not unloosed. Then God touched his person, and brought on him a lingering, fatal disease; the world, however, occupied still too much of his thoughts. His house finally took fire; and as he was carried out of the burning building, he exclaimed: "Blessed be God, I am cured at last." He shortly after died happy in the anticipation of a heavenly inheritance.

(*k*) DIVINITY TAUGHT BY AFFLICTION.—A minister was recovering of a dangerous illness, when one of his friends addressed him thus: "Sir, though God seems to be bringing you up from the gates of death, yet it will he a long time before you will sufficiently retrieve your strength, and regain vigor enough of mind to preach as usual." The good man answered:—"You are mistaken, my friend; for this six weeks' illness has taught me more divinity than all my past studies and all my ten years' ministry put together."

(*l*) EFFECT OF ILLNESS ON DR. CHANDLER.—It used to be said of Dr. Chandler, that, after an illness, he always preached in a more evangeli cal strain than usual. A gentleman who occasionally heard him said to one of his constant auditors: "Pray, has not the doctor been ill lately?" "Why do you think so?" "Because the sermon was more evangelical than he usually preaches when he is in full health."

(*m*) GOD MEANT IT FOR GOOD.—A few years since, says a writer in the Pastor's Journal, I was engaged in a wholesale mercantile business in the city of New-York; but ill health and other circumstances compelled me to close it and remove to the country. My young men were most of them from pious families; some were warm-hearted Christians, and all of them succeeded in finding eligible situations but one. S. was my youngest clerk; his talents were respectable; his conduct, as far as I could judge, was irreproachable; but my best efforts, and those of his friends, could not secure him a situation. After months spent in vain endeavors to find an opening in the business of his choice, and a year occupied on a foreign voyage without success, he returned to the country and engaged reluctantly in a mechanical business, which his father followed, near the place where I had settled. I saw him but seldom; but when I met him as his friend, I was treated with marked coldness. I was at a loss to account for it, and at length demanded an explanation, when I found the whole family considered me culpably to blame in not procuring him a situation in New-York, after I had no longer occasion for his services. It was indeed a mystery even to myself, that the path to manhood chosen by S. and his friends, should be so hedged up as to compel him to walk in another. S. however continued his mechanical pursuits, and, in the providence of God, was directed to the neighborhood of a protracted meeting. He was the child of many prayers, and had more than once lived through an awakening unchanged, though not unaffected. He was now drawn, by an impulse he could not resist, to attend this meeting, feeling that it might be the last strivings of the Spirit. With trembling he took his place on the anxious seat, and, overwhelmed with emotion, he retired from the meeting to a field, where he gave himself away to his Savior, and the Spirit spake peace to his soul. It was but a few days after this happy event, S. returned to our village, (where his parents still reside,) and the humble, meek, and gentle air which his manly countenance had assumed, in place of the haughty, discontented form, was apparent to every one. I was confined to my house by indisposition, and was delighted to welcome him who had scarcely entered my dwelling since his return from the city. He modestly gave me an account of the change in his feelings and happiness, in presence of some members of my family, and solicited a private interview. On retiring with him, he said to me, with tears in his eyes: "*My mind has been sorely troubled by the recollection of some things I did in your store. I was tempted to take sundry small articles, for my own use, without your knowledge or consent, amounting, I should think, to five dollars, and I cannot rest until I have paid you for them!!*" A crowd of reflections rushed into my mind. I felt overwhelmed for a moment with a sense of the goodness of God, in so counteracting all his plans as to save him from the vortex which was opening before him. He had begun to rob his employer, and, as the progress in vice is rapid downward, had not a kind Providence interposed, S. would, in all probability, have become, ere this, a tenant of the state prison, and brought down the gray hairs of his parents with sorrow to the grave. I pointed out to him, as I trust, faithfully and profitably, the finger of God in his rescue, and encouraged him to persevere unto the end. It is now nearly two years since this interview, and S. has continued to give evidence of the sincerity of the change, and bids fair to become an ornament to society and a pillar in the church of Christ.

14. Gratitude for Affliction.

(*a*) GRATITUDE FOR SLAVERY.—In the Southern section of the United States, an African slave, whose name was Jenny, was observed to fail in her labor, and indications of some distress were visible in her countenance. She was asked for the cause; she replied, "Jenny's heart is sick." She was sent from the field, to the house, to obtain relief; but none was gained. She spent her days in silence · only saying, "Jenny's heart is sick." One day she met her mistress, who was very anxious for her case, in the yard, and cried out, "O mistress, Jenny is going to die, and be lost. Who will take care of Jenny's baby when she is gone?" Such was her distress at that moment, that she sunk under its weight motionless at her mistress's feet, who had her taken kindly to her house, and attended with care. Thus she continued for some days, scarcely able to walk. But one day, having got a short distance into a forest, she there cried to God in her distress, and God graciously heard her mourning voice, and poured into her sick heart the balm of Gilead, which gave her immediate relief. On this occasion, when the light broke in on her afflicted soul, and the pardoning love of God in Christ was seen by faith, she said, "All the trees around cry, Glory! and all the angels cry, Glory! and Jenny cry Glory, too!" She now said, when Jenny was in her native country, she had no God, she knew no God! But in America, Jenny has learned there is a God, and that he is hers. In Africa, Jenny had no Jesus, she had no one to tell her of Jesus. But she thanks God that she was ever brought to America to hear of a Savior. In Africa, Jenny was ignorant of sin, and the wrath of God; but in this favored land she has been made acquainted with her sinful and dangerous state, and the way of salvation through a precious Redeemer. Now Jenny lived, and sung, and looked forward to the hope of glory, as the end of sorrows, and certain reward of all who, through faith and patience, wait for the coming of our Lord Jesus unto eternal life. Happy affliction! Blessed African!

(*b*) BLINDNESS A BLESSING.—Mary had learned to read, and at an early age took great delight in her Bible; but before she was eighteen years old, her sight began to fail her, and in a very short time she became totally blind This, it will be thought, must have been a severe trial, at such an age, under any circumstances, but more especially to one who had always derived her chief pleasure and enjoyment from her little stock of books. Mary, however, had learned from her Bible, that "God doth not afflict willingly, nor grieve the children of men;" and she felt assured that he would, in some way or other, make this affliction tend to her eternal good. "Many people pity me," she said one day, to a lady who was talking with her, "and say, it is hard to be blind; but I don't think it at all hard. Perhaps, if I had not lost my sight, I should have grown proud. I was very fond of reading, and I should perhaps have thought too much of knowledge; I might have been puffed up, and therefore the temptation was mercifully taken from me. The Lord knew that I needed some trial, and he chose this for me. I am glad he did, for I should not have known what to have chosen for myself; I am sure I should not have chosen this. What, be blind! No; for then I should not be able to read, or to go about. I should not have chosen any thing that was painful. I sometimes think," she continued, "how many trials this keeps me from, which I should not have known how to bear!"

(*c*) THANKFUL FOR BLINDNESS.—A blind boy, who belonged to the Institution in Dublin, when dying, assured a correspondent of the Tract Magazine that he considered it as one of the greatest mercies of Heaven that he had been deprived of his sight; because this was the means the Lord employed to bring him under the sound of the gospel, which was now the joy and rejoicing of his soul. So much wisdom and truth is there in the beautiful language of the poet:—

> "Good, when he gives, supremely good,
> Nor less when he denies;
> E'en crosses, from his sovereign hand,
> Are blessings in disguise."

(*d*) MARTIN LUTHER'S WILL.—In the last will and testament of this eminent reformer occurs the following remarkable passage:—"Lord God, *I thank thee, that thou hast been pleased to make me a poor and indigent man upon earth.* I have neither house, nor land, nor money, to leave behind me. Thou hast given me wife and children, whom I now restore to thee. Lord, nourish, teach, and preserve them, as thou hast me."

(*e*) A TOKEN OF GOD'S FAVOR.—Mr. Newton had a very happy talent of administering reproof. Hearing that a person, in whose welfare he was greatly interested, had met with peculiar success in business, and was deeply immersed in worldly engagements, the first time he called on him, which was usually once a month, he took him by the hand, and drawing him on one side, into the counting-house, told him his apprehensions of his spiritual welfare. His friend, without making any reply, called down his partner in life, who came with her eyes suffused with tears, and unable to speak. Inquiring the cause, he was told she had just been sent for to one of her children, that was out at nurse, and supposed to be in dying circumstances. Clasping her hands immediately in his, Mr. N. cried, "God be thanked, he has not forsaken you! I do not wish your babe to suffer, but I am happy to find he gives you this token of his favor."

(*f*) KISSING THE OPPRESSOR'S HANDS.—It is related of one, who, under great severity, had fled from the worst of masters to the best, (I mean he had sought rest in the bosom of Jesus Christ, the common friend of the weary and the heavy laden,) that he was so impressed with a sense of the benefit he had derived from his afflictions, that lying on his death-bed and seeing his master stand by, he eagerly caught the hands of his oppressor, and kissing them, said, "These hands have brought me to heaven." Thus many have had reason to bless God for afflictions, as being the instruments in his hands of promoting the welfare of their immortal souls.

(*g*) THE ROAD TO HEAVEN.—Mr. Benn, of Highgate, had long been the subject of a severe affliction, which at length terminated his valuable life, before he had, to human appearance, reached its meridian. The evening before his departure, he desired all his children to come into his chamber; and, placing them around his dying bed, thus addressed them: "You all know that I am soon going to be removed from this world to a better; and I trust that you are walking the same road, and will soon follow me."

To his eldest son he observed, "When you go into the world, and are exposed to persons who, perhaps, will ridicule the Savior's name and the Bible, do not listen to them. Seek that society which will help you to practise your Bible; this book will provide comfort for you when friends forsake you.—Every other comfort in this world has its drawback, and is transitory. When you are in pain or suffering, write upon it, 'The road to Heaven.'"

AGED, THE.

15. Conversion of the Aged.

(*a*) THE YOUNG CONVERT AND HIS AGED MOTHER.—At a village, in the Hastings circuit, (says the Wesleyan Methodist Magazine,) where the Gospel was introduced by the Methodist preachers, a poor laboring man was induced to hear the Gospel. By the blessing of God it proved effectual to his salvation. Having felt the power of divine grace himself, he was anxiously concerned for the spiritual welfare of others. One of the first objects of his solicitude, was his *mother*. She was upwards of ninety years of age; deaf, dim-sighted, and very infirm; totally in the dark as to the nature of true religion, and altogether unconcerned about her best interests. The preaching was removed to her son's cottage, which was situated about a mile from his mother's residence; he wished to bring her under the sound of the Gospel; but *her* infirmities, and *his* poverty, presented considerable difficul ties. She could not walk;—he had no conveyance, and could not afford to hire one. His intense desire for her salvation, however, surmounted all hindrances. He borrowed a cart; put himself in the place of a horse; and regularly *drew* her to his house on the Sabbath morning, and back again to her home in the evening, when the weather would permit. Being thus brought to hear the word of reconciliation, divine light shone into her mind; her conscience was awakened, after a slumber of ninety years; and she began to "call upon the name of the Lord." The God of all grace hearkened to her cry; lifted upon her the light of his countenance; and made her happy in the enjoyment of his salvation. It is a singular fact, that the great change wrought in her mind was the occasion of producing such a change in her appearance, that she looked several years younger than she did a few months before.

(*b*) CONVERTED AT FOURSCORE.—The son of a wealthy grazier, in Rutlandshire, England, was providentially led to a place of worship, where he was deeply and savingly impressed with the love of God. Afterwards he became a frequent attendant, though living at the distance of twenty miles. The old man, his father, just then fourscore, perceived the change which had taken place in his son, who, on inquiry, told him all the circumstances, and the signal blessings which had attended the preaching he had heard. "Son," said the old man, "I wish I could hear the man myself; do you think I can ride as far?" "Father," said he, "if you will go to cousin W.'s over-night, I think you could." The horses were saddled, and off went father and son on Saturday night. On Sunday they both went to church, and the Lord blessed the very first discourse to the old man's heart, and from that day he began to confess Jesus Christ as his strength and Redeemer. During two summers he attended at the same place of worship; but infirmities confining him to his bed, he requested the clergyman to visit him at his own house, where he found him with tears running down his cheeks, whilst he spoke of the hardness of his heart, though it seemed tender as that of a little child. "Mr. C.," said the minister, "how old are you?" "Little more," said he, "than two years old; for I can only reckon my life from the time I knew the Lord Jesus; the fourscore years before were but a life of death." At eighty-four he departed, full of faith and hope, and entered, at the eleventh hour, into the joy of his Lord.

(*c*) CONVERSION OF THE AGED RARE.—In a sermon to young men, delivered at the request of the Philadelphia Institute, Dr. Bedell said: "I have now been nearly twenty years in the ministry of the gospel, and I here publicly state to you, that I do not believe I could enumerate three persons, over fifty years of age, whom I have ever heard ask the solemn and eternally momentous question, 'What shall I do to be saved?'"

16. Reverence for the Aged.

(*a*) THE CHILD'S INQUIRY.—A certain farmer in Connecticut, possessing a small estate, was persuaded by his only son, (who was married and lived with his father,) to give him a deed of the property. It was accordingly executed. Soon the father began to find himself neglected; next removed from the common table, to a block in the chimney corner, to take the morsel of food reluctantly given him. At last the unnatural son resolved one day, to try to break the afflicted heart of his sire. He procured a block and began to hollow it. While at work, he was questioned by one of his own children, what he was doing. "I am making a trough for your grandfather to eat out of," was the reply. "Ah," says the child, "and when you are as old as grandfather, shall I have to make a trough for you to eat out of?" The instrument he was using fell from his hand. The block was cast on the fire; the old man's forgiveness asked, and he was restored to the situation to which his age and worth entitled him.

(*b*) THE OLD WOMAN'S BLESSING.—A gentleman was once passing through a village, and happened to see a poor, feeble old woman let her stick fall, and stand a moment in perplexity, not knowing whether she dared to stoop to pick it up or attempt to reach her home without it. Just by the spot where the accident happened, a group of boys were playing at marbles; some of them took no notice, others rudely marked the poor old woman's distress; but one kind-hearted lad threw down his marbles, ran to her assistance, and helped her into her house. She thanked him, and said, "God Almighty's blessing be upon you, for your kindness to a poor old woman!" The gentleman saw and heard the whole, and made inquiry after the lad, in whom he felt deeply interested. He found that he was already in the Sunday school, and, in all probability, had there learnt the Scriptures, that inculcate reverence to the aged. From that time he had him instructed in writing and accounts at an evening school; when old enough, he assisted in apprenticing him, and in course of time had the satisfaction of seeing him a respectable and flourishing tradesman.

(*c*) THE UNKIND SON REBUKED.—There was once a man who had an only son, to whom he was very kind, and gave every thing that he had. When his son grew up and got a house, he was very unkind to his poor old father, whom he refused to support, and turned out of the house. The old man said to his grandson, "Go and fetch the covering from my bed, that I may go and sit by the way-side and beg." The child burst into tears, and ran for the covering. He met his father, to whom he said, "I am going to fetch the rug from my grandfather's bed, that he may wrap it round him and go a-begging!" Tommy went for the rug, and brought it to his father, and said to him, "Pray, father, cut it in two, the half of it will be large enough for grandfather, and perhaps you may want the other half when I grow a man and turn you out of doors." The words of the child struck him so forcibly, that he immediately ran to his father, and asked forgiveness, and was very kind to him till he died.

(*d*) THE RUSSIAN PRINCESS.—A Russian princess of great beauty, in company with her father, and a young French marquis, visited a celebrated Swiss doctor of the eighteenth century, Michael Scuppack; when the marquis began to pass one of his jokes upon the long white beard of one of the doctor's neighbors who was present. He offered to bet twelve louis d'ors that no lady present would dare to kiss the dirty old fellow! The Russian princess ordered her attendant to bring a plate, and deposited twelve louis d'ors, and sent it to the marquis, who was too polite to decline his stake.

The fair Russian then approached the peasant, saying, "Permit me, venerable father, to salute you after the manner of my country," and embracing, gave him a kiss. She then presented him the gold which was on the plate, saying, "Take this as a remembrance of me, and as a sign that the Russian girls think it their duty to honor old age."

17. AGENTS OF BENEVOLENT SOCIETIES.

(*a*) THE SCOFFER CONFOUNDED. — When the late Rev. Joseph Hughes, A. M., was once travelling in the service of the Bible Society, he found by his side, upon the coach, a grave and respectable looking person. In conversing on topics of general attention, they soon came to the Bible Society. His companion launched forth, in vituperative terms, on its utopian character, and especially on its lavish expenditure; noticing, in a marked way, the needless and extravagant travelling expenses of its vaunted *secretaries*, as well as their enormous salaries. No one, from Mr. Hughes's countenance and manner, could have conjectured that he was a party concerned. "But what," he mildly expostulated, "would be your conclusion, were you informed that their services were gratuitous; and that, with a view of curtailing as much as possible the expense of travelling, they usually, even in very inclement seasons, fix on the outside, as," he added, "one of them is now doing before your eyes?" Need it be added, that both the fact and the tone in which it was announced, with the friendly conversation that ensued, converted an enemy into a friend?

(*b*) ROBERT HALL AS AN AGENT.—The late Rev. Robert Hall of Bristol was much grieved with the want of economy in managing the finances of some of our public institutions. "When you consider, sir," said he, "the sources from which these monies are derived, and the objects to which they are intended to be appropriated, there ought to be no improvident expenditure of any kind. I know Mr. —— who is employed in travelling and collecting for the Bible Society; he puts up at the principal inn in the place where he happens to visit, and rather than exert himself to rise early and travel in the stage coach, I have heard that he takes a post-chaise at the expense of the society. These things ought not to be countenanced. I invariably endeavor to travel on such occasions, sir, outside of the coach, and when, from indisposition, I am compelled to hire a post-chaise, I pay the extra expense out of my own pocket."

18. AMBITION.

(*a*) THE WRESTLER'S REFLECTION.—Philip, king of Macedon, as he was wrestling at the Olympic games, fell down in the sand; and when he rose again, observing the print of his body in the sand, cried out, "O how little a parcel of earth will hold *us*, when we are dead, who are ambitiously seeking after the whole world whilst we are living!"

(*b*) PYRRHUS AND THE PHILOSOPHER.—When Pyrrhus, king of Epirus, was making great preparations for his intended expedition into Italy, Cineas, the philosopher, took a favorable opportunity of addressing him thus:—"The Romans, sir, are reported to be a warlike and victorious people; but if God permit us to overcome them, what use shall we make of the victory?" "Thou askest," said Pyrrhus, "a thing that is self-evident. The Romans once conquered, no city will resist us; we shall then be masters of all Italy." Cineas added, "And having subdued Italy, what shall we do next?" Pyrrhus, not yet aware of his intentions, replied, "Sicily next stretches out her arms to receive us." "That is very probable," said Cineas, "but will the possession of Sicily put an end to the war?" "God grant us success in that," answered Pyrrhus, "and we shall make these only the forerunners of greater things, for then Lybia and Carthage will soon be ours: and these things being completed, none of our enemies can offer any farther resistance." "Very true," added Cineas, "for then we may easily regain Macedon, and make an absolute conquest of Greece; and, when all these are in our possession, what shall we do then?" Pyrrhus, smiling, answered, "Why then, my dear friend, we will live at our ease, drink all day long, and amuse ourselves with cheerful conversation." "Well, sir," said Cineas, "and why may we not do all this now, and without the labor and hazard of an enterprise so laborious and uncertain?" Pyrrhus, however, unwilling to take the advice of the philosopher, ardently engaged in these ambitious pursuits, and at last perished in them.

(*c*) HIGH HOPES OF BONAPARTE.—Bonaparte, referring to the siege of Acre, says: "I see that this paltry town has cost me many men, and occupies much time; but things have gone too far not to risk a last effort. If we succeed, it is to be hoped we shall find in that place the treasures of the pasha, and arms for three hundred thousand men. I will raise and arm the whole of Syria, which is already greatly exasperated by the cruelty of Djezzar, for whose fall you have seen the people supplicate Heaven at every assault. I advance upon Damascus and Aleppo; I recruit my army by marching into every country where discontent prevails; I announce to the people the abolition of slavery, and of the tyrannical government of the pashas; I arrive at Constantinople with armed masses; I overturn the dominion of the Mussulman; I found in the East a new and mighty empire, which shall fix my position with posterity; and perhaps I return to Paris by Adrianople or Vienna, having annihilated the house of Austria." What a wide difference between what he then anticipated and what he subsequently experienced!

(*d*) NAPOLEON AND THE PEASANT BOY.—When Napoleon returned to his palace, immediately after his defeat at Waterloo, he continued many hours without taking any refreshment. One of the grooms of the chamber ventured to serve up some coffee, in his cabinet, by the hands of a child, whom Napoleon had occasionally distinguished by his notice. The emperor sat motionless, with his hands spread over his eyes. The page stood patiently before him, gazing with infantine curiosity on an image which presented so strong a contrast to his own figure of simplicity and peace; at last the little attendant presented his tray, exclaiming, in the familiarity of an age which knows so little distinctions, "Eat, sire; it will do you good." The emperor looked at him, and asked, "Do you not belong to Gonesse?" (a village near Paris.)

"No, sire, I come from Pierrefite."

"Where your parents have a cottage and some acres of land?"

"Yes, sire." "There is happiness," replied the man who was still the emperor of France and king of Italy.

(*e*) NAPOLEON AND THE CHURCH CLOCK.—It is said of Napoleon Bonaparte, that at that period of his life, when the consequences of his infatuated conduct had fully developed themselves in unforeseen reverses, being driven to the necessity of defending himself within his own kingdom with the shattered remnant of his army, he had taken up a position at Brienne, the very spot where he had received the rudiments of his education, when, unexpectedly, and while he was anxiously employed in a practical application of those military principles which first exercised the energies of his young mind in the college of Brienne, his attention was arrested by the sound of the church clock. The pomp of his imperial court, and even the glories of Marengo and of Austerlitz, faded for a moment from his regard, and almost from his recollection. Fixed for a while to the spot on which he stood, in motionless attention to the well-known sound, he at length gave utterance to his feelings; and condemned the tenor of all his subsequent life, by confessing that the hours, then brought back to his recollection, were happier than any he had experienced throughout the whole course of his tempestuous career.

(*f*) THE ACCUSER'S FALL.—One of Artaxerxes' favorites, ambitious of getting a place possessed by one of the king's best officers, endeavored to make the king suspect that officer's fidelity; and to that end, sent information to court full of calumnies against him, persuading himself that the king, from the great credit he had with his majesty, would believe the thing upon his bare word, without further examination. Such is the general character of calumniators. The officer was imprisoned; but he desired of the king before he was condemned, that his cause might be heard, and his accusers ordered to produce their evidence against him. The king did so; and as there was no proof of his guilt but the letters which his enemy had written against him, he was cleared, and his innocence fully confirmed by the three commissioners who sat upon his trial. All the king's indignation fell upon the perfidious accuser, who had thus attempted to abuse the confidence and favor of his royal master.

(*g*) A YOUNG LAWYER'S EXPERIENCE.—A correspondent of the New-York Evangelist, says: I was acquainted with a young man who knew what ambition is in all its madness. He sought to be great, and he sought for nothing else. For years he thought and felt and dreamed about nothing else. For that he labored and *prayed:* yes, though an infidel, he believed in the existence of a God, and he used to pray to him that he would grant him the object of his desires. Often at midnight, when the world was lost in sleep, he would pause from those mental labors which were destroying the energies of his youth and wasting away his life, and pray that God would give him intellectual powers—that he would give him might of mind which would enable him to move and shake the world. He used to tell God that he might deny him any thing else if he would grant him only this. And he was willing to pay any price for it; he was willing to do any thing, or suffer any thing, or sacrifice any thing in order to gain it. And he would promise if God would give him power of intellect that he would exercise it on the side of right and in opposition to wrong. With such feelings he labored ten long years, and oh, how he labored! He toiled night and day. For weeks he would not retire to rest till three or four o'clock in the morning, and then not to sleep. His mind and nervous system were in such a state that he could not sleep. He would lay two or three hours in a dreaming, half-conscious state, and then he would rise and commence his work again. And lest the appetites and indolence of the body might hinder him in his work if he should live with other people, and live as they did, he lived alone, upon bread and water, and had no bed in his room; only a blanket in which he would wrap himself and lie down upon the floor, with a large book under his head for a pillow. He hated every thing calculated to draw him a moment from his studies. Even the kind voice of his poor old mother, entreating him with tears to take some rest or a little food, he hated, and he would scowl upon her and turn madly away.

Thus he lived for many years until a mighty change came over him. In a book he was one day reading, occurred these words: "When all is gained, how little then is won! And yet to gain that little how much is lost!" The words arrested his attention; they sunk deep into his heart, like the voice of a spirit! The whole truth flashed like lightning across his soul. He now beheld the fame he had toiled for, as ABSOLUTELY WORTHLESS. "When all is gained, how little then is won!" said he. "Yes, how little! O, what is it? It is nothing. Fame, O, *what is it?* The breath of *fools* and *devils*. *That* is the object on which I have set my whole heart, and for which I have been laboring. *When all is gained, how little then is won! And yet to gain that little how much is lost!* Yes, HOW MUCH IS LOST! O, how I have been laboring and suffering for it; I have given *all* for it; all of this world, and all of the next."

His whole frame shook under the emotions such thoughts awakened—his hard heart broke, and he *wept!* Yes, he who from childhood up had never shed a tear. He wept burning tears of agony—wept as a man, perhaps, never weeps but once. Rage succeeded to sorrow. "Oh, what a fool I have been," said he; "what a wretched fool—the fool of fools—the greatest fool in the world!" He looked round upon his books and papers, (for he was at this time a lawyer,) and said, "This business I have followed for HONOR, and here it ENDS." And he seized his books and papers and threw them upon the floor and stamped upon them. "Here ENDS THIS BUSINESS," said he. And he went to his trunk and took out his law diploma, and tore it in pieces—seized his axe, knocked down his sign and split it in pieces, and carried them to the middle of the street, and trampled them in the mud. He now felt that he had nothing to live for. He thought there might probably be something in the Christian religion. He examined its evidences, was convinced and converted. And now the ambitious infidel lives to preach the gospel of Christ. Let young men read this and learn a lesson. I would say to them, dread ambition as you would a demon.

19. ANCESTRY.

(*a*) GEORGE III. AND THE PEERAGE.—It is remembered as one of the liberal axioms of George III. that "no British subject is by necessity excluded from the Peerage." Consistently with this sentiment, he once checked a man of high rank, who lamented that a very good speaker in the court of aldermen was of a mean trade, by saying, with his characteristic quickness, "What signifies a man's *trade*? A man of any honest trade may make himself respectable if he will."

(*b*) LORD TENTERDEN'S RETORT.—The obscurity of Lord Tenterden's birth is well known, but he had too much good sense to feel any false shame on that account. We have heard it related of him, that when in an early period of his professional career, a brother barrister, with whom he happened to have a quarrel, had the bad taste to twit him on his origin, his manly and severe answer was, "Yes, sir, I am the son of a barber; if you had been the son of a barber, you would have been a barber yourself."

(*c*) CICERO'S RETORT.—This Roman orator was one day sneered at by one of his opponents, a mean man of noble lineage, on account of his low parentage. "You are the *first* of your line," said the railer; "and you," rejoined Cicero, "are the *last* of yours."

(*d*) DISTINGUISHED MEN OF OBSCURE BIRTH.—"Euripides," says the Cabinet de Terture of Paris, "was the son of a fruiterer, Virgil of a baker, Horace of a freed slave, Anayot of a currier, Voiture of a tax-gatherer, Lamothe of a hatter, Sixtus the Fifth of a swineherd, Fletcher of a chandler, Masillon of a turner, Tamerlane of a shepherd, Greinault of a journeyman baker, Rollin of a herdsman, Molliere of an upholsterer, J. J. Rousseau of a watchmaker, Sir Samuel Romily of a goldsmith, Ben Jonson of a mason, Shakspere of a butcher, Sir Thomas Lawrence of a custom-house officer, Collins of a hatter, Gray of a notary, Beattie of a farmer, Sir Edward Sugden of a barber, Thomas Moore of a grocer, Rembrandt of a miller. These men of genius were not men of leisure; none of them enjoyed a patrimony; and under the regime of our liberal laws, scarcely one amongst them, being neither eligible nor even an elector, could sit in our Chamber of Deputies.

(*e*) THE NOBLEMAN AND THE LION.—Crantz, in his Saxon History, tells us of an Earl of Alsatia, surnamed *Iron* on account of his great strength, who was a great favorite with Edward the Third of England, and much envied, as favorites are always sure to be, by the rest of the courtiers. On one occasion, when the king was absent, some noblemen maliciously instigated the queen to make trial of the noble blood of the favorite, by causing a lion to be let loose upon him, saying, according to the popular belief, that, "if the earl was truly noble, the lion would not touch him." It being customary with the earl to rise at break of day, before any other person in the palace was stirring, a lion was let loose during the night, and turned into the lower court. When the earl came down in the morning, with no more than a night-gown cast over his shirt, he was met by the lion bristling his hair, and growling destruction between his teeth. The earl, not in the least daunted, called out with a stout voice, "Stand, you dog." At these words the lion couched at his feet, to the great amazement of the courtiers, who were peeping out at every window to see the issue of their ungenerous project. The earl laid hold of the lion by the mane, turned him into his cage, and placing his night-cap on the lion's back, came forth without ever casting a look behind him. "Now," said the earl, calling out to the courtiers, whose presence at the windows instantly convinced him of the share they had in this trial of his courage, "Let him amongst you all, that standeth most upon his pedigree, go and fetch my night-cap."

(*f*) JAMES I. AND THE EARL'S GENEALOGY.—King James I., in his progress into England, was entertained at Lumley Castle, the seat of the Earl of Scarborough. A relative of the noble earl was very proud in showing and explaining to his majesty an immensely large genealogical line of the family; the pedigree he carried back rather farther than the greatest strength of credulity would allow. "In gude faith, man," says the king, "it may be they are very true, but I did na' ken before tha Adam's name was Lumley."

ANGER.

20. Anger Indulged.

(*a*) ALEXANDER AND CLITUS.—The folly and danger of anger is seen in the conduct of Alexander. Clitus was a person whom Alexander held very dear, as being the son of his nurse, and one who had been educated together with himself. He had saved the life of Alexander at the battle near the river Granicus, and by him was made Prefect of a province. But he could not flatter. At a feast with the king, when both were doubtless affected by wine, Clitus spoke in high terms of the actions of Philip, preferring them to those of his son. Alexander, transported with anger, seized a javelin and slew him on the spot. But when he became sober and his passion cooled, he was with difficulty restrained from killing himself, for that fault which his sudden fury had led him to commit. He seemed smitten with remorse for the murder, and inconsolable for the loss of his friend.

(*b*) VIOLENCE OF HEROD.—The effect of indulging in anger is seen in the case of Herod, the Tetrarch of Judea. He had so little command over his passion, that upon every slight occasion his anger would transport him to absolute madness. Sometimes he would be sorry and repent of the injuries which he had done when anger clouded his understanding, and soon after commit the same outrages; so that none about him were secure of their lives a moment.

(*c*) THE BOYS AND THE BALL-CLUB.—There were two brothers; Alvah twelve, Michael nine years old. They generally lived together as happily as most brothers do. But sometimes they would quarrel; and when they did get angry with each other they were very furious and reckless of each other's limbs and lives. Their parents were very uneasy at times, lest in a fit of anger one should kill the other. Much they talked to them, and warned them against anger, and against striking each other with fists and clubs, and throwing stones at each other. The boys, when not in anger, appeared loving and kind, and would promise not to strike and throw stones at each other.

One day they were earnestly engaged in a game of ball. Michael had the club, and had just knocked the ball. Alvah caught it—at least, he said he did, and declared it was his turn to knock it. Michael said he did not catch it, but that he wanted to cheat, and should not have the club. Alvah said he would have it. They grew angry, struggling for the club. Then Michael started to run with it. Alvah caught a stone and threw it at him. The stone flew as if winged with the wrath and fury of him who threw it, and struck Michael on the knee. It cut a deep hole right on the joint. In a little while the wound became painfully sore, and Michael soon lost the use of his leg. In time, it turned to a white swelling; and the leg had to be cut off above the knee to save his life.

All this pain and suffering, and maiming for life, merely to decide who should knock a ball! Michael lost his leg to defend his right to keep a ball-club! For this trivial cause, Alvah inflicted on his dear brother unspeakable suffering, and made him a helpless cripple for life. This was a costly fight, and for a worthless object. Anger often produces like results.

(*d*) AN EYE FOR A PIN.—Two boys, named Abel and Asa, were at the same school in New-York, each abou' ten years old; not brothers, but school-mates and class-mates. Both of them had irritable tempers, and had been taught to think they must resent injuries and defend their rights at all hazards. Playing *pin* was a common amusement in the school. They played in this way: Two boys would take a hat and set it down between them, crown upward. Then each boy would lay a pin on top of the crown, and then knock it—first one, and then the other. The one that could knock the pins so that they would lie across each other, had them both. During recess, one day, Abel and Asa were playing pin. They knocked the pins about some time. Both became much excited in the game. Finally, Abel knocked the pins so that, as he said, one lay across the point of the other. Asa denied it. Abel declared they did, and snatched up both pins. Asa's anger flashed in a moment, and he struck Abel in the face with his fist. This excited Abel's wrath. They began to fight—the other boys clustering around, not to part them, but to urge them on. Some cried, "Hit him, Abel!" and some, "Give it to him, Asa!" thus stimulating them to quarrel. The boys seized each other, and finally came tumbling to the ground, Abel on top. Then Abel, in his fury, went to beating Asa in his face, till the blood spouted from his nose and mouth, and till Asa lay like one dead. Then the boys pulled Abel off. But Asa could not get up. The boys began to be alarmed. They were afraid Abel had killed him. The teacher was called. He carried Asa in, washed the blood from his face, and recovered him from his stupor. He examined his face and head, and found them bruised in a shocking manner. One of his eyes was so hurt and swollen he could not open it. And from that day the sight of it grew more and more dim, till it went out in total darkness. So Asa lost an eye, and Abel put it out, merely for a pin!

(*e*) THE LITTLE MURDERER.—Two boys in a southern city, named Augustus and Eugene, were playing top. They had but one top, which they spun alternately. At first they played very pleasantly, but soon became angry and began to speak unkindly. Eugene said, "It is my turn to whirl the top." "No, it is not; it is mine," said Augustus. They grew very angry about it. Augustus at length said to Eugene, "*You lie.*" Eugene struck him. Augustus struck back again. They seized each other in a great rage; and in the scuffle Eugene took a long, sharp knife from his pocket, and stabbed Augustus so that he died in a few moments. Augustus lost his life and Eugene became a murderer, merely to decide whose turn it was to *spin a top!*

21. Anger Subdued.

(*a*) JOHN AND NICETAS.—John, patriarch of Alexandria, had a controversy with Nicetas, a chief man of that city, which was to be decided in a court of justice. John defended the cause of the poor, and Nicetas refused to part with his money. A private meeting was held, to see if the affair could be adjusted, but in vain; angry words prevailed, and both parties were so obstinate that they separated more offended with each other than before. When Nicetas was gone, John began to reflect on his own pertinacity, and although his cause was good, "Yet," said he, "can I think that God will be pleased with this anger and stubbornness? The night draweth on, and shall I suffer the sun to go down upon my wrath? This is impious, and opposed to the apostle's advice." He therefore sent some respectable friends to Nicetas, and charged them to deliver this message to him, and no more: "O sir, the sun is going down!" Nicetas was much affected, his eyes were filled with tears; he hastened to the patriarch, and, saluting him in the most gentle manner, exclaimed, "Father, I will be ruled by you in this or any other matter." They embraced each other affectionately, and settled the dispute instantly.

(*b*) THE SUN IS ALMOST DOWN.—Two good men on some occasion had a warm dispute; and remembering the exhortation of the apostle, "Let not the sun go down upon your wrath," just before sunset one of them went to the other, and knocking at the door, his offended friend came and opened it, and seeing who it was, started back in astonishment and surprise; the other, at the same time, cried out, "The sun is almost down." This unexpected salutation softened the heart of his friend into affection, and he returned for answer, "Come in, brother, come in." What a happy method of conciliating matters, of redressing grievances, and of reconciling brethren!

(*c*) REV. MR. CLARKE'S WAY TO DISPOSE OF ANGER.—It is said of the Rev. Mr. Clarke, of Chesham Bois, that when one observed to him "there was a good deal in a person's natural disposition," he made this answer: "Natural disposition! Why, I am naturally as irritable as any; but when I find anger, or passion, or any other evil temper arise in my mind, immediately I go to my Redeemer, and, confessing my sins, I give myself up to be managed by Him. This is the way that I have taken to get the mastery of my passions."

(*d*) XAVIER'S EXAMPLE.—Francis Xavier sometimes received, in the prosecution of his zealous labors, the most mortifying treatment. As he was preaching in one of the cities of Japan, some of the multitude made sport o him. One, more wanton than the rest, went to him while he addressed the people, feigning that he had something to communicate in private. Upon his approach, Xavier leaned his head to learn what he had to say. The scorner thus gained his object, which was to spit freely upon the face of the devoted missionary, and thus insult him in the most public manner. The father, without speaking a word, or making the least sign of anger or emotion, took out his handkerchief, wiped his face, and continued his discourse, as if nothing had occurred.

By such a heroic control of his passions, the scorn of the audience was turned into admiration. The most learned doctor of the city, who happened to be present, said to himself, that a law which taught men such virtue, inspired men with such unshaken courage, and gave them so perfect a victory over themselves, could not but be from God. Afterwards he desired baptism, and his example was followed by many others. So effectually did the meekness of the missionary promote the success of his work.

22. ANNIHILATION.

(*a*) A TERRIBLE DOCTRINE FOR THE DYING.—A writer in the Connecticut Evangelical Magazine, states that a man of uncommon sagacity and intellect of his acquaintance, was for a long time affected with an apparent debility. But the writer found by conversing with him that he was under conviction. He urged him to repent; but he replied that he could not now part with his worldly schemes. After much solemn conversation they parted. A year after they met, and the writer soon saw in the temper and language of the man, that his seriousness had departed, and that his conscience was seared. He now believed his former state to have been hypochondriac, and said, "Within one week after I detected my folly in being thus anxious for another world, I became well and happy, and have so continued. I now think that all the notions I had concerning the holiness of God, and the rewards of another world, are false. As to sin, it is evident there can be no such thing; nor shall I exist after this body dies, any more than the trees before us will exist, and be happy or miserable." "But," said I, "is it not a gloomy thought that your existence will cease when your body dies?" "As for that," he answered, "I cannot help it, we must make the most of what we have." He seemed determined not to think lest he should be unhappy, and I left him, having in vain attempted to induce a review of his decision.

His life, for years, was what migh be expected from his belie. He seemed to endeavor to erase from his mind all thought of a hereafter. In this state, an awful accident, in a moment, placed before him an eternity, into which he must very soon enter. The powers of his reason were in full strength. And now his beloved scheme of ceasing to exist at death, became his terror. "And have I," said he, "done with existence? shall I presently cease to think, to see, to feel? Am I to exist for a few moments filled with pain, and then lie down to be nothing forever? I am pained for the fruits of my labor; I have labored for nothing; I cannot bid farewell to the earnings of so many years."

On being told by one who did not know his previous opinions, that he certainly should exist; and that the future being of men was indicated by nature, and made sure by Scriptural evidence, an aspect of still greater horror settled on his countenance; and, after a pause of a minute, he replied: "If those Scriptures are true, eternity will be more dreadful to me than the loss of being. I will not believe them; yet how dreadful the idea of sinking into eternal, thoughtless night!" He soon opened his eyes on the realities of another world.

23. ANTINOMIANISM.

(*a*) EFFECT OF ANTINOMIANISM ON A YOUNG LADY.—A young lady, of high family, was called by grace, under the ministry of a pious clergyman of the church of England. The change upon her heart soon became visible. In every good work she was actively engaged. Bible Societies, Missionary Societies, visiting and relieving the sick, teaching a large Sunday School, which her exertions had raised, constituted her constant employment. The floating money she possessed, which had before this been appropriated to dress and worldly amusements, was now consecrated to God, and devoted to carry forward the objects her piety had formed. She was humble, zealous, modest; and lived in the admiration of all who knew her. Henry and Scott were her favorite commentators, and the Bible her constant companion: in every part of Biblical knowledge she made considerable progress. But mark the deadly effects of error upon her mind! Some clergymen, for whom she possessed a high esteem, and to whom she looked with implicit confidence, ran from one error to another; and she as implicitly followed them, and soon became entirely imbued with the Antinomian leaven. Her spirituality of mind, tenderness of conscience, and every truly pious feeling, rapidly declined; and her exertions to promote the cause of God, and the welfare of her fellow-creatures gradually declined also. No books could she read, but such as were of the Antinomian cast; and no preachers could she hear, either of the established church or dissenters, but those of the strongest Antinomian sentiments. In this state she called on a dissenting minister, for whom, in her better days, she had felt a great veneration. He affectionately inquired after the state of her mind, and what were the advantages she had derived from the sentiments she had embraced. She replied, with all the confidence and positiveness that conceit could inspire, "That she was as safe, as to her eternal state, as a saint in heaven." "But," said he, "madam, do you feel yourself as happy and as spiritual in your devotional exercises, as you used to do?" She replied, "I have learned to live without them." "But do you not pray in your closet?" "Pray," said she, "What can I pray for?" Shocked at her reply, he rejoined, "Do you not pray to be favored with a sense of pardoning mercy, and for grace to resist sin?" "Such prayers," answered she, "in my view, would be perfectly absurd; for my sins were imputed to Christ, and pardoned from all eternity; and as to my being kept from sin, I am sure God never designed that I should. I am complete in Christ, and there I rest: all is finished."

Every argument used, elicited similar replies. She proceeded on in this course from bad to worse, and retaining her creed, plunged again into the gayeties of the world. In this state of *professing* religion *without* religion, she remained some years, until God laid her upon the bed of severe affliction. Light broke in again upon her mind; she saw she was destitute of every pious feeling; the errors of her creed appeared in all their fallacy, nor could she derive from it one ray of hope, nor discover one Scriptural evidence of her interest in Christ. The injury she had done to others, by the dissemination of error, the prejudice that had been excited by her conduct against religion, both in the members of her family and others, bore with terrific weight upon her conscience. But the Lord spared her life, and mercifully delivered her from the appalling delusion. In this state, she wrote a most affecting penitential letter to the minister already referred to, saying she could never forgive herself for the reproach she had brought on Christ and his cause, candidly acknowledging, that the sentiments she had imbibed had destroyed all sense of moral obligation in her mind; and had deprived her of all holy and spiritual enjoyment in religion.

(*b*) HILL AND THE ANTINOMIAN.—Rowland Hill would have tried the critical sagacity of the most erudite. His eccentricities are of great notoriety. With many strong points of character, he combined notions prodigiously odd. One of those restless infesters of places of worship, commonly called Antinomians, one day called on Rowland Hill, to bring him to account for his too severe and legal gospel. "Do you, sir," asked Rowland, "hold the ten commandments to be a rule of life to Christians?" "Certainly not," replied the visitor. The minister rang the bell, and on the servant making his appearance, he quietly added, "John, show that man the door, and keep your eye on him until he is beyond the reach of every article of wearing apparel, or other property in the hall!"

24. ANTIQUITY.

(*a*) PRETENSIONS OF THE CHINESE.—It is well known that the Chinese pretend to an excessive antiquity. Their chronology exceeds all bounds of probability: and, could their pretensions be verified, the Mosaic account of the creation must necessarily be discredited. But we have a singular fact to state, which will prove that their boasted antiquity really falls within the limits of the Mosaic chronology. For the evidence we are about to produce, we are indebted to the discoveries of modern astronomy. The Chinese have ever made a point of inserting in their calendar remarkable eclipses, or conjunctions of the planets, together with the name of that emperor in whose reign they were observed. To these events they have also affixed their own dates. There is a very singular conjunction of the sun, moon, and several planets, recorded in their annals, as having taken place almost at the very commencement of their remote history. The far-famed Cassini, to ascertain the fact, calculated back, and decidedly proved, that such an extraordinary conjunction actually did take place in China, February 26th, 1812 years before Christ. This falls four hundred years after the flood, and a little after the birth of Abraham. Here are two important facts ascertained. The one is, that the Chinese are a very ancient nation; and the other, that their pretensions to antiquity beyond that of Moses are unfounded; because this event, which they themselves represent as happening near the beginning of their immense calculations, falls far within the history and chronology of the Scriptures.

52. APOLOGIES.

(*a*) SWIFT AND THE LADY'S DINNER.—A lady invited Dean Swift to a most sumptuous dinner. She said, "Dear Dean, this fish is not as good as I could wish, though I sent for it half across the kingdom, and it cost me so much," naming an incredible price. "And this thing is not such as I ought to have for such a guest, though it came from such a place, and cost such a sum." Thus she went on, decrying and underrating every article of her expensive and ostentatious dinner, and teazing her distinguished guest with apologies, only to find a chance to display her vanity in bringing her trouble and expense into view, until she exhausted his patience. He is reported to have risen in a passion, and to have said, "True, madam, it is a miserable dinner; and I will not eat it, but go home and dine upon sixpence worth of herring."

(*b*) A SENSIBLE HOST.—Lord Carteret, while Lord Lieutenant of Ireland, went one day unattended to Dr. Delany, and told him he was come to dine with him. He thanked his excellency for the honor conferred on him. The dinner was soon in readiness. It was a simple meal, such as was suitable for Dr. D. and his mother. The old lady did the honors of the table. The host made no apology for the entertainment, but said to Lord C.,

> "To stomachs cloyed with costly fare
> Simplicity alone is rare."

Lord C. was highly pleased; for though a courtier, he hated ceremony when he sought pleasure. At the close of the meal, his excellency told Dr. D. that he had always thought him a well-bred man, but had never had so good a proof before. "Others," said he, "on whom I have tried the same experiment, have met me with as much confusion, as if I had come to arrest them for high treason; nay, deprived me of their conversation, by undue attention to the dinner, and then spoiled my meal by fulsome apologies or needless profusion."

26. APOSTACY.

(*a*) APOSTACY AND INTEMPERANCE.—Mr. —— was blessed with a worthy parentage. All that heart could desire was lavished upon him, and especial regard was had to the cultivation of his intellectual powers, which, by nature, were of a superior order. He received a college education, and in early life was supposed to be the subject of a gracious visitation of the Spirit of God. His early Christian experience and deportment gave the cheering promise, that ere long he would be a "burning and a shining light;" but an awful disappointment followed. Instead of devoting himself and all his powers to the work of the ministry, he chose the profession of the law. However unpropitious that profession may be to the growth and energy of true piety, the experience of his worthy father, as well as the lives of several eminent Christian lawyers, were a sufficient guarantee that he too might have served God in the profession of his choice, if his heart had been right. But, alas! the fire of devotion had gone out. Not only was the holy calling of the Christian abandoned, not merely the power of godliness lost, but even the form of religion was in a great measure relinquished, and he became a votary of pleasure, and attached to the bottle.

The subject of this melancholy picture had many engaging qualities; and, in intervals of correct moral deportment, was capable of affording much pleasure to the social circle. At times, too, when conscience raised her voice and lashed him with the stings of remorse, he could chide his wanderings, and cover himself with reproaches. But his, alas! was no the sorrow that worketh repentance unto life; it was the keen remorse, the gnawing anguish of a victim of despair. Mr.—— entered the married state, and although the partner of his bosom did not long continue with him, she left behind her a child, whose tender age, it might have been supposed, would have induced the unhappy man to pause in his ruinous course. But, alas! the endearing relation of father had no charm to break the fatal spell which the god of this world had cast upon his soul. In a little while his own father was stretched upon his dying couch; and his last moments were rendered bitter, not by his own prospects, for he had hope in Christ, but by the character of his ungodly son.

These trying dispensations of Providence had no effect to rouse the unhappy man from the awful lethargy into which he was sunk, and yet his friends were unwilling to give him up for lost. His old companions, some of whom were eminent as preachers of righteousness, expostulated with him. Very many solemn letters were addressed to him. One, who never exchanged a word with him, drew a faithful likeness of his character; the deluded victim saw it in print, and though not a little enraged at the exposure, confessed that the picture was true. In spite of all this, however, he still continued addicted to spirituous liquors, and seemed to place his chief delight in them.

He became, at length, united to an amiable woman, in whose society he might have shared many happy hours, and days, and years, if strong drink had not been dearer to him than all other objects. For a short time he appeared to conduct himself with propriety; but old habits prevailed, and he became their victim with more devotedness than ever. Now and then he would express his deep regret for the wicked course he was pursuing, and appear to desire earnestly that he might be delivered from the horrid temptation; but all his seeming goodness was as the morning cloud, and as the early dew.

Not many weeks previous to the close of this unhappy man's career, he entered into conversation with an old friend, respecting his wicked course of life, and remarked that he desired, above all things, one circumstance to mark h[is] dying hour: "It is," said he, "that I may not possess my reason." "What," rejoined the friend, "to die in a state of derangement, Mr.——! Is it possible that can be your desire?" "It is," replied the victim of despair. "I know what has been my past life; that I have professed religion and apostatized; that I have become an abandoned wretch, lost to all shame and propriety; and I am sure, that if I were to have my reason in my last moments, the retrospect of life would fill me with such insupportable remorse, that I should be a terror to my friends and to myself. I know that I am not, and never shall be, prepared for heaven, and I therefore shall be damned; and I wish that these things may not be in my thoughts in my last moments, but that I may be insensible."

At a time not very distant from the period when he uttered the strange remarks above quoted, he told his wife, in a very grave manner, that he should not long be with her. To others of his family he made the same or similar statements; in all of which he named the day on which he would cease to exist. For a few days after this he appeared to do pretty well, but soon relapsed, and engaging in mirth and festivity, his thoughts of death were all forgotten. Whenever he did speak of death, however, he expressed his horror of dying, associating with it, as he always did, the prospect of bitter remorse for his past wickedness. He was at length attacked by violent illness, which brought on convulsions of the whole frame, long continued, and often repeated for several days, during the whole of which he was deranged, and died as senseless as the brutes.

(*b*) COMPANIONS OF J. A. JAMES.—The Rev. J. A. James relates in his "ANXIOUS INQUIRER AFTER SALVATION DIRECTED AND ENCOURAGED," that he began his own religious course with three companions, one of whom was materially serviceable, in some particulars, to him; but he soon proved that his religion was nothing more than transient devotion. A second returned to his sin, "like a dog to his vomit, and a sow tha is washed to her wallowing in the mire." The third, who was for some time his intimate friend, inbibed the principles of infidelity; and so great was his zeal for his new creed, that he sat up at night to copy Paine's "Age of Reason." After a while he was seized with a dangerous disease: his conscience awoke; the convictions of his mind were agonizing; his remorse was horrible. He ordered all his infidel extracts, the copying out of which had cost him so many nights, to be burnt before his face; and if not in words, yet in spirit—

> "Burn, burn," he cried, in sacred rage,
> "Hell is the due of every page."

His infidel companions and his infidel principles forsook him at once, and in the hearing of a pious friend, who visited him, and to whom he confessed with tears and lamentations his backsliding, he uttered his confessions of sin, and his vows of repentance. He recovered; but, painful to relate, it was only to relapse again, if not into infidelity, yet, at any rate, into an utter disregard to religion.

(*c*) APOSTACY AND SUICIDE.—John Child, of Bedford, England, in early life professed religion, and was for some years zealous in its extension, both by preaching and writing. But yielding to temptation, and indulging a spirit of pride, he became the avowed enemy of the gospel, and wrote a book against the truths he had professed to love. After this, he was brought into a very awful state of mind, absolutely despairing of the mercy of God being extended to him. He was visited by several ministers and others, but without any good effect, and at last committed suicide, by hanging himself in his own house, in the year 1684.

(*d*) SPIRA'S DEATH-BED.—Francis Spira, an Italian lawyer, embraced Christianity, discovered great zeal in its diffusion, and was distinguished for his extensive knowledge of the gospel. When he found that he was likely to suffer for the sake of Christ, he publicly recanted; and soon after being seized with illness, and having the prospect of death before him, he was visited by several eminent Christians, who conversed and prayed with him, but without avail. He died in a state of the most awful despair, declaring the impossibility of his finding mercy at the hands of God.

(*e*) THE APOSTATE BURNED.—Richard Denton, a blacksmith, residing in Cambridgeshire, was a professor of religion, and the means of converting the martyr William Woolsey. When told by that holy man that he wondered he had not followed him to prison, Denton replied, that he could not burn in the cause of Christ. Not long after, his house being on fire, he ran in to save some of his goods, and was burnt to death.

(*f*) CRANMER'S UNWORTHY HAND.—In the bloody reign of Queen Mary of England, Archbishop Cranmer became obnoxious to her persecuting spirit. She was determined to bring him to the stake; but previously employed emissaries to persuade him, by means of flattery and false promises, to renounce his faith. The good man was overcome, and subscribed to the errors of the Church of Rome. His conscience smote him; he returned to his former persuasion; and, when brought to the stake, he stretched forth the hand that had made the unhappy signature, and held it in the flames till it was entirely consumed, frequently exclaiming, "That unworthy hand:" after which he patiently suffered martyrdom, and ascended to receive its reward.

(*g*) APOSTACY DESTROYS THE CONFIDENCE OF WORLDLY MEN.—It is well known that Frederick the Great took pride in having his soldiers well disciplined; and was therefore particularly attentive to the conduct of the subalterns. It is perhaps not so well known, that he sometimes manifested a real respect for religious people; for few men could more clearly discern the excellence of the conduct produced by holy principles. While, therefore, he sneered at Christianity, he sometimes promoted to offices of trust those who consistently maintained it.

A sergeant, of the name of Thomas, who was very successful in training his men, and whose whole deportment pleased the king, was often noticed by him. He inquired respecting the place of the sergeant's birth, his parents, his religious creed, and the place of worship which he frequented. On being informed that he was united with the Moravians, and attended their chapel in William-street, he exclaimed, "Oh! Oh! you are a fanatic, are you? Well, well; only take care to do your duty, and improve your men."

The king's common salutation after this, was, "Well, how do you do? how are you going on in William-street?" His majesty at length, in conversation with Thomas's colonel, mentioned his intention of promoting the sergeant to an office in the commissariat department, upon the death of an aged man who then filled it.

The colonel, in order to encourage Thomas, told him of the king's design. Unhappily this had an injurious effect upon the mind of the sergeant; for, alas! such is the depravity of the human heart, that few can endure the temptation of prosperity without sustaining spiritual loss. Thomas began o forsake the assemblies of his Christian brethren; and when reproved by his minister, he said, "his heart was with him, but he was afraid of offending the king." The minister told him to take good heed that his heart did not deceive him. Soon after the sergeant's religious declension, he was again accosted by the king, with "Well, how do you do? how are your friends in William-street?" "I do not know, please your majesty," was the reply. "Not know! not know!" answered the king; "have you been ill?" "No, please your majesty," rejoined the sergeant; "but I do not see it necessary to attend there so often as I used to do." "Then you are not so great a fanatic as I thought you;" was the royal answer.

In a short time the aged officer died, and the colonel waited upon his majesty to inform him of the vacancy, and to remind him of his intention to raise sergeant Thomas to the situation. "No, no!" said the king, "he shall not have it; he does not go so often to William-street as he used to do." Surprised with this peremptory refusal, the colonel withdrew, and on his return found his sergeant waiting for the confirmation of his appointment. "I do not know what is the matter with the king today," said the cononel, "but he will not give you the situation. He says you do not go so often to William-street as you used to do. I do not know what he means; but I suppose you do." Struck in a moment with the awful impropriety of his conduct, he bowed to the colonel, and departed to humble himself before God. He ever after adored the Divine mercy, which did not leave him fully to realize the Scriptural threatening, "The prosperity of fools shall destroy them."

(*h*) A BACKSLIDER'S WRETCHEDNESS.—Dr. Doddridge was once preaching on the calling and the glorious hopes of the Christian. One of his hearers, after the sermon, addressed him in the following terms: "You have made an excellent and encouraging discourse; but these privileges do not belong to me, nor shall I ever have the least interest in them." "What reason have you for so saying?" asked the doctor; "Jesus is able to save to the uttermost." "I will tell you my circumstances," the man replied, "and then you will not be surprised. I once made a profession of religion, which I supported with great regularity and decorum for several years. I was very strict in the performance of the duties required by the Christian system. None could charge me with immorality of conduct, or the neglect of positive commands; but in the course of time my zeal departed from me, and I became careless and remiss in my walk and conversation. I felt no satisfaction arising from the performance of spiritual duties, and gradually declined my customary observance of them. Instead of praying twice or thrice a day, I only prayed once; the same with respect to family religion; and at last these sacred engagements were entirely omitted, which soon discovered itself by my outward conduct. Ungodly company, and the gratification of sense, became my only enjoyments, in which I could indulge free from those strong convictions of guilt and dreadful apprehension of future misery, which retirement and calm reflection impose upon the mind. Soon after this change took place, I was left guardian to a young lady, whose fortune was committed to my care; but I expended her money, and ruined her reputation. Still I was sensible how far preferable a virtuous life was to a wicked one, and I was careful to instruct my children in the principles of religion. When I returned, one evening, from my sinful pursuits, I asked them, as usual, if they could repeat their lesson. 'Yes,' said the youngest, 'and I have a lesson for you too, papa;' she then read Ezek. xxiv. 13:—'Because I have purged thee, and thou wast not purged, thou shalt not be purged from thy filthiness any more, till I have caused my fury to rest upon thee.' This I considered was to seal my doom, and I now have nothing but a fearful looking for of judgment."

(*i*) SECURITY AGAINST APOSTACY.—"I well remember," says an eminent minister in North Wales, "that when the Spirit of God first convinced me of my sin, guilt, and danger, and of the many difficulties and enemies I must encounter, if ever I intended setting out for heaven, I was often to the last degree frightened; the prospect of those many strong temptations and vain allurements to which my youthful years would unavoidably expose me, greatly discouraged me. And I often used to tell an aged soldier of Christ, the first and only Christian friend I had any acquaintance with for several years, that I wished *I* had borne the burden and heat of the day like *him*. His usual reply was—'That so long as I *feared*, and was *humbly dependent upon God*, I should *never fall*, but certainly prevail.' I have found it so. O, blessed be the Lord, that I can now raise up my Ebenezer, and say, 'Hitherto hath the Lord upheld me.'"

(*j*) FIVE YEARS OF MISERY.—It is said of a Mr. G., that he lay languishing in distress of mind for five years,—during which he took no comfort in meat or drink, nor any pleasure in life; being under a sense of backsliding, he was distressed as if he had been in the pit of hell. If he ate his food, it was not from any appetite, but with a view to defer his damnation, thinking within himself that he must needs be lost so soon as his breath was out of his body. Yet, after all this, he was set at liberty, received great consolation, and afterwards lived altogether a heavenly life. Let not the tempted believer then despond, nor the returning backslider fear lest he should be rejected.

27. APPLAUSE.

(*a*) A CLERGYMAN'S DREAM. The Imperial Magazine contains an account of a remarkable dream related by Rev. R. Bowden, of Darwen, in England, who committed it to writing from the lips of the clergyman to whom it happened. The dream suggests a most solemn and affecting admonition.

A minister of evangelical principles, whose name, from the circumstances that occurred, it will be necessary to conceal, being much fatigued at the conclusion of the afternoon service, retired to his apartment in order to take a little rest. He had not long reclined upon his couch before he fell asleep and began to dream. He dreamed that on walking into his garden, he entered a bower that had been erected in it, where he sat down to read and meditate. While thus employed he thought he heard some one enter the garden; and leaving his bower, he immediately hastened toward the spot whence the sound seemed to come, in order to discover who it was that had entered. He had not proceeded far before he observed a particular friend of his, a clergyman of considerable talents, who had rendered himself very popular by his zealous and unwearied exertions in the cause of Christ. On approaching his friend, he was surprised to find that his countenance was covered with a gloom which it had not been accustomed to wear, and that it strongly indicated a violent agitation of mind apparently arising from conscious remorse. After the usual salutations had passed, his friend asked the relator the time of the day; to which he replied, "Twenty-five minutes after four." On hearing this, the stranger said, "It is only one hour since I died, and now I am damned" "Damned! for what?" inquired the minister. "It is not," said he, "because I have not preached the gospel, neither is it because I have not been rendered useful, for I have many souls as seals to my ministry, who can bear testimony to the truth as it is in Jesus, which they have received from my lips; but it is because I have been seeking the applause of men more than the honor which cometh from above, and verily, I have my reward!" Having uttered hese expressions he hastily disappeared, and was seen no more.

The minister awaking shortly afterward, with the dream deeply graven on his memory, proceeded, overwhelmed with serious reflections, towards his chapel, in order to conduct his evening service. On his way thither he was accosted by a friend, who inquired whether he had heard of the severe loss the church had sustained in the death of their able minister. He replied, "No;" but being much affected at this singular intelligence, he inquired of him the day and the time of the day when his departure took place. To this his friend replied, "This afternoon, at twenty-five minutes after three o'clock."

(*b*) PARMENIDES' AUDIENCE.—To a really wise man, the well weighed approbation of a single judicious character gives more heartfelt satisfaction than all the noisy applauses of ten thousand ignorant though enthusiastic admirers. Parmenides, upon reading a philosophical discourse before a public assembly at Athens, and observing that, except Plato, the whole company had left him, continued, notwithstanding, to read on, and said that Plato alone was audience sufficient for him.

28. ATONEMENT.

(*a*) ATONEMENT FUNDAMENTAL.—The late Thomas, Earl of Kinnoul, a short time before his death, in a long and serious conversation with the Rev. Dr. Kemp, of Edinburgh, thus expressed himself:—"I have always considered the atonement the characteristic of the gospel; as a system of religion, strip it of that doctrine, and you reduce it to a scheme of morality, excellent, indeed, and such as the world never saw; but, to man, in the present state of his faculties, absolutely impracticable.

"The atonement of Christ, and the truths immediately connected with that fundamental principle, provide a remedy for all the wants and weaknesses of our nature. Those who strive to remove those precious doctrines from the word of God, do an irreparable injury to the grand and beautiful system of religion which it contains, as well as to the comforts and hopes of man. For my own part, I am now an old man, and have experienced the infirmities of advanced years. Of late, in the course of a severe and dangerous illness, I have been repeatedly brought to the gates of death. My time in this world cannot now be long, but with truth I can declare that, in the midst of all my past afflictions, my heart was supported and comforted by a firm reliance upon the merits and atonement of my Savior; and now, in the prospect of entering upon an eternal world, this is the only foundation of my confidence and hope."

(*b*) "THIS IS WHAT I WANT."—A certain man, on the Malabar coast had inquired of various devotees and priests, how he might make atonement for his sins; and he was directed to drive iron spikes, sufficiently blunted, through his sandals; and on these spikes, he was directed to place his naked feet, and to walk about four hundred and eighty miles. If through loss of blood, or weakness of body, he was obliged to halt, he might wait for healing and strength. He undertook the journey, and while he halted under a large shady tree, where the gospel was sometimes preached, one of the missionaries came and preached in his hearing from these words, "The blood of Jesus Christ cleanseth from all sin." While he was preaching, the man rose up, threw off his torturing sandals, and cried out aloud, "This is what I want;" and he became a lively witness, that the blood of Jesus Christ does cleanse from all sin indeed.

(*c*) DOCTRINE FIT FOR OLD WOMEN.—The first sermon preached by the late Rev. Robert Hall at Cambridge, after he had become the pastor of the congregation there, was on the doctrine of the atonement, and its practical tendencies. One of the congregation, who had embraced very erroneous views of the gospel, said to him, "Mr. Hall, this preaching won't do for us, it will only suit a congregation of old women." "Do you mean my sermon, sir; or the doctrine?" "Your doctrine." "Why is it that the doctrine is fit only for old women?" "Because it may suit the musings of people tottering upon the brink of the grave, and who are eagerly seeking comfort." "Thank you, sir; for your concession. The doctrine will not suit people of any age, unless it be true; and, if it be true, it is not fitted for old women alone, but is equally important at every age."

(*d*) GOD'S LOVE WONDERFUL.—A missionary, addressing a pious negro woman, said, "Mary, is not the love of God wonderful?" and then enlarging on its manifestation in the atonement of Christ, he made the appeal, "Is it not wonderful?" Mary simply, but we may add, sublimely, replied, "Massa, massa, me no tink it so wonderful, 'cause it is just like Him."

(*e*) THE SCHOLAR'S COMFORT.—"I have taken much pains," says the learned Selden, "to know every thing that was esteemed worth knowing amongst men; but with all my disquisitions and reading, nothing now remains with me to comfort me, at the close of life, but this passage of St. Paul, 'It is a faithful saying, and worthy of all acceptation, that Jesus Christ came into the world to save sinners:' to this I cleave, and herein I find rest."

(*f*) COMMITTING A MILLION SOULS TO CHRIST.—Rev. Mr. H. was for many years co-pastor with the Rev. Matthew Wilks, of the congregations at the Tabernacle and Tottenham-court chapel, London. His venerable colleague, who called upon him a few hours before his death, in a characteristic conversation, said, "Is all right for another world?"

"I am very happy," said Mr. H.

"Have you made your will?"

Mistaking the question—"The will of the Lord be done," said the dying Christian.

"Shall I pray with you?"

"Yes, if you can:" alluding to Mr. Wilks's feelings, at that moment considerably excited.

After prayer, "Well, my brother, if you had a hundred souls, could you commit them all to Christ now?" alluding to an expression Mr. H. frequently used in the pulpit.

With a mighty and convulsive effort, he replied, "A million!"

(*g*) COWPER'S EXPERIENCE.—Cowper, the poet, speaking of his religious experience, says: "But the happy period which was to shake off my fetters and afford me a clear opening of the free mercy of God in Christ Jesus, was now arrived. I flung myself into a chair near the window, and seeing a Bible there, ventured once more to apply to it for comfort and instruction. The first verse I saw was the 25th of the third of Romans; 'Whom God hath set forth to be a propitiation through faith in his blood, to declare his righteousness for the remission of sins that are past, through the forbearance of God.' Immediately I received strength to believe, and the full beams of the Sun of Righteousness shone upon me. I saw the sufficiency of the atonement he had made, my pardon sealed in his blood, and all the fulness and completeness of his justification. In a moment I believed and received the gospel."

(*h*) DES BARREAUX'S POEM.—Des Barreaux, a foreigner of eminent station, had been a great profligate, and afterwards became a great penitent. He composed a piece of poetry after his conversion, the leading sentiment of which was to the following effect:—"Great God, thy judgments are full of righteousness; thou takest pleasure in the exercise of mercy: but I have sinned to such a height that justice demands my destruction, and mercy itself seems to solicit my perdition. Disdain my tears, strike the blow, and execute thy judgments. I am willing to submit and adore, even in perishing, the equity of thy procedure. But on what place will the stroke fall that is not covered with the blood of Christ?"

(*i*) REV. MR. INNES AND THE INFIDEL.—In a conversation which the Rev. Mr. Innes had with an infidel on his sick-bed, he told him that when he was taken ill he thought he would rely on the general mercy of God; that as he had never done any thing very bad, he hoped all would be well. "But as my weakness increased," he added, "I began to think, is not God a just being, as well as merciful? Now what reason have I to think he will treat me with mercy and not with justice? and if I am treated with justice," he said, with much emotion, "WHERE AM I?"

"I showed him," says Mr. Innes, "that this was the *very difficulty* the gospel was sent to remove, as it showed how mercy could be exercised in perfect consistency with the strictest demands of justice, while it was bestowed through the atonement made by Jesus Christ. After explaining this doctrine and pressing it on his attention and acceptance, one of the last things he said to me before leaving him, was, "Well, I believe it must come to this. I confess I see here a solid footing to rest on, which, on my former principles I could never find."

29. AVARICE.

(*a*) A MOTHER MURDERING HER SON.—Two young men of Virginia, who served in the American army during the war, having regularly got their discharge, went home to their friends. One had only a mother living when he left home; when they had got near home, they fell into a conversation on the length of time they had been away, and concluded to try whether their parents would know them; with this impression, each took the nearest path home. The one who had only a mother, came in; and, finding his mother did not know him, he asked for lodging; to whom she replied, she could not lodge him; that there was a tavern not far from the place where he might get lodging, &c. He importuned, but she refused, till at last he told her he had a little money, and he was afraid to lodge in a tavern, lest some person should rob him. He took out his purse and offered it to her keeping. She, struck with the mammon, consented immediately to his staying; accordingly he did, had supper, and still never discovered himself to his mother or any of the family. He was directed to a bed once more in the chamber of her who conceived ... m. How safe he must have thought himself then, compared to the field of battle. But she summoned a negro man, told him the scheme she had planned, hired him to aid her to the stranger's apartment, where they murdered him in his bed. Next day his fellow-soldier came to see his friend; but, on asking for the stranger, could hear nothing of him. He thought it was a trick to plague him, that the old woman denied it, till, hearing her affirm that no stranger had come there the last evening, nor any man, he asked her if she had not a son who went to the war. She said she had. "Well," said he, "I left him within a few miles of this house last evening, and he came here; and he told me he would not make himself known to you, to see if you had forgotten his looks. He must be here." The cruel mother fainted at the sentence, confessed her wickedness, and showed her murdered son, crammed in a closet of the house!! Oh, the love of money, what has it not done; what will it yet do!

(*b*) THE RICH MAN'S VICTORY.—"I could mention the name of a late very opulent and very valuable person," says a writer in the Gospel Magazine, "who, though naturally avaricious in the extreme, was liberal and beneficent to a proverb. He was aware of his constitutional sin, and God gave him *victory* over it, by enabling him to *run away* from it. Lest the dormant love of money should awake and stir in his heart, he would not, for many years before his death, trust himself with the *sight* of his revenues. He kept, indeed, his accounts as clearly and exactly as any man in the world; but he dared not receive, because he dared not look at that gold, which he feared would prove a snare to his affections. His stewards received all, and retained all in their own hands till they received orders how to dispose of it."

(*c*) A LARGE OFFER FOR A FORTNIGHT.—A person who possessed a speculative acquaintance with divine truth, had, by unremitting industry, and carefully watching every opportunity of increasing his wealth, accumulated the sum of twenty-five thousand pounds. But alas! he became engrossed and entangled with the world, and to its acquisitions he appears to have sacrificed infinitely higher interests. A dangerous sickness, that brought death near to his view, awakened his fears. Conscience reminded him of his neglect of eternal concerns, and filled him with awful forebodings of future misery. A little before he expired he was heard to say, "My possessions amount to twenty-five thousand pounds. One half of this my property I would give, so that I might live one fortnight longer, to repent and seek salvation."

(*d*) THE MERCHANT AND THE PEASANT.—A peasant once entered the hall of justice at Florence, at the time that Alexander, duke of Tuscany, was presiding. He stated that he had the good fortune to find a purse of sixty ducats; and learning that it belonged to Friuli the merchant, who offered a reward of ten ducats to the finder, he restored it to him, but that he had refused the promised reward. The duke instantly ordered Friuli to be summoned into his presence, and questioned why he refused the reward. The merchant replied, "that he conceived the peasant had paid himself; for although, when he gave notice of his loss, he said this purse only contained sixty ducats, it in fact had seventy in it." The duke inquired if this mistake was discovered before the purse was found. Friuli answered in the negative. "Then," said the duke, "as I have a very high opinion of the honesty of this peasant, I am induced to believe that there is indeed a mistake in this transaction; for as the purse you lost had in it seventy ducats, and this which he found contains sixty only, it is impossible that it can be the same." He then gave the purse to the peasant, and promised to protect him against all future claimants.

(*e*) SEVERAL AVARICIOUS CHARACTERS.—The greatest endowments of the mind, the greatest abilities in a profession, and even the quiet possession of an immense treasure, will never prevail against avarice. My Lord Chancellor Hardwick, says Dr. King, when worth eight hundred thousand pounds, set the same value on half a crown then as when he was worth only one hundred pounds. That great captain, the Duke of Marlborough, when he was in the last stage of life and very infirm, would walk from the public rooms in Bath to his lodgings, in a cold, dark night, to save sixpence in chair-hire. He died worth more than a million and a half sterling, which was inherited by a grandson of Lord Trevor's, who had been one of his enemies. Sir James Lowther, after changing a piece of silver, and paying twopence for a dish of coffee in George's coffee-house, was helped into his chariot (for he was then very lame and infirm), and went home; some little time after he returned to the same coffee-house on purpose to acquaint the woman who kept it that she had given him a bad halfpenny, and demanded another in exchange for it. Sir James had about forty thousand pounds per annum, and was at loss whom to appoint his heir. I knew one Sir Thomas Colby, who lived at Kensington, and was, I think, a commissioner in the victualling office; he killed himself by rising in the night when he was under the effect of a sudorific, and going down stairs to look for the key of his cellar, which he had inadvertently left on a table in his parlor; he was apprehensive his servants might seize the key and deprive him of a bottle of wine. This man died intestate, and left more than two hundred thousands pounds in the funds, which was shared among five or six-day laborers, who were his nearest relatives.

(*f*) A POOR GUARD.— A courtier busily occupied in ministerial employments, and a member of the chamber of deputies, received from one of "our excellencies" some secret instruction with regard to certain parliamentary consciences, which it was thought might be easily purchased.

The minister happened to mention the name of Mr. X——. "Oh, as to that one," hastily interrupted the political Mercury, I cannot answer for him. I have already sounded him, and he seems to be inaccessible."

"But did you try it with a good bank note in hand?"

"He is said to be wholly incorruptible."

"Agreed—but a good sum"—

"He is conscientious—is virtuous."

"But he loves money very much. I am assured that he is avaricious."

"That is true."

"Very well—very well, my dear sir. Keep on—follow him up. *When virtue is guarded by vice, it is easy to corrupt the sentinel.*"

(*g*) THE JEWISH MOTHER.—One of the nights when Mrs. Siddons first performed at Drury Lane, a Jew boy, in his eagerness to get the first row in the shilling gallery, fell over into the pit, and was dangerously hurt. The manager of the theatre ordered the lad to be conveyed to a lodging, where he was attended by their own physician; but, notwithstanding all their attention, he died, and was decently buried, at the expense of the theatre. The mother came to the play-house to thank the managers, and they gave her his clothes and five guineas, for which she returned a courtesy, but, with some hesitation, added that they had forgotten to return her the shilling which Abraham had paid for coming in!

(*h*) THE MISER IN THE WELL.—An old bachelor, possessed of a fortune of $50,000, meeting a friend one day began to harangue him very learnedly upon the detestable sin of avarice, and gave the following instance of it: "About three years ago," said he, "by a very odd accident I fell into a well, and was absolutely within a very few minutes of perishing before I could prevail upon an unconscious dog of a laborer, who happened to be within hearing of my cries, to help me out for a shilling. The fellow was so rapacious as to insist upon having twenty-five cents, for above a quarter of an hour, and I verily believe he would not have abated me a single farthing if he had not seen me at the last gasp; and I determined rather to die than submit to his extortion!"

(*i*) A LITTLE MORE.—"When I was a lad," says one, "an old gentleman took some trouble to teach me some little knowledge of the world. With this view I remember he once asked me when a man was rich enough? I replied, when he has a thousand pounds. He said, No.—Two thousand? No.—Ten thousand? No.—Twenty thousand? No.—A hundred thousand? which I thought would settle the business; but he still continuing to say No, I gave it up, and confessed I could not tell, but begged he would inform me. He gravely said, When he has a little more than he has, and that is never! If he acquires one thousand, he wishes to have two thousand; then five, then ten, then twenty, then fifty; from that his riches would amount to a hundred thousand, and so on till he had grasped the whole world; after which he would look about him, like Alexander, for other worlds to possess."

(*j*) THE LONG CREDIT.—A wealthy but niggardly gentleman was waited on by the advocates of a charitable institution, for which they solicited his aid, reminding him of the Divine declaration, Prov. xix. 17, "He that hath pity on the poor, lendeth unto the Lord; and that which he hath given will he pay him again." To this he profanely replied, "The security, no doubt, is good, and the interest liberal but I cannot give such long credit." Poor rich man! the day of payment was much nearer than he anticipated. Not a fortnight had elapsed from his refusing to honor this claim of God upon his substance, before he received a summons with which he could not refuse to comply. It was, "This night thy soul shall be required of thee; then whose shall those things be which thou hast provided?"

(*k*) THE BROKEN VOW.—Some years ago, a poor lad came to London, in search of a situation as errand-boy; he made many unsuccessful applications, and was on the eve of returning to his parents, when a gentleman, being prepossessed by his appearance, took him into his employment, and after a few months, bound him apprentice. He so conducted himself during his apprenticeship, as to gain the esteem of every one who knew him; and after he had served his time, his master advanced a capital for him to commence business. He retired to his closet with a heart glowing with gratitude to his Maker for his goodness, and there solemnly vowed that he would devote a tenth part of his annual income to the service of God. The first year his donation amounted to ten pounds, which he gave cheerfully, and continued to do so till it amounted to 500*l*. He then thought that was a great deal of money to give, and that he need not be so particular as to the exact amount: that year he lost a ship and cargo to the value of 15,000*l*. by a storm! This caused him to repent, and he again commenced his contributions with a resolution never to retract; he was more successful every year, and at length retired. He then devoted a tenth part of his annual income for several years, till he became acquainted with a party of worldly men, who by degrees drew him aside from God: he discontinued his donations, made large speculations, lost every thing, and became almost as poor as when he first arrived in London as an errand-boy. "There is," saith Solomon, "that scattereth, and yet increaseth; and there is that withholdeth more than is meet, but it tendeth to poverty."

(*l*) "GIVE ME MY PORTION HERE."—A merchant of ———, engaged in a lucrative trade, was convinced by the Spirit of God that he was an heir of hell, but might, by repentance and faith in Jesus Christ, become an heir of heaven. The "god of this world" tempted him with much earthly gain, and God, in the person of the Holy Ghost, offered him durable riches and righteousness. He was fully convinced, as he said, that the riches of earth and the riches of heaven were set before him, and that he could not obtain both, but might have his choice. He glanced at heaven's durable riches, and then settled his covetous gaze upon earth's glittering gold. He paused, feeling his choice was for eternity, but strangely, madly said, "Give me my portion here." His prayer was answered. His riches were multiplied. But, said he, "I know that to gain the world, I have lost my soul."

BALLS, OR PUBLIC DANCES.

30. They are Incompatible with Prayer.

(*a*) THE BALL AND THE MINISTER.—A pastor was in the frequent habit, during the tours he made in his extensive parish, of stopping for the night in a village inn, and continued his journey the next day. On one occasion he found the principal apartment converted into a ball-room. The host apologized for his not being able to accommodate him as comfortably as usual; but the pastor, without being disconcerted, asked him to have his supper served to him in a corner of the room. When it was ready, he begged the assembly to grant him a few moments silence, that he might, according to his practice, make an audible prayer before partaking of the meal. He accordingly commenced praying, but before he had finished, the dancers had disappeared.

(*b*) THE DEVIL CHEATED.—"Father Hull," now deceased, was a preacher of the old school, S. C. Conference. Passing along the highway one evening, in a strange, wicked country, he called at a good looking house for lodgings. Weary and faint, he sat him down by the fireside. After a while, as night began to close in, companies of well-dressed gentlemen and ladies flocked into his room. One drew out his violin and commenced playing. Away scampered the youngsters, hopping and leaping. It was "a ball!" Here sat the stranger looking silently on. At length a partner was wanted, and one ventured up and asked Mr. Hull if he would take the floor. "Certainly, madam!" said he, rising and walking out on the floor as he spoke; "but I have long made it a rule never to commence any business till I have asked the direction of the Lord, and his blessing upon it. Will you all join in prayer with me?" As he spoke these words, he fell on his knees and began to pray. Some kneeled, others stood, all petrified with astonishment. In the mean time, being a holy, faithful man, and peculiarly powerful in prayer, he seemed to draw the very heavens and earth together. Some groaned, some shrieked aloud, and many fell prostrate, like dead men, on the floor. Truly the place was sweet and awful on account of the divine presence. In short, the dance was turned into a religious meeting, from which many dated their conviction and conversion, and the commencement of a powerful revival. "Behold what a great matter a little fire kindleth!" O, had we more faith and intrepidity, what good we might do! How glorious to attack and drive the devil from his own strong holds.

(*c*) PRAYER AT A PUBLIC DANCE.—Though somewhat eccentric in his manners, Mr. Byne was nevertheless a fearless and faithful servant of the Lord. Not long after he joined the church, he was invited by some of his former companions in sin to attend a dancing party, which he agreed to do *on condition*, expressly understood, that he should give direction to all the exercises of the evening. When the company had collected, (among whom were Mr. Byne and his wife,) a young lady stepped forward and invited the preacher to dance. He accepted her invitation so far as to walk out on the floor with her, when the violin struck up a lively air. Mr. Byne claimed his right to give directions, sung a spiritual song, in which he was joined by several of the party—kneeled down and offered up a fervent and affecting prayer. By the time he concluded his second spiritual song, tears were overflowing from many eyes—the dance was converted into a prayer-meeting, and this was the last frolic ever attempted to be held at that house.

(*d*) THE METHODIST AND THE DINNER PARTY.—In the district which I once travelled, says a writer in the Christian Advocate, on Easter Monday, 1825, a gentleman invited a number of his neighbors to dine with him; and among the rest a good Methodist lady was invited. She accepted the invitation, and attended, without the most distant thought that any thing contrary to her profession would be introduced. In this, however, she was disappointed. For, after dinner, the fiddle was brought in; the company rose to play and amuse themselves by dancing. At length one, with a spirit more daring than the rest, approached her, and asked her to dance. Without a verbal reply, she rose from her seat and accompanied him on the floor. The company was arranged, the fiddler sitting with lifted heel and elbow sprung, and no doubt, the devil laughing in his sleeve, and saying, "Another Methodist safe in my trap." But the good angel whispered, "Not yet, sir." She paused, and then said, "It is my custom to sing some first;" and standing there, she gave out some verse and sang. She then said, "It is my custom to pray some first," and dropped upon her knees and prayed; and no doubt her prayer was the legitimate offspring of a warm heart. Some of the company remained, some ran away, and some trembled and wept. The dance was broken up, the fiddler disappointed, the devil defeated, and the good Methodist lady victorious.

(*e*) THE YOUNG CONVERT'S PRAYER IN THE BALL-ROOM.—In one of the interior counties of Pennsylvania a young man whom, for the sake of distinction, we shall call B——, was convicted of sin and led to inquire anxiously the way to be saved. He was the son of one of the most respectable and wealthy inhabitants of that region of country, but his father was unhappily a bitter opposer of the religion of Christ. Perceiving the state of his son's mind, he determined to leave no means untried to divert his mind from the subject. He hurried him from business to pleasure, and from pleasure to business, with strong hopes that his serious impressions might be driven away, or, at least, that he might be prevented making any public profession of the change of his views. But all these efforts were vain. The Spirit of God had laid hold on his soul, and did not desert him. He was brought to the dust in submission, and found peace in believing in Christ.

About this time a splendid *ball* was got up, with every possible attempt at display, and the youth of the village and surrounding country were all excitement for the festive hall. B—— was invited. He at once declined attending, but his father insisted that he should go. Here was a struggle for the young convert. On the one hand were the convictions of his own conscience, as well as the desires of his heart. On the other, the *command* of a father whom he was still bound to obey. The struggle was long and anxious. At length it was decided—*he determined to go.* His father rejoiced at his decision. His friends congratulated him on having abandoned his new notions and become a man again.

The evening at last arrived. The gay party were gathered in the spacious hall. There was beauty, and wealth, and fashion. The world was there. Every heart seeemed full of gladness, every voice was one of joy. B—— appeared among the rest, with a brow that spoke the purpose of a determined soul. He was the first on the floor to lead off the dance. A cotillion was formed, and as the circle stood in the centre of the room, with every eye fixed on them, what was the astonishment of the company when B—— raised his hands and said, "LET US PRAY." The assembly was awe-struck. Not a word was uttered. It was as silent as the grave, while B—— poured out his heart to God in behalf of his young companions, his parents, and the place in which they lived. With perfect composure he concluded his prayer, and all had left the room *silently*, but *one*. A young lady whom he had led upon the floor as his partner, stood near him bathed in tears. They left the room together, and not long afterwards, she was led to the foot of the cross, having been first awakened by her partner's prayer on the *ball-room floor*. They were soon married, and are still living, active, devoted members of the body of Christ. B—— is an elder in one of the churches near the city of New-York.

31. They Deaden Natural Sensibility.

(*a*) A CORPSE CARRIED TO A BALL.—A writer in the New-York Observer, states that in the place where he resided, in 1840, there was a New Year ball. Invitations were widely extended; and a great gathering of the young, gay, and thoughtless, was anticipated. Notwithstanding the intense cold, many came from a great distance in the country round. There was one couple that set out for the ball, with merry hearts, to ride some twenty miles. The lady was young and gay, and her charms of youth and beauty were never lovelier than when dressed for that new-year ball. Clad too thinly, of course, for the season, and especially for that dreadful day, she had not gone far before she complained of being cold, very cold; but their anxiety to reach the end of the ride in time to be present at the opening of the dance, induced them to hurry on without stopping by the way. Not long after this complaining, she said she felt perfectly comfortable, was now quite warm, and that there was no necessity of delay on her account. They reached at length the house where the company was gathering: the young man jumped from the sleigh and exlended his hand to assist her out; but she did not offer hers. He spoke to her, but she answered not. She was dead—stone dead—frozen stiff—a corpse on the way to a ball!

But the most shocking part of the tale remains to be told. THE BALL WENT ON! The dance was as gay, and the music as merry, as if death had never come to their door.

(*b*) THE CARD-PLAYERS AND THEIR DEAD COMPANION.—During the progress of a ball in one of the towns of New Hampshire, four of the young men retired to play cards. While at their game, one of their number fell down in a fit and expired. But the others rolled his dead body under the table, covered it up with cloaks, and said nothing about it till the ball was over. How do such amusements petrify the better feelings, and make man's heart more hard than that of some of the brutes! For some of the brutes would have shown more sympathy for a dying companion than was exhibited in the case before us.

(*c*) DEATH BUT NO ADJOURNMENT.—A writer in the New-York Observer says: In the village in which I lived for many years, there was a ball but a few steps from my house, and one of the young ladies who was to be there, died suddenly on the very day of the ball. It was proposed by one of the managers to postpone the dance; but the others would not consent; and on it went, although the corpse lay directly in front of the ball-room, and the dim light in the room where it lay could be seen by every dancer, and the sound of the music and dancing disturbed the melancholy watchers. Who can doubt but that such amusements blunt the finer sentiments of our nature, and weaken even the humane feelings of their votaries, to say nothing of their irreligious character and tendency? Congress will adjourn at the announcement of the death of one of their number; but a similar announcement procures not the adjournment of a ball.

(*d*) DANCING DURING A MASSACRE.—The tragical scenes which came under Mr. Fisk's observation while in Greece, had become so common, that they began to be regarded with indifference by many classes of people. Parties of pleasure and vain amusements were revived and engaged in, as though all were peace. Thousands had fled for their lives, and the streets of Smyrna were crimsoned with Grecian blood. It was estimated that 2000 had been massacred, and heavy exactions of money were demanded of others for the privilege of living. The bodies of the slain were frequently seen floating in the bay. In a word, exactions, imprisonment, or death, met the defenceless Greeks in every direction;—and yet, strange to tell, multitudes, only because they were better protected from Turkish violence, went thoughtlessly to the assembly-room and the dance, as though all were peace and security. While the countenance of many gathered blackness through fear, that of others exhibited only the expression of a thoughtless, ill-timed levity.

(*e*) DANCING OVER A FLOOD.—During the month of December, 1847, in the great rise of the Ohio river, a large portion of Cincinnati was overflowed by the water. Multitudes of the inhabitants were driven from their houses in the lower part of the city. Many were subjected to great privations and losses, and many lives lost. In the midst of these scenes of extraordinary and wide-spread wretchedness, Sheriff Weaver, during his charitable tour through the flooded portions of the city, heard music proceeding from a house, of which the upper story and roof only were above the water, and several skiffs were hitched to the windows. Upon rowing up it was discovered that the hall was in full blaze, and the waltz in giddy whirl to merry music, male and female participating. This jolly party seemed unconscious of the danger that threatened themselves, and indifferent to the distress which surrounded them.

32. They prevent Conversion and Ruin the Soul.

(*a*) THE INQUIRY MEETING AND THE BALL-ROOM.—A most interesting work of grace once occur red in the Houston-street Presbyterian church, of the city of New-York. Many anxiously inquired what they should do to be saved. And many made choice of that good part which shall never be taken from them. Among the number who sought the instruction and prayers of the people of God, was the young lady who is the subject of the following sketch.

She listened to the voice of truth, and was troubled. Conscience spoke within her, and would not be utterly silenced. She *felt* that the claims of God must be met, that she must not delay the work of her salvation. Personally and solemnly was she urged to settle the controversy, to renounce the pleasures of sin, and trust in the merits of a crucified Savior. She knew her duty, but she did it not. The next night the "Boz Ball" was to be held, and from this scene of awful solemnity, away she hurries to the chamber of mirth, and joins in the giddy dance. By the sound of the viol and the voice of melody she aims to drown the admonitions of conscience, and she may have succeeded for the moment. Amid the display of fashion, the glare of lights, and the intoxication of the scene, conscience may have slumbered at her post, and suffered the gay transgressor to revel undisturbed in forbidden pleasure. But she only *seemed* to sleep. The voice of admonition and warning came—it came, though the voice of the living preacher was silent. Again she felt, and again is she seen in the meeting for conversation and prayer. Her heart is the seat of ten thousand painful and conflicting emotions. The claims of truth and duty are urged. She would yield, she would follow Jesus, but the world—the theatre—the ball-room—her gay companions—how can she give them up? Unfortunately she was solicited to attend another ball. Satan, as an angel of light, sheds a deceptive radiance over that scene, and suggests that such amusements are innocent, that her seriousness is melancholy, that there is time enough yet. She triumphed over conscience, yielded to the temptation, and went.

She was permitted to return to her dwelling, *but only to die*; to die, too, as she had lived, *without God or hope.*

Mark the facts that fill the last page of her history. On one evening she is in the meeting for inquiry, the next in the ball-room, gayest among the gay, and almost the next *in her coffin!* One week, with a heart as light as air, she goes to a store to purchase trimmings for a ball dress; on the next, her friends go to the same store to *purchase her shroud!*

Thus ended the career of one who loved pleasure more than she loved God. There was no hope in her death! No light to cheer her in the last sad hour!

(*b*) LOSING THE SOUL FOR A BALL.—I was once called, says a venerable clergyman in B——, to visit a young lady, who was said to be *in despair*. She had, at some time previous, been serious, and had, it was hoped, resolutely set her face Zion-ward. In an evil hour some of her former associates, gay, pleasure-loving young ladies, called on her to accompany them to a ball. She refused to go. The occasion, the company, the parade and gayety were all utterly dissonant with her present feelings. With characteristic levity and thoughtlessness, they urged her—ridiculed her "methodism," railed at the cant and hypocrisy of her spiritual guides; and finally so far prevailed, that with a desperate effort to shake off her convictions and regain her former carnal security, she exclaimed, "*Well, I will go if I am damned for it.*"

God took her at her word. The blessed Spirit immediately withdrew His influences, and instead of the anxious sigh and longing desire to be freed from the body of sin and death, succeeded by turns the calmness and horrors of despair.

The wretched victim knew that the Spirit had taken his final leave; no compunctions for sin, no tears of penitence, no inquiries after God, no eager seeking of the "place where Christians love to meet," now occupied the tedious hours.

Instead of the bloom and freshness of health, there came the paleness and haggardness of decay. The wan and sunken cheek, the ghastly glaring eye, the emaciated limb, the sure precursors of approaching dissolution, were there. The caresses of friends, the suggestions of affection, all were unheeded. The consolations of piety, the last resource of the miserable, were to her but the bitterness of death. In this state of mind, I was called to visit her. When I entered the room where she was, and beheld her pale and emaciated, and reflected that the ravages of her form *without* but faintly shadowed forth the wreck and desolation within, I was almost overpowered. Never had I conceived so vivid an idea of the woe and misery of those who have "quenched the Spirit."

I proposed prayer. The word threw her into an agony. She utterly refused. No entreaties of friends, no arguments drawn from the love of God or from the freeness and fullness of atoning blood, could prevail to shake her resolution. I left her without having been able to find an avenue to her heart, or to dart a ray of comfort into her dark bosom. Never shall I forget the dreadful expression of that ghastly countenance—the tones of that despairing voice. The impression is as vivid as though it had been but yesterday. O that all the young, gay, thoughtless ones, who stifle the convictions of conscience and repress the rising sigh; who dance along on the brink of utter reprobation and despair, would read and lay to heart the warning which the last hours and death of this young lady are calculated so forcibly to make.

(*c*) THE FATAL BALL.—The subject of the following narrative was the idolized daughter of a gay and worldly father, who, in spite of the tears and expostulations of a pious mother, to whom such an act seemed little short of sacrilege, led her to the altar of worldly folly—the village dancing-school. She soon excelled all competitors, and was considered the unrivalled belle. At this crisis her father died, and she lent a willing ear to the explanations of divine truth from her mother, which satisfied her understanding and filled her heart with pure and holy emotions. She was on the point of making a public profession of her faith in Christ, when the village in which she lived was agitated with preparations for a splendid ball. The poor widow shuddered as she witnessed the progress of this much dreaded evil: to complete her uneasiness, a brother of her husband, a man of the world, visiting in the family, declared that he would be at the expense of equipping her daughter as his own child, and that she should eclipse all the women of rank and fashion in the ball-room.

The poor girl was at first unwilling to lend an ear to these follies; but she had always delighted in dancing, and on this occasion suffered her better judgment to be overruled. "'Tis but for once, mother," said she, "and to please my uncle—nay, to avoid giving him incurable offence. Believe me, I shall not suffer my head to be turned by one night of gayety. Pray for me, mother, that this compliance with the will of my father's brother may not produce evil consequences." "My child," said the distressed mother, "I dare not so word my supplication. It is in compliance with *your own will* that you thus venture on the tempter's ground, and in this open act of disobedience to your heavenly Father, I cannot lend my aid to excuse or extenuate your guilt. I have prayed, I will still pray, that you may not venture farther in this matter; but if you do, the responsibility must rest with yourself." "But, mother, the Scriptures say themselves, 'there is a time to dance.'" "So they say, in the same place, 'there is a time to make war, and a time to hate.' The wise man means, that all sins and follies will have their seasons; but he does not therefore advocate sin and folly. Oh, beware, my child, and let the same Scriptures teach you, that 'he who hardeneth his neck under reproof shall be destroyed, and *that suddenly*.' These are fearful words for us to part with, my child. Oh, heed my reproof, and do not harden your neck!" "Mother," said the perplexed girl, "I have promised my uncle to go to this unlucky ball, and I cannot break my promise without incurring his resentment. He has been so kind, that it would be ungrateful to thwart him in this trifle." "Oh, my daughter," said the widow, holding her hands to her ears, "let me not hear you use such awful language! Can it be *you* who calls this sin a trifle? Go, if you will; but make no more vain attempts to pervert right reason, lest you add to your own condemnation."

It was indeed with reluctance that the affectionate daughter left her mother, under such circumstances; but she had surrendered her better judgment for the time, and created an imaginary necessity, by which she suffered herself to be controlled. Much admired, she was so often solicited to dance that her blood became painfully overheated; and finding the heat of the ball-room too oppressive, her partner was conducting her into a little back porch. As she swept rapidly along, panting with heat, she encountered a servant entering with a pitcher of water, more than half intoxicated, and as he staggered out of her way, the contents of the pitcher were discharged full in her panting and overheated bosom. The sudden revulsion of physical feeling occasioned by this accident, was almost instantly fatal. A violent ague terminated in convulsions, and before the dawn of day this lovely and interesting girl expired in the arms of her almost distracted mother, breathing with her last gasp the word "SUDDENLY!"

(*d*) THE LAST CALL.—The Rev. Mr. Clark states, that an acquaintance of his was called on to attend a young man's funeral, of whom Mr. C. learned the following facts:—Some time before his death, young G—— had regularly attended the narrator's church, and the truths of religion had made some impression upon his mind. His pastor observed this, and had several interviews with him, but in vain. The influences of the world pressed hard upon him—his convictions were dissipated; and he seemed to gird himself up to tread, with more determined step, the whole round of earthly pleasure. But, in the midst of gay scenes of fashion and amusement, he heard a new note of alarm. He was suddenly laid upon a sick-bed, and brought to the very brink of the grave! He was now overwhelmed with his reflections, and he resolved to enter at once upon a religious course of life. The minister before referred to called to see him at this time, faithfully warned and counselled him; and young G—— faithfully promised, that if raised up from that sick-bed, the Lord should be his God. He was spared, raised up, but his vow was not kept. But a few weeks had passed by, after he left his sick-room, before he was again immersed in the pleasures and follies of the world.

Mr. M——, his ministerial friend, learning his conduct, shortly after called to pay him a visit. G—— had made arrangements to spend the evening of that very day amid a scene of reckless gayety and dissipation. Mr. M——, with the fearlessness of a faithful minister of Jesus Christ, told G—— that the course he was taking would ruin his soul—that his broken vows would one day rise up in judgment against him—that if he now hesitated to repent, this might be the last call that God would ever send him.

After his departure, when G—— found himself alone, and thought of all the past, he could not refrain from tears, which gushed forth amid the bitterness of his soul. He could not but admit the truth of all that had been said to him; still he was undecided. While absorbed in these reflections, and still in this state of indecision, it was announced to him that a gentleman was waiting to see him. It was one of his gay companions. He had called to make some arrangements in reference to the anticipated party. They had not long been discussing their plans before all serious impressions were effaced from young G——'s mind, and he entered the illuminated festal hall that evening with a light and bounding heart. But the *last call* of God had indeed reached his ear, and been rejected, and now he was going like an ox to the slaughter. In the midst of that intoxicating scene of pleasure, where the splendid and gay costume of each passing group was reflected from a hundred brilliant lamps, and where music poured forth her enchanting strains, in the very act of passing through the varied movements of a spirited waltz, young G—— suddenly drooped, and fell lifeless to the floor!

(*e*) THE YOUNG LADY'S CHOICE.—A young lady residing in Waterbury, Ct., made an engagement to attend a ball in a neighboring town. Before the time arrived, a series of religious meetings were held in W., and not a few among the young people were led to reflection, and became hopefully converted. Miss A. was at that time residing in the minister's family, and was very deeply impressed with the necessity of becoming a Christian. Her distress by day and night was so great she could scarcely eat or sleep. She was faithfully conversed and prayed with; but while others found peace in believing, her distress continued. Her friends, who were aware of her engagement, pressed her at once with the question, whether she was willing to give up the ball for the sake of an interest in Christ. For a while she wavered; she wished very much to be saved, and was ready to surrender every thing else; but she thought so much of the ball, and was so anxious to secure the regards of the young man who had invited her, she desired exceedingly to go this once. Here was a controversy with God; a severe struggle between motives of interest and convictions of duty. At length she fully decided to go to the ball. Her serious impressions were speedily dissipated; all anxiety about her soul subsided, and, so far as known, never revived again. That was doubtless the turning point in her history; and that decision sealed her ruin. It is worthy of remark that the conduct of the young man towards her on their way to the ball, led her to a painful discovery of his corrupt character, destroyed her happiness at the ball, and broke up their correspondence forever. She sold her soul for an apple of Sodom: it tempted her eyes,

"But turned to ashes on the lips."

(*f*) DIFFERENCE BETWEEN AMUSEMENT AND PRAYER.—Mary Ann was a beautiful girl, eighteen or nineteen years of age, of an esteemed and intelligent family. Though acknowledging some regard for religion, she believed, with some of its more worldly professors, that it was right to indulge in fashionable amusements. She was very fond of balls and dances.

In the time of a revival, when her young friends were becoming pious, she was urged by her family physician to dedicate her soul to Christ.

"How can I think," said she, "of becoming pious, when, in doing so, I shall debar myself of the privilege of attending balls? Our minister says dancing is wrong. If the Rev. Mr. —— was our pastor, I think I would venture to be pious, for he allows this innocent amusement." "It was in vain that I tried," says the physician, "to convince her of this delusion, and solemnly reminded her, that she would yet see the difference between a life of amusement and a life of prayer. She listened respectfully, and not without a tear, but clung still to her favorite amusement."

Ere long the physician was summoned to her bed-side. He found her dangerously ill with the typhus fever. He alluded to the state of her soul; but she told him she was too weak then to converse with him; yet she requested an interest in his prayers.

After an absence of several hours he returned, and found her on the brink of dissolution. We quote her physician's words for the remainder of the story.

"The patient had fallen into a state of stupor, so fearfully ominous of the fatal termination of the typhus fever. The tongue and lips were covered with a dark tenacious fur, the speech was scarcely intelligible, and the eyes were partially closed. A sort of low murmur or moaning was heard from her half-opened lips. Yet, when called by name, she would open her eyes, and seemed to recognize those around her. She continued in this condition for several hours, during which period she occasionally uttered the most heart-touching and unearthly groans I ever heard from a mortal being. They distressed me—they distressed us all.

"At last, putting my mouth to her ear, I said—Mary Ann, do tell me what mean these unearthly groans which we hear from you?—What is the matter, my dear child? If it is in your power to tell me, do, I beseech you. And never shall I forget the reply. She opened her once beautiful eyes, slowly raised her pale and attenuated hand, and fixing on me a look that made my very soul ache—such was its solemn intensity—she said, with an audibleness of her voice that utterly astonished us all, '*Doctor, Doctor, there is a difference between a life of amusement and a life of prayer. O, it is hard to die without an interest in Christ.*' She closed her eyes, her hand fell, and all was silent. And, my soul, what a silence was that! Soon the earthly anguish of the sufferer was ended—she spoke not again."

33. BANKRUPTCY.

(*a*) THE HONEST DEBTOR.—In the year 1805, a small tradesman, in a country town in Somersetshire, became so much embarrassed, that he thought it no more than an honest part to make known the situation of his affairs to his creditors. The consequent investigation which took place, terminated in an assignment of his effects, which, when sold, produced a dividend of nine shillings and fourpence in the pound, and he received a discharge from all further claims. But, although thus legally acquitted, and with little prospect of realizing his intention, this honest man formed the honorable resolution of, at least, attempting what appeared to him the obligations of unalterable justice, by making up the deficiency to all his creditors. It is true, the sum required was small, not quite ninety pounds; but his means were proportionably inadequate, having now nothing but his daily labor from which it could be obtained, after defraying the necessary expenses; and his wages were discouragingly low, not averaging more than twelve shillings per week. Mean accommodations and clothing, hard fare and hard work, at length enabled him, through the Divine blessing, to accomplish his purpose. The creditors were all paid in full, and they esteemed his integrity so highly, that they thought proper to acknowledge their sense of it by a handsome present.

(*b*) THE INSOLVENT'S QUERY.—I was made acquainted, says a writer in the Fathers' Magazine, with one case that strongly affected me, of a man who had been many weeks under the awakening influences of the Holy Spirit, and at length, when pressed to give up his heart he propounded to his pastor this question: If one had been involved and had failed, and paid his debts by means of the insolvent act, would he, on becoming pious, feel constrained to pay up all he owed? He was answered, as he should be, in the affirmative. But it was perceived from that moment that the man was more than ever troubled, till, after a conflict of several days, he threw off his care about his soul, and has never been disturbed since. And there was not a doubt with any who intimately knew him, but that those dreadful days secured his speedy and fearful damnation. He has probably gone to give in his account.

(*c*) THE HONEST INSOLVENT.—A gentleman of Boston, says a religious journal, who was unfortunate in business thirty years ago, and consequently unable at that time to meet his engagements with his creditors, after more than twenty years of toil, succeeded in paying every creditor, (except one whose residence could not be ascertained,) the whole amount due them. He has in that twenty years brought up and educated a large family—but still he owed one of his former creditors: he was not satisfied to keep another's property; he made inquiry, and received information that the party had died some years since. He again pursued his inquiry respecting the administrator, and ascertained his name and residence, wrote to him, acknowledged the debt, and requested him to inform him of the manner he would receive the money. A few days since he remitted the whole amount, principal and interest.

(*d*) FAILURE OF ROWLAND HILL TO PRACTISE HIS OWN ADVICE.—It was the custom of this eminently useful minister, at the commencement of a new year, to preach an annual sermon for the "Benevolent Society of Surrey Chapel, for visiting and relieving the Sick Poor at their own Habitations," selecting, at the same time, a few of the most remarkable cases to read to his congregation, that had been visited during the preceding year. On one of these occasions, he narrated the afflictive circumstances of a lady, formerly of property and respectability, who had been plunged into the depths of poverty and want, in a time of sickness, through having imprudently become security for some relation or friend; and Mr. Hill took this opportunity of publicly warning and entreating all present to be on their guard against committing so fatal an error. "I would advise all my friends," said he, "to do the same as I do myself, when any request of this kind comes to me. I just walk out of one room into another, and consider what I can afford to *give*, and what I *ought* to *give* to the applicant; then I return and say, 'Here, my friend, I make you a present of this sum, and if you can get a few others to help you in the same way, perhaps you will get over your difficulty.' Then," said Mr. Hill, with emphasis, "I know the *end* of it, but were I to lend my name, or become surety, I know not *how* that might end."

Strange as it may appear, he was waited on a few months after this, by one of the members of the church, soliciting his kind assistance in procuring him a lucrative situation, then vacant in that parish and district, viz., a collector of the king's taxes; the person urged that it would be the making of him and his family, but that he must have two bondsmen for one thousand pounds each. Mr. Hill said, he would consider of it. This petitioner was well known to Mr. Hill; he had long held a confidential situation in his chapel, and was, besides, in a good trade and connection of business, with his friends. There was no reason to doubt his integrity; and he was one that Mr. Hill was desirous to oblige. The result was, he became one of his securities and prevailed on a gentleman at Clapham to be the other; and the situation was obtained. Alas! alas! for poor Mr. Hill and his brother bondsman! In three or four years, the collector was a defaulter to the amount of thousands. The securities were obliged to pay.

(*e*) THE BANKRUPT'S ENTERTAINMENT.—Dr. Franklin relates the following anecdote of Mr. Denham, an American merchant, with whom he once went a passenger to England. "He had formerly," he says, "been in business at Bristol, had failed, in debt to a number of people, compounded, and went to America; there, by a close application to business as a merchant, he acquired a plentiful fortune in a few years. Returning to England in the ship with me, he invited his old creditors to an entertainment, at which he thanked them for the easy compensation they had favored him with; and when they expected nothing but the treat, every man, at the first remove, found under his plate an order on a banker for the full amount of the unpaid remainder, with interest."

(*f*) THE BANKRUPT QUAKER.—A person of the Quaker profession, says a London paper, having through misfortune become insolvent, and not being able to pay more than 11s. to the pound, formed a resolution, if Providence smiled on his future endeavors, to pay the whole amount, and in case of death he ordered his sons to liquidate his debts by their joint proportions. It pleased God, however, to spare his life, and after struggling with a variety of difficulties, (for his livelihood chiefly depended on his own labor,) he at length saved sufficient to satisfy every demand. One day the old man went with a considerable sum to the surviving son of one of his creditors, who had been dead thirty years, and insisted on paying him the money he owed his father, which he accordingly did with heart-felt satisfaction.

34. BEAUTY.

(*a*) THE FATHER'S ADVICE.—A gentleman had two children: the one a daughter, who was considered plain in her person; the other a son, who was reckoned handsome. One day, as they were playing together, they saw their faces in a looking-glass. The boy was charmed with his beauty, and spoke of it to his sister, who considered his remarks as so many reflections on her want of it. She told her father of the affair, complaining of her brother's rudeness to her. The father, instead of appearing angry, took them both on his knees, and with much affection gave them the following advice:—"I would have you both look in the glass every day; you, my son, that you may be reminded never to dishonor the beauty of your face by the deformity of your actions; and you, my daughter, that you may take care to hide the defect of beauty in your person by the superior lustre of your virtuous and amiable conduct."

(*b*) BEAUTY IN THE GRAVE.—A young lady in A——, N. Y., was attacked with the small-pox. She was gay and thoughtless, and had been much admired for her comeliness and beauty. When the disease made its appearance, she became distressed at the thought of losing her beauty, and manifested her concern, by speaking frequently of such a dreadful event. Her mother, with deep solicitude, seemed to sympathize with the daughter in these fearful apprehensions. They conversed on the subject, and spoke of the probable influence which the circumstance would have upon the future prospects of the unfortunate young lady. While dwelling in her mind on this gloomy picture, the messenger of death suddenly and unexpectedly stood before her, clothed in terrors. He bade her silence her wicked complainings, and follow him, and lay her beauty down in the grave. There was no resisting the mandate. She yielded almost instantly to the stern command, and the worms reveled on that beauteous brow, whose fairness she would so sedulously have preserved. The soul—that seemed not to be thought of. No care had been taken to preserve it pure and spotless, or to cleanse it in the fountain of the Savior's blood. What an unsightly thing is *beauty in the grave!*

35. BEGGARS—BEGGARY.

(*a*) THE QUAKER'S CHARITY.—A certain benevolent Quaker in New-York, was asked by a poor man for money as charity, or for work. The Quaker observed—"Friend, I do not know what I can give thee to do! Let me see; thou mayst take my wood that is in the yard, up stairs, and I will give thee half a dollar." This the poor man was glad to do, and the job lasted him till about noon, when he came and told him the work was done, and asked him if he had any more to do. "Why friend, let me consider," said the queer Quaker: "Oh! thou mayst take the wood down again, and I will give thee another half dollar."

(*b*) OBERLIN'S METHOD.—The Rev. John Frederic Oberlin was distinguished by his charity and benevolence, and though scarcely a mendicant was ever seen in the valley of the Ban de la Roche, where he resided, sometimes a pauper from the neighboring communes, attracted by the well-known disposition of the pastor and his people, wandered thither to implore that assistance which, if deserving, he never failed to receive. "Why do you not work?" was Oberlin's usual interrogation. "Because no one will employ me," was the general reply. "Well, then, I will employ you. There—carry these planks—break those stones—fill that bucket with water, and I will repay you for your trouble." Such was his usual mode of proceeding; and idle beggars were taught to come there no more.

(*c*) THE MAYOR'S OPINION.—At a meeting held in London, concerning the houseless poor, the Lord Mayor remarked, that he considered that one of the greatest causes of vagrancy was want of work. For the purpose of preventing this complaint, he would advise the adoption of a plan, which an old friend of his, Mr. Jackson, one of the overseers of the parish of St. Catherine Cree, had tried. He would provide work, whether that work proved a matter of pecuniary advantage or not; and the host of vagrants who hated work would soon disappear, as they had done in the case of his friend, when they found that without working for it, they could get nothing to eat. The case to which his lordship alluded was as follows: Mr. Jackson was considerably annoyed while he was overseer, by the solicitations of great hulking fellows of the parish, who always said they could get no work. "Well, my poor men," he at length said to some of them, "I'll see and get you a little work." He then took them to the church-yard, and ordered them to pick up all the loose stones that were laying about and throw them in a corner. In a few hours all but one got tired, and skulked off. He who remained calculated upon the contrast between his conduct and that of those who departed, and he actually stayed two or three days, which greatly increased his strength. He collected all the small stones he could find, in a corner. As soon as he had done so, he went off to Mr. Jackson, who had paid him most cheerfully, and said he was again at a loss for work. "Say you so, my poor fellow?" said Mr. Jackson; "then I must see what I can do for you. Let me see, there is a sack, fill that with stones from the corner, and carry them off to Bethnal Green, and make haste back for another sack."

The vagrant proceeded upon his new employment with a very ill grace. As soon as he got to White Chapel Church, he shot the contents of his sack into the church-yard, and swearing that he would never, as long as he lived, go into a church-yard again, walked off with the sack, and was never again seen by Mr. Jackson.

The practice has been found an infallible cure for vagrancy in the parish of St. Catherine Cree.

The celebrated Cooke, the miser of Petonville, knew the disposition of beggars well, and drew much benefit from the knowledge. When any beggar came to his gate, and complained of want of work, Cooke set him to digging the garden, but took care to watch from under a window, lest he should run off with the spade. After an hour or two's labor, the workman stuck his spade into the earth and sneaked off. His place was soon supplied by another, who had very little inclination to labor; and thus Cooke managed to have his garden dug entirely over, without a farthing's expense.

BENEFICENCE.

36. Beneficence in Hazarding Life.

(*a*) WRECK OF THE DUTTON.—The following extract of a letter, written by a distinguished naval officer, and published in the "United Service Journal," very forcibly illustrates his benevolent disposition:

"Why do you ask me to relate the wreck of the Dutton? Susan (Lady Exmouth) and I were driving to a dinner party at Plymouth, when we saw crowds running to the Hoe; and learning it was a wreck, I left the carriage to take her on, and joined the crowd. I saw the loss of the whole five or six hundred was inevitable, without somebody to direct them; for the last officer was pulled ashore as I reached the surf. I urged the officers to return, but they refused; upon which I made the rope fast to myself, and was hauled through the surf on board, established order, and did not leave her until every one was saved but the boatswain, who would not go before me. I got safe, and so did he; and the ship went all to pieces. But I was laid in bed for a week, by getting under the mainmast, which had fallen towards the shore; and my back was cured by Lord Spencer's having conveyed to me by letter his majesty's intention to dub me a baronet. No more have I to say, except that I felt more pleasure in giving to a mother's arms a dear little infant, only three weeks old, than I ever felt in my life; and both were saved. The struggle she had to intrust me with the bantling, was a scene I cannot describe; nor need you; and, consequently, you will never let this be visible."

We are informed that the injunction just referred to, was scrupulously regarded till death removed all necessity for secrecy.

(*b*) FRANCIS II. AND HIS FAMISHING SUBJECTS. — One arm of the Danube separates the city of Vienna from a suburban part called Leopold-stadt. A thaw inundated this part, and the ice carried away the bridge of communication with the capital. The population of Leopold-stadt began to be in the greatest distress for want of provisions. A number of boats were collected and loaded with bread: but no one felt hardy enough to risk the passage, which was rendered extremely dangerous by large bodies of ice. Francis II., who was then emperor, stood at the water's edge: he begged, exhorted, threatened, and promised the highest recompenses, but all in vain; whilst, on the other shore, his subjects, famishing with hunger, stretched forth their hands, and supplicated relief. The monarch immediately leaped singly into a boat loaded with bread, and applied himself to the oars, exclaiming, "Never shall it be said that I saw those perish, without an effort to save them, who would risk their all for me." The example of the sovereign, sudden as electricity, inflamed the spectators, who threw themselves in crowds into the boats. They encountered the sea with success, and gained the suburbs just as their intrepid monarch, with the tear of pity in his eye, held out the bread he had conveyed across the water at the risk of his life.

(*c*) THE ARGYLESHIRE FISHERMAN.—Two fishermen, a few years ago, were mending their nets on board their vessel on one of the lakes in the interior of Argyleshire, at a considerable distance from the shore, when a sudden squall upset their boat. One of them could not swim, and the only oar which floated was caught by him that could swim. His sinking companion cried, "Ah, my poor wife and children, they must starve now!" "Save yourself, I will risk my life for their sakes!" said the other, thrusting the oar under the arm of the drowning man. He committed himself instantly to the deep, expecting to perish for the safety of his companion. That moment the boat struck the bottom, and started the other oar by their side, and thus both were enabled to keep afloat till they were picked up.

(*d*) THE HEROIC PEASANT.—The following generous instance of heroism in a peasant, has somewhat even of the sublime in it. A great inundation having taken place in the north of Italy, owing to an excessive fall of snow in the Alps, followed by a speedy thaw, the river Adige carried off a bridge near Verona, except the middle part, on which was the house of the toll-gatherer, who with his whole family thus remained imprisoned by the waves, and in momentary expectation of certain destruction. They were discovered from the banks, stretching forth their hands, screaming, and imploring succor, while fragments of this only remaining arch were continually dropping into the impetuous torrent. In this extreme danger, the Count of Pulverini, who was a spectator, held out a purse of one hundred sequins, as a reward to any adventurer who would take a boat and save this unhappy family. But the risk of being borne down by the rapidity of the stream, and being dashed against the fragment of the bridge, and of being crushed by the falling of the heavy stones, was so great that not one of the vast number of lookers-on had courage enough to attempt such an exploit. A peasant passing along was informed of the promised reward. Immediately jumping into a boat, he, by amazing strength of oars, gained the middle of the river, and brought the boat under the pile, when the whole terrified family safely descended into it by means of a rope. "Courage," cried he, "now you are safe!" By a still more strenuous effort, and great strength of arm, he brought the boat and family to shore. "Brave fellow!" exclaimed the Count, handing the purse to him; "here is your promised recompense." "I shall never expose my life *for money*," answered the peasant; "my labor affords a sufficient livelihood for myself, my wife and my children; give the purse to this poor family who has lost its all!"

(*e*) RESCUING A DROWNING BOY.—The Rev. Mr. Kelly, of the town of Ayr, once preached an excellent sermon from the parable of the man who fell among thieves. He was particularly severe on the conduct of the priest, who saw him, and ministered not unto him, but passed by on the other side; and, in an animated and pathetic flow of eloquence, he exclaimed, "What! not even the servant of the Almighty! he whose tongue was engaged in the work of charity, whose bosom was appointed the seat of brotherly love, whose heart the emblem of pity; did he refuse to stretch forth his hand, and to take the mantle from his shoulders to cover the nakedness of woe? If he refused, if the shepherd himself went astray, was it to be wondered at that the flock followed?" Such were the precepts of the preacher, and he practised what he preached. The next day, when the river was much increased, a boy was swept overboard from a small boat by the force of the current. A great concourse of people were assembled, but none of them attempted to save the boy; when Mr. Kelly threw himself from his chamber window into the current, and at the hazard of his own life saved that of the boy.

(*f*) MARTINEL'S ACHIEVEMENTS.—The life of adjutant Martinel is full of the most striking and sublime exhibitions of a heroic and self-denying benevolence.

In 1820, at Strasburg, a soldier fell into the river Ill, near the sluices of a mill; the place apparently left no chance for help. Hearing the despairing cries of a woman, Martinel, who was passing, threw himself in, with all his clothes on, and without looking to see if there was a chance for his life or not, he swam directly towards the sluice; and there supporting himself by one hand on the post of the water-gate, he attempted to seize with the other, in his passage, the unfortunate being whom a rapid current carried towards the wheel of the mill. He saw him coming, already sunk several feet under the water; it was necessary to quit the support in order to seize him, by which action he would be carried away himself. He, however, quitted it, seized the body, passed under the mill-wheel with him, carried away by the rapidity of the current, and soon reappeared on the other side of the sluice, without having let go of the poor creature, whom he carried to land, and to whom life was restored.

Another time, at Strasburg, he threw himself into greater, and more certain peril. A powder magazine was on fire, and about to blow up. An exalted sentiment of humanity and devotion impelled him on. Immediately above the magazine, (which contained a barrel of powder and a thousand packets of cartridges,) was a large chamber, used as an infirmary, where nine of his poor comrades, soldiers, were confined to their beds. The people flew on all sides. Martinel engaged several men to aid the invalids with him; and he mounted without perceiving that the increasing fire had prevented his companions from following him. He arrived alone at the door of a chamber near that in which the cartridges were kept. He found that by a fatality this door was locked. He made a battering ram of a bench, and burst it open; but, as he was about to rush in, great flames repulsed him. Then his resolution tottered, he recoiled, and was about to redescend. Then he remembered that the fire was approaching the cartridges, and that if his resolution failed him, his companions were about to be blown up. The instinct of his self-preservation then no longer stopped him; he dashed forward, closing his eyes, across the flames, and with clothes, hands, hair, face, blackened and burned, he found with joy that the cartridges were untouched. He pressed onward, and snatched away the heaps of enveloping paper, which the fire was on the point of reaching. He appeared at a window; he cried and called, "Water! water!" His presence in the powder magazine, reassuring his comrades of the imminence of the peril, they mounted; the chamber of cartridges was inundated, and the nine unfortunate invalids were saved.

37. Beneficence in Dying for Others.

(*a*) THE RUSSIAN DRUMMER.—Many years ago, the Baschirs revolted. Near Krasno-Uffimske, in the government of Perm, they had cut in pieces some companies of dragoons, and devised to take the fortress of Atschitskaja, by stratagem. They dressed themselves in the uniforms of the dragoons, mounted their horses, and marched towards the fortress. To keep up the deception of being really Russians, they had spared a drummer, whom they ordered to play the Russian dragoon march. On approaching the fortress, the gates were thrown open; when the drummer, instead of the march, beat the alarm. The garrison then perceived the treacherous artifice, closed the gates, and prepared for resistance. As the Baschirs could not make a regular attack, they were obliged to retreat, when they cut the poor drummer to pieces. His fate he had foreseen, and therefore his voluntary sacrifice was the more striking and praise-worthy.

(*b*) THE HEROIC NEGRO.—The captain of one of Commodore Johnson's Dutch prizes related, that one day he went out of his own ship, to dine on board another; while he was there, a storm arose, which in a short time made an entire wreck of his own ship, to which it was impossible for him to return. He had left on board two little boys, one four, the other five years old, under the care of a poor black servant. The people struggled to get out of the sinking ship into a large boat, and the poor black took his two little children, tied them into a bag, and put in a little pot of sweetmeats for them, slung them across his shoulder, and put them into the boat; the boat by this time was quite full, the black was stepping into it himself, but was told by the master there was no room for him, that either he or the children must perish, for the weight of both would sink the boat. The exalted, heroic negro did not hesitate a moment. "Very well," said he, "give my duty to my master, and tell him I beg pardon for all my faults;" and then plunged to the bottom, never to rise again till the sea shall give up her dead.

(*c*) A SERVANT DYING FOR HIS MASTER.—A gentleman was travelling, with his valet de chambre, in a sledge, through one of the extensive forests of Poland, when they were suddenly attacked by a number of wolves, which leaped furiously at the carriage. The servant, who instantly perceived that either he or his master must fall a victim to their fury, exclaimed, "Protect my wife and children;" and instantly rushing into the midst of them, perished in a moment, and by this generous act saved his master, who fled from the danger, by driving forward with the greatest rapidity.

(*d*) THE DEVOTED NURSE.—The Rev. S. W. Hanna says: On the 10th of June, 1770, the town of Port-au-Prince, in Hayti, was utterly overthrown by a dreadful earthquake. From one of the falling houses the inmates had fled, except a negro woman, the nurse of her master's infant child. She would not desert her charge, though the walls were even then giving way. Rushing to its bed-side, she stretched forth her arms to enfold it. The building rocked to its foundation;—the roof fell in. Did it crush the hapless pair? The heavy fragments fell indeed upon the woman, but the infant escaped unharmed; for its noble protectress extended her bended form across the body, and, at the sacrifice of her own life, preserved her charge from destruction.

(*e*) CAIUS GRACCHUS AND HIS TWO FRIENDS.—Caius Gracchus, who was the idol of the Roman people, and having carried his regard for the lower orders so far as to draw upon himself the resentment of the nobility, an open rupture ensued; and the two extremities of Rome resembled two camps, Opimius the consul on one side, and Gracchus and his friend Fulvius on the other. A battle ensued, in which the consul, meeting with more vigorous resistance than he expected, proclaimed an amnesty for all those who should lay down their arms; and at the same time promised to pay for the heads of Gracchus and Fulvius their weight in gold. This proclamation had the desired effect. The populace deserted their leaders; Fulvius was taken and beheaded, and Gracchus, at the advice of his two friends, Licinius Crassus his brother-in-law, and Pomponius a Roman knight, determined to flee from the city. He passed, on his way, through the centre of the city, and reached the bridge Sublicius, where his enemies, who pursued him close, would have overtaken and seized him, if his two friends had not opposed their fury; but they saw the danger he was in, and they determined to save his life at the expense of their own. They defended the bridge against all the consular troops till Gracchus was out of their reach; but at length, being overpowered by numbers and covered with wounds, they both expired on the bridge which they had so valiantly defended.

38. Self-denying Beneficence, shown by the Rich.

(*a*) THE CONSECRATED FORTUNE. — A minister of the gospel, conversing with Lady Huntingdon about the wants of a family that appeared to be in distress, her ladyship observed, "I can do for them but very little. I am obliged to be a spectator of miseries which I pity, but cannot relieve: for when I gave myself up to the Lord, I likewise devoted to him all my fortune, with this reserve, that I would take with a sparing hand what might be necessary for my food and raiment, and for the support of my children, should they live to be reduced. I was led to this from a consideration that there were many benevolent persons, who had no religion, who could feel for the temporal miseries of others, and help them; but few, even among professors, who had a proper concern for the awful condition of ignorant and perishing souls. What, therefore, I can save for a while out of my own necessaries I will give them; but more I dare not take without being guilty of sacrilege."

(*b*) LADY HUNTINGDON AND THE TRADESMAN. — Lady Huntingdon, with an income of only £1200 a year, did much for the cause of religion. She maintained the college she had erected, at her sole expense; she erected chapels in most parts of the kingdom, and she supported ministers who were sent to preach in various parts of the world. A minister of the gospel, and a person from the country, once called on her ladyship. When they came out, the countryman turned his eyes towards the house, and, after a short pause, exclaimed, "What a lesson! Can a person of her noble birth, nursed in the lap of grandeur, live in such a house, so meanly furnished — and shall I, a tradesman, be surrounded with luxury and elegance? From this moment I shall hate my house, my furniture, and myself, for spending so little for God, and so much in folly."

(*c*) MATTHEW HALE AND THE POOR.—It is said of the excellent Lord Chief Justice Hale that he frequently invited his poor neighbors to dinner, and made them sit at table with himself. If any of them were sick, so that they could not come, he would send provisions to them warm from his own table. He did not confine his bounties to the poor of his own parish, but diffused supplies to the neighboring parishes as occasion required. He always treated the old, the needy, and the sick, with the tenderness and familiarity that became one who considered they were of the same nature with himself, and were reduced to no other necessities but such as he himself might be brought to. Common beggars he considered in another view. If any of these met him in his walks, or came to his door, he would ask such as were capable of working, why they went about so idly.

If they answered, it was because they could not get employ, he would send them to some field, to gather all the stones in it, and lay them in a heap; and then paid them liberally for their trouble. This being done, he used to send his carts, and cause them to be carried to such places of the highway as needed repair.

(*d*) PRINCESS CHARLOTTE'S BENEVOLENCE.—It is related of the lamented Princess Charlotte, that in one of her walks with Prince Leopold, in November, 1816, she addressed a decent looking man, who was employed as a day-laborer, and said, "My good man, you appear to have seen better days." "I have, your royal highness," he replied: "I have rented a good farm, but the change in the times has ruined me." At this reply she burst into tears, and said to the prince, "Let us be grateful to Providence for his blessings, and endeavor to fulfil the important duties required of us, to make all our laborers happy." On her return home, she desired the steward to make out a list of all the deserving families in the neighborhood, with the particulars of their circumstances: orders were given to the household that the whole of the superfluous food should be carefully distributed according to the wants of the poor: and, instead of the usual festivities on the following birth-days of the prince and princess, £150 were sent on each occasion in clothing the poor.

(*e*) THE DUCHESS OF VENTADOUR.—During a scarcity, nearly approaching to famine, which prevailed in France, produced by the dreadful severity of the preceding winter, the Duchess of Ventadour, who had, on account of her exemplary character, been appointed governess of the infant king, Louis XV., not only gave away all her revenue, but, in addition to this borrowed 80,000 francs to relieve the poor. Her steward remonstrated with her, saying, that she passed all the bounds of prudence; but she meekly replied, "Let us give always, and even borrow, while it is necessary, to save the poor from death; we shall never want, neither I nor my family; in my station there is no great hardship in trusting to Providence."

(*f*) EDWARD COLSTON, THE BRISTOL MERCHANT.—Edward Colston, at the age of forty years, became a very eminent East India merchant, prior to the incorporation of the East India Company, and had forty sail of ships of his own, with immense riches flowing in upon him. He still remained uniform in his charitable disposition, distributing many thousand pounds to various charities in and about London, besides private gifts in many parts of the kingdom. In the year 1708, he instituted a very magnificent school in St. Augustine's-back, in Bristol, which cost him £11,000 in the building, and endowed the same with between £1,700, and £1,800 per annum forever. He likewise gave £10 for apprenticing every boy, and for twelve years after his death £10 to put them into business. It has been frequently reported that his private charities far exceeded those in public. "We have heard," says the Bristol (Eng.) Journal, "that one of his ships trading to the East Indies had been missing upwards of three years, and was supposed to be destroyed at sea, but at length she arrived, richly laden. When his principal clerk brought him the report of her arrival, and of the riches on board, he said, as she was totally given up for lost, he would by no means claim any right to her; therefore he ordered the ship and merchandise to be sold, and the produce thereof to be applied towards the relief of the needy, which directions were immediately carried into execution. Another singular instance of his tender consciousness for charity was at the age of forty, when he entertained some thoughts of changing his condition. He paid his addresses to a lady, but being very timorous lest he should be hindered in his pious and charitable designs, he was determined to make a Christian trial of her temper and disposition, and therefore one morning filled his pockets with gold and silver, in order that, if any object presented itself in the course of their tour over London bridge, he might satisfy his intentions. While they were walking near St. Magnus Church, a woman in extreme misery, with twins in her lap, sat begging; and, as he and his intended lady were arm-in-arm, he beheld the wretched object, put his hand in his pocket, and took out a handful of gold and silver, casting it into the poor woman's lap. The lady being greatly alarmed at such profuse generosity, colored prodigiously; so that, when they were gone a little further towards the bridge-foot, she turned to him, and said, "Sir, do you know what you did a few minutes ago?" "Madam," replied Mr. Colston, "I never let my right hand know what my left hand doeth." He then took his leave of her, and for this reason never married to the day of his death, although he lived to the age of eighty-five.

(*g*) MRS. HOWARD'S SPENDING MONEY.—The benevolent John Howard, well known for his philanthropy, especially his attention to prisoners, having settled his accounts at the close of a particular year, and found a balance in his favor, proposed to his wife to make use of it in a journey to London, or in any other excursion she chose. "What a pretty cottage for a poor family it would build!" was her answer. This charitable hint met with his cordial approbation, and the money was laid out accordingly.

(*h*) WHERE IT SHOULD BE.—When a gentleman who had been accustomed to give away some thousands was supposed to be at the point of death, his presumptive heir inquired where his fortune was to be found. To whom he answered, "that it was in the pockets of the indigent."

(*i*) A BENEVOLENT VICAR.—John Baptist Joseph Languet, vicar of St. Sulpice at Paris, sometimes disbursed the sum of a million of livres in charities in a single year. When there was a general dearth in 1725, he sold, in order to relieve the poor, his household goods, his pictures, and some curious pieces of furniture that he had procured with great difficulty.

39. Self-denying Beneficence, shown by the Poor.

(*a*) PEGGY AND THE ONE-POUND NOTE.—Peggy had been consigned by her dying mother in Ireland to the care of an individual, who brought her up as her servant, bestowing upon her only clothes and food as her wages. Her residence with this person led to Peggy's attendance on the ministry of the gospel. It met, in her case, with a heart prepared by Divine influence to receive it: she imbibed it as the thirsty earth the shower. Her appearance became altered, and her whole demeanour highly improved. Her mistress, finding her services increasingly valuable, and fearing that the temptation to high wages might effect a separation, proffered, of her own accord, to give her a small yearly salary. For this she was truly thankful, and some months having elapsed, she came to me, says a Christian minister in London, one evening after service, apparently with great joy, and slipped a piece of paper into my hand—it was a one-pound note. "Peggy," said I, "what is this?" "Your reverence," said she, "it is the first pound that I could ever call my own since I was born. And what will I do with it? Ah! will I forget my country?—No:—it is for poor Ireland—it is for my countrymen to have the blessed, blessed gospel preached to them." I admired her disinterestedness, but thought the sacrifice too great, as I knew she must want such a sum for very important purposes. "Peggy," said I, "it is too much for you to give; I cannot take it." "Oh, your reverence," she replied, with her characteristic energy, "if you refuse it, I would not sleep for a fortnight;" and she went away, leaving the money in my hand, and exclaiming, "God bless my poor country with the ministry of the gospel."

How much does her liberality outshine that of many!

(*b*) THE NEGRESS AND HER NURSE.—A young lady, a visitor of a Bible Association in New-York, found her way to an obscure cellar, where she discovered a colored woman far gone in a consumption, with her aged husband sitting by her bed-side, and another colored woman, about the age of forty, acting in the capacity of nurse and servant. The young lady told them her business. When the sick woman heard that she came on an errand of mercy, her withered and sickly countenance assumed an unwonted glow and brightness. After expressing a steadfast hope of salvation through the merits of the Savior, she gave the following epitome of her life. But a few years before she was a slave in New Orleans: by industry and economy, she and her husband were enabled to purchase their freedom; and in the course of two or three years to lay up about 400 dollars. Sitting at the door of a cottage one morning, she heard that a number of slaves were to be sold by auction that day. She determined to go and see the sale, and, if possible, to buy one of the female captives, and restore her to liberty. "I have so much money," said she, "and if I can make it the instrument of redeeming one of my fellow beings from slavery, then I can say to my soul, depart in peace." She went and purchased one for 250 dollars. "But now," said she, "I must place her under the ministry of the gospel." She took a passage for herself, her husband, and her liberated friend, for New-York. When they landed, she said, "Now you are in a free state, where the privileges of the gospel are enjoyed; all that I ask for my kindness to you is, that you endeavor to seek the favor of God. If you live with me, and with me work for your support, I shall be rejoiced; you are at liberty to do as you please." The liberated woman accepted her invitation, and was found by the young lady, acting as her deliverer's nurse; and enjoying with her the privileges of that heavenly citizenship in which there is neither bond nor free, but all are one in Christ Jesus. Let us cease to eulogize those who have contributed of their abundance for the relief of the wretched; here was an aged, illiterate, degraded daughter of Africa, who gave her all to promote the salvation of one soul.

(*c*) NOT RICH BUT GENEROUS. —A correspondent of the Philadelphia Native American, writes as follows:

The last time I was in Boston, in passing down Hanover, below Fleet-street, I saw a son of Africa sitting on a pile of wood just sawed, and eating, apparently with a keen relish, some fragments of bread which had just been given him for his work. I should probably have passed him without further notice, had I not been struck with the appearance of a woman who was standing a little distance from him, and watching his operations with eager interest. She was a white woman, dressed in the thin garb of poverty, who, in spite of her emaciated and care-worn countenance, looked like one who had seen better days. Curious to know what interest she could take in his movements, I stopped a moment to watch them.

The wood-sawyer, noticing her fixed look, asked her what she wanted.

Pointing to his meal, spread upon the log, she replied, "I have not eaten so much as that in two weeks."

"Well, sit down here, and take a bite," said the kind-hearted negro; "*although I ain't rich, I am generous.*"

With tears in her eyes, that seemed just before already sealed up from weeping, she drew near the humble table. I did not interfere to deprive the wood-sawyer of the pleasure of completing his generous act (*for generous* it *was* in him to share his only meal with another), but after privately slipping a piece of money into the poor woman's hand, I continued my walk.

But I could not shut out the scene from my thoughts, and the words of the African, "not *rich* but *generous,*" kept ringing in my ears. If riches consist in the means of happiness, what a fund of wealth has a man, whom God has blessed with a sympathizing heart: for where is there greater happiness than in blessing another! Many a man that prefaced his sumptuous dinner with a long grace, found no richer blessings at his table, that day, than did the wood-sawyer upon his log.

(*d*) THE SICK MAN'S GIFT.—The Rev. Mr. Holmes, at a Home Missionary meeting in New-York, related the following circumstance:—

Being appointed an agent of this society, I visited one of the towns of Massachusetts, and was accompanied by the minister to a wretched hovel at some distance from the village. It appeared scarcely habitable. We entered, and my name and message were announced to an old and very feeble man, who was lying on a bed of sickness, and, as it proved, of death. His aged wife was also bowing down over the grave. "Before you speak of the agency," said the old man, "I wish you to pray with me; for I am very feeble and full of pain." His request was granted, and the agency afterwards introduced. "My wife," said the aged Christian, "I think we cannot do much, but we must do something for this object. How much shall we give?" The feeble woman replied, "I shall approve of whatever you think proper." "Then go," said the dying saint, "and bring ten dollars." She went, returned, and stooping down over the wretched, hard bed, said, "Mr. Well, I've brought fifteen dollars, and there's enough left to pay for the flour and those other little things." O sir, said Mr. Holmes, that I could bring the hovel and the bed, and the man and his wife, and place them here before the eyes of this vast assembly, and we should never scarcely need to ask for more money.

(*e*) THE HOTTENTOT'S GIFT. --In the year 1813, says the Rev. J. Campbell, after having visited several nations in the interior of Africa, beyond the colony of the Cape of Good Hope, when returning, I halted at the town of Paarl, within thirty-six miles of Cape Town. Here I was requested by friends to relate publicly the state of the nations in the interior of Africa. About one hundred free persons, with some slaves, attended. At the close, several hundred rixdollars were contributed by the white friends present for the Missionary Society.

After the whites had all left the house, a slave woman and her daughter called upon me, and said, "Sir, will you take any thing from a poor slave, to help to send the gospel to the poor things beyond us?" On my saying, "Most certainly I will," she gave me eightpence, and her daughter fourpence. Having done so, they hastily went out, clapping their hands, and ran to some slave men who were waiting to hear the result. On hearing from her that I cheerfully took subscriptions from slaves they rushed into my room, and every one threw down all that he had, to send the gospel to the poor things beyond them!

The immediate cause of this was—their masters had lately built a place of worship for them, where missionaries, when they happened to be in the town, preached to them; and some of their masters would at times read a sermon to them. These tastes of instruction made them desirous that the nations beyond should be favored with the same advantage.

(*f*) THE INDIAN BROOM-MAKER.—Mr. Hooper, one of the assistant missionaries to the Choctaw Nation, relates in his journal the following affecting instance of benevolence while at Steubenville:—"What most of all affected our hearts was, that a poor African, who, it is believed, is a devout servant of God, came forward, and gave a coat, obtained by making brooms after performing his task in the field. Mr. M'Curdy informed us, that both that man and his wife are praying souls. They are slaves. O! is it not truly animating, is it not enough to touch the tenderest sensibilities of the soul, to see an Ethiopian in such circumstances, thus moved at hearing the Macedonian cry, and thus extending the hand of charity? Should every professed disciple of Christ make such sacrifices as did this poor African, at no distant period would the precious gospel be preached to all nations.

(*g*) THE GREENLANDERS' DONATION.—In a very early period of the Moravian mission in Greenland, the Christian natives of that country were told of the demolition of the Indian congregation at Gnadenhutten, in Pennsylvania; they wept bitterly, and at once commenced efforts for their relief. One said, "I have a fine reindeer skin, which I will give." Another, "And I a pair of new reindeer boots, which I will send." "And I," said a third, "will send them a seal, that they may have something to eat and to burn." Their contributions were accepted and sent. Their hearts had been shut by avarice, but the grace of Christ opened them.

(*h*) THE MINISTER'S WIFE AND THE MONUMENT.—A minister in Illinois, on receiving the sad news that the Ceylon missionaries had been obliged, in consequence of the curtailment of funds, to dismiss five thousand scholars from their schools, and that twenty-five dollars would resuscitate a school, resolved to try and raise that sum in his society.

They were a little band, and had already done what they thought they could for Foreign Missions.

He went before his people, related the melancholy intelligence, and told them that he would give five dollars, if they could raise the remaining twenty. The sum was contributed in a few minutes. He then went home and informed his partner of the result. He found that she, too, had been revolving in her mind how she could raise a similar sum. "Well," said her husband, "if you will give up one gratification, you may." It seems they had recently lost a child, and had sent on an order to New-York for a tombstone, which would cost twenty-five dollars. He proposed to dispense with it. Trying though this was to her maternal feelings, she immediately consented, saying that the living children demanded her money more than the one that was dead.

The order was countermanded, and a school in Ceylon was, of course, resuscitated.

(*i*) SKELTON AND HIS BOOKS.—The salary of the Rev. Philip Skelton, an Irish clergyman, arising from the discharge of his ministerial duties and from tuition, was very small; and yet he gave the larger part of it away, scarcely allowing himself to appear in decent clothing. Returning one Lord's day from public worship, he came to a cabin where an awful fire had occurred. Two children had been burnt to death, and a third showed but faint signs of life. Seeing the poor people had no linen with which to dress the child's sores, he tore his linen from his back piece by piece for their use; and cheerfully submitted to the inconvenience to which it exposed him. Some time after this, when a scarcity of food was felt around him, he sold his library, though his books were the only companions of his solitude, and spent the money in the purchase of provisions for the poor. Some ladies hearing of this, sent him fifty pounds, that he might again obtain several of his most valued works; but while he gratefully acknowledged their kindness, he said he had dedicated the books to God, and then applied the fifty pounds also to the relief of the poor.

(*j*) THE DAUGHTER'S PORTION—The Rev. Mr. Rogers, of this country, attended by an officer of the church, called one morning at the house of an excellent woman a widow, who had recently lost, by death, a pious and beloved daughter. As her circumstances were narrow, little was expected from her. Indeed they called upon her chiefly to testify their respect, and to avoid the imputation of either forgetting her person, or despising her mite. To their great surprise, however, when their errand was made known, she presented to them, with much promptness and cordiality, a sum which, for her, was very large—so large, indeed, that they felt and expressed some scruples about accepting it it. She put an end to the difficulty, by saying, with much decision, "You must take it all: I had laid it up as a portion for my daughter; and I am determined that He who has my daughter shall have her portion too."

(*k*) REV. JOHN WESLEY'S PLATE—HIS BENEVOLENCE.—In the year 1776, the Rev. John Wesley received the following letter, in consequence of a recent resolution of the government, that circulars should be sent to all persons who were suspected of having plate, on which they had not paid duty:—

"Reverend Sir,—As the commissioners cannot doubt that you have plate for which you have hitherto neglected to make an entry, they have directed me to send you a copy of the lords' order, and to inform you that they expect that you forthwith make the entry of all your plate, such entry to bear date from the commencement of the plate duty, or from such time as you have owned, used, had, or kept any quantity of silver plate, chargeable by the act of parliament; as in default thereof, the board will be obliged to signify your refusal to their lordships.

"N. B. An immediate answer is desired."

Mr. Wesley replied as follows:—

"Sir,—I have two silver tea-spoons at London, and two at Bristol: this is all the plate which I have at present; and I shall not buy any more while so many around me want bread. I am, sir, your most humble servant,

"JOHN WESLEY."

Perhaps there never was a more charitable man than Mr. Wesley. His liberality knew no bounds, but an empty pocket. He gave away not merely a certain part of his income, but all that he had: his own wants being provided for, he devoted all the rest to the necessities of others. He entered upon this good work at a very early period. We are told, that when he had thirty pounds a year, he lived on twenty-eight, and gave away forty shillings. The next year, receiving sixty pounds, he still lived on twenty-eight, and gave away two-and-thirty. The third year he received ninety pounds, and gave away sixty-two. The fourth year he received one hundred and twenty pounds. Still he lived on twenty-eight, and gave to the poor ninety-two. During the rest of his life he lived economically; and, in the course of fifty years, it has been supposed, he gave away more than thirty thousand pounds.

(*l*) LAVATER HELPING A POOR WOMAN.—The following is an extract from the private diary of the Rev. J. C. Lavater, of Zurich, in Switzerland, dated January 2d, 1769:—

My wife asked me, during dinner, what sentiment I had chosen for the day. "Give to him that asketh thee; and from him that would borrow turn not thou away." "Pray, how is this to be understood?" said she. "Literally: we must take the words as if we heard Jesus Christ himself pronounce them. I am the steward, not the proprietor of my possessions."

Just as I arose from dinner, a widow desired to speak to me. "You will excuse me, dear sir," said she, "I must pay my rent, and I am six dollars short. I have been ill a whole month, and could scarcely keep my children from starving. I have laid by every penny, but I am six dollars short, and must have them to-day or to-morrow; pray hear me, dear sir." Here she presented me a book enchased with silver. "My late husband," said she, "gave it to me when we were betrothed. I part with it with reluctance, and know not when I can redeem it. O, dear sir, cannot you assist me?" "My poor woman, indeed I cannot." So saying, I put my hand in my pocket, and touched my money: it was about two dollars and a half. "It won't do," said I to myself; "and if it would, I shall want it." "Have you no friend," said I, "who would give you such a trifle?" "No, not a soul living; and I do not like to go from house to house; I would rather work whole nights. I have been told that you are a good-natured gentleman; and if you cannot assist, you will, I hope, excuse me for having given you so much trouble. I will try how I can extricate myself; God has never forsaken me; and I hope he will not begin to turn his back on me in my 76th year." The same moment my wife entered the room.

I was—O thou traitorous heart!—I was angry, ashamed, and should have been glad if I could have sent her away under some pretext or other, for my conscience whispered to me, "Give to him that asketh thee." My wife, too, whispered irresistibly in my ear, "She is a pious, honest woman; she has certainly been ill; assist her if you can." "I have no more than two dollars," said I, "and she wants six; how, therefore, can I answer her demand? I will give her something, and send her away." My wife squeezed my hand tenderly, smiling, and beseeching me by her looks. She then said aloud, what my conscience had whispered to me before: "Give to him that asketh thee; and turn not away from him who would borrow of thee." I smiled, and asked her whether she would give her ring in order to enable me to do it. "With great pleasure," said she, pulling off her ring. The old woman was either too simple to observe this, or too modest to take advantage of it: however, when she was going, my wife told her to wait a little in the passage. "Were you in earnest, my dear, when you offered your ring?" said I, as soon as we were in private. "I am surprised that you can ask that question; do you think I sport with charity? Remember what you said a quarter of an hour ago. You have been always so benevolent, and why are you now backward in assisting that poor woman? Why did you not give her what money you had in your purse? Do you not know that there are six dollars in your bureau, and that it will be quarter-day in ten days?" I pressed my wife to my bosom, and dropped a tear. "You are more righteous than I! Keep your ring; you have made me blush!" I then went to the bureau, and took the six dollars. When I was going to open the door, to call the widow, I was seized with horror because I had said, "I cannot help you."—O, thou traitorous tongue! thou deceitful heart!—"There, take the money," said I, "which you want." She seemed at first to suppose it was only a small contribution, and kissed my hand. But when she saw the six dollars, her astonishment was so great, that for a moment she could not speak. She then said, "How shall I thank you? I cannot repay you; I have got nothing but this poor book, and it is old." "Keep your book and the money," said I, "and thank God, and not me. Indeed I do not deserve it, because I have hesitated so long to assist you. Go, and say not one word more."

(*m*) BENEVOLENCE OF JOHN FOX.—John Fox, the celebrated author of the "Book of Martyrs," was remarkable for his liberality to the poor. What was sometimes offered him by the rich, (for he was himself sometimes distressed,) he accepted, but immediately gave it to those who had less than himself. So entirely did he give of his goods to the poor, that when he died, he possessed no ready money. This benevolence was maintained by a sense of the love of Christ, and was shown with a view to his glory. A friend once inquiring of him, if he recollected a poor man, whom he was accustomed to relieve, he replied, "Yes, I remember him well, and would willingly forget lords and ladies to remember such as him."

40. Beneficence with Rule and System.

(*a*) OBERLIN'S PRACTICE.—John Frederic Oberlin, a minister of the Gospel in France, happening to read one day, with more attention than usual, the accounts of the tithes in the Books of Moses, was so struck with some of them, as to resolve from that moment to devote three tithes of all he possessed to the service of God and the poor. The resolution was no sooner made than put into execution, for whatever Oberlin conceived it to be his duty to do, he conscientiously and without delay set about it. From that period till the end of his life, even during the most calamitous seasons of the Revolution, he always scrupulously adhered to the plan, and often said that he *abounded in wealth.*

(*b*) MRS. GRAHAM'S PRACTICE.—Mrs. Graham, of New-York, made it a rule to appropriate a tenth part of her earnings to be expended for pious and charitable purposes; she had taken a lease of two lots of ground, in Greenwich-street, from the Corporation of Trinity Church, with the view of building a house on them for her own accommodation: the building, however, she never commenced: by a sale which her son-in-law, Mr. Bethune, made of the lease in 1795, for her, she got an advance of one thousand pounds. So large a profit was new to her. "Quick, quick," said she, "let me appropriate the tenth before my heart grows hard." What fidelity in duty! What distrust of herself! Fifty pounds of this money she sent to Mr. Mason, in aid of the funds he was collecting for the establishment of a theological seminary.

(*c*) MR. COBB'S COVENANT.—Nathaniel Ripley Cobb, of Boston, displayed the character of a Christian merchant in all its varieties of excellence. He was one of the few noble-hearted men of wealth whose affluence is constantly proved by their munificence. Yet it was not always from what is strictly denominated affluence that he was so benevolent, inasmuch as the vows of God were upon him that he would never become rich; and he redeemed the holy pledge which he had given, by consecrating his gains to the Lord. In November, 1821, he drew up the following remarkable document:—

"By the grace of God, I will never be worth more than fifty thousand dollars.

"By the grace of God I will give one-fourth of the nett profits of my business to charitable and religious uses.

"If I am ever worth twenty thousand dollars, I will give one half of my nett profits; and if I am ever worth thirty thousand, I will give three-fourths; and the whole after fifty thousand dollars.

"So help me God; or give to a more faithful steward, and set me aside. N. R. Cobb, Nov. 1821."

He adhered to this covenant with strict fidelity. At one time, finding his property had increased beyond fifty thousand dollars, he at once devoted the surplus, seven thousand five hundred, as a foundation for a professorship in the Newton Institution for the education of Christian ministers, to which, on various occasions during his short life, he gave at least twice that amount. He was a generous friend to many young men, whom he assisted in establishing themselves in business, and to many who were unfortunate.

(*d*) DR. WRIGHT'S PRACTICE.—Of Doctor Samuel Wright, it is said, that his charity was conducted upon rule; for which purpose he kept a purse, in which was found this memorandum: "Something from all the money I receive to be put into this purse for charitable uses. From my salary as minister, which is uncertain, a tenth part; from occasional and extraordinary gifts, which are more uncertain, a twentieth part; from copy money of things I print, and interest of my estate, a seventh part."

(*e*) THE BEE-HIVE AND THE WALNUT TREE.—The following account is related by Mr. Charles Stokes Dudley, of England:

At one of the meetings for the circulation of the Scriptures, held in Dorsetshire, in 1833, a clergyman, from a distant county, related a circumstance which had fallen under his own immediate observation. A young farmer and his wife, having attended a meeting for the establishment of an auxiliary society, and another held in the evening of the same day for the formation of a ladies' association, became much interested in the object. On returning home, the wife expressed her earnest desire to subscribe a guinea a year to the female branch of the institution; to which her husband replied, that having become himself a contributor of the same sum to the auxiliary society, he thought they could scarcely afford two guineas a year. His wife reminded him that he had given her, a few days before, a guinea to purchase a hive of bees, which she had not yet bought; and that she should much prefer giving the money to the Bible Association. To this arrangement he consented. On the following day, a swarm of bees settled on a tree in their garden, and was soon safely hived. Struck with the circumstance, they immediately determined that the entire produce of those bees, and of the successive swarms from the hive, should be annually contributed to the Bible Society. The circumstance occurred in 1829. In 1830, the sum of £2 was contributed: in 1831, it increased to £10; last year it was £8; and, this year, they fully expected it would be £10 again, if not more.

I had a speedy proof that the relation of this little fact was not in vain. A friend of ours who was present, and under whose hospitable roof I was staying, observing me, on the following morning, admiring a noble walnut tree in his garden, whispered, "That tree belongs to the Bible Society; my wife and I have just dedicated it." I am happy to say, I never saw a tree better laden in my life.

(*f*) FINLEY AND THE AGENT.—"It is true I have but little to give," said Dr. Finley to an agent, "but I consider it a privilege and an honor, so far as the Lord allows, to have something, if it be but a single nail, in every edifice that is going up for Christ."

(*g*) DOING SOMETHING EVERY WHERE.—At one of the anniversaries in London Rev. Richard Knill said :

When I used to travel for the London Missionary Society, I went to Peterborough. A farmer there had read the report of that society. He found that we had 123 missionaries. He sent to Mr. Arundel to say, "I have a great desire to hit out something new." I question whether any member of Parliament would have hit it. He said, "I am determined to have something to do with every tract distributed, every sermon preached, every school established ; and for this purpose I will give a sovereign for each of the missionaries. Here is a check for £123, in order to do something all over the world." That is what I call an enlarged idea. But in the mean time another report came out, and stated that 13 new missionaries had been sent forth. "Well," said he, "I am determined to keep it up ;" and he gave another £13.

41. Beneficence with Industry and Frugality.

(*a*) THE MISER OF MARSEILLES.—An old man, of the name of Guyot, lived and died in the town of Marseilles, in France. He amassed a large fortune by the most laborious industry, and the severest habits of abstinence and privation. His neighbors considered him a miser, and thought that he was hoarding up money from mean and avaricious motives. The populace pursued him, whenever he appeared, with hootings and execrations, and the boys sometimes threw stones at him. He at length died, and in his will were found the following words :—"Having observed from my infancy that the poor of Marseilles are ill supplied with water, which can only be purchased at a great price, I have cheerfully labored the whole of my life to procure for them this great blessing ; and I direct that the whole of my property shall be laid out in building an aqueduct for their use."

(*b*) SAVING A PENNY A WEEK.—My monthly missionary meeting, writes a clergyman in the Missionary Register for 1817, is, indeed, delightful. You would be highly gratified at witnessing the earnest prayers that are there offered up in behalf of the poor heathen, the interest produced by reading the missionary anecdotes, and the uncommon readiness and willingness, in the poor people, to contribute their pence towards so glorious a cause. One of the poorest women (yet one of the richest in the true sense) in the parish, was heard to say, that she would give her penny a week, if she took it from her food ; and she has literally been as good as her word ; for though tea was her only beverage, and often her only meal, she has for some months deprived herself of sugar, in order to contribute her penny, which she does with great regularity every week. But not content with this, as she obtains a livelihood by going about with a basket which contains needles, cotton, etc., she begged me to write a few lines to authorize her to receive any mite which she could collect in her daily travels from house to house, that she might have a chance of getting a penny, even where she could not sell her needles ; and, indeed, I think I may safely say that she is not more gratified when she takes sixpence for herself, than when she receives a penny for the missionary fund. By this means she generally brings in about three shillings every month, in addition to her own fourpence.

Such an instance shames many. True charity begins only with self-denial.

(*c*) I WILL SPIN ONE MORE HANK.—At a meeting held with the view of forming an auxiliary society in aid of Christian missions, the following anecdote was related by one of the speakers : A woman of Wakefield, well known to be in very needy circumstances, offered to subscribe a penny a week to the missionary fund. "Surely you," said one, "are too poor to afford this." She replied, "I spin so many hanks of yarn for a maintenance; I will spin one more, and that will be a penny for the society." "I would rather," said the speaker, "see that hank suspended in the poor woman's cottage, a token of her zeal for the triumph of the gospel, than military trophies in the halls of heroes, the proud memorials of victories obtained over the physical strength of men!"

(*d*) A REFORMED DRUNKARD'S GIFT.—A religious society in Yorkshire (Eng.) had twenty guineas brought to them by a man in low circumstances of life. Doubting whether it was consistent with his duty to his family and the world, to contribute such a sum, they hesitated to receive it, when he answered to the following effect:—"Before I knew the grace of our Lord, I was a poor drunkard: I never could save a shilling; my family were in beggary and rags; but since it has pleased God to renew me by his grace, we have been industrious and frugal; we have not spent many idle shillings, and we have been enabled to put something into the bank, and this I freely offer to the blessed cause of our Lord and Saviour."—This was the second donation from the individual to the same amount.

(*e*) THE MOUNTAIN FARMER.—An agent soliciting funds for a certain benevolent object, called upon the minister of a poor country town, made known his object, and inquired of that minister, whether there were any individuals in his parish, who would contribute for that object. The minister answered, "No." Then, checking himself, he said, "We have, however, one man who considers himself as a steward of the property of God. Perhaps he would give something. You will find him upon the mountain, yonder." The agent toiled up the steep ascent, and approached his dwelling. It was built of logs, and its door was opened by a leather string. He entered and made known the object of his visit. "We have," said the benevolent farmer, "for several years considered all the products of our farm, above what is necessary for the supply of our own wants, as the Lord's property, to be devoted to some good object. We have so disposed of the whole this year, excepting one article, that is our *cheese*. It may be worth twenty or twenty-five dollars. We had not determined to what object to devote it. We will give you that." This man, living in his cabin of logs, and cultivating a small farm upon the mountain, was accustomed to give for purposes of benevolence, about *three hundred dollars yearly*.

(*f*) A NUMEROUS FAMILY.—A pious gentleman in ——, was engaged in a certain branch of business by which he was rapidly increasing his wealth. When he had made about $50,000, Rev. Mr. —— was one day conversing with him, and asked if he had not accumulated property enough for his family, and if he had not now better give up that kind of business? "Oh," said he, "I have not yet made enough to give each of my children a *single leaf of the Catechism*." "Why," inquired the clergyman, "how large is your family?" "About six hundred millions," was his reply. He looks on the whole family of man as his own family, and he is laboring for the salvation of them all.

(*g*) CROUMBIE'S CARE FOR BUSINESS.—The late Mr. John Croumbie, of Haddington (Eng.), some time before his death, calling on one of his customers, his friend said unto him, "I am sure, Mr. Croumbie, you need not care for business." He replied, "It is true, Mrs. ——, but if I were to give over business, I would not be so able to assist the various societies that are formed for diffusing the knowledge of the gospel throughout the world." The same excellent person, in his last illness, after expressing his surprise that some Christians kept back from the support of these institutions, said with peculiar emphasis, "O how I pity the poor heathen, who have nothing to support their minds in the *prospect of eternity!*" His feelings were evidently excited by his own situation, and a conviction of the misery he would feel, if his mind had not been supported by the gospel in the near prospect of entering into an eternal state.

(*h*) THE UNEXPECTED DONATION.—When the money to build Bethlehem hospital was being collected, those who were employed to solicit donations, went to a small house, the door of which being half opened, they overheard the master, an old man, scolding his female servant for having thrown away a match without using both ends. After diverting themselves some time with the dispute, they presented themselves before the old gentleman, and stated the object of their visit; though, from what had just passed, they entertained very little hope of success. The supposed miser, however, no sooner understood their business than he stepped into a closet, from whence he brought a bag, and counted out four hundred guineas, which he presented to them. No astonishment could exceed that of the collectors at this unexpected occurrence; they expressed their surprise, and told the old gentleman that they had overheard his quarrel with his servant. "Gentlemen," said he, "your surprise is occasioned by a thing of very little consequence. I keep house and save money in my own way; the first furnishes me with the means of doing the other. With regard to benevolent donations, you may always expect most from prudent people who keep their own accounts." When he had thus addressed them, he requested them to withdraw without the smallest ceremony, to prevent which he shut the door, not thinking, probably, so much of the four hundred guineas which he had just given away, as of the match which had been carelessly thrown into the fire.

42. Beneficence with Promptitude.

(*a*) THORNTON AND THE POOR CLERGYMAN.—The late Mr. Thornton was applied to, by a respectable clergyman, for some pecuniary assistance. Mr. Thornton having listened to his story, immediately gave him a draft for fifteen pounds.

Whilst the grateful clergyman was still with him, the post letters arrived, and Mr. Thornton begged him not to go till he should see if he had received any news which might interest him. He began, accordingly, to read one of his letters, and, after a considerable pause, said to his friend, "Here is a letter, conveying bad news indeed; I have lost a very valuable ship, and certainly my loss cannot be less than £20,000. You must return me that draft, my dear sir, and to prove that I do not deceive you, read the letter which I have just received.

What could the poor clergyman do? He recalled to mind the condition of his starving and sickly wife and children, and anticipated the grievous disappointment which his returning from Mr. Thornton without assistance would occasion. However, with a heavy heart he handed the draft back to Mr. T., and betook himself to read the letter, by way of concealing his distressed countenance. He soon perceived the loss was even greater than Mr. T. had mentioned, and all his hopes died away.

In the meantime Mr. Thornton had been writing, and when the letter was returned to him, he said, "You see, my dear sir, how unpleasantly I am situated; however here is another paper, which I desire you will put in your pocket. The poor, hopeless clergyman took it, and opening it, found a draft for fifty pounds. He looked at Mr. T., as if doubting the evidence of his senses, but Mr. T. replied, "My dear sir, as the Almighty seems determined to deprive me of that wealth which he gave, and which he has so good a right to take away, I must be speedy, therefore, to give while it is in my possession."

(*b*) LOSING, BUT LIBERAL.—A wealthy merchant, having lost by one shipwreck, to the value of £1500, ordered his clerk to distribute £100 among poor ministers and people; adding, that if his fortune was going by £1500 at a lump, it was high time to make sure of some part of it before it was gone.

(*c*) DR. WILSON AND THE POOR CLERGYMAN.—The benevolent Dr. Wilson once discovered a clergyman at Bath, who, he was informed, was sick, poor, and had a numerous family. In the evening he gave a friend fifty pounds, requesting him to deliver it in the most delicate manner, and as from an unknown person. The friend said, "I will wait upon him early in the morning." "You will oblige me, sir, by calling directly. Think of what importance a good night's rest may be to that poor man."

(*d*) BAXTER'S DELAY AND LOSS.—When Mr. Baxter lost a thousand pounds which he had laid up for the erection of a school, he used frequently to mention the misfortune as an incitement to be charitable while God gives the power of bestowing, and considered himself as culpable in some degree for having so long delayed the performance of a good action, and suffered his benevolence to be defeated for a want of quickness and diligence.

43. Beneficence to Debtors and Robbers.

(*a*) REV. JOHN WESLEY AND HIS LIKENESS.—Mr. Dudley was one evening taking tea with that eminent artist, Mr. Culy, when he asked him whether he had seen his gallery of busts. Mr. Dudley answering in the negative, and expressing a wish to be gratified with a sight of it, Mr. Culy conducted him thither, and after admiring the busts of the several great men of the day, he came to *one* which particularly attracted his notice, and on inquiry found it was the likeness of the Rev. John Wesley. "This bust," said Culy, "struck Lord Shelbourne in the same manner it does you, and there is a remarkable fact connected with it, which, as I know you are fond of anecdote, I will relate to you precisely in the same manner and words that I did to him. 'My lord,' said I, 'perhaps you have heard of John Wesley, the founder of the Methodists?' 'Oh, yes,' he replied; '*he—that race of fanatics!*' 'Well, my lord; Mr. Wesley had often been urged to have his picture taken, but he always refused, alleging as a reason that he thought it nothing but vanity; indeed, so frequently had he been pressed on this point, that his friends were reluctantly compelled to give up the idea. One day he called on me on the business of our church. I began the old subject of entreating him to allow me to take off his likeness. 'Well,' said I, 'knowing you value money for the means of doing good, if you will grant my request, I will engage to give you ten guineas for the first ten minutes that you sit, and for every minute that exceeds that time you shall receive a guinea.' 'What!' said Mr. Wesley; 'Do I understand you aright, that you will give me ten guineas for having my picture taken? Well, I agree to it.' He then stripped off his coat, and lay on the sofa, and in eight minutes I had the most perfect bust I had ever taken. He then washed his face, and I counted to him ten guineas into his hand. 'Well,' said he, turning to his companion, 'I never till now earned money so speedily; but what shall we do with it?' They then wished me a good-morning, and proceeded over Westminster Bridge. The first object that presented itself to heir view was a poor woman crying bitterly, with three children hanging round her, each sobbing, though apparently too young to understand their mother's grief. On inquiring the cause of her distress, Mr. Wesley learned that the creditors of her husband were dragging him to prison, after having sold their effects, which were inadequate to pay the debt by eighteen shillings, which the creditors declared should be paid. One guinea made her happy! They then proceeded on, followed by the blessings of the now happy mother. On Mr. Wesley's inquiring of Mr. Barton, his friend, where their charity was most needed, he replied he knew of no place where his money would be more acceptable than in Giltspur-street Compter. They accordingly repaired thither, and on asking the turnkey to point out the most miserable object under his care, he answered, if they were come in search of poverty, they need not go far. The first ward they entered they were struck with the appearance of a poor wretch who was greedily eating some potato skins. On being questioned, he informed them that he had been in that situation, supported by the casual alms of compassionate strangers, for several months, without any hope of release, and that he was confined for the debt of half a guinea. On hearing this, Mr. Wesley gave him a guinea, which he received with the utmost gratitude, and he had the pleasure of seeing him liberated with half a guinea in his pocket. The poor man on leaving his place of confinement, said, 'Gentlemen, as you came here in search of poverty, pray go up stairs, if it be not too late.' They instantly proceeded thither, and beheld a sight which called forth all their compassion. On a low stool, with his back towards them, sat a man, or rather a skeleton, for he was literally nothing but skin and bone; his hand supported his head, and his eyes seemed to be riveted on the opposite corner of the chamber, where lay stretched out on a pallet of straw a young woman, in the last stage of consumption, apparently lifeless, with an infant by her side, which was quite dead. Mr. Wesley immediately sent for medical assistance, but it was too late for the unfortunate female, who expired a few hours afterwards from starvation, as the doctor declared. You may imagine, my lord, that the remaining eight guineas would not go far in aiding such distress as this. No expense was spared for the relief of the now only surviving sufferer. But so extreme was the weakness to which he was reduced, that six weeks elapsed before he could speak sufficiently to relate his own history. It appeared that he had been a reputable merchant, and had married a beautiful young lady, eminently accomplished, whom he almost idolized. They lived happily together for some time, until, by failure of a speculation in which his whole property was embarked, he was completely ruined. No sooner did he become acquainted with his misfortune than he called all his creditors together, and laid before them the state of his affairs, showing them his books, which were in the most perfect order. They all willingly signed the dividend except the lawyer, who owed his rise in the world to this merchant; the sum was two hundred and fifty pounds, for which he obstinately declared he should be sent to jail. It was in vain the creditors urged him to pity his forlorn condition, and to consider his great respectability; that feeling was a stranger to his breast, and in spite of all their remonstrances, he was hurried away to prison, followed by his weeping wife. As she was very accomplished, she continued to maintain herself and her husband for some time solely by the use of her pencil, in painting small ornaments on cards; and thus they managed to put a little aside for the time of her confinement. But so long an illness succeeded this event, that she was completely incapacitated from exerting herself for their subsistence, and their scanty savings were soon expended by procuring the necessaries which her situation then required. They were driven to pawn their clothes, and their resources failing, they found themselves at last reduced to absolute starvation. The poor infant had just expired from want, and the hapless mother was about to follow it to the grave when Mr. Wesley and his friend entered; and, as I before said, the husband was so reduced from the same cause, that, without the utmost care, he must have fallen a sacrifice; and as Mr. Wesley, who was not for doing things by halves, had acquainted himself with this case of extreme misery, he went to the creditors and informed them of it. They were beyond measure astonished to learn what he had to name to them; for so long a time had elapsed without hearing any thing of the merchant or his family, some supposed him to be dead, and others that he had left the country. Among the rest he called on the lawyer, and painted to him, in the most glowing colors, the wretchedness he had beheld, and which he (the lawyer) had been instrumental in causing; but even this could not move him to compassion. He declared the merchant should not leave the prison without paying him every farthing! Mr. Wesley repeated his visit to the other creditors, who, considering the case of the sufferer, agreed to raise the sum and release him. Some gave one hundred pounds, others two hundred pounds, and another three hundred pounds. The affairs of the merchant took a different turn: God seemed to prosper him, and in the second year he called his creditors together, thanked them for their kindness, and paid the sum so generously obtained. Success continuing to attend him, he was enabled to pay all his debts, and afterwards realized considerable property. His afflictions made such a deep impression upon his mind, that de determined to remove the possibility of others suffering from the same cause, and for this purpose advanced a considerable sum as a foundation fund for the relief of small debtors. And the very first person who partook of the same was *the inexorable lawyer!*"

This remarkable fact so entirely convinced Lord Shelbourne of the mistaken opinion he had formed of Mr. Wesley, that he immediately ordered a dozen of busts to embellish the grounds of his beautiful residence.

(*b*) WASHINGTON'S DEBTOR.—One Reuben Rouzy, of Virginia, owed the general about one thousand pounds. While President of the United States, one of his agents brought an action for the money; judgment was obtained, and execution issuedagainst the body of the defendant, who was taken to jail. He had a considerable landed estate, but this kind of property cannot be sold in Virginia for debts unless at the discretion of the person. He had a large family, and for the sake of his children preferred lying in jail to selling his land. A friend hinted to him that probably General Washington did not know any thing of the proceeding, and that it might be well to send him a petition, with a statement of the circumstances. He did so, and the very next post from Philadelphia after the arrival of his petition in that city brought him an order for his immediate release, together with a full discharge, and a severe reprimand to the agent for having acted in such a manner. Poor Rouzy was, in consequence, restored to his family, who never laid down their heads at night without presenting prayers to Heaven for their "beloved Washington." Providence smiled upon the labors of the grateful family, and in a few years Rouzy enjoyed the exquisite pleasure of being able to lay the one thousand pounds, with the interest, at the feet of this truly great man. Washington reminded him that the debt was discharged; Rouzy replied, the debt of his family to the father of their country and preserver of their parent could never be discharged; and the general, to avoid the pressing importunity of the grateful Virginian, who would not be denied, accepted the money, only, however, to divide it among Rouzy's children, which he immediately did.

(*c*) M. DE SALLO AND THE ROBBER.—In the year 1662, when Paris was afflicted with a long and severe famine, Mons.eur de Sallo, returning from a summer evening's walk accompanied with only a page, was accosted by a man who presented his pistol, and, in a manner far from hardened resolution, asked him for his money. M. de Sallo, observing that he came to the wrong person, and that he could obtain but little from him, added, I have but three pistoles, which are not worth a scuffle, so, much good may it do you with them; but, like a friend, let me tell you, you are going on in a very bad way." The robber took them, and without asking him for more, walked away with an air of dejection and terror.

The fellow was no sooner gone than M. de Sallo ordered his page to follow the robber, to observe where he went, and to bring him an account of all he should discover. The boy obeyed, pursued him throngh several obscure streets, and at length saw him enter a baker's shop, where he observed him change one of the pistoles and buy a large brown loaf; with this salutary purchase the robber went a few doors farther, and, entering an alley, ascended several flights of stairs. The boy crept up after him to the topmost story, where he saw him go into a room which was no otherwise illuminated than by the friendly light of the moon; and, peeping through a crevice, he perceived the wretched man cast the loaf upon the floor, and, bursting into tears, cry out. "There, eat your fill; this is the dearest loaf I ever bought; I have robbed a gentleman of three pistoles; let us husband them well, and let me have no more teazings; for, soon or late, these doings must bring me to ruin." His wife, having calmed the agony of his mind, took up the loaf, and, cutting it, gave four pieces, to four poor starving children.

The page, having thus performed his commission, returned home and gave his master an account of all he had seen and heard. De Sallo, who was much moved (what *Christian* breast can be unmoved at distress like this!), commanded the boy to call him at five the next morning. He rose accordingly, and took his boy with him to show him the way: he inquired of his neighbors the character of a man who lived in such a garret, with a wife and four children; by whom he was informed that he was a very industrious man, a tender husband, and a quiet neighbor; that his occupation was that of a shoemaker, and that he was a neat workman; but was overburdened with a family, and struggled hard to live in such dear times. Satisfied with this account, M. de Sallo ascended to the shoemaker's lodging, and, knocking at the door, it was opened by the unhappy man himself; who, knowing him at first sight to be the gentleman whom he had robbed, prostrated himself at his feet. M. de Sallo desired him to make no noise, assuring him he had not the least intention to hurt him. "You have a good character," said he, "among your neighbors, but you must expect your life will be cut short if you are so wicked as to continue the freedoms you took with me. Hold your hand; here are thirty pistoles to buy leather; husband it well, and set your children a laudable example. To put you out of further temptations to commit such ruinous and fatal crimes, I will encourage your industry. I hear you are a neat workman; you shall therefore now take measure of me and my lad for two pairs of shoes each, and he shall call upon you for them." The whole family seemed absorbed in joy; amazement and gratitude in some measure deprived them of speech. M. de Sallo departed, greatly moved, and with a mind replete with satisfaction at having saved a man from the commission of guilt, from an ignominious death, and, perhaps, from everlasting misery.

Never was a day much better begun; the consciousness of having performed such an action, whenever it recurs to the mind, must be attended with pleasure, and that self-complacency which is more desirable than gold will be ever the attendant on such truly Christian charity

(*d*) A ROBBER BEFRIENDED.—A young man was stopped in a little street in one of the cities of France; his purse or his life was demanded. A courageous and sensible heart soon distinguishes between the voice of the unfortunate wretch, whom misery drags to crime, and that of the villain whose wickedness prompts him to it. The young man felt that it was an unfortunate person whom he ought to save. "What do you ask, miserable creature. what do you ask?" said he in an imposing tone to his aggressor.

"Nothing sir," answered a sobbing voice; "I ask nothing of you."

"Who are you? what do you do?"

"I am a poor journeyman shoemaker, without the means of supporting my wife and four children."

"I do not know whether you speak the truth. Where do you live?"

"In such a street, at a baker's house."

"We shall see, lead the way."

The shoemaker awed by his firmness, led him to his abode as he would have led him to the bottom of a dungeon. They arrived at the baker's. There was none but a woman in the shop.

"Madam, do you know this man?"

"Yes, sir, he is a poor journeyman shoemaker who lives in the fifth story, and who has much difficulty in sustaining his numerous family."

"How can you let him want bread?"

"Sir, we are young people, newly established; we cannot give much; my husband does not wish me to give more than twenty-four cents credit to this man."

"Give him two loaves of bread. Take these two loaves, and mount to your room."

The shoemaker obeys, as much agitated as if he were about to commit some crime, but in a very different kind of trouble. They enter. The wife and children eagerly take the food which is offered them. The young man has seen too much. He goes out, after giving two louis to the baker's wife, with orders to supply the family with bread according to their wants. Some days after he returns to see the children, to whom he has given a second life, and he tells their father to follow him. He conducts his poor protege into a shop, well built and well furnished with tools, and all the necessary materials for working at his trade. "Would you be contented and happy if this shop were yours?"

"Ah sir, but alas!"

"What?"

"I have not the freeman's right, and it costs"—

"Take me to the syndic jury."

The license was bought, and the shoemaker placed in the shop.

The author of so fine an act of humanity, was a young man about twenty-seven years old. It is calculated that the establishment of this workman cost him from three to four thousand livres. He is not known, and useless researches have been made to discover him.

44. Miscellaneous Examples.

(*a*) BAYARD AND HIS HOSTESS.—When Bresse was taken by storm from the Venetians, the Chevalier Bayard saved a house from plunder whither he had retired to have a dangerous wound dressed; and he secured the mistress of the family and her two daughters who were hid in it. At his departure the lady, as a mark of her gratitude, offered him a casket, containing two thousand five hundred ducats, which he obstinately refused; but observing the refusal was very displeasing to her, and not caring to leave her dissatisfied, he consented to accept of her present; and calling to him the two young ladies to take leave of them, he presented each of them with a thousand ducats, to be added to their marriage portion, and left the remaining five hundred to be distributed among the inhabitants who had been plundered.

(*b*) BENEFICENCE OF LUTHER.—Disinterestedness was a leading feature in the character of Luther: superior to all selfish considerations, he left the honors and emoluments of this world to those who delighted in them. The poverty of this great man did not arise from wanting the means of acquiring riches; for few men have had it in their power more easily to obtain them. The Elector of Saxony offered him the produce of a mine at Sneberg; but he nobly refused it; "Lest," said he, "I should tempt the devil, who is lord of these subterraneous treasures, to tempt me." The enemies of Luther were no strangers to his contempt for gold. When one of the popes asked a certain cardinal, why they did no stop that man's mouth with silver and gold; his eminence replied, "That German beast regards not money!" It may easily be supposed, that the liberality of such a man would often exceed his means. A poor student once telling him of his poverty, he desired his wife to give him a sum of money; and when she informed him they had none left, he immediately seized a cup of some value, which accidentally stood within his reach, and giving it to the poor man, bade him go and sell it, and keep the money to supply his wants. In one of his epistles, Luther says, "I have received one hundred guilders from Taubereim; and Schartts has given me fifty; so that I begin to fear, lest God should reward me in this life. But I will not be satisfied with it. What have I to do with so much money! I gave half of it to P. Priorus, and made the man glad."

(*c*) SIR PHILIP SIDNEY.—This eminent man was governor of Flushing, (Neth.) and general of the horse, under his uncle, the Earl of Leicester. His valor, which was esteemed great, and not exceeded by any of his age, was at least equalled by his humanity. After he had received his death wound, at the battle of Zutphen, and was overcome with thirst from excessive bleeding, he called for drink, which was soon brought him. At the same time, a poor soldier, dangerously wounded, was carried along, who fixed his eager eyes upon the bottle just as Sir Philip was lifting it to his mouth. Sir Philip immediately presented it to him, with the remark, "Thy necessity is greater than mine."

(*d*) GEORGE III. AND THE POOR MECHANIC.—The Rev. A. Redford, in his funeral sermon for this benevolent monarch, states that a respectable mechanic, who had the honor and happiness to be personally known to his majesty, was, through affliction in his family, brought into great pecuniary straits. He was advised to present a petition to the king, stating his circumstances. He did so; and his majesty was pleased to appoint a certain hour on the next morning, when he was ordered to be in waiting. He went accordingly to the gate of the queen's lodge, but through diffidence did not ring for admittance. He lingered until the appointed time was past by a few minutes, when the king came out with some attendants. He instantly observed the petitioner, and said rather sharply, "I desired you to be here precisely at such an hour; it is now five minutes past the time; you know that I am punctual." His majesty condescendingly turned back, saying, "Follow me." He proceeded through several rooms, into his private closet; and having shut the door, went to his desk, and took out a purse and gave it to the applicant, and said, "There is money to pay your debts, and a trifle for yourself." The humble petitioner, overwhelmed with the king's goodness, dropped on his knees, and made a stammering effort to thank his king, but a flood of tears prevented him. His majesty instantly put forth his hand, and with considerable emotion exclaimed, "Get up, get up; thank God that I have it in my power to help an honest man."

(*e*) THE DROWNING SAILORS. —Two boats, some time ago, were sent out from Dover to relieve a vessel in distress. The fury of the tempest overset one of them, which contained three sailors, and one of them sunk. The two remaining sailors were floating on the deep; a rope was thrown to one of them from the other boat, but he refused it, crying out, "Fling it to Tom, he is just ready to go down; I can last some time longer." They did so; Tom was drawn into the boat. The rope was then flung to the generous tar, just in time to save him from drowning also.

(*f*) SAVE HIM FIRST.—An accident occurred in a coal pit near Bitton, in Gloucestershire, when six lives were lost. At the moment when the iron handle of the cart, in which the unfortunate men were, snapped asunder, a man and a boy, who were hanging on the rope above, made a sudden spring, and most providentially laid hold of a chain which is always hanging at the side of the pit as a guide. As soon as possible, after the accident was known at the top of the pit, and it was ascertained that some one was clinging to the side, a man was sent down with a rope and noose to render assistance. He came first, in his descent, to a boy named Daniel Harding, and on his reaching him, the noble-minded lad instantly cried out, "Don't mind me, I can still hold on a little; but Joseph Bawn, who is a little lower down, is nearly exhausted; save him first." The person went on, and found Joseph Bawn, as described by his companion, and, after bringing him safely up, again descended and succeeded in restoring the gallant boy to light and safety. When we state that the time which elapsed from the moment of the accident till the boy was brought up was from fifteen to twenty minutes, his fortitude and heroism will be duly appreciated.

(*g*) DR. FOTHERGILL'S GIFT.—Dr. Fothergill, the botanist, remarked, when about purchasing a property which would leave a poor family destitute, that nothing could afford gratification to him which entailed misery upon another; and then gave the property to them.

(*h*) RESIGNING A LEGACY.—Dr. Crow, chaplain to Bishop Gibson, bequeathed him two thousand five hundred pounds; but the bishop, understanding the doctor had left some poor relations, nobly resigned the whole legacy in their favor.

(*i*) THE AUTHOR AND HIS MANUSCRIPTS.—We translate the following anecdote from the Berlin Evangelische Zeitung. To a learned man, particularly if he is much of a recluse, nothing among all *earthly* possessions lies so near the heart, as the manuscript upon which he has spent the flower of youth and the strength of manhood. Regens, a venerable German divine, had, in the year 1809, a very learned manuscript work upon the Prophets, lying in his cloister, and with it many costly books, which he had acquired by the pains and sacrifices of almost a whole life. In another part of the town there lay, after a battle which had shortly before taken place, many persons severely wounded and dying, to whom Regens had afforded divine consolation and refreshment for the mind as well as the body. By means of a heavy bombardment, the town was set on fire in different quarters, and the monastery, in which were the manuscripts and books, was in flames at one and the same time with the buildings in which lay the sick and dying. While others were intent on their own safety and that of their property, this noble disciple of Christ soon decided what he should do; he let his manuscripts, this labor of many years, and the costly books, burn, and carried the sick and dying, upon his own shoulders, forth from the flames!

(*j*) COWPER'S BENEVOLENCE.—"If there is a good man on earth," Lord Thurlow was wont to say, "it is William Cowper." From his childhood, he possessed a heart of the most exquisite tenderness and sensibility. His life was ennobled by many private acts of beneficence; and his exemplary virtue was such, that the opulent sometimes delighted to make him their almoner. In his sequestered life at Olney he administered abundantly to the wants of the poor: and before he quitted St. Alban's, he took upon himself the charge of a necessitous child, in order to extricate him from the perils of being educated by very profligate parents; this child he educated, and afterwards had him settled at Oundle, in Northamptonshire.

45. Beneficence Rewarded by its own Exercise.

(*a*) TESTIMONY OF CATO.—When Cato was drawing near the close of his life, he declared to his friends, that the greatest comfort of his old age, and that which gave him the highest satisfaction, was the pleasing remembrance of the many benefits and friendly offices he had done to others. To see them easy and happy by his means made him truly so.

(*b*) EXAMPLE OF JULIUS CÆSAR.—It was a common saying of Julius Cæsar, that no music was so charming to his ear as the requests of his friends and the supplications of those in want of his assistance.

(*c*) AURELIUS AND ANTONY—Marcus Aurelius tells us that he could not relish a happiness which nobody shared in but himself. Mark Antony, when depressed, and at the ebb of fortune, cried out "That he had lost all, except what he had given away."

(*d*) BURNET'S PLEASURE.—One of Bishop Burnet's parishioners, being in great distress, applied to him for assistance. The prelate requested to know what would serve him, and reinstate him in his trade. The man named the sum, and Burnet told the servant to give it to him. "Sir," said the servant, "it is all that we have in the house." "Well, give it to this poor man; you do not know the pleasure there is in making a man glad."

(*e*) HOWE'S TURN.—During the days of the commonwealth, the Rev. John Howe, one of Cromwell's chaplains, was frequently applied to by men of all parties for protection, nor did he refuse his influence to any on account of difference in religious opinions. One day, the Protector said to him, "Mr. Howe, you have asked favors for every body besides yourself; pray, when does your turn come?" He replied, "My turn, my Lord Protector, is always come when I can serve another."

(*f*) MORE BLESSED TO GIVE THAN RECEIVE.—A gentleman called on Mr. H——, to solicit his aid towards the erection of a Sunday school room in a poor and populous district. Mr. H. contributed, and the gentleman began to thank him for his contribution, when he prevented him by saying, "I beg you will give me no thanks: I thank you for giving me an opportunity of doing what is good for myself. I am thankful to God for the experience I have had, that 'it is more blessed to give than to receive.'"

(*g*) THE EMPEROR AND THE PEASANT.—Alexander, the late Emperor of Russia, in one of his journeys, came to a spot where they had just dragged out of the water a peasant, who appeared lifeless. He instantly alighted, had the man laid on the side of the bank, and immediately proceeded to strip him, and to rub his temples, wrists, &c. Dr. Wyllie, his majesty's physician, attempted to bleed the patient, but in vain; and after three hours' fruitless attempts to recover him, the doctor declared that it was useless to proceed any farther. The emperor entreated Dr. Wyllie to persevere, and make another attempt to bleed him. The doctor, though he had not the slightest hope of success, proceeded to obey the injunctions of his majesty, who, with some of his attendants, made a last effort at rubbing. At length the emperor had the inexpressible satisfaction of seeing the blood make its appearance, while the poor peasant uttered a feeble groan. His majesty, in a transport of joy, exclaimed that this was the brightest day of his life, while tears stole involuntarily down his cheek. Their exertions were now redoubled: the emperor tore his handkerchief, and bound the arm of the patient, nor did he leave him till he was quite recovered.

(*h*) THE COURAGEOUS NURSE.—The typhus fever, in its alarming and contagious form, spread in a certain village. The neighborhood was in consternation, and none but the medical men were willing to venture near the patients. Who then could nurse them? There was one poor woman who was very often ridiculed for her strict religious notions, and for being so very particular in her ways, and for walking in all weathers to attend Divine worship, at a considerable distance. This poor woman alone attended the sufferers, leaving her own children in the care of her eldest son. She nursed and soothed the sick, attended their dying beds, and performed the last decent offices for those who expired. At this time she desired to attend the Lord's table, and her minister heard from her this simple statement, made with much modesty. She wished to be informed whether the principle on which she acted was quite right, as many had blamed her, and she added, "Sir, *I cannot be happy to do otherwise;* besides, I can speak to them a little about their souls." Her own views and feelings were those of a sinner humbled before the cross, subdued to the world, and yielding herself and all she loved into the hands of a gracious Savior.

She persevered in her work and labor of love; she caught the infection, suffered severely, and but just escaped with her life: the effects of the disease remained, and her once comely person was much altered. Yet with *joy of heart* she spoke to her pastor afterwards of her sufferings, and her only sorrow appeared to arise from the sad thought that some of her patients had expired without any apparent change of heart! God mercifully preserved her husband and all her family from the infection. This humble creature did not display these things as a proof that she had faith, but even those who blamed her were constrained to notice its fruits. The grace of God evidently spread its influence in that village, especially among the young; and even those who despised her holy life and conversation, which they called her peculiarities, were constrained to say that she had shown her faith by her works.

(*i*) AN OCCASION OF GRATITUDE.—Not many years since, (says a correspondent of the New-York Evangelist, in 1830,) I had occasion to solicit funds to aid in the prosecution of a work of benevolence. I stepped into the office of a Christian brother, with whom I had a partial acquaintance, and incidentally mentioned the unpleasant business before me, and inquired of him for the residence of a certain benevolent individual, and added that I hoped to get one dollar of him. After receiving directions, I turned to go out: "But stop," said this brother, "suppose you let *me* have the privilege of contributing a little of the money which the Lord has lent me, to this cause. Put down $100 for me." I expressed my surprise that he should contribute so liberally, and remarked that I should feel myself in duty bound not to call on him very soon on a similar errand. "Well then," said he, "my brother, I think you will very much mistake your duty. If you knew *how much pleasure* it gave me to contribute of my substance to the Lord, you would feel no reluctance in calling again. And now let me charge you, when engaged in similar business, never to pass me by. Call, and I think I shall be able to do something; and if not, my prayers shall go with you."

(*j*) FLETCHER'S GRATITUDE.—The Rev. J. W. Fletcher, of Madeley, and his wife, once visited Dublin for a few weeks. After his last sermon, he was pressed to accept a sum of money as an acknowledgment for his important services. He firmly refused it, but his friend continued to urge it upon him. He at length took the purse in his hand, and said, "Well, do you really force it upon me? Must I accept of it? Is it entirely mine? And may I do with it as I please?" "Yes, yes," was the reply. "God be praised, then; God be praised," said he, casting his brimful eyes to heaven; "behold what a mercy is here! Your poor's fund was just out: I heard some of you complaining that it never was so low before. Take this purse; God has sent it you, raised it among yourselves, and bestowed it upon your poor. It is sacred to them. God be praised! I thank you, I heartily thank you, my dear kind brethren."

(*k*) BIBLE SOCIETY IN SALIES.—The church of Salies, (Basses, Pyrenees,) had been without collections for the poor, or those which had been made were so small that no good could be done with their produce. A Bible Society was established. After that time, Christians paid more attention to their Christian duties; the poor's box was richly replenished; system was introduced into the distribution of alms during the rigor of winter; four or five families, who had suffered by fire, were aided; wood was furnished to the poor, food to the aged, clothing to those in infancy, bread was distributed, &c. During the same year, the number of subscribers to the Bible Society was raised from FIFTY TO TWO HUNDRED AND FIFTY.

46. Beneficence Rewarded by Gratitude and Respect.

(*a*) CROMWELL AND THE FLORENTINE MERCHANT.—Francis Frescobald, a Florentine merchant, descended of a noble family in Italy, had gained a plentiful fortune, of which he was liberal-handed to all in necessity; which being well known to others, though concealed by himself, a young stranger applied to him for charity. Signior Frescobald, seeing something in his countenance more than ordinary, overlookod his tattered clothes, and compassionating his circumstances, asked him what he was, and of what country. "I am," answered the young man, "a native of England; my name is Thomas Cromwell, and my father-in-law is a poor shire-man. I left my country to seek my fortune; came with the French army that were routed at Gatylion, where I was page to a footman, and carried his pike and burgonet after him." Frescobald commiserating his necessities, and having a particular respect for the English nation, clothed him genteelly, took him into his house till he had recovered strength by better diet, and, at his taking leave, mounted him on a good horse, with sixteen ducats of gold in his pockets. Cromwell expressed his thankfulness in a very sensible manner, and returned by land towards England; where, being arrived, he was preferred into the service of Cardinal Wolsey.

After the cardinal's death, he worked himself so effectually into the favor of King Henry VIII, that his majesty made him a baron, viscount, Earl of Essex, and, at last, lord chancellor of England. In the meantime, Signior Frescobald, by repeated losses at sea and land, was reduced to poverty; and, calling to mind, without ever thinking of Cromwell, that some English merchants were indebted to him in the sum of fifteen thousand ducats, he came to London to procure payment.

Travelling in pursuit of this affair, he fortunately met with the lord chancellor, as he was riding to court; who, thinking him to be the same gentleman that had done him such great kindness in Italy, immediately alighted, embraced him, and, with tears of joy, asked him if he was not Signior Francis Frescobald, a Florentine merchant. "Yes, sir," said he, "and your most humble servant." "My servant!" said the chancellor. "No; you are my special friend, that relieved me in my wants, laid the foundation of my greatness, and as such I receive you; and since the affairs of my sovereign will not now permit a longer conference, I beg you will oblige me this day with your company at my house to dine with me."

Signior Frescobald was surprised and astonished with admiration who this great man should be, that acknowledged such obligations, and so passionately expressed a kindness for him; but, contemplating awhile his mien, his voice and carriage, he concluded it to be Cromwell, whom he had relieved at Florence; and, therefore, not a little overjoyed, went to his house. His lordship came soon after, and taking his friend by the hand, turned to the lord high admiral, and other noblemen in his company, saying, "Do not your lordships wonder that I am so glad to see this gentleman? This is he who first contributed to my advancement." He then told them the whole story, and holding him still by the hand, led him into the dining-room, and placed him next himself at table. The company being gone, the chancellor made use of this opportunity to know what affair had brought him into England. Frescobald, in a few words, gave him a true state of his circumstances; to which Cromwell replied, "I am sorry for your misfortunes, and I will make them as easy to you as I can; but, because men ought to be just before they are kind, it is fit I should repay the debt I owe you." Then leading him to his closet, he locked the door, and, opening a coffer, first took out sixteen ducats, delivering them to Frescobald, and said, "My friend, here is the money you lent me at Florence, with ten pieces you laid out for my apparel, and ten more you paid for my horse; but considering that you are a merchant, and might have made some advantage by this money in the way of trade, take these four bags, in every one of which are four hundred ducats, and enjoy them as free gifts of your friend." These the modesty of Frescobald would have refused, but the other forced them upon him. He next caused him to give him the names of all his debtors, and the sums they owed, which account he gave to one of his servants, with a charge to find out the men, and oblige them to pay him in fifteen days, under the penalty of his displeasure; and the servant so well discharged his duty, that in a short time the entire sum was paid. All this time, Signior Frescobald lodged in the chancellor's house, where he was entertained according to his merits, was repeatedly invited to continue in England, and an offer of the loan of sixty thousand ducats for four years, if he would trade here; but he desired to return to Florence, which he did, with extraordinary favors from Cromwell.

(*b*) THE WELSH CLERGYMAN AND THE LONDON MERCHANT.—A poor Welsh clergyman had been noticed by a wealthy London merchant, and received an occasional invitation to dinner. After a time, wishing to improve his circumstances, he set up a boarding-school, and was thereby enabled to obtain a bare maintenance for himself and family; while, from unforeseen events, the merchant became reduced in his circumstances.

No sooner did this sad reverse become known to the poor honest Welshman, than he hastened to evince his grateful feelings for the former kindness of the merchant. He sent for one of his sons, and boarded and educated him until he was of age to go out in life. A friend of the merchant afterwards met him, and inquired after his tried friend, the Welsh clergyman. With some emotion, he informed the friend, that he had recently travelled some miles on foot in order to pay a tribute of respect to him, and to his great grief found that he had lately departed this life. "But," said he, "his memory shall be cherished while my life and reason last."

(*c*) THE SERVANT'S OFFER.—During the severe distress which once visited some of the bankers and merchants of London, a man who had lived several years in the service of one of them, sent a note to his former master to this effect:—"Sir, I formerly lived some years in your father's family, and a few in your own. I saved seven hundred pounds. Can it be made of any use to you? If it can, it is yours: take it."

(*d*) DR. L. AND HIS SERVANT.—Dr. L., a respectable gentleman, was confined for some time in the King's Bench Prison; while his fortune, on account of a law-suit, was unjustly withheld from him. During this distress, he was obliged to tell his negro servant, that, however painful to his feelings, they must part; his difficulties being so great, that he was unable to provide for him the necessaries of life. The negro, well known in the King's Bench Prison by the name of Bob, replied, "No, master, we will never part. Many a year have you kept me; and now I will keep you." Accordingly, Bob went out to work as a day laborer; and, at the end of every week, faithfully brought his earnings to his master. These proved sufficient for the support of them both, until, the law-suit being ended, Dr. L. became possessed of a large fortune. He settled a handsome sum on his faithful servant.

(*e*) THE INDIAN AND THE TEAMSTER.—In former times one of the preachers of the Mohegan Indians, situated on the Thames, between Norwich and New London, America, was preaching on the language of Solomon: "Cast thy bread upon the waters; for thou shalt find it after many days," Eccles. xi. 1. To illustrate his subject, and enforce the duty of benevolence, he related a circumstance connected with his early days, as follows:—A certain man was going from Norwich to New London with a loaded team; on attempting to ascend the hill where Indian lives, he found his team could not draw his load; he came to Indian and got him to help him up with his oxen. After he had got up, he asked Indian what there was to pay. Indian told him to do as much for somebody else. Some time afterwards, Indian wanted a canoe: he went up Shetucket river, found a tree, and made him one. When he got it done, he could not get it to the river. Accordingly, he went to a man and offered him all the money he had, if he would go and draw it to the river for him. The man said he would go. After getting it to the river, Indian offered to pay him. "No," said the man, "don't you recollect so long ago helping a man up the hill by your house?" "Yes." "Well, I am the man; there, take your canoe, and go home." So I find it after many days.

(*f*) THE BLACK TRADER AND HIS FRIEND.—In Ramsay's "Essay on the Treatment and Conversion of African Slaves," he tells us, that in 1756 a fire happened in Barbadoes, which burned down a great part of the town and ruined many of the inhabitants. Joseph Rachel, a black trader, happily lived in a quarter that escaped destruction, and showed his thankfulness, by lessening the distresses of his neighbors. Among those who had lost their all by this heavy misfortune, was a man to whose family Joseph, in the early part of his life, owed some obligations. This man, by too great hospitality, had involved his affairs before the fire happened; and his estate lying in houses, that event entirely ruined him; he escaped with only the clothes on his back. Amidst the cries of misery and want which excited Joseph's compassion, this man's unfortunate situation claimed particular notice. The generous temper of the sufferer, and the obligations that Joseph owed to his family, were powerful motives for acting towards him a friendly part.

Joseph held his bond for sixty pounds sterling. "Unfortunate man," said he, "this shall never rise against thee. Never shalt thou apply for the assistance of any friend against my avarice." He got up, ordered a current account that the man had with him, to a considerable amount, to be drawn out, and in a whim that might have called up a smile on the face of charity, filled his pipe, sat down again, twisted the bond, and lighted his pipe with it. While the account was drawing out, he continued smoking, in a state of mind that a mon arch might envy. When finished, he went in search of his friend, with the account discharged, and the multilated bond in his hand. On meeting with him, he presented the papers to him, with this address:—"Sir, I am sensibly affected with your misfortunes: the obligations that I have received from your family give me a relation to every branch of it. I know that your inability to satisfy for what you owe, gives you more uneasiness than the loss of your own substance. That you may not be anxious on my account, accept of this discharge, and the remains of your bond. I am overpaid in the satisfaction I feel from having done my duty. I beg you to consider this only as a token of the happiness that you will impart to me, whenever you put it in my power to do you a good office." One may easily guess the man's feelings, and how much his mind must have been strengthened to bear up against his misfortunes.

(*g*) THE HAZARDOUS BOND.—A person applied to a pious woman, requesting her husband to become bound for an amount which, if ever demanded, would sweep away all his property. On her replying, "My husband will attend, sir, whenever you may appoint;" a bystander asked her, "Do you know what you are engaging to do, and that perhaps this may be the means of leaving you destitute?" She replied, "Yes, I do; but that gentleman found us in the greatest distress, and by his kindness we are surrounded with comforts: now, should such an event take place, he will only leave us where he found us!"

(*h*) THE BROKEN MERCHANT BEFRIENDED.—A merchant resided many years, highly respected, at Canton and Macao, when a sudden reverse of fortune reduced him from a state of affluence to the greatest necessity. A Chinese merchant, to whom he had formerly rendered service, gratefully offered him an immediate loan of ten thousand dollars, which the gentleman accepted, and gave his bond for the amount: this the Chinese immediately threw into the fire, saying, "When you, my friend, first came to China, I was a poor man: you took me by the hand, and, assisting my honest endeavors, made me rich. Our circumstances are now reversed: I see you poor, while I have affluence." The bystanders had snatched the bond from the flames: the gentleman, sensibly affected by such generosity, pressed his Chinese friend to take the security, which he did, and then effectually destroyed it. The disciple of Confucius, beholding the renewed distress it occasioned, said he would accept of his watch or any little valuable, as a memorial of their friendship. The gentleman immediately presented his watch, and the Chinese, in return, gave him an old iron seal, saying, "Take this seal: it is one I have long used, and possesses no intrinsic value: but as you are going to India, to look after your outstanding concerns, should misfortune further attend you, draw upon me for any sum of money you may stand in need of, seal it with this signet, sign it with your own hand, and I will pay the money."

(*i*) THE INDIAN AND HIS FRIEND.—Dr. Dwight, in his travels in New England, states, that soon after the county of Litchfield began to be settled by the English, a strange Indian arrived at an inn, and asked the hostess, as the evening was advancing, to provide him some refreshment; at the same time observing, that from failure in hunting he had nothing to pay, but promising compensation whenever he succeeded.

The plea was, however, in vain: the hostess loaded him with opprobrious epithets, and declared that it was not to throw away her earnings on such creatures as himself, that she worked so hard. But as the Indian was about to retire, with a countenance expressive of severe suffering, a man who sat by directed the hostess to supply his wants, and promised her full remuneration.

As soon as the Indian had finished his supper, he thanked his benefactor, assured him that he should remember his kindness, and engaged that it should be faithfully recompensed whenever it was in his power. The friend of the Indian had occasion, some years after, to go into the wilderness between Litchfield and Albany, where he was taken prisoner by an Indian scout, and carried to Canada. On his arrival at the principal settlement of the tribe, it was proposed by some of the captors that he should be put to death; but, during the consultation, an old woman demanded that he should be given up to her, that she might adopt him for a son who had been lost in the war. Accordingly he was given up to her, and he passed the succeeding winter in her family, amidst the usual circumstances of savage hospitality.

While, in the course of the following summer, he was at work alone in the forest, an unknown Indian came and asked him to go to a place he pointed out, on a given day; and to this he agreed, though not without some apprehension that mischief was contemplated. His fears increased, his promise was broken. The same person repeated his visit, and after excusing himself in the best way he could, he made another engagement, and kept his word. On reaching the appointed spot, he found the Indian provided with ammunition, two muskets, and two knapsacks; he was ordered to take one of each, and he followed his conductor, under the persuasion that, had he intended him injury he might have despatched him at once. In the day-time they shot the game that came in their way, and at night they slept by the fire they had kindled; but the silence of the Indian, as to the object of their expedition, was mysterious and profound. After many days had thus passed, they came one morning to the top of an eminence, from whence they observed a number of houses rising in the midst of a cultivated country. The Indian asked his companion if he knew the ground, and he eagerly said, "It is Litchfield." His guide then recalled the scene at the inn some years before, and bidding him farewell, exclaimed, "I am that Indian! Now I pray you go home."

(*j*) THE SICK ORPHAN AND HIS NEGRO NURSE.—The following anecdote is told by Mr. Ramsay, in his "Essays on the Treatment and Conversion of African Slaves in the British Sugar Islands."

A lieutenant of a regiment, in garrison at St. Christopher's, died, and left his son an orphan boy. A particular family of his acquaintance on the island had promised him, on his death-bed, to take care of his child; but the boy was totally abandoned by them, and forced to remain among the negro children, and live upon such scraps as he could find. In this destitute state, he caught that loathsome disease the yaws, which became an additional reason for their neglecting him. In the ulcerated condition produced by that distemper, a poor female negro, named Babay, found him, took him into her hut, got him cured, and maintained him till he was able to work for himself. The firs money that he earned went to purchase her freedom. He took her home to his house, and as long as she lived afterwards, which was upwards of forty years, he treated her with the greatest kindness and respect. When she died he gave her a most respectable burial, and had a funeral sermon preached on the occasion.

(*k*) THE WELL-SPENT SHILLING.—A gentleman from the country, passing through the streets of the metropolis, saw a poor man who has formerly been employed by him as a laborer, and his circumstances were those of extreme poverty and distress. He had come up to London to seek employment; but, failing to obtain it, was reduced to a state of extreme destitution. The gentleman gave him a shilling and passed on, perhaps scarcely recollecting the circumstance, till it was recalled to his mind by the man himself, whom, about twelve months afterwards, he met again, and whose decent clothing and cheerful looks indicated a favorable change in his circumstances. "Sir," said the poor fellow, "I am bound to bless you, and pray for you as long as I live; that shilling you gave me has been the making of me: bad enough I wanted it for food; but I was resolved first to turn it round: so I went up and down one of the principal streets, and collected as many hare-skins as it would purchase; these I disposed of, and contented myself with such food as the profits would afford, still reserving the shilling as my stock in trade. By degrees I saved a little more, and to you, sir, I am indebted for the foundation of it all. But for your timely aid, I might have perished. May a blessing attend you as long as you live."

(*l*) THE WIDOW AND THE SAVAGES.—On the banks of the Piscataqua, several villages early began to rise as far up as what is now Dover, N. H. Their intercourse with the tawny sons of the forest was not always that of enemies; the latter often came forth to visit their white brethren on terms of friendship; and, on one of those occasions, a squaw, with her infant suddenly taken ill, sought a place for shelter and repose. A widow, alone with her family on the outskirts of the settlement, kindly welcomed them to her humble abode, nursed the sick babe as her own, and, when it was restored to health, sent them on their way with her blessing. That deed of kindness was not lost. Years rolled on; but the Indian did not forget her humble benefactor. Strife arose between the two races; and the Indians prepared to empty upon the place the vials of their wrath. They surrounded it at dead of night; but, before striking a single blow, they sought the poor widow's house, and placed there a guard, lest some of their warriors should, in their ignorance or heedless rage, wreak upon their friend a vengeance aimed only at their foes. This done, they went to their work of fire and blood; nor did they stay their hand until the settlement was in flames, and most of its inhabitants, save the widow and her children, were butchered or made captives.

(*m*) GIVING SIXPENCE A WEEK TO A POOR WOMAN.—The Rev. W. Jay, in his interesting memoirs of his friend and tutor, the Rev. C. Winter, introduces the following fact:

I remember some years ago to have buried a corpse. In the extremity of the audience that surrounded me, I discerned a female, wrinkled with age, and bending with weakness. One hand held a motherless grandchild, the other wiped away her tears with the corner of her woollen apron. I pressed towards her when the service was closed, and said, "Have you lost a friend?" She heaved a melancholy sigh. "The Lord bless her memory!" I soon found the deceased had allowed her, for several years, sixpence per week! O my God! is it possible that the appropriation of a sum so inconsiderable, may cause a widow's heart to sing for joy, and save the child of the needy!

(*n*) BREAD ON THE WATERS.—A benevolent young lady was requested to assist two poor women, who were said to be in great distress. She went, and found two maiden females, advanced in life, dwelling in a small cellar. One was afflicted with a slow consumption; and the other was obliged to spend her whole time in waiting upon her; so that neither of them could earn any thing, and their distress was very great. The young visitor found them in want of all things but confidence in God, and hope in his mercy; and, as a follower of Him who went about doing good, she took effectual means to provide for the wants of these afflicted sisters.

In one of her visits to this abode of misery, she learned that the poor women had once themselves had the pleasure of relieving the poor. Once *they* were rich—once *they* had visited the destitute, fed the hungry, and supported the sick; but, in the war between this country and Great Britain, they lost their father—were deprived of their property in the general disorder of the times; and, when young ladies, were obliged, with their mother, to keep a boarding-house for their maintenance. Some of their boarders were soldiers; and one of them, a young man from Connecticut, never having received his soldier's pay, was unable to discharge the bill for his board. When thus poor, he was taken ill; and, for five or six weeks, these ladies waited upon him with all the kindness which a mother or sister could have done. "They cast their bread upon the waters."—But who was this soldier? And who was the young lady, who went on this errand of mercy to the cellar? The soldier, having fought his country's battles, laid aside his armor, and slept in the tomb. A son of the soldier was married to the young lady. Yes, it was the good pleasure of God, that the wife of the son of the sick soldier should comfort those who comforted him. The aged females were long assisted by the soldier's son. After many days, the bread which they cast upon the waters was returned to them. They had pity upon the poor; and the Lord was pleased, according to his gracious promise, to repay them with interest.

(*o*) THE GRATEFUL SOLDIER. —The Rev. John Craig, a distinguished minister, and colleague of Knox, having gone to reside in Bologna, in a convent of Dominicans, found a copy of "Calvin's Institutes," which God made the means of his conversion to the reformed faith. He was seized as a heretic soon after, and carried to Rome, where he was condemned to be burnt; but, on the evening preceding the day of execution, the reigning pontiff died, and, according to custom, the doors of all the prisons were thrown open. All others were released; but heretics, after being permitted to go outside the walls, were re-conducted to their cells. That night, however, a tumult was excited, and Craig and his companions escaped. They had entered a small inn at some distance from Rome, when they were overtaken by a party of soldiers, sent to apprehend them. On entering the house, the captain looked Craig steadfastly in the face, and asked him if he remembered having once relieved a poor wounded soldier, in the neighborhood of Bologna: Craig had forgotten it. "But," said the captain, "I am the man; I shall requite your kindness; you are at liberty; your companions I must take with me; but, for your sake, I shall treat them with all possible lenity." He gave him all the money he had, and Craig escaped. But his money soon failed him; yet God, who feeds the ravens, did not. Lying at the side of a wood, full of gloomy apprehensions, a dog came running up to him with a purse in its teeth. Suspecting some evil, he attempted to drive the animal away, but in vain. He at length took the purse, and found in it a sum of money which carried him to Vienna.

(*p*) A SUICIDE PREVENTED.—A Piedmontese nobleman, into whose company I fell at Turin, (says Mr. Rages of Italy,) told me his story without reserve, as follows: "I was weary of life, and after a day such as few have known, and none would wish to remember, was lounging along the street to the river, when I felt a sudden check: I turned, and beheld a little boy, who caught the skirt of my coat in his anxiety to solicit my notice, whose look and manner were irresistible. Not less was the lesson he had learned—'There are six of us, and we are dying for food.' Why should not I, said I to myself, relieve this wretched family? I have the means, and it will not delay me many minutes. But what if it does? The scene of misery he conducted me to, I cannot describe; I threw them my purse, and their burst of gratitude overcame me. It filled my eyes, it went as cordial to my heart. I will call again to-morrow, I said. Fool that I was, to think of leaving a world where so much pleasure was to be had, and so cheaply."

(*q*) THE MECHANIC'S SON AND THE REDUCED MERCHANT.—A Philadelphia merchant in former times, whose wealth and importance were only equalled by the goodness of his heart and the purity of his principles, rescued a mechanic from the clutches of poverty, and, what was worse in those days, from the hands of the sheriff. The son of the mechanic was young, but old enough to know his father's benefactor. Many years after this, the merchant fell into difficulties, and at the most trying moment, when all his friends had forsaken him, the mechanic's son, now comparatively wealthy, stepped forward to his relief. "I am much indebted to you," said the reduced merchant. "By no means," said the other; "I have only paid the debt which my father contracted, at the corner of Chesnut-street, thirty years ago, when I was just old enough to know the cause of my poor mother's grief."

The merchant grasped his hand, and burst into a flood of tears.

(*r*) SCATTERING YET INCREASING.—The agent of the N. H. Domestic Miss. Society, was obtaining life subscriptions for the Society in the town of H.

After having obtained a few, he called on Mr. P., a liberal man, who, though not a professor of religion, was ready without urging, to aid every benevolent object. The paper was presented, and he was left to act according to his own judgment. He was in debt, having a large sum to pay out as legacies from his father. But, said he, if I knew what duty was I would do it. He looked at the paper, and laid it down; looked, and laid it down again; but finally took his pen and signed his name, trusting to Providence to bear him through.

One portion of that legacy was to be paid to a brother then residing in a distant part of the country, a minister of the gospel, but who was not in need of more property. This brother came to the residence of the brother who owed the debt, on a visit. Through the mediation of a friend, the subject of the legacy was brought forward. "Name it not," said the minister; "I care nothing about it; let us seek the salvation of the soul of my brother." "No," said that friend, "your brother says he must have this settled; it is a burden to him, it stands in the way of his good." "Well, is my brother a good Society man?" "Yes," was the answer, and then the preceding incident was described to him. "Make out a paper; I am ready to sign any thing, even an acquittance of the whole." And he did it. And his mind was balanced to this act of benevolence to his brother, by the fact that he was so ready to do good, and gave when duty was so doubtful. Had he withholden in that one instance, he would probably have paid ten times the sum which he contributed for life-membership. Trust in the Lord and do good, and verily thou shalt be fed.

(*s*) OBERLIN IN THE FRENCH REVOLUTION.—During the revolution in France, the Ban de la Roche (a mountainous canton in the northeast of that kingdom) alone seemed to be an asylum of peace in the midst of war and carnage. Though every kind of worship was interdicted throughout France, and almost all the clergy of Alsace, men of learning, talents, and property, were imprisoned,—John Frederic Oberlin, pastor of Waldbach, was allowed to continue his work of benevolence and instruction unmolested. His house became the retreat of many individuals of different religious persuasions, and of distinguished rank, who fled thither, under the influence of terror, from Strasburg and its environs, and who always received the most open-hearted and cordial reception, though it endangered his own situation. "I once," says a gentleman, who was then residing at Waldbach, "saw a chief actor of the revolution in Oberlin's house, and in that atmosphere he seemed to have lost his sanguinary disposition, and to have exchanged the fierceness of the tiger for the gentleness of the lamb.

(*t*) DR. DODDRIDGE'S DAUGHTER.—Dr. Doddridge one day asked his little daughter how it was that every body loved her: "I know not," said she, "unless it be that I love every body."

47. Beneficence Rewarded in various ways by Providence.

(*a*) TIBERIUS II. AND HIS TREASURE.—Tiberius II. was so liberal to the poor, that his wife blamed him for it. Speaking to him once of his wasting his treasure by this means, he told her, "he should never want money so long as, in obedience to Christ's command, he supplied the necessities of the poor." Shortly after this, he found a great treasure under a marble table which had been taken up; and news was also brought him of the death of a very rich man, who had left his whole estate to him.

(*b*) "BRING YE ALL THE TITHES."—"Some years ago," says one, "I recollect reading a striking sermon by the late Mr. Simpson, of Macclesfield; the subject, I think, was Christian liberality; but what most forcibly struck my mind, was a passage quoted from Malachi iii. 10: 'Bring ye all the tithes into the storehouse,' &c. I cannot describe how my mind was impressed with the manner in which Jehovah here condescended to challenge his people, when he says, 'And prove me now herewith,' &c. Suffice it to say, that the subject made such an impression, I found it my duty to do more for the cause of God than

I ever had done. I did so, and on closing that year's accounts, I found that I had gained more than in any two years preceding it. Some time afterwards, I thought the Redeemer's cause had an additional claim, as the place in which we worshipped him wanted some repairs. The sum I then gave was £20; and in a very little time afterwards I received £40, which I had long given up as lost."

(*c*) TITHING AND THRIVING.—The Rev. Mr. Whately having in a sermon warmly recommended his hearers to put in a purse by itself a certain portion for every pound of profits of their worldly trades for works of piety, he observed, if they did so, that instead of secret grudging when objects of charity were presented, they would look out for them and rejoice to find them. A neighboring clergyman hearing him, and being deeply affected with what he so forcibly recommended, went to him after the sermon was ended, and asked what proportion of his income he ought in conscience to give. "As to that," said he, "I am not to prescribe to others; but I will tell you what has been my own practice. You know, sir, some years ago, I was often beholden to you for the loan of ten pounds at a time. The truth is, I could not bring the year about, though my receipts were not despicable, and I was not at all conscious of any unnecessary expenses. At length I inquired of my family what relief was given to the poor; and not being satisfied, I instantly resolved to lay aside evey *tenth* shilling of all my receipts for charitable uses; and the Lord has made me so to thrive, since I adopted this method, that now, if you have occasion, I can lend you ten times as much as I have formerly been forced to borrow."

(*d*) THE COVENTRY DOLE.—A singular charity, entitled "The Coventry Dole," has recently been a subject of investigation in Devizes, of which the following is said to be the origin:—

A poor weaver, passing through the place, without money and without friends, being overtaken by hunger and the utmost necessity, applied for charity to a baker, who kindly gave him a penny loaf. The weaver made his way to Coventry, where, after many years of industry, he amassed a fortune; and by his will, in remembrance of the seasonable charity of Devizes, he bequeathed a sum, in trust, for the purpose of distributing, on the anniversary of the day when he was so relieved, a halfpenny loaf to every person in the town, gentle and simple, and to every traveller that should pass through the town on that day a penny loaf.

(*e*) VESSEL SAVED BY A DOLPHIN.—Mr. Colstone, an eminent merchant of Bristol, who lived a century ago, was remarkable for his liberality to the poor, and equally distinguished for his success in commerce. The providence of God seemed to smile, in a peculiar manner, on the concerns of one who made so good a use of his affluence. It has been said, that he never insured, nor ever lost a ship. Once, indeed, a vessel belonging to him on her voyage home, struck on a rock, and immediately sprang a leak, by which so much water was admitted as to threaten speedy destruction. Means were instantly adopted to save the vessel, but all seemed ineffectual, as the water rose rapidly. In a short time, however, the leak stopped without any apparent cause, and the vessel reached Bristol in safety. On examining her bottom, a fish, said to be a dolphin, was found fast wedged in the fracture made by the rock when she struck; which had prevented any water from entering during the remainder of the voyage. As a memorial of this singular event, the figure of a dolphin is carved on the staves which are carried in procession, on public occasions, by the children who are educated at the charity schools founded by Mr. Colstone.

(*f*) A CHILD'S LIFE SAVED BY HER FATHER.—As the Rev. Joseph Davis, an excellent Baptist minister in London, was walking along one of the crowded streets of that city, his attention was arrested by the circumstance that a carriage with several horses was just about to pass over a little girl, who was slowly crossing the road. He strongly felt the danger of the child, and forgetting his own, he ran, snatched her up in his arms, and hastened with her to the side path, when the thought struck him—how would the parents of this dear child have felt, had she been killed!—At this moment he looked in the face of the little girl, which had been concealed from his view by her bonnet, and imagine, if you can, what his feelings were when he discovered that it was his daughter!

(*g*) THE BOLD PETITIONER.—The Romans had a law, that no person should approach the emperor's tent in the night, upon the pain of death; but it once happened, that a soldier was found in that situation, with a petition in his hand, waiting for an opportunity of presenting it. He was apprehended, and going to be immediately executed; but the emperor having overheard the matter in his pavilion, cried aloud, saying, "If the petition be for himself let him die; if for another, spare his life." Upon inquiry, it was found that the generous soldier prayed for the lives of his two comrades who had been taken asleep on the watch. The emperor nobly forgave them all.

(*h*) THE TRAVELLER'S GIFT.—About the year 1797, Mr. M. was travelling from a town on the eastern border of Vermont, to another town on the western side of the same state. Passing over the mountainous part of the country, between the Connecticut and Onion rivers, he perceived the heavens to be gathering blackness; the sound of distant thunder was heard, and a heavy shower of rain was seen to be fast approaching. The traveller was then in a forest; no place of shelter appeared, and he hastened on until he arrived at a small cottage on the extreme border of the woods. The rain just then began to rush down with great violence. He sprang from his horse, pulled off his saddle, and without ceremony went into the house. Surprised to see no family, but a female with an infant child, he began to apologize for his sudden appearance; and hoped she would not be alarmed, but permit him to tarry till the rain had abated. She replied, that she was glad he had happened to come in, for she was always much terrified by thunder. "But why, madam," asked he, "should you be afraid of thunder? It is the voice of God, and will do no harm to those who love him and commit themselves to his care."

After conversing with her for a while on this topic, he inquired if she had any neighbors who were religious. She told him she had neighbors about two miles off, but whether they were religious or not she did not know; only she had heard that some man was in the habit of coming there to preach once a fortnight. Her husband went once, but she had never been to their meetings. In regard to every thing of a religious kind, she appeared to be profoundly ignorant.

The rain had now passed over, and the face of nature smiled. The pious traveller, about to depart, expressed to the woman his thanks for her hospitality and his earnest desire for the salvation of her soul. He earnestly besought her to read her Bible daily, and to give good heed to it, as to "a light shining in a dark place." She, with tears in her eyes, confessed that she had no Bible. They had never been able to buy one. "Could you read one, if you had it?" "Yes, sir, and would be glad to do so." "Poor woman," said he, "I do heartily pity you; farewell."

He was preparing to pursue his journey. But he reflected: "This woman is in very great need of a Bible. Oh that I had one to give her! But I have not. As for money to buy one, I have none to spare: I have no more than will be absolutely necessary for my expenses home. I must go: but if I leave this woman without the means to procure the word of God, she may perish for lack of knowledge. What shall I do?" He recollected the Scriptures, "He that hath pity on the poor, lendeth to the Lord." "Cast thy bread upon the waters, for thou shalt find it after many days." His heart responded, "I will trust the Lord." He took a dollar from his purse, went back, and desired the woman to take it, and as soon as possible procure for herself a Bible. She promised to do so, saying, that she knew where one could be obtained.

He again took his leave, and set off

As there were then but few taverns on the road, he asked for a lodging at a private house, near which he found himself when night overtook him. He had yet a few pieces of change in his pocket; but as a journey of two more days was before him, he purposed to make his supper on a cold morsel which he had with him. But when the family came round their table to take their evening repast, the master of the house very urgently invited the stranger to join with them—not only so, but to crave God's blessing on their meal. He now began to feel himself among friends, and at liberty to speak freely on Divine things. The family appeared gratified in listening to his discourse till a late hour: it was a season of refreshing to their thirsty souls. In the morning, the traveller was urged to tarry till breakfast, but declined, the distance he had to travel requiring him to set off early. His host would take no compensation, and he departed, giving him many thanks. He travelled on till late in the morning, when, finding no public house, he stopped again at a private one for refreshment. While waiting, he lost no time to recommend Christ and him crucified to the family. When ready to depart, he offered to pay the mistress of the house, who had waited upon him very kindly, for his repast, and the oats for his horse; but she would receive nothing. Thus he went on, asking for refreshment as often as he needed it, and recommending religion wherever he called; and always offering, as another traveller would do, to pay his expenses; but no one would accept his money, although it was not known that his stock was so low, for he told them not, and his appearance was respectable: at home he was a man of wealth. "What," thought he, "does this mean? I was never treated in this manner on a journey before." The dollar given to the destitute woman recurred to his mind; and conscience replied, "I have been well paid. It is, indeed, safe lending to the Lord." On the second day after he left the cottage in the wilderness he arrived safely at home; and still had money for the poor, having been at no cost whatever.

About a year and a half after this, a stranger called at the house of Mr. M. for some refreshment. In the course of conversation, he observed that he lived on the other side of the mountain, near Connecticut river. Mr. M. inquired whether the people in that vicinity paid much attention to religion. The traveller replied, "Not much; but in a town twenty or thirty miles beyond the river, with which I am acquainted, there has been a powerful revival. The commencement of it was very extraordinary. The first person that was awakened and brought to repentance, was a poor woman, who lived in a very retired place. She told her friends and neighbors that a stranger was driven into her house by a thunder-storm, and talked to her so seriously, that she began, while listening to his discourse, to feel concerned about her soul. The gentleman was much affected when he found that she had no Bible; and, after he had left the house to go on his journey, returned again, and gave her a dollar to buy one; and charged her to get it soon, and read it diligently. She did so; and it had been the means, as she believed, of bringing her from darkness into light; from a state of stupidity and sin, to delight in the truth and ways of God. The name of this pious man, or the place of his residence, she knew not. But she believed it was the Lord that sent him. At this relation, and the great change which was obvious in the woman, her neighbors wondered much. They were induced to meditate on the goodness, wisdom, and power of God, displayed in this singular event of his providence. They were led to think of the importance of attending more to the Bible themselves; and were finally awakened to a deep concern for the salvation of their souls. As many as thirty or forty are already hopefully converted, and rejoicing in God their Savior." Mr. M., who had listened to this relation with a heart swelling more and more with wonder, gratitude, and joy, could refrain no longer; but, with hands and eyes upraised to heaven, exclaimed, "My God, thou hast paid me again!"

(*i*) THANKSGIVING PRESENTS. --The following anecdote was communicated to the editor of this work, by Capt. S., a late agent of the Am. Bethel Society. The day before thanksgiving, in the State of New-York, I was at F., and just about to return to O., where I resided, when I observed a country sleigh, with a load of chickens, dressed for the market. The thought struck me that there was *this* poor neighbor and *that* poor neighbor in O. who would receive a brace of these fowls from me with a great deal of pleasure, and that if by making such a present, I should add to *their* happiness on thanksgiving day, I should thereby add not a little to my *own*. As the countryman came up, I asked him at what price he would sell them. He was anxious to get home, and offered to dispose of them cheap, and I took the whole eleven pair, though I scarcely knew what I could do with them. My wife was astonished at my load of chickens, when I returned home; but learning my design, she approved of it, and entered with a warm heart into my plans. The next morning I engaged my two little boys to take upon them selves the business of being almoners of their father's bounty; for I have ever felt it important for the development of benevolence in children, that they should be encouraged to take as much part as *possible* in the benevolent projects of their parents. They bore a brace of chickens, along with pork, apples and pies, to this poor family, and the like gift to another poor family, until all but three pair of fowls were disposed of. When they returned their countenances glowed with satisfaction, and in relating the expressions of surprise and gratitude which they had heard that morning from the lips of poverty and want, parents and children wept with delight together. I felt even then repaid for what I had done. But what was most remarkable, followed. About 11 o'clock, some one rapped at the front door with a nice fat turkey, as a present from one of the neighbors to Capt. S. and his family. In a little while a rap was heard at the back door, and who should be there but Capt. A. with a fine round cut of pork, weighing perhaps 20 or 30 pounds, which he insisted on our taking. Then came two braces of fowls, one from one neighbor, and the other from another neighbor, at the same time. And so the gifts kept pouring in until dinner, and even afterwards, till we received precisely as many chickens *as we had given away*, more apples, more pies, more pork, and a turkey besides. Who could but think of the text, "Give and it shall be given unto you, good measure, pressed down, and running over." I could not but feel that God in this case had made a connexion between my giving and receiving, but the blessing bestowed was less a reward than the inward luxury of doing good. The benevolent joy of that day has been tasted over and over again since, by the power of memory, hundreds of times.

(*j*) FINDING A BAG OF MONEY. —A venerable clergyman in the west of England, of the name of Thompson, had annually for many years made it his custom to distribute the overplus of his farm among the poor of his parish, after having supplied the wants of his own household.

One year, however, he was compelled to depart from this plan. His benevolence had led him to engage to give thirty pounds towards the erection of a chapel, in a town whose inhabitants needed more church room. He was compelled, instead of giving his corn to the poor, to sell as much of it as would raise the sum promised. He regretted the circumstance, but it was unavoidable.

Having thus procured the money, he left his home to be the bearer of his own benefaction. On the road he overtook a young lady, mounted on a single horse like himself, whom he accosted with frankness and kindness. They travelled together over a down, and found they were going to the same place. His conversation and manner won much on the respect of the young lady, who listened with attention to his serious and holy conversation. She learned his name, and his residence, and, when they were about to part, was invited by the old clergyman to call upon him at his friend's house in the town.

In the course of the evening, the young lady related with great pleasure, at her friend's where she was on a visit, the very gratifying journey she had travelled, with a clergyman of the name of Thompson.

"Thompson!" exclaimed the lady of the house; "I wish it was Mr. Thompson for whom we have for many years been inquiring in vain. I have money, tied up in a bag by my late husband, due to a person of that name, who desired to leave it till called for. But I suppose he is dead, and his executor, whoever he be, knows nothing of it." It was proposed that the old clergyman should be asked if this were any relation of his. He was sent for, came, and it soon appeared, that the Mr. Thompson, to whom the money was so long due, was his own brother, who had been dead several years, and to whose effects he was executor and residuary legatee.

The money was paid him; he fell on his knees, blessed God, who had thus interposed on behalf of his poor people, hastened to his friend to tell him the joyful news, and as he entered his house exclaimed, "Praise God: tell it in Gath, publish it in Askelon, that our God is a faithful God."

(*k*) BAXTER'S TESTIMONY.—One help to my success, says Baxter, was the relief which my estate enabled me to afford to the poor. The situation which I held, was reckoned at near 200*l.* per annum; but there came only from eighty to ninety pounds to hand. Besides which, some years I had sixty or eighty pounds a year of the booksellers for my books which I wrote. This little, dispersed among them, much reconciled them to the doctrine that I taught. I took the aptest of their children from the school, and sent divers of them to the universities, where, for eight pounds a year, or ten at most, by the help of my friends, I maintained them. In giving the little I had, I did not inquire if they were good or bad, if they asked relief; for the bad had souls and bodies that needed charity most. And this truth I will speak, for the encouragement of the charitable, that what little money I have by me now, I got it almost all, I scarcely know how, *at that time when I gave most;* and since I have had less opportunity of giving, I have had less increase.

(*l*) WHITFIELD AND THE CHURL.—While the Rev. G. Whitfield was preaching on one occasion at Plymouth, he lodged with Mr. Kinsman, a minister of the town. After breakfast on Monday, he said to his friend, "Come, let us visit some of your poor people. It is not enough that we labor in the pulpit; we must endeavor to be useful out of it." On entering the dwellings of the afflicted poor, he administered to their temporal as well as spiritual wants. Mr. K., knowing the low state of his finances, was surprised at his liberality, and suggested that he thought he had been too bountiful. Mr. W., with some degree of smartness, replied: "It is not enough, young man, to pray, and put on a serious face; true religion, and undefiled, is this—to visit the widow and the fatherless in their affliction, and to supply their wants. My stock, it is true, is nearly exhausted; but God, whom I serve, and whose saints we have assisted, will, I doubt not, soon give me a supply." His hopes were not disappointed. A stranger called on him in the evening, who addressed him thus: "With great pleasure I have heard you preach; you are on a journey, as well as myself, and travelling is expensive. Do me the honor to accept this," at the same time presenting him with five guineas. Returning to the family, Mr. Whitfield, smiling, held out the money in his hand, saying: "There, young man, God has speedily repaid what I bestowed. Let this in future teach you not to withhold what it is in the power of your hand to give. The gentleman to whom I was called is a perfect stranger to me; his only business was to give me the sum you see." It is remarkable, that this gentleman, though rich, was notorious for a penurious disposition: but Elijah was fed by ravens.

(*m*) A HUNDRED GUINEAS FOR A BIBLE.—A young girl entered the shop of Mr. B., a bookseller, desiring him to exchange a prayer-book, which she brought with her, for a Bible. He gave her a Bible, and bade her keep the prayer-book also. Some time after, this girl was taken in the service of Rev. Mr. Cecil. On her first coming into the family, Mr. Cecil inquired if she had a Bible; to which she answered in the affirmative, and told him from whom she received it. Mr. Cecil was pleased with the circumstances, and finding out Mr. B., recommended him to his friends. During Mr. Cecil's absence from town, however, Mr. B. became involved in serious pecuniary difficulties, and was compelled to give up his business, and return to a mechanical employment, which he had learned in his youth. The violent exertion attendant on this occupation occasioned a painful illness: he remained some time in a hospital, but at length left, and retired to an obscure lodging, without any adequate means of support for himself and family. To this place Mr. Cecil, on his arrival in town, with difficulty traced him. An early interview took place, and Mr. B., having stated his misfortunes, "Well, B.," said Mr. Cecil, "what can be done for you? Would a hundred guineas be of any service to you?" "I should be truly thankful for such a sum," said B.; "it would be of great use to me, but I cannot expect it." "Well," returned Mr. Cecil, "I am not a rich man, and I have not got a hundred guineas to give you; but," continued he, putting his hand in his pocket, "I have got *one;* here it is at your service, and I will undertake to make it a hundred in a few days." Mr. Cecil represented the case to his friends, fulfilled his promise, and the Bible which B. had formerly given to a child, indirectly procured the means of once more opening his shop, and affording him subsistence.

(*n*) THE KING'S LAST LOAF.—Alfred the Great, who died in the year 900, was of a most amiable disposition, and, we would hope, of genuine piety. During his retreat at Athelney, in Somersetshire, after his defeat by the Danes, a beggar came to his little castle, and requested alms. His queen informed Alfred that they had but one small loaf remaining, which was insufficient for themselves and their friends, who were gone in search of food, though with little hope of success. The king replied, "Give the poor Christian one half of the loaf. He that could feed five thousand men with five loaves and two fishes, can certainly make the half loaf suffice for more than our necessity." The poor man was accordingly relieved, and Alfred's people shortly after *returned with a store of fresh provisions!*

(*o*) THE POOR PHYSICIAN.—A year last November, says a missionary agent, I preached a missionary sermon in the town of ——, and took a subscription. A physician subscribed and paid $5. A gentleman standing by told me that the $5 was all he had, or was worth: that he had lost his property and paid up his debts and moved into town to commence practice, with no other resources than that five dollar bill. He and his wife were obliged to board out, as he was not able to keep house.

I resolved at once that I would keep watch of that man, and see what the Lord would do with him.

About a year after this interview, I visited the place again, and put up with this physician. I found him keeping house in good style. In conversation with him, I brought up the duty of Christian benevolence, and spoke of God's faithfulness to fulfil his promises to the liberal.

He told me he knew a physician who, the last year, gave away the last five dollars he had in the world, resolving to trust the Lord for the future. During the next summer, while the cholera raged in the country, by a series of events guided, as he believed, by the providence of God, most of the practice was thrown into the hands of this physician, and he had taken more than $2,500.

I told him I knew him to be the man referred to, and that I had been keeping watch to see what the Lord would do with him.

Oh, sir, if we would, all of us, only trust in the Lord, and more abundantly give of our substance to aid in spreading the gospel, and throw open our eyes to read the providence, as well as word of *God, we might not only speedily supply the whole world with Bibles, but our hearts would overflow with constant gratitude in view of the evident interpositions of Providence in our behalf.

(*p*) THE STUDENT'S TRICK.—A young man of eighteen or twenty, a student in a university, took a walk one day with a professor, who was commonly called the student's friend, such was his kindness to the young men whom it was his office to instruct.

While they were walking together, and the professor was seeking to lead the conversation to grave subjects, they saw a pair of old shoes lying in their path, which they supposed to belong to a poor man who was at work close by, and who had nearly finished his day's work

The young student turned to the professor, saying, "Let us play the man a trick; we will hide his shoes, and conceal ourselves behind those bushes, and watch to see his perplexity when he cannot find them."

"My dear friend," answered the professor, "we must never amuse ourselves at the expense of the poor. But you are rich, and you may give yourself a much greater pleasure. Put a dollar into each shoe, and then we will hide ourselves."

The student did so, and then placed himself with the professor behind the bushes close by, through which they could easily watch the laborer, and see whatever wonder or joy he might express.

The poor man soon finished his work, and came across the field to the path, where he had left his coat and shoes. While he put on the coat, he slipped one foot into one of his shoes; but feeling something hard, he stooped down and found the dollar. Astonishment and wonder were seen upon his countenance; he gazed upon the dollar, turned it round, and looked again and again; then he looked around him on all sides, but could see no one. Now he put the money in his pocket and proceeded to put on the other shoe, but how great was his astonishment when he found the other dollar! His feelings overcame him; he fell upon his knees, looked up to heaven and uttered aloud a fervent thanksgiving, in which he spoke of his wife, sick and helpless, and his children without bread, whom this timely bounty, from some unknown hand, would save from perishing.

The young man stood there deeply affected, and tears filled his eyes.

"Now," said the professor, "are you not much better pleased than if you had played your intended trick?"

"O dearest sir," answered the youth, "you have taught me a lesson now that I will never forget. I feel now the truth of the words which I never before understood, 'it is better to give than to receive.'"

(*q*) THE SOUTHRON'S LIBERALITY.—A Southern gentleman, gay and worldly, was very friendly to an evangelical church in his neighborhood; and as they were accustomed to hold camp meetings year after year, he had a beautiful plot of his forest land cleared of brush and fallen trees, and fitted up with convenient cabins or booths, for the accommodation of the worshippers, at his own expense. His liberality to the church was such as to attract not a little attention, on account of his being so far from any thing like religion himself. One of his companions one day rallied him on his incongruous benevolence, and inquired why he would make such a fool of himself as to throw away his money in behalf of such an object? His reply in substance was, "You do not understand it; I am no loser by my liberality to the church, but for every *five* dollars I give to them, God's providence in some way brings me back a *hundred!*"

If shrewd-minded, worldly men, like the above, are sometimes clear-sighted enough to see the wisdom of "casting *their* bread on the waters," what shall be said of those professed Christians who are so unbelieving as to regard what is contributed to benevolent efforts, as so much *sacrificed* or utterly thrown away?

(*r*) "GOD LOVETH A CHEERFUL GIVER."—"How is it, Betty," said an elder of the church to a very poor woman in Wales, (who was always observed to contribute something whenever a collection was taken;) how is it that I always see you drop something in the plate? Where do you get it?" "Oh, sir, I do not know," she replied; "the Lord knows my heart and my good-will to his cause; and somehow or other, when a collection is to be made, I am sure to have my penny before me; and when it comes, I put it in the plate."

"Well," said he, "you have been faithful in a little, take this sovereign, and do what you will with it." "A sovereign, sir!" said she; "I never had so much money in my life as a sovereign; what shall I do with it?" "I dare say you will find means of spending it," said he, "if your heart is devoted to the Lord's cause." Soon after this, a man came round to solicit subscriptions for some benevolent object: he went to one of the elders, who gave him half a sovereign, and another gave him five shillings; both of which were regarded as very liberal donations. Not liking to pass by any member of the church, he asked this poor woman what she would do. "Put my name down for a sovereign." "A sovereign!" said he; "why, where did you get a sovereign?" "Oh, sir," said she, "I got it honestly: put my name down for a sovereign." She gave him the sovereign, and in about two weeks from that time she received a letter from Doctors' Commons informing her that a friend *had just left her one hundred pounds!*

(*s*) THE INFIDEL'S DONATION.—In an address before the Indiana Bible Society, the following facts were stated:

An agent once requested an infidel surgeon to make a donation to a benevolent object. He told the agent he did not give money to such objects. He was assured he would be none the poorer for giving. "Do you believe that?" replied the doctor. "Yes, I do." "Well, I will try it," was the answer; and he took out $20, and gave him. The agent requested him to eye the providence of God, and see if it was not soon repaid to him double. He said he would take care to *look out for that.*

When he reached home he found a letter requesting him to come immediately and perform a very difficult surgical operation upon a man worth $200,000 or $300,000. When he had done his work, and was about leaving, the son came to him and said, My father's heart is upon his money, and as he is now very feeble, I fear it may destroy him to be called upon to pay a very heavy bill. I wish the charge you present to him should be small, and I will make up the balance.

He told the son he was willing to make out just such a bill as his father would think right. What do you think he would be willing to pay? He said $200. The surgeon took the $200, and told the agent the next time they met, that the Lord had paid him back *fivefold:* that if he had been *left to himself*, he should not have charged *more* than $100. Such facts might be multiplied without limit.

(*t*) A LOAN TO THE LORD.—"A poor minister," says Rev. Mr. Spencer, of New-York, "once called upon me saying that his horse and carriage were under a mortgage, which was soon to be foreclosed and he had no money to pay it. During the night, on which he stayed at my house, I was much disturbed in thinking over his case. I felt as if I must help him, though my circumstances at first view seemed to forbid the idea. On parting with the good man in the morning, I made him a present of five dollars, which was all the money I had. He hesitated when he saw the amount, and said so large a donation might embarrass me. 'No,' said I; 'it is indeed all I have, but you should have more if I had it: I consider I am lending to the Lord, and have no doubt it will soon be returned again.' The same day, making a call upon one of my parishioners, who paid regularly towards my support, three dollars were unexpectedly put in my hand. And not long after, as I was dining with another family of my congregation, who likewise helped to make up my salary, we were conversing on the reflex benefits of beneficence, and I remarked that all I had ever lent to the Lord, had been paid back in some unexpected way, with the exception of two dollars! Upon this the wife rose up and stepped towards the mantelpiece, while her husband smilingly observed that his wife, a short time ago, had laid up two dollars in the clock for me, and they were now happy to have this opportunity of completing the payment of my recent loan to the Lord!"

(*u*) THE MINISTER'S DONATION.—About the year 1839, says Rev. W. H. Spencer, I attended the Bridgewater Association in Pennsylvania, and was called upon to preach a discourse on Foreign Missions. I felt deeply, and the sympathies of the audience became so enlisted in behalf of the object that an unusually large contribution was taken up.

In the afternoon a warm and excellent discourse was preached by another minister on Home Missions. During his sermon the intrinsic importance of the subject forced itself upon my mind, and led me to agitate the question how much it would be possible to give to the cause myself. I was indeed in a great strait between charity and necessity. I felt desirous to contribute; but then I was on a journey, and I had given so much in the morning, that I really feared I had no more money than would bear my expenses. But when, at the conclusion of the discourse, the speaker said he could hardly expect a large collection after the amount they had given in the morning, my mind was decided; and I arose and stated my convictions of the importance of Home Missions, and for the sake of example, I informed the assembly what were my circumstances, but that I had made up my mind to give a dollar and trust in God to provide. And the result was, that as large a contribution was obtained as in the morning. At the close of the Association I proceeded on my journey; and the next day called on a friend and paid him some forty dollars, which I had collected for him. I was now about 140 miles from home, with scarce a dollar in my pocket; and how my expenses would be met, I could not imagine. But judge my surprise, when on presenting the money to my friend he took a hundred dollars, and adding it to the forty, placed the whole amount in my hand, saying, *he would make me a present of it!* I had, to be sure, rendered him some small services of a similar nature before, but I considered him under no obligations, and was expecting nothing of the kind! Gratitude and joy swelled my bosom; my mind at once recurred to my contribution the day previous, and I felt convinced that I had seen a literal fulfilment of the promise, "Give and it shall be given unto you, good measure pressed down and running over, shall men give into your bosom."

(*v*) THE DAIRYMAN AND THE CHEESE.—The Agent of an Education Society called one day on Mr. S., a member of a church in New Berlin, New-York. Mr. S. was largely engaged in the dairying business. He was a benevolent man, and for some time had given five dollars yearly to the above-named Society. The agent urged him to give twenty dollars instead of five, and told him he believed that if he would contribute this sum, in the exercise of self-denying benevolence, it would soon be returned again, and with large interest too. In proof of this he quoted such passages as these—"The liberal soul deviseth liberal things, and by liberal things shall he stand." "He that watereth, shall be watered also himself," &c. "I do not believe any such doctrine," said Mr. S., "nor agree to any such application of Scripture. However, I will give the twenty dollars." Not many hours after this a neighbor of Mr. S. came to him, and wished him to buy a large amount of cheese of him. The terms were moderate, and the bargain was concluded.

A day or two afterwards a gentleman called on Mr. S. to purchase cheese, and he sold him the lot he had just bought, and at such an advance in the price that he made a hundred dollars by the exchange! Mr. S. was now fully reconciled to the agent's doctrine, and his application of the foregoing promises. He was now constrained to acknowledge that the Lord had indeed rewarded his beneficence, and rewarded it five-fold. He used afterwards to delight in relating the above incident as an illustration of the connection between giving and receiving, which it had led him to recognize —as a proof of the doctrine that he who gives liberally to benevolent objects, other things equal, will be the more liberally supplied with the blessings of Providence himself.

(*w*) THE PHYSICIAN AND THE CHURL.—At the recognition of a church in New-York, in 1847, the following incident was related:—

In a village in the southern part of New-York, the Baptist church had been for some time in a languishing condition. At length a new minister was called to labor with them. The church was poor, and he was supported principally by two or three individuals. With one of these, a physician, he boarded: he was a member of the church, and unusually benevolent, but his wife was an unconverted woman, rather parsimonious, and seemed to take umbrage at every act of her husband's liberality. The church met in a long, low, unfinished building, with the naked rafters overhead. At length a revival of religion occurred, and one of the converts was the physician's wife. Her heart was enlarged, and she said one day to her husband that they must have a new meeting-house. The doctor had about one thousand dollars laid up; and though his wife had often expressed her fears that her husband's generosity would force them to draw upon this little fund, and the family be reduced to want, she now suggested that he had better give the whole sum to the new meeting-house, and leave the result with God. He readily assented, and put down his name on the subscription list for a thousand dollars.

In the same congregation there was a wealthy farmer; his wife was pious and liberal, but he was worldly and avaricious. He was urged to subscribe to the same object; but he would neither give any thing himself or suffer his wife to give. As God would have it, an epidemic not long after made its ravages in the community, and the farmer and his children were taken very sick. The wife, we believe, was the only member of the family who escaped. The pious physician was called upon to attend them in their sickness; their disease was so malignant, and so long continued, that he received at least *one thousand dollars* for his services! So the avaricious farmer had to pay the liberal physician's subscription! The beneficence of the latter was thus amply rewarded, to say nothing of the large sums received from the increase of his practice in the community around him.

Note.—It would be wrong to argue from the foregoing examples that all benevolent efforts, donations, and alms, will be rewarded with the blessings of Providence in the present life. A man may give largely to-day, and die suddenly to-morrow; but then he receives his reward on high. Or, notwithstanding his liberality, God, who loves him as a Father, may see that he needs the moral discipline of adversity, and thus may apply the chastising rod for his spiritual profit. Or a man may give without discretion, or without proper regard to justice, as will be seen at 49*b*, in the case of Goldsmith; or he may give merely from selfish motives, or at least without reference to God's glory, or regard to his promises. In such cases God does not *pledge* himself to grant the liberal any pecuniary or secular advantages in return for their liberality. But still we believe that God has so arranged his government that, as a *general rule*, the more men cherish and develop true benevolence, the more will the blessings of Providence be multiplied upon them. They will see no miracle wrought in their behalf; but God, working in and through natural laws, will often cause the most striking and beautiful connections between men's displays of goodness towards others, and his displays of goodness towards them. The cases alluded to above, are to be regarded as exceptions to the general rule. We heartily agree with the statement of Dr. Harris—and the foregoing incidents illustrate it—that "the most marked interpositions and signal blessings of even earthly prosperity, have attended the practice of Christian liberality in every age. Volumes might be filled with well attested instances of the remarkable manner in which God has honored those who in faith and obedience have devoted their property to Him."

BENEVOLENCE.

48. Benevolence, Want of.

(*a*) LOSING A SEAT IN CONGRESS.—"Sir, bring me a good plain dinner," said a melancholy looking individual to a waiter at one of our principal hotels.

The dinner was brought and devoured, and the eater called the landlord aside, and thus addressed him.—"You are the landlord?" "Yes." "You do a good business here?" "Yes!" (in astonishment.)

"You make, probably, ten dollars a day clear?"

"Yes."

"Then I am safe. I cannot pay for what I have consumed; I have been out of employment seven months; but have engaged to go to work to-morrow. I had been without food four-and-twenty hours when I entered your place. I will pay you in a week." "I cannot pay my bills with such promises," blustered the landlord, and "I do not keep a poorhouse. You should address the proper authorities. Leave me something for security."

"I have nothing."

"I will take your coat."

"If I go into the streets without that, such weather as it is, I may get my death."

"You should have thought of that before you came here."

"Are you serious? Well, I solemnly aver that in one week from now I will pay you."

"I will take the coat."

The coat was left, and a week afterwards redeemed. Seven years after that, a wealthy man entered the political arena, and was presented at a caucus as an applicant for a congressional nomination. The principal of the caucus held his peace; he heard the name and the history of the applicant, who was a member of the church, and one of the most respectable citizens. He was chairman. The vote was a tie, and he cast a negative, thereby defeating the wealthy applicant, whom he met an hour afterwards, and to whom he said, "You don't remember me?"

"No."

"I once ate a dinner at your hotel; and, although I told you I was famishing and pledged my word and honor to pay you in a week, you took my coat and saw me go out into the inclement air, at the risk of my life, without it."

"Well, sir, what then?"

"*Not much. You called yourself a Christian. To-night you were a candidate for nomination, and but for me you would have been elected to Congress!*"

Three years after, the Christian hotel-keeper became bankrupt, and sought a home in Bellevue. The poor dinnerless wretch that was, afterwards became a high functionary in Albany.

(*b*) "I DO NOT MEAN THAT."—A gentleman who had been conspicuous in aiding a missionary collection, was met the following day by one of dissimilar habits, who chided him for the absurd eccentricity of which he deemed him guilty in giving to such an object and in such profusion. It was preposterous, he said, to be sending heaps of money abroad, to be spent, no one knew how, while there were so many unemployed and starving in ——. "I will give —— pounds to the poor of —— if you will give an equal sum;" said the Christian friend. "I did not mean that," replied the objector; "but," continued he, "if you must go from home, why so far? Think of the miserable poor of Ireland." "I will give —— pounds to the poor of Ireland, if you will give the same." "I do not mean that either," was the reply. No, it is neither *this* nor *that*, which this class of objectors exactly mean; but simply to veil their criminal parsimony by excepting against the proceedings of liberal men, whom, if they could not condemn, they must, for very shame, in some degree imitate.

(*c*) THE RECTOR AND THE POOR BOY.—An indigent boy applied for alms at the house of an avaricious rector, and received a dry mouldy crust. The rector inquired of the boy if he could say the Lord's Prayer, and was answered in the negative. "Then," said the rector, "I will teach you that." "Our Father!"—"*Our* Father!" said the boy, "is he *my* Father as well as *yours*?" "Yes, certainly." "Then," replied the boy, "*how could you give your poor brother this mouldy crust of bread?*"

(*d*) FEELING IN THE WRONG PLACE.—A plain, good-hearted, matter-of-fact kind of man, who understood that a poor woman and her family were reduced to extreme distress by the loss of a cow, which was their principal support, generously went round among his neighbors to solicit that aid which he was unable to give himself. He told a plain, simple, and pathetic tale, and received from each a very liberal donation of regret, sorrow, sympathy, &c. But, thought he, this will not buy a cow, and he consequently redoubled his exertions, and to the same effect. He now lost all patience, and after being answered as usual by the son of Midas, with a plentiful shower of sympathetic feeling, "Oho, yes, I don't doubt your feeling, but you don't feel in the right place." "Oh," said he, "I feel with all my heart and soul." "Yes, yes," replied the solicitor, "I don't doubt that either, but I want you to feel in your *pocket*."

49. Benevolence Misdirected.

(*a*) BENEVOLENCE OF LAS CASAS.—One of the most benevolent men, of whom history gives us any account, was Bartholomew Las Casas, bishop of Chiapa. In 1502 he accompanied Orando to Hispaniola, who had been commissioned and sent out as the Spanish governor to that island. He there witnessed, with all the pain of a naturally benevolent heart, the cruel treatment which was experienced by the native inhabitants; the deprivation of their personal rights, the seizure of their lands, their severe toil and inexorable punishment. He was deeply affected; and from that time devoted the whole of his subsequent life, a period of more than sixty years, to exertions in their behalf. Under the impulse of a most unquestionable benevolence, this good man recommended to Cardinal Ximenes, who was at that time head of Spanish affairs, the introduction of *negro slaves* into the West India islands, as one of the best modes to relieve the native inhabitants.

The measures of Las Casas, which tended to introduce enslaved Africans into the Spanish islands, were the results, beyond all question, of an exalted benevolence; but how wofully misdirected was such a benevolence! The injury done by it no human mind can compute.

(*b*) DR. GOLDSMITH AND THE BEGGAR.—A common female beggar once asked alms of Dr. Goldsmith as he walked with his friend up Fleet-street. He generously gave her a shilling. His companion, who knew something of the woman, censured the bard for excess of humanity, adding, that the shilling was much misapplied, for she would spend it in liquor. "If it makes her happy in any way," replied the doctor, "my end is answered." The doctor's humanity was not always regulated by discretion. Being once much pressed by his tailor for a bill of forty pounds, a day was fixed for payment Goldsmith procured the money; bu Mr. Glover calling on him, and relating a piteous tale of his goods being seized for rent, the thoughtless, but benevolent doctor gave him the whole of the money. The tailor called, and was told, that if he had come a little sooner he would have received the money, but he had just parted with every shilling of it to a friend in distress, adding, "I should have been an unfeeling monster not to have relieved distress when in my power." That is no true benevolence which leads a man to be unjust.

BEREAVEMENTS.

50. The Bereaved Comforted.

(*a*) LEGH RICHMOND'S MOTHER.—My mother, says the Rev. Legh Richmond, had six children; three of whom died in infancy. A very affecting circumstance accompanied the death of one of them, which was a severe trial to her maternal feelings. Her then youngest child, a sweet little boy, only just two years old, through the carelessness of his nurse, fell from a bedroom window upon the pavement beneath. I was at that time six years of age, and happened to be walking upon the very spot when the distressing event occurred. I was, therefore, the first to take him up. I delivered into our agonized mother's arms the poor little sufferer. The head was fractured, and he survived the fall only about thirty hours. I still preserve a very lively and distinct remembrance of the struggle between the natural feelings of the mother, and the spiritual resignation of the Christian. She passed the interval of suspense in almost continual prayer, and found God a present help in time of trouble. Frequently during that day did she retire with me; and, as I knelt beside her, she uttered the feelings and desires of her heart to God. I remember her saying, "If I cease praying for five minutes, I am ready to sink under this unlooked-for distress; but, when I pray, God comforts and upholds me: his will, not mine, be done." Once she said, "Help me to pray, my child: Christ suffers little children to come to him, and forbids them not: say something." "What shall I say, mamma? Shall I fetch a book?" "Not now," she replied; "speak from your heart, and ask God that we may be reconciled to his will and bear this trial with patience."

(*b*) SUPPORT FROM THE CROSS.—Dr. Grosvenor's first wife was a most devout and amiable woman. The Sabbath after her death, the doctor expressed himself from the pulpit in the following manner: "I have had an irreparable loss; and no man can feel a loss of this consequence more sensibly than myself; but the cross of a dying Jesus is my support: I fly from *one* death for refuge to *another*." How much superior was the comfort of the Christian divine to that of the heathen philosopher, Pliny the younger, who says, that, in similar distresses, study was his only relief.

(*c*) A LOSS MADE GOOD.—Mr. Patrick Macwarth, who lived in the West of Scotland, whose heart the Lord, in a remarkable way, opened, was, after his conversion, in such a frame, so affected with the discoveries of the love of God, and of the blessedness of the life to come, that for some months together he seldom slept, being so taken up in wondering at the kindness of his Redeemer. His life was distinguished for tenderness of walk, and near communion with God. One day after the death of his son, who was suddenly taken away, he retired alone for several hours, and afterwards appeared so remarkably cheerful, that inquiry was made why he looked so cheerful in a time of such affliction. He replied, 'He had got that in his retirement with the Lord, which, to have it afterwards renewed, he would gladly lose a son every day.'

51. The Bereaved Converted.

(*a*) An impenitent man in Boston was bereaved of a little son. He felt the stroke severely, and his attention was called up to the subject of religion. But his grief at length subsided, and serious impressions wore off. Ere long God took away another little boy from him. His convictions were renewed with his sorrows, and he sought and found comfort in Christ.

Speaking of his experience in a conference and prayer-meeting, he sweetly said, "God in taking away *my* son, revealed to me his own Son, a thousand times more precious than my own."

(*b*) THE YOUTH'S RECOVERY.—A pious clergyman once related the following fact:—When travelling on horseback along a solitary track, in one of the back settlements of America, he overtook a stranger, an Englishman, and delighted with meeting a fellow-countryman in so unusual a spot, joined him and entered into conversation.

My companion, says the narrator, made frequent allusions to his early history, and at last, in answer to my inquiries, gave me the following account:—

"I was the only son of religious parents, who anxiously watched over my expanding mind, and directed me to the God of my fathers. My feelings were naturally strong, and often as I listened to the fond and pious instructions of my mother, or heard a father's prayers ascend to heaven on my behalf, I felt more, far more than I could express.

"My own inclinations and the wishes of my parents, eventually induced me to adopt the profession of a surgeon. Never shall I forget the evening before my departure for town to enter on my preparatory studies; never can I lose the remembrance of my father's affectionate words that evening, almost the last I ever heard from his lips. 'You are about to leave me, my dear child,' he said, with his eyes filled with tears. 'You are about to go into the midst of temptations, but He who has watched over you hitherto, can still preserve you. I have committed you to his care, and He is able to keep what I have committed unto him. Never neglect,' added he, as he presented me with a pocket Bible, 'never neglect this blessed book.' I went up to London, entered with avidity upon the course of studies which were to fit me for my profession, and for a while daily, and even almost hourly, thought of my father's advice, and resolved to follow it. But I was surrounded by infidel fellow-students, who ridiculed religion, despised its precepts, and while they flattered me by complimenting my intellectual powers, regretted that I should be a slave to such antiquated, puritanical notions. At first I endeavored by argument to defend my views, and prove the authenticity of the sacred writings; but I could not withstand their continued raillery, and was at last silent when they touched on the subject. This was my first backward step. I was ashamed of my Lord, and he justly gave me up to be filled with my own ways.

"I became exceedingly profligate, and often made even my thoughtless companions shudder at the depth of my impiety. We had formed among ourselves a select literary society, in which I was giving a course of lectures on the different departments of natural history, with the expressed intention of proving from them the awful doctrines of materialism; when, one evening, at one of our weekly meetings, a hurried note was handed to me, telling me, if I ever wished to see my father again, I must proceed home without delay. I departed immediately by the most rapid conveyance, but the next day and night elapsed before I reached the end of my journey. As I rushed in, the first glance told me my mother was a widow, and I was fatherless. It would be beyond the power of language to express my agony. In spite of the entreaties of my mother, disregarding the absolute commands of the physician, (for the disease which had carried off my beloved parent was infectious,) I flew to his apartment, and throwing myself on the corpse, I, for the first time, found relief in tears. But it was but for a moment. The anxiety of the preceding hours of suspense—the dreadful certainty that had awaited me—the horror and remorse that now filled my awakened conscience, overwhelmed me. I was carried in a swoon from the scene of sorrow; the next morning found me confined to a bed of sickness, in a state of delirium, caused by a burning fever. For three long weeks did my mother watch over me, fearing each day would find her doubly bereft, when the crisis of the disorder passed, and I slowly recovered. Who can describe the gnawing of an awakened conscience, the remorse for my disobedience to my lost father, which, like the worm that never dies, preyed on, and engrossed my mind! In the silence of a sick chamber, the whole course of my backslidings returned to my recollection, and filled me with despair; but

'God passed in mercy by,
(His praise be ever new,) and bade me live.'

"That Bible which I had so long despised, and which now seemed only filled with denunciations of wrath and righteous vengeance, was, under the influences of the blessed Spirit, opened to the eyes of my understanding, as revealing a Saviour for the chief of offenders. I was enabled to flee for refuge to the hope set before me in the gospel, and to cry, 'God be merciful to me a sinner.'"

(*c*) THE ORPHAN SAILOR.—After an absence of several years an American sailor, profane and wicked, returned to his native land, and sought his widowed mother's residence. He knocked, but no one bade him enter. He called, but no answer was returned save the echo of his own voice. It seemed like knocking at the door of a tomb. The nearest neighbor hearing the noise, came and found the youth sitting and sobbing on the steps of the door. "Where," cried he with eagerness, "where is my mother and my brother? Oh, I hope they are not"—

"If," said the stranger, "you inquire for Widow ——, I can only pity you. I have known her but a short time; but she was the best woman I ever knew. Her little boy died of a fever a year ago, and in consequence of fatigue in taking care of him, and anxiety for a long absent son at sea, the good widow herself was buried yesterday."

"O, heavens!" cried the youth, "have I staid just long enough to kill my mother! Wretch that I am—show me the grave—I have a dagger in my bundle—let me die with my mother—my poor, broken-hearted parent!"

"Hold, friend!" said the astonished neighbor, "if you are this woman's eldest son, I have a letter for you, which she wrote a few days before she died, and desired that you might receive it should you ever return."

They both turned from the cottage, and went to the house of the neighbor. A light being procured, the young man threw down his bundle and hat, and read the following short letter, while his manly cheeks were covered with tears.

"My Dearest, only Son.—When this reaches you, I shall be no more. Your little brother has gone before me, and I cannot but hope and believe that he was prepared. I had fondly hoped that I should once more have seen you on the shores of mortality; but this hope is now relinquished. I have followed you by my prayers through all your wanderings. Often, while you little suspected it, even in the dark cold nights in winter, have I knelt for my lost son. There is but one thing that gives me pain at dying; and that is, my dear William, that I must leave you in this wicked world, as I fear, unreconciled to your Maker. I am too feeble to say more. My glass is run. As you visit the sods which cover my dust, Oh, remember that you too must soon follow. Farewell! The last breath of your mother will be spent in praying for you, that we may meet above."

The young man's heart was melted, on reading these few words from the parent whom he so tenderly loved; and this letter was the means, in the hands of God, of bringing this youth to a saving knowledge of the truth "as it is in Jesus," and he became a very respectable and pious man.

52. The Bereaved Rebuked.

(*a*) LADY RAFFLES AND THE NURSE.—One day when Lady Raffles, while in India, was almost overwhelmed with grief for the loss of a favorite child, unable to bear the sight of her other children, or the light of day, and humbled on her couch with a feeling of misery, she was addressed by a poor, ignorant, native woman, of the lowest class, who had been employed about the nursery, in terms not to be forgotten:—"I am come, because you have been here many days shut up in a dark room, and no one dares to come near you. Are you not ashamed to grieve in this manner, when you ought to be thanking God for having given you the most beautiful child that ever was seen? Were you not the envy of every body? Did any one ever see him or speak of him without admiring him? And instead of letting this child continue in this world till he should be worn out with trouble and sorrow, has not God taken him to heaven in all his beauty? For shame!—leave off weeping, and let me open a window."

(*b*) THE WIDOW REPROVED.—Ebenezer Adams, an eminent member of the Society of Friends, on visiting a lady of rank, whom he found, six months after the death of her husband, on a sofa covered with black cloth, and in all the dignity of woe, approached her with great solemnity, and gently taking her by the hand, thus addressed her:—"So, friend, I see then thou hast not yet forgiven God Almighty." This reproof had so great an effect on the lady that she immediately laid aside the symbols of grief, and again entered on the important duties of life.

BIBLE.

53. Historical Facts.

(*a*) THE VENERABLE BEDE.—In the eighth century, a translation of the Gospel of St. John was completed in the Anglo-Saxon language, by the venerable Bede, who was the ornament of the age and country in which he lived. Referring to the time of his education, he says, "From that period I have applied myself wholly to the study of the Holy Scriptures; and in the intervals of the observance of regular discipline, always found it sweet to be either learning, teaching, or writing."

The circumstances of his death, as described by one of his pupils, are interesting:—"Many nights he passed without sleep, yet rejoicing and giving thanks, unless when a little slumber intervened. When he awoke, he resumed his accustomed devotions, and, with expanded hands, never ceased returning thanks to God. By turns," observes his pupil, "we read, and by turns we wept; indeed, we always read in tears. In such solemn joy, we passed fifty days; but, during these days, besides the daily lectures which he gave, he endeavored to compose two works; one of which was a translation of St. John's Gospel into English. It had been observed of him, that he never knew what it was to do nothing; and, after his breathing became still shorter, he dictated cheerfully, and sometimes said, 'Make haste; I know not how long I shall hold out; my Maker may take me away very soon.' On one occasion, a pupil said to him, 'Most dear master, there is yet one chapter wanting; do you think it troublesome to be asked any more questions?' He answered, 'It is no trouble; take your pen, and write fast.' He continued to converse cheerfully, and whilst his friends wept, as he told them they would see him no more, they rejoiced to hear him say, 'It is now time for me to return to Him who made me. The time of my dissolution draws near. I desire to be dissolved, and to be with Christ. Yes, my soul desires to see Christ, my King, in his beauty.' The pupil, before mentioned, said to him, 'Dear master, one sentence is still wanting.' He replied, 'Write quickly.' The young man soon added, 'It is finished!' He answered, 'Thou hast well said; all is now finished! Hold my head with thy hands: I shall delight to sit at the opposite side of the room, on the holy spot at which I have been accustomed to pray, and where, whilst sitting, I can invoke my Father.' Being placed on the floor of his little room, he sang, 'Glory be to the Father, and to the Son, and to the Holy Ghost,' and expired as he uttered the last words."

A copy of some of St. Paul's Epistles, said to be in the handwriting of this venerable man, is preserved in the library of Trinity College, Cambridge.

(*b*) THE BIBLE PROHIBITED.—In the reign of Henry V., a law was passed against the perusal of the Bible in English. It was enacted, "That whosoever they were that should read the Scriptures in the mother tongue, they should forfeit lande, catel, lif, and godes, from theyre neyers for ever; and so be condemned for heretykes to God, enemies to the crowne, and most arrant traitors to the lande."

(*c*) HIGH PRICES OF BIBLES.—Of W. de Howton, abbot of Croxton, it is stated, that he bequeathed to the abbey at his death, in 1274, "a Bible, in nine tomes, faire written, and excellently well glossed by Solomon, archdeacon of Leicester, and paid for it fifty markes sterling," or 33*l.* 6*s.* 8*d.* And in a valuation of books, bequeathed to Merton College, at Oxford, before the year 1300, a Psalter with glosses, or marginal annotations, is valued at ten shillings; and St. Austin, on Genesis, and a Concordantia, or Harmony, are each valued at the same price. Let it be remembered, that these sums should be multiplied by fifteen, to bring them to the present value of money; and, in some instances, the comparative value would be still too low, as in the instance of the laboring men, whose pay, in 1272, was only three halfpence per day, and who must therefore have devoted the earnings of fourteen or fifteen years to the purchase of a Bible. Whitaker, in his "History of Craven," affords the additional information, "that towards the close of the thirteenth, and at the commencement of the fourteenth century, the average wages of a man-servant, with meat and clothing, were only from three to five shillings per annum; that reapers were paid twopence a day; and a sheep sold for a shilling; and thirty quarters of fossil-coal, for seventeen shillings andsix pence." Madox, in his "History of the Exchequer," says, that in 1240, "the building of two arches of London Bridge, cost only twenty-five pounds;" eight pounds less than the Bible bequeathed to the abbey of Croxton, by abbot W. de Howton.

(*d*) LOAN OF A BIBLE.—In 1299, the bishop of Winchester borrowed a Bible, in two volumes folio, from a convent in that city, giving a bond, drawn up in a most formal and solemn manner, for its due return. This Bible had been given to the convent by a former bishop, and in consideration of this gift, and one hundred marks, the monk founded a daily mass for the soul of the donor.

(*e*) THE DEVIL AND DR. FAUSTUS.—Fust (or Faustus) having printed off a considerable number of copies of the Bible, to imitate those which were commonly sold in manuscript, undertook the sale of them at Paris, where the art of printing was then unknown. As he sold his printed copies for sixty crowns, while the scribes demanded five hundred, this created universal astonishment; but when he produced copies as fast as they were wanted, and also lowered his price to thirty crowns, all Paris was agitated. The uniformity of the copies increased the wonder. Informations were given to the magistrates against him as a magician; his lodgings were searched; and a great number of copies being found, they were seized. The red ink, with which they were embellished, was said to be his blood. It was seriously adjudged, that he was in league with the devil; but, on discovering his art, the parliament of Paris passed an act to discharge him from all persecution, in consideration of his useful invention.

(*f*) IGNORANCE OF PRIESTS.—It is very affecting to contemplate the ignorance which existed in Europe before printing was introduced. Stephanus relates an anecdote of a certain doctor of the Sorbonne, who, speaking of the reformers, expressed his surprise at their mode of reasoning, by exclaiming, "I wonder why these youths are constantly quoting the New Testament! I was more than fifty years old before I knew any thing of a New Testament." And Albert, archbishop and elector of Mentz, in the year 1530, accidentally meeting with a Bible, opened it, and having read some pages, observed, "Indeed I do not know what this book is, but this I see, that every thing in it is against us." Even Carolastadius, who was afterwards one of the reformers, acknowledged that he never began to read the Bible till eight years after he had taken his highest degree in divinity. Many other equally striking facts might be introduced, illustrative of the ignorance of the Scriptures which prevailed at that time.

(*g*) LUTHER'S DISCOVERY.—In the year 1507, in the twenty-fourth year of his age, Luther entered into orders, and celebrated his first mass.

In the same year he found, in the library of his monastery, a Latin copy of the Bible, which he eagerly read, and soon became aware that many parts of it had been kept from the people. This was the commencement of his usefulness. What a contrast do those days present to ours! If any are now without a Bible, it must be their own fault; but then it was impossible to obtain one, or to ascertain the nature and tendency of its blessed truths.

(*h*) PRIESTLY TERROR.—The ignorance which prevailed in reference to the Scriptures when Luther was raised up of God to reform the church, in the beginning of the sixteenth century, was indeed surprising. Conrad, of Heresbach, a grave author of that age, relates a fact of a monk saying to his companions, "They have invented a new language, which they call Greek: you must be carefully on your guard against it; it is the matter of all heresy. I observe in the hands of many persons a book written in that language, and which they call the New Testament: it is a book full of daggers and poison. As to the Hebrew, my brethren, it is certain, that whoever learns it becomes immediately a Jew."

(*i*) INCREASE OF BIBLES.—Tindal, to whom we are indebted for the first translation of the New Testament into English, printed it abroad; and on its making its appearance in England, the Popish bishops and clergy obtained, in the year 1527, a royal proclamation, prohibiting the purchase or reading of it. This proclamation only excited the public curiosity, and led to an increased inquiry after the forbidden book. One step which was taken to prevent the circulation of this edition of the Scriptures, at once shows the hand of God in extending his truth, and furnishes an amusing proof of the folly of man in opposing the truth of God. The Bishop of London employed a person to purchase the whole impression of Tindal's version of the New Testament, that he might burn them at St. Paul's Cross. By this means the Reformer was enabled to publish a large and more correct edition, "so that they came over," says Fox, "thick and threefold into England, to the great mortification of the Bishop and his Popish friends."

Of this purchase the following fact is related:—Sir Thomas More, being lord chancellor, and having several persons accused of heresy and ready for execution, offered to compound with one of them, named George Constantine, for his life, upon the easy terms of discovering to him who they were in London that maintained Tindal beyond the sea. After the poor man had obtained as good a security for his life as the honor and truth of the chancellor could give, he told him it was the Bishop of London who maintained him by purchasing the first impressions of his Testaments. The chancellor smiled, and said he believed that he spoke the truth.

(*j*) CRANMER'S BIBLE.—When Archbishop Cranmer's edition of the Bible was printed, in 1538, and fixed to a desk in all parochial churches, the ardor with which men flocked to read it was incredible. They who could, procured it; and they who could not, crowded to read it, or to hear it read in churches, where it was common to see little assemblies of mechanics meeting together for that purpose after the labor of the day. Many even learned to read in their old age, that they might have the pleasure of instructing themselves from the Scriptures. Mr. Fox mentions two apprentices who joined each his little stock, and bought a Bible, which at every interval of leisure they read; but being afraid of their master, who was a zealous papist, they kept it under the straw of their bed.

(*k*) PARLIAMENTARY ENACTMENTS.—At the request of the Romish clergy, severe proclamations were issued by King Henry VIII. against all who read, or kept by them, Tindal's translation of the New Testament; so that a copy of this book found in the possession of any person was sufficient to convict him of heresy, and subject him to the flames. "But the fervent zeal of those Christian days," says the good old martyrologist, Fox, "seemed much superior to these our days and times, as manifestly may appear by their sitting up all night in reading or hearing; also by their expenses and charges in buying of books in English, of whom some gave a load of hay for a few chapters of St. James, or of St. Paul, in English.

In 1543, an act of parliament was obtained by the adversaries of translations, condemning Tindal's Bible, and the prefaces and notes of all other editions. It was therefore enacted, "That no woman, except noblewomen and gentlewomen, who might read to themselves alone, and not to others," (and for which indulgence they were indebted to Cranmer,) "nor artificers, 'prentices, journeymen, serving-men, husbandmen, nor laborers, were to read the Bible or New Testament in English, to themselves or to any others, privately or openly, upon pain of one month's imprisonment."

A similar act was also passed in 1546, prohibiting Coverdale's as well as Tindal's Bible.

(*l*) KING EDWARD AND THE SWORDS.—In the dawning of the glorious day of the Reformation, the Lord raised up the eminently religious King Edward the Sixth, to engage in that excellent work. He had a very high esteem for the Holy Scriptures, according to which this great work was to be squared, and which had been, by the enemies and murderers of souls, long concealed from their forefathers. When, therefore, at his coronation, the swords were delivered to him, as King of England, France, and Ireland; having received them, he said, "There is yet another sword to be delivered to me;" at which the lords wondering, "I mean," said he, "the sacred Bible, which is the sword of the Spirit, and without which we are nothing, neither can we do any thing." And as he prized the word of God himself, so he soon restored it to his people; and that they might all have opportunity to peruse the inspired writings, he ordered a large Bible in English, with the paraphrase of Erasmus on the Gospels, to be set up in every church, in which, at all times, those that could, might go and read; and those that could not read, might go and hear.

(*m*) WILLIAMS AND THE WELSH BIBLE.—Long before the establishment of Bible Societies the Rev. Peter Williams, a pious distinguished clergyman of Wales, seeing that his countrymen were almost entirely destitute of the Bible, and knowing that the work of the Lord could not prosper without it, undertook with holy confidence, though destitute of the means, to translate and publish a Welsh Bible for his countrymen. Having expended all his living, and being deeply involved in debt, with the work unfinished, he expected every hour to be arrested and imprisoned, without the means or hope of release. One morning he had taken an affectionate leave of his family for the purpose of pursuing his pious labors, with an expectation that he should not be permitted to return. When just as he was mounting his horse a stranger rode up and presented him a letter. He stopped and opened it, and found to his astonishment that it contained information that a lady had bequeathed him a legacy of £300 sterling. "Now," says he, "my dear wife, I can finish my Bible, pay my debts, and live in peace at home."

(*n*) THE CZAR AND THE PSALM.—When Alexander, emperor of Russia, came to the throne, few Bibles were found in his empire, and great carelessness in reference to religion almost universally prevailed. A high place in the church soon became vacant, and the emperor appointed his favorite prince Galitzin to fill it. He at first declined the appointment, on the plea of his entire ignorance of religion, but the emperor overruled the objection as of no weight. The prince, on his first interview with the venerable archbishop Platoff, requested him to point out some book which would give him a concise view of the Christian religion. The archbishop, rather surprised at the prince's professed ignorance of religion, recommended the Bible. The prince said he could not think of reading that book. "Well," replied the archbishop, "that is the only book there is, or ever will be, that can give you a correct view of the Christian religion." "Then I must remain ignorant of it: reading the Bible is out of the question." was his reply. The words, however, of the venerable Platoff remained upon his mind, and he shortly afterwards privately bought and read the Bible. The effects were soon visible. He was not known to be "a Bible reader," but his manners were treated with contempt. Nearly every one was now agitated by the threatened invasion by the French. Galitzin was not so. His companions were astonished. Was he become a traitor to his prince? It was impossible; his loyalty was undoubted. At this important crisis, he thought it his duty to acquaint the emperor with the rock on which he rested unmoved at the threatened danger. He requested an interview; it was granted. The invasion was naturally the first subject of conversation; and next, as closely connected with it, the prince's conduct. The emperor demanded upon what principle he remained calm and unmoved, in the midst of universal alarm. The prince drew from his pocket a small Bible, and held it toward the emperor; as he put out his hand to receive it, it fell, and opened at the ninety-first Psalm: "He that dwelleth in the secret place of the Most High, shall abide under the shadow of the Almighty." "Oh that your Majesty would seek this retreat," said the prince, as he read the words of the Psalm. They separated. A day was appointed for public prayer. The minister who preached, took for his subject the ninety-first Psalm. The emperor, surprised, inquired of the prince if he had mentioned the circumstance that occurred at the interview. He assured him that he had not named it. A short time after, the emperor having a few minutes to spare, and perhaps feeling the necessity of Christian support, sent for his chaplain to read the Bible to him in his tent. He came, and began the ninety-first Psalm. "Hold," said the emperor, "who told you to read that?" "God," replied the chaplain. "How?" exclaimed Alexander. "Surprised at your sending for me," continued the chaplain, "I fell upou my knees before God, and besought him to teach my weak lips what to speak. I felt that part of the holy word which I have begun to read clearly pointed out to me. Why your majesty interrupted me I know not." The result was a great alteration in the emperor's conduct, and the manifestation of great zeal in the circulation of the Scriptures.

54. Inspiration of the Bible.

(*a*) WHERE DID HE GET THAT LAW?—In a city in one of the northern states lived a lawyer of eminence and talents. He was notoriously profane. He had a negro boy, at whom his neighbors used to hear him swear with awful violence. One day this gentleman met an elder of the Presbyterian church, who was also a lawyer, and said to him, "I wish, sir, to examine into the truth of the Christian religion. What books would you advise me to read on the evidences of Christianity?"

The elder, surprised at the inquiry, replied: "That is a question, sir, which you ought to have settled long ago. You ought not to have put off a subject so important to this late period of life."

"It is too late," said the inquirer. "I never knew much about it, but I always supposed that Christianity was rejected by the great majority of learned men. I intend, however, now to examine the subject thoroughly myself. I have upon me, as my physician says, a mortal disease, under which I may live a year and a half or two years, but not probably longer. What books, sir, would you advise me to read?"

"The Bible," said the elder.

"I believe you don't understand me," resumed the unbeliever, surprised in his turn: "I wish to investigate *the truth* of the Bible."

"I would advise you, sir," repeated the elder, "to read the Bible. And (he continued) I will give you my reasons. Most infidels are very ignorant of the Scriptures. Now to reason on any subject with correctness, we must understand what it is about which we reason. In the next place, I consider the internal evidence of the truth of the Scriptures stronger than the external."

"And where shall I begin?" inquired the unbeliever. "At the New Testament?"

"No," replied the elder; "at the beginning—at Genesis."

The infidel bought a commentary, went home, and sat down to the serious study of the Scriptures. He applied all his strong and well-disciplined powers of mind to the Bible, to try rigidly but impartially its truth.

As he went on in his perusal, he received occasional calls from the elder. The infidel freely remarked upon what he had read, and stated his objections. He liked this passage—he thought that touching and beautiful—but he could not credit a third.

One evening the elder called, and found the unbeliever at his house, or office, walking the room with a dejected look, his mind apparently absorbed in thought. He continued, not noticing that any one had come in, busily to trace and retrace his steps. The elder at length spoke:

"You seem, sir," said he, "to be in a brown study. Of what are you thinking?"

"I have been reading," replied the infidel, "the moral law."

"Well, what do you think of it?" asked the elder.

"I will tell you what I *used* to think," answered the infidel. "I supposed that Moses was the leader of a horde of banditti; that having a strong mind, he acquired great influence over a superstitious people: and that on Mount Sinai he played off some sort of fireworks, to the amazement of his ignorant followers, who imagined, in their mingled fear and superstition, that the exhibition was supernatural."

"But what do you think *now?*" interposed the elder.

"I have been looking," said the infidel, "into the *nature* of that law. I have been trying to see whether I can add any thing to it, or take any thing from it, so as to make it better. Sir, I cannot. It is *perfect.*

"The first commandment," continued he, "directs us to make the Creator the object of our supreme love and reverence. That is right. If he be our Creator, Preserver, and Supreme Benefactor, we ought to treat him, and *none other*, as such. The second forbids idolatry. That certainly is right. The third forbids profanity. The fourth fixes a time for religious worship, If there be a God, he ought surely to be worshipped. It is suitable that there should be an outward homage, significant of our inward regard. If God be worshipped, it is proper that some *time* should be set apart for that purpose, when all may worship him harmoniously and without interruption. One day in seven is certainly not too much, and I do not know that it is too little. The fifth defines the peculiar duties arising from family relations. Injuries to our neighbor are then *classified* by the moral law. They are divided into offences against life, chastity, property, and character. And," said he, applying a legal idea with legal acuteness, "I notice that the greatest offence in each class is expressly forbidden. Thus the greatest injury to life is murder; to chastity, adultery; to property, theft; to character, perjury. Now the greater offence must include the less of the same kind. Murder must include every injury to life; adultery, every injury to purity, and so of the rest. And the moral code is closed and perfected by a command forbidding every improper *desire* in regard to our neighbors.

"I have been thinking," he proceeded, "where did Moses get that law? I have read the history; the Egyptians and the adjacent nations were idolaters, so were the Greeks and Romans; and the wisest and best Greeks or Romans never gave a code of morals like this. Where did Moses get this law, which surpasses the wisdom and philosophy of the most enlightened ages? He lived at a period comparatively barbarous, but he has given a law in which the learning and sagacity of all subsequent time can detect no flaw. Where did he get it? He could not have soared so far above his age as to have devised it himself. I am satisfied where he obtained it. It came down from heaven. I am convinced of the truth of the religion of the Bible."

The infidel—infidel no longer—he

mained to his death a firm believer in the truth of Christianity.

(*b*) VIEWS OF THE SOUTH SEA ISLANDERS.—The Rev. John Williams, the "Martyr of Erromanga," relates, that at one of the annual missionary meetings in the South Sea Islands, several native speakers addressed the meeting with peculiar effect; but some of the officers and crew of a British man-of-war, who were present, were disposed to regard the natives as mere parrots, saying just what the missionaries had taught them. To satisfy them, Mr. Williams collected some fifteen of the natives together in the afternoon, to have the officers and crew examine them. "I did not," says Mr. W. "give them to understand the purpose for which they were assembled; I only said, 'These gentlemen have some questions to ask you.' The questions were then asked: 'Do you believe the Bible to be the word of God?' They were startled: they had never entertained a single doubt on the subject; but, after a moment's pause, one answered, 'Most certainly we do.' It was asked, 'Why do you believe it? Can you give any reason for believing the Bible to be the word of God?' He replied, 'Why, look at the power with which it has been attended, in the utter overthrow of all that we have been addicted to from time immemorial. What else could have demolished that system of idolatry which had so long prevailed amongst us? No human arguments could have induced us to abandon that false system.' The same question being put to another, he replied, 'I believe the Bible to be the word of God, on account of the pure system of religion which it contains. We had a system of religion before; but look how dark and black a system that was, compared with the bright system of salvation revealed in the word of God! Here we learn that we are sinners; and that God gave Jesus Christ to die for us; and by that goodness salvation is given to us. Now, what but the wisdom of God could have produced such a system as this presented to us in the word of God? And this doctrine leads to purity.' There was a third reply to this question, and it was a rather singular one; but it was a native idea: 'When I look at myself, I find I have got hinges all over my body. I have hinges to my legs, hinges to my jaws, hinges to my feet. If I want to take hold of any thing, there are hinges to my hands to do it with. If my heart thinks, and I want to speak, I have got hinges to my jaws. If I want to walk, I have hinges to my feet. Now here,' continued he, 'is wisdom, in adapting my body to the various functions it has to discharge. And I find that the wisdom which made the Bible, exactly fits with this wisdom which has made my body; consequently, I believe the Bible to be the word of God.' Another replied, 'I believe it to be the word of God, on account of the prophecies which it contains, and the fulfilment of them.'"

(*c*) FIRST CHAPTER OF ROMANS.—Perhaps no part of the Bible occasions more surprise among the heathen, than the first chapter of Romans. Its graphic picture of the follies and the guilt into which men plunge, when God gives them up to a reprobate mind, are instantly recognized as having a counterpart in their own lives. To their minds the great problem is, how came language, so accurate and faithful, to be employed by the sacred writer? Some escape from the difficulty by affirming that the Scriptures have been altered to meet the case. A brahmin once told a missionary that the expression, "Professing themselves to be wise, they became fools," must have been inserted after the arrival of the missionaries in India.

(*d*) WORDS OF DR. YOUNG.—Dr. Cotton was intimate with Dr. Young, and paid him a visit about a fortnight before he was seized with his last illness. Dr. Young was then in his usual health; his venerable appearance, the gravity of his utterance, and the earnestness with which he discoursed about religion, gave him, in Dr. Cotton's view, the appearance of a prophet. They had been delivering their sentiments on Newton's "Dissertation on the Prophecies," when Dr. Young closed the conference thus:—"My friend, there are two considerations upon which my faith in Christ is built as upon a rock

The fall of man, the redemption of man, and the resurrection of man: these three cardinal articles of our religion are such as human ingenuity could never have invented; therefore they must be Divine. The other argument is this:—If the prophecies have been fulfilled, of which there is no doubt, then the Bible must be the word of God; and if the Scriptures are the word of God, Christianity must be true."

(e) AN ARTLESS ARGUMENT.—Naimbanna, a black prince, arrived in England, from the neighborhood of Sierra Leone, in 1791. The gentleman to whose care he was intrusted, took great pains to convince him that the Bible was the word of God, and he received it as such, with great reverence and simplicity. Do we ask what it was that satisfied him on this subject, let us listen to his artless words. "When I found," says he, "all good men minding the Bible, and calling it the word of God, and all bad men disregarding it, I then was sure that the Bible must be what good men called it, the word of God."

(f) REASONING OF THE CHIEFS.—Two Mongul Tartar chiefs went from the borders of China to St. Petersburgh, to examine the arts and manners of the Europeans. They were represented as the most ingenious and noble of their tribes. During their stay, among other things, a German clergyman engaged them to assist him in preparing a translation of the Gospels into the language of their country, and they spent some time every day in study. At length the task was done, the last correction was made, and the book was closed on the table before them. Still they sat, serious and silent. The minister inquired the cause; and was equally surprised and delighted, to hear them both avow themselves converts to the truths of the blessed volume.

"At home," they said, "we studied the sacred writings of the Chinese, and the more we read, the more obscure they seemed; the longer we have read the gospel, the more simple and intelligible it becomes, until at last it seems as if Jesus was talking with us."

This is a very pleasing tribute to the excellence of the Scriptures, and it is just what might be expected from their natural, unpretending style. It is the simple, unvarnished style of truth.

(g) THOMAS PAINE SILENCED.—A gentleman of New-York, who personally knew Thomas Paine, and was repeatedly in his company during the last years of his life, gave the following account of a conversation with him respecting the Bible:—

One evening I found Paine haranguing a company of his disciples, on the great mischief done to mankind by the introduction of the Bible and Christianity. When he paused, I said, "Mr. Paine, you have been in Scotland; you know there is not a more rigid set of people in the world than they are in their attachment to the Bible: it is their schoolbook; their churches are full of Bibles. When a young man leaves his father's house, his mother always, in packing his chest, puts a Bible on the top of his clothes." He said it was true. I continued, "You have been in Spain, where the people are destitute of the Bible, and there you can hire a man for a dollar to murder his neighbor, who never gave him any offence." He assented. "You have seen the manufacturing districts in England, where not one man in fifty can read, and you have been in Ireland, where the majority never saw a Bible. Now, you know it is an historical fact, that in one county in England or Ireland there are many more capital convictions in six months, than there are in the whole population of Scotland in twelve. Besides, this day there is not one Scotchman in the almshouse, state prison, bridewell, or penitentiary of New-York. Now then, if the Bible were so bad a book as you represent it to be, those who use it would be the worst members of society: but the contrary is the fact; for our prisons, almshouses, and penitentiaries are filled with men and women, whose ignorance or unbelief prevents them from reading the Bible." It was now near ten o'clock at night. Paine answered not a word, but, taking a candle from the table, walked up stairs, leaving his friends and myself staring at one another.

(h) YOUNG BUCHANAN AND THE HIGHLANDER.—The late Rev. Claudius Buchanan, shortly after he had visited the principal parts of Europe, was met in the streets of London by an old Highlander, who was an intimate acquaintance of his father. In order to have a little conversation, they went into a public house, and took some refreshments.

Young Claudius gave his countryman a very animated description of his tour, and of the wonders he had seen upon the Continent. The old man listened with attention to his narrative, and then eagerly inquired whether his religious principles had not been materially injured by mixing among such a variety of characters and religions. "Do you know what an infidel is?" said Buchanan. "Yes," was the reply. "Then," said he, "I am an infidel; and have seen the absurdity of all those nostrums my good old father used to teach me in the North; and can *you*," added he, "seriously believe that the Bible is a revelation from the Supreme Being?—"I do."—"And pray tell me what may be your reasons?" "Claude," said the good old Highlander, "I know nothing about what learned men call the *external* evidences of revelation, but I will tell you why I believe it to be from God. I have a most depraved and sinful nature, and, do what I will, I find I cannot make myself holy. My friends cannot do it for me, nor do I think all the angels in heaven could. One thing alone does it,—the reading and believing what I read in that blessed book,—that does it. Now, as I know that God must be holy, and a lover of holiness, and as I believe that book is the only thing in creation that produces and promotes holiness, I conclude that it is from God, and that he is the Author of it."

(i) THE OLD NEGRO'S ARGUMENT.—When the celebrated Tennent was travelling in Virginia, he lodged one night at the house of a planter, who informed him that one of his slaves, a man upwards of seventy, who could neither read nor write, was yet eminently distinguished for his piety, and for his knowledge of the Scriptures. Having some curiosity to learn what evidence such a man could have of their divine origin, he went out in the morning, alone, and without making himself known as a clergyman, entered into conversation with him on the subject. After starting some of the common objections of infidels against the authenticity of the Scriptures, in a way calculated to confound an ignorant man, he said to him, when you cannot even *read* the Bible, nor examine the evidence for, or against its truth, how can you *know* that it is the word of God? After reflecting a moment, the negro replied, "You ask me, sir, how I *know* that the Bible is the word of God:—I *know it, by its effect upon my own heart.*"

(j) MAMGENA'S REASONING.—A poor female Matchappee, named Mamgena, called, says Mr. Campbell, and told me, that when she first heard of the Bible she did not think it was true; but when she found it to describe her heart so exactly, she could not but believe what it said. She was determined, she added, always to live near some place where the word of God was preached; where she might hear about a crucified Saviour, though she should starve.

(k) CONVERSION OF ANUNDO.—Anundo was admitted a pupil in the General Assembly's school, on its opening in August, 1830. In accordance with the system of tuition pursued in the school, he, together with his class-fellows, soon commenced the study of the New Testament. It was not long before his mind became arrested by the Sermon on the Mount. The ideas, the prospects, the images, the illustrations, all were so peculiar, seemed so apposite and so true, that glimpses of light flashed through his soul, and he was often heard to exclaim, 'How beautiful, how tender, how kind, how full of love and goodness! Oh, how unlike the spirit and maxims of Hindooism! *Surely this is the truth!*' Never was there a more striking exemplification of what Owen calls 'the self-evidencing power of the Bible.' As the young man advanced in his acquaintance with its contents, he constantly contrasted its statements with those which the Brahmins rehearsed from their Shasters; and he appeared as it were internally to see and feel that there was truth in the former, and error in the latter. He demanded no *external* evidence to authenticate the divine authority of the Christian Scriptures. To him the reading of them seemed like the presence of the light of day exposing surrounding objects in their true colors: or rather like the sudden admission of the solar rays into a dreary cavern, bringing to view the hideous and loathsome objects with which it had been stored. Not that he disparaged miracles and prophecies; but he declared that these were not *necessary* for *his* conviction; there was something in the whole spirit, and plan, and announcements of the Gospel, that came home to his soul in the light of truth, independent of *external* proofs. Anundo voluntarily applied to Mr. Duff for baptism. His address on the occasion was, in substance, 'What shall I do? I feel that I am a sinner, a great sinner, a sinner that deserves to be eternally punished. What shall become of me? If I die this night, I fear I shall be lost forever, and I know I deserve such a fate. What shall I do? I am troubled, much troubled, day and night I am troubled. But in the Bible I read of God's mercy. May I not trust in it? I sometimes feel that I may, and so try to think and do what is good, when all at once I feel that I am sinning more. Then I read the Bible; I cannot help reading it; and there I find *something that catches me* in a way which I cannot explain. I feel that Christ is the only true Saviour. Last night I could not sleep, and so arose and lighted my lamp, and read the Bible, and it *caught* me; and I am convinced that here is the only way of salvation. May I not then publicly profess my faith in Christ by baptism?"

(*l*) CONDÉ'S ARGUMENT.—Pains had been early taken by some of the Prince of Condé's supposed friends to shake his belief of Christianity; he always replied, 'You give yourselves a great deal of unnecessary trouble; the dispersion of the Jews will always be an undeniable proof to me of the truth of our holy religion.'

TESTIMONIES TO ITS VALUE.

55. Testimony of Distinguished Persons.

(*a*) OF SIR WILLIAM JONES.—Sir William Jones, whose interesting writings on oriental subjects elucidated many obscure points in Scripture history, was a general scholar, and embellished and adorned every subject that passed under his elegant pen. On the blank leaf of his Bible, the following finely conceived description was found written:—"I have regularly and attentively perused these Holy Scriptures, and am of opinion that this volume, independently of its Divine origin, contains more true sublimity, more exquisite beauty, more pure morality, more important history, and finer strains of poetry and eloquence, than can be collected from all other books, in whatever age or language they may have been written. The unstrained application of them to events which took place long after the publication, is a solid ground for belief that they are genuine productions, and consequently inspired."

(*b*) OF DR. AMES.—Fisher Ames, a distinguished American statesman and orator, who died in 1808, was ardently attached to the Bible. He lamented its prevailing disuse in schools, and thought that children should be well acquainted with it, both on account of the all-important truths it contains, and because they would thus learn the English language in its purity. He was accustomed to say, "I will hazard the assertion, that no man ever did, or ever will, become truly eloquent, without being a constant reader of the Bible, and an admirer of the purity and sublimity of its language."

(*c*) OF PATRICK HENRY.—This distinguished man was a native of Virginia, of which state he became governor. He was eminent through life as a statesman and an orator. A little before his death, he remarked to a friend, who found him reading his Bible, "Here is a book worth more than all the other books which ever were printed; yet it is my misfortune never to have, till lately, found time to read it with proper attention and feeling."

(*d*) OF DR. JOHNSON.—Dr. Samuel Johnson is distinguished as a writer on morals; his compositions have seldom been excelled in energy of thought and beauty of expression. To a young gentleman, who visited him on his death-bed, he said, "Young man, attend to the voice of one who has possessed a certain degree of fame in the world, and who will shortly appear before his Maker: read the Bible every day of your life."

(*e*) OF DR. FRANKLIN.—At the time when the celebrated Dr. Franklin lay upon his death-bed, he was visited by a young man who had a great respect for his judgment in all things; and having entertained doubts as to the truth of the Scriptures, he thought that this awful period afforded a suitable opportunity of consulting the doctor on this important subject. Accordingly, he introduced it in a solemn and weighty manner, inquiring of Franklin what were his sentiments as to the truth of the Scriptures. On the question being put, although he was in a very weak state, and near his decease, he replied, "Young man, my advice to you is, that you cultivate an acquaintance with, and a firm belief in, the Holy Scriptures: this is your certain interest."

(*f*) OF WILLIAM COLLINS.—Collins is well known as a celebrated English poet. In the latter part of his life, he withdrew from his general studies, and travelled with no other book than an English New Testament, such as children carry to school. A friend was anxious to know what companion a man of letters had chosen; the poet said, "I have only one book, but that book is the best."

(*g*) OF MONSIEUR BAUTAIN.—M. L. Bautain, a professor of philosophy at Strasburgh, has furnished an account of the power of the Scriptures on his heart:—"A single book has saved me; but that book is not of human origin. Long had I despised it; long had I deemed it a class-book for the credulous and ignorant; until, having investigated the gospel of Christ, with an ardent desire to ascertain its truth or falsity, its pages proffered to my inquiries the sublimest knowledge of man and nature, and the simplest, and at the same time, the most exalted system of moral ethics. Faith, hope, and charity were enkindled in my bosom; and every advancing step strengthened me in the conviction, that the morals of this book are superior to human morals, as its oracles are superior to human opinions."

(*h*) OF COUNT OXENSTEIN.—It is stated, by the celebrated William Penn, that Count Oxenstein, chancellor of Sweden, being visited, in his retreat from public business, by commissioner Whitlock, ambassador from England to Queen Christiana, in the conclusion of their discourse, he said to the ambassador, "I have seen much and enjoyed much of this world; but I never knew how to live till now. I thank my good God, who has given me time to know him and likewise myself. All the comfort I have, and all the comfort I take, and which is more than the whole world can give, is the knowledge of God's love in my heart, and the reading in this blessed book," laying his hand on the Bible. "You are now," he continued, "in the prime of your age and vigor, and in great favor and business; but this will all leave you, and you will one day better understand and relish what I say to you: then you will find that there is more wisdom, truth, comfort, and pleasure, in retiring and turning your heart from the world, in the good Spirit of God, and in reading his sacred word, than in all the courts and favors of princes."

(*i*) OF JOHN LOCKE.—Locke spent the last fourteen years of his life in the study of the Bible; and he wrote "The Common Place Book of the Scriptures," which is an invaluable fruit of his Scripture Studies. These facts of themselves give the strongest proof of the high estimation in which this profound thinker, and acute metaphysician, held the Christian Writings. He admired the wisdom and goodness of God in the method of salvation they reveal; and, it is said, that when he thought upon it, he could not forbear crying out, "O the depths of the riches of the goodness and the knowledge of God!"

He was persuaded, that men would

be convinced of this by reading the Scriptures without prejudice; and he frequently exhorted those with whom he conversed, to a serious study of these sacred writings.

A relative inquired of him, what was the shortest and surest way for a young gentleman to attain a true knowledge of the Christian religion? "LET HIM STUDY," said the philosopher, "THE HOLY SCRIPTURES, ESPECIALLY IN THE NEW TESTAMENT. THEREIN ARE CONTAINED THE WORDS OF ETERNAL LIFE. IT HAS GOD FOR ITS AUTHOR, SALVATION FOR ITS END, AND TRUTH WITHOUT ANY MIXTURE OF ERROR FOR ITS MATTER."

56. Testimony of Infidels.

(*a*) "WE WILL NOT BURN THAT BOOK TILL WE GET A BETTER."—A society of gentlemen, most of whom had enjoyed a liberal education, and were persons of polished manners, but had unhappily imbibed infidel principles, used to assemble at each others' houses, for the purpose of ridiculing the Scriptures, and hardening one another in their unbelief. At last, they unanimously formed a resolution solemnly to burn the Bible, and so to be troubled no more with a book which was so hostile to their principles, and disquieting to their conscience. The day fixed upon arrived; a large fire was prepared; a Bible was laid on the table, and a flowing bowl ready to drink its dirge. For the execution of their plan, they fixed upon a gentleman of high birth, brilliant vivacity, and elegance of manners. He undertook the task; and, after a few enlivening glasses, amidst the applause of his jovial compeers, he approached the table, took up the Bible, and was walking leisurely forward to put it into the fire; but, happening to give it a look, he was seized with trembling; paleness overspread his countenance, and he seemed convulsed. He returned to the table, and, laying down the Bible, said, with a strong asseveration, "We will not burn *that book* till we get a *better*."

Soon after this, the same gay and lively young gentleman died, and on his death-bed was led to true repentance, deriving unshaken hopes of forgiveness and of future blessedness from that book which he was once going to burn. He found it, indeed, the best book, not only for a living, but a dying hour.

(*b*) DIDEROT'S CONFESSION.—It is related, that one day Mr. Beauzet, a member of the French Academy, went to see Diderot, one of the champions of infidelity; he found him explaining a chapter of the gospel to his daughter, as seriously, and with the concern of a most Christian parent. Mr. Beauzet expressed his surprise. "I understand you," said Diderot, "but in truth what better lesson could I give her?"

HAPPY EFFECTS OF THE BIBLE.

57. Morality Promoted.

(*a*) THE TAILOR'S ASSOCIATES.—A Bible was sold, at a reduced price to a tailor, who boarded in a house with several apprentice boys. One of them, having seen it, became very anxious to obtain one on the same terms; and soon saved, from his small earnings, a sufficient sum for its purchase. He became serious, and kept his Bible constantly near him whilst at work. His associates in the same occupation were thoughtless, profane, and constantly disposed to ridicule the book he so much prized. One of them in particular, more wicked than the rest, used sometimes to take it up, and read a passage for sport, or something worse. At length, however, the truth became too powerful for his depraved heart; he began to reflect upon the sin he was committing, soon solicited the boon for himself, abstaining from profaneness, and, in connexion with the owner of the Bible, succeeded in making it finable for any one of their number to utter an oath. The effect upon the whole was remarkable; and several of them became truly anxious about their souls, sincerely praying to be made "wise unto salvation, through faith which is in Christ Jesus."

(*b*) THE RUSSIAN MESSMATE.—A minister at St. Petersburg, writes:

—In the spring of 1829, Timothy, the hawker, called at my house with his wares. My servants, who recommend the Scriptures whenever they have an opportunity, talked with this man on the value of the New Testament, and advised him to buy a copy. "Of what use can it be to me," said he, "when I am not able to read?" "Yes, it may be of great service to you; you can carry it to your lodgings, and have it read to you; or you can send it to your family, some of whom can read it. It will do good: buy one." The man attended to this advice, and carried the book to his lodgings.

We saw nothing more of this man until autumn; when he returned, and earnestly entreated a copy of every kind of book we could give him. "You can form no idea," said he, "of the good that book has done, which I bought here in the spring. There are more than thirty of us who mess together at the same lodgings; and at the time when I first took home the New Testament, these men spent almost every evening at the public house, and returned intoxicated: but now the scene is quite altered; scarcely a man leaves the lodgings in the evening. There are three amongst us who can read; and they take it by turns, and the others sit round and listen to them. There is no drunkenness in our party now."

Oh! what an interesting scene would this group have presented to the eye of an apostle! Thirty poor villagers, collected together from various parts of the country, listening to one of their number reading the words of eternal life: and, from this circumstance, breaking off from their vices, saving their hard earnings for their families, and acting like rational creatures! How true it is, that "godliness is profitable unto all things!"

(*c*) THE MURDERER CONFESSING.—A young German, who, for the crime of murder in the second degree, had been a long time in solitary confinement in America, was repeatedly visited by a German clergyman, to whom he made the most positive declarations of his innocence. After six months had elapsed, on leaving him one evening, the clergyman pointed his attention to three verses in the New Testament, and particularly urged upon him the importance of the truths contained in them. He promised to read them—he did so—and when he threw himself upon his pallet to rest, he found that sleep had forsaken him; he turned again and again, but still there was no rest. The verses had made a deep impression upon his mind, and although he had for six months persisted that he was innocent of the crime of which he stood charged, the first words he uttered to the keeper in the morning were, "I did commit that murder." Being asked what had now induced him to confess, he pointed to the verses; they were as follows:

"If we say that we have no sin, we deceive ourselves, and the truth is not in us. If we confess our sins, He is faithful and just to forgive us our sins, and to cleanse us from all unrighteousness. If we say that we have not sinned we make him a liar, and his word is not in us." 1 John 1: 8–10.

(*d*) COUNTERFEITERS RECLAIMED.—Some few years ago, two women and a man called one evening at the cabin of a schoolmaster, in Ireland, requesting a lodging for the night. The good man had just assembled his family for evening worship, having his Bible before him. He kindly requested the strangers to walk in, and began to read the second chapter of the epistle to the Ephesians. This he did slowly, and with emphasis, that he might secure the attention of his visitors to the important subjects on which it treats. They all appeared to pay attention, particularly the young man, whose countenance indicated the agitation of his mind. When the chapter was ended, he inquired what book that was out of which he had been reading. His host replied, it was the word of God. His agitation immediately increased; and, after remarking that he never before knew there was such a book, he began to inquire the meaning of some of the passages which had particularly arrested his attention; namely, "Dead in trespasses and sins;" "Walking after the course of this world;" "By nature the children of wrath," etc. To all these, the good man, in a plain and simple way, gave answers. The young man heard with the greatest attention, and could not suppress the sigh which indicated what was passing within. He was referred to those parts of Scripture which throw light on the chapter that had been read; and especially on the parts he wished to have explained. Then, looking at his host with great earnestness, he exclaimed, "It is indeed the word of God; it is all true; and my state is fully that which it describes. In this way I have been walking from my childhood; and, in the service of the god of this world, I undertook the journey which has brought me, my wife, and sister, to your house. Oh that our souls may be raised from that death in trespasses and sins in which I have been involved to this moment! I have long followed no other employment, but that of defrauding the ignorant poor at fairs and markets, by passing base money, which I coin; and for this purpose are we come here, on our way to attend the fair which is to be held to-morrow at ——."

58. Conversion of Seamen.

(*a*) LONG-FORGOTTEN TEXT.—A sailor once returned from a voyage flushed with money, and as he had never seen London, he resolved to treat himself with a sight of whatever it contained great or curious. Among other places he paid a visit to St. Paul's. This happened during divine service. When carelessly passing by, he heard the officiating minister utter the words, "Pray without ceasing;" but they then made no impression on his mind: he gratified his curiosity, returned to his marine pursuits, and continued at sea seven years without the occurrence of any thing remarkable in his history.

One fine evening, as he was walking on deck to enjoy the serene air, and while his feelings were soothed by the pleasing aspect of nature, on a sudden the words darted into his mind—"Pray without ceasing." "Pray without ceasing! what words can these be?" exclaimed he. "I think I have heard them before; where could it be?" After a pause, "Oh! it was at St. Paul's in London; the minister read them from the Bible. What! and do the Scriptures say, 'Pray without ceasing?' Oh, what a wretch must I be, to have lived so long without praying at all!" God, who at first deposited this scripture in his ear, now caused it to spring up in a way, and at a time, and with a power peculiarly his own. The poor fellow now found the lightning of conviction flash on his conscience, and seemed to see the gulf of destruction ready to swallow him up. He now began to pray; but praying was not all. "O," said he, "that I had a Bible or some good book!" He rummaged his chest; when lo, at one corner he found a Bible, which his anxious mother had twenty years before put in his chest, and which, till now, he had never opened. He readily embraced it, clasped it to his heart, read, wept, prayed, believed, and became a new man.

(*b*) THE VERSE AND THE TOBACCO.—Says a correspondent of a Religious Tract Society:—On board a vessel at Horsleydown, I found only an old shipkeeper. I asked him whether he could read; he replied, he could. On asking him what books he read, his reply was, "The Bible." I then gave him two tracts, and remarked that I had sometimes seen parts of the Bible in cheesemongers' shops, which I thought very wrong. He said he differed from me: on asking his reason, he stated that he was formerly a great smoker, and on going to purchase some tobacco, it was put up in a part of the Bible. One verse struck him very forcibly; and he was induced to purchase a Bible, and has read it daily to the present time; and, said he, "Blessed be God, I would not part with it, and the hopes I have of salvation, for ten thousand worlds."

(*c*) "WHAT BOOK IS THIS?"—A meeting was once held in Liverpool, for the establishment of a society to supply sailors with Bibles. An active agent of the society having moved the first resolution, said, that as he saw so many sailors around him, he should not ask any one to second his motion, but leave it to some one of the sailors. There was a deathlike silence for some moments; but a poor, old, blind sailor, at the far end of the place, rose, and, in a harsh voice, said, "Sir, there is not an individual present who has greater reason to second this resolution than the person who now addresses you. Before I had arrived at twenty years of age, I led the van in every species of vice and immorality. Our ship was ordered to the coast of Guinea; a violent storm came on, the vivid lightning flashed around, at last it struck my eyes; from that time to the present I have not beheld the light of day; but, sir, though I was deprived of sight, I was not deprived of sin. I was very fond of having books read to me, but, alas! only bad books. At length a Scotchman came to my house, and said, 'I know you are fond of hearing books read, will you hear me read?' I said I had no objection: he read the book to me. I felt interested, and, at the end of his reading, I said, 'Tell me what book you have read.' 'Never mind, said he, 'I will come again and read more; and he came again, and again, and again. At last the tears gushed out from my blind eyes, and I earnestly exclaimed, 'Oh, sir, what book is this?' He said, 'This book is the Bible.' From that time, though blind, I see; I can now discern the way of salvation by a crucified Saviour: from that time to this I have been enabled to follow my Lord; and I second this resolution, knowing the advantages of circulating the sacred volume." Subsequently to this, the poor old man obtained a few shillings a week, which he divided, in various portions, to different religious societies; and gave sixpence a week to a little boy, to read to him the sacred Scriptures, and to lead him about from house to house, and from cellar to cellar, to promote the best interests of others.

(*d*) THE CAPTAIN TURNED PREACHER.—A lady, who was actively engaged in the distribution of the Holy Scriptures and religious tracts, went, on one occasion, to the quay at Plymouth, and requested permission of a captain to go on board a man-of-war in which were about eight hundred men, and many dissipated females. The captain said, "Madam, it will be of no avail; you will only meet with abuse." She answered, "With your leave I'll go." "Certainly, madam," he replied; and she went. Something occurred during the time, which irritated the captain, who swore a most dreadful oath. The lady said, "Sir, as you have granted me one favor, I hope you will confer another." "Certainly, madam," was the reply. "It is then, sir, that you will please to keep from swearing while I am in your ship:" this he complied with. After the lady had gone round the ship, and given away some tracts, (and, to the honor of British sailors be it spoken, they treated her with the greatest respect,) she returned to the captain, who was standing at the entrance of the vessel. She thanked him kindly, and said, "I have yet one more favor to ask of you, sir, which I hope you will comply with." "Yes, certainly, madam," was the reply. "It is this," she said, presenting him with the New Testament, "I desire you will read it through twice." He replied, "I will, madam, for my word's sake."

Some years afterwards, when on a visit to a place about five miles from Plymouth, on the Lord's day, she went to church, where she heard an excellent sermon. As she was returning through the churchyard, a gentleman accosted her, and said, "Do you remember, madam, giving to a captain a New Testament, after distributing some tracts on board a man-of-war, and desiring him to read it twice?" "Yes, sir," she replied. He added, "I am the man to whom you gave it, and I have been preaching to you to-day. Through your instrumentality God has brought me to love that book which once I despised."

(*e*) THE WIDOW'S SON AND HIS BIBLE.—There was a pious widow living in the northern part of England, on whom, in consequence of the loss she had sustained, devolved the sole care of a numerous family, consisting of seven daughters and one son. It was her chief anxiety to train up her children in those virtuous and religious habits, which promote the present happiness and the immortal welfare of man. Her efforts were crowned with the best success, so far as the female branches of her family were concerned. But, alas! her boy proved ungrateful for her care, and became her scourge and her cross. He loved worldly company and pleasure; till, having impoverished his circumstances, it became necessary that he should go to sea. When his mother took her leave of him, she gave him a New Testament, inscribed with his name and her own, solemnly and tenderly entreating that he would keep the book, and read it for her sake. He was borne far away upon the bosom of the trackless deep, and year after year elapsed, without tidings of her boy. She occasionally visited parts of the island remote from her own residence, and particularly the metropolis; and, in whatever company she was cast, she made it a point to inquire for the ship in which her son sailed, if perchance she might hear any tidings of the beloved object who was always uppermost in her thoughts. On one occasion, she accidentally met, in a party in London, a sea captain, of whom she made her accustomed inquiries. He informed her that he knew the vessel, and that she had been wrecked; that he also knew a youth of the name of Charles ——; and added, that he was so depraved and profligate a lad, that it were a good thing if he, and all like him, were at the bottom of the sea. Pierced to her inmost soul, this unhappy mother withdrew from the house, and resolved in future upon strict retirement, in which she might at once indulge and hide her hopeless grief. "I shall go down to the grave," was her language, "mourning for my son." She fixed her residence at one of the sea-ports on the northern coast. After the lapse of some years, a half-naked sailor knocked at her door, to ask relief. The sight of a sailor was always interesting to her, and never failed to awaken recollections and emotions, better imagined than described. She heard his tale. He had seen great perils in the deep, had been several times wrecked, but said he had never been so dreadfully destitute as he was some years back, when himself and a fine young gentleman were the only individuals, of a whole ship's crew, that were saved. "We were cast upon a desert island, where, after seven days and nights, I closed his eyes. Poor fellow, I shall never forget it." And here the tears stole down his weather-beaten cheeks. "He read day and night in a little book, which he said his mother gave him, and which was the only thing he saved. It was his companion every moment; he wept for his sins, he prayed, he kissed the book; he talked of nothing but this book and his mother; and at the last he gave it to me, with many thanks for my poor services. 'There, Jack,' said he, 'take this book, and keep it, and read it, and may God bless you—it's all I've got.' And then he clasped my hand, and died in peace." "Is all this true?" said the trembling, astonished mother. "Yes, madam, every word of it." And then, drawing from his ragged jacket a little book, much battered and time-worn, he held it up exclaiming, "And here's the very book, too." She seized the Testament, descried her own handwriting, and beheld the name of her son, coupled with her own, on the cover. She gazed, she read, she wept, she rejoiced. She seemed to hear a voice, which said, "Behold, thy son liveth." Amidst her conflicting emotions, she was ready to exclaim, "Now, Lord, lettest thou thy servant depart in peace, for mine eyes have seen thy salvation." "Will you part with that book, my honest fellow?" said the mother, anxious now to possess the precious relic. "No, madam," was the answer, "not for any money,—not for all the world. He gave it me with his dying hand. I have more than once lost my all since I got it, without losing this treasure, the value of which, I hope, I have learned for myself; and I will never part with it till I part with the breath out of my body."

(*f*) THE TWOFOLD RESCUE.—The late Rev. Legh Richmond was once speaking at a meeting at Edinburgh, for the advancement of religion among sailors, when he related the following facts:—

"When I reflect on the character and circumstances of seamen, I cannot without peculiar interest recollect the time, when a young man went to sea, whose feelings were ill suited to all the contingencies of a sea-faring life. I remember that the time came when it was said the vessel in which he had sailed had been wrecked, and that the young man was dead, and no intimation had reached the ears of his affectionate parents, of any change in his views as to the things of God. And I remember the time when that young man was so far restored again to his family, that although they saw him not, they heard that he had been saved from the shipwreck. That young man, too, was found by the blessed God while on the ocean with the Bible only, which his father at parting had put into his hand. It was blessed to him in the midst of the carnal companions by whom he was surrounded. This means of grace, without any human instruction, was made effectual to the salvation of his soul. The time came when that young man, who had been a foe to religion, lifted up, in the Bay of Gibraltar, at his mast-head, a Bethel flag, and summoned his sailors to prayer, and prayed with them, and bade the missionary exhort them.—And when I tell you that that young man is *my own son*, you will see that I may well say, God bless the Sailors' Friend!"

(g) THE SPIRITUAL LIFE-BUOY.—Said a youth to one of the secretaries of the Bethel Companies: "I sailed from London in a Scotch vessel for the West Indies, second mate, the most abandoned wretch that ever sailed on salt water, particularly noted for profane swearing. Our captain, though a good seaman, and kind to his ship's company, cared not either for his own soul, or for the souls of his ship's crew. We had been at sea about sixteen days, when one night, during my watch on deck, a sudden puff of wind caused the vessel to give a heavy lurch. Not being prepared to meet it, I was capsized, and came head on against one of the stanchions. Feeling much hurt, I gave vent to my anger, by a dreadful oath, cursing the wind, the ship, the sea, and (awful to mention, the Being who made them. Scarce had this horrid oath escaped me when it appeared to roll back upon my mind with so frightful an image, that I ran aft, and for a moment or two thought I saw the sea parting, and the vessel going down. All that night my awful oath was passing before my eyes like a spectre, and its consequences, my certain damnation. For several days I was miserable; ashamed to say the cause. I asked one of the men for a book; he gave me one of Rousseau's novels. I asked him for a Testament, and he sneeringly answered by asking me if I was going to die. He never troubled himself with these things; he left Bibles and prayer-books to the priests. Several days thus passed in the greatest torment, this dreadful oath always before me, and the devil continually harassing me with the dreadful thought, "I shall be damned, I shall be damned." I could not pray; indeed, I thought it of no use. On the fifth day I was turning over some things in my chest, when I found some trifles I had purchased for sea-stock wrapped in paper—this piece of paper (putting his hand at the same time into his pocket, and from a small red case taking out a leaf containing nearly the whole of the first chapter of Isaiah) oh! how my heart throbbed, when I found it a part of the Bible! But, sir," said he with a tear, "conceive what I felt at these words, 'Though your sins be as scarlet, they shall be white as snow; though they be red like crimson, they shall be as wool!'" He paused to wipe away the tears. Indeed, says the Secretary, my eyes needed wiping too. "O, sir," he continued, "like a drowning man I clung to *this life-buoy;* on this I laid my soul, while the billows were going over me. I prayed, and the Lord was graciously pleased to remove in some measure the great guilt from my conscience, though I continued mournful and bowed down until last evening, on board the Mayflower, I stowed away among the Bethel Company. There the Lord spoke my pardon and peace. I am now like poor Legion, going home to my friends to tell them what great things the Lord has done for me. Farewell, sir." "Farewell, my lad; the Lord go with you."

59. Conversion of the Profligate and Vicious.

(*a*) THE BIBLE AND THE BRANDY BOTTLE.—At an anniversary of a Bible Society in South Carolina, a man was present who had been in the habit of intemperance many years. He had wasted a fortune, and his amiable family were now sharing with him poverty and disgrace. In the evening a director of the Society saw this man in a state of intoxication, and presented him a Bible. He received the drunken man's thanks, who confessed he had no such book at home, and promised to keep it for himself and family to read. Unable to reach his house he slept by the roadside, and in the night awoke, finding his Bible in one pocket and a bottle of brandy in the other. He said to himself, It will not do to carry both home together, and I do not know which to throw away. If I throw away the Bible, I shall die a drunkard, and the devil has me. If I throw away the bottle, I give the lot to God, and I may die a good man. He paused for reflection, and allowed the convictions of duty to contend against habit and inclination. The conflict was a terrible one. Often did he raise his hand to throw away from him the Bible, drink his life out, and let the devil take him. At last conscience prevailed, and taking a hearty draught from the bottle, he dashed it against a tree.

He reached home at the dawn of day, called his family together, told them what he had done, and what he was resolved to do. The morning was spent in reading in his new book with his family, and late on the very same morning they all kneeled around the domestic altar, to offer to Heaven their first united petition. The trembling voice and broken expressions of the father, unaccustomed to pray; the half suppressed emotions of his lovely children, too deeply felt to be silently held in their bosoms, and the loud weeping of his heart-broken companion, overcome with joy and gratitude at the unexpected scene, made an impression on that family which will not be forgotten in eternity. This man now obtained the confidence of the neighborhood; he was exemplary in his morals, a humble and active Christian; and the Lord crowned his temporal affairs with prosperity, and a family once wretched became truly happy.

(*b*) PICKPOCKET AT AN ANNIVERSARY.—The first meeting of the Shoreditch Bible Association was held in the church, which was very much crowded. Some weeks afterwards, the collectors called on a widow, who kept a small grocer's shop, for her subscription, which she had always paid very cheerfully. As they were going away, she said, "Gentlemen, I have got a young man, a lodger, who is always poring over the Bible: I dare say he would subscribe." The collectors were introduced to him to solicit his subscription. He answered, "I certainly will;" and gave them a guinea, and desired them to put down his name as a subscriber of sixpence a week. The gentlemen were astonished, and hesitated at taking so much, and wished to return a part. He answered, "No, I owe my all to the Shoreditch Bible Association." About a month afterwards, the committee wished to increase its number. This young man was proposed and accepted. But when the matter was mentioned to him, he warmly replied, "No, gentlemen, you must pardon me, I am not worthy to form a part of your committee. If you want more money, I will gladly give it; but to act on your committee, I cannot." They in vain pressed the matter, and wished to know his reasons. About a year after, he requested his landlady to desire the gentlemen to wait upon him when they called, (he had regularly paid his subscription through the medium of his landlady,) as he wanted to speak to them; which they did. "Now, gentlemen," said he, "my lips are unsealed. I take my departure for America this week. Here are five guineas. I will now tell you my short history. Two years ago, I was one of the most profligate young men in the city of London. I was a common pickpocket. At your anniversary, seeing the church crowded, I, with several of my companions in iniquity, entered, in order to pursue our sinful practices. From the crowded state of the church, we were separated. I got into the middle aisle, just in front of the speakers. The first words I caught were, 'Thou shalt not steal.' My attention was fixed; my conscience was touched; and tears began to flow. In vain did my companions make their signals to commence our operations. As soon as the meeting closed, I hurried away, threw myself into the first coach I found, drove to my lodgings in the west end of the town, paid my rent, took away all my things, and came into this part of the city, in order to hide myself from my companions; and providentially found this house. I immediately inquired for a Bible; and for the first time in my life began to read it. I found my convictions of the evil of my conduct increased, and I hope I have now found peace and rest in believing on that Saviour whom the Bible reveals."

(*c*) LITTLE JACK AND HIS FATHER.—The substance of the following story was related by the Rev. Mr. S——, at a meeting of the Young Men's Bible Society, of Baltimore, March, 1822.

He stated, that at a meeting of a Bath (England) Bible Association, he was present when there was a call for volunteer speakers, and a stranger came forward and made the following statements. He said, that in the county of Devon, there lived a man, desperately and notoriously wicked, and of so cruel and ferocious a disposition, as in some instances to extinguish his natural affection for his own offspring. One day, taking his little son by the hand, who was big enough to walk, he strolled towards the cliffs, which in those parts overhang the sea, and laid himself down upon the grass. His playful little son meanwhile amused himself with picking up pebbles and throwing them down at the feet of his father, who in a churlish rage, having two or three times bidden him desist without being obeyed, gave vent to his anger, and with a kick, which prostrated the child upon the ground, left the poor creature screaming with anguish and walked away. The unhappy little sufferer having so far recovered as to regain his feet, wandered so near the cliff as to fall over, and was precipitated into the sea; but the air in his dress, (for he still wore infantile garments,) broke the force of his fall, and prevented him from immediately sinking. It happened that the boat of a man-of-war, which was lying in the offing, was just then returning from a watering place, and seeing an object floating on the water rowed up to it, took him in, and carried him on board the ship. The sailors made a pet of him and called him "Little Jack;" and when he had become old enough for the service, made him a powder-monkey, (a title given to those who carry cartridges to the gunners.)

This ship with some others of an inferior size, having had a severe engagement with the enemy, and many being wounded, little Jack, the powder-monkey, was employed to wait upon the surgeon. Among the wounded who were brought from other vessels for surgical aid, was a man, both of whose legs were shot away by a chain shot, and the bones so shattered as to prevent any hope of cure from amputation. Death had indeed already begun to play around his heart. While he lay in these mortal agonies, he fixed his eyes steadfastly upon little Jack, and having yet power to speak, asked the boy who he was, and whence he came? He told him what the sailors had related to him, and which was all he knew of himself. The wounded man, who recognized the features of his son in the boy, was now convinced it must be he. I am, said he, that ungodly and brutal father, who left you upon the cliff, (relating the particulars,) from whence you must have fallen into the sea. Beginning to grow uneasy, I returned to the place where I had left you; but you had disappeared. All my researches proved in vain; I could gain no tidings of you. Supposing that you had perished through my cruelty, I became frantic with grief, and was on the point of putting an end to my existence; but finally, in hopes of finding some relief from my misery, I entered on board a ship-of-war. Having returned from a cruise, while lying in port, a gentleman (a member of a Bible Society) came on board, and asked permission of the captain to distribute some Bibles among the ship's company.

It fell to my lot to receive one, which became the means of my conversion to God; and now I have redemption in the blood of Jesus Christ, even the forgiveness of all my sins. I have but a few moments to live; the pains of death are upon me; I have no will to make, not having any thing to leave you save this Bible, taking it from his bosom and presenting it to him in the language of David to Solomon, "and thou Solomon my son know thou the God of thy fathers; if thou seek him, he will be found of thee; and if thou forsake him, he will cast thee off forever." As he ended the quotation his voice faltered, and he sank in death. The speaker, said Mr. S., admitted that so strange a story might seem incredible, but the tears starting from his eyes, he put his hand into his bosom, drew out a book, and said, "*This is the Bible, and I am Little Jack!*"

(*d*) CUTTING A BIBLE IN PIECES.—A young man, a soldier, who was leading a dissolute life, was often reproved by a pious friend, but to no purpose. At last, his friend gave him a Bible; the young man immediately said, "I will cut it in pieces before your face;" which he instantly did with his sword, and ever after shunned his friend's company. About two years after this had occurred, he was brought to a sick and dying bed, and sent for his friend, and expressed a wish to have a Bible brought to him. He received it, and read it; and one day he clasped the book with both his hands, and exclaimed, "Oh that ever such a wretch as I should be permitted to read this blessed book, which I once cut in pieces! This book has now cut my sins in pieces, and led me to Christ as my Saviour. Oh that I could recall my property and murdered time: all, all should be spent in distributing this blessed book!"

60. Conversion of Infidels.

(*a*) ROCHESTER AND IS. LIII.—It is well known that this extraordinary man was, for many years of his life, an avowed infidel, and that a large portion of his time was spent in ridiculing the Bible. One of his biographers has described him as "a great wit, a great sinner, and a great penitent." Even this man was converted by the Holy Spirit in the use of his word. Reading the fifty-third chapter of Isaiah, he was convinced of the truth and inspiration of the Scriptures, the Deity of the Messiah, and the value of his atonement as a rock on which sinners may build their hopes of salvation. On that atonement he rested, and died in the humble expectation of pardoning mercy and heavenly happiness.

(*b*) THE YOUNG INFIDEL.—The grace of God was manifested in a delightful manner, in the case of a young man at Carlisle. He was an avowed infidel, and his daring acts of violence and outrage exhibited the state of his mind. He fell sick, and his sickness was unto death: having wasted his substance in riotous living, he was now reduced to poverty and destitution. A pious man visited him twice, administered to his temporal necessities, reasoned with him, recommended him to read the Scriptures, and offered to supply him with a Bible; but he obtained nothing but scornful or evasive answers. One of the collectors of the Carlisle Ladies' Bible Association also visited him, and at length succeeded in persuading him to receive a New Testament, with the Book of Psalms. From that time he searched the Scriptures daily and diligently. Through reading them, he became convinced of sin, of righteousness, and of judgment: his blasphemies were changed for praise: he confessed his sins, and professed love to the Saviour. He declared also, that, in the commencement of his illness, he had resolved on destroying himself, seeing that nothing but poverty and death awaited him; but, holding forth the Scriptures, he added, "This blessed book has shown me that it was a temptation of Satan; that God has given to us eternal life, and this life is in his Son." After continuing in this happy state of mind for three or four months, he died; looking for the mercy of God unto eternal life, through the redemption that is in Christ Jesus.

(*c*) THE MOCK DISCUSSION.—The following facts were related by the Rev. Dr Singer, the secretary of the Hibernian Bible Society, at the anniversary of the British and Foreign Bible Society, in 1830:—

Some time since, in a midland county in Ireland, a discussion took place, arising from the operations of the Reformation Society, between a Roman Catholic and a Protestant clergyman. Many farmers and peasants from the neighborhood attended that discussion; and, being under the influence of infidelity, they did so merely for the purpose of ridiculing and censuring the arguments which were brought forward by the two clergymen. Many of the farmers and peasants who attended were themselves deeply read, or, at least, were well acquainted with the writings of infidels; whose works, strange to tell, have been circulated, in print and manuscript, through the country! They ridiculed the circumstance; it amused them; and they said, "we will have a discussion of our own." "You shall be the Roman Catholic," said one, "and I will be the Protestant; and our friends here shall be judges who displays the most ability and ingenuity." They carried their blasphemous object almost into effect: the time was appointed, and they seriously set about preparing for the contest. It was agreed that they should do what they had never done before—read the Scriptures, in order to prepare for the attack. And the result was, that those who did sc became convinced of the truth and excellence of the Bible.

(*d*) CAUGHT WITH GUILE.—Mr. Robert Aitkin, a bookseller of Philadelphia, was the first person who printed a Bible in that city. While he kept a bookstore, a person called on him, and inquired if he had Paine's "Age of Reason" for sale. He told him he had not; but having entered into conversation with him, and found that he was an infidel, he told him he had a better book than Paine's "Age of Reason," which he usually sold for a dollar, but would lend it to him, if he would promise to read it; and after he had actually read it, if he did not think it worth a dollar, he would take it again. The man consented; and Mr. Aitkin put a Bible into his hands. He smiled when he found what book he had engaged to read; but said he would perform his engagement. He did so; and when he had finished the perusal, he came back, and expressed the deepest gratitude for Mr. Aitkin's recommendation of the book, saying it had made him what he was not before—a happy man; for he had found in it the way of salvation through Christ. Mr. Aitkin rejoiced in the event, and had the satisfaction of knowing that this reader of the Bible, from that day to the end of his life, supported the character of a consistent Christian, and died with a hope full of immortality.

(*e*) HALF DESTROYED BIBLE.—A father, residing not far from Columbia, S. C., was about sending his son to College. But as he knew the influence to which he would be exposed, he was not without a deep and anxious solicitude for the spiritual and eternal welfare of his favorite child. Fearing lest the principles of Christian faith, which he had endeavored to instil into his mind, would be rudely assailed, but trusting in the efficacy of that word which is quick, and powerful, he purchased, unknown to his son, an elegant copy of the Bible, and deposited it at the bottom of his trunk. The young man entered upon his college career. The restraints of a pious education were soon broken off, and he proceeded from speculation to doubts, and from doubts to a denial of the reality of religion. After having become, in his own estimation, wiser than his father, he discovered one day, while rummaging his trunk, with great surprise and indignation, the sacred deposit. He took it out, and while deliberating on the manner in which he should treat it, he determined that he would use it as waste paper, on which to wipe his razor while shaving. Accordingly, every time he went to shave, he tore out a leaf or two of the holy book, and thus used it till nearly half the volume was destroyed. But while he was committing this outrage upon the sacred book, a text now and then met his eye, and was carried like a barbed arrow to his heart. At length, he heard a sermon, which discovered to him his own character, and his exposure to the wrath of God, and riveted upon his mind the impression which he had received from the last torn leaf of the blessed, yet insulted volume. Had worlds been at his disposal, he would freely have given them all, could they have availed, in enabling him to undo what he had done. At length, he found forgiveness at the foot of the cross. The torn leaves of that sacred volume brought healing to his soul; for they led him to repose on the mercy of God, which is sufficient for the chief of sinners.

(*f*) AGE OF REASON AND THE BIBLE.—A gentleman was once asked in company, what led him to embrace the truths of the gospel, which formerly he was known to have neglected and despised! He said, "My call and conversion to God my Savior were produced by very singular means:—A person put into my hands Paine's 'Age of Reason.' I read it with attention, and was much struck with the strong and ridiculous representation he made of many passages in the Bible. I confess, to my shame, I had never read the Bible through; but from what I remembered to have heard at church, and accidentally on other occasions, I could not persuade myself that Paine's report was quite exact, or that the Bible was quite so absurd a book as he represented it. I resolved therefore that I would read the Bible regularly through, and compare the passages when I had done so, that I might give the Bible fair play. I accordingly set myself to the task, and as I advanced, I was struck with the majesty which spoke, the awfulness of the truths contained in it, and the strong evidence of its divine origin, which increased with every page, so that I finished my inquiry with the fullest satisfaction of the truth as it is in Jesus, and my heart was penetrated with a sense of obligation I had never felt before. I resolved henceforth to take the sacred word for my guide, and to be a faithful follower of the Son of God.

(*g*) THE DEATH-BED REQUEST.—A young man once went into the shop of a tradesman at Reading, where the subject of the Bible Society was mentioned, when he expressed, in language rancorous and bitter, his hatred of the institution. His passion was too violent to allow at that time a word of remonstrance to be addressed to him. The fact was mentioned to a little girl, a daughter of the tradesman, who was then on her death-bed. She had felt the power of Divine truth, and recommended that they should subscribe for a Bible, and present it to him. The request was attended to, and the Bible was given him, with an account of the dying child's concern for his welfare. He received it with gratitude, carefully perused it, was deeply impressed with its truths, and read it to his fellow-servants. In a word, he became a zealous and consistent advocate for the Divine book, which he had formerly so much opposed.

(*h*) A BIBLE LEFT IN A BARN.—When the committee of a Bible Association, in the state of New-York, were making exertions to supply every destitute family with a copy of the book of God, a distributor called at a house where he met with an angry repulse. The man of the house was full of "cursing and bitterness;" he would not suffer a Bible to be left at his house. "If left any where," said he, "it shall be left at the barn." "Very well," the distributor meekly replied; "I do not know that I could select a better place for it: our blessed Savior once lay in a manger!" He went quickly to the barn, and deposited the sacred treasure in a safe place, with much prayer that it might bless even him who would not allow it to remain in his house. The man, struck with the unexpected reply of the distributor, was led to think of his own rashness and guilt, and especially of the Savior's birth-place. After two or three days his distress became so great, that he went out to the barn in search of the rejected volume. He turned to the passage which records the circumstances connected with the birth of the Redeemer, and wept, and repented, and consecrated himself to God through faith in Christ. The once spurned book now found a place, not only in his house, but its truths were received into his heart, and controlled his life.

(*i*) IT IS NO TASK.—At an annual meeting of the Cambridge Bible Society, the Rev. Professor Scholefield related the following anecdote of Mr. Hone, the well known author of the *Every Day Book*.—Mr. Hone, in the days of his infidelity, was travelling in Wales on foot, and being rather tired and thirsty, he stopped at the door of a cottage where there was a little girl seated reading, and whom he asked, if she would give him a little water. "O yes, sir," she said, "if you will come in, mother will give you some milk and water;" upon which he went in and partook of that beverage, the little girl again resuming her seat and her book. After a short stay in the cottage, he came out and accosted the child at the door, "Well, my little girl, are you getting your task?" "O no, sir," she replied, "I am reading the Bible." "But," said Mr. Hone, "you are getting your task out of the Bible." —"O no, sir, it is no task to me to read the Bible—it is a pleasure." This circumstance had such an effect upon Mr. Hone, tha he determined to read the Bible too, and he was now (said Professor Scholefield) one of the foremost in upholding and defending the great truths contained in that holy book.

61. Conversion of Papists.

(*a*) A CLUSTER OF BLESSINGS. —In the year 1828, a gentleman in London gave the following interesting account:

A few Sabbaths since, I was invited by a serious woman in humble life to visit her daughter, who was too much afflicted to leave her home. In the afternoon I went, and found the lowly dwelling, situated in a small dirty street, inhabited by the poor. From the aspect of the street, I was prepared to enter an apartment of corresponding appearance. I was, however, greatly surprised, on entering, to witness the very opposite to what I had imagined. All was neat and tidy. The poor daughter, who labored under great nervous debility, accompanied with deafness, was too weak to rise, but received me with the greatest respect. Before reading the Scriptures and prayer, which was my errand, I felt an anxiety to hear the outline of the history of a family in which I had already found so much to interest. The mother, with much simplicity, gave me the following account:

"My father was a Roman Catholic, and I was consequently brought up in its superstitions. My husband is a soldier, and has seen much active service, having served in Egypt and at Waterloo. I accompanied him in his campaigns, and, being kept by almighty power, was always noticed by the officers for my propriety of conduct, which procured favors both for my husband and children. At the termination of the late war, we lodged in Westminster, where, during my confinement, I was visited by a gentleman from the Bible Society of that district, who finding I had no Bible, was desirous that I should by small payments procure one; to which I consented. On obtaining it, I frequently read it; and the general impression on my mind was surprise at the many promises it contained. On regaining my strength, I resolved to attend some Protestant place of worship, and, accordingly, occasionally visited some chapels in the neighborhood, but without receiving any permanent benefit. It then pleased God to remove us to our present situation, where I had not long resided before a lady called, and inquired if I should have any objection to a prayer-meeting being held in my apartment. I consented; and such meetings have been held here from that time until now, and have proved a blessing to others in the street. It was at these meetings it pleased the Father of mercies to awaken in my mind a sense of my danger, as a lost sinner, and the consequent necessity of an interest in Christ, the only Savior. My mind became progressively enlightened, and being able to consult the Scriptures, I trust I have increased in knowledge. My afflicted daughter has also tasted that the Lord is gracious, and one child has died in the fear of the Lord; and it was on the very day that the Lord took her to himself that this one was added to a Christian church. So that, instead of the grief which a mother may be expected to feel at the loss of a beloved child, I was lost in gratitude, that on the same day the Lord should introduce one to the church militant, and the other, more happy, to the church triumphant.

"I pray for my husband, and am not without hope that God will answer my prayers. He accompanies me to public worship, joins in domestic worship, which I am obliged to lead, and, as far as external deportment is concerned, is a changed man."

(*b*) HEARING A CHILD READ.—In an Irish school, in London, the children were allowed to take the New Testament home with them at night, to learn from it their lessons for next day. One of the boys read his Testament to his father and mother, who were Roman Catholics, and they felt much interested in what they heard. The wife was taken dangerously ill, and the husband requested a Protestant clergyman to visit her; whom he informed, that, in consequence of hearing the child read the Scriptures, they had renounced Popery, and regularly attended his ministry. "I have reason to thank God and you," said the man, "for teaching my son in the school. I have been all my life in ignorance, sin, and misery, until I heard that book. Now I am taught to put my trust in Christ alone for salvation." The woman, too, gave evidence in life and death of her dependence on the merits and intercessions of Jesus for eternal life. Her husband and son afterwards returned to Ireland, determined, by the Divine help, to make the Bible the only rule of their faith and practice.

(*c*) OPPOSING PROTESTANTISM.—In the short reign of Edward VI., Peter Martyr, under the Prince's patronage, read Divinity lectures at Oxford, and oppo·ed the doctrines of the real presence and other popish dogmas. The papists were alarmed, and began to look eagerly for some polemic champion to oppose him. After much solicitation they prevailed on Rev. Bernard Gilpin, then resident at Oxford, and a Roman Catholic, to enter the lists with Martyr. This engagement led him to study the subject more deeply: he searched the Scriptures, the writings of the fathers, and conferred with a goodly number of divines then living, and the result was a renunciation of popery as indefensible.

(*d*) FRAGMENT OF A TESTAMENT.—In that part of Ireland from which I come, said the Rev. D. Stewart, at a public meeting in London, in 1830, there lived a boatswain of most immoral character, a breaker of the Sabbath, and a profaner of God's holy name. One Sunday, as he and a friend were rowing in a boat up the Liffey, whither they had resorted from the pot-house, they saw something sticking in the mud; which, on approaching, they discovered to be a fragment of the New Testament. The boatswain was, at first, inclined to leave it; but thought, by its means, of ridiculing the sacred truths of religion; and, for that purpose, took it home, read it often, and pondered over it well; which had, at length, an effect far different from that which he had anticipated. It convinced him that the dogmas of Romanism were incompatible with the free circulation of the word of God. This man was induced to attend the controversy then carrying on between the Catholic and Protestant clergy, which led him to think, read, and study. What was the effect? the immediate abandonment of the errors of Romanism, and his exercise of the right of free judgment. He began to grow fond of reading the New Testament, and now prized it beyond all he was worth in the world besides, as it led him to reflect on his past life with horror. He eventually became a true Christian.

(*e*) REPENTANCE BETTER THAN PENANCE.—Among the speakers at the Anniversary of the British and Foreign Bible Society, in May, 1840, was Professor Pelet of Geneva, who made this impressive statement:—

"Among the soldiers of the French army, in which reigns so much levity and infidelity, we have been very successful. Some of them carry the word of God into their own departments, and it is a means of extending the work beyond all that we can tell. A man in a little village in France, when he was young, wished to be a monk. That was prevented. He retired to a forest, where he ate roots which he found there, to imitate John the Baptist; and he bore that name among his acquaintances. There he remained some time, but found no peace to his soul. He went again to his village, sold the property he had, made nine parts of it, and gave eight parts to the poor. He reduced himself to the condition of a simple workman, but yet he found no peace. The church edifice of the village was too little. It was decided to build a new one; and he himself would go to the quarry, to get blocks for the building. He gave them the little money he had remaining, and yet nothing brought comfort to his soul. He sought the Lord but found him not; *till one of the Colporteurs came to his village, and gave him the New Testament.* He read it, and there he found what he had before sought in vain."

62. Conversion of Soldiers.

(*a*) THE BIBLE IN A PRISON-SHIP.—In a report of the Nismes Bible Society, may be found an affecting anecdote of one of their subscribers, who was formerly attached to Bonaparte's army. An officer of the society, struck with the modest zeal of this man in the support of the cause, asked him if his support of the society did not proceed from his knowledge of the incalculable value of the Bible. "It is so," said he; "and I will inform you how it took place. Under the late emperor I was attached to the army; and being taken prisoner, and carried to England, I was confined in one of the prison ships. There, huddled together with my companions, and deprived of every thing that could tend to lessen the miseries of my situation, I abandoned myself to dark despair, and resolved to make away with myself. Under these circumstances, an English clergyman visited us, and addressed us to the following effect:—'My heart bleeds for your losses and privations, nor is it in my power to remedy them; but I can offer consolation for your immortal souls, and this consolation is contained in the word of God. Read this book, my friends; for I am willing to present every one with a copy of the Bible who is desirous to possess it!' The tone of kindness with which he spoke, and the candor of this pious man, made such an impression upon me, that I burst into tears. I gratefully accepted a Bible, and in it I found abundant consolation amidst all my distresses. From that moment the Bible became precious to my soul; out of it I have gathered motives for resignation, and courage to bear up in adversity; and I feel happy in the idea, that it may prove to others what it has proved to me."

(*b*) ONLY VERSE MEMORIZED.—A youth, who had been instructed in a Sunday school, in the southern part of Kent, though the son of a pious widow, was remarkable for thoughtlessness and vice. The clergyman, by whom the school was commenced, felt the deepest sympathy with his mother, but was at length compelled to exclude her son from the school, who soon became, on account of his wicked conduct, the terror of the whole neighborhood.

After a while he entered the army, and went with his regiment to America. While there, one of the sergeants of the regiment visited England, and calling on the poor woman, she made him the bearer of a Bible to her son, and sent an earnest request that he would read one verse of it every day. He received the book and message with great indifference, saying, "I'll try what I can do;" and opening the Bible, added, "Here goes." But mark the happy result. "How strange!" exclaimed he, unable then, for tears, to add more. His eye had caught the only passage he had ever been prevailed upon to commit to memory at the Sunday school: "Come unto me, all ye that labor and are heavy laden, and I will give you rest," Matt. 11 : 28. Such was the happy effect of this text on his heart, that he who had been notorious for swearing, lying, dishonesty, and other vices, now embraced the invitation of the Lord Jesus, and became adorned with Christian excellences. He soon after died on the field of battle, at New Orleans, with his head on the very passage which first arrested his attention! His Bible, stained with his blood, was brought to England.

(*c*) THE POWER OF DIVINE TRUTH.—At a meeting of the London Religious Tract Society, the Rev. James Hill, formerly of Calcutta, related the following fact respecting Captain Connolly, whose overland tour to India had lately been published.

The captain went out a stranger to God, and to true religion; but his sisters were pious ladies, and one of them happened before he went to put into his baggage a Bible. I think he had never read, never looked into it. It so happened, that on his journey to India he was taken captive by a tribe of the Turcomans, through the treachery of his guide. He was made prisoner for a short time. On one occasion he was loading a camel with his own baggage, which had been taken from him, and out dropped the Bible which his sister had given him. He took it up; he had never read it before, and he sat down on a portion of his own baggage, that he was employed in loading upon the camel, and he read of "the unsearchable riches of Christ." His mind was in a state to receive the truth; and he told me in Calcutta, that the first religious impression made on his heart was on that occasion, as he sat amidst the wilds of the Turcoman country.

(*d*) THE BULLET AND THE TEXT.—Dr. John Evans, the author of some excellent sermons on the Christian temper, introduced, on one occasion, a sermon to young people, in the following manner:—Shall I be allowed to preface this discourse with relating a passage concerning an acquaintance of mine, who has been many years dead, but which I remember to have received, when young, from himself? When he was an apprentice in this city, the civil war began; his inclination led him into the army, where he had a captain's commission. It was fashionable for all the men of that army to carry a Bible along with them; which, therefore, he and many others did, who yet made little use of it, and hardly had any sense of serious religion. At length he was commanded, with his company, to storm a fort, wherein they were, for a short time, exposed to the thickest of the enemy's fire. When he had accomplished his enterprise, and the heat of the action was over, he found that a musket ball had lodged in his Bible, which was in his pocket, upon such a part of his body, that it must necessarily have proved mortal to him, had it not been for this seasonable and well-placed piece of armor. Upon a nearer observation, he found the ball had made its way so far in his Bible, as to rest directly upon that part of the first unbroken leaf, where the words of my text are found. It was Eccles. 11 : 9; "Rejoice, O young man, in thy youth; and let thy heart cheer thee in the days of thy youth, and walk in the ways of thine heart, and in the sight of thine eyes; but know thou, that for all these things God will bring thee into judgment." As the surprising deliverance, you may apprehend, much affected him, so a passage, which his conscience told him was very apposite to his case, and which Providence in so remarkable a way pointed to his observation, made the deepest and best impression on his mind; and, by the grace of God, he from that time attended to religion in earnest, and continued in the practice of it to a good old age; frequently making the remark with pleasure, that his Bible had been the salvation both of his body and his soul.

63. Conversion of the Learned and Eminent.

(*a*) THE GOTTINGEN PROFESSOR.—In the summer of 1824, two gentlemen from London, in the course of a tour through Germany, came to Gottingen, where they visited several professors eminent for their meritorious exertions in the promotion of learning. They were received by all in the most friendly manner, but by one in particular, who afforded them some of the most delightful hours they enjoyed on their tour. With the greatest readiness, and in the most obliging manner, he showed his visitors every thing interesting in his house, at the same time gratifying them by many entertaining relations. Having directed their attention to various objects, he left the room, but soon returned with a Bible under his arm, and, with a countenance as grave as it had before been cheerful, he addressed them in nearly the following words: "You must now allow me to relate an extraordinary occurrence. Some years ago, I was in great danger of losing my sight, which had become so bad that I could scarcely distinguish any thing. The prospect of passing the last days of my life in blindness, made me so melancholy, that I resolved to make a tour to Bremen to recover my spirits. On this tour I came to Hanover, where some friends took me into the duke of Cambridge's library, and showed me some Bibles, lately sent by the Bible Society in London as a present to the Duke. Wishing to try whether, in my blindness, I could distinguish the paper and print of those from the common ones, I took one up merely for that purpose, without the least intention of selecting any particular passage; and now see what I read!" He here opened the Bible, and read Isa. 42: 16, "'And I will bring the blind by a way that they knew not; I will lead them in paths that they have not known: I will make darkness light before them, and crooked things straight. These things will I do unto them and not forsake them.' I read this verse, and received spiritual sight." At these words he was so much affected, that the tears ran down his cheeks. "With a cheerful mind I now journeyed back to Gottingen, and my greatest desire was to possess a Bible, in which this verse stood on the same page and in the same place. Shortly afterwards I was visited by a friend from London, to whom I related the occurrence, and immediately received his promise to send me one as soon as possible, which he did." The Bible he continued to esteem as his greatest earthly treasure.

(*b*) CONVERSION OF A DOCTOR OF DIVINITY.—A doctor of divinity in Silesia, to whom the Rev. Mr. Reichardt, a missionary to the Jews, was introduced, was one of the greatest enemies to the gospel; but while he was endeavoring to write against it, and to settle himself more steadfastly in his own principles, it struck him that he had never read his Bible, though he had preached from texts in it. He began to read it; but had not long been reading the first pages, when it struck him that if this book was indeed the truth, then all the edifice he had built for himself must be broken down. This conviction increased, till it pleased the Lord to impress him with the spirit of that book; and he became a truly pious Christian, and the means of turning many from darkness to light.

(*c*) WILBERFORCE'S CONVERSION.—From a speech delivered by Joseph John Gurney, Esq., at the meeting of the British and Foreign Bible Society, in 1834, we learn that Mr. Wilberforce was in the 24th year of his age when he was elected member of parliament for Hull. He afterwards attended the county election, and such was the charm of his eloquence on that occasion, in the large castle area at York, that the people all cried, "We will have that little man for our member." He was then one of the gayest of the gay: not an openly vicious man, but peculiar for his wit, and his distinction in the fashionable circles. His wit became innocuous under Christian principles. He was said to be the "joy and crown of Doncaster races." He went to pay a visit to a relation at Nice, and was accompanied by the Rev. Isaac Milner, afterwards dean of Carlisle. Mention was made of a certain individual who moved in the same rank, an ecclesiastical gentleman, a man devoted to his duty. Mr. W. said, regarding him, "that he thought he carried things too far;" to which Mr. Milner said, he was inclined to think that Mr. W. would form a different estimate on the subject, were he carefully to peruse the whole of the New Testament. Mr. Wilberforce replied that he would take him at his word, and read it through with pleasure. They were both Greek scholars, and in their journey they perused the New Testament together. That single perusal was so blessed to Mr. Wilberforce, that he was revolutionized; he became a new man; and the witty songster, the joy and crown of Doncaster races, proved the Christian senator, and at length became the able advocate for abolishing the slave trade.

64. Conversion of the Heathen.

(*a*) DECREASE OF LAWSUITS.—Lieutenant-colonel Phipps relates the following pleasing narrative:—I was travelling in a remote district in Bengal, and I came to the house of a gentleman belonging to Portugal. I found him reading the Scriptures in the Bengalee to seventy or eighty people, men, women, and children, of that country, who were all very attentive. This gentleman told me that he had been led to employ some of his leisure moments in this way. "And to-morrow," said he, "as you pass my farm, mention my name; and they will procure you a bed; and you will then see the effects of reading the Scriptures." The next day I called at his estate, where I saw one hundred men, women, and children, who had all become converts to Christianity within three or four years. I inquired how they found themselves: they appeared delighted, and thought it a happy thing for them that Europeans had translated the Scriptures, that they might read in their own tongue the wonderful works of God. I had some intercourse, also, with an official person in that district, and I mention it because some persons tell you that nothing is done by the missionaries. I asked the magistrate what was the conduct of these Christians; and he said, "There is something in them that does excite astonishment: the inhabitants of this district are particularly known as being so litigious and troublesome, that they have scarcely any matter but what they bring into the courts of justice; but during three or four years not one of these people has brought a cause against any one, or any one against them." I mention this to show that Christianity will produce, in all countries, peace and happiness, to those who know the truth as it is in Jesus.

(*b*) CUTTING UP AN IDOL FOR FUEL.—Some years ago, Mr. Ward, a Christian missionary, in going through a village near Calcutta, left at a native shop a Bengalee New Testament, that it might be read by any of the villagers. About a year afterwards, three or four of the most intelligent of the inhabitants came to inquire further respecting the contents of the book left in their village. This ended in six or eight of them making a public profession of Christianity. Among these, one deserves particular notice. An old man, named Juggernath, who had long been a devotee to the idol of that name in Orissa, had made many pilgrimages thither, and had acquired such a name for sanctity, that a rich man, in Orissa, was said to have offered him a pension for life, on condition of his remaining with him. On his becoming acquainted with the New Testament, he first hung his image of Khrishnoo, or Juggernath, which he had hitherto worshipped, on a tree in his garden, and at length cut it up to boil his rice. He remained steadfast in his profession of Christianity till his death. Two others being men of superior natural endowments, employed themselves in publishing the doctrines of Christianity to their countrymen in the most fearless manner; while their conduct was such as to secure them universal esteem.

(*c*) THE HINDOO AND THE BITS OF PAPER.—The late Rev. Dr. Corrie, bishop of Madras, was formerly the chaplain of Allahabad. At that time there was no Hindostanee version of the Scriptures; and it was his custom to translate, on small bits of paper, striking passages of Scripture into that language, and every morning distribute these papers at his door. Twenty years afterwards, he received a communication from a missionary at Allahabad, who informed him that a person in ill health had arrived there, and that he had been to visit him. He had come to see his friends, and die among them, after an absence of more than twenty years. The missionary had visited him there several times, and was so astonished at his knowledge of the Scripture, and his impressions of its great realities, that he put the question, "How is it, my friend, that you are so well informed in the sacred Scriptures? You have told me you have never seen a missionary in your life, nor any one to teach you the way of life and salvation!" And what was his answer? He put his hand behind his pillow, and drew out a bundle of well worn and tattered bits of paper, and said, "From these bits of paper, which a sahib distributed at his door, whom I have never seen since, have I learned all. These papers, which I received twenty years ago, and have read every day, till they are thus tumbled and spoiled, are passages of Scripture in the Hindostanee language; from them I have derived all the information on eternal realities which I now possess. This is the source of my information; thus I have derived my knowledge."

(*d*) THE SUTYA-GOOROOS.—About the year 1820, a number of persons were found in a few villages near Dacca, in India, who had forsaken idolatry, and who constantly refused to render to the Brahmins the customary honors. They were said also to be remarkable for the correctness of their conduct, and particularly for their adherence to truth. They were the followers of no particular leader, but from their professing to be in search of a true Gooroo or teacher, they were termed *Sutya-Gooroos*. It was said that they had derived all their principles from a book which was carefully preserved in one of their villages.

Some native Christians resolved to visit the sect of whom they had heard so many remarkable particulars. The singular book from which their principles were derived, was exhibited to the visitors. It was much worn, and was preserved in a case of metal resembling brass. Whence it came no one could tell. On examination, it was found to be a copy of the first edition of the Bengalee New Testament, printed at Serampore in 1800. This copy of a part of the sacred volume seemed to have thus prepared many inhabitants scattered through ten or twelve villages, to receive religious instruction from missionaries, who afterwards labored among them with success.

65. Miscellaneous Conversions.

(*a*) CONVERSION OF AUGUSTINE.—In the spring of the year 372, a young man in the thirty-first year of his age, in evident distress of mind, entered into his garden near Milan. The sins of his youth—a youth spent in sensuality and impiety—weighed heavily on his soul. Lying under a fig-tree, moaning and pouring out abundant tears, he heard, from a neighboring house, a young voice saying, and repeating in rapid succession, "Tolle, lege, Tolle, lege!" take and read, take and read. Receiving this as a divine admonition, he returned to the place where he left his friend Alypius to procure the roll of St. Paul's epistles, which he had, a short time before, left with him. "I seized the roll," says he, in describing this scene, "I opened it, and read in silence the chapter on which my eyes first alighted." It was the thirteenth of Romans. "Let us walk honestly, as in the day; not in rioting and drunkenness, not in chambering and wantonness, not in strife and envying. But put ye on the Lord Jesus Christ, and make not provision for the flesh, to fulfil the lusts thereof." All was decided by a word. "I did not want to read any more," said he; "nor was there any need; every doubt was banished." The morning star had risen in his heart. In the language of Gaussen:—"Jesus had conquered; and the grand career of Augustine, the holiest of the fathers, then commenced. A passage of God's word had kindled that glorious luminary, which was to enlighten the church for ten centuries; and whose beams gladden her even to this present day. After thirty-one years of revolt, of combats, of falls, of misery; faith, life, eternal peace, came to this erring soul; a new day, an eternal day came upon it."

(*b*) THE BIBLE IN THE WAY.—An individual in the interior of this state, says the Charleston Observer, gives the following account of the manner in which he was first arrested by the power of divine truth:

He had been one of those who had paid no regard to the subject of religion. "God was not in all his thoughts," though his awful name was frequently upon his lips in oaths and blasphemies. One morning as he arose, his eyes fell upon the Bible which lay upon a shelf immediately over his washstand, and it seemed to him a silent reprover of his ways. It had long occupied its present position, without exciting the slightest notice. He took it down, brushed the dust from it, and put it back again. The next morning, the first object that arrested his attention was that very Bible, and it continued there morning after morning to reprove him, till he became so much annoyed by its presence, that he resolved to put it out of the way. Taking it down with this view he opened it, and the first passage upon which his eye lighted, was descriptive of his own character. He continued to read, and was troubled and affected by the accuracy with which it delineated his own heart and life. He closed it, returned it to its former position, and engaged in the occupations of the day with a heavy heart. At length, while he was reading it one morning, supposing himself to be unobserved, he turned around to see whether his wife, who had not yet risen, was awake or asleep, and found her bathed in a flood of tears. She had long been anxious for his salvation, and she was much affected at seeing him morning after morning stealing a glance at the word of life. When he saw he was discovered, he remarked, "It is of no use to conceal it any longer. I am a poor miserable sinner, and I find there is no redemption but in Christ Jesus. Will you pray for me? and will you go to the house of God? for from this time forth I am resolved to prepare for heaven." And from that time forth he did become an altered man—a happy, consistent, humble, and devoted Christian. Thus the Bible, casually placed in the way of a wicked man, proved instrumental, through the Spirit, in bringing him to Christ, and in hiding a multitude of sins.

(*c*) THE SPARED LEAF.—In a certain town in Rhode Island, there lived two young men, who were intimately acquainted. The one was truly pious, and the other, a shopman, paid no regard to divine things. On one occasion the shopman took up a leaf of the Bible, and was about to tear it in pieces, and use it for packing up some small parcel in the shop, when the other said, "Do not tear that: it contains the word of eternal life." The young man, though he did not relish the reproof of his kind and pious friend, folded up the leaf, and put it in his pocket. Shortly after this, he said within himself, "Now I will see what kind of life it is, of which this leaf speaks." On unfolding the leaf, the first words that caught his eye were the last in the book of Daniel: "But go thou thy way till the end be: for thou shalt rest, and stand in thy lot at the end of the days." He began immediately to inquire what his lot would be at the end of the days, and the train of thought thus awakened led to the formation of a religious character. By means so various are the purposes of Divine grace accomplished.

(*d*) THE SIXPENCE.—Some time in the latter part of the last century, says Rev. Mr. Grinnell, a missionary from one of the New England Societies was laboring in the interior of the State of New York, where the settlements were very few and far between. This missionary was much devoted to his work, meek and affable, and possessed of a remarkable faculty for introducing the subject of religion to every individual with whom he came in contact. On a hot summer's day, while his horse was drinking from a small brook through which he rode, there came along a poor-dressed, bare-headed, barefooted boy, about 7 years old, and stood looking at the missionary from the bridge just above him.

"My son," said the missionary, "have you any parents?"

"Yes, sir; they live in that house," pointing to a cabin near by.

"Do your parents pray?" "No, sir."

"Why do they not pray?"

"I do not know, sir."

"Do you pray?" "No, sir."

"Why do you not pray?"

"I do not know how to pray."

"Can you read?"

"Yes, sir; my mother has taught me to read the New Testament."

"If I will give you this sixpence, will you go home and read the third chapter of John, and read the third verse over three times?" The little boy said he would; and the missionary gave him the sixpence and rode on.

Some twenty years had elapsed, and the same missionary, advanced in years, was laboring in a sparsely peopled region, in another part of the same state. While on his way to a little village one day, late in the afternoon, he called at a small house, and inquired the distance. "Six miles," was the reply. He then stated that himself and horse were very weary, and inquired if he could not stay all night. The woman of the house objected on account of their poverty, but the husband said, "Sir, you shall be welcome to such as we have."

The missionary dismounted and went in. The wife began to prepare his supper, while her husband proceeded to take care of the horse. As he came in, the missionary addressed him: "Do you love the Lord Jesus Christ?" "That," said the man, "is a great question." "True," said the missionary, but I cannot eat till you tell me." "Sir," said the man, "about 20 years ago, I lived in the interior of this state, and was then about 7 years old. While playing in the road one day, a gentleman in black, rode into the brook near by me, to water his horse. As I stood on the bridge above looking at him, he began to converse with me about praying, and reading the Bible; and told me he would give me a sixpence if I would read the 3d chapter of John and the third verse, three times—"And Jesus answered and said unto him, Verily I say unto thee, except a man be born again he cannot see the kingdom of God." I gave him my promise, took the money, and felt wealthy indeed. I went home, and read as I had promised. That verse produced an uneasiness in my mind, which followed me for days and years, and finally I was led by its influence, as I trust, to love Jesus as my Saviour! "Glory to God!" said the missionary, rising from his seat; "here is one of my spiritual children; the bread cast on the waters is found after many days!"

They took their supper, and talked and sang and prayed and rejoiced together all night long, neither of them having any disposition to sleep. The missionary found him to be poor in this world's goods, but rich in faith, and an heir of the kingdom. Early in the morning they parted, and the missionary went his way inspired with fresh zeal for the prosecution of his pious labors.

66. Benefit to Christians.

(*a*) NOT THE WORLD FOR MY BIBLE.—A poor woman at Gloucester, who had received a Bible from an association a few months before, being asked by the collectors what value she set upon it, replied, "I would not take for it all this world could offer. For," she continued, "since I received my Bible, I have been called to pass through great trials. In those trials my Bible gave me that comfort which the world and all its riches could not; it gave me a hope, through that Saviour whom it reveals, of eternal life beyond the grave—a hope of heaven. This hope has made my sufferings appear light, to what they would have been, if my hope had been in this life only."

(*b*) DAVID SAUNDERS.—"I have led but a lonely life," said David Saunders, ("the Shepherd of Salisbury plain,") "and often have had but little to eat; but my Bible has been meat, drink, and company to me; and when want and trouble have come upon me, I don't know what I should have done indeed, if I had not had the promises of this book for my stay and support."

(c) SCRIPTURE PRACTICALLY USED.—Mr. John Conway, of Monmouthshire, (Eng.) was remarkably subject to nervous affections, which induced a very painful degree of mental depression. He informed Mrs. Conway, that at one season he was so harassed by this affliction, which doubtless was aggravated by the fiery darts of the wicked one, as to render his existence almost insupportable. Relief was sought, and in some measure derived from the following wise expedient: he furnished himself with a variety of Scriptures, eminently expressive of the love and faithfulness of God, and of his great willingness to receive those that are disposed to accept salvation on gospel terms. To these he referred and fled for refuge whenever he found the enemy coming in like a flood; and in the hands of the Spirit, he found them sufficient to lift up a standard against him.

(d) THE DYING SOLDIER.—In the memorable conflict at Waterloo, a soldier, mortally wounded, was conveyed to the rear by a comrade, and at a distance from the battle was laid down under a tree. The dying man requested to have his knapsack opened, that he might obtain from it his pocket Bible. He then requested his comrade to read to him, if but a small portion of it, before he should breathe his last. He was asked what passage he would have read to him, and he fixed upon John 14: 27: "Peace I leave with you, my peace I give unto you: not as the world giveth, give I unto you. Let not your heart be troubled, neither let it be afraid." "Now," said the dying soldier, "I die happy. I desired to have peace with God, and I possess the peace of God which passeth all understanding."

A little while after one of the officers passed near, and seeing him in such an exhausted state, asked him how he felt. He replied, "I die happy, for I enjoy the peace of God which passeth all understanding;" and then expired.

(e) BIBLE IN A COAL MINE.—In one of the coal mines of England, a youth, about fifteen years of age, was working by the side of his father, who was a pious man, and governed and educated his family according to the word of God. The father was in the habit of carrying with him a small pocket Bible, and the son, who had received one at the Sunday school, imitated his father in this.—Thus he always had the sacred volume with him, and whenever he enjoyed a season of rest from labor, he read it by the light of his lamp. They worked together in a newly opened section of the mine, and the father had just stepped aside a short distance to procure a tool, when the arch above them suddenly fell between him and his son, so that the father supposed his child to be crushed. He ran towards the place, and called to his son, who at length responded from under a dense mass of earth and coal. "My son," cried the father, "are you living?" "Yes, father, but my legs are under a rock." "Where is your lamp, my son?" "It is still burning, father." "What will you do, my dear son?" "I am reading my Bible, my father, and the Lord strengthens me." These were the last words of that child; he was soon suffocated.

(f) THE USE OF THE BIBLE—A little boy had often amused himself by looking over the pictures of a large Bible; and his mother one day said to him, "John, do you know the use of the Bible?" He said, "No, mother." "Then, John, be sure you ask your father," was the advice she gave him. Soon afterwards, John ran up to him, and said, "I should like to know, father, what is the use of the Bible?" His father said, "I will tell you another time, John." The boy appeared disappointed, and walked away.

A few days after, the father took his son to a house where was a woman very ill in bed, and began to talk to her; she said that she had suffered a great deal of pain, but hoped that she was resigned to the will of God. "Do you think," said the father, "that God does right to permit you to feel so much pain?" "O, yes," answered the wo man; "for God is my heavenly Father, who loves me; and I am sure that He, who loves me so much, would not permit me to suffer as I do, if it were not for my good." He then said, "How is it that you find your sufferings do you good?" She replied, "My sufferings are good for my soul; they make me more humble, more patient; they make me feel the value of the Savior more, and to pray more, and I am sure all this is good for me." John had been very attentive to this conversation, and the tears stood in his eyes while the afflicted woman was talking. His father looked at him, and then said to the woman, "My good woman, can you tell me what is the use of the Bible?" John was extremely eager to hear her answer. The woman, with a stronger voice than before, said, "O sir, the Bible has been my comfort in my affliction." "There, John," said his father, "now you know one use of the Bible; it can give us comfort when we most need it."

(*g*) BEST PLACE TO LEARN.—Mr. Cecil, during a severe illness, said to a person who spoke of it, "It is all Christ. I keep death in view. If God does not please to raise me up, he intends me better. I find every thing but religion only vanity.—To recollect a promise of the Bible: *this* is substance! Nothing will do but the Bible. If I read authors, and hear different opinions, I cannot say *this* is truth! I cannot grasp it as substance; but the Bible gives me something to *hold*. I have learned more within these curtains, than from all the books I ever read."

(*h*) DR. ELY AND THE NEGRESS.—A little beyond the smoking ruins o' one hundred tenements which had been destroyed by fire, in the city of New-York, Dr. Ely overtook a woman of color; under one arm she carried five large brands, and under the other a quarto Bible. "Poor woman," said he, "have you been burned out too?" "Yes, massa, but blessed be God, I'm alive." "You are very old to be turned out of house and home." "I'm well stricken in years, but God does it; and in dis world 'tis one's turn to-day, and anudder's to-morrow." "Have you saved nothing but the Bible?" "Noting but one trunk o' things; 'ut dis blessed book is wort more as all de rest. It make me feel better than all de rest. So long as I keep dis, I content."

67. Love for the Bible.

(*a*) ANCIENT CHRISTIANS.—We learn, from Chrysostom, that in the primitive church, women and children had frequently the Gospels, or parts of the New Testament, hung round their neck, and carried them constantly about with them. The rich had splendid copies of the sacred writings on vellum, in their libraries and book-cases; but as the art of printing was not known till many ages after, complete copies of the Scriptures were, of course, exceedingly scarce. Children were particularly encouraged in the efforts which they made to commit to memory the invaluable truths of the divine volume. Though in those times the Bible was to be multiplied by no other means than the pen, and every letter was to be traced out with the finger, so repeatedly were the Scriptures copied that many of the early Christians had them in their possession; and they were so copied into their writings, that a celebrated scholar engaged, that if the New Testament, by any accidental circumstances, should be lost, he would undertake to restore it, with the exception of a few verses of one of the Epistles; and he pledged himself to find these in a short time.

(*b*) FELIX, THE MARTYR.—The most excruciating tortures were frequently inflicted on many of the ancient Christians, who refused to deliver up their copies of the Scriptures to the heathen; but all kinds of suffering, and even death itself, were nobly braved by many Christian worthies, to whom the book of God was more precious than life. Felix, an African, being apprehended as a Christian, was commanded, by the civil magistrate of the city, to deliver up all books and writings belonging to his church, that they might be burned. The martyr replied that *it* was better he himself should be burned. The magistrate, therefore, sent him to the proconsul at Carthage, by whom he was delivered over to the prefect of the Prætorium, who was then in Africa. This supreme officer, offended at his bold and candid confession, commanded him to be loaded with heavier bolts and irons; and after being kept in a close and miserable dungeon nine days, ordered him to be put on board a vessel, saying, he should stand his trial before the emperor. In this voyage he lay for four days under the hatches of the ship, between the horses' feet, without eating or drinking. He was landed at Agragentum, in Sicily; and when brought by the prefect as far as Venosa, in Apulia, his irons were knocked off, and he was again asked whether he had the Scriptures, and would deliver them up. "I have them," said he, "but will not part with them." On making this assertion, he was instantly condemned to be beheaded. "I thank thee, O Lord," exclaimed this faithful and heroic martyr, "that I have lived fifty-six years, have preserved the gospel, and have preached the faith and truth. O my Lord Jesus Christ, the God of heaven and earth, I bow my head to be sacrificed to thee, who livest to all eternity."

(c) NOT A TITTLE TO BE ALTERED.—When Valens, the emperor, sent messengers to seduce Eusebius to heresy by fair words and large promises, he answered: "Alas! sirs, these speeches are fit to catch little children; but we, who are taught and nourished by the Holy Scriptures, are ready to suffer a thousand deaths rather than permit one tittle of the Scriptures to be altered."

(d) KING ALFRED AND HIS PSALTER.—King Alfred the Great encountered many difficulties in obtaining scriptural knowledge, which we have never experienced, and manifested an attachment to the sacred volume not often seen now. In those dark ages, learning was considered rather a reproach than an honor to a prince. In addition to which, his kingdom, for many years, was the seat of incessant war. Notwithstanding all this, Alfred found opportunity not only to read the word of God, but actually to copy out all the Psalms of David: which book he constantly carried in his bosom. That he profited greatly from reading the Scriptures is no matter of surprise, when we learn, that, after the example of David, he earnestly sought divine teaching, and prayed that the Lord would open his eyes, that he might understand his law. He frequently entered the churches secretly in the night for prayer; and there lamented, with sighs, the want of more acquaintance with divine wisdom. Having drunk into the spirit of the Bible, and experienced the rich consolation it affords, in setting before the burdened sinner a free and full salvation in Jesus, he wished it published to all around; he therefore commenced a translation of the Psalms into Anglo-Saxon, though he did not, however, live to finish the work.

(e) MARGARET PIERRONE.—Margaret Pierrone, a martyr of the sixteenth century, resided in Valenciennes. She was accused by a wicked female servant, to the Jesuits, because she had not been for many years at the mass, and had kept in her house a Bible, in reading which was her whole delight. The magistrates being informed of it, caused her to be apprehended.

Being in prison the judges called her before them, and said, "Margaret, are you not willing to return home to your house, and there live with your husband and children?" "Yes," said she, "if it may stand with the good will of God." They added further, that they had so wrought with the Jesuits that in doing a small matter she might be set at liberty. "A scaffold shall be erected in the chief place of the city, upon which you are to present yourself, and there to crave pardon for offending the law. Then, a fire being kindled, you must cast your Bible therein to be consumed, without speaking any word at all." "I pray you, my masters, tell me," said Margaret, "is my Bible a good book or not?" "Yes, we confess it is good," said they. "If you allow it to be good," replied the woman, "why would you have me cast it into the fire?" "Only," said they, "to give the Jesuits content. Imagine it to be but paper that you burn, and then all is well enough. Do so much for saving your life, and we will meddle no more with you. You may obtain another whenever you will."

They spent about two hours in endeavoring to persuade her. "By the help of God," answered Margaret, "I will never consent to do it. I will burn my body before I will burn my Bible."

Unable to weaken her resolution, her enemies committed her a close prisoner, to be fed only with bread and water, and none to be permitted so much as to speak to her, thinking by this hard usage to overcome her: but all was to no purpose. A doctor of divinity was frequently sent to her to turn her from her resolution; but he found it too hard a task for him to effect, and often confessed to those who sent him, that he found in her no cause why they should put her to death.

On January 22, 1593, however, she was condemned to be brought upon a stage, erected in the market-place before the town-house, first to see her books burned, then herself to be strangled at a post, and her body dragged to the dunghill without the city. Coming to the place, she ascended the scaffold, and distinctly pronounced the Lord's prayer. Then, seeing her books burned in her presence, she uttered these words, with an audible voice: "You burn there the word of God, which yourselves have acknowledged to be good and holy." Having again repeated the Lord's prayer, she was immediately strangled.

(*f*) MONEY LOST—BIBLE SAVED.—Fox, the martyrologist, informs us of an English sailor, who, being shipwrecked, lost all his property except his Bible, which he was determined to save, and of which he took more care than of his money. Having clung to the wreck until all others on board perished, he committed himself to the sea, with his Bible tied round his neck with a handkerchief. After floating upon the water for a long time, supported by a piece of the mast, he was happily discovered by the crew of another vessel, sitting upon the broken fragment which preserved him from a watery grave; and when thus almost miraculously delivered from starvation and death, he was reading his Bible!

(*g*) TESTAMENT AND HALTER.—When King Henry VIII. had allowed the Bible to be set forth to be read in the churches, immediately several poor men in the town of Chelmsford, in Essex, where the father of William Malden lived, and where he was born, bought the New Testament, and on Sundays sat reading it in the lower end of the church. Many flocked about them to hear them read; and he, among the rest, being then about fifteen years old, came every Sunday to hear the glad and sweet tidings of the gospel But his father, observing it once, angrily fetched him away, and would have him say the Latin matins with him, which much grieved him. And as he returned, at other times, to hear the Scriptures read, his father would still fetch him away. This put him upon the thought of learning to read, that he might search the New Testament himself; which, when he had by diligence effected, he, and his father's apprentice, bought a New Testament, joining their little stocks together; and, to conceal it, laid it under the bed-straw, and read it at convenient times.

One night, having discarded the act of bowing down to the crucifix, in conversation with his mother, she was enraged, and went and informed his father, who, inflamed with anger at hearing that his son denied that worship was due to the cross, went into his son's room, and pulling him out of bed by the hair, beat him most unmercifully. The lad bore all with patience, considering that it was for Christ's sake, as he said, when he related the anecdote in queen Elizabeth's reign. Enraged at this calmness, the father ran and fetched a halter, which he put round his son's neck, and would have hanged him, but for the interference of his mother. Such scenes, doubtless, occurred in many families.

(*h*) OLD ROBERT'S GIRDLE.—A singular instance of attachment to the word of God was shown by a poor and illiterate, but pious and excellent man, the servant of John Bruen, Esq. of Stapleford, in Cheshire. He was most commonly called Old Robert; and though he could neither write nor read, he became mighty in the Scriptures, by means of a curious invention, by which he assisted his memory. He framed a girdle of leather, long and large, which went twice round him. This he divided into several parts, allotting every book in the Bible, in their order, to one of these divisions; then, for the chapters, he affixed points or thongs of leather to the several divisions, and made knots by fives or tens thereupon, to distinguish the chapters of that book; and by other points he divided the chapters into their particular contents, or verses, as occasion required. This he used instead of pen and ink, in hearing sermons, and made so good a use of it, that, coming home, he was able by it to repeat the sermon, and quote the texts of Scripture, &c. to his own great comfort, and to the benefit of others. This girdle Mr. Bruen kept after Old Robert's death, hung it up in his study, and used pleasantly to call it, "the girdle of verity."

(*i*) MORE STUDIED, MORE PRECIOUS.—Dr. Buchanan, in a conversation he had with a friend, a short time before his death, was describing the minute pains he had been taking with the proofs and revisions of the Syriac Testament, every page of which passed under his eye *five* times before it was finally sent to press. He said, he had expected beforehand that this process would have proved irksome to him, but that every fresh perusal of the sacred page seemed to unveil new beauties. Here he stopped, and said he to his friend, as soon as he recovered himself, "I could not suppress the emotion I felt, as I recollected the delight it pleased God to afford me in the reading of his word."

(*j*) PURBLIND MAN'S DEVICE.—Mr. Harris, a London tradesman, whose sight had decayed, procured the whole New Testament, except the book of Revelation, and also the book of Psalms, to be written with white ink on black paper, in letters an inch long, that he might enjoy the consolations of the gospel of Christ.

(*k*) THE SHORT-HAND COPY.—During the persecution of the nonconformists, in the reign of James II., one of them copied out the whole Bible in short-hand for his own use, fearing the re-establishment of popery, and the suppression of the Holy Scriptures.

(*l*) SIX MONTHS' WORK FOR A TESTAMENT.—A young man in Ireland, originally a Roman Catholic, was bound apprentice to a linen weaver. Having learned to read, and a New Testament happening to lie neglected in his master's house, it became the constant companion of his leisure hours. His apprenticeship being finished, he proposed going to see his brother in Castlebar, in the county of Mayo, and begged of his master the New Testament, as a reward for his services. The master, knowing his attachment to the book, refused to give it to him on any other terms than his further servitude for six months. The young man, judging that a copy might be obtained on easier terms at Castlebar, declined this. But, alas! not a Testament was there for sale, in this the principal town of a populous county in Ireland. (1811.) He could not live without it; and accordingly returned and labored half a year for a New Testament.

(*m*) DR. KENNICOTT AND WIFE.—During the time that Dr. Kennicott was employed in preparing his Polyglot Bible, he was accustomed to hear his wife read to him in their daily airings, those different portions to which his immediate attention was called. When preparing for their ride, the day after this great work was completed, upon her asking him what book she should now take, 'Oh,' exclaimed he, 'let us begin the Bible.'

(*n*) BIBLE PRIZED ABOVE FREEDOM.—The Rev. Mr. Fraser, a liberated colored missionary from Antigua, states the following fact:—

The names of Mr. and Mrs. Thwaites are well known in the island of Antigua, as connected with all efforts of practical education. Mrs. Thwaites gave to a girl, who attended one of their Sunday schools, a Bible. Nancy, for that was her name, took home the Bible to the estate to which she belonged. Nancy was ill; the Bible was her constant companion. Nancy got well, and went in and out; but the Bible was always near to her. At length, the overseer asked her what she had got there. She showed it to him. He looked on with admiration, for it was well bound. "Where did you get this?" She told him. "Will you sell this book?" "No, sir; if you will give me my freedom for it, you shall not have it." Let no one think that Nancy did not know the value of freedom. No; it was not that she despised freedom; but it was a stretch of thought in the mind of a slave to find out the most valuable thing with which to compare the Bible; and the most valuable thing to the heart of that negro, was rejected for the Bible.

(*o*) WELSH PEASANTS AND THEIR BIBLES.—When the arrival of the cart, which carried the first sacred load of the Scriptures, sent by the British and Foreign Bible Society, to Wales, in 1806, was announced, the Welsh peasants went out in crowds to meet it; welcomed it as the Israelites did the ark of old; drew it into the town; and eagerly bore off all the copies as rapidly as they could be dispersed. The young people were to be seen spending the whole night in reading it. Laborers carried it with them to the field, that they might enjoy it during the intervals of labor, and lose no opportunity of becoming acquainted with its blessed truths.

(*p*) THE DYING INDIAN BOY.—The missionary, on visiting him, says, "I found him dying of consumption, and in a state of the most awful poverty and destitution, in a small birch-rind covered hut, with nothing but a few fern-leaves under him, and an old blanket over him. After recovering from my surprise, I said, 'My poor boy, I am very sorry to see you in this state; had you let me know, you should not have been lying here.' He replied, 'It is very little I want now, and these poor people get it for me; but I should like something softer to lie upon, as my bones are very sore.' I then asked him concerning the state of his mind, when he replied, that he was very happy; that Jesus Christ, the Lord of glory, had died to save him, and that he had the most perfect confidence in him. Observing a small Bible under the corner of his blanket, I said, 'Jack, you have a friend there; I am glad to see that; I hope you find something good there.' Weak as he was, he raised himself on his elbow, held it in his attenuated hand, while a smile played on his countenance, and slowly spoke, in precisely the following words: 'That, sir, is my dear friend. You gave it me. For a long time I read it much, and often thought of what it told. Last year I went to see my sister at Lake Winnipeg, (about two hundred miles off,) where I remained about two months. When I was half way back through the lake, I remembered that I had left my Bible behind me. I directly turned round, and was nine days by myself, tossing to and fro, before I could reach the house; but I found my friend, and determined that I would not part with it again, and ever since it has been near my breast, and I thought I should have buried it with me; but I have thought since, I had better give it to you, when I am gone, and it may do some one else good."

(*q*) DESIRE FOR THE BIBLE.—Long before the Bibles arrived at Tahiti, says Rev. Mr. Pritchard, many of the people placed in the hands of the missionaries their money to purchase them, that they might not be disappointed when they came to hand. At length a small packing-case, containing thirty Bibles, arrived with Mr. Nott's boxes and trunks from Sydney, New South Wales. Mr. Nott having been taken ill, after his luggage had been put on board, was obliged to remain in Sydney, but sent on most of his things to Tahiti. It was by some means ascertained by the natives that there was a box of Tahitian Bibles at Papeete, in a store kept by an English merchant. They came repeatedly to me, begging that I would open the box and let them have the Bibles, for they would be doing no good lying there, but, in their hands, they might derive benefit from them. I told them Mr.

Nott had sent a letter, stating that not a single box or trunk must be opened till he arrived.

Perceiving that there was no probability of getting them from me, they devised a plan by which they obtained them. Several of the chiefs and one or two members of the royal family went to the store where the Bibles were, and entered, as though they had come to purchase some of the articles there exposed for sale. A few of them stood round the store-keeper, talking to him, that he might not easily perceive what the others were doing, when, all at once, he heard a tremendous crash, and, to his great surprise, he found they had broken the case, and were scrambling for the Bibles. The man begged that they would not take them, stating that they were in his charge, and that he should be blamed if he allowed them to go. His entreaties were all in vain; they had now got them in their possession. They said to the store-keeper, "Don't you fear, we will at once write down the name of each person who has one, and we are willing to pay any price that may be demanded for them, but we will not give them up." We do not attempt to justify the steps taken to obtain the Bibles, but state the fact to show their earnest desire to possess them.

The Queen's secretary succeeded in getting one, and, passing by the missionary's door, he called in to acquaint him with what had taken place, and to show him his *treasure*. The dinner being on the table, the missionary said to him, "Put down your Bible, and dine with us." He replied, "Not to-day, I have better food here; I want to go and feed upon this spiritual food." In general a native does not need much pressing to induce him to partake; but on this occasion he declined the kind invitation, and hastened home to feed upon "the meat which endureth unto eternal life."

(*r*) PEASANT COPYING THE TESTAMENT.—A peasant, in the county of Cork, (Ireland,) understanding that a gentleman had a copy of the Scriptures in the Irish language, begged to see it. He asked whether he might borrow the New Testament in his own tongue, that he might take a copy from it. The gentleman said he could not obtain another copy, and he was afraid to trust it to take a copy in writing. "Where will you get the paper?" asked the gentleman. "I will buy it." "And the pens and ink?" "I will buy them." "Where will you find a place?" "If your honor will allow me your hall, I will come after I have done my work in the day, and take a copy by portions of time in the evening." The gentleman was so struck with his zeal, that he gave him the use of the hall and a light, in order to take a copy. The man was firm to his purpose, finished the work, and produced a copy of the New Testament in writing by his own hand. A printed copy was given to him in exchange, and the written one was placed in the hands of the president of the British and Foreign Bible Society, as a monument of the desire of the Irish to know the Scriptures.

(*s*) THE SPIRITUAL BEGGAR.—Both his hands and his feet had been eaten off by a disease, which the natives call kokovi. But he was industrious and raised food sufficient to support his family. He walked on his knees; he dug the ground with an instrument, and then scraping out the earth with the stumps of his arms, he contrived to place the plant in the hole, and to fill in the earth. Mr. Williams once fell in with him as he was walking along, and found to his astonishment that the poor cripple possessed a wonderful knowledge of the gospel, and a truly Christian spirit. Having never seen him at any place of worship, Mr. Williams asked, "But where did you obtain your knowledge?" "Why," said he, "as the people return from the services, I take my seat by the way-side, and beg a bit of the word as they pass by; one gives me one piece, another another piece, and I collect them together in my heart, and by thinking on what I thus obtain, and praying to God to make me know, I understand a little about his Word." Begging the truth piece-meal from the natives who heard it—this poor cripple obtained a knowledge of the Gospel, that would out thousands, in the most favored parts of Christendom, to the blush!

(*t*) JANE GRAY'S PREFERENCE.—Lady Jane Gray was once asked by one of her feiends, in a tone of surprise, how she could consent to forego the pleasures of the chase, which her parents were enjoying, and prefer sitting at home reading her Bible. She smilingly replied, "All amusements of that description are but a shadow of the pleasure which I enjoy in reading this book."

(*u*) TAHITIAN BIBLE CLASSES.—The Tahitians, says a missionary in 184–, are exceedingly anxious to understand what they read. Hence they have their Bible classes each morning, Saturdays excepted. These they attend soon after sunrise, before they go to the various avocations of the day. None think it beneath their dignity to attend these Bible classes. At Papeete, may be seen Queen Pomare, her mother, her aunt, various chiefs and common people, sitting round their teacher, reading verse by verse alternately, when they are interrogated on each verse as they read it, and if necessary, suitable explanations are given by the teacher. All expect to be interrogated. Queen Pomare would think it very strange if, on account of her being a sovereign, she were not to be interrogated, but merely read her portion. Her Majesty thinks it as important for her to obtain correct views of divine truth, as it is for any of her subjects. Many of them come to our houses with the Bible in their hands, asking for explanations of various passages which they have been reading at home, but not being able satisfactorily to understand them, they at once apply to those who possess a more correct and extensive knowledge of the word of God.

(*v*) THE WOMAN AND THE SHEPHERD BOY.—The late celebrated Robinson, of Cambridge, once said, "We had in our congregation a poor aged widow, who could neither read the Scriptures nor live without hearing them read, so much instruction and pleasure did she derive from the oracles of God. She lived in a lone place, and the family where she lodged could not read; but there was one more cottage near, and in it a little boy, a shepherd's son, who could read; but he, full of play, was not fond of reading the Bible. Necessity is the mother of invention. The good old widow determined to rise one hour sooner in the morning in order to spin one halfpenny more, to be expended in hiring the shepherd's boy to read to her every evening a chapter, to which he readily agreed. This little advantage made her content in her cottage, and even say, 'The lines are fallen unto me in pleasant places.'"

(*w*) BIBLE READ WITH THE LIPS.—At an anniversary of the French and Foreign Bible Society, held in Paris, the secretary related the following interesting fact:

That interesting person, who now lives in a village not far from my house, writes a Christian friend, had lost in her early age the little sight which the bad conformation of her eyes had left her after birth. Her parents, however, had succeeded, while she was yet a child, to make her discern her letters by the use of very large characters; but for a long time past she had not been able even to distinguish the largest letters on the show-bills. She can hardly now make the distinction between light and darkness. Gifted with intelligence and skill, she rejoiced when she learned that God had put it into the hearts of some pious men to offer his word to the blind; and as soon as I was enabled to procure for her the gospel according to Mark, issued from your presses, she began to study it alone with great earnestness. After a few days she could, to my astonishment, read about a page; but she was greatly discouraged, on account of the slowness of her progress.

Her means are very limited, and she is obliged to work for her living. Alone in a small chamber, which she rents, she attends herself to all the necessaries of her life, and cultivates even a little piece of ground, out of which she contrives to raise some vegetables. All this obliterates her sense of touch, which, therefore, is far less delicate than that of other blind, who are less skillful or in easier circumstances, and hence are not obliged to have recourse to this manual labor. One day the idea crosses the mind of this poor girl, that the sensibility of her fingers would be excited were the skin taken off; and immediately (such is her desire to read, and chiefly to read the word of God, which he has taught her to love,) she takes a penknife and begins to skin off the ends of her fingers. But, alas! sensibility excites pain; her touch is not improved; and soon the sores which succeed to the thick skin which she has tried to scrape off, become, for our poor sister, an insurmountable obstacle to the pursuit of her study.

She tries yet, however, but in vain; she must now give it up. In a moment of despair, she takes up the book, and pressing it against her lips, wetting it with her tears, thus addressed it: "Farewell, farewell, sweet word of my heavenly Father, food of my soul! I must part with thee!" But what is her surprise! her lips, more delicate than her fingers, have discerned the form of the letters! she reflects, she tries, at last she cannot doubt any more; she has certainly read, "*Gospel according to Mark!*" Her soul overflowing with gratitude, pours out her thanks before the throne of her Father in heaven. She lies down to rest. All night she perused the holy book, and every where she discovers, in a few moments, not only the form of the letters, but also the sense of the phrases.

68. "Searching the Scriptures."

(*a*) FRENCH BLACKING VENDER AND HIS BIBLE.—An old man, a seller of blacking, took his stand for many years in a very crowded quarter of Paris. A Bible was presented to him. This poor creature was only permitted by the police to sell his blacking after sunset: in the day he was occupied in preparing it; but after standing in the street till late, to obtain 5d. or 7d. by his blacking, he devoted many hours of every night to studying the sacred volume, and reading it to his wife, by the light of a glimmering lamp, till one or two in the morning. It was astonishing to those who visited him how rapidly he proceeded, not merely to read and comprehend, but even to compare different parts of the word of God together. In a few months, at more than seventy years of age, he had obtained such an harmonious view of the Scriptures, as to be much better acquainted with their historical contents than his Christian instructor. When he discovered the doctrine of justification by faith, he was overwhelmed, and could not believe that any one had discovered it before, or, at least, so clearly as himself.

His wife being ill, she was obliged to go to the hospital, and her husband contrived to carry the Bible in a bundle of clothes, that he might read it to her. The priest soon heard of his having the Bible, and attempted to frighten him from reading it, offering him a comfortable support for life, if he would give it up, and return to confession. He replied, "I should then be a hypocrite; I would rather die from want than become one. Since I read this book, I can no longer give up my conscience to another."

(*b*) GEORGE III. AND HIS BIBLE.—It has been stated, by those who had opportunities of acquiring correct information, that of the few books which the king read, the Bible was constantly on the table in his closet, and the commentary which he selected for his private reading, was Matthew Henry's Exposition. A pious female servant, whose office it was to arrange the library room, has been often heard to say, "I love to follow my master in his reading of the Scriptures, and to observe the passages he turns down. I wish every body made the Bible as much their daily study as my good master does."

(*c*) CLUSTER OF EXAMPLES.—The emperor Theodosius wrote out the whole New Testament with his own hand, and read some part of them every day. Theodosius, the second, dedicated a great part of the night to the study of the Scriptures. George, prince of Transylvania, read over the Bible twenty-seven times. Alphonsus, king of Arragon, read the Scriptures over, together with a large commentary, fourteen times.

Sir Henry Wotten, after his customary public devotions, used to retire to his study, and there spend some hours in reading the Bible. Sir. John Hartop in like manner, amidst his other vocations, made the book of God so much his study, that it lay before him night and day. James Bonnel, Esq., made the Holy Scriptures his constant and daily study, he read them, he meditated upon them, he prayed over them. M. De Renty, a French nobleman, used to read daily three chapters of the Bible, with his head uncovered, and on his bended knees.

Lady Frances Hobart read the Psalms over twelve times a year, the New Testament thrice, and the other parts of the Old Testament, once. Susannah, countess of Suffolk, for the last seven years of her life, read the whole Bible over twice annually.

Dr. Gouge used to read fifteen chapters every day; five in the morning, five after dinner, and five in the evening, before going to bed. Mr. Jeremiah Whittaker usually read all the Epistles in the Greek Testament twice every fortnight.

Joshua Barnes is said to have read a small pocket Bible, which he usually carried about with him, a hundred and twenty times over. Mr. Roger Cotton read the whole Bible through twelve times a year.

The Rev. Wm. Romaine studied nothing but the Bible for the last thirty or forty years of his life.

A poor prisoner, being confined in a dark dungeon, had no light, except for a few moments when his food was brought him; he used to take his Bible and read a chapter, saying, he could find his mouth in the dark, when he could not read.

Henry Willis, farmer, aged 81, devoted almost every hour that could be spared from his labor, during the course of so long a life, to the devout and serious perusal of the Holy Scriptures. He had read with the most minute attention, all the books of the Old and New Testament, eight times over, and had proceeded as far as the book of Job in his ninth reading, when his meditations were terminated by death.

(*d*) EXAMPLE OF PRESIDENT ADAMS. — Among men of education and talents, those who have been known as enemies of the Bible have, for the most part, unhesitatingly acknowledged their ignorance of its contents, or at least that they were not familiar with its pages; while the invariable testimony of all who have candidly studied it, has been in favor of its claims to divine authority, and to the sublimity, purity and wisdom of its precepts. The testimony following will be very generally respected.

The venerable John Quincy Adams a short time before his death stated to a friend, that ever since he was thirty years old, he had been accustomed, among the first things, to read the Bible every morning. With few interruptions, he followed the practice over half a century.

69. Familiarity with the Bible.

(*a*) BLIND ALICK.—There was living in 1832, at Stirling, in Scotland, a blind old beggar, known to all the country round by the name of Blind Alick, who possessed a memory of almost incredible strength. Alick was blind from his childhood. He was the son of poor parents, who could do little for him; though, indeed, at that time, wealth could not have done much for the education of one laboring under his privations. Alick was sent by his parents to a common school, to keep him out of mischief, and in order that he might learn something by hearing the lessons of the other children. The only volume then used in such establishments, as a class or reading book, was the Bible; and it was customary for the scholars, as they read in rotation, to repeat not only the number of each chapter, but the number of each verse as it was read. By constantly hearing these readings, young Alick soon began to retain many of the passages of Scripture, and with them the number of the chapter and verse where they occurred. It is probable, that being incapacitated by his sad privation from any useful employment, he may have remained an unusual length of time at this school; and that his father, as was generally the case with the Scottish peasantry, was a great reader of the Bible at home. A constant attendance at church would also contribute to the result. However this may have been, it was observed with astonishment that when Blind Alick was a man, and obliged, by the death of his parents, to gain a livelihood by begging through the streets of his native town of Stirling, he knew the whole of the Bible, both Old and New Testaments, by heart! Many persons of education have examined Alick, and have invairably been astonished at the extent of his memory. You may repeat any passage in Scripture, and he will tell you the chapter and verse; or you may tell him the chapter and verse of any part of Scripture, and he will repeat to you the passage, word for word. Not long since, a gentleman, to puzzle him, read with a slight verbal alteration, a verse of the Bible. Alick hesitated a moment, and then told where it was to be found, but said it had not been correctly delivered; he then gave it as it stood in the book, correcting the slight error that had been purposely introduced. The gentleman then asked him for the ninetieth verse of the seventh chapter of Numbers. Alick was again puzzled for a moment, but then said hastily, "You are fooling me, sirs! there is no such verse—that chapter has but eighty-nine verses." Several other experiments of the sort were tried upon him with the same success. He has often been questioned the day after any particular sermon or speech; and his examiners have invariably found, that had their patience allowed, Blind Alick would have given them the sermon or speech over again.

(*b*) DAVID SAUNDERS.—In conversation with Dr. Stonehouse, David Saunders, who is well known as the subject of Mrs. Hannah More's beautiful tract, "The Shepherd of Salisbury Plain," gave the following narrative of facts concerning himself:—Blessed be God! through his mercy I learned to read when I was a boy. I believe there is no day, for the last thirty years, that I have not peeped at my Bible. If we can't find time to read a chapter, I defy any man to say he can't find time to read a verse; and a single text, well followed and put in practice every day, would make no bad figure at the year's end; 365 texts, without the loss of a moment's time, would make a pretty stock, a little golden treasury, as one may say, from new year's day to new year's day; and if children were brought up to it, they would come to look for their text as naturally as they do for their breakfast. I can say the greatest part of the Bible by heart.

(*c*) REV. DR. MARRYAT.—This eminent man, when but a youth, felt it his duty to store his excellent memory with the words of Divine revelation. He is said to have committed to memory the books of Job, Psalms, Proverbs, Ecclesiastes, Isaiah, and all the lesser prophets, as also the epistles of the New Testament; and, that he might retain this invaluable treasure, he stated that it was his practice to repeat them from memory, without a book, once a year.

(*d*) HON. SAMUEL HUBBARD.—Hon. Samuel Hubbard, of Boston, says the *American Messenger*, had a remarkable acquaintance with the Bible. He had a large Bible class of young men; and in the conversation and discussions which arose, would quote a verse from memory, and add, "I think you will find it in ——," naming the chapter and verse; and the reference would be found invariably correct. Such a knowledge of the Scriptures could have been obtained only by long and faithful study.

(*e*) MISCELLANEOUS EXAMPLES.—Josephus testifies of his countrymen, that if asked concerning the laws of Moses, they could answer as readily as their names.

Erasmus, speaking of Jerome, says, "Who ever learnt by heart the *whole Scripture*, or imbibed or meditated on it as he did?"

Tertullian, after his conversion, was engaged night and day in reading the Scriptures, and got much of them by heart.

Of one Marcus, a primitive Christian, who was well instructed in the morning of life, it is recorded, that he became so expert in the Scriptures, when he was out a youth, that he could repeat the whole of the Old and New Testaments. Of one or two others it is said, that being men of good memories, they got the Scriptures by heart, only by hearing them continually read by others; they not being able to read a single word.

It is related of Beza, one of the reformers, that when he was old, and could not recollect the names of persons and things he had heard but a few minutes before, he could remember and repeat the epistles of St. Paul, which he had committed to memory when he was young.

The celebrated Witsius was able to recite almost any passage of Scripture, in its proper language, together with its context, and the criticisms of the best commentators.

Bonaventure wrote out the Scriptures twice, and learnt most of them by heart.

Zuinglius wrote out St. Paul's Epistles, and committed them to memory.

Cromwell, Earl of Essex, in his journey to and from Rome, learned all the New Testament by heart.

Bishop Ridley thus attests his own practice, and the happy fruit of it: "The walls and trees of my orchard, could they speak, would bear witness, that there I learned by heart almost all the Epistles; of which study, although in time a greater part of it was lost, yet the sweet savor thereof, I trust I shall carry with me to heaven."

Gregory Lopez, a Spanish monk in Mexico, in the sixteenth century, committed to memory both the Old and New Testaments, in the short space of four years, spending four hours a day in memorizing them.

Viscount Carteret, who was Lord Lieutenant of Ireland in 1724, could repeat, from memory, the whole of the New Testament, from the first chapter of Matthew to the end of Revelation. It was astonishing to hear him quote very long passages from it, with as much accuracy as if he were reading a book.

The Rev. Thomas Threlkeld, of Rochdale, in Lancashire, (Eng.) might have been justly called a living concordance to the Holy Scriptures. If three words only were mentioned, except perhaps those words of mere connexion which occur in hundreds of passages, he could immediately, without hesitation, assign the chapter and verse where they could be found; and, inversely, upon mentioning the chapter and verse, he could repeat the words. This power of retention enabled him with ease to make himself master of many languages. Nine or ten he read with critical skill. It is affirmed by a friend, who lived near him, and who was on intimate terms with him, that he was well acquainted with every language in which he had a Bible or New Testament. His powers of reference and quotation were as great and ready in the Hebrew and Greek as in the English.

70. The Bible Neglected or Rejected.

(*a*) DYING WORDS OF SALMASIUS.—Salmasius, one of the most consummate scholars of his time, saw cause to exclaim bitterly against himself. "Oh!" said he, "I have lost a world of time—time, the most precious thing in the world! Had I but one year more, it should be spent in perusing David's Psalms and Paul's Epistles. Oh, sirs," said he, addressing those about him, "*mind the world less and God more.*"

(*b*) BIBLE SOLD FOR DRINK.—During my residence in India, says a correspondent of "The Tract Magazine," I frequently visited a British soldier who was under sentence of death, for having, when half intoxicated, wantonly shot a black man.

In some of my visits to the jail, a number of the prisoners came and sat down with this man to listen to a word of exhortation. In one instance I spoke to them particularly on the desirableness of studying the Bible. "Have any of you a Bible?" I inquired. They answered, "No." "Have any of you ever possessed a Bible?" A pause ensued. At last the murderer broke silence, and amidst sobs and tears confessed that he once had a Bible. "But, oh!" said he, "I sold it for drink. It was the companion of my youth. I brought it with me from my native land, and I have since sold it for drink. Oh, if I had listened to my Bible, I should not have been here!"

Will not the lamentation of this soldier be the bitter lamentation of multitudes in the bottomless pit, to all eternity?

(*c*) DYING WORDS OF SIR THOMAS SMITH.—This eminent man was secretary of state to Queen Elizabeth. A short time before his death he sent to his friends, the bishops of Winchester and Worcester, entreating them to draw from the word of God the plainest and exactest way of salvation; adding, that it was matter of lamentation, that men knew not to what end they were born into the world, till they were ready to go out of it.

(*d*) DEATH OF A BIBLE BURNER.—As the Rev. Mr. ——, a minister in Manchester, England, (1800,) was going to a Sunday school, he was met by a man, who inquired, with much anxiety, whether he was a minister. On being told that he was, "O, sir," he replied, "will you be so kind as to go and see a poor man who is dying, quite in despair?" The minister said, "I am going to a Sunday school; will it not do if I go and see him to-morrow?" "Oh, no," replied the man, "he will be dead before to-morrow." The minister, therefore, instantly complied with his request. When he entered the room, the wretched man, in the agonies of death, cried out that he was undone for ever—that there was no hope for him. At that moment four of his companions came in. When he saw them, he burst forth into a rage of anger, and uttered such dreadful oaths and curses, accusing them as the authors of all his misery, that they instantly left the room, seemingly in surprise and terror. When they were gone, the minister began to talk to him, and repeated some suitable passages of Scripture. "That book," cried the dying man, "might have done for me now, but I have burnt it!" The good minister, knowing the power of prayer, and that many a sinner had found forgiveness, even at the eleventh hour urged him to pray. Instantly he cried out, in accents most dreadful, "I can't pray, and I won't pray!" He then turned his head on his pillow, and expired!

"Should all the forms that men devise,
Assault my faith with treacherous art,
I'd call them vanity and lies,
And bind the Bible to my heart."

(*e*) TOO LATE TO READ.—A person in Birmingham, who lived in the neglect of the worship of God, and of reading the Bible, was, on a Lord's day, sitting at the fire with his family He said he thought he would read a chapter in the Bible, not having read one for a long time. But, alas! he was disappointed; it was too late; for, in the very act of reaching it from the shelf, he sunk down and immediately expired.

(*f*) "I CANNOT PRAY."—A society of infidels were in the practice of meeting together on Sabbath mornings, to ridicule religion, and to encourage each other in all manner of wickedness. At length they proceeded so far as to meet, by previous agreement, to burn their Bibles! They had lately initiated a young man into their awful mysteries, who had been brought up under great religious advantages, and seemed to promise well; but on that occasion, he proceeded the length of his companions, threw his Bible into the flames, and promised, with them, never to go into a place of religious worship again. He was soon afterwards taken ill. He was visited by a serious man, who found him in the agonies of a distressed mind. He spoke to him of his past ways. The poor creature said, "It all did well enough while in health, and while I could keep off the thoughts of death;" but when the Redeemer was mentioned to him, he hastily exclaimed, "What's the use of talking to me about mercy?" When urged to look to Christ, he said, "I tell you it's of no use now; 'tis too late, 'tis too late. Once I could pray, but now I can't." He frequently repeated, "I cannot pray; I will not pray." He shortly afterwards expired, uttering the most dreadful imprecations against some of his companions in iniquity who came to see him, and now and then saying, "My Bible! Oh, the Bible!"

71. Zeal in Circulating the Bible.

(*a*) BOYLE'S BENEVOLENCE.—The Hon. R. Boyle was the seventh son of Richard, earl of Cork. His learning, piety, and beneficence, justly placed him among the most eminent men of the age in which he lived. So profound was his veneration for the Deity, that he never mentioned the Divine name without a visible pause in his discourse. He founded a lecture at St. Paul's for the defence of the Christian religion against infidels; and was at the expense of the translation and printing of 500 copies of the four Gospels and Acts of the Apostles into the Malayan language. He also nobly rewarded Dr. E. Pocock, for the translation of Grotius, "On the Truth of the Christian Religion," into Arabic; of which he printed an edition in quarto, and caused it to be dispersed in the countries where it could be understood. He gave, during his life, £300 to aid the propagation of the gospel, and for translating, printing, and circulating the Scriptures among the American Indians in their vernacular dialects. He caused a font of type to be cast, and the Irish New Testament to be reprinted at his own expense; and afterwards contributed £700 to print an edition of the whole Bible in the same language, besides £100 towards an edition for the Highlands of Scotland. He also contributed £60 towards an edition of the Turkish New Testament; and liberally aided the printing of the Scriptures in the Welsh language. He died in 1691.

(*b*) THE USEFUL FARMER.—In R—— Co. says a colporteur, in 1844, is a plain farmer, of some property, who, when he embraced Christ, six or seven years since, made a willing surrender of *all* to him. Since that time his life has been a series of efforts at home and abroad for the advancement of Christ's kingdom. Much of his time in winter is spent in destitute neighborhoods in his own and adjoining towns, in labors to bring sinners to Christ. When a Bible Depository was established, he undertook to supply the destitute in his region; and let it be sounded in the ears of sluggish Christians, that this faithful servant of his Master has *purchased at his own expense, and distributed with his own hand, between* 500 *and* 600 *Bibles and Testaments within the last two or three years.* Many precious souls have been led to Christ by his efforts. Being a large farmer, he has many Romanists in his employ, over whom he exerts a strong influence. "Treat them kindly and give them Bibles and good books," is his motto. As he came into church, he brought with him three or four of this class and gave them the best seats. On one occasion a Frenchman, who had been in his service, wished to be hired again, giving as a reason, that then he could read his Bible.

(*c*) WHOLE CITY VISITED BY ONE WOMAN.—An intelligent, industrious, and kind-hearted woman in Russia became a Christian. Her labors were transformed into Christian labors; and were followed up with an ardor and perseverance seldom exceeded. In her visits to the poor, she now carried books and tracts, as well as food and raiment; and when she found persons unable to read, which was frequently the case, she made it a point to read to them, and to explain what they could not understand.

Her prompt assistance was, in a great measure, instrumental to a zealous agent becoming extensively engaged in the circulation of the Holy Scriptures. She gave him two of the first Finnish Bibles that ever passed through his hands; and when there was a great demand for the sacred volume in that language, she actually sold her watch, in order to furnish one hundred Bibles to the poor, at reduced prices. This was a noble effort in the cause of God: it augured well as to future usefulness; and the expectations which were excited by it were more than realized. She took the whole city of St. Petersburgh for her sphere, and perambulated it alone; and succeeded beyond all expectations. In the course of a few months, she sold more than one thousand five hundred Bibles, and Testaments, and Psalters; and in this blessed work she continued perseveringly to engage. Hundreds derived advantage from her visits.

72. Miscellaneous.

(*a*) THE SHIPWRECKED CREW. —A narrative was some time ago published in London, of a voyage to the South Seas, in which the author says:

The most valuable thing we preserved from the wreck was our Bible; and I must here state, that some portion of each day was set apart for reading it; and by nothing, perhaps, could I better exemplify its benefits, even in a temporal point of view, than by stating, that to its influence we were indebted for an almost unparalleled unanimity during the whole time we were on the island. The welfare of the community was the individual endeavor of all; and whatever was recommended by the most experienced, was entirely acquiesced in by the rest. If ever a difference of opinion asose, a majority of voices decided the measure, and individual wishes always gave way to the proposals that obtained the largest suffrages. Peace reigned among us; for the precepts of Him who introduced peace and good will towards men, were daily inculcated and practised. If ever there was a fulfillment of the promise, as contained in Eccles. 11: 1, "Cast thy bread upon the waters, for thou shalt find it after many days," this simple fact must bring it home to every contributor to that valuable institution, the Seamen's Bible Society; for it was fulfilled almost to the very letter. The Bible, when bestowed, was thrown by unheeded, it traversed wide oceans, was scattered with the wreck of our frail bark, and was, in deed and in truth, found upon the waters after many days; and not only was the mere book found, but its value was also discovered, and its blessings, so long neglected, were now made apparent to us. Cast away on an island, in the midst of an immense ocean, without a hope of deliverance, lost to all human sympathy, mourned over as dead by our kindred, in this invaluable book we found the herald of hope, the balm of consolation, the dispenser of peace, the soother of our sorrows, and a pilot to the harbor of eternal happiness.

(*b*) THE HINDOO'S REPROOF.—Lukewarmness, or want of zeal, on the part of Christians, in communicating the precious oracles of God to those who are sitting in darkness, is not overlooked by the heathen. "A nayr, of Travancore," says the Rev. Mr. Thompson, "reproached one of our Zillah judges, on the coast, for not giving to the people our Scriptures. The judge had been reading to him some passages from the Malayalim Gospel; when, on his stopping, the man, full of admiration at its divine sentiments, rather abruptly addressed him: 'What, Sir, are these indeed your shasters? Why, why have you not given them to us? We have not kept back ours from you; why have you not given us yours?'" Well might he say this, if his ear had ever caught the sound of those words, "Freely ye have received, freely give;" or if he had ever heard the command, "Go ye into all the world, and preach the gospel to every creature."

(*c*) THE BIBLE AND CRIME.—When a gentleman presented a Bible to a prisoner under sentence of death, he exclaimed, "Oh, sir, if I had had this book, and studied it, I should never have committed the crime of which I am convicted." So it is said of a native Irishman, when he read for the first time in his life, a New Testament which a gentleman had put into his hands, he said, "If I believe this, it is impossible for me to remain a rebel."

(*d*) AN OBJECTION APTLY ANSWERED.—A lady of suspected chastity, and who was tinctured with infidel principles, conversing with a minister of the Gospel, objected to the Scriptures on account of their obscurity and the great difficulty of understanding them. The minister wisely and smartly replied, "*Why, madam, what can be easier to understand than the seventh commandment*, 'Thou shalt not commit adultery?'"

(*e*) INFIDELITY PREVENTED.—A mother of a family was married to an infidel who made jest of religion in the presence of his own children; yet she succeeded in bringing them all up in the fear of the Lord. She was one day asked how she had preserved them from the influence of a father, whose sentiments were so openly opposed to her own. This was her answer. Because, to the authority of a father I did not oppose the authority of a mother, but of God. From their earliest years, my children have always seen my Bible upon my table. This holy Book has constituted the whole of their religious instruction. I was silent that I might allow it to speak. Did they propose a question? did they commit any fault? did they perform any good action? I opened the Bible, and the Bible answered, reproved, or encouraged them. The constant reading of the Scriptures has alone wrought the prodigy that surprises you.

73. BLASPHEMY

(*a*) THE BLASPHEMER DYING A MANIAC.—Among the active followers of Frances Wright, who were accustomed to meet in Concert Hall, in the city of New-York, was a Mr. B—l, remarkable for his deformity, the muscles of one of his legs being contracted. He was a man of more than ordinary intelligence, and frequently participated in the public debates, which were of frequent occurrence at the hall. This man, in one of his harangues, had the impudence to *defy* the Almighty's power, and dared him in the most blasphemous manner to seal his lips. Suddenly, thereafter, he became confused—his tongue faltered—his language became incoherent, and his hearers becoming disgusted, manifested their displeasure, and finishing his address with great difficulty, he sat down, amidst a shower of hisses. A short time subsequent to this event, he died a raving maniac; and his wife, who was a talented skeptic, renounced Infidelity, and united with the church.

(*b*) CHARGING GOD WITH TYRANNY.—About three weeks ago, says the London Methodist Magazine, D. H., of Bowling-street, Westminster, was deprived of a brother and a child, by sudden death; both being taken into eternity within a short period. Previous to their death, he had been accustomed to attend a place of Divine worship; but was sometimes guilty of drunkenness, and while in that state, would frequently rail against the moral government of God. At the death of his brother and child, satanic frenzy seemed to take possession of him. With the most horrid imprecations, too bad to be repeated, he would blaspheme the eternal *Jehovah*, calling him cruel, unmerciful, &c. In this way he proceeded until last Saturday night, (August 15th, 1823,) when intoxicated with rage against the Most High, while getting his supper, he again began to curse and blaspheme most awfully;—calling the Almighty a vindictive tyrant, &c. While thus employed, he was summoned to give an account of the deeds done in the body! His wife perceiving a sudden cessation of his imprecations, looked round, and saw that he was in the agonies of death. Medical assistance was immediately procured; but the spirit had taken its flight.

(*c*) THE FOUR BLASPHEMERS.—In one of the western states there lived four young men, in their exterior, gentlemanly. Two were lawyers, one was a physician, the other a merchant—all avowed infidels.

On a certain occasion, they assembled with some of their associates, agreeably to a previous notice, and held a *mock-meeting*, where they administered to some of their party the ordinance of baptism; then the Lord's supper. They were exceedingly bitter against Christ and his followers.

A short time afterwards one of the

men was taken suddenly ill, and soon became deranged and raged like a maniac. In this state he continued until death closed his earthly existence. The distorted features of the poor man seemed to fill every beholder with terror and dismay.

Very soon after this, another was taken and died in the same way, exhibiting the same terrific appearance; and then another—all apparently visited with the same calamity, sharing the same fate, which seemed to fill the whole neighborhood with alarm. And it is supposed that the last has also gone to give his account for his contempt of the gospel and the ordinances of Christ; for the last intelligence left him in a condition somewhat similar to those who had just gone before him, apparently on the verge of death.

These facts we have from a man who knew the men, gave us their names, the place of their residence, and was himself at the time a fellow-citizen with them. "Surely there is a God, nor is religion vain."

(*d*) THE BLASPHEMOUS SOLDIERS.—On the 4th of August, 1796, between 11 and 12 o'clock in the forenoon, a violent storm of thunder and lightning arose in the district of Montpelier. In a field, about a mile from the town, a body of 900 French soldiers lay encamped. At a small distance from the camp, five of the soldiers were assisting a husbandman in gathering in the produce of the earth for hire. When the storm came on, the party took refuge under a tree, where the five soldiers began to blaspheme God for interrupting them in their labor; and one of them, in the madness of his presumption, took up his firelock, which he happened to have by him, and pointing it toward the skies, said that he would fire a bullet at him who sent the storm! Seized with horror at this blasphemous declaration, the husbandman made all the haste he could to quit their company; but scarcely had he got to the distance of ten paces from the tree, when a flash of lightning struck four of the soldiers dead, and wounded the fifth in such a manner, that his life was despaired of.

(*e*) A DREADFUL FARCE.—About the year 1793, an awful incident occurred at Salem, in the state of New Jersey. There had been a revival of religion, and the pious part of the community had been disturbed with riots and mobs; but, on making application to the civil magistrate, these tumults had been effectually suppressed. The opposers of religion turned their attention to a new method of entertainment, acting in a farcical way at religious meetings, pretending to speak of their experiences, to exhort, etc., in order to amuse one another in a profane theatrical manner. One night a young actress stood upon one of the benches, pretending to speak of her experience; and, with mock solemnity, cried out, "Glory to God, I have found peace, I am sanctified, I am now fit to die." Scarcely had the unhappy girl uttered these words, before she actually dropped senseless upon the floor, and was taken up a corpse. Struck with this awful visitation, the auditors were instantly seized with inexpressible terror, and every face was covered with consternation and dismay.

(*f*) THE TWISTED NECK.—At a general muster in one of the Western States, a wicked man being addressed on the subject of religion was filled with rage, and uttered the horrid declaration that if Jesus of Nazareth was there, he would wring his neck! Suddenly a violent spasm seized the neck of the blasphemer, twisted it round, rolled his eyes nearly out of their sockets, and left him in this frightful position, a living monument of outraged omnipotence. "This fact," says a writer in the Vt. Chronicle, "was stated at a public meeting in this vicinity lately by a respectable gentleman of the bar from Ohio." The meeting referred to, took place in Lebanon, Ohio, and the lawyer referred to was Mr. Latham. His statements having been called in question, Mr. Latham procured a full corroboration of them from the Rev. Ahab Jinks, of Delaware, Ohio, who resided in the immediate vicinity where the circumstance took place. He narrates all the details of the matter more fully, and cites other authorities in the neighborhood where he lives.

(*g*) THE SAILOR'S DEATH.—Some years ago, says a writer in an American periodical, a seaman who accustomed himself to the most horrid imprecations, being on board at sea, took with him a bucket and ascended the shrouds. Proceeding along the yards, "Now," said he, to his shipmates who stood below, "if Jesus was before me, I would heave this bucket at his head!" No sooner dropped these horrid words from his lips, than he fell with tremendous force upon the deck, and was immediately taken up a lifeless corpse. The surviving crew were so impressed by the event, that they were never heard to utter an oath during the remainder of the voyage. This account I have from an eye-witness. May it serve as a solemn warning against the practice of taking God's holy name in vain.

(*h*) THE BLASPHEMER FROZEN TO DEATH.—It was near the close of one of those storms that deposit a great volume of snow upon the earth, that a middle-aged man, in one of the southern counties of Vermont, seated himself at a large fire in a log-house. He was crossing the Green Mountains from the western to the eastern side; he had stopped at the only dwelling of man in a distance of more than twenty miles, being the width of the parallel ranges of gloomy mountains; he was determined to reach his dwelling on the eastern side that day. In reply to a kind invitation to tarry in the house, and not dare the horrors of the increasing storm, he declared that he would go, and that the Almighty was not able to prevent him.

His words were heard above the howling of the tempest. He travelled from the mountain valley where he had rested, over one ridge, and one more intervened between him and his family. The labor of walking in that deep snow must have been great, as its depth became near the stature of a man; yet he kept on and arrived within a few yards of the last summit, from whence he could have looked down upon his dwelling. He was near a large tree, partly supported by its trunk; his body bent forward, and his ghastly intent features told the stubbornness of his purpose to overpass that little eminence. But the Almighty had prevented him—the currents of his blood were frozen. For more than thirty years that tree stood by the solitary road, scarred to the branches with names, letters, and hieroglyphics of death, to warn the traveller that he trod over a spot of fearful interest.

(*i*) I DISPOSE AS WELL AS PROPOSE.—When Bonaparte was about to invade Russia, a person who had endeavored to dissuade him from his purpose, finding he could not prevail, quoted to him the proverb, "Man proposes, but God disposes;" to which he indignantly replied, "I dispose as well as propose." A Christian lady on hearing the impious boast, remarked, "I set that down as the turning-point of Bonaparte's fortunes. God will not suffer a creature, with impunity, thus to usurp his prerogative." It happened to Bonaparte just as the lady predicted. His invasion of Russia was the commencement of his fall.

(*j*) THE FATAL CROWN.—One of the most singular and remarkable deaths of the violent opposers of Christianity occurred at a meeting of the Deistical Society, instituted by Blind Palmer, in the city of New-York. The society had been in a flourishing condition for some time, and its test of merit now consisted in transcendental blasphemy, and he who could excel in this fearful qualification, was entitled to the presidential chair. On a certain occasion, one of their members, a hoary-headed old sinner, had exceeded the rest, and was conducted to his dear-earned seat of distinction; and as his companions in guilt were on the point of placing on his head the coronal of impiety, he fell lifeless on the floor! The society, astounded at the event, disbanded, and the author of this anecdote, himself a member, and an eye-witness, renounced infidelity and embraced Christianity. The above fact is so well authenticated, that there can be no reasonable doubt of its substantial correctness.

(*k*) THE BLASPHEMOUS SAILOR.—The following fact took place in the spring of 1812, at a public house in Rochester, in the county of Kent, (Eng.)

Two wicked sailors meeting at a tavern one day, began to curse and swear, when the more violent of the two, in a tempest of passion, swore that he would kill the other. The awe-struck landlord, raising his voice, said to the sailor who had made the threat, "What if God of a sudden should strike *you* dead, and sink you into hell with his curse upon you!" The sailor replied with a terrible oath, "The Almighty *cannot* do that—give me the tankard of beer—if God *can* do it, I'll go to hell before I drink it up."

With an awful oath he seized the tankard, but instantly fell down and expired!

All blasphemers are not thus suddenly and singularly cut off; but there is a point in every blasphemer's progress in sin, beyond which the forbearance of God cannot be extended to him longer. And how often does God say to such men, in the midst of their awful contempt and mockery of his power, "Thus far shalt thou go and no farther." We do not suppose that any miracle is wrought in such cases; but God, working in and through natural laws, so often causes sudden and awful deaths in immediate connection with bold and impious blasphemy, that we are justified in regarding such a death as a judgment of God, as sent in consequence of the blasphemy.

We mean to say as much as this, that in such cases the sinner's blasphemy and death are so far related to each other, that if the one had not been committed, the other had not occurred; if he had not blasphemed as he did, he had not died as he did.

(*l*) BLASPHEMER DESTROYED.—A writer, *personally knowing to the event*, states that a party of ladies set out on donkeys from Margate, (Eng.) to visit a place a few miles distant. The owner of the animals accompanied them, to assist in urging them forward. When about half way, the party were obliged to have recourse to a farm-yard for shelter, in consequence of a violent storm of thunder and lightning. They were detained some time, and the owner becoming displeased, resolved to quit the party and return with the animals to Margate. As he left the party, he exclaimed, "Damn all the lightning! It shall never prevent me going home!" The expression hardly escaped from his quivering lips, when he was in a moment struck dead on the spot!

(*m*) THE NEWBURG INFIDELS.—During the prevalence of infidelity that occurred in this country after the reign of terror in France, Newburg, New-York, was remarkable for its Deism. Through the influence of "Blind Palmer," there was formed a Druidical Society, so called, which had a high priest, and met at stated times to uproot and destroy all true religion. They descended sometimes to acts the most impious and blasphemous. Thus, for instance, at one of their meetings in Newburg, they burned the Bible, baptized a cat, partook of the sacrament, and one of the number, approved by the rest, administered it to a dog. Now mark the retributive judgments of God towards these blasphemers, which at once commenced falling upon them. On the evening of that very day, he who had administered this mock sacrament, was attacked with a violent inflammatory disease; his inflamed eyeballs were protruded from their sockets; his tongue was swollen; and he died before morning in great bodily and mental agony. Dr. H., another of the same party, was found dead in his bed the next morning. D. D., a printer, who was present, three days after fell in a fit, and died immediately; and three others were drowned in a few days. In short, within five years from the time the Druidical Society was organized, it is a remarkable fact, that all the original members died in some strange or unnatural manner. There were thirty-six of them; and these were the actors in the horrid farce described above. Two were starved to death; seven drowned; eight shot; five committed suicide; seven died on the gallows; one was frozen to death; and three died "*accidentally*."

Of the foregoing statements there is good proof. They have been certified before justices of peace in New-York; and again and again published to the world.

BOOKS RELIGIOUS—USEFULNESS OF.

74. In Effecting Conversions.

(*a*) MR. VENN AND THE HOTEL WAITER.—A year or two after the publication of his COMPLETE DUTY OF MAN, that excellent minister, the Rev. Henry Venn being once at an inn, having held a religious conversation with a waiter, took down his address, which he was very anxious to give, and sent him, upon his return to London, a copy of THE COMPLETE DUTY OF MAN. Many years after this, a friend travelling to see him, brought him a letter from this very person, who then kept a large inn, in the west of England, having married his former master's daughter. His friend told him, that coming to that inn on a Saturday night, and proposing to stay there till Monday, he had inquired of the servants, whether any of them went on Sunday to a place of worship. To his surprise, he found that they were all required to go, at least one part of the day, and that the master, with his wife and family, never failed to attend public worship, and to have family prayer, at which all the servants, who were not particularly engaged, were required to be present. Surprised by this uncommon appearance of religion, where he little expected to find it, he inquired of the landlord by what means he possessed such a sense of the importance of religion. He was told that it was owing to a work which a gentleman had sent to him several years ago, after speaking to him, in a manner which deeply interested him, of the goodness of God in giving his Son to die for our sins. On desiring to see the book, he found it to be THE COMPLETE DUTY OF MAN. Rejoiced to find that his guest was going to pay a visit to Mr. Venn, the innkeeper immediately wrote a letter, expressing, in the fulness of his heart, the obligations which he owed to Mr. Venn, and the happiness which himself, his wife, and many of his children and domestics enjoyed daily, in consequence of the conversation which Mr. Venn had had with him, and the book which he had sent him: and which he had read again and again, with increasing comfort and advantage.

(*b*) PIKE'S "PERSUASIVES."—An elder of a church in Kentucky, on being asked the reason of his deep interest in the volume circulation, replied, that he was presented with a copy of Pike's "Persuasives to Early Piety" eight years since, by the Rev. Mr. Rice, the reading of which God blessed to his conversion. He then loaned it to a young man, Mr. M——, who told him three months after, on his death-bed, that it had led him to the Savior, who was now by grace supporting him in his dying moments. The book was again loaned to another young man, who was persuaded by it to come to Christ in the morning of life, and publicly profess him—giving so much promise by his piety of eminent usefulness, that an individual proposed giving him a liberal education. The same book was placed in the hands of a *fourth* individual, who was a school teacher. After some weeks, the elder, as was his custom, made some inquiries respecting the contents of the book; when the teacher broke out with the exclamation that he had been at war with the book, but that now he had submitted his heart to the Savior, and desired to connect himself with the people of God.

(*c*) THE BOY AND THE SAINTS' REST.—A gentleman in the South was accustomed for years to carry with him volumes and tracts for distribution. Meeting a little boy one day, he told him he could not let him pass without giving him something, though he had nothing suited to his youth. Handing him the Saints' Rest, he said, "This may do you good when you grow up to be a man." He carried it home and gave it to his mother, saying, "Mr. P—— says it may do me good when I get to be a man." He lived to have a family. On losing a member of his family by death, he went to his mother and asked for the book, and read it, but without being specially interested. Some time after he was more deeply affected by the death of his wife and child. He called for the book again, read it with seriousness, and it was the means of leading him to the Savior.

(*d*) THE WELL SPENT DOLLAR.—At a public tract meeting in the Tabernacle, New-York City, when several of the Society's Agents received their instructions, Rev. Mr. S——, who was about to leave for the West, described a destitute family in the Kentucky mountains in a graphic manner, and appealed for aid to send to that and similar families such books as might instruct them in the way of life, and stated that one dollar would supply eight such families with Baxter's Call. A Methodist girl, who earned her bread by her daily toil, gave one dollar after the meeting, and requested that Rev. Mr. S. would take the books to those poor families.

On reaching Kentucky, Rev. Mr. S. joined a colporteur for a few days' excursion, and took eight copies of the Call, writing a sentence in each stating the circumstances of the gift. One of the first abodes at which they called, was that of an aged widow, who had neglected the means of grace, and was surrounded by an irreligious family. It was with difficulty that they gained admittance, and more difficult to secure attention to the object of their mission. At last it was agreed that Baxter's Call should be left, and one of the sons was to read it to his mother. In a few weeks that widow was found in the house of God, a believing penitent; connected herself with the church; adorned her profession, and a few months after died in peace.

The letter containing these facts, and others of interest relative to the other seven books, was given by one of the secretaries to the girl who had contributed the dollar, and rejoiced her heart more than the expenditure of thousands squandered by the wealthy for their worldly gratification.

(*e*) PIKE'S PERSUASIVES AND NOVEL.—I called one afternoon at the house of Mr. T——, writes Mr. S——, a colporteur, to leave a library until my return from another part of the State; and remarked to Miss T—— as I left the house, that I hoped she would avail herself of the opportunity of perusing the books. I am very much obliged, sir, for your kind offer, said she, and would do so with pleasure if I thought they would prove as interesting as the new novels I have just received, at the same time proffering me a favorite one. I selected *Pike's Persuasives to Early Piety*, and requested her to promise on the honor of a Kentuckian, for my sake and that of her pious mother, to read it faithfully through, and the book should be her own. She replied that to her such kind of reading was so dry and insipid, that she was fearful she could not accomplish the task, and should thus cause me to distrust Kentucky veracity. With a little persuasion from the mother, however, she complied with our request.

You may judge what were my feelings, when, on my return, I heard the young lady had united herself with the church; stating that the book, and the circumstances by which it came into her possession, were the means, in the hands of God, of her conviction and conversion. She often laid it aside and took up a novel to wear off the impression—*but her pledge must be redeemed.* O that cruel promise! She read on—the Spirit of God accompanied the perusal of the book; her convictions deepened; and ere she finished reading the volume she was led to the foot of the cross, and enabled to make the language of the last prayer her own.

(*f*) DODDRIDGE AND THE NOVEL READER.—At a meeting of the United Brethren, at E——, last evening, says a colporteur, a clergyman stated that a teacher in S——, Ohio, received a copy of the *Rise and Progress*, and being aware of the nature of the work, laid it aside till he had finished some novels. Having done this, he took up Doddridge one Sabbath morning, and read with his usual haste some of the first chapters, till he came to the one on self-dedication, when he was arrested, and was enabled, he trusts, truly to devote himself to the Lord. He is now *a Missionary in Asia.*

(g) DODDRIDGE AND SHAKSPEARE.—Mr. P——, a valuable officer in one of the churches in Boston, stated at a meeting of the church to consider the expediency of establishing a *concert of reading*, that he came to that city in 1817, when a lad, and entered a store as clerk, where there were two partners. He had been religiously educated, and had a pious praying mother. In the desk of one of the partners he found a copy of Shakspeare's works, and in that of the other the *Rise and Progress.* He read several of the plays of the former, and had thereby a desire to see them acted. He had often left the store at night, and paced back and forth in front of the Federal-street theatre, listening to the clapping and shouts of the multitude, and longed to enter; but his conscience and the thoughts of his mother's prayers deterred him. On other occasions he would read Doddridge, and would be led by that to the Park-street prayer-meeting.

"Thus, for three months," said he, "my mind was swayed first by the influence of one book, and then of the other, and my soul balanced between heaven and hell, till at last the question was decided. *Doddridge's Rise and Progress was the bar which God threw across my pathway to perdition;* and all that I am and hope to be, I owe to the Divine blessing on that precious book!"

(h) THE GOLIATH OF GERMAN INFIDELITY.—A German, Rev. Mr. N——, writing from the West, to an officer of the American Tract Society, communicates the following interesting facts:—

"You will recollect the Sabbath when you heard me preach to the infidels in —— street, and that soon after I recommended to your Board the republication of Bogue's Essay in German. During my stay in New-York I had an interview with that leader of the German infidels, Dr. F——. My host kindly invited him to dine with me. After dinner I had a conversation with him for nearly two hours, in the course of which I showed him the copy of Bogue you gave me, and remarked:—"This little book contains arguments for the Divine authority of the New Testament, which the most unlearned can comprehend, and which in all probability, with all your learning, you have never read. O what a pity! If you would just read this little volume with a sincere desire to know the truth, all your infidelity would soon come to an end!" He affected to smile and laid the book on the mantelpiece; but after he had left me and shut the door, the good Spirit seems to have followed him and brought him back—he asked me if I would not lend him Bogue's Essay. I told him that I would not only lend it to him, but would ask him to keep it, in remembrance of our conversation.

You can imagine my feelings when a few weeks ago I read Dr. F——'s public recantation of infidelity, in which he mentions among other means by which it pleased the Lord to convince him of his evil way, *the reading of your Bogue!* Surely this is great encouragement—the Goliath of German infidelity on his knees, a weeping penitent. What a powerful besom may your Bogue prove in the hand of the Lord, to sweep from this land the mass of infidelity which is constantly imported from Germany!

(i) BAXTER AND BALLOU.—A man between sixty and seventy years of age, "once lived," as he says, "in a place where the society was good—too good for me. I wanted to get away from it. Accordingly I moved to ——, the worst place I could hear of, where I could practice all manner of wickedness without restraint. While thus revelling in sensuality, *Baxter's Call fell into my hands.* I took it up with one of Ballou's works, (for I was a Universalist,) to compare each with the Bible; saw the fallacy of the latter; was powerfully impressed with the truth as it appeared in the former; and was brought as I humbly trust to the foot of the cross, to accept of the offers of mercy, as they are freely made in the Gospel to the chief of sinners."

(j) THE LAD AND THE SAINTS' REST.—Rev. Mr. Willey, of New Hampshire, at a public meeting in Park-street church, Boston, gave the history of a lad in a retired part of the country, to whom a pious lady, after serious conversation, gave 'the Saints' Rest.' He read it, became deeply interested, and carried it to the barn where he was employed, weeping over its pages, and over his hardness of heart, and praying to be saved from the miseries of the lost. But these impressions died away; and some years after, on the Sabbath, in Boston, he wandered into the very church where the meeting was then assembled, where, under the appeals of the venerable Griffin, all his former solicitude for his undying soul was revived, and he was led immediately to apply to a clergyman of the city for the 'Saints' Rest.' After considerable trouble "the long sought volume (said Mr. W.) was found and read,—portions of it time after time during the week. On the Sabbath this youth was seen in this house a weeping stranger, sometimes in one part of it and sometimes in another. It was in that gallery, referring to the west gallery, as he has since ventured to hope, he poured out his soul unto God, and that light began to dawn upon him which has since been as the rising light of day. This youth was the eldest in a family of ten children, *all of whom, together with both parents, have since been brought to hope in the mercy of God*, and to unite with his people; and of the five sons four are in the Christian ministry.

75. In Promoting Revivals.

(*a*) LIFE OF J. B. TAYLOR.—A young business man, a professor of religion, on leaving Detroit in 1841 for the West, procured a copy of the "Life of J. B. Taylor." In pursuing his business his lot was cast in a very wicked community. At length the attention of this young man was called to the book he had purchased. He read it, and was excited to make higher attainments in religion. He attended prayer and conference meetings, and there gave expression to his thoughts and feelings. He did the same in private as opportunity offered. God blessed his labors. The result of the revival which was thus originated and carried forward, was the conversion of some fifty individuals, who became members of the visible church. That young man became a preacher of the gospel to a Presbyterian church.

(*b*) ALLEINE'S ALARM IN COLLEGE.—*Related by the Rev. Dr. Hill, of Va.*—Said the venerable father, "I have abundant cause for interest in this plan of circulating good and pious books. I lost my sainted mother when I was a youth, but not before the instructions which I received from her beloved lips had made a deep impression upon my mind; an impression which I carried with me into a college, (Hampden Sidney,) where there was not then one pious student. There I often reflected, when surrounded by young men who scoffed at religion, upon the instructions of my mother, and my conscience was frequently sore distressed. I had no Bible, and dreaded getting one, lest it should be found in my possession. At last I could stand it no longer, and therefore requested a particular friend, a youth whose parents lived near, and who often went home, to ask his pious and excellent mother to send me some religious books. She sent me *Alleine's Alarm*, an old black book, which looked as if it might have been handled by successive generations for one hundred years. When I got it, I locked my room and lay on my bed reading it, when a student knocked at my door; and although I gave him no answer, dreading to be found reading such a book, he continued to knock and beat the door, until I had to open it. He came in, and seeing the book lying on the bed, he seized it, and examining its title, he said,—"Why H——, do you read such books?" I hesitated, but God enabled me to be decided, and tell him boldly, but with much emotion, "Yes I do." The young man replied with deep agitation, "Oh H——, *you* may obtain religion, but *I* never can. I came here a professor of religion; but through fear, I dissembled it, and have been carried along with the wicked, until I fear that there is no hope for me." He told me that there were two others, who he believed were somewhat serious. We agreed to take up the subject of religion in earnest, and seek it together. We invited the other two, and held a prayer-meeting in my room on the next Saturday afternoon. And O, what a prayer-meeting! We tried to pray, but such prayer I never heard the 'ike of. We knew not how to pray, but tried to do it. It was the first prayer-meeting that I ever heard of. We tried to sing, but it was in a suppressed manner, for we feared the other students. But they found it out, and gathered around the door, and made such a noise that some of the officers had to disperse them. And so serious was the disturbance, that the President, the late excellent Rev. Dr. John B. Smith, had to investigate the matter at prayers that evening, in the prayers' hall. When he demanded the reason of the riot, a ringleader in wickedness got up and stated, that it was occasioned by three or four of the boys holding *prayer*-meeting, and they were determined to have no such doings there. The good President heard the statement with deep emotion, and looking at the youths charged with the sin of praying, with tears in his eyes, he said, "Oh, is there such a state of things in this college? Then God has come near to us. My dear young friends, you *shall* be protected. You shall hold your next meeting in my parlor, and I will be one of your number!" Sure enough, we had our next meeting in his parlor, and half the college was there; and there began the glorious revival of religion, which pervaded the college and spread into the country around. Many of those students became ministers of the gospel. The youth who had brought me Alleine's Alarm from his mother was my friend the Rev. Mr. C. Still, preaching in this State. And he who interrupted me in reading the work, my venerable and worthy friend, the Rev. Dr. H——, is now president of a college in the west. Truly, said Dr. H——, I have good reason to feel a deep interest in the proposed work. May God grant it success."

(*c*) BAXTER'S CALL FORBIDDEN.—Rev. Mr. B——, of the Seventh Day Baptist Church, stated in a public meeting, that after his conversion he requested the teacher of the school which he attended, to grant him the privilege of *reading by himself*, and in a book of his own selection. He chose Baxter's Call; but before he had read it half through, there was so much excitement in the school, in the district, and in the mind of the teacher, that he was forbidden to read from it. Though Baxter was silenced, truth was still upon the heart; and in a few days the teacher and nearly every scholar was converted, besides many in the district.

(*d*) THE JUDGE AND THE LAWYERS.—Judge ——, of Tennessee, who was hopefully converted by a blessing on the perusal of Nelson's Cause and Cure of Infidelity, loaned it to two skeptical lawyers, who were also hopefully converted. They were men of influence, and established meetings at two different points, in connexion with which some two hundred individuals were hopefully converted and gathered into the church. That copy of Nelson was sold them by a colporteur. A member of Congress was among the converts.

(*e*) RESULTS OF READING DODDRIDGE.—In 1807 a clergyman left the city of Hartford for the far West—as far as Whitestown, New-York. He took with him some copies of the "Rise and Progress," and as he stopped at a cabin tavern, he noticed that the woman, who waited on him at the table, was busily engaged in reading. He inquired what book she had, and learned it was the "Rise and Progress," which a neighbor had lent to her, and she was copying out passages that peculiarly fitted her mind. He gave her a copy of the book, which she received with great delight. In 1838, he was passing that way, and, inquiring for this woman by name, he was pointed to an elegant house as her residence. He called on her, and asked her if she remembered him? She did not. "But do you not remember the man who gave you 'Doddridge's Rise and Progress' thirty years ago?" "Oh, yes," said she, "are you the man? Why that book was the means of converting my soul; and it was lent round, and others read it, and we had meetings to read it together; it was read at huskings and bees, and on the Sabbath day, and a revival followed; and by and by we sent for a minister, and formed a church." The church at Wyoming is the fruit of that seed, and that book still lives, and who knows but it may be the means of forming other churches, or raising up other writers like Doddridge, to bless the world?

(*f*) CONVERSION OF A UNIVERSALIST.—In a town in New Jersey where Universalism had a strong hold, the volumes were circulated by two colporteurs from the Princeton Seminary. A Christian friend having purchased Nelson on Infidelity, loaned it to a leading Universalist. He read it eagerly; his attention was arrested; he was soon found in the company of Christians, seeking an interest in their prayers, and became a praying man. His conversion was the beginning of a revival. Others who had embraced the same error followed his example. The influence of the visits and volumes of the colporteurs was manifest in an increased spirit of inquiry and attendance upon public worship; and during the outpouring of the Holy Spirit, nearly seventy were added to the church under the pastoral care of our informant in that place.

76. CARD-PLAYING.

(*a*) MR. SCOTT REFORMED.—The Rev. Thomas Scott, in the early part of his life, was exceedingly fond of cards, but was induced to leave off the practice in the following manner:

One of his parishioners said to him, "I have something which I wish to say to you; but I am afraid you may be offended." "I answered," says Mr. Scott, "that I could not promise, but I hoped I should not." She then said, "You know A— B—; he has lately appeared attentive to religion, and has spoken to me concerning the sacrament; but last night he, with C— D—, and others, met to keep Christmas; and they played at cards, drank too much, and in the end quarreled, and raised a sort of riot. And when I remonstrated with him on his conduct, as inconsistent with his professed attention to religion, his answer was, '*There is no harm in cards—Mr. Scott plays at cards.*' This smote me to the heart. I saw that if I played at cards, however soberly and quietly, the people would be encouraged by my example to go farther; and if St. Paul would eat no flesh while the world stood, rather than cause his weak brother to offend, it would be inexcusable in me to throw such a stumbling-block in the way of my parishioners, in a matter certainly neither useful nor expedient. So far from being offended at the hint thus given me, I felt very thankful to my faithful monitor, and promised her that she should never have occasion to repeat the admonition. That very evening I related the whole matter to the company, and declared my fixed resolution never to play at cards again. I expected I should be harassed with solicitations, but I was never asked to play afterwards.

(*b*) A BLESSING AT A CARD-TABLE.—The Rev. W. Romaine was one evening invited to a friend's house to tea, and after the tea-things were removed, the lady of the house asked him to play at cards, to which he made no objection. The cards were produced, and when all were ready to commence play, the venerable minister said, "Let us ask the blessing of God." "Ask the blessing of God!" said the lady, in great surprise; "I never heard of such a thing to a game at cards." Mr. Romaine then inquired, "Ought we to engage in any thing on which we cannot ask his blessing?" This gentle reproof put an end to the card-playing.

(*c*) ROMAINE'S ADMONITION.—This good man was once addressed by a lady, who expressed the great pleasure she had enjoyed under his preaching, and added, that she could comply with his requirements, with the exception of one thing. "And what is that, madam?" asked Mr. R. "Cards, sir." "You think you could not be happy without them?" "No, sir, I know I could not." "Then, madam, they are your God, and they must save you." This pointed admonition led to serious reflection, and finally to the abandonment of such unworthy pleasures.

(*d*) CARD-TABLE CONVERSATION.—Mr. Locke having been introduced by Lord Shaftesbury to the Duke of Buckingham and Lord Halifax, these three noblemen, instead of conversing with the philosopher, as might naturally have been expected, on literary subjects, sat down to cards. Mr. Locke, after looking on for some time, pulled out his pocket-book, and began to write with great attention. One of the company observing this, took the liberty of asking him what he was writing. "My lord," said Locke, "I am endeavoring, as far as possible, to profit by my present situation; for, having waited with impatience for the honor of being in company with the greatest men of the age, I thought I could do nothing better than write down your conversation; and, indeed, I have set down the substance of what you have said, this last hour or two." This well-timed ridicule had its desired effect; and these noblemen, fully sensible of its force, immediately quitted their play, and entered into conversation more rational, and better suited to the dignity of their characters.

(*e*) A SHREWD REPLY.—Sir Walter Scott says that the alleged origin of the invention of cards produced one of the shrewdest replies he had ever heard given in evidence. It was made by the late Dr. Gregory, at Edinburgh, to a counsel of great eminence at the Scottish bar. The doctor's testimony went to prove the insanity of the party whose mental capacity was the point at issue. On a cross-interrogation, he admitted that the person in question played admirably at whist. "And do you seriously say, doctor," said the learned counsel, "that a person having a superior capacity for a game so difficult, and which requires, in a pre-eminent degree, memory, judgment, and combination, can be at the same time deranged in his understanding?" "I am no card-player," said the doctor, with great address, "but I have read in history that cards were invented for the amusement of an insane king." The consequences of this reply were decisive.

77. CASTE.

(*a*) HINDOO VIEWS OF CASTE.—A Brahmin in Calcutta asked a European gentleman, "What is your order of society in Great Britain, are you divided into castes, or do you eat and drink together, according to circumstances?" The European replied, "We deem it our honor to demean ourselves as brethren in the participation of food at one table, as Providence permits." The Brahmin replied, "That appears to me to be an offence against good morals and good conduct." The gentleman rejoined, "I think I can prove it to you, by a practice of your own, that you are in error. How do you act in the field of Juggernaut? Do you not eat there with the lowest caste of India? There you know no distinction of caste, but all feed at one board." The Brahmin answered, "I can screen myself from the imputation you bring against us, for *there* we are in the presence of our god, there Juggernaut is in our midst, and there we can feast together." "Ah!" said the gentleman, "and I can justify the Christian practice on your own principles, for *we are every where in the presence of our God.*"

78. CENSURE—CENSORIOUSNESS.

(*a*) WESLEY'S GROUNDLESS SUSPICIONS.—Beware, says Mr. Wesley, of forming a hasty judgment concerning the fortune of others. There may be secrets in the situation of a person, which few but God are acquainted with. Some years since I told a gentleman, "Sir, I am afraid you are covetous." He asked me, "What is the reason of your fears?" I answered, "A year ago, when I made a collection for the expense of repairing the Foundry, you subscribed five guineas. At the subscription made this year you subscribed only half a guinea." He made no reply, but after a time asked, "Pray, sir, answer me a question: Why do you live upon potatoes?" (I did so between three and four years.) I replied, "It has much conduced to my health." He answered, "I believe it has. But did you not do it likewise to save money?" I said I did, "for what I save from my own meat, will feed another, that else would have none." "But, sir," said he, "if this be your motive you may save more. I know a man that goes to market at the beginning of every week; there he buys a pennyworth of parsnips, which he boils in a large quantity of water. The parsnips serve him for food, and the water for drink, during the ensuing week, so that his meat and drink together cost him only a penny a week. This he constantly did, though he had two hundred pounds a year, to pay the debts he had contracted before he knew God!" *And this is he whom I set down to be a covetous man!*

CHILDREN.

79. Moral and Religious Influence of Children.

(*a*) THE SWEARER'S DAUGHTER.—The Rev. Mr. Solomon Carpenter held a religious meeting in Sussex county, Mass., at the house of a man who was awfully addicted to swearing, and the minister took occasion to reprove this and other vices. A little girl belonging to the family withdrew, and placed herself behind the door, and began to weep very bitterly. Her father particularly asked her the cause of this, and she told him she was afraid he would go to hell on account of his swearing. He at length promised her that if she would refrain from weeping he would never swear any more. The child was now quiet, and in an ecstasy of joy afterwards told her mother of the promise she had obtained from her father. The unexpected reproof the father had thus received from his daughter was lastingly impressed on his mind; he became a humble penitent, and lived to be a shining light in the Christian community with which he was afterwards connected.

(*b*) FAMILY ALTAR RESTORED.—A man once received from his own child, an infant of three years old, one of the most severe reproofs he ever met with. Family prayer had been, by some means, neglected one morning, and the child was, as it were, out of its element. At length, he came to his father as he sat, and just as the family were going to dinner, the little reprover, leaning on his father's knee, said, with a sigh, "Pa, you were used to go to prayer with us, but you did not to-day." "No, my dear," said the parent, "I did not." "But, pa, you ought; why did you not?" The father had not a word to reply, and the child's rebuke was as appropriate and natural, as if it had been administered by the most able minister in the land; and, it may be said, was as permanently useful.

(*c*) THE DAUGHTER'S LETTER.—Not long ago, writes a gentleman in 1833, as I took some coffee at a house of refreshment, a gentleman who was reading the newspaper, entered into conversation with me. Among other things, we spoke of the Christian Sabbath, when he thus expressed himself:—"Though there is doubtless much ungodliness in England, yet when compared with the Sabbaths on the continent, a Sabbath here is a delightful season. No one can truly value that blessed day until he has been deprived of its enjoyment. When in the army, I felt this deprivation; we had misery in every shape, for, in the Peninsular war, toil, danger, disease, and death, were continually around and among us. The nearer the men appeared to be to eternity, the farther off their thoughts seemed to be from God.

"It was on the Sabbath day that I received a letter from an affectionate daughter, then in England; it alluded to the uncertainty of life, especially to a military man. It pressed on me the consideration of eternal things, and pointed me to Him who, in peace and in war, in health and in sickness, in life and in death, is able to save them to the uttermost that come unto God by him. Every word made a lodgment in my heart. Folding up the letter, and putting a book of prayer in my pocket, I walked out to a distance from the camp, until I came to a solitary ditch; in that ditch, on my knees, I poured out my soul before God, and there, in peace, I spent my Sabbath day."

(*d*) THE CHILD AND HIS CLOSET.—When the late Rev. Thomas Reader, of Taunton, was but a child of eight years old, he felt the importance of religion, and could not be happy without private prayer. One evening, his father's house being full of company, he had not a convenient place for his secret devotions; but unwilling to omit what he knew to be his duty, he went into his father's wool-loft to enjoy the pleasure of communion with God. At first he felt some childish fears, on account of his lonely situation; but afterwards his mind was so filled with God, and the joys of religion, that he forgot the gloominess of the place. During his childhood, a person being on a visit at his father's, Thomas was appointed to sleep with him. After the gentleman had retired to his chamber, the pious little boy knocked at the door, requesting him to let him go through his room to an inner closet, which he used to frequent for the exercise of prayer. The conscience of the visitor severely smote him: "What," thought he, "is this little child so anxious to obtain a place for devout retirement, while I have never prayed in my life?" It led him to serious reflections, which, through the Divine blessing, were the happy means of his conversion; and he afterwards became a true Christian, and a useful minister of the gospel.

(*e*) THE NEGLECTED ALTAR.—A person, who afterwards became a Sunday school teacher near Cambridge, (Eng.) having had his conviction of the necessity and importance of religious duties shaken, began to think lightly of them, and to omit family prayer, which he had been accustomed to perform. A child of his, who had been taught at a Sabbath school, one day said to his parent, with great simplicity, "Father, do you pray in the morning, and let me pray with you." The father was struck with this gentle reproof from his own child, and confessed that he could no longer live in the neglect of family prayer.

(*f*) THE POOR CRIPPLE.—I have seen, says the Rev. J. East, in one of the infant schools at Bath, a helpless cripple filling the post of monitor, while propped up on a high chair for the purpose; and I understood that this poor little boy, who was under the influence of religious principle, had been the means of bringing salvation home to his house, in the conversion of his father and mother, from an ungodly and profligate life, to one of moral correctness and true piety.

(*g*) THE DYING ORPHAN AND HER GRANDMOTHER.—Rosina, an orphan child, at a Moravian missionary station, in North America, being under the care of an old relation, said, the night before her decease, "Dear grandmother, I am baptized and cleansed in our Savior's blood, and shall now soon go to him; but I beg you to seek to be likewise washed, and saved from your sins, by the blood of Christ, that you may become as happy as I am; otherwise, when you go hence, you will not be with the Lord." This exhortation from a dying child made such an impression upon the old woman's heart, that she became anxiously concerned about her salvation, prayed for the remission of her sins in the blood of Jesus, begged for baptism, and was added to the church.

(*h*) THE SAILOR REPROVED.—A very profane and profligate sailor, who belonged to a vessel lying in the port of New-York, went out one day from his ship into the streets, bent on folly and wickedness. He met a pious little girl, whose feelings he tried to wound by using vile and sinful language. The little girl looked at him earnestly in the face, warned him of his danger, and, with a solemn tone, told him to remember that he must meet her shortly at the bar of God. This unexpected reproof greatly affected him. To use his own language, "it was like a broadside, raking him fore and aft, and sweeping by the board every sail and spar prepared for a wicked cruise." Abashed and confounded, he returned to his ship. He could not banish from his mind the reproof of this little girl. Her look was present to his mind; her solemn declaration, "You must meet me at the bar of God," deeply affected his heart. The more he reflected upon it, the more uncomfortable he felt. In a few days his hard heart was subdued, and he submitted to the Savior. He became a consistent follower of the Lamb.

(*i*) THE CHILD AND HER PAPIST FATHER.—Says a correspondent of the Advocate of Moral Reform: I was in the city of P., seated in the study of the brother with whom I had been laboring, when a little German girl, of twelve or fourteen years of age entered the room, and bursting into tears exclaimed, in an animated tone, "Oh, Mr. ——, I am sure the Lord is going to convert my father. I do believe he will be converted now," she added, with so much emotion, as drew from me the inquiry, "Of whom is she speaking?" "Tell the gentleman yourself, my child," said my friend, "what God has done for you, and what he has been trying to do for him."

From the simple story of the girl, I gathered the following. A year and a half before, in her ignorance and sin she had been led to enter the church where my friend was preaching, and while there, the Lord graciously met her, and converted her soul. Full of joy and wonder, she ran home to tell her father, who was a bigoted Catholic, what a Savior she had found; but to her surprise, he became very angry, beat her cruelly, and forbade the mention of the subject again in his house. She continued to attend church, and expressed a wish to join with the people of God in commemorating the dying love of her Savior. He told her if she did, he would beat her to death. With this prospect, she determined to do her duty, putting her trust in Him who hath said, "I will never leave nor forsake thee." When she returned home and told her father what she had done, he beat her most unmercifully, and drove her from the house, telling her never to return, until she had given up her new-fangled religion. Thus forsaken of her father, the Lord took her up; she was provided with a place in a pious family, at service, reserving to herself the first Monday in every month, which day she spent in distributing tracts to all the German families of her acquaintance, and whenever permitted she prayed with them before she left, always taking her father's house in her way, though sure of being beaten, and driven from it. Month after month. she offered the hardened man a tract, at the same time entreating him to think of his poor soul, and offering to pray with him. Although uniformly driven away, with severe blows, she said, "I did not care for the blows, for, sir, my poor father's soul was all I thought of or cared for." In this course she persevered,—how long do you think, indolent Christian? not one month, which many think too long to wait for an answer to prayer; but *eighteen months*, without seeing any fruit of her labor. Two months before I met her, she found, on visiting her father, that he was in tears over his work; he suffered her to read, converse and pray without interruption, and at parting, bade her come again. The next month he was even more tender, and on the day I first saw her, she had seen him again, and she said, "*Oh, how changed was my poor father!* with tears he begged me to forgive him, and pray for him. I told him I had laid nothing up against him, and asked him to pray for himself. He knelt down by my side, but could only say, 'O Lord, forgive, forgive, O Lord, forgive;' and now, sir, I am sure the Lord will hear and convert my poor father."

The next evening, on entering the praying circle, I recognized the voice of the little German girl in the individual who was addressing the throne of grace. Her father was there, inquiring with trembling eagerness the way to the Savior's feet. The father and daughter left the room together that night, rejoicing in the grace which had washed away their stains.

(*j*) LITTLE BOY'S ENTREATY.—While the Rev. Mr. Chambers was once addressing a temperance meeting in Philadelphia, a man who had been occupying a seat in a distant part of the room, arose with a little boy in his arms, scarce six years old, and came forward to the speaker's stand; all gave way for him. He placed his child on the stand, and while the tears were running fast down his cheeks, and with trembling accents, addressed the speaker: "My little boy said to me, 'Father, do not drink any more!' Gentlemen, I have taken my last drink." The effect produced upon the audience beggars all description. The speaker and the whole audience were bathed in tears; and such was the good effects of this example, that *seventeen* others came forward and signed the PLEDGE! Mr Chambers, with tears streaming down his face, caught the boy in his arms, exclaiming, "Well may we say that the grave of Alcohol has been dug by this little boy!"

(*k*) INFANT'S PRAYER ANSWERED.—A drunkard who had run through his property, says Dr. Schnebly, returned one night to his unfurnished home. He entered its empty hall; anguish was gnawing at his heart-strings, and language is inadequate to express his agony as he entered his wife's apartment, and there beheld the victims of his appetite, his lovely wife and darling child. Morose and sullen, he seated himself without a word; he could not speak, he could not look upon them. The mother said to the little angel by her side, "Come, my child, it is time to go to bed;" and that little babe, as was her wont, knelt by her mother's lap, and gazing wistfully into the face of her suffering parent, like a piece of chiseled statuary, repeated her nightly orison; and when she had finished, the child, (but four years of age,) said to her mother, "Dear ma, may I not offer up one more prayer?" "Yes, yes, my sweet pet, pray;" and she lifted up her tiny hands, closed her eyes, and prayed, "O God! spare, oh, spare my dear papa!" That prayer was wafted with electric rapidity to the throne of God. It was heard on high—'twas heard on earth. The responsive "Amen" burst from that father's lips, and his heart of stone became a heart of flesh. Wife and child were both clasped to his bosom, and in penitence he said, "*My child, you have saved your father from the grave of a drunkard. I'll sign the pledge!*"

(*l*) THE CHILD'S REPROOF OF AN IRRELIGIOUS FATHER.—The father of a little boy in Philadelphia, an irreligious man, offered to attend him to the Sabbath school, it being a very rainy day.—"Father, why don't you stay at the school, and go to meeting with me? you ought to go to meeting." The reproof was too powerful to be resisted. His soul was filled with remorse. He left his child at the school-house door, and turned back.

But the arrow of conviction had pierced his soul! He turned back, conscience-smitten, to weep over his sins, with a heart full of sorrow. He returned home immediately, retired to his chamber, bowed his knees in prayer, opened and read his Bible; in doing which he found relief, for the Spirit of the Lord had accompanied the words of the child, and the result was, that from this Sabbath day he determined to consecrate himself to God—to forsake the company of his guilty associates—to abandon the drunkard's bowl, and to lead a new life. He was enabled by divine grace to fulfil his resolution; from that day he established family prayer; became the subject of renewing grace, was baptized, and united with the church, of which he proved a worthy member.

80. Happy Deaths of Pious Children.

(*a*) THE STRONGEST LOVE.—A little girl between six and seven years of age, when on her death-bed, seeing her elder sister with a Bible in her hand, requested her to read respecting Christ's blessing little children. The passage having been read, and the book closed, the child said, "How kind! I shall soon go to Jesus; he will soon take *me* up in his arms, bless me too; no disciple shall keep me away." Her sister kissed her, and said, "Do you love me?" "Yes, my dear," she replied, "but do not be angry, I love Jesus better."

(*b*) DEATH OF DINAH DOWDNEY.—Miss Dinah Dowdney, of Portsea, who died at nine years of age, one day in her illness said to her aunt, with whom she lived, "When I am dead, I should like Mr. Griffin to preach a sermon to children to persuade them to love Jesus Christ, to obey their parents, not to tell lies, but to think of dying and going to heaven. I have been thinking," said she, "what text I should like him to preach from; 2 Kings 4: 26. You are the Shunamite, Mr. G. is the prophet, and I am the Shunamite's child. When I am dead I dare say you will be grieved, though you need not. The prophet will come to see you; and when he says, 'How is it with the child?' you may say, 'IT IS WELL.' I am sure it will then be well with me, for I shall be in heaven singing the praises of God. You ought to think it well too." Mr. G. accordingly fulfilled the wish of this pious child.

(*c*) WILL YOU MEET ME THERE, FATHER?—At a public meeting of the London City Mission, in 1836, the Rev. R. Ainslie related the following fact:—An infided allowed his wife to send their two children to a Sunday school. One of them, not long after, was seized with illness, and it soon appeared, from the nature of the disease, he could not recover. The father came home, on the last evening of the child's life, from an infidel meeting, under the influence of the sentiments and principles usually taught in such societies, when his wife said to him, "James is dying." The father went up stairs, approached the bed-side of his dying child, and while the father was looking upon him, the child said, "Father, I am very happy; I am going to heaven; *will you meet me there, father?*" and immediately expired. This appeal was too much for him. Uttered with so much simplicity, and dictated by the Eternal Spirit, it was engraven upon the tablet of his heart as with a pen of iron upon lead, and sculptured there forever. He made many efforts to efface the impression from his mind, but without effect. He confesses, that he was a drunkard, a blasphemer, and, to use his own language, "the vilest wretch out of hell." The appeal continued to be more and more affecting to him, and on one Sabbath, having driven a party a few miles from town, for he was the driver of a fly, he put up his horses quickly, and went to church One of the lessons for the day was 2 Sam. xiii., containing the reflections of David on the death of his child. When he heard the words, "I shall go to him, but he shall not return to me," he thought, "It is impossible." His past life and infidel ridicule of heaven forbade the hope that he should ever meet his child in that happy world. Still his mind was greatly distressed. He had no pious friend; he could get neither light nor peace in this season of menta anguish. An agent of the City Mission at length called upon him; the man disclosed his state of mind, and the instructions, counsels, and prayers of the agent were blessed by the Holy Spirit: the man has renounced his infidelity — his character is entirely changed; he and his wife are regularly worshippers in the house of God, and he is now cherishing the hope, that he shall meet his child in heaven.

(*d*) THE UNWELCOME VISIT.—A little boy, who was educated in one of the London Hibernian Schools, in the county of Roscommon, was seized by sickness, and confined to his bed. In a few days his dissolution seemed to be near. The parents of the boy being Roman Catholics, sent immediately for the priest, to have the rites of their church administered, which, in their estimation, was the needful preparation for heaven. On the arrival of the priest, the boy seemed much confused, and astonished at his coming. "Your visit," said the boy, "was altogether unnecessary; I have no need of your help or assistance: I have a great High Priest at the right hand of the Majesty in the heavens, able to save to the uttermost all that come unto God by him: He lives for evermore, to make intercession; and He is such a priest as I require." The priest perceiving it to be in vain to reason at such a time, and knowing the boy to have been made acquainted with the Bible, went away. The child requested his parents to send for his schoolmaster, who stated that he never witnessed such a scene; it was altogether unexpected. The boy was always silent; though he was attentive to the instructions given at school, he never once hinted a change in his sentiments. In the course of conversation, he was asked if he was afraid to die. "No," replied the boy; "my Redeemer is Lord of the dead and living; I love him for his love to me, and soon I hope to be with him to see his glory."

(*e*) THE MYSTERIOUS HEARER.—A clergyman in the county of Tyrone had, for some weeks, observed a little ragged boy come every Sunday, and place himself in the centre of the aisle, directly opposite the pulpit, where he seemed exceedingly attentive to the service. He was desirous of knowing who the child was, and for this purpose hastened out, after the sermon, several times, but never could see him, as he vanished the moment service was over, and no one knew whence he came, or any thing about him. At length the boy was missed from his usual situation in the church, for some weeks. At this time a man called on the minister, and told him a person very ill was desirous of seeing him; but added, "I am really ashamed to ask you to go so far; but it is a child of mine, and he refuses to have any one but you; he is altogether an extraordinary boy, and talks a great deal about things that I do not understand." The clergyman promised to go, and went, though the rain poured down in torrents, and he had six miles of rugged mountain country to pass. On arriving where he was directed, he saw a most wretched cabin indeed, and the man he had seen in the morning was waiting at the door. He was shown in, and found the inside of the hovel as miserable as the outside. In a corner, on a little straw, he beheld a person stretched out, whom he recognized as the little boy who had so regularly attended his church. As he approached the wretched bed, the child raised himself up, and stretching forth his arms, said, "His own right hand hath gotten him the victory," Psa. 98:1; and immediately expired!

CHRIST.

81. Divinity of Christ.

(*a*) THE COBBLER'S CONCLUSION.—A poor man, unable to read, who obtained his livelihood by mending old shoes, was asked by an Arian minister, how he knew that Jesus Christ was the Son of God? "Sir," he replied, "I am sorry you have put such a question to me before my children, although I think I can give you a satisfactory answer. You know, sir, when I first became concerned about my soul, and unhappy on account of my sins, I called upon you to ask for your advice, and you told me to get into company, and spend my time as merrily as I could, but not to go to hear the Methodists." "I did so," answered the ungodly minister. "I followed your advice," continued the illiterate cobbler, "for some time; but the more I trifled, the more my misery increased; and at last I was persuaded to hear one of those Methodist ministers who came into our neighborhood, and preached Jesus Christ as the Savior. In the greatest agony of mind, I prayed to Him to save me, and to forgive my sins; and now I feel that he has freely forgiven them!—and by this I know that he is the Son of God."

(*b*) ARIANS CONFOUNDED.—Two of Dr. Priestly's followers, eminent men, once called on an old gentleman of the Society of Friends, to ask what was *his* opinion of the person of Christ. After a little consideration, he replied:—"The apostle says, We preach Christ crucified, unto the Jews a stumbling-block, because they expected a *temporal* Messiah; to the Greeks foolishness, because he was crucified as a malefactor; but unto them which are called, both Jews and Greeks, Christ the power of God, and the wisdom of God. Now, if you can separate the power of God from God, and the wisdom of God from God, I will come over to your opinions."—They were both struck dumb, and did not attempt to utter a single word in reply.

(*c*) THE CAVILLER SILENCED.—Two gentlemen were once disputing on the divinity of Christ. One of them who argued against it, said, "If it were true it certainly would have been expressed in more clear and unequivocal terms." "Well," said the other, "admitting that you believed it, were you authorized to teach it, and allowed to use your own language, how would you express the doctrine to make it indubitable?" "I would say," replied he, "that Jesus Christ is *the true God.*" "You are very happy," rejoined the other, "in the choice of your words; for you have happened to hit upon the very words of inspiration. St. John, speaking of the Son, says, 'This is the true God and eternal life.'"

(*d*) THE INEXPLICABLE CHAPTER.—There was a young man in a school, who had previously indulged the hope of having passed from death unto life, but had not believed in the divinity of Christ. As he was teaching, in the course of his delightful work, a class of children upon a section of the first chapter of John, he knew not how to direct them, or explain to the little listeners what seemed plain to those who believed the Son of God to be a divine person, but on his own principles was inexplicable. This circumstance led him to consider more closely the sacred text, and led him to believe in the supreme divinity of that Savior, whom he had degraded to a finite, created being. Thus, the truth of the inspired volume is made to appear. He that watereth, shall be watered also himself.

(*e*) "THE GOD WAS WITHIN."—While Mr. Kirkland was a missionary to the Oneidas, being unwell, he was unable to preach on the afternoon of a certain Sabbath, and told Peter, one of the head men of the Oneidas, that he must address the congregation. Peter modestly and reluctantly consented. After a few words of introduction, he began a discourse on the character of the Savior. "What, my brethren," said he, "are the views which you form of the character of Jesus? You will answer, perhaps, that he was a man of singular benevolence. You will tell me, that he proved this to be his character, by the nature of the miracles which he wrought. All these, you will say, were kind in the extreme. He created bread, to feed thousands who were ready to perish. He raised to life the son of a poor woman, who was a widow, and to whom his labors were necessary for her support in old age. Are these, then, your only views of the Savior? I will tell you, they are lame. When Jesus came into the world, he threw his blanket around him, but the God was within."

(*f*) THE ROCK OF CALVARY.—In Fleming's Christology it is stated that a deist, visiting the sacred places of Palestine, was shown the clefts of Mount Calvary. Examining them narrowly and critically, he turned in amazement to his fellow-travelers, and said, "I have long been a student of nature, and I am sure these clefts and rents in this rock were never made by nature, or an ordinary earthquake; for, by such a concussion, the rock must have split according to the veins, and where it was weakest in the adhesion of parts; for this," said he, "I have observed to have been done in other rocks when separated or broken after an earthquake; and reason tells me it must always be so. But it is quite otherwise here; for the rock is split athwart and across the veins in a most strange and preternatural manner; and, therefore," said he, "I thank God that I came hither to see the standing monument of a miraculous power by which God gives evidence to this day of the divinity of Christ."

(*g*) CONVICTIONS OF NAPOLEON.—"I know men," said Napoleon at St. Helena, to Count de Montholon, "I know men, and I tell you that Jesus is not a man! The religion of Christ is a mystery, which subsists by its own force, and proceeds from a mind which is not a human mind. We find in it a marked individuality, which originated a train of words and actions unknown before. Jesus is not a philosopher, for his proofs are miracles, and from the first his disciples adored him.

"Alexander, Cæsar, Charlemagne, and myself, founded empires; but on what foundation did we rest the creations of our genius? Upon force. Jesus Christ founded an empire upon love; and at this hour, millions of men would die for him!

"I die before my time, and my body will be given back to the earth, to become food for worms. Such is the fate of him who has been called the great Napoleon. What an abyss between my deep mystery and the eternal kingdom of Christ, which is proclaimed, loved, and adored, and is extending over the whole earth!"

Turning to Gen. Bertrand the emperor added, "If you do not perceive that Jesus Christ is God I did wrong to appoint you general!"

82. Miscellaneous.

(*a*) THE GOD WHO PAID THE DEBT.—A poor negro on the coast of Africa, who felt some concern about his soul, applied to his priest, who gave him various directions, which were all unavailing. He was so distressed in his mind, that he went wandering about from place to place, without meeting with any thing to comfort him. One day as he was sitting in a solitary manner on the beach, some English sailors came ashore to get water. As they were rolling the cask along, one of them heard the moanings of the poor negro, and going up to him said, "Hallo, shipmate! what's the matter with you?" The negro began to tell his tale of wo, in broken language, but was hastily interrupted by the sailor exclaiming, "Oh, I see what's the matter with you; you must go to England, and there you'll hear of the Christian's God, who paid the debt." These words were spoken in a careless and thoughtless manner; but they made an impression on the mind of the negro, and he determined to proceed to England. He traveled a great many miles until he came to an English settlement, where he got leave to work his passage over in a ship that was lying there. During the voyage he would frequently approach one sailor and another, and say, with great simplicity, in a plaintive tone, "Please, massa, you tell me where Christian's God dat pay de debt?" The seamen, who it appears were all irreligious, only laughed at him, and concluded he was mad. The ship arrived at London, and the negro was put ashore at Wapping. Having no money to receive, he wandered from street to street, and whenever he could catch a single passenger, he would stop and say, in the most melancholy manner, "Please, massa, you please tell poor black man where Christian's God dat pay de debt?" Some told him to go about his business, some gave him money, and others, supposing him to be deranged, passed on; but he met no one to answer his question. In this manner he continued to stroll about, as devoid of comfort in England as in his own land.

and frequently would he steal down some by-place, and give vent to his soul in accents like these: "Ah! me no hear of Christian's God dat pay de debt; me walk, walk, day, day, but me no hear. White man tell me in Africa, go to England, but me no find; me go back, me die dere." He saw some people on the Sabbath going into a large house, which he concluded was the temple of the Christian's God; he followed them; he heard a sermon, but he heard nothing about Christ. It was all unintelligible to him, and he still remained the subject of despondency, and still went mourning about. A gentleman accidentally overheard him one day, while he was complaining to himself of his unsuccessful inquiry after the Christian's God. He spoke to him, and directed him to go to such a place that evening, and there he would hear of the Christian's God. He went, and heard a sermon by that gentleman, on the suretiship of Christ, in which he described sin as a debt, and Christ as paying it, and the price he paid, and that he was ascended up to heaven, and had sent him, the preacher, to say to all, "Come unto me all ye that labor," &c. Long before he came to the close of his sermon, the Spirit of God had been pleased to touch the heart of the poor negro, and to enlighten his mind; he started up in the pew, but without making a noise, and in a whispering tone was heard to say, while he clasped his hands together, and the tears ran down his sable cheeks, "Me have found Him! me have found Him! the Christian's God dat pay de debt!" After the meeting the minister had some further conversation with him, and was rejoiced at the state of his mind. An opportunity was afterward taken to send him to Africa.

83. CHRISTIANITY, CHARACTER OF.

(*a*) THE FIRST HOSPITAL.—The first hospital for the reception of the diseased and the infirm was founded at Edessa, in Syria, by the sagacious and provident humanity of a Christian father. The history of this memorable foundation is given by Sozomen, in his account of Ephrem Syrus.

A grievous famine, with all its inseparable evils, having befallen the city of Edessa, its venerable deacon, at the call of suffering humanity, came forth from the studious retirement of his cell, whither he had long withdrawn, that he might devote his latter days to meditation on the deep things of God. Filled with emotion at the sight of the misery which surrounded him, with the warmth of Christian charity, he reproved the rich men of Edessa, who suffered their fellow-citizens to perish from want and sickness; and who preferred their wealth, at once, to the lives of others, and to the safety of their own souls. Stung by his reproaches, and awed by his revered character, the citizens replied, that they cared not for their wealth; but that, in an age of selfishness and corruption, they knew not whom to intrust with its distribution. "What," exclaimed the holy man, "is your opinion of me?" The answer was instant and unanimous: Ephrem was every thing that was holy, and good, and just. "Then," he resumed "I will be your almoner. For your sakes, I will undertake this burden." And receiving their now willing contributions, he caused about three hundred beds to be placed in the public porticoes of the city, for the reception of fever patients: he relieved, also, the famishing multitudes who flocked into Edessa, from the adjoining country; and rested not from his labor of love until the famine was arrested, "and the plague was stayed."

Christianity, therefore, has the honor of erecting the first hospital; and wherever true Christianity has prevailed, her efforts to relieve the wretched, and add to the amount of human happiness have accomplished more in one generation, than paganism or infidelity in a hundred.

(*b*) CHRISTIANITY AND HEATHENISM.—The language of God's word is, "Thou shalt not kill; thou shalt not commit adultery; thou shalt not steal; thou shalt not bear false witness; thou shalt not covet." Now where is there such a code of morality to be found in all the systems of ancient or modern heathen philosophers or politicians? Lycurgus ordained that infants who were deformed or weak, should be destroyed; but God's word says, "Thou shalt not kill." Lycurgus taught his pupils to steal, and rewarded those who could steal in such an artful manner as not to be detected; but the Bible says, "Thou shalt not steal."

Aristippus maintained that it was no harm "to steal, commit adultery and sacrilege; setting aside the vulgar opinion concerning them." The Grecians and many of the ancients practised incest; that is, a man could marry his own sister; and they pretended to derive this practice from gods, feigning that Jupiter married his own sister Juno. Hence many of their great men practised it, such as Cimon, Alcibiades, Darius the Persian, Ptolemy of Egypt, and others; but Moses said, "Thou shalt not marry one that is near akin to thee," and St. Paul required the *incestuous* person to be punished. The laws of Solon allowed of "brothels and prostitution;" but Moses said, "There shall be no harlot in Israel;" and were the principles of this book attended to, there would be none in Christendom. The polite and learned nations of the Greeks and Romans, very generally permitted the custom of exposing infants, and Romulus allowed the Romans to destroy all their female children except the oldest, and even their males if they were deformed. "These practices were common among them, and celebrated at their theatres."

They also had gladiatorial shows in which slaves were obliged to fight with each other, till one or the other fell, mangled with wounds. And so great was the rage for this sport, among both sexes, that no war is said to have been so destructive. Lipsius tells us, "that the gladiatorial shows cost 20 or 30 thousand lives a month, and thus continued for a long course of years, must have destroyed more lives than the ravages of their wars."

(*c*) THE BURMAN'S IMPRESSION.—Mrs. Judson, giving some account in a letter, of the first Burman convert, says:—A few days ago I was reading with him Christ's sermon on the Mount. He was deeply impressed, and unusually solemn. "These words," said he, "take hold on my very heart; they make me tremble. Here God commands us to do every thing that is good in secret, not to be seen of men. How unlike our religion is this! When Burmans make offerings at the pagodas, they make a great noise with drums and musical instruments, that others may see how good they are; but this religion makes the *mind* fear God; it makes it, of its *own accord*, fear sin."

(*d*) THE INFIDEL AND THE ORPHAN SCHOOL.—A mechanic in London, who rented a room very near the Orphan Working School, was unhappily a determined infidel, and one who could confound many a thoughtless Christian with his sophistical reasonings on religion. He, one day, however, said to another man, "I did this morning what I have not done for a long time before; I wept." "Wept!" said his friend; "what occasioned you to weep?" "Why," replied the infidel mechanic, "I wept on seeing the children of the Orphan Working School pass; and it occurred to me, that if religion had done nothing more for mankind, it had at least provided for the introduction of these ninety-four orphans into respectable and honorable situations in life."

(*e*) BYRON'S CONFESSION.—"Indisputably," says Lord Byron, "the firm believers in the gospel have a great advantage over all others, for this simple reason, that if true, they will have their reward hereafter; and if there be no hereafter, they can be but with the infidel in his eternal sleep, having had the assistance of an exalted hope through life, without subsequent disappointment, since, at the worst for them, 'out of nothing, nothing can arise,' not even sorrow."

(*f*) THE TREE JUDGED BY ITS FRUIT.—When Mr. Gutzlaff, in his third voyage to China, went on shore for the first time at a particular place, the people were distrustful, and some of them hinted that the Christian books merely contained the doctrines of western barbarians, which were quite at variance with the tenets of the Chinese sages. Mr. G. did not undertake to contest this point with them, but proceeded to administer relief to a poor man who was almost blind; thus showing the spirit and conduct which the gospel inculcates. The man was affected with this unexpected kindness, and, turning towards Mr. G., said, "Judging from your actions, your doctrines must be excellent; therefore I beseech you give me some of your books; though I myself cannot read, I have children who can." "From this moment," says Mr. G., "the demand for the word of God increased, so that I could never pass a hamlet without being importuned by the people to impart to them the knowledge of divine things. In the wide excursion which I took, I daily witnessed the demand for the word of God."

(*g*) LORD BACON'S OPINION.—Lord Bacon, towards the latter end of his life, said, that a little smattering of philosophy would lead a man to Atheism, but a thorough insight of it will lead a man back again to a first cause, and that the first principle of right reason is religion; and seriously professes, that, after all his studies and inquisitions, he durst not die with any other thoughts than those of religion, taught, as it is professed, among the Christians.

(*h*) LORD CHESTERFIELD'S REPLY TO AN INFIDEL LADY.—Infidels should never talk of our giving up our Christianity, till they can propose something superior to it. Lord Chesterfield's answer, therefore, to an infidel lady, was very just. When at Brussels he was invited by Voltaire to sup with him and Madame C. The conversation happening to turn upon the affairs of England, "I think, my Lord,' said Madame C., "that the parliamen of England consists of five or six hundred of the best informed men in the kingdom?"

"True, madame, they are generally supposed to be so."

"What then can be the reason they tolerate so great an absurdity, as the Christian religion?" "I suppose, madame," replied his lordship, "it is because they have not been able to substitute any thing better in its stead; when they can, I do not doubt but in their wisdom they will readily adopt it."

(*i*) GIBBON'S TESTIMONY.—"While the Roman empire," says Gibbon, "was invaded by open violence, or undermined by slow decay, a pure and humble religion greatly insinuated itself into the minds of men, grew up in silence and sobriety, derived new vigor from opposition, and finally erected the banner of the cross on the ruins of the capital."

Again, he says, "the Christian religion is a religion that diffuses among the people a pure, benevolent, and universal system of ethics, adapted to every condition in life, and recommended as the will and reason of the Supreme Deity, and enforced by the sanction of eternal rewards and punishments."

(*j*) THE MALAY'S TEST OF HONESTY.—A New England sea-captain, who visited "India beyond the Ganges," was boarded by a Malay merchant, a man of considerable property, and asked if he had any tracts which he could part with. The American, at a loss how to account for such a singular request from such a man, inquired, "What do you want of tracts? you cannot read a word of them." "True, but I have a use for them, nevertheless. Whenever one of your countrymen, or an Englishman, calls on me to trade, I put a tract in his way, and watch him. If he reads it soberly and with interest, I infer that he will not cheat me; if he throws it aside with contempt, or a profane oath, I have no more to do with him—I can not trust him."

84. CHURCH, JOINING THE.

(*a*) THE DELAYED BAPTISM.—A young man, by the name of Henry T., from England, was converted in Dartmouth, Mass., about 1835. Before his conversion, he was a very intemperate, profane, abandoned man. His exercises in conversion were marked and clear; and he soon made application for admission into the church. But it fared worse with him than it fared with Saul when he came to Damascus: Christians were not only afraid of him, but they thought he had better wait a month, till the next covenant meeting. They were inclined to think he would turn back to his cups. But he manifested a Christian spirit, and determined not to forsake his brethren or neglect any of the public or private duties of religion. The next covenant meeting came, and Mr. T., full of hope, presented himself for admission again. The confidence of the brethren in the genuineness of his change was decidedly increased by his conduct during the month; but owing to his former habits, some of the brethren hesitated about having him baptized, and they put him off another month. He said he felt anxious to be soon baptized, for he said he might die without receiving the ordinance; still he would patiently submit to the church's decision, and persevere in doing duty. And he did; he was a regular attendant upon public worship; on conference and prayer meetings, and in the latter took a regular and active part. Indeed he often told how much he loved his brethren—those who were so suspicious of him. Another month passed, and another application was made. His conduct had been so exemplary as to secure the confidence of the minister, and all the members of the church in his steadfastness, but that of one of the deacons. He alone objected. When Mr. T. was told he must wait one month longer, he was deeply grieved. "But," said he, "if you never receive me I shall love you still!" This he said as he went out and closed the door.

"That is too much for me," said the deacon; "call him back." He was called back, received a unanimous vote, and united with the church. By pursuing such a course, by overcoming the temptation to quit the church, he had gained the confidence of the church, and confidence in himself; and a candidate is rarely found more happy than he was, when baptized and received into the fellowship of the saints. He proved to be a happy and steadfast Christian.

(*b*) A FATHER CONVERTED.—A few years since, says a correspondent of the New-York Evangelist, during a powerful revival in New England, the Holy Spirit exerted its mighty influence upon a family circle consisting of a father, a mother, and five most interesting children. The mother and her five children were hopefully converted. The father, who was naturally one of the most amiable, retiring, modest men with whom I ever was acquainted, aided his family in attending the numerous meetings, and was not unfrequently seen bowed down and trembling under the power of truth. Still the conversions of his wife and children, in rapid succession, were like so many earthquake shocks to the foundations on which his false hopes had so long rested. But neither the affecting scenes of their distress, nor the ecstasies of their subsequent joy, could melt his heart into contrition. He now felt that he was groping in *a dark path*, and in wretched loneliness; he who should have been the leader of a pious household was left far behind, a subject of prayer, and an occasion of grief to the circle around him. Thus he remained for weeks.

Ere long preparations were made for gathering the fruits of the revival into the church, and a day appointed for the examination of candidates. The mother and her five children, with some sixty others, came before the church, and were propounded for admission into its pale. As the day of admission drew near, the father, who had watched their movements with much concern, expressed his regret to his wife that they should make a profession of religion at present, and requested that they should wait for him. The mother, deeply moved, solicited advice of the pastor and other friends; but, after due deliberation, it was concluded that the path of their duty was plain, and that they were bound to follow Christ. With unusual decision and firmness they resolved to do so. As soon as he knew their decision, he became more earnest in his remonstrances, and used every possible argument, especially with the mother, to dissuade her from her purpose, but in vain. He soon changed his tone of entreaty into that of fearful threatening, warning his wife if she had any affection for him, any regard for the peace of the family, to desist from her purpose and *wait* for him. "No," said the martyr-like woman, "I love you most tenderly, but I love Christ more. I have waited for you for more than twenty years, and now I shall do my duty, and as to the consequences I will leave them with God."

At the close of this interview, which took place Saturday evening, he took his hat, and uttering some threats, left the house, as if never to return to his family again. It was a painful night to mother and children. Might he not become the victim of lasting mania, or in his rage and disappointment suddenly destroy himself? As it afterwards appeared, he retired to his barn, threw himself on the hay-mow, (it being midsummer,) and there rolled and struggled like a wild beast in the net. An awful warfare was waging between an awakened conscience and a desperately rebellious heart. He could not, would not submit. Sabbath morning came—the family, with trembling anxiety for the absent father, prepared to go to the house of God; but, just before the hour of service, his feelings drove him from his hiding place. He was safe, but still unhumbled. He again inquired of his wife if she remained fixed in her purpose, and finding she did, he left the house with dreadful signs of rebellion, throwing out some intimations that he never should return—that fearful consequences might be anticipated. He was soon out of sight, but no out of mind. The family departed; and the father, finding his threats unavailing returned to his house, prepared his person with despatch, and was soon seen placed in the gallery in a situation favorable for witnessing the ceremony he had opposed so vainly. And when the ceremony of reception took place, and the father looked down and saw his wife and five children, with the rest, kneel around the altar, he burst into tears, and his agitation was great. The step was taken, and could not be retraced.

On retiring from the house he felt that he was indeed *alone*. He began to come to himself—to review the dreadful rebellion of his heart which recent events had brought to light. His heart began to break; and in a few hours his soul was made to rejoice in that Savior whom he had so recently persecuted. He now felt deeply thankful that his wife had taken so decided a course; and he considered her uniting with the church, the means, in God's hands, of leading him to repentance.

(*c*) THE AGED BLACKSMITH'S TESTIMONY.—In the year 184–, Mr. W., of R. I., related the following: "Thirty-four years ago I thought God, for Christ's sake, pardoned my sins. My wife and myself thought it duty to follow Christ in baptism, and unite with the people of God. The day arrived on which we were to relate our experience to the church, with a view to becoming members. We were nearly prepared to leave home, when a gentleman called, and wished to transact some business with me. I told my wife to go on—I would be along soon. She went, related her experience, was baptized, and lived and died in the bosom of the church. But I was detained longer than I expected to be, and found, when ready to go, that it was *too late*. The next meeting for the purpose I was again hindered by yielding to worldly business; and by the third meeting I had little inclination to go, and doubted whether I was a Christian. Since then you have heard me profane the name of God, and seen me neglect the house of his worship. But there has never been a single night that I have not, when laying my head upon my pillow, reflected upon the time of my redemption, and endured bitter remorse in view of my disobedience. But the *feeling* which I had on *that afternoon*, has never returned. If I walk, I must go in the dark. And now I am about 'fourscore years old,' and had I the world I would give it, for a return of that impressive sense of my obligation to God which should lead me to do the long neglected duty. O! my friends, as you value your soul's interest, let no earthly consideration prevent the immediate discharge of duty."

(*d*) THE HUSBAND'S CONVERSION.—A woman in Bow, N. H., was converted through the instrumentality of an itinerant minister, and was accordingly anxious to make a public profession of religion by baptism. She wished to have her spiritual father preach in her house, and then administer to her the ordinance. Accordingly she suggested her feelings to her husband. His hatred to the cross was already roused by his wife's conversion, and this proposal kindled it to a fury. "No," said he, "Mr. —— shall never preach in my house." "May he not preach in the yard then?" said she. "No, there is no room for him in the yard." "Well, I suppose you will let us have the barn?" "No, never, for any such purpose." "But we may go into the orchard, perhaps?" "No, he shall not preach any where upon my premises." "Well, we will have the meeting in the road then." "If you suffer him," said the husband, "to baptize you, that breaks up our union; you will never be allowed to enter this house again.' The pious woman, however, was not in the least disposed to yield to any such opposition, and she gave her husband to understand it. Whatever trials might await her, even exile from her family, she stood prepared to abide, rather than neglect her duty and violate God's commands. Her husband found himself baffled. He saw that she was actuated by a new principle, a strong and sublime affection for God and his word, to which she had once been a stranger, and to which he was still a stranger himself. His mind sunk in deep and deeper distress. One day she went up into her chamber, perhaps to pour out her soul in secret before God, when her husband was so overcome by the force of his convictions, that he followed her, and desired her to pray for him. They went to prayer; and as they rose up, and looked out of the window, they saw the before-mentioned itinerant minister approaching. None could be more glad to see him than was the persecuting husband now, or more anxious for an interest in his prayers. He directed him to the Savior, and presented him in the arms of his faith before the throne. The husband was now perfectly willing to have the minister preach in the house, which he did: and he was perfectly willing that his wife should receive baptism, but he wished her to wait a short time, so that they both might receive the ordinance together. She concluded to do so; and two or three weeks after, they were both baptized by the itinerant, on the same day, and received into the fellowship of the church.

(*e*) THE OPPOSING HUSBAND.—When the Rev. Mr. Morton was settled in Manlius, New-York, the church of which he was pastor met together on Saturday afternoon for covenant meeting. A man and his wife who were strangers to Mr. M., were present; and being informed by one of her friends that the lady would like to be baptized, at a suitable time Mr. M. called on her to relate her Christian experience. As she arose to speak she gave her child to her husband, who immediately withdrew with it into the yard before the door. The church heard her narration, and received her as candidate for the ordinance. On the ensuing Sabbath she was baptized. Mr. M. having learned that the woman's husband was offended with him, sought an interview. In answer to the inquiry whether he was offended or no he replied to Mr. M. that he felt very much offended with him, both for baptizing his wife, and also because Mr

Morton had addressed all his discourse to him that morning in the meeting-house. Mr. M. replied firmly, "In baptizing your wife, sir, I had no business to act according to your preferences, for I acted as God's ambassador; and I consider that you have no business to say a word in opposition. I knew not that you had any objections to your wife's joining our church; but if I had, that ought not to have prevented me from doing my duty, nor your wife from doing hers. As to my sermon this morning, if it contained truth adapted to your case, I hope you will apply it: 'if the coat fits you, put it on!' But I advise you, sir, to go home and read your Bible, and repent of your sins, before your iniquity shall be your ruin." The opposer shrunk before Mr. M.'s faithfulness, and the words sunk into his heart. Early the next Tuesday morning, he came to Mr. Morton's residence in great distress of mind. He confessed that since the interview of Sunday he had had no peace; and he desired Mr. M.'s forgiveness and prayers. He stated that he had kept his wife awake all Saturday night, trying to persuade and frighten her out of her purpose of being baptized. But he could not move her; and now he wished to be converted and go and do likewise. Three weeks from that memorable Sabbath Mr. M. baptized him into the fellowship of the church.

(*f*) THE BANISHED DAUGHTER.—In the time of a revival in Harbor Creek, Pa., the daughter of an infidel was happily converted, and on a Saturday afternoon related to the Baptist church her Christian experience, and was received as a canditate for baptism.

She was intending to be baptized on the ensuing Sabbath, and in the morning she made known her intention to her infidel father. He told her angrily that if she went into the water, he would immediately banish her from his house. After consulting with some of her friends, she concluded to defer the matter till some future occasion. At the close of the afternoon service, Rhoda Ann, for that was her name, repaired to the water with the rest of the assembly to witness the baptism of other converts. After the last candidate was immersed, the preacher addressed the assembly, and urged any who might feel it their duty, to relate their experience to the church, most of whom were present; and, if the church so desired, he would baptize any such persons before they left the water. One after another acceded to his request, came before the church, and were accepted and baptized. At length Rhoda Ann stepped forward, and exclaimed with streaming eyes, "I believe it is better to obey God than man!" There was a moral sublimity in the thought and in this new occasion of its utterance, that must have wrought a most thrilling impression upon every mind. Having in a few words given an account of God's gracious dealings with her soul, she too was received and buried with Christ in baptism. On her return home, she found her father absent; but when he came in, some of the members of the family told him of the step Rhoda had taken. Turning to her, he said with firmness, "Rhoda, you remember what I said to you this morning; you must now quit my house." Rhoda solicited the privilege of taking away her clothes and other things with her; and having permission, she soon gathered them together, bade her friends farewell, and started forth upon her cruel exile, between sundown and dark. Soon after she had gone out, her father opened the door and called after her, "Rhoda Ann," said he, "you may come back now. *I want you to understand that I am to be obeyed!*"

Rhoda returned; but from that time her father treated her, as she declared, with greater kindness and tenderness than ever.

85. COMMENTARIES.

(*a*) THE MISTAKEN DIVINES.—Rica, having been to visit the library of a French convent, writes thus to his friend in Persia, concerning what had passed: "Father," said I to the librarian, "what are these huge volumes which fill the whole side of the library?" "These," said he, "are the interpreters of the Scriptures." "There is a prodigious number of them," replied I; "the Scriptures must have been very dark formerly, and be very clear at present. Do there remain still any doubts? Are there now any points contested?" "Are there!" answered he with surprise, "are there There are almost as many as there are lines." You astonish me," said I; "what then have all these authors been doing?" "These authors," returned he, "never searched the Scriptures for what ought to be believed, but for what they did believe themselves. They did not consider them as a book wherein were contained the doctrines which they ought to receive, but as a work which might be made to authorize their own ideas."

86. COMMUNION OF THE LORD'S SUPPER.

(*a*) COL. GARDINER'S ENJOYMENT.—A more devout communicant at the table of the Lord, says Dr. Doddridge, in his life of Colonel Gardiner, has, perhaps, seldom been any where known. Often have I had the pleasure to see that manly countenance softened into all the marks of humiliation and contrition on these occasions: and to discern, in spite of all his efforts to conceal them, streams of tears flowing down from his eyes, while he has been directing them to those memorials of his Redeemer's love. And some, who have conversed intimately with him after he came from that ordinance, have observed a visible abstraction from surrounding objects, by which there seemed reason to imagine that his soul was wrapped up in holy contemplation. And I particularly remember, that when we had once spent a great part of the following Monday in riding together, he made an apology to me for being so absent as he seemed, by telling me that his heart was flown upwards, before he was aware, to Him whom having not seen he loved; and he was rejoicing in him with such unspeakable joy, that he could not hold it down to creature converse.

(*b*) LAYING ASIDE A CROWN.—At the coronation of his Majesty George III, after the anointing was over in the Abbey, and the crown put upon his head with great shouting, the two archbishops came to hand him down from the throne to receive the sacrament. His majesty told them he would not go to the Lord's Supper, and partake of that ordinance, with the crown upon his head: for he looked upon himself, when appearing before the King of kings, in no other character than in that of a humble Christian. The bishops replied, that although there was no precedent for this, it should be complied with. Immediately he put off his crown, and laid it aside: he then desired that the same should be done with respect to the queen. It was answered, that her crown was pinned on her head, that it could not be easily taken off; to which the king replied, "Well, let it be reckoned a part of her dress, and in no other light." "When I saw and heard this," says the narrator, "it warmed my heart towards him; and I could not help thinking, that there would be something good found about him towards the Lord God of Israel.

(*c*) CHILDREN PRESENT.—The

Rev. John Brown, in a narrative of his experience, remarks, "I reflect on it as a great mercy, that I was born in a family which took care of my Christian instruction, and in which I had the privilege of God's worship, morning and evening. About the eighth year of my age, I happened, in a crowd, to push into the church at Abernethy, on a Sacrament Sabbath. Before I was excluded, I heard a minister speak much in commendation of Christ; this, in a sweet and delightful manner, captivated my young affections, and has since made me think that children should never be kept out of church on such occasions."

(*d*) THE COMMUNION PROFANED.—In a speech in the House of Lords, in 1719, Lord Lansdowne said, "The receiving of the Lord's Supper was never intended to be as a qualification for an office; but as an open declaration of one's being and remaining a sincere member of the church of Christ. Whoever presumes to receive it with any other view, profanes it, and may be said to seek his promotion in this world, by eating and drinking his own damnation in the next."

(*e*) THE ESQUIMAUX COMMUNICANTS.—"We can truly say," observes a Moravian missionary, "that among the very considerable number of Esquimaux who live with us, we know of few who are not seriously desirous to profit by what they hear, and to experience and enjoy themselves, that which they see their countrymen possess. Our communicants give us pleasure; for it is the wish of their very hearts to live unto the Lord, and their conduct affords proofs of the sincerity of their professions; thus for example, Esquimaux sisters, who have no boat of their own, venture across bays some miles in breadth, sitting behind their husbands, on their narrow kajacks, in order to be present at the holy sacrament, though at the peril of their lives." What a lesson is this for those who live near, and make any trifling thing an excuse!

(*f*) COLONEL GARDINER'S PREPARATION.—Colonel Gardiner, in a letter, mentions the pleasure with which he had attended a preparation sermon the Saturday before the dispensation of the Lord's Supper. He writes, "I took a walk on the mountains over against Ireland; and I persuade myself, that were I capable of giving you a description of what passed there, you would agree that I had much better reason to remember my God from the hills of Port-Patrick, than David from the land of Jordan, and of the Hermonites from the hill Mizar. In short, I wrestled some hours with the Angel of the covenant, and made supplications to him with floods of tears and cries, until I had almost expired; but he strengthened me so, that like Jacob, I had power with God and prevailed. You will be more able to judge of this, by what you have felt yourself, upon the like occasions. After such a preparatory work, I need not tell you how blessed the solemn ordinance of the Lord's Supper proved to me; I hope it was so to many."

87. COMPANY, EVIL.

(*a*) BURGLARY AND DEATH.—A poor boy, who had been educated in the Stockport Sunday school, England, conducted himself so well, and made much great proficiency in learning, that he was appointed teacher of one of the junior classes. About this time his father died, and his mother, reduced to indigent circumstances, sent him to one of the cotton factories. Here he met with boys of his own age, who were hardened in sin. Through the force of their evil example he lost, by degrees, all his serious impressions; and having thrown off the fear of God, became addicted to intemperance and the commission of petty thefts. His dissolute conduct soon led him into the army

The regiment was sent to Spain, where his habit of excessive drinking was confirmed; and not satisfied with the advantages he reaped as the fruits of many victories, he plundered the innocent and peaceful inhabitants. On the close of the war in the peninsula, he returned home with his regiment: and soon after landing on the coast of Hampshire, he, with others of his companions, whose principles he had vitiated, broke into several houses; till at length he was detected, arraigned at the tribunal of justice, and condemned to an ignominious death at the age of twenty-one.

(*b*) REMORSE AND SUICIDE.—In the year 1832, died in Essex, England, under very painful circumstances, a young man who had once promised to be happy and useful. He was apprenticed to a respectable shopkeeper, who insisted on his always being at home by a certain hour in the evening. For some time he appeared very attentive to his business, and was useful to his master; but he unhappily acquired the habit of walking about the streets in an evening, and soon after formed very improper connexions at a public house. He was seriously admonished, and at times appeared to feel the impropriety of his conduct; but the sins he cherished hardened his heart, and his irregularities became confirmed. At length, his master, on returning from a journey, heard complaints of his conduct, which led him to threaten that unless his conduct was altered, he would cancel his indentures. He now felt that his sins were hastening him to the ruin against which he had often been warned; he had lost alike the confidence of his master and his parents. Stung by the convictions of his guilt, he repaired to his room, when he knew that he would be expected at dinner, and committed suicide; thus rushing into the presence of his Judge uncalled, and every way unprepared. Who can conceive the acuteness of his anguish, when he found himself in the presence of that God whose laws he had trampled under his feet, but from whose wrath he found it impossible to escape!

(*c*) BLAIR'S EXTREMES—Mr. Robert Blair, in a memoir of his life, written by himself, says, "That year (1616,) having, upon an evening, been engaged in company with some irreligious persons, when I returned to my chamber, and went to my ordinary devotion, the Lord did show so much displeasure and wrath, that I was driven from prayer, and heavily threatened to be deserted of God. For this I had a restless night, and resolved to spend the next day in extraordinary humiliation, fasting and prayer; and toward the evening of that day, I found access to God, with sweet peace, through Jesus Christ, and learned to beware of such company; but then I did run into another extreme of rudeness and incivility toward such as were profane and irreligious, so hard a thing is it for short-sighted sinners to hold the right and the straight way."

(*d*) JUDGE BULLER'S CAUTION.—Judge Buller, when in the company of a young gentleman of sixteen, cautioned him against being led astray, by the example or persuasion of others, and said, "If I had listened to the advice of some of those who called themselves my friends when I was young, instead of being a *Judge* of the King's Bench, I should have died long ago a *prisoner* in the King's Bench."

(*e*) ELLIOT'S ADVICE.—The Rev. John Elliot, styled The Apostle of the Indians, was once asked by a pious woman, who was vexed with a wicked husband, and bad company frequently infesting her house on his account, what she should do? "Take," said he, "the Holy Bible into your hand when bad company comes in, and that will soon drive them out of the house."

(*f*) A GOOD EXPEDIENT.—A pious officer of the army, travelling through the Mahratta country, was asked by Judge D——, a religious gentleman, to accompany him to a public dinner, at which the commanding officer of the district, with all his staff, and various other public characters, were expected to meet.

"I expressed a wish to be excused," says the officer, "as I had then no relish for such entertainments, and did not think that much either of pleasure or profit was to be derived from them."

His reply was—"While I feel it my duty to attend on such an occasion, I certainly have as little pleasure in it as you have. But there is one way in which I find I can be present at such meetings, and yet receive no injury from them. I endeavor to conceive to myself the Lord Jesus seated on the opposite side of the table, and to think what he would wish me to do and to say, when placed in such a situation, and as long as I can keep this thought alive on my mind, I find I am free from danger."

88. CONFERENCE MEETINGS.

(*a*) MY BRETHREN, THE LORD IS GOOD.—It is not necessary in our meetings for conference and prayer, that a Christian should speak with a high degree of ability and talent, in order to be a benefit to the meeting. An exhortation with little logical connexion or rhetorical beauty about it, poured from a feeling heart, has often produced more deep and powerful impressions than the most elaborate addresses. A few words even, from a weak and trembling disciple, have frequently done more execution than a long discourse from others.

There was a feeble stammering brother in the southern part of Connecticut, who deemed his gift so small that he usually kept silent in religious meetings. But on one occasion, in the midst of a revival, his emotions were so strong that he could not keep his seat. He rose to give his feelings vent; but all the stammerer could say, was, "MY BRETHREN, THE LORD IS GOOD," and then sat down. But his words fell with power on the hearts of those present, thrilled them like an electric stroke, and gave a fresh and lively interest to the meeting.—Who could not say as much!

(*b*) THE ELECTRIFYING SENTENCE.—In a prayer-meeting, held several years since, in W——, Rhode Island, a person arose, and holding up his right hand, exclaimed, "I am on the Lord's side." The speaker said no more, and as it would seem, felt unable to do so. But the effect was magical. There was an eloquence in that simple sentence and the manner of its utterance, that went home to the minds and bosoms of all present, with kindling, melting energy. Such a happy and lasting impression was produced, that years afterwards it was mentioned again and again, by different persons, to a pastor who was newly settled in the place.

(*c*) DULL CONFERENCE MEETINGS.—Before I knew any thing experimentally of religion, said a young convert in Rhode Island, I used often to attend conference and prayer-meetings, and when Christians were engaged and the time improved, I could not but be interested and carry away impressions strongly in favor of religion. But when they spoke of its being a heavy cross for them to speak or pray before others, I could not understand them. It seemed that if I were such as they professed to be, it would be no cross to me, but a pleasure. And when I attended social meetings where the exercises dragged heavily, I felt uninterested—displeased. As I went away from such meetings, my mind was darkened with skeptical suspicions and doubts. Can these Christians, thought I, have such joy in religion, such love for Christ, as they sometimes express, and yet be so backward and silent? Is their fountain of enjoyment so poor, so inconstant as this? How much can such a religion be worth? Can there be any thing divine and substantial in it? This would be the course of my reflections; such lifeless services not only destroyed my interest in attending such meetings, but shook my confidence in professors of religion, and in religion itself!

CONFESSION.

89 Noble Examples of Confession.

(*a*) Dr. JOHNSON'S CONFESSION.—Ignorant people are generally positive and assuming; and, even when they find themselves in an error, are too proud to acknowledge it; but those who are truly wise, have learned that they are also fallible; they rejoice in an opportunity of having an error corrected, and they can afford to acknowledge it, without risking all their reputation, or any of it, with persons of real judgment.

The celebrated Dr. Johnson, one of the most learned men that England ever produced, one night, rather late, had a dispute in conversation with a Mr. Morgan. Johnson had the wrong side, but did not give up; in short, both kept the field. Next morning, when they met in the breakfast room, Dr. Johnson, with great candor, accosted Mr. Morgan thus: "Sir, I have been thinking on our dispute last night; you were in the right."

(*b*) WASHINGTON'S CONFESSION.—Washington, when stationed in early life at Alexandria, with a regiment under his command, grew warm at an election, and said something offensive to a Mr. Payne, who, with one blow of his cane, brought him to the ground. On hearing of the insult, the regiment, burning for revenge, started for the city; but Washington met them, and begged them, by their regard for him, to return peaceably to their barracks. Finding himself in the wrong, he nobly resolved to make an honorable reparation, and next morning sent a polite note requesting Payne to meet him at the tavern. Payne took it for a challenge, and went in expectation of a duel; but what was his surprise to find instead of pistols, a decanter of wine on the table. Washington rose to meet him, and said with a smile, "Mr. Payne, to err is human; but to correct our errors is always honorable. I believe I was wrong yesterday; you have had, I think, some satisfaction; and if you deem that sufficient, here is my hand—let us be friends." Such an act few could resist; and Payne became from that moment through life, an enthusiastic friend and admirer of Washington.

(*c*) LORD MANSFIELD'S MAXIM.—This eminent judge was never ashamed of publicly retracting any wrong opinion he had entertained, when once convinced of his mistake. He used frequently to say, probably after Dean Swift, who has a similar passage in his writings, "That to acknowledge you were wrong yesterday, was but to let the world know that you are wiser to day than you were then."

CONFESSION OF SIN.

HAPPY EFFECTS OF CONFESSION.

90. Procures Peace of Mind.

(*a*) "I HAVE BEEN DRUNK."—Confession of wrong accomplishes its real object in proportion to its plain, explicit declaration respecting the wrong as committed. If the wrong is public, let the confession be public; if private, let the confession be also. A member of a church in R—— town ship, N. Y., had, according to the practice of the times, been accustomed to indulge in the use of intoxicating drinks. On one occasion he was so overcome as to falter in his step and stammer in his speech. A little time after this, having awaked to a sense of his spiritual declension, he came to the church and made an apparently most sincere and heart-broken confession.

He confessed coldness, worldly-mindedness, neglect of prayer, neglect of the church, and almost all manner of backslidings. Yet he sat down without any alleviation of his distress. Conviction and anguish of spirit increased. He confessed again, and still his trouble increased. At three successive meetings his tears and his sad countenance added interest to his humiliating confessions and still his soul was the more burdened. Finally he arose, and with a full soul, sobbing aloud, said, "I have been drunk. Will you forgive me?" The effect was electrical. Peace and joy filled his soul, and the forgiveness of his brethren and friends beamed on every countenance. Such is the result of a confession that covers the wrong.

91. Prevents Alienation.

(*a*) J. BRADFORD AND J. WESLEY.—Joseph Bradford was for some years the travelling companion of Mr. Wesley, for whom he would have sacrificed health and even life, but to whom his will would never bend, except in meekness. "Joseph," said Mr. Wesley, one day, "take these letters to the post." B. "I will take them after preaching, sir." W. "Take them now, Joseph." B. "I wish to hear you preach, sir; and there will be sufficient time for the post after service." W. "I insist upon your going now, Joseph." B. "I will not go at present." W. "You won't!" B. "No, sir." W. "Then you and I must part." B. "Very good, sir." The good men slept over it. Both were early risers. At four o'clock the next morning, the refractory helper was accosted with, "Joseph, have you considered what I said—that we must part?" B. "Yes, sir." W. "And must we part?" B. "Please yourself, sir." W. "Will you ask my pardon, Joseph?" B. "No, sir." W. "You won't?" B. "No, sir." W. "Then I will ask *yours*, Josepn." Poor Joseph was instantly melted; smitten as by the word of Moses, when forth gushed the tears, like the water from the rock. He had a tender soul; and it was soon observed when the appeal was made to the heart instead of the head.

92. Subdues Enmity and Leads to Conversion

(*a*) AN ANGRY MAN CONVERTED.—A man of my acquaintance, says Dr. Dwight, who was of a vehement and rigid temper, had, many years since, a dispute with a friend of his, a professor of religion, and had been injured by him. With strong feelings of resentment, he made him a visit, for the avowed purpose of quarrelling with him. He accordingly stated the nature and extent of the injury; and was preparing, as he afterwards confessed, to load him with a train of severe reproaches, when his friend cut him short by acknowledging, with the utmost readiness and frankness, the injustice of which he had been guilty; expressing his own regret for the wrong he had done, requesting his forgiveness, and proffering him ample compensation. He was compelled to say that he was satisfied, and withdrew, full of mortification that he had been precluded from venting his indignation, and wounding his friend with keen and violent reproaches for his conduct. As he was walking homeward, he said to himself to this effect: "There must be something more in religion than I have hitherto suspected. Were any man to address me in the tone of haughtiness and provocation with which I accosted my friend this morning, it would be impossible for me to preserve the equanimity of which I have been a witness, and especially with so much frankness, humility, and meekness, to acknowledge the wrong which I had done; so readily ask forgiveness of the man whom I had injured; and so cheerfully promise a satisfactory recompense. I should have met his anger with at least equal resentment, paid him reproach for reproach, and inflicted wound for wound. There is something in this man's disposition which is not in mine. There is something in the religion which he professes, and which I am forced to believe he feels; something which makes him so superior, so much better, so much more amiable, than I can pretend to be. The subject strikes me in a manner to which I have hitherto been a stranger. It is high time to examine it more thoroughly.

with more candor, and with greater solicitude also, than I have done hitherto."

From this incident a train of thoughts and emotions commenced in the mind of this man which terminated in his profession of the Christian religion, his relinquishment of the business in which he was engaged, and his consecration of himself to the ministry of the gospel."

(*b*) THE QUARRELSOME NEIGHBORS.—In a small country town in Massachusetts, there lived two wealthy farmers, whose lands adjoined each other. On some account or other, they became involved in a lawsuit, which both lessened their money, and promoted a spirit of rancor towards each other. After a time, one of these men was convinced of the sinfulness of his past conduct, when, yielding to the influence of the gospel, he became desirous of reconciliation and friendship with his neighbor. With a trembling heart he rapped at the door of the man he had offended, which he had not before entered for six years. Not suspecting who it was, his neighbor invited him in. He went in, took his seat, acknowledged that he had in the affair been much to blame, and entreated forgiveness. The other was much astonished; but maintained his high ground. "I always knew you were to blame, and I never shall forgive you," with much more to the same purpose, was the reply given to him. He again confessed his wrong, asked the pardon of his neighbor, expressed a hope that the Divine Being would forgive him; and added, "We have been actuated by a wrong spirit; and we shall be afraid to meet each other at the bar of God, where we must soon appear." The other became a little softened, and they parted.

The family, when left to themselves, were filled with astonishment. But the mystery was solved when they learned that their neighbor had become a follower of Christ. "What!" said the farmer, "is S— become a Christian? Why should he come and ask my forgiveness? If religion will humble such a man, it is surely a great thing. He said, 'We shall be afraid to meet each other at the bar of God.'" Such reflections as these, with a consciousness of his own ill conduct, occasioned him great distress for several days. At length, he could smother his feelings no longer—he took his hat, and went to see his once hated neighbor. As he entered the door he received a cordial welcome; they took each other by the hand, and burst into tears. He said, "You came to ask my forgiveness the other day, but I find I have been a thousand times worse than you." They retired and prayed together. They became members of the same church, and lived many years in uninterrupted harmony.

93. Heals Divisions and Promotes Revivals.

(*a*) DEACON P. AND SQUIRE M.—The following anecdote, says a correspondent of the Baptist Repository, occurred under the immediate observation of the writer:

A new settlement at the west, was visited by a powerful revival of religion, and most of the heads of families, with many of the youth, were hopefully converted to God; and in a vicinity where the name of Jesus was hardly known, unless in the way of blasphemy, but a short time before, a flourishing church was now organized, and the ordinances of the gospel instituted. A commodious house of worship was soon after erected, and a minister settled, and every thing bore evidence of the happy change with which the vicinity had been visited. Among the subjects of the recent work were two men, in the prime of life, both possessing considerable wealth and influence, upon whom the church principally depended. One of these, whom we shall call Mr. P. was appointed deacon, and the other, whom we shall denominate Squire M., with the assistance of the former, was appointed to manage the secular concerns of the society; and for the first two years things passed on prosperously, and to the mutual satisfaction of all, while the Lord appeared to pour out his blessing upon their efforts. At length, however, from some trifling cause, a coldness or jealousy arose between these two persons, who were regarded as pillars; and the church, aware of how much depended on their efforts, attempted to reconcile them. With regret, however, they saw their efforts unavailing, as their hardness towards each other continued to increase, till at length they broke out into an open quarrel. As their farms lay contiguous to each other, new causes of complaint were continually arising, of a domestic nature, till the church was finally constrained to interfere in their difficulties. This, however, instead of reconciling them, rather seemed to add fuel to the fire, till they were finally compelled to exclude them both from their fellowship. Being now freed from ecclesiastical restraint, they continued to carry on their quarrel in a more open manner, and lawsuit after lawsuit followed each other, till at length they both appeared to become weary of the contest, and for two succeeding years lived like the Jews and Samaritans, not deigning even to speak to each other.

The church, in the meantime, being deprived of their aid, fell into a low and desponding condition; and despairing of being able to support the preaching of the gospel any longer, dismissed their minister, and public worship was finally abandoned altogether.

About this time Deacon P. being at work alone in his field, began to reflect in a serious manner upon his condition, comparing it with what it had formerly been, when he was in fellowship with the church, and living in the line of duty. This was perhaps the first time in three years that he had commenced a candid and impartial examination of his own heart; and however he might have sought to justify his conduct before others, he now saw himself awfully guilty before God. Under a sense of conscious guilt he raised his eyes to heaven, and not only implored grace to enable him to see, but also to perform his duty. Having at length settled the question in his own mind, how often and wherein he had offended in the cause of difficulty before mentioned, he turned his eyes towards Squire M., who also was at work in a neighboring field, and soon came to the following resolution:—"If he has injured me, I will leave him in the hands of a merciful God; but I will go to him, and wherein I have injured him, I will fall upon my knees before him and ask his forgiveness." No sooner had he come to this resolution, than leaving the instrument with which he was employed, he sought the field where Squire M. was at work, and, to the astonishment of the latter, fell down before him, and besought his pardon. Squire M., though somewhat moved at the spectacle, at length replied very coldly, "I am very glad Mr. P. to see you finally sensible of your errors; and must tell you that it is no more than I have long expected. For seriously as you have injured me, I could never fully divest myself of the belief that you had once experienced religion, and therefore always concluded that the Lord would bring you some day or other to own your fault,—I forgive you, though I must tell you that I cannot altogether forget the manner in which you have treated me."

If Squire M. was less affected by his acknowledgment than was expected by the other, it did not disturb him; and he returned to his labor in a more tranquil state of mind than he had experienced in many a weary month. He continued his employment alternately weeping and rejoicing, till late in the afternoon; when happening to turn his eyes towards the field where Squire M. was at work, he saw him approaching; and as he came still nearer, what was his joy when he saw him bathed in a flood of tears. He came up to him, and after seizing his hand with a convulsive grasp, he fell upon his knees and exclaimed, "My much injured friend and brother, can you now forgive me?" After tenderly embracing each other, and weeping and exchanging forgiveness, they retired together to a secret place, and there poured out their united prayers before the throne of mercy. On the following Sabbath they went together to the house of God, and made an humble confession to the church from which they had been excluded, and were again restored to fellowship. This seemed to inspire their brethren with renewed confidence; their former pastor was recalled, public worship was again established, and heaven itself seemed to smile upon their efforts. An extensive revival soon followed, many precious souls were gathered in, and the two returning prodigals have since become, not only a help and comfort to each other, but a blessing to those with whom they are united.

(*b*) REV. MR. W. AND HIS CHURCH.—Difficulty having arisen in the Presbyterian church of R——, N. Y., between the pastor and the people, a council was called. Mr. W. made out charges of slander against five or six of his brethren, and procured his witnesses. They also made out charges against Mr. W. for his improper expressions concerning them. But the council, soon after its organization, decided, for certain reasons, that it was improper for them to act as a council in the case, and so dissolved. Thus the way to adjust the difficulties of the church seemed hedged up. Rev. Mr. L., of Auburn, now rose and delivered a solemn address to the church; and his address was followed by a moving scene. One of the brethren who was complained of by Mr. W. had been to Sherburne, to engage Rev. Mr. Truair, of that place, as an advocate. In that town God was pouring out his Spirit; and Mr. D. returned convicted of his errors. At this interesting moment he came forward, took his pastor by the hand, and made the most humble and melting confession of his faults. Mr. W. as frankly forgave him, and cordially embraced him as a friend and brother. No sooner had he done this than Mr. D. kneeled down and poured out his soul in an appropriate, humble, penitential prayer. Before he concluded, two-thirds of the audience were bathed in tears. He was followed by addresses and prayers from some of the council; and then another was ready to confess his faults, and then another, to the last of the accused; each one taking Mr. Walker by the hand, and receiving forgiveness. He in turn asked their forgiveness wherein he had expressed himself improperly towards them. Pardon was also asked of the church, and cheerfully granted. This opened the door for Mr. W.'s friends, who, one after another, confessed whatever they had said, in an unchristian manner, against the opposite party. Thus two whole days, with the exception of time occupied in hearing two sermons, was spent in mutual confession and forgiveness. Before the council separated they took the papers which contained the charges on both sides, held them up to the view of the audience, declared they were about to make a burnt sacrifice of them, and committed them to the flames. On the evening of the second day, a conference meeting was held, in which several were so deeply impressed as to ask for prayers. From that time a revival of religion commenced. The above facts occurred in R—— in 1819-20.

CONSCIENCE, POWER OF, WITH THE GUILTY.

94. In groundless Suspicions and Alarms.

(*a*) DRAWING A BOW AT A VENTURE.—A Christian minister, writing in 1834, states, that it had been long his practice previously to the commencement of the assizes, which were held in the town of his residence, to preach a sermon applicable to that solemn period. On one of these occasions, his text was 2 Cor. 5: 10: "For we must all appear before the judgment seat of Christ; that every one may receive the things done in his body, according to that he hath done, whether it be good or bad." A particular reference was made, in the course of the sermon, to the solemn proceedings of the judgment, that things done here in darkness would then be brought to light; and it was observed, "Perhaps there are some present this morning who have been engaged in some dark, dishonest transaction, which they suppose is altogether unknown, and will remain for ever concealed. Vain supposition! Let them know that, even *now*, every thing relative to that deed is fully exposed, and if unrepented of, will cover them with disgrace and confusion at the day of universal revelation; God will make their crimes to pass before them and set them in order before their eyes."

The next morning a gentleman called on him and requested a private interview, having something of importance to communicate. Having adjourned to a private apartment, he said, "My business with you, sir, is, I confess, singular, and must appear strange. The discourse you delivered last night has produced an extraordinary impression on Phebe T——. She sent for me early this morning, and most earnestly entreated me to wait upon you, and to intercede with you not to send the officers to apprehend her, for the purpose of conducting her to prison; and the only clue I can obtain from her to explain the cause of her excitement is, that 'you know it all.'"

It may be easily supposed that the minister was astonished at such a communication. The sentence in the sermon was an arrow from the bow drawn at a venture, but it was guided by a hand omniscient and powerful. He replied to his friend, that as he knew of nothing against the person in question, he was altogether at a loss to explain the agitation of her mind; but that he might assure her she should have no officers to trouble her. He also requested him to endeavor to find out the real cause of her distressful feelings.

Her subsequent statement of the case was this:—On a dark evening of one market-day, she had occasion to go out for some article of food, and, in her way, stumbled against something that lay in the road: she turned back for a light, and perceived it was a parcel of considerable size, dropped from a cart. She removed it to her apartment, and suffered it to remain for some time without making any inquiry respecting the owner, for she was unable to read. Curiosity excited her to acquaint herself with the contents of this parcel. She soon found it consisted of various articles of linen and woollen. Having, like Eve, looked and admired, she was tempted to take them for her own use; and, by degrees, the parcel was considerably diminished. No one knew but herself—except ONE, whose piercing eye strikes through the shades of night! and no one was likely to reproach her, except the vicegerent of the Almighty —her conscience!

Phebe T—— was convinced that she had acted wrong; but, as confession alone is insufficient without reparation, the next step was to find out the owner of the parcel, in order to its being restored to him. The direction soon discovered this, and the invoice forwarded with the goods helped to show the deficiency. In a short time the whole was made up, and forwarded to the owner, without the omission of a single article.

(*b*) "DID NOT HE SAY BEANS?" —Two travellers put up for the night at a tavern. Early in the morning they absconded without reckoning with their host, also stealing from him a bag of beans. A few years after they passed that road in company again. Again they asked for lodgings at the same inn. The identical landlord was yet at his post. In the evening the landlord was busy in one corner of the bar-room, talking in a suppressed voice with one of his neighbors, about a swarm of bees. His two dishonest guests were seated in another part of the room, and indistinctly hearing the talk about bees, one says to the other, "Did not he say beans?" "I think he did," was the reply; and quickly they were missing.

(*c*) A NIGHT WITH A DUELLIST.—A duel was fought near the city of Washington, under circumstances of peculiar atrocity. A distinguished individual challenged his relative who was once his friend. The challenged party having the choice of weapons, named muskets, to be loaded with buck-shot and slugs, and the distance ten paces; avowing at the same time his intention and desire that both parties should be destroyed. They fought. The challenger was killed on the spot; the murderer escaped unhurt! Years afterwards, a gentleman was spending the winter in Charleston, South Carolina, and lodged at the same house with this unhappy man. He was requested by the duellist one evening, to sleep in the same room with him, but he declined, as he was very well accommodated in his own. On his persisting in declining, the duellist confessed to him that HE WAS AFRAID TO SLEEP ALONE; and as a friend who usually occupied the room, was absent, he would esteem it a great favor if the gentleman would pass the night with him. His kindness being thus demanded, he consented, and retired to rest in the room with this man of fashion and honor, who some years before had stained his hands in the blood of a kinsman. After long tossing on his unquiet pillow and repeated half-stifled groans, that revealed the inward pangs of the murderer, he sank into slumber, and as he rolled from side to side, the name of his victim was often uttered, with broken words that discovered the keen remorse that preyed like fire on his conscience. Suddenly he would start up in his bed with the terrible impression that the avenger of blood was pursuing him; or hide himself under the covering as if he would escape the burning eye of an angry God, that gleamed in the darkness over him, like lightning from a thunder cloud! For him there was "no rest, day nor night." Conscience, armed with terrors, lashed him unceasingly, and who could sleep? And this was not the restlessness of disease, the raving of a disordered intellect, nor the anguish of a maniac struggling in chains! It was a man of intelligence, education, health, and affluence, given up to himself—not delivered over to the avenger of blood, to be tormented before his time; but left to the power of his own CONSCIENCE, suffering only what every one may suffer who is abandoned of God!

(*d*) LORENZO DOW AND THE THIEF.—The celebrated itinerant preacher, Lorenzo Dow, while travelling on Sunday to the place where he had an appointment to preach, in passing a house overheard a man who was standing at the door, swearing bitterly. Dow went up to him, and inquired the cause. The man answered that he had an axe stolen the night before by some person. "Come along with me to the meeting," said the preacher, "and I will find your axe." The man consented, and when they arrived near the church, Dow stopped and picked up a pretty large stone, which he carried with him into church, and laid upon the front of the pulpit. The subject of his sermon was very well fitted to his particular object, and when in the middle of it, he stopped short, took the stone in his hand, and raising with a threatening attitude, said "A man in this neighborhood had an axe stolen last night, and if the person who stole it doesn't dodge, *I will hit him on the forehead with this stone*," at the same time making a violent effort to throw it, when a person present was observed to dodge his head violently; and it scarce need be added, proved to be the guilty person!

(*e*) BESSUS AND THE BIRDS.—Bessus, a native of Pelonia, in Greece, being one day seen by his neighbors pulling down some birds' nests, and passionately destroying their young, was severely reproved by them for his ill-nature, and cruelty to those who seemed to court his protection. He replied, that their notes were to him insufferable, as they never ceased twitting him of the murder of his father.

95. In Confession and Reparation of Injuries.

(*a*) THE STOLEN SPOON RETURNED.—A well-dressed man called at the tavern of Mr. B., of W., New Hampshire, and asked the landlord whether he kept that house a year before. Mr. B. told him he did. Then, sir, said he, I want to speak to you aside. The tavern keeper followed the man into the farther part of his barn, when, with shame depicted in his face, and embarrassment in his manner, the stranger took from his pocket a silver spoon, and told him, that about a year before he breakfasted at his house, and stole the spoon he then held in his hand. That he, soon after committing the theft, mounted his horse and rode off; but had not gone far before he was strongly inclined to return and replace the spoon on the table; that fear of being seen prevented his doing it. He rode on, continually looking over his shoulder to see if an officer was not in pursuit of him. At length he alighted and buried the spoon under the bridge, thinking that by so doing he should escape detection, and the landlord would not be *much* injured by so small a theft. The man went home to Connecticut; but peace of mind he had lost, and could not find it again at home. After enduring mental torment for a whole year; he, "came to himself," and resolved to return to New Hampshire, and confess his fault, and make restitution. The landlord asked the penitent stranger if he was poor. He said he was not—that he possessed a large estate, and needed nothing this world afforded—that now the spoon was restored, he could breathe freely again, if the landlord would forgive him. The inn-keeper gave him his hand, and compelled him to come in and tarry at his house a night without expense.

(*b*) THE LONG DELAYED RESTITUTION.—The following remarkable instance of the force of conscience occurred, in 1835, in the neighborhood of London. A lady, about thirty-eight years of age, elegantly dressed, entered the shop of Mr. —, a respectable pastry cook, in a state of great mental excitement, and inquired if Mr. — were still alive. On being answered in the affirmative, she, in the most earnest manner, begged to see him. Being engaged in superintending the making of some confectionery, he begged to be excused, and referred her to his daughter, who, he said, would wait upon her. The daughter immediately withdrew with her into the parlor; when, after sitting a few moments in silence, she burst into a flood of tears. When she became more composed, she stated, that upwards of twenty years since, she was a boarder at a highly respectable boarding school in that neighborhood, which school Mr. — had for nearly forty years supplied with pastry, etc.; and while there, she was in the habit of abstracting small articles from his tray, unknown to the person who brought it. She had now been married some years, was the mother of six children, and in the possession of every comfort this world could afford; but still the remembrance of her youthful sin had so haunted her conscience, that she was never happy. Her husband perceiving her unhappiness, had, after many fruitless endeavors, at last got possession of the cause, when he advised her, for the easement of her conscience, to see if Mr. — were alive, and to make him or his family a recompense; and as she was going to leave London on the following day, perhaps for ever, she had then come for that purpose. Mr.—, on being informed of the object of her visit, told her not to make herself any longer unhappy, as she was not the only young lady who had acted in that manner. After begging his forgiveness, which he most readily granted, she insisted on his acceptance of a sum of money, which she said, she believed was about the value of the articles she had stolen; and after remaining about an hour, she departed, evidently much happier.

96. In Confession and Voluntary Submission to Punishment.

(*a*) THE JEWELLER AND HIS SERVANT.—A jeweller, a man of good character, and considerable wealth, having occasion, in the way of business, to travel some distance from his abode, took along with him a servant: he had with him some of his best jewels, and a large sum of money, to which his servant was likewise privy. The master having occasion to dismount on the road, the servant watched his opportunity, took a pistol from his master's saddle, and shot him dead on the spot; then, rifling him of his jewels and money, and hanging a large stone to his neck, he threw him into the nearest canal. With his booty he made off to a distant part of the country, where he had reason to believe that neither he nor his master were known. There he began to trade, in a very low way at first, that his obscurity might screen him from observation; and in the course of many years seemed to rise up, by the natural progress of business, into wealth and consideration; so that his good fortune appeared at once the effect of industry and the reward of virtue. Of these he counterfeited the appearance so well, that he grew into great credit, married into a good family, and, by laying out his hidden stores discreetly, as he saw occasion, and joining to all a universal affability, he was at length admitted to a share of the government of the town, and rose from one post to another, till at last he was chosen chief magistrate. In this office he maintained a fair character, and continued to fill it with no small applause, both as governor and judge; till one day, as he sat on the bench with some of his brethren, a criminal was brought before him who was accused of murdering his master. The evidence came out full; the jury brought in their verdict that the prisoner was guilty, and the whole assembly awaited the sentence of the president of the court (which happened to be himself) in great suspense. Meanwhile he appeared to be in unusual disorder and agitation of mind; his color changed often; at length he arose from his seat, and, coming down from the bench, placed himself just by the unfortunate man at the bar, to the no small astonishment of all present. "You see before you," said he, addressing himself to those who had sat on the bench with him, "a striking instance of the just awards of Heaven, for this day, after thirty years' concealment, presents to you a greater criminal than the man just now found guilty." He then made an ample confession of his heinous offence, with all its peculiar aggravations. "Nor can I," continued he, "feel any relief from the agonies of an awakened conscience, but by requiring that justice be forthwith done against me in the most public and solemn manner." We may easily imagine the amazement of all, especially his fellow-judges. They accordingly proceeded upon his confession, to pass sentence upon him, and he died with all the symptoms of a penitent mind.

(*b*) THE PARRICIDE AND HER HUSBAND.—A man and his wife were executed at Augsburg for a murder, the discovery of which, after a long lapse of time, strongly manifests the impossibility of eluding the all-seeing eye of Providence. The criminal, whose name was Wincze, was originally of Nuremberg, but removed to Augsburg in 1788, where he became a lawyer. In this city he became intimate in the family of M. Glegg, to whose daughter he paid his addresses; but the old gentleman not sanctioning his visits, he met the daughter privately, seduced her, and persuaded her, in order to remove the only obstacle to their union, to administer poison to her father. The horrid plan succeeded; no suspicions were entertained, and their union put him in possession of the old man's wealth. During a period of twenty-one years they lived externally happy, but, in secret, a prey to the greatest remorse. At length, unable to endure any longer the weight of guilt, the wife made confession of the particulars of the atrocious crime which she had been prevailed upon to commit. The husband was apprehended, and both of them received their desert in an ignominious death.

(*c*) THE MURDERER'S REMORSE.—One Sunday evening, says the Frederictown, Md., Expositor, of 1831, a man, who called himself Daniel Shafer, voluntarily came before Michael Baltsell, a magistrate of this city, and requested to be committed to prison, alleging that he had committed a murder during the last winter, in Marietta, Penn.; and that the reproaches of his conscience had become so severe, that he was unable any longer to endure them. His narrative being perfectly coherent, and he himself appearing entirely sane, the magistrate complied with his request and committed him. Since that time, under his direction, communication has been made with the proper authorities in Marietta, and such intelligence received as confirms the horrid tale. His story is, that during the deep snow of last winter, while in a state of intoxication, he entered the house of a widow named Bowers, then living in Marietta, and after violating her person, put her to death by strangling her. The fact of such a person being found dead in her house, about the time stated, is fully substantiated by the accounts received from Marietta; and the whole demeanor of the prisoner since his confinement, as well as his positive declarations, has induced a general belief in the truth of his singular confession.

97. Miscellaneous Examples.

(*a*) MRS. RAMSAY AND THE ROBBERS.—The Rev. Mr. Ramsay, a Methodist clergyman, was wholly dependent for his living on the quarterly collection made by his people, which was barely sufficient, by the greatest economy, to support his family. On the night that one of these collections was taken up, he was obliged to preach six miles distant from his home, and the night was too stormy to allow of his return. During the night, two robbers broke into his house, called up Mrs. Ramsay and her sister, (there were no men living in the house,) and demanded to know where the money was. Mrs. R., in her night dress, lit the candle, and leading the way to the bureau that contained the precious deposit, procured the key, opened the drawer, and pointing out the money as it lay in a handkerchief, said, "This is all we have to live on. It is the Lord's money. Yet, if you *will* take it, there it is." With this remark, she left them, and retired to bed. The next morning, the money, to a cent, was found undisturbed. *Conscience* here was appealed to, and with happy results.

(*b*) THE LUNATIC DUELLIST.—"Some years since," says Dr. Beecher, "I visited the Philadelphia Asylum. In returning from the apartments, I saw a man standing—fixed—immovable—like a pillar. I asked who that was. It was the son of Dr. Rush, who killed a man in a duel. There he stood like a pillar. Sometimes he would wake up to recollection; he would pace off the distance, and give the word 'Fire!' Then cry out, 'He is dead!—he is dead!' This was the power of conscience. It had unsettled reason."

(*c*) DYING FROM REMORSE.—"In my early ministry," says Dr. Beecher, "I was called to attend a neighbor at East Hampton, Long Island. He was skeptical and intemperate. 'Pray for me,' he exclaimed, 'pray for me!—pray for me!' 'You must pray for yourself,' I replied. 'Pray—I cannot pray! I am going straight to perdition!' He lived three days almost without food, and then died—so far as we know—*without any disease*." It was the power of conscience.

(*d*) THE PARRICIDE AND THE PAINTING.—The cruel Al Montaser, having assassinated his father, was afterwards haunted by remorse. As he was one day admiring a beautiful painting of a man on horseback, with a diadem encircling his head, and a Persian inscription, of which he inquired the meaning, he was told that it signified—'I am Shiunyeh, the son of Kosru, who murdered my father, and possessed the crown only six months!'—He turned pale, as if struck by a sentence of death. Frightful dreams interrupted his slumbers, and he died at the early age of twenty-five.

CONSCIENTIOUSNESS.

98. Conscientiousness, Examples of.

(*a*) ROBBING ONE OR ROBBING MANY.—A boy about nine years of age, who attended a Sabbath school at Sunderland, requested his mother not to allow his brother to bring home any thing that was smuggled when he went to sea. "Why do you wish that, my child?" said the mother. He answered, "because my catechism says it is wrong." The mother replied, "But that is only the word of a man." He said, "Mother, is it the word of a man which said, 'Render unto Cæsar the things that are Cæsar's?'" This reply entirely silenced the mother; but his father, still attempting to defend the practice of smuggling, the boy said to him, "Father, whether is it worse to rob one or to rob many ?" By these questions and answers, the boy silenced both his parents on the subject of smuggling.

(*b*) BETTER RULE THAN EXPEDIENCY.—Lord Erskine, when at the bar, was always remarkable for the fearlessness with which he contended against the bench. In a contest he had with Lord Kenyon, he explained the rule and conduct at the bar in the following terms: "It was," said he, "the first command and counsel of my youth, always to do what my conscience told me to be my duty, and leave the consequences to God. I have hitherto followed it, and have no reason to complain that any obedience to it has been even a temporal sacrifice; I have found it, on the contrary, the road to prosperity and wealth, and I shall point it out as such to my children."

(*c*) THE GROCER BOY'S DECISION.—A young lad lived in Boston in 1843, whose mother was a widow, and supported herself by her work and the wages of her son, who was tending the grocery of one who sold ardent spirits. The little fellow had joined the cold water army; and his business of attending the tap-room, and drawing liquors for every loathsome drunkard became in consequence extremely irksome to him. He thought it was not right; he went home one night with a sorrowful heart, and told his mother he thought he was doing wrong, and believed he must quit the grocery. His mother told him that she could not pay her rent and support the little children, without the two dollars a week which he earned; and that he could get no other place. So he went back; but when Saturday night came, he told the grocer he must leave him. "Why?" "I can't feel it right to draw the liquor." "Well," said the grocer, "you and your mother will starve; but you may go." He went home with a heavy heart, and told his mother; and she felt wretchedly enough. But a temperance grocer heard of the case; and on account of the boy's leaving the rum grocer under such circumstances, he became deeply interested in his behalf. He admired the strength of his moral feelings, and accordingly took him into his own employment the next week.

(*d*) THE PUBLISHER CONVERTED.—T—— B——, a publisher, was brought under deep conviction for sin. His conscience reproved him severely, for he was a printer and vender of songs, and similar hurtful trash, in a very large way. On this business he principally depended for the support of himself and his family.

His employment in circulating such injurious publications caused him much trouble, and he consulted some Christian friends, who all advised him to relinquish such a business.

On this subject he afterwards wrote to some friends as follows:—"The great adversary of souls seemed to have much power over me. I thought, if I give up the song business, I might as well give up all, for I shall be sure to be ruined. These were my feelings for three or four months. At length, my sister came to visit me, to whom I made known my distress, and she recommended me to pray. Though I had heard much from the pulpit respecting prayer, it had never taken so much effect as at this time. However, Satan had not done with me; for I may suppose, and have often thought since, he did not like to lose so great a friend as I had been to him, in circulating my trash all over the country; but the Lord, who is sufficient for all things, soon trod him under foot. Having given up a portion of my time, three and sometimes four times a day, to prayer, I shortly after heard a funeral sermon preached from this text, 'What shall it profit a man, if he shall gain the whole world, and lose his own soul? or what can a man give in exchange for his soul?' These words came to my heart with such force, that I determined from that moment never to print any more of my songs. The next morning I went to my work-room, and ordered all the forms of type to be distributed, as I intended never to print any more songs, but to trust to Providence for better means to provide for my family. My mind then seemed relieved from all trouble for a few days: but the constant applications I had from the country for my songs, and the money I was obliged to return, gave me great uneasiness. But the Lord was pleased to give me courage and perseverance to bear up amidst all those trials, and still to look to him for comfort and support, so that in a short time all those angry feelings wore off; and now, if my heart does not deceive me, I feel at peace with that God I so long lived in rebellion against."

(*e*) THE CHIEFS AND THE FILE.—Since the introduction of Christianity into the island of Taheiti, many interesting proofs have been given by the natives, of conscientious principles. Formerly, thieving was considered no crime; but such has been the effect of Christian instruction, that now the very reverse is exemplified. Mr. Ellis mentions the following circumstance, which happened shortly before his arrival there:—

Two Christian chiefs, Tati and Ahuriro, were walking together by the water side, when they came to a place where a fisherman had been employed in making or sharpening hooks, and had left a large file, (a valuable article in Taheiti.) lying on the ground. The chiefs picked it up; and, as they were proceeding, one said to the other, "This is not ours. Is not our taking it a species of theft?" "Perhaps it is," replied the other, "yet, as the owner is not here, I do not know who has a greater right to it than ourselves." "It is not ours," said the former, "and we had better give it away." After further conversation they agreed to give it to the first person they met, which they did, telling him they had found it, and requested that if he heard who had lost such a thing, he would restore it.

(*f*) THE INDIAN AND THE QUARTER OF A DOLLAR.—An Indian, visiting his white neighbors, asked for a little tobacco to smoke, and one of them having some loose in his pocket, gave him a handful. The day following, the Indian came back, inquiring for the donor, saying, he had found a quarter of a dollar among the tobacco. Being told, that as it was given him, he might as well keep it, he answered, pointing to his breast, "I got a good man and a bad man here; and the good man say, it is not mine, I must return it to the owner; the bad man say, why he gave it you, and it is your own now; the good man say, that not right, the tobacco is yours, not the money; the bad man say, never mind, you got it, go buy some dram; the good man say, no, no, you must not do so; so I don't know what to do; and I think to go to sleep; but the good man and the bad kept talking all night, and trouble me; and now I bring the money back, I feel good."

(*g*) ADAM CLARKE'S EARLY SCRUPLES.—A very respectable linen merchant in Coleraine offered Dr. Clarke, when a youth, a situation in his warehouse, which was accepted by him, with the consent of his parents. Mr. B— knew well that his clerk and overseer was a religious man, but he was not sensible of the extent of principle which actuated him. Some differences arose at times about the way of conducting the business, which were settled pretty amicably. But the time of the great Dublin market approached, and Mr. B— was busy preparing for it. The master and man were together in the folding-room, when one of the pieces was found short of the required number of yards. "Come," says Mr. B—, "it is but a trifle. We shall soon stretch it, and make out the yard. Come, Adam, take one end, and pull against me." Adam had neither ears nor heart for the proposal, and absolutely refused to do what he thought a dishonest thing. A long argument and expostulation followed, in which the usages of the trade were strongly and variously enforced; but all in vain. Adam kept to his purpose, resolving to suffer rather than sin. Mr. B— was therefore obliged to call for one of his men less scrupulous, and Adam retired quietly to his desk. These things may be counted little in the life of such a man, but not so in the sight of God. Soon after Mr. B—, in the kindest manner, informed his "young friend," as he seemed always proud to call him, that it was very clear he was not fit for worldly business, and wished him to look out for some employment more congenial to his own mind; adding, that he might depend on his friendship in any line of life into which he should enter.

(*h*) THE QUAKER'S ADVERTISEMENT.—The following account of a Quaker at Falmouth, England, is taken from McDonald's Life of the Rev. J. Benson. It was related by Mr. Woolcraft:

This man, unknown to his family and friends, had joined with some others in fitting out a privateer to act against the French, who had allied themselves to the American States while in arms against Great Britain. The privateer was successful, and when peace was concluded, there was a considerable dividend for the proprietors. The Quaker received his share among the rest; but his conscience reproached him for what he had done. He considered himself guilty of robbery. About this time he was brought by affliction to the gates of death, which greatly increased his distress. He frequently exclaimed, "Oh, that ill-gotten money!" Neither his wife nor friends knew what he meant. At length he resolved, that should the Lord raise him up, he would make restitution to the injured parties, if they could be found. The Lord did raise him up, and he sent his son to Paris with the sum, directing him to advertise in the Paris Gazette, that any person who had suffered by such a privateer, upon coming and proving his losses, would be refunded in proportion to his share in the prizes. This was accordingly done, to the astonishment of all France.

99. Conscientiousness, Want of.

(*a*) WE MUST LIVE.—That was a pertinent and emphatical reply which a Fellow of Emanuel College, in Cambridge, made to a friend of his of the same college. The latter, at the Restoration, had been representing the great difficulties (as they seemed to him) of conformity in point of conscience, concluding, however, with these words, "But we must live." To which the other answered only with the like number of words, "But we must (also) die." A better answer could not possibly be given.

(*b*) A NICK IN THE CONSCIENCE.—When Mr. Nathaniel Heywood, a nonconformist minister, was quitting his living, a poor man came to him, and said, "Ah! Mr. Heywood, we would gladly have you preach still in the church." "Yes," said he, "and I would as gladly preach as you can desire it, if I could do it with a safe conscience." "Oh! sir," replied the other, "many a man now-a-days makes a great gash in his conscience; cannot you make a little nick in yours?"

(*c*) AN APT REJOINDER.—An American minister, who was earnestly exhorted to take a decided stand on the subject of slavery, excused himself by saying, "You know ministers must *live!*" "No," said his friend, "I was not aware of that; I thought they might *die* for the truth's sake!"

100. CONSECRATION TO GOD.

(*a*) THE MINISTER AND THE MERCHANT.—A merchant in one of the towns of the State of New York, says Mr. Finney, was paying a large part of his minister's salary. One of the members of the church was relating the fact to a minister from abroad, and speaking of the *sacrifice* which this merchant was making. At this moment the merchant came in. "Brother," said the minister, "you are a merchant. I suppose you employ a clerk to sell goods, and schoolmasters to teach your children. You order your clerk to pay your schoolmaster out of the store such an amount, for his services in teaching. Now suppose your clerk should give out that *he* had to pay this schoolmaster his salary, and should speak of the sacrifices that he was making to do it, what would you say to this?" "Why," said the merchant, "I should say it was ridiculous." "Well," says the minister, "God employs you to sell goods as his clerk, and your minister he employs to teach his children, and requires you to pay his salary out of the income of the store. Now do you call this *your* sacrifice, and say that *you* are making a great sacrifice, to pay this minister's salary? No, you are just as much bound to sell for God, as he is to preach for God. You have no more right to sell goods for the purpose of laying up money, than he has to preach the Gospel for the same purpose. You are bound to be just as pious, and to aim *as singly* at the glory of God, in selling goods, as he is in preaching the gospel. And thus you are as absolutely to give up your whole time for the service of God, as he does. You and your family may live fully out of the avails of this store, and so may the minister and his family, just as lawfully. If you sell goods from these motives, selling goods is just as much serving God as preaching. And a man who sells goods upon these principles, and acts in conformity to them, is just as pious, just as much in the service of God, as he is who preaches the Gospel. Every man is bound to serve God *in his calling*. the minister by teaching, the merchant by selling goods, the farmer by tilling his fields, and the lawyer and physician by plying the duties of their profession."

(*b*) THE POOR NEGRESS'S DEPOSIT.—A colored woman of Barbadoes, who had been a member of the Moravian church for more than half a century, gave to her pastor a small sum of money, to be returned to her whenever she should want it. When he relinquished his charge, he transferred the deposit to his successor, Mr. Hartvig. The latter perceiving that the poor woman was evidently in want of pecuniary aid, informed her that he had money in his possession which belonged to her. At first she could not believe him; the remembrance of the deposit had apparently faded from her mind. She finally consented to receive enough for her immediate necessities; but Mr. Hartvig wished to know what should be done with the remainder, in case of her death. Her answer was, "*O me belong to the church and me money too!*" There is a volume of instruction in this simple reply. How few Christians seem to feel, that they have given their property, as well as themselves, to the Lord Jesus Christ!

(*c*) THE YOUNG MAN'S GIFT.—Mr. Daniel Clark, an agent employed by a Bible Society, among other interesting facts, related the following, as illustrative of the zeal he met with in the distribution of the Scriptures.

"A young man, who had nothing except what he earned by his labor, came to me, bringing a donation of eight dollars. He said it was the Lord's and he had no right to withhold it. He added, "When I gave myself to God, I also gave him all I had, and all I ever should have. And now the Lord is not dependent upon me. If I do not give it he can easily remove me, and put it into the hands of some one who will give it."

101. CONSISTENCY, CHRISTIAN.

(*a*) "MY MOTHER BELIEVES THE BIBLE."—The son of Selina, the Countess of Huntingdon, whose zeal in the extension of the gospel is well known, was unhappily an unbeliever, but reverenced his pious and venerable mother. "I wish," said a peer to him, "you would speak to Lady Huntingdon; she has just erected a preaching place close to my residence." His lordship replied, "Gladly, my lord; but you will do me the favor to inform me what plea to urge, for my mother really believes the Bible."

(*b*) THE PRINCE'S TRIBUTE.—When Lady Huntingdon became the subject of Divine grace, her change of mind was soon observed by her exalted associates, who endeavored in vain to turn her aside from the path she had chosen. One day at court, the then Prince of Wales asked Lady Charlotte E—, "Where is my Lady Huntingdon, that she is so seldom here?" The lady of fashion replied, with a sneer, "I suppose praying with her beggars." The prince shook his head, and said, "Lady Charlotte, when I am dying, I think I shall be happy to seize the skirt of Lady Huntingdon's mantle, to carry me up with her to heaven."

(*c*) THE DYING MASTER AND HIS SLAVE.—The conscience of the sinner, when aroused, not only accuses himself but his accomplices also. A rich Southern gentleman, careless about his soul, used often to invite his minister, a worldly man and a mere hireling, to hunt, drink wine, play cards, and join parties of pleasure with him.

The poor worldling was taken sick, and his case was pronounced dangerous. His mind was terribly agitated;—he felt unprepared to die. His physician asked him, one day, if he would not send for his minister to converse with him, and offer prayer in his behalf? No, he had no confidence in him: he could hardly bear the mention of his name. He had a poor pious negro servant, by the name of Ben. The master had sometimes overheard him at prayer. "Call for *Ben!*" said he. He came. "Ben," said the dying man, "can't you pray for your poor master?" Down he fell on his knees, and pleaded for the salvation of the sinner's soul; and the prayer, we hope, was answered.

(*d*) THE COVETOUS MAN'S PRAYERS.—About eight years since, (says a correspondent of the N. Y. Evangelist of 1833,) in obtaining subscriptions for a benevolent purpose, I called upon a gentleman in one of our largest cities, who generously contributed to the object. Before leaving, I said to him, "How much, think you, will such an individual subscribe?" "I don't know," said he, "but could you hear that man pray, you would think he would give you all he is worth." I called upon him, but to my surprise, he would not contribute. As I was about to take my leave of him, I said to him, "As I came to your house, I asked an individual what he thought you would probably give. 'I don't know,' said he, 'but could you hear that man pray, you would think he would give you all he is worth.'" The man's head dropped, tears gushed from his eyes, he took out his pocket-book and gave me seventy-five dollars. He could not withstand this argument. His heart relented and his purse opened.

(*e*) THE WAY TO PRESERVE CHURCHES.—The first time I had the pleasure of being in the company of the Rev. John Wesley, (says a correspondent of the N. Y. Evangelist,) was in the year 1783. I asked him what must be done to keep Methodism alive when he was dead, to which he immediately answered,—"The Methodists must take heed to their Doctrine, their Experience, their Practice, and their Discipline. If they attend to their doctrines *only*, they will make the people *Antinomians;* if to the experimental part of religion *only*, they will make them *Enthusiasts;* if to the practical part *only*, they will make them *Pharisees;* and if they do not attend to their discipline, they will be like persons who bestow much pains in cultivating their garden, and put no fence round it, to save it from the wild boar of the forest."

(*f*) INFLUENCE OF HOLY LIVING.—In the town of M——, N. Y., there lived an infidel who owned a saw-mill, situated by the side of the highway, over which a large portion of a Christian congregation passed every Sabbath, in going to and returning from their place of worship. This infidel was accustomed to manage his mill himself, and having no regard for the Sabbath, he was as busy and his mill as noisy on that holy morning as any other. It was soon observed, however, that at a certain time before service this mill would stop and remain silent, and appear to be destitute of the presence of any human being for a few minutes, then pass on with its noise and clatter till about the close of service, when it again ceased for a little time. It was soon noticed that Deacon B—— passed the mill toward the place of worship, during the silent interval. It appeared that the Deacon being (as all other *good* deacons are) *regular* in his

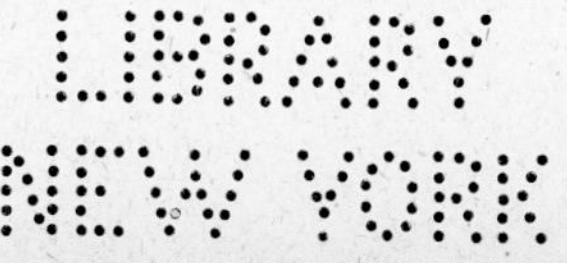

time, the infidel knew just when to stop his mill, so that it should be silent while Deacon B—— was passing, although he paid no regard to the passing of others. On being inquired of, why he paid this marked respect to Deacon B——, the infidel replied, "The Deacon professes just what the rest of you do but he *lives* also such a life, that it makes me feel bad *here*" (putting his hand upon his heart) "to run my mill while he is passing."

102. CONSIDERATION.

(*a*) SPENDING HALF AN HOUR ALONE.—A pious and venerable father had a vain and profligate son; often had he reasoned and expostulated with him, mingling tenderness with advice, and tears with remonstrance; but all was ineffectual. Bad company and vicious habits rendered the unhappy youth deaf to instructions. At last a fatal disorder seized his aged parent, who calling his son to him, entreated him with his dying breath, that he would grant him one small favor, the promise of which would alleviate the pangs of dissolving nature. It was this,—that his son would retire to his chamber half an hour every day for some months after his decease. He prescribed no particular subject to employ his thoughts, but left that to himself.

A request so simple and easy, urged by parental affection from the couch of death, was not to be denied. The youth pledged his honor for the fulfilment of his promise; and, when he became an orphan, punctually performed it. At first, he was not disposed to improve the minutes of solitude, but in time various reflections arose in his mind; the world was withdrawn; his conscience awoke; it reproved him for having slighted a parent who had done so much for his welfare; it renewed the impression of his dying scene; it gradually pointed him to a supreme Cause, a future judgment, and a solemn eternity. God was pleased to sanctify these solitary moments, and to strengthen his convictions. Retirement effected what advice could not do, and a real and permanent change took place. He quitted his companions, and reformed his conduct; virtue and piety filled up the rest of his days, and stamped sincerity on his repentance. To say all in a word—he lived and died a Christian.

103. CONTENTMENT.

(*a*) CATO AND MARIUS CURIUS.—Cato, a pattern of moderation, was very early taught the happy art of contentment, by the following circumstance:—Near his country seat was a cottage, formerly belonging to Marius Curius, who was thrice honored with a triumph. Cato often walked thither, and reflecting on the smallness of the farm and the meanness of the dwelling, used to meditate on the peculiar virtues of the man, who, though he was the most illustrious character in Rome, had subdued the fiercest nations, and driven Pyrrhus out of Italy, cultivated this little spot of ground with his own hands, and, after three triumphs, retired to his own cottage. Here the ambassadors of the Samnites found him in the chimney-corner dressing turnips, and offered him a large present of gold; but he absolutely refused it, remarking, "A man, who can be satisfied with such a supper, has no need of gold: and I think it more glorious to conquer the possessors of it, than to possess it myself." Full of these thoughts, Cato returned home; and taking a view of his own estate, his servants, and his manner of life, increased his labor, and retrenched his expenses.

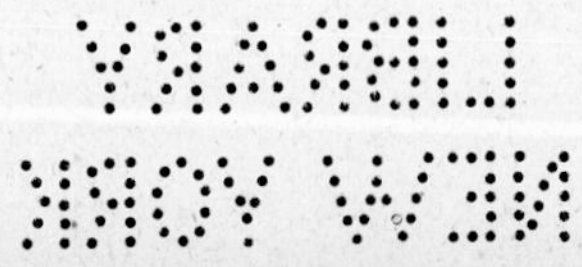

(*b*) HUNTING CONTENT.—Isaac Walton, himself a man of a very cheerful, contented spirit, relates the following anecdote:—

I knew a man that had health and riches, and several houses, all beautiful and well furnished, and would be often troubling himself and his family to remove from one of them to another. On being asked by a friend, why he removed so often from one house to another, he replied, "It was in order to find content in some of them." But his friend, knowing his temper, told him, if he would find content in any of his houses, he must leave himself behind, for content can never dwell but with a meek and quiet soul.

(*c*) THE KING'S ADVICE TO THE STABLE-BOY.—A king, walking out one morning, met a lad at the stable door, and asked him, "Well boy, what do you do? what do they pay you?" "I help in the stable," replied the lad; "but I have nothing except victuals and clothes." "Be content," replied the king, "I have no more." All that the richest possess beyond food, raiment, and habitation, they have but the keeping, or the disposing, not the present enjoyment of. A plough-boy, who thinks and feels correctly, has enough to make him contented: and if a king have a discontented spirit, he will find some plea for indulging it.

(*d*) THE SECRET REVEALED.—An Italian bishop struggled through great difficulties, without repining or betraying the least impatience. One of his intimate friends, who highly admired the virtues which he thought it impossible to imitate, one day asked the prelate if he could communicate the secret of being always easy. "Yes," replied the old man; "I can teach you my secret with great facility; it consists in nothing more than making a right use of my eyes." His friend begged of him to explain himself. "Most willingly," returned the bishop. "In whatever state I am, I first of all look up to heaven, and remember that my principal business here is to get there; I then look down upon the earth, and call to mind how small a place I shall occupy in it, when I die and am buried; I then look abroad into the world, and observe what multitudes there are who are in all respects more unhappy than myself. Thus I learn where true happiness is placed; where all our cares must end; and what little reason I have to repine or to complain.

(*e*) TWO SORTS OF BLESSINGS.—"It is a great blessing to possess what one wishes," said some one to an ancient philosopher, who replied, "It is a greater blessing still, not to desire what one does not possess."

(*f*) THE SHEPHERD OF SALISBURY PLAIN.—Many of our readers are acquainted with that beautiful tract, "The Shepherd of Salisbury Plain." The substance of this narrative is a correct account of David Saunders, of West Lavington, who died about the period of its publication. The conversation represented as passing between the shepherd and a Mr. Johnson, really took place with Dr. Stonehouse, a neighboring clergyman, who afterwards befriended the shepherd on many occasions.

Dr. Stonehouse, who was on a journey, and somewhat fearful, from the appearance of the sky, that rain was at no great distance, accosted the shepherd with asking what sort of weather he thought it would be on the morrow. "It will be such weather as pleases me," answered the shepherd. Though the answer was delivered in the mildest and civilest tone that could be imagined, Dr. S. thought the words themselves rather rude and surly, and asked him how that could be. "Because," replied the shepherd, "it will be such weather as shall please God; and whatever pleases him always pleases me."

Dr. S. was quite satisfied with this reply, and entered into conversation with the shepherd in the following manner:—"Yours is a troublesome life, honest friend." "To be sure, sir," replied the shepherd, "'tis not a very lazy life; but 'tis not near so toilsome, as that which my great Master led for my sake, and he had every state and condition of life at his choice, and chose a hard one, while I only submit to the lot that is appointed me." "You are exposed to great cold and heat," said the gentleman. "True, sir," said the shepherd; "but when I am not exposed to great temptations; and so throwing one thing against another, God is pleased to contrive to make things more equal than we poor, ignorant, short-sighted creatures are apt to think. David was happier when he kept his father's sheep, on such a plain as this, and singing, some of his own psalms, perhaps, than ever he was when he became king of Israel and Judah."

"You think, then," said the gentleman, "that a laborious life is a happy one?"

"I do, sir; and more especially so, as it exposes a man to fewer sins. If king Saul had continued a poor laborious man to the end of his days, he might have lived happy and honest, and died a natural death in his bed at last, which you know, sir, was more than he did."

God blessed Saunders with an excellent wife and numerous offspring; he had sixteen children, and twelve of them, at one time, were "like olive branches round his table." It is not to be supposed that a poor shepherd, with such a family, could be without difficulties, especially as his wife suffered much from sickness.

His wages were but 6*s.* 3*d.* weekly, out of which he was sometimes obliged to pay a boy for assistance; but when times of peculiar necessity occurred, God always raised him up a friend. Dr. (afterwards Sir James) Stonehouse repeatedly assisted him; and sometimes his good neighbors, in humbler life, united to supply his wants. In one of his letters in his old age, he thus writes, with much Christian simplicity:—"As for my part I am but very poorly in body, having very sore legs, and cannot perform the business of my flock without help. As to the things of this world, I have but little share; having my little cot to pray and praise God in, and a bed to rest on: so I have just as much of this world as I desire. But my garment is worn out, and some of my Christian friends think they must put their mites together and buy me one, or else I shall not be able to endure the cold in the winter: so I can say, Good is the Lord! He is still fulfilling his promise, 'I will never leave thee, nor forsake thee.'"

104. CONTROVERSY.

(*a*) EUDAMIDES AND XENOCRATES.—When Eudamides heard old Xenocrates disputing so long about wisdom, he inquired very gravely but archly, "If the old man be yet disputing and inquiring concerning wisdom, what time will he have left to use it?"

(*b*) LUTHER'S PRAYER.—Controversy may be sometimes needful: but the love of disputation is a serious evil. Luther, who contended earnestly for the truth, used to pray: "From a vainglorious doctor, a contentious pastor, and nice questions, the Lord deliver his church!"

(*c*) MELANCTHON AND HIS MOTHER.—Philip Melancthon, being at the conferences at Spire, in 1529, made a little journey to Bretten, to see his mother. This good woman asked him what she must believe amidst so many disputes, and repeated to him her prayers, which contained nothing superstitious. "Go on, mother," said he, "to believe and pray as you have done, and never trouble yourself about religious controversies."

(*d*) DR. SWIFT'S COOLNESS.—When Dr. Swift was arguing one day with great coolness, with a gentleman who had become exceedingly warm in the dispute, one of the company asked him how he could keep his temper so well. "The reason is," replied the dean, "I have truth on my side."

(*e*) NEWTON'S ADVICE TO AN AUTHOR.—Mr. Newton, of London, was a very candid and friendly critic, and was often applied to by young authors for his opinions and remarks, which he would give very candidly, and sometimes under the name of Nibblings. On one of these occasions a practical essay was put into his hand, which he approved; but a letter was appended, addressed to an obscure and contemptible writer, who had said very unwarrantable and absurd things on the subject, and whom therefore the writer attacked with little ceremony. The following is a specimen of some of Mr. Newton's nibblings:—"Were the affair mine, I would take no notice of Mr. ——; but, if I did, it should be with the hope, at least with the desire, of doing good, even to him. This would make me avoid every harsh epithet. He is not likely to be benefited by calling him a fool. The evangelists simply relate what is said and done, and use no bitterness nor severity, even when speaking of Herod, Pilate, or Judas. I wish their manner was more adopted in controversy."

(*f*) THE DEBATING CHURCH.—In the township of Minerva, once flourished a delightful society known for some years as the church of Edessa. It was a congregation of about a hundred and twenty strong, and included sixteen households, besides members of other families. These sixteen families were indeed generally exemplary, but a few of them were known through all the country as houses of prayer and sacred song.

Things progressed most prosperously in this way for some five or six years, and all was peace and brotherly kindness among themselves, while their acts of benevolence, to those without, especially to the destitute and afflicted, won the esteem and admiration of all the surrounding community.

But at length appeared among them a brother from Newfoundland, of good moral reputation and of very respectable attainments. He was well received by the whole church, and for some time they were all exceedingly happy in his company. But, being called upon one afternooon for an address at a prayer meeting, in a place where a number of brethren were wont to convene for cultivating piety and a more perfect acquaintance with the Book of God, he introduced a favorite speculation on the extent of our present and future participation in the sin of Adam; and on the nature and extent of that depravity which has been communicated to all his posterity. Question after question arose about moral evil, its introduction into the universe, and God's designs and provisions, until the prayer meeting became rather a debating club: for there were three young men who took sides with their strange brother, while some of the elder brethren sought to correct some of their alleged aberrations, and to reclaim them from these unprofitable speculations. But their efforts did not avail.

It got into the congregation; and through their inexperience in such matters, both sides of these questions found favor with the different members of the church; and in a little time these opinions were on every one's tongue. Songs and social prayers and works of benevolence were laid aside, and theological debate drank up their energies, and absorbed their thoughts. Alienation of feeling and declension in piety were more and more apparent; and it must have been many years before the blighting influence of their conflicts passed away.

(*g*) WAY TO DISCERN WHO IS WRONG IN ARGUMENT.—A cobbler at Leyden, who used to attend the public disputations held at the academy, was once asked if he understood Latin. "No," replied the mechanic, "but I know who is wrong in the argument." "How?" replied his friend. "Why, by seeing who is angry first."

(*h*) DR. GILL NOT AFRAID TO BE POOR.—After Dr. Gill had written against a gentleman whose publications he considered erroneous, he was waited on by some of his friends, who endeavored to dissuade him from persevering, and among other things, they intimated to him that he might lose the subscriptions of some wealthy persons. "Do not tell me of losing," said the doctor; "I value nothing in comparison with the gospel. I am not afraid to be poor."

105. CONVERSATION BETWEEN CHRISTIANS.

(*a*) WOULD DAVID OR PAUL HAVE TALKED THUS?—It is said of the Rev. John Janeway, an eminently pious and devoted young minister, who died in 1657, that he was greatly distressed on account of the indisposition manifested among Christians to engage in suitable conversation; and that they who should be found encouraging one another in the way to eternal happiness, could satisfy themselves with empty, common, vain stuff; as if Christ, heaven, and eternity, were not of far greater worth than any thing else that usually sounds in the ears and comes from the lips of professors. That the folly of common discourse among Christians might appear more, and that he might discover how little such language did become those that profess themselves followers of Christ, he once sat down silently, and took out his pen and ink, and wrote down in short-hand the discourse that passed for some time together, amongst those who pretended to more than common understanding in the things of God. And, after a while, he took his paper and read it to them, and asked them whether their talk was such as they would be willing God should record. "Oh, to spend an hour or two together, and to hear scarcely a word for Christ, or that speaks people's hearts in love with holiness! Should we talk thus if we believed that we should hear of this again at the day of judgment? Would Enoch, David, or Paul have talked thus? Is this the sweetest communication of saints upon earth? Doth not this indicate our hearts to be very empty of grace, and that we have little sense of those spiritual and eternal concerns upon us?"

(*b*) THE AFFECTING QUESTION.—A number of intimate friends being at dinner together, on the Lord's day, one of the company, in order to prevent improper discourse, said, "It is a question whether we shall all go to heaven or not." This plain hint occasioned a general seriousness and self-examination. One thought, "If any of this company go to hell, it must be myself;" and so thought another, and another; even the servants, who waited at table, were affected in the same manner. In short, it was afterwards found, that this one sentence proved, by the special blessing of God upon it, instrumental to their conversion. What an encouragement is this to Christians, to give a serious turn to conversation, when in company! It should be observed, however, that the Lord's day was not instituted for the visiting and entertainment even of Christians. How is their conduct, who make a point of meeting and feasting on the Sabbath, to be distinguished from the Sunday parties of the profane? Our place of meeting, on that day, is the house of God; and our feast, the rich provisions of the everlasting gospel.

(*c*) COMMUNION WITH SAINTS.—"On Saturday, about ten o'clock," says the Rev. T. Charles, of North Wales, in a letter, "I set out from Bristol. Just as I came to the outside of the gate of the city, I met a dear friend, and one whom Jesus loves. I was exceedingly glad to see him; for I never expected to see him this side of eternity. He had been in a dangerous decline for this half-year; but now, through mercy, he is wonderfully recovered. He has nothing to depend on but Providence; and the Lord put it into the heart of a rich merchant in the city to support and provide for him amply during the whole of his illness; so that, though possessing nothing, he had every thing to enjoy. He turned his horse back, with the intention of accompanying me a mile or two. We talked; and our horses carried us one mile after another, till we had ridden fifteen miles; and both ourselves and our horses wanted some refreshment. His conversation was exceedingly savory, and truly profitable, suited to one who had been, in his own apprehension, and that of others, on the borders of heaven. I cannot look on our meeting, but as a particular appointment and blessing from Providence. We stayed two hours together at the inn, and parted at last with much regret. You would have smiled to see our eyes fixed on each other, till distance obstructed our sight. Communion of saints is a blessing indeed. I would not, for any thing, have it expunged from our creed."

(*d*) MR. HERVEY AND DR. DODDRIDGE.—Mr. Hervey, in a letter, says—"I have lately seen that most excellent minister of the ever-blessed Jesus, Mr——. I dined, supped, and spent the evening with him at Northampton, in company with Dr. Doddridge, and two pious, ingenous clergymen of the Church of England, both of them known to the learned world by their valuable writings; and surely I never spent a more delightful evening, or saw one that seemed to make nearer approaches to the felicity of heaven. A gentleman of great worth and rank in the town, invited us to his house, and gave us an elegant treat; but how mean was his provision, how coarse his delicacies, compared with the fruit of my friend's lips!—they dropped as the honey-comb, and were a well of life."

CONVERSATION, RELIGIOUS, WITH THE IMPENITENT.

106. Way for Humble Christians to be Useful.

(*a*) RELATING A SERMON.—During a revival in M——, says a correspondent of the New-York Evangelist, a minister, who was a stranger to the people, came into the place, and preached on the first Sabbath that he spent there, from the text, "Why will ye die?" Mrs. A——, one of the mothers in Israel, was deeply interested in the subject of the discourse. When she returned home, she still thought of the awful condition of impenitent sinners. She had a near neighbor, the brother of her husband, who was so negligent of the things of religion, that he was seldom seen within the walls of the sanctuary. She felt for this friend. In the evening she called to see him, gave him a relation of the meeting she had attended, told him the text, and as much of the sermon as she could recollect. An arrow of conviction was fixed in his heart, he immediately began to attend the religious meetings, and soon was brought to rejoice in the God of his salvation.

How much good might be accomplished if Christians generally felt as this pious female felt, and like her were faithful to warn sinners, to invite them to Jesus, and entreat them to flee from the wrath to come.

(*b*) THE CHILD AND THE SHOE MAKER.—When Mr. Whitfield was preaching in America, a certain lady in New England became a subject of grace, and a praying, experienced Christian. But she was alone in her exercises; she could influence none to pray with her but her little daughter, between nine and eleven years of age. This child she took into her closet with her, from day to day, a witness to her cries and tears. It pleased God, after some time, to touch the heart of the child, and after sorrow for sin, to give her the knowledge of salvation through the remission of sin. The child, then about eleven years of age, in a transport which is so peculiar to such a blessed experience, said, "O, mother, if all the world knew this! I wish I could tell every body! Pray, mother, let me run to some of the neighbors, and tell them, that they may be happy, and love my Savior too."

"Ah! my dear child," said the mother, "that would be needless; for I suppose if you were to tell your experience, there is not one in many miles but what would laugh at you, and say it was all delusion."

"O, mother," said the child, "I think they would believe me. I must go over to the shoemaker and tell him; he will believe me."

She ran over, and found him at work in his shop. She began by telling him that he must die, and that he was a sinner, and that she was a sinner, but that her blessed Savior had heard her mother's prayers, and had forgiven all her sins; and that now she was so happy she did not know how to tell it! The shoemaker was struck; his tears flowed down like rain; he threw aside his work, and cried for mercy, by prayer and supplication. That alarmed the neighborhood, and in a few months from that time there were above fifty people brought to the knowledge of Jesus, and experienced his power and grace.

107. Influence of Earnestness and Tenderness.

(*a*) YOUNG BUCHANAN AND THE AGED CHRISTIAN.—Dr. Buchanan, in giving an account of his conversion, says;—"It was in the year 1790 that my heart was effectually impressed *in consequence of an acquaintance with a religious man.* This gentleman having called one Sunday evening, out of complaisance I gave the conversation a religious turn. Among other things I asked him whether he believed there was such a thing as divine grace; whether or not it was a fiction imposed by grave and austere persons from their own fancies. He took occasion, from this inquiry, to enlarge much upon the subject; he spoke with zeal and earnestness, and chiefly in Scripture language, and concluded with a very affecting address to the conscience and the heart. I had not the least desire, that I recollect, of being benefited by this conversation; but while he spoke, I listened to him with earnestness; and before I was aware, a most powerful impression was made upon my mind, and I conceived the instant resolution of reforming my life. On that evening I had an engagement which I could not now approve; notwithstanding what had passed, I, however, resolved to go; but as I went along, and had time to reflect upon what I had heard, I half wished that it might not be kept. It turned out as I desired. I hurried home, and locked myself up in my chamber; I fell on my knees, and endeavored to pray."

The result of this interview with his religious friend was made conducive to Buchanan's conversion; and he became one of the most self-denying and useful men in modern times.

(*b*) "HOW DO YOU TREAT MY MASTER?"—Dr. Payson was once going to one of the towns in Maine for the purpose of attending a ministers' meeting, accompanied by a friend, when they had occasion to call at a house on the journey, where Dr. Payson was unknown. The family had just sat down to tea, and the lady of the house, in the spirit of genuine hospitality, invited the strangers to partake of the social repast. Dr. Payson at first declined, but being strenuously urged, he consented. As he took his seat, he inquired if a blessing had been asked; and being answered in the negative, requested the privilege, which was readily granted, of invoking the benediction of Heaven. This was done with so much fervor, solemnity, and simplicity, that it had the happiest effect. The old lady treated the company with the utmost attention, and as Dr. Payson was about to leave, he said to her, "Madam, you have treated me with much hospitality and kindness, for which I thank you sincerely; but allow me to ask, how do you treat my Master? That is of infinitely greater consequence than how you treat me." He continued in a strain of appropriate exhortation, and having done his duty in the circumstances, proceeded on his journey. This visit was sanctified to the conversion of the lady and her household. The revival continued in the neighborhood, and in a short time a church was built, and the regular ordinances of religion established.

(*c*) LADY H. AND THE LABORER.—Lady H. once spoke to a workman who was repairing a garden wall, and pressed him to take some thought concerning eternity and the state of his soul. Some years afterward she was speaking to another on the same subject, and said to him, "Thomas, I fear you never pray, nor look to Christ for salvation." "Your ladyship is mistaken," answered the man. "I heard what passed between you and James at such a time, and the word you designed for him took effect on me." "How did you hear it? "I heard it on the other side of the garden, through a hole in the wall, and shall never forget the impression I received."

(*d*) THE EFFECT OF A TEAR.—In a little village, in the northern part of England, open-air services, for the purpose of preaching the gospel to the ignorant and profligate, had been carried on, during nine successive summer seasons, and not without some salutary effects, as evidenced in the conversion of several. But among others Joseph K——, full of self-righteousness and prejudice, despised in his heart the preacher, his message, and all who loved the truths which he declared.

In the week, he was by necessity associated with two or three, who, since the preaching of the gospel in their village had tasted that the Lord was gracious, and who, as a consequence, ardently longed that others should enjoy the same holy privileges and pleasures as those in which they participated. But Joseph K—— despised all their desires and efforts, because, in his heart, he viewed them only as hypocrites, or as enthusiasts. Many a word in season was dropped by these plain Christians in their daily intercourse with their fellow laborer. But, for a long time, all was to no good purpose: K—— remained insensible, caring for none of these things. During the winter, his master ordered him and John B—— to thrash together in a barn. And often, between the strokes of the descending flail, was many a stroke tenderly aimed at K——'s conscience. However, the only return which he usually made, was a taunting answer as to some people being righteous overmuch, or else a silent yet significantly contemptuous sneer. But his associate in labor was a man of patient, tender spirit, yet of very susceptible feelings. He grieved inwardly at the hardness and impenitency of heart manifested by his neighbor. At length, having, on one occasion, spoken to K—— very kindly about his need of a Savior, and of the things which related to his everlasting peace, and seeing that he disregarded all B——'s counsel, and would have none of his reproof, the fountains of his grief were suddenly broken up, and turning toward a dark part of the barn, a gush of grief burst forth, and betrayed itself, rolling down the cheeks of the poor and pious, yet despised thrasher. But although B—— had turned aside, and endeavored to hide his tears by hastily wiping them away with the rough sleeve of his smock-frock, K—— saw the big round tear glistening in his fellow laborer's eye, who silently, but thoughtfully, soon resumed his work, by diligently plying with his flail the corn which lay spread out on the thrashing floor.

That tear, by the overruling power of God, did more than all the sermons he heard from the preacher under the elm-tree, or all the kind and truly Christian expostulations of his associate in labor. That tear subdued his heart. He melted into tenderness and godly sorrow for his past sins. From that moment he considered.—"What," thought he, "shall John B—— shed tears on my account, and yet I have never shed one tear about my soul's concern?" After much inward conflict, he obtained joy and peace in believing. He began soon to love the minister, and the people, whom before he as heartily despised.

(*e*) THE UNANSWERABLE ARGUMENT.—In the time of a great revival in a certain church and congregation, the pastor urged one of his brethren, an able, skilful lawyer, to go and converse with a scoffing infidel of their acquaintance. "You know," said he, "that Mr. R. comprehends an able argument as well as any of us; and you and I have often seen how his eye will kindle under a compact and well-drawn argument. Now can you not go over, with him, the proofs on which the Christian system rests?"

"I have done that already," said the lawyer, "and he heard me through patiently and then pounced upon my arguments like a tiger on his prey. Then he wound up with bitter reproaches, which made me dread to encounter him again."

One of the elders of the same church had been also to visit the infidel, and met with a like reception, and he had made similar objections to his pastor to visiting the infidel again. But on a subsequent evening he was led by the Spirit of God, to wrestle before the throne with most agonizing prayer in that Infidel's behalf. At intervals he continued all night presenting his case before God, and praying for his conversion and salvation, as a man would pray for a friend's life on the eve of his execution.

Prayer was followed by corresponding effort, and not long after, in the crowded church, Mr. R. stood up, a changed man, to relate his Christian experience!

"I am as a brand," said he, "plucked out of the burning. The change in my views and feelings is astonishing to myself; and all brought about by the grace of God and that *unanswerable argument.*

"It was a cold morning in January, and I had just begun my labor at the anvil in my shop, when I looked out and saw Elder B—— approaching. As he drew near I saw he was agitated—his look was full of earnestness. His eyes were bedimmed with tears. He took me by the hand. His breast heaved with emotion, and with indescribable tenderness, he said, 'Mr. R——, I am greatly concerned for your salvation—greatly concerned for your salvation!' and he burst into tears. He often essayed to speak, but not a word could he utter, and finding that he could say no more, he turned, went out of the shop, mounted his horse, and rode slowly away.

"'*Greatly concerned for my salvation,*' said I audibly, and I stood and forgot to bring my hammer down! '*Greatly concerned for my salvation.*' Here is a new argument, thought I, for religion, which I never heard before, and I know not how to answer it. Had the Elder reasoned with me, I could have confounded him; but here is no threadbare argument for the truth of religion. Religion must move the soul with benevolent, holy, mighty impulses, or this man would not feel as he does. 'GREATLY CONCERNED FOR MY SALVATION'—it rung through my ears like a thunder clap in a clear sky. 'Greatly concerned ought *I* to be for my own salvation,' said I; 'What shall I do to be saved?'

"I went into my house. My poor pious wife, whom I had so often ridiculed for her religion, exclained, 'Why Mr. R——, what is the matter with you?' 'Matter enough,' said I, filled with agony—'Matter enough. Elder B. has rode two miles this cold morning to tell me he was greatly concerned for my salvation. What shall I do?' She advised me to go and see him. No sooner said than done. I mounted my horse and pursued after him. I found him alone in that same little room where he had spent the whole night in prayer for my poor soul. 'I am come,' said I to him, 'to tell you I am greatly concerned for my own salvation.'

"'Praised be God,' said the Elder. 'It is a faithful saying, and worthy of all acceptation, that Jesus Christ came into the world to save sinners, even the very chief;' and he began at that same Scripture and preached unto me Jesus. On that same floor we knelt, and together we prayed, and we did not separate that day till God spoke peace to my soul. And here permit me to say, if you would reach the heart of such a poor sinner as I, you must get your qualification where the good Elder did his, in your closet and on your knees." That converted infidel long outlived the Elder, and was the means of the conversion of many.

(*f*) THE GAY LADY AND HER PIOUS FRIENDS.—A gay, thoughtless young lady, who had not unfrequently indulged in ridiculing "the orthodox," as she was pleased to term those who pretended to any thing more than external morality, after having been in the society of a pious, devoted friend, observed, "Mrs. —— is always *talking religion*, but she does seem to enjoy it so much, that I admire to listen to her, and have been sitting a whole hour to hear her converse."

108. Advantage of Skill and Prudence.

(*a*) MEETING THE IMPENITENT ALONE.—Several young ladies, of a proud, gay and fashionable character, lived together in a fashionable family. Two men were strongly desirous to get the subject of religion before them, but were at a loss how to accomplish it for fear they would all combine, and counteract or resist every serious impression. At length they took this course. They called and sent up their card to one of the young ladies by name. She came down and they conversed with her on the subject of her salvation, and as she was alone, she not only treated them politely, but seemed to receive the truth in seriousness. A day or two after, they called in like manner on another, and then another, and so on till they had conversed with every one separately. In a little time they were all, I believe, every one, hopefully converted. This was as it should be, for then they could not keep each other in countenance. And then the impression made on one was followed up with the others, so that one was not left to exert a bad influence over the rest.

(*b*) TWENTY-ONE YOUNG MEN CONVERTED.—There was a pious woman who kept a boarding house for young gentlemen; she had twenty-one or two of them in her family, and at length she became very anxious for their salvation: she made it a subject of prayer, but saw no seriousness among them. At length she saw that there must be something done besides praying, and yet she did not know what to do. One morning after breakfast, as they were retiring she asked one of them to stop a few minutes. She conversed with him tenderly on the subject of religion, and prayed with him. She followed up the impression made, and pretty soon he was hopefully converted. Then there were two, and they addressed another, and prayed with him, and soon he was prepared to join them. Then another, and so on, taking one at a time, and letting none of the rest know what was going on, so as not to alarm them, till every one of these young men were converted to God. Now if she had brought the subject before the whole of them together, very likely they would have turned it all into ridicule, or perhaps they would have been offended and left the house, and then she could have had no further influence over them. But taking one alone, and treating him respectfully and kindly, he had no such obstacle as arises out of the presence of others.

109. Happy Results Unexpectedly Developed.

(*a*) THE PIOUS WIDOW AND THE SAILOR.—A pious English widow, who resided among ignorant and vicious neighbors in the suburbs of B—, Mass., determined to do what she could for their spiritual benefit; and so she opened her little front room for weekly prayer meetings, and engaged some pious Methodists to aid in conducting them. Much of the seed thus scattered on a seemingly arid soil, produced fruit. One instance deserves special notice.

Among others who attended was a young sailor of intelligent and prepossessing countenance. A slight acquaintance with him discovered him to be very ignorant of even the rudiments of education; but, at the same time he had such manifestly superior abilities, that the widow became much interested in his spiritual welfare, and could not but hope that God would in some way provide for his further instruction, convert him and render him useful.

But in the midst of her anticipations he was suddenly summoned away to sea. He had been out but a short time when the vessel was seized by a British privateer and carried into Halifax, where the crew suffered by a long and wretched imprisonment.

A year had passed away, during which the good woman had heard nothing of the young sailor. Still she remembered and prayed for him with the solicitude of a mother. About this time, she received a letter from her relations, who had settled in Halifax, on business which required her to go to that town. While there, her habitual disposition to be useful, led her with a few friends to visit the prison with Bibles and tracts. In one apartment were the American prisoners. As she approached the grated door, a voice shouted her name, calling her mother, and a youth appeared and leaped for joy at the grate. It was the lost sailor boy! They wept and conversed like mother and son, and when she left she gave him a Bible—his future guide and comfort.

During her stay at Halifax, she constantly visited the prison, supplying the youth with tracts, religious books, and clothing, and endeavoring by her conversation to secure the religious impression made on his mind at the prayer meetings in B—. After many months she removed to a distant part of the provinces; and for years she heard nothing more of the young sailor.

We pass over a period of many years and introduce the reader to Father T—, the distinguished mariner's preacher in the city of B—. In a spacious and substantial chapel, crowded about by the worst habitations in the city, this distinguished man delivered, every Sabbath, discourses as extraordinary, perhaps, as are to be found in the Christian world. In the centre column of seats, guarded sacredly against all other intrusion, sat a dense mass of mariners—a strange medley of white, black, and olive, Protestant, Catholic, and Pagan. On the other seats in the galleries, the aisles, the altar, and on the pulpit stairs, were crowded, week after week, and year after year—the families of sailors, and the poor who had no other temple—the elite of the city—the learned professor—the student—the popular writer—the actor—groups of clergymen, and the votaries of gayety and fashion, listening with throbbing hearts and wet eyes, to a man whose only school had been the forecastle, whose only endowments were those of grace and nature, but whose shrewd sense, keen wit, and glowing fancy, and melting pathos, and energetic delivery would allow none to be inattentive or unaffected in his audience.

In the year 183—, an aged English local preacher moved into the city of B— from the British provinces.

The old local preacher was mingling in a public throng one day with a friend, when they met "Father T—. A few words of introduction led to a free conversation, in which the former residence of his wife in the city was mentioned, and allusion was made to her prayer meeting—her former name was asked by "Father T—;" he seemed seized by an impulse—inquired their residence, hastened away, and in a short time arrived in a carriage, with all his family, at the home of the aged pair. There a scene ensued which must be left to the imagination of the reader. "Father T—" was the sailor boy of the prayer meeting and the prison. The old lady was the widow who had first cared for his soul. They had met once more!

(*b*) "DID YOU EVER DRINK AT THAT GREAT FOUNTAIN?"—A friend of mine, Deacon E., in 1839, was on a visit to Saratoga Springs. One morning, taking a draught at Congress Spring, a lady came to take her usua glass at the same time. The deacon turned to her and asked her, "Have you ever drank at that Great Fountain?" She colored, and looked surprised; bu turned away without a word of reply The next winter Deacon E. was in Rochester, and one evening attended a conference and prayer meeting in the Baptist church. A gentleman invited him to go home with him and see his wife who was very sick. As he entered the room she looked up and smiled, and said, "Don't you know me?" "No,' said he. "Don't you remember asking a woman at Congress Spring, 'Have you ever drank at that Great Fountain?'" "Yes," says he. "Well," said she, "I am the person; I thought at first you were very rude; but your words kept ringing in my ears. They followed me to my chamber, to my pillow. I found no rest till I found it in Christ. I expect to die pretty soon, and go to heaven, and you, under God, are the means of my salvation! Be as faithfu. to others as you have been to me. Never be afraid to talk to strangers on the subject of religion."

(*c*) FAREWELL ADVICE.—Many years ago, a gentleman lived in intimate association with some literary friends, wh met together once a week. In the freedom of this social intercourse, he had ample opportunities of ascertaining their peculiar habits of mind, and remarked, with deep regret, a general alienation from the sentiments and principles of real religion. One of them, in particular, to whom he was on many accounts most attached, scorned the restraints of religion, and abandoned himself to the pleasures of the world. Circumstances at length led the gentleman to leave that place, and on parting with his acquaintance at the corner of the street, he summoned up his moral courage to pronounce the following words:—"We now part, probably to meet no more on earth. We have sometimes discussed, and you have always refused to regard, the appeals of scriptural truth. One word, and I have done. O remember that you have a soul, an immortal soul: will you finally consent to lose it in endless perdition, for the sake of paltry and fleeting indulgences? Farewell."

Each now disappeared from the other, in the crowd of life; and pursued a very different course. Ten, twenty, thirty years elapsed. The gentleman was one day standing at his door, when another gentleman was passing by in great haste; but a momentary glance induced him to stop, and to ask, "Sir, is not your name M—?"

"It is;" and a sudden reminiscence led him to add, "And is not yours G—?"

"You are right. Do you remember what you said at our separation at the corner of S— street, thirty years ago?"

"I have a faint recollection."

"But I have a strong one. I am another man. You left me a man of the world, and an enemy of the cross of Christ: I am now, and have been during many years, a member of a Christian church, and you are the cause. The word was 'in season;' I could not rid myself of it; I was forced by it to reflection; yes, I thought on my ways, and turned to God and happiness."

(*d*) REV. MR. READER AND THE CHILD.—The Rev. Mr. Reader, of Taunton (Eng.), having called, one day, in the course of his pastoral visits, at the house of a friend, affectionately noticed a little girl in the room, about six years of age. Among other things, he asked her if she knew that she had a bad heart, and, opening the Bible, pointed her to the passage where the Lord promises to give a new heart. He instructed her to plead this promise in prayer, and she would find the Almighty faithful to his promise. About seventeen years after, a lady came to him, proposed herself for communion with the church of which he was pastor, and how inexpressible was his delight when he found that she was the very person with whom, when a child, he had so freely conversed, and that the conversation was blessed to her conversion! Taking her Bible, she had retired, as he advised, pleaded the promise, wept, and prayed; and the Lord, in answer to her fervent petitions, gave her what she so earnestly desired, *a new heart.*

(*e*) BISHOP ASBURY AND POOR PUNCH.—Bishop Asbury, in 1798, on his journey to Charleston, S. C., passed a creek in the parish of St.—, on the bank of which sat a slave fishing and humming a ditty. His name was Punch. He was notorious for his vicious character. The pious bishop rode towards him, deliberately proceeded to alight, fastened his horse to a tree, and seated himself by the side of the slave!

As the slave seemed willing, he commenced a minute and personal conversation with him on religion. Punch began to feel, tears ran down his sable cheeks, and he seemed alarmed at his danger, and listened with intentness to the counsels of the singular stranger. After a long conversation, the bishop sung the hymn —

"Plunged in a gulf of dark despair,"

prayed with him, and pursued his journey. More than twenty years elapsed before he again saw or heard of Punch. While on another visit to Charleston he was called upon by an aged and Christian negro, who had travelled seventy miles on foot to visit him. It was the slave he had warned and prayed over on the bank of the creek who had ever since been journeying on the way to heaven. When the bishop left him, on the bank of the stream, he immediately took up his fishing tackle and hastened home in the deepest agitation, pondering over the words of the venerable man. After some days of anguish and prayer, he found peace in believing and became a new man. The change was too manifest not to be discovered by his fellow-servants—it was the topic of his conversation with them incessantly. In his simple way he pointed them to the Lamb of God which taketh away the sins of the world, and many of them became thoroughly penitent for their sins. Throngs of the neglected Africans resorted to his humble cabin to receive his exhortations and prayers. A perverse overseer, who had charge of the plantation, perceiving the increasing interest of the slaves for their souls, and their constant attendance in the evenings at Punch's cabin, determined to put a stop to the spreading leaven. But on coming one night to break up a meeting, he was struck under conviction, fell down under a tree near by, and began to cry for mercy. The negroes gathered around him, and prayed with him till God in his mercy pardoned and comforted him. The overseer now became a co-worker with Punch among them; he joined the nearest Methodist church, and in time became an exhorter, and finally a preacher! Punch had now full liberty to do good among his associates. He exhorted, prayed, and led them on, as a shepherd his flock, and extended his usefulness around the whole neighborhood. After many years he was removed, by the decease of his master and the distribution of the estate, to the parish of A., where he continued to labor for the souls of his fellow bondmen with still greater success. Scores and even hundreds were converted through his instrumentality, and he sustained a kind of pastoral charge over them for years.

110. Various Interesting Conversions.

(*a*) THE MINISTER'S DIRECTION.—A Christian minister some years ago, on returning from preaching in a neighboring village, was asked by an individual to direct him to a certain place. His request was attended to, and when the stranger was thanking him for his kindness, the minister replied, "Take care, my friend, you are in the right way at last." These words appeared long to sound in the man's ears, and, What could the gentleman mean by them? was an inquiry often presented to his mind, and which at length led to the salvation of his soul. Some years had passed away, with all their attendant cares, joys, and sorrows, when the minister was solicited to preach at Ludlow, Salop. After the service, he was requested to visit a member of the church, who was in dying circumstances. As soon as he came near, the dying man fixed his eyes on the countenance of the minister, and, with a peculiarly significant look, and emphatic voice, said, "Sir, I know you! I know you!" "Know me!" replied the minister; "how can that be? for I am a stranger here." "I know you sir," again he replied. "Do you not remember," said he, "some years ago, a person asking you the way to such a place, and your returning with him, putting him in the right path, and when we were parting saying to him, "My friend, take care you are in the right way at last?" "No, I do not," replied the minister; for it had completely escaped his memory. "Yes, you did, sir," rejoined the dying man, "I have not forgotten it, nor ever shall forget it. 'The right way at last;' Oh, sir, am I in that way now? I cannot live long, I feel that I am dying; tell me, Oh, tell me, if I am in the right way." The minister questioned him as to his faith in Christ, and on other important points, to which the dying man returned suitable and satisfactory answers. After which the minister affectionately and earnestly recommended him in prayer to God, and left him. In a few days his mortal career ended.

(*b*) THE PHYSICIAN AND HIS CLERICAL PATIENT.—It would not be easy to calculate the good that might be done, were true religion more prevalent among our medical men, who have constant access to bedsides, which the pious minister, however anxious and willing, is sometimes not permitted to approach.

Dr. — was visiting a gentleman who appeared very much agitated on being informed by him of the nature of his complaint, which Dr. — observing, he said to him, "Sir, you seem very much distressed about your body; do you feel the same anxiety about your soul?" The gentleman was extremely irritated at the question, and the more so as he was a clergyman; but he subsequently thought of it, and told Dr. — that he dated the origin of his anxious concern for salvation to that remark.

(*c*) "A WORD IN SEASON."—The Rev. Peter Mill, a zealous and venerable minister of the Gospel, being on a pedestrian excursion in Yorkshire (Eng.), came to the brink of a large pit, which was so completely covered with the drifted snow as to conceal all danger from the unwary traveller. Just at that imminent moment, when, had he stepped forward, it is more than probable he would have plunged into the gulf of death, a young woman coming up, discovered to him his perilous condition. Grateful to the *First Cause* of his deliverance, he was not unmindful of the *instrument* of it: and desirous of making her some important return for the service she had rendered him, he informed her that he was a minister of Christ, whose office it was to call sinners to repentance. And with much gratitude and earnestness, he exhorted her to flee from the wrath to come, entreating her seriously to consider that her youth was no security from death, and expressing a most ardent desire that he might be the means of saving her *soul* from the *more awful pit* than that from which she had been instrumental in saving his body.

What he said to her was "a word in season;" for, while gratitude sparkled in his eyes, and his countenance expressed more than his tongue could declare, she could not doubt the truth of his assertions; and such was the impression of his discourse on her mind, that she began earnestly to cry, "What must I do to be saved!" She soon obtained ease to her troubled conscience, and an assurance that her sins were pardoned. And about eight weeks after this, she died, happy in the consolations of religion.

(*d*) THE CLERGYMAN CONVERTED.—The excellent Joseph Williams, of Kidderminster, relates, in his diary, that in the year 1754, he was unexpectedly induced to take a journey; and, while out on his way, to ride to Bradford, in Wiltshire, on a stormy night. On a Monday, he called on a clergyman, the vicar of the town, and just as the party, to whom he was thus introduced, was breaking up, a young clergyman, the curate of the parish, came in. A pious friend, who accompanied Mr. Williams, requested him to speak to the curate: and with some reluctance he advanced towards him with the important inquiry, "Sir, how does your soul prosper?" He seemed disconcerted, and replied in a languid manner. Next morning, he sent for Mr. Williams, and told him that the conversation was deeply impressed on his mind, that he feared the state of his soul was bad, and desired some further intercourse. They conversed, they prayed, and, after they separated, kept up a correspondence mutually gratifying. The clergyman afterwards gave abundant evidence of piety, and of great faithfulness to the souls committed to his charge.

111. The Duty Neglected.

(*a*) THE CLERK'S LAMENT.—A writer in the Christian Soldier, gives the following incident which was related to him by an esteemed Christian brother:—

Some few years ago I was clerk in a store in ——. One day a hired man of my employer, whom I knew to be destitute of religion, came into my store. I felt it to be my duty to speak to him upon the subject of his soul's salvation; but my wicked heart invented a thousand excuses. 'He may not receive it kindly, thought I, since I am younger than he; I had better keep silence until a more favorable opportunity.' Conscience told me these excuses were vain, and a voice seemed to say to me, 'Speak to this man;' but I refused to listen.

But mark the sequel. The next day he was taken sick, became deranged, and on the third day, died! O! thought I, that I had listened to the voice of God's Spirit and done my duty. Perhaps I might have saved his soul from perdition; at least I might have cleared my own skirts, and washed my hands in innocence. But now, alas! it is too late! for ever too late! His doom is irrevocably sealed!

(*b*) THE UNFAITHFUL MOTHER.—A Christian minister calling at the house of one of his friends, found him and his wife in deepest distress, from the sudden death of their only child. He attempted to console the distracted parents; but the mother replied, "Ah, sir, these consolations might assuage my grief for the loss of my child, but they cannot blunt the stings of my conscience, which are as daggers in my heart. It was but last week I was thinking, 'My child is now twelve years of age; his mind is rapidly expanding; I know he thinks and feels beyond the measure of his years, and a foolish backwardness has hitherto kept me from entering so closely into conversation with him as to discover the real state of his mind, and to make a vigorous effort to lead his heart to God.' I then resolved to seize the first opportunity to discharge a duty so weighty on the conscience of a Christian parent; but day after day my foolish deceitful heart said, 'I will do it to-morrow.' On the very day that he was taken ill, I had resolved to talk to him that evening; and when he at first complained of his head, I was half pleased with the thought, that this might incline him to listen more seriously to what I should say. But Oh, sir, his pain and fever increased so rapidly, that I was obliged to put him immediately to bed, and as he seemed inclined to doze, I was glad to leave him to rest. From that time he was never sufficiently sensible for conversation; and now he is gone into eternity, and has left me distracted with anxiety concerning the salvation of his precious soul! Dilatory wretch! had it not been for my own sin, I might now have been consoling myself with the satisfactory conviction of having discharged the duty of a Christian parent, and enjoying the delightful assurance of meeting my child before the throne of God and the Lamb. Oh, the cursed sin of procrastination! Oh, the ruinous delusion that lurks in the word *to-morrow!*"

(*c*) DR. CHALMERS AND THE NOBLEMAN.—Dr. Chalmers, on his return from England, a few years ago, lodged in the house of a nobleman, not far distant from Peebles. The doctor was known to excel in conversation, as well as in the pulpit. He was the life and soul of the discourse in the circle of friends at the nobleman's fire-side. The subject was pauperism—its causes and cure. Among the gentlemen present, there was a venerable old Highland chieftain, who kept his eyes fastened on Dr. C., and listened with intense interest to his communications. The conversation was kept up to a late hour. When the company broke up, they were shown up stairs into their apartments. There was a lobby of considerable length, and the doors of the bed-chambers opened on the right and left. The apartment of Dr. C. was directly opposite to that of the old chieftain, who had already retired with his attendant. As the doctor was undressing himself, he heard an unusual noise in the chieftain's room; the noise was succeeded by a heavy groan! He hastened into the apartment, which was in a few minutes filled with the company, who all rushed in to the relief of the old gentleman. It was a melancholy sight which met their eyes. The venerable white-headed chief had fallen into the arms of his attendant in an apoplexy. He breathed for a few moments, and expired. Dr. C. stood in silence, with both hands stretched out, and bending over the deceased. He was the very picture of distress. He was the first to break silence. "Never in my life," said he, in a tremulous voice, "did I see, or did I feel, before this moment, the meaning of that text, 'Preach the word: be instant in season, and out of seasan; reprove, rebuke, exhort, with all long-suffering and doctrine.' Had I known that my venerable old friend was within a few minutes of eternity, I would not have dwelt on that subject which formed the topic of this evening's conversation. I would have addressed myself earnestly to him. I would have preached unto him and you, Christ Jesus, and him crucified. I would have urged him and you, with all the earnestness befitting the subject, to prepare for eternity. You would have thought it, and you would have pronounced it, out of season. But ah! it would have been in season, both as it respected him, and as it respects you."

(*d*) THE DYING DAUGHTER.—A Christian minister, in Yorkshire, had long felt convinced of his sinfulness, in neglecting to converse on spiritual topics with a beloved child. She was brought to the verge of the grave, and was, in his apprehension, an unconverted child. His feelings were painfully distressing; for he felt forcibly the importance of his duty in apprising her of her danger; but till nearly her dying hour he continued to experience the backwardness he had long felt. Repeatedly did he enter her room to address her, and unwilling to add the weight of mental anxiety to her bodily affliction, he as often retired without accomplishing his object. His conscience pained him, for he feared that his misjudging fondness might contribute to her eternal ruin. At length, after repeated petitions for Divine assistance, he once more approached her bed, and pressing her hand, said, in broken words, "Has an eternal state, my dearest daughter, ever engaged your attention?" This was all he could utter. To his astonishment and joy, she immediately replied, "Yes, father; under a sermon that you preached from Romans iii. upon man's lost condition, I was convinced that I was in a state of condemnation. Since that time I have been unable to procure any consolation, and I fear I shall be lost for ever." Her tears for some time prevented her from saying more: but when able to proceed, she told him that she had long wished to make known to him the state of her mind. Overcome with joy at this unexpected answer, he endeavored to convince her of the certainty of salvation to all who, conscious of their depravity, confide in the merits of the Redeemer, for acceptance with God. Her distress was continued for two days longer, when, resting entirely on Christ, every degree of gloom was removed, and she was favored for fifteen days with holy peace and joy. Christ was increasingly precious to her, and her father had the blessedness of witnessing her triumphant departure, in full assurance of hope, in the fifteenth year of her age.

(*e*) AN UNFAITHFUL FATHER.—A father who had a son in college, requested a minister who was going through the town where he was, to call on him and converse with him in reference to the salvation of his soul. The minister called, agreeable to the request of the father, and introduced the subject of religion. He alluded to the feelings and request of the father, who wished him by all means to attend first to the salvation of his soul. The young man replied, "Did my father send such word as that?" "He did," was the reply. "Then," said the young man, "My father is a dishonest man." "But why do you say he is dishonest?" said the minister. "Because," replied the student, "he has often advised me, in regard to the course he would have me pursue in life, how to gain the riches, honors, and pleasures of the world, but he is not the man that has ever manifested any interest in regard to the salvation of my soul, any more than if I had no soul!"

112. COURAGE, MORAL

(*a*) THE BISHOP'S REPLY.—Philip, Bishop of Heraclea, in the beginning of the 4th century, was dragged by the feet through the streets, severely scourged, and then brought again to the governor, who charged him with obstinate rashness, in continuing disobedient to the imperial decrees; but he boldly replied, "My present behavior is not the effect of rashness, but proceeds from my love and fear of God, who made the world, and who will judge the living and the dead, whose commands I dare not transgress. I have hitherto done my duty to the emperors, and am always ready to comply with their just orders, according to the doctrine of our Lord Christ, who bids us give both to Cæsar and to God their due; but I am obliged to prefer heaven to earth, and to obey God rather than man." The governor, on hearing this speech, immediately passed sentence on him to be burnt, which was executed accordingly, and the martyr expired, singing praises to God in the midst of the flames.

(*b*) CHRYSOSTOM IN EXILE.—"When driven from the city, I cared nothing for it. But I said to myself, if the empress wishes to banish me, the earth is the Lord's, and the fulness thereof. If she would saw me in sunder, let her saw me in sunder; I have Isaiah for a pattern. If she would plunge me in the sea; I remember Jonah. If she would thrust me into the fiery furnace; I see the three children enduring that. If she would cast me to wild beasts; I call to mind Daniel in the den of lions. If she would stone me, let her stone me; I have before me Stephen the protomartyr. If she would take my head from me, let her take it; I have John the Baptist. If she would deprive me of my worldly goods, let her do it; naked came I from my mother's womb, and naked shall I return. An apostle has told me 'God respecteth no man's person,' and if I yet pleased men, I should not be a servant of Christ." Even Gibbon cannot refrain from remarking, that these epistles "show a firmness of mind much superior to that of Cicero in his exile."

(*c*) DEATH OF JEROME.—When the executioner went behind Jerome of Prague to set fire to the pile, "Come here," said the martyr, "and kindle it before my eyes; for, if I dreaded such a sight, I should never have come to this place when I had a free opportunity to escape." The fire was kindled, and he then sung a hymn, which was soon finished by the encircling flames.

(*d*) LUTHER'S FORTITUDE.—Vergerio, the Papal nuncio, came to Wirtemberg on the evening of November 6, 1535, with a splendid retinue, and was conducted to the castle with all due honor by the principal governor. The next morning, Luther being introduced, conversed with the nuncio; among other things, on the subject of the council. He said it was not seriously proposed; the pope did but play with them; and, if it were held, it would busy itself only about trifles, such as tonsures and vestments, and not upon faith, and justification, and bringing Christians to the unity of the Spirit and of doctrine; for this would not suit their purpose. He added, that he and his friends felt such an assurance of what they believed, as not to need the determination of a council, though others might do it, who groaned under the oppression of men who did not themselves know what they believed. "But," said he, "call your council; God willing, I will attend it, though I should be burned by it." Vergerio asked where he would have it held. "Where you please," he replied, "at Mantua, at Padua, at Florence, or any where else.' Vergerio asked, "Are you willing it should be at Bologna?" He inquired to whom that city then belonged; and on being told, "To the pope," he exclaimed, "Has the pope seized that place too? Well, I will go even thither." The nuncio, in a courtier-like manner, said something of the pope's visiting Wirtemberg. "Let him come," said Luther; "we shall be glad to see him." "But," said Vergerio, "would you have him come with an army, or unattended?" "As he pleases," replied Luther; "we shall be ready for him either way." The nuncio then inquired whether the ministers in Saxony were consecrated. Luther replied, "Certainly: as the pope will not consecrate them for us, here sits a bishop," (pointing to Pomeranus,) "whom we have consecrated." Much more conversation, says the author of the narrative, passed between them, in which Luther fully explained his views, with the utmost freedom, and even, where the case required, with sharpness of remark. On taking leave, Vergerio said, "See that you be ready for the council." "I will come," replied Luther, "with my life in my hand."

On another occasion, Luther, when making his way into the presence of Cardinal Cajetan, who had summoned him to answer for his heretical opinions at Augsburgh, was asked by one of the cardinal's minions, where he should find a shelter if his patron, the elector of Saxony, should desert him? "Under the shield of Heaven!" was his reply. The silenced minion turned round, and went his way.

(*e*) LUTHER SUMMONED TO WORMS.—When Luther was summoned to attend the diet at Worms, his friends, notwithstanding the safe-conduct granted to him by the emperor Charles V., apprehending danger to his person, would have dissuaded him from going thither. Luther replied, "I am determined to enter the city in the name of the Lord Jesus Christ, though as many devils should oppose me as there are tiles upon all the houses at Worms." He was accompanied from Wirtemberg by some divines, and one hundred horse; but he took only eight horsemen into Worms. When he stept out of the carriage, he said, in the presence of a great number of persons, "God shall be on my side."

(*f*) CASE OF WICKLIFF.—At one period of his life, this eminent reformer's health was considerably impaired by the labor of producing his numerous compositions, and the excitements inseparable from the restless hostilities of his enemies. Being supposed to be in dangerous circumstances, his old antagonists, the mendicants, conceived it next to impossible that so notorious a heretic should find himself near a future world without the most serious apprehensions of Divine anger. While they declared that the dogmas of the reformer had arisen from the suggestions of the great enemy, they anticipated some advantages to their cause, could the dying culprit be induced to make any recantation of his published opinions. Wickliff was in Oxford when this sickness arrested his activity, and confined him to his chamber. From the four orders of friars, four doctors, who were also called regents, were gravely deputed to wait on their expiring enemy; and to these the same number of civil officers, called senators of the city, and aldermen of the wards, were added. When this embassy entered the apartment of the rector of Lutterworth, he was seen stretched on his bed. Some kind wishes were first expressed as to his better health, and the blessing of a speedy recovery. It was presently suggested, that he must be aware of the many wrongs which the whole mendicant brotherhood had sustained from his attacks, especially in his sermons, and in certain of his writings; and, as death was now apparently about to remove him, it was sincerely hoped that he would not conceal his penitence, but distinctly revoke whatever he had preferred against them to their injury. The sick man remained silent and motionless until this address was concluded. He then beckoned his servants to raise him in his bed; and fixing his eyes on the persons assembled, summoned all his remaining strength, as he exclaimed aloud, "I shall not die, but live; and shall again declare the evil deeds of the friars." The doctors and their attendants now hurried from his presence, and they lived to feel the truth of his saying; nor will it be easy to imagine another scene more characteristic of the parties composing it, or of the times in which it occurred.

(*g*) HOOPER AT THE STAKE.—Bishop Hooper was condemned to be burned at Gloucester, in Queen Mary's reign. A gentleman, with the view of inducing him to recant, said to him, "Life is sweet, and death is bitter." Hooper replied, "The death to come is more bitter, and the life to come more sweet. I am come hither to end this life, and suffer death, because I will not gainsay the truth I have here formerly taught you." When brought to the stake, a box, with a pardon from the queen in it, was set before him. The determined martyr cried out, "If you love my soul, away with it: if you love my soul, away with it."

(*h*) LATIMER GOING TO LONDON—In the beginning of the reign

of Queen Mary of England, a pursuivant was sent to bring Bishop Latimer to London, of which he had notice six hours before he arrived. But instead of fleeing, he prepared for his journey to London; and, when the pursuivant was come, he said to him, "My friend, you are welcome. I go as willingly to London, to give an account of my faith, as ever I went to any place in the world. And I doubt not, but as the Lord made me worthy formerly to preach the word before two excellent princes, he will now enable me to bear witness to the truth before the third, either to her eternal comfort or discomfort." As he rode on this occasion through Smithfield, he said, "That Smithfield had groaned for him a long time."

(*i*) KNOX BEFORE THE QUEEN.—The pure heart-searching doctrines which were preached by this Scotch apostle, were then, as they are now, offensive to the carnal heart, and hence he was commanded by the voluptuous court of Mary to desist. Knox, who knew no master and obeyed no mandate that was in opposition to his God and his Bible, paid no attention to this command of the palace. Hearing immediately from the enemies of the cross, who were then, as I fear they are at present, the favorites and friends of the palace, that her orders were disobeyed, the haughty Mary summoned the Scottish reformer into her presence. When Knox arrived he was ushered into the room in which were the queen and her attendant lords. On being questioned concerning his contumacy, he answered plainly that he preached nothing but truth, and he dared not preach less. "But," answered one of the lords, "our commands must be obeyed on pain of death; silence or the gallows is the alternative." The spirit of Knox was roused by the dastardly insinuation that any human punishment could make him desert the banner of his Savior, and with that fearless, indescribable courage which disdains the pomp of language or of action, he firmly replied, "My lords, you are mistaken if you think you can intimidate me to do by threats what conscience and God tell me I never shall do; for be it known unto you that it is a matter of no importance to me, when I have finished my work, whether my bones shall bleach in the winds of heaven or rot in the bosom of the earth." Knox having retired, one of the lords said to the queen, "We may let him alone, for we cannot punish that man." Well, therefore, might it be said by a nobleman at the grave of John Knox, "Here lies one who never feared the face of man."

(*j*) FLETCHER AND HIS NEPHEW.—The Rev. Mr. Fletcher of England, had a very wild and profligate nephew in the army, a man who had been dismissed from the Sardinian service for very bad conduct. He had engaged in two or three duels, and had spent all his money in vice and folly. The wicked youth waited one day on his eldest uncle, General De Gons, and presenting a loaded pistol, threatened to shoot him unless he would that moment advance him five hundred crowns. The general, though a brave man, well knew what a desperate fellow he had to deal with, and gave a draft for the money, at the same time speaking freely to him on his conduct. The young man rode off in high spirits with his ill-gotten money. In the evening, passing the door of his younger uncle, Mr. Fletcher, he called on him, and began with informing him what General De Gons had done; and, as a proof, showed a draft under De Gons' own hand. Mr. Fletcher took the draft from his nephew, and looked at him with surprise. Then after some remarks, putting it into his pocket, said, "It strikes me, young man, that you have possessed yourself of this note by some wrong method; and in conscience, I cannot return it but with my brother's knowledge and approbation." The nephew's pistol was in a moment at his breast. "My life," replied Mr. Fletcher, with perfect calmness, "is secure in protection of an almighty power; nor will he suffer it to be the forfeit of my integrity and your rashness." This firmness drew from the nephew the observation, "That his uncle De Gons, though an old soldier, was more afraid of death than his brother." "Afraid of death!" rejoined Mr. Fletcher, "do you think I have been twenty-five years a minister of the Lord of life, to be afraid of death now? No, sir, it is for *you* to be afraid of death. *You* are a gamester and a cheat; yet call yourself a gentleman! *You* are the seducer of female innocence; and still say you are a gentleman! *You* are a duellist; and for this you style yourself a man of honor! Look there, sir," pointing to the heavens, "the broad eye of Heaven is fixed upon us. Tremble in the presence of your Maker, who can in a moment kill your body, and forever punish your soul in hell."

The unhappy young prodigal turned pale, and trembled with fear and rage. He still threatened his uncle with instant death. Fletcher, though thus threatened, gave no alarm, sought for no weapon, and attempted not to escape. He calmly conversed with his profligate relative; and at length perceiving him to be affected, addressed him in the kindest language, till he fairly disarmed and subdued him! He would not return his brother's draft; but engaged to procure for the youug man some immediate relief. He then prayed for him; and after fulfilling his promise of assistance, parted with him, with much good advice on one side, and many fair promises on the other.

(*k*) THE KING REPROVED.—It is said that Henry the Great of France, took much pleasure in conversing with an honest and religious man of low situation in life, who used great freedom with his majesty. One day he said to the king, "Sire, I always take your part when I hear any man speaking evil of you: I know that you excel in justice and generosity, and that many worthy things have been done by you. But you have one vice for which God will condemn you, if you do not repent, I mean the unlawful love of women." The king, it is said, was too magnanimous to resent this reproof, but he long felt it like an arrow in his bosom; and sometimes said, that the most eloquent discourses of the doctors of the Sorbonne had never made such an impression on his soul, as this honest reproof from his humble friend.

(*l*) HARRIS AND THE SOLDIERS.—Dr. Harris, the minister of Hanwell, (Eng.) during the civil wars, frequently had military officers quartered at his house. A party of them, being unmindful of the reverence due to the holy name of God, indulged themselves in swearing. The doctor noticed this, and on the following Sabbath, preached from these words:—"Above all things, my brethren, swear not." This so enraged the soldiers, who judged the sermon was intended for them, that they swore they would shoot him if he preached on the subject again. He was not, however, to be intimidated; and on the following Sabbath, he not only preached from the same text, but inveighed in still stronger terms against the vice of swearing. As he was preaching, a soldier levelled his carbine at him; but he went on to the conclusion of his sermon, without the slightest fear or hesitation!

(*m*) WESLEY AND THE PAPACY.—Mr. Samuel Wesley, the father of the celebrated Mr. John Wesley, being strongly importuned by the friends of *James the Second*, to support the measures of the court in favor of Popery, with promises of preferment, absolutely refused even to read the king's declaration; and though surrounded with courtiers, soldiers, and informers, he preached a bold and pointed discourse against it from these words:—"If it be so, our God whom we serve is able to deliver us out of thy hand, O king. But if not, be it known unto thee, O king, that we will not serve thy gods, nor worship the golden image which thou hast set up."

(*n*) "TOUCH ME IF YOU DARE."—Some of the Indian chiefs having become the open enemies of the gospel, Mr. Elliot, sometimes called the Apostle of the American Indians, when in the wilderness, without the company of any other Englishman, was, at various times, treated in a threatening and barbarous manner by some of those men, yet his Almighty Protector inspired him with such resolution, that he said,—"I am about the work of the Great God, and my God is with me: so that I fear neither you, nor all the Sachems (or chiefs) in the country. I will go on, and do you touch me if you dare." They heard him, and shrunk away.

(*o*) EXCOMMUNICATING A PRINCE.—William IX, Duke of Aquitaine and Earl of Poitiers, was a violent and dissolute prince, and often indulged himself in improper behavior at the expense of religion. Though he had contracted a very suitable marriage, and one with which he was satisfied for some time, he parted from his wife without reason, to marry another who pleased him better. The Bishop of Poitiers, where he resided, was a holy prelate, named Peter. He could not brook so great a scandal; and having employed all other means in vain, he thought it his duty to excommunicate the duke. As he began to pronounce the anathema, William furiously advanced, sword in hand, saying, "Thou art dead if thou proceedest." The bishop, as if afraid, required a few moments to consider what was most expedient. The duke granted it, and the bishop courageously finished the rest of the formula of excommunication. After which, extending his neck, "Now strike," said he, "I am quite ready." The astonishment which this intrepid conduct produced in the duke, disarmed his fury, and saying ironically, "I don't like you well enough to send you to heaven," he contented himself with banishing him.

(*p*) HINTON AND THE UNWORTHY COMMUNICANT.—A person who was not a member of Mr. James Hinton's church in Oxford, nevertheless enjoyed the privileges of Christian fellowship, as being connected (according to his own statement) with a well known church in London. His conduct was found to be inconsistent; it was ascertained, also, that he had been excluded from the community to which he had declared himself to belong. It was clearly necessary to inform him, therefore, that he could no longer be admitted to the Lord's table. But he was rich, and he was *passionate;* subject, indeed, to paroxysms of rage, on account of which, every one was afraid to interfere with him. The measure was, however, adopted by the church; but when (according to their usual mode) messengers were to be appointed to communicate the result, the deacons would not go; nor would any one go, for all said, it was at the hazard of their lives. "Then," replied Mr. Hinton, "I will go: my life is second to my duty." But no one would even accompany him; and he went alone. The unhappy man's wrath was exceedingly high. When solemnly warned that no such person as he was could "enter into the kingdom of heaven," he seized a large stick, and threatened his reprover's life: to which he replied, "Then, sir, I shall meet you next at the bar of judgment; and you will remember that these were the last words I uttered!" The enraged man immediately threw down his weapon, and ran about the room in agony, crying, "O no, no, no, you shall not charge me with murder!" Mr. Hinton records the deliverance from ——— among his "special mercies."

(*q*) LAVATER AND THE PREFECT.—There lived in the city of Zurich, a person who, though an unworthy character, was a member of its senate. During the time he was prefect over a district of the canton, he had committed innumerable acts of the grossest injustice,—yea, such flagrant crimes, that all the country people reproached and cursed him; but no one dared to prosecute him, as he was related to several members of the Zurich government, and son-in-law to the chief magistrate of the city. Mr. Lavater, the celebrated physiognomist, having often heard of the atrocities of the prefect, committed against even helpless widows and orphans, and having duly examined into them, felt an irresistible desire to plead the cause of the poor and oppressed. He was aware that his supporting this cause would expose him to the frowns of the great and the mighty, and occasion much anxiety to his friends; but conceiving it to be his duty, he determined to proceed. Having prepared himself by earnest prayer, and consulted an intimate friend, he addressed a letter to the prefect, in which he strongly reproached him for his detestable actions, and plainly signified his intention to bring him to public justice, should he not restore his spoils within two months. The time having elapsed, and no restoration having been made, Mr. Lavater proceeded to print a solemn indictment against him, which he caused to be delivered to every member of the Zurich government. At first he concealed his name; but when called upon, he came forward in the most open manner, nobly avowed and fully proved the points of his indictmen before the whole senate,—had the satisfaction to see the wicked prefect (who, conscious of his guilt, had saved himself by flight) solemnly condemned by law, his unjust property confiscated, and restoration made to oppressed poverty and innocence.

113. COURTESY.

(*a*) KING HENRY AND THE POOR CITIZEN.—Henry IV, of France, was standing one day with some of his courtiers, at the entrance of a village, and a poor man passing by, bowed down to the very ground; and the king, with great condescension, returned his salutation just in the same manner; at which one of his attendants ventured to express his surprise, when the monarch finely replied to him,—"Would you have your king exceeded in politeness by one of the lowest of his subjects?"

(*b*) A GOOD REPLY.—When old Zachariah Fox, the great merchant of Liverpool, was asked by what means he contrived to realize so large a fortune as he possessed, his reply was, "Friend, by one article alone, in which thou may'st deal too if thou pleasest—civility."

(*c*) THE POPE AND HIS AMBASSADOR.—It is related of Pope Clement XIV, (Ganganelli,) that when he ascended the papal chair, the ambassadors of the several states represented at his court waited on him with their congratulations. When they were introduced and bowed, he returned the compliment by bowing also; on which the master of the ceremonies told his highness that he should not have returned their salute. "O, I beg your pardon," said the good pontiff, I have not been pope long enough to forget good manners."

(*d*) DR. FURNAM AND THE NEGRESS.—Dr. Furnam was once present in a small company of brethren who had assembled to dine with a common friend, when the usual style by which they addressed each other, was that affectionate appellative of *brother*. Those present were very exact in using this mode of address. While their conversation was in progress, and they were freely *brothering* each other, there came in an aged colored woman, well known for her piety and good character. The brethren present saluted her, one in this manner and another in that—thus: "Well, old woman,' "How-de, mamma;" "How-de, Clarinda," and so on.

When she came to Dr. Furnam, he leaned forward, extended to her his hand, and said: "How do you do, sister Clarinda?" He might have designed his salutation to the old woman as a gentle reproof to those present, who did not seem to feel the true equality in which all who know the religion of Christ stand as brethren.

(*e*) LOUIS XIV AND HIS ANECDOTE.—Louis the XIVth, in a gay party at Versailles, thought he perceived an opportunity of relating a facetious story. He commenced, but ended the tale abruptly and insipidly. One of the company soon after leaving the room, the king said, "I am sure you must all have observed how very uninteresting my anecdote was. I did not recollect till I began, that the turn of the narrative reflected very severely on the immediate ancestor of the prince, or Armigue, who has just quitted us; and on this, as on every occasion, I think it far better to *spoil a good story, than distress a worthy man.*"

(*f*) THE OFFICER'S HAT.—An Englishman, taking the grand tour, towards the middle of the eighteenth century, when travellers were more objects of attention than at present on arriving at Turin, sauntered out to see the place. He happened to meet a regiment of infantry returning from parade, and taking a position to see it pass, a young captain, evidently desirous of making a display before the stranger, in crossing one of the numerous water-courses with which the city is intersected, missed his footing, and trying to save himself, lost his hat. The spectators laughed, and looked at the Englishman, expecting him to laugh too. On the contrary, he not only retained his composure, but promptly advanced to where the hat rolled, and taking it up, presented it with an air of kindness to its confused owner. The officer received it with a blush of surprise and gratitude, and hurried to rejoin his company. There was a murmur of applause, and the stranger passed on. Though the scene of a moment, and without a word spoken, it touched every heart.

On the regiment being dismissed, the captain, who was a young man of consideration, in glowing terms related the circumstance to his colonel. The colonel immediately mentioned it to the general in command; and when the Englishman returned to his hotel, he found an aid-de-camp waiting to request his company at dinner, at head quarters. In the evening he was taken to court, at that time the most brilliant court in Europe, and was received with particular attention. Of course during his stay at Turin he was invited every where; and on his departure he was loaded with letters of introduction to the different States of Italy. Thus a private gentleman of moderate means, by a graceful impulse of Christian feeling, was enabled to travel through a foreign country, then of the highest interest for its society as well as for the charms it still possesses, with more real distinction and advantage than can ever be derived from the mere circumstance of birth and fortune, even the most splendid.

(*g*) A GOOD MAXIM.—It was a maxim of a celebrated minister, "that if a child but lisped to give you pleasure, you ought to be pleased." When occasionally preaching in the villages, he used to be delighted in visiting the poor, and, when solicited, would regale himself with their brown bread and black tea; but took care, at the same time, that they should lose nothing by their attention. "When a poor person shows anxiety to administer to your comfort," he would say, "do not interrupt him. Why deprive him of the pleasure of expressing his friendship?"

(*h*) EASY WAY TO CONFER HAPPINESS.—"If a civil word or two will render a man happy," said a French king, "he must be wretched indeed who will not give them to him." Were superiors to keep this in view, yea, were all mankind to observe it, how much happier would the world be than what it is! We may say of this disposition, "that it is like lighting another man's candle by one's own, which loses none of its light by what the other gains."

(*i*) UNFASHIONABLE BOW.—When Sir William Johnson returned the salute of a negro who had bowed to him, he was reminded that he had done what was very unfashionable. "Perhaps so," said Sir William, "but I would not be outdone in good manners by a negro."

114. CREDULITY.

(*a*) FAITH OF THE COLLIER.—Implicit faith has been sometimes styled *fides carbonaria*, from the story of one who, examining an ignorant collier on his religious principles, asked him what it was that he believed. He answered, "I believe what the church believes." The other rejoined, "What, then, does the church believe?" He replied, readily, "The church believes what I believe." The other, desirous, if possible, to bring him to particulars, once more resumed his inquiry. "Tell me, then, I pray you, what it is which you and the church *both* believe." The only answer the collier could give was, "Why, truly, sir, the church and I *both*—believe the same thing."

CRUELTY.

115. Cruelty Exemplified.

(*a*) CRUELTY OF COMMODUS. —Nothing can be more contrary to nature, to reason, to religion, than cruelty. Hence an inhuman man is generally considered as a monster. Such monsters, however, have existed; and the heart almost bleeds at the recital of the cruel acts such have been guilty of. It teaches us, however, what human nature is when left to itself; not only treacherous above all things, but *desperately* wicked.

Commodus, the Roman emperor, when but twelve years old, gave a shocking instance of his cruelty, when, finding the water in which he bathed too warm, he commanded the person who attended the bath to be thrown into the furnace, nor was he satisfied till those who were about him pretended to put his order in execution. After his succession to the empire, he equalled, if he did not exceed in cruelty, Caligula, Domitian, and even Nero himself; playing, we may say, with the blood of his subjects and fellow-creatures, of whom he caused great numbers to be racked and butchered in his presence merely for his diversion. Historians relate many instances of his cruelty. He caused one to be thrown to wild beasts for reading the life of Caligula written by Suetonius; because the tyrant and he had been born on the same day of the month, and in many bad qualities resembled each other. Seeing one day a corpulent man pass by, he immediately cut him asunder, partly to try his strength, in which he excelled all men, and partly out of curiosity, as he himself owned, to see his entrails drop out at once. He took pleasure in cutting off the feet and putting out the eyes of such as he met in his rambles through the city. Some he murdered because they were negligently dressed; others because they seemed trimmed with too much nicety. He assumed the name and habit of Hercules, appearing publicly in a lion's skin, with a huge club in his hand, and ordering several persons, though not guilty of any crimes, to be disguised like monsters, that by knocking out their brains, he might have a better claim to the title, *the great destroyer of monsters*. He, however, was destroyed in his turn: one of his concubines, whose death he had purposed, poisoned him; but, as the poison did not quickly operate, he was strangled by a wrestler in the thirty-first year of his age.

(*b*) THE TUTOR'S PREDICTION RESPECTING TIBERIUS. — Theodorus Gaddaræus, who was tutor to Tiberius the Roman Emperor, observing in him, while a boy, a very sanguinary nature and disposition, which lay lurking under a show of lenity, was wont to call him, "a lump of clay steeped and soaked in blood." His predictions of him did not fail in the event. Tiberius thought death was too light a punishment for any one that displeased him. Hearing that one Carnulius, who had displeased him, had cut his own throat, "Carnulius," said he, "has escaped me." To another, who begged of him that he might die quickly, "No," said he, "you are not so much in favor as that yet."

(*c*) PETITION OF THE HORSE. —In the days of John, King of Atri, (an ancient city of Abruzzo,) there was a bell put up, which any one that had received any injury went and rang, and the king assembled the wise men chosen for the purpose, that justice might be done. It happened that, after the bell had been up a long time, the rope was worn out, and a piece of wild vine was made use of to lengthen it. Now there was a knight of Atri who had a noble charger, which had become unserviceable through age, so that, to avoid the expense of feeding him, he turned him loose upon the common. The horse driven by hunger, raised his mouth to the vine to munch it, and, pulling it, the bell rang. The judges assembled to consider the petition of the horse, which appeared to demand justice. They decreed that *the knight whom he had served in his youth should feed him in his old age;* a sentence which the king confirmed under a heavy penalty.

116. Cruelty Punished.

(*a*) DEAR-BOUGHT SPORT.—A few years since, at a place near Penzance, some men and boys, accompanied by two young women, having fastened a bullock's horn to the tail of a dog, turned the affrighted animal loose, and followed it with brutal exultations. The dog, pursued by its savage tormentors, ran down a road called Trereife Lane, when meeting a cart drawn by two horses, laden with coals, the horses took fright; the driver, who was sitting on the shafts of the cart, was thrown off, and the wheels passing over his head, he was killed on the spot. The persons who had occasioned this melancholy accident immediately suspended their chase of the dog, and the young women, on coming up, found that the lad, who had been killed by their mischievous frolic, was their brother!

(*b*) THE BLIND MAN'S ENEMY.—Some years ago, there lived in the village of Sutton Basset, in Leicestershire, an elderly man who was quite blind, but who, from his early acquaintance and familiarity with the place pefore this great misfortune befell him, was enabled to find his way about the village and surrounding fields without a guide. He was particularly the butt and jest of a poor sinful woman, who lived near the footpath stile, and who recognized not the hand of God in his affliction. She frequently attempted to impose on him for the mere purpose of plaguing and distressing him, and had one day contrived a very disagreeable vexation, which, to her merriment, succeeded. But, shortly after this, she gave birth to a son, who was born stone blird; and her following chlid, a son, was also born blind; and these two unfortunate youths were living, in 1833, in the above-named village, and obtained a precarious livelihood by opening the gates for passengers, on the roads adjoining the place, with the addition of a small allowance from the parish. They were two fine grown lads, and of about equal size. They were regarded by their neighbors as the objects of God's just displeasure against the wanton and foolish wickedness of their parent. We may be sure sin will find us out: if not always in this world, it will in the next; but even here sinners are not always exempted from punishment.

(*c*) BAJAZET PRONOUNCING HIS OWN SENTENCE.—Tamerlane the Great, having made war on Bajazet, Emperor of the Turks, overthrew him in battle, and took him prisoner. The victor gave the captive monarch at first a very civil reception; and entering into familiar conversation with him, said, "Now, king, tell me freely and truly what thou wouldst have done with me, had I fallen into thy power?" Bajazet, who was of a fierce and haughty spirit, is said to have thus replied: "Had the gods given unto me the victory, I would have enclosed thee in an iron cage, and carried thee about with me as a spectacle of derision to the world." Tamerlane wrathfully replied, "Then, proud man, as thou wouldst have done to me, even so shall I do unto thee." A strong iron cage was made, into which the fallen emperor was thrust; and thus exposed like a wild beast, he was carried along in the train of his conqueror. Nearly three years were passed by the once mighty Bajazet in this cruel state of durance; and at last being told that he must be carried into Tartary, despairing of then obtaining his freedom, he struck his head with such violence against the bars of his cage, as to put an end to his wretched life.

(*d*) CRUELTY OF LOUIS XI.—Philip de Comines, in his "Life of Louis XI," has not concealed the dreadful cruelties and extortions by which he rendered himself one of the most odious monarchs that ever swayed the sceptre of France. Stronger colors could not be employed than those in which he describes his loathsome dungeons, his iron cages, and chain nets

Claude de Seyssel, another historian, says, "That about the places where he was, were seen great numbers of people hanging on trees; and the prisons and other neighboring houses, full of prisoners, which were often heard, both by day and night, to cry out through the torments they endured; besides those who were secretly cast into the rivers." The same historian observes, "That this king carried his absolute power to excess. He caused Tristan, his provost, to take the prisoners who were in the palace gaol, and drown them near the Grange aux Morcier." Mezaria, another historian, relates, "That he had put to death above four thousand, by different punishments, which he sometimes delighted to see. Most of them had been executed without form of law; several drowned with a stone tied to their necks; others precipitated, going over a swipe, from whence they fell upon wheels, armed with spikes and cutting instruments; others were strangled in dungeons; Tristan, his companion and provost of his palace, being at once judge, witness, and executioner."

It is a remarkable fact, that the Bishop of Verdun, who assisted Louis in the invention of his iron cage, was himself put into the first that was made, and confined to it for fourteen days; and that the king himself, not long before his death, was obliged to make himself a close prisoner in one of his strongest castles, from a dread of that thirst for vengeance with which his cruel conduct had inspired, not only his nobles and subjects, but the very members of his own family.

(*e*) A BULL-BAITING.—Improper and cruel amusements are often attended with danger; and the end of such mirth is heaviness. Some years ago, at the termination of a fair, annually held at Rochdale, in Lancashire, it was determined to bait a bull for the gratification of a great number of persons, whose tastes are as savage as their amusements are cruel, and, accordingly, the poor beast was tied to a stake at the edge of the river, near the bridge. The radius of the cord was about six yards, and the animal, in making the circle, was frequently three feet deep in water. The crowd collected to witness this sight was great, and the number of people on and near the bridge made it difficult to pass; the sides of the river were also thronged with spectators of every age and sex, and many were seen near the bull up to their middle in water, jumping with ecstasy at the sport. At every revolution the animal made to disengage himself from the dogs, people were seen tumbling over each other in the mud and water up to the knees, and the shouts of joy occasionally expressed, could only have been equalled by the yell of savages. This sport continued for about three hours, when a considerable portion of the parapet wall leading to the bridge gave way, from the extreme pressure of the crowd, and five persons were killed on the spot. Four other persons died shortly afterwards of the wounds they received, making nine in the whole who lost their lives, besides a considerable number who were severely wounded. The stones being large they fell with overwhelming weight; and from the pressure of the crowd near the wall, numbers of the spectators were precipitated along with the stones on the people below. One woman had her thighs broken, and a young man had his arm completely cut from his body, besides others who were severely bruised.

117. CRUELTY AND BENEVOLENCE COMBINED.

(*a*) TRAJAN'S INCONSISTENCIES. — Who has not heard of the Emperor Trajan, of his moderation, his clemency, his gushing sympathies, his forgiveness of injuries and forgetfulness of self, his tearing in pieces his own robe, to furnish bandages for the wounded—called by the whole world, in his day, "the best Emperor of Rome;" and so affectionately regarded by his subjects, that, ever afterwards, in blessing his successors upon their accession to power, they always said, "May you have the virtue and goodness of Trajan!" yet the deadly conflicts of gladiators who were trained to kill each other, to make sport for the spectators, furnished his chief pastime. At one time he kept up those spectacles for 123 days in succession. In the tortures which he inflicted on Christians, fire and poison, daggers and dungeons, wild beasts and serpents, and the rack, did their worst. He threw into the sea, Clemens, the venerable bishop of Rome, with an anchor about his neck; and tossed to the famishing lions in the amphitheatre the aged Ignatius.

(*b*) CHARACTER OF THEODOSIUS. — Theodosius the Great was a member of the Christian church, and in his zeal against paganism, and what he deemed heresy, surpassed all who were before him. The Christian writers of his time speak of him as a most illustrious model of justice, generosity, benevolence, and every virtue. And yet Theodosius denounced capital punishments against those who held 'heretical' opinions, and commanded intermarriage between cousins to be punished by burning the parties alive. On hearing that the people of Antioch had demolished the statues set up in that city, in honor of himself, and had threatened the governor, he flew into a transport of fury, ordered the city to be laid in ashes, and all the inhabitants to be slaughtered; and upon hearing of a resistance to his authority in Thessalonica, in which one of his lieutenants was killed, he instantly ordered a *general massacre* of the inhabitants; and in obedience to his command, seven thousand men, women and children, were butchered in the space of three hours.

(*c*) DOUBLE CHARACTER OF PLINY.—Pliny the younger, who was proconsul under Trajan, may well be mentioned in connection with the emperor, as a striking illustration of the truth, that goodness and amiableness towards one class of men is often turned into cruelty towards another. History an hardly show a more gentle and lovely character than Pliny. While pleading at the bar, he always sought out the grievances of the poorest and most despised persons, entered into their wrongs with his whole soul, and never took a fee. Who can read his admirable letters without being touched by their tenderness and warmed by their benignity and philanthropy? And yet, this tender-hearted Pliny coolly plied with excruciating torture two spotless females, who had served as deaconesses in the Christian church, hoping to extort from them matter of accusation against the Christians. He commanded Christians to abjure their faith, invoke the gods, pour out libations to the statues of the emperor, burn incense to idols, and curse Christ. If they refused, he ordered them to execution.

(*d*) CHARACTER OF ADRIAN. —The kindness, condescension, and forbearance of Adrian were proverbial; he was one of the most eloquent orators of his age; and when pleading the cause of injured innocence, would melt and overwhelm the auditors by the pathos of his appeals. It was his constant maxim, that he was an emperor, not for his own good, but for the benefit of his fellow creatures. He stooped to relieve the wants of the meanest of his subjects, and would peril his life by visiting them when sick of infectious diseases; he prohibited, by law, masters from killing their slaves, gave to slaves legal trial, and exempted them from torture; yet towards certain individuals and classes, he showed himself a monster of cruelty. He prided himself on his knowledge of architecture, and ordered to execution the most celebrated architect of Rome, because he had criticised one of the emperor's designs. He banished all the Jews from their native land, and drove them to the ends of the earth; and unloosed the bloodhounds of persecution to rend in pieces his Christian subjects.

(*e*) TITUS IN ROME—TITUS IN JUDEA.—Who has not heard of the Emperor Titus—so beloved for his mild virtues and compassionate regard for the suffering, that he was named "The Delight of Mankind;" so tender of the lives of his subjects that he took the office of high priest that his hands might never be defiled with blood; and was heard to declare, with tears, that he had rather die than put another to death. So intent upon making others happy, that when once about to retire to sleep, and not being able to recall any particular act of beneficence performed during the day, he cried out in anguish, "Alas! I have lost a day!" And, finally, whom the learned Kennet, in his Roman Antiquities, characterizes as "the only prince in the world that has the character of *never doing an ill action*." Yet, witnessing the mortal combats of the captives taken in war, killing each other in the amphitheatre, amidst the acclamations of the populace, was a favorite amusement with Titus. At one time he exhibited shows of gladiators, which lasted one hundred days, during which the amphitheatre was flooded with human blood. At another of his public exhibitions he caused five thousand wild beasts to be baited in the amphitheatre. During the siege of Jerusalem, he set ambushes to seize the famishing Jews, who stole out of the city by night to glean food in the valleys: these he would first dreadfully scourge, then torment them with all conceivable tortures, and, at last, crucify them before the wall of the city. According to Josephus, not less than five hundred a day were thus tormented. And when many of the Jews, frantic with famine, deserted to the Romans, Titus cut off their hands and drove them back. After the destruction of Jerusalem, he dragged to Rome one hundred thousand captives, and sold them as slaves, and scattered them through every province of the empire.

DEATH.

18. Readiness for Death.

(*a*) THE MINER BURIED ALIVE.—Charles Greenhough, a native of a populous hamlet in the West Riding of Yorkshire, a humble and pious man, was engaged in the perilous occupation of a miner. One morning, having engaged in family worship, he proceeded to his work and labor, which was to get the iron-stone in one of those pits, which, from their shape, are termed "bell pits." The pit in question was just being finished, and Charles, with four others, were engaged in it, when a tremendous fall of earth threatened them. They simultaneously rushed to the opposite side, which they had scarcely reached, when they were all partially buried. The four companions of poor Charles extricated themselves and each other, and proceeded to use every effort to procure his release, at the peril of their own lives, for a still more dreadful falling in of the side of the pit now threatened them. It was at this awful moment of peril that his Christian calmness and disinterestedness were exhibited. After expressing his conviction that he could not be extricated, he directed them to place a stone to defend his head, which yet remained unburied, and then said, "Escape for your lives! 'tis well I am taken instead of you; for I am ready and you are not!" His few remaining minutes were spent in earnest prayer for his family, and in solemnly commending his departing spirit to the Lord Jesus. The earth then fell, and buried him alive!

(*b*) MR. WESLEY AND THE GERMANS.—In the early part of the career of the Rev. John Wesley, influenced by a desire to do good, he undertook a voyage to Georgia. During a storm on the voyage he was very much alarmed by the fear of death, and being a severe judge of himself, he concluded that he was unfit to die. He observed the lively faith of the Germans, which in the midst of danger, kept their minds in a state of tranquillity and ease, to which he and the English on board were strangers. While they were singing at the commencement of their service, the sea broke over them, split the mainsail in pieces, covered the ship, and poured in between the decks as if the great deep had already swallowed them up. The English screamed terribly: the Ger mans calmly sung on. Mr. Wesley asked one of them afterwards, if he were not afraid. He answered, "I thank God, no." "But were not your women and children afraid?' He replied mildly, "No: our women and children are not afraid to die."

(c) SENTIMENT OF AN AGED CHIEF.—A distinguished Oneida chief, named Skenandoah, having yielded to the instructions of the Rev. Mr. Kirkland, and lived a reformed man for fifty years, said, just before he died, in his hundred and twentieth year, "I am an aged hemlock; the winds of one hundred years have whistled through my branches; I am dead at the top; (he was blind;) why I yet live, the great good Spirit only knows. Pray to my Jesus, that I may wait with patience my appointed time to die; and when I die, lay me by the side of my minister and father, that I may go up with him at the great resurrection."

(d) FEARS OF DEATH VANQUISHED.—A person who lived in the house of a pious friend, often communicated to him his distressing apprehensions. He was not so much disturbed with doubts respecting his interest in Christ, as terrified with the thoughts of dying, and said he thought he should need three or four persons to hold him, if he apprehended death was at hand. His friend proposed Scriptural antidotes to this unreasonable dread; and encouraged him to expect that, as his day, so should his strength be. After a long illness, the time of his departure approached; and he often expressed a wish that his friend could always be with him. Finding himself dying, he repeatedly sent for his friend to pray with him. He felt uneasy, and said, "Satan whispers that I have been a deceiver, and shall die a hypocrite." He asked his friend to pray again with him, after which he cried, "The Lord is come! Praise God, praise God!" He then lifted up both his hands, which, from weakness, he could scarcely raise before, and several times repeated, "Victory, victory, victory, through the blood of the Lamb!" and expired with the unfinished word oı his lips.

(e) SEVERAL EXAMPLES.—*John Dodd*—"I am not afraid to look death in the face. I can say—Death, where is thy sting? Death canno hurt me."

Robert Bolton—"O! when will this good hour come? When shall I be dissolved? When shall I be with Christ?"

Halyburton—"Here is a demonstration of the reality of religion, that I, a poor, weak, timorous man, as much afraid of death as any, am now enabled by the power of grace, composedly and with joy, to look death in the face."

Edward Deering—"As for my death, I bless God I feel and find so much inward joy and comfort to my soul, that if I were put to my choice whether I would die or live, I would a thousand times rather choose death than life, if it may stand with the holy will of God."

John Owen—"Oh! brother Payne, the long-looked for day is come at last, in which I shall see that glory in another manner than I have ever yet done, or been capable of doing."

Risden Darracott—"Well, I am going from weeping friends to congratulate angels and rejoicing saints in heaven and glory. Blessed be God, all is well."

(f) THE PIOUS BOATSWAIN IN THE STORM.—On board an East-Indiaman was a pious boatswain, whom, on this account, the crew looked upon as a strange man. The ship was overtaken with a storm so dreadful, tha after every effort to preserve life, the captain said, 'All that could be done had been done—it was impossible th vessel could weather it.' The shi seemed sinking—the captain withdrew into the cabin—the men were some or their knees, and others with horror hanging on parts of the rigging. All expected the vessel would founder. The boatswain had been very active, and apparently unalarmed, during the whole of the gale. At this moment, when a heavy wave struck the ship, and seemed as if it would instantly sink her, looking up with a smile he exclaimed, 'Blessed be God, all is right!' and h began to sing. The storm afterward abated, and the vessel was saved. Thus, amidst the storm of life, on the dark ocean of death, and amidst the terrors of the judgment day the Christian may still smile and exulting exclaim, 'Blessed be God, all is right!'

(*g*) CECIL'S DYING MOTHER.—My first convictions on the subject of religion, says the Rev. R. Cecil, were confirmed by observing, that really religious persons had some solid happiness among them, which I felt the vanities of the world could not give. I shall never forget standing by the bedside of my sick mother. "Are not you afraid to die?" I asked. "No." "No! Why does the uncertainty of another state give you no concern?" "Because God has said, 'Fear not; when thou passest through the waters, I will be with thee; and through the rivers, they shall not overflow thee.'—'Let me die the death of the righteous.'"

(*h*) BEAUTIFUL REPLY.—A pious Scotch minister being asked by a friend during his last illness, whether he thought himself dying? answered, "Really, friend, I care not whether I am or not; for, if I die I shall be with God; if I live, He will be with me."

(*i*) GEORGE III, AND HIS SEPULCHRE.—At the time his majesty, desiring that himself and family should repose in the same sepulchre, and in one less public than that of Westminster, had ordered the tomb-house at Windsor to be constructed, Mr. Wyatt, his architect, waited upon him with a detailed report and plan of the design, and of the manner in which he proposed to arrange it for the reception of the remains of royalty. The king went minutely through the whole; and when finished, Mr. Wyatt, in thanking his majesty, said apologetically, he had ventured to occupy so much of his majesty's time and attention with these details, in order that it might not be necessary to bring so painful a subject again under his notice. To this the king replied, "Mr. Wyatt, I request that you will bring the subject before me whenever you please. I shall attend with as much pleasure to the building of a tomb to receive me when I am dead, as I would to the decorations of a drawing-room to hold me while living: for, Mr. Wyatt, if it please God that I should live to be ninety or a hundred, I am willing to stay: but if it pleases God to take me this night, I am ready to go!"

(*j*) REMARK OF DR. WATTS.—"I bless God," said Dr. Watts, "I can lie down with comfort to-night, not being anxious whether I awake in this world or another."

119. Happy Deaths of Christians.

(*a*) POLYCARP'S DEATH.—When Polycarp, an ancient bishop of the church at Smyrna, was brought to the tribunal, the proconsul asked him if he was Polycarp; to which he assented. The proconsul then began to exhort him, saying, "Have pity on thine own great age; swear by the fortune of Cesar; repent: say, take away the atheists," meaning the Christians. Polycarp, casting his eyes solemnly over the multitude, waving his hand to them, and looking up to heaven, said, "Take away these atheists;" meaning the idolaters around him. The proconsul still urging him, and saying, "Swear, and I will release thee; reproach Christ," Polycarp said, "Eighty and six years have I served him, and he hath never wronged me; and how can I blaspheme my King who hath saved me?" "I have wild beasts," said the proconsul, "and will expose you to them unless you repent." "Call them," said the martyr. "I will tame your spirit by fire," said the Roman. "You threaten me," said Polycarp, "with the fire which burns only for a moment, but are yourself ignorant of the fire of eternal punishment, reserved for the ungodly." Soon after, being about to be put to death, he exclaimed, "O Father of thy beloved and blessed Son, Jesus Christ! O God of all principalities and of all creation! I bless thee that thou hast counted me worthy of this day, and this hour, to receive my portion in the number of the martyrs, in the cup of Christ."

(*b*) DEATH OF REV. JOHN WESLEY.—The Rev. John Wesley, after a long life of great labor and usefulness, being sixty-five years in the ministry, concluded his course as might have been expected, in peace and holy joy. Having been laid on the bed, from whence he rose no more, he called to those who were with him, to "pray and praise." Soon after he again called upon them to "pray and praise!" and taking each by the hand, and affectionately saluting them, bade them farewell. Attempting afterwards to say something which they could not understand, he paused a little, and then, with all the remaining strength he had, said, "The best of all is, God is with us." And again, lifting his hand, he repeated the same words in a holy triumph, "The best of all is, God is with us."

(*c*) DEATH-BED OF REV. W. DAY.—"The Bible," said the dying saint, "is nothing to me, the Bible is nothing to me, but as it reveals to my soul a covenant Jehovah, Father, Son, and Holy Ghost. There I see perfection. When I look at man—when I look at myself, I see nothing but vileness:—a rent here, a chasm there. It would drive me to despair. Oh when," he wept profusely, "when shall I behold Christ as he is, and cast myself at his feet! He has offered me a pledge of this beyond all your imagination can conceive. I have seen him rising before me in all the majesty of the Godhead. The world has shown me its favors, and has taken them away again. I have enjoyed many tokens of the loving-kindness of my God, and I have at other times been stripped of what I most valued. But, O my God, my Redeemer, thou hast never failed me!" Then stretching out his hands to his family around his bed, he cried, "O Lord, shine forth, shine forth in thy glory upon these dear ones—Thou wilt never leave them—Thou wilt never forsake them."—It was an affecting, a sublime scene. It was like a patriarch standing on the threshold of heaven, looking back to bless his family, and looking forward, earnestly longing to take his last step.

(*d*) "I AM THE LORD THY GOD."—A friend calling on the Rev. Ebenezer Erskine, during his last illness, said to him, "Sir, you have given us many good advices, pray what are you now doing with you own soul?" "I am doing with it," said he, "what I did forty years ago; I am resting on that word, *I am the Lord thy God;* and on this I mean to die." To another, he said, "The covenant is my charter, and if it had not been for that blessed word, *I am the Lord thy God*, my hope and strength had perished from the Lord." The night on which he died, his eldest daughter was reading in the room where he was, to whom he said, "What book is that you are reading, my dear?" "It is one of your sermons, sir." "What one is it?" "It is the sermon on that text, '*I am the Lord thy God.*'" "O woman," said he, "that is the best sermon I ever preached." And it was most probably the best to his soul. A little afterwards, with his finger and thumb he shut his own eyes, and laying his hand below his cheek, breathed out his soul into the hands of his living Redeemer. Happy the man that is in such a state! happy the man whose God is the Lord!

(*e*) "I SHALL SUP WITH CHRIST."—Mr. Robert Bruce, the morning before he died, being at breakfast, having, as he used, eaten an egg, he said to his daughter, "I think I am yet hungry; you may bring me another egg." But having mused a while, he said, "*Hold, daughter, hold, my master calls me.*" With these words his sight failed him: on which he called for the Bible, and said, "Turn to the 8th chapter of the Romans, and set my finger on the words, 'I am persuaded that neither death nor life, &c., shall be able to separate me from the love of God which is in *Christ Jesus* my Lord.'" When this was done he said, "*Now is my finger upon them?*" Being told that it was, he added, "*Now, God be with you, my dear children: I have breakfasted with you, and shall sup with my Lord Jesus Christ this night;*" and then expired.

(*f*) DEATH OF HERVEY.—Dr. Stonehouse, who attended Mr. Hervey during his last illness, seeing the great difficulty and pain with which he spoke, and finding by his pulse that the pangs of death were then coming on, desired that he would spare himself. "No," said he, "doctor, no: you tell me I have but a few minutes to live;

Oh! let me spend them in adoring our great Redeemer. Though my flesh and my heart fail me, yet God is the strength of my heart and my portion for ever." He then expatiated, in the most striking manner, on these words of Paul, "All things are yours, life and death; things present, and things to come; all are yours; and ye are Christ's, and Christ is God's." "Here," said he, "is the treasure of a Christian, and a noble treasure it is. *Death is reckoned in this inventory:* how thankful am I for it, as it is the passage through which I get to the Lord and Giver of eternal life! and as it frees me from all the misery you see me now endure, and which I am willing to endure as long as God thinks fit; for I know he will by and by, in his good time, dismiss me from the body. These light afflictions are but for a moment, and then comes an eternal weight of glory. Oh, welcome, welcome death! thou mayest well be reckoned among the *treasures* of the Christian! To live is Christ, but to die is gain."

(*g*) DEATH OF DR. GOODWIN.—"Ah!" said Dr. Goodwin, in his last moments, "is this dying? How have I dreaded as an enemy this smiling friend!"

(*h*) DEATH OF REV. WILLIAM JANEWAY.—This good man, who was the father of the Rev. John Janeway, being brought to his death-bed, endured great conflict of mind, and entertained many fears as to his future happiness. Under those circumstances, he asked the prayers of his son, who, though he entertained no doubt as to the real piety of his father, was filled with Christian sympathy; and having retired, he spent some time in wrestling with God upon his father's account, earnestly praying that he would fill him with joy unspeakable in believing, and that he would speedily give him some token for good, that he might joyfully and honorably leave this world to go to a better. After he was risen from his knees, he went down to his sick father, and asked him how he felt himself. His father made no answer for some time, but wept exceedingly, to which he was not subject, and continued for some considerable time weeping, so that he was not able to speak. But at last, having recovered himself, with unspeakable joy he burst out into such expressions as these:—"O son, now it is come, it is come, it is come! I bless God I can die; the Spirit of God hath witnessed with my spirit that I am his child. Now I can look upon God as my dear Father, and Christ as my Redeemer. I can now say, This is my Friend, and this is my Beloved. My heart is full it is brimful; I can hold no more. I know *now* what that sentence means,—The peace of God which passeth understanding. That fit of weeping which you saw me in, was a fit of overpowering love and joy, so great that I could not contain myself; neither can I express what glorious discoveries God has made of himself unto me. And had that joy been greater, I question whether I could have borne it, and whether it would not have separated soul and body. Bless the Lord, O my soul, and all that is within me bless his holy name, who hath pardoned all my sins, and sealed the pardon! He hath healed my wounds, and caused the bones which he had broken to rejoice. Oh, now I can die! It is nothing: I bless God I can die. I desire to be dissolved, and to be with Christ." In this delightful frame of soul he shortly after left earth for heaven.

(*i*) HAPPY DEATH OF REV. S. MORELL.—This excellent young minister, when just entering on his important station at Norwich, was called, in the twenty-fourth year of his age, to exchange worlds. On the last day of his life, he remarked, that he should once more wish to commit his soul to God, and then added, "I should like to understand the secrets of eternity before to-morrow morning." His desire was granted. In his last moments he indulged in language like this: "None can know, none conceive the happiness I possess, the peace with which my soul is filled, but the sincere disciple of our Lord Jesus Christ. Redeemer of mankind, give me strength to bear even joy—this joy!"

(*j*) HAPPY SURPRISE OF DEATH.—The Rev. Mr. Hall, of Arnsby, Mr. Evans, of Foxton, and Mr. Christian, of Sheepshead, three eminently pious ministers of the gospel, attended a ministers' meeting at Mr. Woodman's, Sutton, in the Elms, Leicestershire. The day was solemn, and the discourses delivered were very interesting and appropriate. In the evening, these ministers spent their time together in the most agreeable conversation. Amongst other subjects, one of them proposed for discussion, that passage in Job ix. 23, "If the scourge slay suddenly, he will laugh at the trial of the innocent." Deep seriousness pervaded the conversation, while each minister gave his thoughts on the text. When it came to Mr. Christian's turn to speak, he dwelt upon the subject with an unusual degree of feeling. He considered it as referring to the sudden death of the righteous; and was expatiating very largely on the desirableness of such an event, and the happy surprise with which it would be attended, when, amidst a flood of rapturous tears, he took his flight from the world while the words were yet faltering on his tongue!

(*k*) WELCOMING DEATH.—Mrs. Legare, an excellent woman, resided at Charleston, S. C. When she had nearly closed her eyes in death, her physician came and found the family in tears. "Well, doctor," said Mr. Legare, "what do you think of the scene in the next room?" "Indeed, sir," said he, "I know not what to think of it; it is all a mystery to me. I have seen numbers of men in all the vigor of health, and thirsting for martial honor, rush into a field of battle, and in that confused scene put on the appearance of fortitude, not one of whom could face the gradual approaches of death, or a sick bed, without visible horror; but here is a poor emaciated woman, whose whole nervous system is unstrung by long disease, welcoming the grim messenger with the utmost serenity, composure, and joy, though approaching in all the horrors of the most gradual progress imaginable;" (for she was three days in the agonies of death.) "Indeed it is a mystery, and I know not how to account for it." "Do you not, sir?" asked Mr. Legare; "go, then, to Calvary. You see us dissolved in tears but I do not believe there is a tear in the room extorted by grief; no, sir, they are tears of joy." The docto went down stairs, and met a gentleman at the door, who inquired after Mrs. L., to whom he replied, "Just gone, sir." "Well," said he, "Mr. Legare is a philosopher, and I hope he will bear the stroke like one." "Philosophy!" replied the doctor, "I have thought as much of philosophy as any man, but the scene within beats philosophy hollow."

(*l*) DEATH OF MRS. HERVEY.—Mrs. Elizabeth Hervey, the wife of a Missionary in Bombay, died an early but happy death. "I did hope," said she, "that I should be permitted to do something towards elevating the degraded and miserable females of India; but since God decides otherwise, His will be done! In this great conflict, some must fall as soon as they enter the field. Tell my friends that I never have for a moment regretted that I came hither. No! had I foreseen this hour, and all that I have endured since I left America, I should have decided just as I did, if the path of duty had been as plain as it appeared to be."

A friend said to her, he hoped the Saviour would be with her, as she walked through the dark valley of the shadow of death. "If this," said she, "is the dark valley, it has not a dark spot in it; all is light—light!" She had, during most of her sickness, bright views of the perfections of God. "His awful holiness," she said, "appeared the most lovely of all His attributes." At one time, she said she wanted words to express her views of the majesty and glory of Christ. "It seems," said she, "that if all other glory were annihilated, and nothing left but His bare self, it would be enough; it would be a universe of glory!"

(*m*) VARA'S HAPPY DEATH.—Mr. Williams relates, in his "Missionary Enterprises," that a delightful instance of the power of the gospel is to be met with in the history of a chief named Vara, a native of the island of Aimeo. In the time of his ignorance he was a procurer of human sacrifices;

but he became eventually a humble and devoted Christian, and to the day of his death he adorned his profession. He was visited many times in his dying moments by Mr. Orsmond, whose account of his death I will here subjoin.

On seeing his end approach, I said to him, "Are you sorry that you cast away your lying gods, by which you used to gain so much property?" He was aroused from his lethargy, and with tears of pleasure sparkling in his eyes, he exclaimed, "O no, no! What! can I be sorry for casting away death for life? Jesus is my rock, the fortification in which my soul takes shelter." I said, "Tell me on what you found your hopes of future blessedness?" He replied, "I have been very wicked; but a great King from the other side of the skies sent his ambassadors with terms of peace. We could not tell, for many years, what these ambassadors wanted. At length, Pomare obtained a victory, and invited all his subjects to come and take refuge under the wing of Jesus, and I was one of the first to do so. The *blood of Jesus* is my foundation. I grieve that all my children do not love him. Had they known the misery we endured in the reign of the devil, they would gladly take the gospel in exchange for their follies. Jesus is the best King; he gives a pillow without thorns." After a little time I asked him if he were afraid to die; when, with almost youthful energy, he replied, "No, no! The canoe is on the sea, the sails are spread; she is ready for the gale. I have a good Pilot to guide me, and a good haven to receive me. My outside man and my inside man differ. Let the one rot till the trump shall sound, but let my soul wing her way to the throne of Jesus!"

(*n*) NOT KNOWING DAY FROM NIGHT.—My letter was interrupted, writes the Rev. R. Watson, by being called to visit an old follower of Jesus Christ. I have been much profited by the interview. I have not been to instruct, but to be instructed. One of his expressions was: "Days, weeks, and months have rolled round during my affliction, and I have scarcely known the night from the day, nor the day from the night, so rapidly and joyfully have the hours escaped me; I have felt nothing but joy and love; not for a moment have I been impatient or weary, or wished it otherwise with me, so marvellously has God wrought in me. This is the hand of God. This never grew in nature's soil."

(*o*) DEATH OF MR. VENN.—The Rev. T. T. Thomason, who was afterwards a devoted minister of Christ in the East Indies, while at college, paid a visit, in company with two of his young friends, to the excellent Mr. Venn, then languishing in body, but rejoicing in soul, as a strong man to run a race. One of his expressions sunk deep into the mind of Thomason; it was this: "In what a state should I now be, had I only the Socinian's God to trust to!" This extraordinary man did not die like common Christians. The Rev. T. Robinson, of Leicester, visited him in his last illness, and began to speak to him, to use Mr. Robinson's words, "in my poor way." "Oh!" exclaimed Mr. Venn, "that is poor comfort, brother. Here is the passage I build on: 'who hath spoiled principalities and powers, and hath made a show of them openly, triumphing over them in it.'" These words he uttered with an energy and animation peculiar to himself. His mind was filled with the contemplation of a triumph, and he anticipated nothing less than soon meeting a victorious Savior, who shall tread all enemies under his feet.

(*p*) THE DYING COAL-MINER.—Stephen Karkeet, twenty-five years old, whilst employed under ground in a mine, in the parish of Newlyn, was buried alive, by the falling together of the shaft in which he was, at the depth of five fathoms from the surface. The first person who arrived at the spot was a man named George Trevarrow, who called to know if any living being was beneath, when Karkeet answered, in a firm voice, "I feel the cold hand of death upon me; if there is any hope of my being rescued from this untimely grave, tell me; and if not, tell me." Trevarrow at once informed him that there was not a shadow of hope left, as upwards of four tons of rubbish had fallen round and upon him, and he suffocation must inevitably take place before human aid could afford relief. On hearing which, Karkeet exclaimed, "All's well; it is the Lord! let him do what seemeth him good. Tell my dear father and mother not to be sorry as those without hope for me; 'tis now only that I am happy—'tis now that I feel the advantages of a religious life; now I feel the Lord is my stronghold; and now I feel I am going to heaven." Here his voice failed him; he never spake again.

(*q*) THIS IS HEAVEN BEGUN.—The Rev. Thomas Scott, during his last illness, having received the sacrament, at the conclusion of the service, he adopted the language of Simeon, "Lord, now lettest thou thy servant depart in peace, for mine eyes have seen thy salvation." Through the remainder of the day, and during the night, he continued in a very happy state of mind. To one who came in the evening, he said, "It was beneficial to me: I received Christ last night: I bless God for it." He then repeated, in the most emphatic manner, the whole twelfth chapter of Isaiah. The next morning he said, "This is heaven begun. I have done with darkness *for ever—for ever.* Satan is vanquished. Nothing now remains but salvation with eternal glory —*eternal glory.*"

(*r*) DEATH OF MR. JENKS.—As one said to Philip J. Jenks just before he expired, "How hard it is to die," he replied, "O no, no—easy dying, blessed dying, glorious dying." Looking up at the clock, he said, "I have experienced more happiness in dying two hours this day, than in my whole life. It is worth a whole life to have such an end as this. I have long desired that I might glorify God in my death, but O! I never thought that such a poor worm as I could come to such a glorious death."

(*s*) MR. HOLLAND'S DEATH.—Mr. John Holland, the day before he died, called for the Bible, saying, "Come, O come; death approaches, let us gather some flowers to comfort this hour; and turning with his own hand to the 8th chapter of Romans, he gave the book to Mr. Leigh, and bade him read: at the end of every verse, he paused, and then gave the sense, to his own comfort, but more to the joy and wonder of his friends. Having continued his meditations on the 8th of the Romans, thus read to him, for two hours or more, on a sudden he said, "O stay your reading. What brightness is this I see? Have you lighted up any candles?" Mr. Leigh answered, "No, it is the sunshine;" for it was about five o'clock in a clear summer evening. "Sunshine!" said he, "nay, it is my Saviour's shine. Now, farewell world; welcome heaven. The day-star from on high hath visited my heart. O speak it when I am gone, and preach it at my funeral; God dealeth familiarly with man. I feel his mercy; I see his majesty; whether in the body or out of the body, I cannot tell, God knoweth; but I see things that are unutterable." Thus ravished in spirit, he roamed towards heaven with a cheerful look, and soft sweet voice; but what he said could not be understood.

(*t*) DYING WORDS OF HOOKER.—"I have lived," says Hooker, "to see that this world is made up of perturbations; and I have long been preparing to leave it, and gathering comfort for the dreadful hour of making my account with God, which I now apprehend to be near. And though I have by his grace loved him in my youth, and feared him in my age, and labored to have a conscience void of offence towards him, and towards all men; yet, if thou, Lord, shouldst be extreme to mark what I have done amiss, who can abide it?" And therefore, where I have failed, Lord, show mercy to me, for I plead not my righteousness, but the forgiveness of my unrighteousness, through his merits who died to purchase pardon for penitent sinners. And since I owe thee a death, Lord, let it not be terrible, and then take thine own time, I submit to it. Let not mine, O Lord, but thy will be done! God hath heard my daily petitions; for I am at peace with all men; and He is at peace with me. From such blessed assurance, I feel that inward joy which this world can neither give nor take from me. My conscience beareth me this witness, and this witness makes the thought of death joyful. I could wish to live to do the Church more service, but cannot hope for it; for my days are past, as a shadow that runs not." This worthy biographer adds: "More he would have spoken, but his spirits failed him, and after a sharp conflict between nature and death, a quiet sigh put a period to his last breath, and so he fell asleep."

(*u*) DYING WORDS OF DR. PAYSON.—Dr. Payson, upon dying, said, "My God is in this room, I see him, and oh! how lovely is the sight, how glorious does he appear; worthy of ten thousand hearts if I had so many to give." At another time, when his body was racked by inconceivable suffering, and his cheeks pale and sunken with disease, he exclaimed, like a warrior returning from the field of triumph, "The battle's fought! the battle's fought! and the victory is *won!* the victory is won for ever! I am going to bathe in an ocean of purity, and benevolence, and happiness, to all eternity!" At another time he exclaimed, "The celestial city is full in view—its glories beam upon me—its breezes fan me—its odors are wafted to me; its music strikes upon my ear, and its spirit breathes into my heart; nothing separates me from it, but the river of death, which now appears as a narrow rill, which may be crossed at a single step, whenever God shall give permission.

"The sun of righteousness has been gradually drawing nearer and nearer, appearing larger and larger as he approached, and now he fills the whole hemisphere, pouring forth a flood of glory, in which I seem to float like an insect in the beams of the sun; exulting, yet almost trembling, while I gaze on this excessive brightness, and wondering with unutterable wonder, why God should deign thus to shine upon a sinful worm."

120. Unreadiness for Death.

(*a*) THE RABBI'S REASON FOR WEEPING.—When Rabbi Jochanan Ben Zachai was sick, his disciples came to visit him, and when he saw them, he began to weep. They said to him. "Rabbi, the light of Israel, the right hand pillar, wherefore dost thou weep?" He answered, "If they were carrying me before a king of flesh and blood, who is here to-day and to-morrow in the grave, who, if he were angry with me, his anger would not last for ever; if he put me in prison, his prison would not be everlasting; if he condemned me to death, that death would not be eternal; whom I could soothe with words, or bribe with riches; yet even in such circumstances I should weep. But now I am going before the King of kings, the holy and blessed God, who liveth and endureth, who, if he be angry with me, his anger will last for ever; if he put me in prison, his bondage will be everlasting; if he condemn me to death, that death vill be eternal; whom I cannot soothe with words, nor bribe with riches; when, farther, there are before me two ways, the one to hell and the other to paradise, and I know not into which they are carrying me, shall I not weep?"

(*b*) DYING CONFESSION OF BORGIA.—It is said of the celebrated Cesar Borgia, that in his last moments he exclaimed, "I have provided, in the course of my life, for every thing except death; and now, alas! I am to die, although entirely unprepared."

(*c*) I WON'T DIE NOW.—The following affecting account was written, in 1775, by a Christian minister in London, to the Rev. Dr. Ryland, who then resided at Northampton:—A young lady, who was educated at an academy at Bedford, but who afterwards resided in town, became dangerously ill. Her father, a true Christian, procured for her a lodging in the neighbourhood, to try the effects of a change of air. Finding her disorder prevail, he thought it high time for her to be concerned about her soul, and asked her what she thought of eternity. She replied, "Do not talk to me about eternity. You want me out of the way; but I shall live long enough to enjoy all that you have in the world." He left her. Next evening the mistress of the house where she was, said, "Ma'am, I think you look a good deal worse." "Worse! I am much better.

Why do you talk to me about death?" "You certainly are worse; do let the servant sit up with you to-night." "No, I am not about to die." They went to bed; at four in the morning she awoke her servant, who asked, "What is amiss, ma'am?" "Amiss! I'm dying, I'm dying!" The family was called up; the mistress, coming in to see her, was thus addressed: "I won't die now; I am determined I won't die; I will live." Getting worse and worse, she said, "I feel I must die," and in an agony screamed out, "Lord! what must I do?" Her servant replied, "You must turn to the Saviour." She fell back on the bed, and in a moment expired.

(*d*) NOT PREPARED.—A minister was called on to visit a young lady, who was very ill. She was sitting in her room. He asked her how she felt. "Dying, sir; I am going," was the reply. "Be calm," said he; "I hope you will yet recover." "No," said she. "If you feel yourself to be dying, how does your spirit feel in the prospect of another world?" "Not prepared," was the answer. He directed her to the Lord Jesus Christ, as the Saviour of sinners; but in a few moments she looked around her, reclined her head on his hand, and almost instantly expired. How awful! not prepared, and yet entering eternity! Reader, seek the Lord *now*, that you may be always ready to die.

(*e*) PERSECUTOR CONVERTED.—A profane persecutor discovered great terror during a storm of thunder and lightning which overtook him on a journey. His pious wife, who was with him, inquired the reason of his terror. He replied by asking, "Are not you afraid?" She answered, "No, it is the voice of my Heavenly Father; and should a child be afraid of its father?" "Surely," thought the man, "these Puritans have a divine principle in them which the world seeth not, otherwise they could not have such serenity in their souls, when the rest of the world are filled with dread." Upon this, going to Mr. Bolton, of Broughton, near Kettering, he lamented the opposition which he had made to his ministry, and became a godly man ever after.

(*f*) WHO ARE THE COWARDS.—The captain of a ship says, "I am in the habit of reading the Scriptures to the crew. I have suffered much lately at sea; having been dismasted, and nad all my boats washed away, a little to the westward of Cape Clear. I then had an opportunity of seeing who was who; and I found the most unprincipled men the most useless and the greatest cowards in this awful gale, and the Bible men altogether the reverse, most useful and courageous."

(*g*) THE DYING MERCHANT AND HIS PHYSICIAN.—In 1830, a wealthy merchant, who had lived in profanity for many years, heaping up riches and wrath, was suddenly arrested by alarming sickness. The doctor visited him, and found the patient sick unto death. "Am I very sick?" said the alarmed sufferer. "Shall I never recover?" "You are quite sick," said the physician, "and should prepare for the worst." "Cannot I live a week?" asked the merchant. "No," said the doctor, "you will probably continue but a little while." "Say not so," said the dying man; "I will give you a hundred thousand dollars, if you will prolong my life three days." "I could not do it, my dear sir," said the physician, "for three hours!" And the man died within an hour.

(*h*) LOUIS XI AND HIS PHYSICIAN.—Louis XI of France was so fearful of death, that, as often as it came into his physician's head to threaten him with death, he put money into his hands to pacify him. His physician is said to have got 55,000 crowns from him in five months.

(*i*) NO TIME TO DIE.—Mr. D., a gentleman, engaged in an extensive manufacturing business, in one of the midland counties of England, was called to London on business. After being engaged till a late hour on Saturday night, he said to a confidential person in his employment, who had come to town with him, "Well, we cannot settle our accounts to-night, but must do it early in the morning. On Sabbath therefore they were occupied in that work until 3 o'clock in the afternoon, when dinner was announced, Mr. D. said, "Let us eat and drink, for to-morrow we die. Not," added he, "that I have any thought of dying for years to come." After taking his dinner and wine a post chaise was ordered, and Mr. D. sat out for the country. He arrived at home on Monday night. The next morning, when at breakfast with his family, a gentleman called and said, "Mr. D., have you heard of the death of Mr. ——?" "No," said he, "is he dead? It is very different with me; for my part, I am so engaged in business, that I could not find time to die." Immediately after uttering this sentiment, he rose from the table and went into the kitchen; and while stooping in the act of drawing on his boot, he fell down on the floor and expired.

(*j*) SEVERAL EMINENT PERSONS.—The wretchedness of many eminent persons, in the prospect of death, has been very remarkable.

Henry Beaufort, a rich cardinal, in the days of Henry VI, perceiving that death was at hand, exclaimed, "Wherefore should I die, being so rich? If the whole realm would save my life, I am able either by policy to get it, or by wealth to buy it. Will not death be bribed? Will money do nothing?"

Louis XI strictly charged his servants, that when they saw him ill, they should never dare to name death in his hearing.

When Vitellius, a Roman emperor, and a notorious glutton, who at one supper had before him two thousand fishes and seven thousand birds, was in prospect of death, he made himself intoxicated, that he might not be sensible of its pains, or of the mighty change it produced.

121. Miserable Deaths of the Impenitent.

(*a*) THE MONARCH'S LAMENT.—Philip III of Spain, whose life was free from gross evils, professed that he would rather lose his kingdom than offend God willingly; but when he came to the hour of death, considering most seriously the account he would have to render to God, he was led to indulge very anxious fears, and he exclaimed, "Oh! would to God I had never reigned; oh that those years I have spent in my kingdom, I had lived a solitary life in the wilderness! oh that I had lived a life alone with God! How much more secure should I now have died! With how much more confidence should I have gone to the throne of God! What doth all my glory profit, but that I have so much the more torment in my death!"

(*b*) REFUSING TO DIE.—A gentleman in London, when on his death-bed, felt so strong an aversion to dying, and leaving behind him his wealth, that he hastily rose from his bed, went out, and walked in his yard, exclaiming that he would not die! But the unhappy man's strength being soon exhausted, his affrighted friends carried him back to his bed, where he soon expired. Alas! he was destitute of faith in Him who has promised eternal life to his disciples.

(*c*) BEGINNING OF SORROWS.—"Ah! Mr. Hervey," said a dying man, "the day in which I ought to have worked is over, and now I see a horrible night approaching, bringing with it the blackness of darkness for ever. Wo is me! when God called, I refused. Now I am in sore anguish, and yet this is but the beginning of sorrows. I shall be destroyed with an *everlasting* destruction."

(*d*) WOLSEY'S REGRETS.—Cardinal Wolsey, having fallen under the displeasure of his monarch, made the following sad reflection a little before his death:—"Had I but served my God as diligently as I have served my king, he would not have forsaken me now in my gray hairs. But this is the just reward that I must receive for my indulgent pains and study, not regarding my service to God, but only to my prince."

(*e*) NO MERCY FOR ME NOW.—A young man, who had led a wicked life, stifling the voice of conscience, which often reproved him, was at length seized with a violent disorder, which brought him to the grave. During his sickness, he was miserable, as he had been careless and irreligious when in health. A pious neighbor spoke to him of the mercy of God, of the death of the Lord Jesus Christ to make atonement for sin, and of the precious promises which are made to the penitent; saying, "The gospel affords a balm for every wound which sin has made in the soul." "True," said the young man, "but that gospel, despised through my life, affords me no balm in my death. There is no mercy for me now." Soon afterwards he expired.

(*f*) I AM LOST.—Such was the dying and agonizing exclamation of a young man, who a short time before had been expostulated with for neglecting the great and momentous interests of the soul and eternity. The faithful man of God who had thus warned him to prepare to meet his God, thus speaks of the interview:

"I spent half an hour in reasoning with him. He treated me with great respect, acknowledged the necessity of religion, but suggested a thousand difficulties. I left him with a painful conviction, that amidst all the wonderful influences of a revival at that time in progress, he had succeeded in keeping his conscience asleep.

The meeting closed on Sunday night. On Monday morning I found the road alive with horses and vehicles of the returning multitude. After riding about four miles, I perceived a throng about a farm-house before me. I rode rapidly to it, and learned that a young man had been thrown from his horse and dangerously injured. On pressing through the crowd to the chamber where they had placed the sufferer, I found the young man whom I had warned so emphatically the day before. He was shockingly injured, and as I passed into the room, a thrill of dismay seemed to pass over him. A physician soon arrived; he pronounced the case hopeless; and declared he could not survive two hours. Never shall I forget the agonized countenance of the wretched youth when he learned his fate.

"'Must I die?' he exclaimed. 'Is there no hope? Oh! I cannot die, I cannot die!'

"I endeavored to direct him to the cross, and reminded him of the crucified thief.

"'Alas!' he replied, 'he never sinned against such light as I have abused. What shall I do? Pray for me, O pray for me.'

"We knelt down about the chamber, but his agonizing groans struck all with horror and confusion. I arose and endeavored to direct him to the Lamb of God, who taketh away the sins of the world.

"'It is *too late*,' he exclaimed, 'O what would I not give, if I had heeded your warning yesterday, but it is now *too late*; I am lost.'

"His parents and sisters soon arrived; but the scene which followed I will not and cannot describe. The groans of the poor sufferer ceased only with his life. He seemed stunned with the sudden and terrible summons, and unable to command his thoughts sufficiently to pray."

(*g*) DEATH OF CARDINAL MAZARIN.—What a terrific picture does the following passage (from Lardner's Cyclopædia, History of France,) exhibit of the death-bed of a man devoted to the pomp and vanities of the world, and who is at ease in his possessions!

A fatal malady had seized on Cardinal Mazarin, whilst engaged in the conferences of the treaty, and worn by mental fatigue. He consulted Guenaud the physician, who told him he had but two months to live. Some days after, Brienne perceived the Cardinal in his night-cap and dressing-gown tottering along his gallery, pointing to his pictures, and exclaiming, "Must I quit all these?" He saw Brienne, and seized him: "Look at that Correggio! this Venus of Titian! that incomparable Deluge of Caracci! Ah! my friend, I must quit all these. Farewell, dear pictures, that I love so dearly, and that cost me so much!" A few days before his death he caused himself to be dressed, shaved, rouged and painted. In this state he was carried in his chair to the promenade, where the envious courtiers paid him ironical compliments on his appearance. Cards were the amusement of his death-bed, his hands being held by others; and they were only interrupted by the papal nuncio, who came to give the cardinal that plenary indulgence to which the prelates of the Sacred College are officially entitled. Mazarin expired on the 9th of March, 1661.

122. Miscellaneous.

(*a*) DEATH IN THE PULPIT.—The following striking fact is taken from the Edinburgh Advertiser, Dec. 7, 1810. "Died at Waterford, Nov. 4, the Rev. B. Dickinson, minister of the Baptist congregation in that city, while zealously employed in the discharge of his functions. Mr. Dickinson had taken for his text, 2 Cor. v. 10, 'We must all appear before the judgment-seat of Christ;' and had advanced but a short way in its illustration, when he fell down in the pulpit, and instantly expired!" What an impressive lesson to those who preach, and to those who hear the everlasting gospel! And how becoming for every minister to adopt the lines of Baxter:

> "I preach as if I ne'er should preach again,
> And as a dying man, to dying men."

(*b*) A REMARKABLE COINCIDENCE.—The Rev. John Olds, a devoted minister in London, toward the close of the seventeenth century, was suddenly taken ill, immediately after his afternoon prayer, before commencing his sermon, and was removed from the pulpit to glory. And it is remarkable that, on the next Sabbath but one, Mr. Kentish, having just roused the attention of his own congregation, by mentioning in his sermon the sudden death of Mr. Olds, was himself struck with death. Thus each

> "His body with his charge laid down,
> And ceased at once to work and live."

(*c*) CYRUS' EPITAPH.—Cyrus, the Emperor of Persia, after he had long been attended by armies, and vast trains of courtiers, ordered this inscription to be engraven on his tomb, as an admonition to all men of the approach of death, and the desolation that follows it; namely, "O man! whatsoever thou art and whencesoever thou comest, I know that thou wilt come to the same condition in which I now am. I am Cyrus, who brought the empire to the Persians; do not envy me, I beseech thee, this little piece of ground which covereth my body."

(*d*) DEATH PREFERABLE TO SIN.—A man that was addicted to a very wicked course of life, going one Sabbath morning to buy a game-cock for fighting, was met by a good man on his way to a meeting, who asked him where he was going. He related the whole to him, and after much entreaty, was prevailed on to go with him to the meeting, where it pleased God to convince him of his misery. On the Monday morning he went to his work, where he was beset by the rest of the colliers, who swore at him, told him he was going mad, and upbraided him, by saying, that before a month was at an end, he would swear as bad as ever. On hearing this, he kneeled down before them all, and earnestly prayed that God would sooner take him out of the world, than suffer him to blaspheme his holy name; on which he immediately expired.

(*e*) DR. DWIGHT'S MOTHER.—Dr. Dwight's mother lived to be more than a hundred years of age. When she was a hundred and two, some people visited her on a certain day, and while they were with her, the bell was heard toll for a funeral. The old lady burst into tears, and said, 'When will the bell toll for me? It seems that the bell will never toll for me. I am afraid that I shall never die.'

(*f*) THE AVARICIOUS FARMER.—The following fact illustrates the noted line of Dr. Young:

> "All men think all men mortal but themselves.

Mr. A. was a wealthy farmer in Massachusetts. He was about sixty years of age; and it had been his ruling and almost only passion in life to acquire property. His neighbor B. owned a small farm which came too near the centre of A.'s extended domain. It was quite a blot in A.'s prospect--destroyed the regularity of his lands, and on the whole it was really necessary, in his opinion, that he should add it to his other property. B. became embarrassed, and was sued; judgments obtained, and executions issued. A. now thought he should obtain the land, but one execution after another was arranged, and finally the debt was paid off without selling the land. When A. heard of the payment of the last execution, which put an end to his hopes of obtaining the land by this means, he exclaimed, "Well, B. is an old man, and cannot live long, and when he dies I can buy the lot." B. was 58 years old, A. 60! Reader, do *you* ever expect to die?

(*g*) RULING PASSION STRONG IN DEATH.—When the king of Prussia became sensible of the near approach of dissolution, he desired to see his army defile before him for the last time. His bed was accordingly carried to a window, whence by reflection in a mirror he was enabled to take a last adieu of the troops.

Napoleon Bonaparte, under similar circumstances, ordered himself to be seated and arrayed in his military dress that he might meet the king of terrors as he had been accustomed to meet his mortal foes. What a lesson do such instances read to us of the influence of a ruling passion in absorbing the mind to the exclusion of all proper sense of the awful realities of eternity.

(*h*) DYING SILENT.—In the last visit but one which Whitfield paid to America, he spent a day or two at Princeton, under the roof of Dr. Finley, then President of the College at that place. At dinner, the Dr. said, "Mr. W., I hope it will be very long before you will be called home; but when that event shall arrive, I shall be glad to hear the noble testimony you will bear for God." "You would be disappointed, Doctor," said W., "I shall die silent. It has pleased God to enable me to bear so many testimonies for him during my life, that he will require none from me when I die." The manner of W.'s death verifies his prediction.

(*i*) REMARK OF JOHN NEWTON.—Rev. John Newton one day mentioned at his table the death of a lady. A young woman who sat opposite immediately said, "O sir, how did she die?" The venerable man replied, "There is a more important question than that, my dear, which you should have asked first." "Sir," said she, "what question can be more important than "How did she die?" "How did she live?" was Mr. Newton's answer.

(*j*) "I WILL NEVER LEAVE THEE."—Many good people, who feel that the "grace" of God is now "sufficient for" them, are nevertheless disquieted with a fearful apprehension that in death "their hope will be as the giving up of the ghost." It is related of Robert Glover, one of the martyrs, that for several days before his death he was almost overwhelmed with the prospect of martyrdom, and earnestly supplicated for the light of God's countenance, without any sense of comfort. His darkness continued up to the period of his arriving within sight of the stake, when suddenly his whole soul was so filled with consolation, that he could not forbear clapping his hands, and crying out, "He is come! He is come!" He appeared to go up to heaven in a chariot of fire, with little or no apparent sensibility of his cruel death.

123. DEBTS ON MEETING-HOUSES.

(*a*) A CHURCH CONSULTING THEIR CONSCIENCES.—A minister was about to leave his own congregation for the purpose of visiting London, on what was by no means a pleasant errand —to beg on behalf of his place of worship. Previous to his departure, he called together the principal persons connected with his charge, and said to them, "Now I shall be asked, whether we have conscientiously done all that we can for the removal of this debt; what answer am I to give? Brother So-and-so, can you in conscience say that you have?"

"Why, sir," he replied, "If you come to conscience, I don't know that I can." The same question he put to a second, and a third, and so on, and similar answers were returned, till the whole sum required was subscribed, and there was no longer any need of their pastor's wearing out his soul in coming to London on any such unpleasant excursion.

(*b*) REFLEX BENEFITS OF A BIBLE SOCIETY.—An anxious, retired, and diligent country clergyman, waited upon a layman of enlarged, enlightened and truly Christian views, to lay before him the case of his prostrated and embarrassed parish. "If we cannot raise a few hundred dollars," said he, "to pay off a small debt for erecting the church, it will be impossible to get along." "It is exceedingly difficult," was the reply, "to raise money abroad for these purposes; cannot a subscription be raised amongst your own people to pay off the debt?" "I doubt," was the rejoinder, "whether twenty dollars could be collected for the purpose."

The friendly adviser well knew that this could not be owing to absolute pecuniary inability. He paused a moment for reflection, and then asked, very irrelevantly, as the minister thought, whether he had a Bible Society in his parish. "No," said he. "Well, then, go home and set about forming one instantly. If your difficulties are not surmounted by this means, they exceed the measure of my wisdom." In the retirement of his study the expedient appeared at first to the good clergyman absolutely hopeless. He relied much, however, upon the wisdom of his adviser, and reflected that at any rate it was a good work, and the only thing which could relieve his sorrowful reflections by the energy of action. Accordingly he set himself diligently to work, and after encountering many difficulties succeeded in doing something for the Bible cause. But that, though a blessed thing, he considered a mere trifle, when at the end of two years he announced with inexpressible animation and delight to his noble adviser, that his church was paid for, an organ purchased, his family made more comfortable than ever, and that all the affairs of the parish were going on most admirably.

It seems all that was wanted was a lively interest in religious things. Let some of our poor parishes who cannot pay for churches, or feel unable to build them, who have no ministers, or worse still, are starving those they have, try the experiment of getting up vigorous and interesting missionary associations.

(*c*) THE DEACON'S TWO CENTS.—A minister who was urged by his people to go out on a begging excursion, to solicit money to liquidate a debt on their meeting-house, put up on Saturday night with the deacon of a church to which he was to present the subject on the ensuing Sabbath. He seemed to be quite wealthy, and as he treated his guest with great cordiality and kindness, the preacher cherished glowing expectations of a very generous contribution from his purse. On the Sabbath, after setting forth the claims of his object in as forcible and eloquent a manner as possible, the plates were passed around for money. As the deacon sat near the pulpit, the preacher could not resist the temptation of rising up a little and peering over the pulpit to witness the expression of the good man's liberality. As the plate approaches the deacon, he leisurely puts his hand into his pocket. The preacher's heart palpitates with anxiety. But, alas, the deacon just drops from his thumb and fingers two red cents upon the plate and lets it pass! The preacher suddenly sank back into his seat, and hope and faith died within him. The collection, it seems, was small, and the preacher, mortified and indignant, went straight back to his people, told them the story of the two cents, and assured them they must raise the funds needed themselves or send some one else forth to beg besides him. The people caugh his spirit—they determined to solicit no further—increased their subscriptions, and paid their debts themselves.

124. DECREES, DIVINE.

(*a*) THE MOST IMPORTANT DECREE.—A person in the lower ranks, at Lockwinnock, whose life and practice had been every thing but that of a genuine Christian, was, nevertheless, a great speculator on the high points of divinity. This unhallowed humor remained with him to his death-bed, and he was wont to perplex and trouble himself and his visitors with knotty questions on the Divine decrees, and such other topics. Thomas Orr, a person of a very different character, was sitting at his bedside, endeavoring to turn his attention to his more immediate concerns. "Ah, William," said he, "this is the decree you have at present to do with, 'He that believeth shall be saved; he that believeth not shall be damned.'"

DELAY OF REPENTANCE.

125. Causes Regret after Conversion.

(*a*) TESTIMONY OF SEVERAL CHRISTIANS.—Two aged disciples, one eighty-seven years old, one day met. Well, inquired the younger of his fellow-pilgrim, how long have you been interested in religion? "Fifty years," was the old man's reply. Well, have you ever regretted that you began so young to devote yourself to religion? "O no," said he, and the tears trickled down his furrowed cheeks; "I weep when I think of the sins of my youth. It is this which makes me weep now."

Another man of eighty, who had been a Christian fifty or sixty years, was asked if he was grieved that he had become a disciple of Christ. "O no," said he; "if I grieve for any thing, it is that I did not become a Christian before."

A Christian friend visited a woman of ninety, as she lay on her last bed of sickness. She had been hoping in Christ for half a century. In the course of conversation she said, "Tell all the children that an old woman, who is just on the borders of eternity, is very much grieved that she did not begin to love the Savior when a child. Tell them youth is the time to serve the Lord."

Said an old man of seventy-six, "I did not become interested in religion till I was forty-five; and I often have to tell God, I have nothing to bring him but the dregs of old age."

Said another man, between sixty and seventy years of age, "I hope I became a disciple of the Lord Jesus when I was seventeen," and he burst into tears as he added, "and there is nothing which causes me so much distress as to think of those seventeen years—some of the very best portion of my life—which I devoted to sin and the world."

126. Hardens the Heart.

(*a*) THE CONSUMPTIVE'S TESTIMONY.—A few years since, writes the Rev. Jacob Abbot, when spending a Sabbath in a beautiful country town, I was sent for to visit a sick man who was apparently drawing near the grave. I was told, as I walked with the neighbor who came for me toward the house of the patient, that he was in a melancholy state of mind. "He has been," said he, "a firm believer and supporter of the truths of religion for many years. He has been very much interested in maintaining religious worship, and all benevolent institutions; he has loved the Sabbath school, and given his family every religious privilege; but he says he has never really given his heart to God; he has been devoted to the world, and even now, he says, it will not relinquish its hold." "Do you think," said I, "that he must die?" "Yes," replied he, "he must die, and he is fully aware of it. He says that he can see his guilt and danger, but that his hard heart will not feel." This is the exact remark which is made in thousands and thousands of similar cases, and in almost precisely the same language. The eyes are opened, but the heart remains unchanged. We, at length, approached the house: it was in the midst of a delightful village, and in one of those calm still summer afternoons, when all nature seems to speak from every tree, leaf, and flower, of the goodness of God; and to breathe the spirit of repose and peace. I wondered that a man could lie on his bed with the windows all around him opening upon such a scene as this, and yet not feel. As I entered the sick room, the pale and emaciated patient turned towards me an anxious and agitated look, which showed too plainly what was passing within. It was a case of consumption. His sickness had been long and lingering. His strength was now almost gone; he lay gasping for the breath which his wasted lungs could not receive. His eye moved with a quick and anxious glance around the room, saying, by its expression of bright intelligence, that the mind retained its undiminished power. I tried to bring to his case those truths which I thought calculated to influence him, and lead him to the Savior: but he knew all that I could tell him; and I learned from his replies, given in panting whispers, that religious truth had been trying its whole strength upon him all his life; and that, in presenting it to him again now, I was only attempting once more an experiment, which had been repeated in vain almost every day, for forty years. I saw the utter hopelessness of effort, and stood by his bedside in silent despair. He died that night. Reader, if your heart is cold and hard towards God, abandon all hope that the alarm and anxiety of a death-bed will change it. Seek forgiveness NOW.

(*b*) MY HEART IS HARD.—An old man, one day taking a child on his knee, entreated him to seek God *now*—to pray to him—and to love him; when the child, looking up at him, asked, "But why do not *you* seek God?" The old man, deeply affected, answered, "I would, child; but my heart is *hard*—my heart is *hard*."

(*c*) THE OLD MAN'S CONFESSION.—The late Dr. Clark, of Philadelphia, in one of his sermons, illustrates the absurdity of deferring the work of salvation by the following striking fact. He was present on an occasion when a most solemn appeal was made to the young, to seek God without delay; the preacher urging as a motive, that, should they live to be old, difficulties would multiply, and their reluctance to attend the subject would increase with their years. As the reacher descended from the pulpit at the close of the service, an aged man came forward, and extending his hand to him, with much emotion remarked,—"Sir, what you said just now is unquestionably true. I know it from my own experience. When I was young, I said to myself, I cannot give up the world now, but I will by-and-by, when I have passed the meridian of life, and begin to sink into the vale of years; then I will become a Christian; then I shall be ready to attend to the concerns of my soul. But here I am, an old man. I am not a Christian. I feel no readiness nor disposition to enter upon the work of my salvation. In looking back, I oftentimes feel as though I would give worlds if I could be placed where I was when I was twenty years old. There were not half as many difficulties in my path then as there are now." But, though the big tears coursed down his cheeks as he gave utterance to these truths, the emotions that were stirred up within him, like the early dew, soon passed away. He did not turn to God.

127. Grieves away the Holy Spirit.

(*a*) "NOW I AM UNDONE."—A young woman became acquainted with religion in a pious family, but left the situation in which she enjoyed religious privileges, for one much superior as it respects this world; but alas! the master of the house was a lover of pleasure more than a lover of God. Here religious duties were not only neglected, but even ridiculed. She met with no little persecution from her fellow servants this induced her to neglect private prayer and other means of grace. At length she was seldom seen at public worship. A Christian friend perceived her declension by her backwardness to discourse on religious subjects, which she had formerly appeared to love. But she did not return back to the world without considerable checks of conscience. She knew that she was doing wrong, but became hardened by the deceitfulness of sin.

About the twentieth year of her age, she broke a blood-vessel. An apothecary was sent for immediately, but no relief could be afforded. On the day after the circumstance took place, she was visited by the person who had observed her decline in religion, who says: "On asking her how she was, she said, 'Very bad, very bad.' On being asked as to her eternal welfare, she exclaimed, 'That is what I want; my life I care not for, if my sins were pardoned.' When I spoke of the power and willingness of Christ to save lost sinners, she answered, there was no pardon for her. I enlarged on the precious promises of the gospel, but all seemed to aggravate the feelings of her guilty conscience. She burst into tears, and said, 'Oh that I had repented when the Spirit of God was striving with me! but now I am undone.' I again visited her late in the evening of the same day. She was much weaker from the loss of blood, and her countenance bespoke the dreadful horror of her mind, which no doubt hastened her speedy dissolution. On asking her how she felt, she answered, 'Miserable! miserable!' I repeated some encouraging passages of Scripture, but alas! all in vain; her soul labored under the greatest agonies: she exclaimed, 'Oh! how I have been deceived! When I was in health, I delayed repentance from time to time. Oh that I had my time to live over again! Oh that I had obeyed the gospel! but now I must burn in hell for ever. Oh I cannot bear it! I cannot bear it!'

"In this manner she continued breathing out most horrible expressions.

"I reminded her that Jesus Christ would in no wise cast out those sinners who come to him, and that his blood cleanseth from all sin. She said, 'The blood of Christ will be the greatest torment I shall have in hell; tell me no more about it.' I then left her with feelings not to be described. She died next morning at six o'clock. I inquired of the woman who attended her, if she continued in the same state to the last. She said, that she was much worse after I left her, and that they durst not stay in the room with her. She was heard to exclaim several times, about an hour before her end, 'Eternity! eternity! Oh! to burn throughout eternity!'"

(*b*) SEEK RELIGION NOW.—A gentleman called his sons around his dying bed, and gave them the following relation:—"When I was a youth, the Spirit strove with me, and seemed to say, 'Seek religion *now;* but Satan suggested the necessity of waiting till I grew up, because it was incompatible with youthful amusement; so I resolved I would wait till I grew up to be a man. I did so, and was then reminded of my promise to seek religion; but Satan again advised me to wait till middle age, for business and a young family demanded all my attention. 'Yes,' I said, 'I will do so; I will wait till middle age.' I did so; my serious impressions left me for some years. They were again renewed: conscience reminded me of my promises; the Spirit said, 'Seek religion now;' but then I had less time than ever. Satan advised my waiting till I was old; then my children would be settled in business, and I should have nothing else to do; I could then give an undivided attention to it. I listened to his suggestion, and the Spirit ceased to strive with me. I have lived to be old, but now I have no desire as formerly to attend to the concerns of my soul: my heart is hardened. I have resisted and quenched the Spirit; now there is no hope. Already I feel a hell within, the beginning of an eternal misery. I feel the gnawings of that worm that never dies. Take warning from my miserable end; seek religion now; let nothing tempt you to put off this important concern." Then in the greatest agonies he expired.

(*c*) THE FATAL RESOLUTION.—Lydia Sturtevant, was the daughter of pious parents in one of the New England States. She possessed a cultivated mind, buoyancy of spirits, and beauty of person—the ornament of her circle, the admiration of all who knew her.

During the summer of 1824, she had deep religious impressions, and felt that it was unsafe to neglect religion longer. She deliberated, she reasoned, she prayed, and finally made up her mind to the *resolution that she would repent and accept the offer of salvation before the close of* THAT DAY. But the day had its cares and pleasures, its company and business, and the night found her as thoughtless, almost, as she had been for months.

The next morning she had renewed convictions, saw her guilt more clearly, and in great agony of soul, resolved again, "to begin religion before the close of that day." With this new resolution her anxiety somewhat abated, and though she thought often during the day, of the vow she had made, night came again and nothing decisive had been done. The next morning her impressions were again renewed, and she again renewed her resolution; it was dissipated again; and thus she went on resolving and breaking her resolves till she relapsed into her former unconcern. She was not absolutely indifferent; she still expected and resolved to become a Christian, but her resolutions looked forward to a *more distant period*, and she returned to the world with the same interest as before. Some three or four months after this, she was taken sick. It was her last sickness—she was sick only five days—though none thought that she would die till eight hours before she died. About daybreak on the morning of that day, she was informed that her disease would probably prove fatal. The ir elligence was awfully surprising. *The fatal resolution*, as she called it, which she had formed about the same hour of the day, a few months before, was brought, by the opening twilight, afresh to her mind; and her soul was filled with horror at her situation. She saw herself on the brink of eternity—a hardened sinner—her Saviour slighted—the Spirit grieved and gone!

What could she do? The blood was beginning to stagnate, the lungs to falter! Feeble and faint, she raised her haggard eyes and summoned every energy to pray. O, what agony did that prayer express! She called, she begged for mercy, till she sunk into a swoon. As consciousness returned, she began to pray again; then again fainted. On reviving she called on her friends to pray for her; and accordingly all knelt while one engaged in prayer. As they rose Rev. Mr. Phelps, the minister present, began to repeat some promises of Scripture which he thought appropriate to her case. She interrupted him, saying it was too late, and that there was no ardon for her. With her dying breath she charged him to warn the youth of his congregation not to neglect religion as she had done, or "still their convictions by a mere *resolution* to repent." Death soon closed the affecting scene.

(*d*) THE AGED PROCRASTINATOR.—In January, 1825, Mr. H——, of S——, New-York, says a clergyman, called upon me, and taking me by the hand, said, "Sir, do you think there is any mercy in heaven for a man who has sinned more than eighty years?"

"There is mercy," I replied, "for those who repent of sin, and believe on the Lord Jesus Christ."

Still pressing my hand, while tears were flowing over his wrinkled cheeks, and his frame trembling, he more earnestly renewed his inquiry, "*My dear sir, do you believe* that God will forgive a man who has rebelled against him eighty-one years in this world?" Before a word was uttered in reply, he cried out in agony, "I know I shall not be forgiven—I shall die in my sins!"

This caused me to ask how he knew, or what induced him to believe that God would never have mercy on him?

He replied, "I will tell you, and disclose what I never uttered to any human being: When I was twenty-one I was awakened to feel that I was a sinner. I was then intimate with a number of young men, and was ashamed to have them know that I was anxious for my soul. For five or six weeks I read my Bible, and prayed every day in secret. Then *I said in my heart one day, I will put this subject off until I am married and settled in life, and then I will attend to my soul's salvation. But I knew that I was doing wrong.*

"After I was settled in the world, I thought of the resolution I had made, and of my solemn promise to God then to make my peace with him. But as I had no disposition to do so, I again said in my heart, 'I will put off this subject *ten years*, and then prepare to die.'

"The time came, and I remembered my promise; but I had no special anxiety about my salvation. Then did I again postpone, and resolve that if God would spare me through another term of years I would certainly attend to the concerns of my soul. God spared me; but I lived on in my sins; and now I see my awful situation. I am lost. Now I believe that I sinned against the Holy Ghost when I was twenty-one, and that I have lived sixty years since my day of grace was past. "*I know that I shall not be forgiven.*"

When asked if we should pray with him, he replied, "Yes, but it will do no good;" so fearfully certain was he of destruction. He continued in this state for weeks and months. All attempts to urge him to accept of salvation were in vain; this blighting sentiment was ever first in his thoughts. "It will do no good." His feelings were not contrition, or repentance for sin; but the anticipation of wrath to come. And in this state he died.

128. Accompanied by Sudden Death.

(*a*) BOAST NOT OF TO-MORROW.—The Rev. G. Whitfield mentions in his journal, that during his first voyage to Georgia, the ship's cook was awfully addicted to drinking; and when reproved for this and other sins, boasted that he would be wicked till within two years of his death, and would then reform. He died of an illness, brought on by drinking, in six hours.

(*b*) PHILIP HENRY'S WARNING.—Mr. Philip Henry said to some of his neighbors who came to see him on his death-bed, "O make sure work for your souls, my friends, by getting an interest in Christ, while you are in health. If I had that work to do now, what would become of me? I bless God, I am satisfied. See to it, all of you, that your work be not undone when your time is done, lest you be undone for ever."

(*c*) AN INCH OF TIME.—"Millions of money for an inch of time," cried Elizabeth—the gifted, but ambitious queen of England, upon her dying bed. Unhappy woman! reclining upon a couch—with ten thousand dresses in her wardrobe—a kingdom on which the sun never sets, at her feet—all now are valueless, and she shrieks in anguish, and she shrieks in vain, for a single "inch of time." She had enjoyed threescore and ten years. Like too many among us, she had devoted them to wealth, to pleasure, to pride, and ambition, so that her whole preparation for eternity was crowded into a few moments! and hence she, who had wasted more than half a century, would barter millions for an inch of time.

(*d*) THE FATAL THURSDAY.—A few years ago, (says the N. Y. Evangelist of 1831,) there lived in the vicinity of Boston a young lady of amiable character, lovely person, and agreeable deportment; her mind was awakened on the subject of religion: she felt that she was a sinner; and the fearful consequences of the judgment were full in her view. In this trying hour she was urged to repent, at once, without delay. She seemed to think that the terms were hard and peremptory, although they were according to the word of God. When she retired alone, her conscience pressed her, and she came to the conclusion that she would certainly give up her heart to Christ, in *four years*. This, at first, gave her some ease of mind; but she soon reflected that she might not live so long as four years, and then, if she did not repent, she might be lost for ever. She was again alarmed, and resolved to repent in *three* years; at this resolution she was calm for a moment, but reflecting that she might not live this period, she was again alarmed, and again resolved that in *one* year she would cer tainly attend to the concerns of the soul. This was a much shorter time; and on resolving on this period, she was composed for nearly a week; but reflecting again, a whole year seemed a considerable time, and if she should die, she would be lost for ever. Under the pressure of an awakened conscience, she resolved, most solemnly, that on the next *Thursday*, she would give herself to Christ.—This time was so short, and her resolution so solemn, that she seemed to think the work was done. She was after this perfectly at ease; she had made a solemn resolution, and had fixed the time when she would attend to this great concern of salvation; here she rested. But it was a fearful and awful delusion. On *Friday* she was taken ill, and required medical aid; but nothing seemed to arrest the progress and violence of her fever, and she died on *Wednesday;* and the very day she had fixed on, to attend to the interests of her soul, her body was laid in the silent tomb. She had her senses, and knew that she could not live; but she had no hope in the Savior. She said she had rejected and grieved the good Spirit, and it had gone, and would not alarm her, nor give her any hope.

(*e*) TOO SOON—TOO LATE.—A man who would enjoy the pleasures of this world, said, it was *too soon* for him to think of another world. He journeyed, and was taken ill very suddenly, in the middle of the night, at an inn. The people there sent for a clergyman. He came, and the dying man looking him in the face, before he could speak, said to him, "Sir, it is *too late.*" The minister said, "Christ is able to save to the uttermost," and explained the gospel to him; he replied, "Sir, it is too late." The clergyman asked, "Will you allow me to pray with you?" His only reply was, "Sir, it is too late." He died saying, "It is too late." Oh, that all, especially the young, may take warning fron this fact, and seek for salvation before it is too late!

(*f*) AMAZING CONTRAST.—When I was travelling in the State of Massachusetts, writes an American minister, twenty-six years ago, after preaching one evening in the town of ——, a very serious looking young man rose, and wished to address the assembly. After obtaining leave, he spoke as follows:—"My friends, about a year ago, I set out in company with a young man, an intimate acquaintance, to seek the salvation of my soul. For several weeks we went on together, we labored together, and often renewed our engagement, never to give over seeking till we obtained the religion of Jesus. But all at once, the young man neglected to attend public worship, appeared to turn his back on all the means of grace, and grew so shy of me, that I could scarcely get an opportunity to speak with him. His strange conduct gave me much painful anxiety of mind, but still I felt resolved to obtain the salvation of my soul, or perish, making the publican's plea. After a few days, a friend informed me that my companion had received an invitation to attend a ball, and was determined to go. I went immediately to him, and, with tears in my eyes, endeavored to persuade him to change his purpose, and to go with me, on that evening, to a prayer meeting. I pleaded with him in vain. He told me, when we parted, that I must not give him up as lost, for, after he had attended that ball, he intended to make a business of seeking religion. The appointed evening came; he went to the ball, and I went to the prayer meeting. Soon after the meeting opened, it pleased God, in answer to prayer, to turn my spiritual captivity, and make my soul rejoice in his love. Soon after the ball opened, my young friend was standing at the head of the ball room, with the hand of a young lady in his hand, preparing to lead down the dance; and, while the musician was tuning his violin, without one moment's warning, the young man fell backwards dead on the floor. I was immediately sent for to assist in devising means to convey his remains to his father's house. You will be better able to judge what were the emotions of my heart, when I tell you, that that young man was my own brother."

(*g*) FATAL RESOLVE.—A friend was once pressing, on a young lady of fifteen, the importance of thinking of religion; she replied, she would do so when she was older; but added; "I will enjoy the world while I am young." In vain did her friend remind her of the uncertainty of life; she appeared displeased and repeated her resolution.

But mark the result: in about three weeks after, that friend attended her funeral! Oh, reader, think of this fact, and trust not to to-morrow, for "*now* is the day of salvation." Facts like the above are constantly occurring, and call for an instant attention to "the things which make for our peace."

(*h*) DEATH IN THE BALL ROOM.—A young merchant, in one of the large cities of America, was seized with a dangerous illness, which brought him, apparently, to the very confines of the eternal world. In this situation his past neglect of the Savior rushed with power on his conscience, and in the most solemn manner he vowed to lead a new life, if he recovered. Unexpectedly, both to himself and every one else, he gradually attained his former health. During the progress of his recovery, he regarded his vow, and professed decided attachment to the service of God. But when he returned to the business of life, he resumed his gayeties, and indulged in all the vanity of a fashionable life. A friend, who had heard and was deeply affected by his solemn vows when in trouble, reminded him of the affecting scene; he remembered it, and declared his intention of fulfilling all he had said, as soon as he had fulfilled two or three pressing engagements. Then he would give up his soul to the work; *then* he would seek God with all his heart. A few days after the admonition, he attended a fashionable and splendid ball: in the midst of his gayety and mirth, death suddenly entered the festive hall, and the gay and thoughtless merchant fell a corpse. Oh, immortal sinner, beware of delaying attention to the concerns of eternity!

(*i*) THE SIX BROKEN VOWS.—A poor thoughtless man was once taken ill, and sent for the minister of his parish to visit him. He then professed to be very penitent; but he recovered, and again fell into his evil courses. A second time he was ill, and the same promises were held out, but never realized. Six times was this the case in the course of his life. At length, while engaged in sin, he was cut off suddenly, and entered into an eternal world. Reader, "*to-day*" hear the voice of God, and harden not thine heart.

(*j*) THE PRESUMPTUOUS HEIR.—Rev. Mr. Baker, a Free-will Baptist evangelist, was visiting from house to house, in a certain neighborhood, in New England; and met on his walk three young men with axes on their shoulders. He stopped and conversed with them. Two appeared somewhat serious: the third, a gay, frank young man, replied, "You see, sir, that splendid white house on that farm yonder?" "Yes." "Well, sir, that estate has been willed to me by my uncle; and we are now going to do chopping in the woodland that belongs to it. There are some incumbrances on the estate which I must settle, before the farm can be fully mine; and as soon as I have cleared it of these incumbrances I mean to become a Christian." "Ah! young man," said the minister, "beware; you may never see that day; while you are gaining the world, you may lose your soul." "I'll run the risk," said he, and they parted. The three young men went into the woods; and this daring procrastinator, and another, engaged in felling a tree. A dry, heavy limb, hung loosely in the top; and as the tree was jarred by the successive strokes of the axe, it quit its hold, and as it fell crashing through the branches to the earth, it struck the head of the young heir, in its way, and stretched him on the ground a lifeless corpse. Thus were his hopes cut off; and hazarding the delay of months he lost his soul in an hour. His fellow-laborer was converted; for conviction struck his mind when he saw the young heir quivering in death! "I felt then such a horror at the danger of delaying religion, when I thought what he had just said, and saw his end, that I determined to neglect my soul no longer." His example was followed by others; and a great revival ensued.

(*k*) FIVE MINUTES TO CRY FOR MERCY.—In the early part of

my ministry, said the Rev. Mr. T. East, of Birmingham, a woman was in the habit of attending the place of worship in which I preached, who occupied a seat on the stairs, and who was very tenacious of her sitting, not allowing any other person to occupy it. She was observed by her friends, who sought occasion to converse with her on the important subject of religion; but she was very shy and evasive. All they could extract from her was this appalling reply: "Oh, I shall only want five minutes time when I am dying to cry for mercy: and I have no doubt God Almighty will give it me." It was in vain to remonstrate with the woman; this was always her reply. Time passed on. One day, I was walking down the street, when a young woman ran up to me in a state of great agitation and excitement, exclaiming, "O, Mr. East, I have found you; do come to my mother, sir; come this minute, sir: she is dying, she is dying!" I hastened with her to the house, and was astonished to find in the dying sufferer the poor unhappy woman who had attended my place of worship. She was evidently expiring: but, turning her dying eyes towards me, she cried out, "O, Mr. East, I am damned, I am damned!" and expired.

129. Miscellaneous.

(*a*) EXCUSES OF THE GREENLANDERS.—Numbers of the Greenlanders, who had for a time adhered to the Moravian Missionaries, and promised well, drew back, and walked no more with them; while the greater part of those who were wavering, seduced by the concourse of their heathen countrymen, again joined the multitude. One being asked why he could not stay, answered, "I have bought a great deal of powder and shot, which I must first spend in the south, in shooting reindeer;" another, "I must first have my fill of bears' flesh;" and a third, "I must have a good boat, and then I will believe."

(*b*) GREENLANDERS AND THE END OF THE WORLD.—Some of the unconverted inhabitants of Greenland had heard that the world should be destroyed, and, as in that case they should have nowhere to go, they expressed a desire to be converted, that they might go with the believers. "But," added they, with that carelessness and procrastination so natural to man, in the things that belong to eternity, "as the destruction will not happen this year, we will come in next season."

(*c*) ADVICE REJECTED.—When a young man made an open profession of the gospel, his father, greatly offended, gave him this advice,—"James, you should *first* get yourself established in a good *trade*, then think of and determine about religion." "Father," said the son, "Christ advises me differently, he says, 'Seek ye *first* the kingdom of God.'"

(*d*) WORK FOR THE DAY BEFORE DEATH.—Rabbi Eliezer said, "Turn to God *one* day before your death." His disciples said, "How can a man know the day of his death?" He answered them, "Therefore you should turn to God TO-DAY. Perhaps you may die *to-morrow;* thus, every day will be employed in returning."

(*e*) A YOUNG MAN UNDER SENTENCE OF DEATH.—A young man, on whom sentence of death was passed, said, two days before his execution, "I am afraid that nothing but the fear of death and hell makes me seek the Savior now, and that I cannot expect to find him. The words, 'Seek ye the Lord *while* he may be found,' trouble my mind very much, as they show me that there is a time when he may *not* be found."

130. DENIAL OF CHRIST.

(*a*) THE MARTYR'S PRAYER ANSWERED.—David Straiton, one of the Scottish martyrs, was brought to the knowledge of the truth, through the instrumentality of John Erskine of Dun. One day, having retired with the young laird of Laurieston, to a quiet and solitary place in the fields, to have the New Testament read to him, it so happened, that in the course of reading, these words of our Savior occurred, "He that denieth me before men, in the midst of this wicked generation, him will I deny in the presence of my Father and his angels." On hearing them, he became of a sudden, as one enraptured or inspired. He threw himself on his knees, extended his hands, and, after looking for some time earnestly towards heaven, he burst forth in these words, "O Lord, I have been wicked, and justly mayest thou withdraw thy grace from me; but, Lord, for thy mercy's sake, let me never deny thee nor thy truth, for fear of death and corporal pains." The issue proved that his prayer was not in vain. For at his trial and death, he displayed much firmness and constancy in the defence of the truth, and gave great encouragement to another gentleman, Norman Gourlay, who suffered along with him.

(*b*) THE SUBSCRIPTION RECANTED.—"Bishop Jewel," says Fuller, "being by the violence of popish inquisitors, assaulted on a sudden to *subscribe*, he took a pen in his hand, and said, smiling, 'Have you a mind to see how well I can write?' and thereupon underwrit their opinions." Jewel, however, by his cowardly compliance, made his foes no fewer without, and one the more, a guilty conscience, within him. His life being way-laid for, with great difficulty he got over into Germany. Having arrived at Frankfort, by the advice of some friends, he made a solemn and affecting recantation of his subscription, in a full congregation of English Protestants, on a Sabbath morning, after having preached a most tender, penitential sermon. "It was," said he, "my abject and cowardly mind and faint heart, that made my weak hand commit this wickedness." He bitterly bewailed his fall; and with sighs and tears, supplicated forgiveness of the God whose truth he had denied, and of the church of Christ, which he had so grievously offended. The congregation were melted into tears, and "all embraced him as a brother in Christ; yea, as an angel of God."

131. DEPENDENCE ON GOD.

(*a*) THE AGED CHRISTIAN'S ADVICE TO A YOUNG MINISTER.—I well remember, said an eminent minister in North Wales, that when the Spirit of God first convinced me of my sin and danger, and of the many difficulties and enemies I must encounter, if ever I intended reaching heaven, I was often to the last degree in fear; the prospect of the many strong temptations and allurements, to which my youthful years would unavoidably expose me, greatly discouraged me. I often used to tell an aged soldier of Christ, the first and only Christian friend I had any acquaintance with for several years, that I wished I had borne the burden and heat of the day like him. His usual reply was, that so long as I *feared*, and was humbly *dependent upon God*, I should never fall, but certainly prevail. I have *found* it so. O, blessed be the Lord, that I can now raise up my Ebenezer, and say, "Hitherto hath the Lord helped me."

(*b*) HAPPY INFLUENCE OF DANGERS.—At a meeting held in reference to the establishment of schools in the highlands and islands of Scotland, Dr. M'Leod related the following facts:—

A friend of mine happened to be in a boat, by which a poor simple-hearted man from St. Kilda was advancing, for the first time in his life, from his native rock to visit the world; and as he advanced towards the island of Mull, a world in itself in the estimation of the poor St. Kilda man, the boatmen commenced telling him the wonders he was so soon to see. They asked him about St. Kilda; they questioned him regarding all the peculiarities of that wonderful place, and rallied him not a little on his ignorance of all those great and magnificent things which were to be seen in Mull. He parried them off with great coolness and good humor; at length, a person in the boat asked him if he ever heard of God in St. Kilda. Immediately he became grave and collected. "To what land do you belong?" said he; "describe it to me." "I," said the other, "come from a place very different from your barren rock; I come from the land of flood and field, the land of wheat and barley, where nature spreads her bounty in abundance and luxuriance before us." "Is that," said the St. Kilda man, "the kind of land you come from? Ah, then, you may forget God, but a St. Kilda man never can. Elevated on his rock, suspended over a precipice, tossed on the wild ocean, he never can forget his God—he hangs continually on his arm." All were silent in the boat, and not a word more was aked him regarding his religion.

(*c*) THE BEST REFUGE.—"A few years ago," says one, "when an invasion of England by the French was much talked of, the pious Mrs. C—— of L——, heard her pupils relating to each other, where they thought they would conceal themselves on the approach of the enemy, should his threats be realized. With her usual gentleness and condescension, she inquired into, and listened to their little plans. I, (who was one of her pupils,) was the last to point out my hiding-place; having named mine, I added an inquiry where her refuge would be? "My refuge," said she, with a look of devotion and benignity characteristic of her, 'My refuge would be in my God.' I felt reproved; I could not but think hers was the best refuge."

(*d*) GOD UNACKNOWLEDGED.—It has been wisely observed, that we require the same hand to protect us in apparent safety, as in the most imminent danger. One of the most wicked men in the neighborhood of a pious minister, from whom this account was derived, was riding near a precipice, and fell over: his horse was killed, but he escaped unhurt. Instead of thanking God for his deliverance, he refused to acknowledge his hand in it, and attributed his escape to chance. The same man was afterwards riding on a very smooth road; his horse suddenly tripped and fell, threw his rider over his head, and killed him on the spot; while the horse escaped uninjured.

(*e*) THE AGED LADY'S FALL.—An aged mother in Israel residing in S., Rhode Island, says, that once in travelling to and from New-York city, she often lifted up her prayer to God for protection and safety while being whirled along in the railroad cars or borne in the steamboat over the waters of the deep. The desired protection was vouchsafed; and on her return she had safely arrived at the last railroad depot of the journey. Now I seemed to feel, says she, as if all danger had passed, and I omitted to ask God for any further protection as though I could take care of myself. But in passing out of the depot when it was somewhat dark, to walk upon the platform in front, she made a false step, fell to the ground and received a severe injury that confined her to her house for several weeks!

There is no safety for an hour except in God's keeping; and often when we imagine that every natural law is in our favor, we may be in the most imminent peril—within a hair's breadth of the grave.

(*f*) SAYING OF NEWTON.—The Rev. John Newton sometimes said, he had received more damage at his own door than in all the countries he had been in abroad, for he had twice fallen down the steps at his own door, each time spraining a knee. So much injury he had never received abroad. Such a fact shows clearly the necessity of our always living as if exposed to danger, and thus committing ourselves to the Divine protection.

(*g*) THE SHIP'S RETURN.—A ship, which had, on a long voyage, escaped many great dangers from storms, &c., at length arrived safe in port, or harbor. On seeing the safety of the ship, a little boy, who had sailed in it, naturally expressed great joy that they were now, as he thought, out of all danger. In about half an hour after this expression of joy, the poor little fellow fell overboard into the water, and was drowned before any assistance could reach him. Thus many die; they forget God, flatter themselves with security, and then sudden destruction cometh. Our lives are newly loaned to us by God every moment; let us constantly recognize the fact, and so live that living or dying we may be the Lord's.

132. DEPRAVITY.

(*a*) HONESTY TESTED.—A gentleman was once extolling at an extravagant rate the virtue of honesty: what a dignity it imparted to our nature; how it recommended us to the Supreme Being; and confirmed all by a celebrated line from Pope,

"An honest man's the noblest work of God."

"Sir," replied his friend, "however excellent the virtue of honesty may be, I fear there are few men in the world that really possess it." "You surprise me," said the stranger. "Ignorant as I am of your character, sir, I fancy it would be no difficult matter to prove even you a dishonest man." "I defy you." "Will you give me leave, then, to ask you a question or two, and promise not to be offended?" "Ask your questions, and welcome." "Have you never met with an opportunity of getting gain by unfair means?" The gentleman paused. "I don't ask, Have you taken advantage of such an opportunity? but, Have you ever met with such an opportunity? I, for my part, have; and I believe every body else has." "Very probably I may." "How did you feel your mind affected on such an occasion? Had you no secret desire, not the least inclination, to seize the advantage which offered? Tell me without any evasion, and consistently with the character you admire." "I must acknowledge, I have not always been absolutely free from every irregular inclination; but —" "Hold, sir, none of your salvos, you have confessed enough. If you had the desire, though you never proceeded to the act, you were dishonest in heart. This is what the Scriptures call concupiscence. It defiles the soul. It is a breach of that law which requireth truth in the inward parts; and, unless you are pardoned through the blood of Christ, will be a just ground of your condemnation, when God shall judge the secrets of men."

(*b*) A GOD TOO SHARPSIGHTED.—Some of the natives of South America, after listening a while to the instructions of the Catholic missionaries, gave them this cool answer: "You say that the God of the Christians knows every thing, that nothing is hidden from him, that he is every where, and sees all that is done below. Now, we do not desire a God so sharpsighted; we choose to live with freedom in our woods, without having a perpetual observer of our actions over our heads."

(*c*) MILNE'S CONVICTIONS.—Dr. Milne, the pious missionary, in speaking of his conversion, says, "The book which God made use of more especially for convincing me of my sin and misery, was *Boston's Fourfold State*, which I read with the deepest attention. It conducted me to my own heart, discovered the evils which before lay hid in the chambers of imagery; the monstrous ingratitude to God which had marked all my conduct; and the pollution of original and actual sin, with which my soul was contaminated. I saw that I was necessarily under the strongest and most righteous obligations to God, and had never for one hour of my life discharged them, but lived in rebellion against the author of my life; so I was justly under the curse of God's righteous law, and exposed to everlasting misery." Under the tormenting fears of *eternal wrath*, he sometimes wished himself transformed into a stone, or one of the fowls he saw flying over his head in the fields. He was frequent and fervent in prayer, and was, in the mercy of God, led to those means by which he learned how even a vile and guilty creature, such as he was, might be for ever saved.

(*d*) HATING GOODNESS.—"I happened once," says Dr. Cotton Mather, "to be present in the room where a dying man could not leave the world until he lamented to a minister (whom he had sent for on his account), the unjust calumnies and injuries which he had often cast upon him. The minister asked the poor penitent what was the occasion of this abusive conduct; whether he had been imposed upon by any false report. The man made this answer, 'No, sir, it was merely this; I thought you were a good man, and that you did much good in the world, and therefore I hated you. Is it possible, is it possible,' he added, 'for such a wretch to find pardon?'"

(*e*) THERE GOES DR. IVES.—The Rev. and pious Dr. Ives, whose house was on Oxford road, and by which the criminals were carried weekly in carts to Tyburn, used to stand at his window, and say to any young friends who might be near him, pointing out any of the most notorious malefactors, "There goes *Dr. Ives!*"—If an explanation was asked, he took occasion to expound the innate corruption of the human heart; and appealed to the *experience* of his auditors, "whether they had not felt the movements of those very passions, errors, prejudices, lusts, revenge, covetousness, &c., whose direct tendency was to produce the crimes for which these offenders satisfied the claims of public justice, and which were solely prevented from carrying them to the same dreadful fate, by the restraining grace of God."

(*f*) OLD ADAM TOO HARD FOR YOUNG MELANCTHON.—When Melancthon was first converted, he thought it impossible for his hearers to withstand the evidence of the truth in the ministry of the gospel. But after preaching a while, he complained, "that old Adam was too hard for young Melancthon."

(*g*) ERSKINE AND THE CRIMINAL.—The holiest and best men have been usually the most ready to acknowledge the natural depravity of their hearts, and the greatness of their obligations to the free and sovereign grace of God, in preserving or delivering them from the consequences of that depravity.—During the ministry of the Rev. Ralph Erskine, at Dunfermline, a man was executed for robbery, whom he repeatedly visited in prison, and whom he attended on the scaffold. Mr. Erskine addressed both the spectators and the criminal; and, after concluding his speech, he laid his hands on his breast, uttering these words—"But for restraining grace, I had been brought, by this corrupt heart, to the same condition with this unhappy man."

(*h*) THE LAW OF GOD REJECTED BY PAGANS.—"The reason why we hate that law," said some idolaters to a zealous missionary, "is, because it is holy: and therefore it is we destroy it. If it would allow us to rob freely, if it did dispense with our paying the tribute which the king exacts, if it taught us to be revenged of our enemies, and give way to our passions, without being exposed to the consequences of debauchery, we would heartily embrace it; because it so severely curbs our inclinations, therefore we reject it, and do command you the catechist to depart out of the province immediately."

(*i*) BREAKING THE COMMANDMENTS.—A poor negro, a few years ago, thus addressed the late Rev. Mr. Johnson, at Regent's Town, on the western coast of Africa:—

Yesterday morning, when you preach, you show me that the law be our schoolmaster to bring us to Christ. You talk about the ten commandments. You begin at the first, and me say to myself, "Me guilty!" the second, "Me guilty!" the third, "Me guilty!" the fourth, "Me guilty!" the fifth, "Me guilty!" Then you say the sixth, *Thou shalt not kill;* me say, "Ah! me no guilty! me never kill some person." You say, I suppose plenty people live here, who say, "Me no guilty of that!" Me say again in my heart, "Ah, me no guilty!" Then you say, "Did you never hate any person? did you never wish that such a person, such a man, or such a woman was dead!" Massa, you talk plenty about that; and what I feel that time I can't tell you. I talk in my heart, and say, "Me the same person!" My heart begin to beat; me want to cry, my heart heave so much me don't know what to do. Massa, me think me kill ten people before breakfast! I never think I so bad. Afterwards you talk about the Lord Jesus, how he take off our sin. I think I stand the same like a person that have a big stone upon him head, and can't walk—want to fall down. O massa, I have trouble too much; I no sleep all night. (He wept much.) I hope the Lord Jesus Christ will take my sins from me. Suppose he no save me, I shall go to hell for ever.

(*j*) A KEEN REPLY.—John Wesley, in a considerable party, had been maintaining, with great earnestness, the doctrine of *Vox Populi vox Dei*, against his sister, whose talents were not unworthy the family to which she belonged. At last the preacher, to put an end to the controversy, put his argument in the shape of a dictum, and said, "I tell you, sister, the voice of the people *is* the voice of God." "Yes," she replied mildly, "it cried 'Crucify him, crucify him!'" A more admirable answer was perhaps never given.

(*k*) A STRANGE THING.—A friend of Tedyuscung once said to him, when he was a little intoxicated, "There is one thing very strange, and which I cannot account for; it is why the Indians get drunk so much more than the white people." "Do you think strange of that?" said the old chief; "why, it is not strange at all. The Indians think it no harm to get drunk whenever they can; *but you white men say it is a sin, and yet get drunk nevertheless!*"

(*l*) VIRTUE EMBODIED.—Dr. Blair, when concluding a public discourse, in which he had descanted with his usual eloquence on the amiability of virtue, gave utterance to the following apostrophe: "O virtue, if thou wert embodied, all men would love thee."

His colleague, the Rev. R. Walker, ascended the same pulpit, on a subsequent part of the same Sabbath, and addressing the congregation, said, "My reverend friend observed, in the morning, that if virtue were embodied, all men would love her. Virtue has been embodied; but how was she treated? Did all men love her? No; she was despised and rejected of men: who, after defaming, insulting, and scourging her, led her to Calvary, where they crucified her between two thieves." The effect of this fine passage on the audience was very powerful.

(*m*) CONVERSION OF A MORALIST.—Miranda N., says a Christian minister, was about 18 years of age, much distinguished for personal beauty, but more for uncommon sweetness of disposition, and great amiableness of deportment. There was not probably among all the people of my charge, one whose case would have been more promptly cited, and perhaps none so effectively, to disprove the doctrine of the entire sinfulness of the unregenerate heart. She was deservedly a general favorite. She seemed to entertain the kindest affection towards all, and every one who knew her loved her. One evening at an inquiry meeting, held at my house, I noticed, in a full room, a female in great apparent distress. The disturbance she made by her loud sobs, and frequent and painful interruption of the silence of the room, induced me to pass by others and go to her at once. On coming to her seat, I was not a little surprised to find myself by the side of Miranda. The first inquiry I put to to her was this: What has brought you here, M.? With emphasis, she replied

"My sins, sir." With a view to test the reality and depth of her convictions, I then said, "But what have *you* done which makes either your heart or your life appear so heinously sinful?" At this second question she broke out in a voice that reached the extreme part of the room and thrilled through every heart, for she was known and loved by every person there,—"I HATE GOD, AND I KNOW IT. I HATE CHRISTIANS, AND I KNOW IT. I HATE MY OWN BEING. OH THAT I HAD NEVER BEEN BORN!" As she uttered this acknowledgment, she rose and left the room in irrepressible agony. Deeply as I was interested in her case, I could not follow her and leave the many with whom I had yet to converse; but conducted her across the hall into the opposite room, where Mrs. S. was employed in attendance upon a sick child. The remainder of the narrative I received from Mrs. S.

After a little conversation, as I was informed, between Mrs. S. and Miranda, who was walking the room in great distress, her eye lighted upon a copy of Village Hymns, which lay upon the sideboard. She eagerly caught it up, and read at the first page to which she opened, these words:

"There is a fountain filled with blood,
Drawn from Immanuel's veins;
And sinners plunged beneath that flood,
Lose all their guilty stains."

As she finished this verse she dropped the book and exclaimed, "I have found my Savior. This is the Savior I need. O precious Savior!" and many other expressions of the same kind. Her enmity to God was gone. Her burden was removed. Christ was all in all to her.

133. DESPAIR, UNFOUNDED.

(*a*) THE DESPAIRING WOMAN CONVERTED.—A young woman, whom Dr. Gifford visited in prison, and who was to be tried for her life, heard him speak a good while in an awful strain, not only unmoved, but at last she laughed in his face. He then altered his tone, and spoke of the love of Jesus, and the mercy provided for the chief of sinners, till the tears came in her eyes, and she interrupted him by asking, "Why; do you think there can be mercy for me?" He said, "Undoubtedly, if you *can* desire it." She replied, "Ah! if I had thought so, I should not have been here; I have long fixed it in my mind that I was absolutely lost, and without hope, and this persuasion made me obstinate in my wickedness, so that I cared not what I did." She was afterwards tried, and sentenced to transportation, and Dr. Gifford, who saw her several times, had a good hope that she was truly converted before she left England.

(*b*) THE CHRISTIAN IN HELL.—James Rose was resident at Floor, in Northamptonshire, (England,) and was esteemed by all his religious acquaintance, a very humble, pious man. He was a constant and serious attendant on the means of grace, both public and private; and was scarcely ever absent from church meetings. His general conversation showed a mind mortified to the world, and devoted to God. This good man, towards the close of life, was under great darkness and dejection of mind; and in his last sickness was filled with desponding apprehensions as to the safety of his state. These apprehensions he expressed in so affecting a manner, as greatly interested the feelings of his pious friends, and particularly Mr. Petto, the pastor of the church, who frequently visited, conversed, and prayed with him. All this availed nothing; he refused to be comforted, because he thought that the promises of the gospel did not belong to him. As death seemed to approach, he was violently agitated with horror and despair, and addressed his friends that visited him in terms that filled them with great distress. The circumstance occasioned great searching of heart among them. They had been wont to entertain a very high opinion of his personal piety, and could not account for this strange dispensation. However, the day on which he died, a minister who was on a journey, called at Mr. Petto's, not with any view of stopping; but Mr. Petto desired him to alight, for he had a circumstance to relate to him, which was the case of this poor distressed friend, and expressed a wish that he would go and see him, in hopes he might be directed to say something that might be useful. After giving a brief account of the life and conversation of Mr. Rose, expressing the great esteem he had for him, and the concern which his present state of distress gave him, &c., they went to see him. On approaching the bed of the poor dying man, the minister asked him how he was in his mind? "O sir," said he, "*never worse, never worse!* I am in a lost state! just dying, and have no hope! I am as sure that I shall go to hell, as I am of being a man!" The minister replied: "Friend, I am grieved to find you under so much dejection; but however, though I dare not positively say that you will not go to hell, from all the accounts I can gather concerning you, I believe you are not likely to stop there long; for you have loved the company of serious Christians, to converse with them on religious subjects; and you were most in your element when you have been attending at such opportunities. You have been wont to tell of the love and loveliness of Christ—of his matchless grace and condescension in assuming human nature, and obeying and suffering for the redemption and salvation of sinners; and also of the work of the Holy Spirit, in revealing Christ to the souls of sinners, as the only hope set before them in the gospel. Now I would have you to know that, as this was the habitual temper and disposition of your mind, and in all the past part of your life, ever since you knew the Lord Jesus Christ, death will make no change in the habit of your mind. Nay; and if you should even go to hell, you will be the same man; and you will begin to talk on the same subjects. Now, this will never be borne; your company will soon be hateful to the inhabitants of hell, and the devil will soon turn you out again."

This peculiar thought was the means, in the hand of the Spirit, of setting the poor man at liberty; for, with an expressive smile, he exclaimed, "All is well, all is well!" and departed in a few minutes after. Those words had a remarkable accomplishment in him: "Mark the perfect man, and behold the upright; for the end of that man is peace."

(*c*) WILSON AND THE SOLDIER.—One evening, as the Rev. William Wilson of Perth was passing along the streets of that town, three soldiers, then quartered in it, happened to walk behind him, who were indulging in the utterance of the most profane and blasphemous language. One of them, on some frivolous account, declared it to be his wish, that God Almighty might damn his soul in hell to all eternity. Mr. Wilson immediately turned round, and, with a look of dignity and compassion, said, "Poor man, and what if God should say amen, and answer that prayer!" Mr. Wilson passed on. The man seemed to stand petrified, and, on going home to his quarters, was in such distraction of mind and feeling, that he knew not whither to turn for relief. He was soon afterwards seized with fever, under which he continued to suffer the most awful forebodings of eternal misery. His case was so singular, that many Christians went to visit him, to whom he invariably said he was sure of being beyond the reach of mercy, and that God had sent his angel to tell him so. One of them asked him to describe the appearance of the person who had pronounced this doom on him. He did so, and the visitant at once perceiving that it must have been Mr. Wilson, inquired if he would wish again to see him. "Oh," said he, "I would wish above every thing to see him, but he will not come near a wretch like me." Mr. Wilson was soon brought, and told him of the way of salvation through *Christ crucified*, and encouraged him *to flee for refuge to lay hold upon the hope set before him*. His words being accompanied by Divine power, the poor soldier was enabled to believe in Christ, and thus found peace and comfort to his troubled soul. He soon afterwards recovered, and became a very exemplary Christian; and, as he felt the army unfavorable to a religious life, Mr. W. at his request used influence, and procured his discharge. He settled in Perth, became a member of the church, attached himself steadily to Mr. Wilson, and was through life a comfort to him, and an ornament to the Christian profession.

134. DIFFICULTIES IN CHURCHES.

(*a*) FULLER AND HIS CHURCH.—Some years after Mr. Fuller had removed from Soham to Kettering, a difficulty arose between him and some of the members of this church, which grew and increased, till it became formidable. It was expected by both parties, that Mr. Fuller must quit his place, as no means of accommodation presented itself. It was a time of painful suspense to a few, who began to perceive in him the opening of those faculties which afterwards were so conspicuous and useful. In these difficulties, application was made to Dr. Ryland, then of Northampton, Rev. Robert Hall, senior, of Arnsby, and Rev. Jno. Sutcliff, of Almy, to meet at Kettering, and give their advice.

Mr. Hall proposed to be there the day before the meeting; and, if agreeable, to give them a sermon in the evening. The meeting was published, and the people assembled. Mr. Hall came according to appointment, and announced from the pulpit as his text, the following words—"And one went in and told his Lord, saying, thus and thus said the maid, that is of the land of Israel." 2 Kings 5: 4.

After an ingenious and appropriate introduction, he made upon the words two remarks. 1. Much of the trouble and confusion in society originate in the parties misunderstanding each other. 2. A mutual, candid explanation will frequently remove all such difficulties, and restore harmony.

When he had finished the service and pronounced the benediction, a deacon of the church arose and requested, that the members of the church would keep their places, till the congregation were withdrawn. The church being by themselves, he addressed them in purport as follows:—Brethren, we have had much trouble of late; we have been led to think hard of our pastor, and to wish him removed. It occurred to me while Mr. Hall was preaching, is there no misunderstanding among us? There may be, and that may be the cause of our difficulty. As several of his brethren had similar impressions, the business was freely discussed. They came to the conclusion to draw up a list of their complaints, and to add to each a suitable question, which their pastor was requested to answer in writing. They sent messengers with this paper to wait upon him immediately, and request his answers to the questions. After free conversation with him in his study, he furnished them with the required answers, which they carried back to their brethren, who were waiting for them in the meeting-house. They examined them, acknowledged they had been entirely mistaken, and that there was no ground for any difference between them and their pastor. With this report they sent their messengers back to Mr. Fuller, who received them in a Christian spirit, and all the difficulties were done away before the parties slept. He spent the rest of his days with them in usefulness, honor and credit, and few men ever enjoyed more of the affection of a church than himself.

(*b*) THE MISDIRECTED LETTER.—"The Rev. Mr. Bulkley of Colchester, Conn., was famous in his day as a casuist and sage counsellor. A church in his neighborhood had fallen into unhappy divisions and contentions, which they were unable to adjust among themselves. They deputed one of their number to the venerable Bulkley, for his services, with a request that he would send it to them in writing

The matters were taken into serious consideration, and the advice, with much deliberation, committed to writing. It so happened, that Mr. Bulkley had a farm in an extreme part of the town, upon which he intrusted a tenant. In superscribing the two letters, the one for the church was directed to the tenant, and the one for the tenant to the church. The church was convened to hear the advice which was to settle all their disputes. The moderator read as follows: *You will see to the repair of the fences, that they be built high and strong, and you will take special care of the old black bull.* This mystical advice puzzled the church at first, but an interpreter among the more discerning ones was soon found, who said, Brethren, this is the very advice we most need; the direction to repair the fences is to admonish us to take good heed in the admission and government of our members; we must guard the church by our Master's laws, and keep out strange cattle from the fold. And we must in a particular manner set a watchful guard over the *Devil,* the old black bull, who has done so much hurt of late. All perceived the wisdom and fitness of Mr. Bulkley's advice, and resolved to be governed by it. The consequence was, all the animosities subsided, and harmony was restored to the long afflicted church.

(*c*) KILPIN'S METHOD.—When any member of Mr. Kilpin's church at Exeter, came with details of real or supposed injuries, received from a fellow-member, after listening to the reporter, Mr. K. would inquire if they had mentioned these grievances to their offending brother or sister. If the reply was in the negative, and usually it was so, he would then calmly order a messenger to fetch them, remarking, that it would be ungenerous to decide, and unscriptural to act, merely from hearing the statement of one party. This determination always produced alarm, and the request that nothing might be mentioned to the parties implicated. This plan had a peaceful influence, and often produced humility and self-accusation. Assertions and proofs are very different grounds for the exercise of judgment, and are more distinct than angry persons imagine.

135. DISCIPLINE, FAMILY.

135. Disciplining Children in Infancy.

(*a*) THE ROD SUCCESSFUL.—The following fact occurred in the family of a pious minister, who had then a revival in his congregation.

"Electra," said her mother to a little daughter of two and a half years old, playing on the floor, "bring me that apple, my dear." She looked at her mother and said, "No," with indifference, and resumed her play. Her mother rejoined, "bring me that apple instantly;" and was answered, "I wont." Things now became in earnest; and after several more orders and refusals, the case was resigned to the father, who was present and observed the scene. With a tone of authority, and yet benevolence, he reiterated the mandate, "Take that apple to your mother, my child!" Electra arose and went to the place where the apple was, picked up a chip that was near it, returned, threw it into her mother's lap, and was going to her play. Her father here took hold of her, brought her near him, expostulated, warned, and then reordered her. Her sullenness deepened into silence and malignity—*my will be done,* was her deliberate position. Her father took down the provided *birch,* and very dispassionately applied it to the obstinate offender. Electra screamed, and begged, and called for her mother, who first interfered, and then, not succeeding, in a flood of tears left the room. Her father forbore, and tried her again. She walked pouting and sobbing to the apple, stood still near it, and said—she *could* not pick it up. Her father understood the nature of her inability, and its true relation to accountability. He paused for some minutes

Electra looked alternately at the apple and at him, pouted, rubbed her eyes, and said again that she could not pick up the apple. Another whipping was the consequence. Electra screamed louder than ever, begged and *promised.* On this her father tried her again. She went to the apple, stood still, held her eyes to the floor, said and did nothing. Here some sympathetic spectators—friends of the family visiting—began to plead and apologize for the sufferer, and insinuated that it was useless and tyrannous to persist. Her father, with a look, gave them their answer, and his sentiments. He again applied the birch, and let not his soul spare for her crying. As soon as he ceased, while his steady carriage had awed the circle into silence, Electra showed another creature: she ran to the apple, took it up, and brought it to her father. Her actions spoke her obstinacy gone, her pride subdued, her temper humbled, tender, penitent. Her mother was called. As soon as she entered the apartment, "Electra," said her father, "put this apple where it was on the carpet;" she obeyed. Again, said he, "Take it up and carry it to your mother." She obeyed with alacrity and tears. "Come here, my daughter." She came. To the questions, "Are you sorry?" and others like it, she assented; constantly opening her arms and raising her lips for the caresses of her father.

Her mother then began *her confession,* asked pardon for the improper strength of her feelings, and acknowledged that her love for the child was spurious in comparison with that of her husband. The others united in the acknowledgment.

(*b*) THE BALL OF YARN.—M—, was the only child out of five, spared to her parents. The father relates the following incident which occurred when she was two years old. She was diverting herself with a ball of yarn, one day, from which her grandmother was occasionally taking a piece to mend stockings. The old lady wishing to replenish her needle, called upon M— for the ball. For some reason best known to her little self she refused to give it up. The request for the ball was several times repeated but without obtaining it. The father sitting by, reading, interfered and added his *request* that she would give up the ball, but without effect. He then told her decidedly—"Carry the ball to grandma." But instead of obeying she fixed herself in a position of resistance; and with eyes directed to the floor, and her hand grasping the ball more firmly, she stood unmoved. The command was repeated; but the only answer was a shrug of the shoulders, a twitch of the muscles, and a glance of the eye, intimating decidedly "I wont." The command was repeated again, and, to his surprise, the same answer was given. He arose from his seat, and approaching her, repeated the command; but instead of obedience she threw the ball spitefully across the room. He took her by the hand, led her to the ball, told her to take it up and carry it to her grandmother. She refused—he bent her forward and placed her hand on the ball, repeating the command; but instead of obeying she gave it a knock to the other side of the room. He led her to it and repeated the order, placing her hand again on the yarn, and accompanying the order with a threat of punishment; but to no effect. After spending about fifteen minutes in this way, he inflicted several smart blows; but, though she cried lustily, she refused to yield. He repeated the blows two or three times until she stopped crying, and finally submitted. She catches up the ball, and filled with sudden penitence and love, she stretches out her arms, and strives to cling around her father's neck and kiss him. But, to test her sincerity, he requires her first to carry the ball of yarn to grandma. She does so and comes back, but, before he will let her kiss him, he orders her to go and get the ball and bring it to him. She obeys at once. He then orders her to place it in a chair, at another end of the room; she obeys as quickly and returns again. He sends her again for it, and orders her with it thence to another place, and thence to the old lady. All is done as he commands. After these repeated proofs of the reality or her submission, he suffers her to kiss him, and to kiss her grandmother, and then to go to her play again. The father says, he never had much trouble after this event in securing the obedience of that daughter; indeed she was ever afterwards the most affectionate and obedient of his children, though naturally the most decided and self-willed of either of them.

136. Discipline accompanied with Prayer.

(*a*) EFFECTUAL CHASTISEMENT.—A father called to account a little boy, an offender about five years of age. After conversing with him and telling him the guilt and consequences of disobedience, he knelt down and prayed for him, and when he arose, repeated to him a few texts of Scripture, such as,—"He that spareth the rod, hateth his son; but he that loveth him, chasteneth him betimes." "Chasten thy son while there is yet hope, and let not thy soul spare for his crying." "The rod and reproof, give wisdom, but a child left to himself, bringeth his parents to shame." After briefly explaining these passages, the father continued: "You see, my son, what God says; now what is my duty?" "Why, Pa," said the little boy, "it is your duty to punish me: I have done wrong and deserve it." After receiving the chastisement, he embraced and kissed his father with evident thankfulness, and promised never again to disobey him.

(*b*) SIGNIFICANT CONFESSION.—I am acquainted, says the Rev. R. J. Smith, with a young man whose father died when he was but an infant, but whose mother always controlled and governed him. One day in conversation upon this subject, he remarked to me, "Whenever I was guilty of disobeying my mother, and she called me to account, she would talk to me seriously, and then kneel down in prayer and tell God all about my conduct and the consequences of my course. I used to feel at such times as if my heart would burst, and I have often said—"Ma, whip me, but don't talk to me and pray for me." "Ah," said he, "it was the talking and praying that affected me more than the whipping though all were necessary."

(*c*) APPLYING THE WRONG REMEDY.—A gentleman's son, says the Berlin Evangelical Journal, was brought to Mr. Flattich, an aged clergyman, of Wirtemburg, Germany, who was famous as an instructor of youth, with the request that he would place him under his discipline and instruction. "I must give you to understand," said the gentleman, when alone with the minister, "that my son is a desperate lad, upon whom, hitherto, all instructions, all corrections, have been lost. I have admonished him, I have whipped him, I have shamed him before company, but he still remains a desperate boy; praise and blame are equally unavailing." The minister asked whether he had sought for no other remedies. "Yes," said the father, "I confined the boy once to bread and water for two days together." The minister still asked him if he had tried nothing else. "Yes," he replied, "I have exposed him to the cold." Upon being further questioned, he mentioned other measures he had resorted to, without any good effect. He had in vain sought mild methods to bring him to reason; he had, for example, let him go into the company of well-behaved children; but the boy would escape as soon as possible into the society of boys in the street, or else would exhibit rude behavior before the orderly children. Upon this the old clergyman said that all these were not the right remedy; he knew a better remedy for such desperate cases, and that was prayer. He asked him whether he had deliberately and earnestly prayed with his son, and for him. The gentleman said, he must confess he had not done it. Then, observed the clergyman, it need not seem strange that all your pains applied have been in vain. Flattich now tried his remedy upon the boy, and it *succeeded* so well, that, as the writer of this communication knows, from a desperate youth he became an excellent and efficient man.

137. Religious Tendency of Discipline.

(*a*) THE LAD'S PRAYER.—A gentleman's son, in England, of ten or eleven years of age, one day told an untruth, which afterwards came to the knowledge of his father, who determined to chastise him severely for it.

He took the boy and an instrument of correction into a chamber, and there reprimanded him, setting forth the heinousness of the sin against God, and the injury he was doing to his own soul. He then proceeded to the work of correction; though every stroke was doubtless as afflictive to the parent as the child. After this the father left the boy in the room, and made as though he was going down the stairs, shutting the door behind him. But, pausing a little, he returned softly to the door, and waited some time, hearing the sobbing and sighing of the boy. After a while the father heard a movement and began to think of retreating. But after descending a step or two, he heard his son speak, and softly resuming his former station, and looking through the keyhole of the door, he perceived his son on his knees! The boy proceeded to acknowledge his guilt and shame before God, and to pray for forgiveness; thanking God for favoring him with such a father as would not suffer sin upon him. In many similar instances the faithful punishment of disobedient children leads them to be contrite towards their parents for their offences against them; and the transition from *such* penitence in a child religiously educated, to a scriptural repentance towards God, is, comparatively speaking, an easy and natural one. Other things being equal, there can be no doubt of this proposition at least, that a child who is often led humbly to acknowledge and mourn over his offences against his earthly parents, is more likely to be convicted of his sins against his heavenly Father, to confess, forsake, and find mercy.

(*b*) THE CHILD'S GRATITUDE. —A child, who had been trained in the ways of religion, by a parent who was kind, but judiciously firm, as she sunk to rest in peaceful reliance on her Savior's love, affectionately thanked her beloved mother for all her tender care and kindness; but added, "I thank you most of all, for having subdued my self-will." And why so much gratitude for the mother's faithful discipline? Doubtless because the child regarded it as preparatory to the submission of her will to God, and thus instrumental of her salvation.

(*c*) THE INDULGED CHILD.—A mother, says Rev. R. J. Smith, related to me the following instance, illustrating the relation between submission to parental authority, and conversion or submission to the will of God. She had several children, and seemed properly to understand the importance of training them to prompt and cheerful obedience, and, as a consequence, they were early converted to God. One of these children, however, had been from infancy subject to fits, general weakness, and derangement of the physical system. It was the general injunction of her physician, that she should be kept as quiet as possible, and that her will should not be crossed. The mother acted accordingly, and all her whims and desires were freely indulged. But instead of rendering her calm and quiet, this course made her peevish, fretful, and stubborn. After making it a subject of study and prayer, the mother determined to subdue her will, and govern her as she did her other children. She called to her the girl, and confessed to her that the course she had been pursuing towards her was wrong, and told her that now she must depend upon obeying her or she should punish her.

She soon required a certain duty at her hand, but as she was not accustomed to obey, she paid no regard to the requirement. The mother commenced chastising her, and said, for the time it seemed as though the child would be the conqueror. But fully resolved on securing obedience, she persevered until the child yielded. She was penitent, begged her mother to forgive her, and promised in future always to obey her. From this time, she saw that she had not only sinned against her mother, but against God. A few nights after this occurrence, the mother said she was awakened at midnight, with the cry—"Ma, pray for me, for I am a grea sinner." She arose, knelt by her side and commended her to God; and the little girl begged of God, as she had before done of her mother, to forgive her;

and arose with the evidence that her sins were forgiven.

In a short time she was taken violently ill, and failed rapidly. One day she called her mother to her death-bed, extended her hand and said, "Ma, I thank you that you gave me that whipping the other day; if you had not I should have died in my sins and gone to hell; but now I feel that you have forgiven me, and God has forgiven me; and I am going to heaven. She then embraced her mother in her arms and kissed her, and bade her farewell saying, "I shall soon meet you again in heaven," and sweetly fell asleep in Jesus.

If parents do not obtain and keep the mastery of the will, they place an almost insurmountable obstacle in the way of their children ever being converted and saved. They are either never converted, or if converted are given to perpetual backslidings, and make little or no progress in piety. While those whose wills have been subjected to parental authority in early life, are likely to be early converted, and afterwards to prove steadfast in their allegiance and obedience to God.

138. Discipline Withheld.

(*a*) THE RUINED SON.—An only son of pious and respectable parents, says a writer in the Christian Watchman, was sent to school in a neighboring village. He gave early intimations of the truth of Solomon's remark, in Prov. 29: 15. Reports of his improper conduct reached the ears, and pierced the hearts of his fond parents, and called forth repeated expostulations.

I was present one day, when he received a letter from them, written in the bitterness of parental grief. They told him of their anxiety, their sleepless nights, their tears and prayers in his behalf. They warned him of his danger; they implored him to listen to the counsel of an affectionate father, a kind, but heart-broken mother. The son read the letter soberly; sat for a moment as if in deep thought, and the muscles of his face betrayed the working of a troubled conscience. Suddenly springing upon his feet, and with a look of ineffable contempt, he dashed the letter into the fire, exclaiming, "There, now, let the old man and woman warn, write letters, pray and whine: it is of no use: *a good whipping, well laid on, ten years ago, would have done more to save me!*"

While on a journey, in September 1834, I met this same only son, on the public road. He was reeling with intoxication, and pouring forth a torrent of profane and obscene language. Memory instantly reverted to his early days, and to his pious, though misjudging parents, who have since entered their rest. He was the only son; a false tenderness led to indulgence; indulgence fostered the corruptions of his heart, and these led him on to ruin. The whole face of society is marked with examples of the same kind.

139. Miscellaneous.

(*a*) HE NEVER SPEAKS KIND TO ME.—Conversing the other day, says one, with an interesting little girl between six and seven years old, I took occasion to impress upon her mind the debt of gratitude due from her to her Heavenly Parent for bestowing upon her so good and kind a parent, whom every body loves. I was perfectly thunderstruck with her answer. Looking me full in the face with her soft blue eyes, she replied, "He never speaks kind to me." Perhaps this Christian father, harassed with the cares of life, was unconscious that he had roughly checked the fond attention of his child; but could cares or the interruptions of his child excuse unkindness or a total want of tokens of endearment? Will fathers examine their habits on this point?

(*b*) "MY MOTHER NEVER TELLS LIES."—Some females, says the St. Louis Observer, met at the house of a friend, in this city, for an evening visit, when the following scene and conversation occurred:—

The child of one of the females, about five years old, was guilty of rude, noisy conduct, very improper on all occasions, and particularly so at a stranger's house The mother kindly reproved her:

"Sarah, you must not do so."

The child soon forgot the reproof and became as noisy as ever. The mother firmly said,

"Sarah, if you do so again I will punish you."

But not long after, Sarah "did so again." When the company were about to separate, the mother stepped into a neighbor's house, intending to return for the child. During her absence the thought of going home recalled to the mind of Sarah the punishment, which her mother told her she might expect. The recollection turned her rudeness and thoughtlessness to sorrow. A young lady present, observing it, and learning the cause, in order to pacify her said,

"Never mind, I will ask your mother not to whip you."

"Oh," said Sarah, "that will do no good. *My mother never tells lies.*"

Said my informant, who is also a parent, "I learned a lesson from the reply of that child, which I shall never forget. It is worth every thing in the training of a child, to make it feel, that its *Mother never tells lies.*"

(*c*) THE SICK CHILD.—"A child," says Mr. Abbott, "a short time since was taken ill with that dangerous disorder, the croup. It was a child most ardently beloved, and ordinarily very obedient. But in this state of uneasiness and pain, he refused to take the medicine which it was needful without delay to administer. The father finding him resolute, immediately punished his sick and suffering son; under these circumstances, and fearing that his son might soon die, it must have been a most severe trial to the father; but the consequence was, that the child was taught that sickness was no excuse for disobedience: and while his sickness continued, he promptly took whatever medicine was prescribed, and was patient and submissive. Soon the child was well. Does any one say this was cruel? It was one of the noblest acts of kindness which could have been performed. If the father had shrunk from duty here, it is by no means improbable that the life of the child would have been the forfeit."

(*d*) THE COUNT AND HIS FAMILY.—The following account is given by Milner, in his "Church History," of the family order observed by Eleazer, Count of Arian, in the fourteenth century:—I cannot, said the count, allow blasphemy in my house, nor any thing in word or deed which offends the laws of decorum. Dice, and all games of hazard are to be prohibited. Let all persons in my house divert themselves at proper times, but not in a sinful manner. In the morning, reading and prayer must be attended to. Let there be constant peace in my family; otherwise two armies are found under my roof, and the master is devoured by them both. If any difference arise, let not the sun go down upon your wrath. We must bear with something if we have to live among mankind. Every evening, all the family shall be assembled at a godly conference, in which they shall hear something of God and salvation. Let none be absent on pretence of attending to my affairs. I have no affairs so interesting to me as the salvation of my domestics. I seriously forbid all injustice which may cloak itself under color of serving me.

140. DISCIPLINE, CHURCH.

(*a*) THE TWO KEYS.—Once from the pulpit, at an ordination of elders, the late Rev. Mr. M'Cheyne made the following declaration:—"When I first entered upon the work of the ministry among you, I was exceedingly ignorant of the vast importance of church discipline. I thought that my great and almost only work was to pray and preach. I saw your souls to be so precious, and the time so short, that I devoted all my time, and care, and strength, to labor in word and doctrine. When cases of discipline were brought before me and the elders, I regarded them with something like abhorrence. It was a duty I shrank from; and I may truly say it nearly drove me from the work of the ministry among you altogether. But it pleased God, who teaches his servants in another way than man teaches, to bless some of the cases of discipline to the manifest and undeniable conversion of the souls of those under our care; and from that hour a new light broke in upon my mind, and I saw that if preaching be an ordinance of Christ, so is church discipline. I now feel very deeply persuaded that both are of God, that two keys are committed to us by Christ, the one the key of doctrine, by means of which we unlock the treasures of the Bible, the other the key of discipline, by which we open or shut the way to the sealing ordinances of the faith. Both are Christ's gift, and neither is to be resigned without sin."

(*b*) EMPLOYMENT FOR A CHURCH.—A minister of the gospel, in excusing himself and his church for not exerting themselves to instruct and gather in the multitude around them, said, "It is impossible for so large a church as ours, to do much for those out of our body. It takes," said he, "one-third of us to watch the other two-thirds!" What a confession is this! Only one in three possessing the true spirit of Christianity, and he is prevented from being an efficient soldier of the cross, by the lukewarmness and sins of his brethren!

141. DISHONESTY PUNISHED.

(*a*) FEIGNING DEATH AND DYING.—The Gazette de Lyons published the following fact; it happened at Chenas not far from Lyons.—A rich widow, without children, had promised to make her will in favor of her niece. The aunt fell sick, and the niece, as much through attachment as interest, lavished upon her the tenderest as well as the most assiduous cares; however, the aunt died without making a will. The niece was in despair for the loss of her friend and her hopes. She went around, told her story, and asked what could be done. Her perfidious counsellors engaged her to play the old trick of hiding the death, and placing herself in bed, calling for a notary and witnesses, and dictating a convenient testament. She did her part well, and it succeeded wonderfully in a room that was partially darkened. The young girl, sunk in a pillow and curtains, pronounced with a feeble and broken voice, the last will and testament of the aunt; the notary wrote, and the victory was nearly sure, when one of the witnesses, who knew a little more than the others, declared, he would sign no such act; for that the pretended testatrix had been dead for several hours, and he would not be the accomplice of a like deception. The unhappy niece, confounded and overwhelmed, could not support the idea of the consequent shame and punishment of her guilt, and she suddenly expired. She was buried at the same time with her aunt.

(*b*) JOHN EYRE'S NEPHEW.—An anecdote is related of John Eyre, a man whose name is recorded in the annals of crime, as possessing 30,000*l*. and yet being sentenced to transportation for stealing eleven quires of writing paper, which shows, in a striking manner, the depravity of the human heart, and may help to account for the meanness of the crime of which he stood convicted. An uncle of his, a gentleman of considerable property, made his will in favor of a clergyman who was his intimate friend, and committed it, unknown to the rest of the family, to the custody of the divine. However, not long before his death, having altered his mind with regard to the disposal of his wealth, he made another will, in which he left the clergyman only 500*l*., bequeathing the bulk of his large property to his nephew and heir-at-law, Mr. Eyre. Soon after the old gentleman's death, Mr. Eyre, rummaging over his drawers found this last will, and perceiving th legacy of 500*l.* in it for the clergyman, without any hesitation or scruple of conscience, he put it into the fire, and took possession of the whole effects, in consequence of his uncle being supposed to die intestate. The clergyman coming to town soon after, and inquiring into the circumstances of his old friend's death, asked if he had made a will before he died. On being answered by Mr. Eyre in the negative, the clergyman very coolly put his hand in his pocket, and pulled out the former will, which had been committed to his care, in which Mr. Eyre had bequeathed him the whole of his fortune, amounting to several thousand pounds, excepting a legacy of 200*l.* to his nephew.

(*c*) LOSS OF CHARACTER.—Robert Andrews, foreman to a respectable nurseryman at some distance from Philadelphia, who had lived with his employers ten years, and had a good character, one Saturday night, after applying for his wages, claimed pay for a young man up to that day, whom he had discharged some days before. His master said, looking him steadily in the face, "Robert, do you want to cheat me, by asking wages for a man that you discharged yourself eight days ago?" He had no sooner said this, than the miserable conscience-stricken man's blood forsook his face, as if he had been stabbed to the heart. When his master saw him so much affected, he told him that he might still labor as he had done, but that after such a manifestly dishonest attempt, his character, and the confidence in it, were gone for ever. On Monday, Robert made his appearance, but was utterly an altered man. The agitation of his mind had reduced his body to the feebleness of an infant's. He took his spade and tried to use it, but in vain; and it was with difficulty that he reached home. He went to bed immediately; medical aid was procured, but to no purpose, and the poor fellow sunk under the sense of his degradation, and expired on Wednesday forenoon! His neighbors who attended him, say, that a short time before he died, he declared, that the agony consequent on the loss of his character as an honest man, which he had for so many years maintained, was the sole cause of his death.

(*d*) THE HEIR INGENIOUSLY DISCOVERED.—A jeweller who carried on an extensive trade, and supplied the deficiencies of one country by the superfluities of another, leaving his home with a valuable assortment of diamonds, for a distant region, took with him his son, and a young slave, whom he had purchased in his infancy, and had brought up more like an adopted child, than a servant. They performed their intended journey, and the merchant disposed of his commodities, with great advantage; but while preparing to return, he was seized by a pestilential distemper, and died suddenly in the metropolis of a foreign country. This accident inspired the slave with a wish to possess his master's treasures, and relying on the total ignorance of strangers, and the kindness every where shown him by the jeweller, he declared himself the son of the deceased, and took charge of his property. The true heir of course denied his pretensions, and solemnly declared himself to be the only son of the defunct, who had long before purchased his opponent as a slave. This contest produced various results. It happened that the slave was a young man of beautiful person, and of polished manners, while the jeweller's son was ill-favored by nature, and said to be injured in his education, by the indulgence of his parents. This superiority operated in the minds of many to support the claims of the former; but since no certain evidence could be produced on either side, it became necessary to refer the dispute to a court of law. There, however, from a total want of proofs, nothing could be done. The magistrate declared his inability to decide on unsupported assertions, in which each party was equally positive. This caused a report of the case to be made to the prince, who having heard the particulars, was also confounded, and at a loss how to decide the question. At length, a happy thought occurred to the chief of the judges, and he engaged to ascertain the real heir. The two claimants being summoned before him, he ordered them to stand behind a curtain prepared for the occasion, and to project their heads through two openings, when, after hearing their several arguments, he would cut off the head of him who should prove to be the slave. This they readily assented to; the one from a reliance on his honesty, the other from a confidence of the impossibility of detection. Accordingly, each taking his place as ordered, thrust his head through a hole in the curtain. An officer stood in front with a drawn cimeter in his hand, and the judge proceeded to the examination. After a short debate, the judge cried out, "Enough, enough, strike off the villain's head!" and the officer, who watched the moment, leaped towards the two youths; the impostor, startled at the brandished weapon, hastily drew back his head, while the jeweller's son, animated by conscious security, stood unmoved. The judge immediately decided for the latter, and ordered the slave to be taken into custody, to receive the punishment due to his diabolical ingratitude.

142. DISINTERESTEDNESS.

(*a*) ADRIAN AND THE BISHOP.—Terantius, captain to the Emperor Adrian, presented a petition that the Christians might have a temple by themselves, in which to worship God apart from the Arians. The emperor tore his petition, and threw it away, bidding him ask something for himself, and it should be granted. Terantius modestly gathered up the fragments of his petition, and said, with true nobility of mind, "If I cannot be heard in God's cause, I will never ask any thing for myself."

(*b*) CALVIN'S DISINTERESTEDNESS.—This celebrated reformer was remarkable for his disinterestedness. His goods, his books, and his money, were not equal to one hundred and twenty-five crowns, and yet he refused, during his sickness, twenty-five crowns, which the Council of Geneva offered to him, because he was incapable of fulfilling the appointed labors of his office.

(*c*) WHITEFIELD REJECTING AN ESTATE.—It is difficult, in such a world as this, so to live as that "our good" shall not be "evil spoken of." Mr. Whitefield has been charged with mercenary motives: his whole life showed the fallacy and weakness of such a charge. During his stay in Scotland, in 1759, a young lady, Miss Hunter, who possessed a considerable fortune, made a full offer to him of her estate, both money and lands, amounting to several thousand pounds, which he generously refused: and, upon his declining it for himself, she offered it to him for the benefit of his orphan-house. This also he absolutely refused. This incident is given on the authority of his original biographer, Dr. Gillies, who received it from unquestionable testimony.

143. DISOBEDIENCE TO PARENTS.

(*a*) BEGINNING OF EVIL.—A young man was sentenced to the South Carolina penitentiary for four years. When he was about to be sentenced, he stated publicly that his downward course began in disobedience to his parents—that he thought he knew as much of the world as his father did, and needed not his aid or advice, but that as soon as he turned his back upon his home, then temptations came around him like a *drove of hyenas*, and hurried him on to ruin. There is no place so safe and happy as a good home.

(*b*) REASON FOR DISOBEYING.—The American Sunday School

Herald, states, that a little girl, six years old, in a Sunday school, was repeating the fifth commandment. Her teacher endeavored to show her in what way she was to honor her parents, and said, "You must honor your parents by obeying them." "O, ma'am," exclaimed the child, "I cannot keep that commandment." "Why cannot you keep it, my dear?" "Because, ma'am, when my mother tells me to do one thing, my father tells me to do another. Now, just before I came here, my mother told me to stay up stairs and learn my lesson, and my father told me to come down and play: now how could I obey them both? No, no," closing her little hands as if in despair, "no, no, ma'am, it is impossible for me ever to keep that commandment." In such a case, however, a child should obey the father unless he bade her to commit some sin. Neither father or mother should be obeyed then.

(*c*) PHILIP HENRY'S PROPHECY.—The Rev. Philip Henry, speaking once of a wicked son in the neighborhood, that was very undutiful to his mother, charged some of his children to observe the providence of God concerning him; "Perhaps," said he, "I may not live to see it, but do you take notice, whether God do not come upon him with some remarkable judgment in this life, according to the threatening implied in the reason annexed to the fifth commandment;" but he himself lived to see it fulfilled not long after, in a very signal providence.

(*d*) THE DISOBEDIENT PUNISHED.—The Rev. Herbert Palmer, B. D. master of Queen's College, Cambridge, who died in 1647, and who was "a burning and shining light" in his day, was remarkable for his dutiful affection to his parents, not only when he was a child, but during his whole life. He was peculiarly attentive to his pious aged mother; promoting, to the utmost of his power, both her temporal and spiritual comfort, even to the day of her death, which happened not long before his own. He used frequently to enforce this duty in his ministry, observing the emphasis which God puts upon it through the whole of the Scriptures. He used to say that he had noticed the effects of disobedience to parents, so that he scarcely ever knew undutiful children escape some visible judgment of God in the present life; he also thought that the mischiefs which occur in society frequently take their rise in contempt of parental authority.

144. DISTILLERS.

(*a*) THE COLPORTEUR AND DISTILLER.—One day as Mr. R., a colporteur, was passing along the road, a man engaged in making barrels hailed him, stating that as Mr. R. travelled considerably, he should be glad to have him find a purchaser for his distillery; but the colporteur, in the spirit of his Master, began to exhort him to attend to his eternal interests and prepare to give up his final account at the judgment seat. "But what," said he, "shall I do with my still-house?" "Repent, and get your heart right," said Mr. R., "and it shall be shown you what to do with your distillery—you will obtain light on that subject."

After he left the shop, the man, who could not read a line, and, as he afterwards said, had *never before been personally addressed by any Christian on the subject of his soul's salvation*, immediately fell down upon his knees and cried to God for mercy. Some time after, he found peace in Christ. *He gave up his distillery* which cost $1,000; and *his wife, his brother and wife, and his mother, were ere long hopefully converted to God.*

(*b*) THE GRAVE-YARD AND THE DISTILLERY.—An elder of the church in ——, New-York, owned a distillery, and manufactured ardent spirits. The elder was an active Christian, and seemed quite awake to the benevolent efforts of the day. His pastor was grieved that so worthy a man should be engaged in a business which brought ruin temporal and eternal upon his fellow-men: and resolved to give him faithful warning. While visiting the elder at his house, the elder looked to the grave-yard, and said, "I love to look there—it seems to be the way to heaven." "Yes," said the pastor, "and that," pointing to the distillery, "is the way to hell." It was a word in season; and in a few weeks the distillery was levelled to the ground.

145. DOUBTS AND FEARS OF CHRISTIANS.

(*a*) THE CHILD'S PRAYER.—A girl of twelve years of age, in one of the S. Schools of Mass., was known for some time to be very serious, and anxious to have her teacher converse with her about her soul. At length, a beam of joy lighted up her countenance. She said to her superintendent one day, "Oh how I love my Savior!" One Sabbath, soon after this, she came to him, at the close of the school: as he took her by the hand, she burst into tears. "Elizabeth," said he, "do you love the Savior now?" "Yes," said she, "but I have been *tempted* this week. Something seemed to say I was not a Christian, and it made me very unhappy."

"What did you do then?"

"I prayed that I might be delivered from temptation, and then I felt happy."

She gave most decided evidence of being a child of God. Her exercise of mind and her prayers were like those of mature Christians.

(*b*) "REMEMBER TORWOOD."—Mr. Kidd, when minister of Queensferry, a few miles from Edinburgh, was one day very much depressed and discouraged, for want of that comfort which is produced by the faith of the gospel alone. He sent a note to Mr. L., minister of Culross, a few miles off, informing him of his distress of mind, and desiring a visit as soon as possible. Mr. L. told the servant, he was so busy that he could not wait upon his master, but desired him to tell Mr. K. to *remember Torwood!* When the servant returned, he said to his master, "Mr. L. could not come, but he desired me to tell you, to *remember Torwood!*" This answer immediately struck Mr. K., and he cried out, 'Yes, Lord! I will remember *Thee*, from the hill Mizar, and from the Hermonites!" All his troubles and darkness vanished upon the recollection of a day which he had formerly spent in prayer, along with Mr. L. in Torwood, where he had enjoyed eminent communion with God.

(*c*) WORLDLY PROFESSOR'S DEATH-BED.—Sometimes, says the late Rev. R. Cecil, in his valuable "Remains," we have a painful part to do with sincere Christians who have been going too much into the world. I was called upon to visit such a man. "I find no comfort," said he, "God veils his face from me. Every thing round me is dark and uncertain." I did not dare to act the flatterer; I said, "Let us look faithfully into the state of things. I should have been surprised if you had not felt thus. I believe you to be sincere; your state of feeling evinces your sincerity. Had I found you exulting in God, I should have concluded that you were either deceived or a deceiver; for, while God acts in his usual order, how could you expect to feel otherwise on the approach of death than you do feel? You have driven hard after the world; your spirit has been absorbed in its cares; your sentiments, your conversation have been in the spirit of the world. And have you any reason to expect the repose of conscience, and the clear evidence that awaits the man who has walked and lived in close friendship with God? You know that what I say is true."

His wife here interrupted me, by assuring me that he had been an excellent man. "Silence!" said the dying penitent, "it is all true."

(*d*) JOHNSON'S VISIT TO WETHERELL.—The late Rev. Robert Johnson says, "In Bishop Wilton lived a good man, named Thomas Wetherell, much respected, with whom I was intimately acquainted about twenty years ago. I heard that he was ill, and went to Bishop Wilton to see him. On my arrival, I said, 'I am an old friend come to see you. I was afraid you would make your escape to heaven before I had an opportunity.' He replied, 'O, dear sir, I fear I shall never get there. I have lost my way! I have lost my way! Oh, what a stumbling-block am I now, after enjoying confidence for forty years!' I answered, 'I am very sorry that you have turned out so badly. I imagine my visit will not be acceptable. I suppose you have become very wicked, and fond of trifling, vain, worldly company.' He immediately rejoined, 'Oh, no, no! I cannot bear them. I cannot bear them.' I said, 'I am glad of that; and you may be sure of this, that the Lord will not send you to hell among them hereafter, when you so much dislike their ways and company now.'

"He was particularly struck with the manner and language in which I addressed him. 'Come,' said I, 'let me have the history of your complaint.' He proceeded, and said, 'Some time ago, I had a paralytic stroke. I was very ill, but very happy in God. Every one thought I was dying, and I thought so myself; and was full of peace and joy. But, contrary to expectation, I got so far better as to be able to walk about, though unable to work. I never was married; and by frugality and industry I saved about one hundred pounds. But it occurred to me that I might live a considerable time in this debilitated state; my hundred pounds would soon be gone; and I should, after all, become a burden to my friends. I entered into a hurtful train of perplexing reasoning, then of doubt, distrust, and fear. I have grieved the Spirit of God, and he has hid his face from me, and I am troubled. I have lost my confidence in God and am now in darkness and despair.'

"I remarked, 'My dear brother, I clearly see your case. Your mind, as well as your body, is debilitated, and the enemy has taken advantage of your weakness to harass and distress you. In your present circumstances, you are not capable of reasoning with him, or of steadfastly resisting him: he is too cunning for you, and too strong. But lift up your heart to the Lord; venture to look unto Jesus, who will soon bruise him under your feet who is thus painfully bruising your heel. You are just like a musical instrument when all its strings are slackened. If you try to play, there are only discordant sounds; not because it is a bad instrument, but because it is out of tune.'

"He replied with earnestness, 'Do you really think so, sir?' 'Yes, I know that it is so. Because you are so unhinged and slackened in your nervous system, you are ready to imagine that the Lord is disaffected towards you, and that his mercy is clean gone for ever. But, oh, venture to call upon him in your trouble and distress; looking unto Jesus who suffered, being tempted, and who knoweth how to succor them that are tempted; and he will most certainly deliver you, and you shall praise him.'

"We then prayed together, and he was greatly encouraged. In a short time afterwards he was completely set at liberty from all his fears, and was filled with joy and peace in believing."

146. DRESS.

(a) A GOOD CAUSE FOR WEEPING.—A minister calling to visit a lady, was detained a long time while she was dressing. At length she made her appearance, bedizened in all the frippery of fashion and folly. The minister was in tears She asked the cause of his grief; when he replied, "I weep, madam, to think that an immortal being should spend so much of that precious time, which was given her to prepare for eternity, in thus vainly adorning that body which must so soon become a prey to worms."

(*b*) A GOOD RULE.—A lady asked the Rev. John Newton, what was the best rule for female dress and behavior. "Madam," said he, "so dress and so conduct yourself, that persons who have been in your company shall not recollect what you had on." This will generally be the case where singularity of dress is avoided, and where intelligence of mind and gentleness of manners are cultivated.

(*c*) WAY TO BANKRUPTCY.—"It is a lamentable fact," says the author of the 'Wife and Mother,' "that at the present day, there are hundreds of bankrupts or tradesmen on the very verge of bankruptcy, or persons of limited income in embarrassed circumstances, whose difficulties have originated in the fondness of their wives for dress and display, and some of these wives, women professing godliness! Not very long since, a professional man, with an income, perhaps of from two to three hundred a year, on which to support himself, a wife, and one child, was arrested for debt. The stir thus occasioned brought to light his general circumstances, when it appeared, that he owed about twelve hundred pounds, more than half that sum being due to mercers, milliners, and jewellers, for his wife's finery."

(*d*) TWO EXTREMES OF PRIDE.—Diogenes being at Olympia, saw at the celebrated festival some young men of Rhodes, arrayed most magnificently. Smiling, he exclaimed, "This is pride." Afterwards meeting with some Lacedemonians in a mean and sordid dress, he said, "And this is also pride."

Pride is found at the same opposite extremes in dress at the present day.

(*e*) LATHROP AND HIS PARISHIONER.—I was once requested, says Dr. Lathrop, to preach against prevailing fashions. A remote inhabitant of the parish, apparently in a serious frame, called upon me one day, and pressed the necessity of bearing my testimony against this dangerous evil. I observed to him, that as my people were generally farmers in middling circumstances, I did not think they took a lead in fashions; if they followed them, it was at an humble distance, and rather to avoid singularity, than to encourage extravagance; that as long as people were in the habit of wearing clothes, they must have some fashion or other, and a fashion that answered the ends of dress, and exceeded not the ability of the wearer, I considered as innocent, and not deserving reproof. To this he agreed, but said, what grieved him was to see people *set their hearts* so much on fashions. I conceded that as modes of dress were trifles compared with our eternal concerns, to set our hearts upon them must be a great sin. But I advised him to consider, that to set our hearts *against* such trifles, was the same sin, as to set our hearts *upon* them, and as his fashion was different from those of his neighbors, just in proportion as he set his heart *against theirs*, he set his heart *upon his own*. He was therefore doubly guilty of the very sin he imputed to others.

(*f*) DIFFERENT ADVICE OF TWO MINISTERS.—A couple of very gayly dressed ladies being in company with a clergyman, on his being informed that they were professed Christians, were kindly, but very solemnly reproved by him for their extravagance in dress. He reminded them that God had commanded that *women adorn themselves in modest apparel, with shamefacedness and sobriety; not with broidered hair, or gold, or pearls, or costly array, but (which becometh women professing godliness) with good works; whose adorning let it not be that outward adorning of plaiting the hair, and the wearing of gold, or of* PUTTING ON OF APPAREL; *but let it be the hidden man of the heart, in that which is not corruptible, even the ornament of a* MEEK AND QUIET *spirit, which in the sight of God is of great price.* They were somewhat offended, and with the hope of quieting their consciences, went to another clergyman, and asked him, if *he* thought there was any harm in their wearing feathers in their hats, with artificial flowers, &c., &c. He gravely replied, "There is no harm in *feathers* and *flowers*. If you have in your hearts the *ridiculous vanity* to wish to be thought *pretty*, you may as well hang out the SIGN, and let every one know what is the ruling passion of your heart."

(*g*) SWIFT AND THE PRINTER.—Dean Swift was a regular enemy to extravagance in dress, and particularly to that destructive ostentation in the middling classes, which led them to make an appearance above their condition in life. Of his mode of reproving this folly in those persons for whom he had an esteem, the following instance has been recorded. When George Faulkner, the printer, returned from London, where he had been soliciting subscriptions for his edition of the Dean's works, he went to pay his respects to him, dressed in a laced waistcoat, a bag wig and other fopperies. Swift received him with the same ceremonies as if he had been a stranger. "And pray, sir," said he, "what are your commands with me?" "I thought it was my duty sir," replied George, "to wait on you immediately on my arrival from London." "Pray, sir, who are you?" "George Faulkner the printer, sir." "You George Faulkner the printer! why you are the most impudent barefaced scoundrel of an impostor I have ever met with! George Faulkner is a plain sober citizen, and would never trick himself out in lace and other fopperies. Get you gone, you rascal, I will immediately send you to the house of correction." Away went George as fast as he could, and having changed his dress he returned to the Deanery, where he was received with the greatest cordiality. "My friend George," says the Dean, "I am glad to see you returned safe from London. Why, here has been an impudent fellow with me just now dressed in lace waistcoat, and he would fain pass himself off for you, but I soon sent him away with a flea in his ear."

DUELING.

147. Guilt of Dueling.

(*a*) ANNIVERSARY OF A DUEL.—It is related of Lieutenant-Colonel John Blackader, formerly deputy governor of Stirling castle, that though in early life he had been unhappily engaged in a duel, and had killed his antagonist, yet being convinced of its sinfulness, he observed the anniversary of the day with penitence and prayer.

(*b*) GARDINER'S REPLY TO A CHALLENGE.—Colonel Gardiner having received a challenge to fight a duel, made the following truly noble and Christian reply: "I fear sinning, though you know, sir, I do not fear fighting;" thus showing his conviction of a fact too often forgotten, that the most impressive manifestation of courage is to "obey God rather than man."

148. Folly of Dueling.

(*a*) COBBETT'S RECOMMENDATION.—Cobbett, when challenged to fight, recommended the challenger to draw a Cobbett in chalk upon the floor, and if he succeeded in hitting it, to send him instant word, in order that he might have an opportunity of acknowledging that, had the true Cobbett been there, he, in all probability, would have been hit too. But hit or no hit, the bullets could have no effect whatever, he maintained, on the original causes of the quarrel.

(*b*) OCCASIONS OF DUELS.—Colonel Montgomery was shot in a duel about a dog; Captain Ramsay in one about a servant; Mr. Fetherston in one about a recruit; Sterne's father in one about a goose; and another gentleman in one about "an acre of anchovies." One officer was challenged for merely asking his opponent to enjoy the second goblet; another was compelled to fight about a pinch of snuff. General Barry was challenged by a Captain Smith, for declining a glass of wine with him at a dinner in a steamboat, although the General had pleaded as an excuse that wine invariably made his stomach sick at sea; and Lieut. Crowther lost his life in a duel, because he was refused admittance to a club of pigeon shooters! What contemptible folly in men it is to risk their lives in order to settle such trivial disputes as these! And then how does the result of a duel really settle the dispute any more than the result of jumping together from a precipice, or any similar jeopardy of life and limb?

149. Dueling Avoided.

(*a*) ANSWERING A CHALLENGE MATHEMATICALLY.—The eccentric mathematician, Professor Vince, of King's College, Cambridge, being once engaged in a conversation with a gentleman who advocated dueling," is said to have thrown his adversary completely *hors du combat*, by the following cute and characteristic reply to his question: But what could you do, sir, if a man told you to your face, "You lie?" "What could I do? why I wouldn't knock him down, but I'd tell him to prove it. Prove it, sir, *prove it*, I'd say. If he couldn't, he'd be the liar, and there I should have him; but, if he did prove that I lied, I must e'en pocket the affront; and there I expect the matter would end."

(*b*) THE DUELIST OUTWITTED.—The Rev. J. Cooke, of Maidenhead, many years ago, published a very interesting pamphlet, containing the dying confession of a deist, under the title of, "Reason paying homage to Revelation." Soon after its publication, a great commotion was excited in Maidenhead and its neighborhood. The brother of the deceased gentleman conceived himself injured, and sent a message to Mr. Cooke, demanding the satisfaction of a gentleman. Mr. C. replied, "I am quite prepared to give Mr. —— the satisfaction of a Christian gentleman; and, according to the laws of honor, as he has sent the challenge, it rests with me to choose time, place, and weapons. I do not choose to fight with pistols; my weapon is a sword; and if he will meet me in this parlor to-morrow at noon, with any witnesses he may desire, I shall be prepared to meet him with 'the sword of the Spirit, which is the word of God.' My character, my principles, my office, forbid my using any other weapons." It need not be added that his opponent did not admire this method of meeting the challenge, and Mr. C. heard no more of him.

(*c*) MR. SCOTT'S SWORD.—The preaching of the Rev. J. Scott, who had been a captain in the army, having been instrumental in the conversion of a young lady, the daughter of a country gentleman, her father was greatly offended, because she would not join in the usual amusements of their circle. Looking upon Mr. Scott as the sole cause of what he regarded as the melancholy of his daughter, he lay in wait to shoot him. Mr. Scott, being providentially apprised of it, was enabled to escape the danger. The diabolical design of the gentleman being thus defeated, he sent Mr. Scott a challenge. Mr. S. might have availed himself of the law, and prosecuted him; but he took another method. He waited upon him at his house, was introduced to him in his parlor, and, with his characteristic boldness and intrepidity, thus addressed him: "Sir, I hear that you have designed to shoot me, by which you would have been guilty of murder; failing in this, you have sent me a challenge. And what a coward must you be, sir, to wish to engage with a blind man!" (alluding to his being short-sighted). "As you have given me the challenge, it is now my right to choose the time, the place, and the weapon; I therefore, sir, appoint the present moment, the place where we now are, and the sword for the weapon, to which I have been the most accustomed." The gentleman was evidently greatly terrified; when Mr. Scott, having attained his end, produced a pocket Bible, and exclaimed, "This is my sword, sir; the only weapon I wish to engage with." "Never," said Mr. Scott to a friend to whom he related this anecdote, "never was a poor careless sinner so delighted with the sight of a Bible before!"

Mr. Scott reasoned with the gentleman on the impropriety of his conduct, in treating him as he had done, for no other reason but because he had preached the truth. The result was, the gentleman took him by the hand, begged his pardon, expressed his sorrow for his conduct, and became afterwards very friendly to him.

(*d*) THE STAKES UNEQUAL.—Two friends happening to quarrel at a tavern, one of them, a man of hasty disposition, insisted that the other should fight him next morning. The challenge was accepted on condition that they should breakfast together at the house of the person challenged, previous to their going to the field. When the challenger came in the morning, according to appointment, he found every preparation made for breakfast, and his friend with his wife and children ready to receive him. Their repast being ended, and the family withdrawn, without the least intimation of their purpose having transpired, the challenger asked the other if he was ready. "No, sir," said he, "not till we are more on a par; that amiable woman, and those six children, who just now breakfasted with us, depend, under Providence, on my life for subsistence, and, until you can stake something equal in my estimation, to the welfare of seven persons dearer to me than the apple of my eye, I cannot think we are matched." "We are not indeed!" replied the other, giving him his hand. These two persons became firmer friends than ever.

(*e*) HUMOROUS REPLY TO A CHALLENGE.—When the question for the emblems and devices for the *national arms* of the United States, was before the old Congress, a member from the South warmly opposed the eagle as a monarchical bird. The *king* of birds could not be a suitable representative of a people whose institutions were founded in hostility to kings. Judge Thatcher, then representative from Massachusetts, in reply, proposed the *goose*, which he said was a most humble and republican bird, and would in other respects prove advantageous, inasmuch as the *goslings* would do to put on ten cent pieces, &c. The laughter which followed at the expense of the Southerner was more than he could bear. He construed the good humored irony into an insult and sent a challenge. The bearer delivered it to Mr. Thatcher, who read and returned it to him, observing that he should not accept it! "What, will you be branded as a coward?" "Yes, sir, if he pleases; I always was a coward, and he knew it, or he would never have challenged me." The joke was too good to be resisted even by the angry party. It occasioned infinite mirth in the Congressional circles, and the former cordial and gentlemanly intercourse between the parties was soon restored in a manner entirely satisfactory.

150. Dueling Suppressed.

(*a*) GUSTAVUS AND HIS GENERAL.—It was in one of the Prussian campaigns, says Harte, in his Life of Gustavus Adolphus, king of Sweden, that the irrational practice of dueling rose to such a height in the Swedish army, not only among persons of rank and fashion, but even between the common soldiers, that Gustavus published a severe edict, denouncing death against every delinquent. Soon after there arose a quarrel between two officers very high in command, and as they knew the king's firmness in preserving his word inviolable, they agreed to request an audience, and besought his permission to decide the affair like men of honor. His majesty repressed his passion, and under the appearance of pitying brave men who thought their reputation injured, he told them, that though he much blamed their mistaken notions of fame and glory, yet as this unreasonable determination appeared to be the result of deliberate reflection, he would allow them to decide the affair at a time and place specified: "And gentlemen," said he, "I myself will be a witness of your extraordinary valor." At the hour appointed, Gustavus arrived accompanied with a small body of infantry, whom he drew up around the combatants. Having done this, he desired them to fight on till one of them should be killed, and calling the executioner of the army to him, he ordered him, the moment one of them fell, to be ready instantly to behead the survivor. Astonished at such inflexible firmness, the two generals, after pausing a moment, fell upon their knees, and asked the king's forgiveness, who made them embrace each other, and give their promise to continue faithful friends to their last moments; as they both did with sincerity and thankfulness.

(*b*) THE EMPEROR'S LETTER.—The following letter against dueling, written by Joseph, late Emperor of Germany, was published in a collection of his letters, a few years ago at Leipsic.

"General;—I desire you to arrest Count K— and Captain W— immediately. The count is of an imperious character, proud of his birth, and full of false ideas of honor. Captain W—, who is an old soldier, thinks of settling every thing by the sword or the pistol. He has done wrong in accepting a challenge from the young count. I will not suffer the practice of dueling in the army; and I despise the arguments of those who seek to justify it. I have a high esteem for officers who expose themselves courageously to the enemy, and who, on all occasions, show themselves intrepid, valiant, and determined, in attack as well as defence. But there are men ready to sacrifice every thing to a spirit of revenge and hatred. I despise them; such men, in my opinion, are worse than the Roman gladiators. Let a council of war be summoned to try those two officers with all the impartiality which I demand from every judge, and let the most culpable of the two be made an example by the rigor of the law. I am resolved that this barbarous custom, which is worthy of the age of Tamerlane and Bajazet, and which is so often fatal to the peace of families, shall be punished and suppressed, though it should cost me half my officers. There will be still left men who can unite bravery with the duties of a faithful subject. I wish for none who do not respect the laws of the country. JOSEPH."

"Vienna August, 1711."

(*c*) THE DUELISTS AND THE GIBBET.—Frederic the Great is said to have taken the following summary and very successful method of suppressing dueling in his army:

An officer desired his permission to fight a duel with a fellow-officer. He gave his consent, with the understanding that himself would be a spectator of the conflict. The hour of meeting arrived, and the parties repaired to the place of slaughter. But what was their surprise to find a gibbet erected upon the spot. The challenger inquired of Frederic, who was present according to agreement, what this meant. "I intend," said he, sternly, "to *hang* the survivor!" This was enough. The duel was not fought; and by this simple but effectual means, it is said dueling was broken up in the army of Frederic.

151. EDUCATION OF MINISTERS.

(*a*) THE PLOUGHBOY AND THE PRESIDENT.—The president of a well-known college in Kentucky, was one morning, while sitting in his study, astonished by the entrance of a single visitor.

The visitor was a boy of some seventeen years, rough and uncouth in his appearance, dressed in coarse homespun, with thick clumsy shoes on his feet, an old tattered felt hat on his head, surmounting a mass of uncombed hair, which relieved swarthy and sunburnt features, marked by eyes quick and sparkling, but vacant and inexpressive from the want of education. The whole appearance of the youth was that of an untaught, uncultivated ploughboy.

The president, an affable and venerable man, inquired into the business of the person who stood before him.

"If you please, sir," said the ploughboy, with all the hesitancy of an uneducated rustic—"if you please, sir, I'd like to get some larnin'. I heard you had a college in these parts, and I thought if I would work a spell for you, you would help me now and then in gettin' an edication."

"Well, my young friend," replied

the president, I scarcely see any way in which you might be useful to us. The request is something singular."

"Why, I can bring water, cut wood, or black boots," interrupted the boy, his eyes brightening with earnestness. "I want to get an edication—I want to make something of myself. I don't keer how hard I work, only so as to get an edication. I want—"

He paused, at a loss for words to express his ideas, but there was a language in the expressive lip, and glancing eye; there was a language in his manner—in the tone in which these words were spoken, that appealed at once to the president's feelings. He determined to try the sincerity of the youth. "I am afraid, my young friend, I can do nothing for you. I would like to assist you, but I see no way in which you can be useful to us at present."

The president resumed his book. In a moment he glanced at the ploughboy, who sat silent and mute, holding the handle of the door. He fingered his rough hat confusedly with one hand, his eyes were downcast, and his upper lip quivered and trembled as though he were endeavoring to repress strong and sudden feelings of intense disappointment. The effort was but half successful. A tear, emerging from the downcast eyelid, rolled over the sunburnt cheek, and with a quick, nervous action, the ploughboy raised his toil-hardened hand and brushed away the sign of regret. He made a well-meant but awkward mark of obeisance, and opening the door, had one foot across the threshold, when the president called him back.

The ploughboy was in a few minutes hired as a man of all work, and boot-black to the —— college.

The next scene which we give the reader, was in a new and magnificent church, rich with the beauties of architecture, and thronged by an immense crowd, who listened in deathlike stillness to the burning eloquence of the minister of heaven, who delivered the mission of his Master from the altar.—The speaker was a man in the full glow of middle age—of striking and impressive appearance—piercing and intellectual eye, and high intellectual forehead.

Every eye is fixed on him—every lip hushed, and every ear, with nervous intensity, drinks in the eloquent teaching of the orator.

Who in all that throng would recognize in the famed, the learned, the eloquent president of —— college, Pennsylvania, the humble boot-black of —— college, in Kentucky!

(*b*) THE SCHOOLMASTER AND HIS POOR PUPIL.—The following anecdote was related by a gentleman at Utica, at a meeting of the friends of education:—

In the month of December, 1807, Mr. Maynard was teaching school in the town of Plainfield, Mass. One cold blustering morning, on entering his school-room, he observed a lad that he had not seen before, sitting on one of the benches. The lad soon made known his errand to Mr. M. He was fifteen years old; his parents lived seven miles distant; he wanted an education; and had come from home on foot that morning, to see if Mr. M. could help him to contrive how to obtain it.

Mr. M. asked him if he was acquainted with any one in that place. "No." "Can your parents help you towards obtaining an education?"

"No." "Have you any friends that can give you assistance?" "No." "Well, how do you expect to obtain an education?" "I don't know, but I thought I would come and see you." Mr. M. told him to stay that day, and he would see what could be done. He discovered that the boy was possess-of good sense, but no uncommon brilliancy, and he was particularly struck with the cool and resolute manner in which he undertook to conquer difficulties which would have intimidated weaker minds. In the course of the day, Mr. M. made provision for having him boarded through the winter in the family with himself, the lad paying for his board by his services out of school. He gave himself diligently to study, in which he made good, but not rapid proficiency, improving every opportunity of reading and conversation for acquiring knowledge, and thus spent the winter

When Mr. M. left the place in the spring, he engaged a minister who resided about four miles from the boy's father, to hear his recitations; and the boy accordingly boarded at home, and pursued his studies. It is unnecessary to pursue the narrative further. Mr. M. had never seen the lad since; but this was the early history of the Rev. Jonas King, whose exertions in the cause of oriental learning, and in alleviating the miseries of Greece, have endeared him alike to the scholar and philanthropist, and shed a bright ray of glory on his native country.

(*c*) DR. BACON'S ADVICE.—"I received a most useful hint," says Cecil, "from Dr. Bacon, then father of the University, when I was at college. I used frequently to visit him at his living, near Oxford; he would frequently say to me, 'What are you doing? What are your studies?' 'I am reading so and so.' 'You are quite wrong. When I was young, I could turn any piece of Hebrew into Greek verse with ease. But when I came into this parish, and had to teach ignorant people, I was wholly at a loss; I had no furniture. They thought me a great man, but that was their ignorance, for I knew as little as they did, of what it was most important for them to know. Study chiefly what you can turn to good account in your future life.'"

(*d*) THE UNKNOWN PREACHER.–The spontaneous preference which all persons, free from prejudice, are ready to yield, other things being equal, to a preacher who has had the advantages of education, may be illustrated by the following incident:—

In the vicinity of one of our literary institutions, where several young Baptist ministers were at their studies, a church, whose members were violently prejudiced against colleges and college-learned ministers, had passed a vote that they would admit no one from the neighboring institution into their pulpit Shortly after this they sent to a minister then residing near the institution, whom they did not know, but with whose preaching they supposed from information they should be pleased. The minister agreed to attend and preach for them, on the day named in their request. Circumstances, however, prevented his going in person; he therefore engaged a young ministering brother, who had nearly completed his studies at the institution of which he was a member, to go in his stead. This young brother was unknown to any of the church. He came to the place at the hour appointed; and, with a fluent and ready utterance, with a warm heart and fervent spirit, and with a well furnished mind, he delivered his Master's message. The members of the church, who supposed all this while that the preacher was the individual for whom they had sent, and who had never been in a literary institution, were delighted. Their hearts were opened. They pressed him to visit them again, to which he consented. In the meantime, they ascertained who their preacher was, that he was a member of the neighboring institution. But they had committed themselves; he had gained their hearts, and the approbation of their judgment. It was the end of their prejudice against learning in a minister. After this they were ready to admit and act on the principle, that learning cannot MAKE a minister, but that it can greatly increase his power of being useful.

152. EDUCATION, RELIGIOUS.

(*a*) A PIOUS FATHER AND HIS REFRACTORY SON.—A pious, tender father, asked his refractory son, one Sabbath morning, if he was going to attend meeting? The child answered, that he was not. "Why?" said his father. "I have a sore foot," was the answer. "But you shall ride and I will walk." The child being resolved not to go, made many objections, which the father answered in a similar way; until the son, no longer able to hide the opposition of his heart, broke out as follows:—"I will go, but I will not hear one word." He then went away in a passion. But God, who is mighty in wisdom, and seeth not as man seeth, had determined that he *should* hear. His sins were set in order before him, in such a manner, that he was unable to leave the place without assistance. He remained several days in great distress, and then found peace in the blood of Christ. He is now a preacher of the gospel which he so much despised. Those parents who think it will do no good to urge children to attend public worship, may derive from this anecdote a valuable lesson.

(*b*) FIRST IMPRESSIONS.—A respectable lady died in 1845, near Madison, Wisconsin. She was a native of Kentucky, and educated a Protestant. All her family were Protestants. For seven years previous to her death she had no intercourse with Roman Catholics. But when death was approaching she sent a hundred miles for a Catholic bishop, that she might be received into communion and die in the Romish Church. And wherefore? Her feelings were the result of early impressions received while attending a Catholic school at Nazanath, Kentucky! Yet how little many parents think of the depth and permanency of the impressions made on their infant offspring by the school-teacher's instructions or their own! Of all impressions those are most enduring which are the earliest.

(*c*) THE FATHER'S PRAYER. —Of the family of Mr. C——, the following account is given by one of the sons, at the request of a friend:—My father was for many years not only a member, but a living member, of the church of Christ. He had ten children. We were all taught to "fear God and keep his commandments." "The Sabbath day" was "remembered." Well do I recollect, with filial gratitude, how regularly on the Sabbath we were summoned to take our stand around the arm-chair of my father, to repeat the catechism and other religious lessons, and his earnest entreaties that we would "remember our Creator in the days of our youth." His prayers partook much of a wrestling spirit; his whole soul appeared to be in the exercise. I never can forget one request which he pressed with deep and hearty solicitude: "*O Lord! give my children an interest in Christ: whatever else is denied them, deny them not this greatest of all blessings!*" In all my profligate wanderings *that prayer* would ring in my ears, and the image of my praying father would appear to my imagination; and now, with deep emotions of gratitude for God's abounding grace, I can say, every one of their children hope in the mercy of Christ. Two of the sons are officers of churches; and all of us have as many responsibilities as we can faithfully discharge both of a civil and religious character.

(*c*) NO SCOTCH WOMAN THERE.—The Rev. Dr. Waugh was enlarging one evening, at a public Sabbath school meeting, on the blessings of education; and, turning to his native country, Scotland, for proof, told his auditors the following anecdote:—"At board-day at the Penitentiary at Millbank, the food of the prisoners was discussed, and it was proposed to give Scotch broth thrice a week. Some of the governors were not aware what sort of broth the barley made, and desired to taste some before they sanctioned the measure. One of the officers was accordingly directed to go to the wards and bring a Scotch woman, competent to the culinary task, to perform it in the kitchen. After long delay, the board supposing the broth was preparing all the while, the officer returned, and told their honors *that there was no Scotch woman in the house.*"

153. ELOQUENCE, SACRED.

(*a*) INDIANS JUDGING MINISTERS. — Some years ago, three American ministers went to preach to the Cherokee Indians. One preached very deliberately and coolly; and the chiefs held a council to know whether the Great Spirit spoke to them through that man; and they declared he did not, because he was not so much engaged as their head men were in their national concerns. Another spoke to them in a most vehement manner; and they again determined in council that the Great Spirit did not speak to them through that man, because he was mad. The third preached to them in an earnest and fervent manner; and they agreed that the Great Spirit might speak to them through him, because he was both earnest and affectionate. The last was ever after kindly received.

(*b*) TWO WAYS OF TELLING A STORY.—The late Dr. Lathrop, of West Springfield, Mass., related to Mr. Whitefield a fact which the Dr. had personally witnessed; and he related it without much feeling. The same day Mr. Whitefield introduced the story into his sermon, and Dr. Lathrop as he heard it found himself drowned in tears.

(*c*) ELOQUENCE OF STAUGHTON.—The Rev. Dr. Staughton, of Philadelphia, was remarkable for the energy of his delivery, and for the originality of many of his remarks. On one occasion, he was preaching from the words, "God be merciful to me a sinner." His soul kindled, as he proceeded, with intense ardor for the salvation of his assembly. He presented, in a strain of vivid and powerful eloquence, the joy of the angelic hosts on the repentance of one sinner. Perfect silence reigned through the vast audience. There was a moment's pause, and it was obvious, from his countenance and his attitude, that his mind was preparing for some powerful and overwhelming flood of feeling. He proceeded! "Shall I retire with the desponding reflection, that, in all this congregation, there is not one soul humbled before God? Shall angels prepare their wings for flight, and the voice of contrition be unheard? It cannot be. I will cherish the hope that there is, at least, one sinner here whose heart is melted down before the Lord, and trembling at the prospect of future retribution; that there is, even now, one whose agony is on the point of extorting from his lips the cry of the publican." Suddenly throwing up his arm, with a voice full, loud, and rapid, he exclaimed, "Hark!" The effect it is impossible to describe. His arm remained for a time elevated, during which the most awful stillness reigned, interrupted only by an apparently delicate and indescribable breathing, that seemed to pass over the congregation, midway in the edifice. Then, with a grace and energy peculiar to himself, he brought down his hand upon his breast, and repeated the prayer, "God be merciful to me a sinner." The feelings of the assembly were wrought to the highest point, and some time elapsed before they were enabled to breathe freely.

(*d*) MASSILLON'S PREACHING. —When Massillon preached the first Advent sermon at Marseilles, Louis the XIVth paid a most expressive tribute to his eloquence:—"Father, when I hear others preach, I am very well pleased with them; when I hear you, I am dissatisfied with myself."

The first time this great preacher delivered his sermon on the small number of the elect, the whole audience were, in one part of it, in so violent a state of emotion, that almost every person half rose from his seat, as if to shake off the horror of being one of those that would be cast out into everlasting darkness. So remarkably were all his strokes aimed at the heart.

When Baron, the actor, came from hearing one of Massillon's sermons, he said to a person of the same profession, who accompanied him, "Here is an orator; we are only actors."

(*e*) QUITE DIFFERENT PREACHERS.—The different effects produced by pulpit eloquence are well described by the following anecdote of two French preachers. Le Pere Arrius said, "When Le Pere Bourdaloue preached at Rouen, the tradesmen forsook their shops, lawyers their clients, physicians their sick, and tavern-keepers their bars; but, when I preached the following year, I set all thing to rights—every man minded his own business!"

(*f*) PREACHING AS IN THE PRESENCE OF GOD.—The eminence of the Rev. Mr. Brown, of Haddington, both as a preacher and a writer, is well known. On a public occasion, where a man who professed the principles of infidelity was present, two sermons were delivered: the first of them by an ambitious young man, who delivered a very eloquent and florid address; Mr. Brown followed, in one equally remarkable for its simplicity and earnestness. "The first preacher," said the skeptic to one of his friends, "spoke as if he did not believe what he said; the latter, as if he was conscious that the Son of God stood at his elbow."

(*g*) NEWTON'S TRIBUTE TO WHITEFIELD.—In a company of noblemen and gentlemen, at breakfast, Mr. Whitefield having become the subject of conversation, one of the company asked the Rev. John Newton, who was present, if he knew Mr. Whitefield. He answered in the affirmative, and observed, that as a preacher, Mr. Whitefield far exceeded every other man of his time. Mr. Newton added, "I bless God that I lived in his time; many were the winter mornings I got up at four, to attend his tabernacle discourses at five; and I have seen Moorfields as full of lanterns at these times, as I suppose the Maymarket is full of flambeaux on an opera night." As a proof of the power of Mr. W.'s preaching, Mr. Newton mentioned, that an officer at Glasgow, who had heard him preach, laid a wager with another, that at a certain charity sermon, though he went with prejudice, he would be compelled to give something; the other to make sure that he would not, laid all the money out of his pockets; but, before he left the church, he was glad to borrow some, and lose his bet. Mr. Newton mentioned, as another striking example of Mr. Whitefield's persuasive oratory, his collecting at one sermon £600 for the inhabitants of an obscure village in Germany, that had been burned down. After sermon, Mr Whitefield said, We shall sing a hymn, during which those who do not choose to give their mite on this awful occasion, may sneak off." Not one moved; he got down from the pulpit, ordered all the doors to be shut but one, at which he held the plate himself, and collected the above large sum. Mr. Newton related what he knew to be a fact, that at the time of Whitefield's greatest persecution, when obliged to preach in the streets, in one week he received not fewer than a thousand letters from persons distressed in their consciences by the energy of his preaching.

(*h*) HUME'S TRIBUTE TO WHITEFIELD.—An extraordinary attestation to the excellence of Mr. Whitefield, as a preacher, was furnished by Hume, the historian, well known for his infidelity. An intimate friend having asked him what he thought of Mr. Whitefield's preaching, "He is, sir," said Mr. Hume, "the most ingenious preacher I ever heard: it is worth while to go twenty miles to hear him." He then repeated the following passage, which occurred towards the close of the discourse he had been hearing: "After a solemn pause, Mr. Whitefield thus addressed his numerous audience:—'The attendant angel is just about to leave the threshold, and ascend to heaven. And shall he ascend, and not bear with him the news of one sinner, among all this multitude, reclaimed from the error of his ways?' To give the greater effect to this exclamation, he stamped with his foot, lifted up his eyes and hands to heaven, and with gushing tears, cried aloud, 'Stop, Gabriel! Stop, Gabriel! Stop, ere you enter the sacred portals, and yet carry with you the news of one sinner converted to

God.' He then, in the most simple, but energetic language, described what he called a Savior's dying love to sinful man, so that almost the whole assembly melted into tears. This address was accompanied with such animated, yet natural action, that it surpassed any thing I ever saw or heard in any other preacher."

Happy had it been for Mr. Hume, if, in addition to his admiration of the preacher, he had received the doctrine which he taught, and afforded an instance of that conversion to God which Mr. Whitefield so ardently longed for on behalf of his hearers.

(*i*) FRANKLIN'S TRIBUTE TO WHITEFIELD.—The following anecdote, related by Dr. Franklin, which is equally characteristic of the preacher and himself, further illustrates the power of Mr. Whitefield's eloquence:—"I happened," says the doctor, "to attend one of his sermons, in the course of which I perceived he intended to finish with a collection, and I silently resolved he should get nothing from me. I had in my pocket a handful of copper money, three or four silver dollars, and five pistoles in gold. As he proceeded, I began to soften, and concluded to give the copper. Another stroke of his oratory made me ashamed of that, and determined me to give the silver; and he finished so admirably, that I emptied my pocket wholly into the collector's dish,—gold and all. At this sermon there was also one of our club; who, being of my sentiments respecting the building in Georgia, and suspecting a collection might be intended, had, by precaution, emptied his pockets before he came from home. Towards the conclusion of the discourse, however, he felt a strong inclination to give, and applied to a neighbor, who stood near him, to lend him some money for the purpose. The request was made to, perhaps, the only man in the company who had the coldness not to be affected by the preacher. His answer was, "At any other time, friend Hodgkinson, I would lend to thee freely; but not now, for thee seems to be out of thy right senses."

(*j*) SCULPTOR'S OPINION OF WHITEFIELD.—A baronet was one day examining some works of the celebrated sculptor, Mr. Bacon, and observed a bust of Mr. Whitefield among them, which led him to remark, "After all that has been said, this was truly a great man; he was the founder of a new religion." "A new religion, sir!" replied Mr. B. "Yes," said the baronet; "what do you call it?" "Nothing," was the reply, "but the old religion revived with new energy, and treated as if the preacher meant what he said."

(*k*) THE BROKEN HEART.—When Whitefield was preaching at Exeter, a man was present who had loaded his pockets with stones, in order to fling them at that precious ambassador of Christ. He heard his prayer, however, with patience; but no sooner had he named his text, than the man pulled a stone out of his pocket and held it in his hand waiting for a fair opportunity to throw. But God sent a sword to his heart, and the stone dropped from his hand. After sermon he went to Mr. W. and told him, "Sir, I came to hear you this day with a view to break your head, but the spirit of the Lord, through your ministry, has given me a broken heart." The man proved to be a sound convert, and lived to be an ornament to the Gospel.

(*l*) THE SHIPBUILDER'S OPINION OF WHITEFIELD.—A shipbuilder was once asked what he thought of Mr. Whitefield. "Think!" he replied; "I tell you, sir, every Sunday that I go to my parish church, I can build a ship from stem to stern under the sermon; but were I to save my soul, under Mr. W. I could not lay a single plank."

(*m*) THE BLIND MINISTER.—"I was one Sunday travelling through the county of Orange, on the eastern side of the Blue Ridge," says Wirt, in his British Spy, "when my eye was caught by a cluster of horses tied near a ruinous wooden house, in the forest, not far from the roadside. Having frequently seen such objects before, I had no difficulty in understanding that this was a place of religious worship. Curiosity to hear the preacher of such a wilderness induced me to join the congregation. On my entrance, I was struck with his supernatural appearance. He was a tall and very spare old man; his head, which was covered with a white linen cap, his shrivelled hands, and his voice, were all shaking under the influence of palsy; and a few moments ascertained to me that he was perfectly blind. It was the day of the sacrament —his subject was the passion of our Savior; and he gave it a new and more sublime pathos than I had ever before witnessed. When he descended from the pulpit to distribute the mystic symbols, there was a peculiar, a more than human solemnity in his voice and manner, which made my blood run cold, and my whole frame shiver. His peculiar phrases had that force of description, that the original scene seemed acting before our eyes. We saw the very faces of the Jews; the staring, frightful distortions of malice and of rage. But when he came to touch on the patience, the forgiving meekness of our Savior; when he drew to the life his blessed eyes streaming with tears, his voice breathing to God the gentle prayer, 'Father, forgive them, for they know not what they do,'—the voice of the preacher, which had all along faltered, grew fainter and fainter, until his voice being entirely obstructed by the force of his feelings, he raised his handkerchief to his eyes, and burst into a loud and irrepressible flood of grief. The effect was inconceivable. The whole house resounded with mingled groans, and sobs, and shrieks. I could not imagine how the speaker could let his audience down from the height to which he had wound them, without impairing the solemnity of his subject, or shocking them by the abruptness of his fall. But the descent was as beautiful and sublime as the elevation had been rapid and enthusiastic. The tumult of feeling subsided, and a death-like stillness reigned throughout the house, when the aged man removed his handkerchief from his eyes, still wet with the torrent of his tears, and slowly stretching forth his palsied hand, he exclaimed, 'Socrates died like a philosopher,'—then pausing, clasping his hands with fervor to his heart, lifting his 'sightless balls' to heaven, and pouring his whole soul into his tremulous voice, he continued—'but Jesus Christ died like a God.' Had he been an angel of light, the effect could have scarcely been more divine."

(*n*) FLETCHER'S APPEAL.—When the Rev. J. W. Fletcher, of Madeley, was once preaching on Noah as a type of Christ, and while in the midst of a most animated description of the terrible day of the Lord, he suddenly paused. Every feature of his expressive countenance was marked with painful feeling; and, striking his forehead with the palm of his hand, he exclaimed, "Wretched man that I am! Beloved brethren, it often cuts me to the soul, as it does at this moment, to reflect, that while I have been endeavoring, by the force of truth, by the beauty of holiness, and even by the terrors of the Lord, to bring you to walk in the peaceable paths of righteousness, I am, with respect to many of you who reject the gospel, only tying mill-stones round your neck, to sink you deeper in perdition!" The whole church was electrified, and it was some time before he could resume his discourse.

ENEMIES, LOVE TO.

154. Nature of Love to Enemies.

(*a*) THE HAND OF THE AVENGER STAYED.—The following incident is taken from the diary of Hans Egede Saabye, a grandson of the celebrated Hans Egede, first missionary to Greenland.

It has ever been a fixed law in Greenland, that murder, and particularly the murder of a father, must be avenged. About twenty years before the arrival of Saabye, a father had been murdered in the presence of his son, a lad of thirteen, in a most atrocious manner. The boy was not able then to avenge the crime, but the murderer was not forgotten. He left that part of the country, and kept the flame burning in his bosom, no suitable opportunity offering for revenge, as the man was high in influence, and many near to defend him. At length his plan was laid, and with some of his relations to assist him, he returned to the province of the murderer, who lived near the house of Saabye; there being no house unoccupied where they might remain, but one owned by Saabye, they requested it, and it was granted, without any remark, although he knew the object of their coming.

The son soon became interested in the kind missionary, and often visited his cabin, giving as his reason, "*You are so amiable I cannot keep away from you.*" Two or three weeks after, he requested to know more of "the great Lord of Heaven," of whom Saabye had spoken. His request was cheerfully granted. Soon it appeared that himself and all his relatives, were desirous of instruction, and ere long, the son requested baptism. To this request the missionary answered: "Kunnuk"—for that was his name—"you know God: you know that he is good, that he loves you, and desires to make you happy: but he desires also that you should obey him."

Kunnuk answered; "I love him, I will obey him."

"His command is, 'Thou shalt not murder.'" The poor Greenlander was much affected, and silent. "I know," said the missionary. "why you have come here with your relations, but this you must not do, if you wish to become a believer."

Agitated, he answered, "But he murdered my father!"

For a long time the missionary pressed this point, the poor awakened heathen promising to "kill *only one.*" But this was not enough. "Thou shalt do no murder," Saabye insisted was the command of the Great Lord of heaven. He exhorted him to leave the murderer in the hand of God to be punished in another world: but this was waiting too long for revenge. The missionary refused him baptism, without obedience to the command. He retired to consult his friends. They urged him to revenge.

Saabye visited him, and without referring to the subject, read those portions of Scripture and hymns teaching a quiet and forgiving temper. Some days after Kunnuk came again to the cabin of Saabye. "I will," said he, "and will not; I hear, and I do not hear. I never felt so before; I will forgive him, and I will not forgive him." The missionary told him, "When he *would* forgive, then his better spirit spoke; when *he would not* forgive, then his unconverted heart spoke." He then repeated to him the latter part of the life of Jesus, and his prayer for his murderers. A tear stood in his eye. "But he was better than I," said Kunnuk. "But God will give us strength," Saabye answered. He then read the martyrdom of Stephen, and his dying prayer for his enemies. Kunnuk dried his eyes and said, "The wicked men!—He is happy; he is certainly with God in heaven. My heart is so moved; but give me a little time; when I have brought the other heart to silence, I will come again." He soon returned with a smiling countenance, saying, "Now I am happy; I hate no more; I have forgiven; my wicked heart shall be silent." He and his wife, having made a clear profession of faith in Christ, were baptized and received into the church. Soon after, he sent the following note to the murderer of his father: "I am now a believer, and you have nothing to fear," and invited him to his house. The man came, and invited Kunnuk in his turn to visit him. Contrary to the advice of friends, Kunnuk went, and, as he was returning home, he found a hole had been cut in his kajak (or boat) in order that he might be drowned. Kunnuk stepped out of the water, saying, "He is still afraid, though I will not harm him!"

What a noble example of self-conquest! What an illustrious exhibition of the power of the gospel!

(*b*) THE MISSIONARY ASSAILED.–Not many years ago, a missionary was preaching in a chapel to a crowd of idol-loving Hindoos. He had not proceeded far in his sermon, when he was interrupted by a strong native, who went behind the desk, intending to knock him down with his stick. Happily, the blow aimed at the minister fell on his shoulder and did him little, if any, injury. The congregation of hearers was, however, very angry with the offender; and they seized him at the very moment he was attempting his escape. "Now, what shall I do with him?" said the missionary to the people. "What shall I do to him?" "Give him a good beating," answered some. "I cannot do that," said he. "Send him to the Judge," cried others; "and he will receive two years' hard labor on the road." "I cannot follow your advice," said the missionary again; "and I will tell you why. My religion commands me to love my enemies, and to do good to them who treat me injuriously." Then, turning to the culprit, he addressed him in these words: "I forgive you from my heart; but never forget that you owe your escape from punishment to that Jesus whom you persecuted in me."

The effect of this scene on the Hindoos was most impressive. They saw it and marvelled; and, unable any longer to keep silence, they sprang on their feet, and shouted, "Victory to Jesus Christ!" "Victory to Jesus Christ!"

(c) LINKS AND THE MURDERER.—Peter Links, a Namacqua, was the brother of Jacob Links, who was murdered when on a journey into the country with Mr. Threlfall, the Wesleyan missionary. After we heard of his brother Jacob's murder, Peter, when speaking on the subject, said, "Oh that I could find the murderer who took away my brother's life! I would not care what distance I might have to travel; I would not mind any exposure, fatigue, or danger; I would not care what expense I might incur, if I could only lay hold of that man." Being aware that men in their savage state cherish an indomitable spirit of revenge, but believing Peter to be a decidedly pious character, I was a little astonished at his language, and rather hastily inquired, "Well, supposing you could find the man, what would you do to him?" "Do to him?" said Peter; "Mynheer, I would bring him to this station, that he might hear the gospel, and that his soul might be converted to God."

EXHIBITIONS OF LOVE TO ENEMIES.

155. Blessing Enemies.

(a) MUNMOTH AND THE PAPIST.—Bishop Latimer tells us, in his seventh sermon on the Lord's prayer, of a rich man* who had a poor neighbor, whom he treated very kindly. But the alderman became a Protestant and his poor friend became his enemy. Indeed, the poor man would not vouchsafe to speak to him: if he met the rich man in the street, he would go out of his way. "One time it happened that he met him in so narrow a street that he could not shun him, but must come near him; yet for all this, this poor man was minded to go forward, and not to speak with him. The rich man perceiving that, caught him by the hand, and asked him, saying, 'Neighbor, what is come into your heart, to take such displeasure with me? what have I done against you? tell me, and I will be ready at all times to make you amends.'

"Finally, he spoke so *gently*, so *charitably*, and *friendly*, that it wrought in the poor man's heart, so that by and by he fell down upon his knees, and asked his forgiveness. The rich man forgave him, and took him again into his favor, and they loved each other as well as ever they did before. Many a one would have said, Set him in the stocks, let him have bread of affliction, and water of tribulation; but this man did not so. And here you see an example of the practice of God's words; so that the poor man, bearing great hatred and malice against the rich man, was brought, through the lenity and meekness of the rich man, from his error and wickedness, to the knowledge of God's word. I would that you would consider this example well, and follow it."

(b) NARDIN AND HIS ENEMIES.—This excellent pastor of the church

* The rich man here spoken of was Humphrey Munmoth, sheriff and alderman of London.

of Blamont, was so little affected by the unjust proceedings and outrageous conduct to which he was exposed, that the remembrance of it was soon effaced from his mind. If he ever felt any thing like a desire to be avenged, nothing of the kind appeared in the case about to be related. Some time after he had been restored to the ministry, and re-established at Blamont, the intendant of Besançon repaired to the town, and immediately requested to see Mr. Nardin. The latter having complied with his invitation, the other said to him, among several complimentary speeches, "Well, Mr. Nardin, you see yourself well avenged. You ought to be satisfied that your two adversaries, who labored to make you end your days in the dungeons of the mighty Grison, have been shut up there themselves, whilst you have been pronounced innocent." The two persons, indeed, who were most cruelly bent on his destruction, were for some time under confinement in the prisons of Besançon; one as a dealer in contraband commodities, and the other for disturbing certain rights claimed by the Roman Catholics. Mr. Nardin, feeling himself but little flattered by this compliment, replied, in a soft but unhesitating tone, "My religion, my lord, does not permit me to rejoice in the misfortunes of my enemies. I pity them; and wish that a wiser conduct may shelter them from such punishments."

(*c*) BRUEN AND HIS ENEMY.—A gentleman once sent his servant to John Bruen, Esq., of Bruen, requesting him never to set a foot upon his ground; to whom he sent this reply: "If it please your master to walk upon my grounds, he shall be very welcome; but if he please to come to my house, he shall be still more welcome." By thus heaping coals of fire upon his head, he melted him down into love and tenderness, and made him his cordial friend.

156. Doing Good to Enemies.

(*a*) THE UNRULY CATTLE.—The horse of a pious man living in Massachusetts, happening to stray into the road, a neighbor of the man who owned the horse put him into the pound. Meeting the owner soon after, he told him what he had done; "and if I catch him in the road again," said he, "I'll do it again." "Neighbor," replied the other, "not long since, I looked out of my window in the night, and saw your cattle in my meadow, and I drove them out and shut them in your yard; and I'll do it again." Struck with the reply, the man liberated the horse from the pound, and paid the charges himself. "A soft answer turneth away wrath."

(*b*) THE PRINCESS AND THE WARRIOR.—The Bechuanas of South Africa are divided into many different nations or tribes. Two of these nations carried on war for some years, each side trying to kill every man, woman and child of the other nation, and practicing cruelties too horrid for children to hear. The name of the one nation was Barolong, and that of the other Bakueni, or People of the Crocodile.

One day the daughter of the Chief of the Bakueni was gathering berries by the river side; she was some way from her father's village, and all alone; she did not think that any enemy was near, but there was a wicked old warrior of the Barolong nation, creeping along the borders as a spy, and he saw her. She had never done him any harm, but he hated her because she was one of the Bakueni. He crept like a coward upon his hands and knees, and when he was within a few steps of her, he sprang upon her like a tiger, and with his assegai cut off both her hands above the wrists. He mocked at her sufferings, and tauntingly asked, "U tla 'mpona kai? Rumela!" "Where shall you see me again? I salute you." The cries of the poor bleeding girl soon brought her friends from the village, but the wicked old man made off with all speed, and he was far enough away before they reached her. There was no surgeon at hand to dress her wounded arms, so whether she died from pain and loss of blood or not, remains to be told.

At length both nations suffered so dreadfully from war and famine, the they wished to make peace. They killed some cattle, and sat down to eat together, and thus made a treaty of peace. Next season the Bakueni had an abundant crop of corn, but the Barolongs were in great distress. Swarms of locusts ate up the produce of their fields and gardens, and they were obliged to beg food from the people they once meant to destroy.

Among others the old warrior suffered extremely, and he set out on a journey to the Bakueni, in order to save his life. He had a little bag containing a little meal, made from pounded locusts. It was all he could get to eat on his way. He took a pipe and tobacco also, and a walking-stick in his hand, but he was nearly starved, and so weak and thin, that he could not get on fast. He reached the village of the Chief of the Bakueni, and entered the enclosure before the door of the Chief's house. A young woman was sitting near the door. She was dressed in a tiger-skin kaross, which none but the *mofumagari*, or "royal mistress," may wear. The old man addressed his petition to her in the most humble words, and begged her to give him, a poor dog, a little food, as he was dying of hunger. She answered him, "E! U tla 'mpona kai? Rumela!" The old man was stupified by hunger, and did not remember the words.

A servant was cooking food while this was going on. Her mistress turned to her and told her to put some into a dish; then throwing back her kaross, she uncovered her arms. There were no hands, only stumps left. She was the very girl whose hands this same wicked old man had cut off so long before! She said to her servant, "Give the food to that man; he does not deserve it. It was he who cut off my hands when I was a girl; but I will not revenge myself; he is now starving. He little thought that we should thus meet each other." Then speaking to the old warrior, she said, "There; take and eat! U tla 'mpona kai? Rumela!" What the old man felt, it would be difficult to say. The generous conduct of the Chief's daughter has never been forgotten by the Barolong nation. To this day, one of them may be kept from an unkind action by the oppressed party exclaiming, "U tla 'mpona kai? Rumela!"

(*c*) SOUTHEY AND THE BLACK BOY.—Acts of kindness and soft words have an irresistible power, even over an enemy. "When I was a small boy," says Southey, "there was a black boy in the neighborhood, by the name of Jim Dick. I and a number of my playfellows were one evening collected together at our sports, and began tormenting the poor black, by calling him 'negro, blackamoor,' and other degrading epithets: the poor fellow appeared excessively grieved at our conduct, and soon left us. We soon after made an appointment to go a skating in the neighborhood, and on the day of the appointment I had the misfortune to break my skates, and I could not go without borrowing Jim's skates. I went to him and asked him for them. 'O yes, John, you may have them, and welcome,' was his answer. When I went to return them, I found Jim sitting by the fire in the kitchen, reading the Bible. I told him I had returned his skates, and was under great obligations to him for his kindness. He looked at me as he took his skates, and, with tears in his eyes, said to me, 'John, don't never call me blackamoor again,' and immediately left the room. The words pierced my heart, and I burst into tears, and from that time resolved never again to abuse a poor black."

(*d*) THE SLAVE'S CONDUCT EXPLAINED.—A slave in one of the West India Islands, originally from Africa, having been brought under the influence of religious instruction, became so valuable to his owner on account of his integrity and general good conduct, that his master employed him to assist in the management of his plantation. On one occasion, his owner wishing to purchase twenty additional slaves, employed him to make the selection from those who were offered for sale. Soon after commencing his examination of those who were in the market, he fixed his eye intently on an old decrepit slave, and told his master he must take him for one. The master was greatly surprised, and objected, but the slave entreated so earnestly, for this indulgence, that the offer of the seller to add the old man to the twenty, without increasing the price, was accepted. The newly purchased slaves were conducted to the plantation and placed under the charge of the slave, who had made the selection. On the poor old decrepit African he bestowed uncommon care. He took him to his own habitation, and laid him down on his own bed; he fed him at his own table, and gave him drink out of his own cup; when he was cold he carried him into the sunshine; and when he was hot he placed him under the shade of the cocoanut trees. The master, astonished at the careful attention bestowed by him upon his fellow slave, interrogated him on the subject. "Is that old man," said he, "your father, that you take so much interest in him?" "No, massa," answered the poor fellow, "he no my fader." "Perhaps then, he is your elder brother?" "No, massa, he no my broder." "Then he must be your uncle or some other relation." "No, massa, he be no of my kindred at all; he be no my friend."

"Why then do you bestow on him so much care and attention?" "Oh, massa," replied the slave, "he be my old enemy; he sold me to the slave-dealer, and my Bible tell me to love my enemy; when he hunger, feed him, when he thirst, give him drink, and so me only do what my Bible tell me."

(*e*) THE CHEROKEE WOMEN AND THE OSAGES.—A few poor Cherokee women, who had been converted to Christianity, formed themselves into a society for the propagation of the gospel, which was now become so dear to them. The produce of the first year was about ten dollars, and the question was—to what immediate object this should be applied? At length, a poor woman proposed that it should be given to promote the circulation of the gospel in the Osage nation; 'For," said she, "the Bible tells us to do good to our enemies, Matt. 5:44; and I believe the Osages are the greatest enemies the Cherokees have."

(*f*) THE SHIPWRECKED SPANIARDS.—After the dispersion of the Spanish Armada in 1588, Joan Lomes de Medina, who had been general of twenty hulks, was, with about two hundred and sixty men, driven in a vessel to Anstruther in Scotland, after suffering great hunger and cold for six or seven days. Notwithstanding the object for which this fleet had been sent, and the oppressive conduct of the Spaniards to the Scottish merchants who traded with them, these men were humanely treated. Mr. James Melvil, the minister, told the Spanish officer first sent on shore, that they would find nothing among them but Christianity and works of mercy. The laird of Anstruther, and a great number of the neighboring gentlemen, entertained the officers; and the inhabitants gave the soldiers and mariners kail, pottage, and fish;—the minister having addressed his flock, as Elisha did the King of Israel in Samaria, "Give them bread and water."

(*g*) IF THINE ENEMY HUNGER FEED HIM.—During the persecuting times in England, two persons from Bedford went early one morning to the house of a pious man, who rented a farm in the parish of Keysoe, with the intention of apprehending and imprisoning him in Bedford jail for non-conformity. The good man knew their intention, and desired his wife to prepare breakfast, at the same time kindly inviting his visitors to partake with them. In asking a blessing or in returning thanks for the food, he pronounced emphatically these words, "If thine enemy hunger, feed him; if he thirst, give him drink;" by which means the hearts of his persecutors were so far softened that they went away without taking him into custody.

(*h*) PROFITING BY READING THE BIBLE.—A very little girl, who often read her Bible, gave proof that she understood her obligation to obey its precepts. One day, she came to her mother, much pleased, to show her some fruit which had been given to her. The mother said the friend was very kind, and had given her a great many. "Yes," said the child, "very indeed;

and she gave me more than these, but I have given some away." The mother inquired to whom she had given them; when she answered, "I gave them to a girl who pushes me off the path, and makes faces at me." On being asked why she gave them to her, she replied, "Because I thought it would make her know that I wish to be kind to her, and she will not, herhaps, be rude and unkind to me again." How admirably did she thus obey the command to "overcome evil with good!"

(*i*) DR. MATHER'S AMBITION.—It was the laudable ambition of Cotton Mather to say, "He did not know of any person in the world who had done him any ill office but he had done him a good one for it."

(*j*) EXAMPLE OF REV. JOHN BROWN.—The Rev. Mr. Brown of Haddington manifested a singular readiness to forgive his enemies. Notwithstanding the abuse he received from some ministers, when a student, it was remarked, that he was never heard to speak evil of them, nor so much as to mention the affair. A dissenting clergyman, who had used him rudely, being reduced to poverty, he sent him money, and in a way which concealed the benefactor. After the clergyman's decease, he offered to take one of his destitute orphans, and bring him up with his own children. To certain writers who reviled him from the press, he meekly replied, "But now that the fact is committed, instead of intending to resent the injury these reverend brethren have done me, I reckon myself, on account thereof, so much the more effectually obliged, by the Christian law, to contribute my utmost endeavors towards the advancement of their welfare, spiritual or temporal, and am resolved, through grace, to discharge these obligations, as Providence gives me opportunity, for the same. Let them do to, or with me, what they will, may their portion be redemption through the blood of Jesus, even the forgiveness of sins according to the riches of his grace; and call me what they please, may the Lord call them, "The holy people, the redeemed of the Lord."

157. Praying for Enemies.

(*a*) JAMES THE LESS AND THE PHARISEES.—About the year A. D. 63, when Festus was dead and Albinus had not come to succeed him, the Jews, being exceedingly enraged at the success of the gospel, Annanus, son of Annas, it is said, ordered James to ascend one of the galleries of the temple, and inform the people that they had, without ground, believed Jesus of Nazareth to be the Messiah. He got up and cried with a loud voice that Jesus was the Son of God, and would quickly appear in the clouds to judge the world. Many glorified God and believed; but the Pharisees threw him over the battlement. He was sorely bruised, but got upon his knees and prayed for his murderers amid a shower of stones which they cast at him, till one of them beat out his brains with a fuller's club. To the death of this just man some Jews ascribe the ruin of their nation.

(*b*) ADVICE OF MR. LAWRENCE.—Mr. Lawrence once going, with some of his sons, by the house of a gentleman that had been injurious to him, gave a charge to his sons to this purpose: "That they should never think or speak amiss of that gentleman for the sake of any thing he had done against him; but, whenever they went by his house, should lift up their hearts in prayer to God for him and his family." This good man had learned to practise that admirable precept of our Lord, "Pray for them which despitefully use you and persecute you."

(*c*) REV. W. HERRING AND DR. LAMB.—Mr. Herring, one of the puritan ministers, was eminently distinguished for Christian meekness, and for love to his greatest enemies. Dr. Lamb, a violent persecutor of the Puritans, and especially of this good man, being on a journey, unhappily broke his leg, and was carried to the inn where Mr. Herring happened to be staying for the night. Mr. H. was called on to pray that evening in the family, when he prayed with so much fervor and affection for the doctor as to surprise all who heard him. Being afterwards asked why he manifested such respect to a man who was so utterly unworthy of it, he replied, "The greater enemy he is, the more need he hath of our prayers. We must prove ourselves to be the disciples of Christ by loving our enemies, and praying for our persecutors."

(*d*) MR. BURKITT AND HIS INJURIES.—Mr. Burkitt observes in his journal, that some persons would never have had a particular share in his prayers but for the injuries they had done him.

(*e*) OLD GABRIEL AND THE PATROL.—At an anti-slavery meeting, held at Pittsburgh, in Pennsylvania, the Rev. Mr. Dickey, of Ohio, related the following anecdote.

I will relate a case that occurred within the circle of my acquaintance. A slave who could neither read nor write, heard the gospel, and the Spirit of God made it effectual to his conversion. Like all true converts, he felt a missionary spirit. He was anxious for the conversion of his brethren. And, at length, it became his uniform practice, frequently after the toils of the day were over, to walk two or three miles, and hold a meeting among the slaves. On one occasion, this meeting was discovered by the patrol, who are authorized to inflict summary punishment of *ten* lashes upon all slaves they find assembled together, for any reason. This was done immediately with all present, but Old Gabriel. As he was the ringleader, they thought he must be punished more severely; so they took him to the magistrate. As they were tying up his hands, he exclaimed, "Oh this is just the way Pontius Pilate did to my Massa!" Here his persecutors relented. One of them afterwards was troubled in his conscience for what he had done; and after a long time, finding no peace, he went to Old Gabriel, and asked him if he would forgive him. "Forgive you!" said Old Gabriel; "why massa, me have been praying for you ever since you tied me up!"

(*f*) THE DYING NEGRO BOY.—A poor little African negro, only ten years of age, went to hear the preaching of one of the missionaries, and became, through his instrumentality, a convert, to the Christian religion. His master, (an inveterate enemy to missions,) hearing of it, commanded him never to go again, and declared he would have him whipped to death if he did. The poor little boy, in consequence of this mandate, was very miserable He could scarcely refrain from going, yet he knew his death was inevitable if he did. In this critical situation, he sought direction and assistance at the throne of grace, and after having done this, he felt convinced that it was still his duty to attend, but to be careful that he should never interfere with his master's business, and, for the rest, to leave himself in the hands of God. He therefore went, and on his return, was summoned to his master's presence; and after much violent and abusive language, received five-and-twenty lashes, and then in a sarcastic tone of blasphemous ridicule, his master exclaimed "What can Jesus Christ do for you now?" "He enables me to bear it patiently," said the poor child. "Give him five-and-twenty-lashes more," said the inhuman wretch. He was obeyed. "And what can Jesus Christ do for you now?" asked the unfeeling monster. "He helps me to look forward to a future reward," replied the little sufferer. "Give him five-and-twenty lashes more," vociferated the cruel tyrant, in a transport of rage. They complied; and while he listened with savage delight to the extorted groans of his dying victim, be again demanded, "What can Jesus Christ do for you now?" The youthful martyr, with the last effort of expiring nature, meekly answered, "He enables me *to pray for you, massa.*" And instantly breathed his last!

(*g*) SLAVE'S PRAYER OVERHEARD.—A wealthy planter in the South who had a great number of slaves, found one of them reading the Bible, and reproved him for the neglect of his work, saying there was time enough on Sundays for reading the Bible, and that on other days he ought to be in the tobacco house. The slave repeating the offence, he ordered him to be whipped. Going near the place of punishment, soon after its infliction, curiosity led him to listen to a voice engaged in prayer; and he heard the poor black implore the Almighty to forgive the injustice of his master, to touch his heart with a sense of his sin and to make him a good Christian. Struck with remorse, he made an immediate change in his life, which had been careless and dissipated, burnt his profane books and cards, liberated all his slaves, and appeared now to study how to render his wealth and talents useful to others.

158. Examples among the Heathen.

(*a*) PERICLES AND THE RAILER.—Pericles was of so patient a spirit, that he was hardly ever troubled with any thing that crossed him. There was a man who did nothing all the day but rail at him in the market-place, before all the people, notwithstanding Pericles was a magistrate. Pericles, however, took no notice of it, but, despatching sundry cases of importance till night came, he went home with a sober pace. The man followed him all the way, defaming him as he went. Pericles, when he came home, it being dark, called his man, and desired him to get a torch and light the fellow home.

(*b*) EXAMPLE OF CÆSAR.—It is said of Julius Cæsar, that upon any provocation, he would repeat the Roman alphabet before he suffered himself to speak, that he might be more just and calm in his resentments; and, further, that he could forget nothing but wrongs and remember nothing but benefits.

(*c*) EXAMPLE OF ADRIAN.—It is commonly said, that "Revenge is sweet;" but it can only be so to those weak minds that are incapable of bearing an injury. An elevated mind is superior to injuries, and pardons them. The Emperor Adrian, meeting a man who had insulted him before he came to the government, said to him, "Approach, you have nothing to fear; I am an emperor." This is an example well worthy of being imitated by those who are called to return good for evil.

(*d*) EXAMPLE OF EUCLID.—Euclid, a disciple of Socrates, having offended his brother, the brother cried out in a rage, "Let me die, if I am not revenged on you one time or other:" to whom Euclid replied, "And let me die, if I do not soften you by my kindnesses, and make you love me as well as ever." What a reproof to unforgiving professors of Christianity!

(*e*) THE SAYING OF SOCRATES.—Socrates, who was as pure a teacher of morals and as near like a true Christian as any of the ancient heathen, says, "The person who has received an injury must not return it, as is the opinion of the vulgar."

(*f*) PHOCION'S DYING CHARGE TO HIS SON.—Phocion was an Athenian, born some four hundred years B. C., and one of the most upright and benevolent heathen that ever lived. Yet he was condemned to die as a criminal, and denied even a grave in the country to which he had devoted his life. What could be more unjust in the Athenians, than putting their public benefactor to death in such a way as this? They sadly repented their madness afterwards, put the accuser to death, and erected a statue to Phocion's memory. But when Phocion had taken the poison which he was condemned to drink, and was about to die, "*he charged his son, with his last breath, that he should show no resentment against his persecutors.*"

What taught him to feel such forbearance and kindness towards those who had so wickedly wronged him? The voice of conscience—the law God hath written on the heart.

(*g*) THE INDIAN AND THE ENGLISHMAN.—A short time before the war between the English and the Indians in Pennsylvania broke out, an English gentleman, who lived on the borders of the province, was standing one evening at his door, when an Indian came and desired a little food. He answered, he had none for him; he then asked for a little beer, and received the same answer. Not yet discouraged, he begged for a little water; but the gentleman only answered, "Get ye gone for an Indian dog." The Indian fixed his eye for a little time on the Englishman, and then went away.

Some time after, this gentleman, who was fond of shooting, pursued his game till he was lost in the woods. After wandering a while, he saw an Indian hut, and went to it to inquire his way to some plantation. The Indian said, "It is a great way off, and the sun is near going down; you cannot reach it to-night, and if you stay in the woods the wolves will eat you up; but if you have a mind to lodge with me, you may." The gentleman gladly accepted the invitation, and went in. The Indian boiled a little venison for him, gave him some rum and water, and then spread some deer skins for him to lie upon; having done this, himself and another Indian went and lay at the other side of the hut.

He called the gentleman in the morning, telling him that the sun was up, and that he had a great way to go to the plantation, but that he would show him the way. Taking their guns, the two Indians went forward, and he followed. When they had gone several miles, the Indian told him he was within two miles of the plantation he wanted: he then stepped before him, and said, "Do you know me?" In great confusion, the gentleman answered, "I have seen you." The Indian replied, "Yes, you have seen me at your own door; and I will give you a piece of advice: when a poor Indian, that is hungry, and dry, and faint, again asks you for a little meat, or drink, do not bid him get him gone for an Indian dog." So he turned and went away.

Which of these two was to be commended, or which acted most agreeably to the Saivor's golden rule in Matt. vii. 12?

(*h*) THE SLAVE'S REVENGE.—When the Romans besieged Grumentum in Lucania, and the city was reduced to the last extremity, two slaves escaped into the camp of the besiegers. The place was soon afterwards taken by storm, and plundered. The two slaves then ran to the house of their mistress, whom they seized with a kind of violence, and carried off. When they were asked who she was, they answered, she was their mistress, and a most cruel mistress; upon whom they were going to take revenge for all the barbarous treatment they had suffered from her. In this way they compelled her to quit the city, and conveyed her to a safe retreat, where they concealed her with great care; and when the fury of the soldiers was abated, and tranquillity was restored in the city, they brought her back to her house, and obeyed her as before. She gave them their liberty, which was the greatest reward in her power to bestow; but certainly far short of the services they had rendered her.

(*i*) LIVIA'S ADVICE TO AUGUSTUS.—The Emperor Augustus being informed of a conspiracy against his life, headed by Lucius Cinna, was at first moved by resentment to resolve upon the cruelest punishment. But reflecting afterwards that Cinna was a young man of an illustrious family, and nephew to the great Pompey, he broke out into bitter fits of passion. "Why live I, if it be for the god of mercy that I should die? Must there be no end of my cruelties? Is my life of so great a value, that oceans of blood must be shed to preserve it?" His wife Livia, finding him in this perplexity, "Will you take a woman's counsel?" said she. "Imitate the physicians, who, when ordinary remedies fail, make trial of what are extraordinary. By severity you have prevailed nothing. Lepidus has followed Savidienus; Murena, Lepidus; Cœpio, Murena; and Egnatius, Cœpio. Begin now, and try whether sweetness and clemency may not succeed. Cinna is detected. Forgive him; he will never henceforth have the heart to hurt thee, and it will be an act of glory." Augustus was a man of sense; and calling Cinna to a private conference, he spoke as follows: "Thou knowest, Cinna, that having joined my enemies, I gave thee thy life, restored thee all thy goods, and advanced thy fortune equally with the best of those who had always been my friends. The sacerdotal office I conferred upon thee, after having denied it to others who had borne arms in my service. And yet after so many obligations, thou hast undertaken to murder me." Seeing Cinna astonished and silent with the consciousness of guilt, Augustus went on as follows: "Well, Cinna, go thy way; I again give thee that life as a traitor, which I gave thee before as an enemy. Let friendship from this time forward commence betwixt us; and let us make it appear whether thou hast received thy life, or I have given it, with the better faith." Some time after, he preferred Cinna to the cosular dignity, complaining of him that he had not resolution to solicit it. Their friendship continued uninterrupted till the death of Cinna; who, in token of his gratitude, appointed Augustus to be his sole heir. And it is remarkable, that Augustus reaped the due reward of a clemency so generous and exemplary; for from that time there never was the slightest conspiracy or attempt against him.

MOTIVES FOR LOVE TO ENEMIES.

159. It often checks and reforms them.

(*a*) A KISS FOR A BLOW.—I once lived in Boston, says Mr. Wright, and was one of the city school committee.

One day I visited one of the primary schools. There were about fifty children in it, between four and eight years old.

"Children," said I, "have any of you a question to ask to-day?"

"Please tell us," said a little boy, "what is meant by '*overcoming evil with good?*'"

"I am glad," said I, "you have asked that question; for I love to talk to you about peace, and show you how to settle all difficulties without fighting."

I went on, and tried to show them what the precept meant, and how to apply it, and carry it out. I was trying to think of something to make it plain to the children, when the following incident occurred.

A boy about seven, and his sister about five years old, sat near me. As I was talking, George doubled up his fist, and struck his sister on her head, as unkind and cruel brothers often do. She was angry in a moment, and raised her hand to strike him back. The teacher saw her, and said, "*Mary, you had better kiss your brother.*" Mary dropped her hand, and looked up at the teacher as if she did not fully understand her. She had never been taught to return good for evil. She thought if her brother struck her, she, of course, must strike him back. She had always been taught to act on this savage maxim, as most children are. Her teacher looked very kindly at her, and at George, and said again, "My dear Mary, you had better kiss your brother. See how angry and unhappy he looks!" Mary looked at her brother. He looked very sullen and wretched. Soon her resentment was gone, and love for her brother returned to her heart. She threw both her arms about his neck, and kissed him! The poor boy was wholly unprepared for such a kind return for his blow. He could not endure the generous affection of his sister. It broke his heart, and he burst out crying. The gentle sister took the corner of her apron and wiped away his tears, and sought to comfort him, by saying, with most endearing sweetness and generous affection, "*Don't cry, George; you did not hurt me much.*" But he only cried the harder. No wonder. It was enough to make any body cry.

(*b*) PLEDGE OF THE HINDOO BOYS.—Mr. Abbot, a missionary of the American Board of Commissioners for Foreign Missions, had under his care three schools in the villages around Ahmednugger, a city on the peninsula between the Arabian Sea and the bay of Bengal. These schools contained about a hundred Hindoo boys. In one of these, the following scene occurred. The reading lesson on this occasion contained the instructions of our Savior in regard to the manner we should treat those who injure us.

Mr. Abbot says, I asked the boys what their practice was. They said, "We strike those who strike us, and abuse those who abuse us." I asked them what they thought would be the consequence, if, instead of this, they should bless those who curse them. They replied, "Among our people, we should only be abused the more." I told them I thought differently; but as Hindoos were somewhat different from my people, I should like to see the experiment tried. I then explained to them, that however much they were insulted, they must not retaliate; and if they thought they could not endure this, they might sit down. Two or three sat down. After talking a while longer, all got up and said, they would try it one month, and would let any one beat them "till their life began to go," before they would resist. At the next examination, every one declared that they had kept their promise. It was afterwards found that three had failed. I then asked those who had been faithful, if they had suffered in consequence of it. "No," said they, "why should they abuse us now?"

But, said I, what do you do when they abuse you?

One boy said, "When they curse me, I say to them, 'A blessing attend you.'"

Well, what then?

"Then I laugh, and they laugh too."

Another boy said, he "shut his lips tight, and said nothing."

Well, what did the other party do to you?

"O, they turned up their noses, and walked off?"

(*c*) TWO NEIGHBORS AND THE HENS.—A man in New Jersey told me the following circumstances respecting himself and one of his neighbors:—

"I once owned a large flock of hens. I generally kept them shut up. But, one spring, I concluded to let them run in my yard, after I had clipped their wings, so they could not fly. One day, when I came home to dinner, I learned that one of my neighbors had been there, full of wrath, to let me know my hens had been in his garden, and that he had killed several of them, and thrown them over into my yard. I was greatly enraged because he had killed my beautiful hens, that I valued so much. I determined, at once, to be revenged, to sue him, or in some way get redress. I sat down and ate my dinner, as calmly as I could. By the time I had finished my meal, I became more cool, and thought that perhaps it was not best to fight with my neighbor about hens, and thereby make him my bitter, lasting enemy. I concluded to try another way, being sure that it would do better.

"After dinner, I went to my neighbor's. He was in his garden. I went out, and found him in pursuit of one of my hens with a club, trying to kill it. I accosted him. He turned upon me, his face inflamed with wrath, and broke out in a great fury—

"'You have abused me. I will kill all your hens, if I can get at them. I never was so abused. My garden is ruined.'

"'I am very sorry for it,' said I. 'I did not wish to injure you, and now see that I have made a great mistake in letting out my hens. I ask your forgiveness, and am willing to pay you six times the damage.'

"The man seemed confounded. He did not know what to make of it. He looked up to the sky—then down to the earth—then at his neighbor—then at his club—and then at the poor hen he had been pursuing, and said nothing.

"'Tell me, now,' said I, 'what is the damage, and I will pay you sixfold; and my hens shall trouble you no more. I will leave it entirely to you to say what I shall do. I cannot afford to lose the love and good will of my neighbors, and quarrel with them, for hens, or any thing else.'

"'*I am a great fool*,' said the neighbor. 'The damage is not worth talking about; and I have more need to compensate you than you me, and to ask your forgiveness than you mine.'"

(*d*) CRUELTY KILLED BY KINDNESS.—A young woman in Vermont married a poor, but worthy man, against her father's wish. He drove them from his house, and closed his door and heart against them. They came down near Boston, went to work, and prospered. After many years, the father had occasion to come to Boston. He concluded to go and see his daughter, expecting a cold reception. His daughter and her husband received him most kindly and lovingly. After staying with them awhile, he went back to Vermont.

One of his neighbors, hearing where he had been, asked him how his daughter and her husband had treated him.

"I never was so treated before in my life," said the weeping and broken hearted father. 'They have broken my heart—they have killed me—I don't feel as though I could live under it."

"What did they do to you?" asked the neighbor. "Did they abuse you?"

"*They loved me to death*, and killed me with kindness," said he. I can never forgive myself for treating so cruelly my own darling daughter, who loved me so affectionately. I feel as if I should die to think how I grieved the precious child when I spurned her from my door. Heaven bless them, and forgive me my cruelty and injustice to them."

Who does not see in this an infallible cure for difficulties between man and man? There is not a child nor man on earth, who would not feel and say, that that daughter, though so deeply wronged and outraged by her angry father, did right in treating him as she did. That father was her enemy, but she was not his. He hated her, while she loved him.

(*e*) THE REVENGEFUL TENANT.—A gentleman had a garden, in which he took great delight. It was surrounded by the cottages of his tenants and laborers, to whom he justly looked as the protectors of his property, and felt secure, inasmuch as no person could approach his premises but through theirs. He had for some days watched the progress of a fine bed of tulips. "To-morrow," said he, "they will be in full perfection," and he invited a company of friends to witness the display of their beauties. In the morning he hastened to the spot; but to his utter astonishment, the whole bed was a scene of shrivelled desolation. Some unaccountable influence had withered every stem, and each flower lay prostrate and fading on the ground.

A short time afterwards, a bed of ranunculuses shared the same fate; and in succession several other choice and favorite productions. At length, the gentleman became persuaded that the destruction did not proceed from any natural cause, such as blight or lightning, but that it must have been occasioned by the intentional mischief of some treacherous and malignant individual who had access to the grounds. He resolved therefore to watch, and engaged a friend to accompany him for that purpose. After remaining in their station some time, they saw a person come out of one of the cottages, and apply some destructive preparation to the roots of such flowers as were advancing to blossom. The gentleman at once recognized him as a workman whom a few weeks before he had had occasion to reprove, and who thus malignantly gratified his resentment. His friend strongly urged that the offender should be prosecuted, and offered to bear witness against him. But the proprietor replied, "No; I am much obliged by your kindness in remaining with me; I have ascertained the author of the mischief, and am satisfied; I must use another method of dealing with him."

In the morning, the gentleman ordered his servant to purchase a fine joint of meat, and carry it to the cottage of this man, desiring he would enjoy it with his family. This treatment, so contrary to his deserts and expectations, proved the means of effectually humbling and softening his stubborn and malignant heart. The offender presented himself before his injured master, freely confessed his guilt, implored forgiveness, and proved, from that day forward, a most faithful, diligent, and devoted servant. "If thine enemy hunger, feed him; if he thirst, give him drink; for in so doing thou shalt heap coals of fire on his head. Be not overcome of evil, but overcome evil with good."

(*f*) WILLIAM LADD AND HIS NEIGHBOR.—"I had," the Apostle of Peace used to say, in relating the anecdote, "a fine field of grain, growing upon an out-farm at some distance from the homestead. Whenever I rode by I saw my neighbor Pulcifer's sheep in the lot, destroying my hopes of a harvest. These sheep were of the gaunt, long-legged kind, active as spaniels; they would spring over the highest fence, and no partition wall could keep them out. I complained to neighbor Pulsifer about them, sent him frequent messages, but all without avail. Perhaps they would be kept out for a day or tw[illegible]; but the legs of his sheep were lon[illegible] grain more [illegible]empting than the adjoining pasture. I rode by again—the sheep were still there; I became angry, and told my men to set the dogs on them; and if that would not do, I would pay them if they would shoot the sheep.

"I rode away much agitated; for I was not so much of a peace man then as I am now, and I felt literally full of fight. All at once a light flashed in upon me. I asked myself, 'Would it not be well for you to try in your own conduct the peace principle you are teaching to others?' I thought it all over, and settled down in my mind as to the best course to be pursued.

"The next day I rode over to see neighbor Pulsifer. I found him chopping wood at his door. 'Good morning, neighbor!' No answer. 'Good morning!' I repeated. He gave a kind of grunt without looking up. 'I came,' continued I, 'to see about the sheep.' At this, he threw down his axe and exclaimed, in an angry manner: 'Now aren't you a pretty neighbor, to tell your men to kill my sheep? I heard of it; a rich man, like you, to shoot a poor man's sheep!'

"'I was wrong neighbor,' said I; 'but it won't do to let your sheep eat up all that grain; so I came over to say that I would take your sheep to my homestead pasture and put them in with mine; and in the fall you may take them back, and if any one is missing you may take your pick out of my whole flock.'

"Pulsifer looked confounded; he did not know how to take me. At last he stammered out: 'Now, 'Squire, are you in earnest?' 'Certainly I am,' I answered; 'it is better for me to feed your sheep in my pasture on grass, than to feed them here on grain; and I see the fence can't keep them out.'

"After a moment's silence, 'The sheep shan't trouble you any more,' exclaimed Pulsifer. 'I will fetter them all. But I'll let you know that, when any man talks of shooting, I can shoot, too; and when they are kind and neighborly, I can be kind, too.' The sheep never again trespassed on my lot. And, my friends," he would continue, addressing the audience, "remember that when you talk of injuring your neighbor, they will talk of injuring you. When nations threaten to fight, other nations will be ready, too. Love will beget love; a wish to be at peace will keep you in peace. You can overcome evil with good. There is no other way."

(*g*) SUBDUED PRIDE AND SCORN.—A lady in one of the towns of Mass. had repeatedly treated a well disposed young man with marked contempt and unkindness. Neither of them moved in the upper circles of society; but the lady, without cause, took numerous occasions to cast reproachful reflections on the young man as beneath her notice, and unfit to be treated with common respect. This lady had the misfortune to meet with a considerable loss in the destruction of a valuable chaise, occasioned by the running away of an untied horse. She had borrowed the horse and vehicle, and was required to make good the damage. This was a serious draft on her pecuniary resources, and she felt much distressed by her ill fortune. The young man, being of a kind and generous disposition, and determined to return good for evil, instantly set himself about collecting money for her relief. Subscribing liberally himself, and actively soliciting others, he soon made up a generous sum, and before she became aware of his movement, appeared before her and placed his collection modestly at her disposal. She was thunderstruck. He left her without waiting for thanks or commendation. She was entirely overcome, wept like a child, and declared she would never be guilty again of showing contempt, speaking reproachfully of, or treating with unkindness, him or any other fellow-creature. Was there any thing in all this contrary to nature?

(*h*) MR. POWELL AND THE OFFICER.—Mr. Powell, a minister of the gospel, being informed that an officer was come to apprehend him fo preaching the gospel, quietly resigned himself into his hands, requesting only that he might be permitted to join with his wife and children in prayer before he was dragged to prison. With this request the officer complied; and the family being together, the officer was so struck w the ardent and tender prayers of this suffering servant of God for his family, for the church, and for his persecutors in particular, that he declared he would die rather than have a hand in apprehending such a man.

160. It often changes them into friends.

(a) PHILIP AND THE ARGIVE.—Arcadius, an Argive, was incessantly railing at Philip of Macedon. Venturing once into the dominions of Philip, the courtiers reminded their prince that he had now an opportunity to punish Arcadius for his past insolences, and to put it out of his power to repeat them. The king, however, instead of seizing the hostile stranger and putting him to death, dismissed him loaded with courtesies and kindnesses. Some time after Arcadius's departure from Macedon, word was brought that the king's old enemy was become one of his warmest friends, and did nothing but diffuse his praises wherever he went. On hearing this, Philip turned to his courtiers and asked, with a smile: "Am not I a better physician than you?"

(b) ALEXANDER'S VICTORIES.—Alexander the Great being asked how he had been able, at so early an age and in so short a period, to conquer such vast regions and establish so great a name, replied: "I used my enemies so well that I compelled them to be my friends; and I treated my friends with such constant regard that they became unalterably attached to me."

(c) SIGISMOND AND HIS ENEMIES.—Some courtiers reproached the Emperor Sigismond, that instead of destroying his conquered foes he admitted them to favor. "Do I not," replied this illustrious monarch, "effectually destroy my enemies when I make them my friends?"

(d) THE CHINESE MONARCH AND THE REBELS.—A Chinese emperor being told that his enemies had raised an insurrection in one of the distant provinces—"Come, then, my friends," said he, "follow me, and I promise you that we shall quickly destroy them." He marched forward, and the rebels submitted upon his approach. All now thought that he would take the most signal revenge; but were surprised to see the captives treated with mildness and humanity. "How," cried the first minister, "is this the manner in which you fulfil your promise? Your royal word was given that you enemies should be destroyed; and behold you have pardoned them all, and even caressed some of them!" "I promised," replied the emperor, with a generous air, "to destroy my enemies. I have fulfilled my word; for, see, they are enemies no longer; I have made friends of them." Let every Christian imitate so noble an example, and learn "to vercome evil with good."

(e) TAKING CARE OF AN ENEMY'S HAY.—A college professor once related the following fact to his class, in order to show the power of kindness in effecting a change in the disposition and conduct of our enemies towards us.

There were two farmers who lived near neighbors, and whose farms laid side by side. One of these farmers was a pious, good man, of gentle, inoffensive character. The character of the other was just the reverse. His temper was like a tinder, taking fire at every spark that came in his way. He hated his pious neighbor; but more, probably, on account of his piety than any thing else. He was always vexing and tormenting the good man, quarreling about mere trifles, as much as one *can* quarrel who has no one to quarrel with him.

One summer he had mowed down a good deal of grass; and he had gone away from home, leaving it out in the field to dry. But while he was absent there came up a storm of rain. While the clouds were gathering the pious man saw the exposed condition of his neighbor's hay, and it struck him that there was now a fine chance to show a good man's revenge—that is, to return good for evil. So he took with him his hired men, and got his neighbor's hay all safely into the barn. What was the result?

When the quarrelsome man came home, expecting to see his hay all soaked by the rain, and found it had been taken care of by the man he had so much injured, it cut him to the very core. From that hour the evil spirit was cast out of him. No more abuse did he give the good man after that; but he became as obliging and kind to his pious neighbor as the latter had been to him.

(*f*) HOW TO OVERCOME EVIL.—"I once had a neighbor," says Mr. White, "who, though a clever man, came to me one hay-day, and said: 'Esquire White, I want you to come and get your geese away.' 'Why,' said I, 'what are my geese doing?' 'They pick my pigs' ears when they are eating, and drive them away, and I will not have it.' 'What can I do?' said I. 'You must yoke them.' 'That I have not time to do now,' said I; 'I do not see but they must run.' 'If *you* do not take care of them I shall,' said the clever shoemaker, in anger. 'What do you say, Esquire White?' 'I cannot take care of them now; but I will pay you for all damages.' 'Well,' said he, 'you will find that a hard thing, I guess.'

"So off he went, and I heard a terrible squalling among the geese. The next news from the geese was, that three of them were missing. My children went and found them terribly mangled and dead, and thrown into the bushes.

"'Now,' said I, 'all keep still, and let me punish him.' In a few days the shoemaker's hogs broke into my corn. I saw them, but let them remain a long time. At last I drove them all out, and picked up the corn which they had torn down and fed them with it in the road. By this time the shoemaker came in great haste after them.

"'Have you seen any thing of my hogs?' said he. 'Yes, sir; you will find them yonder, eating some corn which they tore down in my field.' 'In your field?' 'Yes, sir,' said I; 'hogs love corn, you know—they were made to eat.' 'How much mischief have they done?' 'O, not much,' said I.

"Well, off he went to look, and estimated the damage to be equal to a bushel and a-half of corn.

"'Oh, no,' said I, 'it can't be.' 'Yes,' said the shoemaker; 'and I will pay you every cent of damage.' 'No,' said I, 'you shall pay me nothing. My geese have been a great trouble to you.'

"The shoemaker blushed, and went home. The next winter, when we came to settle, the shoemaker determined to pay me for my corn. 'No,' said I; 'I shall take nothing.'

"After some talk we parted; but in a day or two I met him in the road, and fell into conversation in the most friendly manner. But when I started on he seemed loth to move, and I paused. For a moment both of us were silent. At last he said: 'I have something laboring on my mind.' 'Well, what is it?' 'Those geese. I killed three of your geese, and shall never rest until you know how I feel. I am sorry.' And the tears came in his eyes. 'Oh well,' said I, 'never mind; I suppose my geese were provoking.'

"I never took any thing of him for it; but whenever my cattle broke into his field after this, he seemed glad; because he could show how patient he could be.

"Now," said the narrator, "conquer yourself, and you can conquer with kindness where you can conquer in no other way."

(*g*) LIVING SWINE FOR DEAD ONES.—There was a Christian in New Jersey, that had a neighbor of such a malevolent and savage character, as made him a plague and terror to those with whom he became offended. Forgiveness, or mercy, nobody expected from him.

One day he found the hogs of his good neighbor in his corn-field. He drove them out, and came to their owner in a storm of passion, making a great bluster, about the damage done to his crop. "If I ever see them in my corn again," said he, "I'll *kill* them—that I will."

On he went, raving and scolding, his eyes flashing fire every word he spoke. But the good man kept calm as a summer's evening, and said nothing but what was kind and good-natured in reply.

Mr. *Wrath*, after he had spent all his fury, went off very much vexed to see that none of it took effect.

The good man shut up his swine at once. But, impatient for their favorite and new-found food, they soon made their escape; and got into the same corn-field again, without the knowledge of their owner.

Mr. *Wrath* discovered them, and at once attacked them with might and main; as much as to say (like a duelist), "Nothing but your blood will give me satisfaction!" He did, indeed, slaughter three or four of them, before they could make their retreat. Then, to cap the climax, and aggravate his neighbor's feelings to the utmost, he put the dead bodies on a sled, or cart, and drew them over to his neighbor's house. He threw them down before the door, saying with sarcastic bitterness, "Your hogs got into my corn again, and I thought I would bring them home!"

The owner of the swine kept perfectly cool, giving no look or word of resentment at the injury done to him. He might have gone to law with Mr. *Wrath*, and, perhaps, made him smart severely for destroying his property and insulting him as he did. But he thought it best to keep out of the law; and every man should think so, except when driven to it by a sense of duty.

The next year he himself had a corn-field situated in a similar way beside the road. Now it so happened that neighbor *Wrath* had some unruly swine running in the street, which got into the good man's corn-field, and committed a depredation similar to that which his had done in Mr. *Wrath's* corn-field the year before. He went to Mr. *Wrath*, and told him what mischief his vagrant swine had done, and requested him to shut them up. But he paid no attention to the request.

Soon after they got into the same field again. The Christian discovered them; and he hit on a good-natured and witty expedient of contrasting his own temper and conduct with those of his neighbor under similar circumstances. Instead of killing them, and carrying them home dead, he caught them, tied their legs carefully, and drew them with his team to their owner's door. "Neighbor," said he, kindly, "*I found your hogs in my corn again, and I thought I would bring them home!*"

Never was a man more completely confounded! He saw the wide difference between his neighbor's conduct and his own; he looked on the *living* swine, but he thought of the *dead* ones! It was too much. He told his neighbor that he was very sorry, and that he would pay all damages the hogs had done. He offered to pay him, too, for the hogs he had killed the year before! "No," replied the other, "I shall make no account of the damages your hogs have done; and I shall take nothing for what you did to mine. I let that pass."

Mr. *Wrath* was completely overcome. He concluded at once to yield, and retreat from a contest where such unequal odds were against him. He was as kind and generous to his Christian neighbor afterwards, as he was mischievous and cruel before.

Thus evil was overcome with good; and wrath made over into friendship.

(*h*) A CHRISTIAN COLONY.—One of thirty or forty New Englanders, who went out to settle in the Western wilderness, related to Mrs. Child the following particulars. They were mostly neighbors, and had been drawn to unite together in emigration from a general unity of opinion on various subjects. For some years previous, they had been in the habit of meeting occasionally at each others' houses, to talk over their duties to God and man, in all simplicity of heart. Their library was the Gospel, their priesthood the inward light. There were then no anti-slavery societies; but thus taught, and reverently willing to learn, they had no need of such agency, to discover their duties to the enslaved. The efforts of peace societies had reached this secluded band only in broken echoes; and non-resistance societies had no existence. But with the volume of the Prince of Peace, and hearts open to his influence, what need had they of preambles and resolutions?

"Rich in God-culture, this little band started for the far West. Their inward homes were blooming gardens; they made their outward in a wilderness. They were industrious and frugal, and all things prospered under their hands. But soon wolves came near the fold, in the shape of reckless unprincipled adventurers; believers in force and cunning, who acted according to their creed. The colony of practical Christians spoke of their depredations in terms of gentlest remonstrance, and repaid them with unvarying kindness. They went farther — they openly announced, "You may do us what evil you choose; we will return nothing but good." Lawyers came into the neighborhood, and offered their services to settle disputes. They answered, "We have no need of you. As neighbors we receive you in the most friendly spirit; but for us your occupation has ceased to exist." "What will you do, if rascals burn your barns, and steal your harvests?" "We will return good for evil. We believe this is the highest truth, and therefore the best expediency."

"When the rascals heard this, they considered it a marvellous good joke, and said and did many provoking things, which to them seemed witty. Bars were taken down in the night, and cows let into the corn-fields. The Christians repaired the damage as well as they could, put the cows in the barn, and at twilight drove them gently home; saying, "Neighbor, your cows have been in my field. I have fed them well during the day, but I would not keep them all night, lest the children should suffer for their milk."

"If this was fun, those who planned the joke found no heart to laugh at it. By degrees a visible change came over these troublesome neighbors. They ceased to cut off horses' tails, and break the legs of poultry. Rude boys would say to a younger brother, "Don't throw that stone, Bill! When I killed the chicken last week, did'nt they send it to mother, because they thought chicken-broth would be good for poor Mary? I should think you'd be ashamed to throw stones at *their* chickens." Thus was evil overcome with good; till not one was found to do them wilful injury.

"Years passed on, and saw them thriving in worldly substance, beyond their neighbors, yet beloved by all. From them the lawyer and the constable obtained no fees. The sheriff stammered and apologized, when he took their hard earned goods in payment for the war tax. They mildly replied, ''Tis a bad trade, friend. Examine it in the light of conscience and see if it be not so.' But while they refused to pay such fees and taxes, they were liberal to a proverb in their contributions for all useful and benevolent purposes.

"At the end of ten years, the public lands, which they had chosen for their farms, were advertised for sale at auction. According to custom, those who had settled and cultivated the soil, were considered to have a right to bid it in at the government price; which at that time was $1 25 per acre. But the fever of land speculation then chanced to run unusually high. Adventurers from all parts of the country were flocking to the auction; and capitalists in Baltimore, Philadelphia, New-York, and Boston, were sending agents to buy up western lands. No one supposed that custom, or equity, would be regarded. The first day's sale showed that speculation ran to the verge of insanity. Land was eagerly bought in at seventeen, twenty-five, and forty dollars an acre. The Christian colony had small hope of retaining their farms. As first settlers, they had chosen the best land; and persevering industry had brought it into the highest cultivation. Its market value was much greater than the acres already sold at exorbitant prices. In view of these facts, they had prepared their minds for another remove into the wilderness, perhaps to be again ejected by a similar process. But the morning their lot was offered for sale, they observed with grateful surprise, that their neighbors were everywhere busy among the crowd, begging and expostulating: "Don't bid on *these* lands! These men have been working hard on them for ten years. During all that time, they never did harm to man or brute. They are always ready to do good for evil. They are a blessing to any neighborhood. It would be a sin and a shame to bid on *their* land. Let them go at the government price."

"The sale came on; the cultivators of the soil offered $1 25; intending to bid higher if necessary. But among all that crowd of selfish, reckless speculators, *not one bid over them!* With out one opposing voice, the fair acres returned to them! I do not know a more remarkable instance of evil overcome with good. The wisest political economy lies folded up in the maxims of Christ."

161. It often leads them to become Christians.

(*a*) RAVENCROSS AND HIS SLAVE.—Mr. Ravencross was a slaveholder in Virginia, and reputed a hard master. His poor distressed slaves were in the habit of meeting at night in a distant hut, for the purpose of worshipping God. He was informed of this, and at the same time put on his guard, as it was suspected their motives for meeting were different from what they held out, and that an insurrection might be the consequence. Under this impression, he determined to prevent their assembling in future, chastised the promoters of this work, and gave positive orders, under the most serious penalty, that they should never assemble again under any pretence whatever, A short time after he was told they had been seen going in a body into the hut. Much displeased at their disobedience, and resolving that night to put a stop to their proceedings, he approached the hut with all the feelings of an offended master. When he reached the door, it was partly open. He looked in; they were on their knees. He listened; there was a venerable old man, who had been long in his service, pouring out his soul in prayer to God. The first words which caught his ear were, "Merciful God, turn my poor massa's heart; make him merciful, that he may obtain mercy; make him good, that he may inherit the kingdom of heaven." He heard no more, but fainted. Upon coming to himself, he wept; went into the sacred hut, knelt by the side of his old slave, and prayed also! From this period he became a true penitent, studied the Scriptures, took orders, and became a shining light. He preached at the General Convention of the Episcopal Church, in the city of Philadelphia, before more than two hundred of the clergy, in the year 1820.

(*b*) THE CRUEL SLAVE-HOLDER CONVERTED.—A slave holder in the South. extremely irascible and severe, found at length a slave as bad-tempered as himself. No severity of punishment could subdue or bow his stern, indomitable spirit; and, even when smarting under the lash, and reeking with blood from head to foot, he would still defy that master to his face, and pour upon him a torrent of bold, fierce, withering imprecations. It was Turk meeting Turk. But the gospel came ere long to that negro's heart; it tamed the tiger into a lamb; and then did that very slave, once so full only of wrath and revenge, make it the burden of his daily prayers, that God would have mercy on his cruel, relentless oppressor. His infidel master, doubting his sincerity, and an utter stranger to his present spirit, treated him with greater severity than ever, and fiercely swore "he'd whip the devil out of the villain;" but the poor slave, even while smarting and writhing, and bleeding under the lash, would fall on his knees, and pray so much the more, "God bless massa! God bless my massa!" This was too much even for depravity like his to bear long; and that very master, under the blessing of God upon such an exhibition of the Christian spirit, good returned for evil, love for hatred, prayers for bloody stripes, at length came himself to pray, and weep, and rejoice in Christ with his much abused, yet still affectionate and devoted, solely because regenerated slave. And when the time came for a public profession of their faith in their common Savior, you might have seen that master and his slave going hand in hand down into the water, there to seal the consecration of themselves to Him whose matchless love it is, rather than his almighty wrath, that subdues rebellious hearts to his sceptre.

(*c*) THE SAILOR CONVERTED.—Kindness and forgiveness to those who insult and abuse us, is often the means, in the hands of God, of making them Christians. You exhibit religion before them in a most attractive and engaging form, if you are known as one of its professors. Besides, when by treating an enemy in this way you have roused his conscience, and led him to feel shame and contrition for what he has done to you, it is natural at such a time that his excited conscience should turn on his sins towards God, and lead him to repentance.

The Holy Spirit, I doubt not, often avails itself of this softened state of the heart, to break it down into penitence before God.

As some rude and irreligious sailors were at work calking a vessel in a certain harbor, they noticed, at a little distance, a very aged and exemplary Christian quietly engaged in his business. He was noted for his generous, peaceful, forgiving disposition.

One sailor says to another, "You can't make that old man angry by any offence you can offer him."

The sailor who was addressed, at once accepted the challenge. He snatched up the bucket of tar that stood by him, ran up to the old man, and very unexpectedly dashed its contents upon him.

He looked up at the sailor with surprise at this wanton and unprovoked act of malignity, and said to him in a mild voice, "Young man, the Savior says, 'Whoso shall offend one of these little ones that believe in me, it were better for him that a millstone were hanged about his neck and that he were cast into the depths of the sea.' Now if I am one of these little ones, you have very much offended me."

The young sailor turned away perplexed and chagrined at the spirit the injured saint exhibited. He felt convinced that the man's religion was of a more sublime, noble and vital character than he had usually thought the Christian religion to be. He came back to his companions confessing that the old man had triumphed.

The image of the old man bearing the marks of his abuse, and looking with so much mingled pity and displeasure at him, was painted indelibly upon his memory. He was gone, but the sailor seemed to see him still! And that mild, but terrible reproof, too, the language still rung in his ear. The more he thought of the old man, the more he thought of the power and beauty of religion. The more he thought of himself, the more ashamed and miserable did he feel. The entire wickedness of his heart and life seemed to come under the review of conscience also. His distress became insupportable.

Some time afterwards he went to see the old man whom he had so wickedly treated; he asked him to forgive him, and to pray for him too. He was very ready to do both; and not long after, if I remember right, the sailor became a hopeful Christian.

There is reason to believe that many sinners might be converted from the error of their ways, if they should meet such a spirit as the sailor did in every professed Christian whom they might insult or abuse.

162. Miscellaneous.

(*a*) LOVE TO ENEMIES OBTAINED BY PRAYER.—There was a man of middle age, of cold, slow, doubting tendency of soul, who obtained, at last a Christian's hope. He hoped his name was in the book of life, but he was a weakly infant. He seemed to grow a little in the course of six or eight years, but slowly. He dreaded his deficiency in one feature of Christian character. The apprehension gave him pain. He read in one section of his Master's letter, "Love your enemies." For a long time, like thousands of others, he concluded he would not hurt them, or fight them, or return evil for evil, and he hoped this was love. He could hear others say of injuries received, "*I can forgive, but I will not forget it;*" and he could see in their case clearly, that this was *Satan's* kind of forgiveness. It made him fear in his own case that he did not *love his enemies.* He remembered that Christ would not accept of a false love. He knew that it did not mean a love of approbation for their sins, but the love of compassion. He tried to feel it, tried again, and for a year, but did not succeed. He read, thought, prayed over the subject. He did not love his enemies. He continued trying for several years. He thought, at times, that his feelings were softer; but he soon found it was not love. At length he found that by mere effect of will he could not move his affections. He became alarmed. He fasted and prayed in earnest; and at an hour when he was not looking for it, at a moment when he was least expecting, *he loved his enemies*. It was a *real love*. He knew it in the same way, reader, that you know *mirth* from *wo*, when you feel it yourself.

When he afterwards forgot the need of this heavenly help, he would sometimes fall again into his former feelings, and be almost as far from loving his enemies as before. But when he threw himself on his knees again, and received the dew of heavenly influence, the drooping grace of love to his enemies was quickened into new life, and bloomed with its wonted beauty and fragance.

(*b*) EXAMPLE OF THE EARLY CHRISTIANS.—Justin Martyr, one of the earliest writers, in his "Apology" to the heathen in behalf of the Christians, says: "We who once hated and murdered one another, we who would not enjoy the hearth in common with strangers, on account of the difference of our customs, now live in common with them, since the appearance of Christ; *we pray for our enemies;* we seek to persuade those who hate us unjustly, that they may direct their lives according to the glorious doctrines of Christ, and may share with us the joyful hope of enjoying the same privileges from God the Lord of all things."

(*c*) EXAMPLE OF ORIGEN.—Origen, one of the greatest scholars and theologians of the Christian church in the third century, when he was cruelly persecuted by Demetrius, and through his efforts excommunicated by the Synod, beautifully exhibited the same mild and forgiving spirit. Speaking, in his defence against the Synod, he mentions wicked priests and rulers thus: "We must pity them rather than hate them, pray for them rather than curse them, for we are created for blessing rather than cursing."

(*d*) THE CARTHAGENIAN CHRISTIANS.—In the time of a great pestilence, Cyprian, Bishop of the church in Carthage, in the third century, exhorts his flock to take care of the sick and dying, not only among their friends, but their foes. "If," says he, "we only do good to our own people we do no more than publicans and heathens. But if we are the children of God, who makes his sun to shine and his rain to descend upon the *just* and upon the *unjust*, who sheds abroad his blessings, not upon his friends alone, but upon those whose thoughts are *far from him*, we must show this by our actions, blessing those who *curse* us and doing good to those who *persecute* us."

Stimulated by their bishop's admonition, the members of the church addressed themselves to the work, the rich contributing their money and the poor their labor. Thus the sick were attended to, the streets soon cleared of the corpses that filled them, and the city saved from the dangers of a universal pestilence.

163. ENVY.

(*a*) ENVY OF DIONYSIUS.—"Dionysius the tyrant," says Plutarch, "out of envy, punished Philoxenius the musician because he could sing, and Plato the philosopher because he could dispute, better than himself."

(*b*) SADNESS OF MUTIUS.—Mutius, a citizen of Rome, was noted to be of so envious and malevolent a disposition, that Publius one day observing him to be very sad, said, "Either some great evil is happened to Mutius, or some great good to another."

(*c*) CAMBYSES AND CALIGULA.—Cambyses, king of Persia, slew his brother Smerdis, out of envy, because he could draw a stronger bow than himself or any of his followers; and the monster Caligula slew his brother because he was a beautiful young man.

"Base envy withers at another's joy,
And hates that excellence it cannot reach"

(*d*) CONVERSION HINDERED.—Mary was one of the first youths

(says a correspondent of the New-York Evangelist) who were awakened during an interesting revival. When many of her companions submitted, she lingered. Her convictions were powerful, her anguish was severe. At length she felt that she must and would submit, and said that she was willing to be in the hands of God. Still all was darkness and trouble within. She remained awhile in this wretched state, and then became calm and joyful. Her evidences of regeneration were bright, and she well adorned the profession which she subsequently made. When her spiritual teacher beheld the smile of joy kindled upon her grief-worn countenance, he said to her, "Mary, what was it that kept you back from Christ?" She replied, "I was unwilling that any of my companions should rejoice in hope, until I did myself. I knew this was wrong, but felt unwilling to mention it, because I thought no other person ever felt so. But I was brought to feel willing, and even anxious, that they should have comfort, if I did not. I felt that I could not claim it, and if I should receive comfort, even at the close of life, it would be a mercy that I did not deserve."

164. ETERNITY.

(*a*) DUMB BOY'S EXPLANATION.—The following question was put in writing to a boy in the deaf and dumb school at Paris: "What is eternity?" He wrote as an answer, "It is the life-time of the Almighty."

(*b*) THE TROUBLESOME WORD.—A lady, having spent the afternoon and evening at cards and in gay company, when she came home, found her servant-maid reading a pious book. She looked over her shoulders and said, "Poor melancholy soul! what pleasure canst thou find in poring so long over that book?" That night the lady could not sleep, but lay sighing and weeping very much. Her servant asked her once and again what was the matter. At length she burst out into a flood of tears, and said, "Oh! it is one word I saw in your book that troubles me: there I saw that word *eternity*. Oh how happy should I be if I were prepared for eternity!" The consequence of this impression was, that she laid aside her cards, forsook her gay company, and set herself seriously to prepare for another world.

(*c*) A GOD—A MOMENT—AN ETERNITY.—How sad it is that an eternity so solemn and so near us should impress us so slightly and should be so much forgotten! A Christian traveller tells us, that he saw the following religious admonition on the subject of eternity printed on a folio sheet, and hanging in a public room of an inn in Savoy; and it was placed, he understood, in every house in the parish:—"Understand well the force of the words—a God, a moment, an eternity. A God who sees thee, a moment which flies from thee, an eternity which awaits thee. A God whom you serve so ill, a moment of which you so little profit, an eternity which you hazard so rashly."

165. ETIQUETTE, UNDUE REGARD TO.

(*a*) SPANISH ETIQUETTE.—Philip the Third was gravely seated by the fireside; the firemaker of the court had kindled so great a quantity of wood that the monarch was nearly suffocated with heat, and his *grandeur* would not suffer him to rise from the chair; the domestics could not *presume* to enter the apartment, because it was against the *etiquette*. At length the Marquis de Pota appeared, and the king ordered him to damp the fires; but *he* excused himself, alleging that he was forbidden by the *etiquette* to perform such a function, for which the Duke d'Usseda ought to be called upon, as it was his business. The duke was gone out, the *fire* burned fiercer, and the *king* endured it rather than derogate from his *dignity;* but his blood was heated to such a degree; that an erysipelas of the head appeared the next day, which, succeeded by a violent fever, carried him off in 1621, in the twenty-fourth year of his age.

The palace was once on fire; a soldier, who knew the king's sister was in her apartment, and must inevitably have been consumed in a few moments by the flames, at the risk of his life rushed in, and brought her highness safe out in his arms; but the Spanish *etiquette* was here wofully broken into! The loyal soldier was brought to trial, and as it was impossible to deny that he had entered her apartment, the judges condemned him to die! The Spanish princess, however, condescended, in consideration of the circumstances, to *pardon* the soldier, and very benevolently saved his life!

(*b*) VICTIM OF ETIQUETTE.—The preposterous degree of etiquette for which the court of Spain has always been remarkable proved the ruin of one of the most illustrious of Spaniards, in the person of the Duke of Ossuna. He was viceroy of Naples, and greatly renowned for his talents as a soldier and a statesman. In consequence of some calumnious reports, he was called to court to give an account of his administration; and on presenting himself to the king, being troubled with the gout and of short stature, he carried, for matter of convenience, his sword in his hand. His majesty, it seems. did not like this *sword-in-hand* style of approaching him, and, turning his back on Ossuna, left the room without speaking. The duke, probably unconscious of the cause of the king's displeasure, was much incensed at this treatment, and was overheard to mutter, "This comes of serving boys." The words being reported to his majesty, an order was given for Ossuna's arrest. He was committed prisoner to a monastery not far from Madrid, and there he continued till his beard reached his girdle. Growing then very ill, he was permitted to go to his house at Madrid, where he died about the year 1622.

166. EXAMPLE, CHRISTIAN.

(*a*) THE MINISTER AND THE INFIDEL.—The Rev. Mr. R. resided in a house where an apprentice lived, who was compelled to hear him preach every Sabbath day, but who always rejoiced when the services of the day were over. He had been drawn into the paths of infidelity, and cherished a malignant hatred to religion and its professors. He considered Mr. R. either as a superior spirit in human form, or a consummate hypocrite, whose exhibitions in the pulpit, and in private life, were alike intended to deceive the spectators for his own purposes. Our young skeptic resolved, however, very closely to watch his conduct. "For several years," said he to the writer of this paper, "I watched him with incessant vigilance. My opportunities of knowing his character were such as occur in the variety and minutiæ of domestic life and family transactions; but his temper, and conduct, and speech, and devotion, were only beautiful representations of the same object—all having one character, and that stamped upon them by Heaven. I began to admire, rather than love him, until a circumstance occurred that produced an indelible impression upon my mind. My apprenticeship was just out, and in a few days I was to set off to a situation in London. He seized an occasion of calling me into his room, warned me of the dangers which I should meet in the metropolis, told me of the duty of prayer, and the pleasures of piety, put into my hands as a parting present, "Doddridge's Rise and Progress," and, kneeling down, commended me fervently to the grace of God, and the guidance of infinite wisdom. This united me to the man for ever. I went to London under the impressions he had made on my mind; did not give way to company, nor launch out into dissipation, but attended the house of God with something like regularity. And a sermon, which I heard Mr. S. preach when he had been recently brought back from the gates of death, was the means of awakening me to a sense of my danger, and of directing me to the cross." Many persons, whom we do not suspect, are watching our temper and general conversation, and the convictions which they receive will tell on their future principles and final destiny. Our Lord knew the power of example was far beyond precept, when he said to his disciples, "Ye are the salt of the earth,"—"ye are the light of the world." Happy are those ministers who can use the same reference as the apostle: "Be ye followers of me, even as I also am of Christ," 1 Cor. xi. 1.

(*b*) PETERBOROUGH AND FENELON.—When Lord Peterborough lodged for a season with Fenelon, Archbishop of Cambray, he was so delighted with his piety and virtue, that he exclaimed at parting, "If I stay here any longer, I shall become a Christian in spite of myself."

(*c*) IRREFUTABLE ARGUMENT.—Mr. Innes, in his work on Domestic Religion, mentions a fact strikingly illustrative of the power of consistent conduct. A young man, when about to be ordained as a Christian minister, stated, that at one period of his life he had been nearly betrayed into the principles of infidelity; "but," he added, "there was one argument in favor of Christianity, which I could never refute—the consistent conduct of my own father!"

(*d*) THE MOTHER'S CONFESSION.—Children, says the Rev. W. Jay, have conveyed religion to those from whom they ought to have derived it. "Well," said a mother one day, weeping, her daughter being about to make a public profession of religion by going to the Lord's table, "I will resist no longer How can I bear to see my dear child love and read the Scriptures, while I never look into the Bible—to see her retire and seek God, while I never pray—to see her going to the Lord's table, while his death is nothing to me!" "Ah," said she to the minister who called to inform her of her daughter's intention, wiping her eyes; "yes, sir, I know she is right, and I am wrong—I have seen her firm under reproach, and patient under provocation, and cheerful in all her sufferings. When, in her late illness, she was looking for dissolution, heaven stood in her face. Oh that I was as fit to die! I ought to have taught her, but I am sure she has taught me. How can I bear to see her joining the church of God, and leaving me behind—perhaps for ever!"

From that hour she prayed in earnest, that the God of her child would be her God, and was soon seen walking with her in the way everlasting.

(*e*) SUCCESS WITH THE IMPENITENT.—It is said of a follower of Christ who lived many years ago in Western New-York, that she had probably been instrumental in the conversion of more sinners than any minister in the same region of country. She was once asked how it was that she, while she was in the habit of speaking to every class of individuals, always spoke with effect without giving offence. Her reply was this: "Whenever such an individual comes within the circle of my influence, I at once set my heart upon saying and doing what I can to secure his salvation. As soon as a fit opportunity presents, my plan is to converse with him on the 'things which concern his peace.' As preparatory to such an event, my aim is to order my entire deportment in his presence so that what I say shall be impressed upon his heart and conscience by all that he has previously seen in me." Here was the secret of her power. What was spoken was always in time, and rendered like "apples of gold in pictures of silver," by its correspondence with her entire character. It is in place for the truly good to urge the practice of goodness upon all around them. Nor is it fitting in any others to engage in this hallowed employment.

EXPERIENCE, CHRISTIAN.

167. Effect of relating, &c.

(*a*) THE CAPTAIN AND THE INFIDEL.—A few years ago, on a voyage to the west of America, a young man sauntering on deck observing one of the sailors more sedate than his companions, stepped up to him, and abruptly asked him: "George, are you not a Christian?" His countenance brightened up as he replied: "I trust that I am; I think I can testify to the goodness of God in giving his Son to die for me." The manner in which he uttered this sentence interested his companion, who requested to know his history. His reply in substance was as follows:

"I have always been a sailor. My father was a sailor before me. My mother was a pious woman; and whenever I went on shore to see her she used to say a great many things to me about my soul. I paid no attention to them; but lived as though I had no soul. I was a fool, as I said in my heart, 'There is no God.' Boldly did I profane his name. Thus I went on from year to year, till I entered a ship that was under a pious captain. He was a good man, and did much for the good of his crew. He read the Scriptures to us, and prayed with us. After some time, however, I began to tremble. The word of God convinced me of sin, and of righteousness, and of judgment to come. I saw my danger, and felt it, too. My sins came up before me, and appeared as mountains that must for ever separate me from peace and happiness. I was a miserable man, and thought I must always be so. At last I opened my heart to the captain. He felt for me, and told me of the mercy of God in Christ Jesus. With tears in his eyes he directed me to behold the Lamb of God which taketh away the sin of the world. My heart broke. Tears of penitence ran down my cheeks; my faith took hold on the Son of God."

At this time the young man who had elicited the narrative was not truly religious. The narrative of the sailor, given with simplicity and deep emotion, went to his heart and brought him to the feet of the Savior. He soon after publicly professed his faith in Christ.

(*b*) THE LAWYER AT THE LOVE-FEAST.—The simple relation of Christian experience always produces a powerful effect upon the hearers. Revivals of religion are often greatly promoted by this means. Some years ago, a young lawyer in Vermont, found his way into a Methodist love-feast. Supposing that he should hear some strange things there, he went prepared to take notes. At the close of the meeting, he arose, and addressed the assembly as follows: "My friends, I hold in my hands the testimony of no less than sixty persons, who have spoken here, this morning, who all testify with one consent, that there is a divine reality in religion, they having experienced its power in their own hearts. Many of these persons I know. Their word would be received in any court of justice. Lie, they would not, I know; and mistaken they cannot all be. I have heretofore been skeptical in relation to these matters. I now tell you that I am fully convinced of the truth, and that I intend to lead a new life. Will you pray for me?" Thus while we "speak that which we do know, and testify to that which we have seen," some will receive "our witness," even if others do not.

168. Every where similar.

(*a*) GOD'S WORK UNIVERSALLY THE SAME.—The eminently pious and learned theologian, Dr. Livingston, related to me, (says, Dr. Alexander,) not many years before his decease a pleasing anecdote, which will serve to illustrate the point under consideration, and which I communicate to the public more willingly, because I do not know that he has left any record of it behind him. While a student at the University of Utrecht, a number of pious persons, from the town and among the students, were accustomed to meet for free conversation on experimental religion, and for prayer and praise, in a social capacity. On one of these occasions, when the similarity of the exercises of the pious, in all countries and ages, was the subject of conversation, it was remarked by one of the company, that there was then present a representative from each of the four quarters of the world. These were Dr. Livingston, from America, a young man from the Cape of Good Hope in Africa, another student from one of the Dutch possessions in the East Indies, and many natives of Europe, of course. It was therefore proposed, that at the next meeting, the three young gentlemen first referred to, together with an eminently pious young nobleman of Holland, should each give a particular narrative of the rise and progress of the work of grace in his soul. The proposal was universally acceptable; and accordingly, a narrative was heard from a native of each of the four quarters of the globe—of their views and feelings, of their trials and temptations, &c. The result was highly gratifying to all present; and I think Dr. Livingston said, that it was generally admitted by those present, that they had never before witnessed so interesting a scene.

(*b*) JOHN NEWTON AND MR OCCAM.—When Mr. Occam, the Indian preacher, was in England, he visited Mr. Newton of London, and they compared experiences. "Mr. Occam," says Mr. Newton, "in describing to me the state of his heart, when he was a blind idolater, gave me, in general, a striking picture of what my own was in the early part of my life; and his subsequent views correspond with mine, as face answers to face in a glass, though I dare say, when he received them, he had never heard of Calvin's name."

FAITH.

169. Nature of Faith.

(*a*) WHAT WE ARE TO BELIEVE.—Rev. Mr. P., of New-York, when settled in B——, N. Y., was called to see a young lady on the brink of the grave. In the course of the conversation he says, "I inquired, 'Do you not *feel* that you are a great sinner before God?' Bursting into an agony of tears and raising her attenuated hands, she cried, 'Oh! yes, that is all that pains me. Oh, I have been *such* a sinner, and God has been so good to me—Christ so good, and I have sinned so much!'

"Being satisfied that she was sincerely penitent for sin, I spoke of the atonement of Christ—its necessity and nature and terms, and asked her if she could see in that plan to save, that there was *room* for her. 'No, not for me, I am such a sinner,' she said, and the fresh torrents of tears attested the sincerity of her confession. Then I told her of the love of Jesus, and besought her by the dying compassion of the Son of God, to believe in his name. But still she refused to trust herself in his hands. Making one more effort, said I, 'Perhaps you do not understand precisely what you are to believe. You say, that you think that Christ is willing to save unto the uttermost all that come unto God, repenting of their sins. You say that you repent. Now, trusting with all your heart in the promises which he has made, believe that he is willing to save *you*.'

"A smile as from heaven played on her pale cheek, as she exclaimed, 'Is that it?' and trusting in Christ, she found joy. Lingering for many weeks afterwards, her faith never wavered; her views of divine things grew brighter and brighter; her confidence in God, deeper and stronger; and as death approached, she welcomed his coming as of a friend.

(b) THE SAILOR'S EXPLANATION.—Mr. Stewart, in his Journal of a Residence in the Sandwich Islands, relates that whilst on board a ship sailing from America to those islands, he felt it his duty to instruct the sailors; and he had several proofs that his labors were not in vain. One sailor, named R——, had been brought to trust in Christ for salvation; and, shortly after, meeting with another who was anxiously inquiring the way of salvation, he thus addressed him: "It was just so with myself once; I did not know what faith was, or how to obtain it; but I know now what it is, and I believe I possess it. But I do not know that I can tell you what it is, or how to get it. I can tell you what it is not: it is not knocking off swearing, and drinking, and such like; and it is not reading the Bible, nor praying, nor being good: it is none of these; for even if they would answer for the time to come, there is the old score still, and how are you to get clear of that? It is not any thing you have done or can do: it is only believing and trusting to what Christ has done; it is forsaking your sins, and looking for their pardon and the salvation of your soul, because he died and shed his blood for sin; and it is nothing else." The most learned divine could not have given a more simple or scriptural exposition of this important subject, or one better adapted to carry conviction to the heart. The simplest terms are the most difficult of explanation, while the unsophisticated feelings of genuine piety find a ready response in every awakened mind.

(c) A VENTURESOME BELIEVING.—The Rev. John Butterworth, a minister of England, speaking of his religious experiences, says, "One day as I was reading in a book called the 'Marrow of Modern Divinity,' a sentence from Luther was quoted, which was this, 'I would run into the arms of Christ, if he stood with a drawn sword in his hand.' This thought came bolting into my mind—'so will I too:' and those words of Job occurred—'Though he slay me, yet will I trust him.' My burden dropped off; my soul was filled with joy and peace through believing in Christ; a *venturesome believing*, as Mr. Belcher calls it, was the means of setting me at liberty; nor have I ever been in such perplexity, respecting my interest in Christ, since that time; though I have had various trials in other respects."

(d) NOTHING BUT TRUE FAITH.—A good man was considerably harassed as to the nature of true faith, and very properly resolved to ask the assistance of his minister. Going to his house, he stated that his fears had been great, that he had sinned beyond the reach of mercy; but that while he was thinking on the subject that portion of Scripture was suggested to his mind, "The blood of Jesus Christ his Son cleanseth us from all sin," and that resting on this truth, he had lost all his anxiety. The minister very properly told him that this was nothing else than true faith.

170. Necessity of Faith.

(a) LUTHER ON PILATE'S STAIRCASE.—For some time after the light of truth began to dawn on the mind of Luther, he submitted to all the vain practices which the Romish church enjoins in order to purchase the remission of sins. One day during his visit to Rome, wishing to obtain an indulgence promised by the pope to any one who should ascend on his knees what is called *Pilate's Staircase*, the poor Saxon monk was slowly climbing those steps, which they told him had been miraculously transported from Jerusalem to Rome. But while he was going through with his meritorious work he thought he heard a voice like thunder speaking from the depth of his heart, "*the just shall live by faith.*" He started up in terror on the steps up which he had been crawling; he was horrified at himself; and struck with shame for the degradation to which superstition had bebased him, he fled from the scene of his folly. This was the decisive epoch in the inward life of Luther.

(b) THE FARMER'S FAITH.—A king of Sweden was under great impressions of spiritual religion for some time before his death. A peasant being prince, on a particular occasion, admitted to his presence, the king, knowing him to be a person of singular piety, asked him, "What he took to be the true nature of faith?" The peasant entered deeply into the subject, and much to the king's comfort and satisfaction. The king, at last, lying on his death-bed, had a return of his doubts and fears as to the safety of his soul; and still the same question was perpetually in his mouth, to those about him, "What is real faith?" His attendants advised him to send for the Archbishop of Upsall: who, coming to the king's bedside, began in a learned, logical manner, to enter into the scholastic definition of faith. The prelate's disquisition lasted an hour. When he had done the king said with much energy, "All this is ingenious, but not comfortable; it is not what I want. Nothing, after all, but the farmer's faith will do for me."

(*c*) RIDDLE'S DYING TESTIMONY.—Mr. Edward Riddle, an aged Christian in Hull, remarked, a few days before his death, to one present, "Some may suppose, that a person at my time of life, and after so long making a profession of religion, has nothing to do but to die and go to heaven; but I find that I have as much need to go to God, through Christ, as a sinner, at the last hour as at the beginning. The blood of Christ, the death of Christ, his victory and fulness, are my only ground of faith, hope, and confidence; there is the same need of him to be the Finisher of my faith, as there was to be the Author of it."

(*d*) DODDRIDGE'S RIGHTEOUSNESS.—"My confidence is," said the pious Dr. Doddridge shortly before his death, "not that I have lived such or such a life, or served God in this or the other manner; I know of no prayer I ever offered, no service I ever performed, but there has been such a mixture of what was wrong in it, that instead of recommending me to the favor of God, I needed his pardon, through Christ, for the same. Yet I am full of confidence; and this is my confidence—there is a hope set before me: I have fled, I still fly, for refuge to that hope."

(*e*) MRS. JUDSON'S EXPERIENCE.—"It is just a year this day," says Mrs. Judson, "since I entertained hope in Christ. About this time in the evening, when reflecting on the words of the lepers, 'If we enter into the city, then the famine is in the city, and we shall die there; and if we sit still here, we die also;' and felt that if I returned to the world, I should surely perish; if I staid where I then was, I should perish; and I could but perish, if I threw myself on the mercy of Christ. Then came light, and relief, and comfort, such as I never knew before."

(*f*) PAYSON'S HAPPINESS.—"Christians might avoid much trouble and inconvenience," says Dr. Payson, "if they would only believe what they profess—that God is able to make them happy without any thing else. They imagine, if such a dear friend were to die, or such and such blessings to be removed, they should be miserable; whereas God can make them a thousand times happier without them. To mention my own case,—God has been depriving me of one blessing after another; but as every one was removed, he has come in, and filled up its place; and now, when I am a cripple, and not able to move, I am happier than ever I was in my life before, or ever expected to be; and if I had believed this twenty years ago, I might have been spared much anxiety."

(*g*) I AM ON THE ROCK.—One day a female friend called on the Rev. William Evans, a pious minister in England, and asked how he felt himself. "I am weakness itself," he replied; "but I am on the *Rock*. I do not experience those transports which some have expressed in the view of death; but my dependence is on the *mercy* of God in Christ. Here my religion *began*, and here it must *end*."

171. Example of Faith.

(*a*) CHALLENGING THE PROMISES.—Mr. John Avery, a minister, having been driven from his native country by the persecution of Archbishop Laud, fled to New England

Upon his arrival, he settled for a short time at Newbury; but, receiving an invitation to Marblehead, he determined upon a removal to that place. Having embarked in a small vessel, together with Mr. Anthony Thacker, another worthy minister, there arose a tremendous storm, by which the vessel struck against a rock, and was dashed to pieces. The whole company, consisting of twenty-three persons, got upon the rock, but were successively washed off and drowned, except Mr. Thacker and his wife. Mr. Thacker and Mr. Avery held each other by the hand a long time, resolving to die together, till, by a tremendous wave, the latter was washed away, and drowned. The moment before this happened, he lifted up his eyes to heaven, saying, "We know not what the pleasure of God may be. I fear we have been too unmindful of former deliverances. Lord, I cannot challenge a promise of the preservation of my life; but thou hast promised to deliver us from sin and condemnation, and to bring us safe to heaven, through the all-sufficient satisfaction of Jesus Christ. This, therefore, I do challenge of thee." He had no sooner uttered these words, than he was swept into the mighty deep, and no more seen. Mr. Thacker and his wife were also washed off the rock; but, after being tossed in the waves for some time, the former was cast on shore, where he found his wife a sharer in the deliverance.

172. Triumphs of Faith.

(*a*) CASE OF REV. DR. AILMER.—This excellent man was rector of Much Hadham, Herts., and died in 1625, heroically closing his own eyelids, and with these words on his lips; "Let my people know that their pastor died undaunted, and not afraid of death! I bless my God, I have no fear, no doubt, no reluctance, but a sure confidence in the sin-overcoming merits of Jesus Christ."

(*b*) CASE OF BISHOP BUTLER.—When this eminent prelate lay on his dying bed, he called for his chaplain, and said, "Though I have endeavored to avoid sin and please God to the utmost of my power, yet, from the consciousness of perpetual infirmities, I am still afraid to die."

"My lord," said the chaplain, "you have forgotten that Jesus Christ is a Savior."

"True," was the answer, "but how shall I know that he is a Savior for me?"

"My lord, it is written, 'Him that cometh to me I will in no wise cast out.'"

"True," said the bishop, "and I am surprised that, though I have read that Scripture a thousand times over, I never felt its virtue till this moment; and now I die happy!"

(*c*) A ROCK TO REST ON.—The Rev. John Rees, of Crown-Street, Soho, London, was visited on his death-bed by the Rev. John Leifchild, who very seriously asked him to describe the state of his mind. This appeal to the honor of his religion roused him; it freshened his dying lamp, and raising himself up in his bed he looked his friend in the face, and with great deliberation, energy, and dignity, uttered the following words:—"Christ in his person, Christ in the love of his heart, and Christ in the power of his arm is the Rock on which I rest; and now (reclining his head gently on the pillow) death, strike!"

(*d*) VENTURING ON CHRIST.—The Rev. Dr. Simpson was for many years tutor in the college at Hoxton, and while he stood very low in his own esteem, he ranked high in that of others. After a long life spent in the service of Christ, he approached his latter end with holy joy. Among other expressions which indicated his love to the Redeemer, and his interest in the favor of God, he spoke with disapprobation of a phrase often used by some pious people, "Venturing on Christ." "When," said he, "I consider the infinite dignity and all-sufficiency of Christ, I am ashamed to talk of venturing on him. Oh, had I ten thousand souls, I would, at this moment, cast them all into his hands with the utmost confidence." A few hours before his dissolution, he addressed himself to the last enemy, in a strain like that of the apostle, when he exclaimed, "O death, where is thy sting?' Displaying his characteristic fervor, as though he saw the tyrant approaching, he said, "What art thou? I am not afraid of thee. Thou art a vanquished enemy through the blood of the cross."

(*e*) ACKNOWLEDGMENT OF STAUPICIUS.—Luther relates concerning one Staupicius, a German divine, that he acknowledged that before he came to understand the free and powerful grace of Christ, he resolved, and vowed a hundred times against a particular sin; yet could never get power over it, nor his heart purified from it, till he came to see that he trusted too much to his own resolutions, and too little to Jesus Christ; but when his faith had engaged against his sin, he obtained the victory.

(*f*) I HAVE SO LEARNED CHRIST.—Of Mr. Stephen Marshall, an eminent divine of the 17th century, Mr. Giles Firman, who knew him in life, and attended him in death, says, "That he left behind him few preachers like himself; that he was a Christian in practice as well as profession; that he lived by faith, and died by faith, and was an example to the believers, in word, in conversation, in charity, in faith, and in purity. And when he, together with some others, conversed with him about his death, he replied, 'I cannot say as one did, I have not so lived that I should now be afraid to die; but this I can say, I have so *learned Christ*, that I am not afraid to die.'"

(*g*) COWPER'S VIEW OF DEATH.—"I have not time to add more," says Cowper the poet, in a letter, "except just to add, that if I am ever enabled to look forward to death with comfort, which I thank God is sometimes the case with me, I do not take my view of it from the top of my own works and deservings, though God is witness that the labor of my life is to keep a conscience void of offence toward him. Death is always formidabie to me except when see him disarmed of his sting by having sheathed it in the body of Jesus Christ."

(*h*) WATTS AND THE PROMISES.—The faith of Dr. Watts in the promises of God was lively and unshaken. "I believe them enough," said he, "to venture an eternity on them." To a religious friend, at another time he thus expressed himself: "I remember an aged minister used to say, that the most learned and knowing Christians, when they come to die, have only the same plain promises for their support, as the common and unlearned, and so," continued he, "I find it. It is the plain promises of the gospel that are my support: and I bless God, they *are* plain promises, which do not require much labor and pains to understand them; for I can do nothing now but look into my Bible for some promise to support me, and live upon that."

(*i*) DEATH OF JOHN HUSS.—When John Huss, the Bohemian martyr, was brought out to be burnt, they put on his head a triple crown of paper, with painted devils on it. On seeing it, he said, "My Lord Jesus Christ, for my sake, wore a crown of thorns; why should not I then, for his sake, wear this light crown, be it ever so ignominious? Truly I will do it, and that willingly." When it was set upon his head, the bishops said, "Now, we commend thy soul to the devil." "But I," said Huss, lifting up his eys to heaven. "do commit my spirit into thy hands, O Lord Jesus Christ; to thee I commend my spirit, which thou hast redeemed." When the fagots were piled up to his very neck, the Duke of Bavaria was officious enough to desire him to abjure. "No," said Huss, "I never preached any doctrine of an evil tendency; and what I taught with my lips I now seal with my blood."

(*j*) A NOBLE REPLY.—In the reign of Charles II, Margaret Wilson, a girl of eighteen, along with an aged widow of sixty-three, was adjudged to die, because she refused to acknowledge the supremacy of any other than Christ in the church. The sentence pronounced against them was, that they should be fastened to stakes driven deep into the oozy sand that covers the beach, and left to perish in the rising tide. The stake to which the aged female was fastened was further down the beach than that of the young woman, in order that, being soonest destroyed, her expiring sufferings might shake the firmness of faith of Margaret Wilson. The tide began to flow—the waters swelled; they mounted from the knee to the waist, and from the waist to the chin, and from the chin to the lip of the venerable matron, and when she was almost stifled by the rising tide, when the bubbling groan of her last agony was reaching her fellow-sufferer further up the beach, one heartless ruffian put to Margaret Wilson the question, "What think you of your friend now?" And what was the calm and noble reply? "What do I see but Christ in one of his members wrestling there? Think you that we are the sufferers? No, it is Christ in us—He who sendeth us not a warfare upon our own charges."

173. FIRMNESS, CHRISTIAN.

(*a*) DEATH PREFERRED TO LYING.—Jerome writes of a brave woman, who being upon the rack, bade her persecutors do their worst, for she was resolved to *die* rather than *lie*.

(*b*) FIRMNESS OF ARETHUSUS.—In the reign of Constantine, there was one Marcus Arethusus, an eminent servant of God, who had been the cause of overthrowing an idol temple; but Julian coming to be Emperor, commanded the people of that place to build it up again. All were ready to do so, only he refused it; whereupon his own people, to whom he had preached, fell upon him, stript off his clothes, then abused his naked body, and gave it up to children and school-boys to be lanced with their penknives; but when all this would not do, they caused him to be set in the sun, his naked body anointed all over with honey, so that he might be bitten and stung to death by flies and wasps. All this cruelty they exercised upon him because he would not do any thing towards rebuilding that idol temple. Nay, they came so far, that if he would give but one half-penny towards the charge they would release him. But with a noble Christian disdain, he refused the offer, though the advancing of one half-penny might have saved his life. In so doing he only lived up to that principle so much commended and so little practised; that Christians should endure the greatest sufferings, rather than commit the least sins.

(*c*) PRINCE OF CONDÉ AND CHARLES IX.—The prince of Condé being taken prisoner by Charles IX, king of France, and put to his choice whether he would go to mass or be put to death, or suffer perpetual imprisonment, his noble answer was, that by God's help he would never do the first, and for either of the latter he left it to the king's pleasure and God's providence.

(*d*) KAPIOLANI'S CONTEMPT OF THE GODDESS.—Owyhee is an island very remarkable for its volcanoes. One of these, named Peli, was long the object of religious worship by the natives, who believed it to be the residence of their gods. This worship has ceased. It has been abolished by the Christian courage of a female of rank, named Kapiolani. She proceeded fearlessly to Peli, accompanied by many friends and dependents. At the first precipice a number of them became alarmed and turned back. At the second, the rest earnestly entreated her to desist from her dangerous enterprise, and to tempt no further the powerful gods of the fires. But she proceeded, saying, "I will descend into the crater, and if I do not return safe, then continue to worship Peli; but if I come back unhurt, you must learn to adore the God that created Peli." With unhesitating step she reached the gloomy abyss, stirred the fiery lake, and completed an achievement seldom equalled in the annals of magnanimity. When she pushed the stick into the glowing lava, the idolatrous natives expected to see her instantly fall a sacrifice to their insulted goddess. Her safety effectually convinced them of their folly.

(*e*) FIRMNESS OF VARIOUS MARTYRS.—Cyprian, when on his

road to suffer martyrdom, was told by the emperor, that he would give him time to consider whether he had not better cast a grain of incense into the fire, in honor of idols, than die so degraded a death. The martyr nobly answered, "There needs no deliberation in the case."

John Huss was offered a pardon when at the stake, about to suffer for his attachment to Christ, if he would recant; his reply was, "I am here ready to suffer death."

Anne Askew, when asked under similar circumstances to avoid the flames, answered, "I came not here to deny my God and Master."

Mr. Thomas Hawkes, an Essex gentleman, said, on a like occasion, "If I had a hundred bodies, I would suffer them all to be torn in pieces, rather than recant."

When the cruel Bonner told John Ardly of the pain connected with burning, and how hard it must be to endure it, with a view of leading the martyr to recant, he replied, "If I had as many lives as I have hairs on my head, I would lose them all in the fire, before I would lose Christ."

Galeazius, a gentleman of great wealth, who suffered martyrdom at St. Angelo, in Italy, being much entreated by his friends to recant, replied, "Death is much sweeter to me with the testimony of truth, than life with its least denial."

(*f*) THE POTTER AND HENRY III.—Bernard de Palissy, a native of Agen, in France, was a maker of earthenware, at Saintes, and distinguished himself by his knowledge and talents. He was a Calvinist, and the French king, Henry III, said to him one day, that he should be compelled to give him up to his enemies, unless he changed his religion. "You have often said to me, sire," was the undaunted reply of De Palissy, "that you pitied me; but as for me, I pity you, who have given utterance to such words as, 'I shall be compelled.' These are unkingly words; and I say to you in royal phrase, that neither the Guises, nor all your people, nor yourself, are able to compel an humble manufacturer of earthenware to bend his knee before statues." Bernard was a man of humor, as well as of courage; and he would sometimes say, alluding to his trade, and his trust in Providence, "My only property is heaven and earth."

(*g*) THE PRAYING NEGRO.—Mr. Knibb relates the following circumstances relative to David, a deacon of his church:—A few years ago, one of the slave members belonging to the Baptist church, at Montego Bay, was banished from his home, and sent to the estate where David lived, to be cured of his praying. By the pious conversation of this exiled Christian negro, David was brought under serious concern for his soul, which ended in his conversion to God. David spoke to his fellow slaves about Jesus, and his love in dying for poor sinners. God, who despises not the humblest instruments, blessed the efforts of this poor negro, and, in a short time, about thirty on the estate began to pray, and at length built a small hut, in which, after the labors of the day, they might assemble and worship God. Tidings of these things reached the ears of the white persons employed on the estate, and David was summoned before his attorney, and asked whether he was teaching the slaves to pray. On replying in the affirmative, the hut was demolished and burnt, and David was stretched upon the earth, and flogged with the cart-whip till his flesh was covered with blood. Next Lord's day I missed my faithful deacon at the house of God. His afflicted wife came, and told me the sad tale of his sufferings, and informed me that his hands were bound, and his feet made fast in the stocks. Often did I inquire after him, and for him, and the same answered was returned, "Massa, him in the stocks:" till one morning, as I sat in my piazza, he appeared before the window. There he stood—I have his image now before me—he was handcuffed, barefoot, unable to wear his clothes from his yet unhealed back; his wife had fastened some of her garments round his lacerated body. I called him in, and said,

"David, David, what have you done?"

With a look of resignation I shall never forget, he replied,

"Don't ask me; ask him that bring me, massa."

Turning to the negro who had him in charge, I said,

"Well, what has this poor man done?"

"Him pray, massa," was the reply; "and buckra send him to the work-house for punishment."

I gave him some refreshment, (for in the state I have described he had walked thirteen miles under a burning sun,) and followed him to the work-house. He was chained to a fellow-slave by the neck, and sent to work on the public roads. The next day I went to visit him again, when I was informed by the supervisor of the work-house, that he had received orders to have him flogged again, as soon as his back was well enough to bear it. In these chains David remained for months; frequently I saw him, but never did I hear one murmur or one complaint except when he heard that the partner of his joys and sorrows was ill on the estate, and he was forbidden to go and see her.

At the end of three months he was liberated, and, returning to the estate, was asked,

"Now, sir, will you pray again?"

"Massa," said the persecuted disciple, "you know me is a good slave; but, if trouble come for dis, me must pray, and me must teach me broder to pray too."

Again he was immured in a dungeon and his feet made fast in the stocks.

(*h*) NOT FOR HIS KINGDOM.—The circumstances of the appointment of Dr. Ken as Bishop of Bath and Wells, were remarkable. King Charles the Second was engaged in erecting a palace at Winchester, and went down with his usual attendants to that city. One of the harbingers employed to arrange lodgings for the party, marked out the doctor's house, which he had in right of his prebend, for the temporary residence of Mrs. Eleanor Gwynne. The doctor, however, absolutely refused her admittance, declaring that "a woman of ill repute was not to be endured for a moment in the house of a clergyman;" and Mrs. G. was, in consequence, compelled to seek an abode elsewhere, to her own great inconvenience, and the indignation of those who urged the doctor to a compliance in the king's name; who, however, could obtain no other reply than the short sentence, "Not for his kingdom." No sooner, however, was application made to King Charles on behalf of another, for the bishopric of Bath and Wells, which became vacant immediately after, than the king promptly replied, "Who shall have Bath and Wells, but the little fellow who would not give poor Nelly a lodging?" Dr. Ken was, in consequence, appointed to the vacant see in the commencement of 1684.

(*i*) CALVIN AND ECKIUS.—Eckius being sent by the Pope, legate into France, upon his return took Geneva in his way, on purpose to see Calvin; and if occasion presented, to attempt reducing him to the Romish church. Eckius went privately to Calvin's house and introduced himself as a stranger who had heard much of his fame, and was come to wait upon him. Calvin invited him to come in, and he entered the house with him; where, discoursing of many things concerning religion, Eckius perceived Calvin to be an ingenuous and learned man, and desired to know if he had not a garden to walk in. To which Calvin replying he had, they both went into it; and there Eckius began to inquire of him, why he left the Roman church, and offered some arguments to persuade him to return; but Calvin could by no means be inclined to think of it. At last Eckius told him that he would put his life in his hands; and then said, he was Eckius the Pope's legate. At this discovery Calvin was not a little surprised, and begged his pardon that he had not treated him with that respect which was due to his quality. Eckius returned the compliment, and told him if he would come back to the Roman church, he would certainly procure for him a Cardinal's cap. But Calvin was not to be moved by such an offer. Eckius then asked him what revenue he had. He told the Cardinal he had that house and garden, and fifty livres per annum, besides an annual present of some wine and corn; on which he lived very contentedly. Eckius told him, that a man of his parts deserved a greater revenue; and then renewed his invitation to come over to the Romish church, promising him a better stipend if he would. But Calvin, giving him thanks, assured him he was well satisfied with his condition.

Eckius accepted Calvin's invitation to dine with him; and after dinner, at the request of Eckius, they visited the church which anciently was the cathedral. On their way Eckius pressed upon Calvin the present of a hundred pistoles to buy him books and to express his respect for him. But as they were coming out of the church, Calvin stopped him a little, and having explained to the persons who accompanied them how he had been presented by the stranger with a purse of gold, he said he would give it to the poor, and so deposited it in the poor-box that was kept there! Eckius was now convinced that all efforts to secure the apostacy of Calvin would be in vain, and made no further attempt.

174. FLATTERY.

(*a*) BEAUTY AND VANITY.—"I once knew," says Mr. Abbott, "a little boy of unusually bright and animated countenance. Every one who entered the house noticed the child, and spoke of his beauty. One day a gentleman called upon business, and being engaged in conversation, did not pay that attention to the child to which he was accustomed, and which he now began to expect as his due. The vain little fellow made many efforts to attract notice, but not succeeding, he at last placed himself full in front of the gentleman, and asked, 'Why don't you see how beautiful I be?

(*b*) THE MONARCH'S PROHIBITION.—One of the first acts performed by George III after his accession to the throne, was to issue an order, prohibiting any of the clergy who should be called to preach before him, from paying him any compliment in their discourses. His majesty was led to this from the fulsome adulation which Dr. Thomas Wilson, Prebendary of Westminster, thought proper to deliver in the chapel royal; and for which, instead of thanks, he received from his royal auditor a pointed reprimand, his majesty observing, "that he came to chapel to hear the praises of God, and not his own."

175 FORBEARANCE.

(*a*) DR. WALL'S INJURERS.—Dr. Wall, sometime Bishop of Norwich, who was as humble and courteous as he was learned and devout, used to say, "I would suffer a thousand wrongs rather than do one; I would suffer a hundred rather than return one; and endure many rather than complain of one, or obtain my right by contending: for I have always observed, that contending with one's superiors is foolish; with one's equals, is dubious; and with one's inferiors, is mean-spirited and sordid. Suits at law may be sometimes necessary, but he had need be more than a man who can manage them with justice and innocence."

(*b*) MAKING A DIFFERENCE.—Rev. Legh Richmond was once conversing with a brother clergyman on the case of a poor man who had acted inconsistently with his religious profession. After some angry and severe remarks on the conduct of such persons, the gentleman with whom he was discussing the case concluded by saying, "I have no notion of such pretences; I will have nothing to do with him." "Nay, brother, let us be humble and moderate. Remember who has said, 'making a difference:' with opportunity on the one hand, and Satan at the other, and the grace of God at neither, where should you and I be?"

(*c*) ELIOT AND HIS BRETHREN.—The attachment of the Rev. John Eliot, usually called "the apostle to the Indians," to peace and union among Christians was exceedingly great. When he heard ministers complain that some in their congregations were too difficult for them, the substance of his advice would be, "Brother, compass them!" "Brother, learn the meaning of those three little words—bear, forbear, forgive." His love of peace, indeed, almost led him to sacrifice right itself.

(*d*) SOUTH SEA ISLANDERS.—On February 2, 1817, Mr. Ellis, a Christian missionary, and his companions, on their voyage to Tahiti, touched at the island of Tubooi, to obtain provisions. Two Europeans, who were on the island, informed them that a canoe, bound for Anaa, one of the Paumotu islands, had recently touched at Tubooi, being driven out of its course by the northerly winds. The people on board the canoe, forty in number, had been to Tahiti, to receive instruction in Christianity, and were returning to their own country. They were intelligent, peaceable, and strict in their observance of the Sabbath. They exerted their influence to persuade the natives of Tubooi to cast away their idols, telling them of the one true God, and the Lord Jesus. The natives, however, treated them as enemies, destroyed their canoe, and forcibly took from them a musket. The Christians, on being asked why they did not resent these injuries, replied, that had they been heathens, they would immediately have fought: but having become Christians, they had embraced a religion opposed to war, and they were afraid of incurring the displeasure of Jehovah by unnecessarily engaging in it. Happy would it be were the inhabitants of the more civilized parts of the world, who profess the Christian religion, to imitate the conduct of the South Sea Islanders.

(*e*) EXAMPLE OF KILPIN.—Mr. Kilpin, of Bedford, father of the Rev. S. Kilpin, of Exeter, was distinguished for many Christian excellences. The following anecdote is related in the life of his son, in reference to his Christian forbearance.

Passing up the street one evening, a drunken man knocked Mr. Kilpin down, and rolled him into the gutter, exclaiming, "That's the place for you, John Bunyan!" The good man arose calmly, and returning to his family, related the circumstance; adding, that the honor of bearing such a name had outweighed the insult.

(*f*) CLAUDE AND THE PRISONER.—In the early part of the last century, when a violent spirit of opposition to true piety raged in France, M. de St. Claude, a man of eminent piety, was imprisoned in the Bastile. At the same time there was a man confined, of so ferocious and brutal a disposition, that no one dared to approach him. He seldom spoke without a volley of oaths and blasphemies, and struck every one who approached him with the utmost violence. Every expedient to humanize this monster had proved in vain, when the governor entreated Claude to undertake the work. His humility would have induced him to decline it, but persuasion prevailed.

Accordingly, the humble Christian was shut up with this human brute, who exhausted his ferocity in revilings, blows, and yet more savage tokens of the barbarity of his disposition. Whilst this treatment continued, silence, patience, and mildness, were the only reply of the man of God. His prayers achieved the rest. The monster, at length, looked on the face of his companion; suddenly threw himself at his feet, and embracing them, burst into a flood of tears; entreating his forgiveness, and besought him to give him instruction in the religion which thus influenced his conduct. He became entirely changed; pious, meek, and cheerful; and, even when his liberty was given him, he could scarcely be prevailed on to leave his Christian friend.

(*g*) THE CONVERTED PRIZE-FIGHTER.—The Rev. Mr. Symes, a Christian missionary in India, baptized a soldier who had been a noted prize-fighter, eminent in the ring in England, a powerful, lion-looking, lion-hearted man. With one blow he could level a strong man to the ground. He was the terror of many in the regiment. That man, to use his own phrase, "sauntered into Mr. Symes's chapel," and heard the gospel, and was alarmed. He returned again and again, and at last light broke in upon his mind, and he became a new creature. The change in such a character was, of course, marked and decisive: the lion was changed into a lamb. Two months after that, in the mess-room, some of those who stood in awe of him before, began to ridicule him. One of them said, "I'll put it to the test whether he is a Christian or not;" and taking a basin of hot soup, he threw it into his breast. The whole company gazed, in breathless silence, expecting that the lion would have started up, and murdered him on the spot; but, after he had torn open his waistcoat, and wiped his scalded breast, he calmly turned round, and said, "This is what I must expect: if I become a Christian, I must suffer persecution." His comrades were filled with astonishment.

(*h*) BISHOP COWPER AND HIS WIFE.—Bishop Cowper's wife, it is said, was much afraid that her husband would prejudice his health by an excess of study. When he was compiling his celebrated dictionary, she got into his study, during his absence, and collected all the notes he had been writing for eight years, and burned them; and when she had acquainted him with the fact, assured of the feeling of kindness in which even this improper act originated, he only remarked, "Woman, thou hast put me to eight years' study more."

(*i*) COTTON MATHER'S LIBELS.—Dr. Cotton Mather was remarkable for the sweetness of his temper. He took some interest in the political concerns of his country and on this account, as well as because he faithfully reproved iniquity, he had many enemies. Many abusive letters were sent him, all of which he tied up in a packet, and wrote upon the cover, "Libels;—Father forgive them."

(*j*) THE TWO STUDENTS.—Two students of one of our Universities had a slight misunderstanding. One of them was a warm-blooded Southron. He conceived himself insulted, and began to demand satisfaction, according to his perverse notions of honor. He was met with a Christian firmness and gentleness. The other calmly told his excited fellow-student he could give only Christian satisfaction in any case; that he was not conscious of having intended him either injury or insult, and that if he could be convinced he had wronged him at all, he was willing to make ample reparation. Fired with chivalrous indignation for a few moments, he discharged a volley of reproachful epithets, and threatened to chastise his cowardly insolence. But nothing could move the other's equanimity. Without the slightest indication of fear or servility, he met his opponent's violence with true heroism, declared that they had hitherto been friends, and he meant to maintain his friendly attitude, however he might be treated, and conjured the threatener to consider how unworthy of himself his present temper, language and conduct were. His manner, look, words, tone, had their effect. The flush of anger turned to a blush of shame and compunction. The subdued Southron stepped frankly forward, reached forth his trembling hand, and exclaimed—"*I have spoken and acted like a fool; can you forgive me?*" "With all my heart," was the cordial response. Instantly they were locked in each other's embrace; reconciliation was complete; and they were evermore fast friends.

176. FORGIVENESS OF INJURIES.

(*a*) PHILIP AND THE AMBASSADOR.—Philip, king of Macedon, discovered great moderation, even when he was spoken to in shocking and injurious terms. At the close of an audience which he gave to some Athenian ambassadors who were come to complain of some act of hostility, he asked whether he could do them any service. "The greatest service thou couldst do us," said Demochares, "would be to hang thyself." Philip, though he perceived al the persons present were highly offended at these words, answered with the utmost calmness of temper, "Go, tell your superiors, that those who dare make use of such insolent language, are more haughty, and less peaceably inclined than those who can forgive them."

(*b*) CRANMER AND THE TRAITORS.—Archbishop Cranmer appeared almost alone, in the higher classes, as the friend of truth in evil times, and a plot was formed to take away his life. The providence of God, however, so ordered it, that the papers which would have completed the plan were intercepted, and traced to their authors, one of whom lived in the archbishop's family, and the other he had greatly served. He took these men apart in his palace, and told them that some persons in his confidence had disclosed his secrets, and even accused him of heresy. They loudly censured such villany, and declared the traitors to be worthy of death; one of them adding, that if an executioner was wanted, he would perform the office himself. Struck with their perfidy, after lifting up his voice to heaven, lamenting the depravity of man, and thanking God for his preservation, he produced their letters, and inquired if they knew them. They now fell on their knees, confessed their crimes, and implored forgiveness. Cranmer mildly expostulated with them on the evil of their conduct, forgave them, and never again alluded to their treachery. His forgiveness of injuries was so well known, that it became a by-word, "Do my lord of Canterbury an ill turn, and you make him your friend for ever."

(*c*) GENERAL OGLETHORPE AND HIS SERVANT.—The Rev. J. Wesley, in the course of his voyage to America, hearing an unusual noise in the cabin of General Oglethorpe, the governor of Georgia, with whom he sailed, stepped in to inquire the cause of it. The general addressed him, "Mr. W. you must excuse me, I have met with a provocation too great for man to bear. You know the only wine I drink is Cyprus wine; I therefore provided myself with several dozens of it, and this villain Grimaldi," (his foreign servant, who was present, and almost dead with fear,) "has drank up the whole of it; but I will be revenged on him. I have ordered him to be tied hand and foot, and be carried to the man-of-war which sails with us. The rascal should have taken care how he used me so, for I never forgive." "Then I hope, sir," said Mr. W. looking calmly at him, "you never sin." The general was quite confounded at the reproof; and putting his hand into his pocket, took out a bunch of keys, which he threw at Grimaldi: "There, villain," said he, "take my keys, and behave better for the future."

(*d*) THE CHRISTIAN'S PERSECUTOR.—"What great matter," said a heathen tyrant to a Christian, while he was beating him almost to death—"What great matter did Christ ever do you?" "Even this," answered the Christian, "that I can forgive you, though you use me so cruelly."

(*e*) MATTHEW HALE'S ENEMY.—A person who had done Sir Matthew Hale a great injury, came afterwards to him for his advice in the settlement of his estate. Sir Matthew gave his advice very frankly to him, but would accept of no fee for it. When he was asked how he could use a man so kindly who had wronged him so much, his answer was, he thanked God, he had learned to forgive injuries.

(*f*) THE NOBLEMAN'S PRAYER.—In 1831, when the cholera first broke out in Hungary, the Sclavack peasants of the North were fully persuaded they were poisoned by the nobles, to get rid of them, and they, in consequence, rose in revolt, and committed the most dreadful excesses. One gentleman was seized by the peasants of the village, among whom he had been, up to that moment, exceedingly popular, dragged from his home to the public street, and then beaten for several successive hours, to make him confess where he had concealed the poison. At last wearied with the trouble of inflicting blows, they carried him to the smith, and applied hot ploughshares to his feet, three several times. As the poor man, exhausted with this dreadful torture, and finding all his entreaties and explanations vain, fell back from weakness, and was apparently about to expire, those beautiful words of our dying Savior escaped from his lips, "Lord, forgive them; for they know not what they do!" As by a miracle, the savage rage of the peasantry was calmed. Struck at once with the innocence of the victim, and enormity of their crime, they fled on every side, and concealed themselves from view.

(*g*) COLORED WOMAN AND THE SAILOR.—A worthy old colored woman in the city of New-York, was one day walking along the street, on some errand to a neighboring store, with her tobacco pipe in her mouth, quietly smoking. A jovial sailor, rendered a little mischievous by liquor, came sawing down the street, and, when opposite our good Phillis, saucily crowded her aside, and with a pass of his hand knocked her pipe out of her mouth. He then halted to hear her fret at his trick, and enjoy a laugh at her expense. But what was his astonishment, when she meekly picked up the pieces of her broken pipe, without the least resentment in her manner, and giving him a dignified look of mingled sorrow, kindness and pity, said, "God forgive you, my son, as I do." It touched a tender cord in the heart of the rude tar. He felt ashamed, condemned and repentant. The tear started in his eye; he must make reparation. He heartily confessde his error, and thrusting both hands into his two full pockets of "*change*," forced the contents upon her, exclaiming, "God bless you, kind mother, I'll never do so again."

177. FORTUNE-TELLING.

(*a*) BYRON AND THE FORTUNE-TELLER.—Lord Byron, when a boy, was warned by a fortune-teller, that he should die in the 37th year of his age. That idea haunted him, and in his last illness, he mentioned it as precluding all hope of his recovery. It repressed, his physician says, that energy of spirit so necessary for nature in struggling with disease. He talked of two days of the week as unlucky days, on which nothing would tempt him to commence any matter of importance; and mentioned as an excuse for indulging such fancies, that his friend Shelley, the poet, had a familiar who had warned him that he should perish by drowning, and such was the fate of that highly gifted but misguided man.

(*b*) THE PENITENT FORTUNE-TELLER.—A reformed gipsy, making a visit to a parish in which one of her children was born, near Basingstoke, entered the cottage of an old couple who sold fruit, &c. Tea being proposed, the old woman expressed her surprise that she had not seen her visitor for so long a time, saying she was glad she was come, as she wanted to tell her many things, meaning future events. She mentioned a great deal that another gipsy woman had told her; on which the reformed one exclaimed—"Don't believe her, dame. It is all lies. She knows no more about it than you do. If you trust to what she says, you will be deceived." The old woman was still more surprised, and asked how she, who had so often told their fortunes, and had promised them such good luck, could be so much altered? The woman, taking her Testament from her bosom, replied, "I have learned from this blessed book, and from my kind friends, 'that all liars shall have their portion in the lake that burneth with fire and brimstone;' and rather than tell fortunes again, I would starve."

178. FRETFULNESS.

(*a*) "I DON'T WANT TO GO TO HEAVEN."—There was a clergyman, who was of nervous temperament, and often became quite vexed, by finding his little grandchildren in his study. One day, one of these little children was standing by his mother's side, and she was speaking to him of heaven.

"Ma," said he, "I don't want to go to heaven."

"Do not want to go to heaven, my son?"

"No, Ma, I'm sure I don't."

"Why not, my son?"

"Why, grandpa will be there, won't he?"

"Why, yes, I hope he will."

"Well, as soon as he sees us, he will come scolding along, and say, 'Whew, whew, what are these boys here for?' I don't want to go to heaven if grandpa is going there."

(*b*) BAIT FOR EVERY AGE.—Mr. Rumsey, a pious physician, speaking of his sinful infirmities, observed, "I have to lament the irritability of my temper in my old age." He had been fond of repeating a conversation which he had in the early part of his life with a pious friend. He observed to this person, that he thought if he arrived at old age, he should be subject to fewer temptations than at an earlier period; but his more experienced friend told him, that "the devil had a bait for every age," and Mr. Rumsey was at length fully convinced of the truth of the remark.

(*c*) THE TWO GARDENERS.—Two gardeners, who were neighbors, had their crops of early peas killed by frost; one of them came to condole with the other on this misfortune. "Ah!" cried he, "how unfortunate we have been, neighbor! do you know I have done nothing but fret ever since. But you seem to have a fine healthy crop coming up already; what are these?" "These!" cried the other gardener, "why these are what I sowed immediately after my loss." "What! coming up already?" cried the fretter. "Yes; while you were fretting, I was working." "What! don't you fret when you have a loss?" "Yes; but I always put it off until after I have repaired the mischief." "Why then you have no need to fret at all." "True," replied the industrious gardener, "and that's the very reason."

179. FRIENDSHIP.

(*a*) PYTHIAS AND DAMON.—When Damon was sentenced, by Dionysius of Syracuse, to die on a certain day, he begged permission, in the interim, to retire to his own country, to set the affairs of his disconsolate family in order. This the tyrant intended peremptorily to refuse, by granting it, as he conceived, on the impossible conditions of his procuring some one to remain as hostage for his return, under equal forfeiture of life. Pythias heard the conditions, and did not wait for an application upon the part of Damon: he instantly offered himself as security for his friend; which being accepted, Damon was immediately set at liberty. The king and all the courtiers were astonished at this action; and therefore, when the day of execution drew near, his majesty had the curiosity to visit Pythias in his confinement. After some conversation on the subject of friendship, in which the tyrant delivered it as his opinion, that self-interest was the sole mover of human actions; as for virtue, friendship, benevolence, love of one's country, and the like, he looked upon them as terms invented by the wise to keep in awe and impose upon the weak, "My lord," said Pythias, with a firm voice and noble aspect, "I would it were possible that I might suffer a thousand deaths, rather than my friend should fail in any article of his honor. He cannot fail therein, my lord: I am as confident of his virtue, as I am of my own existence. But I pray, I beseech the gods, to preserve the life and integrity of my Damon together: oppose him, ye winds, prevent the eagerness and impatience of his honorable endeavors, and suffer him not to arrive, till by death I have redeemed a life a thousand times of more consequence, of more value, than my own; more estimable to his lovely wife, to his precious little children, to his friends, to his country. Oh leave me not to die the worst of deaths in my Damon." Dionysius was awed and confounded by the dignity of these sentiments, and by the manner in which they were uttered: he felt his heart struck by a slight sense of invading truth: but it served rather to perplex than undeceive him. The fatal day arrived. Pythias was brought forth, and walked amidst the guards with a serious but satisfied air, to the place of execution. Dionysius was already there, he was exalted on a moving throne, which was drawn by six white horses, and sat pensive and attentive to the prisoner. Pythias came, he vaulted lightly on the scaffold, and beholding for some time the apparatus of his death, he turned with a placid countenance, and addressed the spectators: "My prayers are heard," he cried, "the gods are propitious; you know, my friends, that the winds have been contrary till yesterday. Damon could not come, he could not conquer impossibilities; he will be here to-morrow, and the blood which is shed to-day shall have ransomed the life of my friend. Oh, could I erase from your bosoms every doubt, every mean suspicion of the honor of the man for whom I am about to suffer, I should go to my death, even as I would to my bridal. Be it sufficient in the mean time, that my friend will be found noble; that his truth is unimpeachable; that he will speedily prove it; that he is now on his way, hurrying on, accusing himself, the adverse elements, and the gods: but I haste to prevent his speed; executioner do your office." As he pronounced the last words, a buzz began to rise among the remotest of the people; a distant voice was heard, the crowd caught the words, and "Stop, stop the execution!" was repeated by the whole assembly: a man came at full speed: the throng gave way to his approach: he was mounted on a steed of foam: in an instant he was off his horse, on the scaffold, and clasped Pythias in his arms. "You are safe," he cried, "you are safe, my friend, my beloved friend: the gods be praised, you are safe, I now have nothing but death to suffer, and am delivered from the anguish of those reproaches which I gave myself for having endangered a life so much dearer than my own." Pale, cold, and half-speechless in the arms of his Damon, Pythias replied in broken accents, "Fatal haste! Cruel impatience! What envious powers have wrought impossibilities in your favor! But I will not be wholly disappointed. Since I cannot die to save, I will not survive you." Dionysius heard, beheld, and considered all with astonishment. His heart was touched, he wept, and leaving his throne, he ascended the scaffold: "Live, live, ye incomparable pair!" cried he: "ye have borne unquestionable testimony to the existence of virtue; and that virtue equally evinces the existence of a God to reward it. Live happily, and with renown: and, Oh! form me by your precepts, as ye have invited me by your example, to be worthy of the participation of so sacred a friendship."

(*b*) THE VICAR AND MASSILLON.—Some years ago, a traveller, passing through Clermont, wished to see the country house in which the celebrated Massillon used to spend the greater part of the year, and therefore applied to an old vicar, who, since the death of the bishop, had never entered the house. He consented, however, to gratify the traveller, notwithstanding the profound grief he expected to suffer from revisiting a place dear to his remembrance. They accordingly set out together, and the vicar pointed out to the stranger the different places of importance. "There," said he, with tears in his eyes, "is the alley in which the excellent prelate used to walk with us; there is the arbor in which he used to sit and read; this is the garden he took pleasure in cultivating with his own hands." Then they entered the house, and when they came to the room where Massillon died, "This," said the vicar, "is the place where we lost him;" and as he pronounced these words his affectionate feelings overcame him, and he fainted away.

(*c*) DR. WATTS' LONG VISIT.—A lady of quality being on a visit to Dr. Watts, the doctor thus accosted her: "Madam, your ladyship is come to see me on a very remarkable day!" "Why is this day so remarkable?" answered the Countess. "This very day thirty years," replied the doctor, "I came to the house of my good friend Sir Thomas Abney, intending to spend but one single week under his friendly roof, and I have extended my visit to his family to the length of exactly thirty years." Lady Abney, who was present, immediately said to the doctor, "Sir, what you term a long thirty years' visit, I consider as the best visit my family ever received."

(*d*) CUDJOE AND MURRAY.—The following account of the conduct of an unenlightened African negro, is furnished in Captain Snelgrave's account of his voyage to Guinea:

A New England sloop, trading there in 1752, left a second mate, William Murray, sick on shore, and sailed without him. Murray was at the house of a black named Cudjoe, with whom he contracted an acquaintance during their trade. He recovered, and the sloop being gone, he continued with his black friend till some other opportunity should offer of his getting home. In the mean time, a Dutch ship came into the road, and some of the blacks, coming on board her, were treacherously seized, and carried off as their slaves. The relations and friends, transported with sudden rage, ran into the house of Cudjoe, to take revenge by killing Murray. Cudjoe stopped them at the door, and demanded what they wanted. "The white men," said they, "have carried away our brothers and sons, and we will kill all white men. Give us the white man you have in your house, for we will kill him." "Nay," said Cudjoe, "the white men that carried away your relations are bad men; kill them when you can take them: but this white man is a good man, and you must not kill him." "But he is a white man," they cried, "and the white men are all bad men, and we will kill them all." "Nay," said he; "you must not kill a man who has done no harm, only for being white. This man is my friend; my house is his post; I am his soldier, and must fight for him; you must kill me before you can kill him. What good man will ever come again under my roof, if I let my floor be stained by a good man's blood?" The negroes, seeing his resolution, and being convinced by his discourse that they were wrong, went away ashamed. In a few days Murray ventured abroad again with his friend Cudjoe, when several of them took him by the hand, and told him they were glad they had not killed him, for he was a good man.

(*e*) COL. BYRD AND THE CHIEF.—It is related in Mr. Jefferson's Notes on Virginia, that Col. Byrd of that state was sent at a certain time to the Cherokee nation to transact some business with them. "It happened," says this writer, "that some of our disorderly people had just killed one or two of that nation. It was therefore purposed in the council of the Cherokees, that Col. Byrd should be put to death in revenge for the loss of their countrymen. Among them was a chief called Silouee, who, on some former occasion, had contracted an acquaintance and friendship with Col. Byrd. He came to him every night in his tent, and told him not to be afraid, they should not kill him. After many days' deliberation, however, the determination was, contrary to Silouee's expectation, that Byrd should be put to death, and some warriors were dispatched as executioners. Silouee attended them, and when they entered the tent, he threw himself between them and Byrd, and said to the warriors, 'This man is my friend; before you can get at him, you must kill me.' On this they returned, and the council respected the principle so much as to recede from their determination.'

GAMBLING.

180. Sustained by Fraud.

(*a*) THE CHEATER CHEATED.—There is no end to the dishonest tricks of professional gamblers. One of these gentry will often deal himself six or seven cards when he should have but five, and if he can make a good hand by laying out the two poorest in his lap he will do so; or if he cannot make a good hand, he will take the two best to help him in his next hand. The following case, which occurred on a western steamboat, shows how men will play more than their number. A gambler was playing with a man whom he mistook for a green Hoosier that knew nothing of playing scientifically. But he was sadly deceived. The gambler, from the beginning played somewhat carelessly, supposing it needed no science to beat the Hoosier; but the gambler lost and commenced playing as scientifically as he could. He still lost, and finally lost nearly all he had, before he quit; and after quitting they went to the bar to drink. The gambler said to the Hoosier, "You beat any man for luck I ever played with; I've lost my money with you, and it makes no difference; I will be honest with you; you did not know it, but I played six cards all the time and your luck beat it." "Well," said the Hoosier, "since you have been so frank, I will also be frank; I have played seven cards all the way through from the word go; besides stocking and palming occasionally for the sake of variety. The gambler was greatly surprised and swore that he would not have supposed, that he much more than knew one card from another; but he was deceived in the man, and it would not have done for him to have shown any anger, as he first confessed having cheated the Hoosier, who was in fact a most expert gambler, and had purposely assumed that disguise.

(*b*) A PRIZE IN A LOTTERY.—The proprietors of lotteries are sometimes swindled through the unfaithfulness of their agents; and thus it happens that a large prize is sometimes drawn and trumpeted forth, which the craft of the proprietors would otherwise have retained. A case, says Mr. Green, came to my knowledge, of a man who drew a capital prize. The mode of effecting this was as follows:—An agent who was stationed in a town some distance from the principal establishment, made two confidents, who doubtlessly acted readily with him from the hope of gain. One of these was the post-master of the town, and the other an acquaintance, a patron of the lottery. The duty of the agent was to transmit to the principal office all unsold tickets, by the first mail that left after the known hour of drawing. This mail also conveyed the lists of the drawing; but, in a regular manner of proceeding, they would not have been accessible to the agent before the departure of the agent with his unsold tickets. By making a confident of the post-master, however, he received the lists as quick as possible after the mail arrived and before it had been assorted. He then examined his unsold tickets, and if any considerable prize remained, he would take it from among the unsold tickets, and despatch the remainder to the principal office, and give the prize to the other confident, each one giving out that the ticket had been sold to him; and accordingly the prize would be claimed and paid though fraudulently obtained. In this particular case the capital prize was drawn, and it appeared that the ticket-holder appropriated all the money to his own use, as he was known to buy much property shortly afterwards. It is believed also by those who were acquainted with the incident that he never divided with the rascally agent; and thus was the cheater cheated, who in his wrath, let out some of the secrets of the manner in which the prize was obtained.

(*c*) THE HORSE-RACE.—Cheats are used in horse-racing as in other species of gambling. There was a man in Kentucky noted for making match races; and a club of men went to the expense of procuring a fast horse in order to beat one he boasted much of. The jockey closed the agreement for the race, with a bet of about two thousand dollars; and the club was very certain of beating the jockey. When the day arrived for the race, and the horses started, the club horse went ahead of the jockey's immediately, and took the inside track nearest the fence. At the first turn, he fell to his knees, and while recovering himself, the slow horse got ahead of him, and after running some distance, the fast horse fell again, and the slow horse won the race. The fast horse became lame from his fall; his owners were much chagrined at their misfortune, and on the next morning, went to the jockey's lodgings in order to close another race with him. The landlord informed them that he had left the night before, soon after the race was over. His sudden departure, after a successful race, excited their suspicions of foul play. They then examined the track and found the jockey had dug a number of small holes on the inside of the track, placing gourds in them and spreading a little loose dirt over them; and when the fast horse ran close to the fence he would tread on these gourds, and would sink and stumble; thus giving the slow the advantage. When this discovery was made, they decided on having a race at all events, and so chased the jockey nearly a hundred miles, but did not succeed in overtaking him.

(*d*) TABLE WITH A HOLLOW LEG.—There are men apparently engaged in business, whose stores are, in the upper apartments, extensive gambling establishments. Of those who go to such places, few ever come out winners; because there are fixed contrivances for cheating those who are invited in to play, of which they are wholly ignorant. A reformed gambler states that he became acquainted with a merchant in New Orleans, who had in his store such a room. He had a great number to play with him, and all of them continually lost. Men who were professed gamblers, here found their tricks and artifices set at nought, and themselves losing at every trial. They became dissatisfied, and suspected some extraordinary trick being used. They combined for the sake of ascertaining, and soon learned from some person in his employment, the whole secret. His table was constructed with a hollow leg, and in that leg, where the knee would rest against it, was fixed a small peg, which would strike against his knee on a small wire being pulled, which was attached to the peg, and passed out under the bottom of the leg and under the floor to the side of the room, thence up stairs directly over the table. And from the centre of a fine moulding in plaster, hung a rich lamp; the moulding was hollow, and so constructed that a man who was a secret partner, could be overhead, and see into the hands below, and give his partner signs from above, previously agreed upon by pulling the wire. This advantage was sufficient to ruin any man who played with him, and enabled him to make money faster than by mercantile business, which in fact he cared nothing about only as a cover for his gambling. This man's establishment was broken up and he fled.

181. Destroys Natural Sensibility.

(*a*) A SCANDALOUS WAGER.—Well did Dr. Nott say, "The finished gambler has no heart—he would play at his brother's funeral—he would gamble upon his mother's coffin." Horace Walpole mentions an anecdote of a man having in his time dropped down dead at the door of White's club house, into which he was carried; the members of the club immediately made bets whether he was dead or not; and upon its being proposed to bleed him, the wagerers for his death interposed, alleging that it would effect the fairness of the bet.

(*b*) A GAME WITH A CORPSE.—The desperate depravity to which gambling reduces its votaries is strikingly illustrated in the case of three gamblers here related. They determined on a game, which was doubtless meant to show their utter contempt of all things sacred in this world and the next. Accordingly they enter at night the charnel house and take from thence a corpse that very day placed in the vault. They bear the deceased into the cathedral, pass within the chancel, light up one of the candles before the altar, seat the grim corpse by the *communion table*, and gathering around the table themselves, proceed to engage in a game of cards!! Shameless, sacrilegious doings that none but gamblers could think of without shuddering!!

The above fact is said by Rev. Wm. B. Tappan of Boston, to rest on good authority and he has accordingly made it the subject of a short poem on gambling.

182. Leads to Bankruptcy and Suicide.

(*a*) NINE HUNDRED DOLLARS FOR A BUTTON.—"I was well acquainted," says Mr. Green, the reformed gambler, "with the circumstance of a young man starting to go to the hot springs of Arkansas. He was a man who had acquired by honesty and industry about nine hundred dollars. He had been in bad health for some time, and concluded to visit the springs to recruit his health. On his arrival at the mouth of White River, he was detained for a boat, and while there he was induced to play cards. I am unable to say at this time, what was the game that he played, but he won some forty or fifty dollars and the game broke up. After the game was broken up, one of the gamblers pulled out a button and bantered the young man to win it at "faro" and he pulled out a quarter and bet it against the button, and the banker won. He tried again and again, until he lost some three or four dollars, to win the button, and then went to bed. The banker had now several persons betting small bets on the game, and had won some eight or ten dollars, and there was quite a noise and bustle going on. The young man, who had quit and gone to bed, got up, and felt a strong propensity to win all. He began betting on the game again, and in a short time lost the whole of his nine hundred dollars trying to win a button; for that was all he could have won, as the man had no money at first but what he had won from the young man. The young man was obliged to make his way home, without his health being benefited, and without his money.

(*b*) THE RUINED MERCHANT.—A writer in the N. Y. Observer for 1831 says: A few years since, the large steamer M—— set out from New Orleans on an upward voyage, having on board much freight, and many passengers. Among them were several merchants who had large amounts in sugar, molasses, coffee, &c., on board. Soon after the boat started they commenced gambling, and continued without intermission until after ten o'clock at night. The captain informed them, that it was contrary to the rules of the boat that they should play in the cabin after that hour. They protested, demurred, and entreated. But he was inexorable. At length he consented to their going to a small private room; but enjoined it upon them that there must be no *fighting*. Four of them renewed the game with excited interest. The captain having occasion to be up all night, went, about three o'clock, into their room. To his surprise he found them just on the point of fighting. Pistols and dirks were drawn! At his interposition and command, their weapons were put up. The cause of the quarrel was this: One merchant had lost all the money he had with him, and all his large cargo on board. The loser desired his merchandise to be estimated at the retail price where he resided, and to which place the boat was bound. But the marble-hearted winner insisted upon the New Orleans price as the basis of the calculation, and which would have left the loser in his debt to a large amount, for which he demanded a due-bill! At the remonstrance of the captain, he ceased to insist upon this, and the bill of lading having been transferred in due form to the winner, the miserable loser went home without a dollar to pay even his passage, to tell (if he could do it) to his wife and children the story of his folly, and to become a *bankrupt!*

(*c*) THE FIREMAN'S STAKES.—A colored fireman, on board a steamboat running from St. Louis to New Orleans, having lost all his money at poker with his companions, staked his clothing, and being still unfortunate, pledged his own freedom for a small amount. Losing this, the bets were doubled, and he finally, at one desperate hazard, ventured his own value as a slave, and laid down his free papers to represent the stake. He lost, suffered his certificates to be destroyed, and was actually sold by the winner to a slave dealer, who hesitated not to take him at a small discount upon his asserted value.

(*d*) THE FATAL GAME.—By the device called *hockelty* in playing *faro*, professional gamesters in the Southern States, have been known to make thousands of dollars out of the uninitiated in a single season. "There is one instance," says J. H. Green, "that I shall never forget. It occurred in New Orleans about the year 1833. A planter, who lived near Vicksburgh, was very fond of play. He went to New Orleans to trade and sell his produce; and while there was invited to a faro bank. He lost, and during his play, he was caught in hockelty for twenty-two hundred dollars at one bet. The dealer had won from him about eighteen thousand dollars, and this bet was the last of his money. The effect of this loss may be more easily imagined than described. In a few moments he drew a pistol and blew out his brains. I have no doubt that the citizens of Warrington, Mississippi, will know the person here spoken of, as I understand his family or relatives lived in or near that place. Such have been the baneful effects of this game, that it was a matter of almost daily occurrence for some one to stab or be stabbed in the vile haunts of these wicked men."

(*e*) LOTTERY AND SUICIDE.—In 1833 an adventurer in lotteries committed suicide in the city of Boston, by drowning himself. The fate of this unfortunate man contains one of those impressive moral lessons, which address us with a power which no uninspired lips can do. He was in the employment of one of the most respectable houses in the city, highly esteemed and respected by the members of it, and in the receipt of a liberal salary. About a year before, he had the misfortune to draw a prize in the lottery, and from that moment his ruin was sealed. The regular earnings of honest industry were no longer enough for him—visions of splendid prizes were continually flitting before his eyes, and he plunged at once into the intoxicating excitement of lotteries. He soon became deeply involved, and his access to the funds of the firm, held out to him a temptation which he could not resist. He appropriated to himself considerable sums from time to time, continually deluded by the hope that a turn of the wheel would give him the means of replacing them. But that turn never came; fortune gave him but one smile, and that was a fatal one. He saw that detection would soon come, and that the punishment and the shame of a felon would succeed to the consideration and respect he had always enjoyed, and he had not courage to wait the moment of disclosure. He sought refuge in death; and added to his other sins the horrible act of self-murder! He left a memorandum which contained an account of the circumstances that made life intolerable to him.

(*f*) SUICIDE OF THE OFFICER OF THE GUARD.—A writer in the London New Monthly Magazine, who resided some time in Paris, relates the following account of a fact which passed under his own observation.

"Though I never in my life won or lost five pounds at play, I was a frequent visitor at Frascati I went as a looker-on, and to confess the truth, for the purpose of indulging in the excitement occasioned by watching the various chances and changes of the game, and their effects upon those who were more seriously interested in them. Upon one occasion, I absolutely grew giddy from anxiety, whilst watching the countenance of an officer of the *Garde Royale*, who stood opposite me, and waiting the turn of a card which was to decide whether he should, at once, return a beggar to his home, or his certain fate be deferred till a few hours, or a few nights later. It appeared to be his last stake. The perspiration was falling from his brow, not in drops, but in a stream. He won; and a friend who accompanied him dragged him out of the room. Some nights afterwards I saw this person again. He was losing considerably, yet he endured his losses with apparent calmness. Once when a large stake was swept from him, he just muttered between his teeth, whilst his lips were curled with a bitter smile, "C'est bien; tres bien." After this, he silently watched the game through five or six deals, but did not play. I concluded he had lost all. Suddenly and fiercely he turned to the dealer, and in a tone of voice almost amounting to a scream, he exclaimed, "C'est mon sang que vous voulez—le voila." He at the same time drew from his pockets two notes of five hundred francs each, and, dashing them down on the table, he rushed into a corner of the room, hid his face, covered his ears with his hands, as if dreading to hear the announcement of the result of his speculation, and literally yelled aloud. It was awful! After a few seconds he returned to his place. His last stake was lost! He twice drew his handkerchief across his forehead, but he uttered not a word. Presently he asked for a glass of *eau-sucre*, and having swallowed it, he slowly walked away. The next morning his servant found him sitting in an arm chair, with his sword thrust to the very hilt, sticking in his throat

183. Miscellaneous.

(*a*) GAMBLERS CONFOUNDED BY A BIBLE.—The Rev. Mr. W., now a Missionary at the Sandwich Islands, a short time before he left this country, took passage from New York to New Haven, in a packet. In the evening a company of fellow passengers, who were quite profane, gathered round a table on which was the only light burning in the cabin, and soon became deeply engaged in gambling. Mr. W., after reflecting some time on the best means of reproving them, drew a Bible from his trunk, and politely requested that he might have a seat at the same table for the purpose of reading. The sight of the Bible at once stopped their swearing; and after gambling in total silence about ten minutes, they all left the table and went upon deck! thus evincing that the silent reproofs of a good man, with the Bible in his hand, are too loud and too pointed for the guilty consciences of gamblers to endure.

184. GENEROSITY.

(*a*) DEMETRIUS AND THE ATHENIANS.—It is related of Demetrius, (surnamed the *Conqueror of cities*,) that having received a marked and undoubted provocation, he laid siege to the city of Athens. The inhabitants made a desperate resistance; but were at last obliged to surrender, in consequence of great scarcity of provisions. Demetrius then ordered them, with the exception of the women and children, to be assembled together in one place, and to be surrounded with armed soldiers. Every one was in the greatest fear, conscious how much they had injured him, and expecting every moment to be put to death. It is not surprising, that they were overwhelmed with joy and admiration, when they heard him with a magnanimity honorable to human nature, thus address them:—"I wish to convince you, O Athenians, how ungenerously you have treated me; for it was not to an enemy that your assistance was refused, but to a prince who loved you, who still loves you, and who wishes to revenge himself only by granting your pardon, and being still your friend. Return to your own homes; while you have been here my soldiers have been filling your houses with provisions."

(*b*) PARKHURST'S GENEROSITY.—Mr. Parkhurst, the celebrated lexicographer, had a tenant who fell considerably behind in the payment of the rent for his farm, which he had taken at five hundred pounds per annum. It was represented to Mr. P. that the rent was too high, and a new valuation was made. It was then agreed that four hundred and fifty pounds should be the annual payment; and when this was done, Mr. P. considering that the rent must always have been too high, unasked, immediately struck off fifty pounds a year from the commencement of the lease, and refunded to the farmer all that he had received more than the above sum. In this act justice and generosity were combined.

(*c*) GLANVILLE AND HIS BROTHER.—The father of that eminent lawyer, Mr. Sergeant Glanville, who lived in the days of Charles II. had a good estate, which he intended to settle on his eldest son; but he proving vicious, and affording no hope of reformation, he devolved it upon the sergeant, who was his second son. Upon his father's death, the eldest son, finding that what he had hitherto considered as the mere threat of his father was really true, became greatly dejected, and, in a short period, his character underwent an entire change. His brother, observing this, invited him, with a party of his friends, to a feast; and after several other dishes had been removed, he ordered one, covered up, to be set before his brother, which, on being examined, was found to contain the writings of the estate. The sergeant then told him that he had now done what he was sure their father would have done, had he lived to witness the happy change they all saw; and that he therefore freely conveyed to him the whole property.

(*d*) THE GENEROUS HEIR.—In the month of September, 1801, W. T. M., dying without a will, his large property, which was chiefly in landed estates, devolved to his eldest son. By this circumstance the eight younger children were unprovided for; but this gentleman, with a generosity seldom equalled, and which does honor to Christianity, immediately made over to his younger brothers and sisters three considerable estates, which were about two-thirds of the whole property. This munificence is the more extraordinary, as he had a young and increasing family of his own. On a friend remonstrating with him on his conduct, his answer was, "I have enough; and am determined that all my brothers and sisters shall be satisfied."

(*e*) A RARE EXECUTOR.—About the year 1772, a grocer, of the name of Higgins, died, and left a considerable sum to a gentleman in London, saying to him, at the time that he made his will, "I do not know that I have any relations, but should you ever by accident hear of such, give them some relief." The gentleman, though thus left in full and undisputed possession of a large fortune, on which no person could have any legal claim, advertised for the next of kin to the deceased; and, after some months were spent in inquiries, he at length discovered a few distant relatives. He called them together to dine with him, and after distributing the whole of the money, according to the different degrees of consanguinity, paid the expenses of advertising out of his own pocket.

185. GOD, EXISTENCE OF.

(*a*) GOD'S SPIRIT AND MAN'S SPIRIT.—As a missionary in India was catechising the children of one of the schools, a Brahmin interrupted him, by saying that the spirit of man and the Spirit of God were one. In order to show him the absurdity of such a declaration, the missionary called upon the boys to refute it, by stating the difference between the spirit of man and God. They readily gave the following answers:—"The spirit of man is created—God is its Creator: the spirit of man is full of sin—God is a pure Spirit: the spirit of man is subject to grief—God is infinitely blessed, and incapable of suffering: these two spirits, therefore," replied the boys, "can never be one."

(*b*) A MUTE'S IDEA OF GOD'S ETERNITY.—One of the deaf and dumb pupils in the institution of Paris, being desired to express his idea of the eternity of the Deity, replied, "It is duration, without beginning or end; existence without bound or dimension; present, without past or future. His eternity is youth without infancy or old age; life without birth or death; to-day without yesterday or to-morrow."

(*c*) LESSON FROM A LEAF.—When the Rev. John Thorpe, of Masborough, in Yorkshire, (Eng.) had preached for about two years, he was greatly harassed with temptations to atheism, which continued, with a few intervals, many months. His distress sometimes, on this account, was so great, as to embarrass his mind beyond description. At length, however, he was happily delivered, by the following occurrence:—

Passing through a wood, with a design to preach in a neighboring village, while he was surveying his hand, a leaf accidentally stuck between his fingers. He felt a powerful impression to examine the texture of the leaf. Holding it between his eye and the sun, and reflecting upon its exquisitely curious and wonderful formation, he was led into an extensive contemplation on the works of creation. Tracing these back to their first cause, he had, in a moment, such a conviction of the existence and ineffable perfections of God, which then appeared, that his distress was removed; and he prosecuted his journey, rejoicing in God, and admiring him in every object that presented itself to his view.

(*d*) STRUCTURE OF THE JOINTS.—Dr. Marshall, a lecturer on anatomy, had deeply studied the construction and laws of man, and was never happier than when explaining them. He once devoted a whole lecture to display the profound science that was visible in the formation of the double hinges of our joints. Such was the effect of his demonstrations, that an inquisitive friend, who had accompanied Dr. Turner to the lecture, with skeptical inclinations, suddenly exclaimed with great emphasis, "A man must be a fool indeed, who after duly studying his own body can remain an atheist."

(*e*) ATHEISTICAL ANATOMIST.—When Galen, a celebrated physician, but atheistically inclined, had anatomized the human body, and carefully surveyed the frame of it, viewed the fitness and usefulness of every part of it and the many several intentions of every little vein, bone and muscle, and the beauty of the whole, he fell into a fit of devotion, and wrote a hymn to his Creator.

GRACE AND MERCY OF GOD.

186. As Revealed in Jesus Christ.

(*a*) FIRST GREENLAND CONVERT.—It is well known that the Moravian missionaries in Greenland labored for several years without any apparent success. They seem to have thought, with many in the present day, that they should first instruct the natives in the existence of God, the crea tion of the world, the nature of their souls, &c.; and all this they did without exciting any degree of attention. On one occasion, however, while one of these good men was occupied in translating the gospels, he was visited by a number of these savages, who were desirous of knowing the contents of the book. He began an address to them by giving them some general scriptural information, and then slid into an account of the sufferings of Jesus; reading them the account of his agony, and speaking much of the anguish which made him sweat great drops of blood.

Now began the Spirit of God to work. One of these men, named Kaiarnack, stepped forward to the table, and said, in an earnest an affecting tone, "How was that? Tell me that once more: for I would fain be saved too!" Never had such language been heard from a Greenlander before. A full statement of the gospel was given: this man became indeed converted to God, and eminently useful. A change took place in the general character of the preaching of the brethren, and their subsequent success is well known.

(*b*) MR. NOTT AND THE SOUTH SEA ISLANDER.—Mr. Nott, missionary in the South Sea Islands, was on one occasion reading a portion of the gospel of John to a number of the natives. When he had finished the sixteenth verse of the third chapter, a native, who had listened with avidity and joy to the words, interrupted him, and said, "What words were those you read? What sounds were those I heard? Let me hear those words again!" Mr. Nott read again the verse, "God so loved," etc., when the native rose from his seat, and said, "Is that true? Can that be true? God love the world, when the world not love him! God so love the world, as to give his Son to die that man might not die! Can that be true?" Mr. Nott again read the verse, "God so loved the world," etc., told him it was true, and that it was the message God had sent to them; and that whosoever believed in him should not perish, but be happy after death. The overwhelming feelings of the wondering native were too powerful for expression or restraint. He burst into tears, and as these chased each other down his countenance, he retired to meditate in private on the great love of God which had that day touched his soul. There is every reason to believe he afterwards enjoyed the peace and happiness resulting from the love of God shed abroad in his heart.

(*c*) "THE SWORD OF THE SPIRIT."—It is related of the Rev. John Wesley, that he was once stopped by a highwayman who demanded his money. After he had given it to him, he called him back, and said, "Let me speak one word to you; the time may come when you may regret the course of life in which you are engaged. Remember this: *The blood of Jesus Christ cleanseth from all sin.*" He said no more, and they parted. Many years afterwards, when he was leaving a church in which he had been preaching, a person came up and asked him if he remembered being waylaid at such a time, referring to the above circumstances. Mr. Wesley replied that he recollected it. "I," said the individual, "was that man; that single verse on that occasion was the means of a total change in my life and habits. I have long since been attending the house of God and the Word of God, and I hope I am a Christian."

(*d*) THE THREE PREACHERS.—The following interesting address was delivered by an Indian, named Johannes, who became one of the missionaries of the United Brethren, in North America:—

Brethren, I have been a heathen, and have grown old amongst them: therefore I know very well how it is with the heathen, and how they think. A preacher once came to us, desiring to instruct us; and began by proving to us that there was a God. On which we said to him, "Well, and dost thou think we are ignorant of that? Now go back again to the place from whence thou camest."

Then, again, another preacher came, and began to instruct us, saying, "You must not steal, nor drink too much, nor lie, nor lead wicked lives." We answered him, "Fool that thou art, dost thou think that we do not know that God and learn it first thyself, and teach the people whom thou belongest to, not to do these things. For who are greater drunkards, or thieves, or liars, than thine own people?" Thus we sent him away also. Some time after this, Christian Henry, one of the Brethren, came to me into my hut, and sat down by me. The contents of his discourse to me were nearly these: "I come to thee in the name of the Lord of heaven and earth. He sends me to acquaint thee, that he would gladly save thee, and make thee happy, and deliver thee from the miserable state in which thou liest at present. To this end he became a man, gave his life a ransom for man, and he shed his blood for man. All that believe in the name of this Jesus, obtain the forgiveness of sin. To all those that receive him by faith, he giveth power to become the sons of God. The Holy Spirit dwelleth in their hearts, and they are made free, through the blood of Christ, from the slavery and dominion of sin. And though thou art the chief of sinners, yet if thou prayest to the Father in his name, and believest in him as a sacrifice for thy sins, thou shalt be heard and saved, and he will give thee a crown of life, and thou shalt live with him in heaven for ever."

When he had finished his discourse, he lay down upon a board in my hut, fatigued by his journey, and fell into a sound sleep. I thought within myself, what manner of man is this? There he lies, and sleeps so sweetly: I might kill him, and throw him into the forest, and who would regard it? But he is unconcerned. This cannot be a bad man; he fears no evil, not even from us, who are so savage; but sleeps comfortably, and places his life in our hands.

However, I could not forget his words; they constantly recurred to my mind; even though I went to sleep, I dreamed of the blood which Christ had shed for us. I thought, This is very strange, and quite different from what I have ever heard. So I went, and interpreted Christian Henry's words to the other Indians. Thus through the grace of God, an awakening took place among us. I tell you therefore, brethren, preach to the heathen Christ, and his blood, and his sufferings, and his death, if you would have your words to gain entrance among them—if you wish to confer a blessing upon them.

187. As Seen in Pardoning the Guilty.

(*a*) THE DEVIL'S CASTAWAYS. —Some ladies called one Saturday morning to pay a visit to Lady Huntingdon, and, during the visit, her ladyship inquired of them if they had ever heard Mr. Whitefield preach. Upon being answered in the negative, she said, "I wish you would hear him; he is to preach to-morrow evening." They promised her ladyship they would certainly attend. They fulfilled their promise; and when they called the next Monday morning on her ladyship, she anxiously inquired if they had heard Mr. Whitefield on the previous evening, and how they liked him. The reply was, "Oh my lady, of all the preachers we ever heard, he is the most strange and unaccountable! Among other preposterous things, would your ladyship believe it, he declared that Jesus Christ was so willing to receive sinners, that he did not object to receive even the devil's *castaways!* Now, my lady, did you ever hear of such a thing since you were born?" To which her ladyship made the following reply: "There is something, I acknowledge, a little singular in the invitation, and I do not recollect to have ever met with it before; but as Mr. Whitefield is below in the parlor, we will have him up, and let him answer for himself." Upon his coming up into the drawing-room, Lady Huntingdon said, "Mr. Whitefield, these ladies have been preferring a very heavy charge aginst you, and I thought it best that you should come up and defend yourself. They say, that, in your sermon last evening, in speaking of the willingness of Jesus Christ to receive sinners, you expressed yourself in the following terms: 'That so ready was Christ to receive sinners who came to him, that he was willing to receive even the devil's castaways.'" Mr. Whitefield immediately replied: "I certainly, my lady, must plead guilty to the charge; whether I did what was right, or otherwise, your ladyship shall judge from the following circumstance. Did your ladyship notice, about half an hour ago, a very modest single rap at the door? It was given by a poor, miserable-looking, aged female, who requested to speak with me. I desired her to be shown into the parlor, when she accosted me in the following manner:—'I believe, sir, you preached last evening at such a chapel.' 'Yes, I did.' 'Ah, sir, I was accidentally passing the door of that chapel, and hearing the voice of some one preaching, I did what I never had been in the habit of doing,—I went in; and one of the first things I heard you say was, that Jesus Christ was so willing to receive sinners, that he did not object to receive the devil's castaways. Do you think, sir, that Jesus Christ would receive me?'" Mr. Whitefield answered her there was not a doubt of it, if she was but willing to go to him. This was the case; it ended in the conversion of the poor creature to God. When she died, she left highly satisfactory evidence that her great and numerous sins had been forgiven, through the atonement of the Lord Jesus.

(*b*) INTENDED SUICIDE'S HYMN.—A gentleman was known by his nearest and dearest friend, his wife, never to lie down upon his pillow some years before his death, or raise his head from it in the morning, without repeating the short hymn annexed to this anecdote; and sometimes he would inadvertently burst into ejaculations in company, when two or three lines of it were distinctly heard before he could recollect himself: the cause at that time was unknown; but, after his decease, a paper was found in his bureau to the following purport: "You will no longer be surprised at my involuntary effusions of feeble gratitude to the Almighty, which broke forth occasionally in gay company, when you shall read that many years since the dread of approaching poverty, disgrace, humiliation, and desertion of friends, had brought me to the fatal resolution of putting an end to my existence. Conscious that I had brought misfortune upon a numerous family by my own imprudence, dissipation, and pride, I considered my punishment as an act of justice. The destined moment arrived; already had I loaded, primed, and cocked; when, strange to relate! though I had not read a page in the Bible for years, a reflection came suddenly across my mind; 'Jesus of Nazareth,' said I to myself, 'was a man (for I disbelieved in his divinity) acquainted with sorrows, endured a life of poverty, was exposed to public scorn and derision, suffered pain of body and agony of mind, and had nothing to reproach himself with, yet this reformer of the morals of mankind, this benefactor to society, this illustrious pattern of fortitude, patience, and humility, was, by an unthankful world, put to death: he was crucified! but he crucified not himself!' Repeating these last words a second time with unusual energy, pride, disdain, shame, and contempt of my inability humbly to imitate this striking example of bearing afflictions manfully, produced a passionate conflict of mind, in which paroxysm I madly flung the pistol some distance from me; to add to the affecting scene, it went off, unheard but by my affectionate wife, who religiously kept the secret: her consolations restored me to temporary tranquillity, but the work of Providence was not yet completed; not a week had elapsed, and settled melancholy was again taking possession of my soul, when a letter announced the death of a distant relation, and summoned me to the reading of his will, by which he had bequeathed me sufficient not only to clear me of all encumbrances, but to enable me, with the assistance of a considerable surplus, to exert my abilities in the line of my profession for the support of my family, and even to aim at a moderate independence, which you will find I have at length acquired."

"Rise, oh my soul! the hour review,
When, awed by guilt and fear,
Thou durst not Heaven for mercy sue,
Nor hope for pity here!

Dried are thy tears, thy griefs are fled,
Dispell'd each bitter care;
For Heaven itself did send its aid,
To snatch thee from despair!

Then here, oh God, thy work fulfil
And from thy mercy's throne

Vouchsafe me strength to do thy will,
And to resist my own.

So shall my soul each power employ
Thy mercies to adore,
While Heaven itself proclaims with joy
One rescued sinner more !"

(*c*) WHITEFIELD'S BROTHER CONVERTED.—Mr. Whitefield, brother of the noted preacher, had fallen into a backslidden state ; but under a sermon preached by his brother in the Countess of Huntingdon's chapel, Bath, it pleased God to arouse him from that state ; after which, however, he became melancholy and despairing. He was taking tea with the Countess of Huntingdon, on a service evening, in the chapel house, and her ladyship endeavored to raise his desponding hopes by conversing on God's infinite mercy through Jesus Christ ; but, for a while, in vain. "My lady," he replied, "I know what you say is true. The mercy of God is infinite : I see it clearly. But, ah ! my lady, there is no mercy for me—I am a wretch, entirely lost." "I am glad to hear it, Mr. Whitefield," said Lady H. "I am glad at my heart that you are a lost man." He looked with great surprise. "What, my lady, glad ! glad at your heart that I am a lost man ?" "Yes, Mr. Whitefield, truly glad ; for Jesus Christ came into the world to save the lost !" He laid down his cup of tea on the table. "Blessed be God for that," said he, "Glory to God for that word," he exclaimed. "Oh what unusual power is this which I feel attending it ! Jesus Christ came to save the lost ! then I have a ray of hope," and so he went on. As he finished his last cup of tea, his hand trembled, and he complained of illness. He went out into the chapel court for the benefit of the air, but staggered to the wall, exclaiming, "I am very ill." A poor old woman, who was going into the chapel, lent him her staff to support him into the house, saying she would call for it when Divine service was over, and inquire after him. But his time was come. Soon after he was brought into the house he expired.

(*d*) MR. FULLER'S SERMON.—When the Rev. Andrew Fuller first visted Scotland, a notoriously wicked and abandoned woman, seeing a number of persons thronging the doors of a chapel, felt her curiosity awakened, and being informed that an Englishman was to preach, she mingled with the crowd, and entered the place. Mr. Fuller took for his text the words, "Come unto me all ye ends of the earth, and be ye saved." "What then," she exclaimed in her heart, "surely there is hope even for me ! Wretch as I am, I am not beyond the ends of the earth." She listened with eager delight, while the good man proclaimed the free salvation of the gospel. Hope sprung up in her heart, a hope which purified as well as comforted ; and the grace of God taught her to "deny ungodliness and worldly lusts, and to live soberly, righteously, and godly, in the present world."

(*e*) "WHO CAN TELL ?"—"I have heard," says Mr. Daniel Wilson, in a sermon of his, "of a certain person, whose name I could mention, who was tempted to conclude his day over, and himself lost ; that, therefore, it was his best course to put an end to his life, which, if continued, would but serve to increase his sin, and consequently his misery, from which there was no escape ; and seeing he must be in hell, the sooner he was there the sooner he should know the worst ; which was preferable to his being worn away with the tormenting expectation of what was to come. Under the influence of such suggestions as these, he went to a river, with a design to throw himself in ; but as he was about to do it, he seemed to hear a voice saying to him, *Who can tell ?* as if the words had been audibly delivered. By this, therefore, he was brought to a stand ; his thoughts were arrested, and thus began to work on the passage mentioned : *Who can tell* (Jonah iii. 9,) viz., what God can do when he will proclaim his grace glorious ? *Who can tell* but such an one as I may find mercy ? or what will be the issue of humble prayer to heaven for it ? *Who can tell* what purposes God will serve in my recovery ? By such thoughts as these, being so far influenced as to resolve to try, it pleased God graciously to enable him, through all his doubts and fears, to throw himself by faith on Jesus Christ, as able to save to the uttermost all that come to God by him, humbly desiring and expecting mercy for his sake, to his own soul. In this he was not disappointed; but aftewards became an eminent Christian and minister; and from his own experience of the riches of grace, was greatly useful to the conversion and comfort of others.

GRATITUDE.

188. Gratitude to God.

(*a*) REV. J. BROWN'S CONFESSION.—"No doubt," said the late Rev. J. Brown, of Haddington, Scotland, "I have met with trials as well as others: yet so kind has God been to me, that I think, if He were to give me as many years as I have already lived in the world, I should not desire one single circumstance in my lot changed, except that I wish I had less sin. It might be written on my coffin, 'Here lies one of the cares of Providence, who early wanted both father and mother, and yet never missed them.'"

(*b*) THE POOR FAMILY'S GRATITUDE.—As a poor pious man was sitting by his little fire, one cold evening, with his wife and children, he said to them, "I have been thinking a great deal to-day about that part of Scripture—'The Son of man hath not where to lay his head.' How wonderful it is, that we, who are so sinful, unworthy, and helpless, should be more favored than he was!" "It is wonderful, indeed, father," said the eldest girl; "for though our house is mean, and our food scanty, compared with the houses and way of living of great folks, yet it seems that Jesus Christ was not so well provided for as we are." "I am right glad to hear you speak in that way, Sarah," said the wife. "How happy we all are in our little dwelling this cold night; and as soon as we wish we have beds to rest ourselves upon: there, sharp and piercing as the frost is, and bleak and stormy as the wind blows, we shall be comfortable and warm; and yet the Son of man, as your father has just told us, 'had not where to lay his head.' Oh! that this thought may make us thankful for our many mercies!" "Tommy," said the father, "reach that hymn, which our dear minister gave you last Sabbath at the Sunday school; and as our hearts are in a good frame, let us try to keep them so by singing it." The whole company, father, mother, and children, then, with a glow of sacred ardor and pleasure, sung the hymn entitled, "The Son of man had not where to lay his head."

(*c*) LOSSES FROM RELIGION.—An aged couple, in the vicinity of London, who in the early part of life were poor, but who, by the blessing of God upon their industry, enjoyed a comfortable independency in their old age were called upon by a Christian minister, who solicited their contributions to a charity. The old lady was disposed to make out some excuse, and to answer in the negative, both for her husband and herself; and therefore replied, "Why, sir, we have lost a deal by religion since we began: my husband knows that very well." And being willing to obtain her husband's consent to the assertion, she said, "Have we not, Thomas?" Thomas, after a long and solemn pause, replied, "Yes, Mary, we *have* lost a deal by our religion! I have lost a deal by my religion. Before I got religion, Mary, I had got a water pail, in which I carried water, and *that* you know I lost many years ago. And then I had an old slouched hat, a patched old coat, and mended shoes and stockings; but I have lost them also long ago. And, Mary, you know that, poor as I was, I had a habit of getting drunk, and quarreling with you; and that you know I have lost. And then I had a burdened conscience, and a wicked heart; and then I had ten thousand guilty feelings and fears: but all are lost, completely lost, and like a millstone cast into the deepest sea. And, Mary, you have been a loser too, though not so great a loser as myself. Before we got religion, Mary, you had got a washing-tray, in which you washed for hire; and God Almighty blessed your industry: but since we got religion, you have lost your washing-tray. And you had got a gown and bonnet much the worse for wear, though they were all you had to wear; but you have lost them long ago. And you had many an aching heart concerning me, at times; but those you happily have lost. And I could even wish that you had lost as much as I have lost, and even more; for what we lose by our religion, Mary, will be our eternal gain." We need not add, the preacher did not go away without substantial proof that Thomas deemed his losses for religion his most weighty obligations to the goodness of Almighty God, as the richest boon of grace on earth, and the most authentic pledge of glory in the world to come.

(*d*) ORIGIN OF THANKSGIVING DAY.—When New England was first planted, the settlers met with many difficulties and hardships, as is necessarily the case when a civilized people attempt to establish themselves in a wilderness country. Being piously disposed, they sought relief from Heaven, by laying their wants and distresses before the Lord in frequent set days of fasting and prayer. Constant meditation, and discourse on the subject of their difficulties, kept their minds gloomy and discontented, and, like the children of Israel, there were many disposed to return to the land which persecution had determined them to abandon.

At length, when it was proposed in the assembly to proclaim another fast, a farmer, of plain sense, rose, and remarked, that the inconveniences they suffered, and concerning which they had so often wearied Heaven with their complaints, were not so great as might have been expected, and were diminishing every day as the colony strengthened; that the earth began to reward their labors, and to furnish liberally for their sustenance; that the seas and rivers were full of fish, the air sweet, the climate wholesome; above all, they were in the full enjoyment of liberty, civil and religious. He therefore thought, that reflecting and conversing on these subjects would be more comfortable, as tending to make them more contented with their situation; and that it would be more becoming the gratitude they owed to the Divine Being, if, instead of a fast, they should proclaim a thanksgiving. His advice was taken; and, from that day to this, they have in every year observed circumstances of public happiness sufficient to furnish employment for a thanksgiving day.

(*e*) APT SAYING OF BOWDLER —Sir W. W. Pepys, in a letter to Mrs. Hannah More, 1825, says, "We are just now reading in an evening a memoir of Mr. John Bowdler, written by his son, which shows him to have been worthy of that excellent family to which he belonged. I have long known and highly respected Thomas Bowdler, but of John I knew nothing, except an admirable saying, which I remember was attributed to him, some years ago, when it was the fashion to lament over the state of this unhappy country. "If," said he, "a man were to go from the northern to the southern extremity of this island, with his eyes shut and his ears open, he would think that the country was sinking into an abyss of destruction: but if he were to return with his ears shut and his eyes open, he would be satisfied that we had the greatest reason to be thankful for our prosperity."

189. Gratitude to Man.

(*a*) "WHY DO YOU PLANT TREES?"—A very poor and aged man, busied in planting and grafting an apple tree, was rudely interrupted by the interrogation, "Why do you plant trees, who cannot hope to eat the fruit of them?" He raised himself up, and, leaning upon his spade, replied, "Some one planted trees before I was born, and I have eaten the fruit; I now plant for others, that the memorial of my gratitude may exist when I am dead and gone."

(*b*) GRATITUDE FOR GRATITUDE.—A complete reverse having taken place in a gentleman's circumstances, by his too great readiness to lend his money to those who deceived him, he was obliged in his old age to dismiss all his domestics. It was, however, his happiness to have one among them, who, knowing the cause, said to him with tears, "I have now, sir, been your servant five-and-twenty years; I have always honored and respected you: you have treated me with the kindness of a master, a father, and a friend. I have saved some scores of pounds in your service, that I might be comfortable in my old age; but I cannot live in peace, while I see you in distress. To you, under the good care of Providence, I owe my life; to you I am indebted for much good instruction, and for the salvation of my soul. I beg you will accept of my purse, and all it contains. He that feedeth the ravens, and letteth not a sparrow fall unheeded to the ground, will not forsake me! I am yet able for service: suffer me to attend your fortunes, and be your servant still." She drew tears from her old master by these and other affectionate expressions; he wept at her generosity, accepted her offer of service, and she remained with him.

Now, reader, mark the result; and be encouraged to every act of kindness to others within your power, especially to those from whom you have derived your best enjoyments, and who may have seen better days. Not long after she had resumed her place, a relation of her master died, and left him a good fortune. How must this have rejoiced the heart of a servant so attached! But one particular yet remains. When her master died, he bequeathed this faithful servant a comfortable maintenance.

(*c*) MR. CATHCART'S DIARY.—Mr. Cathcart, of Drum, was in the practice of keeping a diary, which however included one particular department, seldom to be found in like cases. Mr. Cathcart describes his plan and object in the following words:—"A memorial of acts of kindness, that as memory is liable to fail, and as the kindness and friendship of former times may be forgotten, the remembrance of friendly offices done to the writer or to his family, or to his particular friends, might be preserved, in order that he may himself repay the debt in grateful acknowledgements while he lived, and that his family after him might know to whom their father owed obligations, and might feel every debt of gratitude due by him as obligations on themselves."

(*d*) THE GRATEFUL NEGRO.—An Englishman, a native of Yorkshire, going to reside at Kingston, in Jamaica, was reduced from a state of affluence to very great distress; so much so, that in the time of sickness he was destitute of home, money, medicine, food, and friends. Just in this time of need, an old negro Christian offered his assistance; which being gladly accepted, this "neighbor to him" bought medicine, and administered it himself; furnished nourishment; sat up three nights; and, in short, acted the part of doctor, nurse, and host. Through the blessing of God, the old negro's efforts were rendered successful in the recovery of the sick man: who then inquired what expenses he had been at, and promised remuneration as soon as possible. The generous old Christian replied, "Massa, you no owe me nothing; me owe you much still." "How do you make that out?" said the restored man. "Why, massa, me neber able to pay you; because you taught me to read de word of God!" This reply so affected the man, that he resolved, from that time, to seek the Lord.

HAPPINESS, RELIGIOUS.

190. In Perils and Dangers.

(*a*) CHRISTIAN CALMNESS.—"Some impressions," says a young man, who went out as a missionary to the heathen, "of the importance and necessity of true religion, were made upon my mind at a very early period. The first particular one that I recollect was, I think, when I was about five years of age. There happened one day a very violent storm of thunder and lightning in our neighborhood; on which occasion a few Christian friends, who lived near us, terrified by its violence, came into my father's house. When under his roof, in a moment there came a most vivid flash, followed by a dreadful peal of thunder, which much alarmed the whole company except my father, who turning towards my mother and our friends, with the greatest composure, repeated these words of Dr. Watts:

> "The God that rules on high,
> And thunders when he please;
> That rides upon the stormy sky,
> And manages the seas:
> This awful God is ours;
> Our father and our love," &c.

These words, accompanied with such circumstances, sunk deep into my heart. I thought how safe and happy are those who have the great God for their father and friend; but, being conscious that I had sinned against him, I was afraid he was not my father, and that, instead of loving me, he was angry with me; and this, for some time after, continued to distress and grieve my mind." He then proceeds to say, that these early impressions were succeeded by others which terminated in his conversion.

(*b*) PASSENGERS OF THE KENT.—The efficacy of faith in the word of God, to support the mind in the hour of trouble, has often been the subject of conversation, and its power has been very strikingly illustrated. The writer of the interesting "NARRATIVE OF THE LOSS OF THE KENT EAST INDIAMAN," in 1825, states that, when that vessel was on fire, several of the soldiers' wives and children, who had fled for temporary shelter into the after-cabins on the upper deck, were engaged in prayer and in reading the Scriptures with the ladies, some of whom were enabled, with wonderful self-possession, to offer to others those spiritual consolations, which a firm and intelligent trust in the Redeemer of the world appeared at this awful hour to impart to their own breasts. The dignified deportment of two young ladies, in particular, formed a specimen of natural strength of mind, finely modified by Christian feeling, that failed not to attract the notice and admiration of every one who had an opportunity of witnessing it. On the melancholy announcement being made to them, that all hope must be relinquished, and that death was rapidly and inevitably approaching, one of the ladies above referred to, calmly sinking down on her knees, and clasping her hands together, said, "Even so, come, Lord Jesus!" and immediately proposed to read a portion of the Scriptures to those around her; her sister, with nearly equal composure and collectedness of mind, selected the forty-sixth and other appropriate Psalms; which were accordingly read, with intervals of prayer, by those ladies alternately, to the assembled females.

(*c*) THE CAPTAIN AND THE PILOT.—A pious captain, when sailing down the Mississippi, had the misfortune to have his vessel so much injured, that there was great danger of the loss of both ship and cargo. Though placed in this perilous situation, he manifested a composure which evinced that his mind was stayed on his God, while he omitted nothing that could be done to save the property intrusted to his care.

While in this situation, there came to his aid one of the pilots on that station, who, by his own account, neither feared God nor regarded man; and, after offering his services, began to storm and swear. After a little time, however, he began to contrast his conduct with the captain's and said to himself, "How is it that, while I have nothing at risk, I am swearing as though it were mine; and the captain, who has property and reputation at stake, seems perfectly calm? It must be his religion, and, as I have a Bible on board my boat, I will immediately commence reading it, and see if I can find what his religion is." He did read, and the Spirit of God applied the truth. He became convinced that he was a lost sinner, and that without the religion which he had seen so impressively exhibited, he must be lost. Conviction resulted in conversion; and he afterwards called on the captain, to tell him what the Lord had done for his soul.

191. In Illness.

(*a*) APOSTOLICAL REPLY.—"I was called upon," says the Rev. Mr. Trefit, an American minister, "some years ago, to visit an individual, a part of whose face had been eaten away by a most loathsome cancer. Fixing my eyes on this man in his agony, I said, 'Supposing that Almighty God were to give you your choice: whether would you prefer, your cancer, your pain, and your sufferings, with a certainty of death before you, but of immortality hereafter; or, health, prosperity, long life in the world, and the risk of losing your immortal soul?' 'Ah, sir!' said the man, 'give me the cancer, the pain, the Bible, the hope of heaven; and others may take the world, long life, and prosperity!'"

(*b*) THE CABINET OF JEWELS.—As I entered the apartment where a sick person was confined, says a gentleman in England, she looked at me with a peaceful smile upon her countenance, and, grasping my hand, exclaimed, "I know you are one of the servants of my Lord and Master, by coming with my worthy kind friend. Oh, how good, how very good is my dear Savior, in sending one and another of his children to visit so poor and worthless a sinner as I am! I weep, but they are not the tears of grief, but of gratitude." She requested me to sit down by her bed-side, and said, "As you are a stranger, let me tell you what the Lord my God hath done for my soul. You perceive, dear sir, I am in the furnace; but my happiness is this, that Zion's God sits by as the skilful refiner, watching with an observant eye, that nothing be lost but that which is vile and refuse; and when I am thoroughly tried, I shall come forth like gold seven times purified, either to join the celestial choirs, or to be spared a little longer in the world, that I may honor Him that remembered me in my low estate. And shall I tell you, dear sir, that I have been confined to this bed eighteen months, but not one moment too long; no! thanks be to his dear name, I have had the staff of consolation to support me, as well as his rod to correct me, and every twig of it is an emblem of love."

192. Miscellaneous Examples.

(*a*) ONE OF THE DAYS OF HEAVEN.—Mr. Flavel, at one time on a journey, set himself to improve his time by meditation; when his mind grew intent, till at length he had such ravishing tastes of heavenly joy, and such full assurance of his interest therein, that he utterly lost the sight and sense of this world and all its concerns, so that he knew not where he was. At last, perceiving himself faint through a great loss of blood from his nose, he alighted from his horse, and sat down at a spring, where he washed and refreshed himself, earnestly desiring, if it were the will of God, that he might there leave the world. His spirits reviving, he finished his journey in the same delightful frame. He passed that night without any sleep, the joy of the Lord still overflowing him, so that he seemed an inhabitant of the other world. After this, a heavenly serenity and sweet peace long continued with him; and for many years he called that day "one of the days of heaven!" and professed that he understood more of the life of heaven by it, than by all the discourses he had heard, or the books he ever read.

(*b*) GLORIOUS VIEWS OF GOD.—The Rev. William Tennent had preached one Lord's day morning to his congregation, and in the intermission had walked into the woods for meditation, the weather being warm. He was reflecting on the infinite wisdom of God, as manifested in all his works, and particularly in the wonderful method of salvation through the death and sufferings of his beloved Son. This subject suddenly opened on his mind with such a flood of light, that his views of the glory and the infinite majesty of Jehovah were so inexpressibly great, as entirely to overwhelm him; and he fell almost lifeless to the ground. When he had revived a little, all he could do was to raise a fervent prayer, that God would withdraw himself from him, or that he must perish under a view of his ineffable glory. When able to reflect on his situation, he could not but abhor himself as a weak and despicable worm; and seemed to be overcome with astonishment, that a creature so unworthy and insufficient, had ever dared to attempt the instruction of his fellow men in the nature and attributes of so glorious a Being. Overstaying his usual time, some of his elders went in search of him, and found him prostrate on the ground, unable to rise, and incapable of informing them of the cause. They raised him up, and, after some time, brought him to the church, and supported him to the pulpit, which he ascended on his hands and knees, to the no small astonishment of the congregation. He remained silent a considerable time, earnestly supplicating Almighty God to hide himself from him, that he might be enabled to address his people, who were by this time lost in wonder to know what had produced this uncommon event. His prayers were heard, and he became able to stand up, by holding the desk: and in a most affecting and pathetic address, he gave an account of the views he had of the infinite wisdom of God, and deplored his own incapacity to speak to them concerning a Being so infinitely glorious beyond all his powers of description. He then broke out into so fervent and expressive a prayer, as greatly to surprise the congregation, and draw tears from every eye. A sermon followed which continued the solemn scene, and made very lasting impressions on the hearers

(*c*) ENJOYING GOD.—I have here, said Rev. Mr. Fuller, two religious characters, who were intimately acquainted in early life. Providence favored one of them with a tide of prosperity. The other, fearing for his friend, lest his heart should be overcharged with the cares of this life and the deceitfulness of riches, one day asked him whether he did not find prosperity a snare to him. He paused, and answered. "I am not conscious that I do, for I enjoy God in all things." Some years after, his affairs took another turn. He lost, if not the whole, yet the far greater part of what he had once gained, and was greatly reduced. His old friend being one day in his company, renewed his question, whether he did not find what had lately befallen him to be too much for him. Again he paused, and answered, "I am not conscious that I do, for now I enjoy all things in God." This was truly a life of faith.

(*d*) POOR MAN'S GRATITUDE.—A gentleman of very considerable fortune, but a stranger both to personal and family religion, one evening took a solitary walk through part of his grounds. He happened to come near to a mean hut, where a poor man lived with a numerous family, who earned their bread by daily labor. He heard a continued and pretty loud voice. Not knowing what it was, curiosity prompted him to listen. The man, who was piously disposed, happened to be at prayer with his family. So soon as he could distinguish the words, he heard him giving thanks, with great affection, to God for the goodness of his providence, in giving them food to eat and raiment to put on, and in supplying them with what was necessary and comfortable in the present life. He was immediately struck with astonishment and confusion, and said to himself, "Does this poor man, who has nothing but the meanest fare, and that purchased by severe labor, give thanks to God for his goodness to himself and family; and I, who enjoy ease and honor, and every thing that is pleasant and desirable, have hardly ever bent my knee, or made any acknowledgment to my Maker and Preserver!" It pleased God to make this providential occurrence the means of bringing him to a real and lasting sense of religion.

(*e*) THE FAMILY HERITAGE.—The Rev. W. Thorpe, of Bristol, (Eng.) was once preaching in London, from Rom. viii. 28: "We know that all things work together for good to them that love God, to them who are the called according to his purpose." After remarking that these words were doubtless intended for the common benefit of the Christian church, he added, "But I have looked upon them likewise as a kind of family heritage. They formed the favorite text of my venerated father, who found in it consolation and support in the course of a difficult and laborious ministry. It was no less dear to the heart of my mother, who used to quote it in her easy chair, and on her pillow of rest. When the weight of affliction overcame her feelings in the hour of trial, then she used to say, 'Let me sit down and rest myself, for we know that all things work together for good to them that love God, to them who are the called according to his purpose.' My father was removed in the midst of his pious career, and in the vigor of his manhood, leaving behind him a large and uneducated family, and but little of the goods of earth. My mother was then confined in childbed, having been delivered the day before my father expired. The last words uttered by him to my mother, in this distressing situation were, 'Call the child Christiana; all things must work together for good to them that love God.' To make the measure of sorrow full, it happened that all the rivers of the neighborhood were overflowing at that season, causing on all sides inconvenience, damage, and distress; and the water was a foot deep on the ground-floor of the house! Still she always affirmed that this season of calamity was the happiest period of her life, in which she derived the fulness of consolation from the words of our text. When, a few days after my father had been carried to his place of rest, our house was robbed of every thing that could be borne away, and also of the last quarter's salary which my mother had received; and when, having discovered our loss, my eldest sister ran breathless into her mother's chamber, exclaiming, 'Mother, the thieves have stolen all we had in this world; will this also work together for good?' this Christian replied, 'Yes, for we know that *all* things work together for good to them that love God.' And the result justified her confidence."

(*f*) GLORYING IN TRIBULATION.—Guy de Brez, a French minister, was prisoner in the castle of Tournay, in Belgium. A lady who visited him said, "She wondered how he could eat, or drink, or sleep in quiet." "Madam," said he, "my chains do not terrify me, or break my sleep; on the contrary, I glory and take delight therein, esteeming them at a higher rate than chains and rings of gold, or jewels of any price whatever. The rattling of my chains is like the effect of an instrument of music in my ears: not that such an effect comes merely from my chains, but it is because I am bound therewith for maintaining the truth of the gospel."

(*g*) HOWARD IN TRIALS.—The celebrated philanthropist, Howard, who spent the best part of his life in traveling over all the countries of Europe,—"to plunge into the infection of hospitals,—to survey the mansions of sorrow and pain,—to remember the forgotten, and to visit the forsaken, under all climes,"—was not unhappy amidst his toils. In a letter from Riga, during his last journey, he says, "I hope I have sources of enjoyment that depend not on the particular spot I inhabit; a rightly cultivated mind, under the power of religion and the exercise of beneficent dispositions, affords a ground of satisfaction little affected by *heres and theres.*"

(*h*) SCIENCE AND RELIGION.—It was a usual saying of Pascal, that the sciences produced no consolation in the times of affliction; but the knowledge of Christianity was a comfort both in adversity, and defect of all other knowledge.

(*i*) THE CRIPPLE AND HIS BIBLE.—At a meeting of the Blackheath Auxiliary Bible Society, in the year 1815, Dr. Gregory, of Woolwich, (Eng.), related the following very interesting facts:—More than twelve months ago, I went, pursuant to the request of a poor, but benevolent-hearted woman in my neighborhood, to visit an indigent man deeply afflicted. On entering the cottage, I found him alone, his wife having gone to procure him milk from a kind neighbor. I was startled by the sight of a pale, emaciated man, a living image of death, fastened upright in his chair, by a rude mechanism of cords and belts hanging from the ceiling. He was totally unable to move either hand or foot, having more than four years been entirely deprived of the use of his limbs, yet the whole time suffering extreme anguish from swellings at all his joints. As soon as I had recovered a little from my surprise at seeing so pitiable an object, I asked, "Are you left alone, my friend, in this deplorable situation?" "No, sir," replied he, in a touchingly feeble tone of mild resignation, (nothing but his lips and eyes moving while he spake,) "I am not alone, for God is with me." On advancing, I soon discovered the secret of his striking declaration; for his wife had left on his knees, propped with a cushion formed for the purpose, a Bible, lying open at a favorite portion of the Psalms of David! I sat down by him, and conversed with him. On ascertaining that he had but a small weekly allowance certain, I inquired how the remainder of his wants were supplied. "Why, sir," said he, "'tis true, as you say, seven shillings a week would never support us; but, when it is gone, I rely upon the promise I found in this book: 'Bread shall be given him; his waters shall be sure;' and I have never been disappointed yet; and so long as God is faithful to his word, I never shall." I asked him if he ever felt tempted to repine under the pressure of so long-continued and heavy a calamity. "Not for the last three years," said he, "blessed be God for it;" the eye of faith sparkling and giving life to his pallid countenance while he made the declaration: "for I have learned from this book in whom to believe: and, though I am aware of my weakness and unworthiness, I am persuaded that He will 'not leave me, nor forsake me.' And so it is, that often, when my lips are closed with locked jaw, and I cannot speak to the glory of God, He enables me to sing His praises in my heart."

Gladly would I sink into the obscurity of the same cottage; gladly even would I languish in the same chair; could I but enjoy the same uninterrupted communion with God, be always filled with the same "strong consolation," and constantly behold, with equally vivid perception, the same celestial crown sparkling before me.

(*j*) EXAMPLE OF HALL.—Mr. Hall, after the death of one of his children, appeared as usual in his pulpit on the following Sabbath, and, under the influence of chastened and holy feeling, addressed his congregation from the language of David, after he had been deprived of his son: "I shall go to him, but he shall not return to me." He very properly remarked, that while the child was living, but doomed to die, the afflicted saint fasted, prayed, and wept, if peradventure his days might still be prolonged; but when the event was decided, he evinced his fortitude and deep submission to the will of Heaven. He arose from the earth, changed his mourning attire, and went up to the house of the Lord. The ordinary custom of abstaining from public worship, was accommodating ourselves to the false maxims of the world, and injurious to our spiritual interests. In a season of calamity, whither should we go, but to Him who alone is able to sustain and comfort us, and to the place where he has promised to meet with us and bless us?

(*k*) JOY IN GRIEF.—The Cleveland Herald relates the following touching incident, connected with the burning of the steamboat Vermillion, on Lake Erie:

"Among the sufferers was a young man by the name of ROBINSON, mate of the schooner Ohio. Young and active, he delighted in his profession, and bid fair to become an ornament to it. He had but a day or two before united himself in that 'holiest of ties, wedded love,' to the fair girl of his choice; and was on the way with his bride to spend the 'honey-moon' with his aged mother, who resides in this city, when death, with all its most appalling horrors, came upon them both in a moment, and summoned them hence to that 'bourne from whence no traveller returns.'

"The mother was anxiously expecting their arrival, when the sad news of their untimely fate was communicated to her. Folding her hands upon her breast, and lifting her eyes to heaven, she exclaimed in the spirit of the true Christian,—'The Lord gave, and the Lord hath taken away; blessed be the name of the Lord.'"

(*l*) A SINGULAR BOND.—I have read of a godly man, says Mr. Brooks, who living near a philosopher often strove to persuade him to become a Christian. Oh, but, said the philosopher, I must, or may, lose my all for Christ. To which the good man replied, If you lose any thing for Christ, he will repay it a hundred-fold. Ay, but, said the philosopher, will you be bound for Christ, that if he doth not pay me, you will? Yes, that I will, said the good man! So the philosopher became a Christian, and the good man entered into bond for the performance of covenants. Some time after it happened that the philosopher fell sick. On his death-bed, and holding the bond in his hand, he sent for the party engaged, to whom he gave up the bond, and said, Christ hath paid all, there is nothing for you to pay; take your bond and cancel it; no man shall ever have occasion to say that he has been loser by Christ.

(*m*) GOD WITH THE EXILES —I have read, says Brooks, of a company of poor Christians who were banished into some remote part; and one standing by seeing them pass along, said, that it was a very sad condition those poor people were in, to be thus hurried from the society of men and made companions with the beasts of the field. True, said another, it were a sad condition indeed if they were carried to a place where they should not find their God; but let them be of good cheer God goes along with them, and will exhibit the comforts of his presence whithersoever they go. God's presence with his people is a spring that never fails.

193. HEARERS OF THE GOSPEL.

(*a*) INFLUENCE OF FAULT-FINDING.—The Rev. Mr. Beckwith says:—"I was once conversing with a young and successful minister of the gospel, who related to me the following circumstances. When he was quite a child, he heard a minister preach on repentance. This was on the forenoon of a Sabbath. His feelings were excited, and he had almost determined, before the conclusion of the sermon, to perform the duty without delay. In this state of mind he went to the house of God in the afternoon, and heard the same minister on the judgment. He was still more deeply impressed, and came to the resolution to attend to religion immediately. But, as he passed from the sanctuary, he overheard two professing Christians conversing on the sermon. 'A very solemn discourse,' said one. 'Yes,' replied the other, but—' and he proceeded to make some critical remark, the effect of which was, for that time at least, to erase all serious impressions from the mind of the youth." How often do we witness this evil!

(*b*) BURNING THE BUSHEL——A poor woman went to hear a sermon, wherein, among other evil practices the use of dishonest weights and measures was exposed. With this discourse she was much affected. The next day when the minister, according to his custom, went among his hearers, and called upon the woman, he took occasion to ask her what she remembered of his sermon. The poor woman complained much of her bad memory, and said she had forgotten almost all that he delivered. "But one thing," said she, "I remembered; I remembered to burn my bushel." A doer of the word cannot be a forgetful hearer.

(*c*) THE DEAF WORSHIPER.—"I have in my congregation," said a venerable minister of the gospel, "a worthy aged woman, who has for many years been so deaf as not to distinguish the loudest sound, and yet she is always one of the first in the meeting. On asking the reason of her constant attendance (as it was impossible for her to hear my voice), she answered, 'Though I cannot hear you, I come to God's house because I love it, and would be found in his ways; and he gives me many a sweet thought upon the text when it is pointed out to me: another reason is because there I am in the best company, in the more immediate presence of God, and among his saints, the honorable of the earth. I am not satisfied with serving God in private; it is my duty and privilege to honor him regularly in public.'" What a reproof this is to those who have their hearing, and yet always come to a place of worship late or not at all!

(*d*) "YOU AND ME."—When sitting under the ministry of a devoted servant of God, says a gentleman, he on one occasion preached upon the Diotrephesian spirit. In his usual faithful manner, he pointed out its sad effects upon a church, until in his application he came so close, that I was surprised, knowing, as I did, how delightful the harmony had always been in that church. I soon began to persuade myself, however, that there was a Diotrephes there, but could not satisfy myself who it was. Finally, I ventured to seek information, and turning to a good brother, an elder in the church, I said, Mr. L——, who DOES Mr. S. mean? "*You and me*," was his quick reply. I have never asked since, *who my minister meant*, when he was delivering the message of his Master.

(*e*) FAULT-FINDING AND PRAYING.—Two young men, who were members of the same church in New England, were one day engaged in conversation respecting their minister; when one asked the other, "Are you interested in our pastor's preaching?" "Yes," replied the other, "I am indeed; I derive instruction and profit from his discourses." "Well," said his friend, "I am sure I can't feel so; I am very far from being interested in his labors, or getting any benefit from them." "Perhaps," rejoined the other, "you don't pray for our minister; do you?" "No, I confess I do not." "Well, it strikes me that your neglect of this duty explains your want of interest in his ministry. Now let me urge you to remember him daily in your closet supplications, and I presume the more you are exercised in praying *for* him, the more you will be blessed in hearing *from* him." The fault-finding brother took the advice; and some months afterwards he met with his friend and stated the result. He had given his minister a large place in his petitions, and meanwhile his minister had taken an equally large place in his affections; and if the minister derived no benefit from his praying, he surely derived great benefit from his preaching.

(*f*) DR. CHALMERS' CONGREGATION.—It is well known, that the genius and eloquence of this popular clergyman, during his stay in Glasgow, attracted immense crowds to his church, and the feeling of disappointment when a stranger entered his pulpit, was but too visible for any one to mistake it. On one occasion the Rev. Dr. —— of ——, having made an exchange with Dr. Chalmers, was so struck and irritated, on entering the pulpit, with the reluctant advance of the assembling auditory, and the quick retreat of many from the pews, that he stood up, and addressing the congregation, said, "We will not begin the public worship of God, till the chaff blows off." We need not say that these words had the desired effect, and that the audience became stationary under this severe rebuke.

(*g*) HEARING AND PRAYING.—Mr. Philip Henry notes in his diary the saying of a pious hearer of his own, as what much affected him:—"I find it easier," said the good man, "to go six miles to hear a sermon, than to spend one quarter of an hour in meditating and praying over it in secret, as I should, when I come home."

194. HEAVEN, VIEWS AND FORETASTES OF.

(*a*) DYING SAYING OF PRESTON.—The more you are acquainted with God while you live, the more willing you will be to die, to go to him; for death, to a child of God, is nothing else but a resting with God, in whose bosom he hath often been by holy meditation, when he was alive. Dr. Preston, when he was dying, used these words: "Blessed be God, though I change my place I shall not change my company; for I have walked with God while living, and now I go to rest with God."

(*b*) THREE WONDERS IN HEAVEN.—John Newton said, "When I get to heaven, I shall see three wonders there;—the first wonder will be to see many people there whom I did not expect to see—the second wonder will be to miss many people whom I did expect to see—and the third, and greatest wonder of all, will be to find myself there."

(*c*) DISTINCTIONS OF NO SERVICE.—A distinguished character had an extraordinary mark of distinction and honor sent him by his prince as he lay on his death-bed. "Alas!" said he, looking coldly upon it, "this is a mighty fine thing in this country; but I am just going to a country where it will be of no service to me."

(*d*) "I SHALL KNOW BY NEXT CHRISTMAS."—The author of a pamphlet, entitled, "Circumstantial Details of the Last Moments of Mr. Fox," relates the following particulars:—A nobleman mentioning that he had formed a party of pleasure for Christmas, in which he had included Mr. Fox, added, "It will be a new scene, sir; and I think you will approve of it." "I shall indeed be in a new scene by Christmas next," said Mr. Fox. "My lord, what do you think of the state of the soul after death?" Lord ——, confounded by the unexpected turn of the conversation, made no reply. Mr. Fox continued, "That it is immortal, I am convinced. The existence of the Deity is a proof that spirit exists; why not, therefore, the soul of man? And if such an essence as the soul exists, by its nature it may exist for ever. I should have believed in the immortality of the soul, though Christianity had never existed; but how it acts as separated from the body, is beyond my capacity of judgment. This, however, I shall know by next Christmas."

(*e*) "YOU WILL BE A DUKE BUT I SHALL BE A KING."—A consumptive disease seized the eldest son and heir of the Duke of Hamilton, which ended in his death. A little before his departure from the world, he lay ill at the family seat near Glasgow. Two ministers came to see him, one of whom at his request prayed with him. After the minister had prayed, the dying youth put his hand back, and took his Bible from under his pillow, and opened it at the passage, "I have fought a good fight, I have finished my course, I have kept the faith; henceforth there is laid up for me a crown of righteousness, which the Lord, the righteous Judge, shall give me at that day, and not to me only, but unto all them that love his appearing." "This, sirs," said he, "is all my comfort." As he was lying one day on the sofa, his tutor was conversing with him on some astronomical subject, and about the nature of the fixed stars. "Ah," said he, "in a little while I shall know more of this than all of you together." When his death approached, he called his brother to his bed-side, and, addressing him with the greatest affection and seriousness, he closed with these remarkable words: "And now Douglas, in a little time you will be a duke, but I shall be a king."

(*f*) THE CHILD'S ANSWERS.—A little child, when dying, was asked where it was going; "To heaven," said the child. "And what makes you wish to be there?" "Because Christ is there." "But," said a friend, "what if Christ should leave heaven?" "Well," said the child, "I will go with him."

(*g*) WORDS OF REV. THOMAS HALYBURTON.—"Oh, blessed be God that I was born," said this holy man when dying. "I have a father and a mother, and ten brethren and sisters in heaven, and I shall be the eleventh. Oh, blessed be the day that I was ever born! Oh, that I were where he is! And yet, were God to withdraw from me, I should be weak as water. All that I enjoy, though it be miracle on miracle, would not support me without fresh supplies from God. The thing I rejoice in is this, that God is altogether full; and that in the Mediator, Christ Jesus, is all the fulness of the Godhead, and it will never run out. If there be such a glory in Christ's conduct towards me now, what will it be to see the Lamb in the midst of the throne! My peace hath been like a river. Blessed be God that I was ever born."

(*h*) GLORIOUS THING TO DIE.—Mr. N. R. Cobb, of Boston, so much noted for his benevolence, a short time before his death said: "Within the few last days, I have had some glorious views of heaven. It is indeed a glorious thing to die. I have been active and busy in the world. I have enjoyed it as much as any one. God has prospered me. I have every thing to tie me here. I am happy in my family; I have property enough; but how small and mean does this world appear when we are on a sick bed! Nothing can equal my enjoyment in the near prospect of heaven. My hope in Christ is worth infinitely more than all other things. The blood of Christ, the blood of Christ; none but Christ."

(*i*) DYING WORDS OF MR. H. S. GOLDING.—A little before his death, when his brother said to him, "You seem to enjoy foretastes of heaven," he replied, "Oh, this is no longer a foretaste; this is heaven! I not only feel the climate, but I breathe the fine ambrosial air of heaven, and soon shall enjoy the company!" The last words which he was heard to utter, were, "Glory, glory, glory." He died in the twenty-fourth year of his age.

(*j*) MR. RENWICK'S JOY.—Mr. Renwick, the last of the Scottish martyrs, speaking of his sufferings for conscience' sake, says: "Enemies think themselves satisfied that we are put to wander in mosses, and upon mountains; but even amidst the storms of these last two nights, I cannot express what sweet times I have had, when I had no covering but the dark curtains of night. Yea, in the silent watch, my mind was led out to admire the deep and inexpressible ocean of joy, wherein the whole family of heaven swim. Each *star* led me to wonder what HE must be, who is the star of Jacob, of whom all stars borrow their shining."

(*k*) ADRIANUS AND THE MARTYRS.—One Adrianus, in ancient times, seeing the martyrs suffer such grievous things in the cause of Christ, asked, "What is that, which enables them to bear such sufferings?" One of them replied, "Eye hath not seen, nor ear heard, neither hath it entered into the heart of man, the things which God hath prepared for them that love him." These words were like apples of gold in a '*net-work*' of silver, for they made him not only a convert but a martyr too.

(*l*) THE DYING HOTTENTOT.—An old Hottentot having been taken ill, was visited by Mr. Reid, a missionary. He said, "This is the message of death! I shall now go and see the other country, where I have never been, but which I long to see! I am weary of every thing here! I commit too much sin here. I wish to be free from it; I cannot understand things well here, and you cannot understand me. The Lord has spoken much to me, though I cannot explain it."

195. HOLY SPIRIT, AGENCY OF, IN CONVICTION AND CONVERSION *

(*a*) THE INFIDEL AND THE FIRST CHAPTER OF JOHN.—Francis Junius the younger was a considerable scholar, but by no means prejudiced in favor of the Scriptures, as appears by his own account, which is as follows:—My father, who was frequently reading the New Testament, and had long observed with grief the progress I had made in infidelity, had put that book in my way in his library, in order to attract my attention, if it might please God to bless his design, though without giving me the least intimation of it. Here, therefore, I unwittingly opened the New Testament, thus providentially laid before me. At the very first view, as I was deeply engaged in other thoughts, that grand chapter of the evangelist and apostle presented itself to me, "In the beginning was the Word," &c. I read part of the chapter, and was so affected, that I instantly became struck with the divinity of the argument, and the majesty and authority of the composition, as infinitely surpassing the highest flights of human eloquence. My body shuddered; my mind was all in amazement; and I was so agitated the whole day, that I scarce knew who I was. "Thou didst remember me, O Lord my God, according to thy boundless mercy, and didst bring back the lost sheep to thy flock." From that day God wrought so mightily in me by the power of his Spirit, that I began to have less relish for all other studies and pursuits, and bent myself with greater ardor and attention to every thing which had a relation to God.

(*b*) "OH THE GRACE OF GOD!"—John Dickson was a farmer in the parish of Ratho, near Edinburgh, and was for a long time negligent and irreligious. It pleased God to take away his wife, and it became necessary for him to have a nurse in the house, who happily was a pious woman. When his infant daughter was about twenty months old, she was in the room with her father and several of his profane companions. Most unexpectedly the child repeated, in its infantine tones, "Oh the grace of God!" an exclamation she had often heard from her nurse. The attention of the father was thus excited, the Holy Spirit led him to deep and serious reflections, and thus was his conversion to God effected.

(*c*) "AND HE DIED."—A certain libertine, of most abandoned character, happened to stroll into a church, where he heard the fifth chapter of Genesis read, stating that such and such persons lived so long a time, and yet the conclusion was, they "died;" Seth lived 912 years, "and he died;" Enos, 905, "and he died." The frequent repetition of the words, "he died," notwithstanding the great length of years they had lived, impressed him so forcibly with the thought of death and eternity, that, through Divine grace, he became an exemplary Christian.

(*d*) THE PERTINENT TEXT.—One Sabbath morning, while the Rev. Dr. Bedell, of Philadelphia, was preaching, a young man passed by, with a number of companions, as gay and thoughtless as himself. One of them proposed to go into the church, saying, "Let us go and hear what this man has to say, that every body is running after." The young man made this awful answer, "No, I would not go into such a place if Christ himself was preaching." Some weeks after, he was again passing the church, and being alone, and having nothing to do, he thought he would go in without being observed. On opening the door he was struck with awe at the solemn silence of the place, though it was much crowded. Every eye was fixed on the preacher, who was to begin his discourse. His attention was

* Scripture bids us trace all genuine cases of conviction and conversion to the operations of the Holy Spirit; but in the cases here presented, reason too bids us recognize this divine agency, as the other agencies employed are not those which would naturally produce such results.

instantly caught by the text, "I discerned among the youths a young man void of understanding:" Prov. vii. 7. His conscience was smitten by the power of truth. He saw that *he* was the young man described. A view of his profligate life passed before his eyes, and, for the first time, he trembled under the feeling of sin. He remained in the church till the preacher and congregation had passed out; then slowly returned to his home. He had early received infidel principles, but the Holy Spirit who had aroused him in his folly, led him to a constant attendance on the ministry of Dr. B., who had been the instrument of awakening his mind. He cast away his besetting sin, and gave himself to a life of virtue and holiness. He afterwards declared openly his faith in the Lord Jesus Christ, and his desire to devote himself to his service.

(*e*) "WHAT HAST THOU DONE FOR ME?"—A clergyman in Germany, who had exercised the ministerial office for twelve years, while destitute of faith in, and love to the Redeemer, one day was invited, by a wealthy citizen, one of the members of his congregation, with some other guests, to a collation at his house. Directly opposite to him on the wall, hung a picture of Christ on the cross, with two lines written under it:—

"I did this for thee;
What hast thou done for me?"

The picture caught his attention: as he read the lines they seemed to pierce him, and he was involuntarily seized with a feeling he never experienced before. Tears rushed into his eyes: he said little to the company, and took his leave as soon as he could. On the way home these lines constantly sounded in his ears,—divine grace prevented all philosophical doubts and explanations from entering his soul,—he could do nothing but give himself up entirely to the overpowering feeling: even during the night, in his dreams, the question stood always before his mind, "What hast thou done for me?" He died in about three months after this remarkable and happy change in his temper and views, triumphing in the Savior, and expressing his admiration of his redeeming love.

(*f*) "ME TELL THE GREAT MASSA."—A poor black boy, the property of a slave-holder in Africa, having heard of the preaching of the missionaries, felt a strong desire to go and hear about Jesus Christ. For this purpose he crept secretly away one evening, but being obliged to pass under the window of the house, his master observed him, and called out, "Where are you going?" The poor fellow came back trembling, and said, "Me go to hear the missionaries, massa." "To hear the missionaries, indeed; if ever you go there, you shall have nine and thirty lashes, and be put in irons." With a disconsolate look, the poor black replied, "Me tell Massa, me tell the great Massa." "Tell the great Massa," replied the master, "what do you mean?" "Me tell the great Massa, the Lord in Heaven, that my massa was angry with me, because I wanted to go and hear his word." The master was struck with astonishment, his color changed, and unable to conceal his feelings, he hastily turned away, saying, "Go along, and hear the missionaries." Being thus permitted, the poor boy gladly complied. In the mean time, the mind of the master became restless and uneasy. He had not been accustomed to think that he had a Master in heaven, who knew and observed all his actions; and he at length determined to follow his slave, and see if there could be any peace obtained for his troubled spirit; and creeping unobserved, he slunk into a secret corner, and eagerly listened to the words of the missionary. That day Mr. Kircherer addressed the natives from those words, —"Lovest thou me?" "Is there no poor sinner," said he, "who can answer this question? not one poor slave who dares to confess him?" Here the poor slave boy, unable to refrain any longer, sprang up, and holding up both his hands, while the tears streamed down his cheeks, cried out with eagerness, "Yes, massa, me love the Lord Jesus Christ; me do love him, me love him with all my heart." The master was still more astonished, and he went home convinced of the blessings the gospel brings, and became a decided Christian.

(*g*) THE DEAF MAN'S CONVERSION.—One of the most remarkable cases of conversion in the great revival at Wilton, Ct., in 1822, was that of an aged deaf man. This person had not been able to hear a sermon for thirty years, and had long been totally stupid on the subject of religion. But without knowing there was any such thing as a revival in the place, he became deeply impressed in regard to his soul. How or by what means he could not tell; but he was brought under pungent convictions, and at length led to hope and rejoice in Christ.

(*h*) REMARKABLE INSTANCES OF CONVERSION.—Rev. Roswell Burrows, of Groton, Ct., speaking of a great revival which occurred in 1819, in the Second Baptist church in that town, mentions the following facts, which strikingly exhibit the divine agency in conviction and conversion. Mr. B. says: Convictions have generally taken place in the attendance on the word preached; but in many instances without any special means, and under circumstances seemingly the most forbidding, some of which I would notice.

A Mr. ———, who had not attended any religious meeting for six months or more, and but one day previous was almost blaspheming respecting this work, was taken on his bed at night with such horror as to prevent further sleep, or his taking but little sustenance for several days; when he went to the man he previously hated the most of all men, and made a most humble and penitent confession of secret injuries he had done, earnestly begging his forgiveness, and asking his prayers. He soon after was brought to admire the grace he had despised.

A similar case was that of one who had not attended any religious meetings for perhaps ten years or more, and whose conduct, a little before, had been of the most daring nature.

In two instances, in close succession, he was in imminent danger; he made promises o God if he would spare him he would fear and serve him. He obtained his request in what he thought a miraculous deliverance. In both instances he turned round and laughed, as though in defiance of God! In a few weeks afterwards, without any special means, either of worship, reading or religious instruction, his awful state was set before him.

His distress continued about two weeks, when all hope of forgiveness left him. In his agony of soul he was heard in the woods more than half a mile, which brought his neighbors to the place to learn the cause. They did not approach until they perceived his voice to fail. They went to him and found him prostrate and helpless. Soon after they had carried him to his house, he came to, in as great an ecstasy of joy as any pardoned criminal ever experienced.

(*i*) THE BUTCHER AND HIS WIFE.—The Rev. Mr. Fletcher, the pious vicar of Madely, Eng., relates that going into the pulpit one Sabbath morning, he could recollect no part of his sermon, not even the text. Feeling exceedingly perplexed in his mind, and not willing to dismiss the people without saying any thing, he thought that he would endeavor to make a few remarks upon the morning's lesson, which was respecting the three worthies who were cast into the furnace of fire. Finding uncommon and unexpected enlargement of spirit in so doing, he announced to the congregation at the close, that if there was any person present to whom those remarks more particularly applied, he desired that they would call upon him, in the course of the week. On Wednesday a woman called, and informed him that she had been under serious impressions for some time; but that her husband, who was a butcher, constantly opposed her, and forbid her attending any of the religious meetings, even at the parish church, on Sunday; that on the last Sabbath morning he told her that if she should presume to go to church, he would build up a great fire in the oven, and throw her into it, as soon as she came home. But she resolved to go, and says she, "Sir, while you were speaking of the three young men who were thrown into the fiery furnace, because they would not sin against God, I thought it was just my case, and it pleased the Lord then and there to set my soul at liberty. I went home with a light heart, trusting that the Lord would be with me. When I came near the house, I saw the flames issuing from the oven, and knowing what a man my husband was, I expected to be immediately thrown into it. But what was my amazement upon opening the door, instead of being thrown into the oven, to find my husband upon his knees crying for mercy." Says Mr. Fletcher, "I then knew why I had forgotten my sermon, and was led to speak upon something else."

(*j*) A DIFFICULT CASE.—"It is unphilosophical," says a modern writer, "to introduce divine agency when adequate human means are in exercise." Suppose we should, for argument's sake, grant it; there are still left multitudes of problems, that this writer and kindred errorists will not easily solve; cases where "adequate human means" were not in exercise. Were any such means employed in the following instance?

A young man who was very thoughtless and negligent of religion, and to whom no person had spoken on the subject, as he was standing engaged in an engrossing employment, became suddenly and remarkably impressed with a sense of the being and character of God. His unutterable emotions were not those of fear, but of reverence, solemnity and tenderness. His mental exclamation was, "Oh the being, the majesty, the goodness of God! And how have I neglected Him!" His frame trembled, and tears, floods of tears, gave vent to his feelings.*

Was there any adequate human means here? Do men get excited upon politics, poetry or philosophy in this way? How can any body be so wilfully blind to the operations of God's Spirit, as to say such convictions are all very natural and no special power of God exhibited in them?

(*k*) "THE WIND BLOWETH, &c."—It was on Sunday evening following the old Thanksgiving in Mass., (says a writer in the S. S. Treasury,) that I left my father's house to attend a religious meeting in the neighborhood. The moon, as I distinctly recollect, had just appeared above the horizon, and cast its gentle beams full in my face, while all around was hushed in silent repose. I had walked but a few steps, when a strange solemnity stole in upon my heart. Whence it came I knew not. Why I should feel thus, I could not tell. But I was solemn, I was *grieved:* and as I walked slowly along, my burden increased, for a burden it was, and while I live I shall not forget the spot where I thought I should soon be pressed down to the earth.

At length I reached the place of worship. It was a private house that had seen many a hard winter, the humble abode of a widow in Israel. I entered and took my seat with some boys of my own age; I was then but little more than nine years old. They soon began to whisper and play, wishing me to join them. But I was wounded in spirit. I could not join them. I had no disposition to do so, and wondered that they could act thus in a place so sacred as that seemed to me. I kept silence and wished to remove from their company.

The neighbors having assembled, the services commenced. It was a conference and prayer meeting, the pastor being present and taking an active part. What was said by him, or by others, I cannot tell now, nor have I been able to tell from that day to this. I know that all who took part in the services were much engaged, and the effect on my mind was to increase my seriousness. I wept; I could not refrain from it. My heart was pained. I was in distress. My pious father, I think it was, sitting near me, and seeing my trouble, took me in his arms and labored to quiet me, thinking me unwell. But no, I was not sick. My body was not in pain. The arrows of the Almighty were in my heart, and under his rebuke I trembled.

I do not recollect as any one at the meeting found out the true cause of my sorrow; if so, I was not aware of it After I returned home, however, my aged grandfather, a man that feared God, ascertained it. He was overcome

* See "Letters on Revivals"

by his feelings, as were indeed all in the house. It was a place of tears,—parents and grandparents mingled theirs with mine. But this did not relieve me; nor did I experience essential relief before retiring for the night, though, as I well remember, my father did so far compose himself as to commend me to God in fervent prayer.

I am the more inclined to think that the state of mind described above was the effect of Divine influence, from the fact that nothing had been said to me personally on the subject of religion. There was no revival among the people, and so no chance for the operation of sympathy; a powerful source of influence among children, as I have since had occasion to observe. From that day to this I have loved the church of God, and hoped for salvation through grace in Christ Jesus.

(*l*) THE TWO DUELISTS.—B—— was a member of one of the New England Colleges, from a southern section of the country. He left his class before the completion of the College course, with habits of dissipation. As was anticipated, on his return to the south he plunged into vice without restraint. "My life," to use his own words, "was a continual round of dissipation, criminal in the extreme, and ruinous in its effects both to my body and soul."

But the lowest depth of depravity had not yet been reached. An extract from a letter dated Dec. 1832, will give his own account:—"I continued this course of life, as above described, until a few days before the protracted meeting commenced. And, sir, what think you brought me to a pause? Doubtless you will say, to compose my mind, and to strive for a blessing. Oh! no, sir; it was to prepare myself for *mortal combat* with a fellow being! The time of our meeting was fixed, and it happened to be the day on which the people of God were to assemble together. Within less than half a mile from that solemn assembly, we met, and exchanged shots with pistols. To give you an idea of my utter recklessness and depravity of heart at that time—when I saw the weapon of my antagonist directed towards me, and by one who was esteemed sure and deadly in his aim, the last thought that I recollect was, that I should now have an opportunity of gratifying my *curiosity* respecting the nature of a future state! His ball struck the earth very near my feet—my own passed a few inches from his breast. I returned home to a mother and relations, half dead with grief and anxiety."

Let us turn from this scene to one of a different character. "The *next* day found my antagonist and myself on the same bench at an inquiry meeting, overwhelmed with grief and tears for our sins. The conflict was truly great. For six days I seldom ate or slept. I was at last so much reduced and enfeebled I had scarcely strength to rise from my knees. A consciousness of pardon and acceptance with God was at length obtained—a new song has been put into my mouth."

(*m*) THE PERSECUTED SON.—After his conversion, Dr. Taft was one day in conversation with a young man of a respectable family, with whom he was connected, and had occasion to reprove him for some improper expression of which he had made use. The reproof went to his heart; and thoughtless as he had been, so deeply did he feel it, that passing in an instant from gay to grave, he begged the Doctor to pray with him. The transition was so sudden and unexpected, that at first he thought him in jest, and hesitated to comply. In the end, the young man was convinced of sin, and was brought to God, and became a minister of the Gospel.

(*n*) INFIDEL CONVERTED BY ONE WORD.—In a work entitled, "Religion considered as the only basis of happiness and true philosophy," is mentioned the following incident:—Others, after having doubted all their lives, change in a moment their sentiments. I know a man of great sense and very high character, whose conversion was brought about by a single expression. He was yet in the age of the passions; he had never possessed the least principle of religion; and he prided himself upon being an atheist. One day, in the presence of an ecclesiastic equally distinguished by his eminent virtues and talents, he affected to brave all decorum, which ought at that instant to have constrained him to hold his tongue at least, and after having given him a detail of his sentiments and opinions, he ironically added, that according to every appearance he should never be converted. "Ah!" exclaimed the ecclesiastic, who till then had been silent, "if you could then but *hope!*" He said no more—he got up, and went out. But these words made a deep impression upon the heart of the atheist. He had no difficulty to comprehend their energetic meaning. A crowd of new reflections presented themselves to his mind—he longed to see and converse with the man who had produced in him so strange a revolution. The next day he went and opened to him his heart, asked his advice, hearkened to him with attention, with eagerness, and from that moment renounced forever the vain sophisms of false philosophy. Such is the power of the spirit of grace, it produces the most sudden and surprising changes, and its effects confound the incredulous observer, who professes to be acquainted with the human heart.

(*o*) THE TWO SWISS SOLDIERS.—Two Swiss soldiers, says the Western Recorder, had been brought up in ignorance of the great truths of the gospel. One of them became dangerously sick; and as his life was apparently near its close, began to see that he was a great sinner, to tremble with awful apprehensions about his future state, and to cry for mercy. The other, who was his cousin, had compassion upon him, and finally recollecting himself, he said, not comprehending the import of his own words—"I have heard that there is one Jesus somewhere, who saves sinners; you had better try to find him." It was enough. The sick man recollected indistinctly that he had heard such a name. He sought him; he found him; and contrary to all expectation recovered from his sickness, and became in his turn a successful preacher to his distant relative. Both went on their way rejoicing, ignorant and simple-hearted, knowing scarcely any thing about the subject of religion, excepting as they were taught by the Spirit.

(*p*) A SINGULAR REVIVAL.—In the township of R., in the western par of New York, says a writer in the Ch. Watchman, without any special or known cause, numbers of individuals were suddenly aroused to anxious inquiry and trembling respecting their souls. Some in different parts of the town, without any knowledge of the affections of others, were alarmed by the consideration of their sins. Two men, from different directions, came to a clergyman in the morning, asking What shall we do? About nine o'clock in the same morning, one of the members of the church called upon the same clergyman, to go and visit several anxious individuals in his neighborhood; and before night it was ascertained, that almost the whole population of a considerable district, were solemnly, and with weeping, asking the prayers and instructions of the people of God.

Accompanied by the pastor, on that and the subsequent day, we visited from house to house; but wherever we went the Spirit had preceded us. The whole region was a Bochim. A solemn awe pervaded our soul, and we could not but feel that, "God is in very deed in our midst."

Revivals, thus commencing, are, indeed, *rare;* but where they *do* occur they show very clearly the agency of the Holy Spirit.

196. Holy Spirit Grieved.

(*a*) PRICE OF VAIN AMUSEMENT.—Rev. Caleb Benson, a minister of my acquaintance, was invited by a lady in Plymouth, Mass., to visit her daughter who was lying at the point of death. As he entered the room and commenced with her, he inquired why she wished to see him. She said, she had only consented to see him for the sake of gratifying her friends, that it would do her no good to be visited by him or any other minister. He asked why. She said, the time had been when her mind was powerfully wrought upon by God's Spirit, and occupied with serious thoughts about her eternal welfare. She was convinced then, that she was a guilty, condemned sinner, that she needed pardoning mercy. Her convictions, instead of being of a transient character, had distressed her for months. At length she was invited to be present at a ball, or party of pleasure. She was respectfully and urgently solicited by her young and unconverted acquaintances to attend. But conscience strongly remonstrated—she felt convinced that if she went to that scene of vain amusement, it would be jeopardizing the interests of her soul. Still Satan urged her to accede to their requests. While she was preparing to go, however, and while she was on her way to the place where the gay circle met, she felt that she was doing wickedly, and that if she joined them, perhaps God would leave her to herself, and her soul be lost for ever. She came near the house—she hesitated—doubting whether to go in or not. But at last she yielded to the suggestions of Satan and tremblingly crossed the threshold. But no sooner had she entered and begun to participate in the evening's amusements, than her convictions all left her. Since that time she said, she had had no compunctions of conscience whatever;—powerful preaching, personal appeals, judgments and mercies, and even the firm belief that she must soon die, had not affected her hard heart, or awakened the least anxiety of mind. Her case she said was hopeless. The minister told her that Christ had saved a Manasseh, a Mary Magdalen, the thief upon the cross, the persecuting Saul, and that he was able to save her. Yes, she said, she knew all that; she knew he was able to save all that came unto him for mercy, but she had no desire to come—that the Spirit had taken its flight and left her to hardness of heart, and blindness of mind. Mr. Benson proposed prayer; but she told him his prayers would do her no good. She consented, however, to gratify her friends, that he should pray; "but in prayer," says Mr. Benson, "I had no unction, no liberty. Heaven seemed closed against all my petitions in her behalf." It was a heart-rending case. "You will hear in a short time, Mr. Benson," said she, "that I am gone, but remember that my soul is lost." He visited her afterwards, but gained no satisfaction; the wretched girl died as she had lived, without hope and without God.

(*b*) NO PLACE FOR REPENTANCE.—"I have always believed," said a despairing sinner, just on the brink of eternity, "that there was a horrible thought in dating the possible departure of the Spirit of God from the soul. We shudder at the idea of desertion, without reflecting on its particulars. But it is tolerable while wrapt in the mystery of ignorance—ignorance of its manner, its cause, and its time. And yet, at this very hour, I can look back to the turning point of my hopes. I can remember my struggles under conviction. I can recall the weariness of effort, the distaste, the compunctions which preceded the first bold act of worldliness; and which, in their departure, declared the issue decisive. In all the confusion of my thoughts, there is an unchanging spot in the survey of the past. There it remains and no hand can blot it out. No, you are not to imagine my judgment impaired in such a review. I can deliberately retrace the seasons departed. My return to the world was not designated by an act which the common rules of morality would impeach. But it was by one, which, it is plain, put an end to the struggle. And I could not renew the conflict when I would willingly have done so. Conviction did not leave me. But it sat on my spirits like a lifeless weight, that instead of giving them activity, crushed them down. My judgment is as much convinced as ever. But it avails me nothing. The brightness of a holy law, and that of the world which I am approaching, only render my condition more awful, as the midnight lightning does that of the wrecked mariner, by showing him the impossibility of escape. I can see, I can comprehend, but I can lay hold of nothing, I can compel no play of that interest which the near approach of the Holy Spirit once created in my bosom." We will drop the curtain here, for in less than an hour, the sufferer knew more of eternity than you or I.

(*c*) AWFUL PRAYER ANSWERED.—"About twenty years ago," said a dying man, in G——, New-York, "I was convinced of sin; and so pungent were my convictions, that my life seemed insupportable. Instead of going, as urged by the word and Spirit of God, to him who gives rest to the weary and heavy-laden, I retired to a grove—knelt before God; but instead of pleading for his reconciled favor, prayed that he would unburden my soul, by taking his Holy Spirit from me. My prayer was answered. For I had no sooner risen upon my feet, than my sense of sin and fear of hell were gone. From that day to this, I have had no anxiety about my eternal state. In that grove I prayed away the Spirit of God, and He will never return to offer me pardon and eternal life through the blood of Christ. I know that I shall soon be in hell. Nothing can save me. My doom is sealed, and yet, I am quite indifferent to the future."

HONESTY.

197. Examples of.

(*a*) COLLECTOR AND PEASANT.—M. Drouillard, collector of taxes for the arrondissement of Condom, France,) father of a numerous family, happening to arrive very late in the evening, in the town of Auch, on his way to the receiver-general, in order to convey to that gentleman the sum of six thousand francs in specie, found, on his arrival there, that he had lost the bag containing the money he thus intended to pay.

Though the unfortunate man caused immediate search to be made, no traces of the lost treasure could be discovered. The next morning, he applied to a friend, for the loan of a horse, in order to be enabled to pursue his inquiries with more effect; but his friend's horses happening to be out, that gentleman went himself to a neighbor, named Roussel, a peasant in comparatively low circumstances, to borrow one, mentioning, at the same time, for whom it was wanted, as well as the heavy loss M. Drouillard had sustained.

No sooner had Roussel heard what had happened, than he exclaimed, "Do not give yourself any further trouble; I know where the money is;" and he immediately delivered to him the identical bag containing the six thousand francs.

It appears, that having found this bag, on his return from his daily occupations, he had placed it, though not without some difficulty on account of its weight, upon his horse, and carried it home, without ascertaining how much it contained, or communicating his good fortune to his family; that, the next morning, he had got up at an early hour, and spent about an hour in going to the market place and elsewhere, in order to learn whether any person had made any inquiries about it; and that he was but just then returned home, without having been able to ascertain who had lost it, when he was thus introduced to the delighted owner.

(*b*) TRIBUTE TO M. CORNET.—In Bossuet's funeral oration for M. Cornet, he mentioned the following fact:—One of his friends having a law-suit, M. Cornet exerted his interest in favor of his friend, with a judge who was to try the cause; and it was decided in his favor. Some time afterwards, M. Cornet had doubts of the justice of the decision; and being apprehensive that it had been influenced by his conversations with the judge, he paid to the adversary the whole amount of the sum in dispute.

(*c*) THE POOR HOTEL-KEEPER.—The following interesting anecdote occurs in a German work, entitled, "A Picture of St. Petersburgh."

In a little town, five miles from St. Petersburgh, lived a poor German woman. A small cottage was her only possession, and the visits of a few shipmasters, on their way to Petersburgh, her only livelihood. Several Dutch shipmasters having supped at her house one evening, she found, when they were gone, a sealed bag of money under the table. Some one of the company had no doubt forgotten it, but they had sailed over to Cronstadt, and the wind being fair, there was no chance of their putting back. The woman put the bag into her cupboard, to keep it till it should be called for. Full seven years, however, elapsed, and no one claimed it; and though often tempted by opportunity, and oftener by want, to make use of the contents, the poor woman's good principles prevailed and it remained untouched.

One evening, some shipmasters again stopped at her house for refreshment. Three of them were English, and the fourth a Dutchman. Conversing on various matters, one of them asked the Dutchman, if he had ever been in that town before. "Indeed I have," replied he; "I know the place but too well: my being here cost me once seven hundred rubles." "How so?" "Why, in one of these wretched hovels, I once left behind me a bag of rubles." "Was the bag sealed?" asked the woman, who was sitting in a corner of the room, and whose attention was aroused by the subject. "Yes, yes, it was sealed, and with this very seal here at my watch-chain." The woman knew the seal instantly. "Well, then," said she, "by that you may recover what you have lost." "Recover it, mother! No, no; I am rather too old to expect that: the world is not quite so honest: besides, it is full seven years since I lost the money;—say no more about it, it always makes me melancholy."

Meanwhile, the woman slipped out, and presently returned with the bag. "See here," said she; "honesty is not so rare, perhaps, as you imagine;" and she threw the bag on the table.

(*d*) EPAMINONDAS NOT TO BE BRIBED.—When great presents were sent to Epaminondas, the celebrated Theban general, he used to observe,—"If the thing you desire be good, I will do it without any bribe, even because it is good; if it be not honest, I will not do it for all the goods in the world." He was so great a contemner of riches, that, when he died, he left not enough to discharge the expenses of his funeral.

(*e*) THE HONEST HORSE TRADERS.—Two aged men near Marshalton, Va., traded, or according to Virginia parlance, *swapped*, horses on this condition: that on that day week, the one who thought he had the best of the bargain, should pay to the other two bushels of wheat. The day came, and, strange as it may seem, they met about half way between their respective homes. "Where art thou going?" said one. "To thy house with the wheat," answered the other. "And whither art thou riding?" "Truly," replied the other, "I was taking the wheat to thy house." Each pleased with the bargain, had thought the wheat justly due to his neighbor and was going to pay it.

(*f*) THE TWO FARMERS.—Two neighboring farmers had a dispute respecting the right to a certain meadow, and they could not compromise the matter. An action at law was accordingly brought to determine it. On the day appointed for the trial, one of the farmers, having dressed himself in his Sunday clothes, called upon his opponent to accompany him to the Judge. Finding his neighbor at work on his ground, he said to him, "Is it possible you can have forgotten that our cause is to be decided to-day?" "No," said the other, "I have not forgotten it; but I cannot well spare time to go. I knew you would be there, and I am sure you are an honest man, and will say nothing but the truth. You will state the case fairly, and justice will be done." And so it proved; for the farmer who went to the Judge, stated his neighbor's claims so clearly, that the cause was decided against himself; and he returned to inform his opponent that he had gained the property.

(*g*) THE MAGNANIMOUS NEPHEW.—A farmer in Bucks County, Penn., died and left his farm, stock, &c., to one of his sons: to the other, who had offended him, he bequeathed £600. Notwithstanding the utmost efforts of the poorer brother, he found himself unable to obtain the £600 from his more wealthy brother, and with a family, he was obliged to struggle through life without getting any portion of the money left him by the will of his father. At length the wealthy brother died, and the property fell to an only son. So soon as he got possession of the property, he ascertained the amount of the legacy bequeathed by his grandfather to his uncle; he then added the interest which had accrued all the time the legacy had been withheld, and for the whole amount he forthwith sent a check to his uncle.

(*h*) THE HONEST OSTIAK.—A Russian was travelling from Tobolsk to Beresow. On the road he stopped one night at the hut of an Ostiak. In the morning, on continuing his journey, he discovered that he had lost his purse containing about one hundred rubles.

The son of the Ostiak found the purse, while out a hunting, but instead of taking it up, went and told his father; who was equally unwilling to touch it, and ordered his son to cover it with some bushes.

A few months after this, the Russian returned, and stopped at the same hut, but the Ostiak did not recognize him. He related the loss he had met with.

The Ostiak listened very attentively, and when he had finished, "You are welcome," said he; "here is my son who will show you the spot where it lies; no hand has touched it but the one which covered it over, that you might recover what you have lost."

(*i*) THE TURKISH POSTMAN.—Keppel relates, in his "Journey across the Balcan," that, in the winter of 1828, a Turkish postman was sent to some distant part with a considerable sum of money in specie. The money, in such cases, is carried in bags, which the merchants call "groupes." They are given to the postman, and without receiving any written document as proof of the receipt. This man, on returning from his journey, was applied to by a French house for fifteen thousand piastres; a sum, at that time, equal to fifteen thousand dollars. He made no attempt to evade the demand, but immediately said, "I have doubtless lost the bag, and must therefore pay you as soon as I can raise the money." After maturely thinking of the loss, he returned by the same road, quite confident that if any Mohammedan should find the money, it would be returned to him. He had travelled nearly the whole distance, when he arrived, in a very melancholy mood, at a small, miserable coffee-house, where he remembered to have stopped a few moments on his way. He was accosted at the door, by the café-jee, who called out to him, "Halloo, sheriff! when you were last here, you left a bag, which I suppose to contain gold. You will find it just where you placed it." The postman entered, and discovered the identical bag, evidently untouched, although it must have been left exposed to the grasp of the numerous chance customers of a Turkish café.

(*j*) DISCHARGED FOR HONESTY.—A country gentleman, says the N. E. Galaxy, placed a son with a merchant in —— street. And for a season all went on well. But at length the young man sold a dress to a lady, and as he was folding it up, he observed a flaw in the silk, and remarked, "Madam, I deem it my duty to tell you there is a fracture in the silk." This spoiled the bargain. But the merchant overheard the remark; and had he reflected a moment, he might have reasoned thus with himself, "Now I am safe, while my affairs are committed to the care of an *honest* clerk." But he was not pleased; so he wrote immediately to the father to come and take him home; for, said he, "*he will never make a merchant.*"

The father, who had brought up his son with the strictest care, was not a little surprised and grieved, and hastened to the city to ascertain wherein his son had been deficient. Said the anxious father, And why will he not make a merchant?

Merchant.—Because he has no tact. Only a day or two since, he *voluntarily* told a lady who was buying silk that the goods were damaged, and so I lost the bargain. Purchasers must look out for themselves. If they cannot discover flaws, it will be foolishness in me to tell them of their existence.

Father.—And is this all the fault?

Merchant.—Yes: he is very well in other respects.

Father.—Then I love my son better than ever; and I *thank you* for telling me of the matter; I would not have him in YOUR STORE another day for the world.

198. Honesty the Best Policy.

(*a*) THE POOR BOY AND THE WALLET.—A lad was proceeding to an uncle's to petition him for aid for a sick sister and her children, when he found a wallet containing fifty dollars. The aid was refused, and the distressed family were pinched for want. The boy revealed the fortune to his mother; but expressed a doubt about using any portion of the money. His mother confirmed the doubt, and they resolved not to use it. The pocket-book was advertised, and the owner found. Being a man of wealth, upon learning the history of the family, he presented the fifty dollars to the sick mother and took the boy into his service, and he became one of the most successful merchants in Ohio. Honesty always brings its reward—to the mind, if not to the pocket.

(*b*) THE MASTER AND THE APPRENTICE.—A gentleman, one day conversing with a watchmaker upon the dishonest practices of persons in his way of business, was thus addressed by him: "Sir, I served my apprenticeship with a man who did not fear God, and who consequently was not very scrupulous in the charges which he made to his customers. He used frequently to call me a fool, and tell me I should die in a workhouse, when, in his absence, I used to make such charges as appeared to me fair and honest. In course of time I set up in business for myself, and have been so successful as never to have wanted a shilling, whilst my master, who used to reproach me for my honesty, became so reduced in circumstances as to apply to me for a couple of guineas, and did at length himself actually die in a workhouse."

(*c*) CECIL AND THE ROBBERS.—On one occasion when the Rev. Richard Cecil had to travel on horseback from London to Lewes to serve his churches, instead of leaving town early in the morning he was detained till noon, in consequence of which he did not arrive on East Grinstead Common till after dark. On this common he met a man on horseback who appeared to be intoxicated and ready to fall from his horse at every step. Mr. C. called to him and warned him of his danger, which the man disregarding, with his usual benevolence he rode up to him in order to prevent his falling, when the man immediately seized the reins of his horse. Mr. C. perceiving he was in bad hands endeavored to break away, on which the man threatened to knock him down if he repeated the attempt. Three other men on horseback immediately rode up, placing Mr. C. in the midst of them. On perceiving his danger it struck him, "Here is an occasion for faith!" and that gracious direction also occurred to him: "Call upon me in the time of trouble; I will deliver thee."—Psa. 50: 15. He secretly lifted up his heart to God, entreating the deliverance which he alone could effect. One of the men, who seemed to be the captain of the gang, asked him who he was and whither he was going. Mr. C. here recurred to a principle to which his mind was habituated, that "nothing needs a lie;" he therefore told them very frankly his name and whither he was going. The leader said: "Sir, I know you, and have heard you preach at Lewes. Let the gentleman's horse go. We wish you good-night." Mr. C. had about him sixteen pounds, which he had been to town to receive, and which at that time was to him a large sum.

(*d*) THE SWEEP AND THE WATCH.—A poor chimney-sweeper's boy was employed at the house of a lady of rank to clean the chimney of her chamber. Finding himself on the hearth of the lady's dressing-room, and perceiving no one there, he waited a few moments to take a view of the beautiful things in the apartment. A gold watch, richly set with diamonds, particularly caught his attention, and he could not forbear taking it in his hand. Immediately the wish arose in his mind: "Ah, if thou hadst such a one!" After a pause he said to himself: "But if I take it I shall be a thief. And yet," continued he, "no one sees me. No one? Does not God see me, who is present every where? Should I then be able to say my prayers to him after I had committed this theft? Could I die in peace?" Overcome by these thoughts a cold shivering seized him. "No!" said he, laying down the watch; "I had much rather be poor and keep my good conscience than rich and become a rogue." At these words he hastened back into the chimney.

The countess, who was in the room adjoining, having overheard his soliloquy, sent for him the next morning and thus accosted him: "My little friend, why did you not take the watch yesterday?" The boy fell on his knees, speechless and astonished. "I heard every thing you said," continued her ladyship; "thank God for enabling you to resist this temptation, and be watchful over yourself for the future. From this moment you shall be in my service; I will both maintain and clothe you—nay, more: I will procure you good instruction, that shall ever guard you from the danger of similar temptations." The boy burst into tears; he was anxious to express his gratitude, but he could not. The countess strictly kept her promise, and had the pleasure to see him grow up a pious and intelligent man.

(*e*) THE EARL AND THE FARMER.—A farmer called on the Earl Fitzwilliam, (of Eng.) to represent that his crop of wheat had been seriously injured in a field adjoining a certain wood, where his lordship's hounds had, during the winter, frequently met to hunt. He stated that the young wheat had been so cut up and destroyed, that, in some parts, he could not hope for any produce. "Well, my friend," said his lordship, "I am aware that we have frequently met in that field, and that we have done considerable injury; and if you can procure an estimate of the loss you have sustained, I will repay you." The farmer replied, that, anticipating his lordship's consideration and kindness, he had requested a friend to assist him in estimating the damage, and they thought that as the crop seemed quite destroyed, £50 would not more than repay him. The earl immediately gave him the money. As the harvest, however, approached, the wheat grew, and in those parts of the field which were most trampled, the corn was strongest and most luxuriant. The farmer went again to his lordship, and being introduced, said, "I am come, my lord, respecting the field of wheat adjoining such a wood." His lordship immediately recollected the circumstance. "Well, my friend, did not I allow you sufficient to remunerate you for your loss?" "Yes, my lord, I find that I have sustained no loss at all, for where the horses had most cut up the land, the crop is most promising, and I have, therefore brought the £50 back again." "Ah," exclaimed the venerable earl, "this is what I like; this is as it should be between man and man." He then entered into conversation with the farmer, asking him some questions about his family—how many children he had, etc. His lordship then went into another room, and returning, presented the farmer with a check for £100, saying, "Take care of this, and when your eldest son is of age, present it to him, and tell him the occasion that produced it." We know not which to admire most—the benevolence or the wisdom displayed by this illustrious man; for while doing a noble act of generosity, he was handing down a lesson of integrity to another generation

(*f*) THE BEGGAR AND DR. SMOLLETT.—A beggar asking Dr. Smollett for alms, he gave him through mistake a guinea. The poor fellow perceiving it, hobbled after him to return it; upon which Smollett returned it to him, with another guinea as a reward for his honesty, exclaiming at the same time, "What a lodging has honesty taken up with!"

(*g*) SAVED BY INTEGRITY.—A plain farmer, Richard Jackson by name, was apprehended, during the revolutionary war, under such circumstances as proved beyond all doubt his purpose of joining the king's forces; an intention which he was too honest to deny. Accordingly, he was delivered over to the high sheriff, and committed to the county gaol. The prison was in such a state that he might have found little difficulty in escaping; but he considered himself in the hands of authority, such as it was, and the same conscientiousness—(whether misguided or not, we do not say)—which led him to take up arms, made him equally ready to endure the consequences. After lying there a few days, he applied to the sheriff for leave to go out and work by the day, promising that he would return regularly at night. His character for simple integrity was so well known, that permission was given without hesitation, and for eight months Jackson went out every day to labor, and as duly came back to the prison at night. In the month of May, the sheriff prepared to conduct him to Springfield, where he was to be tried for high treason. Jackson said this would be a needless trouble and expense; he could save the sheriff both, and go just as well by himself. His word was once more taken, and he set off alone, to present himself for trial and certain condemnation. On the way, he was overtaken in the woods by Mr. Edwards, a member of the council of Massachusetts, which at that time was the supreme executive of the state. This gentleman asked him whither he was going. To Springfield, sir, was his answer, to be tried for my life. To this casual interview, Jackson owed his escape. Having been found guilty and condemned to death, application was made to the council for mercy. The evidence and the sentence were stated, and the president put the question whether the pardon should be granted. It was opposed by the first speaker. The case, he said, was perfectly clear; the act was unquestionably high treason, and the proof complete; and if mercy was shown in this case, he saw no reason why it should not be granted in every other. Few governments have understood how just and politic it is to be merciful. This hard-hearted opinion accorded with the temper of the times, and was acquiesced in by one member after another, till it came Mr. Edwards' turn to speak. Instead of delivering his opinion, he simply related the whole story of Jackson's singular demeanor, and what had passed between them in the woods. For the honor of Massachusetts and of human nature, not a man was found to weaken the natural effect of Mr. Edwards' statements on their minds. The council began to hesitate, and when a member ventured to say that *such* a man certainly ought not to be sent to the gallows, a natural feeling of humanity and justice prevailed, and a pardon was immediately made out.

199. HONORS, WORLDLY, VANITY OF.

(*a*) THE SUPERSEDED AMBASSADOR.—In 1664, Sir Richard Fanshawe was ambassador from Charles II. to Madrid. This gentleman had been remarkable for his fidelity to the cause of Charles I, in whose service he had not only endured great privations, but had lost the whole of his family property. The fealty he had shown to the father was shown to the son, who, in rewarding him with an embassy to Spain, by that very elevation only made his fall the greater, for his disgrace in being superseded by another so affected him, that he died of a broken heart; such is the gratitude of princes! Lady Fanshawe's account of their arrival at Cadiz, confirms the truth of the foregoing observations. After mentioning that when they landed they were welcomed by volleys of guns, received by a very large number of people, and met by the governor and his lady, she adds, "When we came to the house where we were to lodge, we were nobly treated, and the governor's wife did me the honor to sup with me. We had a guard who constantly waited on us, and sentries at the gate below, and at the stairs-head above. We were visited by all the persons of quality in that town; our house was richly furnished both my husband's quarter and mine The richness of the gilt and silver plate which we had in great abundance, was fit only for the entertainment of so great a prince as his majesty our master, in the representation of whose person my husband received this great entertainment; yet, I assure you, notwithstanding this temptation, that your father and myself both wished ourselves in a retired country life in England, as more agreeable to our inclinations." But "as never any ambassador's family went into Spain more gloriously, so never went out any so sad;" for the departure of this lady was little else than expulsion from a situation where every earthly honor had been heaped upon her to satiety, and her company was the dead body of her beloved lord! She found, however, strength and consolation where only they are to be found, in God.

(*b*) EXPERIENCE OF WOTTON.—Sir Henry Wotton, in the reign of Queen Elizabeth, who had great honors conferred on him, on account of his near relation to the Queen's great favorite, Robert, Earl of Essex, was very intimate with the Duke of Tuscany, and with James, then King of Scotland, (and afterwards of England,) and had been sent on several embassies to Holland, Germany, and Venice: after all, he desired to retire with this motto, "That he had learned at length, that the soul grew wiser by retirement," and consequently, that a man was more happy in a private situation, than it was possible for him to be with those worldly honors which were accompanied with so many troubles. In short, the utmost of his aim in this life, for the future, was to be Provost of Eton, that there he might enjoy his beloved study and devotion.

(*c*) THE PRIME MINISTER'S MISERY.—On a court day in December, 1795, Sir John Sinclair happened to meet Mr. Secretary Dundas at St. James's, who pressed him to name a day for visiting him at Wimbledon. The day fixed upon chanced to be the last of the year. The party was numerous, and included Mr. Pitt. Sir John remained all night; and next morning, according to Scottish custom, resolved to pay his host an early visit in his own apartment. He found the secretary in the library, reading a long paper on the importance of conquering the Cape, as an additional security to our Indian possessions. His guest shook him by the hand, adding the usual congratulation, "I come, my friend, to wish you a good new year, and many happy returns of the season." The secretary, after a short pause, replied with some emotion, "I hope this year will be happier than the last, for I can scarcely recollect having spent one happy day in the whole of it." This confession, coming from an individual whose whole life hitherto had been a series of triumphs, and who appeared to stand secure upon the summit of political ambition, was often dwelt upon by Sir John as exemplifying the vanity of human wishes.

(*d*) THE SERVANT'S DOCTORATE.—When the University of St. Andrew's, Scotland, *sold her honors*, a certain minister, who deemed that his ministration would be more acceptable, if he possessed what the Germans call the doctor-hat, put £15 in his purse and went to St. Andrew's to "purchase for himself a good degree." His man-servant accompanied him, and was present when his master was formally admitted to the long-desired honor. On his return "the doctor" sent for his servant, and addressed him as follows: "Noo Saunders, ye'll aye be sure to ca' me *the doctor*; and gin ony body spiers at you about me, ye'll be aye sure to say the doctor's in his study, or the doctor's engaged, or the doctor will see you in a crack." "That a' depends," was the reply, "whether ye ca' me the doctor, too!" (The Rev. Dr. started.) "Ay, it's just so," continued the other; "for when I foond that it cost so little, I e'en got a diploma myself, sa ye'll be just good enough to say, 'doctor, put on some coals,' or, 'doctor, bring the whiskey and hot water,' and gin ony body spiers at ye about me, ye'll be aye sure to say, 'the doctor's in the stable,' or, 'the doctor's in the pantry,' or, 'the doctor's digging potatoes,' as the case may be."

200. HOPE, POWER OF.

(*a*) THE SWEEP AND THE CLERGYMAN.—"Passing down Hudson-street in New-York one day," says a clergyman, "a sooty, noisy chimney-sweep crossed my path. I had often noticed this class of persons before; and as I heard their hideous cries and marked their filthy dress and the sooty implements of their calling, I had thought their lot among the most miserable of our race. Pity and curiosity prompted me, as this chimney-sweep was now passing, to address a few kind words. After a salutation I said: 'My friend, this must be a hard life that you live?' 'O, no,' said he, and his eye kindled as he spoke; 'it's not a hard life; it will soon be over, and then we shall have rest.' I was silent for a moment; but recovering from my surprise I replied: 'Yes, indeed, we shall have rest in heaven if we love and serve the Savior on earth. Do *you* love him?' 'I do not wish to presume,' said he, 'but I trust I do love the Savior!' What was my gratification to learn that he was a professor of religion and had been for years a member of a church of the same denomination with myself. And when I told him who I was—a minister of Christ and one of his own brethren—he was full of joy. With a few words of advice and congratulation I passed on. 'O, happy man,' thought I. 'Happier in hope of heaven than the kings of the earth without it. Is not such a hope like an anchor to the soul?'"

(*b*) BISHOP BEVERIDGE AND HIS FRIENDS.—When the pious Bishop Beveridge was on his death-bed he did not know any of his friends or connexions. A minister with whom he had been well acquainted visited him, and when conducted into his room he said: "Bishop Beveridge, do you know me?" "Who are you?" said the bishop. Being told who the minister was, he said that he did not know him. Another friend came who had been equally well known, and accosted him in a similar manner: "Do you know me, Bishop Beveridge?" "Who are you?" said he. Being told it was one of his intimate friends, he said he did not know him. His wife then came to his bedside and asked him if he knew her. "Who are you?" said he. Being told she was his wife, he said he did not know her. "Well," said one of them, "Bishop Beveridge, do you know the Lord Jesus Christ?" "Jesus Christ!" said he, reviving as if the name had produced upon him the influence of a charm; "Oh! yes, I have known Him these forty years; precious Savior, he is my only hope!"

(*c*) REMEMBERING JESUS CHRIST.—A good old minister who died in this country in 1807, at nearly ninety years of age, had lost his recollection and been long incapable of engaging in public services. Towards the last days of his life he was removed to the house of a beloved son, where he was attended to with the most filial affection. On the evening before his death a neighboring minister visited him, but he did not know him. Being told who he was he answered: "No, I do not remember any such person." His beloved son was introduced to him; but no, he did not know him. "I do not remember that I have a son," said the good old man. In short, his memory was so impaired that he knew none of his family or friends about him. At last he was asked: "Do you not remember the Lord Jesus Christ?" On this his eyes brightened; and attempting to lift his hands in the hour of death he exclaimed: "Oh! yes; I do, I do! I remember the Lord Jesus Christ! He is my Lord and my God, by whom I hope to be saved!" May we not be assured that the gracious Redeemer of sinners will not forsake those who thus regard him with a love that even the decay of nature cannot destroy? Blessed are they that put their trust in him! Reader, hast thou done so? If not, what will be thy state when thou comest to die?

(d) WITNESS OF THE SPIRIT. —The celebrated Philip de Morney, prime minister to Henry the IVth of France, one of the greatest statesmen, and the most exemplary Christian of his age, being asked a little before his death, if he still retained the same assured hope of future bliss, which he had so comfortably enjoyed during his illness, he made this memorable reply: "I am," said he, "as confident of it, from the incontestable evidence of the Spirit of God, as ever I was of any mathematical truth from all the demonstrations of Euclid."

(e) THE AFFLICTED SUGAR-BOILER.—A negro named Robert, a sugar-boiler, was dreadfully afflicted for several years; his affliction arose, as was supposed, from a drop of boiling sugar falling on his arm when he was at work. The place broke out, and the sore spread, so that his fingers fell off. The disorder ascended into his head, and his eyes fell out, as also pieces of his skull His feet were likewise affected, and came off. Yet he bore all this with remarkable patience, and, at times, rejoiced in the hope of being received to that place where there is no death, neither sorrow nor crying. The last time I visited him, said the minister, I could not bear to look upon him, but only talked to and prayed with him at his chamber door. When I asked how he was, he said he was just waiting the Lord's time, when he should please to call for him. "Massa," said he, "two hands gone; two eyes gone; two feet gone; no more dis carcase here. Oh, massa! de pain sometimes too strong for me; I am obliged to cry out, and pray to de Lord for his assistance." When he came to close his life, he exhorted all about him to be sure to live to God; and especially his wife, who had remained with him all the time of his affliction; a very rare circumstance then with negroes. But she continued faithful; and he died happy, exhorting her to live to God.

201. HOSPITALITY.

(a) PARK AND THE NEGRESS. —When the celebrated Mungo Park was in Africa, he was directed by one of the native kings to a village to pass the night. He went, but as the order was not accompanied with any provision for his reception, he found every door shut. Turning his horse loose to graze, he was preparing, as a security from wild beasts, to climb a tree, and sleep among the branches, where a beautiful and affecting incident occurred, which gives a most pleasing view of the negro female character. An old woman, returning from the labors of the field, cast on him a look of compassion, and desired him to follow her. She led him to an apartment in her hut, procured a fine fish, which she broiled for his supper, and spread a mat for him to sleep upon. She then desired her maidens, who had been gazing in fixed astonishment on the white man, to resume their tasks, which they continued to ply through a great part of the night. They cheered their labors with a song which must have been composed extempore, as Mr. Park, with deep emotion, discovered that he himself was the subject of it. It said, in a strain of affecting simplicity:—"The winds roared, and the rains fell. The poor white man, faint and weary, came and sat under our tree. He has no mother to bring him milk, no wife to grind his corn." Chorus. "Let us pity the white man, no mother has he," etc. Our traveller was much affected, and next morning could not depart, without requesting his landlady's acceptance of the only gift he had left, two out of the four brass buttons that still remained on his waistcoat.

(b) GETTING AN INVITATION. —Rev. Mr. —— had travelled far to preach to a congregation at ——. After the sermon, he waited very patiently, expecting some one of the brethren to invite him home to dinner. In this he was disappointed. One and another departed, until the house was almost as empty as the minister's stomach. Summoning resolution, however, he walked up to an elderly-looking gentleman, and gravely said—

"Will you go home to dinner with me to-day, brother?" "Where do you live?"

"About twenty miles from this, sir." "No," said the man, coloring, "but *you* must go with *me*." "Thank you—I will cheerfully."

After that time, the minister was no more troubled about his dinner."

(*c*) HOSPITALITY AMONG TURKS.—Mr. Arundel, in his Discoveries in Asia Minor, says: We dismounted at the Oda, a lodging house for travellers, in the village of Cooselare, or Cuselare. It was certainly not a palace, for we shared it with our horses, and there were holes, called windows, without glass or shutters; but the hospitality of our hosts more than compensated for every thing else.

We had trakana soup, pilau, cheese, and petmes, and surprised were we to see our table-cloth, or table-skin, soon after laid, the pancake bread placed all around, and the smoking viands in the midst. It was the more surprising, since we were unexpected guests; and, as the village seemed wretchedly poor, we ventured to ask an explanation; and we learned that our fare was the contribution of many families: the trakana soup was supplied by one, the pilau by a second, the petmes by a third, the bread by a fourth; but all were emulous to feed the famished strangers with as little loss of time as possible: and these were Turks!

(*d*) THE CZAR AND THE PEASANT.—The Czar Ivan, who reigned over Russia about the middle of the sixteenth century, frequently went out disguised, in order to discover the opinion which the people entertained of his administration. One day, in a solitary walk near Moscow, he entered a small village, and pretending to be overcome by fatigue, implored relief from several of the inhabitants. His dress was ragged, his appearance mean; and what ought to have excited the compassion of the villagers and ensured his reception was productive of refusal. Full of indignation at such inhuman treatment, he was just going to leave the place, when he perceived another habitation, to which he had not yet applied for assistance. It was the poorest cottage in the village. The emperor hastened to this, and, knocking at the door, a peasant opened it, and asked him what he wanted. "I am almost dying with fatigue and hunger," answered the Czar; "can you give me a lodging for one night?" "Alas!" said the peasant, taking him by the hand, "you will have but poor fare; you are come at an unlucky time; my wife is in labor; her cries will no let you sleep; but come in, come in; you will at least be sheltered from the cold, and such as we have you shall be welcome to."

The peasant then made the Czar enter a little room full of children; in a cradle were two infants sleeping soundly! A girl three years old was sleeping on a rug near the cradle; while her two sisters, the one five years old, the other almost seven, were on their knees, crying, and praying to God for their mother, who was in a room adjoining, and whose piteous plaints and groans were distinctly heard. "Stay here," said the peasant to the emperor; "I will go and get something for your supper."

He went out and soon returned with some black bread, eggs, and honey. "You see all I can give you," said the peasant; "partake of it with my children. I must go and assist my wife." "Your hospitality," said the Czar, "must bring down blessings upon your house; I am sure God will reward your goodness." "Pray to God, my good friend," replied the peasant, "pray to God Almighty that she may have a safe delivery: that is all I wish for." "And is that all you wish to make you happy?" "Happy! judge for yourself; I have five fine children; a dear wife that loves me; a father and mother both in good health; and my labor is sufficient to maintain them all." "Do your father and mother live with you?" "Certainly; they are in the next room with my wife." "But your cottage here is so very smal.l!" "It is large enough; it can hold us all."

The good peasant then went to his wife, who in about an hour after was happily delivered. Her husband, in a transport of joy, brought the child to the Czar; "Look," said he, "look; this is the sixth she has brought me! May God preserve him as he has done my others!" The Czar, sensibly affected at this scene, took the infant in his arms: "I know," said he, "from the physiognomy of this child, that he will be quite fortunate. He will arrive, I am certain, at preferment." The peasant smiled at the prediction; and at that instant the two eldest girls came to kiss their new-born brother, and their grandmother came also to take him back. The little ones followed her; and the peasant, laying himself down upon his bed of straw, invited the stranger to do the same.

In a moment the peasant was in a sound and peaceful sleep; but the Czar, sitting up, looked around, and contemplated every thing with an eye of tenderness and emotion; the sleeping children and their sleeping father. An undisturbed silence reigned in the cottage. "What a happy chasm! What delightful tranquillity!" said the emperor; "avarice and ambition, suspicion and remorse, never enter here. How sweet is the sleep of innocence!" In such reflections and on such a bed did the mighty emperor of the Russias spend the night! The peasant awoke at the break of day, and his guest, after taking leave of him, said, "I must return to Moscow, my friend; I am acquainted there with a very benevolent man, to whom I shall take care to mention your kind treatment of me. I can prevail upon him to stand godfather to your child. Promise me, therefore, that you will wait for me, that I may be present at the christening; I will be back in three hours at the farthest." The peasant did not think much of this mighty promise; but in the good nature of his heart, he consented, however, to the stranger's request.

The Czar immediately took his leave: the three hours were soon gone, and nobody appeared. The peasant, therefore, followed by his family, was preparing to carry his child to church; but as he was leaving his cottage, he heard on a sudden the trampling of horses and the rattling of many coaches. He knew the imperial guards, and instantly called his family to come and see the emperor go by. They all ran out in a hurry and stood before their door. The horses, men and carriages soon formed a circular line, and at last the state coach of the Czar stopped opposite the peasant's door.

The guards kept back the crowd, which the hopes of seeing their sovereign had collected together. The coach door was opened, the Czar alighted, and, advancing to his host, thus addressed him: "I promised you a godfather; I am come to fulfil my promise: give me your child, and follow me to church." The peasant stood like a statue; now looking at the emperor with the mingled emotions of astonishment and joy; now observing his magnificent robes and the costly jewels with which they were adorned, and now turning to a crowd of nobles that surrounded him. In this profusion of pomp he could not discover the poor stranger who lay all night with him upon straw.

The emperor for some moments silently enjoyed his perplexity, and then addressed him thus: "Yesterday you performed the duties of humanity; today I am come to discharge the most delightful duty of a sovereign, that of recompensing virtue. I shall not remove you from a situation to which you do so much honor, and the innocence and tranquillity of which I envy; but I will bestow upon you such things as may be useful to you. You shall have numerous flocks, rich pastures, and a house that will enable you to exercise the duties of hospitality with pleasure. Your new-born child shall become my ward; for you may remember," continued the emperor, smiling, "that I prophesied he would be fortunate."

The good peasant could not speak; but, with tears of sensibility in his eyes, he ran instantly to fetch the child, brought him to the emperor, and laid him respectfully at his feet. This excellent sovereign was quite affected; he took the child in his arms, and carried him himself to church; and, after the ceremony was over, unwilling to deprive him of his mother's milk, he took him back to the cottage, and ordered that he should be sent to him as soon as he could be weaned. The Czar faithfully observed his engagement, caused the boy to be educated in his palace, provided amply for his farther settlement in life, and continued ever after to heap favors upon the virtuous peasant and his family.

HUMANITY.

202. Humanity Exemplified.

(*a*) CÆSAR AT PHARSALIA.—Julius Cæsar was not more eminent for his valor in overcoming his enemies, than for his humane efforts in reconciling and attaching them to his dominion. In the battle of Pharsalia he rode to and fro, calling vehemently out, "Spare, spare the citizens!" Nor were any killed but such as obstinately refused to accept life. After the battle, he gave every man on his own side leave to save any of the opposite from the list of proscription; and at no long time after he issued an edict, permitting all whom he had not yet pardoned, to return in peace to Italy, to enjoy their estates and honors. It was a common saying of Cæsar that no music was so charming to his ears, as the requests of his friends, and the supplications of those in want of his assistance.

(*b*) A GOVERNOR'S HUMANITY.—When Catharine of Medicis had persuaded Charles IX to massacre all the Protestants in France, orders were sent to the governors of the different provinces to put the Huguenots to death in their respective districts. One Catholic governor, whose memory will ever be dear to humanity, had the courage to disobey the cruel mandate. "Sire," said he, in a letter to his sovereign, "I have too much respect for your majesty not to persuade myself that the order I have received must be forged; but if, which God forbid, it should be really the order of your majesty, I have too much respect for the personal character of my sovereign to obey it."

(*c*) LOUIS XIV AND THE ENGLISH AMBASSADOR.—After the revocation of the famous edict of Nantz, when the Protestants were persecuted in every part of France, an English Ambassador demanded of Louis XIV the liberty of all those who were sent to the galleys on account of their religion. "And what," answered the royal bigot, "would the king of England say, were I to require the release of all his prisoners in Newgate?" "Sir," returned the ambassador, "the king my master would immediately comply with your requisition, if your majesty interposed for them, not as *malefactors*, but as your *brethren*."

(*d*) MEASURING FEELING.—A respectable merchant of London, having been embarrassed in his circumstances, and his misfortunes having been one day the subject of conversation in the Royal Exchange, several persons expressed great sorrow; when a foreigner who was present, said, "I *feel* five hundred pounds for him, what do *you feel?*"

(*e*) HENRY IV AND THE SIEGE.—When Henry IV of France was advised to attempt taking Paris by an assault, before the King of Spain's troops arrived to succor the leaguers, he absolutely protested against the measure, on the principle of humanity. "I will not," said he, "expose the capital to the miseries and horrors which must follow such an event. I am the father of my people, and will follow the example of the true mother who presented herself before Solomon. I had much rather not have Paris, than obtain it at the expense of humanity, and by the blood and death of so many innocent persons."

Henry reduced the city to obedience without the loss of blood, except two or three burgesses who were killed. "If it was in my power," said this humane monarch, "I would give fifty thousand crowns to redeem those citizens, to have the satisfaction of informing posterity that I had subdued Paris without spilling a drop of blood."

(*f*) THE CHILD'S RESCUE.—An English gentleman relates the following affecting fact:

I was once going in my gig up the hill in the village of Frankford, near Philadelphia, when a little girl, about two years old, who had travelled away from a small house, was lying basking in the sun in the middle of the road. About two hundred yards before I got to the child, the teams, five big horses in each, of three wagons, the drivers of which had stopped to drink at a tavern at the brow of the hill, started off, and came nearly abreast, galloping down the road. I got my gig off the road as speedily as I could, but expected to see the poor child crushed to pieces. A young man, a journeyman carpenter, who was shingling the shed by the roadside, seeing the child, and aware of the danger, though a stranger to the parents, jumped from the top of the shed, ran into the road, and snatched up the child when scarcely an inch before the hoof of the leading horse. The horse's leg knocked him down, but he, catching the child by its clothes, flung it out of the way of the other horses, and saved himself by rolling back with surprising agility. The mother of the child, who had apparently been washing, seeing teams coming, and knowing the situation of the child, rushed out, and catching it up just as the carpenter had flung it back, hugged it in her arms, and uttered a shriek such as I never heard before. Then she dropped down as if entirely dead. By the application of the usual means, she was restored, however, in a little while; and I, being about to depart, asked the carpenter if he was a married man, and whether he was a relation of the parents of the child. He said he was neither. "Well then," said I, "you merit the gratitude of every father and mother in the world; and I will show you mine by giving you what I have," pulling out the nine or ten dollars which I had in my pocket. "No, I thank you, sir," said he; "I have only done what it was my duty to do."

(*g*) LESSON TO CONQUERORS—When Edward the Confessor had entered England from Normandy to recover the kingdom, and was ready to give the Danes battle, one of his captains assured him of victory, adding, "We will not leave one Dane alive." To which Edward replied, "God forbid that the kingdom should be recovered for me, who am but one man, by the death of thousands. No: I will rather live a private life, unstained by the blood of my fellow-men, than be a king by such a sacrifice." Upon which he broke up his camp, and again retired to Normandy, until he was restored to his throne without blood.

(*h*) KNOX'S REPLY TO THE PRISONERS.—The prisoners in St. Michael, once consulted John Knox, as to the lawfulness of attempting to escape, by breaking their prison; which was opposed by some of their number, lest their escape should subject their brethren who remained in confinement to a more severe treatment. He returned for answer, that such fears were not a sufficient reason for relinquishing the design, and that they might with a safe conscience effect their escape, provided it could be done "without the blood of any shed or spilt. To the shedding of any man's blood for their freedom he would never consent."

(*i*) ANTHONY'S OPINION OF REVENGE.—Anthony behaved with such lenity towards those who had been engaged for Cassius, that he wrote to the Senate, requesting them to spare the shedding of blood; and requesting this honor to be allowed to his reign, that even under the misfortunes of a rebellion, none had lost their lives, except in the first heat of the tumult. "I wish," said he, "that I could even recall to life many of those who have been killed; for revenge in a prince hardly ever pleases, since even when just, it is considered as severe."

203. Humanity Rewarded.

(*a*) HUMANE DRIVER REWARDED.—A poor Macedonian sol

dier was one day leading before Alexander a mule laden with gold for the king's use; the beast being so tired that he was not able either to go or sustain the load, the mule-driver took it off, and carried it himself with great difficulty a considerable way. Alexander seeing him just sinking under the burthen, and about to throw it on the ground, cried out, "Friend, do not be weary yet; try and carry it quite through to thy tent, for it is all thy own."

(*b*) AGRIPPA AND THAUMASTUS.—When Agrippa was in a private station, he was accused, by one of his servants, of having spoken injuriously of Tiberius, and was condemned by the emperor to be exposed in chains before the palace gate. The weather was very hot, and Agrippa became excessively thirsty. Seeing Thaumastus, a servant of Caligula, pass by with a pitcher of water, he called to him, and entreated leave to drink. The servant presented the pitcher with much courtesy; and Agrippa having allayed his thirst, said to him, "Assure thyself, Thaumastus, that if I get out of this captivity, I will one day pay thee well for this draught of water." Tiberius dying, his successor Caligula, soon after not only set Agrippa at liberty, but made him king of Judea. In this high situation Agrippa was not unmindful of the glass of water given to him when a captive. He immediately sent for Thaumastus, and made him comptroller of his household.

(*c*) TRIUMPH OF METELLUS.—When Nertobrigia was invested by Q. Cæcilius Metellus, the Roman proconsul, Rhetogenes, a chief lord of the place, came out and surrendered himself to the Romans. The inhabitants, enraged at his desertion, placed his wife and children, whom he had left behind, in the breach which the legionaries were to mount. The Roman general hearing of this, and finding that he could not attack the city without sacrificing them, abandoned a certain conquest, and raised the siege. No sooner was this act of humanity known through Tarraconian Spain, than the inhabitants of the revolted cities strove who should first submit to him; and thus was a whole country recovered by one humane act.

(*d*) MERCY BETTER THAN SACRIFICE.—When the Romans had ravaged the province of Azazene, and seven thousand Persians were brought prisoners to Amida, where they suffered extreme want, Acases, Bishop of Amida, assembled his clergy, and represented to them the misery of these unhappy prisoners. He observed that as God had said, "I love mercy better than sacrifice," he would certainly be better pleased with the relief of his suffering creatures, than with being served with gold and silver in the churches. The clergy were of the same opinion. The consecrated vessels were sold; and with the proceeds, the seven thousand Persians were not only maintained during the war, but sent home at its conclusion with money in their pockets. Varenes, the Persian monarch, was so charmed with this humane action, that he invited the bishop to his capital, where he received him with the utmost reverence, and for his sake conferred many favors on the Christians.

(*e*) CLEMENCY OF ALPHONSUS.—The city of Cajeta having rebelled against Alphonsus, was invested by that monarch with a powerful army. Being sorely distressed for want of provisions, the citizens put forth all their old men, women and children, and shut the gates upon them. The king's ministers advised his majesty not to permit them to pass, but to force them back into the city; by which means he would speedily become master of it. Alphonsus, however, had too humane a disposition to hearken to counsel, the policy of which rested on driving a helpless multitude into the jaws of famine. He suffered them to pass unmolested; and when afterwards reproached with the delay which this produced in the siege he feelingly said, "I had rather be the preserver of one innocent person, than be the master of a hundred Cajetas."

Alphonsus was not without the reward which such noble clemency merited. The citizens were so affected by it, that, repenting of their disloyalty, they soon afterwards yielded up the city to him of their own accord.

(*f*) THE ARCHDUKE AND HIS WOUNDED SOLDIERS. — When the Archduke Charles was on his way from Bohemia, to take the command of his army, as he drew near the scene of action, he met a number of wounded men abandoned by their comrades on the road, for want of horses to draw the carriages in their retreat. The prince immediately ordered the horses to be taken from several pieces of cannon that were already retreating, saying that these brave men were better worth saving than a few cannon. When General Moreau, into whose hands the cannon of course fell, heard of this benevolent trait, he ordered them to be restored to the Austrian army, observing that he would take no cannon that were abandoned from such humane motives.

(*g*) HAPPY EFFECTS OF HUMANITY.—The following facts of a young chief of the Pawnee nation, and son of Old Knife, one of the Indians who visited the city of Washington, in America, a few years ago, from the foot of the Rocky Mountains, are highly creditable to his courage, his generosity, and his benevolence. This young warrior, when these events occurred, was about twenty-five years old. At the age of twenty-one, his heroic deeds had acquired for him, among his people, the rank of "bravest of the brave." The savage practice of torturing and burning to death their prisoners existed in this nation. An unfortunate female, taken in war, of the Paduca nation, was destined to this horrible death. The fatal hour had arrived: the trembling victim, far from her home and her friends, was fastened to the stake: the whole tribe was assembled on the surrounding plain, to witness the awful scene. Just when the wood was about to be kindled, and the spectators were on the tiptoe of expectation, this young warrior, who sat composedly among the chiefs, having before prepared two fleet horses, with the necessary provisions, sprang from his seat, rushed through the crowd, loosed the victim, seized her in his arms, placed her on one of the horses, mounted the other himself, and made the utmost speed towards the nation and friends of the captive. The multitude, dumb and nerveless with amazement at the daring deed, made no effort to rescue their victim from her deliverer. They viewed it as the act of their deity, submitted to it without a murmur, and quietly retired to their village. The released captive was accompanied through the wilderness toward her home, till she was out of danger. He then gave her the horse on which she rode, with the necessary provisions for the remainder of her journey, and they parted. On his return to the village, such was the respect entertained for him, that no inquiry was made into his conduct; no censure was passed on it: and, since this transaction, no human sacrifice has been offered in this or any of the Pawnee tribes. Of what influence is one bold act in a good cause!

On the publication of this anecdote at Washington, the young ladies of a female seminary, in that city, presented this brave and humane Indian with a handsome silver medal, on which was engraven an appropriate inscription, accompanied by an address, of which the following is the close:—"Brother, accept this token of our esteem; always wear it for our sake; and, when you have again the power to save a poor woman from death and torture, think of this and of us, and fly to her rescue."

204. HUMILITY.

(*a*) "BY THE GRACE OF GOD I AM WHAT I AM."—Two or three years before the death of John Newton, when his sight was so dim that he was no longer able to read, an aged friend and brother in the ministry called on him to breakfast. Family prayer succeeding, the portion of Scripture for the day was read to him. It was suggested by "Bogatsky's Golden Treasury:" "By the grace of God, I am what I am." It was the good man's custom, on these occasions, to make a few short remarks on the passage read. After the reading of this text, he paused for some moments, and then uttered the following affecting soliloquy :—"I am not what I *ought* to be! Ah! how imperfect and deficient! I am not what I *wish* to be! I abhor that which is evil, and I would cleave to what is good! I am not what I *hope* to be! Soon, soon, I shall put off mortality, and with mortality all sin and imperfection! Yet, though I am not what I ought to be, nor what I wish to be, nor what I hope to be, I can truly say I am not what I once was, a slave to sin and Satan ; and I can heartily join with the apostle, and acknowledge, "By the grace of God, I am what I am!" Let us pray!"

(*b*) MATHER'S RETRACTION.—Dr. Cotton Mather had maintained, with much earnestness, a particular opinion in the prime of life. In advanced age, he re-examined the writings of his opponent which he had replied to, and was convinced of his error. This fact he was careful to acknowledge.

(*c*) REYNOLDS AND THE ORPHAN.—A lady applied to the eminent philanthropist of Bristol, Richard Reynolds, on behalf of a little orphan boy. After he had given liberally, she said, "When he is old enough, I will teach him to name and thank his benefactor." "Stop," said the good man, "Thou art mistaken. We do not thank the clouds for rain. Teach him to look higher, and thank HIM who giveth both the clouds and the rain."

(*d*) THE NOBLEMAN AND THE PRAYER MEETING.—A nobleman was in the habit of attending a prayer meeting in the country village where he lived, and where a few poor people were accustomed to assemble to seek the presence of the Divine Majesty. It was at first customary for these humble persons to make way for him if he came in a little after the appointed time ; but he expressed his unwillingness to receive this mark of respect, saying he should be satisfied to occupy the lowest station. In other places he thought he had a right to claim the distinctions of his rank ; but there he felt himself in the same situation as themselves. Such conduct displayed the genuine feelings of piety, which rising superior to the artificial distinctions of society, rejoices in the fellowship of the body of Christians.

(*e*) LOUIS IX AND THE KITCHEN BOY.—Louis the IXth, king of France, was found instructing a poor kitchen boy ; and being asked why he did so, replied, "The meanest person hath a soul as precious as my own, and bought with the same blood of Christ."

(*f*) OVERLOOKING SELF.—"On a visit to London," says the Rev. J. Campbell, in a letter to a minister. "I was expressing a great desire to see the late Mr. Charles of Bala, with whom I had corresponded for three years concerning a remarkable revival which had taken place under his ministry. Mr. C. happening to be in town at the same time, your father kindly took me to Lady Ann Erskine's, where he resided. We spent there two happy hours. Your father requested Mr. C. to favor us with a brief outline of the circumstances which led to the remarkable revival at Bala, and its surrounding region, its progress, &c. He did so for upwards of an hour. On our leaving him, your father said, 'Did you not observe the wonderful humility of Mr. C. in the narrative he gave ? Never having once mentioned *himself*, though he was the chief actor and instrument in the whole matter." '

(*g*) ELEVATION BY HUMILITY—In the evening of the day that Sir Eardley Wilmot kissed the hand of his majesty, on being appointed chief justice, one of his sons, a youth of seventeen, attended him to his bed-side. "Now," said he, "my son, I will tell you a secret worth your knowing and remembering. The elevation I have met with in life, particularly this last instance of it, has not been owing to any superior merit or abilities, but to my humility ; to my not having set up myself above others, and to a uniform endeavor to pass through life void of offence towards God and man."

(*h*) THE CONVERTED INDIAN.—In the year 1742, a veteran warrior of the Lenape nation and Monsey tribe renowned among his friends for his bravery, and dreaded by his enemies, joined the Christian Indians at Bethlehem, Pa. He was now at an advanced age, full of scars, and all over tattooed with the scenes of the actions in which he had been engaged. All who heard his history thought that it could never be surpassed. This man was brought under the influence of religion; and when he was afterwards questioned respecting his warlike feats, he modestly replied, "that being now taken captive by Jesus Christ, it did not become him to relate the deeds done while in the service of the evil spirit: but that he was willing to give an account of the manner in which he had been conquered."

(*i*) "THE SONS OF GOD."—An individual, says a missionary, employed in the translation of the Scriptures at a station where I resided, on arriving at the passage, "Now are we the sons of God!" etc., 1 John iii. 2, came running to me in great haste, exclaiming, "No, no, it is too much; allow me to render it, 'Now are we permitted to kiss his feet.'" A simple and beautiful representation of those feelings with which Christians should ever contemplate the dignity of their character, and the honor conferred on them.

(*j*) THE PREACHER AND THE FARMER.—The Rev. Mr. R——, in a sermon before a numerous audience, composed in part of preachers, related the following anecdote, illustrative of the influence of humility in subduing a suspicious and repugnant mind.

A young preacher, said he, on going to a distant field of labor, had occasion to stop over night with a farmer, a member of a church, an honest man, but, unhappily, of a peevish, suspicious temper, that had been exasperated by several instances of imposture, in which vagrant men had availed themselves of his hospitality under the character of Christian ministers. The young preacher had just commenced his ministerial career, his appearance was not prepossessing, and he was depressed with anxiety respecting his untried field of labor. It was late in the evening when he reached the gate of the farm-yard. The farmer came forth to meet him with chilling coldness. He made surly inquiries about his name, whence he came, whither he was going, etc., expressing, meanwhile, by his looks his suspicions; and giving very direct intimations about false pretensions, etc. Weary and depressed as was the stranger, he felt a momentary indignation, but, repressing it, he resolved to copy the meekness of his Master, and, by his example, if not otherwise, attempt to cure the perversity of his rustic host. He was pointed to the stable, with permission to feed his horse, and come into the house. As he approached the house he was directed to the kitchen. Some food was spread on a rude table for him. The hired men in the kitchen whispered to each other their surprise that he was not invited into the parlor. Though of humble origin himself, he felt keenly the indignity of his treatment: the pride of his heart for a moment revolted, and he arose to resume his journey, with the prospect of a rainy night: but he suddenly checked his feelings, and, looking to God, resolved to await patiently the result of this strange scene.

It was not long before all were called into another room for family prayers. The preacher followed the hired laborers, and took his seat in a corner. The farmer read a chapter in the Bible. At the end of it he was evidently embarrassed by an inward struggle, not knowing what to do; but, finally, turning to the preacher, he abruptly asked him to pray.

They knelt down, and the young man, oppressed with feelings which prayer could best relieve, poured out his soul and tears before God. A divine influence came down on all present, they sobbed around him. The meek pathos of his tones, the spirituality of his sentiments, the evangelical views involved in the prayer, and its prevailing earnestness, struck all present. The morose farmer, subdued and melted, approached him at the conclusion of the prayer, and, in the presence of the family, with flowing tears, begged his pardon. "I should not have been so suspicious," said he, "but I have been all day under a strong temptation of the adversary—my mind has been irritable—my conduct towards you to-night, is a mystery to myself; I cannot account for it, even by the state of my mind during the day. I have not been myself, or I would not have so treated you. Forgive me, sir. How have you been able to endure it?" "My Lord," replied the youthful preacher, "has said, 'Learn of me, for I am meek and lowly in heart.' It is my ambition to do so. Try, my brother, to learn the same lesson." It was the keenest rebuke that could be given to the farmer; he felt its pertinency, made the humblest acknowledgments, and begged his maltreated guest to tarry at the house several days, and preach to the family and neighbors. His engagements would not allow him to remain so long; but, such was the importunity of his host, that he consented to preach next day. That night he reposed in the best chamber in the house, and his rest was sweetened by the thought that he had conquered a perverse mind by an example of meekness. The next day he preached with deep effect, and went on his journey with the prayers and blessings of the farmer.

"And what do you suppose," said the Rev. Mr. R——, "was the result? The old farmer was a better man ever after: the sermon had a salutary influence on the whole neighborhood, several were awakened, and among them, three of the farmer's children; two of them have since gone safe to heaven. Ah! it is the temper of Christ that fits us for usefulness!"

(*k*) TRUE MISSIONARY SPIRIT.—The Rev. Dr. Morrison, of China, after having for some years labored at Canton, earnestly requested the Directors of the London Missionary Society to send him out a colleague; their attention was directed to Mr. (afterwards Dr.) Milne. A circumstance occurred on his first introduction to the friends of that Society, which at once showed his devotedness to the Savior's cause, and the humble opinion he entertained of himself. On his appearance before the committee at Aberdeen, he seemed so rustic and unpromising, that a worthy member took Dr. Philip aside, and expressed his doubts whether he had the necessary qualifications for a missionary; but added, that he would have no objection to unite in recommending him as a servant to a mission, provided he would be willing to engage in that capacity. "At the suggestion of my worthy friend," says Dr. Philip, "I desired to speak with him alone. Having stated to him the objection which had been made, and asked him if he would consent to the proposal, he replied, without hesitation, and with the most significant and animated expression of countenance, "Yes, sir, most certainly; I am willing to be any thing, so that I am in the work. To be 'a hewer of wood and a drawer of water' is too great an honor for me when the Lord's house is building."

(*l*) "NONE TO SPEAK OF."—Dr. Lathrop was a man of generous piety, but much opposed to the noisy zeal that seeketh the praise of men. A young divine who was much given to enthusiastic cant, one day said to him—"Do you suppose you have any *real religion?*" "None to *speak* of," was the excellent reply.

(*m*) DR. CAREY'S HUMILITY.—When Dr. Carey, the Missionary, was suffering from a dangerous illness, the inquiry was made, "If this sickness should prove fatal, what passage would you select as the text of your funeral sermon?" He replied, "Oh, I feel that such a poor sinful creature as I, is unworthy to have any thing said about him; but if a funeral sermon should be preached let it be from the 51st Psalm, and first verse—'Have mercy upon me, O God, according to thy loving-kindness; according unto the multitude of thy tender mercies, blot out my transgressions.'"

The following extract from the will of this eminent Missionary, is equally illustrative of the general humility of his character. "I direct that my funeral be as plain as possible, and that the following inscription and nothing more be cut out on my grave-stone, viz.

William Carey, born August 17th, 1[illegible];
died——
"A wretched, poor and helpless worm,
On thy kind arms I fall."

205. HYPOCRISY.

(*a*) THE HYPOCRITE'S END.—The following fact is related by the author of Pastoral Letters. N—— was a branch of a pious family, some of whose ancestors were martyrs. She was religiously educated by her pious parents; and her education, particularly her knowledge of history, was extensive. In her study of history the progress of religion had attracted her chief attention. Religious topics were her element; her remarks often evinced the correctness and vigor of her judgment; and she often delighted the social circle by her striking application of the current matters of conversation to the subject of religion. Like the rest of the pious family, she seemed devoted to all the duties of a Christian, with only one exception, and this they wondered at; that she did not attend with them at the Lord's table. All regarded her as an ornament of religion, and urged her to take a part in this ordinance.

In one year N—— lost both her pious parents, and she had just put off mourning, when she was taken desperately ill. Having been on terms of intimacy with the family, I was sent for at her request to visit the dying sister. I certainly went prepared to see a Christian die: but what was my astonishment to behold those features, instead of smiling in death, as I expected, clothed in all the horrors of mental agony! Bidding me sit down, and ascertaining there were no witnesses, she addressed me in nearly these terms: "I am glad you are come: I cannot bear to go out of the world a deceiver, but I am unable to tell the sad secret of my heart to those about me, it would be too much for them to hear. I am not the character my friends have supposed. I am not religious—do not interrupt me—I have talked about religion, my passions have often felt the powers of the world to come, and my imagination roved at large among things unseen; I have amused myself with these matters, and regarded with the interest of an amateur their effects upon minds whom I reckoned of an inferior order, though ennobled by a birth from heaven. But amidst all, my own heart has never loved religion as a personal thing: indeed, I have never concerned myself about it for myself, and now I must die without any of its prospects, and be shut out forever from all its enjoyments."

I paused a moment and began to observe that "Life is the season of hope," and admitting all I heard to be correct, still the Savior's saying, "Whosoever cometh unto me I will in no wise cast out," is equally entitled to credit. But she cut me short, observing, "The vigor of my youth and the strength of my intellect I have wasted in living to myself; I never cared for the divine approbation; and God is justly my adversary. Cast down as I am, I cannot go with a piteous tale of misery to petition for mercy for which I can plead no services, nor live to show any gratitude. I know already what you would say to these sentiments—you would hold out mercy as yet attainable; but my heart revolts at it. Heaven would be no heaven to me on the terms I can only enter it. I have been a worthless idler, and cannot endure to receive the reward of a faithful soldier."

Surprised as I was, I endeavored to enforce the necessity of renouncing such sentiments, and was urging that a good confession, though late, would find acceptance, when she interrupted me with some energy: "No, sir, spare me, spare yourself, my character is finished; what I am that shall I be forever. The tree is even now falling: it is too late to direct where its trunk shall be extended on the earth."

The doctor coming in, I soon after took my leave, intending to renew my visit, but in the morning learned that N—— had expired in the night.

(*b*) HYPOCRITES INACCESSIBLE.—President Edwards remarks, as the result of long and close observation, that, of all sinners, *unconverted professors* of religion are the most hopeless. In his account of the great New England revival in which he labored very extensively, he states that whilst such immense multitudes, and a large proportion of all ages and conditions in life were powerfully wrought upon, and driven to seek refuge from the wrath to come, *unconverted professors* stood alone unmoved.

206. IDLENESS.

(*a*) BLOWING THE BELLOWS.—The happiness to be derived from retirement from the bustle of the city, to the peaceful and rural scenes of the country, is more in idea, than it often proves to be in reality. A tradesman in London, who had risen to wealth from the humble ranks of life, resolved to retire to the country to enjoy, undisturbed, the rest of his life. For this purpose, he purchased an estate and mansion in a sequestered corner in the country, and took possession of it. While the alterations and improvements which he directed to be made were going on, the noise of hammers, saws, chisels, etc. around him, kept him in good spirits. But when his improvements were finished, and his workmen discharged, the stillness every where disconcerted him, and he felt quite miserable. He was obliged to have recourse to a smith upon his estate for relief to his mind, and he actually engaged to blow the bellows for a certain number of hours in the day. In a short time this ceased to afford the relief he desired; he returned to London, and acted as a gratuitous assistant to his own clerk, to whom he had given up his business.

(*b*) DISEASE A RELIEF.—A tradesman who had acquired a large fortune in London, retired from business, and went to reside in Worcester. His mind, without its usual occupation, and having nothing else to supply its place, preyed upon itself, so that existence became a torment to him. At last he was seized with the stone; and a friend, who found him in one of its severest attacks, having expressed his condolence, "No, no, sir," said he, "do not pity me; for I assure you what I now feel is ease compared with the torture of mind from which it relieves me."

(*c*) CLARENDON'S NEIGHBOR.—"When I visited a country neighbor of mine" (says Lord Clarendon) "in the morning, I always found him in bed; and when I came in the afternoon, he was asleep, and to most men besides myself, access was denied. Once walking with him, I doubted he was melancholy, and, by spending his time so much in bed, and so much alone, that there was something that troubled him; otherwise that it could not be that a man upon whom God had poured so many blessings should be so little contented as he appeared to be. To which he answered, 'that he thought himself the most happy man alive in a wife who was all the comfort he could have in this world; that he was at so much ease in his fortune, he did not wish it greater; but he said he would deal freely with me, and tell me, if he were melancholy, (which he suspected himself of,) what was the true cause of it; that he had somewhat *he knew not what to do with; he knew not how to spend his time;* which was the reason he loved his bed so much, and slept at other times, which he said he found did him already no good in his health.'" Lord Clarendon adds, that the unhappy gentleman's melancholy daily increased with the agony of his thoughts, till he contracted diseases which carried him off at the age of thirty-six.

(*d*) IDLENESS AND IRRELIGION.—Dr. Dwight says, "Among all those, who, within my knowledge, have appeared to become sincerely penitent and reformed, I recollect only a single lazy man: and this man became industrious from the moment of his apparent, and, I doubt not, real conversion."

(*e*) THE SPIRITUAL MONK.—A certain brother came to the convent at Mount Sinai, and finding all the monks at work, shook his head and said to the Abbot, "Labor not for the meat which perisheth," and, "Mary hath chosen that good part." "Very well," said the Abbot, and ordered the good brother to a cell and gave him a book to read. The monk retired, and sat hour after hour all day long alone; wondering much that nobody called him to dinner, or offered him any refreshment. Hungry and wearied out, the night at length arrived: he left his solitary cell and repaired to the apartment of the Abbot. "Father," says he, "do not the brethren eat to-day?"

"Oh yes," replied the Abbot, "they have eaten plentifully." "Then how is it, Father," said the monk, "that you did not call me to partake with them?" "Because, brother," replied the Abbot, "you are a *spiritual man*, and have no need of carnal food. For our part, we are obliged to eat, and on that account we work; but you, brother, who have chosen 'the good part,' you sit and read all the day long, and are above the want of the meat that perisheth." "Pardon me, Father," said the monk, "I perceive my mistake."

207. IDOLATRY, FOLLY OF.

(*a*) A BECHUANA'S VIEW OF IDOLATRY.—A Bechuana man, says a missionary, once came into my house and sat himself down. He took up one of our missionary sketches that was lying near him; having looked at it, he concluded that the figures upon it—ugly ones—represented living animals. It never entered into his mind that man would make a thing that never existed. He asked my little daughter Mary, "What game is this?" She said, "They are not game; there are nations that worship these things." "Oh!" said he, "how you tell fibs." She replied, "I am not telling fibs. I heard mamma say so, and my mamma does not tell fibs." He asked her again what game they were, and she again told him that they were things that were worshipped, for they have no name for idols. He burst out into an exclamation of wonder, questioned her again, but received the same answer—that people worshipped these things the same as her papa wished them to worship Jehovah and Jesus. The man was full of amazement, and repeated that she was telling fibs; but she maintained the truth of what she said, and told him to go to her papa. He came to me and said, "Look at that; your daughter says so and so. Is it true?" I said, "It is." Having looked at me with astonishment, he said, "I know you do not tell lies;" and laying the paper down upon a piece of timber that I was planing, he looked at it, put his hands to both sides of his head, and waving it backwards and forwards, said, "The people that make these things of wood and stone,—have they got heads like Bechuanas?" "Yes," I replied, "they have heads." "Have they got legs?" "Yes, they have legs." "Have they got a pair of bellows to breathe through?" (he meant lungs.) "Yes." The man's wonder continued to increase, and he then asked, "Can they talk, and think, and speak? Can they reason? Can they explain a difficult thing? Can they speak in a public meeting like our senators?" On being told that they could do all these things, he said, "After this, never say that the Bechuanas are either foolish or ignorant." Taking from his neck a whistle made of ivory, and carved with some device, perhaps a man's head, or a buffalo, or a giraffe, he looked at the whistle with great reverence, and nodding his head in a very solemn way, he said, "What would my people think if I were to worship that?" Just at that moment, while he was talking with much animation, his staff dropped from his hand He grasped it, and pointing to the picture, he held up his staff and said, "This looks as well as this monster, and I might as well worship my staff just as you worship Jehovah. What would my people think if I were to do so? They would think I was a madman, and would throw me over a precipice, and cover me with stones."

(*b*) THROWING DOWN THE IDOLS.—A native gentleman of India, in relating his history to one of the missionaries, said:—

My father was an officiating priest of a heathen temple, and, was considered in those days, a superior English scholar; and, by teaching the English language to wealthy natives, realized a very large fortune. At a very early period, when a mere boy, I was employed by my father to light the lamps in the pagoda, and attend to the various things connected with the idols. I hardly remember the time when my mind was not exercised on the folly of idolatry. These things, I thought, were made by the hand of man, can move only by man, and, whether treated well or ill, are unconscious of either. Why all this cleaning, anointing, illuminating, etc.? One evening, these considerations so powerfully wrought on my youthful mind, that instead of placing the idols according to custom, I threw them from their pedestals, and left them with their faces in the dust. My father, on witnessing what I had done, chastised me so severely, as to leave me almost dead. I reasoned with him, that if they could not get up out of the dust, they were not able to do what I could; and that instead of being worshipped as gods, they deserved to lie in the dust, where I had thrown them. He was implacable, and vowed to disinherit me, and, as the first step to it, sent me away from his house. He relented on his death-bed, and left me all his wealth.

(*c*) A JEW'S ARGUMENT.—"Some Roman senators examined the Jews in this manner: 'If God had no delight in the worship of idols, why did he not destroy them?' The Jews made answer, 'If men had worshipped only things of which the world had had no need, he would have destroyed the objects of their worship; but they also worship the sun and moon, stars and planets; and then he must have destroyed his worlds for the sake of these deluded men.' 'But still,' said the Romans, 'why does not God destroy the things which the world does not want, and leave those things which the world cannot be without?' 'Because,' replied the Jews, 'this would strengthen the hands of such as worship these necessary things, who would say, Ye allow now that these are gods, since they are not destroyed.'"

(*d*) SERVING GOD WORSE THAN A THIEF.—As Mr. Kincaid was preaching to the people, in Arracan, a man took up manfully on the side of Gaudama, while another man, who had been a great opposer, occasionally threw in a word in favor of Mr K., when the following conversation took place betweenthe two men:

"You have become a disciple of Christ, have you? You join with this foreign teacher, do you, to prove that our god is no god, and that our religion, which has stood a thousand years, is only a cheat and a fable? You are like a dog that is coaxed away by a thief—you may as well lick honey from the edge of a razor as to listen to this foreigner." Very well," replied my new ally, "I have reviled this religion, and this teacher more than you have, but I was a fool with both my eyes shut—this religion is true, and every body would believe it if they knew what it is. We make a god of wood, and then put a rope around his neck, and carry him off to his own place, and then put a fence around him, and keep him there till the white ants eat him up. We would not serve a thief as bad as this. There is as much evidence to prove that Gaudama was a monkey, as that he was a god."

208. IMPRECATIONS ANSWERED.

(*a*) THE PERJURER'S IMPRECATION.—A man once waited on a magistrate near Hitchin, in the county of Hertford, (Eng.) and informed him that he had been stopped by a young gentleman in Hitchin, who had knocked him down and searched his pockets; but not finding any thing, he had suffered him to depart. The magistrate, astonished at this intelligence, despatched a messenger to the young gentleman, ordering him to appear immediately, and answer to the charge exhibited against him. The youth obeyed the summons, accompanied by his guardian and an intimate friend. Upon their arrival at the seat of justice, the accused and accuser were confronted; when the magistrate hinted to the man, that he was afraid he had made the charge with no other view than that of extorting money, and bade him take care how he proceeded; exhorting him, in the most earnest and pathetic manner, to beware of the dreadful train of consequences attending perjury. The man insisted upon making oath to what he had advanced; the oath was accordingly administered, and the business fully investigated, when the innocence of the young gentleman was established, by the most incontrovertible evidence. The infamous wretch, finding his intentions thus frustrated, returned home much chagrined; and meeting soon afterwards with one of his neighbors, he declared he had not sworn to any thing but the truth, calling God to witness the same in the most solemn manner, and wished, if it was not as he had said, his jaws might be locked, and that his flesh might rot upon his bones; when, terrible to relate, his jaws were instantly arrested, and he was deprived of the use of the faculty he had so awfully perverted! After lingering nearly a fortnight, he expired in the greatest agonies, his flesh literally rotting upon his bones.

(*b*) THEN LET IT CRUSH ME TO ATOMS.—I knew a man, says a correspondent of the "Tract Magazine," in 1825, who was very much addicted to swearing, and attempts to convince him of the error of his ways were in vain; all reproof was lost upon him. He was a laborer in a stone quarry, and having one day fastened a stone to a rope, for the purpose of being hoisted up, the man at the top of the quarry said he thought the rope was not strong enough; the man below immediately replied, with a most dreadful oath, "Then let it crush me to atoms." The wretched man had hardly uttered these words, when the stone fell, and hurried his unprepared soul into the presence of his offended God.

(*c*) INSCRIPTION AT DEVIZES.—The following inscription is to be seen in the market-place at Devizes (Eng.);—"The mayor and corporation of Devizes avail themselves of the stability of this building to transmit to future times the record of an awful event, which occurred in this market-place, in the year 1753, hoping that such a record may serve as a salutary warning against the danger of impiously invoking the Divine vengeance, or of calling on the holy name of God, to conceal the devices of falsehood and fraud. On Thursday, the 25th of January, 1753, Ruth Pierce, of Pottern, in this county, agreed with three other women to buy a sack of wheat in the market, each paying her due proportion towards the same. One of these women, in collecting the several quotas of money, discovered a deficiency, and demanded of Ruth Pierce the sum which was wanting to make good the amount. Ruth Pierce protested that she had paid her share, and said, she wished she might drop down dead, if she had not. She rashly repeated this awful wish, when, to the consternation of the surrounding multitude, she instantly fell down and expired, having the money concealed in her hand."

(*d*) THE OPPOSER'S PRAYER.—A candidate for the Christian ministry was once invited to settle in New England. In giving the invitation, there was a general union in the church and society. A few, however, were opposed to the settlement. Among the opposers, one man was exceedingly bitter. This person was open and explicit in expressing the hatred of his heart toward those doctrines, commonly called the doctrines of grace, that were preached by the candidate. A few weeks previous to the ordination, in conversation with some neighbors on the subject of the candidate's settlement among them, the man expressed himself in the following manner:—"I wish I may die before he is settled here." The appointed day approached, and the man remained unrelenting in his opposition. On the morning of the Sabbath preceding the day of ordination, being in usual health and busied in some domestic concern, he was seized in a very surprising manner. In a moment, he was struck into a state of insensibility, speechless, and hopeless. In this melancholy state he continued till Wednesday morning, the day of ordination, when, about two hours before the commencement of the public solemnities, according to his own desire, he expired! His case was so extraordinary as to baffle the attempts of skilful physicians, either to restore him or to satisfy themselves as to the natural cause of his situation.

(*e*) A COCK-FIGHTER'S CURSE.—A person who lived in the parish of Sedgley, near Wolverhampton, (Eng.) having lost a considerable sum by a match at cock-fighting, to which practice he was notoriously addicted, swore in the most horrid manner, that he would never fight another cock as long as he lived; frequently calling upon God to damn his soul to all eternity if he did, and with dreadful imprecations, wishing the devil might fetch him if he ever made another bet. It is not to be wondered at, if resolutions so impiously formed, should be broken; for a while however, they were observed; but he continued to indulge himself in every other abomination to which his depraved heart inclined him. But, about two years afterwards, Satan, whose willing servant he was, inspired him with a violent desire to attend a cocking at Wolverhampton; and he complied with the temptation. When he came to the place, he stood up, as in defiance of Heaven, and cried, "I hold four to three on such a cock." "Four what?" said one of his companions in inquity. "Four shillings," replied he. "I'll lay," said the other. Upon which they confirmed the wager, and, as his custom was, he threw down his hat, and put his hand in his pocket for the money; when, awful to relate, he instantly fell a ghastly corpse to the ground. Terrified at his sudden death, some who were present, for ever after desisted from this infamous sport; but others, hardened in iniquity, proceeded in the barbarous diversion, as soon as the dead body was removed from the spot.

(*f*) BETTING AND DYING.—The following relation of facts was presented to the public, in several of the London newspapers of February 13, 1814:—A melancholy event occurred yesterday evening, between seven and eight o'clock, at the cock-pit, St. Giles's. Whilst preparations were making for the setting-to of the cocks, to engage in this cruel sport, a Mr. Thorpe, from the country, a well-known character, had taken his seat in the front of the pit, and not two minutes before his death, had offered to back the Huntingdon birds for ten guineas. He was observed to lean his head forward, and appeared somewhat ill. He made a kind of moan, and instantly his color changed, and he was a corpse. Surgical aid was immediately procured, but the spark of life was extinct. The body was removed to a neighboring public-house, for the inspection of a coroner's inquest. The wife and sister of the deceased soon arrived to see the body, and the reader may judge of their feelings. It is a fact no less singular than true, that the deceased, half an hour before his death, had said, "The last time I was here, I said, if ever I attended the pit again, I hoped I should die there."

(*g*) THE FATHER'S WISH.—In the neighborhood of Hitchin, in Hertfordshire, there lived a few years ago a laboring man, who having a cross child, frequently wished, with an oath, that his next child might be both deaf and dumb. He afterwards had three children, all of whom were deaf and dumb.

209. INCONSISTENCY OF PROFESSED CHRISTIANS.

(*a*) THE INDIAN'S INFERENCE.—Mr. Brainerd informs us, that when among the American Indians, he stopped at a place where there was a great number, and offered to instruct them in the truths of Christianity. "Why," said one of them, "should you desire the Indians to become Christians, seeing the Christians are so much worse than the Indians? The Christians lie, steal, and drink, worse than the Indians. They first taught the Indians to be drunk. They steal to so great a degree, that their rulers are obliged to hang them for it; and even that is not enough to deter others from the practice. But none of the Indians were ever hanged for stealing; and yet they do not steal half so much. We will not consent, therefore, to become Christians, lest we should be as bad as they. We will live as our fathers lived, and go where our fathers are, when we die." Notwithstanding that Mr. B. did all he could to explain to them that these were not Christians in heart, and that he did not want them to become such as these, he could not prevail on them to accept his doctrine, but left them, mortified at the thought that the wickedness of some, who professed Christianity, should produce such prejudices.

(*b*) "IT IS ALL A FARCE."—I heard, says a Christian minister, an excellent sermon to young people, on a New Year's day, in the morning. The text was, "Redeeming the time, because the days are evil," Eph. v. 16. The minister then went to dine and spend the rest of the day with a party, where the time was spent in feasting, levity, and folly. Late in the evening, one of the party observed, "Really this is a poor way of redeeming the time." "Poh!" said another, "it is all a farce." Let ministers and others beware lest their inconsistencies should lead any to deride the religion they profess.

(*c*) AN ATHEIST QUIETING CONSCIENCE.—An atheist being asked by a professor of Christianity, "how he could quiet his conscience in so desperate a state?" replied, "As much am astonished as yourself, that believing the Christian religion to be true, you can quiet your conscience in living so much like the world. Did I believe what you profess, I should think no care, no diligence, no zeal enough." Alas! that there should still, by Christians, be so much cause given for the astonishment of atheists!

(*d*) UNIVERSALIST'S ARGUMENT.—Said a Universalist to a Calvinist, "Do you believe in eternal punishment?" "Yes," said the Calvinist. "No," said the other, "you do not believe any such thing. Why," continued the Universalist, "do you believe that Mr. S. of —— believes in it? No, he does not believe any such thing." Again the Universalist added, "Do you believe that Rev. Mr —— of —— believes that I am going to hell? He and I have lived here these —— years; he has met me hundreds of times in the streets, and has never said a word to me on the subject—he does not believe any such thing."

(*e*) THE TWO MINISTERS.—As deep and ardent piety exerts its most powerful influence upon those most intimately acquainted, so a want of it will be soonest detected, and most deeply felt, in the domestic circle. This is illustrated by the following facts.

In the village of O—, N. Y., there lived a minister noted for the depth and ardor of his piety. During an interesting revival, his eldest daughter became concerned about her eternal welfare. At an evening meeting, the anxious were invited to occupy a particular seat, in token of their desire for an interest in the prayers of God's people The minister's daughter did not go forward, but upon the arrival of the family at home, she said, "Father, I want you to pray for me." The father inquired why she had not taken the anxious seat. The immediate and earnest reply was, "I had rather you would pray for me, than any body else in the world." At a time of similar interest in the village of P——, there lived a minister who was perhaps equally accounted of in *public*, whose eldest daughter was also convicted of sin. She passed her time as usual, under the paternal roof, but with a sad countenance and heavy heart. Three days passed, while deep distress of soul was daily growing deeper. She then, without the knowledge of her parents, (neither of them having yet inquired after the state of her mind,) wrote a note to a neighboring lady, most earnestly soliciting her to come and pray for her as a poor lost sinner. Christian fathers and mothers! beware you do not destroy the confidence of your children in your piety by your inconsistency, so that when under conviction for sin, and desirous of the prayers of others, they should, in like manner, pass you by.

210. INDUSTRY.

(*a*) CRESSIN'S DEFENCE.—Pliny tells us of one Cressin, who so tilled and manured a piece of ground, that it yielded him fruits in abundance, while the lands around him remained extremely poor and barren. His simple neighbors could not account for this wonderful difference on any other supposition than that of his working by enchantment; and they accordingly proceeded to arraign him for his supposed sorcery, before the justice seat. "How is it," said they, "unless it be that he enchants us, that he can contrive to draw such a revenue from his inheritance, while we, with equal lands, are wretched and miserable?" Cressin was his own advocate; his case was one which required not either ability to expound, or language to recommend. "Behold," said he, "this comely damsel; she is my daughter, my fellow laborer; behold, too, these implements of husbandry, these carts, and these oxen. Go with me, moreover, to my fields, and behold there how they are tilled, how manured, how weeded, how watered, how fenced in! And when," added he, raising his voice, "you have beheld all these things, you will have beheld all the art, the charms, the magic, which Cressin has used!"

The judges pronounced his acquittal, passing a high eulogium on that industry and good husbandry which had so innocently made him an object of suspicion and envy to his neighbors.

(*b*) THE CLERICAL GARDENER.—As Peter the Great, of Russia, was travelling through a village in France, he saw in a garden, belonging to a parsonage, a man in a cassock, with a spade in his hand, digging hard at some beds of vegetables.

The czar, much pleased with the sight, alighted, and asked him who he was. "Sir," answered the man, "I am the clergyman of the village." "I took you for a gardener; why are you employed in this manner?"

"The revenues of my living being but very moderate, I do not choose to be an expense to my parishioners, but wish rather to have it in my power to assist them; they respect me the more when they see that, to procure myself some of the conveniences of life, I improve this garden, and in this humble occupation spend as much of my time as the duties of my ministry will allow."

"You are an honest man," replied the czar; "and I esteem you the more for thinking and acting in this manner; tell me your name." He drew out his tablets, and wrote down the name of the worthy clergyman; and, after telling him who he himself was, and giving him many proofs of kindness, he took leave of him, and returned to his carriage.

When he went back to Moscow, he did not forget this scene, and endeavored to induce the priests in his empire to imitate so virtuous an example.

(*c*) "COME AND GO."—A gentleman in Surrey, (Eng.,) once held a farm worth £200 a year in his own hands, till he was obliged to sell half of it to pay his debts, and let the other half to a farmer, on a lease of 21 years. After a while, the farmer wanted to buy the land. "How is this," said the gentleman, "that I could not live upon the farm, being my own, while you have paid rent, and yet are able to purchase it?" "O," said the farmer, "two words make all the difference: you said *go*, and I say *come;* you lay in bed, or took your pleasure, and sent others about your business; and I rise betimes, and see my business done myself."

(*d*) A DILIGENT STUDENT.—A correspondent of the New York Evangelist gives a striking notice of the *Rev. John A. Sherman*, a Missionary in Benares, upon the Ganges, 500 miles above Calcutta. While at Andover, Mass., though on a passing visit, and in a foreign land, where he wished to notice things around him, he read, during the ten days of his stay, Henry's Life of Calvin, a recent German work in three large octavos, besides much in periodicals, and besides spending considerable time in social intercourse, preaching twice, and delivering a most interesting lecture, of two hours' length, on India.

About two years of his time in India has been spent in Calcutta, in translating and printing the Bible in the Hindostan language, for the British and Foreign Bible Society. While engaged on this translation, he applied himself from four in the morning till eight in the evening, notwithstanding the intense and sultry heat of Calcutta. And strange as it may seem to some, he assigns this very fact of his intense application, as a leading cause of his uninterrupted health and vigor. "The man who would live in India," he says, "must have plenty of work; if not, he will yield to the enervating influence of the climate, and lounge away his days upon the sofa, and consequently be tossing all night on his sleepless couch, for want of the requisite fatigue. Then comes dejection of spirits, and utter prostration of the whole man."

211. IMPULSES.

(*a*) THE TEN COMMANDMENTS AND IMPULSES.—"Several of you," said Rev. R. Robison in a sermon, "know a good old man who departed this life twenty years ago, and who often exhorted you to live by the Ten Commandments, and not by impulses. He used to tell, you know, how he got free from that delusion fifty years before. Then he was pious and poor, and, being only a lad, thought all suggestions in Scripture style came from heaven. Walking in the fields in want of firewood, by the side of a neighbor's hedge, he wished some of it to burn, and the impulse came clothed in Scripture language, "In all this Job sinned not." Believing this suggestion to be the teaching of the Spirit, he began to make free with his neighbor's wood. Presently he discovered his mistake by trying his impulse with the eighth commandment, "Thou shalt not steal," and so got rid of an error which might have led him out of the church into a jail.

INFIDELITY.

CAUSES OF INFIDELITY.

212. Ignorance.

(*a*) GENERAL HAMILTON'S CONFESSION.—A young lawyer, in conversation with Bishop Chase, related the following fact respecting General Hamilton which had occurred but a short time before. The young lawyer had been an infidel, but his mind was now changed, and this narration was given in answer to Bishop Chase's inquiry how the change was brought about. "In pursuit of his professional duties General Hamilton passes from New York to Albany, to attend the highest courts, and Poughkeepsie is his stopping-place for rest and social chat. We young lawyers delight to meet him at Hendrickson's tavern, and there breathe together the atmosphere of wit and satire. Not long since, he passed by: we gathered round him, and he greeted us with his usual cordiality. But there was something altered in his wit—it was solemn, yet more affectionate. At length, to break the spell, I ventured, as erst, a story, the edge of which was ridicule against Christians and their creed. As I finished the anecdote, instead of the loud laugh, and responsive tale, the General gravely asked me, if I knew what I had been talking of? Confusion is the best name I can give my feelings and behavior before the great man at such a question from his lips. Seeing my embarrassment, he said he did not design to give me pain, but by his question, to call my attention to his own case.

"'Not many months ago,' said he, 'I was, as you are, doubtful of the truths of Christianity; but some circumstances turned my thoughts to the investigation of the subject, and I now think differently. I had been in company with some friends of a similar sentiment in New York. I had indulged in remarks much to the disadvantage of Christians, and disparagement of their religion. I had gone further than ever before I had done in this way. Coming home, I stood, late at night, on the door steps, waiting for my servant. In this moment of stillness, my thoughts returned to what had just passed at my friend's and on what I had said there. And what if the Christian religion be true, after all? The thought certainly was natural, and it produced in my bosom the most alarming feelings. I was conscious that I had never examined it—not even with that attention which a small retaining fee requires in civil cases. In this I hold myself bound to make up my mind according to the laws of evidence; and shall nothing be done of this sort, in a question that involves the fate of man's immortal being? Where every thing is at stake, shall I bargain all without inquiry?—Wilfully blinding my own eyes, shall I laugh at that, which, if true, will laugh me to scorn in the day of judgment? These questions did not allow me to sleep quietly. In the morning I sent to my friends, the clergy, for such books as treated on the evidence of Christianity—I read them, and the result is, I believe the religion of Christians to be the truth—that Jesus Christ is the Son of God—that he made an atonement for our sins by his death, and that he rose for our justification.'

"This is the substance of General Hamilton's declaration to me at Hendrickson's, and you may judge how I feel since. As I have followed the General in many other respects, so would I imitate him here."

(*b*) SIR ISAAC NEWTON AND HALLEY.—Sir Isaac Newton set out in life a clamorous infidel; but on a nice examination of the evidences for Christianity, he found reason to change his opinions. When the celebrated Dr. Edmund Halley was talking infidelity before him, Sir Isaac addressed him in these or like words? "Dr. Halley, I am always glad to hear you when you speak about astronomy or other parts of the mathematics, because that is a subject you have studied and well understand; but you should not talk of Christianity, for you have not studied it. I have, and am certain that you know nothing of the matter." This was a just reproof, and one that would be very suitable to be given to half the infidels of the present day, for they often speak of what they have never studied, and what, in fact, they are entirely ignorant of. Dr. Johnson, therefore, well observed, that no honest man could be a Deist, for no man could be so after a fair examination of the proofs of Christianity. On the name of Hume being mentioned to him, "No, sir," said he; "Hume owned to a clergyman in the bishopric of Durham that he had never read the New Testament with attention."

(*c*) CONFESSION OF COUNT STRUENSEE.—From the written and published confessions of many converted infidels, it would be easy to show that the most violent opposers of the Bible are generally those who are most ignorant of its contents. An illustration of this remark may be drawn from the history of the unfortunate Count Struensee, prime minister of Denmark, under Christian VII. whose downfall produced the tragical revolution in the Danish Cabinet of 1772.

This distinguished individual had long been an avowed and zealous infidel, when he was suddenly hurled from the summit of power to the horrors and gloom of a dungeon. During the four months he spent in prison under the pious and zealous instruction of the Rev. Dr. Munter, he became thoroughly convinced of the truth of Christianity, and, as it appeared, a true penitent. In the memorable confession which he wrote before he went to the scaffold, he says, "My former unbelief and aversion to religion, were founded neither upon an accurate inquiry into its truth, nor upon a critical examination of those doubts which are generally made against it. They arose, *as is usual in such cases*, from a very general and superficial knowledge of religion on one side, and much inclination to disobey its precepts on the other, together with a readiness to entertain every objection which I discovered against it." In another place, after having carefully examined the evidences of Christianity and his former objections by the aid of Dr. Munter, he exclaims like a man awakened from a dream, "I never imagined that Christianity was founded on such strong evidences or that they would have convinced me so. After a calm examination I have found them to be unexceptionable, and none, if they only take the proper time, and are not against the trouble of meditating, can ever examine it without being convinced of its truth. Every thing is naturally and well connected, and recommends itself to a mind given to reflection. I never found in Deistical writings a system so well connected, and upon the whole I am inclined to believe there is no such thing as a regular system of infidelity."

213. Corruption of the Heart and Life.

(*a*) THE WAY TO ATHEISM.—I was, says a New England minister, some time before my conversion, under serious impressions on the subject of religion. I had a pious education, and my awakened conscience now alarmed me on account of my danger, and pained me on account of my guilt. I would not submit to God, and I accordingly tried to find relief in Universalism. But I had to wrest and rack the Scriptures so much to support that wretched theory, that I soon became convinced of the absurdity of trying to believe the Bible and disbelieve in future punishment I next threw away the Bible, and tried to find a solid foundation in Deism. But I was still unsatisfied; and my next plunge was into blank and utter Atheism. What presumption! A youth less than eighteen years of age rejecting the Bible, denying the being of a God, and the immortality of the soul! But my belief in all this unbelief, was firm and unshaken. I looked upon myself as possessed of superior wisdom, Christians as simpletons, and religion as downright folly and superstition.

Here I thought I had found relief—then no fear of God, man or devil disturbed me.

I went to board in a pious family. One evening after prayer, Mr. and Mrs——, who were pious persons, entered into personal conversation with me on the subject of religion. I frankly told them it was in vain to talk with me—that I was a downright Atheist. They were astonished and thunder struck at the declaration. After recovering from the shock, they kindly entreated me to review the ground on which I stood, and to seek my soul's salvation. A singularly incongruous exhortation, as some would say, to a person who believed he had no God to pray to, and no soul to be saved. But had they been inspired their words could scarcely have been more adapted to meet my case. Their tenderness had an effect upon me which all the arguments of theologians would not have accomplished. I retired to bed, but not to rest. I was led to look back over my past career; and my progress in skepticism was all revealed before me as under a blaze of light. I saw I had disbelieved, and that because I *wished* to disbelieve. I saw then what I had forgotten.

or never distinctly known before, that I had deceived myself into it, and I beheld the course which I had taken to blind my own eyes. The *self imposition* and *influence of desire* upon my infidel opinions was just as plain to me as any fact in my past life. That review of the process by which I had become an infidel, (a process of which I was previously unconscious,) convinced me of the folly and falsity of infidelity. I was led to renounce its unholy dogmas, and brought step by step to embrace the humbling, and self-denying truths of the gospel. I have often thought that if the infidels of the present day could have the heart in like manner bared before them, and see how its depraved wishes have influenced their judgments, in rejecting religion, they would lose confidence, like myself, in their skeptical notions, and come to a similar happy result.

(*b*) CAUSE OF INFIDELITY AVOWED.—Mr. Wilberforce once told the Rev. Wm. Jay that, some years ago, passing through Dorchester during Carlile's confinement there, he went to see him in prison, and endeavored to engage him in a conversation upon the Scriptures; but he refused: he said he had made up his mind, and did not wish it to be perplexed again; and, pointing to the Bible in the hands of his visitor, he said in an awful manner, "How, sir, can you suppose that I can like that Book? for if it be true, I am undone forever!" "No," said the pious philanthropist, "this is not the necessary consequence, and it need not be; that Book excludes none from hope who will seek salvation by our Lord Jesus Christ."

(*c*) LOOSE LIFE, LOOSE CREED.—It has often been a matter of wonder, that the principles and reasonings of infidels, though frequently accompanied with great natural and acquired abilities, are seldom known to make any impression on thoughtful people. It is said of a deceased gentleman, who was eminent in the literary world, that in early life, he drank deeply into the free-thinking scheme. He, and one of his companions of the same turn of mind, often carried on their conversations in the hearing of a religious, but illiterate countryman. This gentleman afterwards became a true Christian, and felt concern for the countryman, lest his faith in Christianity should have been shaken. One day, therefore, he asked him, whether what had so frequently been advanced in his hearing, had not produced this effect upon him. "By no means," answered the countryman; "it never made the least impression upon me." "No impression upon you!" said the gentleman; "why you must have known that we had read and thought on these things much more than you had any opportunity of doing." "Oh, yes," replied the man; "but I knew also your manner of living; I knew that to maintain such a course of conduct, you found it necessary to renounce Christianity."

(*d*) THEY WISHED IT TO BE SO.—Three young men who were executed in Edinburgh, in 1812, immediately after committing the robberies for which they suffered, had gone to Glasgow; and one evening they heard the family with whom they lodged, employed in the worship of God. This struck their minds exceedingly, and suggested the question,—Whether there is a God, and a world to come? After some discussion, they came to this conclusion,—'That there is no God, and no world to come!'—a conclusion, as they themselves acknowledged, to which they came on this sole ground—and how much infidelity that abounds in the world rests on no better—that *they wished it to be so.*

214. Cure of Infidelity.

(*a*) DR. NELSON'S TESTIMONY.—Dr. Nelson, of Illinois, in his work on Infidelity, says, that for many years he had endeavored to persuade every infidel to read some work on the evidences of Christianity, and he never knew but two instances fail of conviction, and in these he did not know the result for want of opportunity.

(*b*) OPPOSER TURNED APOLOGIST.—Athenagoras, a famous Athenian philosopher in the second century, not only doubted the truth of the Christian religion, but was determined to write against it. However, upon an intimate inquiry into the facts on which it was supported, in the course of his collecting materials for his intended publication, he was convinced by the blaze of its evidence, and turned his designed invective into an elaborate apology, which is still in existence.

(*c*) WEST AND LITTLETON.—Perhaps few events tend more powerfully to impress the mind, as to the overwhelming power of the evidence attending true Christianity, than the fact, that many who have sat down to read the sacred volume with the view of opposing it, have been compelled, by the force of conviction, cordially to embrace its truths. From many instances of this kind we select the following, as related by the Rev. T. T. Biddulph: The effect which was wrought on the mind of the celebrated Gilbert West, by that particular evidence of our Lord's resurrection which was afforded to his apostles, was very remarkable. He and his friend Lord Littleton, both men of acknowledged talents, had imbibed the principles of infidelity from a superficial view of the Scriptures. Fully persuaded that the Bible was an imposture, they were determined to expose the cheat. Mr. West chose the resurrection of Christ, and Lord Littleton the conversion of St. Paul, for the subject of hostile criticism. Both sat down to their respective tasks, full of prejudice, and a contempt for Christianity. The result of their separate attempts was truly extraordinary. They were both converted by their endeavors to overthrow the truth of Christianity. They came together, not, as they expected, to exult over an imposture exposed to ridicule, but to lament their own folly, and to congratulate each other on their joint conviction, that the Bible was the word of God. Their able inquiries have furnished two most valuable treatises in favor of revelation; one entitled, "Observations on the Conversion of St. Paul," and the other, "Observations on the Resurrection of Christ."

(*d*) TAKING THE PART OF THE CHRISTIAN.—The following is from the communication of an American clergyman who writes (in 1827) for a Missionary to be sent to the place referred to in this extract.

A settlement was commenced at S. some ten years ago, by emigrants from various sections of our country, but the largest number, it is believed, were from New England, many of whom were men of intelligence and active industry. There was not a single professor of religion among them, and nearly or quite all had embraced Deistical sentiments, and they manifested a disposition to shut out the gospel from their settlement. They frequently met for the sole purpose of strengthening each other in these sentiments. Nothing, for a time, disturbed them. But, behold the Sovereignty of God! It was suggested by one of their number, as their meetings had been rather dull, "to appoint some one to take the part of the Christian." The plan was approved, and the duty was assigned to my informant. He undertook the defence of Christianity. To this end, it was necessary that he should have a *Bible*, and also that he should *read* it. But to use his own expression, "he thought Christianity should be the last thing he would ever embrace." He was first delighted, then astonished, then alarmed, with his own reasoning. He continued to read, and soon found evidence of the truth of Christianity which his conscience could no longer resist. He was humbled before God, and soon after rejoicing in hope of his mercy; and set himself in good earnest to convince his neighbors of his lost condition. A little church is there organized, but they have no one to break to them the bread of life. What Missionary would not be willing to enter a field like this?

215. Moral Character and Influence of the Doctrines and Supporters of Infidelity.

(*a*) GREATEST TERROR REMOVED.—A servant, upon whom the irreligious conversation continually passing at his master's table, had produced its natural effect, took an opportunity to rob him. Being apprehended, and urged to give a reason for his misconduct, he said, "Sir, I had heard you so often talk of the impossibility of a future state, and that after death there was no reward for virtue, nor punishment for vice, that I was tempted to commit the robbery." "Well, but had you no fear," asked the master, "of the death which the law of your country inflicts upon the crime?" "Sir," rejoined the servant, looking sternly at his master, "what is that to you, if I had a mind to venture that? You had removed my greatest terror; why should I fear the less?"

(*b*) INFIDELS AT THE LORD'S SUPPER.—Collins, though he had no belief in Christianity, yet qualified himself for civil office by partaking of the Lord's Supper; Shaftesbury did the same; and the same is done by hundreds of infidels to this day. Yet these are the men who are continually declaiming against the hypocrisy of priests!

(*c*) DYING TESTIMONY OF A SOCIALIST.—A town missionary, in Birmingham, attended a misguided infidel on his death-bed, and the system of Socialism being referred to, the dying man exclaimed, "Call it not Socialism; call it Devilism! for it has made me more like a devil than a man. I got into company, which led me to Socialism and to drinking. I rejected the Bible, denied the Savior, and persuaded myself that there was no hereafter; and as the result, I acted the part of a bad father and a bad husband. I have the testimony of my master, that I was a steady and respectable man until I listened to the Owenites; but, since that time, I have become a vagabond, and those who formerly knew me have shunned me in the streets. The system of the Owenite is worse than that of Paine." Such was the testimony of a dying victim of Socialism.

(*d*) SEVERAL NOTED INFIDELS.—If we look at the writings and conduct of the principal adversaries of Christianity, we shall form no very favorable opinion of their system, as to its moral effects. The morals of Rochester and Wharton need no comment. Woolston was a gross blasphemer. Blount solicited his sister-in-law to marry him; and, being refused, shot himself. Tindal was originally a Protestant, then turned Papist, then Protestant again, merely to suit the times; and was, at the same period, infamous for vice in general, and the total want of principle. He is said to have died with this prayer in his mouth, "If there be a God, I desire that he may have mercy upon me." Hobbes wrote his "Leviathan" to serve the cause of Charles I; but finding him fail of success, he turned it to the defence of Cromwell, and made a merit of this fact to the usurper, as Hobbes himself unblushingly declared to Lord Clarendon. Morgan had no regard for truth, as is evident from his numerous falsifications of Scripture, as well as from the vile hypocrisy of professing himself a Christian in those very writings in which he labors to destroy Christianity. Voltaire, in a letter now in existence, requested his friend, D'Alembert, to tell for him a direct and palpable lie, by denying that he was the author of the Philosophical Dictionary. D'Alembert, in his answer, informed him that he had told the lie. Voltaire has, indeed, expressed his own moral character perfectly in the following words: "Monsieur Abbe, I must be read; no matter whether I am believed or not." He also solemnly professed to believe the Roman Catholic religion, although, at the same time, he elsewhere professed to doubt the existence of God.

(*e*) FOUR SONS RUINED.—There was a place in New York, called the "Hall of Science," which was opened on Sundays for public lectures: in the day-time lectures were given on some of the sciences, and in the evening a lecture was given in opposition to the Christian or any other religion, and in support of the doctrines of infidelity. In order to show the effect of this institution on the young mind, the N. Y. Evening Journal gives an extract from the register of the House of Refuge, of the progress of a boy in that institution. He was about 16 years of age, and had been a clerk for a merchant in New York, who, on declining business, expressed his great satisfaction at the conduct of the boy. An elder brother had been in the habit of attending the lectures at the Hall of Science, and by degrees became an infidel, and he instilled his notions into the mind of this boy; the consequence of which was that he threw off all restraint and united with loose young men and boys in rioting, &c.; neglected all business; wandered about the streets and slept often in stables, till finally his parents were obliged to send him to the House of Refuge, fearful that he would take to stealing to support himself. The father said that the influence of the doctrines taught at the Hall of Science had ruined his whole family of promising boys, (four in number,) and that hearts almost broken, and much mental misery, had been entailed upon the other portions of his family and relatives.

(*f*) AN INFIDEL FAMILY.—"Mr. J. H.," says a writer in the Christian Mirror, "was an inhabitant of my native town, and with whom and his family I was well acquainted. He was a man of good common sense, and was blessed with more than a common share of intellectual powers. His acquired abilities were considerable, being a great reader, and possessing a tenacious memory. But he was a thorough-going infidel! He early embraced the sentiments of Thomas Paine, whose writings were his oracle. He was often heard to make the most vulgar and blasphemous expressions concerning our blessed Savior, and to revile his religion! He was consistent with his sentiments in all things; and early educated his children to believe and embrace his own opinions, and imitate his practices. The old man lived and died without any thing remarkable befalling him personally. But not so with his family—particularly his sons, of whom he had five, all of whom lived to become men and Infidels. The history of four of them will illustrate the influence of parental instruction and example, and show that infidelity leads to vice and ruin. They were all, without exception, dissipated and given to worldly pleasures in their youth. The eldest son soon became very intemperate. He had a wife, and a large family of little children, dependent on his labor for their support. He removed to Boston, where he soon became a sot and vagabond. The city was obliged to support his family; and after a long fit of drunkenness, he was found dead one morning in the street!

The next son never married. He was a drunkard, a gambler and a spendthrift from his youth. He removed into Vermont, and after a drunken and gambling frolic, he arose one morning and plunged himself from the second story of his boarding-house, which stood upon the bank of the Onion river, into the water and was drowned!

The third son was equally dissipated, and having destroyed his constitution, and squandered his earnings, he took a rope and went and hanged himself! The fourth, being unable to obtain the means to support his dissipation by labor, commenced with purchasing and passing counterfeit money; was soon apprehended, examined and bound for his appearance at court. He obtained bonds which he forfeited, by fleeing his country. What will be the end of the youngest, who is now left in possession of his father's property, time will determine.

INFIDELITY AT VARIANCE WITH THE REASON AND CONSCIENCE OF ITS VOTARIES.

216. Shown by their own Confessions of the Moral Tendency of Infidel Doctrines.

(*a*) WHAT MADE HIM A MURDERER?—Cook, who was executed for a very awful murder at Leicester, (Eng.,) in his confession to the town clerk, alluded to being connected with a society, formed principally of deistical young men, who frequented a public house in that town, in which the writings of Paine, Carlile, and other infidel authors, were taken in and encouraged. He emphatically added, "I considered myself a moral young man, attending, as I did, some place of Christian worship three times a day; till unfortunately, I got connected with the above, and other infidel associations."

(*b*) HUME'S TESTIMONY.—"Disbelief in futurity," says Hume, "loosens in a great measure the ties of morality and may be supposed for that eason to be pernicious to the peace of civil society."

(*c*) HUME AND INFIDELITY IN WOMEN.—It is stated, in the "Life of Dr. Beattie," by Sir W. Forbes, that Mr. Hume was one day boasting to Dr. Gregory, that, among his disciples in Edinburgh, he had the honor to reckon many of the fair sex. "Now tell me," said the doctor, "whether, if you had a wife or a daughter, you would wish them to be your disciples? Think well before you answer me; for I assure you, that whatever your answer is, I will not conceal it." Mr. Hume, with a smile, and some hesitation, made this reply:—"No; I believe skepticism may be too sturdy a virtue for a woman."

(*d*) VOLTAIRE'S CONFESSION.—One day that D'Alembert and Condorcet were dining with Voltaire, they proposed to converse of atheism, but Voltaire stopped them at once. "Wait," said he, "till my servants have withdrawn; I do not wish to have my throat cut to-night."

217. Shown by their Confessions in favor of Christianity.

(*a*) THE TWO TRAVELLERS.—Two men were once travelling in the far west; one was a skeptic, the other a Christian. The former was on every occasion ready to denounce religion as an imposture and professors as hypocrites. According to his own account of the matter, he always *suspected* those who made pretensions to piety, felt particularly exposed in the company of Christians, and took special care of his horse and watch when the saints were around him. They had travelled late one evening and were in the wilderness. They at last drew near to a solitary hut and rejoiced in the prospect of a shelter, however humble. They asked admission and obtained it. But it was almost as dreary and comfortless within, as without; and there was nothing prepossessing in the appearance of its inhabitants. These were an elderly man, his wife, and two sons, sunburnt, hardy and rough. They were apparently hospitable, and welcomed our travellers to such homely fare as the forest afforded; but this air of kindness might be assumed to deceive them; and the travellers became seriously apprehensive that evil was intended. It was a lonely place well suited to deeds of robbery and blood. No help was at hand. The two friends communicated to each other their suspicions, and resolved that on retiring to their part of the hut, they would barricade the door against the entrance of their host, that they would have their weapons of defence at hand, that they would alternate in watching, so that one should be constantly on his guard while his companion slept. Having hastily made their arrangements, they joined the family, partook of the homely meal and spoke of retiring to rest. The old man said it had been his practice in better times and he continued it still, before his family retired, to commend them to God, and if the strangers had no objection he would do so now. The Christian rejoiced to find a brother in the wilderness, and even the skeptic could not conceal his satisfaction at the proposition. The old man then took down a well-worn Bible on which no dust had gathered though age had marked it, and read with emphasis a portion of the Sacred Scriptures. He then supplicated the divine protection, acknowledged the divine goodness, and prayed for grace, guidance, and salvation. He prayed too for the strangers—that they might be prospered in their journey, and when their earthly journey was done, they might have a home in heaven. He was evidently a man of prayer, and that humble cottage was a place where prayer was wont to be made. The travellers retired to their apartment; according to their arrangement the skeptic was to have the first watch during the night; but instead of priming his pistols and bracing his nerves for an attack he was for lying down to sleep as quietly as if he had never thought of danger. His friend reminded him of their engagement, and asked where he had lost his apprehension of danger. Ah; the infidel felt the force of the question and all it implied; and had the frankness to confess that he could not but feel as safe as at a New England fireside, in any house or in any forest where the Bible was read as the old man read it, and prayer was offered as that old man prayed.

(*b*) THE SUICIDE'S MANUSCRIPT.—An avowed infidel, whose language and conduct had been most profane, and who had boldly argued for man's right to kill himself when he found it expedient, swallowed a quantity of opium which put an end to his life. Among his papers was found one, on which was written, "I have this moment swallowed a vial of tincture of opium, consequently my life will be but short. Whether there will be a heaven or a hell, I leave parsons to divine." The part of the manuscript which followed was blotted, and concluded thus: "My hand trembles, my eyes grow dim, I can see to write no more; but he that would be happy should be religious."

(*c*) MASON'S REPLY TO THE SCOFFER.—To a young infidel who was scoffing at Christianity because of the misconduct of its professors, the late Dr. Mason said, "Did you ever know an uproar to be made because an infidel went astray from the paths of morality?" The infidel admitted that he had not. "Then don't you see," said Dr. M., "that, by expecting the professors of Christianity to be holy, you admit it to be a holy religion, and thus pay it the highest compliment in your power?" The young man was silent.

(*d*) BOLINGBROKE'S TESTIMONY.—Lord Bolingbroke, a man of giant intellect, of great political influence during his life, but an avowed infidel, declares that "The doctrine of rewards and punishments in a future state, has so great a tendency to enforce the civil laws and restrain the vices of men, that though reason would decide against it on the principles of theology, she will not decide against it on the principles of good policy." Again he says; "No religion ever appeared in the world, whose natural tendency was so much directed to promote the peace and happiness of mankind, as the Christian. The Gospel of Christ is one continual lesson of the strictest morality, of justice, benevolence, and universa. charity. Supposing Christianity to be a human invention, it is the most amiable, and successful invention, that ever was imposed on mankind for their good."

218. Shown by their Confessions in favor of the Moral Character of Christ.

(*a*) LEGUINIA'S CONFESSION.—"He called himself the Son of God; who among mortals dare to say he was not? He always displayed virtue; he always spoke according to the dictates of reason; he always preached up wisdom; he sincerely loved all men, and wished to do good even to his persecutors; he developed all the principles of moral equality and of the purest patriotism; he met danger undismayed; he described the hard-heartedness of the rich; he attacked the pride of kings; he dared to resist, even in the face of tyrants; he despised glory and fortune; he was sober; he solaced the indigent; he taught the unfortunate how to suffer; he sustained weakness; he fortified decay; he consoled misfortune; he knew how to shed tears with those that wept; he taught men to subjugate their passions, to think, to reflect, to love one another, and to live happily together; he was hated by the powerful, whom he offended by his teaching; and persecuted by the wicked, whom he unmasked; and he died under the indignation of the blind and deceived multitude for whose good he had always lived."

If such was the testimony of the French atheist Leguinia, surely the true Christian is at no loss to enlarge the admirable portraiture.

(*b*) CONFESSION OF ROUSSEAU.—I will confess to you, says Rousseau, in his Treatise on Education, that the majesty of the Scriptures strikes me with admiration, as the purity of the Gospel hath its influence on my heart. Peruse the works of our philosophers, with all their pomp of diction, how mean, how contemptible are they compared with Scripture! Is it possible that a book, at once so simple and sublime, should be merely the work of man? Is it possible that the sacred personage whose history it contains should be himself a mere man? Do we find that he assumed the tone of an enthusiast, or ambitious sectary? What sweetness, what purity in his manner! What an affecting gracefulness in his delivery! What sublimity in his maxims! What profound wisdom in his discourses! What presence of mind, what subtlety, what truth in his replies! How great the command of his passions! Where is the man, where the philosopher, who could so live, and so die, without weakness and without ostentation? When Plato described his imaginary good man, loaded with all the shame of guilt, yet meriting the highest rewards of virtue, he described exactly the character of Jesus Christ; the resemblance was so striking, that all the Fathers perceived it.

What prepossession, what blindness must it be, to compare the son of Sombroniscus to the son of Mary? What an infinite disproportion there is between them! Socrates dying without pain or ignominy easily supported his character to the last; and if his death, however easy, had not crowned his life, it might have been doubted whether Socrates, with all his wisdom, was any thing more than a vain sophist. He invented, it is said, the theory of morals. Others, however, had before put them in practice; he had only to say, therefore, what they had done, and to reduce their examples to precepts. Aristides had been just before Socrates defined justice; Leonidas had given up his life for his country before Socrates declared patriotism to be a duty; the Spartans were a sober people before Socrates recommended sobriety; before he had even defined virtue, Greece abounded in virtuous men. But where could Jesus learn, among his competitors, that pure and sublime morality, of which he only hath given us both precept and example? The greatest wisdom was made known amongst the most bigoted fanaticism, and the simplicity of the most heroic virtues, did honor to the vilest people on earth. The death of Socrates peaceably philosophizing with his friends, appears the most agreeable that could be wished for--that of Jesus expiring in the midst of agonizing pains, abused, insulted, and accused by a whole nation, is the most horrible that could be feared. Socrates, in receiving the cup of poison, blessed the weeping executioner who administered it, but Jesus, in the midst of excruciating torments prayed for his merciless tormentors.

Yes, if the life and death of Socrates were those of a sage, the life and death of Jesus were those of a God. Shall we suppose the evangelic history a mere fiction? Indeed, my friend, it bears not the mark of fiction; on the contrary, the history of Socrates, which nobody presumes to doubt, is not so well attested as that of Jesus Christ. Such a supposition in fact, only shifts the difficulty without obviating it; it is more inconceivable, that a number of persons should agree to write such a history, than that one only should furnish the subject of it. The Jewish authors were incapable of the diction, and of the morality contained in the Gospel, the marks of whose truth are so striking and inimitable, that the inventor would be a more astonishing character than the hero.

(*c*) CONFESSION OF PAINE.—Paine, after scandalizing the account of Christ's supernatural birth in his Age of Reason, uses the following lanuage:

"Nothing that is here said can apply even with the most distant disrespect to the moral character of Jesus Christ. He was a virtuous and amiable man. The morality that he preached and practised was of the most benevolent kind; and though similar systems of morality had been preached by Confucius and by some of the Greek philosophers many ages before; by the Quakers since; and by many good men in all ages, it has not been exceeded by any."

Again, Paine says: "He (Christ) called men to the practice of moral virtues and the belief of one God. The great trait in his character is philanthropy."

Paine, in the first extract, would evidently put Christ on a level with such ancient sages as Socrates and others. The mistake he here commits is sufficiently exposed in the foregoing confession of the infidel Rousseau. If Christ was a virtuous man, then he practised no imposition when he professed to work miracles; and if he wrought miracles, then his doctrines, which his miracles were wrought to confirm, are all true.

219. Shown by Confessions of their Disquietude and Misery.

(*a*) AFRAID THE BIBLE IS TRUE.—The following melancholy case is well authenticated:

Mr. S—, a well-known infidel, said one day to Mr. N—, who had also imbibed the same evil principles, "There is one thing which mars all the pleasures of my life." "Ah," said Mr. N—, "what is that?" "Why," replied Mr. S—, "I am afraid that the Bible is true! If I could know for certain that death is an eternal sleep, I should be happy—my joy would be complete! But here is the thorn that stings me. This is the sword that pierces my very soul. If the Bible is true, I am lost forever! Every prospect is gone! and I am lost forever!"

Mr. S— was just entering on a voyage—sailed not long after—was shipwrecked, and lost! sinking probably into the mighty deep, under all the horrors of absolute despair. Alas! what a dreadful tormentor is a guilty conscience! and how ineffectual are all the opiates of infidelity and licentiousness to assuage its anguish; and if they are so in the time of health and prosperity, what must it be to bear affliction, and to pass the final, solemn test, without the hopes and consolations of the gospel!

(*b*) WE DON'T TELL YOU ALL.—One of the most sensible men I ever knew, says one, but whose life as well as creed had been rather eccentric, returned me the following answer, not many months before his death, when I asked him "whether his former irregularities were not both accompanied at the time, and succeeded afterward by some sense of mental pain." "Yes," said he, "but I have scarce ever owned it until now. We" (meaning we infidels and men of fashionable morals) "do not tell you all that passes in our hearts!"

(*c*) MR. HOBBES AND DEATH.—Mr. Hobbes, the celebrated infidel, in bravado, would often say very unbecoming things of God and the Bible, yet when alone he was haunted with the most tormenting reflections, and would awake in great terror if his candle happened to go out in the night He never could bear any discourse about death, and seemed to cast off all thoughts of it. Notwithstanding all his high pretensions to learning and philosophy, his uneasiness constrained him to confess, as he drew near the grave, that "he was about taking a leap in the dark."

(*d*) ATHEIST'S ACKNOWLEDGMENT.—The example of a perfect Atheist, says Dr. Spence, is very rare, and has seldom been the object of my own experience: one, however, I knew, a jurist and statesman, well learned and of good parts; so well read was he in the Scriptures and divinity in general, that he might have passed for no ordinary theologian. He had, though a speculative unbeliever, maintained several *theses* with great success; on the other hand, he could, in his opinion, account for every appearance in nature, from a theory of matter and motion. Still, says the relator, with all his belief and unbelief, he frankly confessed to me "*that he was unhappy*:" And being then in a state of celibacy, further acknowledged that, "should he ever change his situation, he was determined never to suffer the secrets of his heart to transpire to his wife and children, that in all externals he would strictly conform to the church," adding as one of his philosophical and political reasons, "that it was better to be comforted upon a false ground, than to live *without any consolation*."

(*e*) CONFESSION OF VOLTAIRE.—"Who," says Voltaire, "can, without horror, consider the whole world as the empire of destruction? It abounds with wonders; it also abounds with victims. It is a vast field of carnage and contagion. Every species is without pity pursued and torn to pieces through the earth, and air, and water. In man there is more wretchedness than in all the other animals put together. He loves life and yet he knows that he must die. If he enjoys a transient good, he suffers various evils, and is at last devoured by worms. This knowledge is his fatal prerogative ; other animals have it not. He spends the transient moments of his existence in diffusing the miseries which he suffers : in cutting the throats of his fellow creatures for pay ; in cheating and being cheated ; in robbing and being robbed ; in serving that he might command ; and in repenting of all he does. The bulk of mankind are nothing more than a crowd of wretches, equally criminal and unfortunate ; and the globe contains rather carcasses than men. I tremble at the review of this dreadful picture, to find it contains a complaint against Providence itself: and *I wish I had never been born.*"

220. Shown by their advice to their Friends and treatment of them.

(*a*) THE INFIDEL'S ADVICE.—A man who had been very much connected with infidels, was taken dangerously ill ; and feeling that he could not recover, became alarmed for the safety of his soul. His infidel principles gave him no comfort. He began, for the first time, to examine into the Christian religion. He embraced it, and found it to be the power of God to his salvation, enabling him to triumph over the fear of death. In the mean time, his infidel friends hearing of his sickness, and that he was not likely to recover, showed a degree of feeling and integrity, which, it was hoped, might prove the first step towards their conversion. They were not aware that their dying friend had become a Christian. They called to see him, and actually told him that they came on purpose to advise him now to embrace Christianity : "Because," said they, "if it be false, it can do you no harm ; but if it should prove true, you will be a great gainer."

This, reader, is a fact. It was the united advice of a number of unbelievers to their dying friend.

(*b*) PAINE'S ADVICE TO A TRAVELLER.—A writer in the Western Observer, Bishop McIlvaine, we presume, says :

I have recently been in conversation with a gentleman who personally knew Tom Paine, from whom I have learned some particulars, which it may be useful to repeat. This gentleman states, that when a young man he was driving his father's wagon from Sing Sing to a place in Westchester county, N. Y., when Paine, travelling the same way, requested to be taken in. The young man consenting, they rode about twenty miles together. The fame and talk about "Paine's Age of Reason," had made a skeptical impression on the mind of the youth, and finding himself in the presence of its author, he gladly availed himself of the opportunity to learn more of that sort of reason. In the course of the conversation, Paine positively asserted that he believed the Scriptures to be the word of God, and most seriously charged his auditor not to read his book, or if he did, not to suffer it to have any influence on his mind. He said it did not contain the truth ; that he deeply regretted its publication, and would have given any thing had he never written it. Such was the serious earnestness of Paine in these remarks, and so conclusively did he reason against the principles of his "Age of Reason," that he entirely removed all skeptical impressions from the mind of the young man, (the present informant,) so that the latter has ever since retained a grateful recollection of the conversation, and now says, that such was Paine's earnestness to prevent his being injured by his writings, and to eradicate all such evil impressions as they had already made, that he can never lose the remembrance of it.

(*c*) INFIDEL'S CHOICE OF EXECUTOR.—For the purpose of illustrating the secret respect which is entertained by infidels for a pure and consistent Christianity, we relate the following incidents, which have never appeared in print. They may serve to show that a testimony which under ordinary circumstances would be studiously withheld, may, by the force of circumstances, be extorted.

In one of the flourishing towns of a distant state, resided two gentlemen of high professional standing, but of infidel principles. In habits of the closest intimacy they encouraged each other, not only in a determined opposition to the spread of religion, but in the most profane mockery of its doctrines, institutions, and tendencies. A third individual in the town, likewise possessing influence, but of truly consistent Christian character, was the principal object of their profane jests. They pretended to hold his religion in utter contempt, and often made merry in ridiculing his superstition and fanaticism. How sincere and hearty they were in trusting their own principles may be learned from the sequel. In the course of time one of them was attacked by fatal disease, and died without any happy change in his religious views. On opening his will it was ascertained that he had intrusted the settlement of his estate to the *pious* man, and that his infidel friend was not mentioned as an executor! If an action could speak, this spoke loudly of his distrust of infidel principles, and of his secret confidence in those of Christianity.

221. Shown by their Conduct in Danger.

(*a*) WITHERSPOON AND THE ATHEIST.—The Rev. Dr. Witherspoon, formerly president of Princeton College, N. J., was once on board a packet ship, where, among other passengers, was a professed atheist. This unhappy man was very fond of troubling every one with his peculiar belief, and of broaching the subject as often as he could get any one to listen to him. He did not believe in a God and a future state, not he! By and by there came on a terrible storm, and the prospect was that all would be drowned. There was much consternation on board, but not one was so greatly frightened as the professed atheist. In this extremity, he sought out the clergyman, and found him in the cabin, calm and collected, in the midst of danger, and thus addressed him: "Oh doctor Witherspoon! Doctor Witherspoon! we're all going; we have but a short time to stay. Oh, how the vessel rocks! we're all going; don't you think we are, doctor?" The doctor turned to him with a solemn look, and replied in broad Scotch, "Nae doubt, nae doubt, man, we're a' ganging; but you and I dinna gang the same way."

(*b*) VOLNEY IN A STORM.—Samuel Forester Bancroft, Esq., accompanied Mr. Isaac Weld, jr., in his travels through North America. As they were sailing on Lake Erie, in a vessel, on board of which was Volney, celebrated, (or rather, notorious,) for his atheistical principles. He was very communicative, allowed no opportunity to escape of ridiculing Christianity, and behaved altogether in a very profane manner. In the course of the voyage, a very heavy storm came on, insomuch that the vessel, which had struck repeatedly with great force, was expected to go down every instant. The masts went overboard; the rudder unshipped; and, consequently, the whole scene exhibited confusion and horror. There were many female passengers and others on board; but no one exhibited such strong marks of fearful despair as Volney—throwing himself on deck; now imploring, then imprecating the captain, and reminding him that he had engaged to carry him safe to his port of destination; vainly threatening, in case any thing should happen. One moment he was quite frantic, and raged like a madman; another, in wild consternation, he looked into some of Voltaire's works, which he generally carried in his bosom; then despair took hold on him, and he uttered the most incoherent expressions, and offered a large sum of money to the captain, to prevail on him to attempt what was utterly impossible, namely, to put him ashore in a small boat.

As the probability of their being lost increased, this great mirror of nature, human or inhuman, began loading the pockets of his coat, waistcoat, breeches, and every thing he could think of, with dollars, to the amount of some hundreds; and this, as he thought, was preparing to swim for his life, should the vessel go to pieces. Mr. Bancroft remonstrated with him on the folly of such acts, saying he would sink like a piece of lead, with so great a weight on him; and at length as he became so very noisy and unsteady as to impede the management of the vessel, Mr. Bancroft pushed him down the hatchway. Volney soon came up again, having lightened himself of the dollars, and, in the agony of his mind, threw himself on deck, exclaiming, with uplifted hands and streaming eyes, "Oh, my God! my God!—what shall I do—what shall I do!"—This so surprised Bancroft, that notwithstanding the moment did not very well accord with flashes of humor, yet he could not refrain from addressing him: "Well, Mr. Volney—what! you have a God now?" To which Volney replied, with the most trembling anxiety, "O yes! O yes!" The vessel, however, got safe, and Mr. Bancroft made every company which he went into, echo with this anecdote of Volney's acknowledgment of God. Volney, for a considerable time, was so hurt at his weakness, as he calls it, that he was ashamed of showing himself in company at Philadelphia. But afterwards he said that those words escaped him in the instant of alarm, but had no meaning.

Infidelity, then, will do only ashore, in fine weather; but it will not stand a gale of wind for a few hours.

Infidels and Atheists! how will you weather an ETERNAL STORM?

(*c*) THE INFIDEL AND HIS BOX OF BOOKS.—Infidels are often quite bold in calm weather, but at the first approach of danger their courage vanishes in a moment. During a gale on Lake Erie, the steamer Robert Fulton, among many other vessels, was wrecked and lost. On board that boat, as was related by a passenger, and published in the Religious Herald, was an infidel with a box of books to distribute at the West. He was loud and clamorous in proclaiming his infidelity, till the gale came on—but then, like the rest, he was silent, and waited with trembling anxiety the uncertain fate of the ship. At length they drew near the shore, and attempted to throw out their anchors, when the whole forward part of the boat broke off, and the waves rushed into the cabin. At once the infidel was on his knees crying for mercy—his voice could be heard above the raging elements, begging the Lord to forgive his blasphemies, till a heavy sea swept over the deck, and *carried him and his books to the bottom.*

222. Shown by their Conduct in Death.

(*a*) VOLTAIRE'S LAST HOURS.—In spite of all the infidel philosophers who flocked around Voltaire in the first days of his illness, he gave signs of wishing to return to that God whom he had so often blasphemed. He called for the priest; his danger increasing, he wrote entreating the Abbe Gaultier to visit him. He afterwards made a declaration, in which he, in fact, renounced infidelity, signed by himself and two witnesses. D'Alembert, Diderot, and about twenty others, who had beset his apartment, he would often curse, and exclaim, "Retire; it is you that have brought me to my present state. Begone; I could have done without you all, but you could not exist without me; and what a wretched glory have you procured me!" They could hear him, the prey of anguish and dread, alternately supplicating and blaspheming that God whom he had conspired against; and in plaintive accents would he cry out, "Oh Christ! Oh Jesus Christ!" and then complain that he was abandoned of God and man.

At one time he was discovered by his attendant with a book of prayers in his hand, endeavoring, with a faltering tongue, to repeat some of the petitions for mercy addressed to that Being whose name he had blasphemed. He had fallen from his bed in convulsive agonies, and lay foaming with impotent despair on the floor, exclaiming, "Will not this God, whom I have denied, save me too? Cannot infinite mercy extend to me?"

His physician, Mr. Tronchin, calling in to administer relief, thunderstruck, retired, declaring the death of the impious man to be terrible indeed: the

Mareshal de Richelieu flies from the bed-side, declaring it to be a sight too terrible to be sustained: and Mr. Tronchin, that the furies of Orestes could give but a faint idea of those of Voltaire. He said, "Doctor, I will give you half of what I am worth if you will give me six months' life;" the doctor answered, "Sir, you cannot live six weeks." Voltaire replied, "Then I shall go to hell and you will go with me;" and soon after expired.—Such were the horrors of mind in which this arch-infidel quitted the world, that the nurse who attended him, being many years afterward requested to wait on a sick Protestant gentleman, refused, till she was assured he was not a philosopher; declaring, if he were, she would on no account incur the danger of witnessing such a scene as she had been compelled to witness at the death of M. Voltaire. Bishop Wilson, of Calcutta, mentions that he received this account from the son of the gentleman to whose dying bed the woman was invited.

(*b*) "MOURNING AT THE LAST."—A society of men, who may properly be termed "haters of God," were in the habit of meeting together on Sabbath mornings, to ridicule religion, and to encourage each other in sin. At length they agreed to burn the Bible! They had lately initiated a young man into their awful mysteries, who had been brought up under great religious advantages, but had misimproved them, and now, throwing the holy book into the flames, he declared he would never go to a place of religious worship again. He was soon afterwards taken ill, and was visited by a pious man, who found him in great mental agony. In reference to his conduct, the young man remarked, it all did well enough while in health, and while he could keep off the thoughts of death: but when the Redeemer was mentioned to him, he hastily exclaimed, "What's the use of talking to me about mercy?" When recommended to look to Christ, he said, "I tell you it is of no use now; 'tis too late, 'tis too late. Once I could pray, but now I can't." He frequently repeated, "I cannot pray, I will not pray." When two of his former companions in sin entered his room, and attempted to rally him from his despondency by some of their blustering expressions, he raised himself on his bed, and, with his hands lifted up, invoked the curse of God upon them. Others of the same party afterwards came to see him; but the sight of them could then give him no pleasure. He repeated, and that in a way which no one could hear without shuddering, the same dreadful imprecations.

As death drew near, he lay as if insensible to any thing that was said to him, only rolling about on his bed, and now and then saying, "My Bible! oh the Bible!" He then concealed his face, became violently convulsed, groaned and expired.

How unspeakably awful to reject the word of God! "The wicked is driven away in his wickedness; but the righteous hath hope in his death."

(*c*) GIBBON'S CONFESSION.—The celebrated Gibbon just before his death confessed that when he considered all worldly things, they were all fleeting; when he looked back they had been fleeting; when he looked forward "*all was dark and doubtful.*" Surely no one can wish to be an infidel for the comfort of it.

(*d*) DEATH OF HUME'S MOTHER.—Hume, the historian, received a religious education from his mother, and early in life was the subject of strong and hopeful religious impressions; but, as he approached manhood, they were effaced, and confirmed infidelity succeeded.

Maternal partiality, however alarmed at first, came at length to look with less and less pain upon this declension, and filial love and reverence seemed to have been absorbed in the pride of philosophical skepticism; for Hume applied himself with unwearied, and unhappily with successful efforts, to sap the foundation of his mother's faith.

Having succeeded in this dreadful work, and as he was returning, an express met him in London, with a letter from his mother, informing him that she was in a deep decline, and could not long survive; she said, she found herself without any support in her distress; that he had taken away that only source of comfort upon which, in all cases of affliction, she used to rely, and that she now found her mind sinking into despair; she did not doubt that her son would afford her some substitute for her religion; and she conjured him to hasten to her, or at least to send her a letter, containing such consolations as philosophy could afford to a dying mortal.

Hume was overwhelmed with anguish on receiving this letter, and hastened to Scotland, travelling day and night; but before he arrived his mother expired.

No permanent impression seems, however, to have been made on his mind by this trying event; and whatever remorse he might have felt at the moment, he soon relapsed into his previous hardness of heart. Thus it is that false philosophy restores the sting to death, and gives again the victory to the grave.

(e) END OF NOTED FRENCH INFIDELS.—The following affecting account of the death of several of the leading infidels in France, at the period of the revolution, is extracted from Sir Walter Scott's "Life of Buonaparte," and strikingly shows that deism can afford no help in the hour of trial:

None of all the victims of the reign of terror felt its disabling influence so completely as the despot Robespierre, who had so long directed its sway. The Hotel de Ville, where he and his companions had assembled, was surrounded by about 1500 men, and cannon turned upon the doors. The deserted group of theorists within conducted themselves like scorpions, which, when surrounded by fire, are said to turn their stings on each other, and on hemselves. Mutual and ferocious upbraiding took place among these miserable men. "Wretch! were these the means you promised to furnish?" said Payan to Henriot, whom he found intoxicated, and incapable of resolution or exertion, and seizing on him as he spoke, he precipitated the revolutionary general from a window. Henriot survived the fall only to drag himself into a drain, in which he was afterwards discovered, and brought out to execution. The younger Robespierre threw himself from the window, but did not perish on the spot. Las Basas dispatched himself with a pistol-shot. St. Just, after imploring his comrades to kill him, attempted his own life with an irresolute hand, and failed. Couthon lay beneath the table brandishing a knife, with which he repeatedly wounded his bosom, without daring to add force enough to reach his heart. Robespierre, in an unsuccessful attempt to shoot himself, had only inflicted a horrible fracture on his under jaw.

In this situation they were found, like wolves in their lair, foul with blood, mutilated, despairing, and yet not able to die. Robespierre lay on a table in an ante-room, his head supported by a deal box, and his hideous countenance half hidden by a dirty cloth bound round the shattered chin.

The captives were carried in triumph to the convention, who, without admitting them to the bar, ordered them, as outlaws, for instant execution. As the fatal cars passed to the guillotine, those who filled them, but especially Robespierre, were overwhelmed with execrations, from the friends and relatives of victims whom he had sent on the same melancholy road.

The nature of his previous wound, from which the cloth had never been removed, till the executioner tore it off, added to the torture of the sufferer. The shattered jaw dropped, and the wretch yelled aloud, to the horror of the spectators. A masque, taken from that dreadful head, was long exhibited in different nations of Europe, and appalled the spectators by its ugliness, and the mixture of fiendish expression with that of bodily agony.

(f) LAST DAYS OF THOMAS PAINE,—Paine was nursed in his last illness by a Mrs. Hedden, a very worthy and pious woman, who did her best to serve him not only as a kind attendant, but also as a spiritual counsellor. During the first three or four days, his conduct was tolerable, except that he grew outrageous whenever Madame Bonneville entered the room. About the fifth day his language to Mrs. Hedden was so bad, that she resolved immediately to quit the house, but sensible how necessary she was to his comfort, he made concessions which induced her to remain. Though his conversation was equivocal, his conduct was singular, he would not be left alone night or day; he not only required to have some person with him, but he must see that he or she was there, and would not allow his curtain to be closed at any time; and if, as it would sometimes unavoidably happen, he was left alone, he would scream and cry aloud, until some person came to him. There was something remarkable in his conduct about this period, (which comprises nearly two weeks immediately preceding his death,) particularly when we reflect that Thomas Paine was author of the Age of Reason. He would call out during his paroxysms of distress, without intermission, "O Lord help me, God help me, Jesus Christ help me, O Lord help me," &c., repeating the same expressions without the least variation, in a tone of voice that would alarm the house. On the 6th of June, Dr. Manly, struck by these expressions, which he so frequently repeated, and seeing that he was in great distress of mind, put the following questions to him: "Mr. Paine, what must we think of your present conduct? Why do you call upon Jesus Christ to help you? Do you believe that he can help you? Do you believe in the divinity of Jesus Christ?" After a pause of some minutes he answered, "I have no wish to believe on that subject."

A gentleman of the neighborhood occasionally furnished him with refreshments from his own table, of which a respectable female of the family was the bearer. She being asked by Paine her opinion respecting the Age of Reason, frankly told him that she thought it the most dangerous book she had ever seen; that the more she read the more she found her mind estranged from all good; and that from a conviction of its evil tendency, she had burnt it without knowing to whom it belonged. To this Paine replied, that *he wished all its readers had been as wise as she;* and added, "If ever the devil had an agent on earth, I have been one." Mrs. Bonneville, the unhappy female who had accompanied him from France, lamented to his neighbor her sad case, observing, "For this man I have given up my family and friends, my property and my religion; judge then of my distress, when he tells me that *the principles he has taught me will not bear me out.*"

(*g*) THE ELDER'S VISIT TO PAINE.—The following facts, says a correspondent of the "New York Observer," in 183–, were lately told me by an elder in one of the Presbyterian churches of this city, who visited Paine a few days before his death.

Approaching his bed, my informant saw a loathsome and pitiable object. His face and particularly his nose was greatly swollen and changed by liquor to a dark color. The visitor said to him, "*Mr. Paine, he that believeth on the Lord Jesus Christ shall be saved, but he that believeth not shall be damned.*" "What's that you say!" said the dying man. The visitor repeated the gospel declaration. Paine immediately seized a large black stick, that was lying at his side, nearly the thickness of a man's wrist, and raising it over the head of the visitor, said, with great anger and vehemnce, "*Away with your popish nonsense.*" The very name of Jesus Christ convulsed him with anger. The woman attending him informed the visitor, that he was occasionally visited by persons of like principles and habits with himself, and that his orders were to keep out of his room all who professed any respect for religion. She said that he was a wretched man. That when alone he kept groaning day and night, as if in great distress of mind. She once told him that his groans disturbed her that she could not rest, when he replied, "*I have no rest myself, nor shall you have.*"

(*h*) PAINE'S CONFESSION TO RANDALL.—The Rev. Jedekiah Randall, a most upright and excellent minister of the gospel, formerly of Norwich, Chenango co., N. Y., paid a visit to Thomas Paine on his death-bed, Though Paine was much of the time under the influence of spirituous liquors, and the mere mention of religion would seem to rouse all his vindictive passions against the one who addressed him yet it must be said in his praise, that in this case he seemed to be sober, and listened in a calm and respectful manner to what the minister of Christ had to say. The reply of Mr. Paine was dispassionate, and contained an honest confession, such as a troubled conscience, it seemed, would no longer allow his proud heart to withhold. His words were to this effect:

"Mr. Randall, I never confidently disbelieved in the Christian religion; my unbelief and skepticism were rather assumed than real. And one object of my writing the Age of Reason, was to cripple the power of the corrupt and tyrannical priesthood of the Romish church in France. Should I ever recover from this illness it is my intention to publish another book, disavowing the infidel doctrines contained in the Age of Reason, and expressing my convictions of the truth of the Christian system."

223. Miscellaneous.

(*a*) DEISTICAL HISTORIANS.—Gibbon, who, in his celebrated "History of the Decline and Fall of the Roman Empire," has left a memorial of his emnity to the gospel, resided many years in Switzerland, where, with the profits of his works, he purchased a considerable estate. This property has descended to a gentleman, who, out of his rents, expends a large sum annually in the promulgation of that very gospel which his predecessor insidiously endeavored to undermine.

Voltaire boasted that with one hand he would overthrow that edifice of Christianity which required the hands of twelve apostles to build up. The press which he employed at Ferney, for printing his blasphemies, was afterwards actually employed at Geneva in printing the Holy Scriptures: thus the very engine which he set to work to destroy the credit of the Bible, was employed in disseminating its truths.

It is a remarkable circumstance also, that the first meeting of an Auxiliary Bible Society at Edinburgh, was held in the very room in which David Hume, the infidel, died.

(*b*) INFIDEL PROPHECIES.—Voltaire said "he was living in the twilight of Christianity;" so he was; but it was the twilight of the morning.

Tom Paine, on his return from France, sitting in the City Hotel in Broadway, surrounded by many of our leading men, who came to do him homage, predicted that "in five years there would not be a Bible in America." What would his spirit feel could it now enter the depositories of the American Bible Society?

(*c*) INFIDELS GOING MASKED.—At an infidel convention, held in New York, John A Collins, one of the principal speakers, discoursed at length upon the best means of supporting infidelity. After a series of railings against God and the Bible, and every thing sacred, he used this language; "I never deliver lectures on infidelity; but I am constantly lecturing on the various reforms of the age. I lecture on temperance, on anti-slavery, on peace, on moral reform, on socialism, &c., &c., but wherever I go I lecture on *infidel principles!* Thus our cause is promoted continually."

(*d*) LAST DAYS OF THE GODDESS OF REASON.—In the Paris papers of August 1, 1817, we find among the obituaries the following announcement:—"Died, within these few days, in the hospital of pauper lunatics of Saltpetriere, where she had lived unpitied and unknown for many years, the famous Theroigne de Mericourt, (the Goddess of Reason,) the most remarkable of the heroines of the Revolution." This female (nearly in a state of nudity) was seated on a throne by Fouche and Carnot, in the Champ de Mars, and hailed alternately as the Goddess of Reason and Liberty. There was something remarkable in the history of the latter days of this poor creature, and her life is not without its moral. She who was taught publicly to blaspheme her Creator, and dishonor her sex, was, for the last twenty years of her miserable life, subject to the greatest of human calamities—the deprivation of her *reason*. She repented severely of her horrible crimes, and her few lucid intervals were filled up by the most heart-rending lamentations. She died at the age of fifty-seven.

(*e*) A CONVERTED ATHEIST. —The author of "Philosophy of the Plan of Salvation" gives an account of a man of his acquaintance, who had been a notorious and profane atheist. By the persuasion of pious relatives, who had long prayed for his conversion, he was induced to attend a series of religious meetings, where he was brought to see his condition as a sinner, and to exercise saving faith in the Lord Jesus Christ. "Old things" having now "passed away, and all things become new," the change was so strikingly great, that it was obvious to all who knew him. He immediately sought reconciliation with his enemies, asked their forgiveness, and tried to benefit them by leading them to Christ. He began to visit from house to house, laboring and praying with his neighbors, and inviting them to attend religious worship on the Sabbath. "When converted, one of his first acts, although he had heard nothing of any such act in others, was to make out a list of all his old associates then living within reach of his influence. For the conversion of these he determined to labor as he had opportunity, and pray daily. On his list were one hundred and sixteen names, among whom were skeptics, drunkards, and other individuals as little likely to be reached by Christian influence as any other men in the region. Within two years from the period of the old man's conversion, one hundred of these individuals had made a profession of religion. This account is not exaggerated: the old man is living, and there are a thousand living witnesses to this testimony."

INFLUENCE AFTER DEATH.

224. Influence Beneficial.

(*a*) SERMON EFFECTUAL AFTER EIGHTY-FIVE YEARS.—About the middle of the seventeenth century, the venerable John Flavel, whose excellent practical writings are known to many of our readers, was settled at Dartmouth, where his labors were greatly blessed.

Mr. Flavel's manner was remarkably affectionate and serious, often exciting very powerful emotions in his hearers. On one occasion, he preached from these words:—"If any man love not the Lord Jesus Christ, let him be anathema, maranatha." The discourse was unusually solemn, particularly the explanation of the words *anathema, maranatha*,—"cursed with a curse, cursed of God, with a bitter and grievous curse." At the conclusion of the service, when Mr. Flavel arose to pronounce the benediction, he paused, and said, "How shall I bless this whole assembly, when every person in it, who loveth not the Lord Jesus Christ, is anathema, maranatha?" The solemnity of this address deeply affected the audience, and one gentleman, a person of rank, was so overcome by his feelings, that he fell senseless to the floor.

In the congregation was a lad named Luke Short, then about fifteen years old, and a native of Dartmouth. Shortly after the event just narrated, he entered into the seafaring line, and sailed to America, where he passed the rest of his life.

Mr. Short's life was lengthened much beyond the usual term. When a hundred years old, he had sufficient strength to work on his farm, and his mental faculties were very little impaired. Hitherto he had lived in carelessness and sin; he was now a "sinner a hundred years old," and apparently ready to "die accursed." But one day, as he sat in his field, he busied himself in reflecting on his past life. Recurring to the events of his youth, his memory fixed upon Mr. Flavel's discourse above alluded to, a considerable part of which he was able to recollect. The affectionate earnestness of the preacher's manner, the important truths which he delivered, and the effects produced on the congregation, were brought fresh to his mind. The blessing of God accompanied his meditations: he felt that he had not "loved the Lord Jesus Christ;" he feared the dreadful "anathema;" conviction was followed by repentance, and at length this aged sinner obtained peace through the blood of atonement, and was found "in the way of righteousness." He joined the Congregational church in Middleborough, and to the day of his death, which took place in his 116th year, gave pleasing evidence of piety.

In this case, eighty-five years passed away after the seed was sown, before it sprang up and brought forth fruit. Let the ministers of Christ be encouraged; "in due season they shall reap, if they faint not."

(*b*) OBSCURE WOMAN'S USEFULNESS.—There was once an obscure and pious woman living in a city in the South of England. History is silent respecting her ancestry—her place of birth—or her education. She had an only son, whom in his infancy she made it her great business to instruct, and train up in the nurture and admonition of the Lord. At seven years of age his mother died, and a few years after he went to sea, and became at length a common sailor in the African slave trade. He soon became a great adept in vice—a swearer most horribly profane; and though younger than many of his companions in years he was one of the oldest in guilt. But he could not shake off the remembrance of his pious mother's instructions.—Though dead and in her grave she seemed speaking to him still. After many alarms of conscience and many pungent convictions he became a Christian, and subsequently one of the most successful ministers of the gospel Great Britain ever produced. Of course through the labors of the converted son, we may now trace the influence of the pious mother. In addition to his great ministerial labors, he wrote many evangelical works, and few authors have done more to extend the power of religion. He was highly eloquent and greatly useful in religious conversation; and his hymns, whose use in Divine worship is almost commensurate with the extension of the English language, are of the most elevated and evangelical character. Follow that mother's influence farther. Her son was the means of the conversion of Claudius Buchanan, who subsequently became a minister of the gospel, and went to the East Indies. Here he occupied a responsible station; and his labors in behalf of the English population, and for the improvement of the moral and spiritual condition of the natives, are deservedly ranked among the noblest achievements of Christian philanthropy. His little work entitled "The Star in the East," was the first thing that attracted the attention of Adoniram Judson to a mission in the East Indies. Hence, had it not been for that mother's faithfulness her son might never have been converted, Dr. Buchanan never been converted, nor that train of causes put in operation which are now shedding such a flood of light on Burmah and the surrounding regions.

The converted sailor was also the means of the conversion of Thomas Scott, from the dark mazes of Socinianism to the belief, practice and preaching of evangelical truth. He was a very successful preacher for a good portion of his long life in the metropolis of England,—engaged with vigor and zeal in every enterprise that he thought conducive to the moral welfare and salvation of man. He was, too, the author of a very valuable commentary on the Bible, almost unequalled in its practical tendency and the extent of its circulation. To that pious mother's influence, operating through the efforts of her son, all this is easily traced. Besides, to the connection of her son with the poet Cowper, the evangelical character and great religious influence of Cowper's poetry are doubtless to be mainly attributed. It was by the heavenly counsels and prayers and letters of his clerical friend, that the poet's piety was deepened, and the gloom of his mind dispersed. Again, to this same minister's influence, in connection with that of Doddridge, the conversion of Wilberforce is traced by some. For during fourteen years after he first saw W., and until his conversion, he made

W. the constant subject of his prayers. And with what glorious results was the conversion of Wilberforce fraught to the interests of man! What vast contributions did he make with his princely fortune to objects of benevolence! To his influence, in a great degree, may we impute the abolition of the African Slave Trade, and, in subsequent years, the emancipation of slaves in the British West Indies; for the former step prepared England for taking the latter. In addition to this, Wilberforce was the author of "A Practical View of Christianity," which did much to commend spiritual religion to the higher classes of his countrymen, and which, since his death, has been widely circulated and widely useful. This book was the means of the conversion of Leigh Richmond, the author of the "Dairyman's Daughter," which has been the means of the conversion of thousands!—Such are *some* of the stupendous and glorious results of one holy woman's efforts to educate her son for God—a wide and mighty posthumous influence which an angel might feel honored to exert. Who was she? THE MOTHER OF THE REV. JOHN NEWTON.

(*c*) INFLUENCE OF MR. COBB'S EXAMPLE.—A correspondent of a Methodist paper, published at Richmond, Va., encloses five hundred dollars for missions, and says, "About ten years ago I began the world with what I saved from my wages for attending a store; and about the same time I read in the Christian Advocate an account of certain resolutions of a Mr. Cobb, a member of the Baptist church in Boston, and I concluded, by the grace of God, not only to follow his plan, but also the example and advice of Mr. Wesley, "to make all you can, save all you can, and *give all you can.*"

How powerful is the influence of example! Let every Christian remember that when he lays down a correct principle of action, and carries it into practice, he is influencing others, and he knows not how many, to do the same.

(*d*) THE SICK MAN'S PRAYERS.—A pious man in the western part of New York was sick with a consumption. He was a poor man, and sick for years. An unconverted merchant in the place had a kind heart, and used to send him, now and then, some things for his comfort, or for his family. He felt grateful for the kindness, but could make no return, as he wanted to do. At length he determined that the best return he could make would be to pray for his salvation; he began to pray, and his soul kindled and he got hold of God. There was no revival of religion there, but by and by, to the astonishment of every body, this man came right out on the Lord's side. The fire kindled all over the place, and a powerful revival followed, and multitudes were converted.

This poor man lingered in this way for several years, and died. After his death, I visited the place, and his widow put into my hands his diary. Among other things, he says in his diary, "I am acquainted with about thirty ministers and churches." He then goes on to set apart certain hours in the day and week to pray for each of these ministers and churches, and also certain seasons for praying for the different missionary stations. Then followed, under different dates, such facts as these: "To-day," naming the date, "I have been enabled to offer what I call the prayer of faith, for the outpouring of the Spirit on —— church, and I trust in God there will soon be a revival there." Under another date, "I have to-day been able to offer what I call the prayer of faith, for such a church, and trust there will soon be a revival there." Thus he had gone over a great number of churches, recording the fact that he had prayed for them in faith that a revival might soon prevail among them. Not long after noticing these facts in his diary, the revival commenced, and went over the region of the country, nearly, I believe, if not quite, in the order in which the different places had been mentioned in his diary.

(*e*) INFLUENCE OF DAVIES.—The fruits of this devoted minister of Christ were not ephemeral—they did not end in excitement. *He* went to his rest long since. But the fruits of his ministry still remain, in the consistent piety of those who were reared under the influence of parents brought into the church by his labors. A gentleman in Tennessee says: "The fruits of the great revival in Hanover under the preaching of Samuel Davies, are now spreading and growing in the Valley of the Missisippi. There are many of the children and children's children of those persons, who professed religion in Hanover, under the ministry of that eminent man of God, now scattered in this great valley; and I know of no instance where they go, but an altar is reared for the worship of God in their families and neighborhoods."

This is a kind of greatness—an immortality on earth—which a good man might covet, as he is permitted earnestly to covet "the best gifts."

225. Influence Injurious.

(*a*) THE VILLAGE CURSED.—There is a beautiful village in New England from which Whitefield was driven with such rancorous abuse, that he shook off the dust of his feet and proclaimed that the Spirit of God would not visit that spot, till the last of those persecutors was dead. The good man's language had a fearful truth in it, though he was not divinely gifted with the prophet's inspiration. A consciousness of desertion paralyzed the energies of that church: for nearly a century it was nurtured on the unwholesome food of a strange doctrine; in the very garden of natural loveliness it sat like a heath in the desert, upon which there could be no rain, and not till that whole generation had passed from the earth did Zion appear there in her beauty and strength.

(*b*) HYPOCRITICAL DEFENCE OF PROTESTANTISM.—An affecting account is found among the oral traditions of Lucerne, one of the Catholic cantons of Switzerland. In the days of Luther and Calvin almost half the cantons turned Protestant. The magistrates of Lucerne were about deciding in favor of the Reformers, when a cunning and plausible priest, under the guise of a Protestant exile from one of the German states, obtained an interview with the principal magistrates friendly to the new religion; and under the pretence of defending Protestantism, so caricatured it in its most vulnerable points, as to prejudice the magistrates against it, and secure their adhesion to the Pope with the banishment of all the Protestant preachers from its territory. Lucerne, with its 150,000 inhabitants, has continued Roman Catholic for the last three centuries, while many of the neighboring states are wholly Protestant, and enjoy vastly superior privileges, both civil and religious.

(*c*) APOSTACY OF BRICCONET. When those who stand in a commanding position, at a time when society is agitated by a great moral struggle, fail to do and suffer what duty requires, their influence, even after death, is often signally mischievous. A noted and pertinent example is that of Bricconet, bishop of Meaux in France, in the sixteenth century. Catching the spirit of reform at that time pervading Germany and Switzerland, he zealously opposed some grosser errors and views of the Romish church. Having been twice ambassador to Rome—a bishop—a noble—an intimate friend of the reigning and preceding monarch, he was looked upon as one of the great pillars of the Reformation. A change of government comes, the inquisition is set up, and Bricconet becomes the first object of their vengeance. "The poor bishop," says D'Aubigne, "who had been so sanguine in the hope to see the Reformation gradually and silently winning its way in men's minds, trembled in dismay when he found at the eleventh hour that it must be purchased by life itself. No alternatives were presented him but death or recantation; and to the latter the minions of the pope urged him by the most plausible pretexts. They pretended they too were anxious for a reformation, that all was going on by insensible steps, that many would be won over by his conceding and yielding a little, who would be stumbled by his warm and open opposition to the church. Bricconet heard, considered, his resolution was shaken—he staggered under the cross—he stumbled—he fell! The day of his recantation was a dark day for France. The great conflict then waging in that country between truth and error, was sadly affected by the Bishop's fall. "What his enemies represented as the saving of his country," says the historian, was perhaps the worst of its misfortunes. What might not have been the consequence if Bricconet had possessed the courage of Luther? If one of the most eminent of the French bishops had ascended the scaffold, and there, like the poor of this world, sealed by martyrdom the truth of the gospel, would not France herself have been put upon reflection? Would not the blood of the bishop of Meaux have served, like the blood of Polycarp and Cyprian, as the seed of the church? And should we not have seen these provinces emancipating themselves in the sixteenth century from the darkness in which they are still enveloped? The mournful fall of Bricconet was felt as a shock to the hearts of his former friends, and was the sad forerunner of those deplorable apostacies to which the friendship of the world so often led in another age of French history."

(*d*) PAINE'S "AGE OF REASON."—Though the author of the "Age of Reason" deplored before his death that he had published it, and advised others not to read it, and though its sophistry has been often refuted, that book still exists and perpetuates its author's unholy influence. A noted infidel in New York, once asserted to the editor, that he knew of many who had been made "freethinkers" by reading it. And every year, no doubt, the number it ruins is legion. It has been translated into some of the languages of India; and the Missionaries to those pagan nations find the "Age of Reason" one of the most formidable obstacles to the conversion of the more intelligent classes. Thus, though Paine has been dead for years, his book goes through edition after edition, passes from language to language, misleading men's minds, and corrupting their hearts.

(*e*) INFLUENCE OF HOMER'S ILIAD.—A most pernicious influence is exerted by those writers who array in false and glowing colors the wicked actions of real or imaginary persons. It was the perusal of Homer's Iliad, which celebrates in such moving strains the deeds of bloody and brutal heroes, that helped to make Alexander the wholesale robber and murderer of mankind. Alexander had a perfect passion for Homer. He used to say that Homer's works were the most perfect production of the human mind and the best medicine of the warrior. He always carried with him Aristotle's edition of Homer. He kept it in a golden casket enriched with jewels, and laid it every night, with his sword, under his pillow. Again, reading the Life of Alexander was the means, in part, of making two other bloody heroes, scarce less noted than himself. One was Cæsar, whose highest ambition, we are told, was to walk in the steps of Alexander. Another was Charles XII of Sweden, who longed from his earliest years to imitate the Macedonian conqueror, and who, like him, converted firmness into obstinacy, courage into rashness, and severity into cruelty. Cæsar, again, was the ideal of human greatness that fanned the fire of martial zeal in the bosom of the Turkish Emperor Selymus, who, after defeating and poisoning his father, carried his merciless victories over Egypt and Persia. The highest ambition of Selymus was to imitate Cæsar. These four great conquerors convulsed the world with their crimes, and as they strode on to fame and power, they crushed millions of human hearts in the giant footsteps of their ambition. And how pernicious has been their influence on the world, since their day up to the present time, who can tell? Such have been some of the *ruinous* results, (whatever the *good* results may be) of Homer's writings on mankind since his death; results which the infinite mind can best compute.

226. INGRATITUDE.

(*a*) THE WIDOW AND HER TWO SONS.—In Birmingham, England, once lived a family in humble circumstances. Some of the younger children and their father died, leaving the aged mother with two sons grown up, and able to assist her. This however they refused to do, and she was obliged to apply to the parish for relief; and for some years two shillings a week were allowed her by the overseers, which, with a small sum added by some Christian friends, was all on which she had to subsist.

During this time her youngest son died. He had lived without the fear of God, and died under a sense of his wrath, in deep agonies, both of body and mind, and uttering dreadful expressions.

The eldest son was clever in his business, got forward in the world, and became possessed of considerable property. But he still refused to assist his mother, and even while holding offices of consideration and importance, left her to subsist on her allowance from the parish. This conduct of course was noticed; he was repeatedly spoken to upon the subject; and at length he ordered her name to be taken from the parish books, and allowed her the two shillings a week out of his own pocket, at a time when he possessed thousands of pounds, and was without a family.

One day some friends were assembled, and her case being mentioned, they proposed to remonstrate with the ungrateful son. "No," said an aged minister, "let him alone; if he dies possessed of the property he is now worth, I shall be deceived. God will never suffer such base *ingratitude* to prosper."

In a short time afterwards, the mother was removed to another world. The circumstances of the son at length began to change; repeated losses ensued and finally he became a bankrupt and was reduced to abject poverty.

Sons and daughters, do not forget this lesson.

(*b*) MACEDO AND HIS PRESERVER.—Basilius Macedo, the emperor, exercising himself in hunting, a sport he took great delight in, a great stag, running furiously against him, fastened one of the branches of his horns in the emperor's girdle, and, pulling him from his horse, dragged him a good distance, to the imminent danger of his life; which a gentleman of his retinue perceiving, drew his sword and cut the emperor's girdle asunder, which disengaged him from the beast, with little or no hurt to his person. But observe what reward he had for his pains: "He was sentenced to lose his head for putting his sword so near the body of the emperor," and suffered death accordingly.

(*c*) THE UNGRATEFUL GUEST.—A certain soldier in the Macedonian army had in many instances distinguished himself by extraordinary marks of valor, and had received many marks of Philip's favor and approbation. On some occasion he embarked on board a vessel, which was wrecked by a violent storm, and he himself cast on the shore helpless and naked, and scarcely with the appearance of life. A Macedonian, whose lands were contiguous to the sea, came opportunely to be witness of his distress; and, with all humane and charitable tenderness, flew to the relief of the unhappy stranger. He bore him to his house, laid him in his own bed, revived, cherished, comforted, and for forty days supplied him freely with all the necessaries and conveniences which his languishing condition could require. The soldier, thus happily rescued from death, was incessant in the warmest expressions of gratitude to his benefactor, assured him of his interest with the king, and of his power and resolution of obtaining for him, from the royal bounty, the noble returns which such extraordinary benevolence had merited. He was now completely recovered, and his kind host supplied him with money to pursue his journey. In some time after he presented himself before the king; he recounted his misfortunes, magnified his services; and this inhuman wretch, who had looked with an eye of envy on the possessions of the man who had preserved his life, was now so abandoned to all sense of gratitude as to request that the king would bestow upon him the house and lands where he had been so tenderly and kindly entertained. Unhappily, Philip, without examination, inconsiderately and precipitately granted his infamous request; and this soldier, now returned to his preserver, repaid his goodness by driving him from his settlement, and taking immediate possession of all the fruits of his honest industry. The poor man, stung with this instance of unparalleled ingratitude and insensibility, boldly determined, instead of submitting to his wrongs, to seek relief; and, in a letter addressed to Philip, represented his own and the soldier's conduct in a lively and affecting manner. The king was instantly fired with indignation; he ordered that justice should be done without delay; that the possessions should be immediately restored to the man whose charitable offices had been thus horribly repaid; and having seized the soldier, caused these words to be branded on his forehead, *The Ungrateful Guest;* a character infamous in every age and among all nations, but particularly among the Greeks, who from the earliest times were most scrupulously observant of the laws of hospitality.

(*d*) HANNAH MORE'S VIEW OF INGRATITUDE.—At a dinner party at Bath, the Rev. Mr. Jay, by whom the anecdote was communicated, was lamenting the ingratitude which Mrs. Hannah More had recently met with from a person he had recommended to her beneficence, upon which he received a look from her which silenced him; and after dinner, drawing him into a corner of the room, she said, "You know we must never speak of such things as these before people, for they are always too backward to do good, and they are sure to dwell on such facts to justify their illiberality." She finely added, "It is well for us sometimes to meet with such instances of ingratitude, to show us our motives; for if they have been right, we shall not repent of our doing, though we lament the depravity of a fellow-creature. In these instances also, as in a glass, we may see little emblems of ourselves; for what, after all, is the ingratitude of any one towards us, compared with our ingratitude towards our Infinite Benefactor?"

227. INSTRUMENTALITIES, FEEBLE.

(*a*) DISPUTE ABOUT PAUL AND PLATO.—"I once heard," says Chrysostom, "a Christian disputing in a ridiculous manner with a Greek, and both parties in their dispute refuting themselves. For what the Christian ought to have said, this the Greek asserted; and what one would naturally suppose the Greek would say, this the Christian maintained. The point of controversy was the superiority of Paul or Plato; the Greek endeavoring to show that Paul was unlearned and ignorant; and the Christian in his simplicity being anxious to prove that Paul was more eloquent than Plato. The victory was on the side of the Greek as his argument proved to be the stronger. Now if Paul were a more eloquent teacher than Plato, many would probably object that it was not by grace, but by excellency of speech that he prevailed. Thus the Christian's assertion was in favor of the cause of the Greek, and what the Greek said was in the Christian's favor. For if Paul was uneducated and overcame Plato the victory was brilliant. The former, unlearned as he was, persuaded the disciples of the latter and brought them over to his views, whence it is evident that the Gospel is not the result of human wisdom but of the grace of God."

(b) THE SOUDRAH'S REASONING.—"I am by birth," said a converted Hindoo, when addressing a number of his countrymen, "of an insignificant and contemptible caste; so low, that if a Brahmin should chance to touch me, he must go and bathe in the Ganges for the purpose of purification; and yet God has been pleased to call me, not merely to the knowledge of the Gospel, but to the high office of teaching it to others. My friends, do you know the reason of God's conduct? It is this: if God had selected one of you learned Brahmins, and made you the preacher, when you were successful in making converts, by-standers would have said it was the amazing learning of the Brahmin, and his great weight of character, that were the cause; but now, when any one is convinced by my instrumentality, no one thinks of ascribing any of the praise to me; and God, as is his due, has all the glory."

(c) THE EXHORTER AND THE STRANGERS. — A Baptist church north of Utica, N. Y., being without a pastor, used to help the deficiency by reading sermons and select passages from edifying writers. On these occasions, a warm-hearted though unlettered brother would always at the conclusion, deliver a solemn exhortation. One Lord's day, while pursuing their customary practice, two gentlemen entered and took their seats in the congregation, whose appearance indicated more than ordinary worldly respectability. The brethren became alarmed, lest at the conclusion of the reading, the customary exhorter would mortify them by his rude and unpolished address; and they determined to close the meeting quicker than usual and shut out the exhortation. But the vigilant brother with his zealous spirit was too quick for them; the reading was hardly finished before he was on his feet, and began his warm-hearted appeal. One hung his head and another, but neither daunted or disturbed the speaker. He went on to the end of his message and sat down. The meeting was soon concluded, and several retired with great fears as to the opinions that would be formed of the respectability of the church by the two strangers. Some time after this, at another meeting, one of these individuals presented himself among them, and after a while, to their surprise, rose up to tell what the Lord had done for his soul; and stated the message of the exhorter, as the message of mercy to his soul. How careful should we be not to despise the day of small things.

228. INTEGRITY.

(a) THE TWO OFFERS.—Julius Drusus, a Roman tribune, had a house that in many places lay exposed to the view of the neighborhood. A person came and offered, that for five talents he would so alter it, that it should not be liable to that inconvenience. "I will give thee ten talents," said Drusus, "if thou canst make my house conspicuous in every room of it, that so all the city may behold in what manner I lead my life."

(b) CASE OF MARVELL.—The borough of Hull, in the reign of Charles II, chose Andrew Marvell, a young gentleman of little or no fortune, and maintained him in London for the service of the public. With a view to bribe him, his old school-fellow, the Lord Treasurer Danby, went to him in his garret. At parting, the lord treasurer slipped into his hands an order upon the treasury for £1000, and then went into his chariot. Marvell looking at the paper, called after the treasurer, "My lord, I request another moment." They went up again to the garret, and Jack, the servant boy, was called, "Jack, what had I for dinner yesterday?" "Don't you remember, sir, you had the little shoulder of mutton that you ordered me to bring from a woman in the market?" "Very right. What have I for dinner to-day?" "Don't you know, sir, that you made me lay up the blade bone to broil?"

"Tis so: very right. Go away." "My lord, do you hear that? Andrew Marvell's dinner is provided; there's your piece of paper, I want it not. I knew the sort of kindness you intended. I live here to serve my constituents. The ministry may seek men for their purpose; I am not one."

(c) THE FIRM JURYMAN.—A certain person, being on a jury in a trial of life and death, he was completely satisfied of the innocence of the prisoner; all the other eleven were of the opposite opinion; but he was resolved that a verdict of guilty should not be brought in. In the first place, he spent several hours in trying to convince them; but found that he had made no impression, and that he was exhausting the strength that was to be reserved for another mode of operation. He therefore calmly told them it should now be a trial who could endure confinement and famine the longest, and that they might be quite assured he would sooner die than release them at the expense of the prisoner's life. In this situation they spent about twenty-four hours, when, at length, they all acceded to his verdict of acquittal.

(d) SEWALL AND THE SHOE-BRUSHES.—Judge Sewall, of Massachusetts, who died in 1760, went one day into a hatter's shop, in order to purchase a pair of shoe brushes. The master of the shop presented him with a couple. "What is your price?" said the judge. "If they will answer your purpose," replied the other, "you may have them and welcome." The judge, upon hearing this, laid them down, and bowing, was leaving the shop; upon which the hatter said to him, "Pray, sir, your honor has forgotten the principal object of your visit." "By no means," answered the judge; "if you please to set a price I am ready to purchase: but ever since it has fallen to my lot to occupy a seat on the bench, I have studiously avoided receiving to the value of a single copper, lest at some future period of my life, it might have some kind of influence in determining my judgment."

(e) CATHARINE II AND COUNT MUNICH.—When Catharine the Second ascended the throne of Russia, she solicited Count Munich to accept some marks of her favor, although she knew he had been the most formidable opponent to her accession. "No," said the count, "I am an old man; I have already suffered many misfortunes; and if I purchased a few years of life by compromising my principles, I should make but a bad exchange."

(f) BONNELL'S INTEGRITY.—James Bonnell, Esq., was the accomptant-general of the revenue in Ireland in the seventeenth century, and was equally eminent for his excellences as a man and a Christian. He had many opportunities of improving his fortune, and met with temptations which few but himself would have resisted. He despatched his business with the utmost readiness, and in the most obliging manner, but never once would receive a gratuity or reward. When three pieces of broad gold at one time, and a guinea or two at another, were left on his table by persons whom he had greatly served, he gave it all away among persons who were in want, telling his friends that though he had served others greatly, yet his taking rewards might hereafter bias his judgment, and thus prove a snare to him; and that therefore his principles should be known, and he would take no more than the king allowed him.

(g) FRANKLIN AND HIS PAPER.—Soon after his establishment in Philadelphia, Franklin was offered a piece for publication in his newspaper. Being very busy, he begged the gentleman would leave it for consideration. The next day the author called and asked his opinion of it. "Why, sir," replied Franklin, "I am sorry to say I think it highly scurrilous and defamatory. But being at a loss on account of my poverty, whether to reject it or not, I thought I would put it to this issue,—at night, when my work was done, I bought a two-penny loaf, on which I supped heartily, and then wrapping myself in my great coat, slept very soundly on the floor till morning; when another loaf and mug of water afforded a pleasant breakfast. Now, sir, since I can live very comfortably in this manner, why should I prostitute my press to personal hatred or party passion for a more luxurious living!"

One cannot read this anecdote of our American sage, without thinking of Socrates' reply to king Archelaus, who had pressed him to give up preaching in the dirty streets of Athens, and come and live with him in his splendid courts.—"*Meal, please your Majesty is a half-penny a peck at Athens, and water I get for nothing!*"

(*h*) ANCIENT HERNHUTTER.*—In one of the wars in Germany, a captain of cavalry was ordered out on a foraging party. He put himself at the head of his troop, and marched to the quarter assigned him. It was a solitary valley, in which hardly any thing but woods could be seen. In the midst of it stood a little cottage: on perceiving it he went up, and knocked at the door; an ancient Hernhutter, with a beard silvered with age, came out. "Father," said the officer, "show me a field where I can set my troops a foraging." "Presently," replied the Hernhutter. The good old man walked before, and conducted them out of the valley. After a quarter of an hour's march, they found a fine field of barley: "This is the very thing we want," said the captain. "Have patience for a few minutes," replied the guide; "you shall be satisfied." They went on, and at the distance of a quarter of a league further, they arrived at another field of barley. The troop immediately dismounted, cut down the grain, trussed it up, and remounted. The officer then said to his conductor, "Father, you have given to yourself and us unnecessary trouble: the first field was much better than this." "Very true, sir," replied the good old man, "but it was not mine."

* Better known in this country by the name of Moravians or United Brethren.

INTEMPERANCE.

229. Way to Intemperance.

(*a*) MODERATE DRINKERS BEWARE.—A respectable man, but a moderate drinker, living in the town of Hadlyme, Conn., was urged by the State Temperance Agent some months since to join the temperance society. He said "I am my own master, and can take care of myself. I don't drink but little, and I won't give it up." A short time after this, an appointment was made for an address from the agent.—On the same day, in the evening of which the address was to be delivered, this man in company with a neighbor crossed the river in a small skiff to a grogshop in Cheshire, kept by a professor of religion. There they found several of kindred spirit, and down they sat. Of course the bottle circulated freely; and over it were discussed the merits of temperance societies. Many sage remarks were made about trampling upon individual rights, and invading the liberties of men. The rumselling professor joined them, and thought it outrageous that retailing should be reprobated. Still the bottle goes round, and much ridicule is cast upon the cold water speech that is expected in the evening. Again they drink, and the two friends set out on their return. Now mark the result. In recrossing the river the boat is carried by the current some distance below the landing-place. Arriving at the shore they quarrel, and this man sets out alone to take the boat to its place. He proceeds, gets out into the stream, and is discovered by a negro, who calls him to come ashore, telling him he is intoxicated, and 'tis not safe for him to row the boat alone. "Drunkard!" says he, "I'm as sober as any man." But before the negro could get to his assistance, he tumbled overboard and sunk to rise no more. The race from respectability to a drunkard's end was very short. The exercises of the temperance meeting in the evening were commenced by relating this incident to his fellow townsmen.

(*b*) THE STUDENT'S FALL.—The parents of Henry H—— had placed him in the university of G———, and they hoped, fondly hoped that he would be their stay in their declining years. Oh! how that fond father watched over him while he was pursuing his collegiate studies. And when he received his honors at the university—when he received his honors at the hands of his instructors together with their blessing—when his Alma Mater gloried in having his name enrolled upon her records--then the fond parents received him with open arms, and rejoiced that their son had returned, and had fulfilled all their expectations. In an evil hour he consented to make one of a social party, to celebrate some anniversary. The wine flowed freely and plenteously, and for some time he withstood the jests and banterings of his companions, and refused the proferred glass. At length, by the persuasions of one of his dearest friends, he took the first glass, and finding that his spirits became more bouyant, he took another and another, until Alcohol usurped the throne from which Reason had fled abashed—and the proud scholar fell drunk upon the floor. He, who had so often before bid defiance to the tempter, and had battled manfully against all its arts, had been seduced by his kind friends, and in one short night the toil of years had been swept away! Henry never recovered from that fall. No kind persuasions of his doting parents—no influence that was exerted by his dearest relatives, could save him. Headlong he rushed into the dark abyss of intemperance, and in a few weeks filled *a drunkard's grave!*

(*c*) THE DYING DRUNKARD'S ACCUSATION.—A respectable gentleman at Edinburgh related a most affecting fact, which we will briefly repeat. A religious lady at Edinburgh was sent to visit a woman who was dying, in consequence of disease brought on by intemperance. The woman had formerly been in the habit of washing in the lady's family, and when she came to the dying woman, she remonstrated with her on the folly and wickedness of her conduct, in giving way to so dreadful a sin as that of intemperance. The dying woman said, "You have been the author of my intemperance." "What did you say?" with pious horror, exclaimed the lady; "I the author of your intemperance!" "Yes, ma'am, I never drank whisky till I came to wash in your family: you gave me some, and told me it would do me good. I felt invigorated, and you gave it me again. When I was at other houses not so hospitable as yours, I purchased a little, and by and by I found my way to the spirit shop, and thought it was necessary to carry me through my hard work; and, by little and little, I became what you now see me." Conceive what this lady felt.

(*d*) "THAT FIRST GLASS."—So said a drunkard, after he had waked up from a three weeks' "spree," which had been preceded by several months of total abstinence, which gave hope to his friends that he would entirely reform—and which abstinence was maintained without a pledge. "Why did you give up to drunkenness again, when you had abstained so long?" "O! it was that first glass. When that was done, there was no stopping. The dramseller said, 'Just one glass with me for old acquaintance sake'—and I have been three weeks in his bar-room, drunk day and night." Mortified, ashamed, chagrined beyond measure, his confidence in his own resolution destroyed, this poor man has returned to the gutter. Who ruined this man?

(*e*) TWO OLD MEN'S POSTERITY.—An aged man over whom had rolled a hundred winters (says the N. Y. Evangelist of 1831), died not many years since in New England, who was, in the estimation of all who knew him, pious.—But he had early contracted a fondness for ardent spirits, and drank temperately and daily for the greater part of his life. He gave a little to his children as they grouped around him; and they thought what their father loved must be innocent. But with their growing years a fondness for the stimulus increased, and this aged man lived to mourn the death of half his sons and *forty* descendants, who went down to the grave drunkards. One son yet lives, who was a professor of religion but has been excommunicated,—and is an exile and a drunkard, with a large family who are ruined by his sin.

Another aged man still lives in the

vicinity of the same place, who numbers nearly one hundred descendants, all of whom are temperate persons. He never was in the habit of drinking ardent spirit, nor does he give it to his sons, and his sons' sons, but like Jonadab, he drinks pure water.

What a contrast will the day of judgment disclose, if in one family intemperance continues to roll down like a fiery deluge, and in the other temperance reigns, and descends from generation to generation!

EFFECTS OF INTEMPERANCE.

230. Slavery of Appetite.

(*a*) THE DRUNKARD'S THRALDOM.—The writer of the pamphlet entitled The Confessions of a Drunkard says, "Of my condition there is no hope that I should ever change; the waters have gone over me; but out of the black depths could I be heard, I would cry aloud to all those who have set a foot in that perilous flood. Could the youth to whom the flavor of his first wine is as delicious as the opening scenes of life, or the entering upon some newly discovered paradise, look into my desolation, and be made to understand what a dreary thing it is, when a man shall feel himself going down a precipice with open eyes and a passive will,—to see his destruction, and have no power to stop it, and yet to feel it all the way emanating from himself; to perceive all goodness emptied out of him, and yet not able to forget a time when it was otherwise; to bear about the piteous spectacle of his own ruin:—could he see my fevered eye, feverish with the last night's drinking and feverishly looking forward for this night's repetition of the folly; could he feel the body of death out of which I cry hourly, with feebler and feebler outcry, to be delivered,—it were enough to make him dash the sparkling beverage to the earth in all the pride of its mantling temptation."

(*b*) THE GENERAL'S CONFESSION.—A certain General, and hitherto regarded as a very respectable citizen, had become so intemperate in his habits as to 'mingle strong drink,' three or four times a day. One of his friends visited him and proposed to have a "serious talk," with him on the subject.

The General replied—"Please to hear what I have to say first. I am *sensible* I drink more than is necessary. I am sensible if I persist in my present course the habit will increase upon me, and my respectable standing in society will be lost. I am sensible that my estate will be wasted for want of proper attention. I am sensible that my amiable family will be involved in disgrace and wretchedness. I am sensible that my constitution will be undermined and my health be gone—my countenance will carry marks of depravity—my mind become enfeebled—my soul lost forever except I *repent.* Now, sir, if all these considerations, flashing full conviction on my mind, and sometimes filling me with *horror*, cannot deter me from this detestable habit of drinking, think you that your eloquence is going to do it?" His friend made no reply, but went away sorrowfully. Surely wine is a mocker, and strong drink is raging.

231. Intellectual and Moral Degradation.

(*a*) THE WELSHMAN AND HIS GOAT.—A Welshman was for some time awfully habituated to the vice of drunkenness, but was at length restored to sobriety by the following singular incident. He had a tame goat, which would follow him to the alehouse he frequented. One day, by way of frolic, he gave the animal so much ale that it became intoxicated. What particularly struck the Welshman was, that from that time, though the creature would follow him to the door, he never could get it to enter the house. He was thereby led to see how much his sin had sunk him beneath a beast, and from that period became a sober man.

(*b*) A LONG-BEARDED BEDFELLOW.—The following circumstance happened in one of the towns of Arkansas.—A man had been drinking until a late hour at night before he started for home. Honest folks had long been in bed, and the houses were all shut and dark. The liquor he had taken was too much for him, he did not know where to go. He staggered into an empty wagon shed, and fell on the ground. For a long time he lay in all the unconsciousness of a drunken sleep, and would undoubtedly have frozen, for the snow on the ground showed the night to be very cold, had not others less insensible than himself, been around him.—This shed was a favorite resort for the hogs, which were out when the new comer arrived, but soon returned to their bed. In the utmost kindness, and with the truest hospitality, they gave their biped companion the middle of the bed; some lying on either side of him, and others acting the part of the quilt. Their warmth prevented him from being injured by his exposure. Towards morning he awoke; finding himself comfortable, in blissful ignorance of his whereabouts, he supposed himself enjoying the accommodations of a tavern, in company with other gentlemen. He reached out his hand, and catching hold of the stiff bristles of a hog, exclaimed, "Why, mister, WHEN DID YOU SHAVE LAST?"

(*c*) THE BLASTED GENIUS.—How many of the highest geniuses have passed away from the intellectual firmament, consumed like the burning stars of which astronomers tell us! And how? By the baleful fires of intemperance and lust. Says a distinguished divine, "A story of genius in ruins rises on my mind. In one of the older colleges in Massachusetts, some 20 or 25 years since, there was seen a youth of the highest promise, bearing an honored name, and concentrating in his own intellect the moral power of two generations of his ancestors. He was a prodigy of learning. While others of his class were slowly plodding through the daily tasks in Xenophon, he would be reading the Greek tragedians *con amore.* He seized a language almost by intuition, and his heart entered into the heart of antiquity, as he read the language of the old and buried nations. Called upon by the officers of the college to read dissertations in the chapel upon abstruse and difficult subjects, he was accustomed to read them from blank papers, pouring forth spontaneous bursts of argument that thrilled while they convinced, and charmed while they persuaded. With Euclid, Newton and La Place, he seemed as familiar as with Homer and Eschylus, and he levied large tribute from the lore of every nation under heaven. His person was faultless; his hair like the raven's wing; his eye like the eagle's. By an anomaly in American colleges, he demanded and received his first and second degrees from his Alma Mater on the same day, and on the same evening he was joined in the holy bands of wedlock with one of the most charming nymphs in the vale that embosoms the college. His course was still onward and upward. His profession, the law, led him to the highest office of advocacy in the state. He was Attorney General at an age when most students are admitted to the bar. Suddenly, when as yet no one knew the cause, he resigned his high appointment, giving no reasons. He was a secret drunkard! Too high was his sense of honor, and the importance of his station, to intrust himself longer with the destinies of society. I turn with horror from the years of degradation that followed. He sunk like a mighty ship in mid ocean, not without many a lurch, many a sign of righting once more to plough the proud seas that were destined to entomb him forever. Long since his lovely wife had quitted the home which his vices had made wretched; she had returned to her parents to grieve and to die. But though her husband bowed over her grave, and wept bitterly on the head of the sweet boy she left behind her, he was not permanently affected by the shock. The most distinguished men for talent and piety in the United States wept and prayed over him; and at times he would get the better of the demon that ruled him, and again put forth his gigantic powers. The greatest effort he put forth during this period was the successful advocacy of an important case before the Supreme Court of the United States. Marshall, the patriarch of American judges, gazed with wonder on the barrister, as burst upon burst of eloquence and argument followed. Geo.

W. Briggs, the member of Congress from Massachusetts, seeing his splendid portrait hanging in a conspicuous place at Washington, inquired whose likeness it was; and one of the highest authorities answered—that is the portrait of Talcott, the most brilliant genius—the most talented man in the United States. In his last spasm of temperance he wrote, The Trial and Condemnation of Alcohol: a popular tract, clothed with the forms and phraseology of a criminal court. But after a fatiguing argument before a court in the city of New York, he was over-persuaded by an advocate to take a glass of beer; and he complied. It was his last sober moment, till he was in the agonies of death. As the fabled Phœnix is said to rise from the ashes of its parents, one of the most lovely, eloquent advocates of temperance in the State of New York was the son of this ruined genius; the little one over whom he wept at the grave of his wife.

(*d*) A DRUNKARD'S HEIRS.—U—, of V—, commenced the world a poor man; but by industry and economy he amassed a large property so that he spent the latter part of his life in the luxury often attendant upon wealth when not at the disposal of religious principle. In a pleasant part of his grounds, and at a short distance from his house, he prepared an elegant family tomb, to which were successively committed his own and his wife's remains. Three sons inherited his estate, and lived for a number of years in luxury and lordly independence. Some years since one of these sons was called to bury his wife, whose remains were committed to the same family tomb. This large independent estate is now wasted. These heirs to unearned wealth have nothing which they can call their own, but are dependent on daily labor for the sustenance of their families. The door of the tomb has been thrown down, and for 7 or 8 years these sons have suffered the remains of their parents, and of the wife of one of them, though within a stone's throw of their door, to lie exposed to the open air, and the examination of every intruder; nay, to be scattered upon the floor, and without the door of the tomb; and even to be trampled upon by sheep and other animals that are permitted to graze in the field where the tomb lies. Monumental inscriptions have been defaced, and a mouse has built its nest among the bones of her whose husband lives near by!

And what has been the cause of all this waste of property, this beastly insensibility? Habits of luxury and idleness, but the grand cause of the whole has been *Intemperance.* "*She has cast down many wounded, yea, many strong men have been slain by her. Her house is the way to hell, going down to the chambers of death.*"—Proverbs 7: 26, 27.

(*e*) THE RUINED PREACHER.—A gentleman traveling in Essex, Eng., called at the house of a friend, where he met with a young minister who was just going to preach in the neighborhood. The lady of the house offered him a glass of spirits before he entered upon his work, which he accepted. An elderly man, who was present, thus addressed him:—"My young friend, let me offer you a word of advice respecting the use of liquors. There was a time when I was as acceptable a preacher as you now may be; but by too frequently accepting of the well-designed favors of my friends, I contracted a habit of drinking, so that now I never go to bed sober if I can get liquor. I am, indeed, just as miserable as a creature can be at this side of hell!" About two years after this, the traveler had occasion to call again at the same house, and made inquiry concerning the unhappy old man, when he was informed that he had been some time dead. It was stated that towards the close of his life, he had not drank to the same excess as formerly; but it was only because he could not obtain spirituous liquors.

(*f*) A CLASSMATE'S FATE.—When I commenced a course of study, says a writer in the Pastor's Journal, W. O. was my classmate. His father, after having spent many years of faithful labor in the ministry, had gone to his rest, and his mother had fastened on him her fondest affections, her highest hopes. He was a youth of uncommon promise. His talents were of the first order, and every attention had been paid to their early development. His mind was penetrating and rapid in its movements; his imagination was brilliant; his memory retentive and ready. In his disposition he was amiable and kind—peculiarly capable of winning the affections of all who knew him. He had every desirable facility of improvement—enough of this world's goods to carry him through an extensive course of study, and establish him in professional life. For a while his progress rejoiced the heart of his friends, and awakened the highest expectations. But he took the poisonous cup! He drank it, and his sun went down ere it was fully risen.

Before I left College, for which we commenced our preparation together, I looked out from my window and saw him under its walls,—a dirty, ragged, friendless vagabond. His property had been squandered away—his mother had died of a broken heart, and he was begging worn-out garments to cover his shame. The next that I heard of him was that he was found dead by the wayside. This young man, in point of intellectual endowments and prospects of future eminence, once had few superiors. And had he but dashed from his lips the fatal cup, and swore eternal abstinence, he might now have been standing at the bar of justice, or in the hall of legislation, an object of admiration and envy.

232. Vice and Crime.

(*a*) THE YOUTH'S EXECUTION.—The sheriff, says an old man, took out his watch, and said, "If you have any thing to say, speak now, for you have only five minutes to live." The young man burst into tears, and said—"I have to die. I had only one little brother, and he had beautiful blue eyes, and flaxen hair, and I loved him; but one day I got drunk, for the first time in my life, and coming home, I found my little brother gathering strawberries in the garden, and I became angry with him without cause, and killed him, at one blow with a rake. I did not know any thing about it until the next morning when I awoke from sleep, and found myself tied and guarded, and was told that when my little brother was found, his hair was clotted with his blood and brains, and he was dead. Whiskey has done this. It has ruined me. I never was drunk but once. I have only one more word to say, and then I am going to my final Judge. I say it to young people. *Never*, NEVER! NEVER!! *touch any thing that can intoxicate!*" As he pronounced these words, he sprang from the box and was launched into an awful eternity.

(*b*) HALE'S TESTIMONY.—Lord Chief Justice Hale once remarked, "The places of judication, which I have long held in this kingdom, have given me an opportunity to observe the original cause of most of the enormities that have been committed for the space of nearly twenty years: and by a due observation, I have found that if the murders and manslaughters, the burglaries and robberies, the riots and tumults, the adulteries, and other great enormities that have happened in that time, were divided into five parts, four of them have been the issues and product of excessive drinking, or of tavern and ale-house meetings." The proportion is little less in our own country in the present time.

233. Domestic and Social Wretchedness.

(*a*) THE WINE PARTY.—A company of young men in New Orleans, once assembled around the wine table, for the purpose of enjoying the "feast of reason and the flow of soul." One of the party, who was a mere novice in drinking, while flushed with wine, in an unguarded moment made use of expressions at which one of this social party of *friends* took exceptions, an altercation ensued, and the offended party gave a peremptory challenge to the young man above alluded to. According to a custom handed down to us from the Goths, Huns, Vandals and Teutones, called the code of honor, he was induced to accept. In the morning, when reason had resumed her seat, he found himself in a dreadful situation—duty would have prompted him not to have gone to what is miscalled the "field of honor," but a morbid state of public opinion prompted him to meet his challenger, who was a practised duellist: they met, and this young man fell a victim to a ruthless custom at the first fire. He was borne home mortally wounded to his widowed mother—for he was her only son—and died the following day.

Hardened men were struck mute with grief, and shed tears at his untimely fate; and if men so unused to feel could thus be moved, what must have been the anguish of a mother, when she saw her son borne home in the agonies of death, and who had left her in all the buoyancy of youth, to join in a party of professed friends!!

He was the *only* prop and stay of her declining years. All her hopes and affections were centered in him, and as she gazed upon his manly form during a brief struggle with the "King of Terrors," it seemed as if her heart would break.

The lonely widow followed to the silent tomb the victim of a barbarous custom, who met his death by going to partake of a *social* glass at a WINE PARTY.

(*b*) DEATH OF MRS. S.—Mrs. S—— was once the most admired of all the ladies in her village. She could sing the sweetest, play the prettiest, talk the most enchantingly, dress the most fashionably of all who moved in the gay circles. Her husband was a man of industry, who doted upon her, was anxious at the least depression of spirits, and allowed her every indulgence. When the temperance reform commenced, he was anxious to sign the pledge; but she said it was "well enough for the vulgar, but for people in genteel life it would never do; they could neither go into parties, nor give parties. Besides," said she, "how can I ever sing or dance without one or two glasses of wine to give me a spring?" Time rolled on, when the inquiry began to be made, What is the matter with the beautiful Mrs. S——? On the sidewalk, she was seen to reel to and fro, and in her parties she was now as silly as she was once enchanting. At church, especially in the afternoon of a Sunday, no sermon could keep up her eyelids. Her poor husband saw the change. He devised every method to keep liquor from her, but all in vain. He soon died of vexation and a broken heart. She now gave herself up to brandy and opium; and with a handsome property, no resort was too low, no indulgence too disgusting. For the last two years of her life, few saw her, except as she was stealing away, in the twilight of evening, with a cloak on her head, to the very lowest grog-shops, to fill her bottle. One day her neighbors heard that she was dying. Three respectable women came in to see her, and found her senseless and stupid, just surrendering her lost soul into the hands of her Maker. How awful the scene! If there are any young females who read this, let them be admonished to beware of the exhilarating glass—beware of that pronounced most innocent, "sparkling champagne."

(*c*) THE LITTLE SUICIDE.—A writer in the Vermont Chronicle relates the following as a fact that he learned from good authority: "I wish I was dead," said a little boy one day to his mother. "Why?" asked his kind mother. "Why, the boys all pester me so about father, and I don't want to go again, in the night, to the store after him." His mother talked to him, but thought he did not feel in earnest about it. But one day, when she had returnen from a visit, she inquired for the children, and found all but this boy. She looked, she called, but no answer. She went to the barn as it was just growing dark. She opened the door, and there in one corner, was her little sensitive boy hanging by the neck. She burst into tears. "Oh my son, my son, is it you?"

She felt his cold hands, and he was dead. And at the funeral, his father promised to drink no more rum: "I have for ever done." A long time he kept his promise. One day however, Deacon P. was in the store; and Deacon P. was a good man; he drank but little. He asked for some brandy. And while he drank it, he saw that same man who had been a drunkard looking at him; and he saw too that he was very uneasy; he walked about; he sat down. Again he would go to the door as if going away. He was in silent thought. At length he went to the counter and asked for a little brandy: "I may drink a little as well as Deacon P." He did drink, and became a confirmed drunkard again.

234. Fatal Accidents, Untimely and Awful Deaths.

(*a*) SPONTANEOUS COMBUSTION.—Dr. Peter Schofield, of Upper Canada, gives the following case; a terrible monition to all drunkards. A young man of about 25 years of age, had been an habitual drinker for many years. I saw him about nine o'clock in the evening on which it happened. He was then, as usual, not drunk but full of liquor. About eleven the same evening I was called to see him. I found him literally roasted from the crown of his head to the soles of his feet. He was found in a blacksmith's shop just across the way from where he had been. The owner all of a sudden discovered an extensive light in his shop, as though the whole building was in one general flame. He ran with the greatest precipitancy, and on flinging open the door, found a man standing erect in the midst of a widely-extended, silver-colored blaze, bearing, as he described it, exactly the appearance of the wick of a burning candle, in the midst of its own flame. He seized him by the shoulder and jerked him to the door, upon which the flame was instantly extinguished.

There was no fire in the shop, neither was there any possibility of fire having been communicated to him from any external source. It was purely a case of spontaneons ignition. A general sloughing came on; and his flesh was consumed or removed in the dressing leaving the bones and a few of the larger blood-vessels standing. The blood, nevertheless, rallied around the heart and maintained the vital spark to the thirteenth day, when he died; not only the most loathsome, ill-featured and dreadful picture that was ever presented to human view, but his shrieks, his cries and lamentations were enough to rend a heart of adamant. He complained of no pain of body; his flesh was gone. He said he was suffering the torments of hell; that he was just upon its threshold, and should soon enter its dismal caverns; and in this frame of mind he gave up the ghost.

In all such cases, Prof. Silliman remarks, the entire body becoming saturated with alcohol, absorbed into all its tissues, becomes highly inflammable, as indicated by the vapor which reeks from the breath and lungs of a drunkard; this vapor, doubtless highly alcoholic, may take fire, and then the body slowly consume.

(*b*) LOSS OF THE NEPTUNE.—This ship, carrying 36 men, sailed from Aberdeen, in Scotland, on a fine morn ing in May, with the fairest prospect of good weather and a prosperous voyage. About 11 o'clock the wind arose from the east and swept over the sea with overwhelming violence. In about an hour she was seen standing in, but under such a press of sail as, considering the gale, astonished all on shore. But on she came, now bounding on the top of the sea, and then almost ingulfed in the foaming cavern. The harbor of Aberdeen is exposed to the east, and formed by a pier on one side, and a breakwater on the other, and so narrow at the entrance as not to admit two large ships abreast. All saw that something was wrong on board. One attempt was made to shorten sail, but the ship was then within a cable's length of the shore, and urged on with an impetuosity which no human power could withstand. The wives and families of the men who were thus hastening to death had assembled near the pier; but all stood in silent horror, broke in a moment by the cry, "she's lost!" as the vessel, lashed on by the tempest, passed to the outer side of the breakwater, and struck with awful violence between two black rugged rocks. The cries of the victims were most hor rible. The dreadful crisis had come, and they were lost indeed. A few brave men on shore endeavored to man the life boat, and take it round the breakwater, but it was unavailing. One heavy sea rolling over the wreck for a moment concealed her, and when the people looked again she was gone! Her crew and timbers were hurled against the rocks, and with the exception of one man, who was washed up and lodged on a projecting edge, none escaped of the 36 who had that morning left the shore in health and spirits. From the man who was saved, the melancholy truth was learnt that the crew were *all intoxicated, and could not manage the vessel.*

(*c*) RUM AND RUIN.—The Rev. Mr. Scoresby, preacher to seamen in Liverpool, was for many years the master of a whale ship in the northern seas. He relates the following fact, of which he was an eye-witness. It is given in his own words.

"A collier brig was stranded on the Yorkshire coast, and I had occasion to assist in the distressing service of rescuing a part of the crew by drawing them up a vertical cliff, two or three hundred feet in altitude, by means of a very small rope, the only material at hand. The first two men who caught hold of the rope were hauled safely up to the top; but the next, after being drawn to a considerable height, slipped his hold and fell; and with the fourth and last who ventured upon this only chance of life, the rope gave way, and he also was plunged into the foaming breakers beneath. Immediately afterwards the vessel broke up, and the remnant of the ill-fated crew perished before our eyes. What now was the cause of this heart-rending event? Was it stress of weather, or a contrary wind, or unavoidable accident? No such thing. It was the entire want of moral conduct in the crew. Every sailor, to a man, was in a state of intoxication! The helm was intrusted to a boy ignorant of the coast. He ran the vessel upon the rock at Whitby, and one half of the miserable dissipated crew awoke to consciousness in eternity.

235. The Intemperate Reformed.

(*a*) PERSEVERANCE REWARDED.—A little girl, about eight years old, once took a temperance paper, at a temperance meeting, to see how many she could get to sign it. The next morning she presented it to her father who had been in a drunken frolic for a fortnight, and came home drunk while his little daughter was at the temperance meeting the night before. This cruel father raised his hand and struck his child a blow which leveled her on the floor, and said, "I'll learn you to be saucy to your parents." The little girl got up, and picked up the constitution, which had fallen when she received the blow. She took it with her to school that day and got the teacher and most of the scholars to sign it. When she had leisure she would ask her mother if she might go to such and such a neighbor's and see how many could be got to join the Temperance Society.

Her father could not but see what was doing in the neighborhood. For two weeks he remained at home, and did not use a drop of intoxicating liquor, a thing he had not done for years before. At the end of that period he said to his daughter, "Mary, how many names have you got on your temperance constitution?" "I will bring it and see," she replied. As her father was counting the names she stood between his knees, and when he had looked them over he said, "You have one hundred and fifty." She jumped up on his knee, threw her little arms around her father's neck, and impressed a sweet kiss on his cheek, and said, "Do you sign it too, father, and then there will be one hundred and fifty-one."

The old drunkard's heart was melted. His bosom heaved—his bloated, haggard cheek was wet with the tears of contrition—he pressed his Mary to his heart, and said, "I will sign it;" and at once affixed his name to the constitution and pledge.

(*b*) CURE FOR DRUNKENNESS. A man in Maryland notoriously addicted to this vice, hearing an uproar in his kitchen one evening, had the curiosity to step, without noise, to the door, to know what was the matter, when he beheld his servants indulging in the most unbounded roar of laughter at a couple of his negro boys, who were mimicking himself in his drunken fits; showing how he reeled and staggered; how he looked and nodded, and hickuped and tumbled. The picture which these children of nature drew of him, and which had filled the rest with so much merriment, struck him so forcibly, that he became a perfectly sober man, to the unspeakable joy of his wife and children.

(*c*) THE DRUNKARD AND THE MONKEYS.—A rich drunkard kept two monkeys for his sport. One day he looked into his dining-room, where he and his guests had left some wine, and the two had mounted the table, and were helping themselves generously to the wine—jabbering and gesturing, as they had seen their master and his guests. In a little time they exhibited all the appearance of drunken men. First they were merry, and jumped about, but soon they got to fighting on the floor, and tearing out one another's hair. The drunkard stood in amazement. "What!" said he, "is this a picture of myself? Do the brutes rebuke me?" It so affected his mind, that he resolved he would never drink another drop. And from that day he was never known to be any other than a sober and a happy man.

(*d*) RULING OVER RUM.—Col. B—— was a man of amiable manners and well-informed mind. Being much employed in public business which called him from place to place, ardent spirit was often set before him with an invitation to drink. At first he took a social glass for civility's sake. But at length a habit was formed, and appetite began to crave its customary indulgence. He drank more largely, and once or twice was quite overcome. His friends were alarmed. He was on the brink of a precipice from which many had fallen to the lowest pitch of wretchedness. In his sober hours he saw the danger he was in. Said he to himself one day when alone, "Shall Colonel B—— rule, or shall rum rule? If Colonel B—— rule, he and his family may be respectable and happy; but if rum rule, Colonel B——is ruined, his property wasted, and his family made wretched!" At length, said he, I set down my foot, and said, "Colonel B—— shall rule and rum obey." And from that day Colonel B—— did rule. He immediately broke off from his intemperate habits, and lived to a good old age, virtuous, respected and happy. Let every one who has acquired or is acquiring a similar habit, go and do likewise.

(*e*) REFORMATION OF WM. WIRT.—The distinguished William Wirt, within six or eight months after his first marriage, became addicted to intemperance, the effect of which operated strongly on the mind and health of his wife, and in a few months more she was numbered with the dead. Her death led him to leave the county where he resided, and he moved to Richmond, where he soon rose to distinction. But his habits hung about him, and occasionally he was found with jolly and frolicsome spirits, in bacchanalian revelry. His true friends expostulated with him to convince him of the injury he was doing himself. But he still persisted. His practice began to fall off, and many looked on him as on the sure road to ruin. He was advised to get married, with a view of correcting his habits. This he consented to do, if the right person offered. He accordingly paid his addresses to a Miss Gamble. After some months' attention, he asked her hand in marriage; she replied,—"Mr. Wirt, I have been well aware of your intentions for some time back, and should have given you to understand that your visits and attentions were not acceptable, had I not reciprocated the affection which you evinced for me. But I cannot yield my assent until you make me a pledge never to taste, touch, or handle any intoxicating drinks." This reply to Mr. Wirt was as unexpected as it was novel. His reply was, that he regarded the proposition as a bar to all farther consideration of the subject, and left her. Her course to him was the same as ever—his, resentment and neglect. In the course of a few weeks he went again, and again solicited her hand. But her reply was, her mind was made up. He became indignant, and regarded the terms she proposed as insulting to his honor, and vowed it should be the last meeting they should ever have. He took to drinking worse and worse, and seemed to run headlong to ruin. One day, while lying in the outskirts of the city, near a little grocery or grog-shop, dead drunk, a young lady, whom it is not necessary to name, was passing that way to her home, not far off, and beheld him with his face upturned to the rays of the scorching sun. She took her handkerchief, with her own name marked upon it, and placed it over his face. After he had remained in that way for some hours, he was awakened, and his thirst being so great, he went into the little grocery or grog-shop to get a drink, when he discovered the handkerchief, at which he looked, and the name that was on it. After pausing a few minutes, he exclaimed—"Great God! who left this with me! Who placed this on my face!" No one knew. He dropped the glass, exclaiming, "Enough! Enough!" He retired instantly from the store, forgetting his thirst, but not the debauch, the handkerchief, or the lady, vowing, if God gave him strength, never to touch, taste, or handle intoxicating drinks.

To meet Miss G. again was the hardest effort of his life. If he met her in her carriage, or on foot, he would dodge round the nearest corner. She at last addressed him a note under her own hand, inviting him to her house, which he finally gathered courage enough to accept. He told her if she still bore affection for him, he would agree to her own terms. Her reply was: "My conditions are now what they ever have been." "Then," said the disenthralled Wirt, "I accept them."

They were soon married; and from that day he kept his word, and his affairs brightened, while honors and glory gathered thick upon his brow. His name has been enrolled high in the temple of fame, while his deeds, his patriotism and renown, live after him with imperishable lustre. How many noble minds might the young ladies save, if they would follow the example of the heroine-hearted Miss G., the friend of humanity, of her country, and the relation of La Fayette.

236. Miscellaneous.

(*a*) DRUNKARDS OF THE REVOLUTION.—Benedict Arnold, the traitor who attempted to betray his country, was a rum-seller and a drunkard. Three of the most important defeats of the American army, during the Revolution, were sustained by men who died drunkards. Had a sober crew been on board the Chesapeake, the brave Lawrence would never have had to say to his men, "Don't give up the ship."

(*b*) MR. BISHOP'S DELIRIUM TREMENS.—The delirium tremens is one of the most awful effects of intemperance. Says Mr. Bishop, of New-Haven, "I had been for three weeks beastly drunk. One of my first recollections is that I was forced into my own house. I remonstrated, and was told that I had endeavored to kill a neighbor. As soon as I found an opportunity, I seized a gun and rushed out with the intention of shooting my friend. I was immediately disarmed and forced back into the house. My mind was then seized with a frenzy. I stood in the centre of the room. I thought I heard my old companions without whispering together about appointing a committee to call on me. I refused to see them. It seemed to me they were coming to murder me, and I cried out in the greatest terror. I was then secured and placed in bed. The physician stood at the head of the bed and several of his students were with him. He told me I must be still. They were going to perform on operation. I did not like the appearance of things. The students hung up wires all about the room. I saw them talking with my wife and telling her she had better give her consent. They prepared a machine to flay me alive, and began to cut my flesh with saws, pull off my skin in strings and hang them upon the wires. Then it seemed to me a cage full of wild beasts were let loose upon me. Now a tiger was ready to pounce upon me. At one moment I thought my breast was full of animals. I asked a young man to drag them out, which he did, and every time he drew one out, a horrid sensation of faintness came over me. At length I discovered that all these horrid sensations of sawing and flaying, &c., were occasioned by efforts to wake me up.

I am sometimes asked whether the illusions of the delirium tremens are not always distressing. They are not. At one time I had about five hours of perfect happiness. The asparagus bush which was used to brush off the flies, seemed to me exceedingly beautiful. It was full of the birds of Paradise, and my ears were enraptured with the most delightful music.

But in general the illusion is of the most horrid character. At one time I thought my companions were assaulting me with hooks, which they endeavored to strike into my flesh. I stood on the defence in the centre of the room for seven hours, fighting with all my might until the sweat from my body stood in puddles on the floor. On another occasion I thought my watchers were endeavoring to murder me. I sprang from my bed and ran out, my pulse 170 a minute, and I was brought to death's door. For 18 days I endured the utmost horror of mind. Three times my case was given over as hopeless."

(*c*) GOOD REASON FOR SOBRIETY.—A gentleman on entering a stage coach, rubbing his head, with a yawn said, "My head aches dreadfully; I was very drunk last night." A person affecting surprise, replied, "Drunk, sir! what! do you get drunk?" "Yes," said he, "and so does every one at times, I believe. I have no doubt but you do." "No, sir!" he replied, "I do not." "What! never?" "No, never; and amongst other reasons I have for it, one is, I never find, being sober, that I have too much sense; and I am loth to lose what little I have." This remark put an end to the conversation.

(*d*) LAW OF PITTACUS.—By one of the laws of Pittacus, one of the seven wise men of Greece, every fault committed by a person when intoxicated, was deemed worthy of a double punishment.

237. JEWS.

(*a*) THE RABBI'S CALCULATION.—Dr. South informs us, that a Rabbi, who lived about fifty years before Christ, upon the consideration of Jacob's prophecy, Gen. xlix. 10, and of Daniel's seventy weeks, (Dan. ix.) said, that it was impossible for the coming of the Messiah to be deferred beyond fifty years; a proportion of time vastly different from that of eighteen hundred.

(*b*) A QUESTION FOR JEWS.—Bishop Patrick quotes the following affecting inquiry addressed by Rabbi Samuel Moraccanus to a friend in the eleventh century:

"I would fain learn from thee, out of the testimonies of the law, and the prophets, and other scriptures, why the Jews are thus smitten in this captivity wherein we are, which may be properly termed THE PERPETUAL ANGER OF GOD, because it hath no end. For it is now above a thousand years since we were carried captive by Titus; and yet our fathers, who worshipped idols, killed the Prophets, and cast the law behind their back, were only punished with a seventy years' captivity and then brought home again: but now there is no end of our calamities, nor do the prophets promise any.

"If," says Bishop Patrick, "this argument was hard to be answered then, in his days, it is much harder in ours, who still see them pursued by God's vengeance; which can be for nothing else but rejecting and crucifying the Messiah, the Saviour of the world."

(*c*) THE RABBI'S ADMISSIONS.—A learned rabbi of the Jews, at Aleppo, being dangerously ill, called his friends together, and desired them seriously to consider the various former captivities endured by their nation, as a punishment for the hardness of their hearts, and their present captivity, which was continued sixteen hundred years, "the occasion of which," said he, "is doubtless our unbelief." We have long looked for the Messiah, and the Christians have believed in one Jesus, of our nation, who was of the seed of Abraham and David, and born in Bethlehem, and for aught we know, may be the true Messiah; and we may have suffered this long captivity because we have rejected him. Therefore my advice is, as my last words, that if the Messiah, which we expect, do not come at or about the year 1860, reckoning from the birth of their Christ, then you may know and believe that this Jesus is the Christ, and you shall have no other."

(*d*) THE LEIPSIC STUDENT.—A poor student, of the university of Leipsic, having occasion to undertake a journey to his distant friends, was in want of the money needful for the purpose, and was compelled to go to a Jew, to pawn his Hebrew Bible and Greek Testament. The latter contained the Greek and German text in opposite columns. The Jew, little as he valued this book, was prevailed on to give the student half a rix-dollar for it. During the absence of the student he determined to read it through, with a view of confirming his enmity against Jesus, and to be the better prepared to testify his zeal for the Jewish faith. He concealed it from his family, and commenced its perusal, which, as the young man was absent seven weeks, he had time to do. As he read, he was surprised and impressed, and at times was ready to exclaim, "Oh that Jesus was my Saviour!" When he had gone through the book, he was greatly perplexed and astonished, that he had been able to find nothing to increase his hatred to Jesus, but had rather discovered much that was sublime and heavenly. He now charged himself with folly, and resolved to open the book no more. He adhered to this resolution for several days, but was soon compelled to peruse it a second time, with the determination to be more careful in ascertaining that Jesus and his apostles had deserved the hatred of Jews in all ages. Still he was unable to find what he wished; while he was impressed with the consolation it imparted to the afflicted, and the immortality of glory it revealed, which seemed to remove the anxiety he had long felt on this subject. He was compelled a third time to read the book; and now the history, the doctrines, and the promises of Jesus destroyed his opposition, and melted his soul. He was overcome to tears, and resolved on embracing the doctrines of the cross. He announced his change to a Christian minister, purchased the New Testament of the student, to whom he became a warmly attached friend, and continued to give evidences of being a consistent Christian.

(*e*) THE TRANSLATOR CONVERTED.—When the Rev. Claudius Buchanan was traveling in India, he obtained from the Jews in the interior of that country a very singular copy of the translation of the New Testament into Hebrew, made in the sixteenth century. The translator was a learned rabbi, and the translation is, in general, faithful. The design of the translator was to make an accurate version of the New Testament for the express purpose of confuting it, and of repelling the arguments of his neighbors, the Syrian or St. Thomé Christians. But behold the providence of God! the translator became a convert to Christianity; his own work subdued his unbelief; and he lived and died in the faith of Christ. This manuscript is now in the public library at Cambridge.

(*f*) DEATH-BED OF THE JEW.—In his interesting work, "Judah and Israel," Mr. Frey, a converted Jew, and who for more than forty years has labored among the people as a minister of the gospel, says; "For seven long years, while officiating Rabbi in the synagogue, it was my painful lot to attend the sick and dying; and while I found all of them sensible of their being sinners, and exposed to the wrath of God, I never found one saying, like good old Simeon, 'Now, Lord, lettest thou thy servant depart in peace, for mine eyes have seen thy salvation.'"

(*g*) ROCHESTER'S CONFESSION.—The celebrated Lord Rochester had lived a long while in infidelity, but there was one argument in favor of Christianity which he declared he could never set aside, namely: the existing state and circumstances of the Jews.

238. JUDGMENT DAY.

(*a*) THE DARK DAY AND THE LEGISLATOR.—The 19th of May, 1788, was remarkably dark in Connecticut. Candles were lighted in many houses; the birds were silent, and disappeared; the domestic fowls retired to roost. The people were impressed by the idea that the day of judgment was at hand. This opinion was entertained by the legislature, at that time sitting at Hartford. The house of representatives adjourned: the council proposed to follow the example. Colonel Davenport objected. "The day of judgment," he said, "is either approaching, or it is not. If it is not, there is no cause for an adjournment: if it is, I choose to be found doing my duty. I wish, therefore, that candles may be brought."

(*b*) CHILD'S DREAM OF THE JUDGMENT.—The Rev. Herbert Mends, of Plymouth, Eng., speaking of his early religious impressions, says: "If any particular circumstance might be considered as making a more deep, lasting, and serious impression, than others, it was a dream which I had when at school at Ottery. I felt the apprehension of the approach of the last great judgment day. I well remember all the attending circumstances; and observed that they were perfectly corresponding to the description of that awful event recorded in the Gospel of Matthew. After I had perceived vast multitudes of the human race appearing before the throne of Christ, some being approved and others rejected, I at length beheld my beloved father and mother, and several of the family, summoned to appear. Great agitation was awakened in my breast; but I heard them distinctly examined, and as distinctly heard the Judge say, '*Well done*," &c. At this period, my whole soul was filled with horror indescribable, being conscious that I was not prepared to pass my final scrutiny. At length my name was announced, and I felt all the agonies of a mind fully expecting to be banished from the presence of God, and the glory of his power. The Judge then, with a stern countenance, and in language which struck me with mingled shame and hope, said, 'Well, what sayest thou?' I fell at his feet, and implored mercy, and prayed, 'Lord, spare me yet a little longer, and when thou shalt call for me again, I hope to be ready.' With a smile, which tranquilized my spirits, the Lord replied, "Go, then, and improve the time given thee.' The extreme agitation of my mind awoke me. But so deep was the impression, that I have never forgotten it."

(*c*) CONFIDENCE OF JANEWAY.—"I remember," says the writer of Mr. John Janeway's life, "once there was a great talk that one had foretold that doomsday should be on such a day. Although he blamed their daring folly that could pretend to know that which was hid, yet, granting their suspicion to be true, what then? said he; what if the day of judgment were come, as it will most certainly come shortly? If I were sure the day of judgment were to come within an hour, I should be glad with all my heart. If, at this very instant, I should hear such thunderings, and see such lightenings as Israel did at Mount Sinai, I am persuaded my very heart would leap for joy. But this I am confident of, through infinite mercy, that the very meditation of that day hath even ravished my soul; and the thought of the certainty and nearness of it, is more refreshing to me than the comforts of the whole world."

239. JUSTICE AND EQUITY.

(*a*) SOCRATES AND CHERICLES.—While Athens was governed by thirty tyrants, Socrates the philosopher was summoned to the senate-house, and ordered to go with some other persons they named, to seize one Leon, a man of rank and fortune, whom they determined to put out of the way, that they might enjoy his estate. This commission Socrates flatly refused, and, not satisfied therewith, added his reasons for such refusal: "I will never willingly assist an unjust act." Chericles sharply replied, "Dost thou think, Socrates, to talk always in this high style, and not to suffer?" "Far from it," added he; "I expect to suffer a thousand ills, but none so great as to do unjustly."

(*b*) THEMISTOCLES' PROJECT.—Themistocles having conceived the design of transferring the government of Greece from the hands of the Lacedemonians, into those of the Athenians, kept his thoughts continually fixed on this great project. Being at no time very nice or scrupulous in the choice of his measures, he thought any thing which could tend to the accomplishment of the end he had in view, just and lawful. In an assembly of the people one day, he accordingly intimated that he had a very important design to propose, but he could not communicate it to the people at large, because the greatest secrecy was necessary to its success; he therefore desired that they would appoint a person to whom he might explain himself on the subject. Aristides was unanimously pitched upon by the assembly, who referred themselves entirely to his opinion of the affair. Themistocles taking him aside, told him that the design he had conceived, was to burn the fleet belonging to the rest of the Grecian states, which then lay in a neighboring port, when Athens would assuredly become mistress of all Greece. Aristides returned to the assembly, and declared to them, that nothing could be more advantageous to the commonwealth, than the project of Themistocles; but that, at the same time, nothing in the world could be more unfair. Without inquiring further, the assembly unanimously declared, that since such was the case, Themistocles should wholly abandon his project.

(*c*) CONSCIENTIOUS JUDGE.—Sir Matthew Hale, when chief baron of the exchequer, was very exact and impartial in his administration of justice. He would never receive any private addresses or recommendations from the greatest persons in any matter in which justice was concerned. One of the first peers of England went once to his chamber, and told him "that, having a suit in law to be tried before him, he was then to acquaint him with it, that he might the better understand it when it should come to be heard in court." Upon which Sir Matthew interrupted him, and said "he did not deal fairly to come to his chamber about such affairs, for he never received any information of causes but in open court, where both parties were to be heard alike," so he would not suffer him to go on. Whereupon his grace (for he was a duke) went away not a little dissatisfied, and complained of it to the king as a rudeness that was not to be endured. But his majesty bade him content himself that he was no worse used, and said "he verily believed he would have used himself no better if he had gone to solicit him in any of his own causes."

Another passage fell out in one of his circuits, which was somewhat censured as an affectation of unreasonable strictness; but it flowed from the exactness of the rules he had set himself. A gentleman had sent him a buck for his table that had a trial at the assizes; so, when he heard his name, he asked "if he was not the same person that had sent him venison." And finding that he was the same, he told him "he could not suffer the trial to go on till he had paid him for his buck." To which the gentleman answered "that he never sold his venison, and that he had done nothing to him which he did not do to every judge that had gone that circuit," which was confirmed by several gentlemen then present; but all would not do, for the lord chief baron had learned from Solomon that "a gift perverteth the ways of judgment;" and therefore he would not suffer the trial to go on till he had paid for the present; upon which the gentleman withdrew the record. And at Salisbury, the dean and chapter having, according to custom, presented him with six sugar loaves in his circuit, he made his servants pay for the sugar before he would try their cause.

(*d*) ARISTIDES IN JUDGMENT.—Aristides being judge between two private persons, one of them declared that his adversary had greatly injured Aristides. "Relate rather, good friend," said he, interrupting him, "what wrong he hath done to thee, for it is thy cause, not mine, that I now sit judge of."

(*e*) BANISHMENT OF ARISTIDES.—A tragedy by Æschylus was once represented before the Athenians, in which it was said of one of the characters, "that he cared not more to *be* just than to *appear* so." At these words all eyes were instantly turned upon Aristides as the man who, of all the Greeks, most merited that distinguished character. Ever after he received, by universal consent, the surname of *the Just;* a title, says Plutarch, truly royal, or, rather, truly divine. This remarkable distinction roused envy, and envy prevailed so far as to procure his banishment for ten years upon the unjust suspicion that his influence with the people was dangerous to their freedom. When the sentence was passed by his countrymen, Aristides himself was present in the midst of them, and a stranger who stood near, and could not write, applied to him to write for him in his shell. "What name?" asked the philosopher. "Aristides," replied the stranger. "Do you know him, then," said Aristides, "or has he in any way injured you?" "Neither," said the other; "but it is for this very thing I would he were condemned. I can go nowhere but I hear of Aristides the Just." Aristides inquired no further, but took the shell and wrote his name in it as desired.

The absence of Aristides soon dissipated the apprehensions which his countrymen had so idly imbibed. He was in a short time recalled, and for many years after took a leading part in the affairs of the republic, without showing the least resentment against his enemies, or seeking any other gratification than that of serving his country with fidelity and honor. His disregard for money was strikingly manifested at his death; for though he was frequently treasurer as well as general, he scarcely left sufficient to defray the expenses of his burial.

The virtues of Aristides did not pass without reward. He had two daughters, who were educated at the expense of the state, and to whom portions were allotted from the public treasury.

(*f*) LOCKE'S RESIGNATION.—The integrity of this great man was eminently displayed on several occasions; but the following event, which closed his political life, is worthy of particular notice:—

After the English revolution of 1688, his high name and merits opened to him the prospect of honor and riches, which, however, he declined. King William III pressed him to go on an embassy to one of the principal courts in Europe, which he respectfully refused. His majesty then appointed him to a seat as one of the commissioners of the Board of Trade and Plantations. This post, which was perfectly suited to his talents, he held for some years; but, at length, when the air of London was found to disagree with his health, he resigned the place to the king in person, saying, that his conscience would not permit him to retain a situation the duties of which he could not discharge. The king entreated him to continue in it, telling him that though he could stay in London but a few weeks, his services would be very necessary. Mr. Locke, however, persisted in his resolution; thus relinquishing one thousand pounds a year, which he might have kept till his death. When he was told by a friend that he might have made a composition with any new candidate, and thereby have gained some advantage without giving up the whole income, he replied, "I know it very well, that I might have done so; and that was the very reason why I did not communicate my design to any one. I received my commission directly from the king, and to him I resolved to restore it, that he might have the pleasure of bestowing it upon some worthy man better able to fulfil the duties than myself."

(*g*) MORVILLIERS AND CHARLES IX.—Morvilliers, keeper of the seals to Charles the Ninth of France, was one day ordered by his sovereign to put the seals to the pardon of a nobleman who had committed murder. He refused. The king then took the seals out of his hands, and having put them himself to the instrument of remission, returned them immediately to Morvilliers; who refused to take them again, saying, "The seals have twice put me in a situation of great honor; once when I received them, and again when I resigned them."

(*h*) LOUIS XIV AND HIS CHANCELLOR.—Louis the Fourteenth had granted a pardon to a nobleman who had committed some very great crime. M. Voisin, the chancellor, ran to him in his closet, and exclaimed, "Sire, you cannot pardon a person in the situation of Mr. ——." "I have promised him," replied the king, who was ever impatient of contradiction; "go and fetch the great seal." "But, sire,"—"Pray, sir, do as I order you." The chancellor returns with the seals; Louis applies them himself to the instrument, containing the pardon, and gives them again to the chancellor. "They are polluted now, sire," exclaims the intrepid and excellent magistrate, pushing them from him on the table, "I cannot take them again." "What an impracticable man!" cries the monarch, and throws the pardon into the fire. "I will now, sire, take them again," said the chancellor; "the fire, you know, purifies every thing."

(*i*) ANOTHER BRUTUS.—In the reign of Henry the Eighth, Fitz-Stephen, merchant, Mayor of Galway, sent his only son, as commander of a ship, to Spain, for a cargo of wine. The son kept the money for the purchase of the cargo; and the Spanish merchant, who supplied the wine, sent his nephew to receive the debt. To conceal his fraud, young Fitz-Stephen conceived the plan of murdering the Spaniard; a project, in which he brought the crew to combine. The Spaniard was seized in bed, thrown overboard, and the ship arrived in port.

Some time after, one of the sailors was taken ill, and, being at the point of death, confessed the horrid deed in which he had participated. The father, though struck with horror, shook off the parent, and said, "Justice should take its course." And, as mayor he caused his son to be committed, with the rest of the crew, and the father, like Brutus, sat in judgment on his son, and with his own lips pronounced the sentence which left him childless!

(*j*) FITZ-JAMES AND HIS SOVEREIGN.—It is said of Sir John Fitz-James, that the instant he was seated on the bench, he lost all recollection of his best friends, that would in the least degree have interfered with the administration of justice. A relation once solicited a favor of him. "Come to my house," said he, "and I will deny you nothing; but in the king's court I must do you justice." The attorney-general was weak and criminal enough to request his interest on the part of the king, in a cause to be tried before him. "I will do the king right," he replied. A verdict was given against the crown, and the attorney-general expostulated with Fitz-James, who dismissed the subject by adding, "I could not do his majesty right, if I had not done justice."

(*k*) THE MONARCH AND THE MILLER.—Near Potsdam (Prussia), in the reign of Frederick King of Prussia, was a mill which interfered with a view from the windows of Sans Souci. Annoyed by this inconvenience to his favorite residence, the king sent to inquire the price for which the mill would be sold by the owner. "For no price," was the reply of the sturdy Prussian; and, in a moment of anger, Frederick gave orders that the mill should be pulled down. "The king may do this," said the miller, quietly folding his arms, "but there are laws in Prussia;" and forthwith he commenced proceedings against the monarch, the result of which was, the court sentenced Frederick to rebuild the mill, and to pay besides a large sum of money as compensation for the injury which he had done. The king was mortified, but had the magnanimity to say, addressing himself to his courtiers, "I am glad to find that just laws and upright judges exist in my kingdom." A few years ago, the head of the honest miller's family, who had in due course of time succeeded to the hereditary possession of his little estate, finding himself, after a long struggle with losses occasioned by the war, which brought ruin into many a house besides his own, involved in pecuniary difficulties that had become insurmountable, wrote to the then king of Prussia, reminding him of the refusal experienced by Frederick the Great at the hands of his ancestor, and stating that, if his majesty now entertained a similar desire to obtain possession of the property, it would be very agreeable to him, in his present embarrassed circumstances, to sell the mill. The king immediately wrote, with his own hand, the following reply:—

"My dear neighbor;—I cannot allow you to sell the mill; it must remain in your possession as long as one member of your family exists; for it belongs to the history of Prussia. I lament, however, to hear that you are in circumstances of embarrassment; and therefore send you 6000 dollars (about £1000 sterling) to arrange your affairs, in the hope that this sum will be sufficient for the purpose. Consider me always your affectionate neighbor,

"FREDERICK WILLIAM."

(*l*) THE EFFECTUAL APPEAL.—It is related of Philip, King of the Macedonians, that while one was pleading before him, he dropped asleep, and, waking on a sudden, passed sentence against the righteous cause: upon this the injured person cried out, "I appeal." The king, with indignation, asked, "To whom?" He replied, "From yourself sleeping to yourself waking;" and had the judgment reversed that was against him.

(*m*) PARDON REFUSED TO ROYAL BLOOD.—When a prince of the blood royal of France disgraced nim self, by committing robbery and murder in the streets of Paris, Louis XV would not grant a pardon, though eagerly solicited to do so by a deputation from the Parliament of Paris, who tried him, and suspended their sentence until the royal pleasure should be known. "My lords and counsellors," said the king, "return to your chambers of justice, and promulgate your decree." "Consider," said the first president, "that the unhappy prince has your majesty's blood in his veins." "Yes," said the king, "but the blood has become impure, and justice demands that it should be let out; nor would I spare my own son for a crime, for which I should be bound to condemn the meanest of my subjects." The prince was executed on the scaffold in the court of the grand Chatelet, on the 12th of August, 1729.

(*n*) HENRY V AND THE JUDGE.—One of the favorites of King Henry V, when Prince of Wales, having been indicted for some misdemeanor, was condemned, notwithstanding all the interest he could make in his favor; and the Prince was so incensed at the issue of the trial that he struck the judge on the bench. This magistrate, whose name was Sir William Gascoign, acted with a spirit becoming his character. He instantly ordered the Prince to be committed to prison; and young Henry, sensible by this time of the insult he had offered to the laws of his country, suffered himself to be quietly conducted to jail by the officers of justice. The king, Henry IV, who was an excellent judge of mankind, was no sooner informed of this transaction, than he cried out in a transport of joy, "Happy is the king who has a magistrate possessed of courage to execute the laws; and still more happy in having a son who will submit to such chastisement."

240. JUSTIFICATION BY FAITH.

(*a*) HERVEY'S RECANTATION. —"If it be shameful to renounce error," says Mr. Hervey, "and sacrifice all to truth, I do very willingly take this shame to myself, in a copy of verses which I formerly wrote, sacred to the memory of a generous benefactor. I remember the following lines:

"Our wants relieved by thy indulgent care
Shall give thee courage at the dreadful bar,
And stud the crown thou shalt for ever wear."

These lines, in whatever hands they are lodged, and whatever else of a like kind may have dropt from my pen, I now publicly disclaim; they are the very reverse of my present belief, in which I hope to persevere as long as I have any being. Far be it from me to suppose that any work of mine should, in order to create my peace, or cherish my confidence, be coupled with Christ's most holy acts. I speak the words of our church, and I speak the sense of the prophet, "I will trust, and not be afraid;" wherefore? because I am inherently holy? rather *God* is my salvation; God manifest in the flesh has finished my transgression, and made an end of my sin; and in this most magnificent work will I rejoice. Thy Maker is thy husband: the consequence of which is, all thy debts and deficiencies are upon him, all his consummate righteousness is upon thee."

(*b*) LIBERTY IN DUNGEON.—Mr. Fleming, in his Fulfilling of the Scriptures, relates the case of a man who was a very great sinner, and for his horrible wickedness was put to death in the town of Ayr, Scotland. This man had been so stupid and brutish a fellow, that all who knew him thought him beyond the reach of all ordinary means of grace; but while the man was in prison, the Lord wonderfully wrought on his heart, and in such a measure discovered to him his sinfulness, that after much serious exercise and sore wrestling, a most kindly work of repentance followed, with great assurance of mercy, insomuch, that when he came to the place of execution, he could not cease crying out to the people, under the sense of pardon, and the comforts of the presence and favor of God: "O, He is a great forgiver! He is a great forgiver!" And he added the following words: "Now hath perfect love cast out fear. I know God hath nothing to lay against me, for Jesus Christ hath paid all; and those are free whom the Son makes free."

(*c*) A GLORIOUS POSITION.—Mr. Lyford, a Puritan divine, a few days previous to his dissolution, being desired by his friends to give them some account of his hopes and comforts, he replied, "I will let you know how it is with me, and on what ground I stand. Here is the grave, the wrath of God, and devouring flames, the great punishment of sin, on the one hand; and here am I, a poor sinful creature, on the other; but this is my comfort, the covenant of grace, established upon so many sure promises, hath satisfied all. The act of oblivion passed in heaven is, "I will forgive their iniquities, and their sins will I remember no more, saith the Lord." This is the blessed privilege of all within the covenant, of whom I am one. For I find the Spirit which is promised, bestowed upon me, in the blessed effects of it upon my soul, as the pledge of God's eternal love. By this I know my interest in Christ, who is the foundation of the covenant; and therefore my sins being laid on him, shall never be charged on me."

241. KINDNESS, CONJUGAL.

(*a*) "I WILL NEVER LEAVE YOU."—The wife of a pious man told him one day, that if he did not give over running after the missionaries, a name often applied in the neighborhood where this event occurred, to Christian ministers of different denominations, she would certainly leave him. Finding that he continued obstinate, she on one occasion sent for him from the harvest-field, and informed him that she was about to carry her threats into execution; and that before she left the house, she wished some articles to be divided, to prevent future disputes. She first produced a web of linen, which she insisted should be divided. "No, no," said the husband; "you have been, upon the whole, a good wife to me: if you will leave me, though the thought greatly distresses me, you must take the whole with you; you well deserve it all." The same answer was given to a similar proposal respecting some other articles. At last, the wife said, "So you wish me to leave you?" "Far from that," said the husband; "I would do any thing, but sin, to make you stay; but if you will go, I wish you to go in comfort." "Then," said she, "you have overcome me by your kindness; I will never leave you."

(*b*) THE MIDNIGHT SUPPER.—A married woman was effectually called by Divine grace, and became an exemplary Christian; but her husband was a lover of sinful pleasure. When spending an evening, as usual, with his jovial companions, at a tavern, the conversation happened to turn on the excellencies and faults of their wives; the husband just mentioned pronounced the highest encomiums on his wife, saying she was all that was excellent, only she was a Methodist, "Notwithstanding which," said he, "such is the command which she has of her temper, that were I to take you, gentlemen, home with me at midnight, and order her to rise and get you a supper she would be all submission and cheerfulness!" The company regarded this merely as a vain boast, and dared him to make the experiment, by a considerable wager. The bargain was made, and about midnight the company adjourned, as proposed. Being admitted, "Where is your mistress?" said the husband to the maid-servant, who sat up for him, "She is gone to bed, sir." "Call her up," said he. "Tell her I have brought some friends home with me, and that I desire she would get up, and prepare them a supper." The good woman obeyed the unreasonable summons; dressed, came down, and received the company with perfect civility: told them she happened to have some chickens ready for the spit, and that supper should be got as soon as possible. It was accordingly served up, when she performed the honors of the table with as much cheerfulness as if she had expected company at the proper season.

After supper, the guests could not refrain from expressing their astonishment. One of them particularly, more sober than the rest, thus addressed himself to the lady: "Madam," said he, "your civility fills us all with surprise. Our unreasonable visit is the consequence of a wager, which we have certainly lost. As you are a very religious person, and cannot, therefore, approve of our conduct, give me leave to ask, what can possibly induce you to behave with so much kindness to us?" "Sir," replied she, "when I married, my husband and myself were both unconverted. It has pleased God to call me out of that dangerous condition. My husband continues in it. I tremble for his future state. Were he to die as he is, he must be miserable for ever; I think it, therefore, my duty to render his present existence as comfortable as possible."

This wise and faithful reply affected the whole company. It left a deep impression on the husband's mind. "Do you, my dear," said he, "really think

I should be eternally miserable? I thank you for the warning. By the grace of God, I will change my conduct." From that time he became another man, a serious Christian, and consequently, a good husband.

(*c*) A REFORMED WIFE.—A man once came to the Rev. Jonathan Scott, of Matlock, (Eng.) complaining of his wife. He said she was so exceedingly ill-tempered, and so studiously tormented him in such a variety of ways, that she was the great burden of his life; and, notwithstanding all the kind methods he had used to bring her to a better disposition, she was not at all improved, but grew continually worse and worse. Mr. Scott exhorted him to try what a redoubled affection and kindness would do; observing to him, that the command of Scripture to husbands was, "to love their wives," and that "even as Christ loved the church."

This advice did not appear to satisfy the man; and he went away much dejected, resolving, however, if possible, to follow it; since, though it had not hitherto succeeded, he could not but consider it as founded on the word of God. He accordingly increased his attention; and, as an instance of his kindness, the next Saturday evening brought to his wife his whole week's wages, and, with an affectionate smile, threw them into her lap, begging her entire disposal of them. This did not succeed: she threw the wages in a passion, accompanied with many bitter execrations, at his head; and afterwards continued in the practice of every spiteful and malicious trick that she could devise, or, according to the poor man's own conclusion, that Satan himself could suggest, to make his life miserable.

Some years elapsed, during which he sustained, as patiently as he could, this wicked and undutiful treatment, when Providence favored him with another interview with his kind friend, Mr. Scott. This happened, most opportunely, at a time when a neighbor had been giving him a supposed recipe for the cure of refractory wives; and, as a strong recommendation, mentioned that he had tried it on his own wife with the happiest effects. The man therefore came to Mr. Scott with a countenance bespeaking a considerable degree of confidence, which led Mr. Scott, at first, to hope that his former advice had proved successful; but he was soon informed that, through the extremely vicious disposition of the woman, it had operated in a way precisely the reverse of what was expected from it. Upon being asked, why then he smiled and looked so pleasantly, he said, he believed he had really found out a remedy which, if it should meet Mr. Scott's approbation, would not fail of effecting a cure; for it had been tried by a neighbor of his on a wife, who, though she had been in all respects as bad as his, was, by one application only, become one of the most obedient and affectionate creatures living. "And what is this excellent remedy?" said Mr. Scott. "Why, sir, it is a good horse-whipping! You hear, sir, what good effects have been produced: do you think I may venture to try it?"

Mr. Scott replied, "I read, my friend, nothing about husbands horse-whipping their wives in the Bible, but just the reverse; namely, love, which I before recommended; and I can by no means alter the word of God: but I doubt not, if you persevere, it will be attended with a happy result:" this advice was accompanied with exhortations to more earnest prayer. The man, though he left Mr. Scott both with a mind and countenance very different from those with which he came, resolved to follow his direction, as his esteem for him was very great; and Providence calling Mr. Scott some time after to preach at Birmingham, his old friend, who then resided there, came into the vestry to him after he had concluded the service, and with a countenance expressive of exalted happiness, said, that he should have reason to bless God through eternity for the advice he had given him; and that he had not been induced, by his weak importunities, to alter or relax it; adding that his wife, who then stood smiling with approbation by his side, was not only become a converted woman, through a blessing on his kind attentions to her, but was one of the most affectionate and dutiful of wives.

(*d*) UNKIND HUSBAND REFORMED.—A decent countrywoman, says an English divine, came to me one market day, and begged to speak with me. She told me with an air of secrecy, that her husband behaved unkindly to her, and sought the company of other women: and that knowing me to be a wise man, I could tell what would cure him. "The remedy is simple," said I; "*always treat your husband with a smile.*" The woman thanked me, dropped a curtesy, and went away. A few months after, she came again, bringing a couple of fine fowls. She told me with great satisfaction, that I had cured her husband; and she begged my acceptance of the fowls in return. I was pleased with the success of my prescription, but refused the fee.

(*e*) THE PERSECUTOR'S KIND WIFE.—As I was conversing, says a writer in the New-York Observer, with a pious old man, I inquired what were the means of his conversion. For a moment he paused—I perceived I had touched a tender string. Tears rushed from his eyes, while with deep emotion he replied, "My wife was brought to God some years before myself. I persecuted and abused her because of her religion. She, however, returned nothing but kindness; constantly manifesting an anxiety to promote my comfort and happiness; and it was her amiable conduct, when suffering ill-treatment from me, that first sent the arrows of conviction to my soul. "Temper," added he, "is every thing."

242. KINDNESS, POWER OF.

(*a*) PINEL AND THE LUNATICS.—In 1792, Pinel, who had been for some time chief physician to the Bicetre, or mad-house of Paris, begged repeatedly of the public authorities, to let him remove the chains from the furious. His applications having been unsuccessful, he presented himself before the commune of Paris, and repeating his objections with increased warmth, urged a reform of such monstrous treatment. "Citizen," said one of the members to him, "I will to-morrow go to visit the Bicetre; but wo betide thee, if thou deceivest us, and concealest any of the enemies of the people amongst thy insane."

This member of the commune was Couthon. The next day he went to the Bicetre. Couthon was himself as strange a spectacle as any whom he visited. Deprived of the use of his lower extremities, and compelled to be borne on the arms of others, he appeared, says Pinel, a fraction of humanity implanted on another's body; and from out of this deformity, pronounced in a feeble and feminine voice, merciless sentences proceeded, sentences of death; for death was the only logic that then prevailed. Couthon visited the insane in succession, and questioned them himself; but he received only imprecations amidst the clanking of chains on floors disgustingly filthy from the evacuations of the miserable occupants. Fatigued with the monotony and revolting character of this spectacle, Couthon returned to Pinel. "Citizen," said he, "art thou thyself mad to desire to unchain such animals?" "Citizen," replied Pinel, "I am convinced that these lunatics are intractable only from being deprived of air and liberty, and I expect much from a different course." "Well," said Couthon, "do as thou likest; I leave them to thee; but I am afraid thou wilt fall a victim to thy presumption."

Master of his own actions, Pinel immediately commenced his undertaking, fully aware of its real difficulties; for he was going to set at liberty about fifty furious maniacs, without injurious or dangerous consequences, as he hoped, to the other peaceable inmates of the establishment. He determined to unchain no more than twelve at the first trial; and the only precaution he took, was to have an equal number of strait jackets prepared, made of strong linen with long sleeves, which could be tied behind the back of the maniac, should it become necessary to restrict him from committing acts of violence.

The first person to whom Pinel addressed himself, had been a resident for the longest period in this abode of misery. He was an English captain, whose history was unknown, but who had been chained there for forty years. He was looked upon as the most terrible of all the insane. His attendants always approached him with circumspection; for in a paroxysm of fury, he had struck one of the servants on the head with his manacles, and killed him on the spot. He was confined with more rigor than many of the others, which circumstance, combined with almost total neglect on the part of the keepers, had exasperated a disposition naturally furious. Pinel entered his cell alone, and approached him calmly. "Captain," said he, "if I were to remove your chains, and to give you liberty to walk in the court, would you promise me to be rational, and do harm to no one?" "I promise thee. But thou mockest me; they, as well as thyself, are too much afraid of me." "Assuredly not. I have no fear; for I have six men at hand to make me respected, should it be necessary. But believe my word; be confiding and docile. I will give you liberty, if you will allow me to substitute this strait waistcoat for your ponderous chains."

The captain yielded with a good grace to every thing required of him, shrugging his shoulders, but without uttering a word. In a few minutes his irons were completely removed, and Pinel withdrew, leaving the door of the cell open. Several times the maniac raised himself from his seat, but fell back again; he had kept the sitting posture so long that he had lost the use of his legs. At length, in about a quarter of an hour, and after repeated attempts, he succeeded in retaining his equilibrium, and from the depth of his dark cell advanced staggering towards the door. His first action was to look at the sky, and exclaim in ecstasy, "How beautiful!" Through the whole day he ran about, ascending and descending the stairs, and constantly repeating the exclamation, "How beautiful! how good!" In the evening he returned to his cell, slept tranquilly on a better bed, which had been provided for him; and during the two additional years which he passed in the Bicetre, he had no paroxysm of fury. He rendered himself, indeed, useful in the establishment, by exerting a certain degree of authority over the patients, whom he governed after his own fashion, and over whom he elected himself a kind of superintendent.

But the case of Chevinge, a soldier of the French guards, is looked upon as one of the most memorable feats of that interesting and eventful day. While in the army, he had but one fault—drunkenness; and when in this state he became turbulent, violent, and the more dangerous from his strength being prodigious. Owing to his repeated excesses, he was dismissed from his regiment, and soon dissipated his limited resources. Shame and misery subsequently plunged him into such a state of depression, that his intellect became disordered. In his delirium he thought he had been made a general, and beat those who did not admit his rank and quality; and, in consequence of a violent disturbance thus originating, he was taken to the Bicetre, laboring under the most furious excitement. He had been confined in chains for ten years, and with more severity than most of his fellow sufferers, as he had frequently broken asunder his irons by the sole strength of his hands. On one occasion, when he obtained momentary liberty in this manner, he set at defiance the united efforts of all his keepers to make him re-enter his cell. His strength had, indeed, become proverbial at the Bicetre.

Pinel, on several visits, had discovered in Chevinge an excellent disposition, masked under the excitement incessantly occasioned by cruel treatment. He promised the lunatic to ameliorate his condition, and this promise itself rendered him more tranquil. Pinel at length told him he should be no longer chained; "and to prove the confidence I have in thee," said he, "and that I regard thee as a man adapted for doing good, thou shalt aid me in freeing those unfortunates who have not their reason like thee; and if thou conductest thyself as I have reason to hope, I will take thee into my service, and thou shalt never quit me. Never," adds Pinel, "was there a more sudden and complete revolution. The keepers themselves were impressed with respect and astonishment at the spectacle which Chevinge afforded." Scarcely was he liberated when he was seen anticipating and following with his eye, every motion of Pinel, executing his orders with skill and promptitude, and addressing words of reason and kindness to the insane, on the level with whom he had been but a short time before. This man, whom chains had kept degraded during the best years of his life, and who would doubtless have spent the remainder of his existence in the same wretched condition, became afterwards a model of good conduct and gratitude. Often, in the difficult times of the revolution, he saved the life of Pinel, and on one occasion rescued him from a band of miscreants who were conducting him to the "Lanterne," owing to his having been an elector in 1789. During the time of famine, he left the Bicetre every morning, and returned with supplies of provisions which gold could not at that time procure. His whole life was one of perpetual devotion to his liberator.

In the course of a few days, the shackles were removed from fifty-five lunatics. An unexpected improvement followed from a course previously regarded impracticable and even fatal. The furious mad-men, who monthly destroyed hundreds of utensils, renounced their habits of violence; others, who tore their clothes, and rioted in filth and nudity, became clean and decent; tranquillity and harmony succeeded to tumult and disorder; and over the whole establishment order and good feeling reigned.

(*b*) BUNDY AND THE FEROCIOUS PRISONER.—The power of kindness is seen in the case of Haynes, executed in 1799 at Bristol, Eng. He was heavily ironed, yet so extremely turbulent and outrageous, that the other prisoners stood in fear of him, and were obliged to be constantly on their guard. It became necessary even to call out the military; but this only irritated him, and made him worse. He would expose his naked breast to the soldiers' bayonets, dare them to run him through, and say he would rather be shot dead than surrender himself to them. Yet, when force failed, remonstrance succeeded; for he actually delivered up to the persuasions of a gentleman, a weapon which a file of soldiers were unable to take from him. A pious minister by the name of Bundy, used to visit him, and at length told the keeper he wished to spend the night with the felon. He was warned of his danger; but, moved with compassion, he persisted, and entered the prisoner's cell. Finding him prostrate on the floor under the weight of his irons, he persuaded the keeper to let him have one hand and foot at liberty. The keeper retired late at night, locking after him three massive doors; and Haynes, immediately lifting up his liberated hand, and reaching a clasped knife he had concealed, rushed fiercely towards him, exclaiming with the voice and looks of a demon, "Now thou art in my power, I will kill thee." The man of God thought his end had come; but suddenly recalling the passage, "thou canst have no power over me unless it be given thee from above," was instantly raised above all fear, and calmly met the enraged culprit, to whom he kindly said, "Now, my friend, what harm have I done you, or of what service would my death be to you?" He then spoke of the love of Christ, and assured the felon, that he was ready to receive all, even the most wicked, who came to him. These words of kindness softened the culprit's heart; he threw down the knife, acknowledging his guilt, and burst into tears. Deeply convicted at length of sin, he asked if it was possible for such a sinner as himself ever to be saved? The anguish of his mind was extreme; he would often weep bitterly in view of his sins; and there is reason to hope that he died a sincere penitent.

(*c*) ISAAC HOPPER AND CAIN.—When Isaac Hopper lived in Philadelphia, his attention was drawn to a colored waiter, called Cain, who was remarkable for profanity. Neither persuasion nor rebuke had any effect to change this bad habit. One day Hopper encountered him in the street, quarreling and pouring forth volleys of oaths that made one shudder. Having faith in fines and constables, Hopper took him before a magistrate, who fined him for blasphemy.

Twenty years after, Isaac met Cain, whom he had not seen for a very long time. His outward appearance was much changed for the worse; his garments were tattered, and his person emaciated. This touched the Friend's heart. He stepped up, shook hands, and spoke kindly to the forlorn being. "Dost not thou remember me," said the Quaker, "and how I had thee fined for swearing?" "Yes, indeed, I do; I remember what I paid as well as yesterday." "Well, did it do thee any good?" "No, never a bit; it made me mad to have my money taken from me."

Hopper invited Cain to reckon up the interest on the fine, and paid him principal and interest. "I meant it for thy good, Cain, and I am sorry I did thee any harm."

Cain's countenance changed; the tears rolled down his cheeks; he took the money with many thanks; became a quiet man, and was heard to swear no more.

(*d*) PILLSBURY AND THE GIANT PRISONER.—Mr. Pillsbury, warden of the state prison in Connecticut, once received into the prison a man of gigantic stature, whose crimes had for seventeen years made him the terror of the country. He told the criminal when he came, he hoped he would not repeat the attempts to escape which he had made elsewhere. "It will be best," said he, "that you and I should treat each other as well as we can. I will make you as comfortable as I possibly can, and I shall be anxious to be your friend; and I hope you will not get me into difficulty on your account. There is a cell intended for solitary confinement; but we have never used it, and I should be sorry ever to have to turn the key upon any body in it. You may range the place as freely as I do; if you trust me, I shall trust you." The man was sulky, and for weeks showed only gradual symptoms of softening under the operation of Mr. Pillsbury's cheerful confidence. At length information was brought of the man's intention to break prison. The warden called him, and taxed him with it; the man preserved a gloomy silence. He was told it was now necessary for him to be locked in the solitary cell, and desired to follow the warden, who went first, carrying a lamp in one hand, and a key in the other. In the narrowest part of the passage, Mr. Pillsbury, a small, light man, turned round, and looked in the face of the stout criminal. "Now," said he, "I ask whether you have treated me as I deserve? I have done every thing I could to make you happy; I have trusted you; but you have never given me the least confidence in return, and have even planned to get me into difficulty. Is this kind? And yet I cannot bear to lock you up. If I had the least sign that you cared for me"— The man burst into tears "Sir," said he, "I have been a very devil these seventeen years; but you treat me like a man." "Come, let us go back," said the warden. The convict had free range of the prison as before; and from this hour he began to open his heart to the warden, and cheerfully fulfilled his whole term of imprisonment.

(*e*) AZEL BACKUS AND THE HEATHEN.—At a festival at Ganesa's (Gumputtee's) temple in Ceylon, while the multitude of worshipers, assembled at the temple, were engaged in boiling their rice for an offering, one of them who went for water, fell into the well. As soon as the circumstance was made known to the crowd, they rushed to the well, and among them was the pandarum (priest) of the temple, who, as soon as he had gratified his curiosity, returned to the temple. None among them manifested the least concern for the unfortunate man who was sunk in the water. They looked into the well, and talked about the man in such imminent danger with the most perfect indifference. Not an individual seemed to think assistance could or ought to be rendered, till one of the headmen came to the spot: he exerted all his influence to induce some one to dive into the water, which any person accustomed to swimming might have done with perfect safety, but his efforts were in vain. He then sent for the priest, who was known to be an expert swimmer. At the command of the headman he came, but excused himself from the act of mercy required of him, by saying that he could not absent himself so long from the duties of the temple without sustaining a loss. Just at this moment came to the place a young man, unknown to the crowd, who, as soon as he learned that a fellow being was drowning, threw aside his garment, and leaped into the well. After repeatedly diving, he found the body, and raised it to the surface of the water, from which it was taken by the by-standers. As soon as the noise and confusion occasioned by taking out the lifeless body had subsided, a loud whisper passed along the crowd, "Who is that young man? Who is that good man?" They were not a little surprised, and some of the enemies of Christianity confounded, when they were told that this good Samaritan was Azel Backus, a Christian! This event did not a little towards stopping the mouths, and weakening the strength of some who were arrayed against Christians and the cause in which they are engaged; and is to all, who have any knowledge of Scripture, a striking comment on the words of inspiration, "Overcome evil with good."

(*f*) THE PHYSICIAN AND THE DRAYMAN.—Dr. P—, a Quaker of Philadelphia, was very kind to the poor. In times of sickness, produced by whatever cause, he was always ready and willing to assist them. His benevolence in such cases extended farther than his gratuitous services as a physician. Of course he was beloved.

The streets were frequently somewhat crowded with building materials, so much so as often, at particular places, to prevent two vehicles from passing each other, if the driver of either is disposed to be obstinate.

As the doctor was one day proceeding to visit a patient, his progress was impeded by a dray—the driver of which had stopped his horses in one of those narrow passages. After waiting several minutes, the doctor requested the drayman to allow him to pass. The latter, who had heard of, but did not know the former, poured forth a volley of the vilest abuse upon the "straight coat," and swore he would not move till he thought proper.

"Well, friend," said the doctor, "all I have to observe is this: if thee should get sick, or if thy family should ever be in distress, send for Dr. P., and he will do all he can to assist thee." The heart of the drayman was subdued by the kindness of the man he had abused. He was ashamed of his conduct—stammered an apology, and removed the obstruction as speedily as possible.

How true it is, that "a soft tongue breaketh the bone." If the doctor had cursed the drayman till midnight, he would have received nothing but cursing and blows in return. This may be thought a small matter, but it furnishes a useful lesson.

(*g*) LIFE SAVED BY GOOD NATURE.—A gentleman in Philadelphia, who constantly felt and looked kindly, going out one morning, met a wretched looking man walking hastily with a musket in his hand.

"Good morning, sir," said the gentleman with a smile.

"Good morning," muttered the other; and passed on. Presently the gentleman heard the report of a musket, and soon the cry of murder. It turned out that the man with the musket was insane, and had run out with a musket to kill the first man he should meet, that he might be hanged himself, and thus get rid of this world; but he was asked why he did not kill the first gentleman. "Why he looked so good natured," said he, "that I thought I would not shoot *him*."

(*h*) THE HAYMAKERS.—Two neighbors were getting hay from adjoining lots of marsh land. One had the misfortune to mire his team and load so as to require aid from the other. He called to him for assistance with his oxen and men. But his neighbor felt churlish, and loading him with reproaches for his imprudent management, told him to help himself at his leisure. With considerable difficulty he extricated his load from the mire and pursued his business. A day or two after, his churlish neighbor met with a similar mishap. Whereupon the other, without waiting for a request, volunteered with his oxen and rendered the necessary assistance. The churl felt ashamed of himself. His evil was overcome by his neighbor's good, and he never afterwards refused him a favor.

243. LABOR, DIGNITY OF.

(*a*) CYRUS A GARDENER.—When Lysander, the Lacedæmonian general, brought magnificent presents to Cyrus, the younger son of Darius, who piqued himself more on his integrity and politeness than on his rank and birth, the prince conducted his illustrious guest through his gardens, and pointed out to him their varied beauties. Lysander, struck with so fine a prospect, praised the manner in which the grounds were laid out, the neatness of the walks, the abundance of fruits planted with an art which knew how to combine the useful with the agreeable; the beauty of the parterres, and the glowing variety of flowers exhaling odors universally throughout the delightful scene. "Every thing charms and transports me in this place," said Lysander to Cyrus; "but what strikes me most is the exquisite taste and elegant industry of the person who drew the plan of these gardens, and gave it the fine order, wonderful disposition, and happiness of arrangement which I cannot sufficiently admire." Cyrus replied, "It was I that drew the plan and entirely marked it out; and many of the trees which you see were planted by my own hands." "What!" exclaimed Lysander, with surprise, and viewing Cyrus from head to foot, "is it possible that, with those purple robes and splendid vestments, those strings of jewels and bracelets of gold, those buskins so richly embroidered; is it possible that you could play the gardener, and employ your royal hands in planting trees?" "Does that surprise you?" said Cyrus; "I assure you that, when my health permits, I never sit down to my table without having fatigued myself, either in military exercise, rural labor, or some other toilsome employment, to which I apply myself with pleasure." Lysander, still more amazed, pressed Cyrus by the hand, and said, "You are truly happy, and deserve your high fortune, since you unite it with virtue."

(*b*) LACEDÆMONIANS' SEASONING.—Dionysius the tyrant being at an entertainment given to him by the Lacedæmonians, expressed some disgust at their black broth. "No wonder," said one of them, "for it wants seasoning." "What seasoning?' asked the tyrant. "Labor," replied the citizen, "joined with hunger and thirst."

(*c*) INDUSTRIOUS MONARCH.—It was the custom of Peter the Great to visit the different workshops and manufactories, not only to encourage them, but also to judge what other useful establishments might be formed in his dominions. Among the places he visited frequently, were the forges of Muller, at Istia, ninety versts from Moscow.—The Czar once passed a whole month there; during which time, after giving due attention to the affairs of state, which he never neglected, he amused himself with seeing and examining every thing in the most minute manner, and even employed himself in learning the business of a blacksmith. He succeeded so well, that on one of the last days of his remaining there, he forged eighteen poods of iron, and put his own particular mark on each bar. The boyars and other noblemen of his suite were employed in blowing the bellows, stirring the fire, carrying coals, and performing the other duties of a blacksmith's assistant. When Peter had finished, he went to the proprietor, praised his manufactory, and asked him how much he gave his workmen per pood. "Three kopecks, or an altina," answered Muller. "Very well," replied the Czar; "I have then earned eighteen altinas." Muller brought eighteen ducats, offered them to Peter, and told him that he could not give a workman like his majesty less per pood. Peter refused. "Keep your ducats," said he; "I have not wrought better than any other man; give me what you would give to another; I want to buy a pair of shoes, of which I am in great need." At the same time he showed him his shoes, which had been once mended, and were again full of holes. Peter accepted the eighteen altinas, and bought himself a pair of new shoes, which he used to show with much pleasure, saying,—"These I earned with the sweat of my brow."

One of the bars of iron forged by Peter the Great, and authenticated by his mark, is still to be seen at Istia, in the forge of Muller. Another similar bar is preserved in the cabinet of curiosities at St. Petersburgh.

(*d*) WASHINGTON AND THE CORPORAL.—During the American Revolution, it is said, the commander of a little squad was giving orders to those under him, relative to a stick of timber which they were endeavoring to raise up to the top of some military works they were repairing. The timber went up hard, and on this account, the voice of the little great man was oftener heard, in regular vociferations of "Heave away! There she goes! Heave ho!" An officer, not in military costume, was passing, and asked the commander why he did not take hold, and render a little aid. The latter, astonished, turning round with all the pomp of an emperor, said, "Sir, I am a corporal!" "You are—are you?" replied the officer, "I was not aware of that;" and taking off his hat and bowing, "I ask your pardon, Mr. Corporal." Upon this he dismounted, and lifted till the sweat stood in drops on his forehead. And when finished, turning to the commander, he said, "Mr. Corporal, when you have another such job, and have not men enough, send for your Commander-in-Chief, and I will come and help you a second time." The corporal was thunderstruck! It was Washington.

(*e*) CARTER'S REPLY TO THE TANNER.—The Rev. J. Carter, one of the puritan ministers, once came unexpectedly behind a Christian of his acquaintance, who was busily occupied in his business as a tanner. He gave him a pleasant tap on the shoulder; the good man looked behind him, started, and said, "Sir, I am ashamed that you should find me thus employed." Mr. Carter replied, "Let Christ, when he cometh, find me so doing." "What!" said the good man, "doing thus?"—"Yes," said Mr. C., "faithfully performing the duties of my calling."

An anecdote similar to this is recorded of Dr. Doddringe and one of his friends.

(*f*) SOUTHERN STUDENT AND DR. STUART.—Manual labor is esteemed by many at the South as disgraceful. An anecdote showing to what an extent this sentiment prevails, was related at an anti-slavery meeting at Danvers. A student from one of the southern States, in the Theological Seminary at Andover, had purchased some wood, and was exceedingly embarrassed at being unable readily to obtain some one to saw it for him. He went to Professor Stuart, to inquire what he should do in so unfortunate a predicament. The learned professor replied, that he was in want of a job himself, and he would saw it for him.

244. LAWSUITS AND LAWYERS.

(*a*) THE CZAR AND HIS GOVERNOR.—Peter the Great frequently surprised the magistrates by his unexpected presence in the cities of the empire. Having arrived without previous notice at Olonez, he went first to the regency, and inquired of the governor how many suits were depending in the court of chancery? "None, sire," replied the governor. "How happens that?"

"I endeavor to prevent lawsuits, and conciliate the parties; I act in such a manner that no traces of difference remain on the archives; if I am wrong, your indulgence will excuse me." "I wish," replied the Czar, "that all governors would act on your principles. Go on, God and your sovereign are equally satisfied."

(*b*) GOOD ADVICE OF TWISS.—Mr. Philip Henry relates a remarkable story concerning a good old friend of his, who, when young, being an orphan, was greatly wronged by his uncle. His portion, which was £200, was put into the hands of that uncle; who, when he grew up, shuffled with him, and would give him but £40, instead of his £200, and he had no way of recovering his right but by law. But, before he would engage in that, he was willing to advise with his minister, who was the famous Dr. Twiss, of Newberry. The counsel he gave him, all things considered, was, for peace' sake, and for the preventing of sin, and snares, and troubles, to take the £40 rather than contend; "and Thomas," said the doctor, "if thou dost so, assure thyself that God will make it up to thee and thine some other way, and they that defraud will be the losers by it at last." He did so, and it pleased God so to bless that little which he began the world with, that when he died in a good old age, he left his son possessed of some hundreds a year, whilst he that had wronged him fell into poverty.

(*c*) THE MAGISTRATE'S EXPEDIENT.—A magistrate of Paris established a poor-box in his office; and when he happened to accomplish the pleasantest part of his duty, that of preventing litigation, he invited the parties whom he reconciled, to seal that reconciliation with an alms. In a single year, this worthy functionary collected more than 1400 francs. This ingenious means of beneficence was truly honorable to the inventor.

(*d*) THE UNSETTLED LAW-CASE.—Two neighbors, who were brothers by marriage, had a difficulty respecting their partition fence. Although they had mutually erected a substantial fence, four and one half feet in height on the line separating the sheep pasture of one from the grain field of the other, yet the lambs would creep through the crevices and destroy the grain. Each asserted it to be the duty of the other to chink the fence. After the usual preliminaries of demands, refusals, threats, challenges, and mutual recriminations, they resolved to try the glorious uncertainty of the law; they were, however, persuaded by their friends to the more amicable mode of submitting the defence and final determination to a very worthy and intelligent neighbor, who was forthwith conducted to the scene of trouble, and in full view of the premises: each party in turn, in a speech of some length, asserted his rights, and set forth the law and the facts; at the conclusion of which, the arbitrator very gravely remarked: "Gentlemen, the case involves questions of great nicety and importance, not only to the parties in interest, but to the community at large; and it is my desire to take suitable time for deliberation, and also for advisement with those who are learned in the law, and most expert in the customs of good neighbors; in the meantime, however, I will just clap a billet or two of wood into the sheep holes;" and in ten minutes' time, with his hands, he effectually closed every gap. The parties silently retired, each evidently heartily ashamed of his own folly and obstinacy. The umpire has never been called upon to pronounce final judgment in the case; so the law case remains unsettled to this day.

(*e*) RULE FOR AN ATTORNEY.—A pious attorney, being asked how he could conscientiously plead for some of his clients, replied, "Sir, I have not for many years undertaken a cause which I could not pray for; and I have never lost a case for which I could pray!" If all lawyers would do thus, the oppression of the innocent would be less frequent.

(*f*) ERSKINE'S OPINION.—Lord Erskine, when at the bar, and at the time when his professional talents were most eminent and popular, having been applied to by his friend Dr. Parr for his opinion upon a subject likely to be liti gated by him, after recommending the doctor "to accommodate the difference amicably," concluded his letter by observing, "I can scarcely figure to myself a situation in which a lawsuit is not, if possible, to be avoided."

(*g*) THE LITIGANT'S GRATIFICATION.—A gentleman who had been successively engaged in three professions, that of minister, physician, and lawyer, was asked the comparative advantages of them for acquiring property. He replied, "The man who will give but a fourpence to save his soul, will give twenty-five cents for relief from sickness, and a dollar to have his own will."

(*h*) EXTRAORDINARY LAWYER.—A circumstance is mentioned of Robert Dover, the worthy attorney of Burton on the Heath, on the last leaf of a book of verses to which his portrait is affixed, no less extraordinary than the occasion of writing the poems, namely; that "though he was bred an attorney, he never tried but two causes, having always made up the difference."

(*i*) MATTHEW HALE IN DISGUISE.—The younger of two brothers had endeavored to deprive the elder of an estate of £500 a year, by suborning witnesses to declare that he died in a foreign land. Coming into the court in the guise of a miller, Sir Matthew Hale was chosen the twelfth juryman to sit on this cause. As soon as the clerk of the court had sworn in the jurymen, a little dexterous fellow came into their apartment and slipped ten gold pieces into the hands of eleven of the jury, and gave the miller five, while the judge was known to be bribed with a great sum. The judge summed up the evidence in favor of the younger brother, and the jury were about to give their assent, when the supposed miller stood up and addressed the court with such energetic and manly eloquence, as astonished the judge and all present; unraveled the sophistry to the very bottom, proved the fact of bribery, evinced the elder brother's title to the estate, from the contradictory evidence of the witnesses, and gained a complete victory in favor of truth and justice.

245. LEGACIES.

(*a*) THE RICH MAN'S HEIR.—An old woman, who showed the house and pictures at Towcester, expressed herself in these remarkable words:—"That is Sir Robert Farmer; he lived in the country, took care of his estate, built this house, and paid for it; managed well, saved money, and died rich.—*That* is his son. He was made a lord, took a place at court, spent his estate, and died a beggar!" A very concise, but full account, and fraught with a valuable moral lesson. "He layeth up riches, and knoweth not who shall gather them."

(*b*) THE LOST LEGACY.—We knew a worthy clergyman, says a writer in the New-York Evangelist, who had the cause of religion deeply at heart, and who, by his will, had bequeathed to a benevolent institution a certain bond which he held against an individual then supposed to be rich. At the time of making his will, the bond would have been canceled on demand. But by a reverse of circumstances, the debtor became insolvent; and but a few cents on the dollar were paid on the final winding up of his concerns. This to the benevolent clergyman was a source of much deeper regret, than if he had sustained the same loss in property which he had designed for his own lawful heirs. Instead of accumulating, as he had anticipated, so as to produce a greater ulterior benefit to the cause, it was reduced to a very small pittance. Had he given the money when he had formed his design, it would have effected immediate good, and perhaps yielded, in its advantage to the cause, a far greater per-centage, than any interest upon a bond, had it been perfectly safe.

This incident will serve to illustrate

the importance of doing at once whatever we design for the promotion of the gospel.

(c) THE PRODIGAL REFORMED.—Admiral Williams when a young man, was gay, and so addicted to expensive pleasures, that no remonstrances could reclaim him. When his father died, he met the rest of the family to hear the will read. His name did not occur among the other children, and he supposed the omission was a mark of his father's resentment against him. At the close of it, however, he found that he was mentioned, as residuary legatee, in these words. "All the rest of my estate and effects I leave to my son Peere Williams, knowing that he will spend it all."

On hearing this he burst into tears. "My father," said he, "has touched the right string, and his reproach shall not be thrown away." His conduct from that time was altered, and he became an honor to the Christian profession.

265. LICENTIOUSNESS.

(a) HINT TO YOUNG LADIES. "Why did you not take the arm of my brother last night?" said a young lady to her friend, a very intelligent girl, about 19, in a large town near lake Ontario; she replied, "Because I know him to be a licentious young man." "Nonsense," was the answer of the sister, "if you refuse the attentions of all licentious men, you will have none, I can assure you." "Very well," said her friend, "then I can dispense with them altogether—for my resolution on this point is unalterably fixed." How long would it take to revolutionize society, were all young ladies to adopt this resolution?

(b) THE HAPPY RAKE.—Colonel Gardiner, says Doctor Doddridge, was habitually so immersed in intrigues, that if not the whole business, at least the whole happiness of his life consisted in them; and he had too much leisure for one who was so prone to abuse it. His fine constitution, than which, perhaps, there was hardly ever a better, gave him great opportunities in indulging himself in these excesses; and his good spirits enabled him to pursue his pleasures of every kind in so alert and sprightly a manner, that multitudes envied him, and called him, by a dreadful kind of compliment, "The happy rake." Yet still the checks of conscience, and some remaining principles of an excellent education, would break in upon his most licentious hours; and I particularly remember he told me, that when some of his dissolute companions were once congratulating him on his distinguished felicity, a dog happening at that time to come into the room, he could not forbear groaning inwardly, and saying to himself, "Oh that I were that dog!" Such was then his happiness, and such, perhaps, is that of hundreds more, who bear themselves highest in the contempt of religion, and glory in that infamous servitude which they affect to call liberty.

(c) HIGHWAY TO SUICIDE.—The Rev. John Owen, the eloquent advocate of the Bible Society, after adverting, in a sermon to the young, to the peaceful death of a little girl, mentions the awful end of a youth who had been seduced from the paths of virtue by wicked associates.

Scarcely, says he, had the turf been spread over the mortal remains of this young disciple, when the ground was opened to receive another of our youth, who, awful to relate, had raised his arm, and that with too fatal success, against the precious, the invaluable deposit of his own life. This deluded youth had received the benefit of a Christian education in one of our schools of gratuitous instruction; and, like the happy subject who preceded him into eternity, had been carefully lectured in the house of God on matters which concerned his salvation. But a removal from school to employment was to him, as it unhappily is to too many of our youth, the signal for renouncing his attendance upon the ordinances of religion. The consequence was such that might naturally be apprehended. He fell into the snare of evil company, and became licentious, profligate, and abandoned. Diseased, disgraced, despondent, without any cordial from religious hope, any support in Christian resignation, yielded to the temptation of the destroyer, and completed the measure of his sin, his misery, and his dishonor, by an act of deliberate suicide

Behold then, this victim to his youthful lusts, mangled, cruelly mangled by his own violence; and weltering, with awful publicity, in the stream of blood which his suicidal hands have spilt. Behold—not that you may gratify an unfeeling curiosity, nor yet be convulsed with horror and disgust—but that you may learn the solemn truth which every part of this catastrophy proclaims, "The wages of sin is death!"

247. LOVE, BROTHERLY.

(*a*) A CALVINIST'S LIBERALITY.—"Though a man," says the Rev. John Newton, "does not accord with my views of Election, yet if he give me good evidence that he is effectually called of God, he is my brother. Though he seems afraid of the doctrine of final perseverance, yet if grace enable him to persevere, he is my brother still. If he will love Jesus, I will love him. whatever hard names he may be called by, and whatever incidental mistakes I may think he holds. This differing from me will not always prove him to be wrong, except I am infallible myself."

(*b*) INTIMACY WITH THE PIOUS POOR.—A truly pious man of rank and influence in society, was in the habit of entertaining and admitting to a degree of intimacy, persons of very humble circumstances of life, if they only gave evidence of true religion. A friend of his, who was accustomed to measure every thing according to the standard of this world, pleasantly rallied him on the subject of his associates; intimating his surprise that he should admit to his hospitality and friendship persons of obscure origin, and of little estimation among men. He replied in a tone of unaffected humility, that as he could scarcely hope to enjoy so elevated a rank as they in a future world, he knew not why he should despise them in the present. The reproof came home to the feelings of the proud man, and he was silent; conscience whispering, meanwhile, how dim were his prospects of rising, in the future world, to an equality with the pious poor, if his Christian friend was in danger of falling below them.

(*c*) AN UNBELIEVER CONVINCED.—A man who had for some time attended the meetings of a certain church in the city of New York, came before them to relate his experience, with a view to joining them by baptism. In detailing the exercises of his mind, he stated that what first drew his serious attention to the subject of religion, was observing the unbroken concord and Christian affection existing among the members of the church. It struck him that such a delightful harmony and mutual attachment could not be the effect of natural feeling and self-interest, for it was too pure and too holy. What could produce such a tie of brotherhood but the agency of the Spirit of God! There was no other explanation, and the more he looked upon the church keeping the unity of the spirit in the bond of peace, the more his heart was affected, till he was led to cast himself at the feet of Christ, and pray that his hard and selfish heart might be changed, and that he also might become one of the blessed company of the saints.

If all churches maintained such a fellowship as this, and could always challenge the world with "Behold how these Christians love one another," what multitudes would believe in Christ who now reject him!

(*d*) PLAGUE AT ALEXANDRIA.—A startling instance of the brotherly love of the early Christians, transpired in the great plague that raged in Alexandria, during the reign of Gallienus.

At the first appearance of the symptoms the heathen drove the infected man from their sight; they tore themselves from their dearest connections; they threw their friends half dead into the streets, and left their dead unburied. But in contrast with this cruel selfishness, "the Christians, in the abundance of their brotherly love," as their bishop Dyonysius says, "did not spare themselves, but mutually attending to each other, they would visit the sick without fear, and ministering to each other for the sake of Christ, cheerfully gave up their lives with him. Many died after their care had restored others to health. Many who took the bodies of their Christian brethren into hands and bosoms, and closed their eyes, and buried them with every mark of attention, soon followed them in death."

(*e*) CYPRIAN AND THE CAPTIVES.—The early Christians were remarkable for their brotherly love. When a multitude of Christian men and women in Numidia, had been taken prisoners by a horde of neighboring barbarians, and when the churches to which they belonged were unable to raise the sum demanded for their ransom, they sent deputies to the church that was planted in the metropolis of North Africa. No sooner had Cyprian who was at the head of it, heard a statement of the distressing case, than he commenced a subscription in behalf of the unfortunate slaves, and never relaxed his indefatigable efforts, till he had collected a sum equal to nearly $4,000. This he forwarded to the Numidian Christians, with a letter full of Christian sympathy and tenderness.

"In cases like these," he says in his letter, "who would not feel sorrow, and who would not look upon a brother's sufferings as his own? As the apostle says, when one member suffers, all the members suffer with it. Therefore we must consider the captivity of our brethren as our own captivity. We must see Christ in our captive brethren, and redeem him from captivity who redeemed us from death."

(*f*) THE CONVERT'S DISAPPOINTMENT.—A young lady in Rhode Island, who had been brought up by a pious and devoted mother, and who had always looked up to Christians as patterns of all that was excellent in piety and morality, as forming societies next in their loveliness to that of heaven, was led to repentance, and united with a Christian church. Some time after her baptism, she heard some of the older and leading members of the church, speaking in terms of severity and bitterness respecting the faults and errors of some of the other members; and without appearing grieved at the conduct they so freely censured. Her surprise and disappointment were most painful. Is this, thought she, the boasted fellowship of the church? Can those professors know any thing of the spirit of Christ? She was led to doubt their Christianity; and yet as they had expressed the same attachment to Christ and his cause which she had herself, she was led to think that her own feelings, as well as theirs, were but the kindlings of enthusiasm, the joys of false hopes, and the reveries of an excited imagination. Thus her mind was filled with gloom and despair; she felt she had been most cruelly deceived, and her wretchedness was extreme. She poured out her soul in tears, day and night; but tears proved the food rather than the medicine of her grief. At length she began to be subject to doubts respecting the reality of spiritual religion; she, of course, neglected many of its duties; if she tried to pray, her prayers seemed but foolishness;—at length Jesus Christ became an object of skepticism, and at last she even called in question the existence of a God, And here she remained "in tideless, shoreless wo," till, through the agency of the Providence and Spirit of God, she was led to come to herself, arise and go to her father's house!

Oh! how should such a fact as this urge professed Christians, one and all, to be "kindly affectioned one to another with brotherly love," and to put away from among them "all bitterness, and wrath, and anger, and clamor, and evil speaking, with all malice."

(*g*) WHITFIELD'S OPINION OF WESLEY.—A minister very liberal in his reflections on Mr. Wesley and his followers, being once in company with Mr. Whitfield, expressed his doubt to him concerning Mr. Wesley's salvation, and said, "Sir, do you think when *we* get to heaven, we shall see Mr. Wesley?" "No, sir," replied Mr. Whitfield, "I fear not, for he will be so near the throne, and we shall be at such a distance, we shall hardly get sight of him."

242. LOVE TO CHRIST.

(*a*) THE MORAVIAN PILOT.—In the year 1811, the Moravian missionaries in Labrador determined on the introduction of the gospel in the northern parts of that land. They embarked in company with a Christian pilot whom they had obtained, named Jonathan. The sacrifices which this man made to accompany him were very great. At Hopedale, he was considered the principal person or chief of his nation; but being made a partaker of the same spirit by which the missionary brethren were actuated, he was willing to sojourn among strangers, where he would have no pre-eminence, and to expose himself to unknown hardships and dangers sustained only by the hope that the projected voyage might open the way for the introduction of the gospel among a portion of his countrymen still sitting in darkness and the shadow of death. When any of his countrymen represented to him the danger of the expedition, he used to say, "Well, we will try, and shall know better when we get there:" and once he said, "When I hear people talk about the danger of being killed, I think Jesus went to death out of love to us; what greater matter would it be, if we were to be put to death in his service, should that be his good pleasure?" So effectually had he been taught that Christ died for all, that we who live should not henceforth live unto ourselves, but unto him who died for us, and rose again. Nor was this a mere empty boast; this generous principle of devotedness to Jesus evidently actuated our Esquimaux captain during the severe trials of a most perilous voyage; his cheerful, firm, and faithful conduct, under all circumstances, being quite consistent with his Christian profession.

(*b*) THE HAPPY HINDOO.—The Rev. Eustace Carey, from India, relates a pleasing anecdote of a native Christian whom he was called to visit. Inquiring as to the state of her mind, she replied, "Happy! happy! I have Christ *here*," laying her hand on the Bengalee Bible; "and Christ *here*," pressing it to her heart; "and Christ *there*," pointing towards heaven. Happy Christian! to whatever part of the universe she might be removed, the Lord of the universe was with her, and she was secure of his favor. "Whom have I in heaven but thee? and there is none upon the earth that I desire besides thee. My heart and my flesh faileth, but God is the strength of my heart and my portion for ever.

(*c*) "SHALL WE KNOW EACH OTHER IN HEAVEN.—An old minister, while one day pursuing his studies, his wife being in the room, was suddenly interrupted by her asking him a question, which has not always been so satisfactorily answered. "Do you think we shall know each other in heaven?" Without hesitation, he replied, "To be sure we shall; do you think we shall be greater fools there than we are here?" After a momentary pause, he again proceeded; "But I may be a thousand years by your side in heaven without having seen you; for the first thing which will attract my notice when I arrive there, will be my dear Saviour; and I cannot tell when I shall be for a moment induced to look at any other object."

(*d*) PREFERRING CHRIST TO ORNAMENTS.—In a letter from the Rev. A. Judson, a Christian missionary in Burmah, addressed to American females, is the following anecdote:

A Karen woman offered herself for baptism. After the usual examination I inquired whether she could give up her ornaments for Christ. It was an unexpected blow. I explained the spirit of the gospel, and appealed to her own consciousness of vanity. I then read to her the apostle's prohibition, 1 Tim. 2 : 9. She looked again and again at her handsome necklace, and then, with an air of modest decision, that would adorn, beyond all ornaments, any of my sisters whom I have the honor of addressing, she took it off, saying "I love Christ more than this."

(*e*) LOVING CHRIST BETTER THAN RELATIVES. — A martyr was asked, whether he did not love his wife and children, who stood weeping by him? "Love them!" said he, "yes, if all the world were gold, and at my disposal, I would give it all for the satisfaction of living with them, though it were in prison; yet, in comparison with Christ, I love them not."

(*f*) NONE BUT CHRIST.—John Lambert suffered in the year 1538. No man was used at the stake with more cruelty than this holy martyr. They burned him with a slow fire by inches. But God was with him in the midst of the flame, and supported him in all the anguish of nature. Just before he expired, he lifted up such hands as he had all flaming with fire, and cried out to the people with his dying voice, with these glorious words, "*None but Christ! None but Christ!*" He was at last bent down into the fire and expired.

249. Love to Christ, Assurance of.

(*a*) NAMACQUA GIRL'S LOVE. —I have observed a little Namacqua girl in my house, says Mr. Schmelen, a Christian missionary, about eight years of age, with a book in her hand. very accurately instructing another girl about fourteen. When I asked her if she loved the Lord Jesus, she answered, "Yes, I do; and I desire to love him more." I inquired why she loved him, since she had never seen him; she answered, "He loved me first, and died for me on the cross, that I might live." When I asked her if the Lord Jesus would love the little children, she could not answer me for weeping, and at length fainted away. I had frequently observed this child under deep impressions at our meetings. She is descended from a wild Bushman, and was stolen from her people and country, but has no desire now to return.

(*b*) "LOVEST THOU ME?"—In one of the general associations, held in South and North Wales, of different Sunday Schools to be publicly catechised together, a young girl answered the close questions put by the Saviour to Peter: "Lovest thou me?" When she came to answer the third time, she was overcome by her feelings, and burst into tears, in which she was accompanied by the larger part of the congregation. Silence continued for a few minutes, all the people solemnly waiting her reply, when recovering herself, she cried out, "Thou knowest all things; thou knowest that I love thee!" Happy indeed are those who, by the grace of our Lord Jesus Christ, can thus speak!

(*c*) "EFFECTUAL CALLING." —The Rev. Thomas Doolittle used to catechise the members, and especially the young people of his congregation, every Lord's day. One Sabbath evening, after having received an answer in the words of the Assembly's Catechism, to the question, "What is effectual calling?" and having explained it, he proposed that the question should be answered by changing the words *us* and *our*, into *me* and *my*. Upon this proposal, a solemn silence followed; many felt its vast importance; but none had courage to answer. At length a young man rose up, and with every mark of a broken and contrite heart, by divine grace, was enabled to say, "Effectual calling is the work of God's Spirit, whereby convincing *me* of *my* sin and misery, enlightening *my* mind in the knowledge of Christ, and renewing *my* will, he *did* persuade and enable *me* to embrace Jesus Christ, freely offered *me* in the gospel." The scene was truly affecting. The proposal of that question had commanded unusual solemnity. The rising up of the young man had created high expectations, and the answer being accompanied with proofs of unfeigned piety and modesty, the congregation was bathed in tears. This young man had been convicted by being catechised, and to his honor, Mr. D. says, "From being an ignorant and wicked youth, he had become an intelligent professor to God's glory, and my much comfort."

(*d*) NINE YEARS WITHOUT DOUBTING.—Dea. H. of Southington, Ct., one day said to a friend, "I have scarcely seen an hour for the past nine years, since I professed religion, in which I have not been able to say in holy confidence with Peter, "Lord, thou knowest all things, thou knowest that I love thee!"

250. LOVE TO SOULS.

(*a*) THE COLPORTEUR'S SUFFERINGS.—The following is language held by a Colporteur of the American Tract Society, in Florida :—

"A Colporteur must count the cost, admonished by Him who came to seek and to save that which was lost. Bodily strength and vigor of health are prerequisites. He must be willing to abide with the poorest and most ignorant of our fellow-men, and be content with the humblest fare; cheerfully endure cold and heat, hunger and thirst, labor and fatigue, if souls may be benefited and the kingdom of our Redeemer promoted. Above all, he needs an entire reliance on the Divine aid and guidance and must have his own heart subdued by the Spirit of God.

"Though I have sunk in the bogs, and have extricated myself only by excessive labor; have broken down in the midst of a difficult stream, in the sickly and hot season, and waded out with my boxes of books; have been lost two days in the woods without food for myself or horse; have lain in the wild forest far from any habitation while the storm was raging about me, or only the howling of wolves and of other wild beasts was heard; yet these trials of hunger, thirst, and exposure are of little account, if I can but win souls to Christ."

(*b*) MISSIONARY AMONG LEPERS.—In the south of Africa there was once a large lazar-house, for lepers. It was an immense space, enclosed by a very high wall, and containing fields, which the lepers cultivate. There was only one entrance, which was strictly guarded. Whenever any one was found with the marks of leprosy upon him, he was brought to this gate and obliged to enter in never to return. No one who entered in by that awful gate was ever allowed to come out again. Within this abode of misery, there was multitudes of lepers in all stages of the disease. Dr. Halbeck, a missionary of the Church of England, from the top of a neighboring hill, saw them at work. He noticed two particularly, sowing peas in the field. The one had no hands, the other had no feet,—these members being wasted away by disease. The one who wanted the hands was carrying the other who wanted the feet upon his back, and he again carried in his hands the bag of seed, and dropped a pea every now and then, which the other pressed into the ground with his foot—and so they managed the work of one man between the two.—Two Moravian missionaries, impelled by an ardent love for souls, chose the lazar-house as their field of labor. They entered it never to come out again; and it was said that as soon as these should die, other Moravians were quite ready to fill their place. "Ah! my dear friends," adds the late Rev. Robert M'Cheyne, "may we not blush, and be ashamed before God, that we, redeemed with the same blood, and taught by the same Spirit, should yet be so unlike these men in vehement, heart-consuming love to Jesus and the souls of men?"

(*c*) THE TWO MINERS.—At a meeting of the Wesleyan Missionary Society, the Rev. R. Young, of Truro mentioned a very remarkable fact that had taken place in Cornwall, (Eng.)

"Two men were working together in a mine, and having prepared to blast the rock, and laid the train, the latter became by accident ignited. In a few moments a tremendous explosion they knew was inevitable, and the rock must be rent in a thousand pieces. On perceiving their danger, they both leaped into the bucket, and called to the man on the surface to draw them up. He endeavored to do so, but his arm was found too feeble to raise the bucket while both the men were in it. What was to be done? The burning fuse, which could not be extinguished, was now within a few feet of the powder; a moment or to, and the explosion must take place. At this awful crisis, one of the men, addressing the other, said, "You shall live and I will die; for you are an impenitent sinner, and if you now die, your soul will be lost; but if I die, I know that, by the grace of the Lord Jesus Christ, I shall be taken to himself." And so saying, without waiting for a reply, he leaped out of the bucket and prayerfully waited the result. On the other reaching the surface, he bent over the shaft to ascertain the fate of his companion. At that moment a terrific explosion was heard; a portion of the rock was thrown up and smote him on the forehead, leaving an indelible mark to remind him of his danger and deliverance. But the man of God, when they came to search for him, was found arched over by the fragments of broken rock in the mine, uninjured, and rejoicing in the Lord. This magnanimous miner exhibited in this act an amount of disinterested love and charity which has seldom been equaled, and is never found but in connection with the love of Christ. Here is none of that unholy daring of which we have instances among the heroes of Greece and Rome, who, actuated solely by a love of notoriety, inflicted upon themselves tortures, and even death; but that pure Christian character, which at all hazards, even at the sacrifice of life itself, seeks to save the immortal soul of man. This is the kind of charity we have met this day to elicit, to strengthen, and to direct, and without which it is impossible that the great object of missionary enterprise can ever be accomplished.

(*d*) A PERSECUTOR SAVED.—The Rev. J. Underhill, a worthy and zealous minister of Christ, in Staffordshire, (Eng.) met with much persecution in his work. At one time appointed for public worship, an infuriated mob of more than 500, mostly colliers, collected, some armed with clubs, staves, and stones; others had horns and noisy instruments, determined, as they declared, to drive out the methodists, or to destroy them. While the people, and some ministers, were pursued by the rabble, a gentleman called out fiercely to the rioters, pointing to Mr. Underhill, "There is one of the methodist dogs; take notice of him; do your work well, and I will give you a barrel of ale at the end of it." Two of the ministers narrowly escaped with their lives. Mr. Underhill and a broth'r minister were dragged to a public house; the latter received such a violent blow with a poker from the landlord, that he never entirely recovered from its effects. But, mercifully for the landlord, that was to be his last sin in opposing the gospel. Some time afterwards, these very ministers met the landlord at a house where they supped together; and talking over former scenes of tribulation through which they had together passed, the minister said, "No part appeared so heinous as the conduct of the man who struck me when in quiet custody." He was desired to look on the company, and try to recognize the person. Time had effaced any recollection of his features. Mr. Underhill then said, "Behold, he dippeth with thee in the dish." Here an interesting scene took place. They wept on each other's necks, the landlord bewailing his crime, and entreating forgiveness; and the minister assuring him, that even the loss of life would have been richly repaid by the salvation of one soul.

(*e*) TEARS PREVAILING.—An ungodly youth, who had disregarded the pious advice of his parents, at length consented to accompany them to hear a popular minister, who visited the town in which they lived. The subject of the discourse was, the heavenly state, which was described by the most glowing and attractive representations. On returning home, the young man expressed his admiration of the preacher's talents—"But," said he, turning to his mother, "I was surprised, while the smile of joy was visible on the countenances of all around me, you and my father appeared gloomy and sad, and, more than once in tears. I was the more astonished, because I thought that if any could claim an interest in the subject, you were the happy persons." "Ah, my son," replied the anxious mother, "I did weep, not because I feared my own personal interest in the subject, or that of your affectionate and pious father, but I wept for you: it was the fear that you, my beloved child, would be forever banished from the blessedness of heaven, that caused me to give way to my bursting grief." "I supposed," said the father, turning to his wife, "that those were your reflections. The same concern for our dear son made me weep also." These pointed, yet tender and judicious remarks, found their way to the heart of their child. He felt them keenly; they wounded his hard heart, led him to repentance and to the cross of Christ for mercy and reconciliation, and terminated in his saving conversion.

(*f*) EXPERIENCE OF EDWARDS.—In the life of the Rev. Jonathan Edwards, which is prefixed to his History of Redemption, we find the following paragraphs selected from the narratives of his own religious experience. "I had then abundance of sweet religious conversation in the family where I lived, with Mr. J. Smith, and his pious mother. My heart was knit in affection to those in whom were appearances of true piety; and I could bear the thoughts of no other companions, but such as were holy, and the disciples of the blessed Jesus. I had great longing for the advancement of Christ's kingdom in the world, my secret prayer used to be in great part taken up in praying for it. If I heard the least hint of any thing that happened in any part of the world, that appeared to me in some respect or other to have a favorable aspect on the interest of Christ's kingdom, my soul eagerly catched at it, and it would much animate and refresh me. I used to be earnest to read public news letters, mainly for that end, to see if I could not find some news favorable to the interest of religion in the world."

(*g*) JOY OVER REPENTING SINNERS.—A pious Armenian, calling on Mr. Hamlin, the missionary at Constantinople, remarked that he was astonished to see how the people are waking up to the truth; how, even among the most uncultivated some are seeking after it as for hid treasure.—"Yes," said he, "it is going forward; it will triumph; but alas! I shall not live to see it. Alas! that I am born an age too soon." "But," said Mr. Hamlin, "do you remember what our Saviour said, 'There shall be joy in the presence of the angels of God over one sinner that repenteth?' You may not live to see the truth triumphant in this empire; but should you, through divine grace, reach the kingdom of heaven and be with the angels, your joy over your whole nation repentant and redeemed, will be infinitely greater than it could be on earth." He seemed surprised at this thought; but, after examining the various passages to which I referred him, he yielded to the evidence with the most lively expressions of delight, and seemed to be perfectly enraptured at the thought that our interest in the church of Christ and the progress of his kingdom on earth is something which death cannot touch, and which, instead of ceasing with this life, will only be increased and perfected in another. "Oh fool, and slow of heart," said he, "to read the gospel so many times without perceiving such a glorious truth. If this be so, no matter in what age a Christian was born, nor when he dies."

251. LUXURY.

(a) SUCCESSFUL REPROOF.—The Rev. Mr. S——, an eminent divine of the church of England, happened to dine with several other clergymen, in the house of a pious gentleman. After dinner, the conversation turned on the prevailing faults of professing Christians. Mr. S—— said, that one of the most obvious sins which those of them who are wealthy are apt to indulge in, is the keeping too good tables; that various courses, expensive removes, and luxurious dishes, savored too much of the world, had a tendency to draw away the heart from God, to cherish the desires of the carnal mind, and to make people fond of what is unworthy of a man's attention—good eating; and then, in his plain blunt way, he added, "I cannot help saying, that the dinner we had to-day was not quite agreeable to my ideas of Christian simplicity." The hint was taken, and though Mr. S—— repeatedly afterwards dined in the same house, he never once had occasion to repeat his remark.

(b) CRŒSUS' ADVICE TO CYRUS.—When Cyrus received intelligence that the Lydians had revolted from him, he told Crœsus, with a good deal of emotion, that he had almost determined to make them all slaves. Crœsus begged him to pardon them. "But," said he, "that they may no more rebel or be troublesome to you, command them to lay aside their arms, to wear long vests and buskins, that is, to vie with each other in the elegance and richness of their dress. Order them to drink, and sing, and play, and you will soon see their spirits broken, and themselves changed to the effeminacy of women, so that they will no more rebel, nor give you further uneasiness." The advice was followed, and the result proved how politic it was. While the advice is such as no good man could consistently follow, the incident shows the deteriorating influence of luxury in a very striking light.

(c) DINNER WITH BISHOP BUTLER.—The Rev. John Newton relates, that a friend of his once dined with Dr. Butler, then bishop of Durham; and though the guest was a man of fortune, and the interview by appointment, the provision was no more than a joint of meat and a pudding. The bishop apologized for his plain fare, by saying that it was his manner of living, and that being disgusted with the fashionable expense of time and money in entertainments, he was determined it should receive no countenance from his example. Nor was this conduct the result of covetousness; for, large as were his revenues, such was his liberality to the poor, that he left at his death little more than enough to discharge his debts and pay for his funeral.

252. LYING.

(a) LYING TO CHILDREN.—The Rev. Robert Hall had so great an aversion to every species of falsehood and evasion, that he sometimes expressed himself very strongly on the subject. The following is an instance, stated in his life by Dr. Gregory: Once, while he was spending an evening at the house of a friend, a lady, who was there on a visit, retired, that her little girl of four years old might go to bed. She returned in about half an hour, and said to a lady near her, "She is gone to sleep; I put on my night-cap, and lay down by her, and she soon dropped off." Mr. Hall, who overheard this, said, "Excuse me, madam: do you wish your child to grow up a liar?" "Oh dear, no, sir; I should be shocked at such a thing." "Then bear with me while I say, you must never act a lie before her: children are very quick observers, and soon learn that that which assumes to be what it is not, is a lie, whether acted or spoken." This was uttered with a kindness which precluded offence, yet with a seriousness that could not be forgotten.

(*b*) SUFFERING DEATH WHILE FEIGNING IT.—One day, as Archbishop Leighton was going from Glasgow to Dumblane, there happened a tremendous storm of lightning and thunder. He was observed, when at a considerable distance, by two men of bad character. They had not courage to rob him; but wishing to fall on some method to extort money from him, one said, "I will lie down by the way-side as if I were dead, and you shall inform the archbishop that I was killed by the lightning, and beg money of him to bury me." When the archbishop arrived at the spot, the wicked wretch told the fabricated story: the archbishop sympathized with the survivor, gave him money, and proceeded on his journey. But when the man returned to his companion, he found him really lifeless! Immediately he began to exclaim aloud, "Oh! sir, he *is* dead! Oh! sir, he *is* dead!" On this, the archbishop, discovering the fraud, left the man with this important reflection: "It is a dangerous thing to trifle with the judgments of God!"

(*c*) NOT AT HOME.—Bishop Atterbury was once addressed by some of his right reverend coadjutors to the following effect: "My lord, why will you not suffer your servants to deny you, when you do not care to see company? It is not a lie for them to say you are not at home, for it deceives no one; every body knowing it means only, that your lordship is busy." He replied, "My lords, if it is (which I doubt) consistent with sincerity, yet I am sure it is not consistent with that sincerity which becomes a Christian bishop." What a curious argument it is, that because a falsehood should be known to be such by those who hear it, they are bound to receive it as a truth, or to believe there is no guilt in uttering it!

(*d*) TWO APPEALS.—When Denades the orator addressed himself to the Athenians, "I call all the gods and goddesses to witness," said he, "the truth of what I shall say;" the Athenians, often abused by his impudent lies, presently interrupted him by exclaiming, "And we call all the gods and goddesses to witness that we will not believe you."

(*e*) DISSEMBLER'S INVITATION.—When Dr. Moore was in Paris, in the course of his travels, he one day found a lady of quality, whom he had been in the habit of visiting, manifesting much ill humor, and evidently betraying great agitation of mind. Dr. Moore, who had never before beheld her in such a state of confusion, suspected that some serious calamity had taken place; and, with much sympathetic feeling, inquired into the occasion of her perturbation. The lady, who felt the cause of her vexation in all its magnitude, instantly returned the following reply: "Why, my dear sir, I yesterday sent Comtesse de —— the politest message in the world, begging to have the honor of her company this day at dinner; and behold, the horrid woman, with a rudeness or ignorance of life without example, sends me word that she accepts my invitation!"

(*f*) THE LIAR TAKEN AT HIS WORD.—J—— W—— was a laborer employed on the Liverpool and Manchester railway. During part of the time in which he was thus employed, he lodged at Edge Hill, near Liverpool. There is reason to believe that he was a young man who had "no fear of God before his eyes;" that he was, in the expressive language of an inspired apostle, "without God in the world:" Eph. ii. 12. Becoming acquainted with a young woman, he succeeded in seducing her from the paths of virtue; and soon after, he removed to a new lodging, with a view to avoid the consequences of his conduct. The Almighty, in mercy to the sinner, sent affliction by illness to overtake him, and thus gave him time for repentance, and an opportunity to seek the love and favor of the Lord. But he refused the mercy and hardened his heart. In the course of the last week before he resumed his work, he called upon the person with whom he had formerly lodged, and among other things, asked whether old George (the young woman's father) ever came there to inquire after him. She replied that he did, and mentioned the time of his last inquiry. "Oh," said W—, "when he comes again, tell him that I was killed on the railway; and that I was buried in Childwall churchyard." Childwall is a village about a mile from part of the railway, and about four miles from Liverpool. Within a day or two old George called, and the above iniquitous and awful assertion was made. Deceived by the falsehood, the poor old man went away mourning over the disgrace of his daughter, and the supposed sad end of her base seducer. But the delusion was soon to be dissipated; the lie told, with a view to evade the consequences of previous guilt, was awfully, singularly, literally realized; and the wretched man, who had so impiously trifled with death, was hurried, in a moment, before the bar of his Maker.

On the following Monday morning, May 17, 1830, the laborer returned to work, and on the same day entered upon his everlasting state. Being on the road at the time when an engine, to which several wagons employed to convey rubbish were attached, was passing he was entangled with the apparatus, felled to the earth, and his body so dreadfully mangled, as to occasion instantaneous death. Thus the most affecting, and, to him, important part of his wicked fabrication, was made, by the mysterious providence of God, a solemn reality; and that of which he had no idea when he uttered the language above related, turned out, within a few days, to be a fact, namely, "That he was killed on the railway!"

But there was to be a further literal accomplishment of his words, which, although to him a matter of no consequence after the spirit had quitted the body, should not be passed over unobserved, as it tends to show, in a still more striking manner, that the Supreme Arbiter of life and death does indeed sometimes take men at their word, and fulfil their imprecations, their thoughtless wishes, or their blasphemous expressions, even to the very letter. J— W— had no immediate relations in the neighborhood in which he so unexpectedly expired. But since his removal to Edge Hill, he had lodged with a family who possessed a burial-place in Childwall churchyard. Some of his fellow workmen proposed his interment at Walton, a village three miles north of Liverpool: but others, on account of the nearness of Childwall, urged his burial there: and in a little more than a week after he had deliberately uttered a falsehood to deceive one he had deeply injured, his own awful words were fulfilled.

(*g*) A LIAR'S IMPRECATION ANSWERED.—A few years since, a woman in the Church Gate, Loughborough, (Eng.,) went to purchase a bedstead, which was sold to her for thirteen shillings, and change given her out of a one pound note, which she gave in payment. A short time after, she went again to the shop, and asserted that eighteen pence less than the proper change was given her. This the shopkeeper denied stating the exact coins he had given her. She, however, persisted in her declaration, and said, she wished she might die in his house if she had not spoken the truth. Awful to relate, she was immediately taken ill, was removed to another house, and soon after expired, never once speaking after she had left the shop. The money was found in her pocket, exactly as the shopkeeper had described.

(*h*) NEED OF WATCHING.—Dr. Johnson, giving advice to an intimate friend, said, "Above all accustom your children constantly to tell the truth, without varying in any circumstance." A lady present, emphatically exclaimed, "Nay, this is too much; for a little variation in narrative must happen a thousand times a day, if one is not perpetually watching." "Well, madam," replied the doctor, "and you ought to be perpetually watching. It is more from carelessness about truth than from intentional lying, that there is so much falsehood in the world."

(*i*) LYING, BLASPHEMING, AND DYING.—A poor woman in the workhouse at Milborne Port, (Eng.,) being once charged with having stolen some trivial article, which was missing, wished God might strike her dumb, blind, and dead, if she knew any thing of it. About six o'clock she ate her supper as well as usual—soon after, her speech faltered, her eyes closed, and before seven she was a breathless corpse, without any apparent cause.

253. MARRIAGE.

(*a*) PHILIP HENRY'S ADVICE. —The Rev. Philip Henry used to give two pieces of advice to his children and others, in reference to marriage. One was, "Keep within the bounds of profession." The other was, "Look at suitableness in age, quality, education, temper," etc. He used to observe, from Gen. ii. 18, "I will make him an help meet for him;" that where there is not meetness, there will not be much help. He commonly said to his children, with reference to their choice in marriage, "Please God, and please yourselves, and you shall never displease me;" and greatly blamed those parents who concluded matches for their children without their consent. He sometimes mentioned the saying of a pious gentlewoman, who had many daughters: "The care of most people is how to get good husbands for their daughters; but my care is to fit my daughters to be good wives, and then let God provide for them."

(*b*) MARRYING UNBELIEVERS. —The Rev. S. Kilpin, of Exeter, had witnessed the awful consequences produced in the church of Christ, and in families, from those who professed to be the disciples of Jesus, forming marriages contrary to the command,—"Be not unequally yoked with unbelievers,"—"only in the Lord," etc. As he never shunned to declare the whole counsel of God, this subject was presented to his congregation. The next day, a gentleman, whose name or residence he never knew, called to thank him for the discourse, adding, that his state of mind when he entered Exeter was most distressing, as he was on the very point of complying with a dreadful temptation, which would have embittered his future life. He had been a disciple of Christ, was anxious to consecrate his life to the service of his adorable Master, and had sought a helpmate to strengthen his hands in serving God. A lady, whom he deemed pious, had accepted his addresses; but when every customary arrangement was made, she had dishonorably discarded him. His mind was so exceedingly wounded and disgusted, that he had determined to choose a wife who made no profession of religion, and had fixed on another object for his addresses, with every prospect of success, although he had not as yet mentioned his intention to her. He added, "But the providence of God led me, an entire stranger in this city, to your meeting-house. You may suppose, that your subject arrested my attention. You appeared to be acquainted with every feeling of my soul. I saw my danger, and perceived the temptation, and the certain ruin of my peace if the dreadful snare had not been broken. You, sir, under God, have been my deliverer. By the next Sabbath I should have been bound in honor to an enemy of that Jesus whom I adore; for although she is moral and externally correct, yet she knows the Saviour only in name. I could not leave the city in peace until I had sought to make this communication." They unitedly addressed Him who can deliver, and does deliver his people. Thus, while part of his congregation thought it an unfit subject for the pulpit, at least one person received it as a message from God, by whom it was no doubt sent.

(*c*) CAN I BE HAPPY?—At Southampton, Eng., the labors of the venerable William Kingsbury had been eminently owned and blessed by God, in the conversion of sinners, and the building up of the church. "One Sabbath after the morning service, a respectable-looking elderly woman had come to the vestry, and requested to speak to Mr. Kingsbury. Being introduced, she said, she felt it her duty to take the first opportunity of meeting with him, to state that his ministry had been greatly blessed to her soul, and she hoped to praise God for it to all eternity. Mr. K. observed, that she was quite a stranger to him, he did not recollect having ever seen her before; and asked her where she resided, and how long she had attended his ministry. She replied, that she was a total stranger: having only heard him preach once before, and that more than forty years since, when she resided at Poole in Dorsetshire. She was at that time young, gay, and thoughtless; and on the point of forming a matrimonial connexion with a young man of similar character. According to their usual custom, they set out for a Sunday stroll; and having heard that a stranger was preaching, dropped in out of mere curiosity. The preacher was Mr. Kingsbury; it pleased Almighty God to carry home the word with power to her heart. She returned home, no longer the giddy thoughtless lover of pleasure; but deeply concerned to know what she should do to be saved. Her concern could not escape the notice of her companion, who endeavored to turn the matter into ridicule; but the "King's arrow was sharp in her heart," she could not forget the wound it had inflicted; nor could she find ease until relieved by the application of the "blood of sprinkling." The whole bias of her mind and pursuits now assumed a different direction; the pleasures of the world had no more charms for her; she could no longer idle away the precious hours of the Sabbath; she desired to hold communion with God in his house and ordinances. Under these circumstances, it very naturally occurred to her, "How can I make happy, or be happy with a partner in life, whose views and feelings on the most important of all subjects are the very opposite to my own?" She pursued the inquiry with fervent prayer for Divine direction, and came to the conclusion candidly to state to her lover the change of which she had become the subject; and, though she felt herself bound in honor to fulfil her engagements to him, to appeal to him whether the difference were not likely to be a source of more lasting unhappiness between them, than an honorable dissolution of present engagements by mutual consent. The young man admitted the force of her reasonings; he said he was certain he should never imbibe her religious views, and he feared he should be little inclined to tolerate them; they therefore agreed on a friendly separation. Feeling uncomfortable at residing in the same town with her late companion, and where their intimacy was generally known, she gladly embraced an opportunity of engaging herself to reside with a pious family in the north of England. There she became acquainted with, and was in due time married to one who feared God; with whom she had ever since lived in domestic happiness, and had brought up a family of eight children, every one of whom she had the happiness of seeing walking in the ways of God, and two, or more, filling stations of distinguished usefulness in the Christian church. One of the sons had just returned from abroad in ill health, and was at a hospital near Portsmouth. This had occasioned the mother's journey, to conduct him home; and, being in the neighborhood, she gladly embraced the opportunity of hearing and introducing herself to the minister to whom she felt indebted, under God, in everlasting obligations. Her son, she feared, was in a very precarious state of health; "But," said she, "I have good evidence that he is safe for time and for eternity. Oh, how different are my circumstances and prospects from what they would have been, if I had continued unconcerned about my own soul, or even had married an ungodly man, and become the mother of an ungodly, or at best a divided family!"

(*d*) THE DELUSIVE HOPE.—If there is no relation in life so eminently calculated to promote the happiness of man as a union of "kindred minds," in the matrimonal state; there is, on the other hand, no condition so full of wretchedness as that of two persons who have, without any reflection, indissolubly united themselves and who find subsequently that all their views and feelings are "wide as the poles asunder."

None can think of E. without a feeling of sadness. She was possessed of a high order of intellectual talent, a graceful person and a heart full of those tender sympathies which cannot fail to draw around their possessor, devoted friends. She was, moreover, a Christian. Being addressed by a person who was regarded by her friends as an "eligible match," she at length consented to a union with one who had but little to recommend him, except the position which mere wealth enabled him to occupy. "Although," said she, "he is not professedly pious, he is not openly profligate, and I trust I shall be enabled to exert such an influence, by precept and example, as shall eventuate in great good to his soul." Under this delusive hope, she entered upon her duties as a wife; but soon she discovered that instead of leading her husband to the performance of duty, there was *danger* of being *herself* drawn aside.

In the daily conduct of her husband she saw an exemplification of the truth, that "the natural heart is enmity against God." Bitter was her disappointment when she saw her companion, in following the dictates of his nature, wandering farther and farther from the path of rectitude, and consequently becoming more and more callous to good impressions.

Poor E——! she lived long enough to see him who had sworn to cherish and protect her, a drunkard, a gambler and a suicide. And though "in all her miseries" she never uttered a complaint yet as she laid down to die, wearied and heart-broken by the sorrows of a few brief years, she was doubtless ready to acknowledge in her heart the great error of her life, in disregarding the injunction of the apostle, "Be ye not unequally yoked together with unbelievers; for what fellowship hath righteousness with unrighteousness, and what communion hath light with darkness?"

(e) THE RESULTS OF A MARRIAGE.—The following significant account is condensed from a more detailed statement in one of the publications of the American Tract Society. Mr. R. A., of Maryland, with whom the writer was well acquainted, because hopefully pious at the age of twenty, and joined the church. His life for some time seemed consistent. At length he formed an attachment to a gay young lady, of great personal attractions, but an entire stranger to religion. She was by no means pleased with his religious views, but consented to the marriage in spite of them, thinking that in due time she would be able to cure him of his religious frenzy. She soon commenced the attempt. She urged him to go to places of diversion and amusement—told him that respectable persons would despise and laugh at him for having so much praying and reading in his house. "In fine," said she, "I married you to be happy, but I utterly despair of happiness unless you give up your religion and be like other people." He told her that he never found happiness in the way she proposed, and tried, like a Christian, to reason the case. Finding her efforts to change his mind unavailing, she refused to attend family devotion. He wept and prayed for her in secret. She continued to employ every stratagem her wicked imagination could invent. At length, wearied by her opposition, he gave up family prayer, and resolved that he would try to get to heaven alone. His wife pursued him to the closet, and at last succeeded in driving him to abandon every religious duty. And now that he forsook God, God forsook him; and the corruptions of his heart broke out into greater excesses than before. Some time after a powerful sermon roused his conscience, and he determined once more to enter upon the service of God; but he was still in an enemy's hands, and less able to resist than at first. His wife redoubled her efforts, and gained her point the second time. Now, wholly quitting the company of God's people, he sinned fearfully. In a few years he was laid on a bed of death. He was in awful anguish of mind—full of remorse and despair. He refused to be prayed with, insisting that his doom was already sealed.

Just before his departure, after he had

been rolling from side to side for some time, with horror depicted in every feature, he called to his wife to bring him a cup of cold water; "for," said he, "in one hour I shall be where I shall never get another drop." She brought him the water; he drank it with greediness, and reached back the cup with a trembling hand; then staring her in the face, his eyes flashing with terror, he cried out, "Rebecca, Rebecca, you are the cause of my eternal damnation." He turned over, and with an awful groan left the world.

(*f*) A WISE DECISION.—Eliza Ambert, a young Persian lady, resolutely discarded a gentleman to whom she was to have been married, because he ridiculed religion. Having given him a gentle reproof, he replied "that a man of the world could not be so old fashioned as to regard God and religion." Eliza started, but, on recovering herself, said, "From this moment, sir, when I discover that you do not regard religion, I cease to be yours. He who does not love and honor God can never love his wife constantly and sincerely."

(*g*) ADVICE OF THEMISTOCLES.—An Athenian who was hesitating whether to give his daughter in marriage to a man of worth with a small fortune, or to a rich man who had no other recommendation, went to consult Themistocles on the subject. "I would bestow my daughter," said Themistocles, "upon a man without money rather than upon money without a man."

254. MEEKNESS.

(*a*) DEERING ENDURING INSULT.—Mr. Deering, one of the puritan ministers in the sixteenth century, being at a public dinner, a young man, who sat on the opposite side of the table, indulged in profane swearing, for which Mr. D. sharply reproved him. The young man, taking this as an affront, immediately threw a glass of beer in his face. Mr. Deering took no notice of the insult, but wiped his face, and continued his dinner. The young gentleman presently renewed his profane conversation; and Mr. D. reproved him as before; upon which, but with increased violence, he threw another glass of beer in his face. Mr. Deering continued unmoved, still showing his zeal for the glory of God, by bearing the insult with Christian meekness. This so astonished the young gentleman that he rose from the table, fell on his knees, and asking Mr. Deering's pardon, declared that if any of the company had offered him similar insults, he would have stabbed them with his sword. Here was practically verified the New Testament maxim, "Be not overcome of evil, but overcome evil with good."

(*b*) PERSECUTING HUSBAND SUBDUED.—A woman who had derived spiritual benefit from the discourses of Mr. Robinson of Leicester, was often threatened by her wicked husband for going to St. Mary's church, in which Mr. R. officiated. His feelings were at length wrought up to such a pitch that he declared, with an awful oath, that if ever she went to St. Mary's again, he would cut off her legs. Having sought direction in prayer, she was strengthened to go to the place where oft she had been made joyful in the Lord. On her return from church, she found her husband waiting her arrival, and as soon as she had shut the door, he said in an angry tone. "Where have you been?" She replied, "At St. Mary's." He instantly struck her a violent blow on the face, and she fell to the ground; but rising from the floor, she turned the other side of her face, and in a mild and affectionate manner said, "My dear, if you serve this side the same, I hope I shall bear it with patience." Struck with this meek answer, for she had been a very passionate woman, he said, "Where did you learn that?" She replied, in a gentle manner, "At St. Mary's church, my dear." "Well," said he, "if that is what you learn at St. Mary's, you may go as oft as you like, I will never hinder you again."

This good woman enjoyed her privileges undisturbed, and also had the pleasure, a short time afterwards, of having her husband to accompany her.

(*c*) MEEKNESS OF DODD.—It is said of Mr. Dodd, one of the puritan divines, that a person being enraged at his close and awakening doctrine, raised a quarrel with him, smote him in the face, and dashed out two of his teeth, This meek and lowly servant of Christ, without taking the least offence, held the teeth out in his hand, and said, "See here, you have knocked out two of my teeth without any just provocation; but if I could do your soul good, I would give you leave to dash out all the rest." Thus he was not overcome of evil, but overcame evil with good.

(*d*) MEEKNESS OF M. HENRY.—It is well known, that many of the most eminent ministers of Christ, during the seventeenth century, were the subjects of great persecution. Among others who were thus cruelly treated was the excellent Matthew Henry; but when maligned and reproached, he showed great meekness and patience; and, instead of rendering evil for evil, requited it with good; ever seeking to improve such occurrences for his own advancement in Christian virtue. "How pleasant is it," he would say, "to have the bird in the bosom sing sweetly."

(*e*) MEEKNESS OF LEIGHTON.—Of Bishop Leighton, Bishop Burnet declared that during a strict intimacy of many years, he never saw him for one moment in any other temper than that in which he would wish to live and die.

(*f*) THE MISSIONARIES AND THE HINDOO.—A baboo, (that is, a wealthy Hindoo,) at Chinsurah, sent a message to the missionaries residing there, intimating that a very learned Brahmin was in his house, and that he and his friends very much wished to hear this Brahmin and the missionaries engage in an amicable dispute respecting the merits of Hindooism and Christianity. Two of the missionaries went. The Brahmin opened the debate, charged the missionaries with bad motives, and misrepresented their doctrines in an ill-tempered manner.

The missionaries stated in reply, that Christianity was a religion of love; that God so loved the world as to send his only-begotten Son, the Lord Jesus Christ into it; that the Son of God so loved the fallen race of man as to give his life a sacrifice for their sins; and that missionaries were impelled to leave their beloved relatives and friends, and the comforts of their native home, from the same principle. They then explained the leading truths of Christianity, the substance of which was, that all men every where ought to worship that God that made them, and to worship him alone.

The Brahmin's countenance underwent a change as the missionaries were speaking, and in his rejoinder he said, "I am a Brahmin, and cannot, therefore, be expected to say, that I deem Christianity to be superior to Hindooism; but, in candor, I must say, that the temper of these Christians is superior to that of us Hindoos. Gentlemen," the Brahmin said, turning to the missionaries, "your temper is *boro prarthoneco;*" that is, greatly to be prayed for. "We took our leave," say the missionaries, "convinced that the cause of Christianity had that day risen in the opinion of some influential inhabitants of Chinsurah."

255. MEMORY AND PIETY.

(*a*) PRACTICAL MEMORY.—A minister in Wiltshire, walking near a brook, observed a poor woman washing wool in the stream; which is done by placing it in a sieve, and dipping it in the water repeatedly, until it is white and clean. He engaged in conversation with her, and, from some expressions of regret and gratitude which she uttered, was induced to ask her if she knew him. "O yes, sir," she replied, "and I hope I shall have reason to bless God for you to all eternity. I heard you preach at W——, some years back; and hope your sermon was the means of doing me great good.'

"Indeed, I rejoice to hear it; pray what was the subject?" "Ah, sir, I can't recollect that; mine is such a bad head." "How then can it have done you good, if you don't even remember it?" "Sir, my poor mind is like this sieve; the sieve doesn't hold the water, but it runs through and cleanses the wool: my memory does not keep the words, but, blessed be God, he made them touch the heart: and now I don't love sin; I go whenever I can to hear of Jesus Christ; and I beg of him every day to wash me in his own blood, which cleanses from all sin."

(*b*) TWO THINGS REMEMBERED.—Rev. Mr. Newton, when his memory was nearly gone, used to say, that forget what he might, he never forgot two things,—1st, That he was a great sinner,—2d, That Jesus Christ was a great Savior. Two most important subjects of recollection.

(*c*) NEWTON'S MEMORY OF SCRIPTURE.—Mr. Newton, telling in company one day, how much his memory was decayed, "There," said he. "last Wednesday, after dinner, I asked Mrs. C—— what I had been about that forenoon, for I could not recollect. Why, said she you have been preaching at St. Mary's. Yet it is wonderful, when I am in the pulpit, I can recollect any passage of Scripture I want to introduce into my sermon, from Genesis to Revelation."

256. MERIT OF GOOD WORKS.

(*a*) NIGHT UNDER A HEDGE.—A poor blind man, by the name of Philip (writes a minister from Ireland) who was also very deaf and imbecile, being a member of my congregation, I interested myself to give him particular instructions in the plan of salvation, hoping, by patience, perseverance, and plainness, to make him understand the simplest truths of the Gospel; yet after a long time, and much labor, I found that not the least impression had been made. One day, (after having visited him for a year,) I repeatedly told him that in the Lord Jesus Christ alone was found salvation for sinners, and then begged of him to tell me how he hoped to be saved. He considered for a time, the perspiration pressing through every pore of his face, and replied in the most placid manner I ever witnessed: "Don't you think, sir, that if I was to spend a cold frosty night under a hawthorn bush, it would go a good way towards it?" He afterwards, however, became a humble believer, and trusted in Christ alone for salvation.

How many persons of vastly better advantages, have just as absurd and unscriptural views of the plan of salvation as the subject of the foregoing sketch? Men are much more disposed to attach merit to their own sufferings, than to rely on the sufferings of Christ. But the first principle of salvation for the sinner to learn is, that he cannot save himself.

(*b*) THE NOBLEMAN'S MISTAKE.—The late Rev. C. J. Latrobe visited a certain nobleman in Ireland, who devoted considerable sums to charitable purposes; and, among other benevolent acts, had erected an elegant church at his own expense. The nobleman, with great pleasure, showed Mr. L. his estate, pointed him to the church, and said, "Now, sir, do you not think that will merit heaven?" Mr. Latrobe paused for a moment, and said, "Pray, my lord, what may your estate be worth a year?" "I imagine," said the nobleman, "about thirteen or fourteen thousand pounds." "And do you think, my lord," answered the minister, "that God would sell heaven, even for thirteen or fourteen thousand pounds?"

(*c*) IMPIOUS EPITAPH.—The following epitaph is inscribed upon a monument in one of the Roman Catholic chapels, in the city of Cork:—"J. H. S

Sacred to the memory of the benevolent Edward Molloy, the friend of humanity, the father of the poor; he employed the wealth of this world, only to procure the riches of the next; and leaving a balance of merit on the book of life, he made heaven debtor to mercy. He died 17th October, 1818, aged 90. R J. P." How daring the impiety of making the Creator debtor to his creature!

(*d*) ELLIOT AND HIS LABORS.—When Mr. John Elliot, from advanced age and infirmities, was laid aside from his former employments, he sometimes said, with an air peculiar to himself, "I wonder for what the Lord Jesus lets me live. He knows that now I can do nothing for him." Speaking of his labors among the American Indians, he expressed himself thus:—"There is a cloud, a dark cloud, on the work of the gospel among the poor Indians. The Lord revive and prosper that work, and grant that it may live, when I am dead. It is a work which I have been doing much about. But what have I said? I recall that word. My doings! Alas! they have been poor, and small, and I will be the man that shall throw the first stone at them." He died in 1690, aged eighty-six.

(*e*) UNSUCCESSFUL PREACHING.—"I preached up sanctification very earnestly for six years in a former parish," says the Rev. Mr. Bennet in a letter, "and never brought one soul to Christ. I did the same at this parish, for two years, without having any success at all; but as soon as ever I preached Jesus Christ, and faith in his blood, then believers were added to the church occasionally; then people flocked from all parts to hear the glorious sound of the gospel, some coming six, others eight, and others ten miles, and that constantly. The reason why my ministry was not blessed, when I preached up salvation partly by faith, and partly by works, is, because the doctrine is not of God."

(*f*) HERVEY AND THE PLOUGHMAN.—In the parish where Mr. Hervey preached, when he inclined to loose sentiments, there resided a ploughman, who usually attended the ministry of Dr. Doddridge, and was well informed in the doctrines of grace. Mr. Hervey being advised by his physician, for the benefit of his health, to follow the plough, in order to smell the fresh earth, frequently accompanied this ploughman in his rural employment. Mr. Hervey, understanding the ploughman was a serious person, said to him one morning, "What do you think is the hardest thing in religion?" To which he replied, "I am a poor illiterate man, and you, sir, are a minister: I beg leave to return the question." "Then," said Mr. Hervey, "I think the hardest thing is to deny sinful self;" and applauded at some length, this instance of self-denial. The ploughman replied, "Mr. Hervey, you have forgotten the greatest act of the grace of self-denial, which is to deny ourselves of a proud confidence in our own obedience for justification." In repeating this story to a friend, Mr. Hervey observed: "I then hated the righteousness of Christ: I looked at the man with astonishment and disdain, and thought him an old fool. I have since clearly seen who was the fool; not the wise old Christian, but the proud James Hervey."

(*g*) BISHOP ASBURY'S TESTIMONY.—Bishop Asbury being asked his thoughts on imputed righteousness, observed, "Were I disposed to boast, my boasting would be found true. I obtained religion near the age of thirteen. At the age of sixteen I began to preach, and traveled some time in Europe. At twenty-six I left my native land, and bid adieu to my weeping parents, and crossed the boisterous ocean, to spend the balance of my days in a strange land, partly settled by savages. I have traveled through heat and cold for forty-five years. In thirty years I have crossed the Alleghany mountains fifty-eight times. I have often slept in the woods, without necessary food or raiment. In the southern states I have waded swamps, and led my horse for miles, where I took colds that brought on the diseases which are now preying on my system, and must soon terminate in death. But my mind is still the same, that it is through the merits of CHRIST I am to be saved."

(*h*) WILKINSON'S DYING CONFESSION.—When the venerable Mr. Wilkinson had reached nearly the close of his life, he said to a relative who came to visit him, and who attempted to cheer him by referring to his Christian character, "Ah, you cannot see my heart. It has always been my endeavor not only to abstain from evil, but from all appearance of evil—but I would be jealous of my own heart. The heart is deceitful above all things, and desperately wicked: who can know it? Well, I must do as I have ten thousand times before under such feelings, cast myself entirely on the mercy of God. 'God be merciful to me a sinner'—the vilest of sinners! and, after all I have *received*, a most ungrateful sinner! *I shall never get beyond that prayer*."

(*i*) PRAYER AND GOOD WORKS.—"It has been often observed," says Dr. Owen, in his Doctrine of Justification, "that the schoolmen themselves, in their meditations and devotional writings, speak a language quite different from that which they use in their disputes and controversies; and I had rather learn what men really think on this head from their prayers than from their writings. Nor do I remember that I ever heard any good man, in his prayers, use any expressions about justification, wherein any thing of self-righteousness was introduced. Nor have I observed that any public liturgies (the Mass-Book excepted), guide men in their prayers before God to plead any thing for their acceptance with him, or as the means or condition thereof, but grace, mercy, the righteousness and blood of Christ alone."

(*j*) CHALMERS' CONFESSION.—Dr. Chalmers, who preached the liberal system twelve years, and after this the evangelical, says, "I cannot but record the effect of an actual though undesigned experiment which I prosecuted for upwards of twelve years among you. For the greater part of that time, I could expatiate on the meanness of dishonesty, on the villany of falsehood, on the despicable arts of calumny, in a word, upon all those deformities of character which awaken the natural indignation of the human heart against the pests and disturbers of human society. Even at this time I certainly did press the reformations of honor, and truth, and integrity, among my people; but I never once heard of any such reformations having been effected amongst them. If there was any thing at all brought about in this way, it was more than ever I got any account of. I am not sensible, that all the vehemence with which I urged the virtues and proprieties of social life, had the weight of a feather on the moral habits of my parishioners. And it was not until I got impressed by the utter alienation of the heart in all its desires and affections from God, it was not till reconciliation to Him became the distinct and prominent object of my ministerial efforts, it was not till I took the scriptural way of laying the method of reconciliation before them, it was not till the free offer of forgiveness through the blood of Christ was urged upon their acceptance, and the Holy Ghost given through the channel of Christ's mediatorship to all who ask him, was set before them as the unceasing object of their dependence and their prayers; it was not, in one word, till the contemplations of my people were turned to these great and essential elements in the business of a soul providing for its interest with God, and the concerns of its eternity, that I ever heard of any of those subordinate reformations which I aforetime made the earnest and zealous, but I am afraid, at the same time, the ultimate object of my earlier administrations."

(*k*) CONVERTED MORALIST'S CONFESSION.—In a revival in one of the New England states, one of the subjects was a moralist, who is thus described by an acquaintance:

He was a young gentleman, of good natural abilities, of respectable standing in society, and of irreproachable integrity. In his dealings with others he was accounted strictly honorable, and his exemplary observance of the externals of religion gained him the appellation of "*very* moral." He was also "righteous in his own eyes." Though he gave full credence to the word of God, and professed to believe the necessity of regeneration and justification by the righteousness of Christ, yet he was often heard to assert, that he feared not to enter eternity, and appear before his Judge. He believed that, according to his ability, he had complied with all the requisitions of Jehovah's law, and that the Redeemer would at last receive his soul, and wash it from all its original pollution. One thing however was against him: the discriminating doctrines of the cross were ever offensive.

But the Spirit of the Most High has lately unveiled to him his heart, and taught him the *spirit* of the divine law. His convictions were long and pungent. With tears and heart-rending repentance he confessed his former blindness, his ignorance of himself and of God, and was constrained to cry aloud for the mercy of Heaven to save his soul. The Savior heard him, and appeared for his relief. His joys, though humble, were ecstatic, and his soul seemed to be "filled with the fullness of God." Since that time his triumphing spirit has left the world, and joined the assembly of the redeemed above. In his dying moments he left with a friend the following charge to me:

"Tell —— that his *moral* friend has found himself to be *immoral*, *unholy*, and *unclean*. Tell him also that his friend has found salvation in the blood of Jesus, and is now going to join his Redeemer in the heavens. Tell him to charge the young and giddy that for all their follies God will bring them into judgment—that if they would procure peace of conscience, and solid enjoyment, they must believe in the Infinite Savior, and experience the benefits of the infinite atonement. Tell him to make use of my case in warning sinners to flee from the wrath to come, with the earnest prayer that my death may be the means of converting some soul. Tell him the world is receding. Farewell."

(*l*) THE PLANK OF FREE GRACE.—Mr. M'Laren, and Mr. Gustart, were both ministers of the Tolbooth Church, Edinburgh. When Mr. M'Laren was dying, Mr. G. paid him a visit, and put the question to him, "What are you doing, brother?" His answer was, "I'll tell you what I am doing, brother; I am gathering together all my prayers, all my sermons, all my good deeds, all my ill deeds; and I am going to throw them all overboard, and swim to glory on the plank of Free Grace."

(*m*) POPULAR PREACHING.—A Christian minister once said to a Socinian preacher, "You are always telling people the worth of their good works, flattering them, &c.; now we tell them of their depravity, sinfulness, and danger; yet few come and hear you, while our houses are filled. Can you assign a reason for this?" He said he could not. "Well," said the minister, "I will tell you; there is a conviction on people's minds, that what we preach is truth, and what you preach is falsehood."

(*n*) REASON FOR PREACHING CHRIST.—The Rev. Mr. Venn, an evangelical and faithful minister of Christ, was one day addressed by a neighoring clergyman in nearly the following words: "Mr. Venn, I don't know how it is, but I should really think your doctrines of grace and faith were calculated to make all your hearers live in sin, and yet I must own that there is an astonishing reformation wrought in your parish; whereas I don't believe I ever made one soul the better, though I have been telling them their duty for many years." Mr. Venn was pleased at the clergyman's honest confession, and frankly told him he would do well to burn all his old sermons, and try what preaching Christ would do.

(*o*) PLACE TO LOSE SELF.—A person who had long practised many austerities, without finding any comfort or change of heart, was once complaining to the Bishop of Alst of his state. "Alas," said he, "self-will and self-righteousness follow me every where. Only tell me when you think I shall learn to leave self. Will it be by study, or prayer, or good works?" "I think," replied the bishop, "that the place where you lose self, will be that where you find your Savior."

MINISTERS, CHRISTIAN.

257. Call to the Ministry.

(*a*) DR. DODDRIDGE'S CALL.—When Dr. Doddridge was a young man, and had an earnest desire to engage in the duties of the Christian ministry, he waited upon Dr. E. Calamy on the subject. The doctor advised him to turn his attention to some other pursuit. Young Doddridge felt grieved to receive such advice, but after a few weeks resolved to enter on the study of the law. His mind was yet agitated, and he resolved to devote a morning to special prayer before he formed his final decision. While thus engaged, the postman brought him a letter from Dr. Clarke, telling him he had heard of his difficulties, and was ready to receive him under his care, to prepare him for his future important duties. He very properly regarded this as an instance of the Divine goodness, and to this fact may be attributed, under God, his subsequent usefulness in the Christian church.

(*b*) A KEEN RETORT.—A writer in the Georgetown Baptist Herald, says, "A preacher, not one hundred miles from this, while contending, as he thought, for the "ancient order of things," by ridiculing the doctrine of a call to the ministry, as proof that there is no such call, observed, that he never believed *he* was called to preach,—"*And no person else ever believed it,*" said an acquaintance standing by.

(*c*) THE FARMER BECOMING A MINISTER.—The late Rev. R. Hill writes thus:—A certain farmer, well known to me, was always moral, yet ignorant of the gospel. By reading some of the sermons of the late Mr. Romaine, he was called to the knowledge of the truth. The farmer was a man of good sense and great integrity; and he now conceived his domestics should not live without family worship. In his kitchen the Bible was always as much in sight as the bacon-rack; and when he read the Bible to them, he could not but express the simple feelings of his heart. He wept, and they wept in concert. And in prayer, he found he was not wanting in "the spirit of grace and of supplications." Thus being enabled to tell his own wants before his family, they began to find out their wants also. This answered the end. The family was filled with surprise, and they surprised their neighbors, who stole in to unite in this worship. They now requested him to preach; but the modest farmer resisted the call. He had a gracious sister, who charged him not to fight against God, for that others, besides his own family, were benefited by their attendance. The farmer consented; yet he was no enthusiast, but a solid, pious, thinking man, and had a good knowledge of his Bible: and no man of good sense, though he has neither Greek, Latin, nor logic, will ever talk nonsense. Thus he commenced a preacher, and was wonderfully blessed: quite the apostle, the reformer of the neighborhood. The generous public speedily accommodated the farmer with a convenient place of worship, in the town. The farmer was solemnly ordained to the pastoral charge, and the communion among them was very seriously and largely attended.

258. Industry, Energy, and Devotion to their Work.

(*a*) INDUSTRY OF LUTHER.—From 1517 to 1526, the first ten years of the Reformation, the number of Luther's publications was three hundred; from 1527 to 1536, the second decade, the number was two hundred and thirty-two; and 1537 to 1546, the year of his death, the number was one hundred and eighty-three. His first book was published in November, 1517, and he died in February, 1546, an interval of twenty-nine years and four months. In this time he published seven hundred and fifteen, an average of more than twenty-five a year, or one a fortnight of his public life. He did not go through the manual labor of all this writing, it is true, for many of his published works were taken down from his lips by his friends; and it is also true, that several of the volumes were small enough in size to be denominated pamphlets; but many of them are also large and elaborate treatises. In the circumstances in which he wrote, his translation of the Bible alone, would have been a gigantic task, even if he had his lifetime to devote to it.

(*b*) LABORS OF CALVIN.—Dr. Hoyle, who wrote under the patronage of Archbishop Usher, mentioning Calvin, says, "What shall I speak of his indefatigable industry, almost beyond the power of nature; which, paralleled with our loitering, will, I fear, exceed all credit! It may be the truest object of admiration, how one lean, worn, spent, and wearied body could hold out. He read, every week of the year through, three divinity lectures; every other week, over and above, he preached every day: so that (as Erasmus said of Chrysostom) I know not whether more to admire his constancy, or theirs that heard him. Some have reckoned his yearly lectures to be *one hundred and eighty-six*, and his yearly sermons *two hundred and eighty-six*. Every Thursday he sat in the presbytery. Every Friday, when the ministers met to consult upon difficult texts, he made as good as a lecture. Besides all this, there was scarcely a day that exercised him not in answering, either by word of mouth or writing, the doubts and questions of different churches and pastors; so that he might say with Paul, 'The care of all the churches lieth upon me.' Scarcely a year passed wherein, over and above all these employments, some great volume, in folio, or other size, came not forth."

This celebrated man, even in his dying illness, would not refrain from his labors; but, when his friends endeavored to persuade him to ease himself, he replied, "What! shall my Lord come and find me idle?"

(*c*) DEATH IN VIEW.—Some years ago, the Rev. Dr. Henry Peckwell stepped into a dissecting room and touched one of the dead bodies, forgetting that he had just before accidentally cut his finger. He became diseased and the doctors who were called in pronounced the accident fatal. At that time worship was held at the Tabernacle, Moorfields, on a Friday evening. Conscious of his approaching death, the good man ascended the pulpit, and preached in so powerful a strain as to make many of his audience weep. At the conclusion, he told the audience that it was his farewell sermon,—"not like the ordinary farewell sermons of the world, but more impressive, from the circumstances, than any preached before. My hearers shall long bear it in mind, when this frail earth is mouldering in its kindred dust!" The congregation could not conjecture his meaning, but on the following Sabbath an unknown preacher ascended the pulpit, and informed them that their pious minister had breathed his last on the preceding evening.

(*d*) WAITING THE LORD'S TIME.—When the Rev. George Whitefield was last in America, the Rev. W. Tennent paid him a visit, as he was passing through New Jersey; and one day dined with him, and other ministers, at a gentleman's house. After dinner, Mr. W. adverted to the difficulties attending the gospel ministry; lamented that all their zeal availed but little; said, that he was weary with the burden of the day; and declared the great consolation, that in a short time his work would be done, when he should depart and be with Christ. He then appealed to the ministers if it was not their great comfort that they should soon go to rest. They generally assented, except Mr. T. who sat next to Mr. W. in silence, and by his countenance discovered but little pleasure in the conversation. On which Mr. W. tapping him on the knee said, "Well, brother Tennent, you are the oldest man among us; do you not rejoice to think that your time is so near at hand, when you will be called home?" Mr. T. bluntly answered, "I have no wish about it." Mr. W. pressed him again. Mr. T. again again answered, "No, sir, it is no pleasure to me at all; and if you knew your duty, it would be none to you. I have nothing to do with death; my business is to live as long as I can, as well as I can, and to serve my Master as faithfully as I can, until he shall think proper to call me home." Mr. W. still urged for an explicit answer to his question, in case the time of death were left to his own choice. Mr. T. replied, "I have no choice about it; I am God's servant, and have engaged to do his business as long as he pleases to continue me therein. But now, brother, let me ask you a question. What do you think I should say, if I were to send my man into the field to plough; and if at noon I should go to the field, and find him lounging under a tree, and complaining, 'Master, the sun is very hot, and the ploughing hard; I am weary of the work you have appointed me, and am overdone with the heat and burden of the day. Do, master, let me return home, and be discharged from this hard service?' What should I say? Why, that he was a lazy fellow, and that it his business to do the work that I had appointed him, until I should think fit to call him home."

(*e*) MR. WILKS AND HIS MASTER'S BUSINESS —An aged American minister states, that in the early part of his ministry, being in London, he called on the late Rev. Matthew Wilks. Mr. W. received him with courtesy, and entered into conversation, which was kept up briskly till the most important religious intelligence in possession of each had been imparted. Suddenly there was a pause—it was broken by Mr. W. "Have you any thing more to communicate?" "No, nothing of special interest." "Any further inquiries to make?" "None." "Then you must leave me; I have my Master's business to attend to—good morning." "Here," says the minister, "I received a lesson on the impropriety of intrusion, and on the most manly method of preventing it."

(*f*) BUNYAN'S ZEAL.—Bunyan, with irresistible zeal, preached throughout the country, especially in Bedfordshire and its neighborhood; until, on the restoration of Charles II, he was thrown into prison, where he remained twelve years. During his confinement he preached to all to whom he could gain access; and when liberty was offered to him, on condition of promising to abstain from preaching, he constantly replied, "If you let me out to-day, I shall preach again to-morrow."

(*g*) BAXTER'S LABORS.—The eminently pious Richard Baxter, after he had spent many years in the advancement of the glory of God, by laborious and constant preaching, unceasing pastoral labors, and numerous publications from the press, was yet unwilling to give himself ease, even amidst the infirmities of disease and age. An old gentleman, who heard him preach, related, that when he ascended the pulpit, with a man following him to prevent his falling backwards, and to support him, if needful, in the pulpit, many persons would be ready to say he was more fit for a coffin than for labor; but all this he would soon forget, and manifest the fervor and energy of youth in his labors. It was feared, the last time he preached, that he would have died in the pulpit. And yet, such was his humility, that when reminded of his labors on his death-bed, he replied, "I was but a pen in God's hand, and what praise is due to a pen?"

(*h*) PREPARING FOR THE PULPIT.—Mr. Thomas Shephard was an excellent preacher, and took great pains in his preparations for the pulpit. He used to say, "God will curse that man's labors who goes idly up and down all the week, and then goes into his study on a Saturday afternoon. God knows that we have not too much time to pray in, and weep in, and get our hearts into a fit frame for the duties of the Sabbath."

(*i*) LATIMER'S LABORS.—Every season of a religious revival has been marked by ministerial zeal and diligence. These features eminently distinguished the British reformers. Latimer, in particular, was remarkable for his care in preaching and visiting every part of his diocese, earnestly trying to reform whatever was amiss. Although advanced in life, he traveled continually from place to place, teaching, exhorting, and preaching, to the utmost of his ability. These journeys were mostly performed on foot, with few attend ants, in a plain dress, with a pair of spectacles, and a New Testament hanging at his girdle. Wherever he went he preached to the people; and if he found a number assembled together, and no church at hand, he did not hesitate to preach to them in any place which offered, and sometimes used a hollow tree for a pulpit.

(*j*) IMPOSSIBLE TO STOP PREACHING.—Mr. Cecil tells us that when Mr. Newton had passed eighty years of age, some of his friends feared he might continue his public ministrations too long. They not only observed his infirmities in the pulpit, but felt much on account of the decrease of his strength, and of his occasional depressions. On these things being mentioned to him, he replied, that he had experienced nothing which in the least affected the principles he had felt and taught; that his depressions were the natural result of fourscore years; and that, at any age, we can only enjoy that comfort from our principles which God is pleased to send. "But," it was asked, "in the article of public preaching, might it not be best to consider your work as done, and to stop before you evidently discover that you can speak no longer?" "I cannot stop," said he, raising his voice. "What! shall the old African blasphemer stop while he can speak?"

(*k*) PAYSON'S LOVE FOR PREACHING.—Never has the ruling passion been more strongly exemplified in the hour of death than in the case of this excellent American minister. His love for preaching was as invincible as that of the miser for gold, who dies grasping his treasure. He directed a label to be attached to his breast when dead, with the admonition, "Remember the words which I spake unto you while I was yet present with you;" that they might be read by all who came to look at his corpse, and by which he, being dead, still spoke. The same words were at the request of his people engraved on the plate of the coffin, and read by thousands on the day of his interment.

(*l*) CECIL'S LOVE FOR STUDY. It is recorded of the late Rev. R. Cecil, that he never seemed weary of his studies. They were not only his business, but his enjoyment and recreation, and he used to call them his *rest*. He felt any interruptions of them required acts of self-denial, and always returned to his study with pleasure. Few more carefully aimed to redeem time, and to spend it only in what was worthy of a man and a Christian minister; often repeating—

> For at back I always hear
> Time's winged chariot hurrying near;
> And onward, all before I see
> Deserts of vast eternity.

(*m*) LABORS OF WESLEY.—Among other features in the character of Mr. Wesley, which manifested his devotedness to the great work in which he had engaged, it is said that he ever retained a cheerful insensibility to pain, and even to neglect. As he was traveling with John Nelson, one of his preachers, from common to common, in Cornwall, and preaching to a people who heard him willingly, but seldom or never offered him the slightest hospitality, he one day stopped his horse at some brambles, to pick the fruit. "Brother Nelson," said he, as he did so, "we ought to be thankful that there are plenty of blackberries, for this is the best country I ever saw for getting a stomach, but the worst I ever knew for getting food. Do the people think we can live upon preaching?" "At that time," says his companion, "Mr. Wesley and I slept on the floor; he had a great coat for his pillow, and I had Burkitt's Notes on the New Testament for mine. One morning, about three o'clock, Mr. Wesley turned over, and finding me awake, clapped me on the side, saying, 'Brother Nelson, let us be of good cheer; I have one whole side yet; for the skin is off but on one side.'"

For more than fifty years, in succession, this eminent man generally delivered two, and frequently three or four sermons in a day. But calculating at the lowest estimate, and allowing fifty annually for extraordinary occasions, the whole number, during this period, will be forty thousand five hundred and sixty. To these may be added innumerable exhortations to the societies after preaching, and in other occasional meetings at which he assisted or presided. His journeys, in the work of the ministry, during so long a period, were extraordinary, and probably, on the whole, without a precedent. He traveled about four thousand five hundred miles every year, on an average; and thus, in his long course, he passed over two hundred and twenty-five thousand miles, on his errand of mercy, after he became an itinerant preacher. In addition to all which, the publications which he either wrote, or otherwise prepared for the press, were very numerous. It would have been impossible for him to perform this almost incredible degree of labor, without great punctuality and care in the management of his time. He had stated hours for every purpose, and his only relaxation was a change of employment. His talents for managing complex affairs, and governing a numerous body, dissimilar in its parts, and widely diffused throughout the whole nation, were displayed in the order which he introduced into the societies he had formed, the control which he exercised over them, and the plans he devised and executed for the continuance of that economy which he had established among them.

(*n*) NUMBER OF WHITEFIELD'S SERMONS.—From a memorandum book, in which Mr. Whitefield recorded the times and places of his ministerial labors, it appears that from the period of his ordination to that of his death, which was thirty-four years, he preached upwards of *eighteen thousand sermons*. It would be difficult to tell the many thousand miles that he traveled. It is said that this celebrated man, when advanced in life, finding his physical powers failing him, undertook to put himself upon what he called "short allowance." He preached once only on every day in the week, and three times on the Sabbath!

(*o*) WHITEFIELD'S FIRST VOYAGE TO AMERICA.—There is a most interesting position in which we may look at Whitefield. This was during his first voyage to America, a stripling in his twenty-third year. Perhaps, since Paul's memorable voyage to Rome, the ocean has never exhibited a more surprising spectacle than that furnished by this ship. Such a situation would have paralyzed any ordinary man. A faint and hesitant homage, once on the Sabbath day, from a few of the less obdurate, would be all that such a man could possibly have expected to extort from an assemblage of gentlemen, of soldiers, with their wives and families, and the ship's company. Yet they became pliant as a willow in the hands of this remarkable youth. He accordingly converted the chief cabin into a cloister, the deck into a chapel, and the steerage into a school-room! He so bore down all by love, reason, and Scripture, that we soon behold him, at the request of the captain and officers, with the hearty concurrence of the gentlemen, reading "full public prayers" to them, twice a day, in the great cabin, and expounding every night after the evening prayers, besides daily reading prayers and preaching twice a day on deck to the soldiers and sailors, and increasing the services on Sundays. In addition, he daily catechised a body of young soldiers, and also catechised the women apart by themselves. Nor did all this suffice to expend his zeal, for he commenced a course of expositions on the creed and the commandments; and so convinced was he of the value of catechetical teaching, that on February 3, he writes, "I began to-night to turn the observations made on the lessons in the morning into catechetical questions, and was pleased to hear some of the soldiers make very apt answers." Nor were the children forgotten; a personal friend who accompanied him, a Mr. H—, assumed that as as his department. On February 6, Mr. Whitefield writes, that he was "pleased to see Mr. H— so active in teaching the children. He has now many scholars—may God bless him!"

(*p*) OUSELEY'S ZEAL.—The following beautiful and striking miniature likeness of that great and good man, Gideon Ouseley, is from the pen of Dr. Elliott, editor of the Western Christian Advocate. There was something in Mr. Ouseley's refusing the peerage and estates of his ancestors, and "choosing to suffer afflictions with the people of God," so strange, that we question if his parallel can be found in all history, except in the case of Moses. Blessed man, his reward must be great!

Mr. Ouseley was a marvelous man. He possessed a strong mind, well cultivated with a good university education. He was of a noble family; but became an itinerant Methodist preacher early in life, and for about fifty years kept the field, in labors most abundant. He preached in the Irish and English languages with equal fluency. The Irish language (the opinion of others to the contrary notwithstanding) is the foremost language under heaven for the pulpit. In this he preached with power to those who understood it. His pulpit performances usually amounted to twenty-one each week; two each day, in the open air, and one each evening, in a church, house, barn, &c., as the case might be. He preached thousands of sermons on horseback, in the markets, at horse-races, cock-fights, &c.; and when the multitudes were inclined to leave, which was seldom the case, he followed them in their movements. He was often persecuted, waylaid and beat, so as to be left for dead; but God always raised him up. The Popish clergy hated him to execration; and though many attempts were made on his life, he always escaped, except with the loss of one eye. His violent persecutors mostly came to an untimely end. So manifest was the hand of God in his preservation, that the Papists concluded it would not do to kill him, as by this means he would obtain the reputation of a martyr. He controverted, most freely, the errors of Popery, and exposed them unsparingly, always remembering to point the errorist to the Lord Jesus Christ for mercy. Many thousands were converted from Popery through his instrumentality.

At the death of Sir Gore Ouseley, his uncle, he became heir to his estate and his peerage; but he relinquished both in favor of the next heir, and continued his preaching till death. Few men of the age equaled him for usefulness and labors.

(*q*) TOO MUCH MONEY AND TOO LITTLE LABOR.—Mr. Fletcher accepted the living of Madely in preference to another of more than double the value, which was offered him about the same time; his previous intercourse with the people having excited within him an affection which would not suffer him to be separated from them, and which remained unabated till his death. The circumstances connected with his appointment were remarkable and characteristic. One day Mr. Hill informed him that the living of Dunham, in Cheshire, then vacant, was at his service. "The parish," he continued, "is small, the duty light, the income good, (£400 per annum,) and it is situated in a fine healthy sporting country." After thanking Mr. Hill most cordially for his kindness, Mr. Fletcher added, "Alas! sir, Dunham will not suit me: there is too much money and too little labor." "Few clergymen make such objections," said Mr. Hill; "it is a pity to decline such a living, as I do not know that I can find you another. What shall we do? Would you like Madely?" "That, sir, would be the very place for me." "My object, Mr. Fletcher," rejoined Mr. Hill, "is to make you comfortable in your own way. If you prefer Madely, I shall find no difficulty in persuading the present vicar to exchange it for Dunham, which is worth more than twice as much." In this way he became vicar of Madely, with which he was so perfectly satisfied, that he never afterwards sought honor or preferment.

(*r*) THE SICK MINISTER'S CHOICE.—An eminent divine was suffering under chronic disease, and consulted three physicians, who declared, on being questioned by the sick man, that his disease would be followed by death in a shorter or longer time, according to the manner in which he lived; but they advised him unanimously to give up his office, because, in his situation, mental agitation would be fatal to him. "If," inquired the divine, "I give myself to repose, how long, gentlemen, will you guarantee my life?" "Six years," answered the doctors. "And if I continue in office?" "Three years, at most." "Your servant, gentlemen," he replied; "I should prefer living two or three years in doing some good, to living six in idleness."

(*s*) "LET ME LABOR NOW."—When that zealous and truly apostolic laborer, Mr. Grimshawe, who usually preached from twenty to thirty times a week, was entreated at any time to spare himself, his constant reply was, "Let me labor now, for the hour is at hand when I shall rest."

259. Simplicity of Language.

(*a*) "DEITY! WHO IS HE?"—On one occasion, whilst the late Rev. S. Kilpin was preaching, but not in his own pulpit, he mentioned the great God by the name of "the Deity." A sailor, who was listening, immediately started from his seat, his elbows fully spread, and exclaimed aloud, "Deity! well, who is He? is He our God-a-Mighty?" The attendants were about to turn him out; but the minister stood reproved, and requested him to resume his seat. "Yes, my friend, I did mean the almighty God." The sailor rejoined, "I thought so, but was not quite sure; I never heard that name before." The humbled Minister replied, "You had a right to inquire; I was to blame: whilst delivering God's message of mercy and justice to immortal souls, I ought not to have given my Divine Master a name which prevented the message from being understood." "Thank you, sir," was the sailor's reply; and he looked as though he would have devoured the remaining part of the sermon. After the service, he came and begged pardon for the interruption; and, with a sailor's frankness, requested the kind gentleman to take some refreshment with him, to make it up.

(*b*) LUTHER'S PREACHING.—On one occasion, during the sixteenth century, the principal reformers having been called together, several of them preached. Luther, though unwell, preached with much energy from the words, "Go ye into all the world, and preach the gospel to every creature." Myconius wrote to a friend that he had often heard Luther preach, but on this occasion he seemed not so much to speak as to thunder forth the name of Christ from heaven itself. After Bucer's sermon, he supped with Luther, who, in the course of conversation, commended the discourse of his guest; but added that he himself was a better preacher. Bucer received this apparently rude remark with his accustomed mildness, and readily declared his assent. Luther then spoke seriously, and said, "Do not think that I mean to boast foolishly; I well know my own deficiencies, and that I am unable to deliver such an ingenious and learned discourse as we have this day heard from you; but, when I am in the pulpit, I consider who my hearers are: and because the greater part are an unlearned and simple people, I preach what I think they can understand. But you take a higher flight, so that your discourses suit learned people, but are not understood by our poor people. In this I act like a kind mother, who gives her craving infant the breast, thus feeding it with her own milk as well as she is able, and thinks this better for its nourishment than if mixed with the sweetest and choicest syrups and preparations of art."

(*c*) SIMPLICITY OF WESLEY.—In June, 1790, the Rev. J. Wesley preached at Lincoln: his text was, Luke x. 42: "One thing is needful." When the congregation were retiring from the chapel, a lady exclaimed, in a tone of great surprise, "Is this the great Mr. Wesley, of whom we hear so much in the present day? Why, the poorest might have understood him." The gentleman to whom this remark was made replied, "In this, madam, he displays his greatness; that, while the poorest can understand him, the most learned are edified, and cannot be offended."

(*d*) LEARNING MAKES PLAIN.—The late Rev. Dr. C. Evans, of Bristol, having once to travel from home, wrote to a poor congregation to say that he should have occasion to stay a night in their village, and that if it were agreeable to them, he would give them a sermon. The poor people hesitated for some time, but at length permitted him to preach. After sermon, he found them in a far happier mood than when he first came among them, and could not forbear inquiring into the reason of all this. "Why, sir, to tell you the truth," said one of them, "knowing that you were a very learned man, and that you were a teacher of young ministers, we were much afraid we should not understand you; but you have been quite as plain as any minister we ever hear." "Ay, ay," the doctor replied, "you entirely misunderstood the nature of learning, my friend: its design is to make things so plain that they cannot be misunderstood." Similar was the view of Archbishop Leighton, who says, in one of his charges to his clergy, "How much learning, my brethren, is required to make these things plain!"

(*e*) FEW PLEASED, BUT ONE CONVERTED.—The Rev. John Cotton was an eminent minister of the seventeenth century, who labored for many years at Boston, in Lincolnshire. When at the university of Cambridge, he was remarkable for learning and eloquence; and being called upon to preach at St. Mary's church in that town, high expectations were raised as to the character of the sermon. After many struggles in his own mind, arising from the temptation to display his talent and learning, and from a powerful impression of the importance of preaching the gospel with all simplicity, he at length wisely determined on the latter course. The vice-chancellor and students were not pleased, though a few of the professors commended his style; but his sermon was blessed to the conversion of Dr. Preston, who became one of the most eminent ministers of his day.

(*f*) ROMAINE'S PLAIN PREACHING.—Some persons in the Rev. Mr. Romaine's congregation, thinking his style of preaching too plain and common, had requested him to exhibit a little more learning in the pulpit; accordingly, on a certain occasion, he read his text in Hebrew. "Now," said he, "I suppose scarcely one in the congregation understands that." He then read it in Greek, and added, "Perhaps there may be one or two that understand me now; I will next read it in Latin." He did so and said, "Possibly a few more may comprehend me, but the number is still very limited." He last of all repeated the text in English: "There," he continued, "now you all understand it; which do you think is best? I hope always so to preach, as that the meanest person in the congregation may comprehend me."

260. Fidelity and Boldness.

(*a*) MILLARD AND LOUIS XI.—Oliver Millard, a popular and energetic preacher of the reign of Louis XI, attacked the vices of the court in his sermons, and did not spare even the king himself, who, taking offence at it, sent the priest word, that if he did not change his tone, he would have him thrown into the Seine. "The king," replied Oliver, "is the master to do what he pleases; but tell him that I shall reach Paradise by water sooner than he will with his post-horses." (The establishment of traveling post was instituted by Louis XI.) This bold answer at once amused and intimidated the king, for he let the priest continue to preach as he pleased, and what he pleased.

(*b*) MASSILLON PREACHING.—The eloquence of the celebrated Massillon shone conspicuously in the introduction of a sermon before Louis XIV, king of France, from the words of the Redeemer, Matt. v. 4: "Blessed are they that mourn." The preacher began: "If the world addressed your majesty from this place, the world would not say, 'Blessed are they that mourn.' The world would say 'Blessed is the prince who has never fought, but to conquer; who has filled the universe with his name; who through the whole course of a long and flourishing reign, enjoys in splendor all that men admire—extent of conquest, the esteem of his enemies, the love of his people, the wisdom of his laws.' But, sire, the language of the gospel is not the language of the world."

(*c*) WHITEFIELD AND GRIMSHAWE.—Mr. Whitefield, in a sermon he preached at Haworth, having spoken severely of those professors of the gospel who, by their loose and evil conduct, caused the ways of truth to be evil spoken of, intimated his hope, that it was not necessary to enlarge much upon that topic to the congregation before him, who had so long enjoyed the benefit of an able and faithful preacher; and he was willing to believe that their profiting appeared to all men. This roused Mr. Grimshawe's spirit, and, notwithstanding his great regard for the preacher, he stood up and interrupted him, saying, with a loud voice, "Oh! sir, for God's sake, do not speak so; I pray you, do not flatter. I fear the greater part of them are going to hell with their eyes open."

(*d*) INDIVIDUALITY IN PREACHING.—It is a charge often brought against some faithful ministers, that they direct many of their remarks to certain particular persons. It is certain that this was often done by Mr. Whitefield, and sometimes with very happy effect. He once drew from the conduct of his female servant the picture of a Christian remiss in duty, which painfully distressed her, till he gave her an assurance of his entire forgiveness.

(*e*) RITCHIE AND THE PROFANE SWEARER.—The late Doctor Ritchie, professor of Divinity in the University of Edinburgh, was one day preaching in Tarbolton church, where he was at that time minister, against profane swearing in common conversation, while one of his principal heritors, who was addicted to that sin, was present. This gentleman thought the sermon was designedly addressed to him, and that the eyes of the whole congregation were fixed upon him. Though he felt indignant, he kept his place till the service was concluded, and then waited on the preacher, and asked him to dine with him, as he was quite alone. The invitation being accepted, the gentleman immediately after dinner thus addressed the minister: "Sir, you have insulted me to-day in the church. I have been three times in church lately, and on every one of them you have been holding me up to the derision of the audience; so I tell you, sir, I shall never more enter the church of Tarbolton again, unless you give me your solemn promse, that you will abstain from such topics in future, as I am resolved I shall no more furnish you with the theme of your discourse." Mr. Ritchie heard this speech to a conclusion with calmness, and then looking him steadfastly in the face, thus replied: "Very well, sir, if you took to yourself what I said today against swearing, does not your conscience bear witness to its truth? You say you will not enter the church, till I cease to reprove your sins; if such is your determination, it is impossible you can enter it again, for which of the commandments have you not broken?" On observing his firmness, and feeling that he was wrong in attempting to make the minister of the parish compromise his duty, the gentleman held out his hand to Mr. Ritchie; a mutual explanation took place; and while the minister would abate none of his faithfulness, the heritor endeavored to overcome his evil habits.

(*f*) THE PREACHER AND THE CONSTABLE.—Mr. Maurice, one of the con-conformist ministers in Shropshire, experienced many remarkable deliverances in the providence of God, when in danger of being apprehended by his enemies after his ejection. At one time a constable found him preaching, and commanded him to desist; but Mr. Maurice, with great courage, charged him in the name of the Great God, whose message he was then delivering, to forbear molesting him, as he would answer it at the great day. The constable, awed by his solemn manner, sat down trembling, heard him patiently to the end of his discourse, and then quietly left him.

(*g*) OFFENDING A NOBLEMAN.—Mr. Dod having preached against the profanation of the Sabbath, which much prevailed in his parish, and especially among the more wealthy inhabitants, the servant of a nobleman, who was one of them, came to him and said, "Sir, you have offended my lord to-day." Mr. Dod replied, "I should not have offended your lord, except he had been conscious to himself that he had first offended my Lord; and if *your* lord will offend *my* Lord, let him be offended."

(*h*) FAITHFULNESS TO GOD AND THE KING.—Bishop Latimer having one day preached before King Hery VIII a sermon which displeased his majesty, he was ordered to preach again on the next Sabbath and to make an apology for the offence he had given. After reading his text, the bishop thus began his sermon:—"Hugh Latimer, dost thou know before whom thou art this day to speak? To the high and mighty monarch, the king's most excellent majesty, who can take away thy life if thou offendest; therefore, take heed that thou speakest not a word that may displease; but then consider well, Hugh, dost thou not know from whence thou comest; upon whose message thou art sent? Even by the great and mighty God! who is all-present! and who beholdeth all thy ways! and who is able to cast thy soul into hell! Therefore, take care that thou deliverest thy message faithfully." He then proceeded with the same sermon he had preached the preceding Sabbath, but with considerably more energy. The sermon ended, the court were full of expectation to know what would be the fate of this honest and plain-dealing bishop. After dinner, the king called for Latimer, and, with a stern countenance, asked him how he dared to be so bold as to preach in such a manner. He, falling on his knees, replied, his duty to his God and his prince had enforced him thereto, and that he had merely discharged his duty and his conscience in what he had spoken. Upon which the king, rising from his seat, and takidg the good man by the hand, embraced him, saying, "Blessed be God, I have so honest a servant."

(*i*) "SHORT MEASURE."—The following incident in the life of William Dawson, a very humble, but a very excellent preacher, late of Barnbow, near Leeds, beautifully illustrates the power of the plainly preached word.

"He was preaching in the neighborhood of Leeds, on Dan. v. 27: "Thou art weighed in the balances, and art found wanting." A person who traveled the country in the character of a pedler, and who was exceedingly partial to him as a preacher, was one of Mr. Dawson's auditors. The person referred to, generally carried a stick with him, which answered the double purpose of a walking-stick and a 'yard-wand;' and having been employed pretty freely in the former capacity, it was worn down beyond the point of justice, and procured for him an appellation of 'Short Measure.' He stood before Mr. Dawson, and being rather noisy in his religious professions, as well as ready with his responses, he manifested signs of approbation while the scales were being described and adjusted, and different classes of sinners were placed in them, and disposed of agreeably to the test of justice, truth and mercy,—uttering in a somewhat subdued tone, yet loud enough for those around to hear, at the close of each particular—'Light weight'—'short again,' etc. After taking up the separate characters of the flagrant transgressor of the law of God, the hypocrite, the formalist, etc., Mr. Dawson at length came to such persons as possessed religious light, but little hallowed feeling, and the semblance of much zeal, but who employed false weights and measures. Here, without adverting in his mind to the case of the noisy auditor, he perceived the muscles of his face working, when the report of 'short measure' occurred to him. Resolved, however, to soften no previous expression, and to proceed with an analysis and description of the question, he placed the delinquent, in his singularly striking way, in the scale, when, instead of the usual response, the man, stricken before him, took his stick—the favorite measure, from under his arm—raised one foot from the floor, doubled his knee, and, taking hold of the offending instrument by both ends, snapped it into two halves, exclaiming, while dashing it to the ground, 'Thou shalt do it no more!' So true is it, to employ the language of an eminent minister, 'that no man ever offended his own conscience, but first or last it was revenged upon him for it.'"

(*j*) HACKET AND THE SOLDIER.—Dr. John Hacket was, at the beginning of the civil war, rector of St. Andrew's, Holborn; and when the parliament had forbidden the use of the liturgy, under the severest penalties, Dr. Hacket continued to read, as before, the daily service, and when a sergeant with a trooper rushed into the church, commanding him with threats to desist, he with a steady voice and intrepid countenance continued; on which the soldier, raising a pistol to his head, threatened him with instant death. The undaunted minister calmly replied,—"Soldier, I am doing my duty, do you do yours!" and with a still more exalted voice read on. The soldier, abashed, left the church.

(*k*) BOURDALOUE'S FAITHFULNESS.—The reputation for eloquence which this celebrated preacher very early acquired, reached the ears of Louis the Fourteenth, who sent for him to preach the advent sermon, in 1670, which he did with such success that he was many years retained at court. He was called the king of preachers, and the preacher to kings; and Louis himself said, that he would rather hear the repetitions of Bourdaloue, than the novelties of another. With a collected air, Bourdaloue had little action; he generally kept his eyes half closed, and penetrated the hearts of the people by the sound of a voice uniform and solemn. On one occasion, he turned the peculiarity of his external aspect to a very memorable advantage. After depicting, in soul-awakening terms, a sinner of the first magnitude, he suddenly opened his eyes, and casting them full on the king, who sat opposite to him, he added, in a voice of thunder, "Thou art the man." The effect was confounding. When he had finished his discourse, he went and threw himself at the feet of his sovereign, and said, "Sire, behold at your feet, one who is the most devoted of your servants; but punish him not, that in the pulpit he can own no other master than the King of kings."

(*l*) THE KNIGHT'S COMPLAINT.—During the protectorate, a certain knight, in Surrey, had a lawsuit with the minister of his parish; and whilst the dispute was pending, Sir John imagined that the sermons delivered at church were preached at him. He therefore complained against the minister to Cromwell, who inquired of the preacher concerning the fact; and having found that his sermons were aimed at the common good, he dismissed the complaining knight, saying, "Go home, Sir John, and hereafter live in good friendship with your minister; the word of the Lord is a searching word, and I am afraid it has found you out." It were well, when we feel uncomfortable with the sermons of our ministers, if, instead of complaining of them, we seriously examined our own character, and applied whatever might be suitable to our own case.

(*m*) WALKER AND THE RECTOR.—After the late Rev. Samuel Walker, of Truro, had begun to feel the unspeakable importance of the truth as it is in Jesus, his preaching became of a different character to what it had previously been. When he urged the importance of regeneration, and devotedness to God, those who were living in a sensual and dissipated manner, or who were building their hopes of heaven on the morality of their lives, were offended. Accordingly, some of the most wealthy inhabitants of the town complained of him to the rector, and requested his dismission. The rector promised compliance with their wishes, and waited on Mr. Walker to give him notice to quit his curacy. He was received with much politeness and respect, and Mr. Walker soon took an opportunity, from some passing remark, to explain his views of the importance of the ministerial office, and the manner in which its duties ought to be performed. His sentiments and manner were such, that the rector went away without having accomplished his purpose. He endeavored a second time to effect the wishes of the people, but was again so awed by Mr. W.'s superiority, that he could not speak to him on the subject. Being afterwards pressed by one of the principal persons on the topic, he replied, "Do you go and dismiss him, if you can; I cannot. I feel, in his presence, as if he were a being of superior order, and am so abashed, that I am uneasy till I can retire from it."

(*n*) LATIMER ACCUSED BEFORE HENRY VIII.—Bishop Latimer, in preaching before King Henry the Eighth, spoke his mind very plainly, which some of his enemies thought to make their advantage of, by complaining of him to the king, that they might thus get him out of the way. Soon after his sermon, he and several others being called before the king to speak their minds on certain matters, one of them kneeled before his majesty, and accused Latimer of having preached seditious doctrines. The king turned to Latimer, and said, "What say you to that, sir?" Latimer kneeled down, and turning first to his accuser, said, "What form of preaching would you appoint me to preach before a king? Would you have me to preach nothing concerning a king in a king's sermon? Have you any commission to appoint me what I shall preach?" He asked him several other questions, but he would answer none at all; nor had he any thing to say. Then he turned to the king, and said, "I never thought myself worthy, nor ever sued, to be a preacher before your Grace. But I was called to it, and would be willing, if you mislike me, to give place to my betters. But if your Grace allow me for a preacher, I would desire your Grace to discharge my conscience, give me leave to frame my discourse according to mine audience. I had been a very dolt to have preached so at the borders of your realm as I preach before your Grace." These words were well recieved by the king, as Latimer concluded, because the king presently turned to another subject. Some of his friends came to him with tears in their eyes, and told him, they looked for nothing but that he should have been sent to the tower the same night.

(*o*) USHER AND THE KING.—Dr. Parr, in his Life of Archbishop Usher, relates, that while that prelate was once preaching in the church at Covent Garden, a message arrived from the court, that the king wished immediately to see him. He descended from the pulpit, listened to the command, and told the messenger that he was then, as he saw, employed in God's business, but, as soon as he had done, he would attend upon the king to understand his pleasure, and then continued his sermon.

260. Ingenuity and Wit.

(*a*) KIND OF MINISTER WANTED.—The people of one of the out parishes in Virginia, wrote to Dr. Rice, who was then at the head of the Theological Seminary in Prince Edward, for a minister. They said they wanted a man of first rate *talents*, for they had run down considerably, and needed building up. They wanted one who could *write* well, for some of the young people were very nice about that matter. They wanted one who could *visit* a good deal, for their former minister had neglected that, and they wanted to bring it up. They wanted a man of very *gentlemanly deportment*, for some thought a great deal of that. And so they went on, describing a perfect minister. The last thing they mentioned was,—they gave their last minister $350; but if the Doctor would send them such a man as they had described, they would raise another $50, making it $400. The Doctor sat right down and wrote a reply, telling them they had better forthwith make out a call for old Dr. Dwight, in heaven; for he did not know of any one in this world who answered this description. And as Dr. D. had been living so long on spiritual food, he might not need so much for the body, and possibly he might live on $400.

(*b*) PREACHING ON THE TIMES.—In 1648, it was a question asked of the brethren, at the meetings of ministers, twice in the year, "If they preached the duties of the times?" And when it was found that Leighton did not, he was reproved for his omission; but he replied, "If all the brethren have preached on the *times*, may not one poor brother be suffered to preach on *eternity?*"

(*c*) THE ELEVENTH COMMANDMENT.—At one time Archbishop Usher visited Scotland, and hearing much of the piety of the Rev. Samuel Rutherford, resolved on being a witness of it. Disguised as a pauper, on a Saturday evening, he solicited lodging for the night. Mr. Rutherford took him in, and directed him to be seated in the kitchen. Mrs. Rutherford catechised the servants, as a preparation for the Sabbath; and having asked the stranger the number of the Divine commandments, he answered, *eleven*. The good woman hastily concluded him ignorant, and said, "What a shame it is for you, a man with gray hairs, in a Christian country, not to know how many commandments there are! There is not a child six years old, in this parish, but could answer the question properly." Lamenting his condition, she ordered his supper, and directed a servant to show him a bed in a garret. Mr. Rutherford having heard him at prayer, and finding out who he was, prevailed on the archbishop to preach for him, which he agreed to do, on condition that he should not be made known. Early in the morning Mr. Rutherford changed his clothes, suffered him to depart, and afterwards introduced him to breakfast as a minister on a journey. When in the pulpit, he announced his text—"A new commandment I give unto you, that ye love one another;" and remarked that this might be reckoned the *eleventh* commandment. Mrs. Rutherford, remembering the answer she had received the night before from the stranger, was surprised, and looking at the preacher, almost imagined he might be the pitied traveler. The two holy men spent the evening in delightful conversation, and the archbishop departed, undiscovered, early on the following day.

(*d*) WHITEFIELD AND THE EXECUTION.—During one of the visits which the Rev. George Whitefield paid to Edinburgh, an unhappy man, who had forfeited his life to the offended laws of his country, was executed in that neighborhood. Mr. W. mingled with the crowd that was collected on the occasion, and was struck with the solemnity and decorum which were observable in so awful a scene. His appearance, however, drew the eyes of all upon him, and raised a variety of opinions as to the motives which induced him to join the multitude. The next day being Sunday, he preached to a very large congregation in a field near the city; and, in the course of his sermon, he adverted to the scenes of the preceding day. "I know," said he, "that many of you will find it difficult to reconcile my appearance yesterday with my character. Many of you, I know, will say, that my moments would have been better employed in praying for the unhappy man, than in attending him to the fatal tree; and that, perhaps, curiosity was the only cause that converted me into a spectator on that occasion; but those who ascribe that uncharitable motive to me, are under a mistake. I went as an observer of human nature, and to see the effect that such an example would have on those who witnessed it. I watched the conduct of those who were present on that awful occasion, and I was highly pleased with their demeanor, which has given me a very favorable opinion of the Scottish nation. Your sympathy was visible on your countenances, particularly when the moment arrived that your unhappy fellow-creature was to close his eyes on this world for ever; and then you all, as if moved by one impulse, turned your heads aside, and wept. Those tears were precious, and will be held in remembrance. How different it was when the Savior of mankind was extended on the cross! The Jews, instead of sympathizing in his sorrows, triumphed in them. They reviled him with bitter expressions, with words even more bitter than the gall and vinegar which they handed him to drink. Not one, of all that witnessed his pains, turned his head aside, even in the last pang. Yes, my friends, there was one; that glorious luminary," pointing to the sun, "veiled his brightness, and traveled on his course in tenfold night."

(*e*) HALL'S OPINION OF A SERMON.—A conceited minister having once delivered a sermon in the hearing of Mr. Hall, pressed him, with a disgusting union of self-complacency and indelicacy, to state what he thought of the sermon. Mr. Hall remained silent for some time, hoping that his silence would be rightly interpreted; but this only caused the question to be pressed with greater earnestness. Mr. Hall at length said, "There was one very fine passage, sir." "I am rejoiced to hear you say so. Pray, sir, which was it?" "Why, sir, it was the passage from the pulpit into the vestry."

(*f*) NEWTON'S REPROOF.—The excellent John Newton was faithful and ingenious in administering re proof. He one day heard a minister preach, who affected great accuracy in his discourses, and who occupied nearly an hour on several labored and nice distinctions. Having a high esteem for Mr. Newton's judgment, he inquired of him whether he thought these distinctions were full and judicious. Mr. Newton said, he thought them not full, as a very important one had been omitted. "What can that be?" said the minister; "for I have taken more than ordinary care to enumerate them fully." "I think not," replied Mr. N., "for when many of your congregation had traveled several miles for a meal, I think you should not have forgotten the important distinction which must ever exist between meat and bones."

(*g*) WHITEFIELD AND ELECTIONS.—When Mr. Whitefield was in the zenith of his popularity, lord Clare, who knew that his influence was considerable, applied to him, by letter, requesting his assistance at Bristol, at the ensuing general election. To this request Mr. Whitefield replied, that in general elections he never interfered; but he would earnestly exhort his lordship to use great diligence to make his own particular calling and election sure!

(*h*) THE MINISTER AND THE MUSICIAN.—A musical amateur of eminence, who had often observed the Hon. and Rev. Mr. Cadogan's inattention to his performances, said to him one day, "Come, I am determined to make you feel the force of music,—pay particular attention to this piece." It accordingly was played. "Well, what do you say now?" "Why, just what I said before." "What! can you hear this and not be charmed? Well, I am quite surprised at your insensibility. Where are your ears?" "Bear with me, my lord," replied Mr. Cadogan, "since I too have had my surprise; I have often from the pulpit set before you the most striking and affecting truths; I have sounded notes that might have raised the dead; I have said, Surely he will feel now; but you never seemed to be charmed with my music, though infinitely more interesting than yours. I too have been ready to say with astonishment, Where are his ears?"

(*i*) MR. BROWN AND THE OPPOSER.—Rev. John Brown, of Haddington, was invited to become pastor there, soon after he was licensed to preach. Only one man prevented the call from being unanimous. Being a person possessed of considerable influence, it was greatly feared that he would exert that influence to the injury of the minister and the church. Mr. Brown meeting with this gentleman one day, took him by the hand, and begged him frankly to state his reasons for voting against him. "I am as frank as you are, Mr. Brown," replied he, "and I beg leave to say that my reason for voting against you is a strong one; and it can be told in a word, *I don't think you are a good preacher*." "There we are perfectly agreed," replied Mr. Brown; "I know it as well as you do, my friend, and I say it as frankly as you do, that *I am not a good preacher*. But then," continued Mr. Brown, as he shook his neighbor heartily by the hand, "while you and I are perfectly agreed in this particular, where is the use of you and me setting up *our opinions against the whole parish?*" The man laughed heartily, told Mr. Brown that he had completely disarmed him, that he began to be of his opinion, and that he would not be found opposing the views of the whole parish any longer. He became afterwards Mr. Brown's best friend.

(*j*) MASSILLON AND THE THOUGHTLESS ASSEMBLY.—Massillon, an eminent French preacher, in the first sermon he ever delivered, found, upon his getting into the pulpit, the whole audience in a disposition no way favorable to his intentions; their nods, whispers, or drowsy behavior, showed him that there was no great profit to be expected from his sowing in a soil so barren; however, he soon changed the disposition of the audience by his manner of beginning: "If," said he, "a cause, the most important that could be conceived, were to be tried at the bar before qualified judges; if this cause interested ourselves in particular; if the eyes of the whole kingdom were fixed upon the event; if the most eminent counsel were employed on both sides; and if we had heard from our infancy of this undetermined trial; would you not all sit with due attention and warm expectation to the pleadings on both sides? would not all your hopes and fears be suspended upon the final decision? And yet, let me tell you, you have this moment a cause of much greater importance before you: a cause where not one nation, but all the world are spectators; tried not before a fallible tribunal, but the awful throne of heaven; where not your temporal and transitory interests are the subjects of debate; but your eternal happiness or misery; where the cause is still undetermined; but, perhaps, the very moment I am speaking may fix the irrevocable decree that shall last for ever; and yet, notwithstanding all this, you can hardly sit with patience to hear the tidings of salvation. I plead the cause of Heaven, and yet I am scarcely attended to."

(*k*) PREACHING TO A FARMER.—The Rev. John Cooke, of Maidenhead, once, when traveling, fell in with a rich farmer, who was very unwilling to listen to any serious remarks which he was disposed to make, and at length said, with a sneer, "I don't like religion; and I told you so." "You are not a singular farmer, sir," replied Mr. Cooke. "I have read of one whom you greatly resemble. The farmer to whom I allude, finding his ground very productive, and his barns too small, resolved on building larger barns and filling them; and said to his soul, 'Soul, thou hast much goods laid up for many years; take thine ease, eat, drink, and be merry. But God said unto him, Thou fool! this night thy soul shall be required of thee: then whose shall those things be which thou hast provided?' Luke xii. 19, 20. Now, sir, I think you must see yourself in this picture. Here is a farmer, very rich, living to himself in health, ease, and pleasure, 'without God in the world.' No doubt his neighbors envied and flattered him; but no one dared to reprove so rich a man. And if no one reproved his sins, and many flattered them as virtues, he never heard the truth. This accounts for our Lord's words, 'How hardly shall they that have riches enter into the kingdom of God! But although he thought himself wise, and others wished to be like him, God addresses him differently,—'Thou fool!'

"Why, sir, do you suppose the only wise God called him a fool?" He was silent.

"But, candidly, do not you think he was a fool?"

"I shall not say, sir."

"Well, sir, if you will allow me to hazard an opinion, he appears a fool,—

"1. Because he preferred his body to his soul.

"2. Because he preferred the world to God: 'Eat, drink, and be merry,' was the extent of his aim.

"3. Because he preferred time to eternity: 'Thou hast goods laid up for many years.'

4. "Because he lived as if he should never die; and, whilst presuming on many years, exposed his soul to all the horrors of sudden death, without repentance, without forgiveness, without holiness, and without hope."

(*l*) HAYNES' REPLY TO THE SCOFFERS.—Of Mr. Haynes, the colored preacher, it is said, that some time after the publication of his sermon on the text, "Ye shall not surely die," two reckless young men having agreed together to try his wit, one of them said, "Father Haynes, have you heard the good news?" "No," said Mr. Haynes, "what is it?" "It is great news indeed," said the other, "and, if true, your business is done." "What is it?" again inquired Mr. Haynes. "Why," said the first, "the devil is dead." In a moment the old gentleman replied, lifting up both hands, and placing them on the heads of the young men, and in a tone of solemn concern, "Oh, poor fatherless children! what will become of you?"

(*m*) THE PULPIT WINDOW AND CUSHION REPAIRED.—Rev. Zabeliel Adams at one time exchanged with a neighboring minister—a mild, inoffensive man—who, knowing the peculiar bluntness of his character, said to him, "You will find some panes of glass broken in the pulpit window, and possibly you may suffer from the cold. The cushion, too, is in a bad condition; but I beg of you not to say any thing to my people on the subject; they are poor, &c." "O no! O no!" says Mr. Adams. But ere he left home, he filled a bag with rags and took it with him. When he had been in the pulpit a short time, feeling somewhat incommoded by the too free circulation of the air, he deliberately took from the bag, a handful of the rags, and stuffed them into the windows. Toward the close of his discourse, which was more or less upon the duties of a people toward their clergyman, he became very animated, and purposely brought down both fists upon the pulpit cushions, with a tremendous force. The feathers flew in all directions, and the cushion was pretty much used up. He instantly checked the current of his thought, and simply exclaiming,—"Why, how these feathers fly!"—proceeded. He had fulfilled his promise of not addressing the society on the subject, but had taught them a lesson not to be misunderstood. On the next Sabbath, the window and cushion were found in excellent repair.

(*n*) NEW USE FOR JACOB'S LADDER.—A Welsh clergyman, invited to assist in the ordination of a minister in some part of England, was appointed to deliver the address to the church and congregation; and having been informed that their previous minister had suffered much from pecuniary embarrassment, although the church was fully able to support him comfortably, he took the following singular method of administering reproof.

In his address to the church, he remarked, "You have been praying, no doubt, that God would send you a man after his own heart to be your pastor. You have done well. God, we hope, has heard your prayer, and given you such a minister as he approves, who will go in and out before you, and feed your souls with the bread of life. But now you have prayed for a minister, and God has given you one to your mind, you have something more to do; you must take care of him; and in order to his being happy among you, I have been thinking you have need to pray again. 'Pray again? Pray again? What should we pray again for?' Well, I think you have need to pray again. 'But for what?' Why, I'll tell you. Pray that God would put Jacob's ladder down to the earth again. 'Jacob's ladder! Jacob's ladder! What has Jacob's ladder to do with our minister?' Why, I think, if God would put Jacob's ladder down, that your minister could go up into heaven on the Sabbath evening after preaching, and remain there all the week; then he could come down every Sabbath morning so spiritually minded and so full of heaven, that he would preach to you almost like an angel. 'Oh, yes, that may be all very well; and, if it were possible, we should like it; but, then, we need our minister with us during the week, to attend prayer-meetings, visit the sick, hear experience, give advice, &c., &c., and, therefore, must have him always with us; we want the whole of his time and attention.' That may be, and I will admit the necessity of his daily attention to your concerns; but, then, you will remember, that if he remains here he must have bread and cheese; and I have been told that your former minister was often wanting the common necessaries of life, while many of you can enjoy its luxuries; and, therefore, I thought, if God would put Jacob's ladder down, your present minister might preach to you on the Sabbath, and, by going up into heaven after the services of the day, save you the painful necessity of supporting him."

(*o*) JAY AND THE ANGEL.—When the Edward Irving mania raged, a man calling himself an "Angel of the Church," proceeded from Bristol to Bath, on a special mission to William Jay. The grave, thinking old man, was in his study, and when the "Angel," a man with a dismal countenance, a white cravat, and rusty black trousers, appeared, Mr. Jay asked him his business. "I am the Angel of the Church," said the man. "What church?" asked Mr. Jay. "The Irvingite church at Bristol," replied the angel. "Take off your coat," said Mr. Jay. The angel took off his coat, and Mr. Jay quietly rubbed his shoulder blades. "What are you doing?" asked the angel. "Looking for your wings," was the cool answer of William Jay.

(*p*) WHITEFIELD AND THE SCOFFER.—When the celebrated Whitefield was addressing an immense crowd with his accustomed fervor and eloquence, under the shade of a venerable tree in the meadows at Edinburgh, a poor creature, thinking to turn him into ridicule, had perched himself on one of the overhanging boughs right above the preacher's head, and, with monkey-like dexterity, mimicking his gesticulations, endeavored to raise a laugh among the audience. Guided by the looks of some of his hearers, Whitefield caught a glance of him, but without seeming to have noticed him, continued his discourse. With the skill of a practised orator, he reserved the incident for the proper place and time. He was expatiating at the moment on the power and sovereignty of Divine grace. With gathering force and earnestness he told of the unlikely objects it had often chosen, and the unlooked for triumphs it had achievsd. As he rose to the climax of his inspiring theme, and when in the full sweep of his eloquence, he suddenly paused, and turning round and pointing slowly to the wretch above him, exclaimed, in a tone of deep and thrilling pathos, "Even he may yet be the subject of that free and resistless grace." It was a shaft from the Almighty. Winged by the divine Spirit, it struck the scoffer to the heart, and realized, in his conversion, the glorious truth it contained.

(*q*) BARROW AND ROCHESTER.—The celebrated Lord Rochester one day met Dr. Barrow in the Park, and being determined, as he said, to put down *the rusty piece of divinity*, accosted him by taking off his hat, and, with a profound bow, exclaimed, "Doctor, I am yours to my shoe-tie." The doctor, perceiving his aim, returned the salute with equal ceremony, "My lord, I am yours to the ground." His lordship then made a deeper congee, and said, "Doctor, I am yours to the centre." Barrow replied, with the same formality, "My lord, I am yours to the antipodes;" on which Rochester made another attempt, by exclaiming, "Doctor, I am yours to the lowest pit of hell." "There, my lord," said Barrow, "I leave you," and immediately walked away.

262. Personal Intercourse and Pastoral Labor.

(*a*) DOCTOR SPRING AND THE THOUGHTLESS YOUNG LADY.—Dr. Spring, of New-York, once related, that during the period of a revival of religion in that city, a young lady, the object of high hope, the centre of wide influence, capable of noble things, yet careering on the giddy steep of fashion and folly, created in him no small solicitude, as he would have to give an account for her soul, every avenue to which seemed most sedulously guarded. He delayed the visit of counsel and exhortation; and delayed, till, rebuked by conscience, he could do so no longer. As soon as he called, and was ushered into the saloon, the first and only person whom he saw was this young lady, bathed in tears, who immediately exclaimed, "My dear pastor, I rejoice to see you. I was fearful I was the only one who had escaped your friendly notice." What a rebuke to fear! What an encouragement to hope, and to action!

(*b*) REV. MR. CHARLES' PRACTICE.—When the Rev. Mr. Charles, of Bala in Wales, met a poor man or woman on the road, he used to stop his horse, and make the inquiry, "Can you read the Bible?" He was so much in the habit of doing this, that he became every where known from this practice. "The gentleman who kindly asked the poor people about the Bible and their souls," was Mr. Charles. Meeting one day with an old man, on one of the mountains, he said to him, "You are an old man, and very near another world." "Yes," said he, "and I hope I am going to heaven." "Do you know the road there,—do you know the word of God?" "Pray, are you Mr. Charles?" said the old man. He suspected who he was from his questions. He was frequently thus accosted, when asking the poor people he met with about their eternal concerns. "Pray, are you Mr. Charles?" was often the inquiry. When he had time, he scarcely ever passed by a poor man on the road, without talking to him about his soul, and his knowledge of the Bible. When he found any ignorant of the word of God, and not able to read it, he represented to them, in a kind and simple manner, the duty and necessity of becoming acquainted with it, and feelingly and compassionately set before them the awful state of those who leave the world without knowing the word of God, and the way of saving the soul. He sometimes succeeded in persuading them to learn to read; and the good he thus did was no doubt very great.

(c) PAYSON AND THE LAWYER.—The following rencounter with a lawyer of Portland, who ranked among the first in the place for wealth, and fluency of speech, will show Dr. Payson's insight into character, and also that his conquests were not confined to "weak women and children."

A lady, who was the common friend of Mrs. Payson and the lawyer's wife, was sojourning in the family of the latter. After the females of the respective families had interchanged several "calls," Mrs. —— was desirous of receiving a formal visit from Mrs. Payson; but, to effect this, Mr. Payson must also be invited; and how to prevail with her husband to tender an invitation was the great difficulty. He had been accustomed to associate experimental religion with meanness, and of course felt, or affected, great contempt for the divine, as if it were impossible for a man of his religion to be also a man of talents. He knew, by report, something of Mr. Payson's practice on these occasions, and dreading to have his house a place for what appeared to him gloomy conversation, resisted his wife's proposal as long as he could do so, and retain the character of a gentleman. When he gave his consent, it was with the positive determination that Mr. Payson should not converse on religion, nor ask a blessing over his food, nor offer a prayer in his house. He collected his forces, and made his preparations in conformity with this purpose. When the appointed day arrived, he received his guests very pleasantly, and entered at once into animated conversation; determined, by obtruding his own favorite topics, to forestall the divine. It was not long before the latter discovered his object, and summoned together his powers to defeat it. He plied them with that skill and address for which he was remarkable; still, for some time, victory was inclined to neither side, or to both alternately. The lawyer, not long before, had returned from Washington city, where he spent several weeks on business at the supreme court of the United States. Mr. Payson made some inquiries respecting sundry personages there, and among others, the chaplain of the house of representatives. The counsellor had heard him in the devotional services of that assembly. "How did you like him?" "Not at all; he appeared to have more regard to those around him, than he had to his Maker." Mr. Payson was very happy to hear him recognize the distinction between praying to God, and praying to be heard of men; and dropped a series of observations on prayer, passing into a strain of remark, which, without taking the form, had all the effect on the lawyer's conscience, of a personal application. From a topic so unwelcome, he strove to divert the conversation; and every few minutes would start something as wide from it as the east is from the west. But as often as he wandered, his guest would dexterously, and without violence, bring him back; and as often as he was brought back, he would wander again. At length the trying moment, which was to turn the scale, arrived. The time for the evening repast had come; the servant had entered the parlor with the provisions; the master of the feast became unusually eloquent, resolved to engross the conversation, to hear no question or reply, to allow no interval for "grace," and to give no indication, by the eye, the hand, or the lips, that he expected, or wished for such a service. Just as the distribution was on the very point of commencing, Mr. Payson interposed the question, "What writer has said, 'The devil invented the fashion of carrying round tea, to prevent a blessing being asked?'" Our host felt himself "cornered;" but, making a virtue of necessity, replied, "I don't know what writer it is; but, if you please, we will foil the devil this time. Will you ask a blessing, sir?" A blessing, of course, was asked; and he brooked, as well as he could, this first certain defeat, still resolved not to sustain another by the offering of thanks at the closing of the repast. But in this, too, he was disappointed. By some well-timed sentiment of his reverend guest, he was brought into such a dilemma, that he could not, without absolute rudeness, decline asking him to return thanks. And thus he contested every inch of his ground, till the visit terminated. But, at every stage, the minister proved too much for the lawyer. Mr. Payson retained his character as a minister of religion, and gained his point in every thing; and that, too, with so admirable a tact, in a way so natural and unconstrained, and with such respectful deference to his host, that the latter could not be displeased, except with himself. He not only acknowledged God on the reception of food, but read the Scriptures and prayed before separating from the family; and did it at the request of the master, though made, as in every other instance, in violation of a fixed purpose. The chagrin of this disappointment, however, eventually became the occasion of the lawyer's greatest joy. His mind was never entirely at ease, till he found peace in believing. Often did he revert with devout thankfulness to God, to the visit which had occasioned his mortification; and ever after regarded, with more than common veneration and respect, the servant of God whom he had despised; and was glad to receive his ministrations, in exchange for those on which he had formerly attended.

(*d*) THE INFIDEL'S RETORT.—A preacher perceiving, on one occasion, among his hearers, an individual who was known in the neighborhood as a ringleader of infidelity, was induced to hope that some alteration had taken place in his views. To ascertain whether such was the fact, he called upon him the next day, and told him how happy he had been to see him at the house of prayer the previous evening; the more so, as he had been given to understand that he did not believe the gospel. "Nor you either," said the unceremonious skeptic. "What!" he exclaimed, "do you mean, sir, to call me a hypocrite?" "I call you no ill names, sir," he coolly replied; "but what I mean to say is this; you have known of my infidelity for years, and though I have lived all the while within a short distance of your dwelling, you have never before attempted to enlighten me as to these matters; a thing which, to do you justice, I must believe you would have done, had you thought them as important as your creed would make them. Indeed, I can hardly fancy that you would see me going to hell, and never try to save my soul."

(*e*) MISTAKE OF NEFF.—One day, as Felix Neff was walking in a street in the city of Lausanne, he saw at a distance a man whom he took for one of his friends. He ran behind him, tapped him on the shoulder, before looking him in his face, and asked him, "What is the state of your soul, my friend?" The stranger turned; Neff perceived his error, apologized, and went his way. About three or four years afterwards, a person came to Neff, and accosted him, saying, he was indebted to him for his inestimable kindness. Neff did not recognize the man, and begged he would explain. The stranger replied, "Have you forgotten an unknown person, whose shoulder you touched in the street in Lausanne, asking him, 'How do you find your soul?' It was I; your question led me to serious reflections, and *now I find it is well with my soul.*" This proves what apparently small means may be blessed of God for the conversion of sinners, and how many opportunities for doing good we are continually letting slip, and which thus pass irrevocably beyond our reach. One of the questions which every Christian should propose to himself, on setting out on a journey, is, "What opportunities shall I have to do good?" And one of the points on which he should examine himself, on his return, is, "What opportunities have I lost?"

263. Success in their Labors.

(*a*) THE DAIRYMAN'S DAUGHTER.—Some years ago, a vessel, which was blessed with a pious chaplain, and was bound to a distant part of the world, happened to be detained by contrary winds, over a Sabbath, at the Isle of Wight. The chaplain improved the opportunity to preach to the inhabitants. His text was, "Be clothed with humility." Among his hearers was a thoughtless girl, who had come to show her fine dress, rather than to be instructed. The sermon was the means of her conversion. Her name was Elizabeth Wallbridge, the celebrated DAIRYMAN'S DAUGHTER, whose interesting history, by Rev. Leigh Richmond, has been printed in various languages, and widely circulated, to the spiritual benefit of thousands. What a reward was this for a single sermon preached "out of season!"

(*b*) BERRIDGE AND HICKS.—It is credibly reported of the Rev. John Berridge, the well known vicar of Everton, that in his itinerant labors through the country he preached from ten to twelve sermons a week upon an average, and frequently rode a hundred miles. Nor were such extraordinary exertions occasional, but continued through the long succession of more than twenty years. The success that followed these, as well as his stated labors amongst his own flock, may be estimated from the fact, that he was visited, in the first year after his own spiritual illumination, by a thousand different persons under serious impressions. It is computed, that under his own ministry, and that of Mr. Hicks, a neighboring minister, of whose conversion he had been the instrument, four thousand persons were awakened to a concern for their souls in the space of twelve months.

(*c*) MR. GRIMSHAW'S SUCCESS.—"The last time I was with Mr. Grimshaw," says Mr. Newton, "as we were standing together upon a hill near Haworth, and surveying the romantic prospect around us, he expressed himself to the following purport, and I believe I nearly retain his very words, for they made a deep impression upon me while he spoke:—'When I first came into this country, if I had gone half a day's journey on horseback towards the east, west, north, and south, I could not have met with or heard of one truly serious person; but now, through the blessing of God upon the poor services of the most unworthy of his ministers, besides a considerable number whom I have seen or known to have departed this life, like Simeon, rejoicing in the Lord's salvation; and besides five dissenting churches or congregations, of which the ministers, and nearly every one of the members, were first awakened under my ministry; I have still at my sacrament, if the weather is favorable, from three to five hundred communicants, of the far greater part of whom, so far as man, who cannot see the heart, and who can therefore only determine by appearances, profession, and conduct, may judge, I can give almost as particular an account as I can of myself. I know the state of their progress in religion. By my frequent visits and converse with them, I am acquainted with their several temptations, trials, and exercises, both personal and domestic, both spiritual and temporal, almost as intimately as if I had lived in their families.'"

(*d*) HILL AND THE TWO OLD MEN.—The Rev. Thomas Jackson, of Stockwell, in the memoir of Mr. Hill, furnished to the Evangelical Magazine, states:—Perhaps no man in modern times has been more honored than Mr. Hill, as the instrument of converting souls; his talent appeared more particularly in awakening the careless; instances of which the writer has had many opportunities of witnessing; and he does not remember ever having stayed two days with Mr. H. in any town, without meeting with one person or more to whom his ministry had been made useful. One case, among many, he cannot omit: the scene occurred at Devonport, Devonshire, after Mr. H. had been preaching a missionary sermon to a crowded congregation in the large chapel in Prince's street. The people had withdrawn, and the deacons and a few friends had retired, with Mr. H., into the vestry, when two tall, venerable looking men, upwards of seventy years of age, appeared at the vestry door. After a short pause they entered, arm-in-arm, and advanced towards Mr. H., when one of them said, with some degree of trepidation, "Sir, will you permit two old sinners to have the honor to shake you by the hand?" He replied, with some reserve, "Yes, sir:" when one of these gentlemen, the other hanging on his arm, took his hand, kissed it, bathed it with his tears, and said, "Sir, do you remember preaching on the spot where this chapel now stands, fifty years ago?" "Yes, I do," was the reply. The old man then proceeded to say, "Oh, sir! never can the dear friend who has hold of my arm, or myself, forget that sermon; we were then two careless young men, in his majesty's dock-yard, posting to destruction as fast as time and sin could convey us thither. Having heard that an interesting young clergyman was to preach out of doors, we determined to go and have some fun; accordingly we loaded our pockets with stones, intending to pelt you; but, sir, when you arrived, our courage failed, and as soon as you engaged in prayer, we were so deeply moved that our purpose wavered, and as soon as you began to speak, the word came with power to our hearts; the big tears rolled down our cheeks; we put our hands in our pockets, and dropped the stones one after another. until they were all gone; for God had taken the stone out of our hearts. When the service was over, we retired; but our hearts were too full to speak, until we came near to our lodgings, when my friend at my elbow said, 'John, this will not do; we are both wrong; good night.' This was all he could utter; he retired to his apartment, I to mine; but neither of us dared to go to bed, lest we should awake in hell; and from that time, sir, we humbly hope we were converted to God, who, of his infinite mercy, has kept us in his ways to the present moment; and we thought, sir, if you would permit us, after the lapse of half a hundred years, to have the pleasure of shaking you by the hand. before we go home, it would be the greatest honor that could be conferred on us." Mr. H. was deeply affected; the tears rolled down his venerable cheeks in quick succession; he fell on the necks of the old men quite in the patriarchal style; and there you might have seen them, locked in each others' arms, weeping tears of holy joy and gratitude to the Father of mercies. It was a scene at which Gabriel might have rejoiced, and infidelity must have turned pale. The writer is aware that he cannot do justice to it by his description, though he feels, at this distance of time, something like celestial pleasure in recording what he then witnessed.

(*e*) NEWS FOR A DYING MINISTER.—In the latter part of the last century, a Christian minister at Shrewsbury was brought to the closing scenes of life. He had long grieved over his apparent uselessness in the church of Christ, and when seized with his last illness, this regret was considerably increased. The thought planted thorns in his pillow, and embittered his dying moments. At this very period, two persons, entirely unacquainted with the feelings of the departing minister, applied for communion with the church he had long served, and attributed their conversion to God to his labors. A friend immediately hastened to communicate the intelligence to the venerable man, who listened to the statement with holy joy beaming in his countenance; and then, gathering up his feet into the bed, adopted the language of Simeon, "Now, Lord, lettest thou thy servant depart in peace, for mine eyes have seen thy salvation," and closed his eyes for ever on earthly objects.

(*f*) A CHAIN OF INFLUENCE.—The 31st of January, 1841, when Mr. Jay, of Bath, England, completed fifty years of his ministry, it was observed by his people as a Jubilee. On that occasion the Rev. Timothy East, of Birmingham, stated, that a sermon Mr. Jay preached in London in the early part of his ministry, was blessed to the conversion of a thoughtless and dissolute young man, who became a minister. A sermon preached by that minister thirty-nine years ago, was the arrow of the Almighty that brought Mr.

East to repentance, just as he had determined to leave his native country for ever. And a sermon preached by Mr. East twenty-seven years ago, in London, was the means of the conversion of a careless, gay, and dissipated young man, who was John Williams, the late missionary to the South Seas.

(*g*) THE FAITHFUL PASTOR.—Dr. Gilly relates an anecdote, as it was told him by a well known Irish character, Thaddeus Conolly, who used to spend much of his time in wandering through Ireland, and instructing the lower classes in their native language. "I went," said he, "one Sunday, into a church, to which a new incumbent had been lately appointed. The congregation did not exceed half a dozen, but the preacher delivered himself with as much energy and affection as if he were addressing a crowded audience. After service, I expressed to the clergyman my surprise that he should hold forth so fervently to such a small number." "Were there but one," said the Rector, "my anxiety for his improvement would make me equally energetic." The following year Conolly went into the same church, the congregation was multiplied twenty-fold; a third year he found the church full.

(*h*) THE NEGRO'S ADVICE.—A young minister received a call from two different societies at once, to become their pastor. One was rich, and able to give him a large salary, and was well united; the other was poor, and so divided that they had driven away their minister. In this condition he applied to his father for advice. An aged negro servant who overheard what they said, made this reply: "Massa, go where there is the least money and the most devil." He took the advice, and was made the happy instrument of uniting a distracted church, and converting many souls to Christ.

(*i*) DR. BEECHER'S SERMON TO ONE HEARER.—Dr. Beecher once engaged to preach for a country minister on exchange, and the Sabbath proved to be one excessively stormy, cold, and uncomfortable. It was in mid-winter, and the snow was piled all along in the roads, so as to make the passage very difficult. Still the minister urged his horse through the drifts, put the animal into a shed, and went in. As yet there was no person in the house, and after looking about, the old gentleman—then young—took his seat in the pulpit. Soon the door opened, and a single individual walked up the aisle, looked about, and took a seat. The hour came for commencing service, but no more hearers.

Whether to preach to such an audience, was a question—and it was one that Lyman Beecher was not long deciding. He felt that he had a duty to perform, and he had no right to refuse to do it, because only one man could reap the benefit of it; and accordingly he went through all the services, praying, singing, preaching, and the benediction, with only *one* hearer. And when all was over, he hastened down from the desk to speak to his congregation, but he had departed.

A circumstance so rare was referred to occasionally, but twenty years after, it was brought to the doctor's mind quite strangely. Traveling somewhere in Ohio, the doctor alighted from the stage one day in a pleasant village, when a gentleman stepped up and spoke to him, familiarly calling him by name. "I do not remember you," said the doctor. "I suppose not," said the stranger; "but we once spent two hours together in a house alone in a storm." "I do not recall it, sir," added the old man, "pray when was it?" "Do you remember preaching, twenty years ago, in such a place, to a single person?" "Yes, yes," said the doctor, grasping his hand, "I do, indeed, and if you are the man, I have been wishing to see you ever since." "I am the man, sir; and that sermon saved my soul, made a minister of me, and yonder is my church! The converts of that sermon, sir, are all over Ohio."

(*j*) RESULTS OF HUMBLE EFFORTS.—At one of the anniversaries in New-York, Mr. Todd, of Northampton, Mass., said—

When a boy, Providence sent an humble, unostentatious minister among us—a man who is now laboring in the wilderness at the west, almost unknown.

There was a revival under his preaching—not much said or thought about it, for only a few poor boys and girls were the subjects. It was one among many of similar revivals under the labor of this man. The subjects were poor Sabbath school children: but I can fix my eye upon them, and see two or three of these girls are devoted wives of ministers, two or three of these boys are deacons of churches; two more, at least, ministers of the gospel (of whom the humble individual before you is one). I can point to at least eight new, vigorous, prosperous churches, gathered by these men, and nearly a score of young men from these churches, on the way to the ministry—several powerful revivals of religion, many new Sabbath schools organized, and hundreds of newborn souls, who have begun to sing the song of Moses and the Lamb.

All this can be traced directly to the little seed which this humble man of God cast by the wayside.

264. Trials of Ministers.

(*a*) WAY OF TREATING COMPLAINTS.—A young preacher stated, one day, to the late Mr. Drew, that he had received an anonymous letter, complaining of his pulpit oratory. Mr. Drew said to him, "Do not heed it, any further than to profit by its observations, if true. I have had scores of such letters since I became an author, and often with postage to pay. They never trouble me, and I generally put them into the fire. But these letters are sometimes of use. Our good qualities we may learn from our friends; from our enemies we may chance to discover our defects."

(*b*) DEJECTED MINISTER SATISFIED.—The Rev. Ambrose Morton was generally esteemed a good scholar, and remarkably humble, sanctified, and holy, but was inclined to melancholy, to his own discouragement. In his younger days, when he was assistant to another minister, some good people, in his hearing, speaking of their conversion, and ascribing it under God to that minister's preaching, he seemed cast down, as if he were of no use. A sensible countryman, who was present, and who had a particular value for his ministry, made this observation for his encouragement: "An ordinary workman may hew down timber, but it must be an accomplished artist that shall frame it for the building." Mr. M. therefore rose up, and cheerfully replied, "If I am of any use, I am satisfied." Indeed his preaching was always solid and judicious, and highly esteemed by all but himself; and was especially useful to experienced Christians.

(*c*) SOMETHING MORE AWFUL THAN THE JUDGMENT.—A celebrated preacher of the seventeenth century, in a sermon to a crowded audience, described the terrors of the last judgment with such eloquence, pathos, and force of action, that some of his audience not only burst into tears, but sent forth piercing cries, as if the Judge himself had been present, and was about to pass upon them their final sentence. In the height of this commotion, the preacher called upon them to dry their tears and cease their cries, as he was about to add something still more awful and astonishing than any thing he had yet brought before them. Silence being obtained, he, with an agitated countenance and solemn voice addressed them thus: "In one quarter of an hour from this time, the emotions which you have just now exhibited will be stifled; the remembrance of the fearful truths which excited them will vanish; you will return to your carnal occupations, or sinful pleasures, with your usual avidity, and you will treat all you have heard, 'as a tale that is told!'"

(*d*) MINISTER'S HARVEST DAY.—During the great revival of religion in America, which took place under Mr. Whitefield, and others distinguished for their piety and zeal at that period, Mr. Tennent was laboriously active, and much engaged to help forward the work; in the performance of which he met with strong and powerful temptations. The following is from his own lips:—

On the evening preceding public worship, he selected a subject for the discourse intended to be delivered, and made some progress in his preparations.

In the morning he resumed the same subject, with an intention to extend his thoughts further on it; but was presently assaulted with a temptation that the Bible was not of Divine authority, but the invention of man. He instantly endeavored to repel the temptation by prayer, but his endeavors proved unavailing. The temptation continued, and fastened upon him with greater strength as the time advanced for public service. He lost all the thoughts which he had prepared on the preceding evening. He tried other subjects, but could get nothing for the people. The whole book of God, under that distressing state of mind, was a sealed book to him; and, to add to his affliction, he was "shut up in prayer:" a cloud, dark as that of Egypt, oppressed his mind.

Thus agonized in spirit, he proceeded to the church, where he found a large congregation assembled, and waiting to hear the word; and then he was more deeply distressed than ever; and especially for the dishonor which he feared would fall upon religion through him that day. He resolved, however, to attempt the service. He introduced it by singing a psalm, during which time his agitation increased to the highest degree. When the moment for prayer commenced, he arose, as one in the most painful and perilous situation, and with arms extended to heaven, began with this exclamation, "Lord, have mercy upon me." On the utterance of this petition, he was heard; the thick cloud instantly broke away, and light shone upon his soul. The result was a deep solemnity throughout the congregation; and the house, at the end of the prayer, was a place of weeping. He delivered the subject of his evening meditations, which was brought to his full remembrance, with an overflowing abundance of other weighty and solemn matter. The Lord blessed his discourse, so that it proved the happy means of the conversion of about thirty persons. This day he ever afterwards spoke of as "his harvest day."

(*e*) TEXT FOR A DISCOURAGED MINISTER.—After the Rev. John Clark, of Trowbridge, had been engaged in the ministry for a few years, his mind became greatly depressed with a view of its responsibility, a sense of his own inability, and the want of more success. At length these discouragements were so oppressive, that he assured some Christian friends, one Sabbath afternoon, that he could preach no longer. In vain did they try to remove his difficulties, or to persuade him at least to address the congregation that evening, as no supply could be obtained. He declared his positive inability to preach any more. At this moment a pious old woman applied to speak to the minister. Being admitted, she requested him to preach from that text, "Then I said, I will speak no more in his name: but his word was in my heart as a burning fire shut up in my bones, and I was weary with forbearing, and I could not stay," Jer. 20: 9. She stated that she did not know where the words were, but that her mind was so much impressed with them, that she could not forbear to request him to preach from them that evening. Being satisfied that she was entirely unacquainted with the circumstances which had just transpired, Mr. Clark was assured that Providence had thus interposed that he should continue his ministry. He preached that evening from the text thus given, and never afterwards was greatly distressed on the subject.

(*f*) SERMON THROWN UPON THE FIRE.—Mr. Trowt's anxiety in the anticipation of the public services, had been distressing; and the trepidation of his mind was such, while conducting it, that he went home sorrowful. The aged widow of a minister endeavored to encourage him. "Do not fear," she said: "my husband once came down stairs, complaining, that it was no use for him to attempt to study any longer; and threw what he had written into the fire. I immediately took it out, and said, "No, you ought not to burn it—do not be dejected—God will be better to you than your fears!" Animated by his wife, the good man reentered his study. He composed another sermon on the occasion, which was the means of awakening a person who heard it, to serious attention to religion; and when he afterwards preached the sermon, which he had, in dejection of mind thrown in the fire, that sermon was also attended with a like blessing from God.

(*g*) ROBERT HALL'S FIRST EFFORTS.—Robert Hall, desiring a license to commence preaching, he was appointed to deliver an address in the vestry of Broadmead Chapel from 1 Tim. 4 : 10 : "Therefore we both labor and suffer reproach, because we trust in the living God, who is the Savior of all men : especially of those that believe." After proceeding for a short time, much to the gratification of his auditory, he suddenly paused, and covering his face with his hands, exclaimed, "Oh! I have lost my ideas," and sat down, his hands still hiding his face.

The failure, however, painful as it was to his tutors, and humiliating to himself, was such as rather augmented than diminished their persuasion of what he could accomplish, if once he acquired self-possession. He was therefore appointed to speak again on the same subject, at the same place, the ensuing week.

This second attempt was accompanied by a second failure, still more painful to witness, and still more grievous to bear. He hastened from the vestry, and on retiring to his room, exclaimed, "If this does not humble me, the devil must have me!" Such were the early efforts of him whose humility afterwards became as conspicuous as his talents; and who, for nearly half a century, excited universal attention and admiration by the splendor of his pulpit eloquence.

265. Faults of Ministers.

(*a*) DR. MASON'S CRITICISM.—On one occasion it is related of Dr. Mason, of New-York, that after the delivery of a discourse appointed for the day, and which he and others were expected to criticise, he was observed to remain silent much longer than usual for him on similar occasions, apparently absorbed in thought, and hesitating whether to express his opinion of the performance or not. At length he was appealed to by some one, and asked, whether he had any remarks to make. He arose, and said, "I admire the sermon for the beauty of its style—for the splendor of its imagery—for the correctness of its sentiments—and for the point of its arguments; but, sir, it wanted *one* thing;" and then pausing till the eyes of all were fixed upon him, he added, "It needed to be *baptized* in the name of the Lord Jesus Christ, to entitle it to the name of a CHRISTIAN sermon."

(*b*) DR. DWIGHT AND THE YOUNG CLERGYMAN.—A young clergyman once called upon Dr. Dwight, and inquired respecting the best method of treating a very difficult and abstruse point in mental philosophy, upon which he was preparing a sermon. "I cannot give you any information upon the subject," the doctor replied; "I am not familiar with such topics. I leave them for young men."

(*c*) DEATH-BED ESTIMATE.—A celebrated Irish preacher, distinguished for the eloquence of his pulpit preparations, is said to have exclaimed on his death-bed, "Speak not to me of my sermons; alas! I was fiddling whilst Rome was burning."

(*d*) PREACHING ALMOST EVERY THING.—The Abbé —— preached a fast-day sermon before Louis the Sixteenth, which contained a great deal of politics, finance, and government, and very little of the gospel. "It is a pity," said the king, as he came out of the church; "if the abbé had only touched a little on religion, he would have told us of every thing."

(*e*) NOT DEALING IN SCRIPTURE.—A woman went one day to hear Dr. —— preach, and, as usual, carried a pocket Bible with her, that she might turn to any of the passages the preacher might happen to refer to. But she found that she had no use for her Bible there; and on coming away, said to a friend, "I should have left my Bible at home to-day, and have brought my dictionary. The doctor does not deal in Scripture, but in such learned words and phrases as require the help of an interpreter to render them intelligible."

(*f*) LONG PULPIT EXERCISES—Complaints against long religious ser vices are very frequent. Few things appear so bad to some persons as to be kept in the house of God more than one or two hours. Let us see how it was in the seventeenth century. Mr. Howe was then minister of Great Torrington, in Devonshire. His labors here were characteristic of the times. On the public fasts, it was his common method to begin about nine in the morning, with a prayer for about a quarter of an hour, in which he begged a blessing on the work of the day; and afterwards read and expounded a chapter or psalm, in which he spent about three-quarters of an hour; then prayed an hour; preached another hour; and prayed again for half an hour. After this, he retired, and took a little refreshment for a quarer of an hour or more, the people singing all the while. He then returned to the pulpit, prayed for another hour, gave them another sermon of about an hour's length; and so concluded the service of the day, about four o'clock in the afternoon, with half an hour or more of prayer.

(*g*) A FUNNY PREACHER.—A popular preacher, after a pulpit exhibition of his *wit* to a country congregation, had particularly attracted the attention of a boy who was present. On going home to his mother, he exclaimed, "Well, mother, I shall never forget that preacher—he is the best of all I ever heard!!" "Why so, my boy?" "Oh, mother, because he was so *very funny!*" This anecdote, though short, may be a useful hint to ministers who are in the habit of indulging their natural levity in the pulpit.

(*h*) CRYING IN THE WRONG PLACE.—I remember, (says Foster, in speaking of Robert Hall,) at the distance of many years, with what vividness of the ludicrous he related an anecdote of a preacher long since deceased, of some account in his day and connection. He would, in preaching, sometimes weep, or seem to weep, when the people wondered why, as not perceiving in what he was saying any cause for such emotion, in the exact places where it occurred. After his death one of his hearers happening to inspect some of his manuscript sermons, exclaimed, "I have found the explanation; we used to wonder at the good doctor's weeping with so little reason sometimes as it seemed. In his sermons, there is written here and there on the margins, 'cry here.' Now I really believe the doctor sometimes mistook the place, and that was the cause of what appeared so unaccountable."

(*i*) PAYING LIKE A SINNER.—Several years ago, in North Carolina, where it is not customary for the tavern keepers to charge the ministers for lodging and refreshments, a preacher presumingly stopped at a tavern one evening, made himself comfortable during the night; and in the morning entered the stage without offering to pay for his accommodations. The landlord came running up to the stage, and said, "there was some one in there who had not settled his bill"—the passengers all said they had, except the preacher, who said he had understood that he never charged ministers any thing. "What, you a minister of the gospel, a man of God?" cried the inn-keeper, "you came to my house last night, you sat down at the table without asking a blessing, I lit you up to your room, and you went to bed without praying to your Maker, (for I staid there until you had undressed;) you rose and washed without saying grace, and as you came to my house like a sinner, you have got to pay like a sinner."

(*j*) THE THIRD HEAD.—A certain French preacher, after a long and pompous introduction, said, "I shall now proceed, my hearers, to divide my subject into three parts. 1. I shall tell you about that which I know, and that you do not know. 2. I shall tell about that which you know, and I do not know. 3. And lastly, I shall tell you about that which neither you nor I know." Alas! how much preaching 'comes under the third head.' How often, when Paul supplies the text, has Tully, Plato, Epictetus taught! If there was more simple, plain preaching to the conscience, instead of an ostentatious display of learning, or strife about words to no profit; we should see more faithful, consistent Christians, and more done to advance the mild kingdom of Christ.

(*k*) FALSE AND UNGODLY DELICACY.—The Rev. Dr. Griffin used to relate an anecdote of a clergyman, who said in the course of a sermon, "My dear hearers, unless you repent of your sins and turn unto God, you will go to a place that it would be indelicate to name before so refined an assembly." "Such a man," the doctor would add, "ought to be hurled with indignation from the pulpit." A sentimentalism (for the want of a better word) pervades the minds of many men, and begets a taste that savors far more of false delicacy than real refinement or good sense.

(*l*) SERMON FOR DR. MANTON.—Dr. Harris relates, that while Dr. Manton was minister at Covent Garden, he was called on to preach before the lord mayor, and the companies of the city, at St. Paul's. He studied for the occasion an elaborate discourse, and was heard by the most intelligent part of his congregation with great admiration. But, as he was returning home in the evening, a poor man pulled the sleeve of his gown, and asked if he was the gentleman who had preached before the lord mayor in the morning. On the doctor's replying in the affirmative, the man added, "Sir, I came with the hope of getting some good for my soul, but I was greatly disappointed; for I could not understand a great deal of what you said; you were quite above me." The doctor wept, and replied, "Friend, if I did not give *you* a sermon, you have given *me* one; and, by the grace of God, I will never again play the fool, in preaching before my lord mayor in such a manner."

(*m*) UNDERSTOOD BY FIVE OR SIX.—I remember some years ago, says a writer in the Religious Magazine, to have heard a young minister who was settled in a small obscure town, preach a sermon at an association meeting, which was richly adorned with the graces of finished composition. He was afterwards asked by a senior brother, whether he preached such sermons at home; and having answered in the affirmative, "And how many of your people," it was said, "do you suppose can understand you?" "About five or six," he replied. The avowal produced, as might be expected, among men of piety and experience a mixed emotion of grief and indignation. Nor can we conceive of a more gross and revolting inconsistency, than that of a Christian pastor and teacher pleasing himself and a few fond admirers by picking flowers and wearing pretty garlands, when the sheep of his flock are ready to perish for want of being properly watched and fed. What! will a man who has assumed an office of deep and awful responsibility, spend his time, his strength, and his ingenuity in courting the muses, and canvassing for literary honors, when the souls of his charge are many of them rushing, unprepared, into eternity! Oh, shameful prostitution of the noblest function!

(*n*) THE REFORMER AND THE QUAKER.—A country clergyman was boasting in a large company of the success he had met with in reforming his parishioners, on whom his labors, he said, had produced a wonderful change for the better. Being asked in what respect, he replied that, when he came first among them, they were a set of unmannerly clowns, who paid him no more deference than they did to one another; did not so much as pull off their hat when they spoke to him, but bawled out as roughly and familiarly as though he was their equal; whereas now they never presumed to address him but cap in hand and in a submissive voice, made him the best bow when they were at ten yards' distance, and styled him *your reverence* at every word. A Quaker, who had heard the whole patiently, made answer, "And so, friend, the upshot of this reformation, of which thou hast so much carnal glorying, is, that thou hast taught thy people to worship thyself."

(*o*) BAD EFFECTS OF LEVITY.—An eminent medical practitioner, who is also a man of true piety, was called to attend a patient on the Lord's day, at such a distance from his own place of worship, as to render his attendance there impossible. Not willing, however, to lose the benefit of public worship altogether, he repaired to a neighboring chapel: but as the service was far advanced, and the place much crowded, he could get no farther than the door. The preacher was long and deservedly esteemed in the Christian world, but of that class who are unhappily prone to mingle oddities and witticisms in their discourse. His text was found to be, "Almost thou persuadest me to be a Christian;" and as he proceeded, many ludicrous expressions escaped him, not at all to the taste of his professional hearer. This gentleman was, however, particularly struck with the effect of his mode of preaching on a person who stood near him, who appeared to be a very respectable and intelligent young man. After listening some time with great attention, but with evident and growing indications of uneasiness and disgust, he hastily retired from the scene, muttering in an audible tone, "If *this* be preaching the gospel of Jesus Christ, I know nothing of the meaning of the New Testament. Almost *thou* persuadest me to be an *infidel.*"

266. Miscellaneous.

(*a*) NETTLETON AND THE UNFAITHFUL MINISTER.— The following anecdote of Dr. Nettleton, is a delightful instance of his peculiar tenderness for the ministerial reputation and influence of his brethren. It serves both as a powerful rebuke to that reckless spirit which too often marks the character of flaming zealots, and as a gentle admonition for that reprehensible coldness, which perhaps equally as often prevails in the bosom of the ministry.

Dr. Nettleton was most sensitively careful to sustain the influence of his brethren. He would not, when he knew there was an evident deficiency, do any thing that might tend, in the least degree, to disparage them in the estimation of their people. There was one instance, which I am about to name, in which he showed his delicacy of feeling and address, in a most Christian manner. A clergyman who lived not far from the place where Dr. Nettleton resided, bore the reputation of an indolent and inefficient pastor, and had, in consequence, caused considerable uneasiness amongst his people. Some of the more faithful part of the church who deplored the low state of religion and growing laxity of morals among the youth of the congregation, went to Dr. Nettleton, aud desired him to come and preach to them. To this he would by no means consent, without an express invitation from the pastor, and of that he had little hope. But there happened to be a desert spot on the borders of the town, where religious meetings were seldom held, and where the influence of the pastor did not particularly extend. When he was made acquainted with the fact, he said that he had no objection to go there and hold a few evening meetings with them. He went, and without exciting observation, held several religious meetings. In a short time, a number of the youth were under deep conviction for sin. As soon as he perceived the joyful appearance, he requested all who were under serious impressions, to meet with him the next day, informing them that he had something of an important nature, which he wished to communicate. When they had all met, he advised the young ladies to go that same evening to their pastor, and ask his counsel respecting the present state of their minds; and the young men he advised to go the evening following for the same purpose. They all did as he had prudently directed them; and the effect was so powerfully electric, that the slothful pastor rose up at once, went to work with all his might, preached and labored with assiduous energy, and was the favored instrument in reaping a glorious harvest of souls. As soon as the pastor got thus fairly to work, Dr. N. retired; the pastor ever remained a faithful and useful man.

(*b*) HOW TO HAVE A GOOD MINISTER.—Every church, it is presumed, is desiring a good minister, yet every one may not in their own apprehension be favored with such a blessing. Many churches often feel that their minister is not quite what they desire him to be—not quite the man for the place which he is in. Their eyes are therefore turned away from the minister whose labors they enjoy, to some other man, or to their *beau ideal* of a minister, and they desire a change. For the benefit of such we would relate the following circumstances which we are told are substantially matters of fact.

A young man was settled in a large and popular congregation in New England, under very flattering circumstances. The church and people had settled him with the belief that he was a young man of more than ordinary talents, and with the expectation of his becoming a distinguished man. After a year or two, when the novelty of the thing had worn off, the current seemed to change, and the feeling prevailed that Mr. B—— was not, nor likely to be, quite what they expected. He did not grow as they thought he would; he did not perform that amount of labor which was needed to build up the church and interest the congregation. Things dragged heavily. The young man felt the influence of the chill atmosphere which thus surrounded him. His spirits sunk, his health ran down, and it was whispered around in the society, and in the neighboring towns, that Mr. B—— would probably have to leave, he was not the man for the place, he was not the man of talents which they had anticipated.

While things were in this state, at a meeting of the church when the pastor was absent, (perhaps called to see what should be done,) Mr. O——, an intelligent member of the church arose and said, "Brethren, I think we have been in fault respecting our minister. I think he is a young man of superior talents, and will one day be a distinguished man. But we have not sustained and encouraged him as we should. We have not spoken of him to others with esteem and confidence as we should. We have been standing and looking on, expecting him to raise both himself and us to eminence. Now let us adopt a different course. Let us encourage our minister with our prayers, our sympathies, and efforts. Let us speak of him with esteem and confidence to others, and say that we think him a man of talent, and who bids fair to be a distinguished man."

The thing was agreed upon. The leading men set the example. Very soon every one was speaking in favor of Mr. B——. His people visited him, sympathized with him, encouraged him; and people out of the society began to think how Mr. B—— was rising in the estimation of his people. The young man felt the change. The cold damp chill by which he had been surrounded, and which had benumbed the energies of his soul, was exchanged for a warm genial atmosphere. His spirits rose, his health returned, his energies awoke, and he soon showed to all that he had within him the elements of a man. Several revivals have attended his labors. In the affections of the church and people he has long since firmly established himself. They delight in him as a man of talent, as well as a good man. His name has become honorably enrolled among American authors, and he is one whom his own church, and the churches of New England delight to honor. Reader, Christian, would you have a good minister? Go thou and do likewise.

(*c*) THE MINISTER'S APPEAL.—A minister who was called to preach probationally to a vacant congregation, after sermon was addressed by the deacon of the church, an amiable man, as follows:—"Sir, I should have approved your sermon highly had you closed it without that address to sinners." The young preacher in reply said, "Sir, I cannot preach a sermon without doing it." He was, however, chosen pastor of the church. Some time after, some young persons giving an account of their experience in order to their admission, one of them, the daughter of the said deacon, publicly declared that the Lord had been pleased to make *that* address, which her father had so condemned, the means of her conversion. She lived an ornament to her profession, and died happy in the Lord. The good deacon said, he should never more be an enemy to the free call of the gospel.

267. MISERS.

(*a*) PRODIGAL TURNED MISER.—A young man, of vicious principles and habits, wasted in two or three years a large patrimony in profligacy. When his last means were exhausted, his worthless associates, who called themselves his friends, treated him with neglect. Reduced to absolute want, he one day went out of the house with an intention to put an end to his life; but wandering awhile almost unconsciously, he came to the brow of an eminence which overlooked what were lately his estates. Here he sat down, and remained fixed in thought for some hours, at the end of which he sprang from the ground with a vehement exulting emotion. He had formed his resolution, which was, that all those estates should be his again; he had formed his plan too, which he instantly began to execute. He walked hastily forward, determined to seize the first opportunity to gain money, though it were ever so small a sum, and resolved not to spend, if he could help it, a farthing of whatever he might obtain. The first thing that drew his attention was a heap of coals, shot out of carts on the pavement before a house. He offered himself to put them in the place where they were to be laid, and was employed. He received a few pence for his labor; and then, in pursuance of the saving part of his plan, requested some small gratuity of meat and drink, which was given to him. He then looked out for the next thing that might offer, and went, with indefatigable industry, through a succession of servile employments in different places, of longer and shorter duration, still scrupulously avoiding, as far as possible, the expense of a penny. He promptly seized every opportunity which could advance his design, without regarding the meanness of occupation or appearance. By this method he gained, after a considerable time, money enough to purchase, in order to sell again, a few cattle, of which he had taken pains to understand the value. He speedily but cautiously turned his first gains into second advantages; retained without a single deviation his extreme parsimony; and thus advanced by degrees into larger transactions and incipient wealth. The final result was that he more than recovered his lost possessions, and died an inveterate miser, worth sixty thousand pounds. Happy would it have been for this individual, if he had discovered the same anxiety to recover the heavenly inheritance he had lost, and had pursued it with similar decision and perseverance.

(*b*) DANCER'S MODE OF LIVING—Daniel Dancer, Esq., was remarkable for a miserly disposition. Lady Tempest was the only person who had the least influence on this unfortunate man. She had one day the pleasure of prevailing on him to purchase a hat (having worn his own for thirteen years) from a Jew for a shilling; but, to her great surprise, when she called the next day, she saw the old *chapeau* still covered his head! On inquiry it was found that, after much solicitation, he had prevailed on old Griffiths, his servant, to purchase the hat for *eighteen pence*, which Mr. Dancer bought the day before for a shilling! He generally, in severe weather, laid in bed to keep himself warm; to light a fire he thought expensive, though he had 3000*l*. per annum, besides immense riches! He never took snuff, for that was extravagant, but he always carried a snuff box! This probably he would fill in the course of a month by pinches obtained from others! When the box was full he would barter the contents for a farthing candle at a neighboring green grocer's; this candle was made to last till the box was again full, as he never suffered any light in his house except while he was going to bed. He seldom washed his face and hands but when the sun shone forth; then he would betake himself to a neighboring pool, and used sand instead of soap; when he was washed he would lie on his back, and dry himself in the sun, as he never used a towel, for that would wear, and, when dirty, the washing was expensive. Since his death there have been jugs of dollars and shillings found in the stable. At the dead of night he has been known to go to this place, but for what purpose even *Old Griffiths* could not tell; but it now appears that he used to rob one jug to add to the other.

(*c*) VANDILLE, THE FRENCH MISER.—M. Vandille was the most remarkable man in Paris, both on account of his immense riches and his extreme avarice. He lodged as high up as the roof would admit, to avoid noise or visits; maintained one poor old woman to attend him in his garret, and allowed her only seven sous per week, or a half-penny per day.

His usual diet was bread and milk, and, by way of indulgence, some poor sour wine on a Sunday. This prudent economist had been a magistrate or officer at Boulogne, from which obscurity he was promoted to Paris for the reputation of his wealth, which he lent upon undeniable security to the public funds, not caring to trust individuals with what constituted all his happiness. While a magistrate at Boulogne, he maintained himself by taking upon him to be milk-taster-general at the market, and from one to another filled his belly and washed down his bread without expense to himself.

(*d*) DEATH OF A BANKER.—In December, 1790, died at Paris, literally of want, Mr. Ostervald, a well-known banker. This man felt the violence of the disease of avarice (for surely it is rather a disease than a passion of the mind) so strongly that, within a few days of his death, no importunities could induce him to buy a few pounds of meat, for the purpose of making a little soup for him. "'Tis true," said he, "I should not dislike the soup, but I have no appetite for the meat; what, then, is to become of that?" At the time that he refused this nourishment, for fear of being obliged to give away two or three pounds of meat, there was tied round his neck a silken bag which contained 800 assignats of 1000 livres each. At his outset in life he drank a pint of beer, which served him for supper, every night at a house much frequented, from which he carried home all the bottle corks he could come at: of these, in the course of eight years, he had collected as many as sold for 12 louis d'ors; a sum that laid the foundation of his fortune, the superstructure of which was rapidly raised by his uncommon success in stock-jobbing. He died possessed of 125,000*l.* sterling.

(*e*) ECONOMY OF MR. ELWES.—There have been few persons in whom avarice has predominated more than in the late Mr. Elwes. His mother, indeed, was excessively avaricious; and though she was left nearly 100,000*l.* by her husband, yet she absolutely starved herself to death. Mr. Elwes seemed not less wretched than his mother. At his house at Stoke, in Suffolk, if a window were broken, it was mended by a piece of brown paper, or by patching it with a small bit of glass; and this had been done so frequently, and in so many shapes, that it would have puzzled a mathematician to say what figure they represented. To save fire, he would walk about the remains of an old greenhouse, or sit with a servant in the kitchen! In the advance of the season his morning employment was to pick up chips, bones, or any thing he could find, and carry them home in his pocket for fire! One day he was surprised by a neighboring gentleman in the act of pulling down, with great difficulty, a crow's nest for this purpose; and when the gentleman wondered why he should give himself so much trouble, "Oh, sir," replied Elwes, "it is really a shame that these creatures should do so; do but see what waste they make. They don't care how extravagant they are." He would almost eat any thing to save expense. At a time when he was worth eight hundred thousand pounds, he would eat game at the last state of putrefaction, and meat that no other person could touch! As to his dress, any thing would do. He wore a wig for a fortnight which he had picked up in a rut in the lane when riding with another gentleman. His shoes he never suffered to be cleaned, lest they should be worn out the sooner. As the infirmities of old age, however, came upon him, he began to be more wretched. It is said that he was heard frequently at midnight as if struggling with some one in his chamber, and crying out, "I will keep my money; nobody shall rob me of my property." There are many other remarkable circumstances related of him, but what we have already quoted will afford a striking proof of the vanity of sublunary things, and of the insufficiency of riches to render mankind happy.

(*f*) QUARRELING ABOUT A FARTHING.—Sir Harvey Elwes, the miser, notwithstanding his dislike of society, was a member of a club which occasionally met at his own village of Stoke, and to which belonged two other baronets besides himself, Sir Cordwell Firebras and Sir John Barnardiston. With these three, though all rich, the reckoning was always a subject of the minutest investigation. One day, when they were engaged in settling this difficult point, a wag, who was a member, called out to a friend that was passing, "Step up stairs and assist the poor! Here are three baronets, worth a million of money, quarreling about a farthing."

(*g*) THE PETERSBURGH MISER.—A Russian merchant, who was so immensely rich that on one occasion he lent the Empress Catharine the Second a million of rubles, used to live in a small, obscure room at St. Petersburgh, with scarcely any fire, furniture, or attendants, though his house was larger than many palaces. He buried his money in casks in the cellar, and was so great a miser that he barely allowed himself the common necessaries of life. He placed his principal security in a large dog of singular fierceness, which used to protect the premises by barking nearly the whole of the night. At length the dog died; when the master, either impelled by his avarice from buying another dog, or fearing that he might not meet with one that he could so well depend on, adopted the singular method of performing the canine service himself, by going his rounds every evening, and barking as well and as loud as he could, in imitation of his faithful sentinel.

(*h*) MISER STARVED IN HIS CAVE.—In the year 1762, an extraordinary instance of avarice and peculation occurred in France. M. Foscue, one of the farmers-general of the province of Languedoc, had amassed an immense fortune by grinding the faces of the poor, and by every means, however base and cruel, that could increase his ill-gotten store. This man was ordered by the government to advance a considerable sum of money, but excused himself from complying with the order on the plea of poverty. Fearing, however, that some of the inhabitants of the province, among whom he was very unpopular, would give information to the contrary, and his house be in consequence searched, he determined to hide his money in a way which might elude examination. He dug in his wine-cellar a cave, large and deep, into which he descended by a ladder; at the entrance of which was a spring lock, which, on shutting the door, would fasten of itself. Soon after this M. Foscue disappeared. Diligent search was made for him; the ponds were dragged; and every imaginable method taken to find him, but in vain. A few months after the house was sold; and the workmen beginning to repair it, they discovered a door in the cellar, with a key in the lock. The owner ordered it to be opened, and on going down, they discovered M. F. lying dead on the ground, with a candlestick near him; and on a farther search, they found the vast wealth he had amassed. It was supposed, that when he went into his cave, the door, by some accident, shut after him; and thus, being out of the call of any person, he perished for want of food, and had even gnawed the flesh off both his arms for subsistence.

Such was the wretched end of this oppressive miser, who died in the midst of the immense treasure he had collected, which he neither enjoyed himself, nor would bestow on others. How worthless are the riches of the world if improperly used! What is their value without the favor of God accompanying them?

MISSIONS.

NEED OF MISSIONS.

268. Ignorance of the Heathen

(*a*) SUPERSTITION OF THE CHINESE.—On the 13th of May, 1818, a storm suddenly arose at Pekin, which darkened the heavens, and filled the air with sand and dust. The Emperor was excessively alarmed, conceiving it to be a divine judgment. Anxious to know the meaning of the portentous event, he required of his ministers of state to endeavor to ascertain the cause. In a public document, he reprimanded his astronomers for not having previously informed him when the hurricane was to take place: they had but three days before stated to him, that felicitous stars shed their happy influence around his person, and indicated long life and prosperity.

The Mathematical Board presented their opinion, and affirmed that if this kind of hurricane, accompanied by a descent of dust, continued a whole day, it indicated perverse behavior and discordant counsels between the sovereign and his ministers; and also a great drought and dearness of grain. If the wind should blow up the sand, move the stones, and be accompanied with noise, inundations were to be expected. If the descent of dust should continue but an hour, pestilence may be expected in the southwest regions, and half the population will be diseased in the southeast.

(*b*) THE THREE CRIMINALS. —It is perfectly natural to suppose that those who have little or no knowledge of a future state, should be careless of that life which God has given, during which to prepare for another world. A criminal among the Hindoos being condemned to be hanged on the following day, made a low salaam, or bow, to the judge, and coolly replied, *Buhost atcha*, "Very good." Another, when asked if there was any thing which he particularly wished before leaving the world, answered, "Yes; I never saw a great heap of rupees together; and, of all things, I should like to have that pleasure before I die." A third, when the same question was addressed to him, longed for something more substantial. He said, "Your food is much better than mine; now, before you hang me, pray give me such a good dinner as you have." The indulgence was granted, and he ate with no small appetite. What should be the gratitude of those who have been taught the true end of life, and what zeal should Christians manifest in conveying this knowledge to others!

(*c*) HERE WE ARE LIKE BIRDS OF PASSAGE.—"It is stated in the history of England," says Dr. Philip, in an address delivered at one of the London Anniversaries, "that when the first missionary who arrived in Kent, presented himself before the king, to solicit permission to preach the gospel in his dominions, after long deliberation, when a negative was about to be put upon his application, an aged counsellor, with his head silvered over with gray hairs, rose, and by the following speech obtained the permission which was requested. 'Here we are,' said the orator, 'like birds of passage, we know not whence we come, or whither we are going; if this man can tell us, for God's sake let him speak.' I say, if there are six hundred millions of our fellow-creatures, who, like birds of passage, know not whence they came, nor whither they are going, for God's sake let us send them the gospel, which will tell them whence they came, and which is able to make them wise unto salvation."

(*d*) WHERE SHALL I GO LAST OF ALL?—A Hindoo, of a thoughtful, reflecting turn of mind, but devoted to idolatry, lay on his death-bed. As he saw himself about to plunge into that boundless unknown, he cried out, "What will become of me?" "O," said a brahmin, who stood by, "you will inhabit another body." "And where" said he, "shall I go then?" "Into another." "And where then,"

"Into another, and so on, through thousands of millions." Darting across this whole period as though it were but an instant, he cried, "Where shall I go then?" Paganism could not answer, and he died agonizing under the inquiry, "where shall I go last of all?"

(*e*) THE MIND AND THE HEART.—It is a very instructive fact, that under the highest efforts of reason in other matters, the human mind has been satisfied with the most childish and absurd notions on the subject of religion. The men who erected the pyramids and left behind them those architectural monuments which still excite the admiration of the world, cherished with all their intellectual grandeur the most puerile and degrading notions on the subject of religion. Think of the men who planned and erected the pyramids worshiping cats and onions!

The Phenicians, who claimed the glory of the invention of letters, "and the knowledge of military and naval arts," were accustomed when attacked by enemies, to *chain* the images of their gods to their altars that they might not abandon their city! The men who had in their hands the letters and commerce of the world, worshiped gods which they felt themselves obliged to tie up with chains, lest they should run away through fear! The statesmen, and orators. and poets of ancient Rome, are even now read in the highest schools of Christendom; but think of Cicero and Tacitus and Augustus Cæsar looking into the entrails of a sheep, or watching the flight of birds, to propitiate the gods, or predict the result of a military campaign! This contrast between the mind and the heart becomes more striking when we look at distinguished individuals. Plutarch thought that our souls were made out of the moon, and would therefore return to it. This elegant and discriminating writer of ancient biography, gravely tells us, "that some think the inhabitants of the moon hang by the head to it, or, like Ixion, are tied fast to it, that its motions may not shake them from it; and it ought not to seem surprising that a lion fell out of it, into the Peloponnesus." Even the wise Plato thought the stars required and received nourishment. Seneca was of the same opinion, who says, "hence it is that so many stars are maintained, as eager for their pasture as they are hard worked both by day and night."

This contrast between the mind and the heart is certainly one of the most striking anomalies in human nature. Do we not behold the same anomaly at the present day? Does men's knowledge of religious things keep pace with their general improvement? How often are the most penetrating genius and the largest acquisitions associated with religions opinions that are grossly incorrect and miserably low. What a practical comment is here given us upon the inspired declaration, "They did not like to retain God in their knowledge."

269. Idolatry.

(*a*) IDOLATERS CAN WORSHIP ANY THING.—At Baitenzorg, a village of Java, Messrs. Tyerman and Bennet observed a street occupied exclusively by Chinese. They called at several of the houses and noticed an idol in each. In one, they observed an engraving of the French Emperor Napoleon, in a gilt frame, before which incense was burning. The old man, to whom the picture belonged, in their presence, paid it divine honors, bowing himself in various antic attitudes, and offering a prayer for blessings upon himself and family. When we asked him why he worshiped an European engraving, he replied, "O, we worship any thing."

(*b*) A MECHANIC'S ADVERTISEMENT.—The following advertisement is copied from a Chinese newspaper:—"Achen Tea Chinchin, sculptor, respectfully acquaints masters of ships, trading from Canton to India, that they may be furnished with figure heads of any size, according to order, at one-fourth of the price charged in Europe. He also recommends for private venture, the following idols, brass, gold, and silver: The hawk of Vishnoo, which has reliefs of his incarnation in a fish, boar, lion, and turtle. An Egyptian apis, a golden calf and bull, as worshiped by the pious followers of Zoroaster. Two silver mammosits, with golden ear-rings; an aprimanes for Persian worship · a ram, an alligator, a crab, a laughing hyena, with a variety of household gods on a small scale, calculated for family worship. Eighteen months' credit will be given, or a discount of 15 per cent. for prompt payment of the sum affixed to each article. Direct China Street, Canton, under the Marble Rhinoceros and Gilt Hydra."

(c) A LITTLE HEATHEN BOY AND HIS SISTERS.—"I was much affected," says the Rev. Mr. French, a missionary among the Mahrattas, in India, "by the following incident which occurred in the temple at Pimpulwundee. A little boy, about ten years of age, accompanied by two girls smaller than himself, his sisters probably, came to pay their devotions. The little boy, in a state of almost entire nudity, first washed the idol with water, and then put a little red paint on its forehead, shoulders, and breasts. This being done, he took from the little girl some small flowers, which he laid in various places on the idol; and, to crown all, he threw, after several ineffectual attempts, the idol being taller than himself, a string of flowers over its head. Having finished this part of the ceremony, the three pitiable little creatures commenced circumambulating and bowing to the senseless object which they had thus early been taught to regard as their god. I was much affected, I say, in witnessing this scene, and was led to reflect how different are the circumstances and prospects of the dear children of my native land. There the infant mind is trained in the principles of virtue and salvation. Here it is initiated into the mysteries of iniquity, and swallowed up in the darkness and superstition of idolatry. But it is a blessed thought, to be apprehended only by faith, however, that the infants of India, shall one day speak forth the praises of Immanuel. The Lord hasten that day in his own good time."

Heathen parents take their very young children to the temple of one idol and teach them how to bow and kneel, and wash, and paint, and perform the other ceremonies which are required in the worship of that idol. At another time they take them to the temple of another idol and teach them how to worship that, and so on through all the multitude of their idols; and thus they train their children up to all the wickedness and folly of idol worship.

(d) FESTIVAL OF JUGGERNAUT.—A respectable writer gives the following description of the festival of Juggernaut:—

Loud were the shouts of triumph which greeted our ears as we approached the temple of Juggernaut. Immense were the multitudes that thronged around, and thousands upon thousands would no more have been missed than a single grain from a handful of the finest sand. In a few minutes' space, we stood in front of the idol, raised upon its enormous car, and surrounded by a whole host of priests and devotees.

The first sensations which I experienced, on approaching it, were those of horror and disgust; but, alas! how were these sensations in a tenfold degree increased before the ceremonies of that day were past. The car, or tower, on which the idol was raised, stood at the height of many feet above the ground. Its sides were adorned with massive and enduring sculpture, representing the most lascivious forms and images which the mind of the wicked could suggest. The platform on the top was graced with an innumerable crowd of monsters, half-man, half-beast, in every variety and shape; and in the midst of these, the idol itself, a huge misshapen block of wood, was placed. Its visage was painted black, its mouth was of a bloody color, its arms were of gold, and its apparel was of the richest and most variegated colored silk. There it sat, in horrid, horrid listlessness, upon its elevated throne, while the priests and their assistants bowed themselves before it, and, with the most indecent attitudes and gestures, sought to propitiate its favor and its grace. Loud and long were the shouts of the multitude, as men, women, and children, all pressed forward, to lay, if it might be, even a finger upon the ropes that dragged the stupendous car. Many were the worn-out and travel-soiled pilgrims who were crushed to death in the vain and empty struggle; but loud were the plaudits which they who died received, and a smile remained upon their countenances even in the bitter hour of death.

At length the idol moved. The enormous wheels, upon which it was supported, creaked and groaned beneath its weight, and the deeply indented ground showed the immensity of the pressure that rolled along its surface. In a short space it stopped, and then the worship of the god commenced.

The chief priest advanced, and with many a low salaam began to recite a long roll of obscene and indecent verses. "These are the songs," he exclaimed, "with which the god is delighted. It is but when he is pleased that his car will move." Accordingly it did move a few paces in advance, when again it stopped, and anon a youthful being was brought forward, to attempt, if it might be, something still more lascivious, to propitiate his god. He began to caper—but I cannot, I will not, carry on the horrible description. Fancy cannot picture, the imagination cannot conceive the abominations of this worship. I turned away, in sickness of heart, and in utter loathing and disgust, from the sight; but a loud and renewed shout fell upon my ear, and involuntarily I turned round and saw an emaciated and worn-out pilgrim, with a kind of supernatural strength, and a wild devotion gleaming in his eyes, force his way through the surrounding crowd, and prostrate himself on his face in the very course of the terrific car, and, with outstretched arms and legs, await unmoved the consummation of his fate. On rolled the ponderous wheels, and ere a minute had elapsed, the misguided wretch lay crushed, dismembered, broken, a shapeless mass of flesh, and scarcely to be distinguished from the dust amongst which he was almost concealed from sight. Loud songs of praise accompanied this act of self-devotion, for the multitude believed that the victim would be received as a favored child by Juggernaut, and recalled into life in a state of everlasting happiness and joy.

270. Human Sacrifices.

(*a*) HUMAN SACRIFCES IN ANCIENT BRITAIN.—Maurice, in his "Indian Antiquities," refers thus to the worship practised by the British Druids.

The pen of history trembles to relate the baleful orgies which their frantic superstition celebrated, when, inclosing men, women and children in *one vast wicker image*, in the form of a man, and filling it with every kind of combustibles, they set fire to the huge colossus. While the dreadful holocaust was offering to their sanguinary gods, the groans and shrieks of the consuming victims were drowned amidst shouts of barbarous triumph, and the air was rent, as in the Syrian temple of old, with martial music. Religion shudders at such a perversion of its names and rites, humanity turns with horror from the guilty scene.

Such were our ancestors. To us much has been given, and of us much will be required.

(*b*) HUMAN SACRIFICES AT THE SOUTH SEA ISLANDS.—Mr. Ellis was informed by the inhabitants of Maeva, that the foundation of some of the buildings for the abode of their gods was actually laid in human sacrifices: that every pillar supporting the roof of one of the sacred houses at Maeva, was planted upon the body of a man who had been offered as a victim to the sanguinary deity for whom the temple was erected. The unhappy wretches selected were either captives taken in war, or individuals who had rendered themselves obnoxious to the chiefs or the priests.

(*c*) HABITATIONS OF CRUELTY.—Says Mr. Campbell, for twelve years a missionary in India—

"The human sacrifices which Hindooism demands, are frightful and appalling. Whatever may be the character of the people, and however quiet, and passive, and submissive they appear, their superstition is the most cruel and barbarous that has ever been established. In Goomsoor, a province which has lately fallen into the hands of the British, the horrid scenes which have been discovered, are almost beyond credibility. Whenever a disease raged in the family of the monarch, a human sacrifice was demanded to appease the offended deity, and nothing less precious than the life of an only son would gratify the demon. Immured in houses and in dungeons, there were found hundreds of poor children who had been stolen from the adjoining territories; and for what purpose were they concealed and preserved? that they might be fattened like so many sheep and oxen for the slaughter, and might, at a suitable season, be offered up to the Moloch of the country.

"At the seed-time, the farmers of a district would assemble together; a human victim was selected, was bound as a sacrifice to the altar, and was devoted to the most barbarous death. While the priests proclaim the omens to be propitious, one farmer would come, and with a large knife, would take a slice from the victim, would carry it away to his field, and would press the blood out of it while it was yet warm, and then bury it in the earth. A second, and a third, and a fourth, would come and act a similar part, till the wretched man was sliced in pieces while he was yet alive, and was consigned to various parts of the ground. But why this barbarity? That the favor of Maree might be obtained, and that no curse, nor blight might rest upon their land; and that a richer harvest might arise from fields watered by the blood of sacrifices. Oh! these dark places of the earth are still full of the habitations of cruelty.

"Deeds of blood and atrocity are mixed up with the habits and customs of the people, and fail to produce any great sensation. In England, if a mother strangles her infant, if a father murders his son, if a brother puts a sister to death, a thrill of horror passes through the community, the public voice is lifted up, in loud and terrible denunciations, against such a diabolical act; and the wonder is expressed how such a monster is permitted to live. But in India, such deeds are so common that they have failed to make any impression upon the community, and are often regarded by their authors as actions of merit rather than of infamy."

(*d*) HUMAN SACRIFICES IN AFRICA.—The Ashantees sacrifice human victims, to the number of one hundred, at all their great festivals, some of which occur every twenty-one days. On the death of his mother, the king offered three thousand victims, and at the death of a distinguished captain, twenty-four hundred. At the funeral of a person of rank, it is usual to wet the grave by the blood of a freeman, who is slaughtered unsuspectingly, while assisting in the funeral rites, and rolled into the grave with the corpse. A regular correspondence is supposed by them to be kept up with the invisible world. Hence the king, wishing to send to any of his deceased friends, calls a servant, delivers to him a message, and kills him that he may carry it. Then, if he wishes to make any addition to the message, he calls another slave, and treats him in like manner; and all with the same indifference with which one of us would write a letter and add a postscript.

271. Self-Torture and Self-Murder.

(*a*) DEVOTEES OF JUGGERNAUT.—The facts below are gleaned from Dr. Duff's work on India, and from the organs of missionary societies.

Many of the pilgrims to Juggernaut, from the most distant parts of India, measure the whole distance of their weary pilgrimage with their own bodies on the ground. Some remain all day with their heads on the ground and their feet in the air, some cram their eyes with mud and their mouths with straw. One man may be seen lying with his foot tied to his neck, another with a pot of fire on his breast, and a third enveloped in a net of ropes. At the festival of Charak Pujah, so called, because then is endured the torture of hook swinging so well known, many of the devotees throw themselves down from the top of a high wall, or a scaffold twenty feet high, on iron spikes or knives, that are so thickly stuck in a large bag of straw. At night, numbers of the devotees sit down in the open air, pierce the skin of their foreheads, insert a small rod of iron, to which is suspended a lamp, which is kept burning until the morning dawn. Some have their breasts and arms stuck entirely full of pins, about the thickness of packing needles. Others tie themselves to a wheel, thirty feet in diameter, and raised considerably above the ground—when the wheel turns round, their heads point alternately to the zenith and the nadir—others cover their under lip with a layer of mud, and deposit upon it some small grains, usually of mustard seed, then stretch themselves flat on their backs, exposed to the dripping dews by night and the blazing sun by day. Their vow is, that they will not stir from that position, nor turn, nor move, nor eat nor drink, till the seeds planted begin to sprout; this generally takes place on the third or fourth day. On the day of the great Charak festival, several blacksmiths are stationed in the court of the temple, with sharp instruments in their hands. When the procession reaches the temple, a class of devotees, holding in their hands rods, canes, iron spits, or tubes, approach the blacksmiths. One extends his side, it is instantly pierced through, and in passes one of his rods or canes; another extends his arm, this is perforated, and in passes his iron spit; a third protrudes his tongue, and getting it bored through, he passes in a cord or serpent! These devotees may be seen, in the midst of loud, discordant sounds and frantic dances, pulling backward and forward, through their wounded members, the rods and the canes, the spits and the tubes, the cords and the writhing serpents, till their bodies seem streaming with their own blood!

(*b*) SWINGING ON HOOKS.—Among the Hindoos, particular villages are appropriated for swinging, where the natives assemble at stated seasons. In the centre of an area, surrounded by numerous spectators, a pole from twenty to thirty feet in height is erected, on which is placed a long horizontal beam, with a rope run over a pulley at the extremity. To this rope they fix an iron hook, which, being drawn through the integuments of the foot, the swinger is suspended aloft in the air, amidst the acclamations of the multitude; the longer he is able to bear this painful exertion and the more violently he swings himself round, the greater is the supposed merit. From the flesh giving way, the performer sometimes falls from his towering height, and breaks a limb; if he escapes that accident, from the usual temperance of the Hindoos, the wound soon heals. This penance is generally voluntary, and done from supposed religious motives. Who on reading such descriptions, does not pray that a purer system of faith and morals may soon pervade these vast and populous regions!

(*c*) A HINDOO DEVOTEE.—A Brahmin from the north, says a missionary, has visited these parts, and is now on his way to Cape Comorin, if he has not already reached it. He rolls himself over and over on the bare ground, about three or four miles each day, on his way to the above mentioned place; and it is said that he has traveled in this manner all the way from Benares, in doing which he has consumed nine years and three months. He sets out at dawn, with thick cloths tied round his body and temples; and having reached the village fixed upon, he performs his devotions, and spends the rest of the day with his family, who travel with him in bullock-carts. He is fanned as he rolls along, by his son, a youth of ten or twelve years of age; while the musicians of the village which he leaves, or of that to which he is going, accompany him with music and shouting; thousands of people gazing with admiration upon his progress, and applauding him as "a great soul," a most religious man. When he comes to a tank or river, or other places which he cannot cross by rolling on the ground, he walks through them; and on the other side rolls the same distance along the bank, and back again. When he reaches Cape Comorin he is to set a plantain, and wait there till he offers the fruit of it to the deity whom he worships; after which, they say, he is to ro . back again to Benares, on the other side of the Ghauts. He is a stout man, of about forty years of age, and is said to be not much injured by his devoteeism. The act, instead of being regarded as a waste of time and labor, is praised by the Hindoos generally, as an evidence of the highest wisdom and magnanimity; and yet some of them, enlightened probably by Christianity, regard it as folly; unless, indeed, which is not certain, he derives a splendid profit from it in the offerings of the people. Certain it is that his family maintain a most respectable appearance; but it is said that he was a man of property before he set out on his strange pilgrimage.

(e) BORING THE TONGUE.—At Chinsurah, in the East Indies, there is a famous place of resort, called *Suraishortollah*, or the residence of the Bull-god. This is a square area, on which, beneath the shade of one vast banyan tree, several temples stand, dedicated to several popular idols, to accommodate all classes of comers. Here many self-inflicted or self-chosen cruelties are practised by those who thus hope to merit a place in the Hindoo heaven. A favorite penance is to have the tongue bored through with a large iron spike. A blacksmith is the operator, who is said to be very skillful both in driving a nail and driving a bargain. It sometimes happens that the candidates for this piece of service at his hands are so numerous and impatient, that they are obliged to submit to be arranged in order as they arrive, and wait till each in his turn can be gratified with a wound in the unruly member, which they use, meanwhile, with no small eloquence, to induce him to hasten to their relief, and when he is come, to get the business done as cheaply as they can. The shrewd knave, however, is wise enough to take his time, and extort a larger or a smaller fee, according to the number, rank, or fanaticism of his customers.

(*f*) SUFFERINGS OF A HINDOO DEVOTEE.—A missionary thus describes a singular case of self-torture. The devotee was in the act of measuring his way to Juggernaut by his own body. He never rose upon his feet in traveling. When on his knees, he reached his hands forward to the ground, and thus drew his body onward. Every time he drew himself along thus, he beat his forehead against the ground three times, looking towards the temple, which was now in sight. "When I got sufficiently near," said the missionary, "I called to him; but he did not appear to hear what I said, and continued on his way without paying the least attention. I therefore came up, and succeeded in stopping him; a deep melancholy sat visible upon his countenance, his lips moving in prayer to his god in a low, grumbling tone of voice. When I had surveyed him a few moments, he gave over repeating, and I began to converse with him as well as I was able. I first inquired how far he had come in that manner? He answered, seven hundred and fifty miles. How long have you been on the way? About eight months. He appeared about twenty-one years of age, and was so emaciated by his austerities that his voice was nearly gone: I could but just understand him. I asked him what he expected from this visit to Juggernaut? I was told that he expected almost every thing, particularly that hereby he should get rid of his sins. I then told him about Jesus Christ dying for his sins, and that if he would only believe on Christ, he would immediately find the blessings he sought. He seemed to hear with some attention and surprise. By this time a number of wicked looking Brahmins, from a neighboring temple, were gathered around us, and began to encourage him to proceed."

(*g*) THE FAKEER AND HIS BED OF SPIKES.—The following account of a Hindoo Fakeer, named Purrum Soatuntro, is given by Mr. Duncan, an English gentleman, who saw him at Benares, a large city in India.

When only ten years of age, this man began a life of self-mortification, and used to lie on thorns and pebbles. He went on thus for ten years, and then began to wander about as a fakeer (religious beggar), going from one of their pretended holy places to another. At one place he shut himself up in a cell, where he vowed to do penance for twelve years. There he stayed till vermin gnawed his flesh, and left marks which remained when Mr. Duncan saw him. At the end of a year, the Rajah, or chief of that country, taking pity on him, opened the door of his cell, hoping to persuade him to leave off tormenting himself; but the poor wretch was full of fury to be thus interrupted; and told the Rajah that he should have his curse on his head, (and all the Hindoos dread the curses of these men,) for breaking in upon him. What! Did he think that he was not above such sufferings as these! They were nothing to him! Let the Rajah get him a bed of spikes, that he might lie on it night and day, and show him what he was able to do, and then perhaps he might forgive him. Rajah, frightened at the thought of the curse of this ferocious man lighting on him, got him a bed of spikes; and this bed of spikes became a sort of triumphal car for the wretched man. He set out immediately to take very long journeys; and was drawn on this horrid bed all round the country for thousands of miles, the poor people every where worshiping him as a sort of god. He traveled about in this manner for thirty-five years! Having no longer, as he said, any inclination to roam, he wished to spend the rest of his days in Benares.

But this poor man was so blinded by the prince of the power of darkness, that he was not contented with the supposed merit of his self-torture on the bed of spikes, but he tried to put himself to greater pain. He boasted to Mr. Duncan, that he had caused water to fall on his head, night and day, in the cold season, from a pot with holes in it, placed over him, drop by drop, so that he might be constantly uneasy; and, when the hot weather came, he mortified himself in an opposite manner, by causing logs of wood to be kept burning around him, to make his sufferings from the heat greater!

272. Infanticide.

(*a*) INFANTICIDE IN PEKIN.—In the imperial city, after allowing more than one half for natural deaths, the number of exposed infants is, according to Barrow, about four thousand a year. Some of the scenes he witnessed while at Pekin, were almost incredible. Before the carts go around in the morning to pick up the bodies of infants thrown in the streets—amounting to about four and twenty every night—dogs and swine are let loose upon them. The bodies of those found are carried to a common pit without the city walls, in which the living and the dead are thrown together. This, however, is a small proportion, compared with other places. In some provinces not one out of three is suffered to live.

(*b*) THE CHILDLESS CHIEF.—On one occasion, at Raiatea, one of the Society Islands, six hundred children were assembled. A feast was prepared for them; they marched through the settlement in procession, dressed in European garments, with little hats and bonnets made by those very parents who would have destroyed them had not the gospel come to their rescue. They and their parents occupied the chapel. The appearance of the parents was most affecting. The eyes of some were beaming with delight, as the father said to the mother, "What a mercy it is that we spared our dear girl." Bitter tears rolling down the saddened countenances of others, told the painful tale that all their children were destroyed. A venerable chief, gray with age, could bear the scene no longer; he arose, and with an impassioned look and manner exclaimed, "Let me speak; I must speak. Oh that I had known that the gospel was coming, my children would have been among this happy group; but alas! I destroyed them all. I have not *one* left. I shall die childless, though I have been the father of nineteen children." Sitting down, he gave vent to his agonized feelings in a flood of tears.

(*c*) A BRUTAL FATHER.—Mr. Ellis, in his Missionary Tour, relates the following shocking instance of infanticide. A man and his wife, tenants of Mr. Young, who has for many years held, under the king, the small district of Kukuwaw, situated on the centre of Waiakea bay, resided not far from Maaro's house. They had one child, a fine little boy. A quarrel arose between them on one occasion respecting this child. The wife refusing to accede to the wishes of the husband, he, in revenge, caught up the child by the head and the feet, broke its back across his knee, and then threw it down in expiring agonies before her. Struck with the atrocity of the act, Mr. Young seized the man, led him before the king Tamehameha, who was then at Waiakea, and requested that he might be punished. The king inquired, "To whom did the child he has murdered belong?" Mr. Young answered, that it was his own son. "Then," said the king, "neither you nor I have any right to interfere; I cannot say any thing to him."

(*d*) THE RAJAH'S DAUGHTER.—The wife of a rajah, or native prince of India, had five little girls, who were put to death as soon as they were born, by order of their cruel father. When the sixth was born, the mother began to long very much to have a daughter to love, and she managed to get a servant to take it away, without the rajah knowing any thing about it. He thought that the sixth had been put to death like the rest. The poor mother never dared to send for her little girl. She never saw her again, and died soon after.

Many of the little girls in India are very pretty; they have bright dark eyes, and sweet expressive countenances. This little child grew up a very beautiful girl, and when she was eleven years old, some of her relatives ventured to bring her to her father. They thought that he would be struck with the sight of his sweet child, and that he would love her for the sake of her mother who had died. The little girl fell at his feet, and clasped his knees, and looked up in his face, and said, "My father!" What did that father do? Take her in his arms and kiss her? No! He seized her by the hair of her head, drew his sabre from his belt, and cut off her head at one blow.

273. Cruelty to Parents.

(*a*) CRUELTY TOWARDS THE INFIRM, AMONG SOUTH SEA ISLANDERS.—Before the introduction of Christianity to their islands, the natives often proved themselves destitute of natural affection in their treatment of the infirm. Sometimes the unhappy invalid was buried alive. When this was designed, a pit was dug, bathing was proposed to the sufferer, and the attendents proffered their services to convey him to the beach. Instead, however, of showing him this kindness, they bore him to the pit, and cast him in. Stones and dirt were hurried into the grave, to stifle the voice of the unhappy man. The work of murder was soon performed, and the relatives returned to their dwellings, thankful to obtain relief, by this method, from the cares which humanity enjoins. Sometimes the invalid was destroyed in a more summary manner. Having called out all the visitors, the friends or companions of the sick man armed themselves with spears, and prepared for their savage work. It was in vain that the helpless invalid cried for mercy. So far from being moved by his entreaties, they would amuse themselves with deliberate cruelty, by trying to surpass each other in throwing the spear with dexterity at the miserable suppliant, or rushing upon him, they would transfix him to the couch. So true is it that "the dark places of the earth are full of the habitations of cruelty."

(*b*) THE CONTRAST.—The second evening after we arrived, says Rev. J. Read, missionary to South Africa, we heard late in the evening that an old man and his wife had been carried away by their friends to the top of a precipice, and there left to die from hunger and cold. Early next morning I went to Pala, to request permission to try and save them. Nothing in the world could surprise him so much: he said, their friends had nothing to give them, and there was a law that such persons should not die in one of their houses, nor near the kraal; otherwise the whole neighborhood must break up and leave. He said there was no objection to our sending them food, but he could not allow them to be brought to the kraal. The next day their son came to expostulate against our conduct, saying, that he wished to leave home, and could not go until his father and mother were dead, and that we were preventing them from dying by giving them food. How strong a proof that "the dark places of the earth are full of the habitations of cruelty!"

However, we saved the lives of the

old people for the time, by sending them food daily; so that they recovered and came back to their house; and the interpreter, with our Fingo brother, visited them daily, and made known Jesus unto them. The result eternity alone will tell.

(*c*) FORMER CRUELTY OF SANDWICH ISLANDERS.—In giving an account of the former state of the Sandwich Islands, the missionaries say that the helpless and dependent, whether from age or sickness, were often cast from the habitations of their relatives and friends, to languish and to die—unattended and unpitied. An instance came to their knowledge, in which a poor wretch thus perished within sight of their dwelling, after having lain uncovered for days and nights in the open air, most of the time pleading in vain to his family, still within the hearing of his voice, for a drink of water. And when he was dead, his body, instead of being buried, was merely drawn so far into the bushes, as to prevent the offence that would have arisen from the corpse, and left a prey to the dogs who prowl through the district in the night.

(*d*) HINDOO REVENGE.—A quarrel having arisen between two brothers and a man named Gowrie, the emissaries of Gowrie entered the house of the brothers, in their absence, and carried off forty rupees. On their return, they were informed of the theft by their mother. They immediately led her out to an adjacent rivulet, and one of them severed his mother's head from her body, with the professed view, as entertained by both parent and sons, that the mother's spirit, excited by the beating of a drum during forty days, might for ever haunt, torment, and pursue to death Gowrie and the others concerned with him. The last words pronounced by the mother were, that she would blast Gowrie and those connected with him. Nor is this a solitary case of desperate revenge.

274. Cannibalism.

(*a*) BOYS FATTENED FOR SLAUGHTER.—The Rev. Dr. Carey, of Serampore, writing to a friend in England, a few years ago, had occasion to speak of Sumatra, as an important station for the establishment of a mission, which has since been done. The doctor related, that, a little time before he wrote, he had received very decisive evidence of their being cannibals. He was walking with a gentleman at Serampore, who pointed to a boy, and asked the doctor if he could imagine how he came by him. The reply was, of course, in the negative. He then stated, that he was on the east coast of Sumatra, when, having occasion to go ashore, he saw three little boys. He asked a Malay who they were, and was instantly told that they had been stolen from a neighboring island, and would be sold for food to the Battahs, (a nation inhabiting part of Sumatra,) *as soon as they were fattened.* He asked their price, was told it was 150 dollars, he paid the money, and took them on board his ship for the preservation of their lives! Truly, "the dark places of the earth are full of the habitations of cruelty."

(*b*) CANNIBALISM IN NEW ZEALAND.—Mr. Leigh tells us, that, while he was in the island of New Zealand, he was one day walking with a chief on the beach, and had his attention arrested by a considerable number of people coming from a neighboring hill. He inquired the cause of the concourse, and was told that they had killed a lad, were now roasting him, and then intended to eat him. He immediately proceeded to the place, in order to ascertain the truth of the appalling relation. Being arrived at the village where the people were collected, he asked to see the boy. The natives seemed much agitated at his presence, and particularly at his request, as if conscious of their guilt: it was only after a very urgent solicitation, that they directed him towards a large fire at some distance, where they said he would find him. As he was going to this place, he passed by the bloody spot on which the head of the unhappy victim had been cut off; and, on approaching, he was not a little startled at the sudden appearance of a savage-looking man, of gigantic stature, entirely naked, and armed with a large axe. He was a good deal intimidated, but mustered up as much courage as he could, and demanded to see the lad. The cook, for such was the occupation of this terrific monster, then held up the boy by his feet. He appeared to be about fourteen years of age, and was half roasted. He returned to the village, where he found a great number of natives seated in a circle, with a quantity of coomery (a sort of sweet potato) before them, waiting for the roasted body of the youth. In this company was shown to him the mother of the child, who, with her child, were slaves, having been taken in war. She would have been compelled to share in the horrid feast, had he not prevailed on them to give up the body to be interred, and thus prevented them from gratifying their unnatural appetite.

(*c*) A STRONG-HOLD ASSAILED.—Numerous groups of islands in the Pacific have rapidly yielded to the influence of the gospel. About ninety islands have cast their idols "to the moles and to the bats," and about 400,000 idolaters have nominally (not all truly) embraced Christianity. One of the strongest holds of cannibalism and cruelty is found in the Feejee islands.

When the posts of their temples are erected, human beings are sacrificed, their bodies baked in native ovens, and the flesh eaten by the imbruted worshipers. In 1839 a victorious war party, returning from an exterminating war, placed thirty living children in baskets, and hoisted them up to the mast-head of their canoes, to dangle in the wind as trophies of victory. By the motion of the canoes the helpless victims were dashed against the mast, and their piercing cries were speedily hushed in the silence of death.

So numerous were the victims taken in this war, that the most greedy cannibals were for a time glutted with human flesh! In some instances, this execrable appetite for human flesh has become so strong, that bodies have actually been dug up out of the grave to gratify it! The gospel has assailed this strong-hold. The Wesleyan Missionary Society, (Eng.) from whose quarterly paper these facts are taken, has a successful mission among them; 540 have expressed hope in Christ, and are regular communicants. Nearly 1,000 thousand persons, adults and children, are receiving religious instruction in the schools. Thousands of the natives, who have not embraced Christianity, have been greatly benefited by the gospel. Their manners have been reformed, their morals materially improved. Cannibalism has been abandoned by multitudes, wars are less frequent and less cruel. A few influential chiefs have united with the people of God. One of these was one of the greatest cannibals and warriors that Feejee ever produced. His conversion has astonished his countrymen and gladdened the hearts of the missionaries.

275. Treatment of Females.

(*a*) DISTRESS OF A MOTHER—A missionary in South America reproved an Indian mother for the murder of her female infants. She replied with tears, "I would to God, father, I would to God, that my mother had, by my death, prevented the distresses I endure, and have yet to endure as long as I live. Consider, father, our deplorable condition. Our husbands go out to hunt, and trouble themselves no further. We are dragged along, with one infant at the breast, and another in a basket. They return in the evening without any burden. We return with the burden of our children; and, though tired with a long march, must labor all night in grinding corn, to make *chica* for them. They get drunk, and in their drunkenness beat us, draw us by the hair of the head, and tread us under foot And what have we to comfort us for slavery that has no end? A young wife is brought in upon us, who is permitted to abuse us and our children, because we are no longer regarded. Can human nature endure such tyranny? What kindness can we show to our female children, equal to that of relieving them from such oppression, more bitter a thousand times than death?

I say again, would to God my mother had put me under ground the moment I was born."

(*b*) THE PRIEST'S REASONING.—About the beginning of 1825, Mr. King, an American missionary, spent about six months in Tyre, (of Scripture,) in Syria, and made some efforts to establish a school there for the instruction of Tyrian females. He expected to succeed, when one of the principal priests rose up and said, "It is by no means expedient to teach women the word of God. It is better for them to remain in ignorance, than to know how to read and write. They are quite bad enough with what little they now know. Teach them to read and write, and there will be no living with them." These arguments were sufficient to convince all the Greek and Catholic population of the impropriety of female education.

(*c*) THE HEATHEN ARE WITHOUT NATURAL AFFECTION.—A Hindoo family, after a pilgrimage of nearly two thousand miles on foot, had arrived within about one hundred and fifty miles of the temple of Juggernaut, when the mother was attacked with cholera. The husband immediately forsook her. With an infant at her breast, and reduced as she was, she crawled to a neighboring village, hoping to find a shelter: but every application proved unsuccessful. Denied admittance at every house, she lay, in a stormy night, with her infant, upon the naked ground. Mr. Sutton having been informed of her suffering condition, repaired to the spot, and found mother and infant lying under a tree, drenched with rain. He had her removed, and gave her medicine; but on the second day she died. The infant was almost famished. Mr. S. used every persuasion to obtain for it nourishment and care, but he was unsuccessful. The unfeeling reply of every person was—"It is only a girl." He applied finally to the owner of the village, a wealthy man, and a priest of Juggernaut. The heard-hearted man could coolly say, "If the mother is dead, let the child die too—what else should it do? It is but a girl." At length some milk was procured, and the starving child received the nourishment with the utmost avidity. The heart of the missionary was touched by its look of imploring earnestness and unbounded joy. He resolved to cherish her as his own child She has been brought to this country and placed at a female seminary near Boston.

276. Miscellaneous.

(*a*) "THE HEATHEN HAVE NO GOOD GOD."—A New Zealand chief lay pining on a sick bed. An European visitor inquired whether he ever prayed for the restoration of his health? "No," he replied, "we have no *good* God to address; our god makes us sick and kills us, but gives us nothing. Yours is a good God who hears you when you pray, and bestows good things upon you. Pray for me and I shall get well, yours is a good God. Teach us to know him, for New Zealand people know nothing that is good." So comfortless are the instructions of heathenism, and so unlike the inspired declaration, that "like as a father pitieth his children, so the Lord pitieth them that fear Him."

(*b*) EXAMPLE OF A REVENGEFUL SPIRIT.—The Tahitians, before the introduction of Christianity among them, were as implacable and untiring in their efforts to execute plans of revenge, as savages usually are. Formerly, when one of these islanders had at length succeeded in slaying his enemy, he has bruised the body of his foe to pulp with large stones. He has then spread out the flattened mass to the sun, till it was dried like leather. Then he has glutted his remorseless hatred by wearing the covering thus formed—having made an aperture through the centre for his head—the hands dangling down in front, and the feet behind, till the hideous garment fell in pieces from the revengeful wearer. A practice similar to this, it is said, prevailed among the New Zealanders. How different is the character of the South Sea Islanders now! No people are more harmless, none more kindly affectioned one toward another.

(*c*) PRAYER MILLS OF TARTARY.—The votaries of Lamaism actually use prayer mills. The following is a description of these labor-saving machines, by Zewick.

The *kurdu*, or prayer machine, consists of hollow wooden cylinders of different sizes, filled with Tangud writings. The cylinders are painted with red stripes, and adorned with handsome gilt letters in the Sanscrit character, commonly making a distinct sentence. Each of these is fixed upon an iron axis, which goes through a square frame; this frame is capable of being shut up flat, and is formed upon a small scale, much like a weaver's shearing machine. Where the lower parts of the frame cross, there is a hole in which the axis of the cylinder turns; by means of a string which is attached to a crank in the spindle, the machine can be kept in motion, so that the cylinder turns in the frame like a grindstone upon its axis. Before the fire at Sarepta, we had two large *kurdus* of this kind, with Tangud writings of all sorts, rolled one upon another, round the spindle, in the inside of the cylinder, to the length of some hundred feet. The Moguls believe that it is meritorious respectfully to set in motion, whether by the wind or otherwise, such writings as contain prayers and other religious documents, that the knowledge of these scraps of theology may reach to the gods and bring down their blessing. These prayer mills contain the above named sentence,—a comprehensive request—repeated it may be thousands of times, and thus secure a wonderful multiplication of power. These machines are commonly found in the houses of the Moguls.

We can smile at this worthless device. Is it, however, more absurd than a heartless prayer, offered to the living God, for the coming of his kingdom, and the diffusion of Christianity among the needy heathen?

(*d*) REMORSE OF AN INDIAN.—A young Indian, belonging to one of the most untutored tribes of North America, coveted the distinction of a *brave*. To secure this rank it was necessary, by the usages of his tribe, to kill an enemy. While engaged with a war party, he attacked a little child, and when the child ran into the bushes to escape, he pursued. The child earnestly entreated him to spare his life. But the cries of the helpless fugitive were disregarded; the pursuer struck him with a spear in the breast. The wounded boy persevered in his endeavors to extract the weapon, until he fell and expired. The young man, instead of feeling happy, as he anticipated, after qualifying himself by this cruel act for the rank he coveted, became exceedingly wretched. He could not relieve his mind from painful impressions. The image of the child pleading for life, and his efforts to extract the spear, constantly haunted his imagination. Thus does conscience perform her work even in the dark mind of the savage. The Heathen are thus "a law unto themselves."

BENEFITS OF MISSIONS.

277. Temporal Benefits.

(*a*) A MISSIONARY MAKING PEACE.—On one occasion, when Mr. Nott, a Missionary, and his companions, arrived at the island of Tubooi, the whole of its population were preparing for battle, being engaged in war. The Missionary and his friends stepped forward as mediators, saw the leaders of the contending parties, expostulated with them, brought them together, and reconciled their differences. The contending armies threw down their weapons, cordially embraced each other, went in company to a new building which was devoted to the service of God, and sat side by side to hear the gospel of peace, which was now published to many of them for the first time.

(*b*) THE WILD MEN OF THE JUNGLE.—In the interior of the island of Ceylon there is a tribe of wild men called the Veddahs. When first visited by the Wesleyan Missionaries they seemed to be the lowest specimen of human nature that had been found in all the dark region of heathenism. It is difficult to see how any thing short of idiocy could place them nearer to the brutes. The Missionary thus describes them: "They have no knowledge of God, they have never heard of such a being. They wear scarcely any covering, and have no houses. In dry weather they range the jungle, and often sleep under trees; and in the wet season they creep into the caves, or under overhanging rocks. Their beds are a few leaves; they eat with their fingers, with leaves for dishes. Sunk almost to the brute, they live and die like their shaggy companions of the forest." Even on *this* people the gospel has tried its power. More than fifty families have permanently settled down, forming two pleasant and now Christian villages. They have schoolmasters and Christian teachers. The gospel has given them improvement in civilization and the comforts of home.

Under date of July, 1841, the Missionary writes, "they have already begun to meet together for prayer, and one has become an exhorter. The government agent says that they pray daily, conduct themselves with the greatest propriety, and refrain from all labor on the Sabbath. Twelve months ago *they had never heard of God; now* 200 *have been baptized, and many more are earnestly desiring to embrace the gospel.*"

(*c*) IMPLEMENTS OF WAR CONVERTED TO PEACEFUL AND EVEN SACRED PURPOSES.—Among the natives of the South Sea Islands, war was formerly as prevalent as it now is rare, and the cruelties of their conflicts were of the most revolting description; to specify only their treatment of infant captives, the tender babe was transfixed to the mother's heart by a ruthless weapon; or it was caught by the rough grasp of the warrior and dashed against the rocks; or it was wantonly thrown up in the air and caught upon his spear, where it writhed in agony and died; sometimes the ferocious warrior strung his infant prisoners upon a cord passed through the head from ear to ear, and with a fiend-like pleasure trailed them upon the sand in triumph.

But since Christianity has inculcated her lessons of mercy, war is comparatively unknown.

Says Mr. Ellis—"Often have I seen a gun-barrel or other iron weapon, that has been carried to the forge, submitted to the fire, laid upon an anvil and beaten, not exactly into a ploughshare or a pruning-hook, (for the vine does not stretch its luxuriant branches along their sunny hills,) but beaten into an implement of husbandry, and used by the proprietor in the culture of his plantation. Their weapons of wood also have often been employed as handles for tools; and their implements of war have been converted with promptitude into the furniture of the earthly sanctuary of Jehovah. The last pulpit I ascended in the South Sea Islands was at Rurutu. The stairs that led to it were guarded by rails. I asked my companions where they had procured these rails; and they replied that they had made them with the handles of warriors' spears!"

(*d*) SWARTZ AND THE INHABITANTS OF TANJORE.—In the time of war, the fort of Tanjore, Hindostan, was in a very distressing situation; a powerful enemy was near, and the provisions were insufficient even for the garrison. There was grain enough in the country for their supply, but they had no bullocks to convey it to the fort; the people had lost all confidence in the Europeans, and the rajah in vain entreated their assistance. The only hope left them appeared to be in Mr. Swartz, an eminent Missionary. "We have lost all our credit," said the rajah to an English gentleman; "let us try whether the inhabitants will trust Mr. Swartz." Accordingly he was desired to make a speedy agreement with them, for there was no time to be lost; the sepoys were daily dying in great numbers, and the streets were literally lined with the dead every morning. Mr. Swartz, therefore, sent letters in every direction, promising to pay with his own hands for every bullock that might be taken by the enemy, and in a short time, his benevolent exertions obtained for the perishing inhabitants above a thousand bullocks. He sent catechists and other Christians into the country, at the risk of their lives, who, with all possible haste, brought into the fort a large quantity of rice, by which means it was preserved.

At another time, the inhabitants of the Tanjore country were so miserably oppressed, that many quitted the province. In consequence of their departure, all cultivation ceased, and every one dreaded the calamity of a famine. Mr. Swartz, without delay, entreated the rajah to remove the shameful oppressions, and to recall the inhabitants. His advice was followed, and the rajah endeavored to bring back the people, promising to listen to their complaints, remove their grievances, and that justice should be administered. This, however, proved fruitless; all his efforts were in vain, for the people would not believe him. Mr. Swartz was then requested to write letters to them as before. He cheerfully did so, assuring them that, at his intercession, kindness would be shown them, and that their oppressions should be removed. The people immediately believed his word, and seven thousand men came back in one day, and the rest of the inhabitants soon followed their example. He then exhorted them to exert themselves to the utmost in the cultivation of their lands, which should have commenced in June, but nothing was done even at the beginning of September. The people instantly replied, "As you have shown kindness to us, you shall not have reason to repent of it; we intend to work night and day, to show our regard for you."

(*e*) AN IDIAN TRIBE REFORMED.—At a Methodist missionary meeting in New Hampshire, Bishop Hedding said, that on one of the islands in Upper Canada, that he visited, there was a company, or tribe of Indians, the most filthy and degraded that he ever saw. They were given to intoxication in the worst manner that could be conceived of. They lived a most uncomfortable, miserable life, having scarcely food, raiment, or shelter; but it was to these wretched creatures the gospel was sent, and it became the "power of God to their salvation." They left off entirely their former habits; and when he last saw them, they appeared like another people, had built themselves houses, cultivated farms, and almost all of them were doing well. One circumstance to which he alluded was particularly touching. He said he was explaining to them the intercession of Christ through an interpreter, who was himself a converted Indian, but previously a very bad man, one who, in a passion, had murdered his wife. This was the first time they had ever heard it explained in this way, and the whole tribe were so affected, that they could hardly sit on their seats. For a time, such was the weeping and crying, he could scarcely proceed. The poor murderer was so powerfully overcome at last, that he was unable to interpret any longer.

(*f*) IMPROVED CONDITION OF THE SOUTH SEA ISLANDS.—The Rev. Mr. Orsmond, a Missionary at Eimeo, states that, some years ago, he overheard several chiefs conversing among themselves as follows—

"But for our teachers, our grass on the hill, our fences and houses would have been fire-ashes long ago," meaning that the ravages of war would have continued to desolate the land. "But for the Gospel, we should now have been on the mountains, squeezing moss for a drop of water; eating raw roots, and smothering the cries of our children, by filling their mouths with grass, dirt and cloth. Under the reign of the Messiah we stretch our feet at ease, eat our food, keep our pig by the house, and see children, wife and all at table in the same house. We did not know more than our ancestors, our kings and our parents: and we were all blind, till the birds flew across the great expanse with good seeds in their mouths, and planted them among us. We now gather the fruit and have continual harvest. It was God who put it into the hearts of those strangers to come to us. We have nothing to give them: but we are a people of thorny hands, of pointed tongues, and we have no thoughts." "If God were to take our teachers from us, we should soon be savage again. They are the great roots to the tree on the high hill: the wind strikes it, twists it, but cannot level it to the ground, for its roots are strong. Our hearts delighted in war, but our teachers love peace, and we now have peace."

(*g*) GREAT CHANGE IN RAIATEA.—At a public festival at Raiatea, a South Sea island, some of the chiefs and others addressed the company, in brief and spirited appeals to their memory, of the abominations of past times, and to their gratitude for the glorious and blessed changes which the gospel of Christ had wrought among them. They compared their present manner of feasting, their improved dress, their purer enjoyments, their more courteous behavior, the cleanliness of their persons, the delicacy of their language in conversation, with their former gluttony, nakedness, riot, brutality, filthy customs, and obscene talk. One of the speakers observed, "At such a feast as this, a few years ago, none but kings, or great chiefs, or strong men, could have got any thing good to eat; the poor, and the feeble, and the lame, would have been trampled under foot, and many of them killed in the quarrels and battles that followed the gormandizing and drunkenness." "This," said another, "is the reign of Jehovah,—that was the reign of Satan. Our kings might kill us for their pleasure, and offer our carcasses to the Evil Spirit; our priests and our rulers delighted in shedding our blood. Now, behold, our persons are safe, our property is our own, and we have no need to fly to the mountains to hide ourselves, as we used to do, when a sacrifice was wanted for Oro, and durst not come back to our homes till we heard that a victim had been slain and carried to the marae."

(*h*) THE JUSTICE'S TESTIMONY.—The Rev. Dr. Philip, of the Cape of Good Hope, states, that the honorable Justice Burton informed him, after a circuit tour, that he had made three journeys over the colony as a circuit judge; that, during these circuits, he had nine hundred cases before him, and that only two of those cases were connected with Hottentots who belonged to missionary institutions, and that neither of them were aggravated cases. On a comparison of the population at the Missionary stations with that of the rest of the colony, which was under the jurisdiction of the circuit court, the fact stated by the judge makes the proportion of crimes as one only to thirty-five.

(*i*) THE FOURTH KING.—At a missionary meeting on the island of Rarotonga, one of the Hervey group, in the Pacific Ocean, an old man, a candidate for church fellowship, said, "I have lived during the reign of four kings: in the first we were continually at war, and a fearful season it was, watching and hiding with fear were all our engagements. During the reign of the second we were overtaken with a severe famine, and all expected to perish; then we ate rats and grass, and this wood and that wood. During the third we were conquered, and became the peck and prey of the two other settlements of the island; then if a man went to fish he rarely ever returned, or if a woman went any distance to fetch food, she was rarely ever seen again. But during the reign of this third king we were visited by another king, a great king, a good king, a powerful king, a king of love, Jesus the Lord from heaven. He has gained the victory, he has conquered our hearts; therefore we now have peace and plenty in this world, and hope soon to dwell with him in heaven."

278. Spiritual Benefits.—Remarkable Conversions and Revivals.

(*a*) CONVERSION OF TUAHINE—In a letter from the Rev. Mr. Orsmond, a missionary in the South Seas, he gives the following interesting account:—

A young man named Tuahine, came loitering about my house in an unusual way. Knowing him to be one of the baser sort, I said, "Friend, have you any business with me?" Tears gushed into his eyes—he could at first hardly speak—at length he replied, "You know I am a wicked man. Shame covers my face and holds me back. To-day I have broke through all fear. I want to know, is there room for me? can I expect mercy?" I said, "How came you to have such a thought as that?" His countenance blushed; tears started from his eyes, and he said, "I was at work, putting up my garden fence. It was a long hard work, and only myself to do it. All over dirt and greatly wearied, I sat down on a little bank to rest, and said within myself, I cannot tell why, 'All this great garden, and death for my soul; all this great property, and death for ever! Oh, what shall I do?' I went immediately and bathed; then went to my wife, and told her my thoughts and wishes; she agreed to my desire, and we, on that evening, left our work, and came to this place where the word of God lives, and I have been wishing to speak to you ever since." I was quite affected to hear this tale, gave him all the instruction and encouragement which I conceived the Scriptures warranted, and am happy to say, that the man continues to live happily and worthy of the gospel.

(*b*) THE CONJURER CONVERTED.—Among other converts of Mr. Brainerd's, was a man who had been a most notorious sinner, a drunkard, a murderer, a conjurer; but who at length appeared to be an illustrious trophy of the power and the riches of Divine grace. He lived near the Forks of Delaware, and occasionally attended Mr. Brainerd's ministry; but, for a time, like many others of the Indians, was not at all reformed by the instructions which he enjoyed. About that very time he murdered a promising young Indian, and he still followed his old trade of conjuring, being held in high reputation among his countrymen. Hence, when Mr. Brainerd told them of the miracles of Christ, and represented them as a proof of his Divine mission, and of the truth of his religion, they immediately mentioned the wonders of the same kind which this man had wrought by his magical charms. As he was, in this manner, a powerful obstruction to the progress of the gospel among the Indians, Mr. Brainerd often thought it would be a great mercy if God were to remove him out of the world, for he had little or no hope that such a wretch would ever himself be converted; but He, "whose thoughts are not as our thoughts," was pleased to take a more gracious and a more effectual method of removing the difficulty.

Having been impressed by witnessing the baptism of Mr. Brainerd's interpreter, he followed him to Crossweeksung shortly after, and continued there several weeks during the season of the most remarkable and powerful awakening of the Indians. He was then brought under deep concern for his soul.

His convictions of his sinfulness and misery became by degrees more deep, and the anguish of his mind was so increased, that he knew not what to do, or whither to turn.

After continuing in this state of mind upwards of a week, he obtained such a view of the excellency of Christ, and of the way of salvation through him, that he burst into tears, and was filled with admiration, and gratitude, and praise. From that time he appeared a humble, devout, affectionate Christian.

(*c*) SUCCESS OF MISSIONS IN CEYLON.—During a remarkable effusion of the Holy Spirit upon the several stations on this island, the following scene occurred at Panditeripo:—

On the 13th of February, 1824, while Mr. and Mrs. Scudder were absent, and after the boys of the boarding-school had gone to their room, and were about to lie down to sleep, Whelpley, (a native member of the church,) was induced to exhort them, most earnestly, to flee from the wrath to come. They were roused and could not sleep. By little companies, they went out into the garden to pray, and the voice of supplication was soon heard in every quarter, each one or each company praying and weeping as if entirely alone. More than thirty were thus engaged in a small garden. The cry was, "What shall I do to be saved?" and "Lord, send thy Spirit." In about an hour Dr. Scudder returned, and after waiting awhile, rang the bell for the boys to come in. They came, and with weeping proposed the inquiry, "What shall we do to be saved?" The next day they seemed unmindful of every thing but the salvation of their souls. And soon, under the judicious instructions they received, more than twenty at this place gave en couraging evidence of conversion. This was a specimen of the displays of divine mercy witnessed at the several stations of the mission.

(*d*) THE INDIAN'S REPLY TO THE TRADER.—A trader once endeavoring to persuade the Indian brother Abraham, that the Moravian brethren were not privileged teachers, he replied, "They may be what they will; but I know what they have told me, and what God has wrought within me. Look at my poor countrymen there, lying drunk before your door. Why do you not send privileged teachers to convert them, if they can? Four years ago, I also lived like a beast, and not one of you troubled himself about me; but when the brethren came they preached the cross of Christ, and I have experienced the power of his blood, according to their doctrine, so that I am freed from the dominion of sin. Such teachers we want."

(*e*) A THIEF SAVED.—A Caffre, a fine, tall, athletic young man, addicted to all the debasing and demoralizing customs of his nation, one night resolved to go into the colony for the purpose of stealing a horse, which is a common practice with them. He immediately left home, came into the colony, and watched for an opportunity of accomplishing his purpose, which soon presented itself. He found two horses grazing in a sheltered situation near a bush, and he instantly seized one of them and made off with it as fast as he could. Elated with his success, and rejoicing in the prospect of securing his prize without being detected, he proceeded toward Caffreland, when all at once the thought struck him, "*Thou shalt not steal.*" He could go no farther. He immediately drew up the horse, and said to himself, "What is this? I have frequently heard these words before in the church, but I never felt as I do now. This must be the word of God." He dismounted and held the bridle in his hand, hesitating whether to go forward with the horse or to return back with it, and restore it to its owner. In this position he continued for upwards of an hour. At last he resolved to take the horse back again, which he accordingly did, and returned home a true penitent, determined to serve God. When he reached his dwelling, he could not rest; sleep had departed from him; the arrows of conviction stuck fast in his conscience, and he could not shake them off. The next day he took an ox out of his kraal, or cattle place, and went to the nearest village to sell it, in order that he might buy European clothing with the money, and attend the house of God like a Christian. When he returned home with his clothes, he went to the minister's house, told him all that had taken place, and requested to be admitted on trial as a church member. The minister, cheered with this statement, gladly received him; and after keeping him on trial the appointed time, and finding him consistent in his conduct, a short time ago baptized him; and he is now a full member of the Christian church, and adorning his Christian profession.

(*f*) CONVERSION OF A PRIEST OF BUDDHU.—A young priest, who was a zealous opposer of Christianity, resided in the district of Matura, in Ceylon. This spot is deemed the chief seat of Buddhism on the island. The chief priest resides here, and here also is the principal college of the Buddhist priesthood.

The priest was met incidentally, at the prison of Matura, by Mr. Lalmon, a Wesleyan assistant missionary. Both had come to the place to visit a native man, condemned to die. After some conversation, the missionary challenged the priest to produce a single proof from any of his sacred books, that a Savior for man had come into the world. The priest was highly indignant at the challenge. He went to his temple, and commenced a search for evidence from the Buddhist writings of the doctrine he was required to support. Though he continued his search at times for two years he was unsuccessful.

On visiting a neighboring district he met with another missionary, who gave him a copy of the New Testament, in Cingalese. This he took to his temple and read; but it was four years before the pride of his heart would allow him to divulge the struggle that was going on in his mind. The rank he held in the priesthood, being now second in the Island; his reputation for learning; and the influence he had among the people, were circumstances which induced him so long to resist that light and conviction which the perusal of the Scriptures had conveyed to his mind. The repetition of his visits, however, led to a disclosure of his condition. An alarm was raised, and he found it necessary to fly from the temple and take refuge in the house of the missionary.

The priests wrote a letter to him, which was signed by them all, stating that disgrace would befall them if he became a Christian; that were such a calamity to happen, their religion would receive an incurable wound. To this he paid no regard. In a second communication, they made him an offer of certain temples and emoluments, provided he would not renounce Buddhism. This likewise produced no effect. In a third letter, they declared that if he became a Christian, they would, by some means or other, take his life. This rather startled him at first. But he remained firm to his purpose, and after "learning the way of the Lord more perfectly" from the missionaries, he was publicly baptized in the presence of a very large assembly.

"The conversion of this man," said Mr. Clough, a Wesleyan missionary, "is so impressive an event, that it more than a thousand-fold rewards us for all the toils we have had in translating and publishing the Scriptures in Cingalese."

(*g*) THE BLIND SHALL SEE.—One evening about sundown, says Rev. E. Kincaid, I stopped at a city on the Irawaddy. I sat on the boat, a short distance from the bank, and began to read from my tracts. The people sat down on the shore; some, however, went to the town to say that a foreign teacher had come. The crowd increased, and I read on til sundown. At length a tall young man came wading to the boat, and said, "Teacher, have you the Acts of the Apostles?" Imagine my surprise at hearing such a question in that place. I replied, "Yes." He said again, "Teacher, have you the Gospel of John?" He was evidently well educated; I asked, therefore, "How did you learn about these books?" He told me that long ago his grandfather had obtained them from Mr. Judson, but had lost them in a great fire; and, now hearing of the foreign teacher, the old man had sent him in the hope of getting them agaim. I complied with his request, and he hastened away. A storm soon came upon us, and I removed my boat to the other end of the city, two miles distant.

About eight o'clock in the evening, the young man came again; he had been searching all along the shore for me. On his return to his grandfather, the latter inquired if he had asked the teacher to stay with him; and he had now come to invite me to his house. I went and found the old man seated in the midst of his family. He put out his hand to feel for me, and I perceived that he was blind. His family had read to him, and he spoke of the comfort he had derived from John and the Acts. "The eyes of my body," he said, "are dark; but the eyes of my mind are opened."

(*h*) CONVERSION OF AFRICANER.—One of the most extraordinary instances of the power of divine grace furnished in the annals of missions, is that of Africaner, for many years a chief among the Namacquas, a tribe of people in South Africa. He was pronounced by Mr. Campbell, "the Bonaparte of the interior of South Africa." "His name carried terror along with it for several hundred miles around his residence." He was long engaged in plundering the neighboring tribes, and did not scruple to destroy two missionary settlements.

His character may be learnt more fully from the remark respecting him, recorded by a missionary. "Soldiers are sent, who, it is hoped, will succeed in ridding the country of such a monster, whom neither religion nor government can restrain or subdue."

When Mr. Campbell visited Africa, in 1812, he wrote a conciliatory letter to this man, asking him to allow the missionaries to return to one of the stations, from which they had been driven in terror by his violence. After some delay, he granted the request. The conversation and preaching of a missionary, at this station, had such an effect. that Africaner one day said to him, "am glad that I am delivered. I have long enough been engaged in the service of the devil; but now I am free from this bondage. Jesus hath delivered me: him will I serve, and with him will I abide."

When Mr. Campbell visited Africa the second time, he wrote thus to his friends in England:

Africaner was the man of whom I was most afraid when in that country before, in consequence of the multitude of plunders in which he was engaged. There was a Griqua captain, of a different tribe, between whom and Africaner there were frequent battles. Both of these are now converted to the Christian faith. Africaner, as an act of kindness to Mr. Moffat, traveled with his people a journey of six days across Africa, to convey Mr. Moffat's books and furniture to Lattakoo. Formerly he had gone as far to attack Berend. On this occasion Africaner and Berend met together in my tent, and united in singing praises to the God of peace; and when I recollected the enmity that had formerly existed between them, compared with what I then saw, tears of joy flowed from my eyes. O my friends, after the conversion of Africaner and Berend, let a man be as wicked as he may, despair not of his conversion; for the grace of God is infinite.

It is pleasing to add that, to the day of his death, Africaner maintained the character of a consistent and useful Christion.

(*i*) CONVERSION OF CUPIDO.—Cupido, a Hottentot, was remarkable for swearing, lying, fighting and drunkenness. His vices often laid him on a sick bed. He was sometimes afraid of God, though ignorant of him; and expected that his conduct would prove the destruction of his soul. He begged all he met to point out some mode of deliverance from the sin of drunkenness, supposing that to abandon his other vices would be easy. Some directed him to witches and wizards, whom he found miserable comforters; for they told him that when persons began to make such inquiries it was a sure sign of speedy death. and that his life was not worth a farthing. Others prescribed various medicines, which he found as unavailing as the counsels of the witches. He was providentially led to Graaf Reinet, where he heard, in a discourse from the missionary Vanderlingen, that Jesus Christ, the Son of God, could save sinners from their sins. He said within himself, "That is what I want! That is what I want!" He repaired to the missionaries, expressing his wish to become acquainted with this Jesus. And he told all he met, that he had at last found one who could save sinners from their sins. Upon finding that the preaching of the missionaries fitted his own case, and laid open the secrets of his heart, he said, "This is not of man, but of God." After he had rejoiced in the hope of divine forgiveness, it was his practice to recommend Christ to others, as the only remedy for sin, who could destroy it, as he himself could witness, "both root and branch."

(*j*) CONVERSION OF MIRZA MAHOMED ALI.—Mirza Mahomed Ali, the only son of a venerable Persian Judge, was introduced to the Scottish missionaries at Astrachan, as a teacher. He was found qualified to instruct in Turkish, Persian, and Arabic. Discussions became frequent, and although they often produced in him the most violent rage, he courted their renewal. At length his mind was impressed by the truths of the Gospel, as appears from the following extract from the journal of Mr. McPherson:

"Mahomed Ali, my Arabic teacher, came at his usual hour. On offering a few remarks upon the absurdity of the system of divinity which formed the groundwork of our studies, I was more than surprised to hear him reply, 'I no more believe what is contained in that book,' pointing to the Mohammedan Confession of Faith. He now told me, that his soul was in deep waters, and that he could not sleep at night from reflecting upon his perilous situation, in professing a religion which he was afraid was not the true one."

From this time he appeared to be in great anguish of spirit, while he became more fully convinced of the truth of Christianity. After his conversion, he confessed that the fact of so many Christian missionaries being employed in different parts of the world, had made a deep impression on his heart; that he began to surmise that a religion which could lead men to do so much for their fellow creatures, must be from God; whilst among Mohammedans, none seemed to take any interest in the condition of others, whether they were in the way to heaven or not.

He was much affected with the relation in which he stood to his venerable father. "I am sure," said he, "that my apostacy will bring him down with sorrow to the grave."

A Persian gentleman was sent by Mahomed's father to reclaim him, but the young Christian remained firm.

After this, his father treated him with the utmost harshness. He was confined and beaten severely, until the missionaries applied to the governor, by whose authority he was lodged in safety in the mission house. Afterwards he was publicly baptized.

The convert did not fail to exemplify the meekness of a Christian under the abusive treatment which he endured. When he was brought to the residence of the missionaries, his head still aching from the blows his father had given him, he said, "I have suffered much since I saw you; but Christ Jesus suffered much more." On another occasion, being asked how he felt while his father was beating him, he replied, "O, nothing at all; after he was done, I wept and kissed him."

After his baptism he visited his father. Both of them wept much. The natural affections of the parent's heart were not changed by the son's apostacy, and the son's were only strengthened. The father did not upbraid him, but stated his conviction, that the devil had obtained possession of him, otherwise he never could have forsaken the Prophet, nor his aged parent. He inquired very kindly after his comfort. A few days after, Mahomed Ali received a note from his father, containing these moving appeals :—"O, my unmerciful son, how long wilt thou pain me? I once fondly cherished the hope that when I came to die, I should have laid my head upon your knees, but these hopes are fled."

The afflicted father continued to urge upon his son representations designed to shake his steadfastness, until at last he consoled himself with the Mohammedan tenet, that his son was fated to be an infidel.

The son became a zealous advocate for the Christian faith. His valuable labors proved highly useful to the mission. After the lapse of about two years, however, by some agency that was never divulged, he was prohibited, by an order from the governor-general of the southern provinces of Russia, from engaging in any missionary operations. He was not even allowed to go beyond the boundaries of the city of Astrachan, without leave from the police-master. Nor was this all. He was appointed by the government to the office of teacher in Siberia—an appointment equivalent to exile. On his way to the secluded spot, to which he had been ordered, he passed through Kazan, the seat of one of the Russian universities. A German physician of that place was so much pleased with the young convert, so struck with his talents, and so interested in his history, that he urged the principal persons in the city to procure a change of his destination, and obtain for him an appointment to a professorship in that city. After much delay, the request of the petitioners was granted, and Mahomed Ali, or Alexander Kazem Beg, as he was baptized, was appointed professor of oriental languages in the university of Kazan. He remained steadfast in the faith, adorning the doctrine of God the Savior by a life and conversation becoming the Gospel.

(*k*) HINDOO GIRL SEEKING JESUS.—A little Hindoo girl was one summer's afternoon playing before the door of her father's bungalow, when she was carried off, taken to Calcutta, and sold as a slave. She was a sweet and beautiful little girl, and the lady who bought her soon began to love her very much, and she thought that she would not make her a slave. She had no children of her own, and she liked to have a little girl to play with her and amuse her. She loved her more and more, and as she grew older, she made her her companion.

When this little girl was stolen from her father, she was too young to have learned his religion. The lady who bought her was a Mohammedan, and she brought the little girl up as a Mohammedan too. Thus she lived till she was sixteen years old, and then all at once it came into her mind, she knew not how, or why, that she was a sinner, and needed salvation. She was in great distress of mind, and went to her kind mistress for comfort, but she could not tell her of a Savior. All the lady could do was to try to amuse her, and make her forget her trouble; she hired rope-dancers, jugglers, serpent-charmers, and tried all the sports of which the natives of India are fond, to give her pleasure; these were of no use, and the little girl remained as miserable as ever. Her mistress, deeply grieved at the distress of one whom she loved so dearly, next sent for a Mohammedan priest. He had never felt the want of a Savior, and he could not understand the girl's distress. However, he took her under his care, and did his best. He taught her a long string of prayers in Arabic, a language which she did not understand. She learned the long hard words which had no meaning to her, and she repeated them five times a day, and each time she repeated them, she turned towards Mecca in the east, the birth-place of Mohammed, and bowed her face to the ground.

Did the poor girl find comfort in these dark words and idle ceremonies? No; she felt that there was no forgiveness, no salvation in these. When she had tried these prayers for three long years, the thought struck her that perhaps all this sorrow of mind was a punishment for having left the faith of her fathers, and become a Mohammedan. She set out directly in search of a brahmin or Hindoo priest, and entreated him to receive her back into the Hindoo church How do you think the brahmin answered her? He cursed her in the name of his god. She told him how unhappy she was, and how long she had suffered, and begged him to pity her, but he would not listen. She offered him a large sum of money, and then he was ready to do any thing; so she put herself under his direction, and went again and again. He told her to take an offering of flowers and fruit, morning and evening, to a certain goddess who was some way off, and once a week to offer a kid of the goats as a bloody sacrifice.

In India the people have a language of flowers. Each flower means something; and when you go into a temple, and see the flowers which have been laid on the altar, you may often tell what petitions have been offered. The flowers she brought as her offering signified a bleeding heart. Oh, there was One who would not have refused such an offering! He only could have healed her broken heart, but she knew him not. For a long, long time, did she carry flowers and fruit, morning and evening; and once a week offer a kid of the goats, and sprinkle the blood on herself and on the altar. But she found that "the blood of goats could not take away her sin;" and very often she cried out in her deep distress, "Oh I shall die, and what shall I do if I die without obtaining salvation?" At last she became ill. It was distress of mind which made her ill. Her mistress with deep sorrow watched her beloved companion sinking into an early grave. But one day, as she sat alone in her room, thinking and longing, and weeping, as her custom was, a beggar came to the door and asked alms. Her heart was so full that I suppose she spoke of what she wanted to all whom she met, in hopes that some might guide her. She began talking to the beggar, and used a word which means salvation. The man started and said, "I think I have heard that word before." "Where? oh! where have you heard it?" she eagerly asked. "Tell me where I can find that which I want, and for which I am dying; I shall soon die, and oh, what shall I do if I die without obtaining salvation?" The man told her the name of a charitable institution, where once a week two thousand poor natives were supplied with rice, and before the rice was given out, some Christian teacher used to speak to them. "I have heard it there," he said, "and they tell of one Jesus Christ who can give salvation." "Oh! where is he? Take me to him." The man cared nothing about this salvation himself. He thought she was mad, and he was going away, but she would not suffer him to go till he had given an answer; she dreaded lest she should miss that prize which now seemed almost within her reach. "Well," he said, "I can tell you of a man who will lead you to Jesus," and he directed her to that part of the town where Narraput Christian lived.

Who was Narraput Christian? He was once a rich and proud brahmin, but he had given up all his riches and honors to become a humble disciple of Jesus, and he was now an assistant missionary and preacher to his countrymen. This was the man of whom the beggar spoke.

The Hindoo girl gave the beggar a trifle, and that very evening she set out in search of Narraput Christian, the man who would lead her to Jesus. She went from house to house, and inquired of every one she met, "Where Narraput Christian, the man who would lead her to Jesus, lived?" but no one would tell her. They all knew, but they were worshipers of idols, and they did not choose to tell her. It grew late and dark, and she began to be afraid of being seen out at that hour. Her heart was nearly broken, for she thought she must return as she came, and die without obtaining salvation. She was just turning to go home, when she saw a man walking along the road. She thought she would try once more, so she asked him the same question, "Where Narraput Christian lived, the man who would lead her to Jesus?" To her great joy, he pointed her to the house, and when she reached it she met Narraput himself coming out at the door. She fell at his feet in tears, and wringing her hands in anguish she asked, "Are you Narraput Christian, the man who can lead me to Jesus? Oh take me to him; I shall die, and what shall I do if I die without obtaining salvation?" Narraput did not receive her as the Hindoo priest had done; he raised her kindly from the ground and led her into the house, where his family were met at their evening meal. "My dear young friend," he said, "sit down and tell me all." She told him her history, and as soon as she had done, she rose and said, "Now, sir, take me to Jesus. You know where he is. Oh! take me to him." Ah! if Jesus had been on earth, how willingly would he have received the poor wanderer. She thought he was on earth, and that she might go to him at once; but Narraput knew that though he was not here, he was just as able to pity and welcome her from his mercy-throne in heaven; so he only said, "Let us pray." All knelt down, and as he prayed, the poor Hindoo girl felt that she had found that which she had so long wanted.

(*l*) THE MISSIONARY AND THE PLANTER.—The Rev. Robert Young, missionary in the West Indies, tells the following story:

When I was in the interior of the country, in my former residence in the island, I was waited upon by a white planter, who requested me to go to his estate to teach his negroes morality and industry. I accordingly went, and about three hundred were at once made to assemble in his large hall. I commenced religious worship, and took my stand behind his table. I gave out a hymn, and he assisted me in singing it; and after prayer I gave out a text, which led me to speak against Sabbath-breaking, and another evil very prevalent in that country—two sins of which mine host was notoriously guilty. I perceived that the word was not very acceptable. He evidently withered under the statements I made; he seemed, by his look, to say, "You are traveling beyond your record." But I had possession, and determined to keep it. As soon as I had finished, he rose from his seat, under the influence of great excitement, and said, "I don't believe that. Now stop, my negroes. I brought him here to teach morality and industry—that is, that you are not to steal from your owner, nor to be idle while you are at work; but instead of that, he has been finding fault with me, which, to say the least, is very ungentlemanly conduct. Now," said he, "I will expose the fallacy of all that he has said. He has told you it is wrong to violate the Sabbath; but he must have forgotten that the law respecting the Sabbath was given some thousands of years before the West India Islands were discovered, and therefore it could have no adaptation to that part of the world. And, as regards the other crime of which he has said so much, I, for one, wish you could read your Bibles; for you will find it stated there, that Abraham patronized the very thing that Mr. Young has condemned." And thus, by the most shameful perversion of the Scriptures, he went on to defend his views, and sat down much elated with his performance. I rose and replied, and went further into the subject than I had done before: he rose and replied, and I rose and replied, and we kept up the discussion for two or three hours, to the no small amusement of the negroes, who could no longer subdue their risible powers, but departed with a loud laugh, exclaiming, "Ah! Massa, Parson have been too many for Buckra."

But, hear the sequel. Before I left that country, I saw this same proud planter a humble penitent at the feet of Jesus, putting his confidence alone in that blood which cleanseth from all sin. On my recent visit to the island, I waited upon him, and was delighted to see him. He expressed himself in a way that I cannot here describe: he was walking in the truth, and adorning the doctrine of God his Savior in all things.

(*m*) AN OLD IDOLATER.—One day, while Mr. Wilson, a missionary, was preaching at Raiatea, one of the South Sea Islands, where he had recently introduced the Gospel, an old man stood up and exclaimed, "My forefathers worshiped Oro, the god of war, and so have I; nor shall any thing that you can say persuade me to forsake this way. And," continued he, addressing the missionary, "what do you want more than you have already? Have you not won over such a chief, and such a chief; ay, and you have Pomare himself! what want you more?" "All—all the people of Raiatea; and you, yourself, I want!" replied Mr. Wilson. "No, no," cried the old man; "me—you shall never have me! I will do as my fathers have done; I will worship Oro; you shall never have me I assure you." Little, however, did this poor man understand the power and love of God. Such was the blessed effect of the Gospel on his heart, that, within six months from that time, this stanch, inflexible, inveterate adherent of Oro, the Moloch of the Pacific, abandoned his idol, and became a worshiper of the true God.

(*n*) AND GATHERED OF EVERY KIND.—The Rev. Mr. Coan, writing from the Sandwich Islands some eighteen months after the commencement of the great revival there, thus describes the character of the converts, and the change wrought in them. The entire document may be found in the Herald for 1839.

"Could you get a glimpse of the motley group, as they bend their steps to the house of God, or as they sit around the table of their dying Lord, I am sure that the sight of your eyes would affect, yes, melt your heart. The old and decrepit, the lame, the blind, the maimed, the withered, paralytic, those with eyes, noses, lips and limbs consumed with the fire of their own or their parents' former lust, with features distorted and figures the most deformed and loathsome, these come hobbling upon their staves, and led or borne by their friends, sit down at the table of the Lord. Among this throng you will see the hoary priest of idolatry with hands but recently washed from the blood of human victims, together with the thief, the adulterer, the sorcerer, the manslayer, the highway robber, the blood-stained murderer, and the mother—no, the monster! whose hands have reeked in the blood of her own children. All these meet together before the cross of Christ, with their enmity slain, and themselves washed and sanctified, and justified in the name of the Lord Jesus, and by the Spirit of our God.

279. Striking Exhibitions of Christian Tempers, &c.

(*a*) SOLITARY BUT NOT ALONE.—The following instructive anecdote was told by Rev. R. Moffatt, missionary from Africa, at an anniversary of the London Missionary Society. He and his companions had traveled in the interior all day and night, weary and without food. They approached a village inhabited by the Corannas, who were accustomed to bloodshed and rapine. An individual who met them warned them against entering the village; they would do so at their peril. He pointed them to the heights beyond the town, where he said they could sleep for the night.

"We tied about us the fasting girdle to prevent the gnawing of hunger. We looked at each other, for we were hungry and thirsty, and fatigued beyond measure. At last an individual came; we asked for water. It was refused. I offered two or three buttons remaining on my jacket for a little milk. It was refused with scorn. It was evident something was brewing in the minds of the people, and we had good reason to be alarmed. We lifted up our hearts to God. There we sat; and as we gazed saw a woman descend from the heights. She approached with a vessel in her hand and a bundle of wood. The vessel contained milk; having set them down, she immediately returned. She shortly came back, bringing a vessel of water in one hand and a leg of mutton in the other. She sat herself down and cut up the meat. We asked her name, and if there was any relative of hers to whom we had shown kindness; but she answered not a word. I again asked her to tell me to whom we were indebted; and after repeating the question three or four times, she at last replied, 'I know whose servants ye are, and I love Him, who hath told me, he that giveth a cup of cold water to one of his disciples shall in no wise lose his reward.' Her words seemed to glow while she wept profusely to see one of the servants of Christ. On inquiring into her history, I found she was a solitary lamp burning in that village. I asked her to tell me how she had kept the light of God alive in her soul. She drew from her bosom a Testament, and holding it up she said, 'That is the fountain from which I drink; that is the oil that keeps my lamp burning in this dark place.' I looked at the book; it was a Dutch Testament, printed by the British and Foreign Bible Society. It was given her by a missionary when she left the school! And it was that book that had been the means of her conversion, and had kept alive her piety without any teaching save that of the Holy Ghost, or any Christian fellowship except communion with God."

(*b*) A DISCOURSE ON THEFT LEADS TO THE RESTITUTION OF PILFERED PROPERTY.—Mr. Nott, missionary at Tahiti, preached from the text, "Let him that stole, steal no more." The next morning, when he opened his door, he saw a number of the natives sitting on the ground before his dwelling. He requested an explanation of this circumstance. They answered, "We have not been able to sleep all night; we were in the chapel yesterday: we thought, when we were pagans, that it was right to steal when we could do it without being found out. Hiro, the god of thieves, used to assist us. But we heard what you said yesterday from the word of God, that Jehovah had commanded that we should not steal. We have stolen, and all these things that we have brought with us are stolen goods." One then lifted up an axe, a hatchet, or a chisel, and exclaimed, "I stole this from the carpenter of such a ship," naming the vessel; others held up an *umeti*, or a saw, or a knife; and indeed almost every kind of movable property was brought and exhibited with such confessions. Mr. Nott proposed that they should take the plundered property home and restore it, when an opportunity should occur, to its lawful owners. They all said, "Oh no, we cannot take them back, we have had no peace ever since we heard it was displeasing to God, and we shall have no peace so long as they remain in our dwellings; we wish you to take them, and give them back to the owners when ever they come."

(*c*) THE CONFESSION OF THE MARTYRS.—Fourteen Christians in Madagascar, who, during the persecutions there, had spent two wretched years as fugitives in the mountains, determined to go to the sea side and sail to Mauritius. On their way they were taken prisoners, and conducted to the city.

A deeply interesting circumstance transpired as these Christians were on their way to the capital, after being apprehended. On reaching the town of Beferona, a guard was set upon them. They were told that their manner of traveling was suspicious, and not like that of other people, having lanterns at night, and striking into unusual paths. Three days successively they underwent examination; and, on the third, they resolved to witness the good confession, and therefore made the following declaration, through Andriamanana, one of their number, whom they had appointed as their spokesman: "Since you ask us again and again, we will tell you. We are not banditti nor murderers: *we are* (impivavaka) *praying people; and if this make us guilty in the kingdom of the queen, then whatever the queen does, we submit to suffer.*" "Is this, then," said the interrogator, "your final reply, whether for life or for death?" "*It is our final reply,*" they said, "*whether for life or death.*" "Who," asked the examiner, "sent you from Tananarivo?" "No one," they replied, "we went forth of our own free will." After the Christians made these declarations, it is said that they felt inexpressible peace and joy. They had prayed; they had confessed Christ; and now that concealment was at an end, and they could freely open their overburdened hearts, they said to each other, "Now we are in the situation of Christian and Faithful when they were led to the city of Vanity Fair." And so it proved, when a majority of them underwent the martyr's death after the example of Faithful.

(*d*) A SABBATH-BREAKER REBUKED.—An incident, says a missionary, occurred on the arrival of the United States at Honolulu, worthy of record. The frigate came to anchor on Sabbath morning. Captain Armstrong immediately sent off a lieutenant to make the necessary arrangements for firing a national salute. The lieutenant, in company with the United States consul, called at the residence of governor Kekuanaoa, but he was at church. A note was despatched informing him of the frigate's arrival, and that an officer was ready to make arrangements for a salute. The governor returned an answer that he was at divine service, but would attend to the business on the following day, at nine o'clock, A. M. Hence the quiet of our Sabbath was not disturbed by the discharge of cannon on sea or land. I could not but contrast the conduct of governor Kekuanaoa with that of the commanders of most vessels of war, as well as most of the public men in many parts of Christendom.

(*e*) GOOD FOR EVIL.—When it was known among the islands that Mr. Williams had been killed at Eromanga, the first proposition made by the people was of a character worthy of their Christian profession. It was not to take their clubs and spears, and go, in large numbers, to avenge the death of their beloved friend, who had fallen a victim to the cruel savages on that island; but that native teachers should be sent to carry to those blood-stained shores the gospel of peace, believing that to be the best method that could possibly be adopted to subdue their ferocious spirits, and lead them joyfully to receive and kindly treat European missionaries, who, at some future period, might go to reside among them. Two natives had the moral courage to offer their services for that particular field of missionary enterprise. They were taken thither by Mr. Heath. The chiefs, in whose charge they were left, promised to behave kindly to them and to attend to their instructions.

(*f*) THE HEART OF A NORTH AMERICAN SAVAGE SOFTENED BY THE GOSPEL.—"Whenever I saw a man shed tears," said an Indian, "I used to doubt his being a man. I should not have wept, if my enemies had cut my flesh from my bones, so hard was my heart at that time: that I now weep, is of God, who hath softened the hardness of my heart."

(*g*) A SLAVE'S LOVE FOR PUBLIC WORSHIP.—One of the missionaries in the West Indies gave the following pleasing account to show how highly the converted negroes value their religious privileges:

A slave wished his owner to give him leave to attend with God's people to pray: his answer was, "No, I will rather sell you to any one who will buy you." "Will you," said he, "suffer me to buy myself free, if me can?" "If you do, you shall pay dearly for your freedom, as you are going to pray. Two hundred and fifty pounds is your price."* "Well, massa, it is a good deal of money, but me must pray; if God will help me, me will try and pay you!" For a long time he worked hard, and at last sold all he had, except his blanket, to buy his liberty to pray in public; or in other words, to meet with those who love Jesus Christ.

(*h*) THE CARPENTER AND THE CONVERT.—A carpenter who was building the new church at Waimate, a Missionary station in New Zealand, engaged a native convert to work in his garden, and promised to pay him for his labor. As soon as the native had finished, he went to the carpenter for his wages: but instead of getting paid, another of the European workmen knocked the poor native down, and kicked him very cruelly while lying on the ground. The native bore it all most patiently, not murmuring nor resisting, till the other had ceased his cruelties; but then, starting on his feet, he seized the other by the throat, shook him as if he had been a cat, and brandished a sharp tool over his head, with which he might have taken away his life. "Now," said the native, "you see your life is in my hand; you owe your life to the preaching of the gospel. My arm is quite strong enough to kill you, but my heart is not, because I have heard the missionaries preach the gospel. If my heart were as dark as it was before I heard them preach, I would strike off your head. You owe your life to the preaching of the gospel." He then let the workman go, without having done the least harm to him.

* One hundred and forty pounds was the common price.

(*i*) "IF YOU KILL RIPA I WILL DIE WITH HIM."—Mr. Davies visited a pa at Pateriteri, belonging to two Christian chiefs Perika and Noa, who were brothers. They were expecting an attack from Ripa, a chief of Hokianga. Ripa had made an unjust demand from the two Christian chiefs, and, on their refusal to comply with it, he had marched to attack them. It was at this crisis that Mr. Davies entered the pa, and there he found them surrounded by their armed followers, engaged in solemn prayer—praying especially for the pardon of their enemies—with a white flag hoisted above their heads as a token of their desire for peace.

Mr. Davies then went out to meet Ripa and his party; and how striking was the contrast! With their bodies naked, and their faces painted red, they were listening to addresses urging them on to vengeance and slaughter. The address being ended, they rushed forward toward the pa, yelling frightfully, and dancing their war-dance, bidding bold defiance to the Christians. The Christians were assembled on the other side of the fence opposite the enemy, while one of the Christian chiefs quietly walked up and down between the two parties, telling the enemy they were acting contrary to the word of God; and that his party, though not afraid of them, were restrained by the fear of God from attacking them. Ripa and his party only amounted to twenty; while the Christians were one hundred strong. After many speeches had been made on both sides, one of Ripa's party, in striking at the fence with his hatchet, cut Noa on the head. This Christian chief tried to conceal the wound from his tribe; but some of them saw, by the blood trickling down, that he was wounded, and instantly there was a simultaneous rush from the pa, and every man's musket was leveled. In another moment Ripa and his whole party would have fallen; but Noa, the wounded chief, sprang forward, and exclaimed, "If you kill Ripa I will die with him;" and then, throwing his own body as a shield over Ripa, saved him from destruction. Peace was then made between the two parties, and there was great rejoicing. "Some years ago," adds Mr. Davies, "the very sight of blood would have been a signal for a dreadful slaughter."

(*j*) JOY OF THE REAPER.—A short time since, says Rev. Mr. Goodell, four of our Armenian brethren of the more ordinary class, I mean those whom we have never called upon in our meetings to take an active part, went on a little excursion to a place in the interior, for a change of air. Here they found quite a party of their countrymen; for the place is rather celebrated for its salubrious air and is much frequented in summer. And here, amid much ridicule at first, they established daily prayer-meetings and labored directly for the conversion of those whom they found there. And the result was that during the eight or ten days they remained, they had the happiness of seeing sixteen of those who had lately scoffed, join their little praying circle, and take part in the devotional exercises. These four brethren have just returned with joy to the capital, bringing some of their sheaves with them.

(*k*) THE INSIDE MAN LOVES HIM.—Formerly, says a New Zealand convert, I was in another road, and bore another likeness. When the new road was pointed out to us by the Missionaries, I paid no attention to it. But after these stations were broken up, I began to think about it, and my sins were discovered to me about four thousand (meaning an immense number). They were like an army come up against me to kill me, to slay me, to murder me; they fought against me and caused me great pain, as two men fight against and beat each other, and cause pain. I then began to think of taking to the new religion, and fleeing to Christ. In doing so I found relief. The Spirit, the Comforter, came to my heart, and I felt love, goodness, joy, and peace. I now love Christ. I cannot say that the outside man loves Jesus Christ; but the inside man loves him.

(*l*) A KING'S PRAYER.—Mr. Chamberlain, an American Missionary, giving an account of the opening of a new meeting-house in one of the Sandwich Islands, says, "Probably not fewer than four thousand persons were present, including most of the great personages of the nation. We were exceedingly gratified with the appearance of the King on this occasion, and also of his sister, the Princess Harieta Keopuolani. An elegant sofa, covered with satin damask of a deep crimson color. had been placed for them in the front of the pulpit. The King, in his rich Windsor uniform, sat at one end, and his sister, in a superb dress, at the other. Before the religious services commenced, the King arose from his seat, stepped to a platform in front of the pulpit, directly behind the sofa, called the attention of the congregation, and, addressing himself to the chiefs teachers, and people generally, said that this house, which he had built, he now publicly gave to God, the maker of heaven and earth, to be appropriated to his worship; and declared his wish, that his subjects should worship and serve God, obey his laws, and learn his word. The religious exercises were appropriate; and when these were closed, the Princess arose from her seat, and, taking her stand upon the platform, called the attention of the chiefs and people anew to what her brother had said, and exhorted them to remember and obey. She said God was the King above to whom they should give their hearts, and render constant homage. At the closing exercise of the occasion, the King stood up, and saying, "E pule kakou" (let us pray), addressed the throne of grace. In this act of worship, using the plural number, he gave the house anew to God, acknowledged him as his sovereign, yielded his kingdom to him, confessed his sinfulness, prayed for help, for teaching—supplicated his mercy, as a sinner, needing mercy, pardon, and cleansing—prayed to be preserved from temptation, and delivered from evil. He prayed for the different classes of his subjects: for the chiefs, teachers, learners, and common people; for the missionaries and foreign residents; and concluded, in a very appropriate manner, by ascribing unto God the kingdom, and the power, and the glory, to the world everlasting"

280. Happy Deaths of Missionary Converts.

(*a*) TRIUMPHANT DEATH OF A CONVERTED BRAHMIN.—The following statement was made by the Rev. Mr. Carey, from India, in an address before the American Tract Society, in 1825.

A young Brahmin obtained one of our tracts, and after reading it, he came to us full of anxiety, inquiring, "What shall I do to be saved?" We instructed him out of the Gospel. He came again and again, and at length renounced his idols, and, we have no doubt, gave his heart to Christ. After many weeks he joined a Christian church. But God did not suffer him to remain with us many years. He fell a prey to the cholera. A little before he died, another young native Christian came to see and to comfort him; and as he laid his languishing head on the bosom of his young friend, he broke out in an ecstasy, and said in his native tongue, "Sing, brother, sing." "And what shall I sing?" was the inquiry of his friend. "Sing salvation, salvation through the death of Jesus! Salvation through Jesus Christ." And I believe these were the last words he uttered.

(*b*) THE SIBERIAN LEPER ON HIS DEATH BED.—I heard the other day, said the Rev. Mr. Abeel, at a public meeting, from one of the brethren who had formerly been in Siberia, but was recalled from the field at the elevation of the Emperor Nicholas to the throne, a case of the most thrilling interest. That brother told me, that, as he was passing one day among a collection of Tartar tents, he found a man lying in the last stage of that loathsome disease, the *leprosy*. As the Missionary looked upon him, he lifted up his death-stricken eyes, and fastening them upon his countenance, said, "I know you." "How can that be," replied the Missionary, "have you ever seen me before?" "Oh yes, I have," replied the dying man. "Did you not preach three years ago in such a Bazaar?" "I cannot really tell," replied the Missionary, "I have no particular remembrance of it." "Don't you remember," said the man, in a tone of surprise, "you stood upon the steps of such a house?" "Oh yes," answered the other, "I do remember it now." "And do you remember what you preached there?" "No," said the Missionary, "I have no recollection." "You told us," said the man, "about Jesus who died to save sinners, and that men of every nation might come to him and he would receive and save them: Oh sir, I never heard such things before. I then believed in Jesus; I received him as my Savior, I never heard of him before or since. But now I am dying, and am looking to none other to help me." Penetrated with what he had heard and seen, he went to another tent, and found men drinking. He asked them, "Why do you not go to your brother? he lies there dying with nobody to help him." "Brother!" exclaimed they with indignation, "he is no brother of ours; he is a dog; and has abandoned us, and his soul is going down swiftly to hell." The missionary, thus repulsed, went back to comfort his dying Christian brother. He entered the solitary tent but "the spirit had fled." There lay the follower of the Lamb, dead, and with none to bury him, insomuch that the missionary was obliged to dig a hasty grave, and roll into it the emaciated and half consumed body.

281. Miscellaneous Illustrations

(*a*) EXTENSIVE INTEREST AWAKENED BY THE DISTRIBUTION OF THE NEW TESTAMENT.—The Rev. Mr. Fisher, a chaplain in Bengal, relates the following circumstances respecting a number of Hindoos who were associated together for the purpose of acquainting themselves with the truths of Christianity, in the year 1818.

It was reported that a number of strangers from several villages had assembled in a *tope*, near Delhi, and were busily employed, apparently in friendly conversation, and in reading some books in their possession, which had induced them to renounce caste, to bind themselves to love and associate with one another, and to intermarry only with their own sect, and to lead a strict and holy life. A convert employed by Mr. Fisher visited the spot, and found about five hundred people, men, women, and children, seated under the shade of the trees, employed in reading and conversation. He accosted an elderly man, and said, "Pray who are all these people, and whence came they?" "We are all poor and lowly, and read and love this book." "But what is this book?" "The book of God." "Pray let me look at it, if you please." It proved to be the New Testament, in the Hindoostanee tongue, many copies of which seemed to be in their possession, some printed and others written by themselves. The visitor pointed out the name of Jesus in one of the copies, and inquired, "Who is that?" "That is God. He gave us this book." "When did you obtain it?" "An angel from heaven gave it to us." "An angel?" "Yes—to us he was an angel—but he was a man, a learned pundit." A public reader appears to have been selected by themselves for the express purpose of reading this miraculous book; and their evenings have been habitually spent for many months in this blessed employment, crowds gathering to hear God's book. The ignorance and simplicity of many of them were very striking. They had never heard before of a printed book. All united in acknowledging the superiority of the doctrine of this book to every thing they had hitherto heard or known. An indifference to the doctrine of caste soon manifested itself, and the interference and tyrannical authority of the Brahmins became increasingly offensive. At last it was agreed to separate themselves from the rest of their Hindoo brethren, and to establish a fraternity of their own, choosing four or five, who could read the best, to be public teachers. The number daily and rapidly increasing, especially among the poor, a public meeting was deemed necessary, to which all their congenial associates were invited. A large grove near Delhi was selected for the purpose, and this interesting group had now met for the first time. They seemed to have no particular form of worship, but each individual made daily and diligent use of the Lord's prayer. They resolved to hold such a protracted meeting once a year.

It was found that this remarkable interest among so large a group of inquirers was awakened by the distribution of some new Testaments at Hurdwar.

(*b*) DEMOLITION OF A DEVIL TEMPLE IN TINNEVELLY.—In Sevel, a large and populous village in Southern India, the gospel, says the Rev. Mr. Dent, has publicly triumphed over heathenism. There were a few families there under instruction, of the Shanar tribe. All of them, with three exceptions, joined the congregation; and they then agreed among themselves to demolish their peicoil (or devil temple), and convert it into a place of worship. Soon after, I visited the village, and the people informed me of their intention: I rejoiced exceedingly, that they had come to this determination; and encouraged them to it, by citing a few passages of Scripture that related to the destruction of idolatry. They asked me to come to the spot; and I did so, in order to witness the spectacle. The most forward among our people entered the temple first; and one of them, with an axe in his hand, and with this sentence, "O Christ, help!" in his mouth, gave the chief idol a blow, and severed the head from the body: then came others, and threw down the idols and altars that were therein, demolished the inner courts and walls, and leveled them all to the ground. The idols, broken to pieces, they threw out for public exhibition; saying, "Such are the gods we have ignorantly worshiped and believed all this time! They cannot help themselves; how can they help us?" There was a great crowd of spectators collected together at this place. The heathen of the village were quite angry at this outrage and injustice, as they termed it; and would have made some attempts to recover the gods, but my presence tended considerably to still them. The heathen cried out, "O ye fools, ye madmen! what have ye been doing? Have ye cut down and destroyed the tutelar gods and goddesses of your village? Be sure that you and your families will ere long be visited

Ammen will revenge herself upon you all, shortly." Our people replied: "These are sand and clay, made by our own hands: they can never do us any injury! The Lord Jesus alone is God: Him we all worship, and he will protect us." I had a good opportunity of addressing the crowd on the folly and absurdity of their religion, and of directing them to the Lord Jesus, the Savior of poor lost creatures. The sight was overpowering to me, having never witnessed any thing of the kind before; and I thanked God for this public triumph of Christianity over idols and idolatry in the village. We went afterwards, and had a prayer in that place, which but a little before was a devil-temple, and a nest of all unclean things!

(*c*) SIVA AND HER TEMPLE.—On the 27th of January, 1826, a place of worship was opened at Rammakalchoke, eight miles from Kidderpore: it was crowded: many came from distant villages: there seemed to be an awakening among the inhabitants. Soon after that time, the Lord made bare his arm in a most glorious manner; and the idols of the heathen he began to abolish. On the 20th March the native Christians tore up their idol Siva: it was a massy stone of some hundred pounds' weight. The demolition of the idol produced a wonderful effect on the people: when the "Destroyer," for that is the meaning of the idol's name, was taken out of his temple, the whole village ran together in perfect amazement, one crying one thing, and another another: each individual, however, seemed to say, "Great is Siva of the Hindoos!" The impression, observed Ramjhee, the owner of the temple, was like the shock of an earthquake.

On the 27th of March, the idol was brought to Kidderpore, and presented to the missionaries by its owners, who had turned away from it with abhorrence. Here, indeed, says these good men, we stand amazed; and say, "What hath God wrought!" Never did our most sanguine expectations lead us to think that we should live to behold this obscene idol, in any instance, destroyed before our eyes. This is the first instance that has occurred in Bengal; and it is important to add, that the rooting out of this idol from his dwelling-place by the hands of his owners, and consigning it to destruction, has proceeded from the principles of the gospel.

The temple, in which the idol was placed, has since been taken down by its owners; and, with a part of the materials, they have erected a temple to the one only living and true God. Those very bricks which once inclosed the demon of impurity, serve for the purpose of screening the missionaries from the rays of the sun while preaching to the heathen the unsearchable riches of Christ, in a place which lies nearly in the centre of a number of villages, containing, at least, 20,000 inhabitants.

(*d*) MR. WILLIAMS' CONTRAST—In describing the influence of Christian missions on society, Mr. Williams writes in his "Missionary Enterprises," in reference to Rarotonga, I cannot forbear drawing a contrast between the state of the inhabitants, when I first visited them, in 1823, and that in which I left them, in 1834. In 1823, I found them all heathens; in 1834, they were all professing Christians. At the former period, I found them with idols and maraes; these, in 1834, were destroyed, and, in their stead there were three spacious and substantial places of Christian worship, in which congregations amounting to six thousand persons, assembled every Sabbath day. I found them without a written language; and left them reading in their own tongue the "wonderful works of God." I found them without a knowledge of the Sabbath; and when I left them, no manner of work was done during that sacred day. When I found them, in 1823, they were ignorant of the nature of Christian worship; and when I left them, in 1834, I am not aware that there was a house in the island where family prayer was not observed every morning, and every evening. I speak not this boastingly; for our satisfaction arises not from receiving such honors, but in casting them at the Savior's feet; "for his arm hath gotten him the victory," and, "HE SHALL HAVE THE GLORY."

What has been said of Rarotonga is equally applicable to the *whole* Hervey Island group; for, with the exception of a few at Mengaia, I believe there does not remain a single idolater, or vestige of idolatry, in any one of the islands. I do not assert, I would not intimate, that all the people are real Christians; but I merely state the delightful fact, that the inhabitants of this entire group have, in the short space of ten years, abandoned a dark, debasing, and sanguinary idolatry, with all its horrid rites; and it does appear to me that, if nothing more had been effected, this alone would compensate for all the privations, and labors, and expense, by which it has been effected.

(*e*) CHANGES IN TEN YEARS.—In 1830, Rev. Mr. Williams, of the London Missionary Society, first bore the gospel to the Navigator's Islands. This group lies nearly west from the Society Islands, at a distance of about 700 miles. The war-whoop was one of the first sounds that fell upon his ear. Burning villages marking the warrior's track, met his eye. The mass of the people were debased and vicious, and met together only to pollute and destroy each other.

In March, 1840, a pious Scotch gentleman visited these islands, and gives the following account:—

As we approached and sailed up the harbor, we were gradually surrounded by many canoes; and before we anchored the deck was covered by natives, all anxiously and affectionately greeting the new missionaries who arrived with us. As we passed up to the house of the resident missionary, we observed the large erection, formerly used for holding their savage dances, crowded with women, who were holding a prayer-meeting, and filling the air with notes of praise, in place of their ferocious and abominable war-songs.

The chapel is 100 feet by 27, capable of containing about 1,000 people, for they fill every corner, passages and all, besides standing at the windows outside. You may imagine my feelings, when standing in the midst of reclaimed savages, hearing them sing the praises of Jehovah, seeing them bow the head, and reverently cover the face during prayer; and during sermon seeming to devour the word as it drops from the preacher's lips; while a woman would sob out in spite of her efforts to repress it; and a man would wipe the unbidden tear from his swarthy cheek, so lately marked by all that could express a ferocious heart, but now, meek, humble, and subdued. Oh, how I wish you could be present, to see the fervor of the people, to see their subdued affectionate countenances—those whose hands were deeply stained with blood and murder, washed and purified in the blood of Jesus. In these islands 40,000 have renounced heathenism—more than 20,000 have learned to read!

282. Reflex Benefits.

(*a*) BRITISH SOLDIERS AT MAULMEIN.—In a letter addressed to the British and Foreign Bible Society, by W. Bannister, Esq., of Madras, in 1832, the following facts are related:—

The men of the —th regiment were regarded as amongst the most depraved in the country. Five or six years ago, they were stationed at Maulmein, on the other side of the Bay of Bengal. They had there no divine ordinances, and the Sabbath was scarcely known amongst them. One of the men, in a drunken fit, on one occasion, without any particular provocation, shot a sergeant of his corps, and was subsequently condemned for the crime. Before his execution, a missionary obtained access to him, and, through the blessing of God, was made instrumental in his conversion. He pleaded so affectionately and so earnestly with the prisoner, that the sentinel on guard was led to hearken to what was going forward inside the cell; and was so much affected by what he heard, that he requested, as a favor, to be admitted, whenever the missionary visited the condemned man. This soldier not only attended himself, but he told his comrades of the manner in which the missionary conversed with the criminal in such affecting terms, that many others were led to attend; and after seeing their comrade die in peace through Christ, notwithstanding the offence he had committed, they requested the missionary to come to their barracks and talk to them in the same way. This he, of course, very gladly did; and, ere long baptized about one hundred of them, as he believed, in the faith of Christ. Many of these men remained faithful to the solemn profession they had made, and became diligent students of the Bible.

(*b*) EMBARKATION OF MISSIONARIES AND THE OBJECTING SPECTATOR.—A man of the world stood upon the wharf, and saw a devoted company of foreign missionaries go abroad. "He saw the son, the daughter, the brother, and the sister, the relation, and the friend, with Christian spirit and self-denial, give the parting hand, and he protested against it." These, said he, are just such spirits and talents as we need at home, and it is not right, to send them away from the country, when we need them so much at home. But the Spirit of the Lord was there; and the spirit exhibited by these missionaries was made the means of his conversion, and he afterwards, with his own money, educated more pious young men for the ministry, than sailed in that missionary company.

(*c*) FULLER AND HIS CHURCH REWARDED.—"There was a period of my ministry," said this devoted man to a friend, "marked by the most pointed systematic effort to comfort my serious people: but the more I tried to comfort them, the more they complained of doubts and darkness. Wherever I went among them, one lamentation met my ear, 'Ah! sir, I can get no comfort. I am unable to appropriate any of the great and precious promises to myself, I looked for light and behold darkness.' I knew not what to do, nor what to think, for I had done my best to comfort the mourners in Zion. I was therefore at my wit's end. At this time it pleased God to direct my attention to the claims of the perishing heathen in India; I felt that we had been living for ourselves, and not caring for their souls. I spoke as I felt. My serious people wondered and wept over their past inattention to this subject. They began to talk about a Baptist mission. The females, especially, began to collect money for the spread of the Gospel. We met and prayed for the heathen, met and considered what could be done amongst ourselves for them, met and did what we could. And, whilst all this was going on, the lamentations ceased. The sad became cheerful, and the desponding calm. No one complained of a want of comfort. And I, instead of having to study how to comfort my flock, was myself comforted by them. They were drawn out of themselves. Sir, that was the real secret. God blessed them while they tried to be a blessing."

(*d*) MISSIONARY SOCIETY IN A THEOLOGICAL SEMINARY.—"It may not be improper for me to observe," says the Rev. Dr. Alexander, respecting the Society of Inquiry of the Theological Institution at Princeton, "that in my opinion, no part of the exercises in the Theological Seminary, has been attended with more manifest good effect than those which appertain to the proceedings of this Society."

(*e*) INFLUENCE OF A PARTICIPATION IN MISSIONS ON BAPTIST CHURCHES IN ENGLAND.—"After the departure of our brethren,—the first Baptist Missionaries to India"—says the brief narrative of the Baptist Mission, "we had time for reflection. In reviewing the events of a few preceding months, we were much impressed. The thought of having done something towards enlarging the boundaries of our Savior's kingdom, and of rescuing poor heathens and Mahomedans from under Satan's yoke, rejoiced our hearts. We were glad, also, to see the people of God offering so willingly; some leaving their country, others pouring in their property, and all uniting in prayers to Heaven for a blessing. A new bond of union was formed between distant ministers and churches. Some who had backslidden from God were restored; and others who had long been poring over their unfruitfulness, and questioning the reality of their personal religion, having their attention directed to Christ and his kingdom, lost their fears and found that peace which in other pursuits they had sought in vain. Christians of different denominations discovered a common bond of affection: and instead of always dwelling on things wherein they differed, found their account in uniting in those wherein they were agreed. In short, our hearts were enlarged: and if no other good had arisen from the undertaking, than the effect produced upon our own minds, and the minds of Christians in our own country, it was more than equal to the expense."

(*f*) PROPERTY SAVED BY A MISSIONARY BOX.—On the 14th of July, 1814, the three brigs, Eliza, Mary, and Irish Miner, sailed together from Limerick, all bound for London. Early on the 26th they fell in with the American armed ship of war Whig, commanded by James Clark, Esq. Capt. Clark was first on board the Mary of Waterford, and after examining his prize, he gave orders to take some supplies for the Whig, and then to set fire to the Mary, which was instantly complied with. After seeing her in a blaze, Capt. Clark went in his boat on board the brig Eliza, Capt. Davis. When he found her loaded with a cargo of no use to him, he gave orders immediately to set fire to her, and when the preparations were making to carry the order into execution, (which would not take three minutes time,) Capt. Clark accidentally went below into the cabin, where Capt. Davis was overwhelmed with trouble, bundling up his clothes to follow his men, who by this time had been put in chains, on board the Whig. After Capt. Clark had observed all about the cabin, and took away a heap of charts and nautical and religious books, he cast his eye on the "*Missionary Box*," and asked what it meant. Capt. Davis consequently told him the whole. He paused a little, with one end of his stick on the little box, and then broke silence. "Captain, we Americans are not at war with you nor the like of you; but with your —— government (please excuse the expression) we are at war. Captain, as your cargo belongs to your government, I will utterly destroy it: but neither you nor your vessel will I by any means hurt." With that, he ordered fifty of his men to come on board, which they did, and threw 637 sacks of corn overboard, and threw salt water over what was left for ballast so as utterly to spoil it; and when Capt. Clark understood, by the register of the Irish Miner, that part of her belonged to Capt. Davis, of the Eliza, he spared her altogether and her cargo: so that I look upon it, that the Missionary box, actually saved two vessels and one cargo. The above, I assure you, is altogether authentic.

I am, gentlemen, with respect,

Yours truly,

THOMAS PROPERT,

Master of the brig Brothers, of Pembroke.

Cardiff Roads, May 17, 1814.

The above is an extract from a letter to the Editors of the Evangelical Magazine.

Capt. Davis was a member of a Methodist church. He was in the habit of putting into the box 6d., his mate 3d., his men 1d. each, every Monday morning.

(*g*) INFLUENCE OF MISSIONS ON COMMERCE.—There is, says Mr. Dibble, one result of the missionary effort, which is often overlooked; the safety secured to ships in the Pacific that visit to refit or recruit at the different groups of islands. In former times there was not an island in all Polynesia where a ship could touch without imminent peril. There is scarcely a group of islands with which is not connected some tale of massacre. Now, throughout the whole of Eastern Polynesia, except, perhaps, the Marquesas Islands, ships may anchor, refit, and recruit; and the seamen may wander in safety over the fields, and through the groves. If the missions in the Pacific had been sustained entirely by our government and the governments of Europe, it would have been a small expenditure compared with the mere commercial advantages which have been gained—a far more economical expenditure than characterizes most of our national enterprises. What does it require to support one man-of-war or one exploring squadron? Yet how limited the results in comparison; how small, I say, if we look merely at the commercial benefit to the world!

(*h*) AN ENGLISH SEAMAN CONVERTED AT OTAHEITE.—Before the mission to the islands of the South Seas had proved successful, an English seaman, on board a trading vessel, called at Otaheite, and, through the blessing of God upon the efforts of the missionaries, was there called to the knowledge of the truth. Afterwards he was removed to a man-of-war, and became the happy instrument, by his example and conversation, of bringing thirteen or fourteen of his companions to a sense of their lost state and their need of salvation by Jesus Christ.

(*i*) VARIOUS REVIVALS IN CONSEQUENCE OF THE MONTHLY CONCERT.—The establishment of the monthly concert in this country was soon followed by great reflex spiritual blessings to the churches and congregations.

In a narrative of the state of religion within the bounds of the General Assembly of the Presbyterian Church, published, May, 1816, we find the following:

"By the last General Assembly it was recommended to the churches to join in monthly concerts of prayer, for the extension of the triumphs of the gospel. This recommendation has met with very general attention: Christians of other denominations have cordially united with us in this interesting service. God has been entreated by his people; he has answered their petitions, and blessed their souls. Several conversions to God in individual cases, and several revivals of religion in societies, may be traced to these seasons of social prayer."

In a narrative of the extensive revivals of religion in Massachusetts, Connecticut, and New Hampshire, the monthly concert is particularly noticed among other means by which these interesting seasons were promoted.

The General Association of Mass., in their Report for 1816, say: "In Sandisfield, a special attention to religion, which is traced to the monthly concert of prayer as its origin, has very recently changed the religious aspect of that people. A hope is entertained of two hundred, that they have passed from death unto life."

"It is understood in this body, that the monthly concert, attended in this and in foreign countries, has been blessed as a very great means of promoting religious attention in many places. In several instances, this concert is mentioned as the means of extensive revivals. While churches have met to pray for a world lying in wickedness, they have been led to realize their own need of those divine influences which they have attempted to implore for others." "Such is the nature of prayer; we cannot pray for others without being benefited ourselves."

(*j*) HOW TO MULTIPLY MINISTERS.—A writer in the St. Louis Observer, relates the following facts as having occurred in New England:—"One who mourned over the march of sin, said to an old man, 'Alas, for our destitution; within the bounds of our association fifty ministers might labor; we have not ten who are sound, both in health and in faith. We need forty more pressingly. How shall we get them? What shall we do?' He was somewhat surprised to hear his aged friend say, with slow severity—'Send one half of the best you have away! Send five of your ten across the ocean! He that watereth shall be watered also himself. For fifty years you have paid scarcely the least attention to our Captain's last charge, *preach to every creature*. Half were not sent, but some were sent, and their number of ministers and communicants was doubled, and doubled again, within the recollection of a middle-aged man."

HINDERANCES TO MISSIONS.

283. Bad Example and Influence of Nominal Christians.

(*a*) FIRST MISSIONARIES TO THE SANDWICH ISLANDS OPPOSED BY EUROPEANS.—When the first missionaries from America reached the Sandwich Islands, in the spring of 1820, an effort was made by some of the foreigners to have their landing and establishment at the Islands forbidden by the government. With this view, their motives were misrepresented by them to the king and chiefs. It was asserted, that while the ostensible object of the mission was good, the secret and ultimate design was the subjugation of the Islands, and the enslavement of the people: and by way of corroboration, the treatment of the Mexicans, and aborigines of South America and the West Indies, by the Spaniards, and the possession of Hindostan by the British, were gravely related. It was in consequence of this misrepresentation, that a delay of eight days occurred before the missionaries could secure permission to disembark. In answer to these allegations, the more intelligent of the chiefs remarked,—"The missionaries speak well; they say they have come from America only to do us good: if they intend to seize our islands, why are they so few in number? where are their guns? and why have they brought their wives?" To this it was replied, "It is true their number is small; a few only have come now, the more fully to deceive. But soon many more will arrive, and your islands will be lost." The chiefs again answered, "They say that they will do us good; they are few in number; we will try them for one year, and if we find they deceive us, it will then be time enough to send them away." Permission to land was accordingly granted. Mr. Young, it is said, was the only foreigner who advocated their reception.

(*b*) REMARK OF A NORTH AMERICAN INDIAN.—The missionary David Brainerd, in a tour among the Indians of North America, visited a place, then called Minnissinks. Here he offered to instruct the people in the truths of Christianity. The king, to whom he addressed himself for leave, laughed, and turning upon his heel, went away. Mr. Brainerd followed him into his house, and renewed his request; but he referred the business to another, who appeared to be a man of good natural parts. "Why," said he, "should you desire the Indians to become Christians, seeing the Christians are so much worse than the Indians? The Christians lie, steal, and drink worse than the Indians. They first taught the Indians to be drunk. They steal to that degree, that their rulers are obliged to hang them for it; and that is not enough to deter others from the practice. But none of the Indians were ever hanged for stealing, and yet they do not steal half so much; we will not consent, therefore, to become Christians, lest we should be as bad as they. We will live as our fathers lived, and go where our fathers are, when we die."

(*c*) THE CHINESE AND EUROPEAN IDOLATRY.—The more intelligent Chinese object to many parts of the Catholic system, particularly to what they call preaching down *Chinese idolatry*, and preaching up *European idolatry*, for they say, they have more reason to worship their own saints, than those of Europe, of whom they know nothing; they are willing to lay aside the worship of images wholly, but will not exchange them for those of Europe.

They are also offended at the indulgences sold for money, for this, they say, is *priestcraft*.

"I knew a merchant (says a gentleman who resided among them) who threw off his (Catholic) religion in consequence of being denied to eat pork in Lent, without paying the church, which he was not then disposed to do; and without it he understood he was to be damned, which startled him; upon this, he inquired, why he might not as well eat the flesh as fish fried in pork fat, which all the Christians in Macao were allowed to do? He therefore told the Padre, that if his salvation depended on so nice a point as the difference between fat and lean, he should no longer be of that religion, and so returned to paganism. He often asked why the English did not send Padres, who worshiped no images, and teach their religion, for it would be better approved."

284. Prejudices and Persecutions of the Heathen.

(*a*) FIRMNESS OF A HINDOO WOMAN UNDER PERSECUTION.—The Rev. Mr. Sutton, a Baptist missionary, related the following account at a public meeting in New-York.

A Hindoo woman, who professed to have been converted, applied to him for

Christian baptism. He had tried her state of feeling, by representing to her the sufferings which must necessarily follow a renunciation of her heathenish creed; he set before her the loss of caste, the wrath of her husband, the disgrace, misery, and persecution, she would probably be called to endure. "I know all this," she replied. "I considered about that before I came to you. I am ready and willing to bear it all: I am ready to sacrifice all to my Lord. Surely, sir, I cannot endure any thing in comparison to what he suffered for me."

Such was converting grace in Hindoostan, and such the pure spirit of martyrdom it could infuse into the bosom of a despised Gentoo woman. She was baptized; her husband swore to destroy her: she applied to the judge to get her child restored to her, but the judge decided against her, her child was torn from her, she was stripped of all her clothing in open court, her husband went to the high priest of Juggernaut, who performed her funeral rites, as though she were dead: and she was considered by the law and by all her former friends as a dead woman. But she endured it all, and endured it patiently, for the love she bore to Jesus of Nazareth, who had had mercy upon her.

(*b*) THE HINDOO'S SACRIFICE.—By the native law of India, the renunciation of idolatry involves the loss of all hereditary property; hence many who sport with its absurdities and practically disregard its rites, keep hold of their possessions, and retain the badge of Hindooism to their dying day. But the conscience of a Christian will not sanction such a compromise, and if he has patrimonial riches to relinquish, he must renounce them, and become poor. This was exemplified in the case of a Hindoo convert, who for some years has labored as an evangelist, and who sacrificed an income of 3,900 dollars per annum, rather than conceal his principles. And where a convert has no sacrifice of wealth to make, the dearer *treasures of the heart* must be relinquished. His dishonored father will disown him, his frantic mother will curse the hour that gave her such a son; by the wife of his bosom he will be despised and forsaken, and even his children, around whom his lacerated heart still lingered as the last earthly objects of interest and hope, will often be torn from his embrace.

(*c*) PERSECUTIONS IN GREENLAND.—The Moravian missionaries in Greenland endured much mockery and opposition from the rude inhabitants, when communicating to them the knowledge of divine truth. When the missionaries told them they meant to instruct them about the will of God, they were met by the taunt, "Fine fellows, indeed, to be our teachers! We know very well you yourselves are ignorant, and must be taught by others!" If they tarried more than one night with them, they used all their endeavors to entice them to participate in their wanton and dissolute sports: and when they failed in this, they mocked and mimicked their reading, singing, and praying, practising every kind of droll antic; or they accompanied their devotions by drumming or howling hideously. Nor did the poverty of the brethren escape their keenest ridicule, or most cutting sarcasms. They even pelted them with stones, climbed upon their shoulders, destroyed their goods, and maliciously tried to spoil their boat, or drive it out to sea.

(*d*) EARLY BAPTIST MISSIONARIES' TRIALS.—"I have generally," says one of the Baptist missionaries in India, "been three or four hours every day in actual contact with the people. Frequently I go and return in good spirits, but sometimes I am low enough. Good spirits are commonly necessary to dealing with my poor people, for there is generally a great deal among them that is very provoking. I frequently tell them that it is a regard to their welfare that leads me to do as I do; and the declaration is received with a sneer. On two or three occasions, a number of little children have been officiously seated before me, as an intimation that I say nothing worthy the attention of men. The people often call after me as I go about: one cries, 'Juggernaut! Juggernaut!' another perhaps says with a contemptuous smile

'Won't you give me a book?' Soon after, perhaps a third says, 'Sahib! I will worship Jesus Christ!' and a fourth exclaims, 'victory to Juggernaut the Ruler!' Among these infatuated people, I fear that the utmost propriety in spirit and demeanor would be no protection from very frequent insults. In spite of the most affectionate addresses of which am capable, and in the midst of them, the people, in malicious derision, shout, 'Juggernaut! Juggernaut!' and seem determined, as it were, with one heart and voice, to support their idols, and resist Jesus Christ. I hope he will, ere long, act for himself; and then floods of pious sorrow will stream from the haughtiest eyes, and the grace now scorned will be sought with successful earnestness."

(*e*) A CHOCTAW INDIAN AND HIS ENEMIES.—The Rev. Mr. Cushman, a missionary among the Choctaw Indians, in a letter, dated March, 1833, writes:—

That you may have a clear view of the trials and temptations to which the Christian Indians are exposed, I will relate one circumstance. A man in this neighborhood, who is very deaf, gave evidence of piety, and was received into the church. His example as to industry and Christian deportment was worthy of imitation; and his unblemished character no doubt rendered him a more desirable prey for the enemy. At length he was besieged by them, and every art and stratagem was made use of, till he finally parleyed with the tempter and drank a little. Their prey was taken. He finally drank till he became completely intoxicated. After he became sober, his wife, who appears to be truly pious, told him that they had professedly set out together in the road to heaven; that they had walked together for a while; but that he had now turned out in the road to hell. She told him further, that if he would continue to go on in that way, he must go alone, and they could walk together no more; for she could never leave the bright path that she had found. She then fell upon her knees, and prayed in the most melting, fervent manner, for the soul of her poor husband. This touched his heart. He melted also, confessed his sin, and resolved never more to taste the accursed thing. After this he was again attacked by the enemy. He was requested to drink, but refused. It was urged that he had drank once, and he might as well drink again. He still refused. Finally, every thing was said that could be thought of to influence him to drink, but he stood firm. Having failed in all this, they seized him and held him fast, and forced whisky into his mouth, but as often as this was repeated, he ejected it without swallowing a drop. Finding all their efforts fail, one said, "This man has done nothing amiss, and he now takes all this ill treatment patiently and we do wrong to use him so; if he has a mind to be a Christian, let him be a Christian."

285. Privations and Perils of Missionaries.

(*a*) MISSION HOUSE ASSAILED.—The mission house at Lahaina, one of the Sandwich Islands, was assailed by English seamen. The Rev. Mr. Stewart writes thus from the scene of this outrage:

"How great was my astonishment, at the peculiar circumstances in which I found our inestimable and beloved friends Mr. and Mrs. Richards! How was I surprised to meet, at my first approach to the house, the presented bayonet, and to hear the stern challenge of the watchful sentry, 'who goes there?'—and when I assured him that I was a friend, how inexplicable to my mind was the fact of receiving the cordial embraces of my brother, not in the peaceful cottage of the missionary, but in the midst of a garrison, apparently in the momentary expectation of the attack of a foe, and to find the very couch on which was reclining one, who, to us, has been most emphatically a sister, surrounded by the muskets and the spears of those, known to the world only by the name of savages! My first thoughts were that a revolt of the island against the general government had taken place, in which our friends had been seized, and were guarded as captives—or that some formidable party of unfriendly natives had risen with the determination of destroying them, and that they were protected by the higher chiefs—but as soon as an explanation could be given, I learned that their peril was from false brethren, if the outcasts of a civilized and Christian country can be designated by such terms. The seamen of a large ship, at anchor at Lahaina, exasperated at the restraints laid on their licentiousness through the influence of the mission, had carried their menaces and open acts of violence against Mr. and Mrs. R. to such an extent as to cause the chiefs to arm a body of men to defend them at the hazard of life. At that very hour, three boats' crews, amounting to near forty men, were on shore with the sworn purpose of firing their houses and taking their lives. But as every thing, when I left them, was in a posture to secure their safety, it is unnecessary for me to go further into particulars."

(*b*) SUFFERINGS OF DR. JUDSON.—The sufferings of Dr. Judson, missionary to Burmah, while imprisoned, during the war between Burmah and Bengal, are thus described by himself, in a letter dated Feb. 25, 1826:

"I was seized on the 8th of June, 1824,—and in company with Dr. Price, three Englishmen, one Armenian, and one Greek, was thrown into the 'death prison' at Ava, where we lay eleven months—nine months in three pair, and two months in five pair of fetters. The scenes we witnessed and the sufferings we underwent, during that period, I would fain consign to oblivion. From the death prison at Ava, we were removed to a country prison at Oung-ben-lay, ten miles distant, under circumstances of such severe treatment, that one of our number, the Greek, expired on the road; and some of the rest, among whom was myself, were scarcely able to move for several days. It was the intention of the government, in removing us from Ava, to have us sacrificed, in order to ensure victory over the foreigners; but the sudden disgrace and death of the adviser of the measure prevented its execution. I remained in the Oung-ben-lay prison for six months, in one pair of fetters; at the expiration of which period I was taken out of irons, and sent under a strict guard to the Burmese head-quarters at Mah-looan, to act as interpreter and translator. Two months more elapsed, when, on my return to Ava, I was released, at the instance of Moung-shaw-loo, the north governor of the palace, and put under his charge. During the six weeks that I resided with him, the affairs of government became desperate, the British troops making steady advances on the capital: and after Dr. Price had been twice despatched to negotiate for peace, (a business which I declined as long as possible,) I was taken by force and associated with him. We found the British above Pahgan: and on returning to Ava with their final terms, I had the happiness of procuring the release of the very last of my fellow prisoners; and on the 21st inst. obtained the reluctant consent of government to my own final departure from Ava with Mrs. Judson.

"On my first imprisonment, the small house which I had just erected, was plundered, and every thing valuable confiscated. Mrs. J., however, was allowed to occupy the place, which she did until my removal to Oung-ben-lay, whither she followed. Subsequently to that period, she was twice brought to the gates of the grave; the last time with the spotted fever, while I was absent at Mah-looan. She had been senseless and motionless several days, when the providential release of Dr. Price at the very last extremity gave an opportunity for such applications as were blest to her relief. Even little Maria, who came into the world a few months after my imprisonment, to aggravate her parents' woes, and who has been, from very instinct, it would seem, a poor, sad, crying thing, begins to brighten up her little face, and to be somewhat sensible of our happy deliverance."

Some conceptions can be formed of the sufferings of Dr. Judson during his imprisonment at Ava, from the following statement:

The white prisoners were all put inside of the common prison, in five pairs of irons each; and where they were so crowded with Burman thieves and robbers, that they had no sufficient room to lie down. There were at the time near one hundred prisoners, all in one room, without a window or a hole for the admittance of air, and the door half closed. This, too, was after the severe hot season had commenced.

(*c*) NARROW ESCAPE OF L. C. DEHNE, MORAVIAN MISSIONARY TO SOUTH AMERICA.—In Nov. 1757, the Carribbee Indians set out with the intention of executing their resolution, long since determined upon, of murdering me. One day, while I sat at my dinner table, I saw fifty men approaching in their canoes, who presently after surrounded my cabin. Some were armed with iron hoes and mattocks; others carried swords and such like instruments. Going out, I spoke to them in the Arawak language, and bade them welcome in a friendly manner. They answered roughly that I should speak the Carribbee tongue. In the meantime, I took care to observe which of them was their commander. Perceiving that I did not understand the Carribbee, after some consultation in this language, they ordered their interpreter to step forth and ask me in Arawak, "Who gave you permission to build and to live here?" Ans. "The governor." "Why have you come upon our land?" I now stepped up to the chief and thus frankly addressed him: "I have brethren living on the other side of the ocean, who, when they heard that Indians lived here who were ignorant of their Creator, have sent me to you in love, that I should first learn your language, and then tell you about the true God. At some future time, you may expect to see more of my brethren come here on the same errand." "I suppose you are a Spaniard?" "No." "Or a Frenchman?" "No." "Are you a Dutchman, then?" "Yes, I came from Holland, and a good way further off. In short, I am one of the Brethren that love you, and live on the other side of the ocean." "Well, didn't you hear that the Indians were going to kill you?" "Yes, but I did not believe it, and you have those among you, who have been to see me and know that I love them." "That is true; and they have also told me that you were a Christian very different from other white people." "Well, if you knew that I loved you, how could you think of killing me?" He replied, laughing, "Well, indeed, I never thought of that." Upon this, all changed their savage natures and walked off. In this manner the Savior helped me on from day to day, insomuch, that at the close of the year, I found much cause for praise and thankfulness to the Giver of every good and perfect gift. During this period, I suffered much outward distress, and often I rose in the morning without knowing what I should eat, or where I should procure food; yet whenever I was perfectly destitute, undoubtedly according to the direction of Him who fed Elijah by the brook Cherith, Waraus or other Indians came and shared their "Casavi" with me.

(*d*) NARROW ESCAPE OF COUNT ZINZENDORF.—This zealous friend of missions visited the Indians along the course of the Susquehannah river, to promote among them the establishment of Moravian missions. In one of these visits, he had occasion to encamp several days, with a few Moravian brethren, among the Shawanese, a very depraved and cruel tribe. Conrad Weiser, a man well acquainted with the customs and manners of the Indians, had accompanied the Count to this spot, and had left him for a short time, promising to return. The Shawanese thought that, as Europeans, the Count and his companions came either to trade or buy land; and, though he endeavored to explain the true aim of his coming, they were not satisfied that his intentions were such as he described.

It appeared afterwards that the savages had conspired to murder him and his whole company. But the design was mercifully frustrated. Conrad Weisser, who was absent, and who could know nothing of the plot, became so uneasy that he could not prolong his stay. He was thus brought back providentially, to the party marked out for destruction, just in time to discover the treacherous plan, and by his influence and dexterity to prevent its execution. Thus, while Count Zinzendorf, unconscious of danger, retired frequently to his tent, to pray for the savages around him, and while he enjoyed no security except such as the entrance of his tent, fastened by a pin, furnished, the shield of Providence extended over him its ample protection.

(*e*) A MISSION FAMILY BURNED ALIVE.—On the 24th of November, 1755, the Moravian Mission at Gnadenhuetten, not far from Bethlehem, in North America, was broken up by a most destructive assault from Indians under French influence.

While the mission family were at supper, an uncommon barking of dogs was heard. Presently a gun was fired. Upon this, several ran to the door, to ascertain the nature of the disturbance. As soon as the door was opened, the Indians fired upon the unsuspecting missionaries. Martin Nitschman was instantly killed. His wife and some others were wounded, but fled with the rest up stairs into the garret, and barricaded the door with bedsteads. One of the missionaries escaped by a back window, another by a rear door. The savages pursued those who had taken refuge in the garret, and strove hard to force the door. Finding it too well secured to be thus opened, they set fire to the house. The building was soon in flames. A boy and the wife of a missionary who had escaped by the window, leaped from the roof, and escaped unhurt and without observation. Mr. Fabricuis leaped also from the roof, but before he could escape, he was perceived and murdered. The rest, eleven in number, were burnt alive in the house. Mrs. Senseman was seen by her unhappy husband, who had escaped, standing with folded hands, surrounded by the flames; and she was heard to say, "'Tis all well, dear Savior."

(*f*) ARRAIGNMENT OF A MISSIONARY AT AVA.—In the month of November, 1836, Mr. Kincaid was summoned from his home to the palace. The early hour and other circumstances indicated that a fearful storm hung over the mission at Ava. Nor was he mistaken in this apprehension. On reaching the royal court, he was confronted with a list of charges, of which the substance is as follows.

The American teacher is stirring up divisions among the people, teaching them to despise the religion of their country, and to follow a religion which the king, the princes and noblemen do not approve. He is not contented to live quietly in the Golden City, as other foreigners do, but in the city and all places around, is giving books and preaching a foreign religion, and his object is to bring into contempt and destroy the religion which has been revered for ages.

After some replies had been made by Mr. K., one of the functionaries told him publicly, that they were determined to stop the distribution of books and preaching. Mr. K. remonstrated on the violence of this proceeding, and then said, "You will allow Papists and Mussulmans to follow their religion unmolested, and converts from among the Burmans are not disturbed." They cried out most violently, "No Burmans enter the Papist and Mussulman religions, and those people do not give books or preach." Mr. K. asked, "Do you intend to drive me out of the country?" One of the leading men replied, "No, but you must promise to give no more books, and not go about preaching." "I cannot make such a promise." "You must promise." "I fear God more than earthly kings, and cannot promise: if you cut off my arms, and then my head, I dare not promise." They then said he was not fit to live in the empire, and must be sent off. The court became exceedingly violent. Although Mr. K. had reason to expect the worst consequences, his personal liberty was not abridged. His labors however were, for a length of time, crippled by the opposition of the government.

(*g*) A MISSIONARY "PERPLEXED, BUT NOT IN DESPAIR."—A missionary and his wife had been located by an English society in the colony at the Cape of Good Hope, or among the Bushmen on its borders. The opposition they met with from the colonists destroyed all hope of success. Means failed from the society; the wife of the missionary was sick, and he must either find means to return to England, or penetrate the vast wilderness for many hundred miles. While he was making it a matter of prayer, his wife, regardless of her own comfort, desired that they should of their own means, procure the common conveyance of the country, and depart in search of a settlement in the wilderness. The missionary consented willingly. They traveled over four hundred miles, but met with no encouragement of attaining their object. Almost despairing, they encamped one night, and, upon rising in the morning, they discovered a savage chief, with his train, not far distant. The blacks advanced and addressed them. They had been deputed by their tribe, and were then on a journey of five hundred miles to the colony, where they desired to procure a missionary! As may be supposed, the man of God hesitated not, but returned with the savage chief to preach the Gospel to his tribe.

(*h*) ROMANCE OF MISSIONARY LIFE.—Mr. Hinsdale, writing from Mosul under date of January 4th, 1842, gives the following picture of what must be a Missionary life in that country.

Earnestly as I long to greet more laborers in this field, yet I feel constrained to repeat the sentiment, long since expressed by my esteemed associate, Dr. Grant. I should regret to see any one come to labor here, who cannot cheerfully and even joyfully make up his mind to endure toils, and hardships, and weariness, and hunger, and self-denial, and peril in almost every form, for these must be the portion of the first Missionaries here, and especially of those who may be stationed among the mountains. It is no small step to come down from the refined circles, to which our young brethren in the ministry have been accustomed, and relinquish the conveniences, not to say luxuries, by which they have been surrounded, to sleep in a mud hut, or in the stable with his horses, with a quilt or rug spread upon the clay floor for his bed and covering, surrounded perhaps with six or eight natives with even fewer accommodations than himself; to exchange the well arranged table for the simple sheep-skin spread upon the floor, or rather ground; to dip his large wooden spoon into one common dish with half a dozen hungry Koords or Yezidees, or Nestorians; to drink the pure and often impure mountain water from a simple gourd-shell; to sit on the clay floor, with a fire in the centre of the room, and neither fire-place nor chimney; to come down to these and various attendant inconveniences, is no small step, and requires no ordinary degree of self denial.

(*i*) WESLEYAN MISSIONARY AT FEJEE.—When the Wesleyan Missionaries ventured among the cannibal Fejeeans, they found them sunk to the lowest depths of degradation. Soon after Mr. Hunt had settled on Somasoma, the heathen party brought several dead bodies and laid them opposite to Mr. Hunt's house; there they baked them, and there they ate them. The Missionary, shocked at these proceedings, closed his door and blinds. One of the heathen chiefs went to Mr. Hunt, and insisted upon his opening them again, and intimated that if he thought proper to reside in their country, he must put up with their customs; if he insulted them in any way, he might expect a place in the oven. An American ship of war was at anchor at a neighboring island. When the captain heard of this circumstance, he took up his anchor and sailed to Somasoma, with a view of removing Mr. Hunt and family to some other island where they would not be exposed to such imminent danger. Mr. Hunt thanked the captain for his kind and humane conduct in thus coming to remove him, but begged respectfully to decline accepting his kind offer, stating that he was willing still to hazard his life in the cause of Christ. He considered the circumstance of their being so exceedingly depraved as an additional reason for remaining to diffuse that gospel which, accompanied with the divine blessing, would soon improve their condition.

286. Zeal for Missions.

(*a*) HOW TO GIVE.—At a Missionary meeting held among the negroes in the West Indies, these three resolutions were agreed upon:

1. We will all give something.

2. We will all give as God has enabled us.

3. We will all give willingly.

As soon as the meeting was over, a leading negro took his seat at a table, with pen and ink, to put down what each came to give. Many came forward and gave, some more and some less. Amongst those that came was a rich old negro, almost as rich as all the others put together, and threw down upon the table a small silver coin. "Take dat back again," said the negro that received the money, "Dat may be according to de first resolution, but it not according to de second." The rich old man accordingly took it up, and hobbled back to his seat again in a great rage. One after another came forward, and as almost all gave more than himself, he was fairly ashamed of himself, and again threw down a piece of money on the table, saying, "Dare! take dat!" It was a valuable piece of gold; but it was given so ill-temperedly, that the negro answered again, "No! Dat won't do yet! It may be according to de first and second resolution, but it not according to de last:" and he was obliged to take up his coin again. Still angry at himself and all the rest, he sat a long time, till nearly all were gone, and then came up to the table, and with a smile on his face, and very willingly, gave a large sum to the treasurer. "Very well," said the negro, "dat will do; dat according to all de resolutions."

(*b*) THE COLORED WOMAN'S EXAMPLE.—In one of the eastern counties of New-York there lived a colored female, who was born a slave, but she was made free by the act gradually abolishing slavery in that state. She had no resources except such as she obtained by her own labor. On one occasion she carried to her pastor *forty dollars;* she told him that she wished him, with two dollars of this sum to procure for her a seat in his church; eighteen dollars she desired to be given to the American Board; and the remaining twenty dollars she requested him to divide among other benevolent societies according to his discretion. With such a spirit pervading the church, how soon would the gospel be carried to every creature!

(*c*) AN ADMONITION FROM A HEATHEN.—A Chinese, says Rev. Mr. Dean, who one year ago was a worshiper of idols, and had then never heard of the gospel, has joined us for the last seven months in observing the monthly concert of prayer at Hong Kong, and has given, monthly, one dollar to the cause of missions. He commenced giving the sum when he was a day laborer, and when his entire income amounted to less than twenty-five cents a day; out of which he purchased his food and clothing.

(*d*) "THY KINGDOM COME."—A little girl sent about ten shillings to a gentleman, for the purchase of some missionary tracts; and in her letter she says, "She who takes this freedom to ask so much of a stranger, began this letter with a trembling hand. She is indeed young in years and in knowledge too, and is not able to talk much with a gentleman on religion; but her mother has taught her, almost eleven years, to say, '*Thy kingdom come*;' and she believes she cannot be saying it sincerely if she does nothing to help it on among the heathen. This thought emboldens her to write to a stranger, almost as though he were a friend."

(*e*) GIFT OF A POOR BLIND GIRL.—A poor blind girl, in England, brought to a clergyman 30 shillings for the missionary cause. He objected, "You are a poor blind girl, and cannot afford to give so much." "I am indeed blind," said she, "but can afford to give these 30 shillings, better perhaps than you suppose." "How so." "I am, sir, by trade a basket maker, and can work as well in the dark as in the light. Now, I am sure in the last winter, it must have cost those girls who have eyes more than 30 shillings for candles, to work by, which I have saved; and therefore hope you will take it for the missionaries."

(*f*) THE NEGRO'S OFFERING.—The following pleasing circumstance is related in a letter from the Rev. E. Davies, of New Amsterdam. It is delightful to witness such proofs of Christian devotedness among the negroes of the West Indies, whose temporal condition was once so unfavorable to their spiritual interests:

There has been a considerable increase in the income of the station during the past year. That increase has been chiefly owing to a great effort which the people are now making towards a new chapel. In many instances I was obliged to restrain their liberality. One incident occurred which I shall never forget. In calling over the names, to ascertain how much they could give, I happened to call the name of "Fitzgerald Matthew." "I am here, sir," he instantly replied; and at the same time, I saw him hobbling with his wooden leg out of the crowd, to come up to the table-pew, where I was standing. I wondered what he meant, for the others answered to their names without moving from their places. I was, however, forcibly struck with his apparent earnestness. On coming up, he put his hand into one pocket and took out a handful of silver wrapped in paper, and said, with a lovely kind of abruptness, "That's for *me*, massa." "Oh," I said, "keep your money at present, I don't want it *now;* I only wanted to know how much you could afford to give; I will come for the money another time." *"Ah, massa," he replied, "God's work must de done, and I may be dead;" and with that he plunged his hand into another pocket and took out another handful of silver*, and said, "That's for my *wife*, massa." Then he put his hand into a third pocket, and took out a somewhat smaller parcel, and said, "That's for my *child*, massa;" at the same time giving me a slip of paper, which somebody had written for him, to say how much the whole was. It was altogether near £3 sterling—a large sum for a poor field negro with a wooden leg! But his expression was to me worth more than all the money in the world. I have heard eloquent preachers in England, and felt, and felt deeply, under their ministrations, but never have I been so impressed with any thing they have said, as with the simple expression of this poor negro. Let me never forget it; let it be engraved on my heart; let it be my motto in all that I take in hand for the cause of Christ—"God's work must be done, and I may be dead."

(*g*) ONE STICK OF WOOD PER MONTH.—Mr. Hitchcock, a missionary at Kaluaaha, a little town on Molaki, one of the Sandwich Islands, describing his monthly concerts in 1834, reports that there were seldom less than 100 persons present. "Most of those who attend," he added, "have, during the past year, been in the habit of contributing, for benevolent purposes, *one stick of wood each per month.* And I can assure you that it is no uninteresting sight to see men, women, and sometimes children, bringing their humble offerings on their shoulders from the distance of one, two or more miles. The men go into the mountains, and get the sticks, both for themselves and their wives; but the latter bring and present their own. Though the people are superlatively poor, yet their contributions in one year in this way will amount to not far from twenty dollars."

(*h*) A WIDOW AND HER TWO SONS.—The Rev. Mr. James, of Birmingham, England, stated at an anniversary of the London Missionary Society, that an association was formed for missionary purposes among his people several years before, and that on this occasion, among the other contributors, a youth of sixteen years of age came forward to enroll his name. When he was requested to state how much he wished to subscribe, he replied with some diffidence, "myself." He was the eldest son of an unfortunate widow, to whom seven other children looked for support. The proffer of the young man could not be received without the mother's consent. It was scarcely to be expected that her oldest son would be yielded up for the missionary service, when his exertions might soon prove useful to his widowed parent, in her indigent circumstances. The inquiry was made, whether the son could be allowed to give himself to the missionary cause? "Let him go," was the prompt reply of the devoted mother. "God will provide for me and my babes, and who am I, that I should be hus honored to have a son a missionary to the heathen?"

The young man, after obtaining an education, repaired to India, where he labored successfully and died.

(i) THE MOTHER OF A MISSIONARY.—When the Lord's supper was first administered in the Bengalee language, at Union Chapel, Calcutta, a missionary, Rev. J. B. Warden, spoke of the advantages of a religious education. After speaking farther of his departure, he said:

"A pious and affectionate mother, who I trust still survives, may perhaps be with us in spirit. Among the sweetest ingredients which are mingled in her present cup of consolation, stands this the foremost, that she has a son, an oldest son employed as a missionary to the heathen.

"When I was about to quit my country and home, for these distant lands, she told me in accents never to be forgotten, that as I should not be present at her dying hour to share her parting blessing, and divide with my dear brothers and sisters, the small patrimony which Providence might enable her to divide to her offspring, as a pledge that her affectionate sympathies and tender concern would follow me to the distant scene of my missionary labors, she said, I have a silver cup, which has been handed down to each other by generations now no more, and produced at the annual festivals of the domestic circle, and this I give you to employ for a very different purpose. When God shall graciously crown your labors, or those of your dear companions with success among the heathen, let this cup be employed as the sacramental cup, from which the first convert may drink the emblem of the Savior's blood." He presented the cup to the infant church.

(j) REV. MR. COX GOING TO AFRICA.—A short time before Mr. Cox, an American missionary, sailed to Africa, he visited the University at Middletown. In conversation with one of the students, he said, "If I die in Africa, you must come after me and write my epitaph." To which the other replied, "I will; but what shall I write?" "Let a thousand missionaries die before Africa be given up," was the reply. In this spirit he died.

(k) MISSIONARY ZEAL OF A POOR WOMAN.—Rev. W. S. Plumer addressing the Virginia Bap. Ed. Society, related the following fact.

A poor woman had attended a missionary meeting a few years since. Her heart was moved with pity. She looked around on her house and furniture to see what she could spare for the mission. She could think of nothing that would be of any use. At length she thought of her five children, three daughters and two sons. She entered her closet, and consecrated them to the mission. Two of her daughters are now in heathen lands, and the other is preparing to go. Of her sons, one is on his way to India, and the other is preparing for the ministry, and inquiring on the subject of a missionary life.

(l) ZEAL OF MARY PERTH.—Mary Perth, a black woman, kept an inn at Sierra Leone during the latter part of her life. In her early days she had been a slave in North America, and had to labor from sunrise to sunset; yet, during the interval of night, she used, twice or thrice a week, to walk seven or eight miles, with a child on her back, to teach a few slaves of her acquaintance to read, that they might be able to study the Scriptures for themselves.

(m) ZEAL OF A FEMALE SERVANT.—A small chapel was a few years ago built on the Barrackpore road, Calcutta; the circumstances attending the erection are interesting in a high degree, and afford a pleasing example of zeal and devotedness to God, in the lower walks of life. It was built and finished, with conveniences which no other of the society's chapels possessed, by an aged Portuguese female, a member of the church meeting in the Lal Bazar Chapel, who had been all her life a servant, and in the receipt of very moderate wages. Yet her earnings seem to have been greater than her wants; for, out of her small pittance, she was able to save a sum, which she thought could not be better employed than by erecting a Bengalee chapel, in which the word of life might be regularly preached to the perishing heathen. Ground was accordingly procured, though with some difficulty, in the situation already mentioned, and a commodious little chapel erected; which she herself frequently visited, to see it kept clean and neat, and fit for the worship of God. When the whole was completed, she wrote a letter to one of the missionaries, in which, with a simplicity and a knowledge of her own heart truly Christian, she confessed the struggle which had taken place in her mind between good and bad motives; but, at the same time, renounced all idea of merit on account of what she had done. Besides building and furnishing the house, she also defrayed the monthly rent of the ground, and the ordinary expenses of lighting, &c., which attended Divine worship.

(*n*) ZEAL OF ELLIOT.—Soon after the settlement of the Non-conformists in New-England, Mr. Elliot felt himself strongly disposed to attempt the conversion of the native Indians He was affected with that sentiment which is expressed on the seal of the Massachusetts colony; a poor Indian, having a label from his mouth, with these words: "Come over and help us." He was further induced to enter upon this work, by the following sentence in the royal charter: "To win and incite the natives to the knowledge and obedience of the only true God, and Savior of mankind, and the Christian faith, is our royal intention, the adventurers' free professions and the principal end of the plantation."

In the prosecution of his efforts to evangelize the Indians, he endured many hardships. In a letter to a friend he says: "I have not been dry night nor day, from the third day of the week to the sixth, but so traveled; and at night pull off my boots, wring my stockings and on with them again, and so continue. But God steps in and helps."

After having formed, with the greatest difficulty, a grammar of the Indian language, he wrote, in a letter to a friend, "Prayers and pains through faith in Christ Jesus will do any thing."

Such was the perseverance of Elliot in his great work, that on the day of his death, in his 80th year, the "apostle of the Indians" was found teaching the alphabet to an Indian child at his bedside. "Why not rest from your labors, now?" said a friend. "Because," said the venerable man, "I have prayed to God to render me useful in my sphere; and now that I can no longer preach, he leaves me strength enough to teach this poor child his alphabet."

(*o*) ROBERT BOYLE'S INTEREST IN MISSIONS.—About the year 1680, the Hon. Robert Boyle evinced rare zeal for the diffusion of Christianity. He ordered five hundred copies of the Gospels and the Acts to be translated and printed in the Malayan tongue, and sent to the East at his own charge; and a considerable number of Pococke's Arabic translations, to be distributed in every country in which that language was spoken. He also contributed large sums to the translation of the Welsh and Irish Bibles. At the same time he rendered valuable aid to the missionary Elliot in his endeavors to evangelize the aborigines of North America. This great man did not disdain the enterprise of imparting Christianity to the pagan world.

(*p*) ZEAL OF TWO BOYS IN CANADA.—There are two little boys in Canada, the elder of whom is about ten years old, and the younger about eight. Two years ago their father gave them the use of a small garden spot, and told them they might have all they could get by the sale of vegetables, or whatever else they might choose to raise upon it. He said he would put the land in order and help them to plant it; and then they must take all the care of it themselves. The proposition was accepted; the land was planted, and the little fellows, with zeal and faithfulness, fulfilled their part of the bargain.

When the time came for selling green corn and vegetables, these boys opened a regular account with as many families as they could supply, and, like business men, entered all the items upon their little day-book, from which every thing was duly posted to their ledger. At the close of the season, the accounts were all drawn off and collected. From the money thus raised, they paid their contributions to the Bible, Tract, and Home Missionary Societies, and other benevolent institutions, and then each of them gave five dollars to the American Board.

The plan succeeded so well, that last year, the contract was renewed with their father. Now, however, they took into partnership their little brother, about six years old, who thought he could help a little. The business was pursued in the same way as before. When the agent of the American Board visited their father, a few months ago, the three little boys brought him their books, and showed their accounts for the season, and then put into his hand three half eagles, (fifteen dollars,) as the portion of their income which they had consecrated to foreign missions!

(*q*) A POOR WOMAN GIVING A FARTHING A DAY.—A poor wo-woman just after a misionary meeting, called at the lodging of a minister, who had been engaged at the meeting, and told him she had been prevented from attending it, but hoped she was not too late to present a little contribution she wished to make to the Society. The poverty of her appearance induced the minister to say, he feared she could not afford to give any thing; but the poor woman assured him that though she was a widow, and had four children to support by the mangle which she worked, she had contrived to save a little; and that she should be much grieved, if he should refuse to take it. She then untied a bundle she had brought with her, and produced three hundred and thirty farthings, saying, that she had laid by one farthing every day for the year past, excepting those days in which illness prevented her from working.

(*r*) A KING A NURSING FATHER.—When Messrs. Tyerman and Bennett, in their visit to the southern islands, held a large missionary meeting, previously to their departure for the Marquesas Islands, at which several persons offered to accompany them as missionaries, to introduce the gospel where it was at present unknown; after some offers of this kind had been accepted, Hautia, the regent of the island, who was virtually king, and held valuable hereditary possessions upon it, and received large contributions to support his royal state, both from chiefs and people, rose; his noble countenance betrayed much agitation of spirit, and he hesitated for awhile to unburden his mind in words. At length, with an air of meekness and humility, which gave inexpressible grace to the dignity of the high-born highland chief, he said, "I have a little speech, because a thought has grown up in my heart, and it has grown up also in the heart of Hautia Vahine (his wife). But, perhaps, it is not a good thought; yet I must speak it; and this is our thought: If the missionaries, and the deputation, and the church of Huahine, think that I and my wife would be fit companions for Auna and his wife, to teach the good word of God to those idolatrous people, who are as we *were*, and cause them to become as we *are* here; and in Tahiti, and Eimeo, and Raiatea, and Borabora, we should be rejoiced to go; but, perhaps, we are not worthy, and others may be better suited for the blessed work; yet we should love to go."

This declaration produced a most extraordinary sensation throughout the whole assembly; as the speaker had given good evidence of his true Christianity. When, however, it was represented to him that his usefulness where he was in the church, as the superintendent of the schools, and in the exertion of his influence among his subjects, was far more extensive than that of any other person could be; and that, though it was well that this thought was in his heart, yet he could not on these accounts be sent, he was deeply affected, and replied, "Since you say so, perhaps it is the Lord's will that we should not go to the Marquesas, but stay in Huahine; perhaps we may serve him better here. Be it so; and yet I wish that it had fallen to me and my wife to go." Oh, what a lesson is this to Christians.

(*s*) ZEAL OF DR. PHILIP.—An English clergyman was once invited to take the pastoral charge of a large and wealthy congregation. One of his first inquiries on coming among them, was, what they had done in aid of benevolent Societies. "What does your subscription for foreign missions amount to?" "We have not given any thing for that object." "And for the Bible Society?" "Nothing." "I cannot stay with such a church," said the clergyman. The members of the congregation, who were extremely anxious to secure his services, remarked that he could himself open subscriptions for these different religious societies on the spot. He took them at their word, and set himself immediately to work. He organized several associations among his people, and collected, the first year, six hundred pounds sterling (nearly $3,000.) During the same year, he sent from his own church, eleven members to be missionaries; before he left his charge, he had sent out twenty, and finally devoted himself to the missionary work. This clergyman is known to all friends of the cause. It was Dr. Philip, afterwards Superintendent of the London Society's missions at the Cape of Good Hope.

(*t*) CONSCIENTIOUS ZEAL OF CONVERTED PAGANS.—Missionary associations were formed among the converted islanders of the South Seas, to aid the London Missionary Society. The contributions consisted of oil, cotton, arrow-root, and swine. Such articles were subscribed "*to buy money with.*"

When an auxiliary association was formed at Huahine, the people were cautioned against making donations merely from a sense of constraint. Still, a native brought a pig to the treasurer, Hautia, and throwing the animal down at his feet, said, in an angry tone, "Here is a pig for your society." "Take it back again," replied Hautia, calmly, "God does not accept angry pigs." He then explained the objects of the society, and urged upon the consideration of the native the fact, that "The Lord loveth a cheerful giver." The man was deeply chagrined at the unyielding refusal of the treasurer. In Tahiti, on a similar occasion, a person brought a quantity of cocca-nut oil to Pomare, in a like bad spirit, exclaiming, "Here are are five bamboos of oil, take them for your society." "No," said the king, "I will not mix your angry bamboos with the missionary oil, take them away."

Are no dollars cast into the treasury of the Lord with a wrong spirit?

(*u*) HENRY PALMER, OR THE MISSIONARY AND THE SOLDIER.—A writer in the London Record, in urging the duty of ministers of the Gospel in England to volunteer as missionaries to Canada, relates the anecdote which we give below, with the following preamble: "I have often felt wounded and grieved, by hearing the privations of missionaries much harped upon. Soldiers and sailors go to inhospitable climes at the call of duty—neither whining nor simpering is set up for them; a merchant also crosses boisterous seas, in pursuit of honorable trade, perchance; but as soon as a minister leaves home for a foreign field of labor, immediately do we hear of his self-devotedness, and a puling sympathy is extorted for the self-denying man. Surely this is not right."

"Some years since, the late much esteemed Charles Macarthy, Governor of Sierra Leone, being in England and much in want of faithful men to labor in that sickly climate, when there had just been a great mortality among the missionaries, attended the Committee of the Church of England Society in London, and thus in substance addressed them:—'Gentleman, I need not tell you how many of your zealous and devoted missionaries have recently fallen a sacrifice to the deadly climate of Sierra Leone; and it grieves me to find that you have not on your list any volunteers to supply the place of those men of God who have just been cut off by disease. But, gentlemen, I have just been at the Horse Guards, and on inquiring there whether there were any officers ready to proceed to that sickly station, a list containing several hundred names was immediately handed to me of individuals anxious to accompany me on my return; and is it possible that there is not one man in England willing to go forth with his life in his hand to preach the gospel to the poor perishing negroes?' A young friend who had left the army, where he had greatly distinguished himself, and had studied for the ministry, was sitting in a retired part of the room; the words of Sir Charles reached his heart; he offered himself and was accepted, as a missionary under that Society, and soon after proceeded to Sierra Leone, where, through his instrumentality, a goodly number of poor negroes were turned from the service of dumb idols to that of the living and true God, who learned to bless the name of Henry Palmer while he lived, and who doubtless will be his crown of rejoicing throughout eternity."

(*v*) DR. CAREY'S LABORS.—Dr. Carey completed the translation of the entire Scriptures, in seven of the principal languages of India, viz., the Sungskit, the Bengalee, the Hindu, the Ooria, the Mahratta, the Panjabee, and the Assamese. In addition, he completed the translation of the New Testament in twenty-two more, and portions of both Testaments in several others, besides superintending the printing of the translations in other languages still. These early translations made in the first stages of acquaintance with the languages of the East, were necessarily very imperfect; but they show what a single individual may accomplish in very difficult circumstances, under the influence of the love of souls, when it becomes the master passion.

(*w*) CAREY, MARSHMAN, AND WARD'S DONATIONS.—Those who are most intimately acquainted with missions, set the highest estimate on their importance. Missionaries, as all must admit, are best qualified to form a correct judgment in reference to the value of the means employed, to bless and save the heathen around them. And they are willing to sacrifice the enjoyments of refined society—to live an exile from kindred, and friends, and home—to suffer poverty, shame, imprisonment, and even death, in order to carry forward the work in which they are engaged. If their situation is such that they can acquire property in connection with their labors, they are ready to lay it out in behalf of the mission to which they are attached. For instance, the Rev. Messrs. Carey, Marshman, and Ward, (missionaries at Calcutta and Serampore,) each of them gave about £1500, in all about $20,000 a year, which they acquired by their printing establishment, to be expended in efforts for the spiritual welfare of the pagans around them.

(*x*) GOOD REASON FOR SELLING A FARM.—Near the close of a Missionary meeting at Syracuse, N. Y. a minister made the following statement:—A member of his church, when first commencing business in the world, had purchased a dairy farm, for which, by industry and economy, he had been able to pay all the purchase money, and on which he continued to thrive. It was, however, remote from any village, and the enjoyment of the religious and social privileges could only be procured by considerable effort. In due time another farm was purchased, more favorably situated and furnished with much more convenient and pleasant buildings, to which they removed. This farm was also paid for, and a third purchased. During all this time his contributions for benevolent purposes were very small, and all solicitation was met by him with the plea that he was in debt. Nevertheless, he and his companion were under the influence of religious principle, and frequently conversed with each other respecting a return to the old dairy farm, in order that, by the sale of one of the others, they might be in better circumstances to aid the cause of Christ. These discussions, however, always terminated adversely to any change, by the recollection, that they were occupying a very comfortable home, surrounded with all the enjoyments of life, and the old farm house was dilapidated and remote from every enjoyment.

This good couple were at the missionary meeting until the morning of the last day, when it became necessary for them to return home. On parting with their pastor, the brother said to him, "I wish you to understand that I have now fully determined to sell one of my farms immediately. I have become convinced at this meeting, that it is my duty. After hearing what I have of the spiritual necessities of our country I can no longer be voluntarily in debt, so as to prevent my doing my duty in the cause of Christ." "And I," said his weeping wife, "have become equally convinced of my duty; we conversed on this subject late last night, and are agreed as to what we shall do. I am now willing to part with all the comforts of our present home, if necessary, and return to the dairy farm and make cheese as long as I live, that I may be able to do something in spreading the gospel of Christ."

The effect of this relation was powerful. Few who heard it could refrain from tears, or fail to resolve that they would attempt, by some means, more effectually to aid the good cause.

(*y*) THE KAREN WOMAN'S RUPEE.—Mr. Kincaid records the following touching incident, in his journal in the Magazine for November, 1841:—

Some time since, I went to the house of an aged female who worshiped God. For several months she had been unable to leave the house, and is fast wearing out with consumption. She has four children, but one is blind and another is deaf. She is very poor too. The house might have been worth fifteen rupees, and all there was in it fifteen more. She could talk but little, on account of her cough, but expressed great anxiety for the eternal welfare of her children. After about an hour spent in conversation and prayer, I rose up to take leave, when the poor old woman bid me remain a little longer. She crept along to another part of the house, and returning soon, she put into my hand a rupee. I could not comprehend what she meant, and said, what is to be done with this? "This is very little," she replied, "but it is all I have, and it is to help in the cause of Christ." "But you are old, and infirm, and poor." "Yes, but I love Christ, and this is very little." Surely, I thought, here, in the midst of poverty and decrepitude, is a converted heathen, exercising the enlightened faith which works by love, purifies the heart, and overcomes the world. For days I could not cease reflecting on the expression, "This is to help the cause of Christ." When I thought of the withered hand, and wrinkled face of her who gave it, that rupee was magnified a thousand times beyond its real value.

The same rupee was brought to this country, and its exhibition by agents of benevolent societies, in connection with the above affecting incident, has awakened in thousands of hearts, a deeper interest in missions, holier emotions, and firmer purposes of Christian benevolence.

(*z*) JOHN WESLEY'S REPLY TO THE UNBELIEVER.—When John Wesley was about going to Georgia as a Missionary to the Indians, an unbeliever said to him, "What is this, sir? are you one of the knights-errant? How, pray, got Quixotism into your head? You want nothing: you have a good provision for life, and in a way of preferment: and must you leave all to fight windmills—to convert savages in America?" He answered willingly and calmly, "Sir, if the Bible be not true, I am as very a fool and madman as you can conceive; but, if it is of God, I am sober-minded. For he has declared, 'There is no man who hath left house, or friends, or brethren, for the kingdom of God's sake, who shall not receive manifold more in the present time, and in the world to come everlasting life.'"

287. MOTHERS, PIOUS, INFLUENCE OF.

(*a*) ALFRED THE GREAT AND HIS ALPHABET.—Alfred the Great had reached his twelfth year before he had even learned his alphabet. An interesting anecdote is told of the occasion on which he was first prompted to apply himself to books. His mother had shown him and his brothers a small volume, illuminated in different places with colored letters, and such other embellishments as were then in fashion. Seeing that it excited the admiration of her children, she promised that she would give it to the boy who should first learn to read it. Alfred, though the youngest, was the only one who had spirit enough to attempt obtaining it on such a condition. He immediately went and procured a teacher, and in a very short time was able to claim the promised reward. When he came to the throne, notwithstanding his manifold duties, and a tormenting disease, which seldom allowed him an hour's rest, he employed his leisure time either in reading or hearing the best books. His high regard for the best interests of the people he was called to govern, and the benevolence of his conduct, are well known.

(*b*) DODDRIDGE AND THE DUTCH TILES.—It is related of Mrs. Doddridge, that, when her son Philip was quite a little boy, she used to teach him Scripture history from the Dutch tiles of the fireplace, on which there were pictures of subjects taken from the Bible. Philip never forgot those early instructions, and probably to them, under God, his future usefulness may be traced.

(*c*) PIOUS MOTHER'S PRODIGAL SON.—A pious mother had a prodigal son. He was about to leave her and go to sea. As a last resource, she placed a Bible in his chest, with a prayer to God for his blessing upon it. Year after year passed away, and nothing was heard of the wanderer. But the eye of his mother's God was upon him. A long time after, a clergyman was called to visit a dying sailor. He found him penitent and prepared to die. He had in his possession a Bible, which he said, was given to him by a dying shipmate, who, expiring in the hope of the glory of God, gave it to him with his parting blessing. On the blank leaf was found written the name of John Marshall, the pious mother's prodigal son. He was the brother of Mrs. Isabella Graham, whose interesting memoirs have profited many readers.

(*d*) THE SAILOR'S DYING MOTHER.—During the last illness of a pious mother, when she was near death, her only remaining child, the subject of many agonizing and believing prayers, who had been roving on the sea, returned to pay his parent a visit.

After a very affecting meeting, "You are near port, mother," said the hardy-looking sailor, "and I hope you will have an abundant entrance."

"Yes, my child, the fair haven is in sight, and soon, very soon I shall be landed

'On that peaceful shore,
Where pilgrims meet to part no more.'"

"You have weathered many a storm in your passage, mother; but now God is dealing very graciously with you, by causing the winds to cease, and by giving you a calm at the end of your voyage."

"God has always dealt graciously with me, my son: but this last expression of his kindness, in permitting me to see you before I die, is so unexpected, that it is like a miracle wrought in answer to prayer."

"O mother!" replied the sailor, weeping as he spoke, "your prayers have been the means of my salvation, and I am thankful that your life has been spared till I could tell you of it."

She listened with devout composure to the account of his conversion, and at last, taking his hand, she pressed it to her dying lips, and said, "Yes, thou art a faithful God! and as it hath pleased thee to bring back my long-lost child, and adopt him into thy family, I will say, 'Now lettest thou thy servant depart in peace; for mine eyes have seen thy salvation.'"

(*e*) NOW I LAY ME DOWN TO SLEEP.—A venerable minister, in New Hampshire, lodging at the house of a pious friend, observed the mother teach some short prayers and hymns to her children. "Madam," said he, "your instructions may be of far more importance than you are aware: my mother taught me a little hymn when a child, and it is of use to me to this day, I never close my eyes to rest, without first saying,

'Now I lay me down to sleep,
I pray thee, Lord, my soul to keep
If I should die before I wake,
I pray thee, Lord, my soul to take.'"

(*f*) THE SICK SAILOR AND HIS MOTHER.—A clergyman, at a public religious meeting, related the following anecdote, illustrative of the power of practical maternal faith:

He was at the time the seamen's chaplain, at a southern port. In the course of duty, he was called to the sick bed of a sailor, apparently at the gates of death from the effects of his licentiousness. He addressed him affectionately upon the state of his soul. With an oath, the sick man bid him begone, and not harass his dying bed. The chaplain, however, told him plainly he would speak, and he must hear, for his soul was in danger of eternal death. The man, however, remained sullen and silent, and even pretended to sleep, during his faithful address and prayer. Again and again the visit was repeated with similar ill success. One day, however, the sick man made use of an expression, by which the chaplain suspected he was a Scotchman. To ascertain the fact, the chaplain repeated a verse of that version of the Psalms, still in use among the churches in Scotland:

> " Such pity as a father hath
> Unto his children dear,
> Like pity shows the Lord to such
> As worship him in fear."

The chords of his heart vibrated to the well known language. Tears came into his eyes. The chaplain improved his advantage. Knowing the universality of religious instruction among the Scotch, he ventured an allusion to his mother. The poor prodigal burst into tears. He admitted himself to be the child of a praying mother, who had often commended him to God. He had left her long before, to become a wanderer on the face of the great deep. No longer he repelled the kind attentions of the chaplain; and after his recovery, his instructor had the satisfaction of seeing him give evidence that he was a humble, penitent child of God.

(*g*) I'LL GO TO THE MEETING.—Mr. Abbott relates, in his "MOTHER AT HOME," that a gentleman in one of the most populous cities of America, was once going to attend a seamen's meeting in the Mariners' Chapel. Directly opposite that place there was a sailors' boarding-house. In the doorway sat a hardy weather-beaten sailor, with arms folded and puffing a cigar, watching the people as they gradually assembled for worship. The gentleman walked up to him, and said, "Well, my friend, won't you go with us to meeting?" "No," said the sailor bluntly. The gentleman, who, from the appearance of the man, was prepared for a repulse, mildly replied, "You look, my friend, as though you had seen hard days: have you a mother?" The sailor raised his head, looked earnestly in the gentleman's face, and made no reply.

The gentleman, however, continued: "Suppose your mother were here now, what advice would she give you?" The tears rushed into the eyes of the poor sailor; he tried for a moment to conceal them, but could not; and hastily brushing them away with the back of his rough hand, rose and said, with a voice almost inarticulate through emotion, "I'll go to the meeting." He crossed the street, entered the door of the chapel, and took his seat with the assembled congregation.

(*h*) GREAT TRUTHS EARLY COMMUNICATIED.—The mother of Dr. Samuel Johnson was a woman of great good sense and piety: and she was the means of early impressing religious principles on the mind of her son. He used to say, that he distinctly remembered having had the first notice of heaven, "a place to which good people go," and hell, "a place to which bad people go," communicated to him by her, when a little child in bed with her; and that it might be the better fixed in his memory, she sent him to repeat it to her man-servant. The servant being out of the way, this was not done; but there was no occasion for any artificial aid for its preservation. When the doctor related this circumstance, he added, "that children should be always encouraged to tell what they hear, that is particularly striking, to some brother, sister, or servant, immediately before the impression is erased by the intervention of new occurrences."

(*i*) PIOUS MOTHERS AND MINISTERS.—Several young men who were associated in preparing for the Christian ministry, felt interested in ascertaining what proportion of their number had pious mothers. They were greatly surprised and delighted in finding that, out of one hundred and twenty students, more than a hundred had been blessed by a mother's prayers, and directed by a mother's counsels to the Savior. Though some of these had broken away from all the restraints of home, and, like the prodigal, had wandered in sin and sorrow, yet they could not forget the impressions of childhood, and each was eventually brought to Jesus, and proved a mother's joy and blessing.

(*j*) SPOT WHERE MY MOTHER KNEELED. — Every one who has thought on the subject, must know how great is the influence of the female character, especially in the sacred relations of wife and mother. I have a vivid recollection, says the Rev. R. Knill, in his MEMOIR OF MRS. LOVELESS, of the effects of maternal influence. My honored mother was a religious woman, and she watched over and instructed me as pious mothers are accustomed to do. Alas! I often forgot her admonitions; but, in my most thoughtless days I never lost the impressions which her holy example had made on my mind. After spending a large portion of my life in foreign lands, I returned again to visit my native village. Both my parents died while I was in Russia, and their house is now occupied by my brother. The furniture remains just the same as when I was a boy, and at night I was accommodated with the same bed in which I had often slept before, but my busy thoughts would not let me sleep. I was thinking how God had led me through the journey of life. At last, the light of the morning darted through the little window, and then my eye caught a sight of the spot where my sainted mother, forty years before, took my hand and said, "Come, my dear, kneel down with me, and I will go to prayer." This completely overcame me. I seemed to hear the very tones of her voice. I recollected some of her expressions, and I burst into tears, and arose from my bed, and fell upon my knees just on the spot where my mothe· kneeled, and thanked God that I had ·ıce a praying nother. And oh! if every parent could feel what I felt then, I am sure they would pray with their children as well as pray for them.

(*k*) RANDOLPH SAVED FROM ATHEISM.—John Randolph, the eccentric but influential statesman, once addressed himself to an intimate friend in terms something like the following: —"I used to be called a Frenchman, because I took the French side in politics; and though this was unjust, yet the truth is, I should have been a French atheist, if it had not been for one recollection, and that was, the memory of the time when my departed mother used to take my little hands in hers, and cause me on my knees to say, 'Our Father which art in heaven.'"

(*l*) THE MOTHER'S HAND.—When I was a little child, said a good man, my mother used to bid me kneel beside her, and to place her hand upon my head while she prayed. Before I was old enough to know her worth, she died, and I was left much to my own guidance. Like others, I was inclined to evil passions, but often felt myself checked, and, as it were, drawn back by the soft hand on my head. When I was a young man, I traveled in foreign lands, and was exposed to many temptations; but, when I would have yielded, that same hand seemed to be upon my head and I was saved. I appeared to feel its pressure as in the days of my happy infancy, and sometimes there came with it a voice in my heart—a voice that must be obeyed—"Oh, do not this wickedness, my son, nor sin against thy God."

(*m*) A MOTHER CONSTANT IN PRAYER.—In the vicinity of Philadelphia, there was a pious mother, who had the happiness of seeing her children in very early life, brought to the knowledge of the truth; walking in the fear of the Lord, and ornaments in the Christian church. A clergyman, who was traveling, heard this circumstance respecting this mother, and wished very much to see her, thinking that there might be something peculiar in her mode of giving instruction, which rendered it so effectual. He accordingly visited her, and inquired respecting the manner in which she discharged the duties of a mother in educating her children. The woman replied, that she did not know that she had been more faithful than any Christian mother would be, in the religious instruction of her children. After a little conversation, she said, "While my children were infants on my lap, as I washed them, I raised my heart to God, that he would wash them in that blood which cleanseth from all sin; as I clothed them in the morning, I asked my heavenly Father to clothe them with the robe of Christ's righteousness; as I provided them food, I prayed that God would feed their souls with the bread of heaven and give them to drink of the water of life. When I have prepared them for the house of God, I have pleaded that their bodies might be fit temples for the Holy Ghost to dwell in. When they left me for the week-day school, I followed their infant footsteps with a prayer, that their path through life might be like that of the just, which shineth more and more unto the perfect day. And as I committed them to the rest of the night, the silent breathing of my soul has been, that their heavenly Father would take them to his embrace, and fold them in his paternal arms.'

(*n*) A MOTHER'S USEFULNESS THROUGH HER POSTERITY.—E—H— was born in Massachusetts, in 1737. His parents carefully instructed him in the principles of the Gospel. His father was an eminently godly man, but naturally of a very hasty spirit. His mother was remarkable for Christian meekness, and was his principal religious instructor. When a child he was accustomed to pray that he "might possess the grace of his father and the meekness of his mother." At the age of seven he gave evidence of being born again. His whole life was eminently devoted to God. In the things of this world he was poor, but in Christian character and influence rich. Having for some time sustained the office of deacon of a church in B—, and afterwards of a church in P—, Vermont, at the earnest solicitation of the latter he obtained license to preach, and entered on the pastoral office, which he reputably sustained more than twenty years. The church, while under his care, experienced repeated seasons of "refreshing from the presence of the Lord," and large accessions. Many bore joyful testimony to the powerful influence in favor of godliness every where exerted by him as he moved on in his Master's work. Especially in his family do we find striking proof of the benefits of the early religious training he himself received under the instructions of his mother. He had ten children who came to mature age; three sons and seven daughters. *Nine* of them gave evidence of piety. The tenth was not pious. This child was put to a trade at the usual age, where nothing like a Christian influence was exerted over him, and his habits became vicious. The children of Mr. H. reared *sixty* children, *thirty-six* of whom were known to have made a Christian profession; nearly all between the ages of ten and twenty.

(*o*) THE CONVERTED STUDENTS AND THEIR MOTHER.—"In a college of ——," says a correspondent of the N. Y. Evangelist of 1831, "there has lately been an extensive revival. Having myself a praying mother, it occurred to me to inquire of the subjects of the revival, whether their mothers were pious. I did so, and found that scarcely one sinner was brought into the fold of Christ, who was not blessed with a pious, prayerful mother. This is a *fact*, and oh! that mothers would let it make the proper impression on their hearts."

(*p*) THE YOUNG INFIDEL AND HIS MOTHER.—"Where parental influence does not convert," says Richard Cecil, "it hampers—it hangs on the wheels of evil. I had a pious mother, who dropped things in my way—I could never rid myself of them. I was a professed infidel; but then I liked to be an infidel in company, rather than when alone—I was wretched when by myself. These principles and maxims spoiled my pleasure. With my companions I would sometimes stifle them; like embers, we kept one another warm. Besides, I was a sort of hero; I had beguiled several of my associates into my opinions, and I had to maintain a character before them: but *I could not divest myself* of my better principles. I went with one of my companions to see ——: he could laugh heartily, but I could not: the ridicule on regeneration was high sport to him—to me it was none; it could not move my features. He knew no difference between regeneration and transubstantiation—I did. I knew there was such a thing. I was afraid and ashamed to laugh at it. Parental influence thus cleaves to a man—it harasses him—it throws itself constantly in his way."

(*q*) MY MOTHER'S PRAYERS AND COUNSELS.—A young man, on whose mind the doctrines of religion had been early impressed by his pious mother's instructions, at length went to sea, and became an abandoned and miserable creature. He was thrown into prisons and workhouses, and into dens of wretchedness and vice: but into all these places his faithful mother followed him with her prayers and tears, till she died, leaving him in prison, convicted of crime. Here he was an object of so much dread, that not one of the keepers ventured to approach him alone. In about six months, however, the tiger began to grow tame, and his inquiry was, "What shall I do to be saved?" Mr. Bradford questioned him about his feelings, and he informed him, that for two months he had paced his room, with sleepless nights, in agony and remorse, save when exhausted nature would sometimes overcome his horrible convictions. Mr. B. inquired what particular cause had led him to his present feelings. He replied, "My mother's prayers and counsels! Her last words to me were, 'William, there is no other name given under heaven among men, whereby you can be saved, but the name of Jesus Christ.'" His mother's prayers were answered, and this man became a consistent follower of the Lamb.

(*r*) THE AGED PRISONER AND HIS DECEASED MOTHER.—The chaplain of the prison at Weathersfield says:

"A man of fifty, who has been a wanderer over almost the whole earth, and a partaker in almost every sin that can be named, and who has also met with much which we should think was calculated to make him solemn, told me that nothing in his whole life has ever made him feel serious, but *what his mother said to him just before her death.* She resided in Trenton, New Jersey, and was a sincere, warm-hearted Christian. When she found herself dying, she sent for her son, then a lad of twelve years old, to come to her chamber. As he approached her bed, she took his hand, and spoke to him with maternal tenderness and fidelity. Telling him she must soon leave him, she earnestly besought him by every moving consideration, so to love the Savior, and so to take care of his soul, as to meet her in heaven. She continued to clasp his hand until hers became cold in death. For nearly half a century afterwards, this man was pressing onwards through a course of crime, too revolting for description. Yet he assured me, that amidst his lowest and darkest descents into the vortex of sin, he could never utterly drive from his mind the last words of his mother, and *was never able to think of them without solemn emotion.* This struck me with some surprise, and appeared to me a remarkable proof of the deep and lasting impression a pious mother may make upon the mind of her child."

MURDERERS.

288. Misery, Detection and Punishment of.

(*a*) REV. E. ERSKINE AND THE MURDERER.—The Rev. Ebenezer Erskine, after traveling, at one time, toward the end of the week, from Portmoak to the banks of the Forth, on his way to Edinburgh, was, with several others, prevented by a storm from crossing that frith. Thus obliged to remain in Fife during the Sabbath, he was employed to preach, it is believed, in King horn. Conformably to his usual practice, he prayed earnestly in the morning for the Divine countenance and aid in the work of the day; but suddenly missing his note-book, he knew not what to do. His thoughts, however, were directed to the command, "Thou shalt not kill;" and having studied the subject with as much care as the time would permit, he delivered a short sermon on it in the forenoon. Having returned to his lodging, he gave strict injunctions to the servant that no one should be allowed to see him during the interval of worship. A stranger, however, who was also one of the persons detained by the state of the weather, expressed an earnest desire to see the minister; and having with difficulty obtained admittance, appeared much agitated, and asked him, with great eagerness, whether he knew him, or had ever seen or heard of him. On receiving assurance that he was totally unacquainted with his face, character, and history, the gentleman proceeded to state, that his sermon on the sixth commandment had reached his conscience; that he was a *murderer;* that being the second son of a Highland laird, he had some time before, from base and selfish motives, cruelly suffocated his elder brother, who slept in the same bed with him; and that now he had no peace of mind, and wished to surrender himself to justice, to suffer the punishment due to his horrid and unnatural crime. Mr. Erskine asked him if any other person knew any thing of his guilt. His answer was, that so far as he was aware, not a single individual had the least suspicion of it; on which the good man exhorted him to be deeply affected with a sense of his atrocious sin, to make an immediate application to the blood of sprinkling, and to bring forth fruits meet for repentance; but at the same time, since, in providence, his crime had hitherto remained a secret, not to disclose it, or give himself up to public justice. The unhappy gentleman embraced this well intended counsel in all its parts, became truly pious, and maintained a friendly correspondence with Mr. Erskine in future life.

(*b*) THE MURDERER AND HIS SINGULAR WOUND.—A gentleman who was very ill, sending for Dr. Lake, of England, told him that he found he must die, and gave him the following account of the cause of his death. He had, about a fortnight before, been riding over Hounslow-heath, where several boys were playing at cricket. One of them, striking the ball, hit him just on the toe with it, looked him in the face, and ran away. His toe pained him extremely. As soon as he came to Brentford, he sent for a surgeon, who was for cutting it off. But unwilling to suffer that, he went on to London. When he arrived there, he immediately called another surgeon to examine it, who told him his *foot* must be cut off. But neither would he hear of this; and so, before the next day, the mortification seized his *leg*, and in a day or two more struck up into his *body*. Dr. Lake asked him, whether he knew the boy that struck the ball? He answered, "About ten years ago, I was riding over Hounslow-heath, where an old man ran by my horse's side, begged me to relieve him, and said he was almost famished. I bade him be gone. He kept up with me still; upon which I threatened to beat him. Finding that he took no notice of this, I drew my sword, and with one blow killed him. A boy about four years old, who was with him, screamed out, 'His father was killed!' His face I perfectly remember. *That boy it was who struck the ball against me, which is the cause of my death.*"

(*c*) MURDER TRACED TO THE RIGHT SOURCE.—Nicholson, the murderer of Mr. and Mrs. Bonar, at Chiselhurst, in Kent, who paid the forfeit of his life to the violated laws of his country, declared solemnly in writing, after sentence of death was passed upon him, that he had no previous malice towards the parties, nor intention to murder them, five minutes before he committed the horrid deed; but that suddenly, as he awoke, the thought suggested itself to his mind, and which he can only account for by confessing, "that he had long lived in utter forgetfulness of God, and was in the habit of giving way to the worst passions of the human heart."

(*d*) MURDER REVEALED BY A DOG.—Mr. Clarke relates an account of two French merchants, who were traveling to a fair, and while passing through a wood, one of them murdered the other, and robbed him of his money. After burying him, to prevent discovery, he proceeded on his journey. The dog of the person murdered remained, however, by the grave of his master; and, by his loud and continued howling, attracted the notice of several persons in the neighborhood, who, by this means, discovered the murder. The fair being ended, they watched the return of the merchants. The murderer no sooner appeared in view, than the dog sprung furiously upon him. He was apprehended, confessed the crime, and was executed.

(*e*) MURDER REVEALED BY A NAIL.—When Dr. Donne, afterwards dean of St. Paul's, took possession of the first living he ever had, he walked into the churchyard as the sexton was digging a grave; and on his throwing up a scull, the doctor took it into his hands to indulge in serious contemplation. On looking at it, he found a headless nail sticking in the temple, which he secretly drew out, and wrapped it in the corner of his handkerchief. He then asked the grave-digger whether he knew whose skull it was? He said he did; adding, it had been a man's who had kept a brandy shop; a drunken fellow, who, one night, having taken two quarts of ardent spirits, was found dead in his bed the next morning. "Had he a wife?" "Yes." "Is she living?" "Yes." "What character does she bear?" "A very good one; only her neighbors reflect on her because she married the day after her husband was buried." This was enough for the doctor, who, in the course of visiting his parishioners, called on her: he asked her several questions, and, among others, of what sickness her husband died. She giving him the same account, he suddenly opened the handkerchief, and cried, in an authoritative voice, "Woman, do you know this nail?" She was struck with horror at this unexpected question, instantly acknowledged that she had murdered her husband, and was afterwards tried and executed.

(*f*) MURDERER DETECTED BY HIS OWN REMARK.—How many murders have been disclosed after the lapse of years, and the perpetrators of them brought to condign punishment! Of this, the case of Eugene Aram, of Knaresborough, is a remarkable instance. Descended from an ancient Yorkshire family, he had cultivated his talents with so much care, that he acquired a knowledge of Latin, Greek, Hebrew, and Chaldee, and was conversant with history, antiquity, botany, and poetry; but he associated with low and depraved company, and in conjunction with Daniel Clark, a shoemaker, and Richard Housman, a flax-dresser, it was agreed to make use of Clark's credit to borrow a quantity of silver plate and other valuables from their neighbors, and then to abscond. Having accomplished their object, they met on the evening of February 7, 1744, to make a division; and either to prevent detection, or to increase their own share of the plunder, Aram and Housman murdered Clark, and concealed his body in St. Robert's Cave. No trace of the perpetrators of the deed occurred till fourteen years afterwards, when a skeleton was discovered at Thistle Hill, near Knaresborough, which was at first supposed to be Clark's. Housman, who was then living, rejected the supposition, and taking up one of the bones, said, "This is no more one of Daniel Clark's bones than it is mine." Suspicion was immediately excited against Housman, who at length confessed his participation in the murder, but that Aram was the perpetrator. Aram, who at that time resided at Lynn, in Norfolk, was forthwith apprehended, tried, and executed. What an illustration of the text, "Be sure thy sin will find thee out!"

(*g*) REMARKABLE DISCOVERY OF FRATRICIDE.—In the beginning of 1815, a circumstance took place that excited much interest in Paris. A surgeon in the army, named Dautun, was arrested at a gambling house, in the Palais Royal, on the testimony of a scar on his wrist. Some time before, the officers of the night had found, while passing their rounds, in the different parts of the city, four parcels tied up. One contained the head, another the trunk, a third the thighs, and a fourth the legs and arms of a man. In the teeth, tightly compressed, was a piece of human flesh, apparently torn out in the dying struggle. The parts were collected, and put together in their regular order, and exhibited for a number of days at the Morgue. The mystery which enveloped this dark transaction excited considerable interest, and numbers went to view the corpse. The general conviction was, that the deceased must have been murdered; but for a number of weeks no light was thrown upon the circumstance. When the body could not be kept any longer, a cast in plaster was taken, fully representing the murdered victim, which remained for some time exposed to the public. Dautun happened to be engaged in gambling at the Palais Royal; he played high and lost: calling for liquor, and being angry because the waiter was somewhat tardy, Dautun emptied the glass and threw it at him. It was shivered into a thousand pieces, one of which entered into Dautun's wrist under the cuff of his coat. The spectators gathered round, and learning the accident, wished to see the gash; he drew down his sleeve, and firmly pressed it round his wrist; they insisted on seeing it, he obstinately refused. By this course the bystanders were led to suppose that something mysterious was involved in this conduct, and they determined at all events to see his wrist. By force they pushed up his sleeve, and a scar recently healed, as if made by tearing out of flesh, appeared. The landlord had been at the Morgue, had seen the murdered man with the flesh between the teeth, and it struck him in a moment that the flesh was torn from this man's wrist. Charging them to keep him safe, he hastened to call in the legal authorities, and arrested him. Dautun afterwards confessed, that being quartered at Sedan, and without money, he came to Paris to try some adventure. Knowing that his brother had a large sum by him, directly on his arrival he went to his lodgings, in a retired part of the city, about eight in the evening. He entered the house, unnoticed by the porter, and passing to his apartment, found his brother asleep. He immediately commenced his work of death; his brother waking up, defended himself, but being in a feeble state of health, he was speedily overpowered. In the struggle he tore out the flesh. Being killed, Dautun cut up the body, tied it up in four parcels as before mentioned, secured the money, and retired.

He also confessed, that eleven months before this he had murdered an aunt, who was living with a second husband, to obtain money. Her husband was arrested and imprisoned for a number of months, but as nothing appeared to criminate him, he had been discharged.

(*h*) MURDER DISCOVERED BY GUN WADDING.—A M. Martin was murdered at Bilguy in France, which was soon after discovered in a most singular manner. The crime was committed on the 9th of February, on the high road, at one o'clock in the afternoon. The shot entered M. Martin's heart, and he fell down dead. He was returning from collecting, and had only 130 francs about him, of which he was robbed, as well as of his watch and ring. The charge of the gun was rammed down with a written paper. This had been carefully taken up, and carried away with the body. The writing was still legible. On this piece of paper there were words which are used in glass manufactories, and a date of nearly fifteen years preceding. Upon this single indication, the magistrate went to the owner of the glass manufactory at Bilguy, examined his books, and succeeded in finding an article relative to the delivery of some glass, of which the paper which had been found was the bill of parcels. The suspicion immediately fell on the son-in-law of this individual, who had been out of the country for ten years. Orders were given to arrest the suspected person. When the officers came to him, he confessed the deed on the spot, and even showed where the watch and ring were, which were found under the thatch of his house.

(*i*) A MURDERER'S HORROR OF MIND.—Some years ago, a man of the name of Cooper died in Gloucestershire. He had long endured great horror of mind; and, about an hour previous to his death, he mentioned the cause of it, which was, that, about forty years before, he had assisted another man, of the name of Horton, who died two years before Cooper, in murdering one Mr. Rice, a surveyor of the roads, whose body they threw into a well, where it was found soon after; but the murderers were not discovered till he made them known.

(*j*) GUILTY SAILORS DETECTED.—Some years ago, a ship, named the Earl of Sandwich, sailed from London to Vera Cruz, where she discharged her lading. She then sailed to Oratavo, and took in a cargo of wine, a quantity of Spanish dollars, gold, jewels, &c., and sailed for London. On the voyage, four of the crew combined to put the rest of their companions to death, which they at length effected in the most cruel manner. When they had nearly reached Waterford, they put their treasures in a boat, and sunk the ship. They now thought themselves secure, as the dead could tell no tales, and no one could search the bottom of the sea for evidence. On landing, they buried the bulk of their property in the sand, reserving a portion for present use. Wherever they went, they were remarkable for their prodigality, and the ship which they had consigned to the sea, was cast on shore near Waterford. This occasioned much speculation; and suspicion pointed out the guilty parties, who were living at Dublin in great gayety. They were at length separately examined, their guilt established, and due punishment awarded.

(*k*) MURDERER AND PEASANT GIRL.—Judge Helmanots, in the department of Lips, sent a peasant girl with money to Golnitz. Not far from that village, a countryman joined her, and inquired where she was going? She replied that she was going with 200 florins to Golnitz. He was going there too, he said, and would accompany her; and here he took a path which he stated would shorten their journey two leagues. At length, arriving at the brink of an excavation, (once worked as a mine,) he stopped short and cried out to the girl. "Behold your grave; give me the money instantly." She complied; but fell down on her knees and prayed him to spare her life. He refused, but happening to turn away his head, she sprang upon him, threw him into the cavity, and ran and told the villagers. Several men returned with her, provided with ladders; and descending into the hole, found the countryman dead, with the money which he had taken from the girl in his possession. Near him lay three dead female bodies in a state of putrefaction. It is probable that these were victims to the rapacity of the same villain. In a girdle which he had round his body, was discovered a sum of 800 florins in gold.

(*l*) A MILLER FOUND GUILTY OF MURDER.—In the early part of the seventeenth century, a man near Lutterworth, (Eng.,) was missing, and immediately after a miller suddenly left the neighborhood. About twenty years afterwards, the miller returned to the town to visit some friends, and the man who then occupied the mill, having occasion at that time to dig deep in the ground adjoining the mill, discovered a corpse. Attention was excited; suspicion as to murder having been committed began to exist; some of the old people remembered the sudden disappearance of their neighbor, and the hasty manner in which the former miller had left the town. This led to his apprehension, and on a close examination, he acknowledged the murder, and received the punishment of death.

(*m*) A DOG AND THE MURDERER OF HIS MASTER.—The fame of an English dog has been deservedly transmitted to posterity by a monument in basso relievo, which still remains on the chimney piece of the grand hall at the castle of Montargis, in France; the sculpture represents a dog fighting with a champion, and was occasioned by the following circumstances:—

Aubri de Mondidier, a gentleman of

family and fortune, traveling alone through the forest of Bondi, was murdered and buried under a tree. His dog, an English bloodhound, would not leave his master's grave for several days, till at length, compelled by hunger, he went to the house of an intimate friend of the unfortunate Aubri's at Paris, and by his melancholy howling seemed desirous of expressing the loss they had both sustained. He repeated his cries, ran to the door, then looked back to see if any one followed him, returned to his master's friend, pulled him by the sleeve, and with dumb eloquence entreated him to go with him.

The singularity of all the actions of the dog; his coming there without his master, whose faithful companion he always had been; the sudden disappearance of his master; and, perhaps, that divine dispensation of justice and events which will not permit the guilty to remain long undetected, made the company resolve to follow the dog, who conducted them to the tree, where he renewed his howl, scratching the earth with his feet, to signify that that was the spot they should search. Accordingly, on digging, the body of the unfortunate Aubri was found.

Some time after the dog accidentally met the assassin, who is styled, by all historians that relate this fact, the Chevalier Macaire; when, instantly seizing him by the throat, it was with great difficulty he was made to leave his prey.

Whenever he saw him after, the dog pursued and attacked him with equal fury. Such obstinate virulence in the animal, confined only to Macaire, appeared extraordinary to those persons who recollected the dog's fondness for his master, and, at the same time, several instances wherein Macaire had displayed his envy and hatred to Aubri de Mondidier.

Additional circumstances increased suspicion, which at length reached the royal ears. The king (Louis VIII.) sent for the dog. He appeared extremely gentle, till, perceiving Macaire in the midst of twenty noblemen, he ran directly towards him, growled, and flew at him as usual.

In those times, when no positive proof of a crime could be procured, an order was issued for a combat between the accuser and accused. These were denominated the judgment of God, from a persuasion that Heaven would sooner work a miracle than suffer innocence to perish with infamy.

The king, struck with such a collection of circumstantial evidence against Macaire, determined to refer the decision to the chance of war; or, in other words, he gave orders for a combat between the chevalier and the dog. The lists were appointed in the aisle of Notre Dame, then an unenclosed, uninhabited place; Macaire's weapon was a great cudgel.

The dog had an empty cask allowed for his retreat, to recover breath. The combatants being ready, the dog no sooner found himself at liberty than he ran round his adversary, avoiding his blows, menacing him on every side, till his strength was exhausted; then springing forward, he griped him by the throat, threw him on the ground, and forced him to confess his crime before the king and the whole court. In consequence of which the chevalier, after a few days, was convicted on his own acknowledgment, and beheaded on a scaffold in the aisle of Notre Dame.

The above curious recital, is translated from the *Memoirs sur les Duels*, and is confirmed by many judicious critical writers, particularly Julius Scaliger and Montfaucon, neither of them relators of fabulous stories.

(*n*) MURDERER DISCOVERED BY A JOKE.—The Rev. H. G Keene states, in his "Persian Stories," that the following narrative was related by a person of authority and reputation, who was one of the party. A vessel set sail from Bassorah to Bagdad, with several passengers on board. In the course of the voyage, the sailors, by way of a joke, put a man in irons as he lay asleep, and he became a subject of diversion to the whole party, till they drew near the capital. But when the sailors wanted to let him loose, the key was nowhere to be found, and after a long and fruitless search, they were compelled to send for a blacksmith to knock off the fetters. When, however, the blacksmith came, he refused to do what they wanted, till he had the authority of the magistrate; for he thought the man might be some criminal whom the officers of justice had laid hold of, and that his friends wished to favor his escape. To the magistrates they accordingly went, who sent down one of his attendants to see into it. But the officer, when he had heard their story, and had taken the evidence of some of the most respectable among the passengers, shook his head, and with a look of solemnity, said, it was much too serious a case for him to decide. So they repaired in a body to the magistrate, and carried the poor captive with them. So strange a procession was sure to attract notice; and a crowd soon collected about them, each curious to know the prisoner's offence, and to catch a sight of him: till, at length, one man, springing forward, seized the captive by the throat, and exclaimed, "Here is the villain I have been looking for these two years; ever since he robbed and murdered my poor brother." Nor would he quit his hold till they came before the magistrate; and the murder being clearly proved, the man, who had been confined in joke only, was given up to death, as a punishment for the blood that he had shed.

(*o*) THE FATAL ELOPEMENT.—A young lady, named D'Aumont, was executed in the city of Lyons, for the supposed murder of her uncle, the Chevalier de la Poulone, with whom she had lived in the most affectionate harmony from her infantile years. Having conceived a passion for a deserving young officer quartered in the town, and between whom and the young lady a mutual affection subsisted, she came to a determination of eloping with him unknown to her uncle, and only admitted one female servant to her confidence. It unfortunately happened, that the servant was leagued with a private soldier, who meditated the plan of murdering the chevalier, with a view of plundering the house, on the night the intended elopement should take place, in order that the unhappy niece should be judged the perpetrator of the horrid deed, which was accordingly effected with every degree of barbarity. The young lady and the officer were immediately pursued, taken, and committed to prison. The former was tried, and executed, on the false evidence of the female servant, and the officer, her husband, was cashiered, and sent to the gallies for life.

Some time after, the servant being taken ill, threatened to divulge the whole matter before a magistrate; to prevent which, the soldier, who had married her, put an end to his wife's existence; but, at length, feeling sincere remorse for these repeated murders, he voluntarily surrendered himself up to justice, confessed the whole affair, and was publicly executed, amidst the execrations of the enraged multitude.

What adds to the dreadful recital is, that the young lady who was executed, was not less remarkable for her beauty, than her unaffected piety, and sweet simplicity of manners. A broken heart soon terminated the existence of the wretched officer, who died in six weeks after the execution of the most amiable sufferer, in the most excruciating tortures.

(*p*) THE DOGS AND THE MURDERERS.—A laboring man of Tobolski, in Siberia, who had deposited in a purse of skin, which he wore at his breast, the hard-earned savings of his life, was murdered by two of his companions, for the sake of his little treasure. The murderers escaped to a neighboring forest followed by two dogs belonging to the deceased, which would not quit them. The wretches did every thing to appease them, but in vain. They then endeavored to kill them, but the dogs were upon their guard, and continued to howl dreadfully. Reduced to despair, the murderers, at the end of two days, returned to Krasnojarsk, and delivered themselves into the hands of justice.

(*q*) MURDER CONFESSED IN A DREAM.—The following is translated from a respectable publication at Bâsle, Switzerland:—

A person who worked in a brewery quarreled with one of his fellow-workmen, and struck him in such a manner that he died upon the spot. No other person was witness to the deed. He then took the dead body and threw it into a large fire under the boiling-vat, where it was in a short time so completely consumed, that no traces of its existence remained. On the following day, when the man was missed, the murderer observed, very coolly, that he had perceived his fellow-servant to have been intoxicated, and that he had probably fallen from a bridge which he had to cross in his way home, and been drowned. For the space of seven years after no one entertained any suspicion of the real state of the fact. At the end of this period the murderer was again employed in the same brewery. He was then induced to reflect on the singularity of the circumstance that his crime had remained so long concealed. Having retired one evening to rest, one of the other workmen, who slept with him, hearing him say in his sleep, "It is now fully seven years ago," asked him, "What was it you did seven years ago?" "I put him," he replied, still speaking in his sleep, "under the boiling-vat." As the affair was not entirely forgotten, it immediately occurred to the man that his bedfellow must allude to the person who was missing about that time, and he accordingly gave information of what he had heard to a magistrate. The murderer was apprehended; and though at first he denied that he knew any thing of the matter, a confession of his crime was at length obtained from him, for which he suffered condign punishment.

(*r*) THE SERGEANT AND THE DRUMMER BOY.—Jarvis Mutcham was pay-sergeant in a regiment, where he was so highly esteemed as a steady and accurate man, that he was permitted opportunity to embezzle a considerable part of the money lodged in his hands for the pay of soldiers, bounty of recruits, then a large sum, and other charges, which fell within his duty. He was summoned to join his regiment from a town where he had been on the recruiting service, and this, perhaps, under some shade of suspicion. Mutcham perceived discovery was at hand, and would have deserted, had it not been for the presence of a little drummer lad, who was the only one of his party appointed to attend him. In the desperation of his crime, he resolved to murder the poor boy, and avail himself of some balance of money to make his escape. He meditated this wickedness the more readily, that the drummer, he thought, had been put as a spy on him. He perpetrated his crime, and, changing his dress after the deed was done, made a long walk across the country to an inn on the Portsmouth road, where he halted, and went to bed, desiring to be called when the first Portsmouth coach came. The waiter summoned him accordingly; but long after remembered, that when he shook the guest by the shoulder, his first words as he awoke were, "I did not kill him." Mutcham went to the seaport by the coach, and instantly entered as an able-bodied landsman or marine, I know not which. His sobriety and attention to duty gained him the same good opinion of the officers, in his new service, which he had enjoyed in the army. He was afloat for several years, and behaved remarkably well in several actions. At length, the vessel came into Plymouth, was paid off, and some of the crew, among whom was Jarvis Mutcham, were dismissed as too old for service. He and another seaman resolved to walk to town, and took the route by Salisbury. It was when within two or three miles of that celebrated city, that they were overtaken by a tempest, so sudden, and accompanied with such vivid lightning, and thunder so fearfully loud, that the obdurate conscience of the old sinner began to be awakened. He expressed more terror than seemed natural for one who was familiar with the war of elements, and began to look and talk so wildly, that his companion became aware that something more than usual was the matter. At length, Mutcham complained to his companion that the stones rose from the road and flew after him. He desired the man to walk on the other side of the road of the highway, to see if they would follow him when he was alone. The sailor complied, and Jarvis Mutcham complained that the stones still flew after him, and did not pursue the other. "But what is worse," he added, coming up to his companion, and whispering, with a tone of mystery and fear, "who is that little drummer boy, and what business has he to follow us so closely?" "I can see no one," answered the seaman. "What! not see that little boy with the bloody pantaloons!" exclaimed the secret murderer, so much to the terror of his comrade, that he conjured him, if he had any thing on his mind to make a clear conscience, as far as confession could do it. The criminal fetched a deep groan, and declared he was unable longer to endure the life he had led for years. He then confessed the murder of the drummer; and added, that as a considerable reward had been offered, he wished his companion to deliver him up to the magistrates of Salisbury, as he would desire a shipmate to profit by his fate, which he was now convinced was inevitable. Having overcome his friend's objections to this mode of proceeding, Jarvis Mutcham was surrendered to justice accordingly, and made a full confession of his guilt. But before the trial the love of life returned. The prisoner denied his confession, and pleaded not guilty. By this time full evidence had been procured from other quarters. Witnesses appeared from his former regiment to prove his identity with the murderer and deserter, and the waiter remembered the ominous words which he had spoken, when he awoke him to join the Portsmouth coach. Jarvis Mutcham was found guilty, and executed. When his last chance of life was over, he returned to his confession, and with his dying breath averred, and truly, as he thought, the truth of the vision on Salisbury plain.

(*s*) FATHER AND MOTHER MURDERING THEIR OWN SON. —A seafaring man called at a village on the coast of Normandy, and asked for a supper and a bed; the landlord and lady were elderly people, and apparently poor. He entered into a conversation with them, invited them to partake of his cheer, asked many questions about them and their family, and particularly of a son who had gone to sea when a boy, and whom they had long given over as dead. The landlady showed him to his room, and when she quitted him, he put a purse of gold into her hand, and desired her to take care of it till morning, pressing her affectionately by the hand. She returned to her husband, and showed the accursed gold; for its sake they determined to murder the traveler in his sleep, which they accomplished, and buried the body.

Early in the morning came two or three relations, and asked, in a joyful tone, for the traveler who arrived the night before. The old people seemed greatly confused, but said he had risen early and gone away. "It is your own son," said they, "who has lately returned to France, to bless your old age, and he resolved to lodge with you, one night, unknown, and then judge of your conduct to wayfaring mariners"——

Language is incapable of describing the horror of the murderers, when they learned that they had dyed their hands in the blood of their long lost child. They confessed their crime, the body was found, and the murderers expiated their offence with their lives.

289. MUSIC.

(*a*) CHEERFUL CHURCH MUSIC. —When the poet Carpani inquired of his friend Haydn, how it happened that his church music was always so cheerful, the great composer made a most beautiful reply. "I cannot," said he, "make it otherwise, I write according to the thoughts I feel; when I think upon God, my heart is so full of joy that the notes dance and leap, as it were, from my pen: and since God has given me a cheerful heart, it will be pardoned me that I serve him with a cheerful spirit."

(*b*) THE SOLDIER UNPREPARED TO SING.—Mr. Cooper, a missionary in the East Indies, had been on one occasion preaching on Justification, at a military station on the Malabar coast; and on giving out the hymn at the end of the service, which was the 109th of the first book of Watts, he paused and remarked, that if any one who did not come to Christ for the bestowment of this righteousness, joined in the singing of this hymn, he was only insulting God. One of the soldiers who was hearing him said, he was as if thunderstruck: "What a wretch must I be," said he, "that I am prohibited from joining in the praises of God!" He went to the barracks under this impression, and found that, without an interest in Christ, he was a wretch indeed; and now, to all human appearance, he has fled for refuge to that atonement he had formerly neglected.

(*c*) THE NOBLEMAN'S DAUGHTER.—A nobleman of great wealth, Lord ——, was a man of the world. His pleasures were drawn from his riches—his honors and friends. His daughter was the idol of his heart. Much had been expended in her education: and well did she repay, in her intellectual endowments, the solicitude of her parents. She was highly accomplished, amiable in her disposition, and winning in her manners. They were all strangers to God. At length Miss —— attended a Methodist meeting in London, was deeply awakened, and soon happily converted. Now she delighted in the service of the sanctuary and social religious meetings. To her the charms of Christianity were overpowering; frequenting those places where she met with congenial minds animated with similar hopes, she was often found in the house of God.

The change was marked by her fond father with awful solicitude. To see his lovely daughter thus infatuated, was to him occasion of deep grief, and he resolved to correct her erroneous notions on the subject of the real pleasures and business of life. He placed at her disposal large sums of money, hoping she would be induced to go into the fashions and extravagances of others of her birth, and leave the Methodist meetings, but she maintained her integrity. He took her on long and frequent journeys, conducted her in the most engaging manner, in order to divert her mind from religion; but she still delighted in the Savior. After failing in many projects which he fondly anticipated would be effectual in subduing the religious feelings of his daughter, he introduced her into company under such circumstances that she must either join in the recreation of the party or give high offence. Hope lighted up the countenance of the infatuated but misguided father, as he saw his snare about to entangle in its meshes the object of his solicitude. It had been arranged among his friends, that several young ladies should, on the approaching festive occasion, give a song, accompanied by the piano forte. The hour arrived—the party assembled. Several had performed their parts to the great delight of the party, who were in high spirits: Miss —— was now called on for a song, and many hearts beat high in hope of victory. Should she decline, she was disgraced. Should she comply, their triumph was complete. This was the moment to seal her fate. With perfect self-possession she took her seat at the piano forte, ran her fingers over its keys, and commenced playing and singing in a sweet air, the following words:

> No room for mirth or trifling here,
> For worldly hope or worldly fear,
> If life so soon is gone;
> If now the Judge is at the door,
> And all mankind must stand before
> The inexorable throne;
>
> No matter which my thoughts employ,
> A moment's misery or joy;
> But Oh! when both shall end!
> Where shall I find my destined place?
> Shall I, my everlasting days,
> With fiends or angels spend?

She arose from her seat. The whole party was subdued. Not a word was spoken. Her father wept aloud. One by one they left the house. Lord —— never rested till he became a Christian. He lived an example of Christian benevolence—having given to benevolent Christian enterprises, at the time of his death, nearly half a million of dollars.

(*d*) THE PIRATE AND THE ZENAIDA DOVES.—The following interesting fact is related by Audobon in his Ornithological Biography. In speaking of the Zenaida dove, he says, —"A man who was once a pirate assured me, that several times, while at certain wells dug in the burning shelly sands of the well known Key, which must be here nameless, the soft and melancholy cry of the doves awoke in his breast feelings that had long slumbered, melted his heart to repentance, and caused him to linger at the spot in a state of mind, which he only who compares the wretchedness of guilt with the happiness of former innocence, can truly feel. He said he never left the place without increased fears of futurity, associated as he was, although I believe by force, with a band of the most desperate villains that ever annoyed the Florida coast. So deeply moved was he by the notes of any bird, and especially by those of a dove, the only soothing sounds he ever heard during his life of horrors, that through these plaintive notes, and them alone, he was induced to escape from his vessel, abandon his turbulent companions, and return to a family deploring his absence. After paying a parting visit to those wells, and listening once more to the cooings of the Zenaida dove, he poured out his soul in humble supplication for mercy, and once more became what one has said to be "the noblest work of God," an honest man. His escape was effected amidst difficulties and dangers; but no danger seemed to him comparable with the danger of one living in the violation of human and divine laws; and now he lives in peace in the midst of all his friends.

(*e*) IRREVERENCE IN THE CHOIR.—The result of my observations, says a minister of the gospel, is, that there is a great lack of devotion, (not to say of common good breeding) in the choirs of all our denominations. Especially is this manifested by smiling and whispering, and looking over tune books in the time of sermon. I once, in a strange church, had before me a leader, who formally took up his tune book, as soon as I had named the text, and began poring over it. Seeing some little boys of the Sunday school, similarly engaged, I took occasion mildly to reprove them, and noticed that he offender in the gallery took the hint and amended his manners. A thousand times would I prefer the *Precentor*, as I have seen him in the Presbyterian churches at the South, in the front of the pulpit, rise and lead the congregation, to the best trained, most exact, scientific, undevout choir in the land.

(*f*) LUTHER'S OPINION OF MUSIC.—"Music," says Luther, "is one of the fairest and most glorious gifts of God, to which Satan is a bitter enemy; for it removes from the heart the weight of sorrows and the fascination of evil thoughts. Music is a kind and gentle sort of discipline; it refines the passions and improves the understanding. Even the dissonance of unskillful fiddlers serves to set off the charms of true melody, as white is made more conspicuous by the opposition of black. Those who love music are gentle and honest in their tempers. I always loved music," adds Luther, "and would not, for a great matter, be without the little skill which I possess in the art."

(*g*) WRATH OF AMURATH SUBDUED.—Sultan Amurath, a prince notorious for his cruelty, laid siege to Bagdad; and, on taking it, gave orders for putting thirty thousand Persians to death, notwithstanding they had submitted and laid down their arms. Among the number of the victims was a musician, who entreated the officer to whom the execution of the sultan's order was intrusted to spare him for a moment, that he might speak to the author of the dreadful decree. The officer consented, and he was brought before Amurath, who permitted him to exhibit a specimen of his art. Like the musician in Homer, he took up a kind of psaltery which resembles a lyre, and has six strings on each side, and accompanied it with his voice. He sung the capture of Bagdad and the triumph of Amurath. The pathetic tones and exulting sounds which he drew from the instrument, joined to the alternative plaintiveness and boldness of his strains, rendered the prince unable to restrain the softer emotions of his soul. He even suffered him to proceed, until, overpowered with harmony, he melted into tears of pity and repented of his cruelty. In consideration of the musician's abilities, he not only directed his people to spare those among the prisoners who yet remained alive, but also to give them instant liberty.

(*h*) REFRESHMENTS IN THE ORGAN LOFT.—Many years ago, says a writer in a New-York paper, I boarded, when a very young man, with a family at the South, the head of which was an organist in the church. Not being attached to any church or to any form, I willingly attended divine service with him now and then, and for convenience sat with him in the organ loft. As I do not mention names or places, it is no breach of confidence to reveal the secrets with which I became acquainted, as connected with the choir. The loft was railed in, and furnished with substantial thick crimson curtains, which, when drawn, were sufficient to exclude vulgar eyes from the hallowed interior.

It was the custom, when the excellent ritual of devotion was gone through, and the rector had named the text, for the singers to draw the curtain around them and read or sleep, as it suited them best. In very warm weather they also took care to be supplied with *refreshments*, and thus the tedious half hour allotted to the sermon was pretty easily consumed without much weariness. I recollect that one very warm Sabbath afternoon, the singers had *water-melons* and *lemonade* wherewith to console themselves, and it happened that one of the gentlemen in handing a slice to a lady singer overset the lemonade jug. This might not have been of much consequence had the *floor* of the organ loft been liquor-tight. But there were many chinks in it, and the lemonade trickled through pretty freely, down into the broad aisle, to the discomfiture of the rector and such of his congregation as were wakeful enough to notice passing events.

(*i*) EFFECTS OF MUSIC ON BISHOP BEVERIDGE.—Bishop Beveridge observes, that, of all recreation, he found music to be the bes and especially when he played himself. "It calls in my spirits," says he, "composes my thoughts, delights my ear, recreates my mind, and so not only fits me for after business, but fills my heart at the present with pure and useful thoughts."

(*j*) THE CLERGYMAN'S FAMILY.—An excellent clergyman, possessing much knowledge of human nature, instructed his large family of daughters in the theory and practice of music. They were all observed to be exceedingly amiable and happy. A friend inquired if there was any secret in his mode of education. He replied, "When any thing disturbs their temper I say to them *sing*, and if I hear them speaking against any person, I call them to sing to me, and so they have sung away all causes of discontent, and every disposition to scandal." Such a use of this accomplishment, might serve to fi a family for the company of angels. Young voices around the domestic altar, breathing sacred music at the hour of morning and evening devotion, are a sweet and touching accompaniment.

290. NOBILITY.

(*a*) SCHILLER'S ESTIMATE.—Schiller, the German poet, had a patent of nobility conferred upon him by the Emperor of Germany, which he never used. Turning over a heap of papers one day, in the presence of a friend, he came to his patent, and showed it carelessly to his friend with this observation, I suppose you did not know I was a noble; and then buried it again in the mass of miscellaneous papers in which it had long lain undisturbed. Schiller's friend might have answered, after this action, "If I did not before know you were noble, I know it now."

(*b*) A SIGNIFICANT QUESTION.—At the commencement of the first revolution in France, a gentleman of Dauphine, anxious to support the interests of the aristocracy, said, "Think of all the blood the nobles of France have shed in battle!" A commoner replied, "And what of the blood of the people poured forth at the same time? Was that water?"

NON-RESISTANCE,* SAFETY AND OTHER BENEFITS OF

291. Prevents and Disarms Aggression.

(*a*) RAYMOND THE TRAVELER.—Raymond, a celebrated European traveler, bears the following testimony:

Speaking of the Spanish smugglers, he says: "These smugglers are as adroit as they are determined, are familiarized at all times with peril, and much in the very face of death. Their first movement is a never-failing shot, and certainly would be an object of dread to most passengers; for where are they to be dreaded more, than in deserts, where crime has nothing to witness it, and the feeble no assistance? As for myself, *alone and unarmed*, I have met them without anxiety, and have accompanied them without fear. We have little to apprehend from men whom we inspire with no distrust or envy, and every thing to expect in those from whom we claim only what is due from man to man. The laws of nature still exist for those who have long shaken off the laws of civil government. At war with society, they are sometimes at peace with their fellows. The assassin has been my guide in the defiles of the boundaries of Italy; the smuggler of the Pyrenees has received me with a welcome in his secret paths. Armed, I should have been the enemy of both; unarmed, they have alike respected me. In such expectation, I have long since laid aside all menacing apparatus whatever.

(*b*) ROBERT BARCLAY AND THE ROBBERS.—Robert Barclay, the celebrated apologist of the Quakers, and Leonard Fell, a member of the same Society, were severally attacked by highwaymen in England, at different times. Both faithfully adhered to their non-resistance principles, and both signally triumphed. The pistol was leveled at Barclay, and a determined demand made for his purse. Calm and self-possessed, he looked the robber in the face, with a firm but meek benignity, assured him he was *his* and every man's friend, that he was willing and ready to relieve his wants, that he was free from the fear of death through a divine hope in immortality, and therefore was not to be intimidated by a deadly weapon; and then appealed to him, whether he could have the heart to shed the blood of one who had no other feeling or purpose but to do him good. The robber was confounded; his eye melted; his brawny arm trembled; his pistol fell to his side; and he fled from the presence of the non-resistant hero whom he could no longer confront.

(*c*) A CHILD'S PLEA FOR LIFE.—At the close of a battle, a soldier of the victorious army, more ferocious and reckless from the bloody work of the day, chanced to find a small boy on the field, and, very much from the habit of assailing whatever came in his way, lifted his sword to cleave him down, when the little fellow, looking up in his face, exclaimed, "*O sir, don't kill* ME, *I'm so little.*" That simple appeal went to the warrior's heart; and returning his sword into its scabbard, he galloped away without harming the child. Some men there possibly may be who would have killed him; but scarce one man in a million would so outrage his own nature.

(*d*) REV. MR. LEE AND THE GENERAL.—Says General P. of Virginia, "When I was a young man I went to hear Mr. Lee preach at —— meeting-house. There was a very large crowd in attendance, and a great many could not get into the house. Among others I got near the door, and being fond of show and frolic, I indulged in some indiscretion, for which Mr. Lee mildly but plainly reproved me. In an instant all the bad feelings of my heart

* By the use of this word we do not mean to have it understood that we take the ground of those technically called "Non-resistants" in our time. On the extent of Christ's precept, "Resist not evil," there is much difference of opinion. But on that precept all will find the following facts an interesting comment. Alas that our Master's precept is so little regarded!

were aroused. I was deeply insulted, and felt that my whole family was disgraced. I retired from the crowd to brood over the insult, and meditate revenge. It was not long before I resolved to whip him before he left the ground. I kept the resolution to myself; and watched with the eager intensity of resentment, the opportunity to put it in execution. But the congregation was dismissed and dispersed, and I saw nothing of the preacher. How he escaped me I could never learn. But I 'nursed my wrath to keep it warm;' and cherished the determination to put it into execution the first time I saw Mr. Lee, although long years should intervene. Gradually, however, my feelings subsided; and in the lapse of a few years the whole affair faded away from my mind. Thirteen years passed over me, and the impetuosity of youth had been softened down by sober manhood. I was standing upon the downhill of life!

On a beautiful morning in the early spring, being from home on business, I saw, a few hundred yards before me, an elderly looking man jogging slowly along in a single gig. As soon as I saw him, it struck me, that's Jesse Lee. The name, the man, the sight of him, recalled all my recollections of the insult, and all my purposes of resentment. I strove to banish them all from my mind. But the more I thought the warmer I became. My resolution stared me in the face; and something whispered *coward* in my heart if I failed to fulfil it. My mind was in a perfect tumult, and my passions waxed strong. I determined to execute my resolution to the utmost; and full of rage I spurred my horse, and was soon at the side of the man that I felt of all others I hated most. I accosted him rather rudely with the question, "Are you not a Methodist preacher?" "I pass for one," was the reply, and in a manner that struck me as very meek. "Ain't your name Jesse Lee?" "Yes: that's my name." "Do you recollect preaching in the year —— at —— meeting-house?" "Yes; very well." "Well, do you recollect reproving a young man for some misbehavior?" After a short pause for recollection, he replied, "I do." "Well," said I, "I am that young man; and I determined I would whip you for it the first time I saw you. I have never seen you from that day to this; and now I intend to carry out my purpose."

As soon as I had finished speaking, the old man stopped his horse, and looking me full in the face, said, "You are a younger man than I am. You are strong and active; and I am old and feeble. I have no doubt but, if I were disposed to fight, you could whip me very easily; and it would be useless for me to resist. But as a man of God I must not strive! So as you are determined to whip me, if you will just wait, I will get out of my gig, and get down on my knees, and you may whip me as long as you please." "Never," said the old general, "was I so suddenly and powerfully affected. I was completely overcome. I trembled from head to foot. I would have given my estate if I had never mentioned the subject. A strange weakness came over my frame. I felt sick at heart, ashamed, mortified and degraded, I struck my spurs into my horse, and dashed along the road with the speed of a madman. I am now old: few and full of evil have been the days of the years of my life, yet I am not without hope in God. I have made my peace with him who is the 'judge of the quick and dead;' and hope ere long to see that good man of God with feelings very different from those with which I met him last."

(*e*) INDIAN AND THE QUAKER MEETING.—A little before the revolutionary war, there were a few families of Friends, who had removed from Dutchess county, and settled at Easton, then in Saratoga county, New-York. These requested the favor of holding a religious meeting, which was granted. The section of country proved to be one which was so much distressed by scouting parties from both the British and American armies, that the American government, unable to protect the inhabitants, issued a proclamation, directing them to leave their country: and they did generally go.

Friends requested to be permitted to exercise their own judgment, (saying, "You are clear of us in that you have warned us,") remained at their homes, and kept up their meeting.

Robert Nisbet, who lived at that time at East Hoosack, about thirty miles distant, felt a desire to walk through the then wilderness country, and sit with Friends at their week-day meeting. As they were sitting in meeting, with their door open, they discovered an Indian peeping round the door post. When he saw Friends sitting without word or deed, he stepped forward and took a full view of what was in the house: then he and his company, placing their arms in a corner of the room, took seats with Friends, and so remained till the meeting closed.

Zebulon Hoxie, one of the Friends present, then invited them to his house, put a cheese and what bread he had on the table, and invited them to help themselves: they did so, and went quietly and harmlessly away.

Before their departure, however, Robert Nisbet, who could speak and understand the French language, had a conversation with their leaders in French. He told Robert, that they surrounded the house, intending to destroy all that were in it; "but," said he, "when we saw you sitting with your door open, and without weapons of defence, we had no disposition to hurt you—we would have fought for you." This party had human scalps with them.

(*f*) WHITE FEATHER OF PEACE.—A family of Quakers from Pennsylvania, settled at the west in a remote place, then exposed to savage incursions. They had not been there long before a party of Indians, panting for blood, started on one of their terrible excursions against the whites, and passed in the direction of the Quaker's abode; but, though disposed at first to assail him and his family as enemies, they were received with such openhearted confidence, and treated with such cordiality and kindness, as completely disarmed them of their purpose. They came forth, not against such persons, but against their enemies. They thirsted for the blood of those who had injured them; but these children of peace, unarmed and entirely defenceless, met them only with accents of love, and deeds of kindness. It was not in the heart even of a savage to harm them; and, on leaving the Quaker's house, the Indians took a white feather, and stuck it over the door, to designate the place as a sanctuary not to be harmed by their brethren in arms. Nor *was* it harmed. The war raged all around it; the forest echoed often to the Indian's yell, and many a white man's hearth was drenched in his own blood; but over the Quaker's humble abode gently waved the white feather of peace, and beneath it his family slept without harm or fear.

(*g*) CHRISTIANS WHO WOULD NOT FIGHT.—"I have read," says Mrs. Chapman, "of a certain regiment ordered to march into a small town, (in the Tyrol, I think,) and take it. It chanced that the place was settled by a colony who believed the gospel of Christ and proved their faith by works. A courier from a neighboring village informed them that troops were advancing to take the town. They quietly answered, 'if they *will* take it, they must.' Soldiers soon came, riding in with colors flying, and fifes piping their shrill defiance. They looked round for an enemy, and saw the farmer at his plough, the blacksmith at his anvil, and the women at their churns and spinning wheels. Babies crowded to hear the music, and boys ran out to see the pretty trainers, with feathers and bright buttons, 'the harlequins of the nineteenth century.' Of course none of these were in a proper position to be shot at. 'Where are your soldiers?' they asked. 'We have none,' was the brief reply. 'But we have come to take the town.' 'Well, my friends, it lies before you.' 'But is there nobody here to fight?' 'No, we are all Christians.' Here was an emergency altogether unprovided for by the military schools. This was a sort of resistance which no bullet could hit; a fortress perfectly bomb-proof. The commander was perplexed. 'If there is nobody to fight with, of course we can't fight,' said he. 'It is impossible to take such a town as this.' So he ordered the horses' heads to be turned about, and they carried the human animals out of the village, as guiltless as they entered, and perchance somewhat wiser. This experiment on a small scale indicates how easy it would be to dispense with armies and navies, if men only had faith in the religion they profess to believe."

(*h*) INDIANS AND THE SHAKERS.—About the year 1812, Indiana was the scene of Indian hostilities; but the Shakers, though without forts or arms, lived in perfect safety while the work of blood and fire was going on all around them. "Why," said the whites afterwards to one of the Indian chiefs, "why did you not attack the Shakers as well as others?" "What!" exclaimed the savage, "we warriors attack a peaceable people! We fight those who won't fight us! Never; it would be a disgrace to hurt *such* a people."

(*i*) INHABITANTS OF THE LOOCHOO ISLANDS.—These islands are in the neighborhood of the Chinese Sea. They have been visited by several navigators, and, among others, by Captain Basil Hall. He states that they have neither forts, men-of-war, garrisons, arms, nor soldiers, and appear to be quite ignorant of the art of war. They are kind, hospitable, courteous, and honest, and acquainted with some of the mechanical arts. Well, what has been their fate? Reasoning on the rash premises of the opponents of peace principles, we should predictate their utter destruction. But have they been destroyed? Quite the contrary. They have been preserved in peace, safety, and happiness. "The olive branch" is planted on their shores, and they sit beneath it, "no man daring to make them afraid."

(*j*) QUAKERS IN THE IRISH REBELLION.—Perhaps the severest test to which the peace principles were ever put, was in Ireland, during the memorable rebellion of 1798. During that terrible conflict, the Irish Quakers were continually between two fires. The Protestant party viewed them with suspicion and dislike because they refused to fight or to pay military taxes; and the fierce multitude of insurgents deemed it sufficient cause of death, that they would neither profess belief in the Catholic religion nor help them fight for Irish freedom. Victory alternated between the two contending parties, and, as usual in civil war, the victors made almost indiscriminate havoc of those who did not march under their banners. It was a perilous time for all men; but the Quakers alone were liable to a raking fire from both sides. Foreseeing calamity, they had, nearly two years before the war broke out, publicly destroyed all their guns, and other weapons used for game But this pledge of pacific intentions was not sufficient to satisfy the government, which required warlike assistance at their hands. Threats and insults were heaped upon them from all quarters; but they steadfastly adhered to their resolution of doing good to both parties and harm to neither. Their houses were filled with widows and orphans, with the sick, the wounded and the dying, belonging both to the loyalists and the rebels. Sometimes when the Catholic insurgents were victorious, they would be greatly enraged to find Quakers' houses filled with Protestant families. They would point their pistols and threaten death, if their enemies were not immediately turned into the street to be massacred. But the pistols dropped, when the Christian mildly replied. "Friend, do what thou wilt, I will not harm thee, or any other human being." Not even amid the savage fierceness of civil war, could men fire at one who spoke such words as these. They saw that this was not cowardice, but bravery very much higher than their own.

On one occasion, an insurgent threatened to burn down a Quaker house unless the owner expelled the Protestant women and children who had taken refuge there. "I cannot help it." replied the Friend; "so long as I have a house, I will keep it open to succor the helpless and distressed, whether they belong to thy ranks, or to those of thy enemies! If my house is burned I must be turned out with them, and share their affliction." The fighter turned away and did the Christian no harm.

Whichever party marched into a village victorious, the cry was, "Spare the Quakers! They have done good to all and harm to none." While flames were raging, and blood flowing in every direction, the houses of the peacemakers stood uninjured.

It is a circumstance worthy to be recorded, that during the fierce and terrible struggle, even in counties where Quakers were most numerous, but one of their society fell a sacrifice.

That one was a young man, who, being afraid to trust peace principles, put on a military uniform, and went to the garrison for protection. The garrison was taken by the insurgents, and he was killed. "His dress and arms spoke the language of hostility," says the historian, "and therefore invited it."

(*k*) THE BISHOP AND DUKE.—Luther gives an account of a duke of Saxony, who made war unnecessarily upon a bishop of Germany. At that period ecclesiastics could command military resources, as well as the secular nobility. But the weapons of the good bishop were not carnal. The duke thought proper, in a very artful way, to send a spy into the company of the bishop, to ascertain his plan of carrying on the contest. On his return, the spy was eagerly interrogated by the duke. "O, sir," replied he, "you may surprise him without fear, he is doing nothing, and making no preparation." "How is that," asked the duke; "what does he say?" "He says he will feed his flock, preach the word, visit the sick; and that, as for this war, he should commit the weight of it to God himself." "Is it so?" said the duke; "then let the devil wage war against him; I will not."

(*l*) PACIFIC POLICY OF PENN.—The case of William Penn, is perhaps the fullest and fairest illustration of pacific principles in their bearing on the intercourse of nations. His colony, though an appendage to England, was to the Indians an independent State. They knew no power above or beyond that of Penn himself; and they treated his colony as another tribe or nation. Their king had himself expressly abandoned these Quakers entirely to their own resources. "What!" said Charles II to Penn, on the eve of his departure, "venture yourself among the savages of North America! Why man, what security have you, that you will not be in their war-kettle within two hours after setting your foot on their shores?" "The best security in the world," replied the man of peace. "I doubt that, friend William; I have no idea of any security against those cannibals, but a regiment of good soldiers with their muskets and bayonets; and I tell you beforehand that, with all my good will to you and your family, to whom I am under obligations, I will not send a single soldier with you." "I want none of thy soldiers; I depend on something better." "Better! on what?" "On the Indians themselves, on their moral sense, and the promised protection of God."

Such was the course of William Penn; and what was the result? In the midst of the most warlike tribes on this continent, the Quakers lived in safety while all the other colonies, acting on the war-policy of armed defence, were involved almost incessantly in bloody conflicts with the Indians. Shall we ascribe this to the personal tact of William Penn? Shrewd he doubtless was; but the success of his policy was owing mainly, if not entirely, to its pacific character. Penn was only an embodiment of his principles, and the efficacy of these is strikingly exhibited in the fact that Pennsylvania, during all the seventy years of her peace policy, remained without harm from the Indians, but suffered as soon as she changed that policy, the same calamities with the other colonies.

(*m*) THE CHRISTIAN INDIANS.—The following anecdote is related by a writer of Graham's Magazine. A large body of Indians had been converted by the Moravian missionaries, and settled in the west, where their simplicity and harmlessness seemed a renewal of the better days of Christianity. During the Revolutionary war these settlements, named Lichtenan and Guadenhutten, being located in the seat of the former Indian contests, were exposed to outrage from both parties.

Being, however, under the tuition and influence of the whites, and having adopted their religion, and the virtuous portion of their habits, they naturally apprehended that the hostile Indians, sweeping down upon the American frontier, would take advantage of their helplessness, and destroy them as allies of the whites. Subsequent events enable us to compare the red and white man, and determine which is the savage. A party of two hundred Hurons, fiercely approached the Moravian Indian town. The Christian Indians conducted themselves, in this trying extremity, with meekness and firmness. They sent a deputation with refreshments to their approaching foes, and told them, that by the word of God, they were taught to be at peace with all men, and entreated for themselves, and their white teachers, peace and protection. And what replied the savage, fresh from the wilds, and panting for blood? Did he mock to scorn the meek and Christian appeal? Did he answer with the war whoop, and lead on his men to the easy slaughter of his foes? What else could be expected from an Indian? Yet such was *not* the response of the red warrior. He said he was on a war party, and his heart had been evil, and his aim had been blood; but the words of his brethren had opened his eyes. He would do them no harm. "Obey your teachers," said he, "worship your God and be not afraid. No creature shall harm you."

292. Effects the Reformation of Aggressors.

(*a*) OBERLIN AND THE CONSPIRATORS.—M. Oberlin was appointed minister of the Ban de la Roche, France, in the year 1767: he was then twenty-seven years of age. His parish was a very rude and ignorant district, secluded from the rest of the province. His predecessor, an excellent individual, had commenced the execution of several plans which were likely to improve the moral and religious state of his parish. M. Oberlin determined to carry on and extend these measures as far as he could, to the great satisfaction of those who had approved them; but the greater part of the inhabitants were resolved to oppose the designs of their excellent pastor, and laid a plan to waylay him, and treat him with such severity as might effectually deter him from continuing his admonitions. Their pastor was informed of this intention, and that an approaching Lord's day was fixed for the perpetration of their wicked design. On that day he took for his text the words of our Lord, Matt. v. 39, "Resist not evil: but whosoever shall smite thee on thy right cheek, turn to him the other also." In the course of his sermon he spoke of the Christian patience with which we ought to suffer injuries. After service the conspirators assembled at the house of one of their number, and were probably amusing themselves with the idea that their minister would himself soon have to put in practice the lessons he had just given. While conferring upon the execution of their plan, the door suddenly opened, and to their great astonishment, M. Oberlin himself stood in the midst of the assembly. "Here am I, my friends," said he, with a calmness which inspired even the most violent with respect; "I am aware of your intentions with regard to me. You intend to beat me, and to chastise me for acting in a manner which you disapprove. If I have broken the rules of conduct which I have laid down for you to follow, then punish me. I would much rather give myself up to you, than to have you guilty of the baseness of lying in wait for me." This simple address produced an immediate effect. The peasants, ashamed of themselves, entreated his pardon, and promised that they would not again doubt his affection for them. From that period he was enabled to pursue his benevolent designs, and, eventually, a most pleasing change was effected.

(*b*) HENRY C. WRIGHT AND HIS ASSAILANT.—The following incident in the life of Henry C. Wright shows his admirable consistency, and the salutary influence of non-resistance on the offender. He was in a hotel in Philadelphia, and there engaged in a conversation on non-resistance. An officer present became enraged and struck him. Mr. Wright took no notice of the assault, but proceeded with his remarks. In a few moments the officer struck him again. Friend Wright still preserved his equanimity, and continued the conversation. His assailant struck him a third time, and nearly knocked him down. He recovered himself, and though much injured by the blows of his opponent, took him by the hand and said, "I feel no unkindness towards you, and hope soon to see you at my house." He then left the company and returned home. Mr. Wright saw his assailant much sooner than he expected, for he was called up at dawn next morning, by the very man who had struck him the previous evening. He exclaimed, as he entered the house, "Can you forgive me? I have been in agony all night. I thought you would strike again, or I never should have struck you." "He that is slow to anger is better than the mighty; and he that ruleth his spirit than he that taketh a city."

(*c*) THE METHODIST NON-RESISTANT.—The Rev. John Pomphret, an English Methodist minister, always advocated the *practical applicability* of the "peace doctrine,"—"If a man will sue thee at law, and take away thy coat, let him have thy cloak also; and if he compel thee to go with him a mile, go with him twain,"—always declaring that if he should be attacked by a highwayman, he should put it in practice. Being a cheesemonger, (he preached without wages,) on his return from market one day, after he had received a large amount of money from his customers for the purpose of replenishing his year's stock, he was accosted by a robber, demanding his money, and threatening his life if he refused. The reverend peaceman coolly and kindly replied, "Well, friend, how much do you want, for I will *give* it to you. and thus save you from the crime of committing highway robbery?" "Will you *certainly* give me what I require?" asked the robber. "I will, in truth, if you do not require more than I have got," replied the non-resistant. "Then I want fifteen pounds," (about seventy-five dollars.) The required sum was counted out to him, and in gold, instead of in bank-bills, which, if the numbers had been observed, the reverend father, by notifying the bank, could have rendered uncurrent, besides leaving the robber liable to detection in attempting to pass them, telling him at the same time *why* he gave the gold instead of bank-notes; and saying, "Unfortunate man, I make you *welcome* to this sum. Go home. Pay your debts. Hereafter, get your living honestly."

Years rolled on. At length the good preacher received a letter, containing principal and interest, and a humble confession of his sins, from the robber, saying that his appeals waked up his slumbering conscience, which had given him no rest till he had made both restitution and confession, besides wholly changing his course of life.

293. Transforms Aggressors into Friends.

(*a*) THE SUBDUED HATTER.—When I was in the hatting business, says Mr. Hanchett, I employed a man by the name of Jonas Pike, from Massachusetts, who was a most excellent workman in the manufacture of hats. But he was one of that kind of journeymen who would have their trains, as they were familiarly called amongst us in that day. Therefore, as a natural consequence, he was without comfortable clothing the most of the time. After he got a shop he would work very industriously until he had earned from twenty to thirty, and sometimes forty dollars worth of clothing; (for he was always in want of clothing when he commenced work;) and then he would get on one of his trains, and dispose of every article of his clothing that would fetch six cents, expending all for whisky. When all was gone, and he began to cool off a little, he would be very ugly; sometimes he would fret and scold, and then he would coax and plead, to have me trust him a hat or something else, that he might sell, and thereby get more whisky. When I refused him, he would become very angry and threaten to whip me, which I told him he might do as soon as he pleased. But said he, "I will not do it in your own shop; if I had you out of doors I would thrash you like a sack."

After hearing him repeat these sayings several times, I walked out at the door. I then spoke to him, saying, "I am now out of the shop, thou canst whip me if thou wishest to do so very much;" at which he stepped out of the shop, came furiously towards me, squaring himself for a box, and struck me a blow on the breast, at which I put my hand upon my cheek, and held it down to him, saying, "Now strike here, Jonas." He now looked at me with surprise and astonishment, then turning round, saying at the same time, with an oath, "If you will not fight, I will let you alone," he went into the shop, sat down and was quiet. He got sober and went to work, and ever after was affectionate and kind, and very peaceable with me. I employed him several times afterwards to work for me, and he was always very peaceable and obliging.

(*b*) THE GENERAL'S EXPERIMENT WITH THE INDIANS.—The following anecdote is related of General ——. He was engaged on a tour to the northwest, some time after the war of 1812–15, for the purpose, among other objects, of selecting and obtaining from the Indians a site for a military post. He was attended by a small party, and they were unarmed. Before he had succeeded in his object, the Indians conceived a design for murdering him and his party; and they accordingly fixed the time for carrying their purpose into execution. A trader who resided on the spot, communicated the plot to the general, and proposed, as the only possible chance of escape, that he should take shelter in his house, supposing that he might perhaps have interest with them sufficient to keep them from breaking into his house to perpetrate the intended massacre. The general received the intelligence—his own observation of the countenances and movements of the Indians left him no room to doubt its correctness; but he was unwilling to accept the offer of the trader. He thought it would derogate from the character he had obtained, to leave his tent and take shelter in a private house. His situation was perilous.

The h ur had almost arrived, and there was no possibility of escape or defence. In this extremity, he determined on a bold experiment. With the aid of the trader, though not without difficulty, he succeeded in collecting the chiefs in council; but their menacing countenances gave evidence of the determination they had formed. At that critical moment, the assembly exhibited a most interesting scene. The general, with his little handful of men, all unarmed, in the heart of the Indian country, was surrounded by many times their own number of Indians, determined on their work of death, equipped for the horrid purpose, and waiting for the signal of onset.

The general arose with composure. He told them the object of his visit—that *their* happiness was also contemplated—that he came among them as brothers. He had brought no forces, nor even arms, with which to defend himself. "You see," said he, "I have nothing but this," stretching out his hand with his cane. He reminded them that he was in the midst of their people, and he looked to them for protection.

They had listened with increasing attention to his discourse thus far. But here they would no longer remain in silent attention. They leaped from their seats, and rushing to him with all the ardor of friendship, they caught him in their arms, hugged him, gave him every assurance of protection, and during his hasty stay among them, fully realized their promises.

(*c*) THE REVOLUTIONARY SOLDIER.—A beloved brother, now dead, (says a writer in a Massachusetts journal,) related to me a circumstance of his life, which I think is worth preserving. He was a soldier in the revolutionary war. After he came here, he became religious, and was convinced that all "wars and fightings" are contrary to the Gospel of Christ. His zeal in advocating his principles, stirred up the enmity of a wicked man in the neighborhood, who threatened, when his son came home from the army, he would flog him.

Sure enough, when the son came home, the old man told such stories to him about this brother, that it excited him to that degree, that he came to the house where my brother lived, in a rage, determined to fight. My brother expostulated with him, and endeavored, by all the means in his power, to allay his anger, and deter him from his purpose; but all would not do; fight he must, and fight he would. "Well," says the brother, "if we must fight, don't let us be like cats and dogs, fighting in the house; so go out into the field." To this he assented. When they had got into the field, and the young bully had stripped himself for the fight, my brother looked him in the face, and said, "Now you are a great coward." "Coward! don't call me a coward." "Well, you are one of the greatest cowards I ever saw." "What do you mean?" "I mean as I say; you must be a very great coward to go fighting a man who will not fight you." "What, don't you mean to fight me?" "Not I; you may fight me as much as you please, I shall not lift up a finger against you." "Is that your principle?" "Yes, it is; and I mean to be true to it." The spirit of the young soldier fell; and, stretching out his arm, he said, "Then I would sooner cut off that arm than I would strike you." They then entered into an explanation, and parted good friends.

294. Non-Resistance and Trust in God.

(*a*) THE PIOUS CAPTAIN AND THE PIRATE SHIP.—Capt. S——, of W——, Massachusetts, relates, that on a voyage to Brazil, in the spring of 1833, while sailing near Cape St. Roque, he descried, one morning, in the distance, a suspicious looking vessel, under a press of canvas, standing toward him. From several circumstances, he was led to imagine that she was occupied by pirates, who were advancing to plunder and murder. Still, not being certain of the fact, he concluded to keep the vessel on her course. The suspicious schooner continued to gain upon him, and soon, by the help of the glass, he saw her deck covered with men, and a long eighteen pounder on a swivel, so prepared as to turn in any direction desired. She was evidently a faster sailer than his own vessel; he concluded, therefore, that if he turned out of his course, he would at length be overtaken, and from the pirates, excited and exasperated by a long chase, little mercy could be expected. The captain was a professed Christian, a strong believer in the *providence of God*, and emphatically a *man of peace*. Instead of fighting with carnal weapons, he determined to fight him with spiritual ones. Having religious tracts on board, he determined, as soon as the schooner came along side, to go on board, and present his tracts to the captain and crew, and preach to them in a bold, but affectionate manner, appropriate truths from the Gospel of Christ. He ordered all the hands to go down below, but the man at the helm. This he did partly to keep them from being agitated and from agitating his own mind, and partly to do away with all appearance of opposition against the approaching foe. Then, committing his men and himself to God, he patiently awaited the pirate's arrival. The schooner came nearer and nearer, till at length even the figures of the men could be distinctly seen by the naked eye. A fearful crisis was fast coming. But still the captain never shrunk nor veered from his course for a moment. Suddenly the pirates altered their course, hauled the vessel upon the wind, and stood away as rapidly as sail and surge could carry them! From the fact that they saw no men on board but Capt. S. and the helmsman, and no manifestations of fear, the pirates might have been led to suspect that there was a large armed force below, or some other decoy prepared; and thus concluded it dangerous to attempt their hostile design. Whatever process of thought it was, however, which led them to retreat, who will fail to recognize in that process an overruling Providence, protecting in this instance, as in many others, the man who resists not evil, but in the hour of threatened violence depends not on his own arm, but on God's?

(*b*) QUAKERS IN THE FRENCH AND INDIAN WAR.—The reader of American history will recollect, that in the beginning of the 18th century a desultory and most dreadful warfare was carried on by the natives against the European settlers; a warfare that was provoked—as such warfare has almost always originally been—by the injury and violence of the [nominal] Christians. The mode of destruction was secret and sudden. The barbarians sometimes lay in wait for those who might come within their reach, on the highway or in the fields, and shot them without warning, and sometimes they attacked the Europeans in their houses, "scalping some, and knocking out the brains of others." From this horrible warfare the inhabitants sought safety by abandoning their houses, and retiring to fortified places, or to the neighborhood of garrisons; and those whom necessity still compelled to pass beyond the limits of such protection, provided themselves with arms for their defence. But amidst this dreadful desolation and universal terror, the *Society of Friends*, who were a considerable portion of the whole population, were steadfast to their principles. They would neither retire to garrisons, nor provide themselves with arms. They remained openly in the country, whilst the rest were flying to the forts. They still pursued their occupations in the fields or at their homes, without a weapon either for annoyance or defence. And what was their fate? They lived in security and quiet. The habitation, which, to his armed neighbor, was the scene of murder and of the scalping knife, was to the unarmed Quaker a place of safety and of peace. *Three* of the Society were however killed. And who were they? They were three who abandoned their principles. Two of these victims were men who, in the simple language of the narrator, "used to go to their labor without any weapons, and trusted to the Almighty, and depended on his providence to protect them, (it being their principle not to use weapons of war to offend others, or to defend themselves;) *but a spirit of distrust* taking place in their minds, they took weapons of war to defend themselves, and the Indians, who had seen them several times without them and let them alone, saying, they were peaceable men and hurt nobody, therefore, they would not hurt them—now seeing them have guns, and supposing they designed to kill the Indians, they therefore shot the men dead. The third whose life was sacrificed was a woman, "who had remained in her habitation," not thinking herself warranted in going "to a fortified place for preservation," neither she, her son, nor daughter, nor to take thither the little ones: but the poor woman after some time began to let in a slavish fear, and advised her children to go with her to a fort not far from their dwelling. She went; and shortly afterwards "the bloody, cruel Indians, lay by the way, and killed her."

(*c*) QUAKER'S HOUSE PRESERVED.—A most remarkable case occurred at the siege of Copenhagen under Lord Nelson. An officer in the fleet says, "I was particularly impressed with an object which I saw three or four days after the terrific bombardment of that place. For several nights before the surrender, the darkness was ushered in with a tremendous roar of guns and mortars, accompanied by the whizzing of those destructive and burning engines of warfare, Congreve's rockets. The dreadful effects were soon visible in the brilliant lights through the city. The blazing houses of the rich, and the burning cottages of the poor, illuminated the heavens; and the widespreading flames, reflecting on the water, showed a forest of ships assembled round the city for its destruction. This work of conflagration went on for several nights; but the Danes at length surrendered; and on walking some days after among the ruins, consisting of the cottages of the poor, houses of the rich, manufactories, lofty steeples, and humble meeting-houses, I descried, amid this barren field of desolation, a solitary house unharmed; all around it a burnt mass, this alone untouched by the fire, a monument of mercy. 'Whose house is that?' I asked. 'That,' said the interpreter, 'belongs to a Quaker. He would neither fight, nor leave his house, but remained in prayer with his family during the whole bombardment.' Surely, thought I, it *is* well with the righteous. God *has* been a shield to thee in battle, a wall of fire round about thee, a very present help in time of need."

(*d*) CITY OF REFUGE.—During the rebellion in Ireland, in 1798, the rebels had long meditated an attack on the Moravian settlement at Grace-Hill, Wexford county. At length they put their threat in execution, and a large body of them marched to the town. When they arrived there, they saw no one in the streets nor in the houses. The brethren had long expected this attack, but true to their Christian profession, they would not have recourse to arms for their defence, but assembled in their chapel, and in solemn prayer besought Him, in whom they trusted, to be their shield in the hour of danger. The ruffian band, hitherto breathing nothing but destruction and slaughter, were struck with astonishment, at this novel sight. Where they expected an armed hand, they saw it clasped in prayer—where they expected weapon to weapon, and the body armed for the fight, they saw the bended knee, and humble head, before the altar of the Prince of Peace. They heard the prayer for protection; they heard the intended victims asking mercy for their murderers: they heard the song of praise, and the hymn of confidence, in the "sure promise of the Lord." They beheld in silence this little band of Christians; they felt unable to raise their hand against them; and, after lingering in the streets, which they filled for a night and a day, with one consent they turned and marched away from the place, without having injured an individual, or purloined a single loaf of bread. In consequence of this signal mark of protection from heaven, the inhabitants of the neighboring villages brought their goods, and asked for shelter in Grace-Hill, which they called the City of Refuge.

295. NOVELS.

(*a*) NOVELS RIGHTLY DISPOSED OF.—Mr. Nicholas Ferrar, a very learned and pious man, who lived early in the seventeenth century, on the third day before his death, summoned all his family around him, and then desired his brother to go and mark out a place for his grave, according to the particular directions he then gave. When his brother returned, saying it was done as he had wished, he desired them all, in the presence of each other, to take out of his study three large hampers full of books, which had been locked up for many years: "They are comedies, tragedies, heroic poems, and romances; let them be immediately burnt upon the place marked out for my grave; and when you have so done, come back and inform me." When information was brought him that they were all consumed, he desired that this might be considered as the testimony of his disapprobation of such books, as tending to corrupt the mind of man, and improper for the perusal of every serious and sincere Christian.

(*b*) NOVEL WRITER'S TESTIMONY.—Dr. Goldsmith, who had himself written a novel, in writing to his brother, respecting the education of his son uses this strong language: "Above all things, never let your son touch a novel or romance. How delusive, how destructive are those features of consummate bliss! They teach the youthful mind to sigh after beauty and happiness, that never existed; to despise the little good that fortune has mixed in our cup, by expecting more than she ever gave; and in general—take the word of a man who has seen the world and studied it more by experience than by precept—take my word for it, I say that such books teach us very little of the world."

(*c*) SIN CURSING AFTER REPENTANCE.—A young lady in one of the large cities, (says the N. Y. Evangelist), of good native talent, was once condemning her folly, in terms of deepest regret, for cultivating her taste for novel reading. She had lately become pious, and now found to her sorrow, that her imagination had become so fascinated, and her taste so vitiated by this pernicious reading, that she could fix on nothing permanent, and said she, "Were it in my power, I could make any earthly sacrifice, could I thirst after the Bible, as I have after novels; and the greatest daily cross I am called to take up, is to pass by a novel without reading it. I would say it as a warning to all my sex, beware of this fatal rock; beware of wasting not only days but nights, to make yourselves fools all the rest of your days, if not absolutely wretched." This is a frank confession, which might be made by multitudes who are ciphers in society, because they have no fund within; for novels ever so attentively read, will furnish none.

(*d*) HALL'S OPINION OF MISS EDGEWORTH.—"Miss Edgeworth," says Robert Hall, "is the most irreligious writer I ever read; not so much from any direct attacks she makes on religion, as from a universal and studied omission of the subject. In her writings you meet a high strain of morality. She delineates the most virtuous characters, and represents them in the most affecting circumstances in life; in distress, in sickness, and even in the immediate prospect of eternity, and finally sends them off the stage with their virtue unimpaired; and all this without the remotest allusion to religion. She does not directly oppose religion, but makes it appear unnecessary, by exhibiting a perfect virtue without it. No works ever produced so bad an effect on my own mind. I did not expect to find any irreligion in Miss Edgeworth's writings. I was off my guard; their moral character disarmed me. I read nine volumes of them at once; but I could not preach with any comfort for six weeks after reading them. I never felt so little ardor in my profession, or so little interest in religion. She was once called to account for the character of her works, and asked her reasons for representing a mere ideal morality, without attributing any influence to religion. She said, that if she had written for the lower classes, she should have recommended religion; but that she had written for a class for whom it was less necessary. How absurd! She seemed to think that the virtues of the higher orders of society, stand in no need of religion, and that it was only designed as a curb and a muzzle for the brute.

(*e*) HANNAH MORE'S OPINION.—Many works of fiction (says Hannah More,) may be read with safety, some even with profit; but the constant familiarity even with such as are not exceptionable in themselves, relaxes the mind that wants hardening, dissolves the heart which wants fortifying, stirs the imagination which wants quieting, irritates the passions which want calming, and above all, disinclines and disqualifies for active virtues, and for spiritual exercises. The habitual indulgence in such reading, is a silent, mining mischief.

296. OBEDIENCE TO PARENTS.

(*a*) CECIL'S OBEDIENCE.—When the Rev. Richard Cecil was but a little boy, his father had occasion to go to the India House, and took his son with him. While he was transacting business, the little fellow was dismissed, and told to wait for his father at one of the doors. His father on finishing his business went out at another door, and entirely forgot his son. In the evening, his mother, missing the child, inquired where he was; on which his father, suddenly recollecting that he had directed him to wait at a certain door, said, "You may depend upon it, he is still waiting where I appointed him." He immediately returned to the India House and found his dear boy on the very spot he had ordered him to remain. He knew that his father expected him to wait, and therefore he would not disappoint him.

(*b*) FIRST STEP TOWARDS RUIN.—It was stated, at a meeting of the American Prison Discipline Society as the result of the examinations made by that institution into the history and career of the various criminals confin ed in the prisons of the United States, that in almost all cases their course of ruin began in disobedience to parents. This was followed by intemperance, and that made way for all other crimes. The statement was made by the secretary of the society, the Rev. Louis Dwight, whose opportunity for observation dad certainly been very great.

297. OMNIPRESENCE AND OMNISCIENCE OF GOD.

(*a*) GOD IS PRESENT.—The celebrated Linnæus always testified, in his conversation, writings, and actions, the greatest sense of God's omniscience; yea, he was so strongly impressed with the idea, that he wrote over the door of his library, *Innocui vivite, Numen adest;* —Live innocently, God is present.

(*b*) THIEF FORGETTING TO LOOK UP.—A man, who was in the habit of going to a neighbor's corn-field to steal the grain, one day took his son with him, a boy eight years of age. The father told him to hold the bag, while he looked if any one was near to see him. After standing on the fence, and peeping through all the corn-rows, he returned to take the bag from the child, and began his sinful work. "Father," said the boy, "you forgot to look somewhere else." The man dropped the bag in a fright, and said, "which way, child?" supposing he had seen some one. "You forgot to look up to the sky, to see if God was noticing you." The father felt this reproof of the child so much, that he left the corn, returned home, and never again ventured to steal; remembering the truth his child had taught him, that the eye of God always beholds us.

(*c*) WHERE AND WHERE NOT IS GOD?—A child, six years of age, being introduced into company, was asked, by a clergyman, where God was, with the offer of an orange. "Tell me," replied the boy, "where he is not, and I will give you two."

(*d*) THOUGHT FOR A FREE-THINKER.—Collins, the freethinker, or deist, met a plain countryman going to church. He asked him where he was going. "To church, sir." "What to do there?" "To worship God." "Pray, whether is your God a great or a little God?" "He is both, sir." "How can he be both?" "He is so great, sir, that the heaven of heavens cannot contain him; and so little that he can dwell in my heart." Collins declared, that this simple answer from the countryman had more effect upon his mind than all the volumes which learned doctors had written against him.

PAPACY.

298. Fanaticism and Cruelty.

(*a*) BONNER'S TREATMENT OF CRANMER.—After Archbishop Cranmer had been condemned, in the beginning of Queen Mary's reign, to suffer death, they proceeded afterwards to degrade him. To make this appear as ridiculous as possible, they put on him an episcopal habit made of canvas and old rags; Bonner, in the meantime, by way of insult and mockery, called him *Mr. Canterbury*, and such like. He bore all with his wonted fortitude and patience; telling them, the degradation gave him no concern, for he had long despised these ornaments. When they had stript him of all his habits, they put upon his jacket an old gown, threadbare and ill-shaped, and a townsman's cap, and so delivered him to the secular power, to be carried back to prison, where he was kept entirely destitute of money, and totally secluded from his friends. Such was the iniquity of the times, that a gentleman who gave him a little money to buy some provisions, narrowly escaped being brought to trial for it.

(*b*) THE IRISH LAD AND THE PRIEST.—The following striking anecdote of a papal priest and a clergyman's son, was related by William Digby Seymour, Esq., a young Irish barrister, at an Anniversary of the "Irish Society of London."

The boy was taking a walk, when a father-confessor of an adjoining parish met him; and when he had spoken awhile with him, he said, "You're a smart lad you young heretic! Do you know, I'd eat meat nine Fridays running to coax you into Maynooth?" "Would you?" replied the youngster; "I'd do more; I'd fast every Friday of my life to coax Maynooth into the Shannon." The priest was surprised at this sally. He spoke with the lad some minutes longer, and, when going off, he presented him with a half-crown, saying, he gave because the other was "the very picture of his poor, dear, departed grandmother!" The boy took the half-crown, and said, he would put it into his papa's collection box for the Irish Society. This enraged the priest. The face of the holy father, proceeded Mr. Seymour, blazed till ignition was momentarily threatened: an anathema of pious vengeance burst from his lips:—'My curse,—the Virgin's curse—the curse of Peter and Paul,—the curse of the Church and martyrs, be upon that Society!" he shouted; "may a blight and a blast be upon it! It took from me the best Catholic in my parish to be a Scripture-reader last week, and he'll steal them all from me before this time twelvemonth. So, you young reprobate, you're going to abuse my kindness this way! You'll not take your life and your half-crown together from this till you swear on this blessed cross (taking one from his breast) that you will not give my money to such an infernal purpose." So saying, and with a furious imprecation, he sprang off the saddle. It was truly a wild and painful scene! There stood the weeping boy and the man! the boy so bewildered as to forget restoring the coin; the priest so frenzied with religious ardor as to forget he was before a child. There they stood, for a moment only The savage man had an Irish heart; the tears of childhood fell upon that breast and melted it to softness. The priest re-mounted his horse and bade the last adieu forever. The priest's curse fell where it was uttered. The arrow touched not the Society, for the breath of God's blessing wafted it aside. The priest has since been gathered to them that sleep. He died a penitent. Oh! may he awake to glory. But what of the boy? Some kind voice here may ask—"What of the boy?" He lives, my friends; he lives to muse full oft on that eventful scene. He lives to pray for the Society he much loved then, and loves much now. He lives to thank England's people for their zeal in that Society's behalf, and to urge them to continue in the noble work of giving Irishmen the Bible; of giving children their Father's will in a copy they can understand; of giving the bondmen of Rome the Magna Charta of Protestant liberty. Full of gratitude for the past, and full of hopes for the future, it is he who now addresses you.

(*c*) DON PEDRO'S CONFESSION.—Don Pedro, one of the Spanish captains taken by Sir F. Drake, being examined before the Lords of the Privy Council as to what was their design of invading us, replied, "To subdue the nation and root it out." "And what meant you," said the lords, "to do with the Catholics?" "To send them good men," says he, "directly to heaven, and you heretics to hell." "For what end were your whips of cord and wire?" "To whip you heretics to death." "What would you have done with the young children?" "Those above seven years old should have gone the way their fathers went: the rest should have lived in perpetual bondage, branded in the forehead with the letter L. for Lutheran."

(*d*) DECLARATION OF FRANCIS I.—Francis I, king of France used to declare, "that if he thought the blood in his arm was tainted with the Lutheran heresy, he would have it cut off; and that he would not spare even his own children if they entertained sentiments contrary to the Catholic Church."

(e) WORKING ON SAINT'S DAY.—A historian who lived at the period of the Norman conquest, in mentioning some kings of England before Alfred, was apprehended for working on a saint's day; and, being asked why he gave such offence to religion, his reply was, "I am a poor man, and have nothing but my labor to depend upon; necessity requires that I should be industrious, and my conscience tells me there is no day but the Sabbath which I ought to keep sacred from labor." Having thus expressed himself, he was committed to prison, and being brought to trial, was, by his iniquitous judges, condemned to be burnt.

(f) THE INDIAN'S DISLIKE OF HEAVEN.—The Spaniards, by their cruelty to the natives of the island of Cuba, rendered themselves odious, and excited in the minds of the inhabitants the strongest prejudices against their religion. A chief, who had been condemned to be burnt, when brought to the stake was exhorted to embrace Christianity, assured that thereby he would be admitted to heaven. The chief asked if there were any Spaniards in heaven. "Yes," said the priest who attended him, "but they are all good ones." The chief replied, "I cannot bring myself to go to a place where I should meet with but one; therefore, do not speak to me any more of your religion, but let me die."

(g) DRUNK WITH THE BLOOD OF THE SAINTS.—According to the calculation of some, about two hundred thousand suffered death in seven years, under Pope Julian; no less than a hundred thousand were massacred by the French in the space of three months; the Waldenses who perished, amounted to one million; within thirty years, the Jesuits destroyed nine hundred thousand; under the Duke of Alva, thirty-six thousand were executed by the common hangman; a hundred and fifty thousand perished in the inquisition; and a hundred and fifty thousand by the Irish massacre; besides the vast multitude of whom the world could never be particularly informed, who were proscribed, banished, burned, starved, buried alive, smothered, suffocated, drowned, assassinated, chained to the galleys for life, or immured within the horrid walls of the Bastile, or others of their church or state prisons. According to some, the whole number of persons massacred since the rise of Papacy, amounts to fifty millions!

(h) WAY THEY WOULD SERVE HERETICS.—A correspondent of the Protestant Vindicator, says:

A lady who lived in Kingston, U. C., told me she formerly belonged to the *Roman church*. A large family Bible had been given her, a heretic Bible, or the *word of God*, in which were entered the names of all her family, her marriage, births, &c., and for which she felt much veneration and regard. The Vicar General or Priest came to her house, saw the venerable book, asked what it was, of which he obtained a complete history—he said, "For shame!—What! you pretend to be a good Catholic, and have a vile *heretic* Bible in your house—I am astonished at you: send it out—send it out immediately, or the thing will bring a *curse* upon you, and all your family. She said she wished to keep it, on account of the names of all her family being inserted in it. He replied, oh! never mind that, you must not keep the foolish thing in your house, it will spoil *you*, and all *your children*. He left the house in a rage, and then sent a person, who demanded and really took from her, her valuable treasure, her Bible.

She also sent some of her children to a Protestant Sunday School—they *consequently* had Tracts, and Sunday School books given to them. He took away all the poor children's books—had a *fire* kindled in some part of the Popish chapel; called a meeting, and *himself* tore the little books to pieces, leaf after leaf: and threw them into the flames, saying, thus we serve *heretic* books, and *thus* ought *all heretics* to be served.

(i) KILL THEM ALL.—The Albigensian war, in the beginning of the thirteenth century, commenced with the storming of Bezières, and a massacre in which fifteen thousand persons, or according to some accounts, sixty thousand, were put to the sword. Not a living soul escaped, as witnesses assure us. It was here that a Cistercian Monk, who led on the Crusaders, being asked if the Catholics were to be distinguished from heretics, answered, "Kill them all! God will know his own."

(*j*) THE HERMIT OF LIVRY.—In the forest of Livry, three leagues distant from Paris, and not far from the site of an ancient abbey of the order of St. Augustin, lived a hermit, who having chanced in his wanderings to fall in with some of the men of Meaux, had received the truth of the Gospel into his heart. The poor hermit had felt himself rich indeed that day in his solitary retreat, when, along with the scanty dole of bread which public charity had afforded him, he brought home Jesus Christ and his grace. He understood from that time how much better it is to give than to receive. He went from cottage to cottage in the villages around, and as soon as he crossed the threshold, began to speak to the poor peasants of the gospel, and the free pardon which it offers to every burdened soul, a pardon infinitely more precious than any priestly absolution. The good hermit of Livry was soon widely known in the neighborhood of Paris; many came to visit him at his poor hermitage, and he discharged the office of a kind and faithful missionary to the simple-minded in all the adjacent districts.

It was not long before intelligence of what was doing by the new evangelist reached the ear of the Sorbonne, and the magistrates of Paris. The hermit was seized—dragged from his hermitage—from his forest—from the fields he had daily traversed,—thrown into a dungeon in that great city which he had always shunned,—brought to judgment,—convicted,—and sentenced to "the exemplary punishment of being burnt by a slow fire."

In order to render the example the more striking, it was determined that he should be burnt in the close of Notre Dame; before that celebrated cathedral, which typifies the majesty of the Roma Catholic Church. The whole of the clergy were convened, and a degree of pomp was displayed equal to that of the most solemn festivals. A desire was shown to attract all Paris, if possible, to the place of execution. "The great bell of the church of Notre Dame swinging heavily," says an historian, "to rouse the people all over Paris." And accordingly from every surrounding avenue, the people came flocking to the spot. The deep-toned reverberations of the bell made the workman quit his task, the student cast aside his books, the shop-keeper forsake his traffick, the soldier start from the guard-room bench,—and already the close was filled with a dense crowd, which was continually increasing. The hermit attired in the robes appropriated to obstinate heretics, bareheaded, and with bare feet, was led out before the doors of the cathedral. Tranquil, firm, and collected, he replied to the exhortations of the confessors, who presented him with the crucifix, only by declaring that his hope rested solely on the mercy of God. The doctors of the Sorbonne, who stood in the front rank of the spectators, observing his constancy, and the effect it produced upon the people, cried aloud—"He is a man foredoomed to the fires of hell." The clang of the great bell, which all this while was rung with a rolling stroke, while it stunned the ears of the multitude, served to heighten the solemnity of that mournful spectacle. At length the bell was silent,—and the martyr having answered the last interrogatory of his adversaries, by saying that he was resolved to die in the faith of his Lord Jesus Christ, underwent his sentence of being "burnt by a slow fire." And so, in the cathedral close of Notre Dame, beneath the stately towers erected by the piety of Louis the younger, amidst the cries and tumultuous excitement of a vast population, died peaceably, a man whose name history has not deigned to transmit to us,—"the hermit of Livry."

(*k*) OCCURRENCE IN CUBA.—In December, 1830, (says a traveler,) I went to Cuba, with an intention of remaining at Havanna some months in the transaction of business. On one of the Popish festival days, about the new-year, I was walking alone, when I met two shaven-crowned Jesuits in their long cloaks—one bearing an image of the Virgin Mary, and the other carrying in his hand a crucifix. They immediately assailed me, and insisted that I should fall down on my knees to honor the image. I resisted their demand to comply with this baneful abomination. In consequence of my refusal, one of the priests struck me several times with the crucifix. When I attempted to ward off the blows, the other Jesuit came to his assistance; upon which I laid hold of the image, and the idol was almost pulled to pieces in the scuffle. In a very short time, a number of Spaniards with their knives and dirks came around me, and after threatening to take my life upon the spot, dragged me to prison. Then the monks, who judged the cause, condemned me to be kept on board a Spanish man-of-war for life; but the consul, to whom I applied for protection, preserved me, so that my punishment was changed to pay thirty-four dollars fine, and to be reshipped back to America.

299. Hostility to the Bible.

(*a*) ADVICE OF THE BOHEMIAN BISHOPS.—It is stated, in the life of Ridley the reformer, that, in October, 1553, a closet council of Roman bishops was held at Bononia, to advise the pope as the best means of checking the progress of the reformation. After making many very curious concessions, the bishops of Termulæ, Capralæ, and Thessalonica, thus concluded their address to Pope Julius III:—"But we have reserved the most considerable advice, which we could at this time give your highness, to the last. And here you must be awake, and exert all your force to hinder, as much as you possibly can, the gospel from being read, (especially in the vulgar tongue,) in all the cities that are under your dominion. Let that little taste of it which they have in the mass serve their turn, nor suffer any mortal to read any thing more; for as long as men were contented with that little, things went to your mind, but grew worse and worse from the time that they commonly read more. This, in short, is the book that has, beyond all others, raised these storms and tempests, in which we are almost driven to destruction. And really, whosoever shall diligently weigh the Scripture, and then consider all the things that are usually done in our churches, will find that there is a great difference between them; and that this doctrine of ours is very unlike, and in many things quite repugnant to it."

(*b*) PRIEST BURNING THE BIBLE.—In the year 1833, a poor family in Ireland, of the name of M'Gennis, was greatly distressed by the painful illness of a young girl, who, after lingering some time, gave signs of approaching dissolution. She was attended by the priests of the Romish church, to which the family belonged, one of whom discovered, shortly before her decease, that she had repaired for support and comfort in her affliction to a forbidden source. In the wretched hut was a Bible, which the sufferer had received as a reward, at a Protestant minister's free school; and the priest commanded that it should be instantly destroyed. The dying girl shuddered; the aged parent entreated that the book might be spared; but he was inexorable, and demanded that it should be burned in his presence. The father now declared that it should not be done under his roof; and the incensed priest, rushing from the hut with the Bible in his hand, placed it upon a fire of turf, kindled in the open air, and thus deliberately destroyed it in the daytime, in the presence of numbers, and in the high road! Nor is this a solitary case.

(*c*) ENOUGH BAD BOOKS ALREADY.—The following is from "*Les Archives du Christianisme*," a French religious monthly publication:

We can attest the truth of the following fact. At a sale, made after the death of the minister of the village of Dosenheim, (Lower Rhine,) when the books of the deceased were about to be sold, the Romish minister of a neighboring parish seized a volume, declaring that there were enough of bad books in the world already, and this should not be sold. It was not sold, and the reader will be more afflicted than surprised, to hear, that this bad book (as he called it) was the New Testament of our Lord and Savior Jesus Christ!

(*d*) "SINCE ADAM WAS A BOY."—Who would belong to a church which withholds from its members the inspired volume? We copy the following fact from a periodical called "The Thistle," published in 1836:

Not long since, when priest W., of Corofin, was passing by some men and boys who were engaged in breaking stones for a new road, now in progress in the neighborhood of Carhue, he said, that the road there would be of great use; "and it is a long time," said he, "since there was a road in this place." "Not since Adam was a boy," remarked one of the men. "And when was that? can you tell me?" said priest W. "No, sir, I cannot," replied the man. The same question was asked of several persons, and a similar reply given. At length the priest turned to a young boy, and said, "Can you tell me, my lad, when Adam was a boy?" "Sir, Adam never was a boy; God created him man, and made him perfect also." "Are ye not ashamed," said the priest, "to be excelled by a young boy like this?" "No," answered one of those appealed to, "we are not; that boy reads the Scriptures, and has them explained to him; that is what is not done to us, and we are prevented from reading them ourselves." Priest W. rode away without making any reply.

(*e*) THE ARROGANT AVOWAL.—An English officer, who was once at Valenciennes, states the following fact, which came under his own observation. A number of Bibles in French had been sent from England to the above city, for sale or distribution. Many of the people received them with gratitude, and read them with avidity; but the priest getting information of the matter, ordered all the Bibles to be returned. The English officer, who was acquainted with him, asked the reason of this, to which he gave the following truly *Popish* reply:—"*I* teach the people every thing that is necessary for them to know!"

(*f*) THE PRIEST OUTWITTED.—An elderly female, of the Roman Catholic persuasion, residing near Montreal, in Canada, having obtained a Bible, was visited by her priest, who earnestly endeavored to prevail on her to give it up. Finding he could not persuade her to relinquish her treasure, he attempted to induce her to sell it; offering first five, then ten, fifteen, and at last twenty dollars. The good woman, after refusing these offers, at length consented to sell it for twenty-five dollars. The priest agreed, the money was paid, the obnoxious volume was given up, and he departed in triumph. But the old woman set off immediately to Montreal, and, with the priest's twenty-five dollars, purchased twenty-five new Bibles, for herself and her neighbors.

300. Idolatry.

(*a*) VIRGIN OF GAUDALOUPE.—About ten years after what the Spaniards call "*The Conquest*," the celebrated apparition of the Virgin de Gaudaloupe, made its appearance in the following manner. Adjacent to the city of Mexico is a hill entirely barren; an Indian accidentally passing heard sounds of music, and, at the same time, saw an aerial female figure in a praying attitude. The Indian, alarmed at the vision, fled; but passing near the hill a few days afterwards, the same strange occurrence again took place. The figure called him by name, and told him to repair to the spot on a certain day, and he would find her picture buried under a heap of roses;—he did so, and met with it as directed. The Indian carried this mysterious figure to the Bishop of Mexico, who was, of course, in the secret. A solemn conclave of the clergy took place, and the Bishop, with the most profound reverence, knelt before the picture and named it Neuestra Senora de Gaudaloupe. A magnificent church was built for her reception, and she received the exalted title of "*Patroness of Mexico*," which she enjoys to the present day. This is the origin of the Virgin de Gaudaloupe, conformably to the records of the church now existing at Mexico. The original picture is still exhibited in the Virgin's Church; it is painted on a cloth of linen manufacture, called "*Uangochi,*" composed of coarse threads spun from the fibres of the aloe (Agava Americana) and woven very wide apart. The Indians and the Creoles say, that he picture is miraculous, because, as you approach it, the painting becomes less visible, and when quite close all traces of the picture disappear; their blind superstition not permitting them to discover that the open texture of the material upon which it is painted, is the cause of this disappearance.

A priest told the writer of the above, another circumstance respecting the Virgin, respecting another part of the miracle, viz., that the picture was found under a heap of roses in the winter season, and on a spot where those flowers had never bloomed. It never occurred to the priest that, a few leagues from this barren hill the climate was quite different and where roses grow throughout the year. Consequently the persons who painted the picture of the Virgin did not require any celestial aid to procure a bed of roses.

In such veneration do the Indians and lower order of Creoles (and indeed many of the middling and higher classes,) hold their patroness, that they have paintings of her in all their houses, invoke her in all their prayers, and implore her assistance in all their difficulties.

(*b*) NEW-FOUND IMAGE.—Says the Rev. Blanco White, "I will tell you what happened at Madrid, during a residence of three years which I made in that most Roman Catholic capital. In one of the meanest parts of the town the ragged children, who are always running about the streets, found an old picture which had been thrown, with other rubbish, upon a dunghill. Not knowing what the picture was, they tied to it a piece of rope, and were dragging it about, when an old woman in the neighborhood looked at the canvas, and found upon it the head of a Virgin Mary. Her screams of horror at the profanation which she beheld scared away the children and the old woman was left in possession of the treasure. The gossips of the neighborhood were anxious to make some amends to the picture for the past neglect and ill-treatment, and they all contributed towards the expense of burning a lamp, day and night, before it, in the old woman's house. A priest getting scent of what was going on took the scratched virgin under his patronage, framed the canvas, and added another light. All the rich folks who heard of this new-found image came to pray before it, and gave something to the priest and the old woman, who were now in close partnership. In a very short time the amount of the daily donations enabled the joint proprietors of the picture to build a fine chapel, with a comfortable house adjoining it for themselves. The chapel was crowded from morning till night; not a female, high or low, but firmly believed that her life and safety depended upon the favor of that particular picture: the rich endeavored to obtain it by large sums of money for masses to be performed, and candles to be burned before it; and the poor stinted their necessary food to throw a mite into the box which hung at the door of the chapel. I do not relate to you old stories; I state what I myself have seen."

(*c*) ST. PETER'S TOE.—I have seen people, says a traveler, of all ranks and ages prostrate themselves before the statue of St. Peter at Rome, and after saying a short prayer most humbly kiss his toe. To such an extent is this carried, that the great toe of the image (it is so wretched a thing I can hardly call it a statue) is from time to time worn away, and the brazier is called in to supply another, that the toe-worshipers may not miss the object of their adoration. But a letter would not suffice to tell of half the instances that I have seen acted before my eyes of the most degrading superstition and image-worship.

(*d*) "IT IS NOT MY FAULT."—In Lisbon the priests once found or pretended to have found an image, dug up from the earth, and proclaimed it to be the effigy of an eminent saint; it was accordingly set up in one of the churches, where crowds of devotees assembled to offer their devotions. To his saintship was also referred the decision of the disputed point, "who was the legitimate monarch of Portugal," The officiating priest put the question in an audible voice, "Is Don Pietro the lawful sovereign of these realms?" The saint shook his head as a negative indication. "Is Don Miguel the Sovereign?" The image nodded assent. This was repeated on various occasions to increased congregations, and was considered by the multitude as an astonishing miracle. At one time in the presence of our informant, the first inquiry had been replied to as usual; to the second no answer was returned; upon which the priest several times repeated the question, and at length assumed great vehemence of manner, when a boy popped out his head from behind the curtain, and exclaimed, "It is not my fault, sir, *the string is broken.*"

(*e*) CORONATION OF THE VIRGIN.—The following is a translation of a proclamation for the coronation of an image of the Virgin:—

"The most reverend chapter of St. Peter's at Rome, in compliance with the will of the count Alexander Sforza Pallavicini, is accustomed to distribute every year certain crowns of gold, to decorate the brows of those images of the blessed Virgin, the most celebrated either for their antiquity, their wondrous works, (query, prodigies or miracles?) or for their popularity, in order to increase ever more and more the worship of such images, and to excite the piety and devotion of the faithful towards the great mother of God.

"Now the above-mentioned most reverend chapter, having listened to the claims urged in favor of the image of the immaculate conception, which is adored in the church of Jesu Vecchio, in Naples, represented by a little wooden statue, three feet high, with an infant Jesus in its arms; and having found these claims to be supported by satisfactory evidence and solid documents, have judged it right to award a golden crown, not only to the image of the Virgin, but also to that of the infant Jesus in her arms. With this decision the supreme pontiff, Leo XII, has signified his approbation in his apostolic brief, (query, bull?) issued on the 2nd of December, 1826; and he has not only signified his approval of this act, but has been pleased to grant an abundant portion of grace and indulgence to all who shall assist in the ceremony of the coronation, or be present in the church on that great day." Then follow the order to the archbishop to do it, and the approbation of the king of Naples, as well as all the prayers and hymns that are to be said or sung to this little wooden image, before and after the coronation, etc. etc.

(*f*) INFANT JESUS AT ROME.—I went forth, says a gentleman on the continent, in 1825, at half past four in the morning, to see an exhibition, which is made at one of the first cathedrals in Rome, (St. Mary the greater,) of the infant Jesus in the cradle. The splendid edifice was brilliantly illuminated, and crowded to excess: a large body of priests, richly arrayed, with a mitred bishop at their head were engaged in performing mass. When this was over, they moved in procession to one of the chapels, at the side of the nave, which from the lights, the marbles, the paintings, and the gilded and jeweled altar, presented a gorgeous spectacle; hence they shortly issued, and made a procession round the church bearing the crucifix, and a large vase of glass, about the size of a cradle, which had on its cover the golden image of a child, and contained also a representation of a new-born infant, in wax. Returning to the chapel, the priests commenced another mass. With some difficulty we got admission to the chapel: a cordon of soldiers being drawn round the entrance, and the multitude pressing to see through the open gates the exhibition within. We found, under the altar-piece, a representation of the birth of Christ, consisting of figures in some material as white as alabaster; the infant was seen lying in the manger, with rays of gold round its head, and two oxen feeding near it. On one side, the virgin mother, with clasped hands, was worshiping the child; and on the opposite side was another figure in the same attitude. But what surprised me most was to hear occasionally, a short plaintive cry, evidently proceeding from that part of the chapel where the child was, and so exactly resembling the cry of an infant, that I supposed there must be a living child in the place. I was confirmed, by the opinion of those around me, as to the quarter from whence the cry proceded; and I can therefore only conjecture that it was a contrivance of the priests to impress more vividly upon the minds of the multitude, the scene which they wished to represent!

301. Indulgences.

(*a*) ST. PETER'S AT ROME.—Pope Julius II began the building of the magnificent church at Rome, but left it unfinished. His successor, Leo X, was desirous to complete this superb edifice, but being involved in debt, and finding the apostolic treasury exhausted, he had recourse to the selling of indulgences, a gainful traffic, for the procuring a sufficient sum of money. Accordingly, in 1517 he published general indulgences throughout all Europe, to such as would contribute to the building of St. Peter's. The sum of *ten shillings* was sufficient to purchase the pardon of sins, and the ransom of a soul from purgatory!

(*b*) ABSOLUTION IN ADVANCE.—When Tetzel was at Leipsic, in the sixteenth century, and had collected a great deal of money from all ranks of the people, a nobleman, who suspected imposition, put the question to him, "Can you grant absolution for a sin which a man shall intend to commit in future?" "Yes," replied the frontless commissioner; "but on condition that proper sum of money be actually paid down." The noble instantly produced the sum demanded; and in return received a diploma, sealed and signed by Tetzel, absolving him from the unexplained crime, which he secretly intended to commit. Not long after, when Tetzel was about to leave Leipsic, the nobleman made inquiry respecting the road he would probably travel, waited for him in ambush at a convenient place, attacked and robbed him; then beat him soundly with a stick, sent him back to Leipsic with his chest empty, and at parting, said, "This is the fault I intended to commit, and for which I have your absolution."

(*c*) SHOEMAKER OF HAGENAU.—The dealers in indulgences had established themselves at Hagenau in 1517. The wife of a shoemaker profiting by the permission given in the instruction of the commissary-general, had procured against her husband's will, a letter of indulgence, and had paid for it a gold florin. Shortly after, she died; and the widower omitting to have mass said for the repose of her soul the curate charged him with contempt of religion, and the judge of Hagenau summoned him to appear before him. The shoemaker put in his pocket his wife's indulgence, and repaired to the place of summons. "Is your wife dead?" asked the judge. "Yes," answered the shoemaker. "What have you done with her?" "I buried her and commended her soul to God." "But have you had a mass said for the salvation of her soul?" "I have not—it was not necessary;—she went to heaven in the moment of her death." How do you know that"—"Here is the evidence of it." The widower drew from his pocket the indulgence, and the judge in presence of the curate, read, in so many words, that in the moment of death, the woman who had received it would go, not into purgatory, but straight into heaven. "If the curate pretends that a mass is necessary after that," said the shoemaker, "my wife has been cheated by our holy father the Pope; but if she has not been cheated, then the curate is deceiving me." There was no reply to this defence, and the accused was acquitted. It was thus that the good sense of the people disposed of these impostures.

(*d*) CROSS IN SWITZERLAND—In Switzerland, says Bishop Wilson we actually saw on a cross, by the road side, this notice: "The archbishop of Chamberry and the bishop of Geneva grant forty days' indulgence to all those who shall say before this cross a Pater, and an Ave-Maria, with an act of contrition, 1819."

(*e*) BLACKAMOOR VIRGIN.—At Dijon, as I walked along, wrote the Rev. Dr. Wilson, bishop of Calcutta, in 1823, I observed on all the churches an immense placard. I stopped, from mere curiosity, to see what it was. It was an advertisement of a new edition of the History of the Miraculous Image of Notre Dame, at Dijon. I hurried to the church, and looked all around: I saw a gaudily embellished building, filled with altars, and pictures, and statues, but no image that I could discover. I went out and inquired of an elderly woman. She took me up to an altar on which was the statue of the Virgin, resembling that of a blackamoor, and decked out with tawdry ornaments. I afterwards bought the book; it positively asserts that various miracles have been performed by this wretched figure! Nay more, indulgences are granted to all who worship this image, and a society is formed to celebrate feasts to her honor. As the image is black, the author attempts to prove, very gravely, that the Virgin Mary was of a swarthy complexion!

302. Confession and Absolution.

(*a*) FREE SPOKEN AMBASSADOR.—After the death of Charles VI, the Spanish Ambassador, Don Pedro Rouguillo, at his first audience of the new king James VI, being requested to state freely his opinion of the state of affairs in England, his excellency told James, "that he saw several priests about his majesty, who would importune him to alter the established religion in England, but prayed him not to hearken to their advice, lest his majesty should repent of it when it was too late." The king being a good deal displeased with this counsel, asked the ambassador with some zeal, "whether it was not customary in Spain to advise with their confessors?" "Yes, sir," replied the ambassador, "we do so, and that's the reason our affairs succeed so ill."

(*b*) A PENITENT ROGUE.—A Roman Catholic, who had filled up the measure of his iniquities, as far as he dared, went to the priest, to confess and obtain absolution. He entered the apartment of the priest, and addressed him: "Holy father, I have sinned."

The priest bid him kneel before the penitential chair. The penitent was looking about and he saw the priest's gold watch lying upon the table within his reach. He seized it and put it in his bosom. The priest approached him and requested him to acknowledge the sins for which he wished absolution.

"Father," said the rogue, "I have stolen, and what shall I do?"

"Restore," said the priest, "the thing you have stolen, to its rightful owner."

"Do you take it?" said the penitent.

"No, I shall not," said the priest; "you must give it to the owner."

"But he has refused to take it."

"If this be the case you may keep it."

The priest granted him full absolution.—The penitent knelt and kissed his hand, craved his benediction, crossed himself, and departed with a *clear* conscience, and a very valuable gold watch into the bargain.

303. Inquisition.

(*a*) WHITE AND HIS MOTHER.—Blanco White remarks, "Believe a man, who has spent the best years of his life where Roman Catholicism is professed without the check of dissenting opinions, where it luxuriates on the soil which fire and sword have cleared of whatever might stint its natural and genuine growth; a growth incessantly watched over by the head of the church, and his authorized representatives, the inquisitors."

He then states, "I had a mother, remarkable for the powers of her mind, and the goodness of her heart. No woman could love her children more ardently, and none of those children was more vehemently loved than myself. But the Roman Catholic creed had poisoned in her the purest source of affection. I saw her during a long period unable to restrain her tears in my presence. I perceived that she shunned my conversation, especially when my university friends drew me into topics above those of domestic talk. I loved her, and this behavior cut me to the heart. In my distress I applied to a friend to whom she used to communicate all her sorrows: and, to my utter horror, I learned, that suspecting me of anti-catholic principles, my mother was distracted by the fear that she might be obliged to accuse me to the Inquisition, if I incautiously uttered some condemned proposition in her presence! To avoid the barbarous necessity of being the instrument of my ruin, she could find no other means but that of shunning my presence! Did this unfortunate mother overrate or mistake the nature of her Roman Catholic duties? By no means. The Inquisition was established by the supreme authority of her church, and under that authority she was enjoined to accuse any person whatever, whom she might overhear uttering heretical opinions. No exception was made in favor of fathers, children, husbands, wives; to conceal was to abet their errors, and thus doom two souls to eternal perdition! A sentence of excommunication, to be incurred by the fact of having thus acted, was annually published against all persons, who having heard a proposition, directly or indirectly, contrary to the Roman Catholic faith, omitted to inform the inquisitors of it. Could any sincere Roman Catholic slight such a command?" Protestants, what think ye of such a system?

(*b*) ADMIRAL PYE AND THE INQUISITORS.—Admiral Pye of England, having been on a visit to Southampton, and the gentleman under whose roof he resided observing an unusual intimacy between him and his secretary, inquired into the degree of their relationship, as he wished to pay him suitable attention. The admiral informed him that they were not related, but their intimacy arose from a singular circumstance, which, by his permission, he would relate. The admiral said, when he was a captain, he was cruising in the Mediterranean. While on that station he received a letter from shore, stating that the unhappy author of the letter was by birth an Englishman; that, having been a voyage to Spain, he was enticed, while there, to become a Papist, and, in process of time, was made a member of the Inquisition; that there he beheld the abominable wickedness and barbarities of the Inquisitors. His heart recoiled at having embraced a religion so horribly cruel and so repugnant to the nature of God; that he was stung with remorse to think that, if his parents knew *what* and *where* he was, their hearts would break with grief; that he was resolved to escape if he (the captain) would send a boat on shore at such a time and place; but begged secrecy, since, if his intentions were discovered, he should be immediately assassinated. The captain returned for answer that he could not with propriety send a boat, but if he could devise any means to come on oard, he would receive him as a British subject and protect him. He did so; but, being missed, there was soon raised a hue and cry, and he was followed to the ship.

A holy inquisitor demanded him, but he was refused. Another, in the name of his *holiness the pope*, claimed him, but the captain did not know him or any other master but his own sovereign, King George. At length a third *holy brother* approached. The young man recognised him at a distance, and, in terror, ran to the captain, entreating him not to be deceived by him, for he was the most *false*, *wicked*, and *cruel* monster in all the Inquisition. He was introduced, the young man being present; and, to obtain his object, began with the bitterest accusations against him; then he turned to the most fulsome flatteries of the captain; and, lastly, offered him a sum of money to resign him. The captain treated him with apparent attention; said his offer was very handsome, and, if what he affirmed were true, the person in question was unworthy of the English name or of his protection. The holy brother was elated; he thought his errand was accomplished. While drawing his purse-strings, the captain inquired what punishment would be inflicted upon him. He replied that it was uncertain; but as his offences were atrocious, it was likely that his punishment would be exemplary. The captain asked if he thought he would be burned in a *dry pan*. He replied, that must be determined by the *holy Inquisition*, but it was not improbable.

The captain then ordered the great copper to be heated, but no water to be put in. All this while the young man stood trembling; his cheeks resembling death; he expected to become an unhappy victim to avarice and superstition. The cook soon announced that the orders were executed. "Then I command you to take this fellow," pointing to the inquisitor, "and *fry him alive* in the copper." This unexpected command thunderstruck the holy father. Alarmed for himself, he rose to be gone. The cook began to bundle him away. "Oh, good captain! good captain! spare, spare me, spare me!" "Have him away!" replied the captain. "Oh no, my good captain!" "Have him away! I'll teach him to attempt to bribe a *British commander* to sacrifice the life of an *Englishman* to gratify a herd of bloody men." Down the inquisitor fell upon his knees, offering him all his money, and promising never to return if he would let him begone. When the captain had sufficiently alarmed him, he dismissed him, warning him never to come again on such an errand. What must have been the reverse of feelings in the young man to find himself thus happily delivered! He fell upon his knees in a flood of tears before the captain, and poured out a thousand blessings upon his brave and noble deliverer. "This," said the admiral to the gentleman, "is the circumstance that began our acquaintance. I took him to be my servant; he served me from affection; mutual attachment ensued; and it has inviolably subsisted and increased to this day."

304. Praying to and for the Dead.

(*a*) BEATIFICATION OF ST. JULIAN.—The following account is given in a letter from Rome, dated May 28, in the year 1825:—

"On Whitmonday was beatified, in St Peter's at Rome, a Spanish Franciscan friar, named St. Julian da St. Agostino. The church was hung with crimson damask, illuminated with wax candles, and ornamented with large paintings, representing several miracles ascribed to him while living, as well as after his decease. One of them afforded considerable amusement. It represented St. Julian, who it seems was cook to his convent, in the act of taking several half-roasted birds from a spit, and restoring them to life, clothing them miraculously with feathers, and enabling them to fly away! The *Te Deum* was sung, and followed by a prayer addressed to this new saint. High mass concluded the ceremony; and in the afternoon the pope entered the church, and prayed before the portrait of the new St. Julian."

(*b*) BUONAVANTURA'S BEATIFICATION.—When Dr. Moore was at Rome, in 1775, a new saint, called St. Buonavantura, was added to the list. Dr. M. was present at the first part of the ceremony usual on these occasions, which is called the beatification of a saint, and has given a full account of the particulars. For several days previously, a very large picture of the proposed saint was hung up in front of St. Peter's church, and printed papers announcing the ceremony were distributed, particularly by the Franciscan monks, of whose order he had been a member. On the day fixed for the solemnity, the pope with many cardinals and other ecclesiastics attended; a long discourse was pronounced by a Franciscan friar, setting forth the devotions, penances, and charitable actions of the saint, and enumerating the miracles he had performed when alive, and those effected after his death by his bones. The most remarkable among these, was his replenishing a lady's cupboard with bread, after her housekeeper had, by the saint's desire, given to the poor all the loaves she had in the family.

This orator was opposed as usual by another, who is called the advocate for the devil, and objects to the miracles of the saint, his life and conduct, etc. etc. This controversy was drawn out to a great length; but at length the claimant was admitted to the privileges of beatification, which Dr. M. says the church of Rome considers "as entitling the saint to more distinction in heaven than before; but he has not the power of freeing souls from purgatory till he has been canonized, and therefore is not addressed in prayer till he has obtained the second honor." We may here observe, that the pope decrees who are to be considered as saints, and thus professes to know who are in heaven.

(*c*) SHRINE OF THOMAS A BECKET.—The shrine of Thomas a Becket, at Canterbury, was once profitable. It was valued abundantly more than the shrine of the Virgin Mary, or of Christ; for, in one year, there was offered at Christ's altar, £3 2s. 6d., at the Virgin's, £63 5s. 6d., but at St. Thomas's, £832 12s. 3d. And the next year was offered at Christ's, NOTHING; at the Virgin's, £4 1s. 8d., but at Becket's, £954 6s. 3d. A jubilee of fifteen days was ordained for Becket, at Rome, every fiftieth year, and indulgence was granted to all that would visit his shrine. In the sixth jubilee, in 1420, 100,000 strangers visited his tomb; and brought with them immense wealth.

(*d*) FLOGGING THE RELICS.—Galbert, monk of Marchiennes, informs us of a strange act of devotion in his time, and which is indeed attested by several contemporary writers. When the saints did not readily comply with the prayers of their votaries, they flogged these relics with rods in a spirit of impatience; a chastisement which they supposed would bend the saints into compliance!

(*e*) PAPAL BLASPHEMY.—During the great drought of the summer of 1824, in Spain, prayers were offered up in all the churches for rain, and amongst others in that of the village of Las Cabezas de San Juan, in Andalusia, where the unfortunate Riego proclaimed the constitution. But it was in vain that the patron St. Nicholas was invoked and worshiped, not a drop of rain fell. However, on a Sunday, as the faithful were at their devotions in his church, they perceived a letter in the hands of the saint. Some of the most devout approached to take it, but though St. Nicholas was of no more yielding material than wood, yet he raised the hand that held the letter, which appeared an unequivocal sign that he was unwilling to deliver it. The Curè, being informed of the circumstances, came in full canonicals to the saint, and prayed him humbly to give him the letter, which the saint, by lowering his hand, acceded to; and the Curè took the missive and read it to the assembly, to their infinite edification. The letter was composed in the following terms:—

Abodes of the Blessed, May 1, 1824.

"MY BELOVED NICHOLAS,—I have heard your continual prayers to me, to send down rain upon your country: you have no doubt forgotten the crimes with which your *rebel village* is stained, and which are the cause of the drought which afflicts unfortunate Spain. It is in vain that you ask for water; at present it is impossible for me to oblige you. Except rain, ask any thing else you wish from

Your ever Affectionate,
THE ETERNAL FATHER!!"

305. Miracles.

(*a*) GREAT CURE BY RELICS OF DOGS AND CATS.—When the reformation was spreading in Lithuania, Prince Radzivil was so affected that he went in person to visit the Pope, and pay him all possible honors. His holiness, on this occasion, presented him with a box of precious relics. Having returned home, the report of this invaluable possession was spread; and, at length, some monks entreated permission to try the effect of these relics on a demoniac who had hitherto resisted every kind of exorcism. They were brought into the church with solemn pomp, deposited on the altar, and an innumerable crowd attended. After the usual conjurations, they applied the relics. The demoniac instantly became well. The people called out, "*A Miracle!*" and the prince, lifting up his hands and eyes to heaven, felt his faith confirmed. In this transport of pious joy, he observed a young gentleman, who was keeper of this rich treasure of relics, to smile, and appear by his motions to ridicule the miracle. The prince, with violent indignation, took our young keeper of the relics to task; who, on promise of pardon, gave the following secret intelligence concerning them:—He assured him, that in traveling from Rome he had lost the box of relics; and that, not daring to mention it, he had procured a similar one which he had filled with the small bones of dogs and cats, and other trifles, similar to what was lost. He hoped that he might be forgiven for smiling, when he found that such a collection of rubbish was idolized with such pomp, and had even the virtue of expelling demons. It was by the assistance of this box that the prince discovered the gross imposition of the monks and demoniacs, and he afterwards became a zealous Lutheran.

(*b*) THE AUTOMATON JESUS.—In the monastery at Isenach, (says Luther,) stands an image which I have seen. When a wealthy person came hither to pray to it (it was Mary with her child), the child turned away his face from the sinner to the mother; but if the sinner gave liberally to that monastery, then the child turned to him again; and if he promised to give more, then the child showed itself very friendly and loving, and stretched out its arms over him in the form of a cross. But this picture and image was made hollow within, and prepared with locks, lines, and screws; and behind it stood a knave to move them,—and so were the people mocked and deceived, who took it to be a miracle!

(*c*) MIRACLE OF THE OMELET.—A priest in extreme poverty resolved to get credit for a miracle. He put the yolks of several eggs in a hollow cane, and stopped the end with butter; then, walking into an alehouse, he begged to fry a single egg for his dinner. The smallness of his repast excited curiosity, and they gave him a morsel of lard. He stirred the lard with his cane, and, to the wonder of the surrounding peasants, produced a handsome omelet.—This miracle established his fame; he sold omelets and got rich by his ingenuity.

(*d*) THE MONK AND THE MAGPIE.—St. Anthony is thought to have had a great command over fire, and power of destroying by that element those who incurred his displeasure. A certain monk of St. Anthony one day assembled his congregation under a tree where a magpie had built her nest, into which he had found means to convey a small box filled with gunpowder, and out of the box hung a long thin match that was to burn slowly, and that was hidden among the leaves of the trees. As soon as the monk or his assistant had touched the match with a lighted coal, the friar began his sermon; in the mean while the magpie returned to her nest, and finding in it a strange body which she could not remove, she fell into a passion and scratched with her feet most vehemently. The friar affected to hear without emotion, and continued his sermon with great composure, only he would now and then lift up his eyes towards the top of the tree, as if he wanted to know what was the matter. At last, when he judged that the match was near reaching the gunpowder, he pretended to be out of patience; he cursed the magpie, wished St. Anthony's fire might consume her, and went on again with his sermon. But he had scarcely proceeded two or three periods, when the match on a sudden produced its effect, and blew up the magpie with its nest; which miracle wonderfully raised the character of the friar, and proved afterwards very beneficial to him and his convent.

(*e*) A MARTYR MAKING OFF WITH HIS HEAD.—Among the many strange things related in the Roman breviary for the edification of the faithful, is the following, concerning Dionysius, the Roman saint:

Dionysius, having now passed his hundredth year, was struck with the axe on the seventh of the ides of October; concerning whom tradition relates that he took up his head, when cut off, and carried it in his hands two miles, &c. *Die* ix. *Octobris*.

Think of this, reader; "a man running two miles with his head in his hands!"

(*f*) PLAYING THE DEVIL.—A singular occurrence took place abou 1824, in a village called Artes, nea

Hostalreich, about twelve leagues from Barcelona. A constitutionalist being at the point of death, his brother called on the curate, and requested him to come and administer the sacrament. The curate refused, saying, "Your brother is a constitutionalist, that is to say, a villain, an impious wretch, and an enemy to God and man; he is damned without mercy, and it is therefore useless for me to confess him!" "But who told you that my brother was damned?" "Who told me?" replied the curate; "why, God himself!" "What!" cried the astonished Spaniard, "has God spoken to you?" "Yes," answered the curate with assurance; "God spoke to me during the sacrifice of the mass, and told me your brother was damned to all the devils." It was in vain that the brother had reiterated his entreaties, the curate was inexorable. A few days after, the constitutionalist died, and the brother returned to the curate to beg him to perform the funeral ceremonies on the body. The curate refused, saying, "The soul of your brother is now burning in hell, as I told you before. It would be in vain for me to take any trouble about interring his body, for during the night the devils will come and carry it away, and in forty days you yourself will meet with the same fate." The Spaniard not giving implicit credit to this diabolical visit, watched during the night by the body of his brother with his pistols loaded. Between twelve and one o'clock a knock was heard at the door, and a voice exclaimed, "I command you to open, in the name of the living God;—open, if not, your instant ruin is at hand." The Spaniard refused to open, and shortly after, he saw enter by a window, three able-bodied devils, covered with skins of wild beasts, having the usual quantity of horns, claws, and spiked tails, who set about carrying off the coffin containing the body. Upon this the Spaniard fired, and shot one devil dead. The others took to flight; he fired after them, and wounded both, one of whom died in a few minutes, the other escaped. In the morning, when the people went to church, there was no curate to officiate, and it was shortly after discovered, on examining the two defunct devils, that one was the curate, the other the vicar; the wounded devil was the sacristan, who confessed the whole diabolical affair.

(*g*) GIVING SIGHT TO THE BLIND.—In the Life of Mary Queen of Scots, by Henry Glassford Bell, Esq., we find the following account of a pretended miracle upon a blind boy. The author was certainly not induced to give this account from any partiality to the Scottish Reformers, of whom he speaks in no friendly terms. The miracle is in good keeping with many related in the Roman Breviary, and is a fulfillment of the prophecy of Paul the Apostle concerning "lying wonders," 2 Thess. ii. 9.

"There was a chapel in the neighborhood of Musselburgh, dedicated to the Lady of Loretto, which, from the character of superior sanctity it had acquired, had long been the favorite resort of religious devotees. In this chapel a body of the Catholic priests undertook to put their religion to test by performing a miracle. They fixed upon a young man who was well known as a common beggar in the streets of Edinburgh, and engaged to restore to him, in the presence of the assembled people, the perfect use of his eyesight. A day was named on which they calculated they might depend on this wonderful interposition of divine power in their behalf. From motives of curiosity, a great crowd was attracted at the appointed time to the chapel. The blind man made his appearance on the scaffold erected for the occasion. The priests approached the altar, and after praying very devoutly, and performing other religious ceremonies, he who had previously been stone blind, opened his eyes and declared he saw all things plainly. Having humbly and gratefully thanked his benefactors, the priests, he was permitted to mingle among the astonished people and receive their charity. Unfortunately, however, for the success of this deception, a gentleman from Fife, of the name of Colville, determined to penetrate, if possible, a little further into the mystery. He prevailed upon the subject of the recent experiment to accompany him to his lodgings in Edinburgh. As soon as they were alone, he locked the chamber door, and either by bribes or threats contrived tc win from him the whole secret. It turned out that in his boyhood this tool in the hands of the designing had been employed as a herd by the nuns of the convent of Sciennes, then in the neighborhood of Edinburgh. It was remarked by the sisterhood that he had an extraordinary facility in 'flipping up the lid of his eyes, and casting up the white.' Some of the neighboring priests, hearing accidentally of this talent, imagined that it might be applied to good account. They accordingly took him from Sciennes to the monastery near Musselburgh, where they kept him till he had made himself an adept in this mode of counterfeiting blindness, and till his personal appearance was so much changed that the few who had been acquainted with him before, would not be able to recognize him. They then sent him to Edinburgh to beg publicly, and make himself familiarly known to the inhabitants as a common blind mendicant. So far every thing had gone smoothly, and the scene at the chapel of Loretto might have had effect on the minds of the vulgar, had Colville's activity not discovered the gross imposture. Colville, who belonged to the congregation, instantly took the most effectual means to make known the deceit. He insisted upon the blind man's appearing with him next day at the cross of Edinburgh, where the latter repeated all he had told Colville, and confessed the iniquity of his own conduct, as well as that of the priests. To shelter him from their revenge, Colville immediately afterward carried him off to Fife, and the story with all its details being speedily disseminated, exposed the Catholic clergy to more contempt than ever."

306. Transubstantiation.

(*a*) GETTING A WORLD OF MERIT.—An anecdote was related by the celebrated Mr. Maclaurin, professor of mathematics in the university of Edinburgh, which most impressively illustrates the implicit confidence of the Roman Catholics in the dogmas of their creed, however opposed to reason they may appear.

When Mr. Maclaurin was traveling in France, he accidentally fell into the company of a learned Jesuit, with whom he traveled several leagues. After some mathematical conversation, the Jesuit discovered and lamented his heretical principles, and kindly offered his assistance to bring him into the Roman Catholic faith. Mr. Maclaurin embraced his offer, and the conversation turned upon transubstantiation. After a lengthened discussion of some hours, the Jesuit embraced him, and said, "My dear Mr. Maclaurin, you are the best, the truest friend I ever met with. How happy am I in this blessed opportunity of your conversation! I shall never forget the obligation under which I am laid to you, above all men living!" Mr. Maclaurin was surprised, and began to hope that he had convinced the Jesuit of his errors, and requested him to tell him in what the obligation consisted. "Why, really," replied the Roman Catholic, "you have made this doctrine of transubstantiation so very absurd and ridiculous, that for the future I shall have a world of merit in believing it."

(*b*) GOD EATEN BY MICE.—A man who lives fifty miles below Quebec, (says the Canadian Missionary Record,) mentioned that he had a Testament, and that a neighbor had one too, about whom he related the following circumstance:

A protracted meeting having been held here, several priests came to see this man, who, hearing of their coming, took a *house fly*, and put it on a plate on the table, with a thread tied to it. When the priests entered, the man received them very politely, thanking them for their attention to his soul's interest. They had a long conversation, in the course of which, he referred to his want of faith in the power of the priest; but pointing to the fly, he said, "I have been told that you can work miracles; now, if you will cause that fly to drop down dead, while I am looking at it, I will then go to confess." The priests refused, saying that they would not work a miracle for the sake of one person. "But my soul is very precious," said the man, "and if you love me as you say, you should do all in your power to bring me back to the church." During the conversation, speaking of the Host, he asked the priest to take some of the consecrated wafer, and put it in a cupboard with a number of mice, and if at the end of two weeks, it remained uneaten, then he would believe that it was God; otherwise he would remain as he was, for he could not think that God would allow himself to be eaten by mice.

(*c*) BELIEVING IN AN IMPOSSIBILITY,—"Do you believe in transubstantiation?" said a Protestant to a Papist. "Yes, I do," was the reply.—"Why," said the other, "the thing is impossible." "And I," said the Papist, "believe it *because* it is impossible!"

(*d*) PRIESTS SUPERIOR TO ANGELS.—In the reign of the "bloody Mary," the popish bishop of London publicly preached the doctrine, that priests were superior to angels. "The dignity of priests," said that impious prelate, "by some means passeth the dignity of angels, because there is no power given to any of the angels to make the body of Christ, which the least priest may do on earth, and the highest angel in heaven cannot do: wherefore, priests are to be honored before all kings of the earth, princes, and nobles. For a priest is higher than a king, happier than an angel, and maker of his Creator"

(*e*) LADY JANE GREY'S SARCASM.—It is related of lady Jane Grey, that being, when very young, at Newhall, in Essex, the seat of Mary, afterwards queen, and walking near the chapel with lady Anne Wharton, she observed her companion, as they passed, bow to the elements on the altar. Affecting surprise at the motion of her friend, she asked, "Is the lady Mary in the chapel?" "No," replied her companion, "I bend to Him who made us all." "How is that?" retorted Jane, "can he be there who made us all, and yet the baker made him?" It is asserted that this sarcastic remark laid the foundation of Mary's hatred to this lovely woman.

307. Purgatory.

(*a*) HABEAS ANIMAM FOR PURGATORY.—The Rev. Blanco White relates, that, in Spain, besides masses, bulls, prayers, and penances, the pope has established eight or ten days in the year, on which every Spaniard, (for the grant is confined to Spain,) by kneeling at five different altars, and there praying for the extirpation of heresy, is entitled to send a species of *habeas animam* writ to any of his friends in purgatory; that is, to require their deliverance as a reward for what he has done.

(*b*) "I'LL TAKE BACK MY MONEY.—An Italian noble being at church one day, and finding a priest who begged for the souls in purgatory, gave him a piece of gold. "Ah! my lord," said the good father, "you have now delivered a soul." The count threw upon the plate another piece. "Here is another soul delivered," said the priest. "Are you positive of it?" replied the count. "Yes, my lord," replied the priest, "I am certain they are now in heaven." "Then," said the count, "I'll take back my money, for it signifies nothing to you now; seeing the souls are already got to heaven, there can be no danger of their returning to purgatory."

(*c*) HEAVY DEMAND ON PATIENCE.—Mr. Temple, a Missionary of Malta, relates of a native of that island, that, "not long after he came into our family he was visited by a disease which reduced him so low, that his physician, a Roman Catholic, told him it was proper to confess himself, receive the host, and thus prepare himself for death. He was at that time sick in his own family, for he has a wife and children. According to the advice of the doctor, he sent for a priest, and confessed himself, a thing which he had not done for a long time before.

"A few evenings ago when he came to prayers, I asked him what the priest said to him. As he now detests the whole system, he seemed quite willing to tell me all about it. He said he confessed to the priest as many of his sins as he could recollect, and then asked his confessor what he must do as he felt that he must soon die.

"The priest told him that, should he be spared, he must, as soon as his health would permit, kiss the ground fifteen times a day, for eight days together, must hear one mass a day during the same period, and recite a certain part of the Rosary a great many times for eight days; this was the penance enjoined by the confessor. 'But,' said the poor man, 'what shall I do if I die and cannot perform this penance?' 'Oh,' replied the confessor, 'have patience and go to purgatory.'

"I have never detected this man in a falsehood, and I have no doubt he told me the truth concerning this affair."

(*d*) DISTRICTS IN PURGATORY.—A woman and two children, says Dr. Brownlee, called on a lady in Broadway, New-York, to ask alms. The woman was dressed in black, and said that she was left a widow, with the children she had accompanying her, in distressed circumstances, and she urged her request for alms with considerable earnestness. The lady informed her that she could give her no money, but offered her food and articles of clothing if she might need them. But these would not do; the widow wanted money, and she insisted so earnestly on the gift of money, that the lady asked her into the house, and entered into conversation with her, when she drew from the widow the following story:

"My husband," said she, "died a few weeks ago, and since that I've had no peace. Priest —— called on me soon after, and reproved me for not paying over to him the sum of money necessary for his release from that place of torment. I asked him how much that would be. 'Oh,' said he, 'we have had different prices for different souls. For saying mass for some we have one hundred dollars, for others fifty, and for others less. The least sum I can accept for praying the soul of your departed husband out of that place of torment is *twenty-four dollars.*' And now he gives me no peace because you know I have not the money, and what can I do for the soul of my poor husband?"

The lady took a Bible, and handing it to the afflicted widow, said to her, "Here, take this Bible, and go to the priest you speak of, and request him to fold down a leaf on that place which teaches the doctrine of purgatory, and then you bring the Bible back to me, and I will give you the whole amount you want to pay for the praying your husband out of that place of torment."

The poor Romanist was delighted with this proposal. She took the Bible and made off in great haste to the priest; but she was not gone a great while; she soon returned more sorrowful than before. She told the lady, in great distress, that she carried the Bible to the priest, and informed him how he could put her in the way of obtaining the whole amount necessary to procure the release of her husband's soul from the torments of purgatory. But, alas! instead of turning down a leaf in her Bible upon the place where it teaches the doctrine of purgatory, he flew into a violent rage, and ordered her from his presence, saying, "See that the twenty-four dollars are forthcoming, or I'll put you under penance for having in your presence that heretical book, and your husband shall never be released from purgatory till the money is paid down; and, mind you! no other priest but myself can pray him out, for he is *in my district!*"

(*e*) INSCRIPTION AT MENTZ.—In the year 1738, Mr. John Wesley traveled in Germany, and spent a night or two at Mentz. While there, he went into the great church, and spent an hour, and copied the following from a paper on the door.

"*A full release for the poor souls in purgatory.*

"His Papal Holiness, Clement XII hath this year, 1738, on the 7th of August, most graciously privileged the Cathedral Church of St. Christopher, in Mentz, so that every priest, as well secular as regular, who will read mass at an altar for the soul of a Christian departed on any holiday, or any day within the octave thereof, or on two extraordinary days, to be appointed by the ordinary, of any week in the year, may each time deliver a soul out of the fire of purgatory."

(*f*) THE ARMENIAN'S REASONING.—Rev. Mr. Dwight of Constantinople says, "The subject of purgatory was introduced in a company of eight or ten Armenians, by one of their number who had frequent intercourse with papists. He remarked he had one difficulty in regard to it which none of them could solve. "According to the papal notions," said he, "all who die in the church have certain venial sins upon them, for which they must suffer in purgatory, according to the number and nature of those sins; some for a year, some for a hundred years, and some for ten thousand, &c. And this shall be the case up to the very time when the judgment day shall come. At that day what will be done with those who have not served out their time in purgatory? For example, what will be done with those who died the week or day previous to the judgment? Some of them may require the action of the purgatorial fires for a week, and some for a year, and some for a hundred years, and some for a thousand, or ten thousand, before they can atone for their sins and be sufficiently purified for heaven. Let the believers in purgatory decide what is to be done with these cases at the judgment, when all that are in their graves shall rise, and the righteous are to be forever separated from the wicked; the latter to go away into everlasting punishment, and the former into life eternal."

308. Relics.

(*a*) RELICS AT HALLE.—Halle, in Saxony, so remarkable for the hospital erected by the celebrated Francke, seems to have been, in the dark ages of Popery, like Athens of old, a "city full of idols," Acts xvii. 16, (marginal reading.) The churches contained forty-two entire bodies of Romish saints, and more than 8,000 smaller relics! A work, published by the authority of the archbishop, contains engravings of more than 200 vases in which these relics were kept. Some of them are particularly specified, as earth from a field at Damascus, where Adam was formed from the dust of the ground! Several bones and part of the standard of St. George; pieces of Noah's ark; portions of the bodies of several patriarchs and prophets; the rods of Moses and Aaron; clothing which had belonged to the Virgin; and a piece of the skin of Bartholomew! Among the entire bodies was one of the infants slain by Herod; also seventeen bodies of the companions of St. Ursula, who were, by mistake, said to have been 11,000 in number, instead of one named Undecimilla; also the glass or mirror used by these virgin martyrs, with much more of the like trumpery. On the Sunday next after the eighth of September, in every year, these relics were carried in solemn procession, and exhibited to the people. To all such as beheld them with devotion upon this occasion, offering prayers, and giving money to the collegiate church, indulgences, or pardon of sins, were promised, for 29,245,120 years, and 220 days. We are not told by what process of calculation this extraordinary number was ascertained; but the authorized writer might well boast that a great treasure was to be obtained at a small price, had not the treasure, even if obtained, been utterly worthless. There was, however, a qualifying clause; the indulgences were only to be obtained by those who were "suited to deserve them;" an expression which, as Seckendorf observes, would be as unintelligible to the people, as the millions and hundreds of thousands spoken of in the calculation. Into what fearful delusions do mankind fall, when they forsake the simple truths of the Bible!

(*b*) SINGULAR RELICS.—We are sometimes told of the harmless character of Popery, and are assured that the Roman Catholic system is, in reality, little different from that of Protestantism. Let our readers, however, be assured of the following facts:

When the monasteries were suppressed at the time of the reformation, there were found in one of them as many relics as could be named in several sheets of paper. Among others, there was an angel with one wing that brought over the spear's head which pierced the Redeemer's side. There were also some of the coals that roasted St. Lawrence, the parings of St. Edmund's toes, St. Thomas à Becket's penknife and boots, with as many pieces of the Savior's cross as would make a large whole one, a piece of St. Andrew's finger, set in an ounce of silver, with many others of equal veracity. Some of the images were broken; among which was one, that, by means of springs, was made to move the head, hands, and feet: this had proved very profitable. Some of the blood of a duck was found in a phial, which was thick on one side, and thin on the other: the people were taught to believe this was the blood of Christ; and on their paying a considerable sum, the thin side of the phial was turned towards them, and hey were permitted to see the blood.

(*c*) RELICS AT AIX LA CHAPELLE.—Dr. Raffles, in his tour through Europe in 1817, visited the church of the Minorites, in Aix La Chapelle. After describing sundry antiquities, among which were "the remains of one of the children whom Herod killed in the hope of destroying Christ," he proceeds:

"All this was interesting, but the cream of the antiquities yet remained. We were conducted to the vestry, or robing place of the priest, where a young man whose province it is to expose these wonders to the gaze of the credulous, threw open the curiously painted doors of an immense recess, where in an instant we were dazzled with a profusion of gold and precious stones, wrought into various forms, to contain or emblazon the precious and sacred relics.

* * * * We were shown, 1. The girdle of Jesus Christ, brought from Jerusalem, by Charlemagne, and with that monarch's seal annexed to it. 2. Girdle of the Virgin Mary, derived from the same quarter. 3. A bone of the Virgin Mary's father. 4. A bit of the cord with which Jesus was bound when he was scourged. 5. A prickle from the crown of thorns. 6. A bit of the sponge with which they supplied the vinegar. 7. A bit of one of the nails by which he was fastened to the cross. 8. And lastly, some *sweat* which fell from him in the garden of Gethsemane. To this may be added a link of the chain with which Peter was chained at Rome! a bit of the bone of Simeon's arm, with which he embraced the infant Jesus!! a rib of St. Stephen!!! and a tooth of St. Thomas!!!!"

I thought of the sailor, who, after his messmates had told some wonderful stories of what had been found in the bellies of whales and sharks, and such monsters, determining to outstrip them all, said he had once been present at the catching of a fish, out of whose belly, when opened, there came a ship, with all its masts and rigging, and the whole of the crew.

(*d*) A PHIAL OF DARKNESS.—A traveler on the continent visiting a celebrated cathedral, was shown by the Sacristan among other marvels, a dirty opaque phial. After eyeing it some time, the traveler said, "Do you call this a relic?" "Sir," said the Sacristan indignantly, "it contains some of the darkness that was spread over the land of Egypt."

309. Moral Tendency of Papacy.

(*a*) CONSOLING TO PIRATES.—Several Spanish pirates were once taken and brought into Boston, tried and sentenced to death. They were, it seems, Catholics; and on the day of their execution they were attended by a Spanish priest. As they arrived at the foot of the gallows, the priest turned to the captain, and with much gravity exclaimed:

"SPANIARDS, ASCEND TO HEAVEN."

(*b*) NUNNERY AT BARDSTOWN.—The following appeared in 183—, in various religious journals of this country. No place in Kentucky is more famous among papists, and no place more detestable in part to Protestants than Bardstown in Kentucky. It is the hotbed of all popish abominations.

Not long since, a young lady of Kentucky, whose parents reside in the vicinity of Bardstown, was induced to enter upon the noviciate for a conventual life: and finally she became a nun. The "Lady Superior" immediately began to explain the secrets of the priestcraft—and among other delectable things inculcated for the young lady's belief, the vast superiority of a nun's enjoyments over those of common women, for that they were often visited by angels in white robes, with whom they had holy intercourse; and persuaded the thoughtless and credulous girl to believe it. When the nun was fully prepared, the Abbess informed her victim, that she had a revelation from heaven, and that the nun might speedily expect a visit from one of the angels, cautioned her not to be alarmed, and above all to submit herself to the "White robed Angel's" commands. Almost immediately after, at night, while in her bed, she saw by the moonlight, a figure dressed in white enter her dormitory. She instantly sat up, and began to cross herself, and to mutter her Ave Marys. The "White robed Angel," proceeded towards her, and the nun instantly perceived that instead of a white robed visitant from heaven her associate was real flesh and blood,—even a priest from the neighboring Jesuit seminary. By some means, she suddenly extricated herself from his grasp; and before he could execute his nefarious design, she escaped from the nunnery, whether by the window or by the door I do not remember; and with the fleetness of a deer, in her night dress, she fled to her father's house; and for ever abandoned all intercourse with those who, to use her own expression, represent themselves as "White robed Angels from heaven."

(c) THE HARLOT'S HOME.—A Roman Catholic young woman, says a Montreal paper, received serious religious impressions, and determined, after a diligent examination of the Scriptures, to renounce the Romish Church.

The priest of her parents deprived them of the partial Sacrament of the Lord's Supper, and declared that he would continue to do so, until they had prevailed upon their daughter to return to their church—he also expressed a desire to receive a call from the young woman. She called accordingly upon him, and informed him that her parents were not concerned in her change of views, but had done all in their power to bring her back to Popery.

In the conversation which followed, the priest exerted himself to persuade her that she was in error, but in vain. At length, he inquired if she was willing to enter into the church, and before the altar, ask God to bless her in her present course. She replied that she was, and they proceeded together to the church, where she poured out her heart in unaffected and earnest prayer that God would smile upon her endeavors to know and do his will, and that he would bring her parents to see the errors into which they had fallen.

The priest, amazed at her resolution and steadfastness, seemed to experience a sudden change, and told her to go forward—if she thought she was right, to continue as she had begun. This she has done, and is now on the point of connecting herself with a Protestant church, as a believer in Christ.

In the early stages of her seriousness, a young man, a Romanist, was authorized by her parents, to decoy her back into the bosom of Popery, by the offer of marriage, but the attempt was unsuccessful. Afterwards, when she became more confirmed in her views, this young man came to her employer, with a burdened conscience, which he hoped to relieve in a measure by confession, and declared that he had been authorized by her parents—a priest consenting—to offer his hand to the young woman, and if he could not succeed in making her a Roman Catholic by any other means, to *seduce her*.

We could not believe this except on the most credible testimony. As it is, we cannot doubt. A harlot, we might infer, is more at home in the Roman Catholic than in the Protestant Church, in the view of Romanists themselves; but it is most distressing to find that such criminal and detestable acts are employed, and that the interests of immortal souls are sacrificed that the ranks of Popery may be kept unbroken.

Who is not aroused from his sleep?

What Protestant can stand by inactive, and witness the perpetration of such enormities in the sacred name of religion? We have another fact of much the same description, but we reserve it for a future occasion.

(*d*) WHERE NUNS PUT THEIR CHILDREN.—A captain of a vessel, says the Philadelphian for 184—, stated some time since, that when in port in a Catholic country, an old nunnery was torn down, for the purpose of rebuilding, and although every exertion was made by the holy *father* to suppress the curiosity of the people, a number flocked round the ruins, and some few examined them, when it was discovered that a large vault was under the building, wherein was a large number of INFANTS' BONES. When this discovery was made known, the populace insisted that they should be brought out; the bones were then laid out on a plain near the ruins, and examined by several physicians, who at once pronounced them to be *human bones*. Our informant, whose name we possess, states that he was among the number who witnessed the dreadful sight.

(*e*) A NUNNERY ABANDONED.—"In the rear of Alleghany town," says the Richmond Telegraph for 184–, "and in full view of Pittsburg, is a Catholic Nunnery, one of those schools of superstition, tyranny, and pollution, which are rising up, as by enchantment, in every part of the West. An event has recently occurred which has induced the whole sisterhood, with the priest, to abandon the buildings. A gentleman, residing at the East, had a daughter in the nunnery to be educated, with the expectation that she was to visit him occasionally. Much time elapsed, no visit was made, and not being able to get any satisfactory information respecting his daughter, he came to the nunnery to see her. The lady superior told him she was not at home; he insisted on knowing where she was, and was finally told that she was sick in bed, and could not be seen; he demanded a sight of her in a spirit which the lady superior thought it imprudent to attempt to resist; and being shown to her room, behold, there was his once healthy and promising daughter, *with an infant*. His indignation was so aroused, that he uttered some threats in regard to the safety of the establishment; and the next morning not an individual was found there."

(*f*) SINGULAR METHOD OF PROSELYTING.—The following anecdote is current in Germany, and illustrates the disguises often assumed by Jesuits to forward Popery. When the Duke and Duchess of Anhalt Cothen embraced the Romish faith, the court followed their example, with the exception of one maid of honor, who adhered to her Protestant principles. Shortly after, a young gentleman arrived from Vienna, who won the affections of the lady, but informed her, that being a Roman Catholic, he could not ally himself to a heretic. She consented, after a struggle, to forsake Protestantism, but fainted when her recantation was made. The lover then informed her, that he had paid his addresses to her for the good of her soul, marriage being out of the question, as he was a priest and a Jesuit—a fact of which she was convinced, when taking off a wig which he wore, he showed her the tonsure or shaven crown, which is a distinguishing mark of popish priests.

310. Miscellaneous.

(*a*) DYING WORDS OF POPE PIUS V.—It is said of Pius Quintus, that when dying he cried out in despair: "When I was in low condition, I had some hopes of salvation; but when I was advanced to be a cardinal, I greatly doubted it; but since I came to the popedom, I have no hope at all."

(*b*) PAPAL INSPIRATION.—A Roman Catholic curé, in France, once ventured to ask a Protestant, "Upon what do you build your belief, since you have no authority for your faith?" The reply was, "Upon the Bible; if the apostles had left behind them any infallible successors, it would have been unnecessary to bequeath to us so many instructions in writing."

"The apostles! and why are you to place greater reliance on the apostles than on their successors?"

"Because the apostles were inspired by the Holy Ghost."

"Well! and we too are inspired."

"Are you inspired?"

"Yes! I repeat—We too are inspired!"

"Then why do you require to be further instructed in the college of the Jesuits?"

The priest was confounded.

(*c*) SURPRISE AT THE TRUE VERSION.—The Rev. Mr. Temple, one of the American missionaries at Malta, has related the following fact:—My teacher, a native of Italy, came into my room one morning, and took up a tract, then lying on my table, and immediately cast his eyes upon the ten commandments, which I had inserted at the end. As soon as he had read the second commandment, he expressed much astonishment, and asked whether this was part of the decalogue. I immediately showed him this commandment in Archbishop Martini's "Italian Translation of the Latin Vulgate." He could not suppress his feeling of surprise on reading this in the Italian Bible, and in a version, too, authorized by the Pope. "I have lived," said he, "fifty years; have been publicly educated in Italy; have had the command of a regiment of men, and fought in many campaigns; but, till this hour, I never knew that such a commandment as this was written in the pages of the Bible."

(*d*) THE POPE ANGRY.—Pope Julius, sitting at dinner one day, and pointing to a peacock which he had not touched, "Keep," said he, "this cold peacock for me against supper, and let me sup in the garden; for I shall have guests." When supper came, the peacock was not brought to the table, on which the Pope, after his wonted manner, fell into an extreme rage. One of his cardinals, sitting by, desired him not to be so moved with a matter of such small weight. "What!" said the Pope, "if God was so angry for an apple, that he cast our first parents out of Paradise for the same, why may not I, being his Vicar, be angry for a peacock, since a peacock is a greater matter than an apple?"

(*e*) ST. JANARIUS AND THE HORSES.—We were present to-day, say the author of "Rome in the Nineteenth Century," written in 1818, at one of the most ridiculous scenes I ever witnessed, even in this country. It was St. Anthony's blessing of the horses; which began on that saint's day, and, I understand, lasts for a week. We drove to the church of the saint, near Santa Maria Maggiore, and could scarcely make our way through the streets, from the multitude of horses, mules, asses, cows, sheep, goats, and dogs, which were journeying along to the place of benediction; their tails, heads, and necks, decorated with bits of colored ribbon and other finery, on this—their unconscious gala day. The saint's benediction, though nominally confined to horses, is equally efficacious, and equally bestowed upon all quadrupeds; and I believe there is scarcely a brute in Rome, or in the neighborhood, that has not participated in it. An immense crowd were assembled in the wide open space in front of the church: and from the number of beasts and men, it looked exactly like a cattle fair. At the door stood the blessing priest, dressed in his robes, and wielding a brush in his hand, which he continually dipped into a huge bucket of holy water that stood near him, and spirted at the animals as they came up, in unremitting succession, taking off his little skull-cap, and muttering every time in Latin, "By the intercession of blessed Anthony the abbot, these animals are freed from evil, in the name of the Father, Son, and Holy Spirit, Amen." The poor priest had such hard work in blessing, that he was quite exhausted and panting, and his round face looked fiery red with his exertions. The rider, or driver of the creature, always gave some piece of money, larger or smaller, in proportion to his means or generosity; and received an engraving of the saint, and a little metallic cross: however, all animals might be blessed gratis. Several well-dressed people, in very handsome equipages, attended with out-riders, in splendid liveries, drove up while we were there; and sat uncovered till the benediction was given. Then, having paid what they thought fit, they drove off, and made way for others. One adventure happened, which afforded some amusement. A countryman having got a blessing on his beast, and therefore putting his whole trust in its power, set off from the church-door at full gallop; and had scarcely gone a hundred yards, before the ungainly animal tumbled down with him, and he rolled over his head into the dirt. He soon got up, however, and shook himself, and so did the horse, without either seeming to be much the worse. The priest seemed not a whit out of countenance at this catastrophe; and some of the standers-by exclaimed, with entire steadfastness of faith, that, "but for the blessing, they might both have broken their necks!"

311. PATIENCE.

(*a*) TORTURED NOBLEMAN.—When the Mexican emperor, Gatimozin, was put upon the rack by the soldiers of Cortes, one of his nobles, who lay in tortures at the same time, complained bitterly to his sovereign of the pains he endured. "Do you think," said Gatimozin, "that I lie upon roses?" The nobleman ceased moaning, and expired in silence. "When a Christian," adds the pious Bishop Horne, "thinks his sufferings for sin, in sickness, or pain, &c., intolerable, let him remember those of *his* Lord, endured patiently on that bed of sorrow, the *cross*, and he will think so no longer."

(*b*) TRIBULATION WORKETH PATIENCE.—There was a little boy who was so crippled that he could not open his Bible, which he had always before him. A gentleman asked him why he was so fond of reading it. "I like to read the Bible," said he, "because it tells me of Jesus Christ." "Do you think you have believed on Jesus Christ?" "Yes, I do." "What makes you think so?" "Because he enables me to suffer my afflictions patiently."

(*c*) PATIENT MINISTER.—Mr. Rivet, a learned and pious divine, was an instance of extraordinary patience under excruciating pains, which he bore for many days. "You see," says he, "through the grace of God, I am not tired: I wait, I believe, I persevere. Patience is much better than knowledge. I am no more vexed with earthly cares: I have now no desire but after heavenly things. I have learnt more divinity in these ten days, than in fifty years before. This body is feeble, but the spirit is strong and enriched. Far be it from me that I should murmur. How small are these pains in comparison of that grace, through which I bear, with a quiet mind, whatsoever it pleaseth God to lay upon me! The body, indeed, suffers, but the soul is comforted and filled abundantly."

(*d*) PATIENCE OF SARAH PARBECK.—One of the most remarkable instances of patience on record is to be found in the case of Miss Sarah Parbeck, of Salem, Mass. A lady visiting her in 1845, thus describes her interview:

"The door was opened by a very old lady, wrinkled and bowed down with age, who invited us to enter. The room was so dark, that before my eyes were accommodated to the change, I could only see a figure dressed in white, sitting upon the bed and rocking to and fro. This motion was attended by a sound like the click of wooden machinery, which arose, as I afterwards discovered, from the bones as they worked in their loosened sockets. As we approached, she extended her hand to my companion, and said in a painful but affectionate voice, 'Eliza, I am very glad to see thee;' and then asked my name and place of residence. She had just given me her hand, when a spasm seized her, and it was twitched suddenly from my grasp. It flew some four or five times with the greatest violence against her face, and then, with a sound which I can only compare to that made by a child who has been sobbing a long time, in catching its breath, she threw up both her arms, and with a deep guttural groan was flung back upon her pillow, with a force inconceivable to one who has not witnessed it. The instant she touched the bed, she uttered that piercing shriek again, and sprung back to her former position, rocking to and fro, with those quick, heart-rending groans which I had heard while standing at the door. It was several minutes before she could speak, and then there was none to answer her. Both my companion and myself were choked with tears. Her poor mother went to the other side of the bed, and smoothed the coverlid, and rearranged the pillows, looking sadly upon her poor child, writhing in torture which she could not alleviate. I became faint, and trembled with a sudden weakness; a cold perspiration stood upon my face. The objects in the room began to swim about me, and I was obliged to take hold of the bedside for support. I have been in our largest hospitals, and have spent hours in going from room to room with the attending physician. I have witnessed there almost every form of human suffering, but I had never beheld any thing to be compared to that now before me. She afterwards told me, as if in apology for her screams, that when she was hurled back upon her pillow both shoulders were dislocated, and as they sprung back into their sockets, the pain was far beyond endurance, and extorted from her these shrieks.

"Her sentences were broken, uttered with much difficulty, and frequently interrupted by the terrible spasm I have described above. Yet this was her 'quiet' state; this the time when she suffered *least*. Day after day, night after night, *fourteen weary years* have dragged themselves along, whilst her poor body has been thus racked. No relief; no hope of relief, except that which death shall give. When I asked her if her affliction did not at times seem greater than she could bear, 'O! never,' she replied. 'I cannot thank God enough for having laid his heavy hand upon me. I was a thoughtless sinner, and had he not in his mercy afflicted me, I should probably have lost my immortal soul. I see only his kindness and love. The sweet communion I have with my Savior more than compensates me for all I suffer. I am permitted to feel, in a measure, in my poor body, what he suffered to save me, and my soul can never grow weary in his praise.' This last sentence, I must say, gave me an argument which put doubts of the verity and power of religion to flight more effectually than all the evidences which the wisdom of man has arrayed against the skeptic; and I could not but exclaim, 'If this be delusion, let me be deluded!'

"She spoke in the most tender terms of her Savior's love. Her conversation was in heaven, from whence also she looked for her Savior, knowing that he should change her body of humiliation, and fashion it like unto his glorious body. I shall never forget the tones and language in which she entreated my sobbing companion to give that Savior her heart. As she recovered from a spasm, I said to her, 'Do you not often desire to depart, and be with the Savior you love so fervently?' She had hardly recovered her exhausted breath, but replied with great decision, 'By the grace of God *I have never had that wish*. Though death will be a welcome gift when my Father sees fit to bestow it upon me, yet, thanks to his supporting grace, I can wait his time without impatience. He sees that there is much dross to refine away, and why should I wish against his will?'

"I remained by her side for more than an hour; such, however, were the attractions of her discourse, that I was unconscious of the time. I know not when I have been so drawn towards a fellow Christian, and never had I been led to such delightful contemplations of our Savior's character; his faithfulness and love. I remarked to her, as I turned to go away, 'God has made you a powerful preacher, here upon your bed of pain.' 'O,' she replied, 'if he will make me the instrument of saving but a single soul, I am willing to live and suffer here until my hair is gray with age.' I noticed some bottles standing upon a small table, and asked her if she found any relief from opiates. 'Through God's kindness,' she answered, 'I probably owe the preservation of my life thus far to an extract made from black drop.' 'Does it enable you to sleep?' 'O no,' she replied, 'I have not known sleep for a very long time.' 'What!' I cried, 'do you never rest?' A severe spasm here seized her, and it was some time before she could answer me; she had been attacked in this way some twelve or fifteen times whilst conversing with us, and frequently in the midst of a reply. When she recovered, she said the physicians thought she obtained rest in her 'long spasm,' which lasted for more than an hour. 'During that time,' she continued. 'I am dead to every thing but a sense of the most extreme anguish. I see and hear nothing; I only feel as though I was being crushed in pieces by some immense weight.' This was her rest! The rack! Yet, through all this suffering, the smiles of God penetrate to her heart. She sees him just, and acknowledges his love."

(e) SUFFERING PATIENTLY FOR CHRIST.—Negrino and Paschali exercised their ministry in Calabria, in comforting the persecuted Waldensians among the woods and mountains. But when the sufferers were closely hunted, the preachers were not likely to escape. At the instance of the inquisitor, they were both apprehended. Negrino was starved to death in prison at Casueza. At this place Paschali was detained in confinement eight months, whence he was sent prisoner to Naples, with a view of being conducted to Rome. The patience with which he endured the cross, appears from the sensible and ardent letters which he addressed to the persecuted church of Calabria, to his afflicted spouse Camilla, and to the church of Geneva. In one of these he thus describes his journey from Cosenza to Naples:

"Two of our companions had been prevailed on to recant; but they were no better treated on that account, and we know not what they will suffer at Rome, whither they are to be conveyed, as well as Marquet and myself. The Spaniard, our conductor, wished us to give him money to be relieved from the chain by which we were bound to one another; yet, in addition to this, he put on me a pair of handcuffs, so strait that they entered into the flesh, and deprived me of all sleep; and I found that, if at all, he would not remove them until he had drawn from me all the money I had, amounting only to two ducats, which I needed for my support. At night, the beasts were better treated than we, for their litter was spread for them, while we were obliged to lie on the hard ground, without any covering; and in this condition we remained for nine nights. On our arrival at Naples we were thrust into a cell, noisome in the highest degree, from the damp, and the putrid breath of the prisoners."

He was next sent in bonds to Rome, at which place his brother arrived from Coni, with letters of recommendation, to ask his liberty. With difficulty this brother obtained an interview with him, in the presence of a judge of the Inquisition. He gives the following description of this first interview:

"It was hideous to see him, with his bare head, and his hands and arms lacerated with the small cords with which he was bound, like one to be led to the gibbet. On advancing to embrace him, I sunk to the ground. 'My brother,' said he, 'if you are a Christian, why do you distress yourself thus? Do you know that a leaf cannot fall to the ground without the will of God? Comfort yourself in Christ Jesus, for the present troubles are not to be compared with the glory to come.'"

At last, on the 8th of September, 1560, he was led to the conventual church of Minerva, to hear his process publicly read; and the next day, the 9th of September, he appeared, with the greatest fortitude, in the court adjoining the castle of St. Angelo, where he was burnt in the presence of the pope and a party of cardinals.

(f) ERETRIUS AND HIS FATHER.—A youth named Eretrius was for a considerable time a follower of Zeno. On his return home, his father asked him what he had learned? The boy replied, that would hereafter appear. On this, the father being enraged, beat his son; who bearing it patiently, and without complaining, said, "This have learned—to endure a parent's anger."

312. PATRIOTISM.

(*a*) THE ROMAN AMBASSADORS.—Ptolemy Philadelphus, king of Egypt, having sent to desire the friendship of the Roman people, an embassy was dispatched from Rome the following year, in return for the civilities of Ptolemy. The ambassadors were Q. Fabius Garges, Cn. Fabius Pictor, with Numerius his brother, and Q. Ogalnius. The disinterested air with which they appeared sufficiently indicated the greatness of their souls. Ptolemy gave them a splendid entertainment, and took that opportunity to present to each of them a crown of gold, which they received because they were unwilling to disoblige him by declining the honor he intended them; but they went the next morning and placed them on the heads of the king's statues erected in the public places of the city. The king likewise having tendered them very considerable presents at their audience of leave, they received them as they had the crowns; but, on their arrival at Rome, before giving the Senate an account of their embassy, they deposited all those presents in the public treasury, and made it evident, by so noble a conduct, that in serving the republic they had proposed no other advantage to themselves than the honor of having well done their duty. The republic, however, would not suffer itself to be exceeded in generosity of sentiments. The Senate and people came to a resolution, that the ambassadors, in consideration of the services they had rendered the state, should receive a sum of money equivalent to that they had deposited in the public treasury. This indeed was an amiable contest; and one is at a loss to know to which of the antagonists to ascribe the victory. Where shall we now find men who devote themselves in a similar manner to the public good, without any interested expectations of selfish advantage?

(*b*) THE CORSICAN AND HIS UNCLE.—A striking display of the character of the legislator, and of the subject, was related by Paoli to Mr. Boswell, when he visited Corsica. "A criminal," said he, "was condemned to die. His nephew came to me with a lady of distinction, that she might solicit his pardon. The nephew's anxiety made him think that the lady did not speak with sufficient force and earnestness. He therefore advanced, and addressed himself to me, 'Sir, is it proper for me to speak?' as if he felt that it was unlawful to make such an application. I bade him go on. 'Sir,' said he, with the deepest concern, 'may I beg the life of my uncle? If it is granted, his relations will make a gift to the state of a thousand zechins. We will furnish fifty soldiers in pay during the siege of Furiana. We will agree that my uncle shall be banished, and will engage that he shall never return to the island.' I knew the nephew to be a man of worth, and I answered him, 'You are acquainted with the circumstances of this case: such is my confidence in you, that if you will say, that giving your uncle a pardon would be just, useful, or honorable for Corsica, I promise you it shall be granted.' He turned about, burst into tears, and left me, saying in his native language, 'I would not have the honor of our country sold for a thousand zechins.' His uncle suffered."

(*c*) PATRIOTIC MOTHER.—History furnishes many examples of mothers, led away by the seductive attractions of honor, riches, and grandeur, to sacrifice the true happiness of their children, in the hope of securing the future fortune and rank of their posterity. Russia, however, furnishes one instance of a mother who opposed the elevation of her child to the highest dignity, with the utmost anxiety. During the interregnum that succeeded the unfortunate reign of Chowski, in 1610, the Russian nobles agreed to give the crown to a near relation, on the maternal side, of the Czar Fedor Iwanovitch. They accordingly invited young Michael Romanof and his mother to Moscow, but they both refused to attend;

the mother even went further; she wrote to her brother Cheremetef, to beg of him to oppose the elevation of his nephew to a throne, since his extreme youth rendered him incapable of undertaking so important a charge. The election, however, proceeded, and Michael Romanof was chosen Emperor. When the deputies repaired to Kostroma, to announce to the new sovereign the choice they had made of him, his mother begged a private interview with the plenipotentiaries, before she introduced them to her son. They consented, and met her in the church, where, with tears, she renewed her entreaties, and begged of them to choose some person more able to govern the people than her son. She was informed that, having decided, the nobles would not revoke their choice. "Well, then," said she, "I must content myself with soliciting you to take my child under your guardianship; he has not been educated in the difficult art of governing mankind; but you have elected him—you insist on him for your monarch, and if he does not fulfil your expectations, you alone will be answerable to God for the events of which your choice may be the cause; but as for me, I have done my duty to my God, my country, and my child."

(*d*) WASHINGTON AND HIS FRIENDS.—An anecdote is told of the great Washington, which exhibits, in a fine light, the distinction between public duty, and private friendship. During his administration as President of the United States, a gentleman, the friend and the companion of the general, throughout the whole course of the revolutionary war, applied for a lucrative and very responsible office. The gentleman was at all times welcome to Washington's table; he had been, to a certain degree, necessary to the domestic repose of a man, who had for seven years fought the battles of his country, and who had now undertaken the task of wielding her political energies. At all times, and in all places, Washington regarded his revolutionary associate with an eye of evident partiality and kindness. He was a jovial, pleasant, and unobtrusive companion. In applying for this office, it was accordingly in the full confidence of success; and his friends already cheered him on the prospect of his arrival at competency and ease. The opponent of this gentleman, was known to be decidedly hostile to the politics of Washington; he had even made himself conspicuous among the ranks of opposition. He had, however, the temerity to stand as candidate for the office to which the friend and the favorite of Washington aspired. He had nothing to urge in favor of his pretensions, but strong integrity, promptitude, and fidelity in business, and every quality which, if called into exercise, would render service to the state. Every one considered the application of this man hopeless; no glittering testimonial of merit had he to present to the eye of Washington; he was known to be his political enemy; he was opposed by a favorite of the general's; and yet, with such fearful odds, he dared to stand candidate. What was the result? The enemy of Washington was appointed to the office, and his table companion was left destitute and dejected. A mutual friend, who interested himself in the affair, ventured to remonstrate with the president on the injustice of his appointment. "My friend," said he, "I receive with a cordial welcome; he is welcome to my house, and welcome to my heart; but, with all his good qualities, he is not a man of business. His opponent is, with all his political hostility to me, a man of business; my private feelings have nothing to do in this case. I am not George Washington, but President of the United States; as George Washington, I would do this man any kindness in my power; but as President of the United States, I can do nothing."

313. PEACE-MAKERS.

(*a*) TRUE PEACE-MAKER.—When Mr. Welch accepted of the call to Ayr, he found the wickedness of the people, and their hatred to religion so great, that no one would let him a house, till Mr. John Stewart, an eminent Christian, and some time provost of Ayr, accommodated him with an apartment in his house, and became his lasting friend. Mr. Welch first addressed himself to the arduous task of healing their divisions, uniting their factious parties, and putting an end to their daily battles, which were so desperate, that no one could walk in the street even in the day-time, without the most imminent danger of being wounded. His method was this: after he had put a helmet on his head, he would go between the parties of fighting men, already covered with blood; but he never took a sword, which convinced them that he came not to fight, but to make peace. When he had brought them, by little and little, to hear him speak, and to listen to his arguments against such inhuman proceedings, he would order a table to be spread in the street, and, beginning with prayer, persuade them to profess themselves friends, and to sit down, and to eat and drink together; which, when done, he would finish this labor of love with singing a psalm. Thus, by degrees, laboring among them in word and doctrine, for he preached every day, and setting them a good example, he brought them to be a peaceable and happy people; and he grew, at length, in such esteem among them, that thev made him their counsellor, to settle all their differences and misunderstandings, and would take no step of importance in civil affairs without his advice.

(*b*) ENVIABLE REPUTATION.—John Dickinson, Esq., of Birmingham, was often called by way of distinction, "The Peace-maker;" and such was his anxiety to keep the bonds of peace from being broken—such was his solicitude to heal the breach when made, that he would stoop to any act but that of meanness—make any sacrifice but that of principle—and endure any mode of treatment, not excepting even insult and reproach. From the high estimate in which his character was held, he was often called upon to act as umpire in cases of arbitration, and it was but rarely, if ever, that the equity of his decisions was impeached. On one occasion, two men were disputing in a public-house about the result of an arbitration, when a third said, "Had John Dickinson any thing to do with it?" "Yes," was the reply. "Then all was right, I am sure;" and in this opinion the whole party concurred, and the disputation ceased.

(*c*) PACIFIC MINISTER.—George Wishart, one of the first Scottish martyrs at the time of the reformation, being desired to preach on the Lord's day, in the church of Mauchline, went thither with that design; but the sheriff of Ayr had, in the night time, put a garrison of soldiers into the church to keep him out. Hugh Campbell, of Kinzeancleugh, with others in the parish, were exceedingly offended at this impiety, and would have entered the church by force; but Wishart would not suffer it, saying, "Brethren, it is the word of peace which I preach unto you; the blood of no man shall be shed for it this day. Jesus Christ is as mighty in the fields as in the church, and he himself, while he lived in the flesh, preached oftener in the desert and on the seaside, than in the temple of Jerusalem." Upon this the people were appeased, and went with him to the edge of a moor, on the south-west of Mauchline, where, having placed himself upon a mound of earth, he preached to a great multitude. He continued speaking for more than three hours, God working wondrously by him, insomuch that Laurence Ranken, the Laird of Shield, a very profane person, was converted by his discourse. The tears ran from his eyes, to the astonishment of all present; and the whole of his after life witnessed that his profession was without hypocrisy.

314. PERJURY.

(*a*) FORSWEARING A DEBT.—At a Justice's Court, held at Mayslick, Kentucky, says an eye-witness, a cause came on to be heard, wherein the sum in dispute was 75 cts. due to the plaintiff, a tavern-keeper for whisky.

Neither party having any testimony to introduce, Mr. S——, one of the justices, for the purpose of obtaining some knowledge of the situation of the claim, permitted the parties to go into a free conversation, on the subject of their dealings.

After considerable affirmation on one side, and denial on the other, the plaintiff told the defendant, if he would swear he had paid for two half pints, he would strike them out of his account; defendant said he would, and asked Mr. S—— to administer the oath, but he being conscious from prior confessions of the defendant, that it was impossible it could be so, said to him, I feel a delicacy in doing so, and you had better pay it; it's a trifling sum, I would not take the trouble to swear for it. Something at that moment called the attention of Mr. S—— from the subject, and before he again had fixed his eyes on the defendant, he had stept to Mr. Y——, another of the magistrates, in the other corner of the room, and had sworn in the most solemn manner, to the payment of the money, of which he immediately informed Mr. S——.

Until this awful period, the defendant had retained his usual appearance of health and vigor; but, alas! no sooner had he turned about to inform Mr. S—— of his successful attempt to commit the horrid crime of perjury, than a death-like paleness was visible on his countenance; the people in the room simultaneously remarked, with astonishment, the change so instantaneously effected in his appearance. Mr. S—— himself remarked, when relating the circumstance, that he had the appearance of a man already two days dead. Judgment was entered for fifty cents, and he retired from the scene of his guilt. But wretched infatuated mortal! he could not retire from *conscious guilt.* He took neither refreshment nor sleep that night; but appeared restless, (as his wife relates,) and rolled in his bed from side to side, like one bereft of every earthly enjoyment. Morning came; but with it brought no relief to his perturbed bosom. Still taking no food, after breakfast he went to the field, where a number of reapers had met to cut his grain; he gave them some incoherent directions relative to the harvest, and returned to his house. The whole day was spent in thoughtful musings, and apparent agony of mind: and another night was spent like the preceding. In the morning, a short time after he had left his bed, he was seen running upon all-fours through the door-yard, and exclaiming. "John Johnston (the name of the constable who attended the trial) and the Devil are after me." He was picked up by some men who were about the house, and set down on the step of the door. In a few minutes he suddenly started from his seat, and again commenced running upon his hands and feet as before; and exclaiming most awfully, "John Johnston and the Devil are after me." In this manner he made his way into a small field of corn which stood open to the door-yard, and as he ran between the rows of corn, he tore up a number of hills by the roots, and whilst thus engaged, and before he could be reached by his pursuers, in the act of tearing up a cornhill, he suddenly and instantaneously expired.

(*b*) THE SENATOR'S OATH.—Mr. J. Taygart was elected a Senator from the county of Columbiana to the second General Assembly of the State of Ohio. He appeared and made the necessary oaths, and took his seat. In a few days he became melancholy, which soon progressed to insanity. In his insane ravings he disclosed that he was not thirty years of age when he took the oath of office and his seat; and that his conscience upbraided him with the crime of perjury in taking an oath to support the constitution, and at the same moment taking a seat in violation of its provisions. From this insanity he never recovered, and survived its commencement but a few months.

(*c*) STENNETT AND HIS ENEMIES.—Dr. Samuel Stennett dwelt in the castle of Wallingford, (Eng.) where no warrant except that of the Lord Chief Justice could reach him; and the house was so situated that religious assemblies could meet there without any danger of legal conviction, unless informers were admitted, which care was taken to prevent. A justice of peace in the neighborhood, highly incensed at this, resolved, together with a clergyman, upon a conviction of the offence by suborning false witnesses. Several persons, therefore, were hired to swear they had heard prayer and preaching at the castle, though they never had been present. Mr. Stennett finding an indictment laid against him on the Conventicle Act, and being well assured that nothing but perjury could support it, resolved to traverse it; and accordingly did so. The assizes were held at Newbury; and when the time approached, his adversaries greatly triumphed in their expected success. But the scene was suddenly changed. News came to the justice that his son at Oxford was gone off with a player: this prevented one perjurer from attending. The clergyman, who was determined to be present, and boasted of the service that would be done to the church by prosecution, was removed by sudden death. One of the witnesses who lived at Cromast, was prevented by a violent disease, of which he subsequently died. Another of them fell down and broke his leg, and so was hindered. In short, of seven or eight persons who were engaged in this design, only one was left capable of appearing. He was a gardener, who had frequently been employed by Mr. Stennett at day-labor, who had never been admitted into the meeting. This man was expected to be a very material witness, and was kept in liquor several days for that purpose. But coming to his reason just as the assizes drew near, he went about town exclaiming against his ingratitude and perjury, and refused to go. So when Mr. Stennett came to Newbury, neither prosecutor or witnesses appearing against him, he was of course discharged.

315. PERSECUTION.

(*a*) DIOCLESIAN'S CONFESSION.—Dioclesian, the last and the worst of the Roman persecuting emperors, observed, that the more he sought to blot out the name of Christ, the more legible it became; and that whatever of Christ he thought to eradicate, it took the deeper root, and rose the higher in the hearts and lives of men.

(*b*) THE HIGHEST HONOR.—One of the witnesses of the truth, when imprisoned for conscience' sake in Queen Mary's persecution of the Church, is said to have thus written to a friend: "A prisoner for Christ! What is this for a poor worm? Such honor have not all his saints. Both the degrees which I took in the University, have not set me so high as the honor of becoming a prisoner of the Lord."

316. PERSECUTORS, END OF.

(*a*) END OF HEROD THE GREAT.—The disease of which Herod the Great died, and the misery which he suffered under it, plainly showed that the hand of God was then in a signal manner upon him; for not long after the murders at Bethlehem, his distemper, as Josephus informs us, daily increased in an unheard-of manner. He had a lingering and wasting fever, and grievous ulcers in his entrails and bowels; a violent colic, and insatiable appetite; a venomous swelling in his feet; convulsions in his nerves; a perpetual asthma, and offensive breath; rottenness in his joints and other members; accompanied with prodigious itchings, crawling worms, and intolerable smell: so that he was a perfect hospital of incurable distempers.

(*b*) DEATH OF JULIAN.—The Roman Emperor Julian, a determined enemy of Christianity, was mortally wounded in a war with the Persians. In this condition, we are told that he filled his hand with blood, and casting it into the air, said, "O Galilean! thou hast conquered." During this expedition, one of Julian's followers asked a Christian of Antioch, "What the carpenter's son was doing?" "The Maker of the world," replied the Christian, "whom you call the carpenter's son, is employed in making a coffin for the emperor." In a few days after, news came to Antioch of Julian's death.

(*c*) NERO, DOMITIAN, AND OTHERS.—Persecutors, and others who have unjustly shed the blood of their fellow-creatures, have often, in the righteous providence of God, met with a violent death, or been visited by signal judgments. Nero was driven from his throne, and perceiving his life in danger, became his own executioner; Domitian was killed by his own servants; Hadrian died of a distressing disease, which was accompanied with great mental agony; Severus never prospered in his affairs after he persecuted the church, and was killed by the treachery of his son; Maximinus reigned but three years, and died a violent death; Decius was drowned in a marsh, and his body never found; Valerian was taken prisoner by the Persians, and, after enduring the horrors of captivity for several years, was flayed alive; Dioclesian was compelled to resign his empire, and became insane; Maximianus Herculeus was deprived of his government, and strangled; Maximianus Galerius was suddenly and awfully removed by death; and Severus committed suicide.

(*d*) DEATH OF CHARLES IX. - Charles IX of France was a cruel and persecuting monarch, (witness the massacre at Paris in 1575,) and died in a very wretched state. He expired, bathed in his own blood, which burst from his veins, and in his last moments he exclaimed, "What blood!—what murders!—I know not where I am!—how will all this end?—what shall I do?—I am lost forever!—I know it!"

(*e*) THE EARL'S BOAST.—Felix, earl of Wurtemburg, one of the captains of the Emperor Charles V, being at supper at Augsburg, in company with many who were threatening the sorest punishments on the persons of the pious Christians of that day, swore, before them all, that before he died he would ride up to his spurs in the blood of the Lutherans. That same night he was choked, probably by the bursting of a blood-vessel, which filled his throat, and at once removed him from the world.

(*f*) THE EMIGRANT'S PERSECUTORS.—A number of persons, in the north of England, once determined to emigrate to South Africa. They had a great dread of what they called *Methodism*, and refused to allow a young man, who was reputed to belong to that body of Christians, to go with them. They had not, however, been many days at sea, before it was discovered, that notwithstanding their most strenuous endeavors to prevent the exportation of Methodism, they had got an excellent old man aboard, who privately exhorted his fellow passengers to fear God, and flee from the wrath to come. The flame of persecution was now lighted up; and Mr. C., the leader of the party, availed himself of every opportunity to annoy and injure poor Mr. P. In the course of the passage, his wife and son were taken alarmingly ill; but, so bitter was the spirit which prevailed against him, that it was with difficulty he obtained even the medicines provided by government, which their state rendered absolutely necessary. The above-mentioned gentleman, who had the affairs of the party almost wholly under his control, frequently threatened not only to deprive him of the land to which he was legally entitled, but of all the privileges of the settlement, unless he kept his religion to himself. In his menaces and designs, this petty Nero was supported by three or four others, who were influenced by a similar spirit. The earth, however, is the Lord's, and "though hand join in hand, the wicked shall not go unpunished." Two only of those persecutors lived to see the settlement. The death of one was occasioned by intemperance and dissipation while at sea. The head of the party himself fell sick immediately after his arrival at Algoa Bay, and there expired, in dreadful agony, both mental and bodily. He therefore never set foot on the land which he had so arrogantly affected to command. Another of his comrades was taken off suddenly, and carried to the grave along with him! A fourth, being some time afterward provoked by his companion, the only survivor of the five, presented his fowling-piece at him, and lodged the contents in his breast; for which he was, of course, arrested, and conveyed to prison in Graham's Town. But his spirit and conduct having apparently rendered life burdensome, and filled his dungeon with insufferable gloom, the unhappy wretch hung himself in his cell! "Woe unto the wicked! it shall be ill with him; for the reward of his hands shall be given him: but say ye to the righteous, it shall be well with him; they shall eat the fruit of their doings."

The poor old Methodist now began, more earnestly than ever, to call all around him to repentance, and actually became the virtual head of the party; he obtained favor in the eyes of the people, and was ever after looked up to as their chief counsellor in all matters of importance. His rustic cottage was no sooner built than converted into a place of worship, wherein Divine service was regularly performed, until, by steady zeal and praiseworthy exertions, they were enabled to erect a neat little chapel, which constitutes a lasting honor to his memory. This good man is now no more; but, although dead, by his works he still speaketh; and his name is held in the highest estimation by all who knew him.

(*g*) THE CONSTABLE'S ADMONITION.—In 1682, some soldiers came to break up a meeting where Mr. Browning, who had been ejected from Desborough, in Northamptonshire, was, and to apprehend him. The constable of the place, who was present, admonished them to be well advised in what they did, "For," said he, "when Sir —— was alive, he eagerly persecuted these meetings, and engaged eight soldiers of the country troop to assist him, whereof myself was one. Sir —— himself is dead; six of the soldiers are dead; some of them were hanged, and some of them broke their necks, and I myself fell off my horse and broke my collar-bone, in the act of persecuting them. This has given me such a warning, that, for my part, I am resolved I will never meddle with them more."

(*h*) END OF BISHOP GARDINER.—On the day of the martyrdom of Ridley and Latimer, Gardiner waited with impatience for the account of their burning, having arranged that messengers should be dispatched to inform him as soon as the pile should be set on fire. He delayed sitting down to his dinner till he received the desired intelligence, which arrived about four o'clock. He now sat down to his dinner, and, as Fox remarks, "He was not disappointed of his lust, but while the meat was yet in his mouth the heavy wrath of God came upon him." While at table he felt the first attacks of a mortal disease, the effect of vices in which he had long indulged; and though, for some days afterwards, he was able to go out and attend the parliament, his illness rapidly increased, until, as was stated by one of his contemporaries, he became so offensive, "that it was scarcely possible to get any one to come near him." The sufferings of his mind were not less painful than those of his body. He frequently exclaimed, "I have sinned like Peter, but I have not wept like him." He endured these protracted pains longer than Ridley and Latimer had suffered, lingering in this state till the 13th of November, during which time it is recorded, that, "he spake little but blasphemy and filthiness, and gave up the ghost with curses in his mouth, in terrible and inexpressible torments." What were the sufferings of the martyrs compared with these?

317. PHYSICIANS.

(*a*) HUMANITY OF WALKER.—The following anecdote of Dr. Walker, well known as the director of the London Jennerian and Vaccine Institutions, is extracted from his memoir.

While our troops were using the weapons of destruction, Dr. Walker was busily employed in saving life. His work of vaccination being completed, he attended the sick of the British navy, and of the Turkish army. The sense of weariness while engaged in these works of mercy, he seems hardly to have known; being assisted by his friend General Sir John Doyle, in prosecuting these labors of goodness. The following extract of a letter from that worthy officer speaks volumes. "The general can never forget the impression made upon him by the extraordinary situation in which he first made an acquaintance with that amiable and benevolent individual, Dr. Walker. The day after the action, near Alexandria, where the brave Abercrombie fell, the general was riding over the field of battle, attended by two orderly dragoons, to see if there were any wounded, French or English, who had escaped notice the evening before; when, on turning round a wall near the sea-side, he was struck with an appalling sight of more than a hundred French soldiers, with their officers, huddled together, desperately wounded by grape and cannon shot from an English brig of war. From being collected in the recess of the wall, they had escaped notice on the previous day of search, and were exposed to the night air, and with undressed wounds. Here the general saw a man, evidently English, in the garb of a Quaker, actively employed in the heavenly task of giving his humane assistance to those poor brave sufferers; giving water to some, dressing the wounds of others, and affording consolation to all. Upon inquiry he found the benevolent individual to be Dr. John Walker, who was himself almost exhausted, having been thus nobly employed from day-break, without any assistance."

(*b*) FOTHERGILL'S GENEROSITY.—A worthy clergyman, a friend of Dr. Fothergill, was, in the early part of his life, settled in London upon a curacy of 50*l*. per annum. An epidemical disease seized upon his wife and five of his children. In this state of distress he earnestly desired the doctor's advice, but dared not apply for it, from a consciousness of being unable to reward him for his attendance. A friend kindly offered to accompany him to the doctor's, and give him his fee. They took advantage of his hour of audience; and, after a description of the several cases, the fee was offered and rejected, but a note was taken of his place of residence. The doctor assiduously called from day to day, till his attendance was no longer necessary. The curate, anxious to return some grateful mark of the sense he entertained of his services, strained every nerve to accomplish it; but his astonishment was great, when the doctor, instead of receiving the money he offered, put ten guineas into his hand, desiring him to apply to him without hesitation in future difficulties.

(*c*) THE SURGEON'S REPLY.—M. Boudon, an eminent surgeon, was one day sent for by the Cardinal Du Bois, Prime Minister of France, to perform a very serious operation upon him. The cardinal, on seeing him enter the room, said to him, "You must not expect to treat me in the same rough manner, as you treat your poor miserable wretches at your hospital of the Hôtel Dieu." "My lord," replied M. Boudon with great dignity, "every one of those miserable wretches, as your eminence is pleased to call them, is a prime minister in my eyes."

(*d*) DR. SMITH'S METHOD.—The benevolent and eccentric Dr. Smith when established in a practice equal to that of any physician in London, did what few physicians perhaps in great practice would have done. He set apart *two days for the poor in each week.* From those who were really poor, he never took a fee; and from those who were of the middling ranks of life, he never would take above half a guinea! yet so great was the resort to him, that he has in one day received fifty guineas at half a guinea only from each patient!

(*e*) EXAMPLE OF SALTER.—"The functions of a simple, earnest and skilful country surgeon," says Coleridge, "living in a small town or village, and circulating in a radius of ten miles, are, and might always be made, superior in real, urgent, and fitting relief, to the Lady Bountiful. I often think with pleasure of the active, *practical* benevolence of Salter. His rides were often sixty, averaging more than thirty miles every day over bad roads and in dark nights: yet not once has he been known to refuse a summons, though quite sure that he would receive no remuneration, nay, not sure that it would not be necessary to supply wine or cordials, which in the absence of the landlord of his village, must be at his own expense. This man was generally pitied by the affluent and idle, on the score of his constant labors, and the drudgery which he almost seemed to court. Yet with little reason; for I never knew the man more to be envied, or more cheerful, more *invariably* kind, or more patient; always kind from real kindness and delicacy of feeling; never even for a moment angry.

(*f*) "WILL YOU TRUST MY FATHER?"—An aged Christian who had long been an invalid and was dependent on Christian charity for her support, on sending for a new physician who had just come into the place, and united with the same church of which she was a member, said to him, "Doctor, I wish to put myself under your care, but I cannot do it unless you will *trust my father.*" "Well, ma'am," replied the physician, "I believe your Father is rich; *I may safely trust Him*"—

(*g*) GOLDSMITH'S PATIENT.—A poor woman understanding that Dr. Goldsmith had studied physic, and hear of his great humanity, solicited him in a letter to send her something for her husband, who had lost his appetite and was reduced to a most melancholy state. The good natured poet waited on her instantly, and, after some discourse with his patient, found him sinking in sickness and poverty. The doctor told him they should hear from in an hour, when he would send them some pills which he believed would prove efficacious. He immediately went home and put ten guineas into a chip box, with the following label; "These must be used as necessities require; be patient, and of good heart." He sent his servant with this prescription to the comfortless mourner, who found it contained a remedy superior to any thing Galen or his tribe could administer.

(*h*) THE TWO PHYSICIANS.—Is it possible, says a writer in the American Messenger for 1847, for physicians in full practice to be as regular in attendance on public worship as other men? That physicians frequently plead their business as an excuse for neglecting a regular attendance in the house of God is certainly true, but is this a valid plea? does their business justify their neglect? The following conversation which I chanced to overhear the other day, between two physicians, may throw some light upon the subject. They are both in large practice in one of our northern cities.

Dr. L. How happens it, Doctor B., that you are so regular in your attendance upon the public and social meetings of the church? I hear that you are seldom absent, at least I always see you there when I am. There must be some secret about it, for your practice is as extensive as mine, if not more so, and with all my diligence I cannot make out to attend half the time. I really should like to know how you manage it. I often wish that I could so arrange my business as *never* to be absent.

Dr B. You are frequently called in

consultation with your medical friends, are you not?

Dr. L. Certainly I am, once or twice every day, and sometimes oftener.

Dr. B. Are you in the habit of meeting your consultations punctually?

Dr. L. I am, and am seldom obliged to make a draft upon the fifteen minutes' grace usually allowed?

Dr. B. That is all the secret I have about the matter. *I have always made it a rule punctually and promptly to meet my consultations*, and I feel that I have at least two every Sabbath in the house of God, and God who loveth the gates of Zion more than all the dwellings of Jacob, has for more than thirty years enabled me, with very few exceptions, to meet them.

Dr. L. thanked Dr. B. and thought he should profit by the hint, and in the hope that others may likewise, this paragraph is given to the Messenger.

318. POWER, ARBITRARY, CORRUPTING INFLUENCE OF.

(*a*) XERXES ANGRY WITH THE HELLESPONT.—When the force of the current had carried away the temporary bridge which Xerxes had caused to be thrown over the Hellespont, on his grand expedition into Greece, he was so enraged, that he not only ordered the heads of the workmen to be struck off, but, like a madman, inflicted lashes upon the sea, to punish it for its insolence; he, moreover, affected to hold it in future under his control, by throwing fetters into it! "A striking proof," adds the historian, "how much the possession of despotic power tends not only to corrupt the heart, but even to weaken and blind the understanding."

(*b*) EFFECTS OF POWER ON NERO.—The beginning of Nero's reign was marked by acts of the greatest kindness and condescension; by affability, complaisance, and popularity. The object of his administration seemed to be the good of his people; and, when he was desired to sign his name to a list of malefactors that were to be executed, he exclaimed, "I wish to heaven I could not write!" He was an enemy to flattery; and when the Senate had liberally commended the wisdom of his government, Nero desired them to keep their praises till he deserved them. But mark the corresponding tendency of arbitrary power! This was the wretch who afterwards assassinated his mother, who set fire to Rome, and destroyed multitudes of men, women, and children, and threw the odium of that dreadful action on the Christians. The cruelties he exercised towards them were beyond description, while he seemed to be the only one who enjoyed the tragical spectacle. "The heart is deceitful above all things and desperately wicked; who can know it?" Arbitrary power is dangerous, and who shall be trusted with it?

(*c*) CATO, THE MODEL AND THE MONSTER.—No man has ever lived who was more celebrated for his scrupulous observance of the most exact justice, and for the illustration furnished in his life of the noblest natural virtues, than the Roman Cato. His strict adherence to the nicest rules of equity—his integrity, honor, and incorruptible faith—his jealous watchfulness over the rights of his fellow citizens, and his generous devotion to their interest, procured for him the sublime appellation of "The Just." Towards *freemen* his life was a model of every thing just and noble: but to his slaves he was a monster. At his meals, when the dishes were not done to his liking, or when his slaves were careless or inattentive in serving, he would seize a thong and violently beat them, in presence of his guests. When they grew old or diseased, and were no longer serviceable, however long and faithfully they might have served him, he either turned them adrift and left them to perish, or starved them to death in his own family. No facts in his history are better authenticated than these. And what so vitiated his feelings and conduct towards these slaves, but the fact that over *them* he exercised arbitrary power?

(*d*) A WOMAN WITH TWO FACES.—A lady, now in the West Indies, was sent in her infancy to her friends, near Belfast, in Ireland, for education. She remained under their charge from five to fifteen years of age, and grew up every thing which her friends could wish. At fifteen, she returned to the West Indies—was married—and after some years paid her friends near Belfast a second visit. Towards white people, she was the same elegant and interesting woman as before; apparently full of every virtuous and tender feeling; but towards the colored people she was like a tigress. If Wilberforce's name was mentioned, she would say, "Oh, I wish we had the wretch in the West Indies, I would be one of the first to help to tear his heart out!"—and then she would tell of the manner in which the West Indian ladies used to treat their slaves. "I have often," she said, "when my women have displeased me, snatched their baby from their bosom, and running with it to a well, have tied my shawl round its shoulders and pretended to be drowning it: oh, it was so funny to hear the mother's screams!!"—and then she laughed almost convulsively at the recollection.

What but the exercise of despotic power could have thus steeled her sensibilities and corrupted her mind?

(*e*) WEST INDIA PLANTER.—A planter of the West Indies, who was owner of a considerable number of slaves, treated them with the utmost cruelty, whipping and torturing them for the slightest fault. One of the unfortunate victims of his cruelty, thinking any change preferable to slavery under such a barbarian, attempted to make his escape among the mountain Indians; but, unfortunately, was taken, and brought back to his master. Poor Arthur (so he was called) was immediately ordered to receive three hundred lashes, when stripped; which were to be given him by his fellow slaves, among whom happened to be a new negro, just brought from Africa, and who had been purchased by the planter the day before. This slave, the moment he saw the unhappy wretch destined to the lashes, flew to his arms, and embraced him with the greatest tenderness; the other returned his transports, and nothing could be more moving than their mutual bemoaning each other's misfortunes. Their master was soon given to understand that they were countrymen and intimate friends; and that Arthur had formerly, in a battle with a neighboring nation, saved his friend's life at the extreme hazard of his own. The new negro, at the same time, threw himself at the planter's feet with tears, beseeching him, in the most moving manner, to spare his friend, or, at least, to suffer him to undergo the punishment in his room, protesting he would rather die ten thousand deaths, than lift his hand against him. But the wretch, looking on this as an affront to the absolute power he pretended over him, ordered Arthur to be immediately tied to a tree, and his friend to give him the lashes; telling him, too, that for every lash not well laid on, he should himself receive a score. The new negro, amazed at a barbarity so unbecoming a human creature, with a generous disdain refused to obey him, at the same time upbraiding him with his cruelty; upon which the planter, turning all his rage on him, ordered him to be immediately stripped, and commanded Arthur, to whom he promised forgiveness, to give his countryman the lashes he had been destined to receive himself. This proposal too was received with scorn, each protesting he would rather suffer the most dreadful torture than injure his friend. This generous conflict, which must have raised the strongest feelings in a breast susceptible of pity, did but the more inflame the monster, who now determined they should both be made examples of; and to satiate his revenge, was resolved to whip them himself. He was just preparing to begin with Arthur, when the new negro drew a knife from his pocket, stabbed the planter to the heart, and the following instant struck it to his own.

West India slavery was fruitful in such atrocities. And why produce such results? Because it placed arbitrary power in the master's hand, making him a despot on the small scale.

(*f*) SELLING ONE'S OWN CHILD.—A person who resided in a slaveholding country, sold a black woman and her mulatto child to a negro trader. The woman knew nothing of the sale until she and her child were taken possession of by the purchaser. She was, it appears, a female of spirit, and as she was now out of the hands of her former master, and must go, she knew not whither, she took occasion to vent her indignant feelings in language that showed at once the courage of the Roman matron, as it respected herself, and the heartless villany of a slave-dealer, when applied to him. Walking toward him with her child in her arms, she interrogated him as follows: "Well, sir, I am sold, am I?" "Yes," was the reply. She continued—"This gentleman, I suppose, then, is my master." He answered in the affirmative. "Well, now," she proceeded, "I will tell you to your face, that you are one of the most wicked, unmanly, cold-hearted creatures, that I ever heard of. *Here, sir, is your own child—your own flesh and blood—which, together with its mother, you have sold for money!! Look at it, sir.* Your features are in its face—your blood runs in its veins—and yet, you've *sold it*—away! I cannot bear the sight of you." And these results were the legitimate fruits of the illegitimate and irresponsible authority which the tyrant exercised over her and her offspring.

319. POWER, VANITY OF.

(*a*) CYRUS' CROWN.—Cyrus, the Persian king, was accustomed to say, that did men but know the cares he had to sustain, he thought no man would wish to wear his crown.

(*b*) GILIMEX VICTORIOUS.—Gilimex, king of the Vandals, when he was led in triumph by Belisarius, cried out, "Vanity of vanities, all is vanity."

(*c*) WORDS OF CHARLES V.—Charles V, emperor of Germany, whom of all men the world judged most happy, cried out, in reference to whatever is generally considered good and great, "Get you hence, let me hear no more of you."

(*d*) ALEXANDER'S TEARS.—The conquests of Alexander the Great could not satisfy him; for when he had conquered the whole of one known world, he sat down and wept because he knew of no other world to conquer.

(*e*) SKETCH OF MENZIKOFF.—Menzikoff, who was at first a pastry cook, accidentally coming into favor of Peter the Great, rose with a rapidity beyond example. He was loaded with honors, and frequently appeared in public as vice-czar, the emperor assuming the rank of a private person. It is not very surprising, that so extraordinary and sudden an elevation should cause Menzikoff sometimes to forget that he was a man. His enemies trembled at his presence; for, as his power was great, so was his revenge. After the death of his imperial master, to whom he was warmly attached, he remained faithful to Catherine; and upon her decease, he placed the crown upon the head of Peter III, son of the unfortunate Alexis, and grandson of his benefactor. It is said he had formed the ambitious design of marrying his daughter to this young prince. The sun of prosperity, however, which had hitherto shone in meridian splendor upon Alexander Menzikoff, was now fast sinking into the darkest gloom. The Dolgoroukis, a noble family who hated him, were artful, pliable, and insinuating; Peter was young, unsuspicious, and easily imposed upon by the frank and apparently disinterested friendship of the younger branches of the family. The ruin of the man who had placed him on the throne, was now, at the instigation of the Dolgoroukis, resolved on, and the fall of Menzikoff was even more rapid than his rise. As he had seldom shown mercy, so little was shown to him. His banishment to Berezof was attended with every aggravation that could be imagined. Previous to this fatal sentence, he had been deprived of his dignities, his pensions, his employments. This blow was quickly followed by another; he was banished the court, and desired to confine himself to his country house at Oranienburg. On his way thither he was overtaken by a messenger, accompanied by a party of dragoons, who brought the fatal mandate of banishment to Siberia. Berezof is situated near the mouth of the Oby; during six months in the year there is no actual daylight, and the earth is covered with frost and snow. What a situation for persons who had been used to every luxury, every indulgence! The Princess Menzikoff died on the journey, and was buried on the banks of the Wolga. She had always very weak eyes, and they were so affected by the cold and her excessive weeping, that she lost her sight before the half of her journey was completed. This unfortunate family were treated like the worst of criminals.—Their dresses were twice changed; first to the coarsest woolen, then to the coarsest stuffs. After being used to walk upon the softest carpets, clothed in the richest attire, and to travel with every possible convenience, they were now exposed to cold, and all the inclemencies of the weather, in small wooden carts made without springs, and which are always used to convey criminals to their place of exile. Menzikoff and one of his daughters lived to reach Berezof, but to end their days in that place of solitude.

When Menzikoff found his death approaching, he called his children to his bedside, and thus addressed them: "My children, I draw near to my last hour; death, the thoughts of which have been familiar to me since I have been here, would have nothing terrible in it, if I had only to account to the Supreme Judge for the time I have passed in misfortune. Hitherto your hearts have been free from corruption. You will preserve your innocence better in these deserts than at court: but should you return to it, recollect only the examples which your father has given you here."

On the accession of the Empress Anne to the throne, Menzikoff's younger daughter, and his son, returned to Russia; and the Dolgoroukis felt, in their turn, all the horrors they had contributed to inflict on the Menzikoffs; with this aggravation, that the same person who conducted them to Berezof, carried with him the recall of Menzikoff and his family.

PRAYER.

NATURE OF PRAYER.—SCRIPTURAL PRAYER.

320. Praying with Faith.

(*a*) MINISTER LEARNING TO PRAY.—A curious case occurred in one of the towns in the western part of the state of New-York. There was a revival there. A certain clergyman came to visit the place, and heard a great deal said about the prayer of faith. He was staggered at what they said, for he had never regarded the subject in the light they did. He inquired about it of the minister who was laboring there. The minister requested him, in a kind spirit, to go home and take his Testament, look out the passages that refer to prayer, and go round to his most praying people, and ask them how they understood those passages. He said he would do it, for though these views were new to him, he was willing to learn. He did it, and went to his praying men and women, and read the passages without note or comment, and asked them what they thought. He found their plain common sense had led them to understand these passages, and to believe that they mean just as they say. This affected him, and then the fact of his going round and presenting the promises before their minds, awakened a spirit of prayer in them, and a revival followed.

(*b*) PRAYER FOR A DYING CHILD.—A clergyman, concluding a sermon to youth, took occasion to press upon parents the duty of parental faith, and illustrated its power in the following manner:

About two-and-twenty years ago, a little circle were met around the couch of an apparently dying infant; the man of God, who led their devotions, seemed to forget the sickness of the child, in his prayer for his future usefulness. He prayed for the child, who had been consecrated to God at his birth, as a man, a Christian, and a minister of the word. The parents laid hold of the horns of the altar, and prayed with him. The child recovered, grew towards manhood, and ran far in the ways of folly and sin. One after another of that little circle ascended to heaven; but two, at least, and one of them the mother, lived to hear him proclaim the everlasting gospel. "It is," said the preacher, "no fiction; that child, that prodigal youth, that preacher, is he who now addresses you."

(*c*) GOOD REASON FOR PRAYING.—A little girl, about four years of age, being asked, "Why do you pray to God?" replied, "Because I know he hears me, and I love to pray to him." "But how do you know he hears you?" Putting her little hand to her heart, she said, "I know he does, because there is something *here* that tells me so."

(*d*) SECRET OF THE NEGRO'S COMFORT.—A negro slave in Virginia, whose name we will call Jack, was remarkable for his good sense, knowledge of the leading truths of the gospel, and especially for his freedom from all gloomy fears in regard to his future eternal happiness. A professing Christian, a white man, who was of a very different temperament, once said to him, "Jack, you seem to be always comfortable in the hope of the gospel. I wish you would tell me how you manage it, to keep steadily in this blessed frame of mind." "Why, massa," replied Jack, "I just fall flat on the promise, and pray right up." We recommend Jack's method to all desponding Christians, as containing, in substance, all that can be properly said on the subject. Take ground on the promises of God, and plead them in the prayer of faith—pray "right up."

321. Praying with Submission.

(*a*) BOLINGBROKE AND LADY HUNTINGDON.—Lord Bolingbroke once asked Lady Huntingdon, how she reconciled prayer to God for particular blessings, with absolute resignation to the Divine will. "Very easily," answered her ladyship; "just as if I were to offer a petition to a monarch, of whose kindness and wisdom I had the highest opinion. In such a case, my language would be, I wish you to bestow on me such or such a favor; but your majesty knows better than I, how far it would be agreeable to you, or right in itself to grant my desire. I therefore content myself with humbly presenting my petition, and leave the event of it entirely to you."

(*b*) THE CHILD RESTORED.—A Christian widow in London saw with great alarm, her only child taken dangerously ill. As the illness increased she became almost distracted, from a dread of losing the child; at length it became so extremely ill, and so convulsed, that she kneeled down by the bed, deeply affected, and in prayer said, "Now, Lord, thy will be done." From that hour the child began to recover, till health was perfectly restored.

322. Praying with Importunity and Earnestness.

(*a*) A MOTHER'S INTERCESSION.—A Christian minister in Somersetshire, Eng., stated, that on the evening when the first permanent impressions were made on his mind, his pious mother was detained at home. She spent the time devoted to public worship, in secret prayer for the salvation of her son; and so fervent did she become in these intercessions, that she fell on her face, and remained in fervent supplication till the service had nearly closed. Her son, brought under the deepest impressions by the sermon of his father, went into a field after the service, and there prayed most fervently for himself. When he came home, the mother looked at her son with a manifest concern, anxious to discover whether her prayers had been heard, and whether her son had commenced the all-important inquiry, "What shall I do to be saved?" In a few days the son acknowledged himself to be the subject of religious impressions; impressions which lay the foundation of all excellence of character here, and of all blessedness hereafter.

(*b*) MY HEART TALKED.—A child, six years old, in a Sunday school, said, "When we kneel down in the school-room to pray, it seems as if my heart talked." Vain are words, if the heart pray not.

(*c*) "WHY, SIR, I BEGGED."—A little boy, one of the Sunday school children, in Jamaica, called upon the missionary, and stated that he had lately been very ill; and in his sickness often wished his minister had been present to pray with him. "But, Thomas," said the missionary, "I hope you prayed." "Oh yes, sir." "Did you repeat the collect I taught you?" "I prayed." "Well, but how did you pray?" "Why, sir, I begged."

323. Praying with Constancy and Perseverance.

(*a*) "PRAY WITHOUT CEASING."—A number of ministers were assembled for the discussion of difficult questions, and among others it was asked, how the command "to pray without ceasing" could be complied with. Various suppositions were started, and at length one of the number was appointed to write an essay upon it, to read at the next monthly meeting; which being overheard by a female servant, she exclaimed, "What! a whole month wanted to tell the meaning of that text! It is one of the easiest and best texts in the Bible." "Well, well," said an old minister, "Mary, what can you say about it? Let us know how you understand it; can you pray all the time?" "O yes, sir." "What! when you have so many things to do?" "Why, sir, the more I have to do, the more I can pray." "Indeed; well, Mary, do let us know how it is; for most people think otherwise." "Well, sir," said the girl, "when I first open my eyes in the morning, I pray, Lord, open the eyes of my understanding; and while I am dressing, I pray, that I may be clothed with the robe of righteousness; and when I have washed myself, I ask for the washing of regeneration; and as I begin to work, I pray, that I may have strength equal to my day. When I begin to kindle the fire, I pray, that God's work may revive in my soul; and as I sweep out the house, I pray, that my heart may be cleansed from all its impurities; and while preparing and partaking of breakfast, I desire to be fed with the hidden manna, and the sincere milk of the word; and as I am busy with the little children, I look up to God as my Father, and pray for the Spirit of adoption, that I may be his child, and so on all day: every thing I do furnishes me with a thought for prayer." "Enough, enough," cried the old divine, "these things are revealed to babes, and often hid from the wise and prudent." "Go on, Mary," said he, "pray without ceasing; and as for us, my brethren, let us bless the Lord for this exposition, and remember that He has said, 'The meek will he guide in judgment.'" The essay, as a matter of course, was not considered necessary after this little event occurred.

(*b*) WHITEFIELD'S PRAYERS FOR HIS BROTHER.—One Lord's day morning, Mr. Whitefield, with his usual fervor, exhorted his hearers to give up the use of the means for the spiritual good of their relations and friends *only with their lives*; remarking that he had had a brother, for whose spiritual welfare he had used every means. He had warned him and prayed for him; and apparently to no purpose, till a few weeks ago, when his brother, to his astonishment and joy, came to his house, and with many tears declared, that he had come up from the country, to testify to him the great change that divine grace had wrought upon his heart; and to acknowledge with gratitude his obligation to the man whom God had made the instrument of it. Mr. Whitefield added, that he had that morning received a letter which informed him, that on his brother's return to Gloucestershire, where he resided, he dropped down dead as he was getting out of the stage coach, but that he had previously given the most unequivocal evidence of his being a new man in Christ Jesus—"Therefore," said Mr. Whitefield, "let us pray always for ourselves and for those who are dear to us, and never faint."

(*c*) TWO WOMEN PRAYING.—In the county of A. there lived, remote from a village, two pious females, who had been recently united with husbands opposed to the gospel of Christ. These young women beheld, with the keenest sensation, the dear partners of their lives pursuing a path which must soon end in everlasting death. Each had often carried her troubles and sorrows to the throne of grace, and laid them before One who knew the anxiety of her heart, and each had often shed the silent tear. As a great intimacy had existed between those young females, they jointly agreed to spend one hour daily in praying for their husbands. They continued this prayer for seven years without any visible effect. At length, with hearts full of anguish, they met to mingle together their sorrows. Their inquiry was, shall we no longer pray for our dear partners—must they, Oh, must they be for ever miserable? They concluded that although their prayers had not been answered, yet they would persevere even unto the end of life, in the course they had adopted; and if their husbands would go down to destruction, they should go loaded with their prayers. They moreover resolved to renew their strength, and to pray more earnestly than ever. Thus they continued for three years longer. About this time one of them was awakened in the night by the mental distress of her husband. Sleep had departed from his eyes, distress and anguish had seized his soul, for the prayers of these females had come up in remembrance before the throne of God; and the man who could once ridicule the tender anxieties of a distressed wife, was how upon his knees in the greatest agony. Now, with earnestness, he entreated her to pray for him; for, said he, the day of grace is almost over, and the door of mercy is ready to be closed against me for ever. His distress, and the hope of the wife, continued to increase. As soon as the day dawned she went with an overflowing heart to tell her praying companion, that God was about to answer their petitions. But great was her surprise, to meet her friend coming on the same errand, to tell her what God was doing for her own husband.

Thus after ten years' perseverance in calling mightily upon God, these Christian females had the unspeakable satisfaction of seeing both their husbands brought on the same day to realize their undone condition, and about the same time to accept, as it is hoped, the offers of mercy.

324. Miscellaneous.

(*a*) THE PUBLICAN'S PRAYER.—A Hottentot of immoral character, being under deep conviction of sin, was anxious to know how to pray. He went to his master, a Dutchman, to consult with him; but his master gave him no encouragement. A sense of his own wickedness increased, and he had no one near him to direct him. Occasionally, however, he was admitted with the family at the time of prayer. The portion of Scripture which was one day read by the master, was the parable of the Pharisee and the Publican. While the prayer of the Pharisee was read, the poor Hottentot thought within himself, "This is a *good* man; there is nothing for me;" but when his master came to the prayer of the Publican—God be merciful to me a sinner—"This suits me," he cried; "now I know how to pray!" With this prayer he immediately retired, and prayed night and day for two days, and then found peace. Full of joy and gratitude, he went into the fields, and as he had no one to whom he could speak, he exclaimed, "*Ye hills, ye rocks, ye trees, ye rivers,* hear what God has done for my soul!—he has been merciful to me, a sinner."

(*b*) PHILIP HENRY'S PROMISE. —The following remark of Rev. Philip Henry, after he had been engaged in ardent prayer for two of his children, that were dangerously ill, is so expressive of the *simplicity* and *tenderness* of Christian faith and love, as to recommend itself to the hearts of those who walk with God: "If the Lord will be pleased to grant me this my request concerning my children, I will not say as the beggars at our door used to do, 'I'll never ask any thing of him again;' but, on the contrary, he shall hear oftener from me than ever; and I will love God the better, and love prayer the better as long as I live."

UNSCRIPTURAL PRAYER.

325. Praying without Submission.

(*a*) THE BOY AND HIS DEAD B.RD.—"What occasions that melancholy look?" said a gentleman to one of his young favorites, one morning. He turned away his face, to hide a tear that was ready to start from his eyes. His brother answered for him, "Mother is very angry with him," said he, "because he would not say his prayers last night; and he cried all day, because a sparrow died of which he was very fond. The little mourner hastily turned round, and looking at me exclaimed, "I could not say *thy will be done*, because of my poor bird." The gentleman took him by the hand, and pointing to his school-fellows, "Mark the observation," said he, "from the youngest present, only six years old; for it explains the nature of prayer, of which, perhaps, some of you are ignorant. Many persons repeat words, who never prayed in their lives. My dear boy, I am very glad to find you were afraid to say to God what you could not say truly from your heart; but you may beg of him to give you submisssion to his will."

(*b*) MR. AND MRS. MART AND THEIR SON.—Mr. Edmund Calamy relates, in his life, that some persons of the name of Mart, in whose family he resided for some time, had a son who discovered the most wicked and impious disposition. When confined in prison, he wrote letters professing penitence; but, as soon as he had an opportunity, he returned to his former sins.

This young man had been the darling of both his father and mother; and the latter had set her affections upon him to so great a degree, that when she saw him a monster of wickedness, she became deranged, and attempted to destroy herself, which she at length effected. So far from being suitably impressed with this awful event, her son now proceeded to greater lengths in wickedness. At length he professed to be sorry for his depraved course, and applied to the Rev. Samuel Pomfret to intercede for him with his father. He was made ready for sea, but unhappily became connected with a gang of villains, and, on the very night before he was to set sail, he robbed Mr. Pomfret, was pursued, tried, and condemned to die.

On the Sabbath preceding the Wednesday on which he was condemned to die, his father entreated Dr. Calamy to accompany him that evening to his cell in Newgate, to converse with his unhappy son, and to give his opinion as to the propriety of seeking to obtain his pardon. The doctor went, and found him in a very awful state of mind, resenting different things which he conceived his father had done wrong, and saying that he might obtain a pardon for him if he would but part with some of his money. In vain did the doctor expostulate with him on the improper feelings he manifested, and entreat him to humble himself before God on account of his sins, as the only way of engaging his friends to obtain for him a reprieve. His reply was, "Sir, I scorn any thing of that nature; and would rather die with my company." The doctor reasoned with him on the existence of a hereafter, charged him with the death of his mother, taxed him with the murder of some persons abroad, whose blood he had actually shed, and showed him the heavy punishment he must endure in an eternal world unless he turned to God, repented of his sins, and prayed for pardon through the atonement of the Lord Jesus. He admitted the truth of all these things, but was filled with trifling unconcern. He frankly said that he had no hope of being better in his character, and that, on the contrary, he was satisfied she should grow worse. The next morning he was visited by Dr. Jekyl, who asked him whether, during the whole time he had been confined in Newgate, he had once bowed his knees to the great God, making it his earnest request to him to give him a sense of his sins, and to create in him a tender heart: he admitted that he had not, nor did he think it of any use. He was promised that if he would engage to pray morning and evening for the grace of God, an effort should be made, with every probability of success, for a reprieve, and subsequently a pardon. But he would make no engagement, and was hung on the day appointed.

On the day of his execution, the father of this unhappy young man told Dr. Calamy, that when the culprit was a very young child, and their only child, he was exceedingly ill with a fever, and that both his wife and himself, thinking their lives were bound up in the life of the child, were exceedingly importunate with God in prayer that his life might be spared. A pious mother expostulated with him on the vehemence he manifested, and said she dreaded the consequence of his praying in such a way, and that it became him to leave the matter to an infinitely wise God. At length the father said, "Let him prove what he will, so he is but spared, I shall be satisfied." The old man added, "This I now see to have been my folly. For, through the just hand of God, I have lived to see this wretched son of mine a heart-breaking cross to them that loved him with the greatest tenderness, a disgrace to my whole family, and likely to bring my gray hairs with sorrow to my grave. I read my sin very distinctly in my punishment; but must own that God is righteous in all his ways, and holy in all his works."

(*c*) "I CANNOT BEAR IFS."—It is of great importance that we should entreat the Spirit of God to enable us to pray as we ought. It is quite possible to ask for what may appear to us good things, but which, if we had them, would prove evil. Rachel, indulging a petulant disposition, said, "Give me children, or I die:" her desire was granted, and as the result she died.

The late Mr. Kilpin, of Exeter, writes, "I knew a case, in which the minister, praying over a child apparently dying, said 'If it be thy will, spare ——.' The poor mother's soul yearning for her beloved, exclaimed, 'It must be his will! I cannot bear *ifs*. The minister stopped. To the surprise of many the child recovered; and the mother, after almost suffering martyrdom by him while a stripling, lived to see him hanged before he was two-and-twenty! Oh! it is good to say, 'Not my will, but thine be done.'"

326. Various Examples.

(*a*) PRAYER WITHOUT EFFORT.—At a boarding school in the vicinity of London, a Miss ——, one of the scholars, was remarked for repeating her lessons well; a school-fellow rather idly inclined, said to her one day, "How is it that you always say your lessons so perfectly?" She replied, "I always pray that I may say my lessons well." "Do you?" said the other; "well, then, I will pray too:" but, alas! the next morning she could not even repeat a word of her usual task. Very much confounded, she ran to her friend, and reproached her as deceitful: "I prayed," said she, "but I could not say a single word of my lesson." "Perhaps," rejoined the other, "you took no pains to learn it!" "Learn it! learn it!" answered the first, "I did not learn it at all. I thought I had no occasion to learn it, when I prayed that I might say it."

(*b*) ABUSE IN PRAYER.—Mr. John Kilpin, father of the Rev. Samuel Kilpin, of Exeter, having from some cause displeased a member of the church; at a prayer meeting, his offended brother used most unbecoming expressions respecting him in prayer. On his family's offering their sympathy and expressing resentment, he said, with a mind unruffled, "I was not the least hurt on my own account; such *talking* never goes any higher than the ceiling; the God of love never admits it as *prayer*."

(*c*) PRAYERS TOO SELFISH.—A man once complained to his minister, that he had prayed for a whole year that he might enjoy the comforts of religion, but found no answer to his prayers. The minister replied, "Go home now, and pray, Father, glorify thyself." Reader, are you one of those who find no profit in calling upon God? Ask yourself if your prayers are not all selfish.

(*d*) OBJECTS OF PRAYER.—A gentleman conversing with his friend respecting the exercises of his own mind, before and after conversion, observed that there was a great difference as to the *objects* of prayer. "When I was," said he, "only a nominal Christian, I used to pray *to my family*, if any strangers were present I prayed *to them*, when I was alone I prayed *to myself*—but since I have been renewed by divine grace, in all my prayers I pray to God!"

(*e*) PRAYING TO MAN.—In the town of——, in Connecticut, there lived Mr. S—, an elderly man of undoubted piety, and one whose catholic and Christian spirit led him to associate with the people of God of all denominations. He circulated to some extent, among Congregationalists, Baptists and Methodists; attended many of their prayer meetings, and was frequently invited to conduct them. Every Christian loved Father S—. One evening he was to conduct a meeting for prayer, and had opened it with reading a portion of Scripture, after which he proposed to lead in prayer. He had nearly finished his chapter, when elder L—, a Baptist minister of high-toned Calvinistic sentiments, entered and took his seat near him. The thought crossed his mind, "Now I am rather moderate in some of my views, and I must try to shape my prayer so as not to give offence to good brother L—." With this thought in his mind, he kneeled and commenced with a few words of address to the Deity—became confused, and stopped. A second and third attempt were made with similar results. No one except the Baptist brother could conjecture what it was that occasioned the embarrassment of father S—. At length he exclaimed, "I don't know what ails me, I can't pray a bit!" "I know what ails you," said Mr. L—, "you are trying to pray to *me*; pray to God and you will get along well enough." "I believe you are right," said the old gentleman, "I will try once more." He did so, and succeeded to the edification of all present.

(*f*) SAYING PRAYERS SEVENTY YEARS.—A poor old man, when a child of three years of age, had been taught by his mother to repeat a prayer every night, which he did till he was seventy-three years old; and not a little proud was he to say that he had not omitted saying his prayers every night for seventy years! At this advanced age, it pleased God to afflict him severely; he was led by the Holy Spirit to see that he was a poor sinner, who had been living in the form of godliness, but had never felt its power. He was enabled to spend the last few years of his life in humble dependence on the grace of Christ; and when he referred to himself, he would often add, "I am the old man who said his prayers for seventy years, and yet all that time never prayed at all."

(*g*) IRREVERENCE IN PRAYER.—An aged minister told me, says a correspondent of the Morning Star, that when he was a young man, he had, on a certain occasion, been praying in a family, and in his prayer he had made a very frequent and energetic use of the terms of *good God* and *God Almighty*. At the close of his prayer, a little child about four years of age, came to his mother and said, "Mother, I don't like to hear that minister pray!" Why, inquired the mother. "Because," said the child, "he swears so when he prays." This reproof from the child, broke the minister of swearing when he prayed. Prayer is *petition*: and no one would use the name of a ruler, to whom he was making a petition in as harsh a manner as many use the name of the great God.

(*h*) A LONG PRAYER.—Rev. Mr. —— while traveling through one of the western States, stopped for the night at the house of a worthy member of a church. When Mr. —— entered the house, the old gentleman was about commencing family worship. Mr. —— being seated, he who was the head of the family proceeded with worship; and after having read and sung the usual length of time, he, together with all who were present, kneeled in prayer. Mr. — thought the prayer extremely long, but being much fatigued with the day's journey, supposed that his impression with regard to its length might have arisen, in some degree, from that circumstance. After having made a slight change in his attitude, he endeavored to compose himself, and wait patiently until the service should end. But the prayer continuing for near an hour, he could no longer control his impatience; but turning to a son of the old gentleman, who was kneeling or reclining near him, asked him if his father was not almost through with his prayer. The youth inquired if he had yet got to the Jews? Mr. — replied that he believed not. Well, said he, he is not half done yet.

OCCASIONS OF PRAYER.

327. Secret Prayer.

(*a*) MELANCTHON'S EXPERIENCE.—When Melancthon was entreated by his friends to lay aside the natural anxiety and timidity of his temper, he replied, "If I had no anxieties, I should lose a powerful incentive to prayer; but when the cares of life impel to devotion, the best means of consolation, a religious mind cannot do without them. Thus trouble compels me to prayer, and prayer drives away trouble."

(*b*) EXAMPLE OF MASON.—It is a fact which deserves the attention of all, that many of the most eminent men of the world have left behind them the most decisive testimony to the importance and value of true religion. Sir John Mason, who had been a privy counsellor to four successive monarchs, and was connected with the most important transactions of the state for thirty years, in the evening of his life declared, "Were I to live again, I would exchange the court for retirement, and the whole life I have lived in the palace for one hour's enjoyment of God in my closet. All things now forsake me, except my God, my duty, and my prayers."

It is said further of this eminent man, that at the close of life he observed, that the result of his observation and experience might be comprised in three short sentences:—Seriousness is the greatest wisdom; temperance the best physic; and a good conscience the best estate."

(*c*) PHILIP HENRY'S PRACTICE.—In the life of Philip Henry, it is said, "He and his wife constantly prayed together, morning and evening." He made conscience of closet worship, and abounded in it. It was the caution and advice which he frequently gave to his children and friends, "Be sure you look to your secret duty; keep that up, whatever you do; the soul cannot prosper in the neglect of it. Apostacy generally begins at the closet door."

(*d*) GRIMSTONE'S HABIT.—Sir Harbottle Grimstone, master of the rolls, an eminent lawyer, a just judge, and a person of large fortune, who lived in the 17th century, was a very pious and devout man, and spent, every morning and evening, at least an hour in meditation and prayer. And even in winter, when he was obliged to be very early on the bench, he took care to rise soon enough to have the time he usually devoted to these exercises.

(*e*) THE THREE METHODS.—The celebrated Haydn was in company with some distinguished persons. The conversation turned on the best means of restoring their mental energies, when exhausted with long and difficult studies. One said, he had recourse in such a case, to a bottle of wine—another that he went into company. Haydn being asked what he would do, or did do, said that he retired to his closet and engaged in prayer—that nothing exerted on his mind a more happy and efficacious influence than prayer. Haydn was no enthusiast.

(*f*) PAYING FOR PRAYING.—An aged burgomaster, traveling to Germany, stopped at an inn on the borders of that country and Holland. He observed that the servant girl who laid the cloth, and made other preparations for his supper, performed these offices neatly and with much alacrity, and he commended her, saying also, "I trust that, while you show yourself so careful in the performance of the common duties of your station, you are not less diligent in observing the duties and privileges of a Christian." The girl, who was quite ignorant of religion, replied by asking what he meant; upon which he entered more particularly into an explanation of his meaning, dwelling especially on the importance of prayer, as he found that she lived in entire neglect of it. Her countenance and manner indicated a strict adherence to truth, and he told her that if, when he again passed through the place, she could assure him that she had knelt down every night and morning, and uttered a short prayer, he would give her a ten-guilder piece, (a gold coin, value 16*s.* 8*d.*) After some hesitation the girl agreed, and asked what the prayer was, the repetition of which was to procure her a larger sum than she had ever before possessed at one time. The burgomaster told her, "Lord Jesus, convert my soul." At first, the girl hesitated, and sometimes thought that she might omit the repetition of these words, the full meaning of which she did not understand. A better feeling, however, induced her to continue, and also to inquire the meaning of these words.

About six months afterwards, the old gentleman returned; he went to the same inn; another girl laid his supper cloth; he inquired for her predecessor in vain. He then asked for the landlord, who told him that five months back the girl alluded to had been seized with such a praying fit, that he found she would no longer do for his service, and that she was then living with a private family in the neighborhood. In the morning the old gentleman sought for and found her; and said he was come to fulfil his promise. She immediately recognized him, but decidedly refused his offered money, saying, "I have found a reward much richer than any sum of gold."

(*g*) A SECRET OF SUCCESS.—Edward Lee, of Manchester, Massachusetts, was for several years a sailor, and apparently hardened in sin, but he became converted, and then all his energies were devoted to the service of Jesus Christ. Quitting the sea for the sake of being more useful, he took up his residence in his native village; and the time which could be spared from his labors on the farm, he employed in behalf of God's glory, and the salvation of souls. For thirty years he kept up a weekly prayer-meeting every Thursday afternoon in his own house. It was his rule to visit all the families in the village once in a year, to inquire after their spiritual welfare. The houses of affliction and sorrow were always sure of his visits and his prayers. In his own house, in the field, and on his journeys, wherever he could warn and plead with the impenitent, he was sure to do so. One night, putting up at an inn where a country ball had commenced, he got permission to enter the room, and addressed the company with such moral power and energy, that dancing was abandoned, and the evening, begun in mirth and folly, was spent in holy exhortation, and closed with prayer.

Mr. Lee gave away one eighth of his income, yet left enough to support his widow for thirty years after his death. Wonderful example of piety! What was the secret of his high attainments? He was a man of prayer! A few days before he died, he pointed his Christian friends to a spot on the floor, and observed that for more than thirty years, with the exception of ten days' illness, he had risen from his bed at night, and prayed for a dying world's salvation. His minister used to say, "I am but a babe to brother Lee: I prize his prayers more than gold."

(*h*) A SHEEPCOT FOR A CLOSET.—Dr. Milne, a laborious and useful Missionary in China, in his early years attended a Sabbath evening school, which was taught in the neighborhood of his residence. Here his knowledge of evangelical truth increased, and considerable impressions of its importance were made upon his mind. Sometimes he used to walk home from the school alone, about a mile over the brow of a hill, praying all the way. At this time he began the worship of God in his mother's family; and also held some meetings for prayer, with his sisters and other children, in a barn that belonged to the premises.

When removed from the immediate care of his mother, the providence of God placed him near to the spot where one of those persons lived, who, though poor in this world, are rich in faith, and heirs of the kingdom. He used sometimes to go to his house, at the hour of prayer, when he and his family bowed the knee and worshiped God, at the foot of their domestic altar. After reading a chapter in the Bible, he was accustomed to make some remarks upon it, both for the instruction of his children, and as a preparation for the solemn exercise of prayer; these remarks interested young Milne very much, and showed him a beauty in the word of God, which he never saw before. From this time, more particularly, he began to discover an excellence in religion, which led him to choose it as the only object deserving the supreme attention of an immortal creature. As the family in which he lived were strangers to religion themselves, and derided all others who made it their concern, he was very unpleasantly situated. The only place he found for retirement, where he could be quiet and unnoticed, was a sheepcot in which the sheep were kept in winter. Here, surrounded with his fleecy companions, he often bowed the knee on a piece of turf, which he carried with him for the purpose. Many hours did he spend there, in the winter evenings, with a pleasure to which before he was a stranger; and, while some of the members of the family were plotting how to put him to shame, he was eating in secret of that bread "which the world knoweth not of."

(*i*) SANCTUARY IN THE GROVE.—A correspondent of the N. Y. Evangelist remarks: While it is a subject of regret, that many professors of religion are so conformed to the world, as exceedingly to limit their usefulness, it is very refreshing to the spirits of holy ones, to meet with here and there a disciple living above the world, and at the same time shedding a holy influence on all around. Of this latter and better sort of Christians, I knew a man who departed this life at the advanced age of 94 years. His *whole business*, while I knew him, and as I have been told for about 80 of the last years of his life, had been to serve God and enlarge the kingdom of Christ on earth. His conversation was spiritual beyond that of any other man I ever knew. It was exceedingly difficult to interest him in any other subject than that of religion. The cause of his high spiritual attainments consisted in the fact, that he was more than any other person of my knowledge, a man of prayer.

On the day of his burial, when many friends were assembled to commit his remains to the tomb, the subject of his spirituality and holy living, became a topic of conversation. Said one, who was more intimately acquainted with the deceased than the rest, if you will take a short walk, I will let you into the great secret of our departed friend's holy life, and triumphant death. To this proposition a number of the relatives conceded. They were conducted along a narrow beaten footpath into a grove some fifty rods from the house. This grove was the chosen place for many years of this holy man for prayer and meditation. Soon after entering the grove, they came to the devoted spot, the sanctuary where the holy man had carried on his intercourse with the upper world. The very impress of his knees, as he bowed before the Mighty One of Israel, was distinctly visible. He supported himself in this attitude by two saplings, one on either side, which, by long and frequent use were worn smooth like polished steel. The place was often afterwards visited by the curious, and was ever regarded as one of the best mementoes of the worth of this departed saint. This footpath and the prints of the knees and hands were visible for some two or three years after the good man entered his *rest;* but are now overgrown and forgotten.

(*j*) PRAYER OF THE CONDEMNED SOLDIER.—During the unhappy commotions in Ireland, a private soldier in the army of Lord Cornwallis, was daily observed to be absent from his quarters and from the company of his fellow-soldiers. He began to be suspected of withdrawing himself for the purpose of holding intercourse with the rebels; and on this suspicion, probably increased by the malice of his wicked comrades, he was tried by a court-martial, and condemned to die. The Marquis hearing of this, wished to examine the minutes of the trial; and not being satisfied, sent for the man to converse with him. Upon being interrogated, the prisoner solemnly disavowed every treasonable practice or intention, declared his sincere attachment to his Sovereign, and his readiness to live and die in his service:—he affirmed that the real cause of his frequent absence was, that he might obtain a place of retirement for the purpose of private prayer; for which his Lordship knew he had no opportunity among his profane comrades, who had become his enemies merely on account of his profession of religion. He said, he had made this defence on his trial; but the officers thought it so improbable, that they paid no attention to it. The Marquis, in order to satisfy himself as to the truth of his defence, observed that if so, he must acquire some considerable aptness in this exercise. The poor man replied, that as to ability, he had nothing to boast of. The Marquis then insisted on his kneeling down and praying aloud before him; which he did,—and pouring forth his soul before God with such copiousness, fluency, and ardor, that the Marquis took him by the hand, and said, he was satisfied that no man could pray in that manner who did not live in the habit of intercourse wtth his God. He not only revoked the sentence, but received him into his peculiar favor, placing him among his personal attendants.

328. Family Prayer.

(*a*) FAMILY PRAYER ESTABLISHED BY A CHILD.—The Rev. John Baily, an eminent divine of the 17th century, was so honored of God as to be made the instrument of the conversion of his own father, while he was yet a child. His mother was a very pious woman, but his father was a wicked man. The good instructions and frequent prayers of the former, were so blessed to the soul of little John, that he was converted to God while very young: and having a remarkable gift in prayer, his mother wished him to pray in the family. His father, overhearing him engaged in this exercise, was so struck with remorse and shame at finding his child, then not above eleven or twelve years of age, performing that duty in his house, which he had neglected himself, that it brought on a deep conviction of his wretched state, and proved, through the Divine blessing, the means of his conversion.

(*b*) AN INFIDEL CONVERTED.—Mr. Abbott states, in his "MOTHER AT HOME," that a gentleman from England brought a letter of introduction to a gentleman in America. The stranger was of accomplished mind and manners, but an infidel. The gentleman to whom he had brought letters of introduction, and his lady, were active Christian philanthropists. They invited the stranger to make their house his home, and treated him with every possible attention. Upon the evening of his arrival, just before the usual hour for retiring, the gentleman, knowing the peculiarity of his friend's sentiments, observed to him, that the hour had arrived in which they usually attended family prayers; that he should be happy to have him remain and unite with them, or, if he preferred, he could retire. The gentleman intimated that it would give him pleasure to remain. A chapter of the Bible was read, and the family all knelt in prayer, the stranger with the rest. In a few days the stranger left this hospitable dwelling, and embarked on board a ship for a foreign land. In the course of three or four years, however, the providence of God again led that stranger to the same dwelling. But oh, how changed! He came the happy Christian, the humble man of piety and prayer. In the course of the evening's conversation he remarked, that when he, on the first evening of his previous visit, knelt with them in family prayer, it was the first time for many years that he had bowed the knee to his Maker. This act brought to his mind such a crowd of recollections, it so vividly reminded him of a parent's prayers, which he had heard at home, that he was entirely bewildered. His emotion was so great, that he did not hear one syllable of the prayer which was uttered, from its commencement to its close. But God made this the instrument of leading him from the dreary wilds of infidelity to the peace and the joy of piety. His parents had long before gone home to their eternal rest; but the prayers they had offered for and with their son, had left an influence which could not die. They might have prayed ever so fervently for him, but if they had not prayed with him, if they had not knelt by his side, and caused his listening ear to hear their earnest supplications, their child might have continued through life an infidel.

(*c*) FAMILY WORSHIP IN CEYLON.—At the annual meeting of the British and Foreign Bible Society, in 1826, the Rev. W. B. Fox, a Missionary from Ceylon, said, that as he was traveling in a jungle, in the dead of the night, which is the usual time for journeying, he heard a voice reading. He drew near to the cottage, and found that the party was reading the word of God. He put aside the leaves, of which the cottage was composed, and saw the whole group, consisting of three or four generations, sitting on the ground, while a youth was reading the 14th of St. John. He waited in silence, to see the result: and, at the conclusion, the boy began to invoke the Divine blessing on what he had read; and one of the petitions was very remarkable: he prayed that God would make larger the ears of his grandmother. Mr. F. supposed, from this circumstance, that his poor relative was so deaf that she could not hear those truths which he admired himself. He added, that these instances were formerly rare, but they were now spreading over the whole land; and though he was no prophet, yet he would venture to predict, that nothing like half a century would pass, ere it would be said, that there were no heathen temples, and no idols remaining in Ceylon.

(*d*) LOSS OF FAMILY PRAYER.—A young lady, the child of pious parents, had arrived at the years of maturity apparently without having any salutary impression made on her mind, either by the instructions she had received, or the examples she had witnessed. In this state of mind she received the addresses of a gentleman destitute of religion, and who, probably, had not possessed her early advantages. He was moral, respectable, and honorable in social life, and had no idea that any thing more was necessary. In due time they were married.

The worth of any blessing is often best taught by its loss. The very first day of her residence in the house of her husband, the young lady was struck with horror and distress at the omission of family prayers; and that the family separated at night, and met in the morning, and no Bible was called for; no expressions of gratitude offered for protection and refreshment through the night; no supplication for provision, direction, and support through the day. She felt desolate and uncomfortable; and that which she had so long disregarded in the house of her father, seemed now absolutely essential to her comfort. The deficiency was the means of awakening in her mind deep and serious convictions of her sin, in having failed to improve the privileges with which she had so long been favored. She was led to tremble at her awful state of guilt and danger as a sinner before God; she humbly and earnestly sought mercy through the blood of the cross, and found joy and peace in believing. Now, the instructions and admonitions of her pious parents, which had so long seemed to be like good seed rotting beneath the clod, began to spring up and yield fruit.

She said, "The God of my parents shall be my God;" and she gave herself up to him in a covenant never to be forgotten! She could not now be insensible to the best interests of her husband and family; these became matter of deep solicitude and fervent prayer. Her pious endeavors were blessed: her husband was awakened to discern the things that belonged to his everlasting peace, and was made a partaker of the grace of God in truth. Their household was soon numbered among those in whose tabernacles is heard the voice of rejoicing and salvation. They became eminently pious, exemplary, and useful characters, and trained up their children in the nurture and admonition of the Lord.

(*e*) FAMILY PRAYER ABANDONED AND RESUMED.—A pious tradesman, conversing with a minister on family worship, related the following instructive circumstances respecting himself:

When I first began business for myself, I was determined, through grace, to be particularly conscientious with respect to family prayer. Accordingly, I persevered for many years in the delightful practice of domestic worship. Morning and evening, every individual of my family was ordered to be present; nor would I allow my apprentices to be absent on any account. In a few years, the advantages of these engagements manifestly appeared; the blessings of the upper and nether springs followed me; health and happiness attended my family, and prosperity my business. At length, such was the rapid increase of trade, and the importance of devoting every possible moment to my customers, that I began to think whether family prayer did not occupy too much of our time in the morning. Pious scruples arose respecting my intentions of relinquishing this part of my duty; but, at length, worldly interests prevailed so far as to induce me to excuse the attendance of my apprentices, and, not long after, it was deemed advisable, for the more eager prosecution of business, to make the prayer with my wife, when we rose in the morning, suffice for the day.

Notwithstanding the repeated checks of conscience that followed this base omission, the calls of a flourishing concern, and the prospect of an increasing family, appeared so imperious and commanding, that I found an easy excuse for this fatal evil, especially as I did not omit prayer altogether. My conscience was now almost seared with a hot iron; when it pleased the Lord to awaken me by a singular providence.

One day I received a letter from a young man who had formerly been my apprentice, previous to my omitting family prayer. Not doubting but I continued domestic worship, his letter was chiefly on this subject; it was couched in the most affectionate and respectful terms: but judge of my surprise and confusion, when I read these words: "O, my dear master, never, never shall I be able sufficiently to thank you for the precious privilege with which you indulged me in your family devotions! O, sir, eternity will be too short to praise my God for what I learned there. It was there I first beheld my lost and wretched state as a sinner; it was there that I first knew the way of salvation; and there that I first experienced the preciousness of 'Christ in me, the hope of glory.' O, sir, permit me to say, never, never neglect those precious engagements: you have yet a family, and more apprentices, may your house be the birth-place of their souls!" I could read no further; every line flashed condemnation in my face. I trembled, I shuddered, I was alarmed lest the blood of my children and apprentices should be demanded at my soul-murdering hands.

Filled with confusion, and bathed in tears, I fled for refuge in secret. I spread the letter before God. I agonized, and—but you can better conceive than I can describe my feelings; suffice it to say, that light broke in upon my disconsolate soul, and a sense of blood-bought pardon was obtained. I immediately flew to my family, presented them before the Lord, and from that day to the present I have been faithful, and am determined, through grace, that whenever my business becomes so large as to interrupt family prayer, I will give up the superfluous part of my business and retain my devotion: better to lose a few shillings, than become the deliberate murderer of my family, and the instrument of ruin to my own soul.

(*f*) RYLAND AND THE INKEEPER'S FAMILY.—The Rev. John Ryland, of Northampton, being on a journey, was overtaken by a violent storm, and compelled to take shelter in the first inn he came to. The people of the house treated him with great kindness and hospitality. They would fain have showed him into the parlor, but being very wet and cold, he begged permission rather to take a seat by the fireside with the family. The good old man was friendly, cheerful, and well stored with entertaining anecdotes, and the family did their utmost to make him comfortable: they all supped together, and both the residents and the guest seemed mutually pleased with each other. At length, when the house was cleared, and the hour of rest approached, the stranger appeared uneasy, and looked up every time a door opened, as if expecting the appearance of something essential to his comfort. His host informed him, that his chamber was prepared whenever he chose to retire. "But," said he, "you have not had your family together." "Had my family together! for what purpose? I don't know what you mean;" said the landlord. "To read the Scriptures, and to pray with them," replied the guest: "surely you do not retire to rest in the omission of so necessary a duty." The landlord confessed that he had never thought of doing such a thing. "Then, sir," said Mr. R., "I must beg you to order my horse immediately." The landlord and family entreated him not to expose himself to the inclemency of the weather at that late hour of the night; observing, that the storm was as violent as when he first came in. "May be so," replied Mr. R., "but I had rather brave the storm than venture to sleep in a house where there is no prayer. Who can tell what may befall us before morning? No, sir, I dare not stay." The landlord still remonstrated, and expressing great regret that he should offend so agreeable a gentleman, at last said, he should have no objection to "call his family together," but he should not know what to do when they came. Mr. R. then proposed to conduct family worship, to which all readily consented. The family was immediately assembled, and then Mr. R. called for a Bible; but no such book could be produced. However, he was enabled to supply the deficiency, as he always carried a small Bible or Testament in his pocket. He read a portion of Scripture, and then prayed with much fervor and solemnity, especially acknowledging the preserving goodness of God, that none present had been struck dead by the storm, and imploring protection through the night. He earnestly prayed that the attention of all might be awakened to the things belonging to their everlasting peace, and that the family might never again meet in the morning, or separate at night, without prayer. When he rose from his knees, almost every individual present was bathed in tears, and the inquiry was awakened in several hearts—"Sir, what must we do to be saved?" Much interesting and profitable conversation ensued. The following morning, Mr. R. again conducted family worship, and obtained from the landlord a promise, that however feebly performed, it should not in future be omitted. This day was indeed the beginning of days to that family; most, if not all of them, became decided and devoted followers of the Lord Jesus Christ, and were the means of diffusing a knowledge of the gospel in a neighhorhood which had before been proverbially dark and destitute.

(*g*) GOOD EXAMPLE OF A MAYOR.—Sir Thomas Abney was the beloved friend of the celebrated Dr. Watts, who found in his house an asylum for more than thirty-six years. This knight was not more distinguished by his hospitality than his piety. Neither business nor pleasure interrupted his observance of public and domestic worship. Of this a remarkable instance is recorded: upon the evening of the day that he entered on his office as lord mayor of London, without any notice, he withdrew from the public assembly at Guildhall after supper, went to his house, there performed family worship, and then returned to the company.

(*h*) HOWARD'S PRACTICE.—Mr. Howard, the philanthropist, never neglected the duty of family prayer, even though there was but one, and that one his domestic, to join in it; always declaring, that where he had a tent, God should have an altar. This was the case. not only in England, but in every part of Europe which they visited together, it being the invariable practice, wherever, and with whomsoever he might be, to tell Tomasson to come to him at a certain hour, at which, well knowing what the direction meant, he would be sure to find him in his room, the doors of which he would order him to fasten; when, let who would come, nobody was admitted till this devotional exercise was over. "Very few," says the humble narrator, "knew the goodness of this man's heart."

(*i*) THE DISCOURAGED FATHER.—The Rev. A. D. Merrill states that there was once a pious father with seven children, who had maintained the worship of God in his family, until all his children had grown up to manhood, and womanhood, and not one of them had been as yet converted to God. At last the old man's faith began to fail, in relation to the promise; and growing "weary and faint in his mind," he resolved to give up his family worship, and confine his devotions to the closet, and to leave his children to do as they pleased. But before he finally proceeded to do this, he concluded to call his children together once again, to pray with them, and explain to them his reasons for this course. Being assembled, and taking up the "old family Bible," from which he had so often read to them "the words of eternal life," he thus addressed them:—"My children, you know that from your earliest recollection I have been accustomed to call you together around this altar, for family worship. I have endeavored to instruct you in the ways of the Lord, and to imbue your minds with the truth. But you have all grown up, and not one of you is converted to God. You are yet in your sins, and show no signs of penitence. I feel discouraged, and have concluded to make no further efforts for your salvation—to demolish my family altar—to confine my own devotions to my closet, and thus to endeavor still to work out my own salvation, while I leave you to yourselves." Upon his speaking thus, first one and then another fell upon their knees, until they were all bowed before God, and besought him, that he would not do as he had resolved, but, that he would still continue to pray for them, and that he would do it now; for they were now ready to give their hearts to God. He bowed with them. The Spirit descended according to the promise, and before they rose from their knees, they were all made happy in God. One of their number who was married, and away from home, upon returning on a visit, and hearing what great things the Lord had done for the rest of the family, likewise immediately submitted to God, and thus were they all saved, and the covenant promise fulfilled.

(*j*) FAMILY PRAYER BY TWO DAUGHTERS.—A gentleman residing in the western part of the state of New-York, had sent two of his daughters to Litchfield, to be educated. While they were there, God was pleased to bless the place with a revival of religion. The news of it reached the ears of their father. He was much troubled for his daughters, "apprehensive," to use his own words, "lest their minds should be affected, and they be frightened into religion."

Alive, as he thought, to their happiness, and determined to allay their fears, and quiet their distresses, he sent a friend to Litchfield, with positive orders to bring them immediately home, that they might not be lost to all happiness and hope, and consigned to gloom and despondency.

The messenger departed on this errand. But they had already chosen Christ for their portion, and had resolved that, whatever others might do, they would serve the Lord.

They returned to their father's, not overwhelmed, as he expected, with gloom and despondency, but with hearts glowing with gratitude to God, and countenances beaming with serenity and hope. Indeed, they rejoiced in the Savior.

Soon after their return home, they were anxious to establish family worship. They affectionately requested their father to commence that duty. He replied, that he saw no use in it. He had lived very well more than fifty years without prayer, and he could not be burdened with it now. They then asked permission to pray with the family themselves. Not thinking they would have confidence to do it, he assented to the proposition.

The duties of the day being ended, and the hour for retiring to rest having arrived, the sisters drew forward to the stand, placed on it the Bible; one read a chapter—they both kneeled—the other engaged in prayer. The father stood, and while the humble fervent prayer of his daughter was ascending to heaven, his knees began to tremble; he also kneeled, and then became prostrate on the floor. God heard their prayer, and directed their father's weeping eyes, which had never shed tears of penitence before, to the Lamb of God, who taketh away the sin of the world.

Happy family! a believing father, and believing children! whose God is the Lord!

(*k*) "SIR, WHO HAVE YOU BEEN TALKING WITH?"—There lived in the town of —— in Vt. (says a correspondent of the Christian Mirror,) a man who had a large family of children. He was poor; and unable to keep them at home, he put some of them away from home to live. It was the favored lot of a little girl, I think, about eight years of age, to fall into a family, where daily prayers were offered up to Almighty God. Prayer she was unacquainted with. The subject was new to her. At home she never heard a prayer. An astonishment seized her, when she saw her master, night and morning, standing in one corner of the room, talking, as she termed it, with something that she could not see. An anxiety swelled in her little bosom to know who it could be. Unwilling to ask any one of the family with whom she lived, yet solicitous to know, she obtained leave to go home. She had hardly reached the lonely cottage, before she asked her mother who it was that her master talked with, when standing in the corner of the room night and morning. She told her that she did not know, being herself a heathen though in a Christian land. Not satisfied, she asked her father, who answered in a thoughtless and inhuman manner, "The devil I suppose." The little inquisitive child returned uninformed to her master, where she witnessed the same promptitude and holy ardor as before. Not many days had elapsed, before she summoned fortitude enough to put the question.

One morning, after her master had been talking with the unknown being, she stepped up before him, and said, "Sir, who have you been talking with this morning?" The question was so unexpected, and from such a source, that at first he felt unable to answer her; and was unusually impressed with the importance of the duty of prayer, and the weight of obligation resting upon him to approach God aright. But after recollecting himself a little, he said, and that with reverence, "I have been trying to talk with God." "God!" said she with astonishment, "where is he? where does he live?" &c. Many questions of a similar nature she put with much interest and feeling to which her master gave her such answers as were calculated to awaken the liveliest feelings of her mind, in regard to Jehovah. After she had learned all her little mind could contain of divine things, she desired to go home and see her parents, with an earnestness that could not be resisted. Go she must; leave was granted: she went home to her father's cottage, a place where prayer was not wont to be made, with her little bosom beating with a high tone of pious feeling in view of the importance of prayer. She went to her father, and said, "Father, pray." She urged with warmth a compliance; but he utterly refused. She then went to her mother and asked her to pray; but with no better success. She could not endure it any longer; her feelings must vent themselves in words. She said, let us pray.

She knelt down and prayed, and it appears to me, that scripture was fulfilled. "The effectual fervent prayer of the righteous availeth much." In answer to her prayer, both of her parents were brought under conviction, which terminated in hopeful conversion to God. And this was the beginning of an extensive revival of religion.

(*l*) SELF-CONVICTED COMMITTEE.—In a certain church, there were four brethren, heads of families, who were generally known to neglect the important social Christian duty of Family Prayer. The subject being introduced at a church meeting, it was proposed to appoint a committee to wait upon two of these brethren, and labor with them on this subject. When the committee was nominated, who should be named, but the two other brethren who were known by many to be guilty of the same neglect. They tried to shift off the appointment and excuse themselves, without, however, stating the true reason of their reluctance ; but it was all in vain, the vote was put, and these two were appointed the committee. They were now in rather an awkward situation—pretty sort of persons, thought they, to be appointed to labor with others for the neglect of family prayer, when we are guilty of the same ourselves. The result, however was good. The two brethren got together to talk the matter over, and concluded that they could not very well converse with the others, till they had reformed themselves. After conversing together, and reflecting alone, they were each convicted of the guilt of their criminal neglect. They assembled their families, confessed to them their guilt, re-established at once the family altar, and the Lord came down and blessed their souls. They were then ready to go and converse with the other two delinquents; they told them how they had been equally guilty, how they had repented of their sinful neglect, and how the Lord had blessed them and their families in erecting afresh the broken down family altar, and entreated them to do the same. The consequence was, that family prayer was immediately re-established in these families also, and at the next church meeting, the committee reported with tears in their eyes, that they had been successful in reclaiming not only their brethren, but also themselves, from the guilt and the inconsistency of those professedly Christian heads of families who call not upon the name of the Lord.

(*m*) THE SON'S ADMONITION.—My father, says Prof. B., was one of those still men who, much as he thought of company, carried on *his* part of conversation in brief questions and monosyllabic answers. He had deceived himself into the belief that his talents were not such as to make it his duty to conduct family worship. With this view, he had lived for more than forty years, in every *other* respect a consistent Christian. A son, who, at the time referred to, was preparing for the ministry, and already licensed to preach, was spending a vacation at home—the last evening of his stay had arrived—the family Bible, as usual, is placed before him on the stand, with a request to lead in prayer. The thought occurred, that now for a year or more, whatever devotion might be *felt*, no voice of prayer could be heard in the family, except from the lips of strangers who should turn in for the night. The thought affected him, and endeavoring to use such a manner as would become him in addressing a father almost threescore years and ten, he said—"Father, I delight to lead in this exercise when at home, but I am affected with the thought that there is to be no more prayer here, until I shall return. How is it that you have never established family prayer? I know the diffidence of your nature—I know that it would be hard to overcome it—but would it not have been attended with satisfaction to yourself, and a blessing to the family worth a far greater sacrifice? You can ask a favor of a neighbor—to do the same thing with God, is prayer: and he greatly mistakes, who thinks that the best prayer is that clothed in the most fluent language." The old man was affected—said he knew that it was so—and then gave an account of his feelings and practice in this respect since the commencement of his Christian course. Tears glistened in the eyes of some unaccustomed to weep for sin, and the father's expression gave encouragement to hope that the suggestion would not be in vain, and that an altar would still be erected, whence incense and a pure offering should daily rise to Heaven. On the day following, before leaving, the son mentioned the scene of the previous evening to the minister of the place, who took an opportunity to add his influence to what had been said, and it proved effectual. The man whose voice, though for forty years a professed Christian and a father, had never been heard in prayer by his children, at the age of threescore years and ten, commences the discharge of that duty in his family, and so far as I know never ceases until the infirmities of age render it impossible. His children, ten in number, who had not before, have since professed the religion of Christ, though I cannot say how much the father's prayers had to do with this result.

(*n*) FAMILY WORSHIP ESTABLISHED BY A CHILD.—A boy, about fourteen years of age, who had learned, at one of the schools belonging to the Gælic Society, the value of his own soul, was deeply impressed with the importance of family religion. As none of the family could read but himself, he intimated his intention of establishing family worship. No answer was made, no opposition started, and as little encouragement given. Still he made the attempt. He read the Scriptures, and prayed for himself, and for all present. The rest of the family looked on. Alone he continued to worship God in this manner for some time, the others being merely spectators; but at length, one after another sunk down on their knees beside him, until the whole domestic circle united in the hallowed exercise; the gray-headed father kneeling down beside his child, and joining in his artless aspirations to God the Father of all.

(*o*) A FAMILY CONVERTED.—A man in the western country removed into a new town and took the first measures to establish religious meetings. The Lord blessed his exertions; a church was formed of which he was chosen deacon, and a minister was settled His family grew up around him, but none of his children were converted, and he felt great anxiety lest *family prayer* should cease after he should be removed. He lived to be upwards of seventy years old, and all the time his constant prayer was, that God would have mercy on his children and not suffer the lamp of piety to go out in his house. One of the sons moved into the family mansion to take care of the old man, as his wife was dead. He still kept up family prayer as usual, never forgetting to pray for his son, that he might be converted and take his place at the family altar. A revival commenced in the town and the minister heard that there was something unusual at the old family mansion. He called to see them; in one room he beheld six or seven persons weeping, distressed for their sins, and the old man kneeling in one corner with his eyes and hands lifted up to heaven, crying to God to have mercy on his children. The minister attempted to address them, but found every thing he attempted to say far beneath the subject. God was there doing his own work—to this God he kneeled and prayed and then left them. The result was that the son, and several of his children were converted, and the good old man could say with Simeon, "Now Lord lettest thou thy servant depart in peace, for mine eyes have seen thy salvation.'

329. Giving Thanks at Meals.

(*a*) DON'T LET US FORGET.—At Lebanon, in the state of New York, there dwelt a certain man, about fifty years of age, who had not only lived a very careless life, but was an open opposer of the gospel plan of salvation, and of the work of God in the late revival of religion in that part of the country; he was, however, brought under serious convictions in the following manner:—One day there came into his house a traveler with a burden on his back; the family being about to sit down to dinner, the stranger was invited to partake with them, which he accordingly did. When the repast was finished, and the members of the family were withdrawing from their seats, the stranger said, "Don't let us forget to give thanks to God." He accordingly gave thanks, and departed. The man of the house felt reproved and confounded. The words of the stranger were fastened on his mind by the power of God. He was led to reflect on his wickedness in being unmindful of God, and in neglecting prayer and thanksgiving; he was also led to reflect on his manifold sins, which soon appeared to him a burden infinitely greater than that which the traveler bore. He found no relief until he sought in that very way which he used formerly to despise, through the peace-speaking blood of the Lord Jesus Christ.

(*b*) REBUKE ADMINISTERED.—Very salutary impressions have frequently been produced upon the minds of foreigners by the pious example of the native converts. I was on one occasion dining on board an English ship of war with Queen Pomare, other members of the royal family, and several chiefs. A large table was prepared on the quarter-deck. All being seated, the plates were soon abundantly supplied, but not one of the natives attempted to eat. The captain was greatly surprised at this, and said to me, "Mr. Pritchard, I fear we have not provided such food as the natives like; I don't see one of them begin to eat." I replied, "You could not have provided any thing that the natives would like better; the reason why they do not commence eating is simply this, they are accustomed always to ask a blessing." Before I could say any thing more, the captain evidently feeling a little confused, said, "I beg your pardon, Mr. Pritchard: please to say grace." I immediately "said grace," when the natives soon gave proof that they liked the food, which had been provided. One of the officers from the end of the table looked at the captain very significantly, and said, "We have got it to-day!" And then addressing himself to me he said, "Mr. Pritchard, you see what a *graceless* set we are." All the gentlemen seemed to feel the rebuke thus unintentionally given.

(*c*) THE KING OF TOOBOW.—The king of the island of Toobow, one of the Friendly Islands, avowed an attachment to Christianity. In the early part of 1823, he went on board a British vessel, to pay a visit to the captain and unconsciously conveyed a very forcible practical reproof to the party. He sat down at the captain's table to partake of some refreshment; though food was placed before him, he made a very observable pause; and when asked why he did not begin, he replied that he was waiting till a blessing had been asked on their food. The reproof was felt; and the party were ashamed at being rebuked by a man whose intellectual attainments they considered far inferior to their own. They rose, and the king gave thanks previously to their commencing the repast.

330. Social and Public Prayer.

(*a*) PRAYER MEETING ABANDONED.—In former times, there was a neighborhood some few miles from Philadelphia, where the inhabitants did not, it would seem, enjoy but seldom the blessings of a gospel ministry. Still, some of them were professors of religion, and for a long time they met together in a school-house in the capacity of a conference and prayer meeting. The spirit of religion, however, was so low among them, that their meetings were conducted with little interest and attended by a scanty number. At length, at the close of a lifeless service, some one proposed that the meetings thereafter should be abandoned. All assented but an aged mother in Israel, who, after a vain remonstrance, assured them that the worship of God should be kept up there, though she might have to keep it up alone. On the ensuing Sabbath she accordingly bent her solitary steps to the deserted sanctuary. She read a portion of Scripture, sang a hymn, and knelt down to weep and pray over the desolation of Zion. While engaged in this exercise, two men happened to be strolling by, and overhearing prayer, went in. What was their surprise on entering, to find but a single Christian present, where they expected to find an assembly. They took their seats and waited till she had got done. As she rose from her knees, seeing strangers present, she asked them to engage in prayer. They had probably never prayed in their lives, and accordingly, they peremptorily refused. Having, therefore, we presume, addressed them faithfully on the subject of religion, she sung another hymn, and once more addressed the throne of grace. At the close of the services, she gave out an appointment for a prayer meeting in the same place on the ensuing Sabbath. These men were not slack in publishing their singular visit to the school-house, or in circulating the notice of another meeting which was to be held there the next Lord's day. When the time arrived, some came from shame, perhaps, and more from curiosity, and so the school-house was filled! The Spirit of the Lord now began to work; Christians confessed their lukewarmness and devoted themselves afresh to the service of God; and sinners began to inquire, "What shall we do to be saved?" Indeed, there was a precious revival; and as the result, a church was constituted, and remains as a monument of that Christian woman's faithfulness to this day. One of the converts became a minister of the gospel, and labored in the western part of Pennsylvania, and was, perhaps, instrumental in the conversion of many souls. Despise not the day of small things. Keep up the prayer meetings.

(*b*) A PRAYER MEETING OF FORTY YEARS.—Mr. W——, of ——, N. Y., (says the writer of a tract,) was a plain man, a farmer, with a very limited common-school education. But he studied the Bible diligently, not to theorize, but that he might know the will of God, and do it. His piety was consistent, humble, meek, benevolent, active, uniform. He was acknowledged by all to be an every-day Christian.

At a time when the church was small and but two or three brethren lived in his vicinity, he consulted his pastor and established a neighborhood prayer meeting, to be held on Sabbath evening in the district school-house. In the circle of attendance there were sixteen or eighteen families, in very few of which the domestic altar had ever been erected. The meeting was commenced in the year 1800. Mr. W—— led it for twenty years, when, with a hope full of immortality, and a faith which triumphed over death, he entered his eternal rest.

Others were raised up, who have also gone to their reward. And after the lapse of forty years, when but two of the original heads of families yet live, the prayer meeting, which no heat or cold, no darkness or storm, breaks up, is still sustained and cherished with warm affection.

During the first year of the meeting, several parents and a few youth were brought publicly to profess Christ.—Then succeeded a long and severe trial of faith and perseverance. For fourteen years very few were added to the church, and "the ways of Zion mourned." Thoughtlessness and mirth prevailed. Few came to the prayer meeting, but it was never relinquished. Mr. W—— and one or two others, now in heaven, were always at their post, to pray and speak a word for the Redeemer, to warn sinners of the error of their way, and beseech them to become reconciled to God.

During the fourteenth year of this spiritual dearth, these individuals became so deeply affected in view of the condition of the impenitent, and so anxious that "Zion might arise and shine," that after others had retired from the school-house, they frequently remained one, two, or three hours in prayer. In the opening spring their hopes revived. The meetings became full and solemn. Their cries had reached heaven, and the Holy Spirit came down. One evening, a youth who had been deeply impressed for several days, could no longer suppress his feelings. He gave vent to his burdened heart by a single expression of warning to his companions, which carried conviction to several other minds, and from that hour a deep solemnity pervaded the neighborhood, and resulted in a glorious and powerful work of grace. The means, blessed of God, were personal conversation, family visiting, and more frequent prayer meetings, all conducted among themselves, with very little ministerial help.

The revival continued for two years, and spread not only through that congregation, but into neighboring churches, and hundreds renounced their sins and consecrated themselves to God. In this district nearly every family had now erected a family altar, and nearly every adult was rejoicing in hope of the glory of God. Other seasons of refreshiug have been enjoyed, and eternity alone can make known the number of souls that nave been and will be converted in answer to the prayers offered in that school-room. Some whole households down to the second and third generations, give evidence that they will be united in the great family above. And as another result, not less than ten men have been raised up in these families to preach the blessed gospel.

(*c*) THE AGED LADY AND THE PRAYER MEETING.—A pious old lady, (says the Religious Intelligencer,) in a country town, has long been in the habit of attending religious conference meetings, for, like many others, she had often found them refreshing. It happened, however, as in many other places, religion had got to a low ebb—the ways of Zion mourned because few came to her solemn feasts—the love of Christians had waxed cold—the wise and the foolish were alike asleep, and they gave up conference meetings entirely. I am inclined to think, however, that it was because they gave up these meetings and neglected other duties, that they became so cold and stupid; be that as it may, the old lady could not bear to give them up; she spoke to one and another of the brethren to introduce them again; but with one accord they replied, "We have worn them quite out, nobody will attend." Not satisfied, the old lady said she would go, if nobody else went. Accordingly, the next Wednesday evening she took her hymn-book and walked some distance to the school-house where the meetings used to be held—here she prayed, and sung, and prayed. On her way home she stopped at a neighbor's house to rest. "Where have you been?" said the neighbor. "Why, I have been to conference." "To conference! I didn't know there was one—who was there?" "O, God was there, and I was there, and we have had a good conference; and there is to be another next Wednesday evening."—Accordingly, next week the old lady went as before; but what was her joy and surprise to find the house was crowded; her pious zeal had admonished professors; Christians were awakened; sinners were alarmed; and verily, God was there, and from that time has been carrying on a glorious work of grace in that place.

(*d*) DR. FRANKLIN'S PROPOSAL.—While the important question of the representation of the American States in the senate was the subject of debate, and the states were almost equally divided upon it, Dr. Franklin moved that prayers should be attended in the convention every morning, and in support of his motion, thus addressed the president:

"Mr. President: The small progress we have made after four or five weeks of close attendance and continual reasonings with each other, our different sentiments on almost every question, several of the last producing as many noes as ayes, is, methinks, a melancholy proof of the imperfection of the human understanding. We indeed seem to feel our own want of political wisdom, since we have been running all about in search of it. We have gone back to ancient history for models of government, and examined the different forms of republics, which, having been originally formed with the seeds of their own dissolution, now no longer exist; and we have viewed modern states all around Europe, but find none of their constitutions suitable to our circumstances. In this situation of this assembly, groping, as it were, in the dark, to find political truth, and scarcely able to distinguish it when presented to us, how has it happened, sir, that we have not hitherto once thought of humbly applying to the Father of lights, to illuminate our understandings? In the beginning of the contest with Great Britain, and when we were sensible of danger, we had daily prayers in this room for Divine protection. Our prayers, sir, were heard, and they were graciously answered. All of us who were engaged in the struggle, must have observed frequent instances of a superintending Providence in our favor. To that kind Providence we owe this happy opportunity of consulting in peace, on the means of establishing our future national felicity. And have we now forgotten that powerful Friend? or do we imagine we no longer need his assistance? I have lived, sir, a long time, and the longer I live, the more convincing proofs I see of this truth—that God governs in the affairs of men. And if a sparrow cannot fall to the ground without his notice, is it probable that an empire can rise without his aid? We have been assured, sir, in the sacred writings, that 'except the Lord build the house, they labor in vain that build it.' I firmly believe this; and I also believe, that without this concurring aid, we shall succeed in this political building no better than the builders of Babel; we shall be divided by our little partial local interests, our projects will be confounded, and we ourselves shall become a reproach and a by-word to future ages. And what is worse, mankind may hereafter, from this unfortunate instance, despair of establishing governments by human wisdom, and leave it to chance, war, or conquest. I therefore beg leave to move, that henceforth prayers, imploring the assistance of Heaven, and its blessings on our deliberations, be held in this assembly every morning before we proceed to business; and that one or more of the clergy of this city be requested to officiate in that service."

What a lesson to the legislators of other nations!

(*e*) FORGETTING THE OFFENCE.—A person came to Mr. Longdon one day and said, "I have something against you, and I am come to tell you of it." "Do walk in, sir," he replied; "you are my best friend: if I could but engage my friends to be faithful with me, I should be sure to prosper; but, if you please, we will both pray in the first place, and ask the blessing of God upon our interview." After they rose from their knees, and had been much blessed together, he said, "Now I will thank you, my brother, to tell me what it is that you have against me." "Oh," said the man, "I really don't know what it is; it is all gone, and I believe I was in the wrong."

PRAYER ANSWERED.

331. Prayer Answered by God's Providential Control of Material and Animal Agencies.

(*a*) THE PILGRIM FATHERS AND THE DROUGHT.—It is well known, that many of the good men who were driven from England to America, by persecution, in the seventeenth century, had to endure great privations. A numerous party, who came out about 1620, were for a time supplied with food from England, and from the natives of the western wilderness. But as these resources were uncertain, they began to cultivate the ground. In the spring of 1623, they planted more corn than ever before, but by the time they had done planting, their food was spent. They daily prayed, "Give us this day our daily bread;" and, in some way or other, the prayer was always answered. With a single boat and fishing-net they caught bass, and when these failed, they dug for clams. In the month of June, their hopes of a harvest were nearly blasted by a drought, which withered up their corn, and made the grass look like hay. All expected to perish with hunger.

In their distress, the pilgrims set apart a day for humiliation and prayer, and continued their worship for eight or nine hours. God heard their prayers, and answered them in a way which excited universal admiration. Although the morning of that day was clear, and the weather very hot and dry during the whole forenoon, yet before night it began to rain, and gentle showers continued to fall for many days, so that the ground became thoroughly soaked, and the drooping corn revived.

(*b*) THE SOUTH SEA ISLANDERS.—About the time when the Gospel was beginning to make its way in

Ra atea, a canoe, with four men in it, was upset at sea, and the men were thrown into the water, where, though nearly amphibious, they must have been drowned, the waves drifting them to and fro, unless speedily carried to shore, or taken up by some vessel. Two of the men having embraced Christianity, immediately cried out, "Let us pray to Jehovah; for he can save us." "Why did you not pray to him sooner?" replied their pagan comrades: "here we are in the water, and it is useless to pray now." The Christians, however, did cry mightily unto their God, while all four were clinging for life to their broken canoe. In this situation, a shark suddenly rushed towards them, and seized one of the men. His companions held him as fast and as long as they could; but the monster prevailed, and hurried the unfortunate victim into the abyss, marking the track with his blood. He was one of the two who were idolaters. After some time, the tide bore the surviving three to the reef, when, just as they were cast upon it, a second shark snatched the other idolater with his jaws, and carried off his prey, shrieking in vain for assistance, which the two Christians, themselves struggling with the breakers, could not afford him. This circumstance very naturally made a great impression upon the minds of their countrymen, and powerfully recommended to them the "God that heareth prayer."

(c) LUTHER'S PRAYER FOR MELANCTHON.—At a certain time Luther received an express, stating that his bosom friend and co-worker in the reformation, Philip Melancthon, was lying at the point of death; upon which information he immediately set out upon the journey of some 150 miles, to visit him, and upon his arrival, he actually found all the distinctive features of death; such as the glazed eye, the cold clammy sweat, and insensible lethargy, upon him. Upon witnessing these sure indications of a speedy dissolution, as he mournfully bent over him, he exclaimed with great emotion, "Oh, how awful is the change wrought upon the visage of my dear brother!" On hearing this voice, to the astonishment of all present, Melancthon opened his eyes, and looking up into Luther's face, remarked, "Oh Luther, is this you? Why don't you let me depart in peace?" Upon which Luther replied, "O no, Philip, we cannot spare you yet." Luther then turned away from the bed, and fell upon his knees, with his face towards the window, and began to wrestle with God in prayer, and to plead with great fervency, for more than an hour, the many proofs recorded in Scripture of his being a prayer-hearing and prayer-answering God; and also how much he stood in need of the services of Melancthon, in furthering that cause, in which the honor and glory of God's great name, and the eternal welfare of unnumbered millions of immortal souls, were so deeply interested; and that God should not deny him this one request, to restore him the aid of his well tried brother Melancthon. He then rose up from prayer, and went to the bedside again, and took Melancthon by the hand. Upon which Melancthon again remarked, "Oh, dear Luther, why don't you let me depart in peace?" To which Luther again answered, "No, no, Philip, we cannot possibly spare you from the field of labor yet." Luther then requested the nurse to go and make him a dish of soup, according to his instructions. Which being prepared, was brought to Luther, who requested his friend Melancthon to eat of it. Melancthon again asked him, "Oh, Luther, why will you not let me go home, and be at rest?" To which Luther replied as before, "Philip, we cannot spare you yet." Melancthon then exhibited a disinclination to partake of the nourishment prepared for him. Upon which Luther remarked, "Philip, eat, or I will excommunicate you."—Melancthon then partook of the food prepared, and immediately grew better, and was speedily restored to his wonted health and strength again, and labored for years afterwards with his coadjutors in the blessed cause of the reformation.

Upon Luther's arrival at home, he narrated to his beloved wife Catharine the above circumstances, and added, "God gave me my brother Melancthon back in direct answer to prayer;" and added further, with patriarchal simplicity, "God on a former occasion gave me, also, you back, Kata, in answer to my prayer."

(*d*) PRAYER FOR FAIR WEATHER.—In the life of the Rev. Robert Blair, a Scottish minister of the seventeenth century, the following passage occurs:

"There having been incessant rain for a month in harvest, the corn was growing a finger length in the sheaves, and the whole crop was in hazard of perishing. In this deplorable situation, the people resolved solemnly, by humiliation and fasting, to beseech the Lord to avert the threatened famine. When the day came, it rained heavily from morning till night; so that the Lord seemed to be thrusting out their prayers from him. But that same night he sent a mighty wind, which did fully dry the corn and check the growing; and this wind continuing to blow fair for two days, the people ceased, neither night nor day, till the whole corn was got in. During these two days, I and two neighboring ministers were continuing our supplications and thanksgivings to the Lord for his great mercy."

(*e*) PRAYING FOR A LUNATIC.—Richard Cook, a pious man, during Mr. Baxter's residence at Kidderminster, went to live in the next house to him. After some time he was seized with melancholy, which ended in madness. The most skillful help was obtained, but all in vain. While he was in this state, some pious persons wished to meet to fast and pray in behalf of the sufferer; but Mr. Baxter, in this instance, dissuaded them from it, as he apprehended the case to be hopeless, and thought they would expose prayer to contempt in the eyes of worldly persons, when they saw it unsuccessful. When ten or a dozen years of affliction had passed over Richard Cook, some of the pious men referred to would no longer be dissuaded, but fasted and prayed at his house. They continued this practice once a fortnight for several months; at length the sufferer began to amend, his health and reason returned, and, adds Mr. Baxter, "he is now as well almost as ever he was, and so hath continued for a considerable time."

(*f*) TWO CHRISTIANS IN AVA.—The Rev. Eugenio Kincaid states, that among the first converts in Ava, were two men who had held respectable offices about the palace. Some time after they had been baptized, a neighbor determined to report them to government, and drew up a paper setting forth that these two men had forsaken the customs and religion of their fathers, were worshiping the foreigner's God, and went every Sunday to the teacher's house, &c. He presented the paper to the neighbors of the two disciples, taking their names as witnesses, and saying that he should go and present the accusation on the next day. The two Christians heard of it, and went to K. in great alarm, to consult as to what they should do. They said if they were accused to government, the mildest sentence they could expect would be imprisonment for life at hard labor, and perhaps they would be killed. K. told them that they could not flee from Ava, if they would; that he saw nothing he could do for them, and all that they could do was to trust in God. He then knelt with them, and besought God to protect them, and deliver them from the power of their enemies. They also prayed, and soon left K., saying that they felt more calm, and could leave the matter with God. That night the persecutor was attacked by a dreadful disease in the bowels, which so distressed him, that he roared like a madman; and his friends, as is too often the case with the heathen, left him to suffer and die alone. The two Christians whom he would have ruined, then went and took care of him till he died, two or three days after his attack. The whole affair was well known in the neighborhood, and from that time not a dog dare move his tongue against the Christians of Ava. Is there no evidence in this of a special providence, and that God listens to the prayers of his persecuted and distressed children?

(*g*) ELLIOTT'S PRAYER FOR FOSTER.—Among many remarkable instances of the prevalence of prayer, which Dr. Mather in his Magnalia, mentions, the following anecdote of the celebrated Elliott deserves notice, which give in Dr. Mather's own words. There was a godly gentleman of Charlestown, one Mr. Foster, who, with his son was taken captive by the Turks. Much prayer was employed, both publicly and privately, by the good people here, for the redemption of that gentleman, but we were at last informed, that the bloody prince in whose dominion he was now a slave, was resolved, that in his lifetime, no prisoner should be released, and so the distressed friends of this prisoner now concluded, "*our hope is lost.*" Upon this, Mr. Elliot in some of his next prayers before a very solemn congregation, broadly begged, "*Heavenly Father, work for the redemption of thy poor servant, Foster; and if the Prince who detains him, will not, as they say, dismiss him, as long as himself lives; Lord, we pray thee to kill that cruel Prince: kill him and glorify thyself upon him.* And now behold the answer: the poor captive gentleman quickly returns to us, that had been mourning for him as a lost man, and brings us news that the Prince was come to an untimely death, by which means he was now set at liberty."

(*h*) THE COVENANTER'S PRAYER.—Mr. Alexander Peden, a Scotch Covenanter, with some others, had been, at one time, pursued both by horse and foot, for a considerable way. At last, getting some little height between them and their persecutors, he stood still and said, "Let us pray here, for if the Lord hear not our prayer and save us, we are all dead men." He then prayed, saying, "O Lord, this is the hour and the power of thine enemies, they may not be idle. But hast thou no other work for them than to send them after us? Send them after them to whom thou wilt gi'e strength to flee, for our strength is gane. Twine them about the hill, O Lord, and cast the lap of thy cloak over puir auld Saunders, and thir puir things, and save us this ae time, and we will keep it in remembrance, and tell to the commendation of thy guidness, thy pity and compassion, what thou didst for us at sic a time." And in this he was heard, for a cloud of mist immediately intervened between them and their persecutors; and in the meantime, orders came to go in quest of James Renwick, and a great company with him.

(*i*) THE FRENCH ARMAMENT.—The destruction of the French armament, under the Duke d'Anville, in the year 1746, ought to be remembered with gratitude and admiration by every inhabitant of this country. This fleet consisted of forty ships of war; was destined for the destruction of New England, was of sufficient force to render that destruction, in the ordinary progress of things, certain; and sailed from Chebucto, in Nova Scotia for this purpose.

In the meantime, our pious fathers, apprised of their danger, and feeling that their only safety was in God, had appointed a season of fasting and prayer to be observed in all their churches. "While Mr. Prince was officiating" in this church (Old South Church) on this fast day, and praying most fervently to God, to avert the dreaded calamity, a sudden gust of wind arose, (the day had till now been perfectly clear and calm,) so violent as to cause a loud clattering of the windows. The Rev. pastor paused in his prayer, and looking round upon the congregation with a countenance of hope, he again commenced, and with great devotional ardor, supplicated the Almighty God to cause that wind to frustrate the object of our enemies, and save the country from conquest and popery. A tempest ensued in which the greater part of the French fleet was wrecked on the coast of Nova Scotia. The Duke D'Anville the principal general, and the second in command, both committed suicide. Many died with disease, and thousands were consigned to a watery grave. The small number that remained alive, returned to France without health and without spirits. "And the enterprise was abandoned, and never again resumed."

(*j*) VESSEL SAVED BY PRAYER.—The following striking anecdote is recorded in the diary kept at Freidensburg, a settlement of the Moravians, in St. Croix:—

In March, 1819, Mr. Bell, a captain of a ship from Philadelphia, who is a religious man, living some time in this island, paid us several visits. One day he brought with him another captain from Baltimore, by the name of Boyle. Having for some time conversed on religious subjects, the latter inquired whether any of our family were on board an English vessel, with only six guns, and twenty-two men, which in the year 1814 was attacked by a North American privateer, of fourteen guns, and one hundred and twenty men, on her voyage to St. Thomas; and which, after a most desperate conflict beat off the American enemy. He added, that he supposed very fervent prayer had been offered up on board the vessel. Sister Ramock answered, that she was on board the English vessel, and could assure him that *there was.* "That I believe," replied the captain, "for I felt the effects of your prayers!" He then informed us, that he was the captain who commanded the privateer. "According to my wild way of thinking, at that time, I was determined to strain every nerve to get possession of the British vessel, or sink her; but she was protected by a higher power, against which all my exertions proved vain." This disappointment and defeat astonished him: but when he afterwards heard, that missionaries were on board the English vessel, it struck him, that the fervent prayers to God had brought them protection and safety. This led him to a further thought about these things; and at length, by God's mercy, to a total change of mind. On his making this statement, we joined him in thanking the Lord for his goodness. From this authentic fact, we learn that under all circumstances, however bad and hopeless, it is the Christian's duty to pray and not to faint; to exercise faith and hope in that Almighty Jehovah, whose ear is never heavy that he cannot hear, nor his hand shortened that he cannot save.

(*k*) THE INDIAN MOTHER'S PRAYER.—"Pummehanuit, an Indian of prime quality, on Martha's Vineyard, and his wife, had buried their first five children successively, every one within ten days of their birth, notwithstanding all their use of powows and of medicines to preserve them. They had a sixth child, (a son,) born about the year 1638, which was a few years before the English settled on the Vineyard. The mother was greatly perplexed with fear that she should lose this child like the former; and utterly despairing of any help from such means as had been formerly tried with so little success, as soon as she was able, with a sorrowful heart, she took up her child and went out into the field, that she might weep out her sorrows. While she was musing on the insufficiency of all human help, she felt it powerfully suggested to her mind that there is one Almighty God who is to be prayed unto, that this God had created all the things that we see—and that the God who had given being to herself, and all other people, and given her child unto her, was easily able to continue the life of her child.

Hereupon, this poor pagan woman resolved, that she would seek unto this God for that mercy, and did accordingly. The issue was, that her child lived, and her faith in Him who thus answered her prayer was wonderfully strengthened, the consideration whereof caused her to dedicate this child unto the service of that God who had preserved his life, and educated him, as far as might be, to become the servant of God.

Not long after this, the English came to settle on Martha's Vineyard; and the Indians who had been present at some of the English devotions, reported that they assembled together, and that the man who spoke among them often looked upwards. This woman, from this report, presently concluded that their assemblies were for prayers, and that their prayers were unto that very God whom she had addressed for the life of her child. She was confirmed in this when the gospel was not long after preached by Mr. Mayhew to the Indians; which gospel she readily, cheerfully, and heartily embraced. And in the confession that she made publicly at her admission into the church, she gave a relation of the preparation for the knowledge of Christ, wherewith God had in this remarkable way favored her. Her child, whose name was Japhet, became afterwards an eminent min ister of Christ. He was pastor of an Indian church, on Martha's Vineyard ; he also took much pains to carry the gospel unto other Indians on the main land, and his labors were attended with much success."

(*l*) THE GUARDED HOUSE.—When the year 1814 began, troops of Swedes, Cossacks, Germans, and Russians, were within half an hour's march of the town of Sleswick ; and new and fearful reports of the behavior of the soldiers were brought from the country every day. There had been a truce, which was to come to an end at midnight of the 5th of January, which was now drawing near.

On the outskirts of the town, on the side where the enemy lay, there was a house standing alone, and in it there was an old pious woman, who was earnestly praying, in the words of an ancient hymn, that God would raise up a wall around them, so that the enemy might fear to attack them.

In the same house dwelt her daughter, a widow, and her grandson, a youth of twenty years. He heard the prayer of his grandmother, and could not restrain himself from saying, that he did not understand how she could ask for any thing so impossible, as that a wall should be built around them, which could keep the enemy away from their house. The old woman, who was now deaf, caused what her grandson said to be explained to her, but only answered that she had but prayed in general for protection for themselves and their town people. "However," she added, "do you think that if it were the will of God to build a wall around us, it would be impossible to him ?"

And now came the dreaded night of the 5th of January ; and about midnight the troops began to enter on all sides. The house we were speaking of lay close by the road, and was larger than the dwellings near it, which were only very small cottages. Its inhabitants looked out with anxious fear, as parties of the soldiers entered one after another, and even went to the neighboring houses to ask for what they wanted ; but all rode past their dwelling. Throughout the whole day there had been a heavy fall of snow—the first that winter—and towards evening the storm became violent to a degree seldom known. At length came four parties of Cossacks, who had been hindered by the snow from entering the town by another road. This part of the outskirts was at some distance from the town itself and therefore they would not go further ; so that all the houses around that where the old woman lived, were filled with these soldiers, who quartered themselves in them ; in several houses there were fifty or sixty of these half-savage men. It was a terrible night for those who dwelt in this part of the town, filled to overflowing with the troops of the enemy.

But not a single soldier came into the grandmother's house ; and amidst the loud noises and wild sounds all around, not even a knock at the door was heard, to the great wonder of the family within. The next morning, as it grew light, they saw the cause. The storm had drifted a mass of snow, to such a height, between the roadside and the house, that to approach it was impossible. "Do you not now see, my, son," said the old grandmother, "that it was possible for God to raise a wall around us ?"

Does not this story remind us of the words—"The angel of the Lord encampeth round about them that fear Him and delivereth them !" Does it not seem as if the snow had been gathered together as by angels' hands to form a defence for that house where one dwelt who thus feared God and trusted in him ?

(*m*) THE TIDE RETARDED.—"In the number of providential interpositions in answer to prayer," says Le Clerc, "may be placed what happened on the coast of Holland, in the year 1672. The Dutch expected an attack from their enemies by sea, and public prayers were ordered for their deliverance. It came to pass, that whem their enemies waited only for the tide, in order to land, the tide was retarded, contrary to its usual course, for twelve hours ; so that their enemies were obliged to defer the attempt to another opportunity, which they never found, because a storm arose afterwards, and drove them from the coast."

332. Prayer answered by God's Providential Control of Men's Minds.

(*a*) THE WELL-TIMED LOAF.—A lady, who had just sat down to breakfast, had a strong impression on her mind, that she must instantly carry a loaf of bread to a poor man, who lived about half a mile from her house, by the side of a common. Her husband wished her either to postpone taking it till after breakfast, or to send it by a servant; but she chose to take it immediately herself. As she approached the hut, she heard the sound of a human voice, and wishing to discover what was said, she stepped unperceived to the door. She heard the poor man praying, and among other things he said, "O Lord, help me; Lord, thou wilt help me; thy promise cannot fail: although my wife, myself, and children, have no bread to eat, and it is now a whole day since we had any. I know thou wilt supply me, though thou shouldst again rain down manna from heaven." The lady could wait no longer, but opening the door, "Yes," she replied, "God has sent you relief. Take this loaf, and be encouraged to cast your care upon Him who careth for you; and whenever you want a loaf of bread, come to my house."

(*b*) SLAVE'S PRAYER.—A missionary in India, passing one day through the school-room, observed a little boy engaged in prayer, and overheard him say, "O Lord Jesus, I thank thee for sending big ship into my country, and wicked men to steal me, and bring me here that I might hear about thee, and love thee; and now, Lord Jesus, I have one great favor to ask thee, please to send wicked men with another big ship, and let them catch my father and my mother, and bring them to this country, that they may hear the missionaries preach, and love thee." The missionary in a few days after, saw him standing on the sea shore, looking very intently as the ships came in. "What are you looking at, Tom?" "I am looking to see if Jesus Christ answer prayer." For two years he was to be seen day after day, watching the arrival of every ship. One day, as the missionary was viewing him, he observed him capering about, and exhibiting the liveliest joy. "Well, Tom, what occasions so much joy?" "O, Jesus Christ answer prayer—father and mother come in that ship;" which was actually the case.

(*c*) FRANCKE'S SCHOOL AT HALLE.—The conduct of the eminent and justly celebrated Francke, in the establishment of the hospital and school for the poor, at Halle, near Glaucha, in Saxony, is well known. Having no permanent funds to meet the expenses, it may be easily supposed that the good man would frequently be reduced to great difficulties; at such times the interpositions of the providence of God were truly remarkable. About Easter, 1696, he knew not where to obtain money for the expenses of the ensuing week; but when their food was reduced to the very last morsel, one thousand crowns were contributed by some entirely unknown person. At another time, all their provisions were exhausted, and the good minister wisely presented his requests to the God of mercy, who careth even for the ravens when they cry. When prayer was over, just as he was taking his seat, a friend from a distance arrived with fifty crowns, which was shortly followed by twenty more. At another period, the workmen wanted thirty crowns, when he remarked that he had no money, but that he trusted in God; scarcely had he uttered the sentence, when, in this moment of necessity, the precise sum arrived.

"Another time," says Francke, "all our provision was spent; but, in addressing myself to the Lord, I found myself deeply affected with the fourth petition of the Lord's prayer, 'Give us this day our daily bread;' and my thoughts were fixed in a more especial manner upon the words 'this day,' because on the very same day we had great occasion for it. While I was yet praying, a friend of mine came before my door in a coach, and brought the sum of four hundred crowns!"

(*d*) THE LUNATIC RESTORED.—The following particulars, says the Columbian Star, are communicated by a friend, who received the information immediately from one of the brethren who attended the prayer meeting.

The daughter of a very eminent Christian, and a deacon of the Baptist church at Birmingham in England, married a respectable merchant of the city of Bristol (distant from each other about 100 miles), and at a subsequent period (such was the will of Providence) by one sudden and unexpected loss at sea, he was nearly ruined. This news gave such a shock to his amiable companion, that she was rendered altogether insane, and that to such a degree, that it was necessary to confine her in order to prevent her from doing herself and others harm. Her distressed situation was immediately communicated by a letter to her father, who on receiving it, like one of old, "conferred not with flesh and blood," but presented the case before his heavenly Father; and in the evening gathered together at his house many of his brethren in the church for the purpose of pleading with God in her behalf. It was a season of solemn and united supplication to the Lord. He answered prayer; for a few days after a letter was received by her father informing him that on such an hour, her reason returned, she sat up in bed, her bands of confinement were removed, and she was, as it were, in an instant restored to her usual health. That evening and that hour of restoration, were the *same evening*, and the *same hour* when many were gathered together and prayer was made unto God for her.

333. Prayer answered by the Agency of the Holy Spirit in various interesting Conversions.

(*a*) THE PRAYING SISTERS.—Two young men, members of a family the greater number of whom were devoted to God, left the house of their widowed mother, to reside in a distant state. After a little while they imbibed exceedingly erroneous views of religion, and were thus exposed to the utmost danger. Their sisters heard of their errors, and resolved to seek their deliverance from them by earnest prayer. They agreed separately to spend half an hour at sunset every Saturday evening in fervent supplication for their brothers. The hearer of prayer was not unmindful of their requests. The two brothers were awakened to a sense of their danger, and hopefully converted to God.

(*b*) AN INFIDEL CONVERTED.—A writer in the Christian Witness, speaking of the conversion of some of Abner Kneeland's followers, says: One is so remarkable that we cannot forbear relating it to our readers. The subject of it is a young man, engaged in a public establishment, and in the employ of a pious individual. His former efforts to introduce his baneful doctrines into the establishment, were a source of great annoyance to his employer. He embraced every opportunity to expose to visitors his utter contempt of all the sacred things of the gospel.—His bold blasphemies, and his scornful sneers, were alike shocking to decency and religion. The vile print which weekly disseminates its moral poison through our community, he contrived as frequently as possible to bring under the notice of the visitors of the establishment, though his employer as vigilantly sought to destroy it, whenever introduced there.—Withal, he was given to occasional fits of intemperance, in which his treatment to his family rendered him a terror, where he ought to have been a comfort and support. His great usefulness in the establishment, alone reconciled his employer to the utterance of his wicked principles, and his vicious conduct. To manifest his contempt for the ordinances of religion, and his open defiance of the God of the Bible, he laid a wager with his profane companions, that he would attend a Methodist prayer meeting in his neighborhood, and go forward to be *prayed for*. And now mark how God brings good out of evil. He went—and his hardihood carried him through the accomplishment of his wicked purpose. But perhaps his conscience was not so much at ease as his demeanor indicated; perhaps the rude impertinence of his blasphemy startled even his own proud heart, and awakened his attention to the things he was endeavoring to ridicule; perhaps his character and purposes were known to "the sons of God," so that they adapted their supplications to the dreadful enormity of his sins. Whatever may have been the immediate influence by which he was moved, certain it is that the Spirit of God strove with him, and subdued the stubborn rebellion of his heart. Conscience arose in its intended and outraged majesty; and like Esau, when he had lost his birthright, he "lifted up a great and bitter cry." He went forth from the house of prayer, his spirit bowed within him, and his very frame sympathizing in its strong commotion. He has found peace in believing. The influence of his change wrought upon her with whose happiness his principles had hardly less to do than with his own; and they both entered on probation as candidates for full communion in the denomination by whose pious instrumentality the husband was first called to the knowledge of the truth.

(*c*) THE BEGGAR'S PRAYER. A wealthy merchant in this country once gave the following account:—As he was standing at his door, a venerable gray-headed man approached him and asked an alms. He answered him with severity, and demanded why he lived so useless a life. The beggar answered that "age disabled him for labor and he had committed himself to the providence of God, and the kindness of good people." The rich man was at this time an infidel. He ordered the old man to depart, at the same time casting some reflections on the providence of God. The venerable beggar descended the steps, and kneeling at the bottom offered up the following prayer:—"O my gracious God, I thank thee that my bread and water are sure; but I pray thee, in thy intercession above, to remember this man; he hath reflected on thy providence. Father! forgive him, he knows not what he saith." Thus the present scene ended. The words, "Father! forgive him, he knows not what he saith," constantly rung in the ears of the rich man. He was much disconcerted the following night. The next day, being called on business to a neighboring town he overtook the old man on the road. As he afterwards confessed, the sight almost petrified him with guilt and fear. He dismounted, when an interesting conversation ensued. At the close of it the old man remarked:—"Yesterday, I was hungry, and called at the door of a rich man. He was angry, and told me he did not believe in the providence of God, and bid me depart; but at the next house I had a plentiful meal. And this, mark ye! was at the house of a *poor woman*." The wealthy man confessed, that at this moment he was pierced with a sense of guilt. He then gave some money to the poor man, of whom he never could hear afterwards; yet the sound of these words being impressed on his mind by the last interview—"He knows not what he saith,"—never left him, till he was brought to Christian repentance.

(*d*) MOTHER PRAYING FOR A SON AT A BALL.—When I was about 18 years of age, says a blind preacher, there was a dancing party in Middleboro, Mass., which I was solicited to attend, and act as usual, in the capacity of musician. I was fond of such scenes of amusement then, and I readily assented to the request. I had a pious mother; and she earnestly remonstrated against my going. But at length, when all her expostulations and entreaties failed in changing my purpose, she said: "Well, my son, I shall not forbid your going; but, remember that all the time you spend in that gay company, I shall spend in praying for you at home." I went to the ball, but I was like the stricken deer, carrying an arrow in his side. I began to play; but my convictions sunk deeper and deeper, and I felt miserable indeed. I thought I would have given the world to have been rid of that mother's prayers. At one time I felt so wretched and so overwhelmed with my feelings, that I ceased playing and dropped my musical instrument from my hand. There was another young person there who refused to dance; and, as I learned, her refusal was owing to feelings similar to ny own, and perhaps, they arose from a similar cause.

My mother's prayers were not lost. That was the last ball I ever attended, except *one*, where I was invited to play again, but went and prayed and preached *instead*, till the place of dancing was converted into a Bochim, a place of weeping. The convictions of that wretched night never wholly left me, till they left me at the feet of Christ, and several of my young companions in sin ere long were led to believe and obey the gospel also.

(*e*) THE PRAYING MOTHER AND HER SIX DAUGHTERS.—In a sea-port town in New England, lived a pious mother, who had six daughters. At the age of sixty, she had been for many years the subject of disease, which confined her to her house, and almost to her room. To a Christian friend she remarked, "I have not for these many years known what it is to go to the house of God, in company with his people, and to take sweet counsel with them. But I have another source of grief greater than this; one that weighs down my spirits day and night, while disease and pain bear my body towards the grave. I have six daughters; two are married and live near me, and four are with me; but not one of them is pious. I am alone. I have no one for a Christian companion. Oh that even one of them were pious, that I might walk alone no longer!" Such was her language. She was evidently a woman of a sorrowful spirit, beseeching the Lord with much entreaty. Soon after this, a revival of religion commenced in the neighborhood, of which her four single daughters were among the first subjects. A fifth was soon added to the number, but the other, the eldest, was unmoved. "Mother," said one of the converts, "let us all unite in observing a day of fasting and prayer for our unawakened sister." The agreement was made; the day was observed. Of this, the subject of their prayers had no knowledge; but on the same day, while engaged in her domestic concerns at home, her mind was solemnly arrested; and she was soon after added to the Christian sisterhood. The praying mother lived a few years to enjoy their Christian society They surrounded her dying bed, received her last blessing, commended her spirit to God, and followed the faith and patience of that mother who was first removed to inherit the promises.

(*f*) PRAYING AN HOUR DAILY EIGHTEEN MONTHS.—A poor woman, at Berwick St. John, in Wiltshire, England, the wife of a day laborer, being called by the grace of God, her husband became a bitter persecutor; and, because his wife would not relinquish the service of God, he frequently turned her out of doors in the night, and during the winter season. The wife, being a prudent woman, did not expose this cruelty to her neighbors, but, on the contrary, to avoid their observations, she went into the adjacent fields, and betook herself to prayer. Greatly distressed, but not in despair, her only encouragement was, that with God all things are possible; she therefore resolved to set apart one hour every day, to pray for the conversion of her persecuting husband. This she was enabled to do, without missing a single day, for a whole year. Seeing no change in her husband, she formed a second resolution to persevere six months longer, which she did up to the last day, when she retired at about twelve o'clock as usual, and, as she thought, for the last time. Fearing that her wishes, in this instance, might be contrary to the will of God, she resolved to call no more upon him; her desire not being granted, her expectation appeared to be cut off. That same day her husband returned from his labor in a state of deep dejection, and, instead of sitting down as usual to his dinner, he proceeded directly to his chamber. His wife followed, and heard, to her grateful astonishment, that he who used to mock, had returned to pray.

He came down stairs, but refused to eat, and returned again to his labor until the evening. When he came home, his wife affectionately asked him, "What is the matter?"

"Matter enough," said he, "I am a lost sinner. About twelve o'clock this morning," continued he, "I was at my work, and a passage of Scripture was deeply impressed upon my mind, which I cannot get rid of, and I am sure I am lost."

His wife encouraged him to pray, but he replied, "O wife, it is of no use, there is no forgiveness for me!" Smitten with remorse at the recollection of his former conduct, he said to her, "Will you forgive me?" She replied, "Oh yes." "Will you pray for me?" "Oh yes, that I will." "Will you pray for me *now?*" "That I will, with all my heart." They instantly fell on their knees and wept, and made supplication. His tears of penitence mingled with her tears of gratitude and joy. He became decidedly pious, and afterwards greatly exerted himself to make his neighbors acquainted with the way of salvation by Christ Jesus.

(*g*) A WRITTEN PRAYER ANSWERED.—Captain Mitchell K. was from early life accustomed to the sea. He commanded a merchant ship that sailed from Philadelphia. After his marriage, he again went to sea, and one day committed to writing, while in a highly devotional frame of mind, a prayer for the temporal and eternal happiness of his beloved wife and unborn babe. This prayer, nearly filling a sheet of paper, was deposited, with his other writings, at the bottom of an old oak chest. The captain died before the completion of the voyage, in the year 1757, and his instruments, papers, etc., were returned to his wife. Finding they were generally what she could not understand, she locked up the chest for the inspection and use of her babe, (who proved to be a son,) at some future period. At eighteen, this son entered the army, and in 1775 marched for Boston. He gave the reins to his lusts, and for many years yielded to almost every temptation to sin. At last, he was called to the death-bed of his mother, who gave him the key of his father's chest, which, however, he did not open, lest he should meet with something of a religious kind, that would reprove his sins and harass his feelings. At length, in 1814, when in his fifty-sixth year, he determined to examine its contents. When he reached the bottom, he discovered a paper neatly folded, and endorsed—"The prayer of Mitchell K for blessings on his wife and child, August 23, 1757." He read it. The scene, the time, the place and circumstances under which it was written and put there, all rushed upon his mind, and overwhelmed him; for often had his widowed mother led him to the beach, and pointed to him the direction on the horizon, where she had traced the last glimpse of flowing canvas that bore his father from her, never to return. He threw the contents back into the chest, folded up the prayer, and put it in the case with his father's quadrant, locked up the chest, and determined never again to unlock it. But his father's prayer still haunted his imagination, and he could not forget it. His distress then became extreme, and a woman with whom he sinfully lived entreated to know the cause. He looked on her with wildness, and replied, "I cannot tell you." This only increased her solicitude; he entreated her to withdraw; as she left the room, she cast an anxious and expressive look on him, and he instantly called her back. He then, with all the feelings which an awakened guilty conscience could endure, told her the cause of his agonies—his father's prayer found in the old oak chest. She thought him deranged, his neighbors were called in to comfort him, but in vain. The prayer had inflicted a wound which the great Physician of souls only could heal. From that period he became an altered man. He married this woman, whom he had formerly seduced; united himself to the church of Christ, manumitted his slaves; and lived and died a humble, exemplary Christian.

(*h*) PRAYER FOR THREE SISTERS.—A young lady, who afterwards became the wife of an American missionary, immediately after her own conversion, began to pray and use means for the salvation of her three younger sisters. She began and continued to act systematically. A little season was devoted every week to pray with and for them. At length, He who is both a prayer-hearing and a prayer-answer ing God, who has said, "Ask, and ye shall receive," and who never said, "Seek ye me in vain," condescended to give her a gracious answer. The three sisters were brought to bow to the sceptre of Jesus, and to take upon them the profession of his name. After their conversion, the prayer-meeting became doubly interesting to all; and it was continued by the three, for whom it was first established, and the mother occasionally united with them. If all Christians were thus devoted to prayer, how much good might be effected!

(*i*) "I KNOW WHAT IS THE MATTER."—A gay, dissipated young man, went one day to his pious mother, and said, "Mother, let me have my best clothes, I am going to a ball tonight." She expostulated with him, and urged him not to go, by every argument in her power. He answered, "Mother, let me have my clothes, I will go, and it is useless to say any thing about it." She brought his clothes; he put them on, and was going out. She stopped him, and said, "My child, do not go." He said he would; she then said to him, "My son, while you are dancing with your gay companions in the ball-room, I shall be out in that wilderness praying to the Lord to convert your soul." He went; the ball commenced; but instead of the usual gayety, an unaccountable gloom pervaded the whole assembly. One said, "We never had such a dull meeting in our lives;" another, "I wish we had not come, we have no life, we cannot get along;" a third, "I cannot think what is the matter." The young man instantly burst into tears, and said, "I know what is the matter; my poor old mother is now praying in yonder wilderness for her ungodly son." He took his hat, and said, "I will never be found in such a place as this again," and left the company. To be short, the Lord converted his soul. He became a member of the church—was soon after taken ill—and died happy.

(*j*) A FATHER AND HIS FRIENDS PRAYING.—The Boston Christian Herald relates the following instance of the efficacy of prayer A gentleman in Boston had an impenitent son in Vermont, for whose salvation he felt extremely anxious, and calling on some of the brethren of the church, made known to them his feelings, and requested them to go with him and pray that his son might be converted to God. He prevailed on his brethren, and they joined him in prayer.

Not long after this, his son knocked at his father's door in Boston; his father went to the door, and his son on seeing him, exclaimed, weeping, "I have come to see you that you might rejoice with me for what the Lord has done for my soul." His father inquired at what time his mind was first arrested—he replied on such an evening, about eight o'clock. His father remembered it was the same time, at which he and his brethren engaged in prayer for his son, and he greatly rejoiced with him in the goodness of God.

(*k*) THE WIFE'S LAST PRAYER.—In a revival that occurred some years ago in New England, several hardened men, past the meridian of life, became as little children, and were admitted to the church. The case of one excited peculiar attention. He had been moral, indeed, but ignorant of religion, while most of his family had become members of the church. He had withstood the gospel so long that Christians seemed to regard his case as hopeless, and forgot him in their efforts and supplications. But his wife had long been faithful in entreating him, and for years had made him the subject of many prayers. And now she felt moved once more to enter her closet in his behalf and submit his case, with an agonizing effort, fully and finally to God's disposal, and there lay down forever the burden of her anxiety on his account. After long wrestling, she came at length from the place of her intercessions, and finding him at the door engaged with his axe, she begged him in a *farewell* entreaty, for *her* sake if not for his own, to go immediately and pray for the salvation of his soul. He seemed amazed, like Saul of Tarsus when the voice came from Heaven. He stood a moment trembling—the axe fell from his hand—and he replied, "*I will.*" He went to a retired place, remained till some time in the evening, and when he returned he was under deep convictions. He began from this time to attend all the meetings for prayer and worship. But his feelings were unknown to Christians, and at the close of the solemn meetings, he would linger behind, standing apart, neglected, and gazing at the group of happy converts, a lame old man waiting beside the pool and none to help him into the healing waters. His wife watched his course, and said but little. At length the light broke gradually in upon his soul. His life exhibited a marvelous change. He attended every meeting, old as he was, with the zeal of a young convert; he confessed Christ before men, and resolved to erect a family altar. After knowing such a fact what wife could cease praying for a husband's conversion?

(*l*) PRAYER FOR AN ABSENT BROTHER.—A lady in New-York was one day called on by her pastor, who found her earnestly telling her newly converted husband, of the assurance she felt that the Lord had heard her prayer for the conversion of an absent brother, who was engaged in mercantile business at the South. The husband, though recently brought to Christ in answer to her prayers, smiled incredulously at what he considered her enthusiasm. The pastor pointed out some passages of Scripture which warranted the pious woman, as he thought, in exercising such feelings and expectations, though he himself was but half convinced that the sequel would confirm her sanguine hopes. Her own confidence, however, was strengthened; she felt more than ever assured that God had heard her supplications.

This lady had previously done all she could by writing to awaken her brother to a sense of his condition as a sinner, and then had besieged the throne of grace in his behalf. The result was that as soon as a letter could come from the South, she received a letter from him, informing her that on that same afternoon, at the same time she was bowing her knees in his behalf in her closet, and her soul set at rest concerning him, he, thousands of miles away from his sister, entered into his chamber grieving over his sins. There he made a full surrender—there he knelt in sorrow, but arose rejoicing in Christ.

(*m*) PRAYER MEETING FOR THE CONSUMPTIVE.—A young lady who had for several successive terms been connected with a Seminary in H., Mass., was taken sick with consumption. Her amiable disposition and attractive manners had won for her the esteem and love of both teacher and classmates. But amiable and morally good as she was, she was entirely destitute of that grace which would have added lustre to all her virtues. She was not a Christian. She now found herself upon a sick bed, death staring her in the face, "without God and without hope in the world." The several clergymen in the place, visited and conversed with her day after day, and yet, believer as she was in the revealed truths of the Gospel, she still appeared unaffected. Several weeks passed on; her disease in the meantime had been making rapid inroads upon her constitution, and it was now thought that she could survive but a short time. Her friends renewed their efforts to bring her to Christ. They plainly, but affectionately told her of the danger to which she was exposed, and urged her as she valued her soul, to secure its salvation. She appeared to have clear intellectual views of her case, and expressed a strong desire that *God* would bring her to repentance, but seemed disinclined to make any effort for herself. The pious students in the Seminary, and some of her classmates in an especial manner, felt deeply interested in her case, and one of them, a young man, proposed to several of his companions, that they should commence a series of prayer-meetings for the purpose of making special effort for her conversion, and continue them until she was by the blessing of God converted. And the ensuing evening they met, a little band of the faithful followers of the Redeemer, and he, true to his promise, met with them. Each in his turn, feelingly and fervently presented her case before God, pleading with him to have mercy upon her, and bring her to a saving knowledge of his grace.

The meeting at length closed, and they parted to meet again the next evening. But they had prayed in "faith believing," and he who has promised to hear and answer such prayer, had by his Spirit been operating upon that young lady's heart, even at the very time that others were interceding for her; and the next morning, these pious students had the satisfaction of hearing that Miss D—— had acknowledged God as her Savior, and was rejoicing in the hope of immortal life. She was converted while they were praying for her. She gave abundant evidence of the genuineness of her conversion, and died soon after, exclaiming "Jesus is precious."

(*n*) THE PIOUS LAD AND HIS PERSECUTING FATHER. — In 1828 or 9, a lad in Kentucky was hopefully converted, whose father was a decided enemy of the gospel of Christ; and while his affectionate son entreated him with tears to seek the favor of his Maker, he turned away with scoffing and profaneness.

It is true that the Christian character shines most beautiful in adversity. It gathers fragrance from affliction. So it was in the instance before us. This lad had learned in the school of Christ; and though he received in return the unkindest treatment, he continued his entreaties to his ungrateful parent.

The father at length became enraged, and in a fit of passion told his son to quit his religion, or he should quit his father's house. He gave him until the next morning to decide the question.

The night, as we may well suppose, was spent by this young disciple in laying his complaints before God; and He whose ear is never closed to the supplications of humble and contrite hearts, was graciously pleased to afford him relief.

The morning came. The father, firm to his purpose, demanded of the son if he had made his decision. "Yes, father,' said the faithful boy, "*I am decided to serve God—to serve him as long as I live—and I feel assured, that 'when my father and my mother forsake me, then the Lord will take me up.'*"—The inflexible father directed him to the door—to leave his house forever. The son begged permission to pray with his parents once more, before he bade them a final adieu. So reasonable a request could not be refused. He kneeled down and prayed. The fullness of his soul was poured out, and his ardent cries went up to the throne of God. The Holy Spirit descended, and both father and mother fell upon the floor, under the oppressive weight of their sins.

When the lad rose from his knees, the hearts of his parents relented; hey besought him to tell them what they should do to be saved. In the spirit of the gospel he directed them to the Lamb of God which taketh away the sins of the world. There was no need of his entreaties now. God had opened their eyes to see the enormity of their guilt, and they could never have peace till they found it in the hopes of the gospel. These hopes they were soon led to cherish, and at the time this account was related, they were adorning the church of Christ.

334. Prayer Answered by the Agency of the Holy Spirit, in Various Interesting Revivals.

(*a*) ASSURANCE OF A REVIVAL'S APPROACH.—There was a woman in New Jersey, in a place where there had been a revival. She was very positive there was going to be another. She insisted upon it, that they had had the former rain, and were now going to have the latter rain. She wanted to have conference meetings appointed. But the minister and elders saw nothing to encourage it, and would do nothing. She saw they were blind, and so she went forward and got a carpenter to make seats for her, for she said she would have meetings in her own house. There was certainly going to be a revival. She had scarcely opened her door for meetings, before the Spirit of God came down in great power. And these sleepy church members found themselves surrounded all at once with convicted sinners. And they could only say, "Surely the Lord was in this place and I knew it not." The reason why such persons understand the indication of God's will, is not because of the superior wisdom that is in them, but because the Spirit of God leads them to see the signs of the times. And this not by revelation, but they are led to see that converging of providences to a single point, which produces in them a confident expectation of a certain result.

(*b*) THE POOR BLACKSMITH'S POWER WITH GOD.—In a certain town, says Mr. Finney, there had been no revival for many years; the church was nearly run out, the youth were all unconverted, and desolation reigned unbroken. There lived in a retired part of the town, an aged man, a blacksmith by trade, and of so stammering a tongue that it was painful to hear him speak. On one Friday, as he was at work in his shop, alone, his mind became greatly exercised about the state of the church, and of the impenitent. His agony became so great, that he was induced to lay aside his work, lock the shop door, and spend the afternoon in prayer.

He prevailed, and on the Sabbath, called on the minister and desired him to appoint a conference meeting. After some hesitation, the minister consented, observing, however, that he feared but few would attend. He appointed it the same evening, at a large private house. When evening came, more assembled than could be accommodated in the house. All was silent for a time, until one sinner broke out in tears, and said, if any one could pray, he begged him to pray for *him*. Another followed, and another, and still another, until it was found that persons from every quarter of the town were under deep convictions. And what was remarkable, was, that they all dated their conviction at the hour when the old man was praying in his shop. A powerful revival followed. Thus this old stammering man prevailed, and, as a prince, had power with God.

(*c*) REVIVAL WITHOUT A MINISTER.—The following facts were stated by Rev. Mr. Crane, at a missionary meeting in New-York city.

Not four miles from my residence, said Mr. Crane, in the western part of this state, there was to be found a few years since, a most abandoned and profligate set of men, who disregarded religion and despised its power. In the course of Providence, a professor of religion from Connecticut happened to come amongst them. He mourned over their state, and wet his couch with his tears. He prayed unceasingly that he might see the souls of those around him saved. One was finally brought to a knowledge of the truth, and with him joined in prayer. A revival of religion followed; and soon there were to be numbered fifteen professing Christians. In answer to their prayers another increase was experienced; a proposal was then made to send for a missionary that should labor amongst them. To this the aged father of the colony objected, trusting that He who had helped them thus far, would not permit them to fail. No minister came among them until their number amounted to fifty-four, and they were able to build a church, and settle one with a salary adequate to his support. All this without any preaching, other than the example and prayers of a single Christian.

335. Various Examples of the Power of Prayer.

(*a*) DR. MASON AND THE DYING UNITARIAN.—The Rev. Dr. Mason, of New-York, was once requested to visit a lady in dying circumstances, who, together with her husband, openly avowed infidel principles, though they attended on his ministry. On approaching her bedside, he asked her if she felt herself a sinner, and perceived the need of a Savior. She frankly told him, she did not; and that she wholly disbelieved the doctrine of a Mediator. "Then," said the doctor, "I have no consolation for you; not one word of comfort. There is not a single passage in the Bible that warrants me to speak peace to any one who rejects the Mediator provided for lost sinners. You must abide the consequences of your infidelity." Saying that, he was on the point of leaving the room, when some she said, "Well, but doctor, if you cannot speak consolation to her, you can pray for her." To this he assented, and kneeling down by the bedside, prayed for her as a guilty sinner, just sinking into hell; and then arising from his knees, he left the house. A day or two after, he received a letter from the lady herself, earnestly desiring that he would come and see her without delay. He immediately obeyed the summons; but what was his amazement, when, on entering the room, she held out her hand to him, and said, with a benignant smile, "It is all true; all that you said on Sunday is true. I have seen myself the wretched sinner which you described me to be in prayer. I have seen Christ that all-sufficient Savior you said he was; and God has mercifully snatched me from the abyss of infidelity in which I was sunk, and placed me on the Rock of ages. There I am secure; there I shall remain. I know in whom I have believed!" All this was like a dream to him; but she proceeded, and displayed as accurate a knowledge of the way of salvation revealed in the gospel, and as firm a reliance on it, as if she had been a disciple of Christ for many years. Yet there was nothing like boasting or presumption—all was humility, resignation and confidence. She charged her husband to educate their daughter in the fear of God; and, above all, to keep from her those novels and books of infidel sentimentality, by which she had been nearly brought to ruin. On the evening of the same day, she expired in fullness of joy and peace in believing.

(*b*) THE MURDERERS OVER-AWED.—Maree, a Polynesian, was a man of fine natural talents, and was not destitute of acquired ones; being able to read and write well, and acquainted with some of the first rules of arithmetic. He was possessed of a surprising memory, a quick perception, and a good understanding, with a sound and penetrating judgment; while, to crown all, he was a man of genuine piety and ardent zeal in the Savior's cause. He was one of the first who publicly embraced Christianity among these islanders, and, before it became general, his life was often in jeopardy, through his profession of it. More than one attempt was made, by a number of wicked men, to shoot him, and a little praying company who used to meet with him that they might together worship the true God. On one occasion, these men having found him and his little party at prayer in a place appropriated for the purpose, leveled their muskets at them, with a view to execute their cruel design, when, as though withheld by an unseen hand, their attention was arrested by the prayers offering up by the intended victims of their fury. The effect was instantaneous and powerful. Abandoning their murderous purpose, they went in and sat down with Maree and his company, confessed what their intention had been, and told them not to be afraid, as they should not molest them any more; which promise they kept.

(*c*) "SHOW THEM THY CROSS."—Says a pastor in one of the Middle States, during a pleasing and powerful revival of religion, having but very few male members to take part in the prayer meetings, I was accustomed occasionally to call on one or two females, to whom the voice of the community by general consent seemed to have conceded the propriety of the exercise in such meetings. While one was thus engaged, all was solemnity, anxiety, and agony, with twenty or more anxious souls around us. She prayed, "*Show them thy* CROSS *and lead them to it; enable them to see the* SUFFERER *there, and the blood thou hast shed in their behalf.*" These words came like the rising sun upon the mind of an intelligent man then in agony among the anxious, and were like balm to his soul. His guilt and danger were in full view, but now he saw the ground of hope and safety, and gladly resorted to it, submitted, believed and rejoiced; and before he left the house told us of the relief and peace he had found. But while these words seemed to give life to one, they at the same moment smote another.

There was standing a little on one side, an intelligent, influential, but stubborn young man, observing all that passed; and as these words of that prayer fell upon his ear in all the feeling earnestness in which they were uttered, he said they came like a bolt from heaven; his muscles relaxed, his knees gave way, and he sank upon the seat by him as weak as water. He passed through a season of deep distress, obtained peace with the former, became an active, devoted and efficient Christian; and is now a leading member of a prosperous church, and superintendent of a flourishing Sabbath School.

(*d*) NONE PRAYS FOR ME.—A writer in the N. Y. Evangelist says:

Whilst a meeting of much interest was going on in a certain country town in Virginia, Mr. K., a pious young man, selected a young lawyer who was a noted scorner, and made him the subject of special prayer. About two days afterwards, the young lawyer came to the house where the pastor was. I myself was in the same house at this time, but being particularly engaged I requested the pastor to speak to him. "O," says he, "he is not serious." Yes, I replied, he must be, or he would not come here. "I know him better than you do," said the pastor, "he is a scorner. There is no hope of him." The young lawyer was permitted to depart, I believe without a single religious remark having been made to him. My conjectures were true. He was then under awakening influences, and a few days afterwards he professed conversion!

Perhaps two weeks after that, this young lawyer was riding along the road on his way to a protracted meeting, about to be held in an adjacent county. Before he reached the place he fell in with another young man, Mr. P., going to the same meeting. Religious conversation was introduced, and the hopefully converted sinner spoke freely of the change of views and feelings which he had experienced, and ascribed them, under God, to the prayers of his friend, Mr. K., who selected him as the subject of special prayer. "Ah," said Mr. P., "I had friends once who used to pray for me; but I have been so careless, so wicked, they don't think it worth while to pray for me now. They have all given me up. There is not one, I suppose, on earth, who remembers me in prayer." "O, yes," replied the young lawyer, "there is one I know." "Who is it?" quickly asked Mr. P. "The very same who prayed for me, has made you the subject of special prayer." "Is it possible!" said Mr. P.; and throwing himself back, he had well nigh fallen from the horse upon which he was riding. From that moment he waked up to the claims of his undying soul. A few days after, with great joy, he was telling to all around, what a dear Savior he had found!—Blessed be God, the effectual fervent prayer of a righteous man availeth much.

(*e*) A DUEL BROKEN UP.—A pious young man in the army, not having a place in the barracks in which he was quartered, wherein he could pour out his soul unto God in secret, went for this purpose one dark night into a large field adjoining. Here he thought that no human being could see or hear him. But that God whose thoughts and ways are superior to ours, ordained otherwise. Two wicked men belonging to the same regiment, in whose hearts enmity had long existed against each other, were resolved, as they said, to end it that night in battle. They chose the same field to fight in, where the other had gone to pray. The field, however, was large, and they might have taken different ways; but they were led by Providence to the same spot where the young man was engaged in his delightful exercise. They were surprised at hearing, as they thought, a voice in the field at that time of night; and much more so when they drew nearer, and heard a man at prayer. They halted, and gave attention; and the effect of the prayer was to turn their mutual aversion into love. They took each other instantly by the hand, and cordially confessed that there remained no longer in either of their breasts hatred against each other.

(*f*) A BALL BROKEN UP.—In a certain place, where there had for a long time been no revival, there was to be a splendid ball. There were three very pious and devoted Christians in the village who mourned over the excessive dissipation and folly of the rising generation, and especially over the coming ball. They naturally feared it would do much to deepen the disrelish of the youth for sacred things, and to entrench them more securely in the charmed circle of worldlines and vanity. They knew no means to prevent the ball, and they determined on the evening of the dance, to meet together and carry the case to God, and beseech Him to confound this artful scheme of Satan to delude and ruin the young. They prayed with earnestness, and with faith, wrestling as Jacob did with the angel of God. Ere long they arose from their knees, believing their supplications had found audience in heaven. How was it? Soon after the ball commenced, a young lady was led out on the floor to dance, and being struck with an awful sense of her guilt and madness, she fell down on her knees, and in the utmost agony and horror of conscience, began to cry to God to have mercy on her soul. Confusion, sadness, and dismay spread like fire through all the circle, music and mirth suddenly ceased, and all returned to their homes. Was not this the finger of God? Was not this the work of the Holy Spirit? Was not His promise verified to the two or three, who were agreed as touching one thing?

(*g*) SCHOOLMASTER PREPARING TO PRAY.—A minister relates a very extraordinary fact, which he had from a gentleman of respectability. In one of the Southern cities, an instructor was wanted to take the charge of a school. A gentleman well qualified by talents, made application for the situation, and was appointed. On becoming acquainted with the duties which he must perform, he found, to his surprise, that one of the requisitions which were made on the instructor was, that he must daily open the school by prayer. As he was an infidel in his opinions, this was to him an appalling condition. How could he, with his peculiar views, attempt to pray to a God, in whose existence and attributes he did not believe? Here was a mortal struggle As, however, he greatly coveted the situation, to which at his own request he had been appointed, he came to the conclusion he would endeavor to surmount the difficulty, by learning in some way a form of prayer. The time drawing near when he must open the school, he retired to a forest of woods in the vicinity, where he might be perfectly free in expressing himself audibly and without interruption, resolving to do so as if it were the first day of opening the school. He commenced, but before leaving the woods, light darted on his mind, and conviction arrested his conscience. He became deeply sensible of the being and perfections of Almighty God, against whom he had transgressed in denying his existence; and when the season arrived for commencing his duties as a teacher, he had become a true Christian, and he prayed with the unction and penitence of the publican. He became the instrument of the conversion of a number of his pupils, and was afterwards an acceptable and highly popular preacher of the gospel.

(*h*) PRAYER ON HORSEBACK—A young lady, says a writer in the Pastor's Journal, in making a visit to one of her acquaintance, took an unfrequented path through a deeply shaded grove; and as the day was very warm, after pursuing her walk some distance up a somewhat steep acclivity, she stopped to rest her on a beautiful mossy bank. While seated there, the tones of a human voice very unexpectedly broke upon her ear. On turning her eye the way from whence it came, she saw Deacon M—— on horseback, making his way up the same hill. The thought occurred to her that she would retire from the sight of the road, let him pass, and remain undiscovered. This she did. As Deacon M—— approached leisurely on his horse, she was wondering what could be his object in being so busily employed in talking to himself, as she could distinctly discover that no fellow mortal accompanied him. As he drew nearer, and she could hear his voice more plainly, she ascertained that he was engaged in prayer. The only sentence that left a distinct impression on her mind was.

"O Lord have mercy on the dear youth in this place." He passed on, praying, till the sounds which came from his lips died away on her ear. But an impression was made upon her heart, as it may be hoped, which will never die away, but prepare her to mingle in the symphonies of the redeemed in ascribing salvation to God and the Lamb. A new discovery respecting Christians was at this instant made to her. "Is this the manner," she reflected with herself, "in which they live, and pass on their way about the town? Do they thus pray for the youth? How unlike a Christian have I lived! I have never prayed in this manner: I have seldom thought of the souls of others, and cared but very little for my own. While others pray for me, I live without prayer for myself."

Her sins, particularly her neglect of prayer to Him who is every where, now became a distressing burden to her. Soon, we have had reason to hope, there was joy among the angels of God over her as a penitent, and over many others in the town. She was first awakened in a revival.

336. Miscallaneous Facts Respecting Prayer.

(*a*) MASSA, YOU NO UNDERSTAND IT.—There once lived in one of our large cities a poor colored woman, named Betty, who had been confined by sickness for nearly twenty years. By the few friends that knew her she was familiarly called poor Betty. Betty had seen comfortable days. She had long been blind, and was said to be 105 years old.

Mr. B. was a man of wealth and business in the same city. His signature was better than silver on the exchange, because it was more easily transferred. His sails whitened the ocean, his charity gladdened many hearts, and his family gave impulse to many benevolent operations. Notwithstanding the pressure of business, Mr. B. often found time to drop in and see what became of poor Betty. His voice, and even his step had become familiar to her, and always lighted up a smile on her dark wrinkled face. He would often say some pleasant things to cheer this lonely pilgrim on her way to Zion.

One day Mr. B. took a friend from the country to see Betty. As he stopped and entered the cottage door, he said, "Ah, Betty, you are alive yet." "Yes, tank God," said Betty. "Betty," said he, "why do you suppose God keeps you so long in this world, poor, and sick, and blind, when you might go to heaven and enjoy so much?"

While Mr. B.'s tone and manner were half sportive, he yet uttered a serious thought which had more than once come over his mind. *Now comes the sermon.*

Betty assumed her most serious and animated tone and replied, "Ah, massa, you no understand it. Dare be two great things to do for de church; *one be to pray for it, toder be to act for it.* Now, massa, God keep me alive to pray for de church, and he keep you alive to act for it. Your great gifts no do much good, massa, without poor Betty's prayers."

For a few moments Mr. B. and his friend stood silent, thrilled, and astonished. They felt the knowledge, the dignity, the moral sublimity of this short sermon. It seemed to draw aside the veil a little, and let them into heaven's mysteries. "Yes, Betty," replied Mr B., in the most serious and subdued tones, "your prayers are of more importance to the church than my alms." This short sermon preached by poor Betty, was never forgotten by Mr. B. or his friend. It made them more prayerful, more submissive in afflictions.

(*b*) GOD LESS CRITICAL THAN MEN.—"My grandfather," says Mr. Orton, "once solicited a very excellent but modest minister to pray in his family when there were several others present; he desired to be excused, alleging that he had not thought of it, and there were so many other ministers present." My grandfather replied, "Sir, you are to speak to your master, and not to them, and my Bible tells me, he is not so critical and censorious as men are."

337. PRIDE.

(*a*) HOWARD AND THE COUNTESS. — The eminently great and good Howard, the philanthropist, neither wanted courage or talent to administer reproof where he thought it was needed. A German count, governor of Upper Austria, with his countess, called one day on a man who had excited so large a share of the public attention. The count asked him the state of the prisons within his department. Mr. Howard replied, "The worst in all Germany;" and advised that the countess should visit the female prisoners. "I," said she, haughtily; "I go into prisons!" and rapidly hastened down stairs in great anger. Howard, indignant at her proud and unfeeling disposition, loudly called after her, "Madam, remember that you are a woman yourself, and you must soon, like the most miserable female prisoner in a dungeon, inhabit but a small space of that earth from which you equally originated."

(*b*) THE CHIEF'S INQUIRY.— A petty African prince who was visited in his cell by an English traveler, folded his arms with an air of imperial consequence, as he sat upon the floor, and demanded of his guest, "What do they think of me in Europe?"

(*c*) THE CONQUEROR CONQUERED. — Tigranes, an ancient monarch of Pontus, furnishes a striking instance of the uncertainty of worldly possessions. At the beginning of his reign his dominions were small; but he overthrew many cities of Parthia and Greece, conquered the whole of Syria and Palestine, and gave laws to the Scenites of Arabia: he acquired an authority which was respected by all the princes of Asia, and was honored by the people almost with adoration. His pride was inflamed and supported by the immense riches he possessed, by the excessive and continual praises of his flatterers, and by a prosperity which had never known an interruption. He knew no law but his own will, and assumed the title of king of kings! So far did he carry his pride as to be waited on by crowned heads. He never appeared in public without the attendance of four kings on foot, two on each side of his horse; these persons performed for him the meanest services, especially when he gave audience to foreign ambassadors. On such occasions they were compelled to appear in the habits and posture of slaves. Such pride is universally hateful, and is sure to be ultimately punished. Tigranes was compelled to resign his dominions to Pompey, who only restored to him a small part of his power.

(*d*) THE ANGRY MONK.—"I remember," says a keen writer, "when at Tivoli, near Rome, conversing with a monk, who with a face of much sorrow told me, that he was a great rascal and the chiefest of sinners, worse than Judas Iscariot, and altogether vile. I said to him in reply, 'Alas, my poor friend, it is but too true,' and then the man got very angry, and would not talk with me any more!"

(*e*) THE PEDANT SILENCED —At a dinner party one of the company challenged any person to start a question to which he could not give a satisfactory answer. All were silent, till a worthy clergyman said, "This plate furnishes me with a question—Here is a fish that has always lived in salt water; pray tell me why it should come out a fresh fish, and not a salt one?" The boaster was silenced: nor was there one in the room who envied him his feelings.

(*f*) SOCRATES AND ALCIBIADES.—One day, when Alcibiades was boasting of his wealth and the great estates he had in possession, which generally feed the pride of young people of high rank Socrates carried him to a geographical map, and asked him to find Attica. It could scarcely be perceived upon the draught; he found it, however, though with much difficulty; but upon being desired to point out his own estate there, "It is too small," said he, "to be distinguished in so little a space." "See, then," replied the phi losopher, "how much you are affected about an imperceptible point of land!"

(*g*) AFFECTED HUMILITY AND REAL PRIDE. — Thomas à Becket, who was afterwards primate of England, was a strange compound of affected humility and real pride. While he performed the lowly office of washing the feet of thirteen beggars every morning, his supercilious, obstinate, and turbulent spirit assumed a proud, overbearing, spiritual authority over his sovereign, whom he was in the habit of treating with all the insolence of a licensed censor.

(*h*) THE BOASTER BECOMING AN IDIOT.—Simon Tournay affords a memorable and affecting proof of the truth of that scripture, "Professing themselves to be wise, they became fools." In 1201, after he had excelled all Oxford in learning, and had become so eminent at Paris as to be made chief doctor of the Sorbonne, he was so puffed up with foolish pride as to hold Aristotle superior to Moses and Christ, and yet but equal to himself. In his latter days, however, he grew such an idiot as not to know one letter in a book, or to remember one thing he had ever done.

(*i*) TRIUMPHING BEFORE THE BATTLE.—"Nothing," says Bishop Horne, "can be got, but much may be lost, by triumphing before a battle. When Charles V invaded France, he lost his generals and a great part of his army by famine and disease; and returned baffled and thoroughly mortified from an enterprise which he began with such confidence of its happy issue that he desired Paul Jovius, the historian, to make a large provision of paper sufficient to record the victories which he was going to acquire."

(*j*) THE GAY GIRL'S DEATH.—A young lady, eighteen years of age, in the city of New-York, was brought up by her parents in all the gayety and follies of youth; by them encouraged to ornament her person, and engage in every vain amusement. When she was taken ill, three physicians were sent for immediately, who pronounced her to be near her dying hour. No sooner was their opinion made known to her, than she requested as a favor, that all her gay companions might be collected with haste. They were soon around her bed, when she told them she was going to die—described the awful manner in which they had spent their precious time, and exhorted them all to repentance before it was too late, in a very affecting manner. She then, turning to her father and mother, addressed to them, in the presence of her acquaintances, these heart-rending words: "You have been the unhappy instruments of my being; you fostered me in pride, and led me in the paths of sin; you never once warned me of my danger, and now it is too late. In a few hours you will have to cover me with earth; but remember, while you are casting earth upon my body, my soul will be in hell, and yourselves the cause of my misery!" She soon after expired.

(*k*) FINE CLOTHES AND THE DEATH-BED.—A young lady, about twenty years of age, had been born to a rich inheritance, and was the only child of parents who were exceedingly fond of her. Nothing was spared to complete her education, as a lady of fashion. As she grew up she answered all her mother's hopes in making a display in the fashionable world. But the hour of sickness came—it was a dreadful hour, for it was the termination of all her hopes. The minister was called in. He talked of death, judgment, and eternity. She had never heard such language addressed to her, and she trembled. In her dying hour, she called for some of her fine clothes. When they were brought, she looked up to her mother, and said, "These have ruined me. You never told me I must die. You taught me that my errand into this world was to be gay and dressy, and to enjoy the vanities of life. What could you mean? You knew I must die and go to judgment. You never told me to read the Bible, or to go to church, unless to make a display of some new finery. Mother, you have ruined me. Take them away, and keep them as a remembrance of your sin, and my sad end." She died in a few moments after.

PROFANITY.

338. Profanity Sinful.

(*a*) SWEARING AT A CHILD FOR SWEARING.—A profane father in one of the New England States, one day learned that his little son had uttered some blasphemous expressions—doubtless a second edition of his own. But the father had no fancy for having his child coming forward so fast in his own footsteps. He called the child to account for his vicious conduct—reproved him severely for his profanity, and then commenced whipping him and scolding him at the time. While whipping his son for his profanity, he swore several profane oaths himself!

(*b*) THE PEASANT'S QUERY.—An elector of Cologne (who was likewise an archbishop) one day swearing profanely, asked a peasant, who seemed to wonder, what he was so surprised at. "To hear an archbishop swear," answered the peasant. "I swear," replied the elector, "not as an archbishop, but as a prince." "But, my lord," said the peasant, "when the prince goes to the devil, what will become of the archbishop?"

(*c*) HOWARD'S OPINION.—As he was standing one day near the door of a printing-office, he heard some dreadful volleys of oaths and curses from a public house opposite, and buttoning his pocket up before he went into the street, he said to the workmen near him, "I always do this whenever I hear men swear, as I think that any one who can take God's name in vain can also steal, or do any thing else that is bad."

(*d*) ROMAINE'S REPROOF.—The Rev. William Romaine, of London, in crossing the Black Friar's bridge, came up with a man who, in a style of unusual and fearful impiety, called upon God "to damn his soul for Christ's sake!" Mr. Romaine, laying his hand upon the blasphemer's shoulder, said: "*My friend, God has done many things for Christ's sake, and perhaps he will do* THAT *too;*" and passed on. The roof, quite as original as the imprecation, went to the wretch's heart; and was the occasion of his "turning from the power of Satan unto God," and becoming an exemplary follower of that Redeemer whom he had been in the habit of insulting. "A word spoken in due season, how good is it!" The power of Jesus to save, how mighty! His grace, how free!

339. Profanity Rebuked, Suppressed, Abandoned.

(*a*) ROWLAND HILL AND THE CAPTAIN.—Once when I was returning from Ireland, says Rowland Hill, I found myself much annoyed by the reprobate conduct of the captain and mate, who were both sadly given to the scandalous habit of swearing. First, the captain swore at the mate—then the mate swore at the captain—then they both swore at the wind—when I called to them with a strong voice for fair play. "Stop! stop!" said I, "if you please, gentlemen, let us have fair play: it's my turn now." "At what is it your turn, pray?" said the captain. "At swearing," I replied. Well, they waited and waited until their patience was exhausted, and then wanted me to make haste and take my turn. I told them, however, that I had a right to take my own time, and swear at my own convenience. To this the captain replied, with a laugh, "Perhaps you don't mean to take your turn?" "Pardon me, captain," I answered, "but I do, as soon as I can find the good of doing so." My friends, I did not hear another oath on the voyage.

(*b*) MR. CLARK AND HIS WORKMEN.—Mr. A. Clark, of Edinburgh, was accustomed, previous to engaging a workman, to put this question directly to him, "Are you a swearer in common conversation? for if you are, you shall not work with me. I am determined to permit none in my shop to take the sacred name of God in vain, before whose presence angels bow down and adore."

(*c*) THE MERCHANT AND HIS CAPTAIN.—A merchant in one of our seaports, on fitting out a ship for India, told the captain, at the time of making the contract for the voyage, that there must be no swearing among the crew; that he (the captain) must engage not to swear himself, nor permit others to be profane; that he must do as he pleased, with respect to taking command of the ship on these terms; but if he accepted the employment, it would be expected, that he should rigidly adhere to the stipulation, and that it should be known, as the law of the ship, that no profaneness should be indulged. The captain seemed to have no objection to reforming, but inquired, "How can I suddenly break off an inveterate habit?" "I will take care that you be reminded of your duty," said the owner. "Wear the ring that I will give you, and let the law of the vessel be explicitly known." Accordingly he procured a ring for the captain, with this motto engraved upon it, "SWEAR NOT AT ALL." The vessel soon sailed, and after performing the voyage returned to the seaport from whence he sailed. On being inquired of respecting the subject, the supercargo declared, that there had been no profaneness on board excepting a little within the first twenty days after sailing. At the close of this short period, the old habit was entirely destroyed; and during the remainder of the voyage, both in sea and in port, the success of the experiment was complete.

This single fact is of inestimable value, and it shows how groundless are the palliations of profaneness, and how easy it is to do good, when a person is seriously engaged in it, is influenced by principle, and acts with decision.

(*d*) THE CAPTAIN'S REQUEST.—"My lads," said a captain, when about to take command of a ship, reading his orders to the crew on the quarter-deck, "there is one law I am determined to make, and I shall insist on its being kept. It is a favor, indeed, I will ask of you, and which, as a British officer, I expect will be granted by a crew of British seamen. What say you, my lads? are you willing to grant your new captain one favor?" "Ay ay," cried all hands, "let's know what it is, sir." "Well, my lads, it it this: that you must allow me to swear the first oath in this ship. No man on board must swear an oath before I do: I am determined to swear the first oath on board. What say you, my lads, will you grant me this favor?" The men stared, and stood for a moment quite at a loss what to say. "They were taken," one said, "all aback." "They were brought up," said another, "all standing." The appeal seemed so reasonable, and the manner of the captain so kind and prepossessing, that a general burst from the ship's company answered, "Ay, ay, sir," with their usual three cheers. Swearing was thus wholly abolished in the ship.

(*e*) COLONEL GARDINER PUTTING DOWN PROFANITY.—During Colonel Gardiner's residence at Bankton, the Commander of the King's forces, with several colonels and gentlemen of rank, one day dined with him. When the company assembled, he addressed them with a great deal of respect, and yet with a very frank and determined air, and told them that he had the honor in that district to be a Justice of the Peace, and, consequently, that he was sworn to put the laws in execution, and, among the rest, those against swearing; that he could not execute upon others with any confidence, or approve himself as a man of impartiality and integrity to his own heart, if he suffered them to be broken in his presence by persons of any rank whatever; and that, therefore, he entreated all the gentlemen who then honored him with their company, that they would please to be on their guard; and that if any oath or curse should escape them, he hoped they would consider his legal animadversion upon it as a regard to the duties of his office, and dictates of his conscience, and not as any want of deference to them. The commanding officer immediately supported him in this declaration, as entirely becoming the station in which he was, assuring him he would be ready to pay the penalty if he inadvertently transgressed; and when Col onel Gardiner on any occasion stepped out of the room, he himself undertook to be the guardian of the law in his absence; and, as one of the inferior officers offended during this time, he informed the colonel, so that the fine was exacted and given to the poor, with the approbation of the company.

(*f*) THE TRAVELER AND THE SAILOR.—From the tract entitled "The Christian Traveler," (one of the most interesting and profitable tracts ever published,) we take the following scene which transpired on board a vessel on one of the western lakes. The young man, a mechanic, and the hero of the scene, had, at the breakfast table, with almost inimitable wisdom and propriety, obtained leave of the captain to attempt to put an end to the profanity of the sailors, one of the best means to reprove the captain himself for his own sin in this respect. Mark the manner in which the attempt was executed.

"As soon as breakfast was over, the oldest and most profane of the sailors seated himself on the quarter-deck to smoke his pipe. The young man entered into conversation with him, and soon drew from him a history of the adventures of his life. From his boyhood, he had followed the ocean. He had been tossed on the billows in many a tempest; had visited several missionary stations in different parts of the world, and gave his testimony to the good effects of missionary efforts among the natives of the Sandwich Islands. Proud of his nautical skill, he at length boasted that he could do any thing that could be done by a sailor.

'I doubt it,' said the young man.

'I can,' answered the hardy tar, 'and will not be outdone, my word for it.'

'Well, when a sailor passes his word he ought to be believed. I know a sailor who resolved to stop swearing; and did so.'

'Ah!' said the old sailor, 'you have anchored me; I'm fast—but I can do it.'

'I know you can,' said the young man, 'and I hope you will anchor all your ship-mates' oaths with yours.'

"Not a word of profanity was afterwards heard on board the vessel. During the day, as opportunity presented itself, he conversed with each sailor singly, on the subject of his soul's salvation, and gained the hearts of all."

(*g*) AN OLD MAN'S REBUKE.—A good old man was once in company with a gentleman, who occasionally introduced into conversation the words "devil, deuce," etc., and who, at last, took the name of God in vain. "Stop, sir," said the old man, "I said nothing while you only used freedoms with the name of your own master, but I insist upon it that you shall use no freedoms with the name of mine."

(*h*) SLAVE CURING HIS MASTER.—An American planter had a favorite domestic negro, who was ordered to stand opposite to him and to wait at table. His master was a profane person, and often took the name of God in vain. Whenever he did so, the negro made a low and solemn bow. On being asked why he did this, he replied, that he never heard this great name mentioned, but it filled his whole soul with reverence and awe. His master took the hint without offence, and was reclaimed from a very sinful and pernicious practice by his pious slave. The poorest Christian may thus be encouraged in the faithful discharge of duty. A word spoken in due season, how good is it!"

(*i*) GEORGE III AND THE ARCHITECT.—A pious architect, having some business with his majesty George III, attended at one of his palaces, and was shown into a room where a nobleman afterwards came, and used much impious and blasphemous language, for which the gentleman felt it his duty to rebuke him. The peer became very angry, so that the king came into the room to inquire the cause of the noise, when the nobleman informed him that he had been insulted by the other person; but upon the architect explaining that he only rebuked him for profaneness and blasphemy, his majesty said, he had his approbation for what he had done, as he did not allow blasphemy in his dwelling. He afterwards desired the architect to sit down, to forget his royalty, and freely tell him the ground of his hope of salvation, which he stated to be the sacrifice and work of the Lord Jesus Christ. The king said, that also was the ground of his dependence.

(*j*) WASHINGTON'S OPINION.—"Many and pointed orders have been issued against the unmeaning and abominable custom of swearing; notwithstanding which, with much regret, the general observes that it prevails, (if possible,) more than ever. His feelings are continually wounded by the oaths and imprecations of the soldiers, whenever he is in hearing of them. The name of that Being, from whose bountiful goodness we are permitted to exist and enjoy the comforts of life is incessantly imprecated and profaned, in a manner as wanton as it is shocking. For the sake, therefore, of religion, decency, and order, the general hopes and trusts that officers of every rank will use their influence and authority to check a vice which is as unprofitable as wicked and shameful. If officers would make it an inviolable rule to reprimand, and (if that won't do) to punish soldiers for offences of this kind, it would not fail of having the desired effect."

(*k*) WREN AND HIS WORKMEN.—When this eminent architect was building St. Paul's Cathedral, he caused the following notice to be affixed to several parts of the structure:—"Whereas among laborers and others, that ungodly custom of swearing is so frequently heard, to the dishonor of God and contempt of his authority; and to the end that such impiety may be utterly banished from these works, which are intended for the service of God, and the honor of religion; it is ordered that profane swearing shall be a sufficient crime to dismiss any laborer that comes to the call; and the clerk of the works, upon a sufficient proof, shall dismiss him accordingly: and if any master, working by task, shall not, upon admonition, reform the profanation among his apprentices, servants, and laborers, it shall be construed his fault, and he shall be liable to be censured by the commissioners."

(*l*) THE SWEARER AND HIS BOY.—A man in the state of New-York, who was extremely addicted to profane swearing, was one day at work with a yoke of oxen near his house. The oxen not working to suit him, he began whipping them severely, at the same time uttering vollies of most horrid blasphemous oaths. The oxen breaking loose from their burthen, ran to the house, while the owner in a passion pursued them, and coming up with them at the house, began whipping them again, and swearing horridly as before. His little boy, at this time just old enough to begin to talk, began to prattle his profane oaths over after him. No sooner did the father hear this, than his feelings were wrought up to a lively sensibility. He paused for a moment, dropt his whip, sat down and wept bitterly. A flood of keen reflections at once rushed upon his convicted conscience, which produced such an effect, that he found no rest to his mind, day nor night, until his sins were forgiven and washed away in the blood of Christ, which took place a few weeks afterwards.

(*m*) CHRYSOSTOM'S DIRECTION.—Chrysostom proposes a singular method to facilitate the leaving off this practice of customary swearing. "Would'st thou know," says the father, "by what means thou may'st be rid of this wicked custom of swearing, I'll tell thee a way, which if thou'lt take, will certainly prove successful. Every time, whenever thou shalt find thyself to have let slip an oath, punish thyself for it by missing the next meal. Such a course as this, though troublesome to the flesh, will be profitable to the spirit; and cause a quick amendment; for the tongue will need no other monitor to make it take heed of swearing another time, if it has been thus punished with hunger and thirst for its former transgression, and knows it shall be so punished again if ever it commits the like crime hereafter."

340. Profanity, Punishment of.

(*a*) SUDDEN VENGEANCE.—There was, in a populous Swiss village, a pious and excellent clergyman, who preached and lived with such holy zeal and exemplary piety, that many were converted under his ministry. But there lived in the same place a wicked and abandoned man, who not only slighted all the means of grace, but turned the most serious matters into ridicule, and made a laughing-stock of the preacher's expressions. One morning, he went early to the public house, and began to intoxicate himself with liquor, profaning the name and word of God, and ridiculing the term conversion. "Now," said he, "I myself will become a convert," turning himself from one side to the other, and dancing about the room with a variety of foolish gestures. He quickly went out, and falling down the stairs, broke his neck, and expired, exhibiting an awful monument of God's most righteous vengeance, which sometimes, even in this life, overtakes those that profane his holy name.

(*b*) THE COAL MERCHANT'S DEATH.—A coal merchant at Brigg, in Lincolnshire, had occasion to send a boat to Barton, with a cargo of coals, and ordered one of his men to take charge of it. As the boat was leaving the wharf, a person civilly accosted the man, asking where he was going. "I am going to hell," said he, with an oath. Awful to relate, he died suddenly, before he reached Barton!

(*c*) THE LAST OATH.—Two soldiers, at Chatham, (Eng.) once laid a trifling wager which could swear most oaths. After one of them had uttered many shocking ones, he hesitated a short time, and said, he could think of one more, which should be his last, but was instantly struck speechless, and so remained for about three hours, when he died. His body was, by order of his officers, made a public spectacle to the populace, soldiers, and sailors, as a warning to them.

(*d*) DEATH FROM PROFANITY AND ANGER.—A person of considerable property and eminence in the city of N——, who lived in habits of impiety and profaneness, was seized by an indisposition, which induced him to call a medical gentleman; but being disappointed for a time, by his absence from home, he fell into a violent agitation, which was vented in horrid imprecations. As soon as the medical gentleman arrived, he was saluted with a volley of oaths. The violence of his agitation broke a blood-vessel; so that oaths and blood continued to flow from his mouth, till he could speak no longer; and in this situation he expired.

(*e*) THE INTOXICATED HORSEMAN.—The following event, says a correspondent of the Charleston Intelligencer, occurred in my native town: A young man, about twenty years of age, of the name of G——, on a public day, being somewhat intoxicated, rode down the main street with considerable rapidity, and meeting a friend, he reined in his horse, which was skittish, in order to converse with him. Not many words had passed, when the young man's friend requested him to turn about and go with him to the "North Woods." "*I'll go to hell first!*" was the reply. The words hardly escaped his lips, when his horse suddenly reared himself on his hind legs, and pitching backwards, fell on his rider, and crushed him to death! He was taken up a corpse, and carried into an adjoining house, where I saw him. He was taken at his word! Oh! where is his soul?

PROVIDENCE.

IN BESTOWING TEMPORAL BLESSINGS.

Preserving Life.

By the Control of Material and Animal Agencies.

341. Preserving from Fires, Famines, and Similar Dangers.

(*a*) PREACHING DURING A PLAGUE.—The great plague in London, in the year 1665, gave occasion for the display of the piety and zeal of several of the ejected ministers, and of the providence of God in preserving them from the contagion, when prosecuting their ministerial labors in the midst of it. The Rev. Thomas Vincent was at this period tutor of an academy at Islington, but determined to leave his situation, and devote himself to the spiritual instruction of the people in London, where many of the pulpits were deserted. His friends vainly endeavored to dissuade him from the dangerous enterprise. He agreed, however, to follow the advice of his reverend brethren in and about the city. When they were assembled, he told them his resolution, and assured them that it had been the result, of much serious thought. He had carefully examined the state of his own soul, and could look death in the face with comfort. He thought it absolutely necessary that the vast numbers of people then dying, should have some spiritual assistance, and that he could never again have such a prospect of ministerial usefulness as now presented itself. He added, that he had solemnly devoted himself to God and souls upon this occasion; and that, therefore, he hoped none of them would endeavor to weaken his hands in this work. Encouraged by the ministers, who prayed for his protection and success, he entered on his labors with fortitude and diligence. During all the time of the plague, he preached every Sabbath in some of the parish churches. He chose the most moving and important subjects, and treated them in the most pathetic and searching manner. The awfulness of the judgment then before the eyes of all, gave great force to his addresses, and a very general inquiry was always made where he would preach the next Sabbath. Many learned from him the necessity of salvation, and the way to heaven through the blood of Christ. He visited all who sent for him, and it pleased God to take especial care of his life; for though in this year there died in London, of the plague, 68,596, including seven persons in the family in which he lived, he continued in perfect health all the time, and was a useful minister to a numerous congregation at Hoxton for upwards of twelve years afterwards. Thus were the promises in the ninety-first Psalm fulfilled to this servant of God.

(*b*) ESCAPE FROM AN EARTHQUAKE.—The following epitaph is said to have been copied from a tomb, in the vicinity of Port Royal, Jamaica:—

"Here lieth the body of Louis Caldy, Esq., a native of Montpelier, in France, which country he left on account of the revocation. He was swallowed up by the earthquake which occurred at this place in 1692, but, by the great providence of God, was, by a second shock, flung into the sea, where he continued swimming till rescued by a boat, and lived forty years afterwards."

How wonderful are the judgments of God, and his ways "past finding out."

(*c*) REV. T. RABAN'S ESCAPES.—During the life of this worthy man, who was a Christian minister for many years at Yardley Hastings, England, he was several times preserved from threatened death. On one occasion, being in an unfinished building two stories high, his foot slipped, and he fell to the ground upon an axe the edge of which stood upright: it cut his hat but not his head, and he suffered but little injury.

At another time, a large piece of timber, on which he had set his foot, heaved up, and fell with him into a saw-pit, and an anvil of a hundred pounds weight connected with it, fell upon him, but it only slightly bruised his leg. A still more remarkable preservation was afforded him. As he was assisting in raising a beam in a mill, the rope slipped, and the beam under which he stood fell with him the height of four stories, and yet he was saved. And, once more: he was driving a team with a load of hay down a narrow lane; when, attempting to pass on to the other side of the wagon, he fell, and was thrown under one of the wheels; but calling out to the horses, they instantly stopped.

But while God thus preserves the lives of his servants, that they may accomplish his designs, he often removes them in a way not expected, when those designs are accomplished. Mr. Raban was to learn by experience the truth of his friend Cowper's statement:

"Safety consists not in escape
From dangers of a frightful shape;
An earthquake may be bid to spare
The man that's strangled by a hair."

After preaching one Lord's day, and walking home, his foot slipped over a pebble, and he broke his leg, which in a few weeks brought on his death.

(*d*) THE LOST AND FOUND.—A youth, sixteen years of age, the son of a respectable Christian minister, was bathing some years ago in the river Mersey. The tide was returning, and having ventured too far into the water for the purpose of swimming, he was carried down the current to the distance of three or four miles. All hope of reaching the shore vanished; and, at the moment he was about to give up the struggle, he was providentially perceived by the crew of a vessel bound from Liverpool to Dublin. When brought on board, every means was kindly used to restore nature: the youth recovered, and was carried to the port of the Irish capital. In the meantime, a person to whom he was known, and who had seen him go into the water, returning, and finding his clothes on the shore, but seeing nothing of his person, concluded he was drowned, and carried the afflictive intelligence to his parents. A reward was offered for the body, and suitable mourning was ordered.

On the arrival of the vessel at Dublin, the youth was humanely furnished, by the crew, with such articles of clothing as they could spare; and the captain gave him a piece of silver, and put him on shore. The singularity of his dress restrained him from making known his situation to those who, from respect to his father, would gladly have rendered him assistance. He therefore inquired for a vessel bound to Liverpool, and having providentially met with one, was received on board, and reached the place of his destination on the very day of the following week that he was supposed to have been lost. No sooner did he get on shore than he hastened to his father's house. Nothing could have been more unexpected to the sorrowing parents than the appearance of their son. The mourning which they had ordered was, that evening, to be brought home, and worn on the following day. The children, at the sight of their brother, shrieked with fear: the surprise was too great for the delicate frame of his affectionate mother; before she could embrace her son, she fainted away; and the father, more collected and composed, wept tears of joy.

(*e*) THE WALDENSES AND THE WHEAT.—It is well known, that, in the year 1686, the Duke of Savoy was prevailed on by Louis XIV to expel the Waldensian Christians from their native valleys. In 1689, eight or nine hundred of these persons, through great difficulties, returned. Dr. Calamy, in his "Life and Times," relates, that M. Arnauld, their minister and leader, told him that when they had nearly reached their houses, pursued by a number of their enemies, they were in great danger of dying from want of provisions. Such, however, was the kindness of God to them, that a sudden thaw removed in one night a mass of snow from the fields, when they discovered a considerable quantity of wheat, standing in the earth, ready for the sickle, that had been suddenly covered with snow, and which now as unexpectedly left it. On this corn they lived till other sources supplied them with food.

(*f*) MISSIONARY AND THE SEAL.—Nathaniel, an assistant to the Moravian missionaries in Greenland, when engaged in the seal-fishery, being in company with another brother, who was yet inexperienced in the management of a kayak (a Greenland boat), he met a Neitsersoak, the largest kind of seal, which he killed. He then discovered his companion on a flake of ice, endeavoring to kill another of the same species, and in danger; he, therefore, left his dead seal, kept buoyant by the bladder, and hastened to help his brother. They succeeded in killing the seal; but suddenly a strong north wind arose, and carried off both the kayaks to sea; nor could they discover any kayaks in the neighborhood. They cried aloud for help, but in vain. Meanwhile the wind rose in strength, and carried both the kayaks, and also the piece of ice, swiftly along with the waves. Having lost sight of the kayaks, they now saw themselves without the least hope of deliverance. Nathaniel continued praying to his Savior, and thought with great grief of the situation of his poor family, but felt a small degree of hope arising in his breast. Unexpectedly, he saw his dead seal floating towards him, and was exceedingly surprised at its approaching against the wind, till it came so near the flake of ice, that they could secure it. But how should a dead seal become the means of their deliverance? and what was now to be done? All at once, Nathaniel resolved, at a venture, to seat himself upon the dead floating seal; and by the help of his paddle, which he had happily kept in his hand when he joined his brother on the ice, to go in quest of the kayaks. Though the sea and waves continually overflowed him, yet he kept his seat, made after the kayaks, and succeeded in overtaking his own, into which he crept, and went in quest of that of his companion, which he likewise found. He also kept possession of the seal; and now hastened in search of the flake of ice, on which his companion was most anxiously looking out for him; having reached it, he brought him his kayak, and enabled him to secure the other seal, when both returned home in safety. When relating his dangerous adventure, he ascribed his preservation, not to his own contrivance, but to the mercy of God alone.

(*g*) THE FALLEN TREE.—About the year 1830, while a young man of the town of Wells, Maine, was at work in the woods alone, he felled a tree which struck a large log, lying up some distance from the ground. When the tree struck the log, the butt bounded, struck the man, carried him some distance, plunged him into a deep snow and fell across his stomach, confining him there. The log across which the tree fell, served as a fulcrum, being so near the middle of the tree as to prevent it from lying so heavily upon him as to give much immediate distress. His feet were so completely confined that he had no power to move them; his hands being the only means with which he could do the least towards extricating himself, which he used in the best possible manner he was capable of; but he was utterly unsuccessful in his efforts to raise the body of the tree, or beating away the snow. Now feeling in some degree that all hopes of being delivered from that state of confinement also were vain, he cast his eyes toward heaven, when he saw a large limb, which had broken from the tree while falling, suspended in the air by the branch of another tree, and at the distance of thirty or forty feet above him, apparently directly over his head. What must have been his feelings while thus confined, and viewing that threatening death hanging directly over him, and expecting every moment it would fall and terminate his existence?

While he thus lay, with his eyes fastened upon the limb, waiting for the result he thought must soon take place, the twig by which it was suspended gave way—the limb fell and struck the snow about one foot from his head. He immediately thought to use that as a lever, by which to raise the tree;

the effort proved successful, and he made his escape without any material injury.

(*h*) WESLEY'S ESCAPE FROM FIRE.—Mr. Wesley, father of the Rev. John Wesley, was roused from sleep by the cry of fire from the street; but, little imagining that the fire was in his own house, he opened his bed-room door, and found the place full of smoke, and that the roof was already burned through. Directing his wife and two girls to rise and flee for their lives, he burst open the nursery-door, where the maid was sleeping with five children. She snatched up the youngest, and bade the others follow her. the three eldest did so; but John, who was then six years old, was not awakened, and in the alarm was forgotten. The rest of the family escaped—some through the windows, others by the garden door; and Mrs. Wesley, to use her own expression, "waded through the fire." At this time John, who had not been remembered till that moment, was heard crying in the nursery. The father ran to the stairs, but they were so nearly consumed that they could not bear his weight; and being utterly in despair, he fell upon his knees in the hall, and, in agony, commended the soul of the child to God. John had been awakened by the light; and finding it impossible to escape by the door, climbed up a chest that stood near the window, and he was then seen from the yard. There was no time for procuring a ladder; but one man was hoisted on the shoulders of another, and thus he was taken out. A moment after the roof fell in. When the child was carried out to the house where his parents were, the father cried out, "Come, neighbors, let us kneel down; let us give thanks to God! He has given me all my eight children: let the house go, I am rich enough." Mr. Wesley remembered this providential deliverance through life with the deepest gratitude.

(*i*) THE WIDOW AND THE TURK.—During the struggle of the Greeks to regain their liberty, a body of Turks were, in 1824, encamped in a part of Greece, and committed every kind of outrage upon the inhabitants One of these barbarians, an officer, had pursued a Greek girl, who took refuge in the house of a widow. The widow met him at the door, and mildly attempted to dissuade him from forcing his way in to seize the girl. Enraged, he drew his sabre; but when in the act of attempting to cut down the widow, it snapped in two pieces before it reached the victim. The wretch paused, yet drew a pistol, to accomplish his purpose, but it missed fire; and when in the act of drawing a second, he was forcibly dragged away by one of his companions, who exclaimed, "Let her alone. Do not you see that the time is not yet come?" Resolved, however, on taking some revenge, he carried off her infant child to the camp; but, as though Providence designed to frustrate all his designs on this occasion, whilst he was asleep, the child was carried back to the widow by one of his own men.

(*j*) THE MARTYR SAVED.—It is related, in the memoirs of the celebrated William Whiston, that a Protestant, in the days of Queen Mary, of the name of Barber, was sentenced to be burned. He walked to Smithfield, was bound to the stake, the fagots were piled around him, and the executioner only waited the word of command to apply the torch. At this crisis, tidings came of the queen's death; the officers were compelled to stay proceedings till the pleasure of Elizabeth should be known; and thus the life of the good man was spared, to labor, with some of his descendants, successfully in the service of the Lord Jesus and his church.

(*k*) THE SPANISH ARMADA.—When the Spaniards, on the defeat of their Invincible Armada, stung with disappointment, and wishing to detract from the honor which our brave defenders had acquired, exclaimed, that the English had little reason to boast, for if the elements had not fought against them, they would certainly have conquered us; the enlarged and vivid mind of Queen Elizabeth improved the hint. She commanded a medal to be struck, representing the Armada scattered and sinking in the back-ground; and in the front, the British fleet riding triumphant, with the following passage as a motto round the medal: "Thou didst blow with thy wind, and the sea covered them." It becomes us to say in reference to this, as well as many other national deliverances, "Blessed be the Lord, who hath not given us as a prey to their teeth."

842. Preserving from Persecutors and other Enemies.

(*a*) JOACHIM AND THE WALDENSES.—Maximilian, the emperor of Germany, conversing one day in his coach with Johannes Crato, who was his principal physician, and a learned Protestant, was lamenting the divisions of Christians, and asked Crato which party, in his opinion, approached the nearest to apostolic simplicity. Crato replied, that he thought that honor belonged to the brethren called Picards, (these were also called Waldenses and Albigenses.) The emperor said, "I think so, too." This being reported to them, afforded them much encouragement, and induced them to dedicate to him a book of their devotions; for, during the preceding year, God had marvelously preserved him from the guilt of their blood. Joachim a Novo Domo, chancellor of Bohemia, went to Vienna, and would give the emperor no rest until he procured for him a mandate for the revival of a former persecuting ordinance against them. Having obtained his commission, as he was leaving Vienna, and passing a bridge over the Danube, the bridge gave way and fell; when Joachim and all his retinue were plunged into that great river; and all were drowned except six horsemen and one young nobleman, who perceiving his lord in the water, caught hold of his gold chain, and held him up till some fishermen came to their assistance; but they found Joachim dead, and his box containing the persecuting mandate had sunk beyond recovery. The young nobleman was so affected by the hand of God in this affair, that he joined the brethren in their religion, and the persecution dropped.

(*b*) THE MERCHANT AND THE CRIMINAL.—A gentleman in an extensive line of business, in a distant part of the country, left his house with an intention of going to Bristol fair; but, when he had proceeded about half way, he was taken ill, and detained several days. As the fair by this time was in a considerable degree over, he returned home. Some years after, the same gentleman, happening to be at the place where the assizes for the county were held, was induced to be present at the execution of a criminal. While he was mixed with the crowd, the criminal perceived him, and expressed a desire to speak with him. On the gentleman approaching him, he asked, "Do you recollect at such a time intending to be at Bristol fair?" "Yes, perfectly well." "It is well that you did not go, for I and several others, who knew that you had a considerable sum of money about you, had resolved to waylay and rob, and then murder you, to prevent detection."

(*c*) GILPIN'S FALL.—When this zealous minister was on his way to London, to be tried before the popish party, he broke his leg by a fall, which put a stop for some time to his journey. The person in whose custody he was, took occasion from this circumstance to retort upon him an observation he used frequently to make, "That nothing happens to the people of God but what is intended for their good;" asking him, "whether he thought his broken leg was so." He answered meekly, "I make no question but it is." And so it proved; for before he was able to travel, Queen Mary died. Being thus providentially preserved from probable death, he returned to Houghton through crowds of people, who expressed the utmost joy, and blessed God for his deliverance.

(*d*) THE CHILD AND THE LION.—The Rev. John Campbell relates a singular escape of a Bushman child from being devoured by a lion. The child was only four years of age, and was sleeping beside its parents in a half open hut. About midnight the child awoke, and sat by a dull fire. The father happening to awake about the same time, looked at his child, and while looking, a lion came to the opposite side of the fire. The child, ignorant of its danger, was not afraid, but spoke to it, and sportingly threw live cinders at it, on which the lion snarled, and approached nearer, when the child seized a burning stick, and playfully thrust it into its mouth, when the lion scampered off as fast as it could run. The father witnessed all this, but was afraid to interfere, lest he, as well as his child, should have been torn to pieces by the ferocious animal.

(*e*) THE CZAR AND THE NOBLEMAN'S DINNER.—Alexander Menzikoff, who rose to the highest offices of state in Russia, during the reign of Peter the Great, was born of parents so excessively poor, that they could not afford to have him taught to read and write. After their death, he went to Moscow to seek for employment, where he found an asylum with a pastry-cook. He had a very fine voice, and soon became known in that great city, from the musical tone of his cry when vending his master's pastry in the street. His voice also gained him admission into the houses of many noblemen; and he was fortunate enough one day to be in the kitchen of a great lord with whom the emperor was to dine. While Menzikoff was there, the nobleman came into the kitchen, and gave directions about a particular dish, to which he said the emperor was very partial; into this dish he dropped (as he thought unperceived) a powder. Menzikoff observed it, but taking no notice, immediately left the house; and when he saw the emperor's carriage coming, he began to sing very loud. Peter, attracted by his voice, called him, and bought all the pies he had in his basket. He asked some questions of Menzikoff, and was so much pleased with his answers, that he commanded him to follow him to the nobleman's house, and wait behind his chair. The servants were surprised at this order, but it proved of the greatest importance to Peter; for when the nobleman pressed his royal guest to take of this favorite dish, his new servant gently pulled him by the sleeve, and begged he would not touch it till he had spoken to him. The emperor immediately withdrew with Menzikoff, who informed his imperial master of his suspicions. The czar returned to the company, and suddenly turning to his host, pressed him to partake of the favorite dish. Terrified at this command, he said, "It did not become the servant to eat before his master." The emperor then offered it to a dog, who greedily devoured its contents, and shortly afterwards expired in the greatest torments!

343. Preserving from Animals or by means of them.

(*a*) DU MOULIN AND THE SPIDER.—During the awful massacre at Paris, by which so many Christians were removed from the present world, the celebrated Moulin crept into an oven, over the mouth of which a spider instantly wove its web; so that when the enemies of the Christians inspected the premises, they passed by the oven, with the remark, that no one could have been there for some days. So easily can the blessed God devise means for the safety of his servants!

The memoirs of the late Rev. E. White, of Chester, by the Rev. Dr. Fletcher, of Stepney, relate a very similar anecdote of one of the ancestors of that pious and useful minister.

(*b*) A HEN SUPPORTING A CHAPLAIN.—In the melancholy Bartholomew massacre, in France, for three days every Protestant who could be found was put to death. By order of the king, Admiral de Coligny was murdered in his own house, but Merlin, his chaplain, concealed himself in a hayloft. It is recorded in the acts of the next synod, of which he was a moderator, that though many in similar circumstances died of hunger, he was supported by a hen regularly laying an egg near his place of refuge.

(*c*) GRESHAM AND THE GRASSHOPPER.—Sir Thomas Gresham, who built the Royal Exchange in London, was the son of a poor woman, who, while he was an infant, abandoned him in a field. By the providence of God, however, the chirping of a *grasshopper* attracted a boy to the spot where the child lay; and his life was, by this means, preserved. After Sir Thomas had, by his unparalleled success as a merchant, risen to the pinnacle of commercial wealth and greatness, he chose a grasshopper for his crest; and becoming, under Queen Elizabeth, the founder of the Royal Exchange, his crest was placed on the walls of the building in several parts, and a vane, or weathercock, in the figure of a grasshopper, was fixed on the summit of the tower.

(*d*) THE EAGLE'S NEST AND THE CHILD.—Sir Robert Sibbald relates, that a woman in the Orkney Islands, having left her child of about one year old, in a field, while she went to some distance, an eagle passing by took up the infant by its clothes, and carried it to her nest on a neighboring rock; which being observed by some fishermen, they instantly pursued the eagle, attacked her nest, and brought back the child unhurt.

(*e*) THE HOTTENTOT AND THE LION.—In the year 1829, a Hottentot, in South Africa, went out on a hunting excursion, accompanied by several other natives. Arriving on an extensive plain, where there was abundance of game, they discovered a number of lions, also, which appeared to be disturbed by their approach. A prodigiously large male immediately separated himself from the troop, and began slowly to advance towards the party, the majority of whom were young, and altogether unaccustomed to rencontres of so formidable a nature; the very appearance of the lion made them tremble.. While the animal was yet at a distance, they all dismounted to prepare for firing; and, according to the custom on such occasions. began tying their horses together by means of the bridles, with the view of keeping the latter between them and the lion, to attract his attention, until they were able to take deliberate aim. His movements, however, were too swift for them. Before the horses were properly fastened to each other, the monster made a tremendous bound or two, and suddenly pounced upon the hind parts of one of them; which, in its fright, plunged forward, and knocked down the poor man who was holding the reins in his hand. His comrades instantly took flight, and ran off with all their speed; and he, of course, rose as quickly as possible, in order to follow them. But no sooner had he regained his feet, than the lion, with a seeming consciousness of his superior might, stretched forth his paw, and striking him just behind the neck, immediately brought him to the ground again. He then rolled on his back, when the lion set his foot upon his breast, and lay down upon him. The poor man now became almost breathless, partly from fear, but principally from the intolerable pressure of his terrific load. He endeavored to move a little to one side, in order to breathe; but feeling this, the lion seized his left arm, close to the elbow, and continued to amuse himself with the limb for some time, biting it in different places down to the hand, the thick part of which seemed to have been pierced entirely through. All this time the lion did not appear to be angry, but merely caught at his prey, like a cat sporting with a mouse that is not quite dead; so that there was not a single bone fractured, as would in all probability have been the case had the creature been hungry or irritated. Whilst writhing in agony, gasping for breath, and expecting every moment to be torn limb from limb, the sufferer cried to his companions for assistance, but cried in vain. On raising his head a little, the beast opened his dreadful jaws to receive it, but providentially the hat slipped off, so that the points of the teeth only just grazed the surface of the skull. The lion now set his foot upon the arm from which the blood was freely flowing; his fearful paw was soon covered with it, and he again and again licked it clean! But this was not the worst; for the animal then steadily fixed his flaming eyes upon those of the man; smelt on one side, and then on the other, of his face; and, having tasted the blood, he appeared half inclined to devour his helpless victim. "At this critical moment," said the poor man, "I recollected having heard that there was a God in the heavens, who was able to deliver at the very last extremity, and I began to pray that he would save me, and not allow the lion to eat my flesh and drink my blood." Whilst thus engaged in calling upon God, the beast turned himself completely round. On perceiving this, the Hottentot made an effort to get from under him; but no sooner did the creature observe his movement than he took fast hold of his right thigh. This wound was dreadfully deep, and occasioned the sufferer most excruciating pain. He again sent up his cry to God for help; nor were his prayers in vain. The huge animal soon afterwards quietly relinquished his prey, though he had not been in the least interrupted. Having risen from his seat, he walked majestically off, to the distance of thirty or forty paces, and then lay down in the grass, as if for the purpose of watching the man. The latter being happily relieved of his load, ventured to sit up, which circumstance immediately attracted the lion's attention; nevertheless it did not induce another attack, as the poor fellow naturally expected; but as if bereft of power, and unable to do any thing more, the lion again rose, took his departure, and was seen no more. The man seeing this, took up his gun, and hastened away to his terrified companions, who had given him up for dead Being in a state of extreme exhaustion, from loss of blood, he was immediately set upon his horse, carried away, and by the use of suitable means, soon recovered.

(*f*) THE SAILOR AND THE CROCODILE.—Campbell, the sailor, being at sea, felt, one evening when near the shore, a disposition to bathe. His companions would have dissuaded him from it, as they had recently seen several sharks; but being partly intoxicated, he would not listen to their persuasions. Nearly as soon as he was in the water, his companions saw an alligator directing his course towards him, and considered his escape from death totally impossible. They fired at the alligator, but in vain. Campbell became aware of his danger, and immediately made for the shore. On approaching within a short distance of some canes and shrubs that covered the bank, and while closely pursued by the alligator, a ferocious tiger sprung towards him, at the very instant he was about being devoured by his first enemy. At this awful moment he was preserved. The eager tiger overleaped him, fell into the grasp of the alligator, and, after a long struggle, was killed by him. Campbell was conveyed to his vessel, gratefully returned thanks to Providence which had preserved him and from that period a marked change was observed in his character.

(*g*) RUGGLES AND THE INDIANS.—This worthy man, who was an American minister, had a remarkable preservation from death. While he was once preaching, a party of Indians came suddenly upon the congregation, scattered them, and carried him away into the forest. At night, he was left under the charge of two women, while the men went to rest; but his female keepers, as well as the dogs, falling asleep, he took the opportunity to make his escape. He had not gone far before he heard the alarm cry, and the crashing of the bushes behind warned him that the enemy were already in close pursuit of him. In his distress he crept, with little hope of safety, into a hollow tree, at whose foot there happened to be an opening, through which he could squeeze his body, and stand upright within. The Indians soon rushed by in full chase, without stopping to search his retreat; and, what is more extraordinary, their dogs had previously smelled about the root of the tree, and ran forward without barking, as though they had discovered nothing.

(*h*) THE TRAVELER AND THE STRANGE DOG.—A gentleman, says the London Methodist Magazine, traveling in Cornwall, observed a strange dog following him on the road, which, notwithstanding every effort he used to drive him back, claimed acquaintance with him.

Being benighted in a lonely place, he called at the first inn he met with, and desired to be accommodated with a room. After supper the gentleman retired to rest. No sooner had he opened the door, than the before mentioned dog rushed in. After some fruitless efforts to drive the dog away, the gentleman permitted him to stay in the room; thinking he could do him no harm

When the gentleman began to prepare for bed, the dog ran to a closet door, and then ran back to him, looking very wistfully at him. This the dog did several times, which so far excited the curiosity of the gentleman, that he opened the closet door; and to his great terror, saw a person laid with his throat cut. Struck with horror, he began to think of his own state. To attempt to run away he supposed would be unsafe. He therefore began to barricade the door with the furniture of the room, and laid himself on the bed with his clothes on. About midnight two men came to the door and requested admittance, stating that the gentleman that slept there the preceding night, had forgotten something and was returned for it. He replied, the room was his, and no one should enter his room until morning. They went away, but soon returned with two or three other men, and demanded entrance; but the gentleman, with an austere voice, threatened if they did not desist, he would defend himself. Awed apparently by this bold reply, they left him and disturbed him no more.

In the morning he inquired for a barber; one was immediately sent for, when the gentleman took the oppportunity of inquiring into the character of his host. The barber replied, he was a neighbor, and did not wish to say any thing to his disadvantage. The gentleman still urged his inquiry, assuring him he had nothing to fear, till the barber said, "Sir, if I must tell the truth, they bear a very bad character, for it has been reported, that persons have called here, who have never been heard of afterwards." Can you, said the gentleman keep a secret? On his answering in the affirmative, the gentleman opened the closet door, and showed him the person with his throat cut; he then directed the barber to procure a constable, and proper assistance with all speed, which was done immediately, and the host and hostess were both taken into custody, to take their trial at the next assize. They took their trial and were found guilty of the murder, condemned and executed. The dog was never seen by the gentleman afterwards.

672

(*i*) ESCAPE FROM BUFFALOES AND A PANTHER.—Mr. Hunter, in the narrative of his life among the western Indians, says, "In one of my excursions, while seated in the shade of a large tree, situated on a gentle declivity, with a view to procure some mitigation from the oppressive heat of the noonday sun, I was surprised by a tremendous rushing noise. I sprang up, and discovered a herd I believe of a thousand buffaloes, running at full speed directly towards me; as I supposed to beat off the flies, which at this season, inconceivably trouble some of those animals.

"I placed myself behind the tree, so as not to be seen, not apprehending any danger, because they ran with too great rapidity and too closely together, to afford any one of them any opportunity of injuring me while protected in this manner. "The buffaloes passed so near me on both sides that I could have touched several merely by extending my arm. In the rear of the herd, was one on which a huge panther had fixed, and was voraciously engaged in cutting off the muscles of its neck. I did not discover this circumstance till it had nearly passed beyond rifle shot distance, when I discharged my piece and wounded the panther. It instantly left its hold on the buffalo, and bounded with great rapidity towards me. On witnessing the result of my shot, the apprehensions I suffered can hardly be imagined. I had, however, sufficient presence of mind to retreat, and secrete myself behind the trunk of the tree, opposite to its approaching direction. Here, solicitous for what possibly might be the result of my unfortunate shot, I prepared both my knife and tomahawk, for what I supposed a dreadful conflict with this terrible animal. In a few moments, however, I had the satisfaction to hear it in the branches of the tree over my head. My rifle had just been discharged, and I entertained fears that I could not reload it, without discovery, and yet exposing myself to the fury of its destructive rage. I looked into the tree with the utmost caution, but could not perceive it, though its groans and vengeance-breathing growls, told me tha it was not far off, and also what I had to expect, in case it should discover me. In this situation, with my eyes almost constantly upwards to observe its motions, I silently loaded my rifle, and then creeping softly round the tree, saw my formidable enemy resting on a considerable branch about thirty feet from the ground, with his side fairly exposed. I was unobserved, took deliberate aim, and shot it through the heart. It made a single bound from the tree to the earth and died in a moment afterwards.

(*j*) CHILD CARRIED AWAY BY AN EAGLE.—A peasant with his wife and three children, had taken up his summer quarters in a chalet, and was pasturing his flock on one of the rich Alps which overhang the Durance. The oldest boy was an idiot, about eight years of age; the second was five years old, and dumb; and the youngest was an infant. It so happened, that the infant was left one morning in charge of his brothers, and the three had rambled to some distance from the chalet before they were missed. When the mother went in search of the little wanderers, she found the two elder, but could discover no traces of the babe. The idiot boy seemed to be in a transport of joy, while the dumb child displayed every symptom of alarm and terror. In vain did the terrified parent endeavor to collect what had become of the lost infant. The antics of the one and the fright of the other explained nothing. The dumb boy was almost bereft of his senses, while the idiot appeared to have acquired an unusual degree of mirth and expression. He danced about, laughed, and made gesticulations as if he were imitating the action of one who had caught up something of which he was fond, and hugged to his heart. This, however, was some slight comfort to the poor woman; for she imagined that some acquaintance had fallen in with the children, and had taken away the infant. But the day and night wore away and no tidings came of the lost child. On the morrow, when the parents were pursuing their search, an eagle flew over their heads, at the sight of which the idiot renewed his antics, and the dumb boy clung to his father, with shrieks of anguish and affright. The horrible truth then burst upon their minds, that the miserable infant had been carried off in the talons of a bird of prey, and that the half-witted elder brother was delighted at his riddance of an object of whom he was jealous.

On the morning on which the accident happened, an Alpine yager,

> "Whose joy was in the wilderness—to breathe
> The difficult air of the iced mountain's top,"

had been watching near an eagle's seat under the hope of shooting the bird upon her return to her nest. The yager, waiting in all the anxious perseverance of a true sportsman, beheld the eagle slowly winging her way toward the rock, behind which he was concealed. Imagine his horror, when, upon her nearer approach, he heard the cries and distinguished the figure of an infant in her fatal grasp. In an instant his resolution was formed—to fire at the bird at all hazards, the moment she should alight upon her nest, and rather to kill the child, than leave it to be torn to pieces by the horrid devourer. With a silent prayer, and a steady aim, the mountainer poised his rifle. The ball went directly through the head or heart of the eagle, and in a minute afterward, the gallant hunter of the Alps had the unutterable delight of snatching the child from the nest, and bearing it away in triumph. It was dreadfully wounded by the eagle in one of its arms and sides, but not mortally; and, within twenty-four hours after it was first missed, he had the satisfaction of restoring it to its mother's arms.

(*k*) THE IMPORTUNATE INTRUDER.—Sir Harry Lee, in Ditchlong, in Oxfordshire, ancestor of the late earl of Litchfield, had a mastiff which guarded the house and yard, but had never met with the least particular attention from his master, and was retained for his utility only, and not from any particular regard. One night as his master was retiring to his chamber, attended by his *faithful* valet, an Italian, the mastiff silently followed him up stairs, which he had never been known to do before, and to his master's astonishment, presented himself in his bed room. Being deemed an intruder, he was instantly ordered to be turned out; which being complied with, the poor animal began scratching violently at the door, and howling loudly for admission. The servant was sent to drive him away. Discouragement could not check his labor of love, or rather providential impulse; he returned again, and was more importunate than before to be let in. Sir Harry, weary of opposition, bade the servant open the door, that they might see what he would do. This done, the mastiff, with a wag of his tail, and a look of affection at his lord, deliberately walked up, and crawling under the bed, laid himself down as if desirous of taking up his night's lodging there. To save farther trouble, but not from any partiality for his company, the indulgence was allowed. About the hour of midnight the chamber door opened, and a person was heard stepping across the room. Sir Harry started from his sleep; the dog sprung from his covert, and, seizing the unwelcome disturber, fixed him to the spot! All was dark, and Sir Harry rung his bell in great trepidation, in order to procure a light. The person who was pinned to the floor by the courageous mastiff roared for assistance. It was found to be the *valet*, who little expected such a reception. He endeavored to apologize for his intrusion, and to make the reasons which induced him to take the step appear plausible; but the importunity of the dog, the time, the place, and the manner of the valet, all raised suspicion in Sir Harry's mind, and he determined to refer the investigation of the business to a magistrate. The perfidious Italian, alternately terrified by the dread of punishment, and soothed with the hope of pardon, at length confessed that it was his intention to murder his master, and then rob the house. This diabolical design was frustrated only by the dog, who had perhaps providentially overheard some expressions in soliloquy or conversation, from the valet, respecting his contemplated crime.

(*l*) KICHERER AND THE ASSASSIN.—This name will remind the reader of the first Missionary to the African Hottentots. During his early residence among them, he was visited by a man who had been sentenced at the Cape of Good Hope to death, but had effected his escape; and who, making great pretensions to religion, imposed on Mr. K. and induced him to receive him into his house. He slept in a room immediately adjoining that of the Missionary, and rose during the night with the design of murdering him, and of making his escape, with the property on the premises, to a distant place. At the moment he was proceeding to the bedside of this good man, Mr. K. was suddenly awoke in a fit of terror, and unconsciously cried out, as though aware of the design of this wicked man, who, in consequence, became alarmed, and fled.

(*m*) DREAM OF THE SERVANT.—Mr. Williams, an eminently pious man, who lived at Kidderminster in the last century, records in his diary a remarkable interposition of the providence of God, in preserving his family and property from devouring flames. One of his servants dreamed that a neighbor's house was on fire, and through the agitation which the dream occasioned, she made a little noise, which awoke Mrs. W. who was sleeping in a room below. On awaking, she found her room filled with smoke; and when Mr. Williams arose and examined the house, he found part of one of the lower rooms on fire; which, but for the singular manner in which they had been disturbed, would have speedily placed the whole family in danger; and, as the house was not that year insured, have deprived the good man of nearly all he possessed.

BY THE CONTROL OF MIND.

344. In Overruling Involuntary Affections and Dreams.

(*a*) THE SOLDIER AND THE JEWELER.—During the late French war, the French and Prussian troops met in Lubec. The inhabitants could not anticipate any thing but plunder and murder.

Among others, a very pious jeweler determined to fly to God for refuge. All his gold and silver articles being placed upon a table, he requested all the members of his family to unite with him in prayer. While on their knees, a French soldier burst open the door of the house, and stood still, until the jeweler closed the solemn exercise. He then invited the soldier to the table, saying, "Sir, take of these articles whatever you please." "No!" said the soldier, I will take nothing; but shall continue with you as a guard, until we march away. At night, a bed was offered to the soldier, but he declined accepting it, preferring to remain in the room below, in order to be ready at any moment for defending the jeweler against plunderers. The French after some days withdrew. The soldier of course joined his troops. Stationed in another city, he was quartered at the house of an intimate friend of the jeweler, to whom he related the occurrence, adding, I never knew what fear was, until I unexpectedly saw the jeweler and his family upon their knees praying. Such was the degree of terror with which I was struck, that I could not move from the sill of the door until the jeweler came to me! God protects his children.

(*b*) THE MISSIONARIES AND THE MURDERERS.—Soon after the Moravian brethren had commenced their zealous and disinterested labors in Greenland, a number of murderers, excited by the angekoks, or sorcerers, threatened to kill the Missionaries, and entered their house for that purpose, at a time when all were absent, excepting one, named Matthew Stach. When they arrived, they found him engaged in the work of translation, in which he went on, without showing any marks of fear, though uncertain as to their intention. After they had sat awhile, their leader said, "We are come to hear good." "I am glad of it," replied the Missionary, and silence being obtained, he sang, prayed, and then proceeded: "I will not say much to you of the Creator of all things—you know there is a Creator;"—to this they all assented except one. "You also know that you are a wicked people." "Yes!" was the unanimous reply. "Now, then," resumed the Missionary, "I will tell you what is most necessary to know." He then proceeded to declare the incarnation and death of Jesus; spoke of his resurrection from the dead; and assured them, that he would be the final Judge of all men. He then solemnly appealed to the leader of the banditti, as to the account he would render of his murders and other crimes at the last day, and entreated him immediately to accept the mercy offered him by the Lord Jesus. After he had done, a woman, whose brother they had murdered, spoke of the efficacy of the Savior's atonement, told them she felt it, and exhorted them no longer to resist the truth. They heard all this with attention, walked for some time before the house with their hands folded, and towards evening retired, without offering either violence or insult.

(*c*) HILL AND HIS GARDENER.—The Rev. Rowland Hill had great reason to rejoice in the consistent lives, and zealous devotion to God, of many of his people at Wotton. There was amongst them a person of the name of Rugg, of a piety so deep, and of a life so useful and unblemished, that even his enemies admired and were awed by his character. Mr. Hill's gardener at Wotton, who had always passed for an honest, quiet sort of man, was at length discovered to have been the perpetrator of several burglaries, and other daring robberies in the neighborhood, though he had, till caught in the fact, never been even suspected. He was tried at Gloucester, condemned, and executed. It need scarcely be said that his master visited him in gaol. During his interview with him there, he confessed the many crimes of which he had been guilty. "How was it, William," he inquired, "that you never robbed me, when you had such abundant opportunity?" "Sir," replied he, "do you recollect the juniper bush on the border against the dining room? I have many times hid under it at night, intending, which I could easily have done, to get into the house and plunder it; but, sir, I was afraid: something said to me, He is a man of God: it is a house of prayer; if I break in I shall surely be found out: so I never could pluck up courage to attempt it." In another conversation, he told him, "Sir, I well knew that old Mr. Rugg was in the habit of carrying a deal of money in his pocket: times and times have I hid behind the hedge of the lane leading to his house: he has passed within a yard of me, when going home from the prayer-meeting, again and again; I could not stir; I durst not touch so holy a man. I was afraid. I always began to tremble as soon as he came near me, and gave up the thought altogether, for I knew he was a holy man."

(*d*) RUFFIANS FRIGHTENED BY PRAYER.—A lady in one of our large cities had been in the habit of attending religious meetings in the evening. When she had no one to accompany her, she would go alone, although frequently admonished of her danger. On her return one evening from the place of worship, in crossing a public walk which lay in her way home, she was met by two ruffians, who stopped before her, and presenting a pistol to her breast, demanded her watch and money. Although alone as they supposed, there was one present in whom she trusted, that the wretches did not see, and at whose approach others like them once "went backward and fell to the ground." As she had no arm of flesh to protect her, she instantly fell upon her knees before them, and with uplifted hands cried out, "Now, Lord Jesus, help!" The affrighted assassins fled.

(*e*) BUNYAN AND THE JAILER.—The respectability of Bunyan's character and the propriety of his conduct, while in prison at Bedford, appear to have operated very powerfully on the mind of the jailer, who showed him much kindness, in permitting him to go out and visit his friends occasionally, and once to take a journey to London.

The following anecdote is told respecting the jailer and Mr. Bunyan:—It being known to some of his persecutors, in London, that he was often out of prison, they sent an officer to talk with the jailer on the subject; and, in order to discover the fact, he was to get there in the middle of the night. Bunyan was at home with his family, but so restless that he could not sleep; he therefore acquainted his wife that, though the jailer had given him liberty to stay till the morning, yet, from his uneasiness, he must immediately return. He did so, and the jailer blamed him for coming in at such an unseasonable hour. Early in the morning the messenger came, and interrogating the jailer, said, "Are all the prisoners safe?" "Yes." "Is John Bunyan safe?" "Yes." "Let me see him." He was called, and appeared, and all was well. After the messenger was gone, the jailer, addressing Mr. Bunyan, said, "Well, you may go in and out again just when you think proper, for you know when to return better than I can tell you.

(*f*) THE DROWNING LADY.—A gay lady in New England once had occasion to go to a neighboring town, where she had often been before. In the immediate vicinity was a stream which she had to go near, and which at this period was high. With a view of showing her courage to a young person whom she had taken with her as a companion, she went into the stream with her horse, and in a very little time was thrown into the water,—had already sunk once or twice to the bottom, and felt that she was within a few moments of an eternal world, without being prepared for so great a change.

It so happened, that a young man in another neighboring town had felt a powerful impression on his mind that morning, that he would visit the same place. He had no business to transact; but, being forcibly impressed with the importance of going thither, he invited a young man to accompany him. Arriving at the side of the stream just as the young ladies were about to cross it, they saw it was improbable that they could ford it; yet, as the ladies went, they determined to follow.

By the time the young lady was thrown from her horse, the others had nearly reached the opposite shore; but, perceiving her danger, one of them immediately followed her on his horse, and in the last moment of life, as it then appeared, she caught hold of the horse's leg; he thus secured her, and snatching hold of the other drowning young lady, she was saved also. After the use of proper remedies they recovered; and the young gentlemen, believing that the design of their coming from home was now answered, returned back.

The impressions made on the mind of this young lady were permanent, and she was led to reflect on the sins she had committed against God, to pray for the pardon of her guilt, and to devote herself to the Divine service. She embraced the mercy of the Lord, believing in the Redeemer, who alone saves from the wrath to come.

In the same town with herself lived a young gentleman, who had often spent his hours in vain conversation with her. On her return home, he went to congratulate her on her escape, and to his surprise, found she attributed her deliverance to the power of God, and urged him to seek that grace which they had both neglected. Her serious conversation was blest to his conversion, and he became a faithful minister of Jesus Christ.

(*g*) WISHART AND THE FORGERY.—The name of this eminent man is well known in Scotland, where he acted a distinguished part in the reformation of religion, which rendered him a constant object of the hatred of the popish party. Cardinal Benson frequently formed plans to take away his life. At one time, he procured a letter to be sent to him as from an intimate friend, the laird of Kinnier, in which he was requested to come to him without delay, as he had been seized with sudden illness. In the meantime, the cardinal had provided sixty men to waylay him, and deprive him of life.

The letter having been delivered by a boy who also brought a horse to convey him on his journey, Wishart set out, but suddenly stopping by the way, avowed to the friends who had accompanied him, his strong conviction that God did not will that he should proceed; for that there was treachery in this business. They went forward without him, and discovered the whole plot, by which means his life was preserved.

(*h*) KNOX AND THE ASSASSIN.—This celebrated Scotch reformer had many surprising escapes from the malicious designs of his enemies. He was accustomed to sit at the head of the table in his own house, with his back to the window; on one particular evening, however, he would neither himself sit in his chair, nor allow any one else to do so. That very night a bullet was shot in at the window purposely to kill him; it grazed the chair in which he usually sat, and made a hole in the foot of the candlestick.

(*i*) DOD'S SINGULAR VISIT.—It is recorded of Mr. Dod, one of the Puritan ministers, that being one evening late in his study, his mind was strongly inclined, though he could assign no reason for it, to visit a gentleman of his acquaintance, at a very unseasonable hour. Not knowing the design of Providence, he obeyed and went. When he came to the house, after knocking a few times at the door, the gentleman himself came, and inquired if he wanted him upon any particular business. Mr. Dod having answered in the negative, and signified that he could not rest till he had seen him, the gentleman replied, "O, sir, you are sent of God at this very hour, for I was just now going to destroy myself!" and immediately pulled the halter out of his pocket, by which he had intended to commit the horrid deed, which was thus prevented.

(*j*) THE LOST WOMAN.—A poor woman residing in a village in Bedfordshire, had occasion to go to another village, about three miles distant; and as she could not return before evening, it was agreed that her husband, who was a laboring man, should meet her as she returned home.

The night being extremely dark, she unfortunately missed her way, and her endeavors to find the path only led her so much the farther from it. Bewildered and alarmed, she wandered she knew not whither. In this distressing situation she walked about for some time, until completely fatigued and exhausted.

At this moment it was strongly impressed upon her mind to sit down, and wait the return of morning, which she accordingly did; and on extending her feet in order to obtain as much relief as possible for her weary limbs, they splashed in some water.

Ignorant of her real situation, and without one ray of light to direct her, her feelings may be more easily conceived than described; with the utmost anxiety she awaited the dawn of day, which discovered her perilous situation, on the bank of a deep river, the Ouse, into which another step would inevitably have plunged her.

Being a pious woman, she first acknowledged, with unfeigned gratitude, the hand of her gracious Preserver, and then made the best of her way home.

345. In Overruling Voluntary Acts and Affections.

(*a*) THE SOLDIER'S SHIELD.—Samuel Proctor was trained up in the use of religious ordinances, and in early life felt some religious impressions. He afterwards enlisted as a soldier in the first regiment of foot guards, and was made a grenadier. Notwithstanding this, the impressions made upon his mind continued; and the fear of the Lord, as a guardian angel, attended him through the changing scenes of life. There were a few in the regiment who met for pious and devotional exercises; he cast in his lot among them, and always carried a small pocket Bible in one pocket, and his hymn-book in the other. He took part in the struggle on the plains of Waterloo in 1815. In the evening of June 16th, in the tremendous conflict on that day, his regiment was ordered to dislodge the French from a wood, of which they had taken possession, and from which they annoyed the allied army. While thus engaged, he was thrown a distance of four or five yards by a force on his hip, for which he could not account at the time; but, when he came to examine his Bible, he saw, with overwhelming gratitude to the Preserver of his life, what it was that had thus driven him. A musket-ball had struck his hip where his Bible rested in his pocket, and penetrated nearly half through that sacred book. All who saw the ball, said that it would undoubtedly have killed him, had it not been for the Bible, which served as a shield. The Bible was kept as a sacred treasure, and laid up in his house, like the sword of Goliath in the tabernacle. "That Bible," said Proctor, "has twice saved me instrumentally—first, from death in battle, and second from death eternal."

(*b*) POWELL SAVED BY FIDELITY.—This good man was one of those devoted ministers, who, in the seventeenth century, were grievously persecuted. In an account of the trials and mercies he experienced, he tells us, that two of the enemies of religion on one occasion severely beat him, one of whom, with a cudgel, greatly wounded him; but his life was preserved. At another time, four armed men waylaid him, intending to kill him, but were unexpectedly discovered by two strangers, who dispersed them. One of these persecutors that very day became, under Mr. Powell's preaching, convinced of his sin, and refrained ever after from persecution. At another period, a poor man took an oath to kill him; but, after several ineffectual attempts to accomplish his purpose he went to hear Mr. P. deliver a sermon, in which the mercy of Christ as the Savior of sinners was so powerfully exhibited, that his heart was melted; he entreated Mr. P. to pray for him and become his friend. On another occasion Mr. P. was apprehended while preaching; and on his way to the justice of peace, he so preached as to be the instrument of causing one of his greatest enemies to weep. When he arrived at the house of the magistrate, who was not at home, he preached even there, and the impression on the minds of his two daughters was such, that they became his intercessors, and he was released.

(*c*) ESCAPE OF GEN. WASHINGTON.—Major Ferguson, who commanded a rifle corps in advance of the hussars under Kniphausen, during some skirmishing a day or two previous to the battle of Brandywine, was the hero of a very singular incident, which he thus relates in a letter to a friend. It illustrates, in a most forcible manner, the overruling hand of Providence in directing the operations of a man's mind, in moments when he is least of all aware of it.

"We had not lain long, when a rebel

officer, remarkable by a hussar dress, pressed towards our army, within a hundred yards of my right flank, not perceiving us. He was followed by another, dressed in dark green and blue, mounted on a bay horse, with a remarkably high cocked hat. I ordered three good shots to steal near to them, and fire at them; but the idea disgusting me, I recalled the order. The hussar, in returning, made a circuit, but the other passed within a hundred yards of us, upon which I advanced from the wood towards him. Upon my calling, he stopped; but after looking at me, he proceeded. I again drew his attention, and made signs to him to stop, leveling my piece at him; but he slowly cantered away. As I was within that distance at which, in the quickest firing, I could have lodged half a dozen balls in or about him, before he was out of my reach, I had only to determine; but it was not pleasant to fire at the back of an unoffending individual, who was acquitting himself very coolly of his duty; so I let him alone.

"The day after, I had been telling this story to some wounded officers who lay in the same room with me, when one of the surgeons, who had been dressing the wounded rebel officers, came in, and told us, that they had been informing him that General Washington was all the morning with the light troops, and only attended by a French officer in a hussar dress, he himself dressed and mounted in every point as above described. I am not sorry that I did not know at the time who it was."

(*d*) TEMPTED CHRISTIAN SAVED.—About the year 1808, a young lady, walking out late on a winter's evening, on the Kentish coast, was alarmed by overhearing a conversation of some Irish laborers, which proved she was in danger of being robbed, if not murdered. She resolved to return to the village she had just left, which she accomplished, though pursued by one of the men, from whom she was mercifully delivered.

Agitated and distressed, she determined to stay at the village for the night, and went to the house of a baronet in pursuit of a pious woman, who, in the absence of the family, always slept in it. She was surprised that, for a long time, her rap at the door was not answered; and still more to find, when entrance was permitted, all the doors she had to pass with her friend fastened; nor was her astonishment lessened, when she learned that the good woman was entirely without food, or firing. However, she stayed for the night, and, in the morning, went home.

Ten years rolled along, during which time the old woman treated her young friend with much kindness; the former had buried several of her family, and was about to leave the neighborhood. Previous to this, she called on her friend, reminded her of the circumstances, which, indeed, she had never forgotten; and then, under a promise of secrecy during her life, divulged the following facts:—

For some time before the events first alluded to occurred, the poor old lady, though a pious woman, had been the subject of many temptations. Melancholy and doubting, Satan at last prevailed on her to attempt to take away her life. And so nearly was this purpose accomplished, that, at the time this young lady sought admission to the house, she had locked up all its doors, and was passing down the yard to throw herself into the sea! She recognised the hand of God in this interposition to save her life, lived to his praise for twelve or fourteen years after this event, and at length died in the full hope of immortality, through the mediation of the Lord Jesus.

(*e*) AUGUSTINE'S MISTAKE.—Posidonius, in his life of Augustine, relates, that the good man, going on one occasion to preach at a distant town, took with him a guide to direct him in the way. This man, by some unaccountable means, mistook the usual road, and fell into a bye-path. It afterwards proved, that in this way the preacher's life had been saved, as his enemies, aware of his journey, had placed themselves in the proper road with a design to kill him.

(*f*) THE SADDLE BAG IN THE WRONG BOAT. — The Rev. T.

Charles, who was well known as a holy and useful minister in Wales, had once a remarkable escape from death. In one of his journeys to Liverpool, his saddle-bag was, by mistake, put into a boat different from that in which he intended to go, which made it necessary to change his boat, even after he had taken his seat. By this change, so contrary to his intentions, he was graciously preserved; for the boat in which he meant to sail was lost, and all its passengers were drowned.

(*g*) DR. COLE'S COMMISION.—It is related, in the papers of Richard earl of Cork, that towards the conclusion of Queen Mary's reign, a commission was signed for the persecution of the Irish Protestants; and, to give greater weight to this important affair, Dr. Cole was nominated one of the commission. The doctor in his way to Dublin, stopped at Chester, where he was waited upon by the mayor; to whom, in the course of conversation, he imparted the object of his mission, and exhibited the leather box which contained his credentials. The mistress of the inn, where this interview took place, being a Protestant, and having overheard the conversation, seized the opportunity, while the doctor was attending the mayor to the bottom of the stairs, of exchanging the commission for a dirty pack of cards, on the top of which she facetiously turned up the knave of clubs. The doctor, little suspecting the trick, secured his box, pursued his journey, and arrived in Dublin on the 7th of October, 1558. He then lost no time in presenting himself before lord Fitzwalter and the privy council; to whom, after an explanatory speech, the box was presented, which to the astonishment of all present, was found to contain only a pack of cards! The doctor, greatly chagrined, returned instantly to London, to have his commission renewed: but while waiting a second time on the coast for a favorable wind, the news reached him of the queen's decease, which prevented the persecution, that would have otherwise proved so awful a calamity. Queen Elizabeth was so much gratified with these facts, which were related to her by Lord Fitzwalter on his return to England, that she sent for the woman, whose name was Elizabeth Edwards, and gave her a pension of forty pounds a year during her life.

(*h*) HOWARD AND THE HIGHWAYMAN. — John Howard, Esq., the eminent philanthropist, always set a very high value on the Sabbaths he spent in England; and, during his absence on the continent, he deeply deplored the want of Christian privileges. That he might not increase the labor of his servants, nor prevent their attendance on Divine worship, he usually walked to the chapel, where he attended, at Bedford, though at a distance of nearly three miles from his residence. So regularly did he pursue this practice, that an idle and dissolute man, whom he had reproved for his sins, determined to avail himself of this opportunity to waylay and murder him. But Divine Providence remarkably interposed to preserve so valuable a life, by inclining him that morning to go on horseback a different road, by which means his valuable life was prolonged.

(*i*) GREENLAND MISSIONARIES FED.—When the Moravian missionaries first went, in the last century, to labor in Greenland, they were called to endure the most painful and distressing trials, both in reference to the indifference of the heathen, and the want of food. Famine, of the most afflictive kind, almost constantly threatened them. But in the darkest hours, God always appeared in some way or other, for their help. On one occasion, He disposed a Greenlander, a perfect stranger to them, to travel forty leagues to sell them some seals, the flesh of which, with oatmeal and train oil, was a delicacy to them compared with the old tallow candles on which they sometimes lived. At another time, when they had just returned from a toilsome excursion, in which they could obtain no food, a Greenlander brought them word that a Dutch ship was lying at some distance to the south, the captain of which had letters for them. On sending to the ship, they found a cask of provisions sent them by a kind friend at Amsterdam, with the proposal to send more if they needed. At another period, they were returning home empty in their frail boat, when a contrary wind forced them on a desolate island, where they were compelled to remain all night. Here they shot an eagle, and thus obtained food, and also quills for writing.

(*j*) MRS. ERSKINE'S RELEASE.—There is a remarkable circumstance connected with the history of Ralph Erskine—a fact well authenticated in the part of Scotland where his family lived. His mother "died and was buried," some years before he was born. She wore on her finger at the time of her death a rich gold ring, which, from some domestic cause or other, was much valued by the family. After the body was laid in the coffin, an attempt was made to remove the ring, but the hand and the finger were so much swollen that it was found impossible. It was proposed to cut off the finger, but the husband's feelings revolted at the idea. She was therefore buried with the ring on her finger. The sexton, who was aware of the fact, formed a resolution to possess himself of the ring. Accordingly on the same night he opened the grave and coffin.—Having no scruples about cutting off the finger of a dead woman, he provided himself with a sharp knife for the purpose. He lifted the stiff arm, and made an incision by the joint of the finger. The blood flowed—and the woman arose and sat up in her coffin! The grave digger fled with affright, while the lady made her way from her narrow tenement and walked back to the door of her dwelling, where she stood without and knocked for admittance. Her husband, who was a minister, sat conversing with a friend. When the knock was repeated he observed, "were it not that my wife is in her grave, I should say that was her knock." He arose hastily and opened the door. There stood his dear companion, wrapped in her grave clothes, and her uplifted finger dropping blood. "My Margaret!" he exclaimed. "The same," said she—"Your dear wife, in her own proper person, do not be alarmed."

The lady in question, lived seven or eight years after this occurrence, and became the mother of several children, among whom was the person above spoken of.

(*k*) WISHART AND THE PSALM.—The Covenanters, in the time of the civil wars were exceedingly fond of singing psalms. When the great Montrose was taken prisoner, his chaplain, Wishart, the elegant historian of his deeds, shared the same fate with his patron, and was condemned to the same punishment. Being desired on the scaffold to name what psalm he wished to have sung, he selected the 119th, consisting of twenty-four parts. In this he was guided by God; for before two thirds of the psalm was sung a pardon arrived.

IN BESTOWING VARIOUS BLESSINGS.

346. In Overruling Benevolence.

(*a*) "THERE IS THAT SCATTERETH," &c.—During the siege of the Protestant city of Rochelle, under Louis XIII and Cardinal Richelieu, the inhabitants endured great miseries before they yielded to an honorable capitulation, the terms of which were, however, far from being kept by their enemies. One of the many touching incidents of the siege is recorded by Merivault. "He gives the names of the parties chiefly concerned," says Smedley; "and the narrative is marked by an air of truth, which renders its authenticity undoubted. During the height of calamity among the Rochellois, some charitable individuals, who had previously formed secret magazines, relieved their starving brethren without blazoning their good deed. The relict of a merchant, named Prosni, who was left in charge of four orphan children, had literally distributed her stores, while any thing remained, among her less fortunate neighbors; and whenever she was reproached with profusion and want of foresight by a rich sister-in-law of less benevolent temper, she was in the habit of replying, 'The Lord will provide for us.' At length, when her stock of food was utterly exhausted, and she was spurned with taunts from the door of her relative, she returned home destitute, broken-hearted, and prepared to die, together with her children. But it seemed as if the mercies once displayed at Zarephath were again to be manifested; and that there was still a barrel and a cruse in reserve for the widow, who, humbly confident in the bounty of Heaven, had shared her last morsel with the supplicant in affliction. Her little ones met her at the threshold with cries of joy. During her short absence, a stranger, visiting the house, had deposited in it a sack of flour; and the single bushel which it contained was so husbanded as to preserve their lives till the close of the siege. Their unknown benefactor was never revealed; but the pious mother was able to reply to her unbelieving kinswoman, 'The Lord hath provided for us.'"

(*b*) ANDERSON AND THE MERCHANT.—This worthy man, formerly minister at Walton-upon-Thames, being the subject of persecution in England, in the year 1662, and apprehensive of the ascendency of Popery, removed to Middleburgh, in Zealand. The little money he took with him was soon expended, and he was reduced with his family to very great want, which his modesty would not allow him to make known. In this perplexity, after he had been at prayer one morning with his family, his children asked for some bread for their breakfast; but he having none, nor money to buy any, they all burst into tears. While they were thus sorrowing together, the door bell was rung; Mrs. Anderson went to the door, where she was met by a man who presented a small parcel, saying it had been sent by a gentleman, and that some provision would be sent in shortly. When they opened the paper, they found it to contain forty pieces of gold. Soon afterwards a countryman arrived, with a horse-load of whatever could contribute to their comfort. These supplies were continued at intervals to his dying day, without his knowing where they came from. It afterwards appeared, that these kindnesses were shown by a pious merchant at Middleburgh; who observing a grave English minister frequently walk the streets with a dejected countenance, inquired privately into his circumstances, and sent him the gold by his apprentice, and the provision by his country servant, saying, "God forbid that any of Christ's ambassadors should be strangers, and we not visit them; or in distress, and we not assist them;" at the same time expressly charging them to conceal his name.

(*c*) THE MINISTER'S STARVING FAMILY.—A clergyman of the state of New-York, (says the Religious Museum,) through a misapprehension of a leading member, was precipitately deprived of his pulpit, which involved a large family in necessity. At supper, the good man had the pain of beholding the last morsel of bread placed upon the table, without the least means or prospect of a supply for his children's breakfast. His wife, full of grief, with her children, retired to her bed. The minister chose to sit up and employ his dark hours in prayer, and reading the promises of God. Some secret hope of supply pervaded his breast; but when, whence, or by whom, he knew not. He retired to rest, and in the morning appeared with his family, and performed the duty of prayer. It being the depth of winter, and a little fire upon the hearth, he desired his wife to hang on the kettle, and spread the cloth upon the table. The kettle boiled—the children cried for bread—the afflicted father, standing before the fire, felt those emotions of heart unknown to those whose tables are replenished with affluence.

While in this painful state, some one knocked at the door, entered, and delivered a letter into the minister's hand. When the gentleman was gone, the letter was opened, and to the minister's astonishment, it contained a few bank bills with a desire of acceptance. So manifest an interposition of Divine goodness could not but be received with gratitude and joy; and should be a lesson to others to trust in that Savior who hath said, "Verily thou shalt be fed;" Psalm 37: 3. "I never will leave thee nor forsake thee;" Heb. 13: 5.

This remarkable occurrence being communicated to the editor, who having an intimacy with the gentleman said to be the hand that offered the sea sonable relief, was determined the next time he made him a visit to introduce the subject, and if possible, to know the reason that induced the generous action. The story being told, the gentleman discovered a modest blush, which evinced the tenderness of his heart. On interrogation, he said, "he had frequently heard that minister; on a certain morning he was disposed for a walk; thought in the severity of the winter season a trifle might be of service as fuel was high; felt a kind of necessity to enclose the money in a letter, went to the house, found the family adjusted as was described; delivered the paper and retired; but knew not the extreme necessity of the minister and his family until this moment.

(*d*) KNOLLYS' DELIVERANCE.—The Rev. Hanserd Knollys suffered much persecution for his conscientious attachment to the truth. In the early part of his ministry, he emigrated from England to America, the common asylum at that time, for all who wished to enjoy liberty of conscience. There he sojourned four years, but returned in 1641, at the earnest request of an aged father. On his arrival in England he was reduced to great straits, but experienced the goodness of Providence in a peculiar manner. The following particulars are extracted from his own account. "I was still poor and sojourned in a lodging till I had but sixpence left, and knew not how to provide for my wife and child. Having prayed to God and encouraged my wife to trust in him, and to remember former experiences, and especially that word of promise, 'I will never leave thee nor forsake thee,' I paid for my lodging and went out, not knowing whither God's good hand would lead me to receive something towards my present subsistence. About seven or eight doors from my lodgings, a woman met me in the street, and told me she came to seek me, and her husband had sent her to tell me that there was a lodging provided and prepared in his house by some Christian friends for me and my wife. I told her my present condition and went along with her to the house. There she gave me twenty shillings which Dr. Bastock, a late sufferer, had given her for me, and some linen for my wife, which I received, and told her husband I would fetch my wife and child and lodge there. I returned with great joy, and my wife was greatly affected with this seasonable and suitable supply. After we had returned praises to God, we went to our new lodgings, where we found all things necessary provided for us, and all charges paid for fifteen weeks." When the time was expired, he undertook a school, and by the blessing of God was successful in bringing up a large family creditably, and though several times imprisoned for religion, continued the laborious and esteemed pastor of a poor church, for fifty years, till he went to his reward, Sept. 19th, 1691, aged ninety-two years.

(*e*) ERSKINE'S DELIVERANCES.—Rev. Henry Erskine was often in great straits and difficulties. Once when he and his family had supped at night, there remained neither bread, meal, flesh, nor money, in the house. In the morning the young children cried for their breakfast, and their father endeavored to divert them, and did what he could at the same time to encourage himself and wife to depend upon that Providence that hears the young ravens when they cry. While thus engaged, a countryman knocked hard at the door, and called for some one to help him off with his load. Being asked whence he came, and what he would have, he told them he came from Lady Reburn with some provisions for Mr. Erskine. They told him he must be mistaken, and that it was more likely to be for another Mr. Erskine in the same town. He replied, no, he knew what he said, he was sent to Mr. Henry Erskine, and cried, "Come, help me off with my load, or else I will throw it down at the door." Whereupon they took the sack from him, and on opening it, found it well stored with fish and meat.

At another time, being at Edinburgh, he was so reduced that he had but three half pence in his pocket. When he was walking about the streets, not knowing what course to steer, one came to him in a countryman's habit, presented him with a letter in which were enclosed several Scotch ducatoons, with these words written, "Sir, receive this from a sympathizing friend. Farewell." Mr. Erskine never could find out whence the money came.

At another time, being on a journey on foot, his money fell short and he was in danger of being reduced to distress. Having occasion to fix his walking stick in some marshy ground, among the rushes, he heard something tinkle at the end of it; it proved to be two half crowns, which greatly assisted in bearing his charges home. In days of persecution and poverty God wonderfully interposes for his people.

347. In Overruling Various Acts and Affections.

(*a*) THE BUTCHER AND THE REDEMPTIONER.—A person in Holland, who had made a considerable fortune in Philadelphia, as a butcher, went on board a ship from Amsterdam, which carried a number of German Redemptioners,* for the purpose of purchasing one to assist him in his business.

After examining the countenances of several of the passengers, without being able to please himself, his attention was arrested by the tranquil and composed countenance of a man advanced in years, but with much appearance of strength and activity.

Not less pleased with the tenor of the conversation of his fellow countryman, than with his exterior, he described the purpose for which he wanted a servant, and obtained the man's consent to purchase his indentures, providing he would also purchase those of his wife, who had accompanied him.

The parties then went ashore to complete the business, attended by the captain; and upon the names of the persons being mentioned, to insert them in the writings, they were found to be the name of the purchaser's father and mother: and, upon further inquiries, he ascertained them to be, in fact, his father and mother, the latter declaring, that if he was their son, he had a remarkable mole upon his left arm, which proved to be the case.

Nothing could surpass the joy of all parties. The providence of God had snatched the venerable pair from poverty and servitude, and conducted them to plenty and independence, under the protection of an affectionate son.

He, it appeared, had run away from his parents when quite a boy, and, from the continual wars in Europe, neither party had heard of the other since that period.

(*b*) MR. NEWTON'S HABIT.—"Nothing was more remarkable," says the biographer of Mr. Newton, "than his constant habit of regarding the hand of God in every event, however trivial it might appear to others. In walking to his church, he would say, 'The way of man is not in himself, nor can he conceive what belongs to a single step. When I go to St. Mary Woolnoth, it seems the same whether I turn down Lothbury, or go through the Old Jewry; but the going through one street, and not another, may produce an effect of lasting consequence. A man cut down my hammock in sport, but had he cut it down half an hour later, I had not been here, as the exchange of crew was then making. A man made a smoke on the sea-shore, at the time a ship passed, which was thereby brought to, and afterwards brought me to England.'"

(*c*) AN OLD PERSON.—The Rev. Dr. Bedell relates, that while Bishop Chase, of Ohio, was at the house of a Mr. Beck, in Philadelphia, he received a package from Dr. Ward, the Bishop of Sodor and Man, making inquiries relating to certain property in America, of which some old person in his diocese was the heir. The letter had gone to Ohio, followed him to Washington, then to Philadelphia, and found him at Mr. Beck's: when he read it to Mr. B., the latter was in amazement, and said, "Bishop Chase, I am the *only* man in the world who can give you information. I have the deeds in my possession, and have had them forty-three years, not knowing

* A redemptioner is a person who engages to article himself, by indenture, for an agreed number of years, to some one who may want him, on his arrival in America: and the captain receives the sum paid for the services of the individual so articled, as passage and subsistence money.

what to do with them, or where any heirs were to be found." How wonderful, that the application should have been made to Bishop Chase, and he not in Ohio, but a guest in the house of the only man who possessed any information on the subject!

(*d*) THE LORD WAS THEIR BANKER.—Mr. Philip Henry, one of the non-comformist ministers, when silenced from preaching, by the act of uniformity, took comfort himself, and administered comfort to others, from the passage, "Let mine outcasts dwell with thee, Moab." "God's people," he observed, "may be an outcast people, cast out of men's love, their synagogues, their country; but God will own his people when men cast them out; they are *outcasts*, but they are *his*, and some way or other he will provide a *dwelling* for them." Shortly before his death, the same pious man observed, that, though many of the ejected ministers were brought very low, had many children, were greatly harassed by persecution, and their friends generally poor and unable to support them; yet, in all his acquaintance, he never knew, nor could remember to have heard of, any non-conformist minister in prison for debt.

(*e*) HAPPY MEETING.—After the battle of Talavera, among the prisoners sent to France was an interesting child, about seven years old, concerning whom one of the English officers received an account, that he was the son of a sergeant M'Cullum, who had served in the 42d Highland regiment, under Sir John Moore, in the Peninsula, and was killed in the battle of Corunna. The child's engaging manners had greatly won upon several persons, one of whom, as he passed through Toboso, immediately took him under his protection, and obtained leave to bring him to England, having a recommendation to the Duke of York. His royal highness, from what he had heard, felt such an interest in the boy, that, when brought into his presence, he took him on his knee, conversed with him in the French and German languages, which the child knew, and made arrangements promptly for his admission into the Military Asylum, at Chelsea. It being necessary to obtain the signature of Lord Huntly before the boy could be admitted, the officer and his little protegé were proceeding to Richmond House for that purpose, when, on reaching Charing Cross, he perceived a soldier, in the Highland uniform, walking before him: he quickened his pace, and soon overtook this man, who happened to belong to the 42d regiment. On inquiring of him if he had been acquainted with sergeant M'Cullum, who was killed the year before at Corunna, he replied, "Sir, I did not know any man of that name who was killed; but will you be so good, sir, as to tell me why you have asked that question?" "Because," said the officer, pointing to the boy, "that is his child, whom I found in Spain." "O sir," said he, rushing over to the boy, "he is my child! Jamie, don't you know me?" The scene, as may be supposed, was truly affecting. The feelings depicted in the soldier's countenance, on the sudden discovery of his long-lost child, together with the rush of thought upon the past scenes of the boy abroad, so overcame the officer, that he was obliged to retire into an adjoining shop, to give vent to his emotions.

(*f*) THE CAPTIVE AND HER FAVORITE HYMN.—In the year 1754, a dreadful war broke out in Canada, between the French and the English. The Indians took part with the French, and made excursions as far as Pennsylvania, where they plundered and burned all the houses they came to, and murdered the people. In 1755, they reached the dwelling of a poor family from Wirtemberg, while the wife and one of the sons were gone to a mill, four miles distant, to get some corn ground. The husband, the eldest son, and two little girls, named Barbara and Regina, were at home. The father and his son were instantly killed by the savages, but they carried the two little girls away into captivity, with a great many other children, who were taken in the same manner. They were led many miles through woods and thorny bushes, that nobody might follow them. In this condition they were brought to the hab itations of the Indians, who divided among themselves all the children whom they had taken captive.

Barbara was at this time ten years old, and Regina nine. It was never known what became of Barbara; but Regina, with a little girl of two years old, whom she had never seen before, were given to an old widow, who was to them very cruel. In this melancholy state of slavery these children remained nine long years, till Regina reached the age of nineteen, and her little companion was eleven years old. While captives, their hearts seemed to have been drawn towards what was good. Regina continually repeated the verses from the Bible, and the hymns which she had learnt when at home, and she taught them to the little girl. They often used to cheer each other with one hymn from the hymn book used at Halle, in Germany:

> "Alone, yet not alone am I,
> Though in this solitude so drear."

They constantly hoped that the Lord Jesus would, some time, bring them back to their Christian friends.

In 1764, the hope of these children was realized. The merciful providence of God brought the English Colonel Bouquet to the place where they were in captivity. He conquered the Indians, and forced them to ask for peace. The first condition he made was, that they should restore all the prisoners they had taken. Thus the two poor girls were released. More than 400 captives were brought to Colonel Bouquet. It was an affecting sight to see so many young people wretched and distressed. The colonel and his soldiers gave them food and clothes, brought them to the town of Carlisle, and published in the Pennsylvania newspapers, that all parents who had lost their children might come to this place, and in case of their finding them, they should be restored. Poor Regina's sorrowing mother came, among many other bereaved parents, to Carlisle; but, alas! her child had become a stranger to her; Regina had acquired the appearance and manner, as well as the language of the natives. The poor mother went up and down amongst the young persons assembled, but by no efforts could she discover her daughters. She wept in bitter grief and disappointment. Colonel Bouquet said, "Do you recollect nothing by which your children might be discovered?" She answered that she recollected nothing but a hymn, which she used to sing with them, and which was as follows:

> "Alone, yet not alone am I,
> Though in this solitude so drear;
> I feel my Savior always nigh,
> He comes the weary hours to cheer.
> I am with him, and he with me,
> Even here alone I cannot be."

The colonel desired her to sing this hymn. Scarcely had the mother sung two lines of it, when Regina rushed from the crowd, began to sing it also, and threw herself into her mother's arms. They both wept for joy, and the colonel restored the daughter to her mother. But there were no parents or friends in search of the other little girl: it is supposed they were all murdered; and now the child clung to Regina, and would not let her go; and Regina's mother, though very poor, took her home with her. Regina repeatedly asked after "the book in which God speaks to us." But her mother did not possess a Bible; she had lost every thing when the natives burnt her house.

(*g*) THE CAPTIVE'S RELEASE.—"In the war called Braddock's war," says a writer in the Christian's Advocate, "my father was an officer in the British Navy. One night as they were running close to the coast of Barbary, the officers on deck heard some person singing. A moment convinced them that he was singing the Old Hundred psalm tune. They immediately conjectured that the singer was a Christian captive, and determined to attempt his rescue. Twenty stout sailors, armed with pistols and cutlasses, manned the ship's boats and approached the shore. Directed by the voice of singing and prayer, they soon reached the abode of the Christian captive. It was a little hut at the bottom of his master's garden on a small river. They burst open the door, and took him from his knees, and in a few moments he was on the ship's deck frantic with joy. The account he gave of himself was, that his name was McDonald; that he was a native of Scotland; and had been a captive eighteen years, he had obtained the confidence of his master, was his chief gardener, and had the privilege of living by himself. He said he was not at all surprised when they burst open his door, for the Turks had often done so, and whipped him when on his knees."

(h) THE BROTHERS' MEETING.—A gentleman residing near Marlborough, went to New-York to get a hand to work for him on his farm. He chanced to have recommended to him, a young man who had just emigrated from Germany, and through hired persons (as the German could not speak English,) he engaged to work for him, and brought the young man over to his residence. At dusk the gentleman sent to a neighbor for a German who had been working there a long time, having emigrated from Germany many years since, and whose steady habits had, as much as any thing, influenced him in retaining the young man, to come and talk with the new work-hand. The German who was sent for, came and seated himself by the fire, back of the other, who was drinking his tea. The family were waiting for the meal to be finished, expecting to here some regular Dutch talk; nor did they wait in vain, for the moment the young man turned from the table, his eyes were fixed on the other German. Both stood a moment, regarding each other—and then rushed into each other's arms—they were brothers, and had met for the first time in many years. The kind feeling, the unbounded joy, the repeated embrace, were worthy of lovers. These two honest Dutchmen did talk real Dutch that night, and will probably do so a long time, as they work on farms that adjoin each other.

IN CONVERSIONS.

348. Overruling Misfortunes and Bereavements.

(a) GAME OF FOOT-BALL.—Vavasor Powell, an eminent minister of the seventeenth century, being appointed to preach on a certain day, in a meadow, near Treozaron, Cardigan shire, a number of idle persons, enemies to religion, agreed to meet at the same time and place, to play at foot-ball, and thereby create a disturbance. Among them was a young man of respectable family in that neighborhood, lately returned home from school, who being nimble-footed and dextrous at the game, had obtained possession of the ball, intending to kick it in the face of the preacher. At this instant, another person ran towards him, and tripped up his heels. By the fall his leg was broken; and after lying on the ground in great agony, he expressed a wish to see the minister, to whom, on his arrival, he confessed his wicked intention, and acknowledged that the just judgment of God had befallen him.

Mr. Powell, having represented to him the evil and danger of sin, preached the power and grace of the Savior; and, at the request of the young man, accompanied him to his father's house. So great was the change produced in him by means of this affliction, that on his recovery he began to preach, and was for many years the most laborious and useful minister in those parts. His name was Morgan Howell.

(b) THE INFIDEL CONVERTED.—The conversion of Dr. Vanderkemp was preceded by a very remarkable interposition of the providence of God, in the preservation of his life. He was sailing on the river near Dort, in company with his wife and daughter, when a violent storm arose, and a water-spout broke on the boat, by which it was instantly overset. Mrs. and Miss Vanderkemp were immediately drowned; and the survivor, clinging to the boat, was carried down the stream nearly a mile; no one daring, in so dreadful a storm, to venture from the shore to his assistance. A vessel then lying in the port of Dort, was by the violence of the storm driven from her moorings, and floated towards the part of the river in which he was, just ready to perish; and the sailors took him from the wreck. Thus remarkably was a life preserved, which was afterwards to be employed for the advantage of mankind, and for the propagation of that faith which he had labored to destroy. The sudden loss of his earthly comforts, and his long struggle against a painful death, softened his hard heart, shook the infidel principles he had hitherto cherished, and ended in the consecration of his life to the cause of God.

(*c*) THE WRECKED SAILOR'S CONSECRATION. — A ship, says Rev. John Blain, was wrecked amongst the rocks, near Cape Horn. While the winds fiercely blowed, and the foaming billows dashed the timbers in pieces, one seaman reached a lonely, barren rock. The day passed slowly away. He stretched his eye to the east and west, to the north and south, over the deep, dark, and ever restless waters—but no friendly sail appeared! The sun disappeared, and he sat down to pass in solitude the lonely night. His shipmates were cold and silent in their watery graves. The waves dashed against the rock, the winds passed swiftly onward, the lamps of night shed their dismal light on the bosom of the deep—but no human voice sounded in his ear, no brother's hand administered to his wants. Hunger and thirst made strong demands, but he had no means to relieve them. The bread and the water were entombed with his companions. Nor had he any consolation to draw from a future world. The Bible and the Redeemer had been neglected, and he was strangely indifferent. Another day came and passed, and another night. On the third night, as he lay on his back, gazing into the starry heavens, he began to think about *God* and *eternity*, his past life, and the interests of his soul. But all was dark. His skin was peeling from his face, his teeth all loose, his thirst almost intolerable, and death seemed to stand by his side. He had never prayed, nor did he know how to pray. A single commandment was all he remembered, and that commandment his dear mother taught him when a child. And how should he meet that mother and his God in a future world? His sins passed in review, and pressed on his guilty conscience, while bitter tears of repentance began to roll down his scalded cheeks. Without knowing wha the Lord required of him, he rose, stood on his kness, lifted his feeble hands towards heaven, and there on that lonely rock, far, far away from home and friends, he submitted all to God, and most solemnly promised, if his life was spared, he would *learn* and do whatever God required. From that consecrated and blessed hour, peace flowed into his soul—Christ was his Savior, and hope entered within the vail. The next day the life-boat from a passing ship took him from the Bethel rock. He landed in Boston, found the sailor's friend, and the sailor's home, and listened to the gospel of peace. Father Taylor gave him a Bible, which he read with prayerful attention. He came to New-York—visited different churches, searched for truth, remembered his solemn vow, and in February, 1843, while I was preaching in the Baptist Tabernacle, he offered himself to the church. On hearing his experience, every heart felt—every eye wept. Bro. Wm. W. Everts baptized him, welcomed him to the church, and *he went on his way rejoicing.*

(*d*) CURE FOR NERVOUS EXCITEMENT.—A friend once told me that, amongst other symptoms of high nervous excitement, he had been painfully harassed by the want of sleep. To such a degree had this proceeded, that if in the course of the day any occasion led him to his bed-chamber, the sight of his bed made him shudder at the idea of the restless hours he had passed upon it. In this case it was recommended to him to endeavor, when he lay down at night, to fix his thoughts on something at the same time vast and simple—such as the wide expanse of ocean, or the cloudless vault of heaven; that the little hurried and disturbing images that flitted before his mind might be charmed away, or hushed to rest, by the calming influence of one absorbing thought. Though not at all a religious man at the time, the advice suggested to his mind, that if an object at once vast and simple was to be selected, none could serve the purpose so well as that of God. He resolved then to make the trial, and to think of Him.

The result exceeded his most sanguine hopes; in thinking of God he fell asleep. Night after night he resorted to the same expedient. The process became delightful; so much so, that he used to long for the usual hour of retiring, that he might fall asleep, as he termed it, in God. What began as a mere physical operation, grew by imperceptible degrees into a gracious influence. The same God who was his repose at night, was in all his thoughts by day. And at the same time this person spoke to me, God, as revealed in the gospel of his Son, was "all his salvation," so inscrutable are the ways by which God can "fetch home again his banished."

(*e*) THE STUDENT AND HIS MOTHER'S LETTERS.—Among the students in an Academy in Massachusetts in 1845, was one, who was the son of a pious mother, but whose father was a professed believer in the doctrine of the final and universal restoration of all men, and openly rejected and ridiculed true religion. Yet, notwithstanding Mr. F.'s (the young man's father) hostility to religion, he had permitted his son to be trained up in the Sabbath school, where the true principles of the gospel had been so instilled into his young mind that all the sophistical arguments used by his father were unable to move him. But at the period of which we are speaking, the young man was a stranger to God experimentally.

The second week after he entered school, he received a letter from his mother, in which she warned him of the danger to which he exposed himself by living in rebellion against God, and urged him to repent. He thought but little of the letter, and, being a close student, applied himself to his books, entirely regardless of the concerns of his soul. Two weeks passed and another letter came, containing the same warning and expostulations as the first. And thus she continued, for some months, to write to her impenitent son, using every argument a mother's love and concern for his soul could suggest to persuade him to become a Christian. Still his mind remained unaffected.

In the meantime a protracted meeting was being held in the village where the academy was located. The young man had frequently been solicited to lay aside his books and attend it. This he refused to do, saying, he did not feel at all interested in the meetings, nor had he the least concern for his soul; besides, it was more profitable for students to attend to their books, than spend their time in that manner.

Two weeks had passed since he received his mother's last letter; he went to the post-office for another, and found one with the post-mark of his native village upon it; but on opening it, instead of seeing the familiar hand of his mother, his eye rested on characters scarcely legible. What could this mean? He began to read, and soon learned that his mother by accident had been deprived of the use of her right hand, and had written with her left, still presenting to him the important theme of his salvation. This touched a chord in the young man's heart, and he said, "If my sins are the cause of so much grief to my mother, there must be something wrong, and by the grace of God I will forsake them, and begin *now* to seek my soul's salvation." That evening he went to the prayer-meeting; and when "the anxious" were requested to come forward to the altar that Christians might pray for them, he was among the first there. But as he afterward stated, he had no conviction for sin, though he knew he was a sinner, and without repentance could not be saved. It was love for his mother alone which prompted him to take the step he had, and love for her led him still further. For several successive evenings he was seen upon the anxious seat, yet there appeared to be no change wrought in him. At length, one evening he rose up, and stated what his feelings had been, and added, that he now began to desire religion because he believed it to be the "power of God unto salvation."

Conviction from this time began to roll in upon his mind, and he saw himself as he never had done before, a lost and condemned creature, without God and without hope. His distress of mind was great, and his trials unusual.

severe. But he heard a voice saying, "Behold the Lamb of God which taketh away the sins of the world," and like Andrew he went to meet Him and became his disciple, and one of the brightest ornaments of religion among the many who were hopefully converted at that time.

349. Overruling Intended or Actual Persecution.

(*a*) INTENDED MURDERER AND THE SERMON.—Mr. Bradbury possessed an ardent zeal in the cause of civil and religious liberty, and had many admirers. This exposed him to the hatred of the popish faction, whose designs in respect of the Jacobitish succession he had often exposed. They once employed a person to take away his life. To make himself fully acquainted with Mr. Bradbury's person, the man frequently attended at places of worship where he preached, place himself in front of the gallery, with his countenance steadfastly fixed on the preacher. It was scarcely possible, in such circumstances, wholly to avoid listening to what was said. Mr. Bradbury's forcible way of presenting divine truth awakened the man's attention; the truth entered his understanding, and became the means of changing his heart. He came to the preacher with trembling and confusion, told his affecting tale, gave evidence of his conversion, became a member of Mr. Bradbury's church, and was, to his death, an ornament to the gospel which he professed.

(*b*) WHITEFIELD'S PERSECUTORS.—When this distinguished minister was once at Plymouth, four gentlemen came to the house of one of his particular friends, kindly inquiring after him, and desiring to know where he lodged. Soon afterwards, Mr. Whitefield received a letter, informing him that the writer was a nephew of Mr. S—, an attorney at New-York; that he had the pleasure of supping with Mr. Whitefield at his uncle's house, and desired his company to sup with him and a few friends at a tavern. Mr. Whitefield sent him word, that it was not customary for him to sup abroad at taverns; but he should be glad of the gentleman's company to eat a morsel with him at his lodging: he accordingly came and supped, but was observed frequently to look around him, and to be very absent in mind. At last he took his leave, and returned to his companions in the tavern; and on being asked by them what he had done, he answered, that he had been used so civilly, that he had not the heart to touch him. Upon which another of the company, a lieutenant of a man-of-war, laid a wager of ten guineas that he would do his business for him. His companions, however, had the precaution to take away his sword. It was now about midnight, and Mr. Whitefield, having that day preached to a large congregation, and visited the French prisons, had gone to bed, when the landlady came and told him that a well-dressed gentleman desired to speak with him. Mr. Whitefield imagining it was somebody under conviction, desired him to be brought up. He came, and sat down by the bed-side, congratulated him upon the success of his ministry, and expressed much concern at being detained from hearing him. Soon after, he broke out into the most abusive language, and in a cruel and cowardly manner beat him in his bed. The landlady and her daughter, hearing the noise, rushed into the room and laid hold of him; but he soon disengaged himself from them and repeated his blows upon Mr. Whitefield, who being apprehensive that he intended to shoot or stab him, underwent all the surprise of a sudden and violent death. Afterwards a second came into the house, and cried out, from the bottom of the stairs, "Take courage, I am ready to help you!" But, by the repeated cry of "murder!" the alarm was now so great, that they both made off. "The next morning," says Mr. Whitefield, "I was to expound at a private house, and then to set out for Bideford. Some urged me to stay and prosecute; but, being better employed, I went on my intended journey, was greatly blessed in preaching the everlasting gospel, and, upon my return, was well paid for what I had suffered, curiosity having led perhaps two thousand more than ordinary to see and hear a man that had like to have been murdered in his bed. And I trust, in the five weeks that I waited for the convoy, hundreds were awakened and turned unto the Lord."

(*c*) THE POINTED SERMON.—In the year 1743, the Rev. George Whitefield had resolved to come to this country, and had engaged his passage in a ship that was to sail from Portsmouth; but as the captain afterwards refused to take him, "for fear of his spoiling the sailors," he was obliged to go to Plymouth. While staying there, he frequently preached, and an attempt having recently been made to murder him in his bed, much attention was excited, and many thousands flocked to hear him. While he was one day preaching, Mr. Tanner, who was at work as a ship-builder, at a distance, heard his voice, and resolved, with five or six of his companions, to go and drive him from the place where he stood; and for this purpose they filled their pockets with stones. When, however, Mr. T. drew near, and heard Mr. Whitefield earnestly inviting sinners to Christ, he was filled with astonishment, his resolution failed him, and he went home with his mind deeply impressed. On the following evening, he again attended, and heard Mr. Whitefield on the sin of those who crucified the Redeemer. After he had expatiated on their guilt, he appeared to look intently on Mr. Tanner, as he exclaimed with energy, "Thou art the man!" These words powerfully affected Mr. T.; he felt his iniquities to be awfully great, and in the agony of his soul he cried, "God be merciful to me a sinner." The preacher then proceeded to proclaim the free and abundant grace of Jesus, which He commanded to be preached among the very people who had murdered him; on hearing which, Mr. T. was encouraged to hope for mercy, and he surrendered himself to Christ. This sermon was made eminently useful to many other persons.

(*d*) THE "HELL-FIRE CLUB."—The Rev. John Cooke, of Maidenhead, (Eng.) was once called on to preach at the opening of a chapel. Six years afterwards, a man came to him after preaching at Bristol, and told him that, at the period first referred to, he belonged to an awfully wicked society, called, "The hell-fire club," the members of which always endeavored to coin a new oath for each evening on which they met, the chairman deciding who had the preference. As this man was walking towards his club, he was asking himself what sin he had not committed, resolving he would commit it before he went to bed. His attention was arrested by the lights of the chapel, and the voice of the preacher. After some hesitation, whether he should enter the chapel for sport now, or as he returned from the club, he determined on the former. He entered as the preacher was repeating his text, "All manner of sin and blasphemy shall be forgiven unto men; and whosoever speaketh a word against the Son of man, it shall be forgiven him: but whosoever speaketh against the Holy Ghost, it shall not be forgiven him, neither in this world, neither in the world to come." He described the nature of the sin; the reason why it was unpardonable; showed who had not committed it, and proved that their sins might be pardoned. The man went home, locked himself in his bedroom, fell on his knees, thanked God he was out of hell, and prayed for the pardon which he was delighted to know he might yet receive, though he had often wished to die, that he might know the worst of hell. He read, prayed heard the gospel, looked by faith t Christ, and soon enjoyed a sense of pardon, and the privilege of friendship with God. In his case he considered,

"Jehovah here resolved to show
What his Almighty grace could do."

(*e*) MR. WHITEFIELD AND THE TRUMPETER.—On one occasion, during Whitefield's residence in America, a black trumpeter, belonging to an English regiment, resolved to interrupt him during a discourse which he was expected to deliver in the open air. At the hour appointed for the sermon, he repaired to the field where it was to be preached, carrying his trumpet with him on purpose to blow it with all his might about the middle of the sermon. He took his stand in front of the minister, and at no great distance. The concourse that attended became very great, and those who were towards the extremity of the crowd pressed forward, in order to hear more distintly, which caused such a pressure at the place where the trumpeter stood, that he found it impossible to raise up the arm which held the trumpet at the time he intended to blow it. He attempted to extricate himself from the crowd, but found this equally impossible, so that he was kept within hearing of the gospel as securely as if he had been chained to the spot. In a short time, his attention was arrested, and he became so powerfully affected by what the preacher presented to his mind, that he was seized with an agony of despair, and was carried to a house in the neighborhood. When the service was over, he was visited by Mr. Whitefield, who tendered some seasonable counsels; and the poor trumpeter from that time became an altered man.

(*f*) WHITEFIELD AND THE FIDDLER.—John Skinner, of Houndscroft, in Gloucestershire, (Eng.,) was a strolling fiddler, going from fair to fair, and supplying music to any party that would hire him. Having determined to interrupt that great and successful minister of Christ, Mr. Whitefield, he obtained a standing on a ladder raised to a window near the pulpit; he remained a quiet, if not an attentive hearer, till the text was named, when he intended to begin his annoying exercise on the violin. It pleased God, however, while he was putting his instrument in tune, to convey the word spoken with irresistible power to his soul; his attention was diverted from his original purpose, he heard the whole sermon, and became altogether a new man.

(*g*) THE WIDOW AND HER SON.—A minister from England being at Edinburgh, was accosted very civilly by a young man in the street, with an apology for the liberty he was taking: "I think, sir," said he, "I have heard you at Spafield's chapel." "You probably may, sir; for I have sometimes ministered there." "Do you remember," said he, "a note, put up by an afflicted widow, begging the prayers of the congregation for the conversion of an ungodly son?" "I do very well remember such a circumstance." "Sir," said he, "I am the very person; and, wonderful to tell, the prayer was effectual. Going on a frolic with some other abandoned young men, one Sunday, through the Spafields, and passing by the chapel, I was struck with its appearance, and hearing it was a Methodist chapel, we agreed to mingle with the crowd, and stop for a few minutes to laugh and mock at the preacher and the people. We had only just entered the chapel, when you sir, read the note, requesting the prayers of the congregation for an afflicted widow's son. I heard it with a sensation I cannot express. I was struck to the heart; and, though I had no idea that I was the very individual meant, I felt that it expressed the bitterness of a widow's heart, who had a child as wicked as I knew myself to be. My mind was instantly solemnized. I could not laugh; my attention was riveted on the preacher. I heard his prayer and sermon with an impression very different from that which had carried me into the chapel. From that moment, the truths of the gospel penetrated my heart; I joined the congregation; cried to God in Christ for mercy, found peace in believing, and became my mother's comfort, as I had long been her heavy cross.

(*h*) THE PERSECUTING FATHER AND HIS DAUGHTER.—During a series of religious meetings, held in the school-house of a small village, a very little girl became much interested for the salvation of her soul. Her father, a hater of holiness, who lived next door to the place of meeting finding that his little daughter was much interested in the meetings, and had been forward to be prayed for, strictly forbade her again entering the "house of prayer." The poor little girl was much oppressed, and knew not what to do, but obeyed her father until the next meeting was nearly half through, then slipping out without his knowledge, and getting through a hole in the back yard fence, she hastily ran to the meeting. It was some time before her father missed her, but when he found her gone, he went immediately to the meeting, where she was on her knees, with others whom the people of God were praying for. So enraged was he, that he went directly forward, and took her in his arms, to carry her from the place. As he raised her from her knees, she looked up with a heavenly smile, and said, "It is too late now, pa; I have given my heart to the Savior." This was too much for the hardened sinner: he too sunk on his knees, while he was prayed for; and very soon he found that Savior he had in vain attempted to shut out from his daughter's heart.

350. Overruling various forms of Wickedness.

(*a*) WORD OF GOD POWERFUL.—An eminently pious curate, in England, was accustomed, on account of the village in which he resided being at a great distance from the church, to preach on the sabbath evening in his own house. On his return from his stated parochial duties, one sabbath afternoon, he was warned by one of his neighbors to keep a strict look-out against two suspicious characters then lurking in the village, as there was some reason to apprehend that they intended that night to rob his house. They contrived however, by some means, to get within his premises while the people were assembling in considerable numbers for worship, and concealed themselves in a retired part of the house; but not being far from the room where the worthy man was preaching, they could distinctly hear his voice. The sword of the Spirit pierced their hearts; they were not only convinced of the wickedness of their meditated burglary, but of the awful criminality of sins committed against God, and left their dark retreat under the most pungent sense of guilt. From this time, an effectual change was wrought in their minds and conduct, and the pious clergyman, after several years, could bear testimony that by their unblamable lives, they adorned the gospel of Christ.

(*b*) THE NEGRO'S SERMON.—A worthy and excellent bishop of the Episcopal church was in early life an immoral and dissipated man. Dining one evening with a party of gentlemen, they sat late over their wine, and with a view to promote merriment, this young man sent for one of his slaves, who was in the habit of preaching to his companions in slavery, and ordered him to preach a sermon to the company. The good man hesitated for a time, but at length began to address them. Instead of the mirth, however, which they anticipated from the ignorance and simplicity of the poor man, the piety and fervor of his discourse produced a contrary effect. The solemn truths he delivered sank deeply into the hearts of some of the company, and, through the Divine blessing, carried conviction to the heart of his master, who now seriously inquired after the way of salvation; which having learned, he began from a sense of duty to publish the grace of Christ, and became an ornament to the Christian ministry.

(*c*) THE SCOFFER CONVERTED.—When the Rev. G. Whitefield and J. Wesley commenced their zealous and successful labors, there was a very prevalent disposition to oppose and misrepresent them. Many of the public-houses became places where their doctrines and zeal were talked of and ridiculed. Mr. Thorpe, and several other young men in Yorkshire, undertook at one of these parties to mimic the preaching of these good men. The proposition met with applause; one after another stood on a table to perform his part, and it devolved on Mr. T. to close this very irreverent scene. Much elated, and confident of success, he exclaimed, as he ascended the table, "I shall beat you all." Who would have supposed that the mercy of God was now about to be extended to this transgressor of his law! The Bible was handed to him; and, by the guidance of unerring Providence, it opened at Luke 13: 3. "Except ye repent, ye shall all likewise perish." The moment he read the text his mind was impressed in a most extraordinary manner; he saw clearly the nature and importance of the subject; and as he afterwards said, if he ever preached with the assistance of the Holy Spirit, it was at that time. His address produced a feeling of depression in his auditors; and, when he had finished, he instantly retired to weep over his sins: he associated with the people of God; and became a useful minister of the New Testament, and died at Masborough, in 1776.

(*d*) TAKING OFF THE METHODIST.—The Rev. Mr. Madan was educated for the bar. His conversion to God arose from the following circumstances. Some of his companions, when assembled one evening at a coffee-house, requested him to go and hear the Rev. John Wesley, who, they were informed, was to preach in the neighborhood, and then to return and exhibit his manner and discourse for their entertainment. With that intention he went to the house of God. Just as he entered the place, Mr. Wesley read as his text, "Prepare to meet thy God," Amos 4: 12, with a solemnity of accent which excited his attention, and produced a seriousness which increased as the good man proceeded in exhorting his hearers to repentance. Mr. Madan returned to the coffee-room, and was asked by his companions if he had taken off the old methodist. He replied, "No, gentlemen, but he has taken me off;" and from that time forsook their company, associated with true Christians, and became an eminently good man.

(*e*) A SINGULAR MOTIVE FOR ATTENDING CHURCH.—A young man of the city of Norwich, (Eng.,) about eighteen years of age, was walking one morning with several companions, who had agreed on that day to take their pleasure. The first object that attracted attention was an old woman, who pretended to tell fortunes. They immediately employed her to tell theirs, and that they might qualify her for the undertaking, first made her thoroughly intoxicated. The young man, of whom mention was first made, was informed, among other things, that he would live to a very old age, and see his children, grandchildren, and great-grandchildren growing up around him. Though he had assisted in intoxicating the old woman, he had credulity enough to be struck with those parts of the prediction which related to himself. "And so," said he, when alone, "I am to see children, grandchildren, and great-grandchildren! At this age, I must be a burden to the young people. What shall I do? There is no way for an old man to render himself more agreeable to youth, than by sitting and telling them pleasant and profitable stories. I will then," thought he, "during my youth, endeavor to store my mind with all kinds of knowledge. I will see and hear, and note down every thing that is rare and wonderful, that I may sit, when incapable of other employments, and entertain my descendants. Thus shall my company be rendered pleasant, and I shall be respected, rather than neglected, in old age. Let me see, what can I acquire first? Oh! here is the famous methodist preacher, Whitefield; he is to preach, they say, to-night—I will go and hear him."

From these strange motives the young man declared he went to hear Mr Whitefield. He preached that evening from Matthew, 3: 7. "But when he saw many of the Pharisees and Sadducees come to his baptism, he said unto them, O generation of vipers, who hath warned you to flee from the wrath to come?" "Mr. Whitefield," said the young man, "described the Sadducees' character; this did not touch me; I thought myself as good a Christian as any man in England. From this he went to that of the Pharisees. He described their exterior decency, but observed, that the poison of the viper rankled in their hearts. This rather shook me. At length, in the course of his sermon, he abruptly broke off; paused for a few moments; then burst into a flood of tears; lifted up his hands and eyes, and exclaimed, 'Oh, my hearers! the wrath's to come! the wrath's to come!' These words sunk into my heart, like lead in the waters; I wept, and, when the sermon was ended, retired alone. For days and weeks I could think of little else. Those awful words would follow me wherever

I went, 'The wrath's to come! the wrath's to come!'" The issue was, that the young man soon after made a public profession of religion, in a little time became an eminent preacher, and he himself related these circumstances to the late Rev. Andrew Fuller of Kettering.

(*f*) PLAYING BALL ON THE SABBATH.—The following interesting facts were related to the Rev. Dr. Conder, of London, by an old gentleman, who remembered when a boy to have heard them from the great-grandfather of that gentleman:—

I used, said he, when young, to accompany my father to Royston market, which Mr. Conder also frequented. The custom of the worthy men in those days was, when they had done their marketing, to meet together, and take needful refreshment in a private room, where, without interruption, they might talk freely about the things of God—how they had heard on the Sabbath day, and how they had gone on the week past, etc. I was admitted to sit in a corner of the room. One day, when I was there, the conversation turned upon the question, "By what means God first visited their souls, and began a work of grace upon them?" It was your great-grandfather's turn to speak, and his account struck me so, that I never forgot it. He told the company as follows:—"When I was a young man, was I greatly addicted to foot-ball playing; and, as the custom was in our parish, and in many others also, the young men, as soon as church was over, took a foot-ball and went to play. Our minister often remonstrated against our breaking the Sabbath, which, however, had but little effect; only my conscience checked me at times, and I would sometimes steal away and hide myself from my companions. But being dextrous at the game, they would find me out, and get me among them. This would bring on me more guilt and horror of conscience. Thus I went on sinni g and repenting a long time, but had no resolution to break off from the practice, till, one Sabbath morning, our minister acquainted his hearers that he was very sorry to tell them, that by order of the king (James I.) and his council, he must read them the following paper or relinquish his living. This was the Book of Sports, forbidding the ministers or churchwardens, or any others, to molest or discourage the youth, in what were called their manly sports and recreations on the Lord's day, etc. While our minister was reading it, I was seized with a chill and horror not to be described. Now, thought I, iniquity is established by a law, and sinners are hardened in their sinful ways! What sore judgments are to be expected upon so wicked and guilty a nation! What shall I do? Whither shall I flee? How shall I escape the wrath to come? —And thus God convinced me that it was high time to be in earnest about salvation. And from that time, I never had the least inclination to take a foot-ball in hand, or to join my vain companions any more: so that I date my conversion from that time, and adore the grace of God in making that to be an ordinance for my salvation, which the devil and wicked governors laid as a trap for my destruction."

This, continued the narrator, I heard him tell: and I hope with some serious benefit to my own soul.

(*g*) THE ROBBER AND THE STOLEN SERMONS.—A minister, had been preaching one evening, in a village at some distance from his home; when, on his return, he was stopped by a footpad, who presented a pistol, and demanded his money. The minister allowed him to take his watch and his money; and the thief, feeling some papers in his pocket, took them also away with him, saying, that for any thing he knew, there might be bank notes among them. These papers were, howeve·, manuscript sermons, written out at length in a fair and legible hand. Some months afterwards, a respectable looking man called upon the same minister, recalled to his recollection the robbery, stated that he had been the robber, restored the watch and a sum of money equivalent to that which he had taken away, and stated the cause of his making restitution was, that upon looking over the papers, he found a a sermon on the words, "Thou shalt not steal." The singularity of this circumstance induced him to read it; and the impression produced by its warnings upon him was so powerful, that he abandoned his profligate courses, became an altered man, devoted himself to industrious labor, and took the earliest opportunity of restoring the property he had stolen.

(*h*) DRUNKARD SAVED FROM SUICIDE.—An aged Christian in Berwick upon the Tweed, England, gave a visiter of the poor the following account of his conversion. He said, that previous to the Lord's meeting with him, he was a notoriously wicked character, and, among many other vices, he was much addicted to drinking to excess. On a certain occasion, he had, what he termed, *broke out*, and had been in a state of intoxication for, I think he said, a fortnight. When the effects of the liquor left him, and he began to come to himself, his spirits sunk unusually low, and guilt and remorse preyed on his mind so much, that he was driven to despair, and felt himself so miserable, that he determined on the rash act of putting an end to his existence; he accordingly procured a rope to hang himself. At that time, his wife, who was a truly pious woman, was at Spafields chapel. A thought came into his mind, that he should like his wife to know his fate soon after he was dead; this induced him to go round the back of the chapel, to seek for a convenient place to commit the fatal deed, expecting that when the congregation came out he should be found dead, and that his wife would be informed. When passing the back of the chapel, with the rope in his pocket, the sound of the minister's voice caught his ear, and induced him to go and look in at the door. At the instant the minister was preaching, in a very animated manner, on the efficacy of the blood of Christ to cleanse the guilty conscience, stated that the Savior was able and willing to save the vilest rebels, and then gave a most pressing invitation to the chief of sinners, saying,

"Come and welcome, come and welcome,
All that feel your need of him."

These and similar sentences so penetrated his heart, that they produced feelings which are easier conceived than described.

When the service was over, he went home, fell on his knees, and cried for mercy. His wife was, at first, astoned at the wonderful change; but, on inquiry, she found the Lord had answered her prayer in behalf of her husband.

(*i*) THE THREE SCOFFERS.—In a sea-port town on the west coast of England, notice was once given of a sermon to be preached there one Sunday evening. The preacher was a man of great celebrity; and that circumstance, together with the object of the discourse being to enforce the duty of strict observance of the Sabbath, attracted an overflowing audience. After the usual prayers and praises, the preacher read his text, and was about to proceed with his sermon, when he suddenly paused, leaning his head on the pulpit, and remained silent for a few moments. It was imagined that he had become indisposed; but he soon recovered himself, and, addressing the congregation, said that before entering upon his discourse, he begged to narrate to them a short anecdote. "It is now exactly fifteen years," said he, "since I was last within this place of worship; and the occasion was, as many here may probably remember, the very same as that which has now brought us together. Amongst those who came hither that evening, were three dissolute young men, who came not only with the intention of insulting and mocking the venerable pastor, but even with stones in their pockets to throw at him as he stood in the pulpit. Accordingly, they had not attended long to the discourse, when one of them said impatiently, "Why need we listen any longer to the blockhead?—throw!" But the second stopped him, saying, "Let us first see what he makes of this point." The curiosity of the latter was no sooner satisfied, than he, too, said. "Ay, confound him, it is only as I expected—throw now!" But here the third interposed, and said, "It would be better altogether to give up the design which has brought us here." At this remark his two associates took of fence, and left the place, while he himself remained to the end. Now mark, my brethren," continued the preacher, with much emotion, "what were afterwards the several fates of these young men? The first was hanged, many years ago, at Tyburn, for the crime of forgery; the second is now lying under the sentence of death, for murder, in the jail of this city. The third, my brethren" — and the speaker's agitation here became excessive, while he paused, and wiped the large drops from his brow—"the third, my brethren, is he who is now about to address you!—listen to him."

(*j*) THE INFIDEL'S SERMON TO THE PIRATES.—A native of Sweden, residing in the South of France, had occasion to go from one port to another in the Baltic Sea. When he came to the place whence he expected to sail, the vessel was gone. On inquiring, he found a fishing boat going the same way, in which he embarked. After being for some time out to sea, the men observed that he had several trunks and chests on board, concluded he must be very rich, and therefore agreed among themselves to throw him overboard. This he heard them express, which gave gave him great uneasiness. However, he took occasion to open one of his trunks which contained some books. Observing this, they remarked among themselves that it was not worth while to throw him into the sea, as they did not want any books, which they supposed was all the trunks contained. They asked him if he were a priest. Hardly knowing what reply to make, he told them he was; at which they seemed much pleased, and said they would have a sermon on the next day, as it was the Sabbath.

This increased the anxiety and distress of his mind, for he knew himself to be as incapable of such an undertaking, as it was possible for any one to be, as he knew very little of the Scriptures; neither did he believe in the inspiration of the Bible.

At length they came to a small rocky island, perhaps a quarter of a mile in circumference, where was a company of pirates, who had chosen this little sequestered spot to deposit their treasures. He was taken to a cave, and introduced to an old woman, to whom they remarked that they were to have a sermon preached, the next day. She said she was very glad of it, for she had not heard the word of God for a great while. His was a trying case, for preach he must, still he knew nothing about preaching. If he refused, or undertook to preach and did not please, he expected it would be his death. With these thoughts he passed a sleepless night. In the morning his mind was not settled upon any thing. To call upon God, whom he believed to be inaccessible, was altogether vain. He could devise no way whereby he might be saved. He walked to and fro, still shut up in darkness, striving to collect something to say to them, but could not think of even a single sentence.

When the appointed time for the evening arrived, he entered the cave where he found the men assembled. There was a seat prepared for him, and a table with a Bible on it. They sat for the space of half an hour in profound silence; and even then, the anguish of his soul was as great as human nature was capable of enduring. At length these words came to his mind,—"Verily, there is a reward for the righteous: verily, there is a God that judgeth in the earth." He arose and delivered them: then other words presented themselves, and so on till his understanding became opened—his heart enlarged in a manner astonishing to himself. He spoke upon subjects suited to their condition; the rewards of the righteous—the judgments of the wicked—the necessity of repentance, and the importance of a change of life. The matchless love of God to the children of men, had such a powerful effect upon the minds of these wretched beings, that they were melted into tears. Nor was he less astonished at the unbounded goodness of Almighty God, in thus interposing to save his spiritual as well as his natural life, and well might he exclaim,—"This is the Lord's doings, and marvelous in our eyes." Under a deep sense of God's goodness, his heart became filled with such thankfulness, that it was out of his power to express. What marvellous change was thus suddenly brought about by Divine interposition! He who a little before disbelieved in communion with God and the soul, became as humble as a little child. And they who were so lately meditating on his death, now are filled with love and good will towards each other, particularly towards him; manifesting affectionate kindness, and willing to render him all the assistance in their power!

The next morning they fitted out one of their vessels, and conveyed him where he desired. From that time he became a changed man. From sentiments of infidelity he became a sincere believer in the power and efficacy of the truth as it is in Jesus.

351. Overruling Dreams and Involuntary Affections.

(*a*) THE MOUNTAINEER'S DREAM.—A man who has long lived in an obscure place, on one of the mountains in Berkshire county, Mass., (says the New-York Evangelist of 1831), who had been taught to read the Bible in childhood, but had not been to any religious meeting, or had a Bible in his house for many years, began last spring to dream every night whole chapters of what he had read in early life, and to think of what he had dreamed during the day. This he did several nights and days in succession, till the truth thus brought to mind, effected a deep conviction of sin, which resulted in his hopeful conversion.

(*b*) THE BACKSLIDER'S DREAM.—A young gentleman being reproved by his mother for being religious, made her this answer: "I am resolved by all means to save my soul." Some time after he fell into a lukewarm state, during which time he was sick and nigh unto death. One night he dreamed that he saw himself summoned before God's angry throne, and from thence hurried into a place of torments: where, seeing his mother full of scorn, she upbraided him with his former answer; why he did not save his soul by all means. This was so much impressed on his mind when he awoke, that, under God, it became the means of his turning again to him; and when any body asked him the reason why he became again religious, he gave them no other answer than this: "If I could not in my dream endure my mother's upbraiding my folly and lukewarmness, how shall I be able to suffer that God should call me to an account in the last day, and the angels reproach my lukewarmness, and the devil aggravate my sins, and all the saints of God deride my folly and hypocrisy?"

(*c*) THE FATHER'S DREAM OF JUDGMENT.—"In January last," said a pious father in writing to his friends, "I dreamed that the day of judgment was come. I saw the Judge on his great white throne, and all nations were gathered before him. My wife and I were on the right hand; but I could not see my children. I said, I cannot bear this; I must go and seek them. I went to the left hand of the Judge, and there found them al standing in the utmost despair. As soon as they saw me, they caught hold of me and cried, 'O! father, we will never part.' I said, 'my dear children, I am come to try, if possible, to get you out of this awful situation.' So I took them all with me, but when we came near the Judge I thought he cast an angry look, and said, 'What do thy children with thee now? they would not take thy warning when on earth, and they shall not share with thee the crown in heaven; depart, ye cursed.' At these words, I awoke bathed in tears. A while after this, as we were all sitting together on a Sabbath evening, I related to them my dream. No sooner did I begin that first one, and then another, yea, all of them, burst into tears, and God fastened conviction on their hearts. Five of them are rejoicing in God their Savior; and I believe, the Lord is at work with the other two, so that I doubt not he will give them also to my prayers.

(*d*) HILL'S REPLY TO THE CONVERT.—A candidate for admission to church membership under the Rev. Rowland Hill being required to give some account of his first impressions as to the evil of sin, and the need of the gospel, related a *dream* by which he had been affected and led to serious inquiry, to the hearing of sermons, &c. When he had ended, Mr. Hill said, We do not wish to despise a good man's dreams by any means; but we will tell you what we think of the dream, *after we have seen how you go on when you are awake.*

352. Overruling various Feelings, Actions, and Events.

(*a*) GUTHRIE AND THE PAPIST.—Mr. Guthrie, an eminent minister in Scotland, was one evening traveling home very late. Having lost his way on a moor, he laid the reins on the neck of his horse, and committed himself to the direction of Providence. After long traveling over ditches and fields, the horse brought him to a farmer's house, into which he went, and requested permission to sit by the fire till morning, which was granted. A popish priest was administering extreme unction to the mistress of the house, who was dying. Mr. Guthrie said nothing till the priest had retired: then he went forward to the dying woman, and asked her if she enjoyed peace in the prospect of death, in consequence of what the priest had said and done to her. She answered, that she did not; on which he spoke to her of salvation through the atoning blood of the Redeemer. The Lord taught her to understand, and enabled her to believe the message of mercy, and she died triumphing in Jesus Christ her Savior. After witnessing this astonishing scene, Mr. Guthrie mounted his horse, and rode home. On his arrival, he told Mrs. Guthrie he had seen a great wonder during the night. "I came," said he, "to a farm-house, where I found a woman in a state of nature; I saw her in a state of grace; and left her in a state of glory."

(*b*) THE DYING MINISTER'S DISSOLUTE SON.—Mr. Nathan Davies, the eldest son of a respectable Christian minister in Wales, was a youth of wild and dissolute conduct, and thereby occasioned much grief to his pious parents. Neither the mild nor the severe methods used to reclaim him had the desired effect. At length, a period arrived when the aged and venerable father must die; and, like Jacob, he desired that his children should be called to his bedside, to receive his dying admonitions. Having addressed them all, one by one, except the profligate son, in a very affectionate and solemn manner, he concluded by warning them to shun the bad example and wicked ways of their eldest brother, and advised them to act towards him with caution and forbearance, adding, that he feared they would experience from him nothing but sorrow and trouble. He then dismissed them, and soon after died.

The circumstance of the father's silence made a deeper impression on the mind of Nathan than all the reproofs and exhortations he had before received; and, to use his own expression, he thought at the time that his heart would have burst. He was then about twenty-seven years of age; and, through the Divine blessing, a great change became visible in him; he abandoned his former ways and companions, became a serious hearer of the word, and, in a short time, a member of the church over which his late father had been pastor. A few years afterwards he was called to the ministry, succeeded his father in the pastoral office, and was blessed in it with eminent success until the day of his death, which took place in the year 1726.

(*c*) HOWE AND HIS ENEMY.—When the melancholy state of the times compelled this excellent man to quit the public charge of his beloved congregation at Torrington, in Devonshire, impressed with a sense of duty, he embraced every opportunity of preaching the word of life. He and Mr. Flavel used frequently to conduct their secret ministrations at midnight in different houses in the north of Devonshire. One of the principal of these was Hudscott, an ancient mansion belonging to the family of Rolle, between Torrington and Southmolton. Yet, even here, the observant eye of malevolence was upon them. Mr. Howe had been officiating there, in a dark and tempestuous wintry night, when an alarm was made that information had been given, and a warrant granted to apprehend him. It was judged prudent for him to quit the house; but in riding over a large common, he and his servant missed their way. After several fruitless efforts to recover it, the attendant went forward to seek for a habitation, where they might either find directions or a lodging. He soon discovered a mansion, and received a cheerful invitation to rest there for the night. But how great was Mr. Howe's surprise, to find, on his arrival, that the house belonged to his most inveterate enemy, a country magistrate, who had often breathed the most implacable vengeance against him, and, as he had reason to believe, was well acquainted with the occasion of his traveling at such an hour. However, he put the best face he could upon it, and even mentioned his name and residence to the gentleman, trusting to Providence for the result. His host ordered supper to be provided, and entered into a lengthened conversation with his guest; and was so delighted with his company, that it was a very late hour before he could permit him to retire to his chamber. In the morning, Mr. Howe expected to be accosted with a commitment, and sent to Exeter; but, on the contrary, he was received by the family at breakfast with a very hospitable welcome. After mutual civilities, he departed to his own abode, greatly wondering to himself at the kindness of a man from whom he had before dreaded so much.

Not long after, the gentleman sent for Mr. Howe, who found him confined to his bed by sickness, and still more deeply wounded with the sense of sin. He acknowledged that, when Mr. Howe came first to his door, he inwardly rejoiced that he had an opportunity of exercising his malice upon him, but that his conversation and his manner insensibly awed him into respect. He had long ruminated on the observations which had fallen from the man of God, and was become a penitent, earnestly anxious for the blessings of eternal life. From that sickness he recovered, became an eminent Christian, a friend to the conscientious, and an intimate companion of the man whom he had threatened with his vengeance.

(*d*) THE DUMB SERMON EFFECTUAL.—The Rev. William Tennant once took much pains to prepare a sermon, to convince a celebrated infidel of the truth of Christianity. But, in attempting to deliver this labored discourse, he was so confused, as to be compelled to stop, and close the service by prayer. This unexpected failure, in one who had so often astonished the unbeliever with the force of his eloquence, led the infidel to reflect that Mr. T. had been, at other times, aided by a Divine power. This reflection proved the means of his conversion. Thus God accomplished by silence what his servant wished to effect by persuasive preaching. Mr. Tennant used afterwards to say, his dumb sermon was one of the most profitable sermons that he had ever delivered.

(*e*) THE DRUNKARD'S CONVERSION.—In a regiment of soldiers stationed at Edinburgh, there was a sergeant named Forbes, a very abandoned man, who got in debt for liquor wherever he could. His wife washed for the regiment, and thus obtained a little money. She was a pious woman, but all her attempts to reclaim him were long unsuccessful. During one of Mr. Whitefield's visits to that city, she offered her husband a sum of money if he would for once go and hear him. This was a strong inducement, and he engaged to go. The sermon was in a field, as no building could have contained the audience. The sergeant was rather early, and placed himself in the middle of the field, that he might file off when Mr. Whitefield ascended the pulpit; as he only wished to be able to say that he had seen him. The crowd, however, increased; and when Mr. Whitefield appeared, they pressed forward, and he found it impossible to get away. The prayer produced some impression on his mind, but the sermon most deeply convinced him of his sinfulness and danger. He became an altered man, and proved the reality of his conversion, by living for many years with the strictest economy, in order to liquidate the claims of every one of his creditors.

(*f*) THE MATHEMATICIAN CONFOUNDED.—A young man, who had graduated at one of the first colleges in America, and was celebrated for his literary attainments, particularly his knowledge of mathematics, settled in a village where a faithful minister of the gospel was stationed. It was not long before the clergyman met with him in one of his evening walks, and after some conversation, as they were about to part, addressed him as follows: "I have heard you are celebrated for your mathematical skill; I have a problem which I wish you to solve." "What is it?" eagerly inquired the young man. The clergyman answered, with a solemn tone of voice, "What shall it profit a man, if he shall gain the whole world, and lose his own soul?" The youth returned home, and endeavored to shake off the impression fastened on him by the problem proposed to him, but in vain. In the giddy round of pleasure, in his business, and in his studies, the question still forcibly returned to him, "What shall it profit a man, if he shall gain the whole world, and lose his own soul?" It finally resulted in his conversion, and he became an able advocate and preacher of that gospel which he once rejected.

(*g*) THE MERCHANT TURNED PREACHER.—Peter Waldo was a citizen and opulent merchant of Lyons, and at one period a believer of the errors of popery. Being in company, however, with some friends, one of whom suddenly fell dead to the ground, he was aroused to the importance of religious truth, and led to inquire seriously after it. So deeply was he impressed with the superior value of eternal things, that he gave up his mercantile occupations, distributed his wealth to the poor, exhorted his neighbors to seek the bread of life, and became a most eminent minister in the Waldensian churches, who are thus designated from him.

(*h*) THE ACTRESS AND THE COTTAGER'S FAMILY.—An actress in one of the English provincial or country theatres, was one day passing through the streets of the town in which she then resided, when her attention was attracted by the sound of voices, which she heard in a poor cottage before her. Curiosity prompted her to look in at an open door, when she saw a few poor people sitting together, one of whom, at the moment of her observation, was giving out the following hymn, which the others joined in singing:—

> "Depth of mercy! can there be
> Mercy still reserved for me?"

The tune was sweet and simple, but she heeded it not. The words had riveted her attention, and she stood motionless, until she was invited to enter, by the woman of the house, who had observed her standing at the door. She complied, and remained during a prayer which was offered up by one of the little company; and uncouth as the expressions sounded, perhaps, to her ears, they carried with them a conviction of sincerity, on the part of the person then employed. She quitted the cottage, but the words of the hymn followed her. She could not banish them from her mind, and at last she resolved to procure the book which contained it. She did so, and the more she read it, the more decided her serious impressions became. She attended the ministry of the gospel, read her hitherto neglected and despised Bible, and bowed herself in humility and contrition of heart, before him whose mercy she now felt she needed, whose sacrifices are those of a broken heart and a contrite spirit, and who has declared, that with such sacrifices he is well pleased.

Her professsion she determined at once and for ever to renounce; and for some little time excused herself from appearing on the stage, without, however, disclosing her change of sentiments or making known her resolution finally to leave it.

The manager of the theatre called upon her one morning, and requested her to sustain the principal character in a new play which was to be performed the next week for his benefit. She had frequently performed this character to general admiration; but she now, however, told him her resolution never to appear as an actress again, at the same time giving her reasons. At first he attempted to overcome her scruples by ridicule, but this was unavailing; he then represented the loss he should incur by her refusal, and concluded his arguments by promising, that if to oblige him, she would act on this occasion, it should be the last reques of the kind he would ever make. Unable to resist his solicitations, she promised to appear, and on the appointed evening went to the theatre. The character she assumed required her, on her first entrance to sing a song; and when the curtain drew up, the orchestra immediately began the accompaniment. But she stood as if lost in thought, and as one forgetting all around her, and her own situation. The music ceased, but she did not sing; and supposing her to be overcome by embarrassment, the band again commenced. A second time they paused for her to begin, and still she did not open her lips. A third time the air was played, and then, with clasped hands, and eyes suffused with tears, she sang, not the words of the song, but,

> "Depth of mercy! can there be
> Mercy still reserved for me?"

It is almost needless to add, that the performance was suddenly ended; many ridiculed, though some were induced from that memorable night to "consider their ways," and to reflect on the wonderful power of that religion which could so influence the heart, and change the life of one hitherto so vain, and so evidently pursuing the road which leadeth to destruction.

It would be satisfactory to the reader to know, that the change in Miss —— was as permanent as it was singular; she walked consistently with her profession of religion for many years, and at length became the wife of a minister of the gospel of our Lord Jesus Christ.

(*i*) THE CHRISTIAN'S GLOOMY DEATH.—A pious parent had three sons, who, notwithstanding all his admonitions and instructions, mingled with many prayers and tears, grew up to manhood in skepticism and profligacy. The father lay dying; and, conceiving that it might perhaps produce a good impression on the minds of his abandoned children, to let them see how a Christian dies, the friends of the family introduced them to the bedside of their expiring parent. But, to their unspeakable grief, the good man died without any expressions of Christian confidence, and appeared destitute of those strong consolations which believers in Jesus usually experience in the closing scene. It was now apprehended that the effect of this melancholy circumstance on the young men would be to confirm them in their prejudice against religion, and afford them, in their opinion, a sufficient evidence that it is all a cunningly devised fable. However, it was not so: the ways of God are not as our ways, neither are his thoughts as our thoughts. A few days after the funeral, the younger brother entered the room in which the other two were; and observing that he had been weeping, they inquired the cause of his grief, "I have been thinking," said he, "of the death of our father." "Ah," said they, "a dismal death it was; what truth or reality can there be in religion, when such a man as he died in such a state of mind?" "It has not affected me in this way," replied the younger brother; "we all know what a holy life our father led, and what a gloomy death he died; now I have been thinking, how dreadful our death must be, who lead such a wicked life!" The observation was like an arrow to their consciences; and they began to be alarmed. They repaired to the ordinances of religion, which, in their father's life time they had neglected, and ultimately became as eminent for piety as their exemplary parent had been.

(*j*) SAY YOUR PRAYERS IN FAIR WEATHER.—A sea captain of a profligate character, who commanded a vessel trading between Liverpool and America, during the last war, once took on board a man as a common sailor, to serve during the voyage, just as he was leaving port. The new comer was soon found to be of a most quarrelsome, untractable disposition, a furious blasphemer, and, when an opportunity offered, a drunkard. Besides all these disqualifications, he was wholly ignorant of nautical affairs, or counterfeited ignorance to escape duty. In short, he was the bane and plague of the vessel, and refused obstinately to give any account of himself, or his family, or past life.

At length a violent storm arose, all hands were piped upon deck, and all, as the captain thought, were too few to save the ship. When the men were mustered to their quarters, the sturdy blasphemer was missing, and my friend went below to seek for him; great was his surprise at finding him on his knees, repeating the Lord's prayer with wonderful rapidity, over and over again, as if he had bound himself to countless reiterations. Vexed at what he deemed hypocrisy or cowardice, he shook him roughly by the collar, exclaiming, "*say your prayers in fair weather.*" The man rose up, observing in a low voice, "God grant I may ever see fair weather to say them."

In a few hours the storm happily abated, a week more brought them to harbor, and an incident so trivial passed quickly away from the memory of the captain; the more easily, as the man in question was paid off the day after landing, and appeared not again.

Four years more had elapsed, during which, though the captain had twice been shipwrecked, and was grievously hurt by the falling of a spar, he pursued without amendment a life of profligacy and contempt of God. At the end of this period, he arrived in the port of New-York, after a very tedious and dangerous voyage from England.

It was on a Sabbath morning, and the streets were thronged with persons proceeding to the several houses of worship, with which that city abounds—but the captain was bent on far other occupation, designing to drown the recollection of perils and deliverances, in a celebrated tavern which he had too long, and too often frequented.

As he walked leisurely towards this goal, he encountered a very dear friend, a quondam associate of many a thoughtless hour. Salutations over, the captain seized him by the arm, declaring that he should accompany him to the hotel "I will do so," replied the other, with great calmness, "on condition that you come with me first for a single hour into this house, (a church,) and thank God for his mercies to you on the deep. The captain was ashamed to refuse, so the two friends entered the temple together. Already all the seats were occupied, and a dense crowd filled the aisle; and by dint of personal exertion, they succeeded in reaching a position right in front of the pulpit, at about five yards distance. The preacher, one of the most popular of the day, riveted the attention of the entire congregation, including the captain himself, to whom his features and voice, though he could not assign any time or place of previous meeting, seemed not wholly unknown, particularly when he spoke with animation. At length the preacher's eye fell upon the spot where the two friends stood. He suddenly paused—still gazing upon the captain, as if to make himself sure that he labored under no optical delusion—and after a silence of more than a minute, pronounced with a voice that shook the building, "*say your prayers in fair weather.*"

The audience were lost in amazement, nor was it until a considerable time had elapsed, that the preacher recovered sufficient self-possession to recount the incident with which the reader is already acquainted, adding, with deep emotion, that the words which his captain uttered in the storm, had clung to him by day and by night after his landing, as if an angel had been charged with the duty of repeating them in his ears—that he felt the holy call as coming direct from above, to do the work of his crucified Master—that he had studied at college for the ministry. and was now, through grace, such as they saw and heard.

At the conclusion of this affecting address, he called on the audience to join in prayer with himself, that the same words might be blessed in turn to him who first had used them. But God had outrun their petitions—the captain was already His child, before his former shipmate had ceased to tell his story. The power of the Spirit had wrought effectually upon him, and subdued every lofty imagination. And so, when the people dispersed, he exchanged the hotel for the house of the preacher, with whom he tarried six weeks, and parted from him to pursue his profession, with a heart devoted to the service of his Savior, and with holy and happy assurances which advancing years hallowed, strengthened, and sanctified.

(*k*) CONVERSION OF THE HALDANES.—The Rev. James Haldane (pastor of one of the Baptist churches in Edinburgh, Scotland), says Rev. Mr. Turnbull, was a junior member of a highly respectable and wealthy family. In his youth, he became connected with the British navy, and rose to the post of captain, in one of his majesty's war ships. On one occasion, being engaged in a warmly contested battle, he saw the whole of his men on deck swept off by a tremendous broadside from the enemy. He ordered another company to be "piped up" from below, to take the place of their lost companions. On coming up, they saw their mangled remains strewn upon the deck, and were seized with a sudden and irresistible panic. On seeing this, the captain jumped up, and swore a horrid oath, imprecating the vengeance of Almighty God upon the whole of them, and wishing that they might all sink to hell. An old marine, who was a pious man, stepped up to him, and respectfully touching his hat, said:—"Captain, I believe God hears prayer; and if God had heard your prayer just now, what would have become of us?" Having spoken this, he made a respectful bow, and retired to his place. After the engagement, the captain calmly reflected upon the words of the old marine, and was so deeply affected by them, that he devoted his attention to the claims of religion, and was subsequently converted to God.

Of course he informed his brother Robert of his change of views, but instead of being gratified by it, his brother was greatly offended, and requested him never to enter his house till he had changed his views. "Very well, Robert," said James, "but I have one comfort in the case, and that is, you cannot prevent my praying for you;" and holding out his hand, he bade him good-bye. His brother Robert was much affected by this; he could not get rid of the idea that his brother was constantly praying for him. He saw the error of his ways, and after much investigation and reflection, became a decided Christian.

Some years afterwards, Robert Haldane made a journey to the Continent and settled for some time in Geneva. He was much affected with the low spiritual condition of the Protestant church there, which had become infected with the rationalistic and neological views prevalent in Germany. Indeed, the clergy themselves, had so far departed from the faith of the Reformation, as to reject almost all the fundamental doctrines of the gospel, particularly the divinity of Christ, and the doctrine of atonement. Mr. Haldane made himself acquainted with the students attending the divinity school in Geneva, and invited a number of them to his house, and, by free conversation, endeavored to teach them the gospel, and the nature of spiritual religion. This he frequently repeated, till at last, God blessed his efforts to the conversion of ten or twelve of them. Among them were *Felix Neff*, subsequently pastor in the high Alps, and one of the purest and most devoted men that ever lived. *Henry Pyt*, another well-known and truly pious man, and *Henry Merle D'Aubigne*, well known throughout the literary and religious world, as the author of the History of the Reformation, and President of the New Evangelical School of Theology in Geneva.

353. Trust in Providence.

(*a*) THE WIDOW'S PRAYER ANSWERED.—A correspondent of THE TRACT MAGAZINE gives the following account as she had it from the lips of a pious widow of her acquaintance:

"One evening we were eating our supper, we had nothing but bread, and of that not sufficient to satisfy our hunger. 'Mother,' said little John, when he was finishing his last morsel, 'what shall we do to-morrow morning? there is no bread in the house; we shall have no breakfast.' I answered him, 'Do not fear, John: God has not forsaken us: let us pray to him, and be assured he will remember us.' I made him kneel down by my side, and prayed to God, that he would in his goodness have pity upon us, and give us bread for the morrow. I then put my child to bed, telling him to go to sleep quietly, and to depend upon his God, who never forgot those who put their trust in him. I myself went to bed, firmly believing that my God had heard my prayer, and, commending myself to the protection of our Lord Jesus Christ, I slept comfortably till four in the morning, when John woke me; 'Mother,' said he, 'is the bread come?' Poor little fellow! he had but a scanty supper, and was very hungry. 'No,' I answered, 'it is not yet come, but be quiet, and go to sleep again; it will come.' We both went to sleep: I was awakened a little before six in the morning by some one rapping at my window. 'Dame Bartlet,' said a woman, 'you must get up immediately, Mrs. Martin's dairymaid is taken very ill, and you must come and milk her cows:' here then was bread for us. I went to Mrs. Martin's, and milked her cows, and afterwards sat down in the kitchen to breakfast; but I thought of my child, and could not eat. Mrs. Martin observing me, said, 'You do not eat your breakfast, Dame Bartlet.' I thanked her, and told her I had left a little boy at home in bed, very hungry; if she would permit me, I should prefer carrying my breakfast home to him. 'Eat your breakfast now,' was the kind answer of Mrs. Martin; 'you shall carry some breakfast home to your little boy besides.' Mrs. Martin then gave me a basket of provisions, sufficient for myself and child for two or three days. As I returned home, I could not but thank my God, and feel grateful to him, and my kind benefactress: I rejoiced my little boy's heart by a sight of my breakfast. He got up directly, eager to partake of Mrs. Martin's kindness: after a good breakfast, I made him kneel down again by my side, whilst I returned thanks to our gracious God, who had heard our prayers the evening before, and who had given us a kind benefactress. When we rose, I took him in my lap, and said to him, 'Now, John, I hope what has happened to us will be remembered by you through your whole life. Last evening we had eaten all our bread, we had none left for this morning; but we prayed to God that, through his mercy, and for the sake of his Son Jesus Christ, he would give us our daily bread. God has heard us, and has given us bread: may this teach you through life to put your trust and faith in your heavenly Father. I most earnestly pray to God that you may never forget this.'"

Dame Bartlet concluded her interesting narrative by adding, "And, madam, I have never wanted bread since. I am blessed in my son, who is now a man; he is dutiful and good to me, and has never forgotten the pains his mother took with him in his childhood; nor the exhoration I then gave him, to trust in God."

(*b*) THE PERSECUTED WOMAN FED.—A pious woman in the days of persecution, used to say, she should never want, because her God would supply her every need. She was taken before an unjust judge for attending the worship of God. The judge, on seeing her, tauntingly said, "I have often wished to have you in my power, and now I shall send you to prison, and then how will you be fed?" She replied, "If it be my heavenly Father's pleasure, I shall be fed from your table." And that was literally the case; for the judge's wife being present at her examination, was greatly surprised with the good woman's firmness, and took care to send her victuals from her table, so that she was comfortably supplied all the time she was in confinement; and the other found her reward, for the Lord was pleased to convert her soul, and give her the blessings of his salvation.

(*c*) "BREAD SHALL BE GIVEN THEE."—In a large and populous village, in one of the hundreds, or wapentakes of Yorkshire, England, lived a poor, but honest and pious man, whose name was Jonathan. He was an afflicted man, and much paralyzed by disease. He had a wife, and two or three children, whose chief dependence in life was upon his small earnings. Jonathan was patient, industrious, and persevering in his efforts to provide for himself and for his household, all of whom were content with homely fare. At the time the writer of this account knew him, he might be from forty to fifty years of age. Amongst other occurrences of his life, he says, I distinctly recollect the following, which he related to me:—

During the time of harvest, while employed in gathering the fruits of the earth, he accidentally slipped from the top of a barley-mow, and sprained one or both of his ankles; in consequence of which he was confined to his room and bed for some weeks. It is unnecessary to state, that in the meantime, his family must have felt the loss of his weekly labor and income. His wife, on one occasion, went up stairs into his room weeping. "What is the matter?" said Jonathan, "what is distressing thee?" "Why, the children are crying for something to eat, and I have nothing to give them," was the affecting reply. "Hast thou faith in God?" asked Jonathan. "Dost thou believe in his providence, and in his word? Has he not said, 'Bread shall be given thee, and thy water shall be sure?' Isa. xxxiii. 16. Kneel down," he continued, "at the bedside, and pray to God. Tell him how thy children are circumstanced; that they have no bread; that thou hast nothing wherewith to buy them any; and I will also pray. Who can tell what God may do? He heareth prayer."

Jonathan and his wife prayed earnestly together; they pleaded the promises of God, and waited the result. Soon after, a person came to the door with a loaf of bread. She came from a house in the immediate neighborhood of Jonathan, the occupier of which was one of several branches of a family who were proprietors of very extensive iron works, carried on in the village where Jonathan lived. No sooner did the good woman receive the loaf of bread, than she ran to Jonathan to tell him how God had answered their prayer. "Now," said Jonathan, "before any thing else be done, kneel down at the bedside, and return thanks to God for having heard our prayer." She did so: they praised his name together: and then ate their food with gladness and with singleness of heart. Not many hours elapsed before another kind interposition of Providence presented itself. A second visitor brought them a joint of meat. When this was told Jonathan, he replied to his wife, "Aye! see! God is even better than his word! He promised bread, and he sends flesh in addition. Kneel down, and thank him again."

(*d*) THE FARMER AND THE SOLDIERS.—Soon after the surrender of Copenhagen to the English, in the year 1807, detachments of soldiers were, for a time, stationed in the surrounding villages. It happened one day that three soldiers, belonging to a Highland regiment, were sent to forage among the neighboring farm-houses. They went to several, but found them stripped and deserted. At length they came to a large garden, or orchard, full of apple trees, bending under the weight of fruit. They entered by a gate, and followed a path which brought them to a neat farm-house. Every thing without bespoke quietness and security; but as they entered by the front door, the mistress of the house and her children ran screaming out by the back. The interior of the house presented an appearance of order and comfort superior to what might be expected from people in that station, and from the habits of the country. A watch hung by the side of the fireplace, and a neat book-case, well filled, attracted the attention of the elder soldier. He took down a book: it was written in a language unknown to him, but the name of Jesus Christ was legible on every page. At this moment, the master of the house entered by the door through which his wife and childen had just fled.

One of the soldiers, by threatening signs, demanded provisions: the man stood firm and undaunted, but shook his head. The soldier who held the book approached him, and pointing to the name of Jesus Christ, laid his hand upon his heart, and looked up to heaven

Instantly the farmer grasped his hand, shook it vehemently, and then ran out of the room. He soon returned with his wife and children laden with milk, eggs, bacon, etc., which were freely tendered; and when money was offered in return, it was at first refused. But as two of the soldiers were pious men, they, much to the chagrin of their companion, insisted upon paying for all they received. When taking leave, the pious soldiers intimated to the farmer that it would be well for him to secrete his watch: but, by the most significant signs, he gave them to understand that he feared no evil, for his trust was in God; and that though his neighbors, on the right hand and on the left, had fled from their habitations, and by foraging parties had lost what they could not remove, not a hair of his head had been injured, nor had he even lost an apple from his trees.

"The angel of the Lord encampeth round about them that fear him, and delivereth them."

(*e*) INCIDENTS IN STILLING'S LIFE.—In youth, Stilling was extremely poor, destitute of the common comforts and necessaries of life. After a long season of anxiety and prayer, he felt satisfied that it was the will of God that he should go to a university, and prepare himself for the medical profession. He did not at first make choice of a university, but waited for an intimation from his heavenly Father; for as he intended to study simply from faith, he would not allow his own will in any thing. Three weeks after he had come to this determination, a friend asked him whither he intended to go. He replied he did not know. "O," said she, "our neighbor, Mr. T., is going to Strasburg, to spend the winter there, go with him."

This touched Stilling's heart; he felt that this was the intimation he had waited for. Meanwhile, Mr. T. entered the room, and was heartily pleased with the proposition. The whole of his welfare now depended on his becoming a physician; and for this, a thousand dollars at least were requisite, of which he could not tell in the whole world where to raise a hundred. He nevertheless fixed his confidence firmly on God, and reasoned as follows:

"God begins nothing without terminating it gloriously. Now, it is most certainly true, that he alone has ordered my present circumstances, entirely without my co-operation. Consequently, it is also most certainly true, that he will accomplish every thing regarding me in a manner worthy of himself."

He smilingly said to his friends, who were as poor as himself—"I wonder from what quarter my heavenly Father will provide me with money?" When they expressed anxiety, he said—"Believe assuredly that he who was able to feed a thousand people with a little bread lives still, and to him I commend myself. He will certainly find out means. Do not be anxious, the Lord will provide."

Forty-six dollars was all that he could raise for his journey. He met unavoidable delay on the way; and while at Frankfort, three days' ride from Strasburg, he had but a single dollar left. He said nothing of it to any one, but waited for the assistance of his heavenly Father. As he was walking the streets and praying inwardly to God, he met Mr. L., a merchant from the place of his residence, who says to him, "Stilling, what brought you here?"

"I am going to Strasburg, to study medicine."

"Where do you get your money to study with?"

"I have a rich Father in heaven."

Mr. L. looked steadily at him, and inquired—"How much money have you on hand?"

"One dollar," said Stilling.

"So," said Mr. L. "Well, I'm one of your Father's stewards," and handed him thirty-three dollars.

Stilling felt warm tears in his eyes; says he—"I am now rich enough, I want no more."

This first trial made him so courageous, that he no longer doubted that God would help him through every thing.

He had been but a short time in Strasburg, when his thirty-three dollars had again been reduced to one, on which account he began again to pray very earnestly. Just at this time, one morning, his room-mate, Mr. T., says to him, "Stilling, I believe you did not bring much money with you," and offered him thirty dollars in gold, which he gladly accepted, as an answer to his prayers.

In a few months after this, the time arrived when he must pay the lecturer's fee, or have his name struck from the list of students. The money was to be paid by six o'clock on Thursday evening. Thursday morning came, and he had no money, and no means of getting any. The day was spent in prayer. Five o'clock in the evening came, and yet there was no money. His faith began almost to fail; he broke out into a perspiration; his face was wet with tears. Some one knocked at the door. "Come in," said he. It was Mr. R., the gentleman of whom he had rented the room.

"I called," said Mr. R., "to see how you like your room?"

"Thank you," said Stilling, "I like it very much."

Says Mr. R.—"I thought I would ask you one other question; have you brought any money with you?"

Stilling says he now felt like Habakkuk when the angel took him by the hair of the head to carry him to Babylon. He answered "No; I have no money."

Mr. R. looked at him with surprise, and at length said, "I see how it is; God has sent me to help you."

He immediately left the room, and soon returned with forty dollars in gold.

Stilling says he then felt like Daniel in the lion's den, when Habakkuk brought him his food. He threw himself on the floor, and thanked God with tears. He then went to the college, and paid his fee as well as the best.

(*f*) THE WALKING BIBLE.—Of a good man who from his love to the sacred volume, and his extensive knowledge of its contents, was called "the walking Bible," it is recorded, that when he was very young, he was, with his parents, oppressed with great poverty. In the garden in which their cottage, or rather hovel stood, there was a large pear-tree, more venerated for its age than valued for its fruitfulness. The mother requested him to cut it down for firewood. He heard the request in silence; she repeated it, and he still hesitated. At length he said, "Mother, I ought to obey you, but I must first obey God. The tree is not ours. It belongs to our landlord: and you know that God says, 'Thou shalt not steal.' I therefore hope you will not make me cut it down." She desisted; for a day or two longer they endured the cold, when she peremptorily renewed her demand that the tree should be cut down. He then said, "Mother, the good Being has often helped us, and supplied our want when we have been in trouble. Let us wait till this time to-morrow. Then, if we do not find some relief, though I am sure it will be wrong, yet if you make me do it, I will cut down the tree in obedience to your command." She yielded, and he, in his simple manner, retired, and in secret earnestly prayed to God to interfere, and prevent them from displeasing him by a transgression of his holy law. He sallied forth the next morning, and wandering about found a man whose cart wheel had broken under a heavy load of coal. He told his distress to the man, who was induced to leave the coals for him to carry away, with the understanding that whenever he called for the money, if the family were able, they should pay it. He never after, however, made his appearance.

(*g*) REV. S. WELLES' CONFIDENCE IN GOD.—The Rev. Samuel Welles, a Christian minister of the seventeenth century, constantly trusted the good providence of God, and was once told by a doctor of divinity that he lived better on Providence than the doctor himself with all his income. Though this good man had ten or eleven children, he declared that he had no anxiety about their support, for God would surely provide. On this principle he acted in leaving a situation which brought him 200*l*. a year for one that yielded only 100*l*. per annum, that his usefulness might be increased; and afterwards for the same reason refused a living of 300*l*.

(*h*) THE SUFFERERS AT SIGATEA.—During the 17th century, while the Rev. John Cotton was minister of Boston, intelligence reached that town of the distress of the poor Christians at Sigatea, where a small church existed, the members of which were reduced to great extremity of suffering by persecution. Mr. Cotton immediately began to collect for them, and sent the sum of £700 for their relief. It is remarkable, that this relief arrived the very day after they had divided their last portion of meal, without any prospect than that of dying a lingering death, and immediately after their pastor, Mr. White, had preached to them from Psalm xxiii. 1, "The Lord is my Shepherd; I shall not want."

(*i*) THE DYING MINISTER'S FAMILY.—"I have known," says an English writer, "wonderful proofs of the faithfulness of the Lord in answering the prayers of parents who left young and helpless families behind. A friend of mine in the west of England, (a faithful laborious minister, but who, I believe, never was master of five pounds at a time,) was dying.

His friends advised him to make his will; he replied, "I have nothing to leave but my wife and children, and I leave them to the care of my gracious God." Soon after this he died, happily. But there appeared no prospect of support for his family at this time. The Lord, however, stirred up a man, who had always despised his preaching, to feel for the deceased minister's poor, destitute family, and he so exerted himself, that he was the means of £1,600, being raised by subscriptions for them; and the clergy of Exeter, who had never countenanced his preaching, gave his widow a house and garden for life, so that she lived in far greater plenty than in her husband's lifetime. Why was all this? It was in answer to the prayers of the good man, who committed his wife and family to that God who could *supply all their needs*, and who he knew was able to open the doors of relief for them.

354. Miscellaneous.

(*a*) A BIRD'S FLIGHT DECIDING THE SPREAD OF MOHAMMEDANISM.—The great drama of a nation's politics, and the most mighty changes in the history and character of mankind, may hinge on circumstances of the most trivial nature. One of the most remarkable instances of this sort is found in the history of Mohammed. When his pursuers followed hard upon him to take his life, they were turned away from the mouth of the cave in which he had the moment before taken shelter, by the flight of a bird from one of the shrubs that grew at its entry! For they inferred that if he had recently passed that way, the bird must previously have been frightened away, and would not now have made its appearance. It is a striking remark of the historian, that this bird, by its flight on this occasion, changed the destiny of the world—instrumental as it was in perpetuating the life of the false Prophet, and with him the reign of that superstition which to this day hath a wider ascendency over ourspecies than Christianity itself. Such are the links and concatenations of all history. It is well that God has the management, and that what to man is chaos, in the hands of God is a sure and unerring mechanism.

(*b*) SKEPTICAL SAILOR CONVINCED—A careless sailor, on going to sea, replied to his religious brother in words like these: "Tom, you talk a great deal about religion and Providence; and if I should be wrecked, and a ship was to heave in sight and take me off, I suppose you would call it a merciful Providence. It's all very well, but I believe no such thing; these things happen like other things, by mere chance, and you call it Providence, that's all." He went upon his voyage, and the case he put hypothetically was soon literally true; he was wrecked, and remained upon the wreck three days, when a ship appeared, and, seeing their signal of distress, came to their relief. He returned, and, in relating it, said to his brother, "Oh! Tom, when that ship hove in sight, my words to you came in a moment into my mind; it was like a bolt of thunder. I have never got rid of it, and now I think it no more than an act of common gratitude to give myself up to Him who pitied and saved me."

(*c*) COMPLAINING AGAINST PROVIDENCE.—A person with not very ample means of support, was burthened with a large family. A neighbor had just called to tell him of a friend who had got a prize in a lottery, when he was also informed of the birth of his twelfth child. He exclaimed, peevishly, "God sends meat to others, children to me." It so happened, that God, at whose government he had so impiously murmured, sent him those riches he longed for. But as he sent him the wished-for wealth, he deprived him of the children he had complained of. He saw them one by one go to the grave before him; and in advanced life, and great affluence, when he endured the stroke of having his last beloved daughter taken from his eyes, he bitterly remembered (it is hoped with salutary bitterness) his former rebellious murmurings against God.

355. PUNCTUALITY.

(*a*) WASTING OTHERS' TIME.—A committee of eight ladies, in the neighborhood of London, was appointed to meet on a certain day at twelve o'clock. Seven of them were punctual; but the eighth came hurrying in, with many apologies for being a quarter of an hour behind time. The time had passed away without her being aware of it; she had no idea of its being so late, etc. A Quaker lady present, said, "Friend, I am not so clear that we should admit thine apology. It were matter of regret that thou shouldst have wasted thine own quarter of an hour; but here are seven besides thyself, whose time thou hast also consumed, amounting in the whole to two hours, and seven-eighths of it was not thine own property."

(*b*) MELANCTHON'S EXAMPLE.—It is said of Melancthon, the celebrated reformer and colleague of Martin Luther, that when he made an appointment, he expected not only the hour, but the minute to be fixed, that the day might not run out in the idleness of suspense.

(*c*) WILLIAM PENN'S EXAMPLE.—Few men have been more distinguished for vigorous exertions of various kinds, than the worthy and well known William Penn. If we consider the number of books which he wrote and published, the number and difficult active engagements in which he was occupied, and the almost incessant troubles and interruptions to which he was subject, we shall wonder how it was possible for him to accomplish what he did. He who reads attentively the life of this eminent man, written by Mr. Clarkson, will find that the secret of his extraordinary despatch in study, writing and business, was his punctuality.

(*d*) BLACKSTONE'S EXAMPLE.—Of Sir William Blackstone we are informed, that in reading his lectures, it could not be remembered that he ever made his audience wait, even for a few minutes, beyond the time appointed. Indeed punctuality, in his opinion, was so much a virtue, that he could not bring himself to think perfectly well of any who was notoriously defective in this practice.

(*e*) WAY TO PROMOTE PUNCTUALITY. — The residence of the Rev. David Brown in Calcutta, was at a considerable distance from the Mission Church, where he preached; but no weather ever deterred him from meeting the people at the stated periods of Divine service. And when on any occasion, and even in cases of indisposition he was urged to postpone the service, he would not consent; for, he would observe, "If the hearers once find a minister to be irregular in his attendance on them, they will become irregular in attending him; but when my congregation sees that no inconvenience whatever makes me neglect them, they will be ashamed to keep away on any frivolous pretext."

(*f*) EXAMPLE OF WASHINGTON.—When General Washington assigned to meet congress at noon, he never failed to be passing the door of the hall while the clock was striking twelve.—Whether his guests were present or not, he always dined at four. Not unfrequently new members of congress, who were invited to dine with him, delayed until dinner was half over, and he would then remark, "gentlemen, we are punctual here." When he visited Boston in 1788, he appointed eight A. M. as the hour when he should set out for Salem, and while the Old South church clock was striking eight, he was mounting his horse. The company of cavalry, which volunteered to escort him, were parading in Tremont-street, after his departure, and it was not until the President reached Charles River Bridge, that they overtook him. On the arrival of the corps, the President, with perfect good nature, said, "Major, I thought you had been too long in my family, not to know when it was eight o'clock." Captain Pease, the father of the stage establishment in the United States, had a beautiful pair of horses which he wished to dispose of to the President, whom he knew to be an excellent judge of horses. The President appointed five o'clock in the morning to examine them. But the captain did not arrive with the horses until a quarter after five, when he was told by the groom that the President was there at five and was then fulfilling other engagements. Pease, much mortified, was obliged to wait a week for another opportunity, merely for delaying the first *quarter of an hour*.

(*g*) BREWER'S PUNCTUALITY.—The Rev. S. Brewer was distinguished for punctuality. When a youth in college, he was never known to be a minute behind time in attending lectures of the tutors, or the family prayers, at which the young men who boarded in private families were expected to assemble. One morning the students were collected; the clock struck seven, and all rose up for prayer; but the tutor observing that Mr. Brewer was not present, paused awhile. Seeing him enter the room, he thus addressed him; 'Sir, the clock has struck, and we are ready to begin; but as you were absent, we supposed the clock was too fast, and therefore waited."—The clock was actually too fast by some minutes.

(*h*) CURING A CONGREGATION.—A punctual minister once had the misfortune to succeed a tardy man who had had the congregation in charge for some years. He despaired of reforming them in great matters if he could not reform them in small. He found them in the habit of meeting at twelve o'clock though the hour appointed and agreed upon was eleven. The preacher knew his duty and begun at the minute. The first day after his settlement his sermon was well nigh closed before most of his congregation arrived. Some actually arrived just at the benediction. They were confounded. He made no apology. He only asked the seniors if they would prefer any other time than eleven o'clock and he would be sure to attend. A few weeks passed and the house was regularly full and waiting for the minute. The preacher never failed in twenty years, except in a few cases of indisposition, to commence at the hour appointed. His congregation became as punctual and circumspect in other matters as in their attendance at church; for it is almost impossible to be habitually punctual in one class of duties and to be remiss in all others.

PUNISHMENT OF THE WICKED, NOT IN THIS LIFE.

356. Because their Remorse is not Commensurate with their Guilt.

(*a*) THE TWO GREEK PIRATES,—Two Greeks, notorious for their piracies and other crimes, were, in 1829, tried and condemned, and three days after executed at Malta. In the course of the trial, it appeared that the beef and anchovies, on board one of the English vessels which they pirated, were left untouched, and the circumstances under which they were left appeared to the court so peculiar, that the culprits were asked the cause of it. They promptly answered that it was at the time of the great fast, when their church ate neither meat nor fish. They appeared to be most hardened and abandoned wretches, enemies alike to their own and every other nation, and yet rigidly maintaning their religious character: and while they were robbing, plundering, and murdering and stealing the women and children of their countrymen, and selling them to the Turks, and committing other atrocious deeds, they would have us understand that they were not so wicked as to taste meat or fish, when prohibited by the canons of their church! Had a single drop of the blood of the murdered been, by means of the blows inflicted, spattered on their lips, and thus by chance passed into their mouth, they would probably have felt in continual danger of the fire that shall never be quenched, until they could have visited some church, confessed and done penance for having tasted something of an animal nature in the season of a fast. I do not know, indeed, says Mr. Goodell, that they would have manifested such ignorance and superstition, but it would have given me no surprise to hear that they did; and moreover, that they derived their principal hopes of success, in their villainous and horrid traffic, from a strict attention to the requirements of their religion.

(*b*) THE PIRATE GIBBS.—This man, whose name was for many years a terror to commerce with the West Indies and South America, was at last taken captive, tried, condemned, and executed in the city of New-York. He acknowledged before his death that when he committed the first murder and plundered the first ship, his compunctions were severe, conscience was on the rack, and made a hell within his bosom. But after he had sailed for years under the black flag, his conscience became so hardened and blunted, that he could rob a vessel and murder all its crew and then lie down and sleep as sweetly at night as an infant in its cradle. His remorse diminished as his crimes increased. So it is generally. If therefore remorse in this life is God's way of punishing crimes, the more they sin the less he punishes them! How absurd!

(*c*) THE SHEPHERD AND THE PRIEST.–A Neapolitan shepherd came in anguish to his priest, saying, "Father have mercy on a miserable sinner. It is the holy season of Lent; and while I was busy at work, some whey spurting from the cheese-press flew into my mouth, and, wretched man, I swallowed it. Free my distressed conscience from its agonies by absolving me from my guilt!" "Have you no other sins to confess?" said his spiritual guide. "No; I do not know that I have committed any other." "There are," said the priest, "many robberies and murders from time to time committed on your mountains, and I have reason to believe that you are one of the persons concerned in them." "Yes," he replied, "I am, but these are never accounted as a crime; it is a thing practised by us all, and there needs no confession on that account." Was not this straining at a gnat and swallowing a camel with a witness?

(*d*) REV. HENRY WARD BEECHER'S TESTIMONY.—"I remember the time when I swore the first oath It seemed as though every leaf on the trees and every blade of grass were vocal in their condemnation of my sin. The very sky seemed to lower upon me, and all Nature raised the note of reproof. But in after days, under the demoralizing influence of bad company, I became able to use profane language without a blush—without the least remorse of conscience; and finally without being conscious of the language I employed."

357. Because Tender Consciences are most Troublesome when Violated.

(*a*) KILPIN'S THEFT OF A PENNY.—The Rev. Samuel Kilpin, a minister of Exeter, (Eng.,) says, in his life:—When seven years old, I was left in charge of my father's shop. A man passed, crying, "Little lambs, all white and clean, at one penny each." In my eagerness to get one, I lost all self-command, and taking a penny from the drawer, I made the purchase. My keen-eyed mother inquired how I came by the money. I evaded the question with something like a lie. In God's sight it was a lie, as I kept back the truth.

The lamb was placed on the chimney shelf, and was much admired. To me it was a source of inexpressible anguish; continually there sounded in my ears and heart, "Thou shalt not steal; thou shalt not lie." Guilt and darkness overcame my mind; and in sore agony of soul I went to a hay-loft, the place is now perfectly in my recollection, and there prayed and pleaded, with groanings that could not be uttered, for mercy and pardon. I entreated for Jesus' sake. With joy and transport I left the loft from a believing application of the text, "Thy sins, which are many, are forgiven." I went to my mother, told her what I had done, and sought her forgiveness, and burned the lamb, while she wept over her young penitent.

If such was young Kilpin's misery and remorse in stealing a penny, then, in justice, he who steals a pound should suffer more, provided remorse of conscience in this life gives every sinner his due punishment. But thieves and robbers who have for years pursued their path of crime, can and do steal hundreds of pounds, and have no such sense of guilt and sorrow for it as young Kilpin had for his theft of a penny.

(*b*) STEALING A LAMB AND ASKING A BLESSING OVER IT.—Thomas D. had a large family, and lived in the parish of M——, (Eng.) Time was when he loved his Bible, attended his church, and endeavored to instruct his children in the fear of God.

In the year 1826 work was very slack, and Thomas struggled hard against poverty and sickness. His trials were very great; and, instead of taking those trials to the Lord in prayer, he sunk into a low state, little short of desperation. This was Satan's opportunity. When Thomas was reduced to this strait, and feared that his wife and little ones would be famished, he meditated and planned a step, at which he would formerly have shuddered: he resolved on stealing a lamb from the flock of a neighboring farmer. This, after many inward struggles, was accomplished, and that too without detection. The lamb was killed, and brought home. To the inquiries of his wife, Thomas gave an evasive answer, and part of the stolen provision was cooked for supper. The poor woman called her husband from the loom when it was ready, and he was about to follow his usual custom of asking a blessing; his tongue faltered, and he could not do it; but snatching up the dish from his astonished family, he went with it to the farmer's house, and confessed his guilt. "My life," said he, "is yours, or if you spare it, I will try to pay you for the lamb." The farmer was touched at his tale of misery, and the voluntary confession of the theft. He told the poor fellow to take the dish and its contents back to his cottage, and freely forgave him what he had done.

What made the thief's conscience so sensitive and his compunctions so severe? Because he so seldom violated it, while those accustomed to such violations would have felt little compunction, if at all.

(*c*) THE YOUNG CONVERT AND HIS BROTHER'S SLED.—It is often the case that some comparatively slight deviation from duty on the part of the Christian causes him more remorse of conscience than he outbreaking sins of the impenitent. Rev. Mr. D., of Michigan, states that soon after his conversion, when a boy some fourteen years of age, he was standing at the door, and in a playful mood, pulling back and forth a sled belonging to his younger brother. The child saw him, and cried aloud as if some great outrage was being done to his property. Upon this Mr. D. was so much exasperated, that he hastily snatched up the sled and threw it over the fence. To most impenitent persons who should do such a deed, it would cause little afterthought or regret. But not so with the young convert. His conscience severely accused him; his convictions before his conversion were scarce more absorbing and severe. He felt he had treated his little brother unkindly and maliciously—acted inconsistently with his profession—above all, he had sinned, as he felt, against God. His agony of mind was distressing and awful; and it was not till he had wept and prayed, confessed his sins to God, to his brother whom he had injured, and his mother who had witnessed his conduct, that he felt forgiven or found relief to his conscience. Did that young convert suffer more than he deserved? Then he suffered unjustly, and the present retribution of conscience is evidently imperfect. Did he suffer no more than he deserved? Thousands of hardened sinners commit offences a hundred-fold more flagrant and feel little or no compunction. Justice, therefore, is not done in this life, and it must be done in another.

358. Because they take Delight in their Wickedness.

(*a*) THE BLASPHEMOUS THANKSGIVING.—One of the most horrid circumstances attending the dreadful massacres of the Protestants under Charles IX of France, was, that when the news of this event reached Rome, Pope Gregory XIII instituted the most solemn rejoicing, giving thanks to Almighty God for this glorious victory over the heretics!

(*b*) BONAPARTE'S DELIGHT IN MASSACRE.—"Bonaparte," says Sir Robert Wilson, "having carried the town of Jaffa by assault, many of the garrison were put to the sword, but the greater part flying into the Mosques, and imploring mercy from their pursuers, were granted their lives. Three days afterwards, Bonaparte, who had expressed much resentment at the compassion manifested by his troops, and determined to relieve himself from the maintenance and care of 3800 prisoners, ordered them to be marched to a rising ground near Jaffa, where a division of French infantry formed against them. When the Turks had entered into their fatal alignment, and the mournful preparations were completed, the signal gun fired. Volleys of musquetry and grape instantly played against them, and Bonaparte, who had been regarding the scene through a telescope, when he saw the smoke ascending, could not contain his joy.

359. Because they often Die in the very act of Sin.

(*a*) DEA. EATON AND THE INFIDEL.—Dea. Eaton, a missionary on the Erie canal, once came in contact with an infidel on a canal boat, who urged him into a dispute about the divinity of Jesus Christ. At first he proposed to argue the question on the ground of the Scriptures, but being confounded by Dea. Eaton's reading 1 John, chapter v., he declared that the Bible was nothing but man's invention. "I saw," says Dea. E., "that he appeared to be very angry, and left him; but during the whole afternoon, whenever he had an opportunity, he would vent some of his spite upon me. When we came to Syracuse, where we changed packets, I thought I should stop, and was bidding the passengers farewell. Among the rest I shook hands with the infidel's wife, and said to her, 'I hope you will alter your belief before I see you again.' He saw me talking to her, and coming along, struck off my hand with which I held hers, and said, 'Let the woman alone. If you wish to atack any one, try me, but don't abuse the woman."

I asked his pardon, and told him I intended no abuse to any one. I finally concluded to go in the packet, and as the boat started many of the passengers went on deck, and among the rest the infidel and his wife. I was in the cabin when a man came down in great haste, and inquired for a bottle of camphor; he said a man had fainted on deck. Without knowing who it was, it struck me immediately that it was the infidel, and that God had destroyed him. I went on deck, and sure enough the infidel was dead. A gentleman with whom he was conversing, said he was railing against me, and saying I was spunging my living, when he fell in a moment with a half-uttered curse on his lips. They were trying to bring him back to life, but I saw that there were no hopes that he would ever breathe again. He was dead the moment he reached the deck, and then presented the most awful object I had ever looked upon. His eyes were open, and his countenance indicated woful despair. It was a solemn moment, as still as the house of death. One of the boatmen said to me, "It will not do to fight against God."

(*b*) DYING WHILE BLASPHEMING.—A minister in a small seaport town in Scotland, once furnished an account of a man, who for many years was master of a coasting vessel, and an inhabitant of that place. In his younger days he made a profession of religion; and, among the small but respectable body to which he belonged, he was deemed an eminent Christian. He afterwards became a deist!—nay, a professed atheist, and made the existence of the Deity and a future state the subjects of his ridicule and profane mockery. For horrid swearing and lewdness he had perhaps few equals in Scotland. One night, in a public house, when swearing awfully, in a rage, he was summoned into eternity in a moment, by the rupture of a blood-vessel.

Was he punished for his blasphemy before his death? If not, then he was punished afterwards.

(*c*) DYING DEAD DRUNK.—George Davidson, aged about 36 years, of Fryeburg village, Maine, had been in the habit, for a long time, of drinking to excess occasionally; and, though he was provident when free from this bane of society, he had, with his wife and children, lived a wretched life. For a week prior to his death, he was intoxicated every day, and abused his family unmercifully. That morning he said to his wife, with a horrible oath, "When I drink another glass of rum, I hope God Almighty will strike me dead!" He immediately visited the public house; drank rum while there; filled his jug; and, returning, beat his wife, and threw her on the floor, though her peculiar situation demanded the most kind and affectionate treatment from her husband. About two o'clock in the afternoon, he took his "jug," and going to another room, said, "I swear I will drink till I die, let it be longer or shorter." His wife expostulated, when he replied with a most awful oath that he would do it. Before three o'clock his spirit had fled, and where, ye drunkards, do ye think it went? The Bible says, that no drunkard shall enter the kingdom of God, 1 Cor. vi. 10. Gal. v. 21. What will be the reward of those who are summoned to the bar of eternal justice with an oath on the tongue? Will such a man at once be happy in the presence of God? Will he say to such, "Come, ye blessed?"

360. Punishment, Future.

(*a*) FUTURE FEELINGS OF THE RIGHTEOUS. — The pious mother of an unworthy son, whose misconduct had brought upon her that species of decline familiarly termed a broken heart, sent for him before her death, and addressed him in this remarkable language: "My dear Charles, how tenderly I have loved you, is but too evident from the state to which you now see me reduced; and so long as I remain in this body, I shall not cease to love you, and to pray for you, with all a mother's anxiety; but the period is approaching when I shall hear the sentence of even your eternal destruction with a majestic composure and an entire complacency, arising from a feeling identified only with perfect purity and infinite rectitude." The impression this appeal made, was never effaced; it was the means of effecting a permanent change of character.

(*b*) PRESIDENT N— AND THE RESTORATIONIST.—President N— once preached a discourse near Schenectady, in which he set forth the intense and eternal torment of the finally impenitent. One of our modern restorationists heard the discourse, and having "an itching palm" to show his knowledge of futurity and divine dispositions, he followed the President to the house, where he took tea after the exercises of the day were closed, and introduced himself by saying to Mr. N——, "Well, sir, have been to hear you preach, and have come here to request you to prove your doctrine." "I thought I had proved it, for I took the Bible for testimony," was the reply. "Well, I do not find any thing in my Bible to prove that the sinner is *eternally damned*, and I do not believe any such thing?" "What do you believe." "Why I believe that mankind will be judged according to the deeds done in the body, and those that deserve punishment will be sent to hell, and remain there until the debt is paid," &c. Says Mr. N—, "I have but a word to say to you; and first—For what did Christ die? And lastly—there is a straight road to heaven; but if you are determined to go round through hell to get there, I cannot help it." The man took his leave, but his mind was "ill at ease." *There is a straight road to heaven*, still rang in his ears; he went home, read his Bible attentively, and was soon convinced of and acknowledged his error; and after a suitable time, united with the followers of the Lamb.

(*c*) A CLOSE QUESTION.—A pious minister of respectable talents, now in the Methodist connexion, was previously a preacher among the Universalists. The incident which led him seriously to examine the grounds of that doctrine is striking and singular. He was amusing his little son by telling him the story of the "Children in the Wood." The boy asked, "What became of the little innocent children?" "They went to heaven," replied the father. "What became of the wicked old uncle?" "He went to heaven too." "Won't he kill them again, father?" said the boy.

(*d*) MR. HALLOCK'S REPLY TO A FRIEND.—A clerical brother of like sentiments with Mr. Hallock, who had just lost a dear son without the consolation of strong hope in his case, once put this question, with rather peculiar emphasis: "Do you not sometimes doubt, Mr. Hallock, whether a holy and benevolent God will inflict eternal punishment upon a part of mankind?" He promptly replied, "No, sir; if a man should tell me that he had just seen Canton meeting-house in flames, and I should hasten to the spot and find it not so, would he be able afterwards to look me in the face? So, if there is to be no everlasting punishment for any of our race, how could Christ, after his many positive declarations to the contrary, hold up his head before his people in the future world?"

361. QUARRELS.

(*a*) ARISTIPPUS AND ÆSCHINES.—Aristippus and Æschines having quarreled, Aristippus came to his opponent and said:—"Æschines, shall we be friends?" "Yes," he replied, "with all my heart." "But remember," said Aristippus, "that I being older than you, do make the first motion." "Yes," replied Æschines, "and therefore I conclude that you are the worthiest man; for I began the strife, and you began the peace."

(*b*) THE WORTHIEST MAN.—Rev. John Clark, of Frome (Eng.), was a man of peace. He was asked one day, by a friend, how he kept himself from being involved in quarrels. He answered, "By letting the angry person always have the quarrel to himself." This saying seems to have had some influence on some of the inhabitants of that town; for, when a quarrel has been likely to ensue, they have said, "Come, let us remember old Mr. Clark, and leave the angry man to quarrel by himself." If this maxim were followed, it would be a vast saving of expense, of comfort, and of honor to thousands of the human race.

(*c*) PEACE PRESERVED BY PRAYER. — Mr. Johnston of West Africa, in one of his journals, relates the following very pleasing and instructive incident: "In visiting a sick communicant, his wife, who was formerly in our school, was present. I asked several questions, viz. if they prayed together, read a part of the Scriptures (the woman can read), constantly attended public worship, and lived in peace with their neighbors. All these questions were answered in the affirmative. I then asked if they lived in peace together. The man answered, 'sometimes I say a word my wife no like, or my wife talk or do what I no like, but when we want to quarrel we shake hands together, shut the door, and go to prayer, and so we get peace again.' This method of keeping peace quite delighted me."

(*d*) THOMAS, GERALD, AND THE CANDY.—These boys lived in Rhode Island, and were brothers. One cold day, when the ground was frozen, they were out driving a hoop. Both boys were following and driving the same hoop. This is rather dangerous, as the boys, running one behind the other, and both driving the same hoop, are liable to run on to each other, and fall. As they were driving their hoop down the street, running as fast as they could, Gerald, the younger, being behind, Thomas hit his foot against a stone, and fell headlong upon the frozen ground — coming down with violence upon his bare hands and face. Gerald, being close behind, and running fast, could not stop, but came down with his whole weight on Thomas. This hurt Thomas still worse. He was angry at Gerald for falling on him. They both rose. Thomas, in his wrath, began to scold and storm at his brother, and beat him. What did Gerald do? Did he cry out, and strike back? He did no such thing. He put his hand into his pocket hurriedly, fumbled about, and soon drew out a stick of candy, and thrust it into his brother's mouth, as he was scolding and beating him. Thomas instantly stopped, and looked confused and ashamed. His brother urged him to take the candy. He took it and began to eat—sorry enough that he had struck his affectionate and generous brother.

Thus his wrath was disarmed, and his blows stayed, by the love and kindness of his gentle-hearted brother.

A stick of candy is a better weapon to fight with, and more sure to gain a victory, than a stick of wood, or a fist.

(*e*) THE YOUNG LAD AND HIS BOAT. — A young, lad says Mr. Wright, was once rowing me across the Merrimack river in a boat. Some boatmen, going down the river with lumber, had drawn up their boat and anchored it on the spot where the boy wished to land me.

"There!" he exclaimed, "those boatmen have left their boat right in my way."

"What did they do that for?" I asked

"On purpose to plague me," said he; "but I will cut it loose, and let it go down the river. I would have them know I can be as ugly as they can."

"But, my lad," said I, "you should not plague them because they plague you. Because they are ugly to you, it is no reason why you should be to them. Besides, how do you know they did it to vex and trouble you?"

"But they had no business to leave it there—it is against the rules," said he.

"True," I replied, "and you have no business to send their boat down the river. Would it not be better to ask them to remove it out of the way?"

"They will not comply, if I do," said the angry boy, "and they will do so again."

"Well, try it for once," said I. "Just run your boat a little above, or a little below theirs, and see if they will not favor you, when they see you disposed to give way to accommodate them."

The boy complied; and when the men in the boat saw the little fellow quietly and pleasantly pulling at his oars, to run his boat ashore above them, they took hold and helped him, and wheeled their boat around, and gave him all the chance he wished.

Thus, by submitting pleasantly to what he believed was done to vex him, the boy prevented a quarrel. Had he cut the rope, at that time and place, and let their boat loose, it would have done the boatmen much damage. There would have been a fight, and many would have been drawn into it. But the boy, who considered himself the injured party, prevented it all by a kind and pleasant submission to the injury.

362. REASON, INSUFFICIENCY OF.

(*a*) "WHAT IS GOD?"—Simonides, a heathen poet, being asked by Hiero, king of Syracuse, *What is God?* desired a day to think upon it; and when that was ended, he desired two; and when these were past, he desired four days; thus he continued to double the number of days in which he desired to think of God, before he would give an answer. Upon which the king expressed his surprise at his behavior, and asked him, What he meant by this? To which the poet answered, "The more I think of God, he is still the more dark and unknown to me."

(*b*) THE DEIST CONFOUNDED.—A deist, on a visit to his friends, among other topics of conversation, enlarged considerably on the sufficiency of reason, separate from Divine assistance, to guide us to happiness. To whom the relative present, who was a farmer, made the following reply:—"Cousin, when you were about fourteen years of age, you were bound apprentice to your trade, and having served the appointed time, you soon became a master, and have now continued in business about twelve years. I wish to know whether you could not prosecute your trade at this time to greater advantage than when you first embarked in it as a master?" The tradesman admitted that his experience in business was of considerable value to him; but asked, what relation that had to the present topic of discourse. The farmer answered, "You were come to the perfect use of your reason, and had been for a long time taught how to manage your trade; and if, therefore, your reason without experience was insufficient to preserve you from many errors, in so plain and easy a business as yours, how can you imagine that it should be sufficient, without Divine assistance, to guide you to heaven?" The deist was confounded.

(*c*) PAINE'S REGRET.—When Thomas Paine resided in Bordentown, in the state of New Jersey, he was one day passing the residence of Dr. Staughton, when the latter was sitting at the door. Paine stopped, and after some remarks of a general character, observed, "Mr. Staughton, what a pity it is that a man has not some comprehensive and perfect rule for the government of his life." The doctor replied, "Mr. Paine, there is such a rule." "What is that?" Paine inquired. Dr. S. repeated the passage, "Thou shalt love the Lord thy God with all thy heart, and thy neighbor as thyself." Abashed and confounded, Paine replied, "Oh, that's in your Bible," and immediately walked away.

(*d*) ETHICS ASIDE FROM THE BIBLE.—De Luc, speaking of the superior efficacy of positive laws, compared with the mere precepts of any system of moral philosophy, gives us the following narrative.—"Some time ago I was conversing upon this subject with a very celebrated man, (the late Sir John Pringle,) who had been professor of *moral philosophy* in the university of Edinburgh; he was advanced in years, and had lived much in the world. At that time I was still rather a friend to teaching *rational morality*, thinking it was useful to bring men acquainted with their duty in every possible way. I had just read a work of this nature, entitled '*Of an Universal Moral, or Man's Duties founded upon*

Nature;' and as he had not read it, I offered to lend it to him. I cannot express the tone in which he refused this offer, but you will have some idea of it when you come to know the motives upon which he did it. 'I have been,' said he, 'for many years professor of this pretended science; I have ransacked the libraries and my own brain to discover the foundation of it; but the more I sought to persuade and convince my pupils, the less confidence I began to have myself in what I was teaching them; so that at length I gave up my profession and turned to medicine, which had been the first object of my studies. I have nevertheless continued from that time to examine every thing that appeared upon the subject, which, as I have told you, I could never explain or teach so as to produce conviction; but at length I have given up the point, most thoroughly assured, that without an express divine sanction attached to the laws of morality, and without positive laws, accompanied with determinate and urgent motives, men will never be convinced that they ought to submit to any such code, nor agree among themselves concerning it. From that time I have never read any book upon morality but the *Bible*, and I return to that always with fresh delight.' "

363. RECONCILIATION TO GOD.

(*a*) PROOF OF BEING A CHRISTIAN.—The simplicity of youthful conversion was illustrated in the case of a child thirteen years old, some time ago, in New-York. "Mother," said this girl, "can you know whether or not I am a Christian by my feelings?" "My dear," replied her mother, "I must first know what your feelings are." The daughter smiled, and said, "Well, then, you know, when you have been angry with a person, and it is all made up, how happy you feel. Now I have been a long time angry with God, and it is all *made up*, and I feel so happy." Thus she expressed a sense of reconciliation to God through Christ Jesus.

(*b*) PEACE WITH GOD AND CONSCIENCE.—"When I used to go," said a man who formerly lived in sin, "to all kinds of fairs, and revels, and horse-races, I was never happy. As I was coming home through the woods at night, the rustling of a leaf would frighten me; terrified by I knew not what, fleeing when no man pursued, I galloped home as fast as my horse could carry me. Now, if I go to visit a poor dying man, or if I have been enjoying the word of life, I come home in a calm and peaceful frame of mind. I find that the Lord is present with me; and as I walk my horse gently along, I look up and see the bright stars above my head, and am happy in the assurance that the God who made them all is mine in Christ. O, what a mercy!—the loneliness of the wood, the rustling of the leaves, the stillness of night, no longer alarm me. I am, I trust, reconciled to my God, and at peace with him and my own conscience, through the death of his Son. He that fills the heavens with his glory, and the earth with his mercies, condescends to dwell in, and to comfort my poor sinful heart."

364. RELIGION. REFORMING POWER OF.

(*a*) THE DISCHARGED SOLDIER.—Wherever religion has spread its banners and enrolled its armies, order, discipline, and efficiency have characterized its followers. A discharged soldier had been a notorious Sabbath-breaker. He was often met on that day, ragged and barefoot, accompanied with one or two of his children, in a similar condition, strolling with a gun or a fishing pole to his accustomed employment of the day. His house was the picture of wretchedness. After the lapse of a few years, a gentleman in the town where he lived, noticed, one Sabbath morning, a decent wagon proceeding to church with a well-dressed family. He thought he knew the driver, who appeared to be the head of the family, and accosted him. He was not mistaken. It was the identical Sabbath-breaker and idler. He had become a religious man, which his appearance evinced, while his tongue confessed it. His house was found to exhibit economy and industry. Its windows, which were once stuffed with rags, were now glazed. His children attended the Sunday school. He was himself respectable, clean, and thriving; at peace with his own mind, and living peacably with his neighbors. Such are some of the trophies of religion, showing itself, as indeed it is, profitable unto all things, having promise of the life that now is, and of that which is to come.

(*b*) METHODISTS ACCUSED AND ACQUITTED.—In an early period of the ministry of the Rev. John Wesley, he visited Epworth, in Lincolnshire, where his father had formerly been minister, but found the people greatly opposed to what they considered his new notions. He tells us, in his journal, that many persons were convinced of the importance of the truths he delivered from the tombstone of his father, some of whom were conveyed in a wagon to a neighboring justice of the peace, to answer for the heresy with which they were charged. Mr. Wesley rode over also: when the magistrate asked what these persons had done, there was a deep silence; for that was a point their conductors had forgotten. At length, one of them said, "Why, they pretend to be better than other people; and, besides, they pray from morning to night." He asked, "But have they done any thing besides?" "Yes, sir," said an old man, "An't please your worship, they have *convarted* my wife. Till she went among them, she had such a tongue: and now she is as quiet as a lamb." "Carry them back, carry them back," replied the justice, "and let them convert all the scolds in the town."

(*c*) SAVAGE WARRIOR CONVERTED.—It is related, in Abbott's American Religious Magazine, that as Dr. Cornelius was riding through the wilderness of the west, he met a party of Indian warriors, just returning from one of their excursions of fire and blood. One of these warriors, of fierce and fiend-like aspect, led a child of five years of age, whom they had taken captive.

"Where are the parents of this child?" said Dr. Cornelius.

"Here they are," replied the savage warrior, as with one hand he exhibited the bloody scalps of a man and a woman, and with the other brandished his tomahawk in all the exultation of gratified revenge.

That same warrior became a disciple of Jesus Christ, a humble man of piety and of prayer. His tomahawk was laid aside, and was never again crimsoned with the blood of his fellow men. His wife became a member of the same church with himself, and their united prayers ascended, morning and evening, from the family altar. Their daughters were amiable and humble, and devoted followers of the blessed Redeemer, trained up under the influence of a father's and a mother's prayers, for the society of angels and saints.

(*d*) LION CHANGED TO A LAMB.—"Do you remember," said an Indian convert to a Missionary, "that a few years ago, a party of warriors came to the vicinity of the tribe to whom you preach, and pretending friendship, invited the chief of the tribe to hold a talk with them?"

"Yes," replied the Missionary, "I remember it very well."

"Do you remember," continued the Indian, "that the chief, fearing treachery, instead of going himself, sent one of his warriors to hold the talk?"

"Yes," was the reply.

"And do you remember," proceeded the Indian, "that warrior never returned, but that he was murdered by those who, with promises of friendship, had led him into their snare?"

"I remember it all very well," replied the Missionary.

"Well," the Indian continued, weeping with emotion, "I was one of that band of warriors. As soon as our victim was in the midst of us, we fell upon him with our tomahawks, and cut him to pieces."

This man became one of the most influential members of the Christian church, and reflected with horror upon those scenes in which he formerly exulted. He gave his influence and his prayers, that there might be glory to God in the highest, peace on earth, and good will among men.

(*e*) "IS JACK BETTER FOR THE PREACHING?"—A person who had expressed doubts, whether the negroes received any real advantage by hearing the gospel, was asked, whether he did not think one named Jack was better for the preaching? He replied, "Why, I must confess that he was a drunkard, a liar, and a thief, but, certainly, he is now a sober boy, and I can trust him with any thing; and since he has talked about religion, I have tried to make him drunk, but failed in the attempt."

(*f*) DISPLAY OF DIVINE GRACE.—"It is now fifteen years," says the Rev. Risdon Darracott, in a letter, "since I was settled in this place, (Wellington,) and though I found religion at a very low ebb, it pleased God, by my poor ministration, to revive it soon on my first coming, and to continue it, more or less, in a flourishing state to this day. Every year there have been additions, and, in some years, very large, to the Church, of such as I hope will be saved. Upwards of two hundred have been taken into communion, upon a credible profession, since my settlement; many of them the most profligate in the places round us, whose change has been so remarkable, that the world at once bears their testimony to, and expresses their astonishment of it. Many of them so very ignorant, as not to know the plainest and most common principles of religion; yea, were not able to read a letter, who are now making the word of God their daily study and delight; many who never prayed in all their lives, and lived without God in the world, who have attained to such a gift in prayer, as to be engaged, on particular occasions, in public, to the pleasure and edification of all present, and whose houses, which were once dens of thieves, are now become Bethels, in which family worship is constantly and seriously performed. O, my dear sir, rejoice with me, and let us exalt his name together!"

(*g*) RELIGION ON SHIP-BOARD.—"I have lately had the honor," said Captain Parry, at a public meeting in 1826, "and I may truly say the happiness, of commanding British seamen under circumstances requiring the utmost activity, implicit and immediate obedience, and the most rigid attention to discipline and good order; and I am sure, that the maintenance of all these was, in a great measure, owing to the blessing of God upon our humble endeavors to improve the religious and moral character of our men. In the schools established on board our ships in the winter, religion was made the primary object, and the result was every way gratifying and satisfactory. It has convinced me, that true religion is so far from being a hinderance to the arduous duties of that station in which it has pleased Providence to cast the seaman's lot, that, on the contrary, it will always incite him to their performance, from the highest and most powerful of motives; and I will venture to predict, that in proportion as this spring of action is more and more introduced among our seamen, they would become such as every Englishman would wish to see them. To this fact at least, I can, on a small scale, bear the most decided testimony; and the friends of religion will feel a pleasure in having the fact announced, that *the very best seamen* on board the Hecla—such, I mean, as were always called upon in any case of extraordinary emergency—were, *without exception*, those who had thought the most seriously on religious subjects; and if a still more scrupulous selection were to be made out of that number, the choice would fall, *without hesitation*, on two or three individuals possessing dispositions and sentiments *eminently Christian*."

365. REMORSE.

(*a*) JUDGED AND CONDEMNED.—The venerable Bede tells us of a certain great man, who was exhorted to repent of his sins, during a season of illness: he answered that he would not repent yet; for, should he recover, his companions would laugh at him on account of his religion. Getting worse, the subject was again pressed on his attention, when he replied, "It is too late now, for I am judged and condemned."

(*b*) A PRESENT HELL.—An avowed infidel, who had been accustomed to scoff at the Holy Scriptures, to exercise his profane wit in ridiculing the justice of God, and the future punishment of the wicked, and had strenuously denied that there was a hell, with his last quivering breath exclaimed, "Now I know that there is a hell, for I feel it."

(*c*) SABAT'S WRETCHEDNESS.—After poor Sabat, an Arabian, who had professed faith in Christ by means of the labors of the Rev. Henry Martyn, had apostatized from Christianity, and written a book in favor of Mohammedanism, he was met at Malacca, by the Rev. Dr. Milne, who proposed to him some very pointed questions; in reply to which he said, "I am unhappy! I have a mountain of burning sand on my head! When I go about, I know not what I am doing." It is indeed "an evil thing and bitter to forsake the Lord our God."

(*d*) A MODERN JUDAS.—John Diazius, a native of Spain, having embraced the Protestant faith, came afterwards to Germany, where he visited Malvinda, the Pope's agent there. Having attempted in vain to bring him back to the church of Rome, Malvinda sent to Rome for his brother Alphonsus Diazius, who, hearing that his brother was become a Protestant, came into Germany with an assassin, resolving either to draw him back to Popery, or to destroy him. Alphonsus finding his brother so steadfast in his belief of the truths of the gospel, that neither the promises nor threats of the Pope's agent, nor his own pretensions of brotherly love, could prevail on him to return to Popery, feigned to take a most friendly and affectionate farewell, and then departed. Having soon returned, he sent in the ruffians who accompanied him, with letters to his brother, himself following behind, and while his brother was reading them, the assassin cleft his head with a hatchet which they purchased on the way from a carpenter; and, taking horse, they both rode off. Alphonsus, though highly applauded by the Papists, became the prey of a guilty conscience. His horror and dread of mind were so insupportable, that, being at Trent during the general council, like another Judas, he put an end to his life by hanging himself.

(*e*) A MARTYR'S CROWN LOST.—James Le Fevre, of Etables, did not outwardly depart from the church of Rome, yet at the bottom of his heart he was a Protestant. He was protected by the Queen of Navarre, sister to Francis I; and, dining with her in company with some other learned men, whose conversation pleased the queen, he began to weep: and when the queen asked him the reason of it, he answered, "the enormity of his sins threw him into that grief! It was not the remembrance of any lewdness he had been guilty of, and with regard to other vices, he felt his conscience easy enough; but he was pricked in his conscience, that having known the truth and taught it to several persons who had sealed it with their blood, he had the weakness to keep himself in an asylum far from the places where crowns of martyrdom were distributed." He went to bed, where he was found dead a few hours after.

(*f*) DEATH OF JOHN RANDOLPH.—John Randolph of Roanoke, was near his end. Dr. —— was sitting by the table, and his man John sitting by the bed, in perfect silence, when he closed his eyes, and for a few moments seemed, by his hard breathing, to be asleep. But as the sequel proved, it was the intense working of his mind. Opening his keen eyes upon the doctor, he said, sharply, "*remorse*"—soon afterward more emphatically, "REMORSE"—presently at the top of his strength, he cried out, "REMORSE." He then added, "*Let me see the word.*" The doctor not comprehending his desire, made no reply. Randolph then said to him with great energy, "*Let me see the word. Show me it in a Dictionary.*" The Dr. looked round and told him he believed there was none in the room. "*Write it then,*" said Randolph. The Dr. perceiving one of Randolph's engraved cards lying on the table, wrote the word in pencil under the printed name, and handed it to Randolph. He seized it, and holding it up to his eyes with great earnestness, seemed much agitated. After a few seconds, he handed back the card, saying, "Write it on the other side." The Dr. did so, in larger letters. He took it again, and after gazing earnestly upon it a few seconds, returned it, and said, "Lend John your pencil, and let him put a stroke under it." The black man took the pencil and did so, leaving it on the table. "Ah!" said the dying man, "*Remorse*, you don't know what it means! you don't know what it means." But added presently, "I cast myself on the Lord Jesus Christ for mercy."

366. REPENTANCE.

(*a*) LITTLE BOY'S FALSEHOOD.—"A man," says the Rev. J. Todd, "who is now a minister of the Gospel, gave me the following account. I tell it to you in order to show you what repentance is. 'I had one of the kindest and best of fathers; and when I was a little white-headed boy about six years old, he used to carry me to school before him on his horse, to help me in my little plans, and always seemed trying to make me happy; and he never seemed so happy himself, as when making me happy. When I was six years old, he came home one day, very sick. My mother, too, was sick, and thus nobody but my two sisters could take care of my father. In a few days he was worse, very sick, and all the physicians in the region were called in to see him. The next Sabbath morning early, he was evidently much worse. As I went into his room he stretched out his hand to me and said, "My little boy, I am very sick. I wish you to take that paper on the stand, and run to Mr. C.'s, and get me the medicine written on that paper." I took the paper and went to the apothecary's shop, as I had often done before. It was about half a mile off; but when I got there, I found it shut, and as Mr. C. lived a quarter of a mile further off, I concluded not to go to find him. I then set out for home. On my way back I contrived what to say. I knew how wicked it was to tell a lie, but one sin always leads to another. On going in to my father, I saw that he was in great pain; and though pale and weak, I could see great drops of sweat standing on his forehead, forced out by the pain. O then I was sorry I had not gone and found the apothecary. At length he said to me, "My son has got the medicine, I hope, for I am in great pain." I hung my head and muttered, for my conscience smote me, "No, sir, Mr. Carter says he has got none!" "Has got none! Is this possible?" He then cast a keen eye upon me, and seeing my head hang, and probably suspecting my falsehood, said, in the mildest, kindest tone, "*My little boy will see his father suffer great pain for the wan of that medicine!*" I went out of the room, and alone, and cried. I was soon called back. My brothers had come, and were standing—all the children were standing round his bed, and he was committing my poor mother to their care, and giving them his last advice. I was the youngest, and when he laid his hand on my head and told me "that in a few hours I should have no father; that he would in a day or two be buried up;—that I must now make God my father, love him, obey him, and always do right and *speak the truth*, because the eye of God is always upon me"—it seemed as if I should sink; and when he laid his hand upon my head again and prayed for the blessing of God the Redeemer to rest upon me, "soon to be a fatherless orphan," I dared not look at him I felt so guilty. Sobbing, I rushed from his bed-side, and thought I wished I could die. They soon told me he could not speak. O how much would I have given to go in and tell him that I had told a lie, and ask him once more to lay his hand on my head and forgive me! I crept in once more and heard the minister pray for "the dying man." O how my heart ached. I snatched my hat and ran to the apothecary's house and got the medicine. I ran home with all my might, and ran in, and ran up to my father's bed-side to confess my sin, crying out, "O here father,"—but I was hushed: and I then saw that he was pale, and that all in the room were weeping. *My dear father was dead!* And the last thing I ever spake to him was *to tell a lie!* I sobbed as if my heart would break; for his kindnesses, his tender looks, and my own sin, all rushed upon my own mind. And as I gazed upon his cold, pale face, and saw his eyes shut, and his lips closed, could I help thinking of his last words; "My little boy will see his father suffer great pain for the want of that medicine;" I could not know but he died for the want of it.

"'In a day or two he was put into the ground and buried up. There were several ministers at the funeral, and each spoke kindly to me, but could not comfort me. Alas! they knew not what a load of sorrow lay on my heart. They could not comfort me. My father was buried, and the children all scattered abroad, for my mother was too feeble to take care of them.

"'It was twelve years after this, while in college, that I went alone to the grave of my father. It took me a good while to find it; but there it was, with its humble tomb-stone, and as I stood over it, I seemed to be back at his bed-side, to see his pale face, and hear his voice. Oh! the thought of that sin and wickedness cut me to the heart. It seemed as if worlds would not be too much to give, could I then only have called loud enough to have him hear me ask his forgiveness. But it was too late. He had been in the grave twelve years, and I must live and die, weeping over the ungrateful falsehood. May God forgive me.'"

(*b*) KILPIN'S PENITENT SON.—Rev. Samuel Kilpin gives the following account of his son:—On one occasion, when he had offended me, I deemed it right to manifest displeasure, and when he asked a question about the business of the day, I was short and reserved in my answers to him. An hour or more elapsed. The time was nearly arrived when he was to repeat his lessons. He came into my study, and said, "Papa, I cannot learn my lessons except you are reconciled. I am very sorry I have offended you, I hope you will forgive me: I think I shall never offend again."

I replied, "All I want is to make you sensible of your fault; when you acknowledge it, you know all is easily reconciled with me."

"Then, papa," said he "give me the token of reconciliation, and seal it with a kiss." The hand was given, and the seal most heartily exchanged on each side.

"Now," exclaimed the dear boy, "I will learn Greek and Latin with any body;" and was hastening to his study.

"Stop, stop," I called after him, "have you not a heavenly Father? If what you have done has been evil, he is displeased, and you must apply to him for forgiveness."

With tears starting in his eyes, he said, "Papa, I went to him first: I knew that except he was reconciled, I could do nothing;" and with tears fast rolling down his cheeks, he added, "I hope, I hope he has forgiven me, and now I am happy!" I never had again occasion to look at him with a shade of disapprobation.

(*c*) MOST DELIGHTFUL EMOTION.—"Which is the most delightful emotion?" said an instructor of the deaf and dumb to his pupils, after teaching them the names of our various feelings. The pupils turned instinctively to their slates, to write an answer ; and one with a smiling countenance wrote *Joy*. It would seem as if none could write any thing else ; but another with a look of more thoughtfulness, put down *Hope*. A third with beaming countenance wrote *Gratitude*. A fourth wrote *Love*, and other feelings still, claimed the superiority on other minds. One turned back with a countenance full of peace, and yet a tearful eye, and the teacher was surprised to find on her slate, "*Repentance* is the most delightful emotion." He returned to her with marks of wonder, in which her companions doubtless participated, and asked, "Why ?" "Oh," said she, in the expressive language of looks and gestures, which marks these mutes—"It is so delightful to be humbled before God !"

(*d*) A GREAT SINNER AND NO SINNER.—A woman professing to be under deep conviction, went to a minister, crying aloud that she was a sinner; but when he came to examine her in what point, though he went over and explained all the ten commandments, she would not own that she had broken one of them.

367. Repentance on Death-beds.

(*a*) DEATH WILL NOT WAIT FOR EXPLANATION.—Mr. Wilcox in his sermon mentions the following incident. A young man in the vigor of health, with the fairest prospect of a long and prosperous life, was thrown from a vehicle, and conveyed to the nearest house, in a state that excited instant and universal alarm for his safety. A physician was called. The first question of the wounded youth was, "Sir, must I die ? must I die ? deceive me not in this thing." His firm tone and penetrating look demanded an honest reply. He was told he could not live more than an hour. He waked up, as it were, at once, to a full sense of thedreadful reality. "Must I then go into Eternity in an hour ? Must I appear before my God and Judge in an hour ? God knows that I have made no preparations for this event. I knew that impenitent youth were sometimes cut off thus suddenly, but it never entered my mind that I was to be one of the number. And now what shall I do to be saved ?" He was told that he must repent and believe on the Lord Jesus Christ. "But how shall I repent and believe ? There is no time to explain the manner Death will not wait for explanation. The work must be *done*. The whole business of an immortal being in this probationary life is now crowded into one short hour—and that is an hour of mental agony and distraction." Friends were weeping around, and running to and fro in the frenzy of grief. The poor sufferer, with a bosom heaving with emotion, and an eye gleaming with desperation, continued his cry of "What shall I do to be saved ?" till, in less than an hour, his voice was hushed in the stillness of death.

(*b*) MR. BOOTH'S TESTIMONY.—"I pay more attention," says Mr. Booth, "to people's lives than to their deaths. In all the visits I have paid to the sick during the course of a long ministry, I never met with *one*, who was not previously serious, that ever recovered from what he supposed the brink of death, who afterwards performed his vows, and became religious, notwithstanding the very great appearance there was in their favor when they thought they could not recover."

(*c*) TESTIMONY OF AN AMERICAN PHYSICIAN. — A certain American physician, whose piety led him to attend not only to people's bodies, but to their souls, stated that he had known a hundred or more instances in his practice, of persons who, in prospect of death, had been hopefully converted, but had subsequently been restored to health. Out of them all he did not know of more than three who devoted themselves to the service of Christ after their recovery, or gave any evidence of genuine conversion. If therefore they had died as they expected, their hopes of heaven would have proved terrible delusions.

(*d*) TESTIMONY OF AN ENGLISH PHYSICIAN.—A pious English physician once stated that he had known some three hundred sick persons who, soon expecting to die, had been led, as they supposed, to repentance of their sins, and saving faith in Christ, but had eventually been restored to health again. Only ten of all this number, so far as he knew, gave any evidence of being really regenerated. Soon after their recovery, they plunged, as a general thing, into the follies and vices of the world. Who would trust, then, in such a conversion ?

REPROOF OF SIN.

368. Faithfulness and Firmness in Reproving.

(*a*) LATIMER'S REPROOF.—Latimer was obliged to attend the parliament and the convocation, but he always avoided meddling in state affairs, and never stayed in London longer than he could help. Once he was in town on new-year's day, at which season it was customary for the bishops and nobility, then at court, to make presents to the king: some of the former gave considerable sums of money, in proportion to their expectations; but Latimer's gift was more simple, and highly characteristic of himself. It was a New Testament, with a leaf doubled down at Hebrews xiii. 4: "Whoremongers and adulterers God will judge!" Henry the Eighth, forcibly as he must have felt this rebuke of his sins, did not appear offended, but manifested decided kindness to his reprover. Bad men seldom despise those whose holy and consistent character condemns their wicked conduct.

(*b*) POINTED REPLY TO A YOUTH.—An eminent man is said to have been so remarkable for his reverence of the Divine name, that even the bold blasphemer was awed before him, and could not swear. A youth, who was his nephew, one day said to him, "Sir, I believe some parts of the Bible." The uncle replied, "Great condescension in you, no doubt, to believe any thing your Maker has said. Vain boy! whether you believe it or not, that word with which you trifle, shall judge you in the last day."

(*c*) "SIR, I FEAR GOD."—On one occasion, the Rev. A. Fuller, when traveling in the Portsmouth mail, was much annoyed by the profane conversation of two young men who sat opposite to him. After a time, one of them, observing his gravity, accosted him with an air of impertinence, inquiring, in rude and indelicate language, whether, on his arrival at Portsmouth, he should not indulge himself in a manner corresponding with their own vicious intentions. Mr. Fuller, lowering his ample brows, and looking the inquirer full in the face, replied in a measured and solemn tone, "Sir, I fear God." Scarcely a word was uttered during the remainder of the journey.

(*d*) IRRELIGION REPROVED.—A man was tried at Cambridge, for a robbery committed on an aged lady, in her own house. The judge was Baron Smith, who maintained a consistent profession of religion. He asked the lady if the prisoner at the bar was the person who robbed her? "Truly, my lord," said she, "I cannot positively say it was he, for it was rather dark when I was robbed; so dark that I could hardly discern the features of his face." "Where were you when he robbed you?" "I was in a closet that joins to my bed-chamber, and he had got into my house while my servant had gone out on an errand." "What day of the week was it?" "It was the Lord's day evening, my lord." "How had you been employed when he robbed you?" "My lord, I am a Protestant dissenter; I had been at the meeting that day, and had retired into my closet in the evening for prayer, and meditation on what I had been hearing through the day." When she uttered these words, the court, which was crowded with some hundreds of persons, including many young men, rung with a peal of loud laughter. The judge looked round the court as one astonished, and with a decent solemnity laid his hands upon the bench, as if going to rise, and, with great emotion, spoke to the following effect: "Where am I? Am I in the place of one of the universities of this kingdom, where it is to be supposed that young gentlemen are educated in the principles of religion, as well as in all useful learning? and can such persons laugh in so improper a manner on hearing an aged Christian relate that she retired into her closet on a Lord's day evening, for prayer and meditation! Blush, and be ashamed, all of you, if you are capable of it, as well you may." And then turning to the lady, he said, "Do not be discouraged, madam, by this piece of rude and unmannerly, as well as irreligious conduct; you have no reason to be ashamed of what you have on this occasion, and in this public manner, said. It adds dignity to your character, and shame belongs to those who would expose it to ridicule."

(*e*) THE SERVANT AND THE SABBATH-BREAKER.—When Rev. John Fletcher was residing, as a tutor, in the family of Thomas Hill, Esq., of Tern Hall, in Shropshire, (Eng.,) though he felt the importance of religion, he was far from being an open and decided servant of Christ. On one Sabbath evening, a servant coming into his room to make up his fire, observed he was writing music, and looking at him with serious concern, said, "Sir, I am sorry to see you so employed on the Lord's day." At first his pride was offended, and his resentment excited, at being reproved by a servant; but, upon reflection, he felt that the reproof was just. He immediately put away his music, and from that hour became a strict observer of the Lord's day.

(*f*) THE SABBATH SCHOOL GIRL AND HER PROFANE FATHER.—In the town of W—, Connecticut, there was a pious little girl belonging to the Sabbath School, whose father was an opposer of religion. One day he had several men to assist him in haying. They indulged in profanity and scoffing at religion; and their employer rather encouraged them in it. The little girl overheard them, and was so shocked and grieved at their conduct, that she went into the meadow and asked them if they did not know it was wicked to use such profane language? This drew forth their ridicule, and so exasperated her father that he gave her a severe rebuke, and sent her back into the house. She returned as commanded; but retired to her closet and prayed for those who had abused her. In the course of the day she overheard their profanity again, and resolved again to reprove them whatever might be the results.

As she addressed them the second time in her artless manner, her father became so angry he told her: "My daughter, we don't want any of your religion here; if you say any thing more upon that subject, you must quit my house. Now return and attend to your business." The little girl returned; but resolved rather to quit the paternal roof than to do violence to her conscience. She went back to her chamber, and having prayed to God, proceeded to tie up her clothes, and then put on her bonnet and went out, scarce knowing whither she went.

She went first to the field to bid her father farewell, and fell at his feet, saying, "Pa, I must leave you. I am going away, but I shall pray for you." She immediately left the field, and passing over the hill was soon out of sight. The unfeeling father now began to reflect on what he had done; and his torpid conscience began to awake. He could not work; and after some time he threw down his scythe and started in pursuit of his daughter. As he was hurrying on to overtake her, he came near to a grove, and as he listened he heard a voice in the adjacent field. He crept softly along to the stone wall and listened again: the woods were still, he heard it again. It was the voice of prayer—the voice of his little daughter praying for her father's salvation! The stubborn heart of the father was melted; he hastened over the wall to his daughter; and clasping her in his arms asked her to pray for him, "for," said he, "I am a great sinner." O! it was an affecting scene, one that must have awakened the joy of angels! He carried his little daughter home in his arms, and ere long obtained forgiveness of his sins, and father and child were soon rejoicing together in the blessings of the Christian's hope.

369. Proper Spirit in Reproving.

(*a*) THE PIOUS SAILOR'S REBUKE.—A merchant and a ship owner, of the city of New York, stood at the entrance of his store, conversing with a gentleman on business. A pious sailor belonging to one of his vessels approached the store with the design of entering it, but observing the door was occupied, modestly stepped aside, not willing to interrupt the conversation.

As he stood waiting patiently an opportunity to pass into the store, he overheard profane allusions made to Christ, and turning to look he perceived it was his employer that was speaking. Instantly he changed his position, and stood in front of the gentleman with his head uncovered, and his hat under his arm, and addressed his employer in the following language. "Sir, will you forgive me if I speak a word to you?" The gentleman recognizing in the sailor one of the crew of the vessel recently arrived, and supposing he might have something to communicate affecting his interests, kindly encouraged him to speak on. Without further hesitation, the sailor proceeded: "You won't be offended then, sir, with a poor ignorant sailor, if he tells you his feelings." The gentleman again assured him he had nothing to fear. "Well then, sir," said the honest-hearted sailor with emotion, "will you be so kind as not to take the name of my blessed Jesus in vain; he is a good Savior—he took my feet from the pit and the miry clay, and established my going. O sir! don't, if you please, take the name of my Jesus in vain, he never did any one any harm, but is always doing good." The rebuke was not lost upon him for whom it was intended; a tear suffused his eye, and he replied to his urgent request, "My good fellow, God helping me, I never will again take the name of your Savior in vain." "Thank you, sir," said this faithful witness of Christ, and putting on his hat he walked away.

(*b*) THE YOUNG MAN NEAR PHILADELPHIA.—A young man in the vicinity of Philadelphia, was one evening stopped in a grove, with the demand, "your money or your life." The robber then presented a pistol to his breast. The young man, having a large sum of money, proceeded leisurely and calmly to hand it over to his enemy, at the same time setting before him the wickedness and peril of his career. The rebukes of the young man cut the robber to the heart. He became enraged, cocked his pistol, held it to the young man's head, and with an oath, said, "Stop that preaching, or I will blow out your brains." The young man calmly replied,—"Friend, to save my money, I would not risk my life; but to save you from your evil course, I am willing to die. I shall not cease to plead with you." He then poured in the truth still more earnestly and kindly. Soon the pistol fell to the ground; the tears began to flow; and the robber was overcome. He handed the money all back with the remark, "I cannot rob a man of such principles."

(*c*) DR. JOHNSON AND PROFANITY.—Dr. Johnson never suffered an oath to pass unrebuked in his presence. When a libertine, but a man of some note, was once talking before him, and interlarding his stories with oaths, Johnson said, "Sir, all this swearing will do nothing for our story; I beg you will not swear." The narrator went on swearing: Johnson said, "I must again entreat you not to swear." He swore again, and Johnson indignantly quitted the room.

370. Skill and Prudence in Reproving.

(*a*) THE OPPOSING MILLER REPROVED.—An active and skillful young minister in the village of J—, was told of a miller, who, with more than usual profaneness, had repelled every attempt to approach him on the subject of religion, and had discouraged the hopes and efforts of the few serious persons in his vicinity. Among other practices of sinful daring, he uniformly kept his windmill, the most striking object in the hamlet, going on the Sabbath. In a little time, the minister determined to make an effort for the benefit of the hopeless man. He undertook the office of going for his flour the next time himself. "A fine mill," said he, as the miller adjusted his sack to receive the flour; "a fine mill indeed; one of the completest I have ever seen." This was nothing more than just—the miller had heard it a thousand times before; and would firmly have thought it, though he had never heard it once; but his skill and judgment were still gratified by this new testimony, and his feelings conciliated, even towards the minister. "But, oh!" continued his customer, after a little pause, "there is one defect in it!" "What is that?" carelessly asked the miller. "A very serious defect too." "Eh!" replied the miller, turning up his face. "A defect that is likely to counterbalance all its advantages." "Well, what is it?" said the miller, standing straight up, and looking the minister in the face. He went on: "A defect which is likely to ruin the mill." "What is it?" rejoined the miller. "And will one day no doubt destroy the owner." "And can't you say it out?" exclaimed the impatient miller. "It goes on the Sabbath!" pronounced the minister, in a firm, and solemn, and monitory tone. The astonished man stood blank and thunderstruck; and remained meek and submissive under a remonstrance and exhortation of a quarter of an hour's length, in which the danger of his state and practices, and the call to repentance towards God, and faith in our Lord Jesus Christ, were fully proposed to him.

(*b*) DR. GIFFORD'S REPROOF OF PROFANITY.—As the Rev. Dr. Gifford was one day showing the British Museum to some strangers, he was much shocked by the profane language of a young gentleman belonging to the party. Taking down an ancient copy of the Septuagint, he showed it to the youth; on which he exclaimed, "Oh! I can read this." "Then," said the doctor, "read that passage," pointing to the third commandment. The reproof went home to his conscience, and he immediately refrained from swearing.

(*c*) THE SURGEON AND HIS PATIENT.—Mr. Meikle, a gentleman of eminent piety, was a surgeon at Carnwath, in Scotland. He was once called to attend a gentleman who had been stung in the face by a wasp or bee, and found him very impatient, and swearing, on account of his pain, in great wrath. "O doctor," said he, "I am in great torment; can you any way help?" "Do not fear, replied Mr. M., "all will be over in a little while." Still, however, the gentleman continued to swear, and at length his attendant determined to reprove him. "I see nothing the matter," said he, "only it might have been in a better place." "Where might it have been?" asked the sufferer. "Why, on the tip of your tongue."

(*d*) POINTED REBUKE OF PROFANITY.—A minister traveling in a stage coach, had the mortification of being shut up for the night with a naval officer, who was much addicted to swearing. At length the conversation turned on the topic of the day, the Boulogne flotilla; when the officer observed, "If one of our ships meet with them, "she will send them all to the devil." "There is a great deal of propriety, sir," said the minister, "in your observation; for as it is probable there are many profane swearers on board the French ships, should these men die in their sins, they will certainly go to the devil."

(*e*) WESLEY, AND A YOUNG OFFICER.—The Rev. John Wesley once traveled in a stage coach with a young officer, who swore and uttered curses upon himself in almost every sentence. Mr. W. asked him if he had read the Common Prayer Book; for, if he had, he might remember that collect beginning, "O God, who art ever more ready to hear than we are to pray, and art wont to give more than either we desire or deserve." The young gentleman, who had contracted a very common, but despicably vulgar and sinful habit, had the good sense to make the application, and behave accordingly.

(*f*) HOWE AND THE NOBLEMAN.—At the time when the Conformity Bill was debated in Parliament, Mr. Howe passed a noble lord in a chair in St. James's Park, who sent his footman to call him, desiring to speak with him on this subject. In the conversation, speaking of the opponents of the dissenters, he said, "D—n these wretches, for they are mad." Mr. Howe, who was no stranger to the nobleman, expressed great satisfaction in the thought that there is a God who governs the world, who will finally make retribution to all according to their present characters; "And he, my lord, has declared he will make a difference between him that sweareth, and him that feareth an oath." The nobleman was struck with the hint, and said, "*I thank you, sir, for your freedom. I take your meaning, and shall endeavor to make good use of it.*" Mr. Howe replied, "My lord, I have more reason to thank your lordship for saving me the most difficult part of a discourse, which is the *application.*"

(*g*) MEMNON AND HIS SOLDIER.—During the war between Alexander the Great and Darius, King of Persia, a soldier in the army of the latter, thought to ingratiate himself with Memnon, the Persian General, by uttering the fiercest invectives against Alexander: Memnon gently struck the fellow with his spear, and answered, "Friend, I pay you to fight against Alexander, not to revile him."

(*h*) MR. HOWE AND THE PROFANE.—The excellent Mr. Howe being at dinner with some persons of fashion, a gentleman expatiated largely in praise of King Charles I., introducing some harsh reflections upon others. Mr. Howe, observing that the gentleman mixed many oaths with his discourse, told him that, in his humble opinion, he had omitted a singular excellence in the character of that prince. The gentleman eagerly desired him to mention it, and seemed all impatience to know what it was. "It was this, sir," said Mr. Howe; "he was never heard to swear an oath in common conversation." The hint was as politely received as given; and the gentleman promised to break off the practice.

At another time, passing two persons of quality, who were talking with great eagerness, and imprecating curses on each other repeatedly; Mr. H. said to them, taking off his hat in a respectful manner, "I pray God save you both;" for which handsome reproof they immediately returned him thanks.

(*i*) PROFANITY SILENCED.—As a minister was on his way from one town to another, for several miles his ears were assailed by oaths too awful to mention: how to stop it he was at a loss to know: at last, having looked to God for direction, he asked the gentlemen if they would grant a stranger a particular favor. They all agreed that if it were in their power, they would grant it. Being assured that it was in their power, the minister begged that what he was going to say to them might not give offence. They all agreed that whatever he said should not. Seeing their curiosity excited, he mildly told them that he was astonished to hear so many oaths uttered, and would esteem it a great favor if they would refrain from them. One of the gentlemen made this reply, "You have acted wisely in making us promise to perform, and also not to be angry; and we, as gentlemen, will endeavor to keep our word. I believe you are correct in disliking swearing; it is a very bad custom, and it is a pity there should be so much of it; for my own part, I am not one who swears as some do." The minister, glad to hear this confession, said that he was unacquainted with the meaning of some common oaths, but would briefly explain the meaning of some words he heard repeated by them and they would be better able to judge as to their propriety; accordingly he went over word by word, explaining each, when they all agreed they were wrong in using them, and promised to refrain in future. It is gratifying to know that they did as they said. One loquacious gentleman, who had interlarded almost every sentence with oaths, now sat silent; even the coachman ceased to add an oath in calling to his horses. The conversation turned upon useful subjects and the minister inwardly thanked God for the word spoken in season. One of their friends, who was riding inside, wishing to enjoy the fine evening breeze, proposed getting on the outside, and the minister offered to give him his place. "No, no," cried more than one, "you must not leave us, you must remain, for your company is highly necessary." It is pleasing to say that for nearly forty miles, except once, they kept to their promise: and when he left the coach, they thanked him for his company, and hoped they should not forget his advice. How important is it to use prudence with zeal!

(*j*) REPLY TO A SABBATH BREAKER.—One Lord's day, a few children were gathered round the porch of a village church, waiting for the commencement of public worship, when a wagon, with a number of persons in it who were going out on pleasure, stopped, and one of the men called out to the children, "Halloo there, what sort of religion do you have there?" One of the young lads replied, "A sort of religion that forbids our traveling on the Sabbath."

(*k*) TARRYING AT JERICHO.—A very young clergyman, who had just left college, presented a petition to the King of Prussia, requesting that his Majesty would appoint him inspector in a certain place where a vacancy had just happened. As it was an office of much consequence, the King was offended at the presumption and importunity of so young a man, and instead of any answer to the petition, he wrote underneath, "2 Book of Samuel, Chap. x. ver. 5," and returned it. The young clergyman was eager to examine the quotation, but, to his great disappointment, found the words, "Tarry at Jericho until your beards be grown."

(*l*) THE DEIST AND THE QUAKER.—A gay young man, traveling in a stage coach to London, forced his deistical sentiments on the company by attempting to ridicule the Scriptures; and, among other topics, made himself merry with the story of David and Goliath, strongly urging the impossibility of a youth like David being able to throw a stone with sufficient force to sink into the giant's forehead. On this he appealed to the company, and particularly to a grave Quaker gentleman, who sat silent in one corner of the carriage. "Indeed, friend," replied he, "I do not think it at all improbable, if the Philistine's head was as soft as thine." This grave rebuke reduced the young man to silence.

(*m*) REPROOFS FROM DR. WAUGH.—At one of the half-yearly examinations at the Protestant Dissenters' Grammar School, at Mill Hill, the head master informed the examiners that he had been exceedingly tried, by the misconduct and perverseness of a boy who had done something very wrong; and who, though he acknowledged the fact, could not be brought to acknowledge the magnitude of the offence. The examiners were requested to expostulate with the boy, and try if he could be brought to feel and deplore it. Dr. Waugh was solicited to undertake the task; and the boy was, in consequence, brought before him. How long have you been in the school, my boy?" asked the doctor. "Four months, sir." "When did you hear from your father last?" "My father's dead, sir." "Ay! alas the day! 'tis a great loss, a great loss, that of a father. But God can make it up to you, by giving you a tender, affectionate mother." On this the boy, who had previously seemed as hard as a flint, began to soften. The doctor proceeded: "Well, laddie, where is your mother?" "On her voyage home from India, sir." "Ay! good news for you, my boy: do you love your mother?" "Yes, sir." "And do you expect to see her soon?" "Yes, sir." "Do you think she loves you?" "Yes, sir, I am sure of it." "Then think, my dear laddie, think of her feelings when she comes here, and finds that, instead of your being in favor with every one, you are in such deep disgrace as to run the risk of expulsion: and yet are too hardened to acknowledge that you have done wrong. Winna ye break your poor mother's hear think ye? Just think o' that, my lad The poor culprit burst into a flood of tears, acknowledged his fault, and promised amendment.

On one occasion, a young minister having animadverted, in the presence of

Dr. Waugh, on the talents of another minister, in a manner which he thought might leave an unfavorable impression on the minds of some of the company, Dr. W. observed, "I have known Mr. —— many years, and I never knew him to speak disrespectfully of a brother in my life."

At another time, in a company of nearly forty gentlemen, a student for the ministry entertained those around him with some ungenerous remarks on a popular preacher in London. Dr. Waugh looked at him for some time with pity and grief depicted in his countenance, and when he had thus arrested the attention of the speaker, he mildly remarked, "My friend, there is a saying in a good old book which I would recommend to your consideration: 'The spirit that dwelleth in us lusteth to envy.'"

(*n*) THE CLERGYMAN AND THE PROFLIGATE.—A clergyman having made several attempts to reform a profligate, was at length repulsed with, "It is all in vain, doctor; you cannot get me to change my religion." "I do not want that," replied the good man; "I wish religion to change you."

(*o*) WESLEY'S REQUEST OF THE OFFICER.—John Wesley, having to travel some distance in a stage coach, fell in with a pleasant tempered, well informed officer. His conversation was sprightly, and entertaining, but frequently mingled with oaths. When they were about to take the next stage, Mr. Wesley took the officer apart, and after expressing the pleasure he had enjoyed in his company, told him he was thereby encouraged to ask of him a very great favor. "I would take a pleasure in obliging you," said the officer, "and I am sure you will not make an unreasonable request." "Then," says Mr. Wesley, "as we have to travel together some time, I beg that if I should so far forget myself as to swear, you will kindly reprove me." The officer immediately saw the motive, and felt the force of the request, and smiling said, "None but Mr. Wesley could have conceived a reproof in such a manner."

(*p*) A NOBLEMAN REPROVED BY HIS SERVANT.—A nobleman seeing a large stone lying near his gate, ordered his servant, with an oath, to send it to hell. "If," said the servant, "I were to throw it to Heaven, it would be more completely out of your lordship's way."

(*q*) WHERE YOU OUGHT TO HAVE BEEN.—A clergyman who was in the habit of preaching in different parts of the country, was once at an inn, where he observed a horse-jockey trying to take in a simple gentleman, by imposing upon him a broken winded horse for a sound one. The parson knew the bad character of the jockey, and, taking the gentleman aside, told him to be cautious of the person he was dealing with. The gentleman finally declined the purchase, and the jockey, quite nettled, observed, "Parson, I would much rather hear you preach than see you privately interfere in bargains between man and man, in this way." "Well," replied the parson, "if you had been where you ought to have been last Sunday, you might have heard me preach." "Where was that?" inquired the jockey. "In the State Prison," returned the clergyman.

371. Happy Effects of Reproving.

(*a*) SUCCESSFUL REBUKE OF PROFANITY.—When the Rev. Mr. K—— was settled in his congregation of S——, they could not furnish him with a manse, or even with lodgings. In these circumstances, a Captain P—, in the neighborhood, though a stranger to religion, generously took him into his family, and gave him his board, it is believed, gratuitously. But our young clergyman soon found himself in very unpleasant circumstances, owing to the captain's usual practice of profane swearing. Satisfied of his duty, however, he determined to perform it at all hazards. Accordingly, one day at table, after a very liberal volley of oaths from the captain, he observed calmly, "Captain, you have certainly on the present occasion made use of a number of very improper terms." The captain, who was rather a choleric man, was instantly in a blaze. "Pray, sir, what improper terms have I used?" "Surely, captain, you must know," replied the clergyman, with greater coolness, "and having already put me to the pain of hearing them, you cannot be in earnest in imposing upon me the additional pain of repeating them." "You are right, sir," resumed the captain, "you are right. Support your character, and we will respect you. We have a parcel of clergymen around us here, who seem quite uneasy till they get us to understand that we may use any freedom we please before them, and we despise them." It ought to be known, that the captain never afterwards repeated the offence in his presence, and always treated Mr. K—— with marked respect, and befriended him in all his interests.

(*b*) ALLEINE'S REPROOF.—The Rev. Joseph Alleine was very faithful and impartial in administering reproof. Once, when employed in a work of this kind, he said to a Christian friend, "I am now going about that which is likely to make a very dear and obliging friend become an enemy. But, however, it cannot be omitted; it is better to lose man's favor than God's." But, so far from becoming his enemy for his conscientious faithfulness to him, he rather loved him the more ever after, as long as he lived.

(*c*) THE FAITHFUL YOUNG INDIAN.—At a meeting of a missionary society in Philadelphia, at which two Indian chiefs were present, and addressed a very large audience, the Rev. Mr. Finley, in the concluding part of his speech, related one or two very interesting anecdotes, to show the progress of the revival, and the depth of solid piety among the Wyandots. In one of his tours he took with him an Indian youth of zeal and piety. On setting out, he told him it was possible, when he got among sinful and wicked company, that he might forget his God, and again betake himself to the paths of folly and sin. "But," said he, calling him by his name, "I would rather preach your funeral sermon than see you depart from the paths of piety." They proceeded, and in their tour came to the house of a very wealthy merchant, where they remained for some time. The merchant had two or three clerks, who were giddy, gay young men. The Indian boy was put to sleep in a room with these clerks. Before retiring to bed, he knelt down to pray. The others began to disturb and torment him, but he heeded them not. This continued for some time: at length, one night when they were become so bad as to disturb him very much, the youth remonstrated, pointed out the wickedness of their conduct, and concluded by saying, that they were really worse than any Indian in all the Wyandot tribe of Upper Sandusky, observing, that Indians would be ashamed of such conduct, as they had more common sense, virtue, and piety. This appeal came home with keen conviction to the hearts of the young men. The effect was deep and lasting, the reproof was blessed to them, and they became humble and devoted Christians.

(*d*) MARTIN AND THE GOWNSMAN.—When the Rev. Henry Martyn was at college, he was called to visit a family in great distress on account of the expected death of the husband and father. Some of the family, lest the agony of their grief should add to the distress of the dying man, had removed to another house, where Martyn found a gownsman reading a play to them with a view to their consolation. He very properly rebuked him with some severity for this great impropriety, and was led to fear, from the manner in which his reproof was received, that some unpleasant results might follow. But mark the goodness of God, in blessing the means employed for the advancement of his glory. When this gownsman again saw Martyn, it was to thank him for his faithful admonition, which proved the means of a saving change of heart; and these two holy men labored together in India in extending the knowledge of the Lord Jesus.

372. Miscellaneous.

(*a*) FULLER'S SEVERITY.—The natural temper of the Rev. Andrew Fuller, of Kettering, though neither churlish nor morose, was not distinguished by gentleness, meekness, or affability. He could rarely be faithful without being severe; and, in giving reproof, he was often betrayed into intemperate zeal. Once, at a meeting of ministers, he took occasion to correct an erroneous opinion, delivered by one of his brethren; and he laid on his censure so heavily, that Dr. Ryland called out vehemently, in his own peculiar tone of voice, "Brother Fuller! brother Fuller! you can never admonish a mistaken friend, but you must take up a sledge hammer and knock his brains out!"

(*b*) JUDGE REPROVED BY A LOOK.—An eminent judge of Virginia, once said to a friend, that the most cutting reproof he had ever received for profaneness, was without words. He happened to be crossing a ferry with Dr. John H. Rice. On account of shallows, the boat could not be brought to land, and they were carried to the shore by the black ferryman. One of these was so careless as to suffer Judge H.'s clothes to become wetted, and the latter expressed his anger by an imprecation. Dr. Rice, without saying a word, turned to him his large speaking eye, with sorrowful expression. "I never so felt a reproof," said the judge, "in my life; and instantly begged his pardon. 'Ask pardon of God,' said Dr. Rice. I shall never forget it." At this time Judge H. was entirely ignorant who his reprover was.

373. RESTITUTION

(*a*) A PENITENT YOUTH.—A draper in Yarmouth, England, discovered that a lad in his service had stolen his property. He was tried, found guilty, and sentenced to seven years' transportation; but, on account of some favorable traits in his character, application was made to the Secretary of State, and the punishment was mitigated to five years' imprisonment in the Millbank Penitentiary. At the expiration of three years, his conduct induced the authorities to release him, when he went at once to Yarmouth, called on his former employer, and, in the spirit of a sincere penitent, expressed his sorrow for his dishonesty and ingratitude to so good a master, and said, "Sir, I have taken care of the money that I took away, and am now come to return your property." The gentleman was surprised at this announcement; and seeing him put his hand in his pocket, began to expect to receive from him a few pounds. Great was his astonishment, when the lad handed to him £102 16*s.* 6*d.*

(*b*) A PENITENT YOUNG JEW.—A young Jew, who had been admitted into an asylum for the benefit of that nation, near Dusseldorf, in the Prussian dominions, after having long given pain by his improper behavior, became very deeply impressed under a sermon, preached by the Rev. Mr. Schmidt, and afterwards furnished evidence that his impressions were deep and abiding.

In the course of one of his sermons, the minister, to whom we have referred, was led to speak of persons who glory in their shame, and even boast of their crimes in having robbed or defrauded their neighbors. This young man became visibly affected, turned pale, fell into fits, and was carried out of the place. He was afterwards visited by the minister, to whom he exclaimed, "I am lost; lost without remedy." In the course of the conversation, he confessed that he had robbed a widow of one thousand dollars, and that his life had been one whole series of awful crimes. The minister did not attempt to palliate his sins, but explained to him the atonement of Jesus, and the efficacy of his blood to take away all sin, encouraging him in this way to seek pardon. This at length afforded him rest. He now felt it his duty to travel to the residence of the widow, to acknowledge his crime, and thus to subject himself to the punishment of the law. When he was last heard of, he had set out on his journey, with the determination that, if the widow did not prosecute him, he would, by his labor, pay the debt due to her.

(c) SIXTY POUNDS RESTORED. -A gentleman residing in the vicinity of York once received an anonymous letter, appointing a meeting in the oat-market, when, as the letter stated, something would be communicated for his advantage. The gentleman kept the appointment, and was accosted by a respectable looking man, who proposed that they should go to an inn together. The gentleman consented; and having entered a private room, they both sat down at a table, when the stranger presented his new friend with sixty pounds, which he said was his property. The gentleman refused to take it without an explanation; but the stranger then presented him with sixty pounds more, and said that this was also due besides, as interest for the money, simple and compound, during the time he held his property. He afterwards gave the following explanation to the gentleman: "More than twenty years ago, you had an uncle, whose property you now possess: his age and infirmities rendered it expedient for him to have a housekeeper to manage his affairs. My sister was that housekeeper. Some time after his death she found sixty pounds folded up in one of her trunks, which she believed to have belonged to him at the time of his death. She sent for me, gave it into my hands, and requested that I would restore it to you, as the lawful heir of her master's property. This I promised to do, but being embarrassed in my circumstances at the time, I made use of it for my own purposes. I now make the proper restitution. I do it to the utmost, and with pleasure; and I do assure you that this transaction has taken a very heavy weight from my distressed mind." Various circumstances then occurred to the gentleman's mind, which left no doubt of the truth of the stranger's story.

(d) STOLEN WATCH RESTORED.—As a gentleman in London entered his house, he found a well dressed female sitting on the stairs, who asked pardon for the liberty she had taken, saying, that hearing the alarm of a mad dog, she had taken refuge in his house, and had almost fainted away. On hearing her story, the gentleman gave her some refreshment, when she recovered and walked off, thanking him for his civility. In the evening his lady missed a gold watch, which she had left hanging at the head of her bed; the servants said no person had been in that room since they had made up the bed, when they were certain the watch was there. It was, therefore, concluded that this female was the thief.

Fifteen years afterwards, the guard of the York mail coach called with a small parcel, saying, that a gentleman had given him five shillings to deliver it. On opening the parcel, it was found to contain the lost watch, and a note from a female, saying, that as the gospel had changed her heart, she desired to return the watch to its rightful owner.

(e) THE SURPLUS CHANGE RETURNED.—In the course of the forenoon of yesterday, says the New York Statesman, for 183–, a person called at the office of Messrs. Beers and Bunnell, and handed to Mr. Beers the sum of twenty dollars, stating that it was from a young man who, in changing money for his master, received that sum above what he should have received, at Beers and Bunnell's office, and, without saying any thing of it to his master, appropriated it to his own use. The person who handed in the money declined giving the name of the conscience-struck young man, but observed that he was lying on a bed of sickness, probably of death, and that he could not rest in view of the hereafter, till the money had been returned as evidence of his bitter contrition.

(f) THE DISHONEST CLERK. —A young man, says a writer in the N. Y. Evangelist, went into one of our large cities and offered his services to a man in important public business. Here he labored for years, having the entire confidence of his employer. But he performed a hard service at small wages, and was many times deprived of his rest all night. At length the thought thwarted his mind, that the entire confidence placed in him gave him opportunity *to do himself justice.* This evil thought was the opening wedge.

He laid by from time to time such sums as he supposed would make up the defect in his wages, till before he quitted the man it amounted to some hundreds of dollars. He then went into another part of the country to thrive on his earnings, and as he still supposed, *honest earnings.* There, though still in rather humble life, he thrived well, and was esteemed and respected, till within a few years since. The Spirit of God came down upon the people where he lived. He became awakened, and at length obtained a hope in the mercy of God, and took his seat with those who felt as he did. But his conscience was slumbering over the scenes of olden time. He was happy because God suffered past scenes to be forgotten. He had never pondered on the doctrine of retribution, and went sailing on to heaven with fair breeze and sails all filled.

At length, however, he became cast down and disconsolate, and the mystery was that no one could get from him the secret of his distress, not even his beloved wife. What could the matter be?

At length, when he could keep the fire shut up in his bones no longer, he sought an interview with his pastor. He watched a long time to find him entirely alone, and where he could not be overheard while he opened his whole heart. There was a very sequestered spot in a deep glen, where the pastor used to retire to hold uninterrupted communion with God. There this wretched man met him and told him all his heart—the length, and breadth, and height, and aggravation of his sin. And what must he do? He could not disclose the matter to his wife. It would ruin his family. He dare not seek and could not find the man he had wronged—the disclosure would imprison him. Indeed he was in the grave by this time, and whether any heir of his was living, to whom the debt could be refunded, so that God would forgive him and let him live, demanded a doubt.

At length the pastor set out to seek the heirs, if they could be found, that the money might be refunded to them. On his way he called on the writer of this and gave me the whole story. After going from street to street and house to house many days, till it seemed to him impossible that he should ever find the object of his chase, he entered a lonely and humble habitation, where he found the only surviving daughter and child of the injured man. And to her at that time he was indeed an angel of mercy. She had been, as he presumed, in better circumstances, but was brought to poverty, and was then a widow poor and needy. He paid her some two hundred dollars, and will perhaps come on similar errands of mercy hereafter. The widow he found trying to support her half famished family by sewing.

(*g*) THE INFIDEL AND HIS EMPLOYER.—Mr. C— an avowed infidel, was for many years in the employ of a worthy and respectable mechanic, in a small village in R. I. He was a man of steady habits and a good workman, and consequently had secured the favor and confidence of Mr. A—, his employer. It was Mr. A—'s custom to settle with his workmen but once a year.

At one time, a few months before the time for settlement arrived, Mr. C— was in want of some money, and called at Mr A—'s counting-room, and asked him for twenty-five dollars. The money was handed him, but, through negligence, no charge made against him. At the expiration of the year, Mr. C— went to receive the remainder of his wages, but perceiving the $25 was forgotten by his employer, received the whole amount credited him.

Years passed on, and a revival of religion took place in that village, and among those who were hopefully converted was the infidel C—. But no sooner had the Spirit of God wrought a work of grace in his heart, than he began to think of the injury he had done his employer, and he felt that he ought to confess his sin and make restitution. But unsubdued pride at first prevented his doing this. At length, convictions for this sin came with such overwhelming force as to threaten destruction to his peace of mind, and he went to Mr. A—, confessed his guilt, paid him back the $25, and went on his way rejoicing. He remained afterwards a consistent follower of Christ.

(*h*) PAINFUL EFFECTS OF A JOKE.—A gentleman in ——— attended the preaching of Dr. Clarke, and was deeply convinced of sin. With strong prayer and tears he sought pardon, but found not. Being confined by sickness soon after, he sent for Dr. Clarke, who came; but learning how long he had mourned, and with what earnestness he had sought salvation, he secretly wondered at God's so long withholding freedom from such deep repentance; and finding the lamp of life burning low, and mental agony hurrying on its extinction, with tender but firm language he said, "It is not often, Mr. ——, that God thus deals with a soul so deeply humbled as yours, and in his own appointed way seeking redemption. Sir, there must be a cause. You have left something undone which it is your duty and interest to have done. God judge between you and it."

Fixing his eyes intently on Dr. Clarke, the gentleman gave the following narration: "In the year —— I was at ——, and took my passage in the ship —— for England. Before sailing, some merchants put on board a small bag of dollars, which were given in charge to the captain for such and such parties. I saw the transaction, and noticed the captain's carelessness, who left the bag day after day rolling upon the locker. For the simple purpose of frightening him, I hid it. He made no inquiries, and we arrived at ——. I still retained it till it should be missed. Months passed, and still no inquiry was made. The parties to whom it had been consigned came to the captain for it. He remembered receiving it in charge, but no more. It must have been left behind. Search was made, letters written, but it could not be found. All this occupied some months. I had now become alarmed and ashamed to confess, lest I should implicate my character.

"The captain was sued, and, having nothing to pay, was cast into prison. He maintained his innocence as to the theft, but confessed his carelessness. He languished two years in prison, and died. Guilt had by this time hardened my mind. I strove to be happy in the amusements of the world, but all in vain. Under your preaching the voice of God broke in upon my conscience. I have agonized at the throne of mercy for the sake of Christ for pardon; but God is deaf to my prayer. I must go down to the grave unpardoned, unsaved."

Dr. Clarke suggested to the dying penitent that God claimed from him not only *repentance*, but *restitution*. The widow and fatherless children still lived. The gentleman readily consented. The sum, with interest and compound interest, was made up and given to the widow, to whom the circumstances were made known. The dying man's mind was calmed, and soon, in firm hope of pardon, he died.

(*i*) THE PURSE RESTORED.—Forty-two years ago, says a writer in the Boston Mercantile Journal of 183–, my father was a poor man, with a wife as industrious as himself, and one child, and he worked early and late for a support. One dollar then in his purse made him feel richer than he now feels with a title to a good farm.

Returning home one day with a purse containing ten silver dollars in his pocket, he lost it on the road. Long and diligent was the search for it, but in vain, as a neighbor had picked it up and appropriated it to his own use. It must, however, have been a fire in his bosom; for how could he travel that road, or pass the house of his neighbor, without feeling the lashes of a guilty conscience?

Recently he has been brought under the influence of that gospel which teaches man to do justly. He went to his neighbor, confessed the injury done, asked his forgiveness, restored the money, promised the accumulated interest of forty two years, and any other remuneration in his power. "Not a wink," said he, "could I sleep last night; nor could I rest till I had made confession and restitution."

374. RICHES.

(*a*) RICHES AND COVETOUSNESS.—A respectable widow lady, with a very small income, which she was obliged to eke out by the produce of her own industry and ingenuity, was remarkable for her generous liberality, especially in contributing to the cause of religion. When any work of pious benevolence was going forward, her minister hesitated to call on her, lest her liberal spirit should prompt her to contribute beyond her ability; but she was always sure to find out what was in hand, and voluntarily to offer a donation equal to those of persons in comparative affluence, accompanied by a gentle rebuke to her minister for having passed her by. In process of time, this lady came into the possession of an ample fortune, greatly to the joy of all who knew her willing liberality. But it was with no small degree of regret that her minister observed she no longer came forward unsolicited towards the cause of Christ, and that when applied to, she yielded her aid but coldly and grudgingly, and sometimes excused herself from giving at all. On one occasion she presented a shilling to the same cause to which she had formerly given a guinea, when in a state of comparative poverty. The minister felt it his duty to expostulate with her, and remind her of her former generosity when her means were so circumscribed. "Ah! sir," she affectingly replied, "then I had the shilling means, but the guinea heart; now I have the guinea means, but only the shilling heart. Then, I received from my heavenly Father's hand, day by day, my daily bread, and I had enough, and to spare; now, I have to look to my ample income, but I live in constant apprehension that I may come to want!" Can any reader be at a loss to decide which was the time of her poverty and which of her riches?

(*b*) AFFECTING CONTRAST.—I once accompanied a friend, wrote the Rev. S. Kilpin, in 1830, to see the princely abode of a certain nobleman, and was much struck with the splendor of the place. The castle stood on the side of a beautiful river, the water of which, as it rushed over some large fragments of an old bridge, glittered in the sunbeams. The warder opened the massy gate at the lodge, and we proceeded up an avenue hewn through the solid rock, whose sides were festooned with different shrubs and lichens. The towers and battlements were high and strong; the smoothly shaven lawn wide and green; the pleasure grounds extensive; and the broad, dark, and flat branches of the goodly cedars swept gracefully the very grouud.

But if the outside of the castle was fair to gaze upon, the inside of it was still more worthy of attention. Almost every room was ornamented with valuable paintings, hung with curious tapestry, and adorned with costly vases; statues of marble stood in niches in the hall, and in the avenues leading from one apartment to another; the armory was filled with coats of mail, helmets, spears, and various ancient instruments of warfare; and some thousands of volumes were arranged in the library. The pomp and splendor of the whole were enough to make any one believe that the possessor of such a mansion must be a rich man; and yet, at the moment that I was walking through his castle, he himself was not permitted to enter it! His constitution was decayed; his conduct had diminished his resources, so that his own castle was, for a season, closed against him. How then could he be a rich who had neither health of body nor peace of mind?

Now, it happened, at the time of which I am speaking, that I knew a man who was considered poor, who lived at no great distance from the castle. He dwelt near the road side, and though he had neither turrets, nor lawns, nor goodly cedars, yet his cottage was a comfortable abode; the green before his door was very pleasant, and the fruit trees in his little garden were covered with blossoms.

He had neither paintings, statues, nor

vases; nor would they have made him more happy had he possessed them. A sampler, which had been wrought by his wife in her youthful days, hung framed and glazed opposite the window; and a painted tea-tray was placed upright upon a table against the wall: these were the principal decorations of his humble abode. His library was not like that of the castle, for it consisted only of about half-a-dozen books, one of which was the Bible, and a few tracts. He was a hard-working man, had an excellent constitution, which he did not abuse; and, what was better than all, he was a reader of his Bible, and a humble and sincere disciple of Jesus Christ. He had health of body and peace of mind.

(*c*) THE MERCHANT AND THE "WHITE STONE."—In the strait between Johor and Rhio, there is a small white rock, called the "White Stone," very little elevated above the water, and so exactly in the centre of the passage, that many vessels, unacquainted with it, have been wrecked upon it. A Portuguese merchant passing this strait, in a vessel of his own, richly laden with gold and other valuable commodities, asked the pilot when this rock would be passed: but each moment appearing to him long until he was secure from the danger, he repeated his question so often, that the pilot impatiently told him the rock was passed. The merchant, transported with joy, impiously exclaimed, that "God could not now make him poor." But in a little while, the vessel struck on the White Stone, and all his wealth was ingulfed in the abyss; life alone remained, to make him feel his misery and his punishment.

(*d*) "IT WILL NOT DO."—Mr. Jeremiah Burroughs, a pious minister, mentions the case of a rich man, who, when he lay on his sick-bed, called for his bags of money; and having laid a bag of gold to his heart, after a little he bade them take it away, saying, "It will not do! it will not do!"

(*e*) THE RICH MAN'S PORTION.—A nobleman, who lived in the neighborhood of the Rev. Mr. D——, one day asked him to dine with him. Before dinner they walked into the garden, and after viewing the various productions and rarities with which it abounded, his lordship exclaimed, "Well, Mr. D——, you see I want for nothing: I have all that my heart can wish for." As Mr. D—— made no reply, but appeared thoughtful, his lordship asked him the reason. "Why, my lord," said the old man, "I have been thinking, that a man may have all these things, and go to hell after all. The words powerfully struck the nobleman, and through the blessing of God terminated in his conversion.

(*f*) THE NOBLEMAN AND THE COTTAGER.—A nobleman in the north of England once said to a gentleman who accompanied him in a walk, "These beautiful grounds, as far as your eye can reach, those majestic woods on the brow of the distant hills, and those extensive and valuable mines belong to me; yonder powerful steam engine obtains the produce of my mines; and those ships convey my wealth to other parts of the kingdom." "Well, my lord," replied the gentleman, "do you see yonder little hovel that seems but a speck in your estate? there dwells a poor woman who can say more than all this, for she can say, 'Christ is mine.' In a very few years your lordship's possessions will be confined within the scanty limits of a tomb; but she will then have entered on a far nobler inheritance than your lordship now possesses—an inheritance incorruptible, undefiled, and that fadeth not away, reserved in heaven for those who are kept by the power of God through faith unto salvation."

(*g*) CHOOSING AFFLICTION.—The Rev. H. Venn once told his children, that he would take them to see one of the most interesting sights in the world. He would not tell them what it was; but in the evening led them to a miserable hovel, whose ruinous walls and broken windows showed an extreme degree of poverty and want. "Now,' said he, "my dear children, can any one that lives in such a wretched habitation as this be happy? Yet this is not all; a poor young man lies there on a miserable straw bed, dying of disease, at the age of nineteen, consumed with fever, and afflicted with nine painful ulcers." "How wretched!" they all exclaimed. He then led them into the cottage, and addressing the poor dying young man, said, "Abraham Midwood, I have brought my children here to show them that it is possible to be happy in a state of disease, and poverty, and want: now, tell them if it is not so." The dying youth, with a sweet smile, replied, "Oh! yes, sir; I would not change my state with that of the richest person on earth, who has not those views which I have. Blessed be God! I have a good hope, through Christ, of being admitted into those blessed regions where Lazarus now dwells, having long forgotten all his sorrows and miseries. Sir, this is nothing to bear whilst the presence of God cheers my soul, and whilst I can have access to him, by constant prayer, through faith in Jesus. Indeed, sir, I am truly happy, and I trust to be happy through eternity; and I every hour thank God, who has brought me from a state of darkness into marvelous light, and has given me to enjoy the unsearchable riches of his grace."

(*h*) CECIL'S RICH HEARER.—Mr. Cecil had a rich hearer, who, when a young man had solicited his advice, but who had not, for some time, had an interview with him. Mr. C. one day went to his house on horseback, being unable to walk, and, after the usual salutations, adressed him thus:—"I understand you are very dangerously situated!" Here he paused, and his friend replied, "I am not aware of it, sir." "I thought it was probable you were not; and therefore I have called on you. I hear you are getting rich; take care, for it is the road by which the devil leads thousands to destruction!" This was spoken with such solemnity and earnestness, that it made a deep and lasting impression.

(*i*) FULLER'S QUESTION.—"This morning," says Mr. Fuller, "I have read another of Edwards' sermons, on *God the Christian's Portion*, from Psalm lxxiii. 25. The latter part comes very close, and I feel myself at a loss what to judge as to God's being my chief good. He asks, whether we had rather live in this world rich and without God, or poor and with him? Perhaps I should not be so much at a loss to decide this question as another; namely, had I rather be rich in this world, and enjoy but *little* of God; or poor and enjoy *much* of God? I am confident the practice of great numbers of professing Christians declares that they prefer the former; and in some instances I feel guilty of the same thing."

(*j*) "POSSESSING ALL THINGS."—A lady in England, more than seventy years of age, who had long been known as an "Israelite indeed," was called, in the providence of God, to pass her last days in a *poor-house*.

She was visited one day by a Wesleyan minister; and while in conversation with her on the comforts, prospects, and rewards of religion, he saw an unusual lustre beaming from her countenance, and the calmness of Christian triumph glistening in her eye. Addressing her by name, he said, "Will you tell me what thought it was that passed through your mind, which was the cause of your appearing so joyful?' The reply of the "old disciple" was "*Oh! sir, I was just thinking what a change it will be from the* POOR-HOUSE TO HEAVEN!"

375. RIDICULE.

(*a*) LAUGHED OUT OF RELIGION.—A poor man, who had heard the preaching of the Gospel, and to whom it had been greatly blessed, was the subject of much profane jesting and ridicule among his fellow workmen and neighbors. On being asked if these daily persecutions did not sometimes make him ready to give up his profession of attachment to Divine truth, he replied, "No; I recollect that our good minister once said in his sermon, that if we were so foolish as to permit such people to laugh us out of our religion, till at last we dropped into hell, they could not laugh us out again."

(*b*) LANDLADY'S GIFT TO ADMIRAL COLPOYS.—Admiral Colpoys, who rose to that high station as the effect of his meritorious exertions, used to be fond of relating, that on first leaving an humble lodging to join his ship, as a midshipman, his landlady presented him with a Bible and a guinea, saying, "God bless you, and prosper you, my lad; and as long as you live, never suffer yourself to be laughed out of your money or your prayers." The young sailor carefully followed this advice through life, and had reason to rejoice that he did so; while thousands have unavailingly regretted that they pursued a different course.

376. ROBBERS—ROBBERY.

(*a*) ROBBERY ITS OWN PUNISHMENT.—The only sailor who perished in the Kent Indiaman was present in the hold very shortly after the commencement of the fire which destroyed the vessel, when, availing himself of the confusion, he hastened to the cabin of the second mate, forced open a desk, and took from thence four hundred sovereigns, which he rolled up in a handkerchief, and tied round his waist; but in attempting to leap into one of the boats, he fell short, and the weight of his spoils caused him immediately to sink! Unhappy sailor! of what avail were his four hundred sovereigns when he lifted up his eyes in an eternal world, and stood before the righteous Judge as a self-convicted robber? What if he had gained the whole world, and could have put it round him? It would only have sunk him deeper and quicker into the bottomless pit. How many millions of immortal souls have gone down to this abyss, loaded with ill-gotten wealth!

(*b*) WARNING TO YOUTH.—The St. Louis Reveille contains an account of the death of a young man by the name of Leak, who, although only twenty-two years of age, had made himself notorious in crime. He was arrested for robbing a store, having been betrayed by one of his companions in crime. He plead his own case before the jury, and besought them to deal lightly with him, for he was both young in years and in the knowledge of crime. The jury leaned to the side of mercy, and instead of ten, alloted him four years in the state penitentiary. A struggle now commenced in the felon's heart which finally ended in suicide.

Nashville, the seat of the state prison, was the home of his childhood, and his aged mother lived there, highly respected; his brother and sisters, also, the former being a respectable merchant of that city. He spoke frequently on the trip up, of how hard it would be for him to pass his mother's door in chains, on his way to prison, and said he would rather die than undergo the ignominy. The companions of his childhood, his schoolmates, he said, would gather about him and look upon his wretched felon carcass until their eyes would burn into his heart. To his wretchedness of mind was added sickness of body, and at length, when eight miles above Cairo, on the Ohio river, the miserable felon, bearing the manacle badges of his wickedness upon his person, plunged into the river and ended his guilty career. "Truly the way of the transgressor is hard."

(*c*) ROBBER SON RECLAIMED.—The following is related of Mr. John Welsh. He was, it is said, a most hopeless and extravagant youth. He frequently played truant; and, at last, while very young, he left his studies, and his father's house, and went and joined himself to the thieves on the *borders* of the then two kingdoms, who lived by robbery and plunder. After he had suffered many hardships among them, and, like the prodigal in the gospel, began to be in great misery, and no man gave unto him, he took the prodigal's resolution to return home to his father's house. He made Dumfries in his way homeward, where lived a Mrs. Forgath, his father's cousin: he earnestly entreated her to bring about a reconciliation for him with his father.

He had not been long with this lady, before his father came, providentially, to visit her; to whom, after conversing a while, she said, "Cousin, have you heard any thing of your son John?" "Oh! cruel woman!" said the father, with grief, "how can you mention his name to me? The first news I expect to hear of him, is, that he is hanged for a thief." She answered, "Many a profligate boy has become a virtuous man;" and endeavored to comfort him, but in vain. At length, he asked her if she knew whether his lost son was yet living. She answered, "Yes, he is yet alive, and I hope he will make a better man than he was a boy," at the same time she introduced him to his father. The youth came in weeping, and threw himself at his father's feet, beseeching him, for Christ's sake, to pardon his misbehavior, and earnestly, and with much apparent sincerity, promising future amendment. His father reproached and threatened him; but, upon the importunities of Mrs. Forgath, he was persuaded to a reconciliation. He then besought his father to send him to college, saying, "that if ever he misbehaved again, he would be content that his father should disclaim him forever." His father granted him his request; and, after a little time spent there, not only a thorough reformation, but a saving conversion, took place in him; and he was so diligent a student, that, in much less time than could be expected, he went through all his necessary studies, and entered early into the ministry. He became one of the most extraordinary characters of his age.

377. RULE, GOLDEN, THE.

(*a*) GOLDEN RULE VIOLATED.—The manner in which some professed Christians violate the golden rule in their business transactions, is deeply to be regretted as evidence of the bluntness of their moral perceptions, as a disgrace to the cause of true religion, and a stumbling-block to the impenitent. The correspondent of a certain religious journal says, "I passed an American eagle and a Spanish doubloon to a countryman, for value received, as I had given full value for them. True, I had heard from a gentleman broker, that they were of suspicious character, and probably base metal merely baptized in gold. But as I did not *certainly know* that they were base coins, ought I to have offered them to persons who were not judges of them, without any intimation of the report? I also passed in silence a $50 bank note of doubtful character, to a farmer, which I had unsuspectingly received in a fair sale of the necessaries of life; but not *knowing* it to be a counterfeit, I did not altogether condemn myself, as I had said nothing in commendation of it But on reading some of your remarks I fear I have done wrong. Pray what is your opinion?" The editor promptly replies, "My opinion is that you did a moral wrong. You have not done to another what you would have done to you?" And the editor's reply is the heartfelt response of every enlightened, conscientious Christian, who will, for a moment, make the case of the "countryman" and "farmer," who were deceived by the money, their own.

Take another instance of the violation of the same precept. "I heard," says a Western Preacher, "a conversation between a father and a son, both members of the same church, in the presence too of both their families. "My son," said he, "you got cheated in that horse: he stumbles wretchedly, and will certainly go blind. You ought to sell him the first opportunity." "Yes, father, I was deceived: but he is a good looking horse; and I think by putting him into the hands of your auctioneer I can sell him for cost." "You ought then to do it soon," replied his father, "or perhaps you will lose by the transaction." "I will send him to town to-morrow, and let the bidder do as I did—trust to his own eyes and judgment, for I will not warrant him." "You ought not to warrant him for two reasons—first, because the thing is wrong in itself; and in the next place, you might be made to pay the damages. Honesty is the best policy, my son. Remember that." Strange that professed Christians should talk in this manner! Fluently and conscientiously passing a cheat upon themselves, and acting the villain under the guise of honesty and fair dealing. How differs such a transaction in principle from robbery? Touch such a transaction with the golden rule, and its true character and deformity will be at once apparent, like those of Satan at the touch of Ithuriel's spear.

(*b*) TEDYNSCUNG AND HIS FRIEND.—Tedynscung was a celebrated chief among the Delaware Indians of North America, about 1780. The efforts of the Christian missionaries had been the means of diffusing much scriptural knowledge among the native Indians, and their doctrines were frequently the subject of conversation among them. One evening, Tedynscung was sitting by the fireside of his friend, who mentioned the golden rule to him as very excellent, "For one man to do to another as he would the other should do to him!" "It is impossible; it cannot be done," said the Indian chief. After smoking his pipe, and musing for about a quarter of an hour, Tedynscung again gave his opinion, and said, "Brother, I have been thoughtful on what you told me. If the great Spirit that made man would give him a new heart, he could do so as you say, but not else."

SABBATH, THE CHRISTIAN.

BENEFITS OF THE SABBATH.

378. Physical Benefits to Domestic Animals.

(*a*) THE DROVERS AND THEIR SHEEP.—Two neighbors in the state of New-York, each with a drove of sheep, started on the same day for a distant market. One started several hours before the other, and traveled uniformly every day. The other rested every Sabbath. Yet he arrived at the market first, with his flock in a better condition than that of the other. In giving an account of it, he said that he drove his sheep on Monday about seventeen miles, on Tuesday not over sixteen, and so lessening each day, till on Saturday he drove them only about eleven miles. But on Monday, after resting on the Sabbath, they would travel again seventeen miles, and so on each week. But his neighbor's sheep, which were not allowed to rest on the Sabbath, before they arrived at the market, could not travel without injury more than six or eight miles in a day.

(*b*) WAY TO EXPEDITION.—At a tavern in Pennsylvania, a man who had arrived the evening before, was asked on Sabbath morning whether he intended to pursue his journey on that day. He answered, "No." He was asked, "Why not?" "Because," said he, "I am on a long journey, and wish to perform it as soon as I can. I have long been accustomed to travel on horseback, and have found that, if I stop on the Sabbath, my horse will travel farther during the week than if I do not."

(*c*) THE VICTORIOUS TRAVELER.—A gentleman started from Connecticut with his family for Ohio. He was on the road about four weeks, and rested every Sabbath. From morning to night others, journeying the same way, were passing by. Before the close of the week he passed them. Those who went by late on the Sabbath he passed on Monday; those who went by a little earlier he passed on Tuesday; and so on, till before the next Sabbath he had passed them all. His horses were no better than theirs, nor were they better fed. But having had the benefit of resting on the Sabbath, according to the command of God and the law of nature, they could out-travel those who had violated that law.

(*d*) MANUFACTURERS AND THEIR TEAMS.—A manufacturing company, which had been accustomed to carry their goods to market with their own teams, kept them employed seven days in a week, as that was the time in which they could go to the market and return. But by permitting the teams to rest on the Sabbath, they found that they could drive them the same distance in six days, that they formerly did in seven, and with the same keeping preserve them in better order.

(*e*) THE TEAMSTER AND HIS HORSES.—A gentleman in Vermont, who was in the habit of driving his horses twelve miles a day seven days in a week, afterwards changed his practice, and drove them but six days, allowing them to rest one. He then found that, with the same keeping, he could drive them fifteen miles a day, and preserve them in as good order as before. So that a man may rest on the Sabbath, and let his horses rest, yet promote the benefit of both, and be in all respects the gainer.

(*f*) EXPERIMENT WITH CATTLE.—A number of men started together from Ohio, with droves of cattle for Philadelphia. They had often been before, and had been accustomed to drive on the Sabbath as on other days. One had now changed his views as to the propriety of traveling on that day. On Saturday he inquired for pastures. His associates wondered that so shrewd a man should think of consuming so great a portion of his profits by stopping with such a drove a whole day. He stopped, however, and kept the Sabbath. They, thinking that they could not afford to do so, went on. On Monday he started again. In the course of the week he passed them, arrived first in the market, and sold his cattle to great advantage. So impressed were the others with the benefits of thus keeping the Sabbath, that ever afterwards they followed his example.

379. Physical Benefits to Man.

(*a*) PHYSICIANS OF ROCHESTER.—Dr. F. Backus and seven other respectable physicians of Rochester, New-York, have given the following testimony: "Having most of us lived on the Erie Canal since its completion, we have uniformly witnessed the same deteriorating effects of seven days' working upon the physical constitution, both of man and beast, as have been so ably depicted by Dr. Farre." They are more sickly than others, bring upon themselves, in great numbers, a premature old age, and sink to an untimely grave.

(*b*) EXPERIMENT IN A MILL.—The experiment was tried in a large flouring establishment. For a number of years they worked the mills seven days in a week. The superintendent was then changed. He ordered all the works to be stopped at eleven o'clock on Saturday night, and to start none of them till one o'clock on Monday morning, thus allowing a full Sabbath every week. And the same men, during the year, actually ground thousands of bushels more than had ever been ground, in a single year, in that establishment before. The men, having been permitted to cleanse themselves, put on their best apparel, rest from worldly business, go with their families to the house of God, and devote the Sabbath to its appropriate duties, were more healthy, moral, punctual and diligent. They lost less time in drinking, dissipation and quarrels. They were more clear-headed and whole-hearted, knew better how to do things, and were more disposed to do them in the right way.

(*c*) RESULT OF EXPERIENCE—In the year 1839 a committee was appointed in the legislature of Pennsylvania, who made a report with regard to the employment of laborers on their canals. In that report, they say, in reference to those who had petitioned against the employment of the workmen on the Sabbath, "They assert, *as the result of their experience*, that both man and beast can do more work by resting one day in seven, than by working on the whole seven." They then add, "Your committee feel free to confess, that *their own experience* as business men, farmers, or legislators, corresponds with the assertion."

(*d*) EXPERIMENT IN THE LAST WAR.—An experiment was tried on the northern frontier of the United States, during the last war. When building vessels, making roads, and performing other laborious services, the commander stated that it was not profitable to employ the men on the Sabbath, for it was found that they could not, in the course of the week, do as much work.

(*e*) BRITISH HOUSE OF COMMONS.—In the year 1832, the British House of Commons appointed a committee to investigate the effects of laboring seven days in a week, compared with those of laboring only six, and resting one. That committee consisted of Sir Andrew Agnew, Sir Robert Peel, Sir Robert Inglis, Sir Thomas Baring, Sir George Murray, Fowell Buxton, Lord Morpeth, Lord Ashley, Lord Viscount Sandon, and twenty other members of Parliament. They examined a great number of witnesses, of various professions and employments. Among them was John Richard Farre, M. D., of London; of whom they speak as "an acute and experienced physician." The following is the testimony:

"I have practised as a physician between thirty and forty years; and during the early part of my life, as the physician of a public medical institution. I had charge of the poor in one of the most populous districts of London. I have had occasion to observe the effect of the observance and non-observance of the seventh day of rest during this time. I have been in the habit, during a great many years, of considering the *uses* of the Sabbath, and of observing its *abuses*. The abuses are chiefly manifested in labor and dissipation. Its use, medically speaking, is that of a day of rest.

"As a day of rest, I view it as a day of *compensation* for the inadequate restorative power of the body under *continued* labor and excitement. A physician always has respect to the preservation of the restorative power; because, if once this be lost, his healing office is at an end. A physician is anxious to preserve the balance of circulation, as necessary to the restorative power of the body. The ordinary exertions of man *run down* the circulation every day of his life; and the first general law of nature, by which God prevents man from destroying himself, is the alternating of day and night, that repose may succeed action. But, although the night apparently equalizes the circulation, yet it does not sufficiently restore its balance for the attainment of a *long* life. Hence, one day in seven, by the bounty of Providence, is thrown in as a day of compensation, to perfect by its repose the animal system.

"I consider, therefore, that, in the bountiful provision of Providence for the preservation of human life, the sabbatical appointment is not, as it has been sometimes theologically viewed, simply a precept partaking of the nature of a political institution, but that it is to be numbered amongst the *natural* duties, if the preservation of life be admitted to be a duty, and the premature destruction of it a suicidal act."

(*f*) NEW HAVEN MEDICAL ASSOCIATION.—At a regular meeting of the New Haven Medical Association, composed of twenty-five physicians, among whom were the professors of the Medical College, the following questions were considered:

1. Is the position taken by Dr. Farre in his testimony before the committee of the British House of Commons, in your view, correct?

2. Will men who labor but six days in a week be more healthy and live longer, other things being equal, than those who labor seven?

3. Will they do more work, and do it in a better manner?

The vote on the above was *unanimously in the affirmative*; signed by Eli Ives, chairman, and Pliny A. Jewett, clerk.

(*g*) MINISTER OF MARINE IN FRANCE.—The minister of marine in France has addressed a letter to all the maritime prefects, directing that no workman, except in case of absolute necessity, be employed in the government dock-yards on the Sabbath. One reason which he gives is, that men who do not rest on the Sabbath do not perform as much labor during the week, and, of course, that it is not profitable to the state to have labor performed on that day. Another reason is, that it is useful to the state to promote among the laboring classes *the religious observance of the Sabbath.*

(*h*) THOROUGH EXPERIMENT WITH LABORERS.—Nor is it true that men who labor six days in a week, and rest on one, are more healthy merely, and live longer than those who labor seven; but *they do more work, and in a better manner.* The experiment was tried in England upon two thousand men. They were employed for years, seven days in a week. To render them contented in giving up their right to the Sabbath, as a day of rest, *that birthright of the human family,* they paid them double wages on that day, eight days' wages for seven days' work. But they could not keep them healthy, nor make them moral. Nor can men ever be made moral, or kept most healthy in that way. Things went badly, and they changed their course —employed the workmen only six days in a week, and allowed them to rest on the Sabbath. The consequence was, that they did more work than ever before. This, the superintendent said, was owing to two causes, viz.: *demoralization of the people* under the first system, and *exhaustion of bodily strength,* which was visible to the most casual observer. Such a course will always demoralize men, and diminish their strength.

380. Intellectual Benefits.

(*a*) TESTIMONY OF WILBERFORCE.—The celebrated Wilberforce ascribes his continuance, for so long a time, under such a pressure of cares and labors, in no small degree, to his conscientious and habitual observance of the Sabbath. "O what a blessed day," he says, "is the Sabbath, which allows us a precious interval wherein to pause, to come out from the thickets of worldly concerns, and give ourselves up to heavenly and spiritual objects. *Observation and my own experience have convinced me that there is a special blessing on a right employment of these intervals.* O, what a blessing is Sunday, interposed between the waves of worldly business, like the divine path of the Israelites through Jordan. There is nothing in which I would recommend you to be more strictly conscientious than in keeping the Sabbath holy. By this I mean not only abstaining from all unbecoming sports, and common business, but from consuming time in *frivolous conversation, paying or receiving visits,* which, among relations, often leads to a sad waste of this precious day. I can truly declare that to me *the Sabbath has been invaluable.*"

(*b*) MAKING BRIEFS ON SUNDAY.—The distinguished Dr. Wilson, Pastor of the first Presbyterian Church in Philadelphia, for a number of years before he became a preacher of the gospel, was an eminent lawyer in the State of Delaware. He was accustomed when pressed with business, to make out his briefs and prepare for his Monday's pleading on the Sabbath. But he so uniformly failed, during the week, in carrying out his Sunday plans, that it arrested his attention. As a philosopher, he inquired into the cause of his uniform failure, and came to the conclusion that it might be, and probably was on account of his violation of the Sabbath by employing it in secular business. He therefore, from that time, abandoned the practice of doing any thing for his clients on that day. The difficulty ceased. His efforts on Monday were as successful as on other days. Such were the facts in his case, and many others have testified to similar facts in their experience.

(*c*) TESTIMONY OF A FINANCIER. — A distinguished financier, charged with an immense amount of property during the great pecuniary pressure of 1836 and 1837, said, "I should have been a dead man, had it not been for the Sabbath. Obliged to work from morning till night, through the whole week, I felt on Saturday, es pecially Saturday *afternoon*, as if I *must* have *rest*. It was like going into a dense fog. Every thing looked dark and gloomy, as if nothing could be saved. I dismissed all, and kept the Sabbath in the good old way. On Monday it was all bright sunshine. I could see through, and I got through. But had it not been for the Sabbath, I have no doubt I should have been in the grave."

(*d*) FRUITFUL CAUSE OF INSANITY.—A distinguished merchant, who, for twenty years did a vast amount of business, remarked to Dr. Edwards: "Had it not been for the Sabbath, I have no doubt I should have been a maniac long ago." This was mentioned in a company of merchants, when one remarked, "That is the case exactly with Mr. ——. He was one of our greatest importers. He used to say that the Sabbath was the best day in the week to plan successful voyages; showing that his mind had no Sabbath. He has been in the Insane Hospital for years, and will probably die there." Many men are there, or in the maniac's grave, because they had no Sabbath. They broke a law of *nature*, and of nature's God, and found "the way of the transgressor to be hard." Such cases are so numerous that a British writer remarks, "We never knew a man work seven days in a week who did not kill himself or kill his mind."

(*e*) DR. SEWALL'S OPINION.—Thomas Sewall, M. D., professor of pathology and the practice of medicine in the Columbian College, Washington, D. C., remarks: "While I consider it the more important design of the institution of the Sabbath to assist in religious devotion, and advance men's spiritual welfare, I have long held the opinion that one of its chief benefits has reference to his *physical* and *intellectual* constitution; affording him, as it does, one day in seven for the renovation of his exhausted energies of body and mind; a proportion of time small enough, according to the results of my observation, for the accomplishment of this object. I have remarked, as a general fact, that those to whom the Sabbath brings the most *entire* rest from their habitual labors, perform the secular duties of the week more vigorously, and better than those who continue them without intermission. I have no hesitation in declaring it as my opinion, that if the Sabbath were universally observed as a day of devotion, and of rest from secular occupations, *far more work of body and mind would be accomplished, and be better done; more health would be enjoyed, with more of wealth and independence, and we should have far less of crime, and poverty and suffering.*"

381. Providential Benefits.

(*a*) THE CONSCIENTIOUS ESQUIMAUX.—In December, says Mr. Barsoe, the Missionary, a pleasing circumstance occurred; it showed the reverence of our Esquimaux for the Lord's day. Owing to the state of the weather during the preceding month, but few seals had been taken; and Saturday, the second of December, was the first day on which the state of the ice permitted our people to go out on the seal-hunt. Considering the great uncertainty which ever attends this occupation, the inducement to pursue it on the following day, in the hope of securing a better provision for their families, was any thing but slight. We were, therefore, not a little pleased to learn that a meeting of fathers of families had been convened on the Saturday evening, and that it had been resolved that they would none of them go out on the ensuing day of the Lord, but would spend it in a manner becoming the disciples of Christ, who were invited thankfully to commemorate his coming into the world to save sinners. They expressed their belief that their Heavenly Father was able to grant them, on Monday, a sufficiency for the supply of their wants. The meeting they closed with the singing of some verses, during which they felt the presence and peace of their Lord and Savior. Their confidence in God was not put to shame. On Monday the weather proved so favorable that they captured no fewer than one hundred seals; but in the course of the following night the frost became so intense as to close all the bays and inlets, and to preclude any further attempts to take seals.

(*b*) THE CONVERTED BAKER.—A baker, who had long been accustomed to attend to his business on the Lord's day, having had his attention drawn to religion, and having felt its power, became desirous of associating with a body of Christians; who, however, declined to receive him, unless he relinquished baking on the Sabbath. The struggle in his mind was long and painful, as a considerable part of the support of his family was derived from his occupation on that day, but he at length yielded to the claims of duty; and, by refusing to serve his customers on the Lord's day, gave them offence, and became reduced to great poverty. His Christian friends urged him to persevere, assuring him that God would not forsake him. He was enabled to do so, and Providence interposed in his behalf. His customers gradually returned to him, and at length he was favored with a larger share of business than had ever before fallen to his lot.

(*c*) STATEMENT OF CAPTAIN SCORESBY.—"It is a little remarkable," says Captain Scoresby, in his voyage to Greenland, "that during the whole of this voyage, no circumstance ever occurred to prevent us engaging in public worship on the Sabbath day. In a few instances, the hour of worship could not be easily kept, but opportunity was always found of having each of the services in succession on a plan adopted at the commencement of the voyage. And it is worthy of observation, that in no instance, when on fishing stations, was our refraining from the ordinary duties of our profession on the Sunday ever supposed, eventually, to have been a loss to us; for we in general found, that, if others who were less regardful, or had not the same view of the obligatory nature of the command respecting the Sabbath day, succeeded in their endeavors to promote the success of the voyage, we seldom failed to procure a decided advantage in the succeeding week. Independently, indeed, of the divine blessing on honoring the Sabbath day, I found that the restraint put upon the natural inclinations of the men for pursuing the fishery at all opportunities, acted with some advantage, by proving an extraordinary stimulus to their exertions when they were next sent out after whales. Were it not out of place here, I could relate several instances in which, after our refraining to fish upon the Sabbath, while others were thus successfully employed, our subsequent labors succeeded under circumstances so striking, that there was not, I believe, a man in the ship who did not consider it the effect of the divine blessing."

(*d*) THE SHOP-KEEPER AND HER CUSTOMERS—Mrs. Sarah Thorp, of Buckingham, (Engl.,) was left a widow with four small children, and with nothing to support herself and them but the profits of small chandler's shop, an annuity of ten pounds per annum, left to poor widows, and making a little lace. While in this state, a Mr. Cooper came to the church, and sounded an alarm to formal professors, moralists, and the profane. Mrs. Thorp soon became convinced of the impropriety of keeping her shop open on the Lord's day, and determined at all events to shut it up, and told her customers, in the week preceding, of her intention, and begged of them to come for what they wanted on the Saturday. At first they took very little notice of it, but went on Sunday as usual; but Mrs. Thorp shut herself in a back room, and paid no attention to the door. The ensuing week they came again, and were very much displeased, saying they must have victuals on Sunday as well as on the other days; and if they could not be served by her they would go where they could. She said she should be sorry to lose their custom, but she had served on the Lord's day too long. Many of her customers left her, and, for a time, she was much straitened in her circumstances; but this did not continue: the Lord blessed her business with increase, so that in a little time she took the house adjoining to her own, keeping the shop for her increasing stock, as before this she had lived in the shop. Finding her business still increase, she was enabled to send to London for goods, which she had hitherto taken from a superior shop in the town. After this, she went to the gentleman of whom she had received her annuity, and told him the Lord had so blessed her in her circumstances, that she had now no need of it, and begged he would confer it on some one who was in greater necessity. The Lord still continued to bless her; she at length bought the house and shop, and lived comfortably in them the remainder of her days.

(*e*) THREE SHIPHOLDERS.—"Several years ago," says a correspondent of the N. York Evangelist, "there lived in one of our seaports, A. B. and C., all of whom were owners of merchant vessels. Each of these men loaded a ship at the same time, which was to go first to Egypt, and then to the Baltic, - one of the Russian ports. All being loaded, they waited for a favorable wind. The harbor was so situated that there was no egress for ships except the wind blew in a particular direction. On Sabbath morning the wind was fair. The masters of the vessels went to their respective owners for sailing orders. A. and B. immediately had their ships put to sea; but C. told the master that he must remain in port till the next day. Before Monday morning the wind had changed, and remained contrary till the next Sunday, when it again came round fair. The master of the vessel again repaired to the house of C. to procure the ship's papers, and sailing orders. But, to his astonishment, C. remarked that his ship must not leave port on the Sabbath. The captain attempted to reason the point with him, but all in vain. He said if his ship never sailed it should not put to sea on the Lord's day. He was willing to trust in Divine Providence. Some time during the following week the ship sailed. It arrived in Egypt just as the ships of A. and B. were about to sail for the Baltic. In the meantime information had circulated through the country that American vessels were in port, wishing to sell their cargoes, and purchase a certain kind of their produce, which, if I mistake not, was rice. The desired article was brought in such abundance that the market was glutted by the time C.'s ship arrived. In consequence of this his cargo was sold at an advanced price, and his ship loaded at a much better rate than the others. C.'s vessel then proceeded on her voyage up the Baltic. The ships were to dispose of their rice in the Russian port, and load for home with iron. C.'s ship arrived in the Baltic after those of A. and B. had purchased their freight, and nearly loaded. Fortune, or to speak more properly, Providence operated here much as it did in the Mediterranean. Abundance of iron was brought to market, and there were enough purchasers for the rice. All these ships reached America about the same time, that of C. having cleared as much by the voyage as both the others. Thus C. found by experience, that "in keeping God's commands there is great reward," even in this world.

(*f*) THE HIDE TRADERS AND THE SABBATH.—I was in command of a vessel, says Capt. S., of V——, Mass., engaged in the Hide trade, between N—— and a port in Brazil. In performing one of those voyages, several occurrences took place strictly providential, and illustrative of the benefits to be derived from a concientious regard to the Sabbath.

The custom of the Brazilian port, was to load vessels on the Sabbath. This labor was performed by *gangs* of negroes, under the direction of *stevedores*. These stevedores were few in number; and, in times of great hurry of business, in order to an equitable division of their services, the vessels were accustomed to take their turns in the order in which they were reported as ready to receive cargo. If, when the time came round for a particular vessel to load, she was not ready, her name was transferred to the bottom of the list. It was my lot to experience some of the effects of this custom.

My turn came to load. The work commenced and continued till Saturday night, when I ordered the *hatches* closed, and forbid any work being done on board till Monday morning. The *stevedore* and his *gang*, muttering curses, left the vessel, threatening to do no more work on board.

Monday came. I made application to the commission merchant, and was informed that I had lost my turn in loading, and must wait until it came round again, and that the *stevedore* and his *gang* had gone on board another vessel.

To aggravate my disappointment, I found that a hostile feeling had sprung up against me, and was participated in by all around. The merchant was studiously polite and respectful as before, but no longer familiar. Masters of vessels avoided my society. Evil disposed persons busied themselves in doing me secret injuries, cutting my rigging in the night time, and in other ways showing their malice. Our devotional exercises, morning and evening, were interrupted, and our efforts to do good derided and mocked.

Thus things went on, until our turn came round again; when, there being no other vessel ready to load, we were left to do our work in our own way. The loss of time, occasioned by the refusal to load on the Sabbath, amounted to several weeks; but after all was it in fact a loss? The result will show.

It was now Saturday night again, the lading of the ship was completed, and we were ready for sea.

The Sabbath dawned, and with it came a fresh and fair wind. Shall we improve it, and violate the day, and that too after so many sacrifices to promote its sanctification? It was not to be thought of, and hoisting the Bethel flag as an invitation for our shipmates to come on board, we spent the day in devotional exercises. It was a happy Sabbath to all on board.

Monday morning early we were under sail for the lower harbor, several miles distant. On our way, we passed two brigs aground with lighters along side discharging their hides in order to lighten them and get them off. *They* left the upper harbor on the Sabbath, and here they were, and like to be until the next fair wind had blown itself out. On reaching the lower harbor we found to our surprise, lying at anchor, upwards of forty sail of shipping waiting for a wind. Among them were all the vessels that had cleared for the last month or more, including every vessel that had obtained an advantage over us in respect to loading.

We had now to obtain a pilot and get to sea when the wind came fair and before it had spent itself. These were by no means matters easy to be accomplished. Pilots were few, and vessels many, and here, too, the principle of rotation was rigidly enforced. The winds, meanwhile, when fair, were short-lived and feeble, and the *bar* at the entrance of the harbor, too dangerous to pass without a pilot.

But He who had sustained us through previous trials for his name's sake, did not forsake us now. A pilot who had been on a long visit to the *interior*, returned to the sea-board and resumed his duties on the very day we reached the outer harbor, and presenting himself on board, offered to pilot us to sea.

Tuesday morning found us, with a fair wind, a pilot on board, and under way at day-light. We were the second vessel over the *bar*, and among the first to arrive in the United States.

The getting out of cargo, its exposure and sale, were matters of no little interest. We *then* found that "in keeping the commandments of God there is great reward." Our cargo, owing to the delay in getting it on board, received unusual attention at our hands, and was in perfect shipping order when stowed away, and came out in the same good condition.

The cargoes of the other vessels came out very differently, with a loss in some cases of 20, 30, and even 50 per cent. This loss was occasioned in part by hurrying the hides on board in the first instance without their being thoroughly dried, in order to greater dispatch, and in part to the unusual detention of the vessels at the port of lading. From these two causes combined, and the activity of the *wevils* that took possession of the hides, and riddled them through and through, several of those voyages turned out splendid failures.

(*g*) FOUR FISHING VESSELS.—Capt. Bourne states that about 1829, he went out from Rhode Island in a brig on a fishing voyage along the coast of Labrador, with a crew of thirteen men. Three other vessels, with larger crews, from the same state, accompanied him. When they arrived upon the ground, Captain B. determined that he and his crew should sacredly regard the Sabbath; but the other crews prosecuted their employment on that day the same as on others. After fishing with them in company for two weeks, and finding it in some respects quite disagreeable, he parted from them, and went farther north, and fished in company with English vessels, who pursued the same course respecting the Sabbath day which he did himself. Trusting in that Providence which favors those who regard the true and right, he was not disappointed. He and his men succeeded in getting a "full voyage," cured their fish and sold it some four weeks sooner than any of the Sabbath-breaking vessels that accompanied them. What was better, Capt. B. and his crew made more profits to a share in less time, than those who profaned the Sabbath and wore themselves out by laboring hard seven days in the week.

(*h*) SABBATH-KEEPING FISHERMEN.—A gentleman, says Dr. Edwards, who resides in a fishing town, and who has made extensive inquiries, remarks, "Those who fish on the Sabbath do not, ordinarily, take any more, during the season, than those who keep the Sabbath. They do not make more money, or prosper better for this world.

One man followed fishing eight years. The first four he fished on the Sabbath. The next four he strictly kept the Sabbath, and is satisfied that it was for his advantage in a temporal point of view. Another man, who was accustomed for some years to fish on the Sabbath, afterwards discontinued it, and found that his profits were greater than before. Another man testifies that, in the year 1827, he and his men took more fish by far than any who were associated with them, though he kept the Sabbath and they did not. It was invariably his practice to rest from Saturday till Monday. Though it was an unfavorable season for the fisheries, he was greatly prospered in every way, and to such an extent that many regarded his success as almost miraculous.

Examples like the above might be multiplied to almost any extent. So far as I can learn by diligent inquiry, all who have left off fishing on the Sabbath, *without an exception*, think the change has been for their temporal advantage.

(*i*) IMPORTANT TESTIMONY.—A gentlemen, says Dr. Edwards, belonging to a fishing town, which sends out more than two hundred vessels in a year, writes as follows: "I think it may safely be stated that those vessels which have not fished on the Sabbath have, taken together, met with *more than ordinary success*. The vessel whose earnings were the highest, the last year and the year before, was one on board which the Sabbath was kept by refraining from labor, and by religious worship. There is one firm which has had eight vessels in its employ this season. Seven have fished on the Sabbath, and one has not. That one has earned seven hundred dollars more than the most successful of the six. There are two other firms employing each three vessels. Two out of the three, in each case, have kept the Sabbath, and in each case have earned *more than two-thirds of the profits*."

(*j*) SAD END OF SABBATH-BREAKERS.—A distinguished merchant, in a large city, said to Dr. Edwards, "It is about thirty years since I came to this city; and every man through this whole range, who came down to his store, or suffered his counting-room to be opened on the Sabbath, has lost his property. There is no need of breaking the Sabbath, and no benefit from it. We have not had a vessel leave the harbor on the Sabbath for more than twenty years. It is altogether better to get them off on a week day than on the Sabbath." It is better even for this world. And so with all kinds of secular business. Men may seem to gain for a time by the profanation of the Sabbath; *but it does not end well*. Their disappointment, even here, often comes suddenly.

382. Examples of the Conscientious, &c.

(*a*) MATTHEW HALE'S EXAMPLE.—The following declaration of Sir Matthew Hale is an illustration of this truth:

"Though my hands and my mind

have been as full of secular business, both before and after I was judge, as, it may be, any man's in England, yet I never wanted time in six days to ripen and fit myself for the business and employments I had to do, though I borrowed not one minute from the Lord's day to prepare for it, by study or otherwise. But, on the other hand, if I had, at any time, borrowed from this day any time for my secular employment, I found it did further me less than if I had let it alone; and therefore, when some years' experience, upon a most attentive and vigilant observation, had given me this instruction, I grew peremptorily resolved never in this kind to make a breach upon the Lord's day, which I have now strictly observed for more than thirty years."

(*b*) WASHINGTON'S EXAMPLE.—In one of the towns of Connecticut, when the roads were extremely bad, Washington, the President of the United States, was overtaken one Saturday night, not being able to reach the village where he designed to rest on the Sabbath. Next morning, about sun-rise, his coach was harnessed, and he was proceeding forwards to an inn, near the place of worship which he proposed to attend. A plain man, who was an informing officer, came from a cottage, and inquired of the coachman, whether there was any urgent reason for his traveling on the Lord's day. The general, instead of resenting this as impertinent rudeness, ordered the driver to stop, and with great civility explained the circumstances to the officer, commending him for his fidelity, and assuring him that nothing was farther from his intention than to treat with disrespect the laws and usages of Connecticut, relative to the Sabbath, which met his most cordial approbation. How many admirers of Washington might receive instruction and reproof from his example!

(*c*) SENTENCE WORTHY OF REMEMBRANCE.—A man who had been accustomed to go with the cars on week days, informed his wife that he had been requested to go with the cars on the Sabbath. She replied, "I take it for granted that you do not intend to go." Such was her confidence in her husband, that she took it for granted that he would not do a wicked thing for money. He told her that, if he should not go, he might lose his place; that he had no other employment, the times were hard, and he had a family to support. "I know it," said she, "but I hope you will not forget that, if a man cannot support a family by keeping the Sabbath, he certainly cannot support them by breaking it"—a sentence which ought to be written in letters of gold, and held up to the view of all Christendom. "I am very glad," said the man, "that you think so. I think so myself. That was what I wanted—to see whether we think alike." He told the superintendent that he liked his situation, and should be very sorry to lose it, but that he could not go with the mail on the Sabbath; that he wished to attend public worship, and go with his children to the Sabbath-school. He did not lose his place, nor did he suffer in a pecuniary point of view. He prospered more than before, and lived to bear his testimony, not only to the duty, but to the utility, even for this world, of keeping the Sabbath.

(*d*) JOHN ADAMS AND THE SABBATH.—The elder John Adams, while President of the United States, as he was returning from the country to his family in Boston, was interrupted by a New England snow storm, which effectually blocked up his way. He was then at Andover, twenty miles from Boston, where his family, as he had learned, were waiting his arrival. Sabbath morning, the roads became for the first time passable. On the question of going to Boston that day, it was the opinion of the clergyman of the place, that the circumstances of his detention, and the sickness of his family would justify his traveling on the Sabbath. His reply was, that the justifiable occasion in this case would not prevent the bad influence of his example on those who might see him traveling on the Sabbath, without knowing the cause. He therefore decided to wait till Monday.

(*e*) HAPPY EFFECTS OF DECISION.—In one of the ports near the southern shore of Lake Erie, the little band of Christians were often disturbed by the arrival and departure of steamboats and stages, especially by one chiefly owned in the village, which left the port regularly every Sabbath morning. The Presbyterian minister exerted himself both in public and private to enlighten the people, and show them the duty of keeping the Sabbath holy; and publicly announced his determination to do his best to have the Sabbath-breaker as promptly disciplined as any other sinner.

One Saturday night about sunset, an estimable member of his church called to ask his advice. He said he had business to a large amount that must be done at the bank in B—, on Wednesday, or a sad loss of credit and money would be the consequence; that he had calculated to go in a boat on Friday; but storms had prevented it coming in, that the stage would go on the Sabbath, and not again till Tuesday; that the boat then in the harbor would go out in the morning, but no other boat was expected for some days. And now what should he do? He was not rich, and a delay would cost him a serious loss. He had subscribed beyond his means (and such was the fact,) for building a meeting-house, and supporting the minister, and economized in every way possible to meet his debts.

He was told that his case was a hard one; but that the circumstances of it would not justify him in breaking the command of God; that he had better lose a hundred dollars, or go on horseback, or even on foot to the next port (50 miles) than break the Sabbath. Seeing that his minister was inflexible, he relinquished his Sabbath voyage, called on several others in town in similar circumstances, mostly professed Christians, told them his determination, and invited them to go with him in extra stages early on Monday morning. This they did, and had a pleasant and profitable trip.

The steamboat lost by that single circumstance upwards of one hundred and twenty dollars. And the proprietors of the boat immediately changed the day of leaving the port from Sunday to Thursday. And the following year, their boat was regularly laid by every Sabbath through the season.

EVILS OF SABBATH-BREAKING.

383. Vice and Crime.

(*a*) ENGLISH CRIMINALS.—A gentleman in England, who was in the habit, for more than twenty years, of daily visiting convicts, states that, almost universally, when brought to a sense of their condition, they lamented their neglect of the Sabbath, and pointed to their violation of it as the *principal cause* of their ru . That prepared them for, and led them on, step by step, to the commission of other crimes, and finally to the commission of that which brought them to the prison, and often to the gallows. He has letters almost innumerable, he says, from others, proving the same thing, and that they considered the violation of the Sabbath the great cause of their ruin. He has attended three hundred and fifty at the place of execution, when they were put to death for their crimes. And nine out of ten who were brought to a sense of their condition attributed the greater part of their departure from God to their neglect of the Sabbath.

(*b*) TESTIMONY OF CRIMINALS.—A gentleman, who was conversant with prisoners for more than thirty years, stated, that he found in all his experience, both with regard to those who had been capitally convicted and those who had not, that they referred to the violation of the Sabbath as the chief cause of their crimes; and that this has been confirmed by all the opportunities he has had of examining prisoners. Not that this has been the only cause of crime; but, like the use of intoxicating liquors, it has greatly increased public and private immorality, and been the means, in a multitude of cases, of premature death.

(*c*) A WARDEN'S TESTIMONY.—A gentleman, who has had charge of more than one hundred thousand prisoners, and has taken special pains to ascertain the causes of their crimes says, that he does not recollect a single case of capital offence where the party had not been a Sabbath-breaker. And in many cases they assured him that Sabbath-breaking was the first step in their downward course. Indeed, he says, with reference to prisoners of al classes, *nineteen out of twenty have neglected the Sabbath and other ordinances of religion.* And he has often met with prisoners about to expiate their crimes by an ignominious death, who earnestly enforced upon the survivors the necessity of an observance of the Sabbath, and ascribed their own course of iniquity to a non-observance of that day.

Says the keeper of one of the largest prisons, "*Nine-tenths of our inmates are those who did not value the Sabbath, and were not in the habit of attending public worship.*"

(*d*) VOICE FROM AUBURN PRISON.—Of twelve hundred and thirty-two convicts who had been committed to the Auburn State Prison previously to the year 1838, four hundred and forty-seven had been watermen, either boatmen or sailors—men who, to a great extent, had been kept at work on the Sabbath, and thus deprived of the rest and privileges of that day. Of those twelve hundred and thirty-two convicts, only twenty-six had conscientiously kept the Sabbath.

(*e*) CRIMINALS IN MASS. STATE PRISON.—Of one hundred men admitted to the Massachusetts State Prison in one year, eighty-nine had lived in habitual violation of the Sabbath and neglect of public worship.

(*f*) SUSPICIOUS APPRENTICE.—A distinguished merchant, long accustomed to extensive observation and experience, and who had gained an uncommon knowledge of men, said, "When I see one of my apprentices or clerks riding out on the Sabbath, on Monday I dismiss him. Such an one cannot be trusted."

(*g*) MURDERERS IN NEWGATE.—In the evening, says a writer in an English Magazine, I stepped into St. Sepulchre's, Snow-hill. Dr. Rudge, a preacher of some note in the metropolis, is evening lecturer here and we had a sermon from him in behalf of a parochial charity, by which fifty-one poor boys of the parish are supported and educated. He took occasion to remark, that his official situation (as chaplain to Newgate) often led him to hear the confessions of malefactors, under sentence of death; and that in almost every instance, they ascribed their ruin to their desertion of the house of God, and the violation of the day of rest.

384. Various Evils.

(*a*) LESSON FOR YOUNG MEN.—Seven young men, in a town in Massachusetts, started in the same business nearly at the same time. Six of them had some property or assistance from their friends, and followed their business seven days in a week. The other had less property than either of the six. He had less assistance from others, and worked in his business only six days in a week. He is now (1845) the only man who has property, and has not failed in his business.

(*b*) "THE FINGER OF GOD."—A man who ridiculed the idea that God makes a difference in his providence between those who yield visible obedience to his laws and those who do not, had been engaged, on a certain Sabbath, in gathering his crops into his barn. The next week he had occasion to take fire out into his field in order to burn some brush. He left it, as he supposed, safely, and went in to dinner. The wind took the fire and carried it into his barn-yard, which was filled with combustibles, and, before he was aware of it, the flames were bursting out of his barn. He arose in amazement, saw that all was lost, and fixing his eyes on the curling flames, stood speechless. Then, pointing to the rising column of fire, he said, with a solemn emphasis, "That is the finger of God."

(*c*) FAILURES OF SABBATH-BREAKERS.—The following fact, communicated by a respectable merchant of New-York, is well worthy of notice:—"I have particularly observed," says the gentleman, "that those merchants in New-York who have kept their counting-rooms open on the Sabbath day, during my residence there (twenty-five years), have failed without exception."

In another part of the country an old man remarked, "I can recollect more than fifty years; but I cannot recollect a case of a man, in this town, who was accustomed to work on the Sabbath, who did not fail or lose his property before he died."

(*d*) WAY WHICH WORKS BEST.—A distinguished mechanic, in a part of the country where the Sabbath was disregarded, had been accustomed for a time to keep his men at work on that day. He was afterwards at work for a man who regarded the Sabbath, and who, on Saturday, was anxious to know what he intended to do; and therefore asked, "What do you expect to do to-morrow?" He said, "I expect to stop, and keep the Sabbath. I used to work on the Sabbath, and often obtained higher wages than on other days. But I so often lost, during the week, more than all I could gain on the Sabbath, that I gave it up years ago. I have kept the Sabbath since, and I find it works better." It does work better. And all who make the experiment will, in due time, find it so.

(*e*) MORE LOSSES THAN GAINS.—"I used," said the master of a vessel, "sometimes to work on the Sabbath; but something would happen, by which I lost so much more than I gained by working on the Sabbath, that on one occasion, after having been at work and met with some disaster, I swore most profanely that I never would work again, or suffer my men to work on that day. And I never have." He finds it works better. He does not swear now. He has induced many others not to swear, and not to break the Sabbath. He finds that in the keeping of God's commands there is great reward. All who obey them will find the same.

(*f*) OLD MAN'S REMARK.—An old gentleman in Boston remarked, "Men do not gain any thing by working on the Sabbath. I can recollect men who, when I was a boy, used to load their vessels down on the Long Wharf, and keep their men at work from morning to night on the Sabbath day. But they have come to nothing. Their children have come to nothing. Depend upon it, men do not gain any thing, in the end, by working on the Sabbath."

(*g*) THE PEDLER'S EXPERIENCE.—The Rev. Dr. Benedict, of Plainfield, gave a writer in the Connecticut Observer, the following account a few years before his death.

Soon after he left college he had occasion to travel southward as far as the State of North Carolina. Being unacquainted with the way, he was desirous of finding some one to accompany him. A man who had frequently traveled that road in the business of a pedler, was about to commence the journey, and informed him that it would afford him pleasure to be his companion and guide. They accordingly set out together. At the close of the week Mr. B. remarked to his companion, that the journey thus far had been pleasant to him; "but," added he, "I know not how I shall do next week, provided you intend to continue your journey on the Sabbath. I cannot proceed till Monday, and if you leave me, I shall probably lose my way." The man replied, "I have not traveled on the Sabbath for several years, though my business leads me to take long journeys. I formerly did; but I always lost more than I gained by the practice. Some hinderance or accident would occur on the following week, which convinced me that it is for my interest to rest upon the Sabbath."

385. Sabbath-breaking Unnecessary.

(*a*) SABBATH-KEEPING MILL-OWNER.—At the second annual meeting of the Society for Promoting the due Observance of the Lord's Day, the Rev. H. Stowell stated, that at a large meeting, which was held at Manchester, (Eng.,) to petition the legislature on the better observance of the Sabbath, a leading spinner came forward, and said, that there was nothing more common than to hear from his brother spinners and master manufacturers this assertion, "If you stop the mill altogether on Sunday, you must frequently stop it on Monday also; because, if the engine gets out of order, or any other necessary repair be required, it must be done on the Sunday, or the mill cannot proceed on the Monday." Now, all this seems mighty plausible, said the good man, but I can prove it to be false; for in my mill I never suffer a stroke to be struck on the Sabbath; and on one occasion, my boiler had suffered a misfortune on a Saturday, and I feared the mill must stop on the Monday, but determined to try what could be done. I sent for a leading engineer, and said to him, "Can you have the mill ready to work on Monday morning?" "Yes, certainly I can." "But then," said I, "you mean to work on Sunday?" "Of course, sir." "But," said I, "you shall not do it in my mill." "But I cannot mend the boiler, if I do not," said he. I said, "I do not care, you shall not work in my mill on Sunday. I would rather that my mill stood the whole of Monday, than that the Sabbath should be violated in it!" The man said, "You are different from all other masters." I said, "My Bible, not the conduct of others, is my rule; and you must do it without working on Sunday, or I will try to get somebody else." This had the desired effect: they set to work, and worked till twelve o'clock on the Saturday night, and began again at twelve o'clock on the Sunday night; and the repairs were finished, and the mill was in full work, at the usual hour on Monday morning.

(*b*) THE DRUGGIST'S CONFESSION.—A chemist and druggist once remarked to an American author, "There was a time when I used to court business on the Lord's day; and, sheltering myself under the alleged necessity of being at hand to supply medicine in case of illness, I employed myself in preparing a quantity of tinctures, weighing packets of soda-water powders, and many such like things, not because they were needed, but really for the sake of saving time on other days. At that time I did take more money on the Sabbath than on any other day, no a penny in a shilling of which was for matters of real necessity. When I began to see it my duty to act differently, and refused to sell, on the Sabbath, perfumery, cigars, and other matters, of mere luxury and fancy, I offended a few of my customers, and expected to find that I had seriously injured my business; but in a little time people fell into my arrangements, and left off coming for such things. I now enjoy my Sabbaths undisturbed, except in cases of real need, to which, of course, I readily attend. Every customer whom I would wish to return has come back to me; and, taking into account the saving of Sunday expenses, which almost invariably countervail Sunday gains, I can say, with humble thankfulness, that my prosperity is now greater than ever."

(*c*) THE PHYSICIAN AND HIS PATIENTS.—A distinguished practitioner was harassed with calls on the Sabbath—his Sabbaths were broken—he was detained from public worship; it was a trial to him to be obliged to serve his patrons so often and so constantly on the Sabbath. At length he adopted this expedient: he let it be known that he viewed the Sabbath as the Lord's day—sacred to his worship, and that he must regard his calls upon the sick on that day as works of *necessity and mercy, and that he should make no charge for his services on that day.* He supposed that people would not call on him in these circumstances, that they would have too much goodness to ask his services gratuitously, and that he should have few calls and be free to attend public worship. But to his surprise it increased the evil;—if his services were to be given on the Sabbath, every body wanted him on the Sabbath; and he was sent for here and there and all about. There was no keeping the Sabbath so. *He accordingly changed the tables, and gave out that he should make a double charge for travels and visits on the Sabbath*, and of course it would cost as much again to be sick on the Sabbath as any other day of the week. This expedient had the desired effect; he could do up his business Saturday night, and with the exception o a few extreme cases, he could have hi

Sabbaths for religious uses, and regularly attend public worship.

(*d*) THE MINISTER HIRING HIS NEIGHBOR.—An eminent minister in Wales, hearing of a neighbor who followed his calling on the Lord's day, went and aked him why he broke the Sabbath. The man replied, that he was driven to it, by finding it hard work to maintain his family. "Will you attend public worship," said Mr. P., "if I pay you a week day's wages?" "Yes, most gladly," said the poor man. He attended constantly, and received his pay. After some time Mr. P. forgot to send the money; and recollecting it, called upon the man and said, "I am in your debt." "No, sir," he replied, "you are not." "How so," said Mr. P., "I have not paid you of late." "True," answered the man, "but I can now trust God; for I have found that he can bless the work of six days for the support of my family, just the same as seven." Ever after that he strictly kept the Sabbath, and found that in keeping God's commands, there is not only no loss, but great reward.

386. SABBATH-BREAKERS REPROVED.

(*a*) THE BLIND MAN AND HIS WIFE.—A pious man came into western New-York, from one of the New England States. He was then perfectly blind. He had a near relative in this country, who advised him to leave or sell his farm, and come and reside with him, to be taken care of. He then had a wife of a similar religious character, (since dead.) They accepted the proposal of their relative and came; and, coming from society highly refined and moral, they were not prepared to encounter the disadvantages, and real evils, which attended a society the reverse of this. Their first Sabbath in "York state," he declared, would never be forgotten. No sooner was its sacred dawn ushered in, than shooting and other recreations commenced in the immediate vicinity of his relative, while the latter, being a merchant, dealt out the whisky to all who applied. Consequently the day was trampled on, and its hallowed hours spent in dissipation. Before breakfast, which was delayed to receive a party of visitors from another town, this devoted pair resolved to seek some retreat from the noise and profaneness, fled into an adjacent wood, the wife taking the Bible and leading her blind husband. Here, in the deep solitude of the forest, they spent the first Sabbath in fasting and prayer, and reading the Word of God. After the Sabbath was past, they informed their relative, they could not live with him if such were the manner of spending the Sabbath, in amusements and dissipation. They must have a house of their own. He replied, that it would avail nothing, for people would visit him on the Sabbath. Mr. D—— said firmly, that he would risk their visits to him. Accordingly a house was provided. The first Sabbath in their new residence, two of their neighbors called to see them, one of whom was a magistrate. His wife was reading the Bible. After passing the usual compliments, and providing seats, she went on reading aloud. Before the chapter was finished, one of the visitors left, and before the close of the second, the other left. But he was not troubled with visitors. He commenced visiting some of his ungodly neighbors, and conversing with them on the subject of religion, his wife leading him. Soon they began to hold meetings on the Sabbath, and many attended. The wife read sermons, and the husband prayed and exhorted. One wicked man, whose shop was opposite the meeting, set open his door, and worked in order to disturb it. The next Sabbath, this same man came into the meeting, fell on his knees, confessing his sins and asking forgiveness. The Lord came down by his Spirit on that wicked neighborhood, and forty became the members of a church, afterwards formed in that place, as the fruits of that re vival. There was no regular preaching in the place previously, and it was evidently through the instrumentality of this blind man and his wife. That church, the writer is acquainted with. It is quite flourishing. They have built a handsome house of worship, and settled a minister to break unto them the bread of life.

(*b*) MR. CRUDEN AND THE GARDENER.—Mr. Cruden, during the last year of his life, lived in terms of the strictest intimacy with the Rev. David Wilson, minister of the Presbyterian congregation, Bow Lane, London. The two friends were in the habit of paying frequent visits to Mr. Gordon, a pious nurseryman in the neighborhood of the metropolis. One evening Mr. Gordon informed Mr. Wilson, that a young Scottish gardener in his employment, who usually attended divine service at Bow Lane, sometimes absented himself from public worship without a sufficient cause, and was besides rather indolent, desiring the minister to admonish him. The young man was accordingly called into the parlor, and Mr. Wilson concluded a solemn address with these words: "Remember the Sabbath day, to keep it holy." "Have you done, sir?" said Mr. Cruden. "Yes," replied Mr. Wilson. "Then," rejoined Mr. Cruden, "you have forgotten one-half of the commandment: Six days shalt thou labor, and do all thy work, &c.; for if a man does not labor six days of the week, he is not likely to rest properly on the seventh."

(*c*) THE LOST MOTION.—A motion was once made in the House of Commons for raising and embodying the militia, and, for the purpose of saving time, to exercise them on the Sabbath. When the resolution was about to pass, an old gentleman stood up, and said, "Mr. Speaker, I have one objection to make to this; I believe in an old book called the Bible." The members looked at one another, and the motion was dropped.

SABBATH SCHOOLS.

VARIOUS SALUTARY INFLUENCES, ETC.

387. In Promoting Religious Knowledge and Intellectual Culture.

(*a*) THE "TENNESSEE TESTAMENT."—In the year 1831, a young man from Tennessee, apparently about twenty-two years of age, wandered into a Sabbath school in the State of Illinois, and after having gazed awhile upon the objects that surrounded him, seated himself near one of the classes that was then engaged in recitation. He was noticed by the superintendent as apparently much interested in what he heard, and at the close, was asked whether he would like to join the school. He replied promptly in the affirmative. Next Sabbath a place was assigned him in one of the classes; and after he had been there a few weeks, the superintendent offered him a library book, but he refused to take it, assigning as a reason that he was compelled to labor during the week for his livelihood, that he had little time for reading, and all he could spare from his work he wished to spend in reading his Testament. He was then holding one in his hand, which had been given him from the library; and as he spoke of his Testament, his countenance brightened, and he said, with much apparent feeling, "This Testament is worth twenty Tennessee Testaments." The superintendent was at first at a loss for his meaning; but a moment's reflection made it obvious. He had read the Testament in Tennessee, and loved it; but when he came to study it in the Sabbath school so much new light was thrown upon it by the instruction of the superintendent and his teacher, that the one which he used in the Sabbath school seemed to him a new book, and worth twenty of the Testaments which he had been accustomed to read in Tennessee.

(*b*) DAUGHTER EXPLAINING THE BIBLE.—A teacher called at a neighbor's house, and the parents being absent, questioned the children about the creation, the flood, &c. They appeared much surprised at the questions, and were as unable to answer them as though they had related to another planet. *They did not attend the Sabbath school.*

In the same neighborhood lived another child, whose age was about the average age of those children just mentioned, and her advantages, excepting the Sabbath school, of which she was a member, were no better than theirs. As her father called on the superintendent to inquire the meaning of a certain passage of Scripture, he remarked that he was in the habit of asking his daughter the meaning of obscure portions of the Bible, and that he seldom failed of obtaining a satisfactory explanation.

(*c*) A SCHOLAR BECOMING BLIND AND DEAF.—A writer in "The Children's Friend," for 1838, states that while attending an eminent surgeon to have an operation performed on one of his eyes, a friend of his led into the same room a young woman who was completely blind and deaf. This sad condition had been brought on suddenly, by a violent pain in the head. Her case was examined by a number of surgeons then present, all of whom pronounced it incurable. She was led back to the house of my friend, when she eagerly inquired what the doctor said about her case, and whether he could afford her any relief. The only method by which her inquiries could be answered was by tapping her hand, which signified No; and by squeezing it, which signified Yes; for she could not hear the loudest noise, nor distinguish day from night. She had to receive for her answer on this occasion, the unwelcome tap, No. She burst into tears, and wept aloud in all the bitterness of despair. "What!" said she, "shall I never again see the light of day, nor hear a human voice? Must I remain incapable of all social intercourse—shut up in silence and darkness while I live?" Again she wept. The scene was truly affecting. Had she been able to see, she might have been pointed to the Bible as a source of comfort. Had she been able to hear, words of consolation might have been spoken, but, alas! those channels to the mind were closed, to be opened no more in this world. Her friends could pity, but they could not relieve; and what made her case still more deplorable, she was an orphan, had no father or mother, or brother or sister, to pity and care for her. She was entirely dependent upon a few pious friends for her support. This she felt, and continued to weep, 'll my friend, with great presence of mind, took up the Bible, and placed it to her breast. She felt it, and said, "Is this the Bible?" She was answered that it was. She held it to her bosom, and said, "This is the only comfort I have left, though I shall never be able to read it any more;" and began to repeat some of its promises, such as, "Cast thy burden on the Lord, and he will sustain thee." "As thy day is, so shall thy strength be." "Call upon me in the day of trouble, and I will deliver thee." "My grace is sufficient for thee," etc. In a moment she dried her tears, and became one of the happiest persons I ever saw. She never seemed to deplore her condition afterwards. I have many times heard her speak of the strong consolations she felt.

Happily for this young woman, she had been taken, when a very little girl, to a Sunday School, where she enjoyed the only opportunity she ever had of learning to read the Bible, and where she had committed to memory those passages of Scripture which now became her comfort. With great gratitude she used to speak of her teachers, who, she said, not only taught her to read, but took pains to instruct her in the things that belonged to her eternal peace. "What would have become of me, had I not then been taught the way of salvation, for now I am deprived of all outward means?" was her constant language.

(*d*) MILITARY PENSIONER.—An aged man in America, a military pensioner, who commenced his Christian life at threescore years and ten, was induced to join a Sabbath school. Speaking of the benefits derived from the school, he said he had been in the habit of reading the Bible from his youth, and had read it through many times, and thought he understood it tolerably well; but when he joined the Sabbath school, he found it was necessary to do something more than read the Bible. He had to *search* the Scriptures. And it led him to observe, that we are nowhere commanded to read the Bible, but every where directed and encouraged to "*search* the Scriptures."

388. Influence in Promoting Attendance on Public Worship.

(*a*) LEADING PARENTS TO WORSHIP.—A little girl one Sabbath morning was much affected under the sermon, and on her return home, earnestly entreated her mother would accompany her to chapel in the evening to hear how delightfully the minister talked about Jesus Christ. The child was so intent on this object that she made the request with tears, and the mother, at last, consented to accompany her importunate girl to the chapel. The preacher chose for his text, "I am not ashamed of the gospel of Christ; for it is the power of God unto salvation," Rom. i. 16. The woman was seriously and effectually impressed by the word of God, was led earnestly to seek salvation, and obtained mercy by faith in Christ Jesus. The wife now naturally became anxious for the salvation of her husband, and persuaded him also to attend the chapel. He also submitted to the influence of the truth, and both the parents became grateful to God for the child whose importunity led them to hear the gospel of salvation.

(*b*) DYING GIRL AND HER FATHER.—A little girl went to the Peter-street, Wardour-street, Sunday school, Westminster, for about two years: her conduct and conversation were always very exemplary. Her parents paid little or no regard to religion; but when, on a Sunday, her father was going out to take his pleasure she would often say, "Father, the people are going and coming out of church, why do you not go?" and such like expressions. Her death was caused by an accident, some boiling liquid being thrown over her, on the 20th of November, 1821. She lingered until the next day, and then died, aged eight years. She bore the anguish with great patience and resignation; and about two hours before her death, she said to her father, "I am going to heaven; I hope you will go to chapel, that you may go to heaven when you die;" and he solemnly promised to do as she requested. He accordingly attended public worship, and the first discourses he heard all seemed to be directed only to and for him. He then had reason to remember his dear child, and her words; and a radical change ensued He constantly attended there; the word of eternal life was blessed to his soul, and he became a communicant. There was also a change at home; the mother generally attended with her husband. Thus, through the instrumentality of this little girl, a whole family was brought near to God.

(*c*) A SCHOOL'S INFLUENCE.—In a town in Massachusetts there was a large neighborhood, where many of the inhabitants were accustomed to spend the Sabbath in hunting, fishing, drunkenness, and profaneness. There was only one professor of religion in the place. She went to the church with which she was connected, three or four miles distant, and asked if something could not be done to serve her neighbors? A few teachers were sent out to commence a Sabbath school there. One year after, most of the inhabitants had found their way to the house of God, where they afterwards attended regularly; and one old man who had lived *eighty* years, zealously declaring to all around him, that the "wicked shall *not* be turned into hell with all the nations that forget God," erected the family altar, and gave pleasing evidence that he had commenced a new life. The whole moral character of that neigborhood is radically changed.

389. In Promoting Benevolence and other Virtues.

(*a*) THE LITTLE GIRL AND THE LOST POCKET-BOOK.—A gentlemen jumping from an omnibus in the city of New-York, dropped his pocket-book, and had gone some distance before he discovered its loss; then hastily returning, inquired of every passenger whom he met, if a pocket-book had been seen. Finally, meeting a little girl of ten years old, to whom he made the same inquiry, she asked, "what kind of a pocket-book?" He described it—then unfolding her apron, "Is this it?" "Yes, that is mine; come into this store with me." They entered, he opened the book, counted the notes, and examined the papers. "They are all right," said he; "fifteen notes of a thousand dollars each; had they fallen into other hands, I might never have seen them again; take then, my little girl, this note of a thousand dollars, as a reward for your honesty, and a lesson to me, to be more careful in future." "No," said the girl, "I cannot take it; I have been taught at Sunday school not to keep what is not mine, and my parents would not be pleased if I took the note home, they might suppose I had stolen it." "Well, then, my girl, show me where your parents live." The girl took him to an humble tenement in an obscure street, rude, but cleanly; he informed the parents of the case; they told him their child had acted correctly. They were poor, it was true, but their pastor had always told them not to set their hearts on rich gifts. The gentleman told them they must take it, and he was convinced they would make a good use of it, from the principle they had professed.

The pious parents then blessed their benefactor, for such he proved, they paid their debts which had disturbed their peace, and the benevolent giver furnished him employment in his occupation, as a carpenter, enabling him to rear an industrious family in comparative happiness. This little girl became he wife of a respectable tradesman of New-York, and had reason to rejoice that she was born of pious parents, who had secured their daughter's happiness by sending her to Sunday school.

(*b*) ORIGIN OF A MISSIONARY SOCIETY.—The Rev. Richard Knill writes, in January, 1837,—"There is a town in England where the Sunday scholars are showing their love to the heathen; a beautiful description of which was sent to me by their minister. I give it in his own words:—

"'But you should have been with us last Sabbath, for God has turned his hands upon the little ones. You remember, when you were here, I told you that the young people, who were flocking around you, composed my spiritual family, and that they had raised a Sabbath school Missionary Society. How it happened, I cannot precisely relate; but a few months ago the children began to be very desirous to have a society of their own, and one little girl came to her teacher, and told her, with tears, that she had been praying to God a great while to put it into the heart of her mother to give her a penny, to send the news of salvation to the children of the poor heathen. I knew the complaints which had been made respecting the contributions of older persons, but what could I do? If the love of Christ had been enkindled in the breasts of those of tenderest years, was it for me to strive to quench it? Thirty or forty of the dear little creatures met privately in the vestry, on Sabbath morning, for prayer, and to read the rules of the society, and I never expect to have more sublime or more tender emotions excited in my bosom, until I join the company of the redeemed, than I felt when I looked upon this part of the army of Jesus, who met at the footstool of divine mercy, to grasp in their feeble hands the banners of the cross, and who stood prepared to wage war against the rulers of spiritual wickedness in high places. Oh! what an unspeakable mortification it must be to the prince of darkness, to be conquered by such helpless instruments as these!'"

(*c*) BRITISH CONSUL AND SABBATH SCHOOL BOY.—The following anecdote is copied from a New-York paper, of July, 1818, in which it appears as a communication to the editor:

"This moment the British consul has related to me an anecdote too interesting to be suffered to pass unnoticed. A few days since, a young man, about nineteen years of age, called at the consul's office, and made himself known as one whom, but a few years before, the consul had taken into his own Sunday school, in the north of Ireland. He was then a poor, little, helpless, wretched outcast. No father owned him for a son; but the Sunday school was to him as a father, a sister and a brother. The precepts of religion and morality, which he learned there, have taken deep root in his heart, and are now ripened into abundance of fruit. He put into the consul's hand more than one hundred dollars, the little earnings he had laid up, to be remitted to his destitute mother, the forlorn daughter of shame and sorrow."

(*d*) BOY RESISTING TEMPTATION.—On a Sabbath afternoon, a little boy, eight years of age, was in the sick chamber of his afflicted father, reading aloud a chapter in the Bible, when two persons called in to see the father; they requested that the child might be permitted to finish the chapter, which being done, one of the visitors praised him highly for his reading, and gave him sixpence, desiring him to go and buy some cakes, and divide them with his brothers and sisters. "What, to-day!" exclaimed the child with astonishment, for he had been taught to reverence the Sabbath; "none but wicked people keep open shop to-day, and I must not go and buy of them."

"But mother will give you leave for once," returned the injudicious visitor, because you have been such a good boy, and read your chapter so well."

The parents, of course, expressed their positive and entire objection to such a practice, and the child steadily refused to receive the money. But on the persons taking their leave, the little boy was desired to go down stairs with them and open the street-door; when his mistaken friend renewed her temptation, slipping the sixpence into his hand, saying, "There, now you can run and buy what you like, your mother will not miss you." "No," replied the child, "but if she should not, it is God's commandment that says, 'Remember the Sabbath day to keep it holy.'" So saying, he laid the sixpence on the step, and shut the door; there it was found by the servant, some hours afterwards; when, on inquiry being made, the little boy confessed that the visitor had again offered him the money, and that he had refused it. It was from the other lady, who was grieved at the impropriety of her friend's conduct, while she admired that of the child, that the parents were afterwards informed of the firm and proper reply. The boy's next concern was, how to return the money; for the idea of retaining it for his own use, even on another day, seemed never to have entered his mind. After a little consideration, he inquired if it would be right to purchase with it a little book on the subject of keeping holy the Sabbath day; his proposal being agreed to, a suitable book was named, but as the price was a shilling, the boy cheerfully contributed the remaining sixpence from his own little store; and the following day a book was purchased, and sent to his mistaken friend; with his earnest prayers that a divine blessing might accompany it.

(*e*) DEATH-BED CONTRIBUTION.—A girl nine years of age united with the school in T——, in the summer of 1834. She had not the privilege of parental religious instruction. Her residence was two or three miles from school. On one Sabbath in August, when notice was given in the school that the next Sabbath would be *contribution-day*, she was present. But it was her *last Sabbath*. She went home under the influence of that disease which during the week, hurried her into eternity.

While on her bed of sickness, she remembered the contribution-day, and spoke of the *luxury of giving*. Twice she had been present on the contribution Sabbath, and had put her cent into the box. She called for the *cent* which she had laid aside for the Sabbath, gave it to her mother, and told her that if she died before the next Sabbath, to carry it to her teacher, that it might be put into the Sabbath school contribution trunk. On the next Sabbath, her soul was in eternity; but her *cent*, like the poor widow's two mites, was cast into the treasury of the Lord.

(*f*) LITTLE BOY AND HIS TRACT.—A little boy, belonging to a

Sabbath school in London, having occasion every Sunday to go through a certain court, observed a shop always open for the sale of goods. Having been taught the duty of sanctifying the Lord's day, he was grieved at its profanation, and for some time seriously considered if it was possible for him to do any thing to prevent it. At length he determined on leaving a tract, "ON THE LORD'S DAY," as he passed by. On the next Sabbath, coming the same way, he observed that the shop was shut up. He stopped, and pondered whether this could be the effect of the tract he had left. He ventured to knock gently at the door; when a woman within, thinking it was a customer, answered aloud, "You cannot have any thing; we don't sell on the Sunday." The little boy still begged for admittance, encouraged by what he had heard, when the woman recollecting his voice, opened the door, and said, "Come in, my dear little fellow: it was you who left the tract here last Sabbath against Sabbath breaking, and it frightened me so, that I did not dare to keep my shop open any longer; and I am determined never to do so again while I live."

(*g*) SCHOLAR AND THE SICK WOMAN.—A gentleman, near London, went to visit a woman who was sick. As he was going into the room, he saw a little girl kneeling by the side of the poor woman's bed. The little girl rose from her knees as soon as she saw the gentleman, and went out of the room. "Who is that child?" the gentleman asked. "O sir!" said the sick woman, "that is a little angel, who often comes to read her Bible to me, to my great comfort; and she has just now given me sixpence." The gentleman was so pleased with the little girl's conduct, that he wished to know how she had learned to love the word of God, and to be so kind to poor people. Finding that she was one of the scholars of a neighboring Sunday school, he went to the school, and asked for the child. She felt rather afraid when she was called to the gentleman; but he was very kind to her, and asked her if she was the little girl that had been to read the Bible to the sick woman. She said she was. The gentleman said, "My dear, what made you think of doing so?" She answered, "Because, sir, I find it said in the Bible, that "pure religion and undefiled before God and the Father is this—to visit the fatherless and widows in their affliction.'" "Well," said he, "and did you give her any money?" "Yes, sir." "And where did you get it? "Sir, it was given me as a reward."

(*h*) LITTLE PEACE-MAKER.—A gentleman, once speaking at a Bible Society meeting, stated, that a little time previously he had called in at one of the Sunday schools in Southwark; and as he was looking over one of the classes, the teacher took him aside and said, "Sir, Lucy, whom you have just noticed, is one of the most extraordinary children I ever knew." "How so?" said he. "Why, sir, she is remarkably diligent, gentle, and, above all, remarkably humble. She is very forgiving to those who have injured her; and there never is a quarrel in the school but she interferes, and is not satisfied until she has reconciled the parties. I am almost afraid of loving her too much." After school the gentleman addressed her: "Lucy, I am pleased to hear you give great satisfaction to your teacher. What is it makes you so desirous to oblige your schoolfellows, and settle their disputes?" She blushed, and hesitated some time; and at last said, in a meek voice, "Sir I hope it is because our Savior has said, 'Blessed are the peace-makers.''

(*i*) SCHOLARS AND THEIR SICK TEACHER.—A number of boys, who had been taught in a Sabbath school near Sheffield, England, met in a field; and instead of spending their money in oranges, on what is called Shrove-Tuesday, they agreed to give all they had to their teacher, who they knew was in great distress. They tied up the money in an old cloth; and, when it was dark, they opened his door, and threw it into the house. Inside of the parcel was a small piece of paper, on which was written, "Trust in the Lord, and do good, and verily thou shalt be fed."

(*j*) THE BOY AND HIS FARTHINGS.—At the anniversary of a

Sunday school, at Copthall, a village in Essex, on Sunday, Oct. 5, 1834, whilst the collection was making, a little boy, about seven years of age, put a bag upon the plate. As it was rather heavy, the collector was curious to ascertain its contents. On examination, it was found to contain two hundred and eighty-five farthings, or five shillings and elevenpence farthing. Upon inquiry, it was found that the boy was in the habit of going on errands for his mother, and was allowed the farthings in change, to be disposed of as he pleased, which he perseveringly saved, and generously gave to the support of the Sunday school.

(*k*) SATURDAY EVENING SCHOOL.—The following anecdote is extracted from a letter from Baltimore, dated July, 1818:—

A short time since, the mother of one of the girls attending my school accosted me in the street, and said she had been wishing to see me for some time. I replied, "I am glad to see you; what do you want with me?" "Sir, I live in a little village about three miles from Philadelphia. We have no Sabbath school there; but my little girl attends yours; and as she has derived a great deal of good from it, she tried to get some of our neighbors' girls to go with her, but she could not prevail on them to go, it being so far off; and so, about two months ago, she began with a Saturday evening school." "A Saturday evening school!" "Yes, sir; and she has now about thirty little girls attending regularly; my house is quite filled with them." "What is the age of your daughter?" "She is only twelve, sir." "And how does she conduct her school?" "In the same way that you do: she goes through all the exercises of a Sabbath school; and as she has no tickets to reward them with, she is the more diligent during the week to get her lesson well, that she may receive her tickets, and with these she rewards her own scholars." After getting her address, I desired her not to say any thing of our meeting, and I would endeavor to be at her house next Saturday. I went, and oh! how was I delighted with the fervency of this dear child, in offering up the first prayer! I remained concealed; and witnessed the whole duties of the school, conducted with all the gravity of an aged matron.

(*l*) SOLDIER GIVING AWAY HIS PENSION.—At the annual meeting of the Sunday School Union, in 1822, the Rev. George Marsden stated, that as a gentleman, who by the providence of God had become reduced in his circumstances, was walking along the street, he was met by an old soldier, who immediately recognized him, and mentioned the pleasure he felt in having been one of his Sabbath scholars. The soldier had heard of the circumstances which had reduced his former teacher to distress, and thus addressed him: "You were my teacher; I have a pension from Government; I can work a little, and will willingly give my pension for your relief."

(*m*) THREE SCHOLARS AND THEIR MOTHER.—Three boys attended a Sunday school in London for some time; at length their father died, and their mother was taken so dangerously ill, that, being very poor, she was obliged to be removed to the workhouse. The two elder boys had employment, by which they earned a few shillings each per week. On the mother's removal, the three boys consulted together what they should do; and they calculated that what they could earn would be sufficient to provide them with food, and to pay the rent of the room which had been tenanted by their mother. They asked the landlord if he would let them stop in the room, if they paid the weekly rent regularly; to this he cheerfully consented. Some weeks passed on, and the third boy got a situation, and the two eldest obtained an advance in their wages on account of their diligence and good conduct. By this time their mother had nearly recovered her health; the three boys again consulted together, and found that their earnings would enable them to maintain their mother, and they resolved upon trying to do it. They accordingly made application to the parish officers, and their mother was restored to her house: and, by prudence and economy, the boys managed to maintain the family, and to pay their rent regularly. The boys acknowledged that it was by their attendance at the Sunday-school that they had been taught to feel for their parent, and to arrange their earnings so as to relieve the parish from any further charge on her account.

390. In Reforming Neighborhoods.

(*a*) TESTIMONY OF A JUSTICE.—A justice of the peace, near Bristol, England, in 1820, speaking of the neighborhood in which a Sunday school had been established, said, that formerly it was dangerous even to go through the parish, in consequence of the ignorant and depraved state of the inhabitants; but now he saw such an alteration for the better, and was so pleased with the sight of the children, that on one occasion he invited them all to his house, and gave them refreshment.

(*b*) CHANGE IN THE SINGING OF THE STREETS.—The teachers in a New England Sabbath school, in 1830, were fully convinced of the good influence their school had exerted on the population with whom they labored. Before its establishment, and even some time afterwards, it was no uncommon thing to hear songs and dancing tunes on Sabbath mornings, in the street where the school is located; but during the year then closed, it was not remembered that one instance had occurred; but, on the contrary, they were often heard singing psalms and hymns.

(*c*) SUNDAY SCHOLAR AND DANCING.—The Sunday school at Sheriff Hill, Newcastle, was established in the year 1813, and the circumstances attending its establishment were rather singular. A dancing school had, at that time, been opened there, and many seemed desirous of attending it. Some Christian colliers conversing on the subject, down in the pit, and endeavoring to devise some means for stopping the progress of iniquity, it occurred to one of them, that the most effectual way would be to begin a Sunday school. When they came up from the pit, they spoke to one of the agents of the colliery, who expressed himself favorable to the undertaking, and very handsomely gave them permission to teach in the very room where the dancing was taught. They went home full of gratitude to the Lord, who had so far opened a way for them. They next canvassed the whole village, taking down the names of such children as wished to come: sixty-five agreed to attend. They had, however, neither books nor forms for the school; but the Lord raised up a kind friend, who supplied them with both. The school was then opened, and was soon filled. The dancing was laid aside, and the children were employed in reading their Bibles and singing hymns.

391. In Counteracting and Removing Infidelity.

(*a*) THE INFIDEL AND CHILD.—A man, who was once a decided infidel, said he desired to bless God for Sunday schools. They had been, he observed, the means of saving his soul. His brother-in-law and sister had, with much entreaty, persuaded him to send his little boy to the Sunday school. The child had often heard the superintendents enforce the duty and importance of prayer, to which he had listened attentively. One Sunday morning, while his mother was dressing his little brother, this boy was missing, and on inquiring of him where he had been, he replied, he had been saying his prayers: and added, "Mother, does my father ever pray?" She informed his father what the child had said. The father, having lived in the neglect of prayer, felt condemned; conviction seized his mind: he sought the Lord, and found him, to the joy of his soul.

(*b*) THE INFIDEL'S OBJECTION.—In conversation with a pious woman, an infidel manifested great hostility to Sabbath schools. He said it took possession of the minds of the young and made impressions which they could not get rid of! Such was the case with him, in reference to the instructions of his mother. Although he did not believe in the religious instructions she inculcated when he was a child, yet he could never get rid of it. It was always troubling him. The good woman then told him, if that was the case, she would do all that she could to encourage Sabbath schoo.s, and extend their influence to the utmost.

(c) THE INFIDEL AND HIS DAUGHTER.—A deist whose infidelity was shaken by the conversation of his little daughter, who attended a Sabbath school, was induced to attend the preaching of the gospel. The Holy Spirit accompanied it with his blessing. On the following November 5th, he convened his family together, and having made a bonfire of his infidel books, they all joined in singing that hymn, "Come let us join our cheerful songs," &c.

(d) AN INFIDEL'S ALARM.—An infidel in the town of B., New-York, used to ridicule religion and rail against it. On one occasion he observed, "of all religions that ever cursed the world, the Christian religion is the worst. But," said he, as if he was considering what he could do to stop its progress; "but," said he, "what I shall do to put down these infernal Sunday schools, I *don't know*, I'M AFRAID OF THEM!" That which so alarms the fears of some infidels, should encourage the hopes and nerve the hands of all Christians; and for the very reasons such infidels would pull down Sunday schools, Christians should strive to build them up.

MORAL AND RELIGIOUS INFLUENCE ON PUPILS.

392. In Preventing and Removing Crime and Vice.

(a) SABBATH SCHOOLS AND PRISONERS.—Jos. Lancaster says:

"I was naturally desirous of gaining information and instruction from a venerable man of seventy-two, who had in a series of years, superintended the education of 3,000 poor children; who had been actively engaged in visiting both the city and the county prisons, whereby he had gained an ample opportunity of knowing if any of the scholars were brought in as prisoners: and who on appealing to his memory, which, although at an advanced age, is strong and lively, could answer—'None!'"

In a letter to the editors of the New-York Observer, in 1829, the chaplain of the State Prison attests the following important fact:—

"I have lately made a pretty thorough inquiry among the convicts here, for the purpose of learning who, and how many, have ever enjoyed the advantages of a Sabbath school. The result is, that out of more than five hundred convicts, not one has been found who has ever been, for any considerable time, a regular member of a Sabbath school: and not more than two or three who have ever attended such a school at all.

(b) SCHOLAR LEARNING HONESTY.—A colored boy, living with Dr. M——, of P——, was sent by a little boy in the family with six cents to buy a top for him. On his return, he told the child that the top had cost twelve cents, and that he had paid the other six from his own money. He was repaid, and no more was thought of the affair.

Some time after, the colored boy was introduced to a Sunday school; and having learned some valuable lessons, he one day said to his master's son, "I gave but six cents for that top, and not twelve, as I told you; but I did not know then, as I do since I have been to a Sunday school, how wicked such things are." Handing him six cents from his pocket, he said, "I have been saving them for you, one by one—take them, they are yours."

(c) YOUNG CRIMINAL REFORMED.—The following interesting account appeared in the Christian Guardian of 1823, and was furnished by a gentleman, who visited on the Sabbath the city prison, in the Newgate of Dublin, for the purpose of affording religious instruction to the prisoners:—

One youth I gave up as a hopeless case; he pretended he could not read, but I discovered he read better than any of them. He endeavored to pick my pockets, and to pull my coat whenever I happened to turn round, and has pierced me with pins more than once. I bore it all patiently; and, instead of causing him to be punished, I expostulated with him on the folly and wickedness of his ways. I also gave him two or three suitable tracts, which he promised to read.

Cold weather coming on, he had no coat or shoes, a common thing in the prison, where some, indeed, were almost naked. I promised him an old coat and a pair of shoes, if he would become more attentive. The bribe was too tempting to be refused; and, after two or three weeks of trial, I sent him the coat and shoes. He continued promising for some time, but there was nothing in his conduct which could induce a person to hope for an entire reformation. It is the duty of teachers, when they meet with such a scholar, to present him in fervent prayer before the throne of grace; yet, at the same time, to watch over him, and to lose no opportunity of communicating suitable advice. This was the method adopted on the occasion, and I trust it was not unavailing. However, the term of his confinement expired, and he was released. Shortly after, I had occasion to leave town; and, on my return, having been reading the whole of the day, I went out in the evening to enjoy a walk. My spirits were unusually low. I proceeded along one of the public roads for some time; but the noise and bustle not suiting my feelings, I turned up a narrow private road, shaded by trees on both sides, and interspersed here and there with neat whitewashed cottages. On passing one of them, I heard the clicking noise of a busy loom, and the singing of a light-hearted weaver. When I had passed about fifty paces, the door opened, and a neatly-dressed young man called after me by name. Not recognising him, I did not reply, but proceeded. He ran after me, and stopped me. I looked at him. "Do you not know me, sir?" said he. "No, indeed I do not." "Do you not recollect your scholar at Newgate, James ——?" I looked at him from head to foot; but the neatly-combed hair, the clean face, new shirt, and plain and comfortable suit of clothes, had so metamorphosed him, that it was with difficulty I could recognize him. Taking me most affectionately by the hand, and with tears in his eyes, he said, "Sir, I saw you passing by, and could not refrain from coming out to ask your pardon for all my unkindness to you; and to thank you for all that you and the other young gentlemen said to me while in Newgate. It was a sad place, but I thank God that ever I was put into it. I shall count that day the happiest in my life. I should have been now, perhaps, living in wickedness, and probably come to the gallows at last. When I got out, I was friendless, and without a home. But reflecting on what was often told me in Newgate, that Christ is the Friend of sinners, and ever willing to receive the vilest, I prayed to him to support and assist me. I shuddered at the idea of going to rob and pilfer again, and determined to work. I got some work, and some clothes too; and I have now employment enough at this cottage; and I pass away my time very happily."

(*d*) SABBATH SCHOOLS TOO LATE.—"Sabbath schools would have saved me from the gallows; but they were fifteen years too late for me," muttered the abandoned Gibbs, a few days before his execution. But the history of this pirate is not the only one that furnishes occasion for such a declaration. Hundreds before him, who have shed innocent blood, might as justly have said, if we had been instructed in Sabbath schools, they would have saved *us* from this ignominious death on the scaffold!

(*e*) REPORTS OF THIRTY-FIVE SCHOOLS.—In the reports of 35 schools of Mass., in 1829, it was definitely stated, that no individual from their number had ever been arraigned before a civil tribunal for immoral conduct; while only two from all the schools in the State, are mentioned, who had been arrested: and these attended the Sabbath school, irregularly, for a very short time.

393. Conversions.

(*a*) FAITHFULNESS REWARDED.—During a single week, in 1842, there were six hopeful conversions in one class of ten or twelve boys, in the Pearl-street Baptist Sabbath school in the city of Albany. The teacher, G. T. C., had for three or four weeks felt an unusual anxiety for their salvation, which led him to be faithful in his in struction, and fervent in prayer for them. He held several prayer meetings at his house with them, to which other scholars were invited, and at one or two meetings they continued almost "all night" in prayer. One Sabbath, one of them, who had found peace the night before, called on the teacher at 4 o'clock in the morning to tell him how joyful he felt in loving the Savior, and he was so happy he could not wait until he should see him in the Sabbath school. When the school assembled in the P. M., they all came forward and told what the Lord had done for them, and affectionately invited their associates to come to the Savior and taste the joys they felt. Such a scene, and such a circumstance would be interesting at any time, but at that time particularly so, from the fact that in the rest of the school, and in the church, there was a lamentable coldness, while the ways of Zion mourned, and few came to her solemn feasts.

(*b*) REV. MR. CHARLES' TESTIMONY.—The excellent Rev. T. Charles, of Bala, England, informed the general meeting of the Sunday School Union, in 1813, that, throughout the country in which he resided, they received most of the members into their churches from Sunday schools; and that, during the preceding year, nearly one hundred persons had been received into Christian communion from the Sunday schools in the town of Bala.

(*c*) GREAT CHANGE IN A FAMILY.—The Rev. Mr. Hoover, in addressing a meeting of the Philadelphia Sunday School Union, thus spoke:—

"If you had accompanied me in a walk through this district, two years ago, I could have led you to a house, or rather a hovel, not far from this spot, which was unfit to be the residence of man or beast. There you would have seen a widow with her seven children, in the rags of poverty, and with the impress of misery on their countenances; the room and its occupants forming a scene of wretchedness seldom surpassed. If you will go with me to-morrow, I will show you the same house, but no longer a miserable tenement. Within, you shall behold the same widow, and the same seven children; but clothed in comfortable raiment, and peace smiling in their faces. The Sabbath school teacher has been there, and he has led them to the place of holy instruction. God has visited them in the plenitude of his grace, and five of those seven children give joyful evidence that they have passed from death unto life."

(*d*) "FROM THE TOP OF THE ROCKS I SEE HIM."—The Rev. T. T. Biddulph, of St. James's Church, Bristol, England, mentioned from the pulpit, about 1818, that a boy, some years before, behaved so ill in the St. James's Sunday school, that neither kindness nor severity appeared to have any effect on him. At length the teachers were very reluctantly obliged to expel him. For several years they heard nothing of him, and had almost forgotten the circumstance of his expulsion. Lately, however, as a clergyman, who had been a teacher in the school, was sitting in his study, in a distant country village, a sailor knocked at the door. On being admitted, he said to the clergyman, "I suppose that you have forgotten me, sir?" "Yes," said the Rev. Henry Poole, "I have, if I ever knew you." "Do you remember a wicked boy named James Saunders?" "Oh, yes," said he, "I have cause to remember him; he gave me much trouble and anxiety. What do you know of him?" "I am the lad!" "You are grown so, and so much altered, I could not have believed it. Well, James, what account can you give of yourself?" "A very sorry one, sir. When I was expelled from the school, I left the city, and wandered, I scarcely knew or cared where. At length I found myself at the sea-side. Weary of living by lying and stealing, I got on shipboard; and after sailing in various parts of the world, I was shipwrecked in a hurricane in the Bay of Honduras. After swimming till my strength failed me, I gave myself up for lost. In the middle of a dark night, I came to my senses, and found myself on a rock half covered with water. I looked around and called out for my shipmates, and found that two of them were circumstanced like myself, every moment expecting a watery grave.

For the first time since I left the school, you, sir, darted into my mind. I thought of your kindness, of my base ingratitude, and of some of the sacred truths you took so much pains to fix in my memory; particularly that passage in Numbers xxiii. 9, 'From the top of the rocks I see him.' In my extremity, I looked to the Savior, of whom I had heard so much, but whom I had so long slighted and despised. I knelt down, up to my waist in water, and cried mightily, that God would be the rock of my heart, and my portion for ever. I found your words true, that 'praying breath was never spent in vain.' On the day breaking, we discovered some pieces of the wreck, on which we ultimately succeeded in reaching the shore. Then many precious truths which you had taught me from the Bible came fresh into my memory; though I had almost forgotten during my career of iniquity, even that there was such a book. I thought, sir, you would be glad to find that all your care and anxiety on my behalf was not lost; I therefore walked from my ship to thank you, in the best manner I can, for your former kindness to me."

Knowing the cunning adroitness of the lad, Mr. Poole was half inclined to discredit him. He inquired the name of his captain, to whom he wrote, and ascertained that since this young man had sailed with him, his conduct had been so correct and exemplary, that whenever he knew James Saunders was on deck, he made himself perfectly easy, knowing that the duties of the ship would be faithfully attended to. Many months afterwards, Mr. Poole received a letter from the captain, saying that poor James Saunders, in a distant part of the world, was seized with a fever; that during its progress he sent for the sailors, read to them while he was able out of the Bible, exhorted them to cleave to the Rock of ages that never moves, to take example by him, though one of the vilest of sinners, who had found mercy and grace to help in every time of need; and commending them all to Jesus, he fell asleep in Him without a struggle.

The new school rooms at Bristol, accommodating from five to six hundred children, being in debt several hundred pounds, some gentlemen of the committee, and other friends to the institution, had lent the money wanted, upon loan, in sums to suit their convenience, and had received bills for their respective amounts bearing interest. The day after narrating the above incident, Mr. Biddulph received from a member of his congregation a letter, inclosing one of these bills for fifty pounds, requesting Mr. B. to burn it, as the above anecdote had amply repaid both the principal and interest on it. Another of the congregation, who held three similar fifty pound bills, sent them with a like request. Surely this is encouragement for every person connected with Sunday schools, to persevere amidst discouragements.

(*e*) TWO ORPHAN SCHOLARS. —Some years ago, two little boys, decently clothed, the elder about thirteen years of age, and the younger eleven, called at a lodging house for vagrants, in Warrington, to stay for the night. The keeper of the house, very properly, took them to the Vagrant Office to be examined, that, if proper objects, they might be relieved. The account they gave of themselves was very affecting, but no doubt was entertained of its truth. It appeared, that but a few weeks had elapsed since these poor little wanderers had resided with their parents in London. The typhus fever, however, in one day, carried off both father and mother, leaving them orphans. Immediately after their parents were buried, the children, having an uncle in Liverpool, resolved to go and throw themselves upon his protection; and, tired and faint, they arrived in the town of Warrington, on their way thither.

Two bundles contained their little all. In the youngest boy's was found neatly covered and carefully preserved, a Bible. The keeper of the lodging house said to the boy, "You have neither money nor meat, will you sell me this Bible? I will give you five shillings for it." "No," exclaimed he; "I'll starve first." "The keeper then said, "there are plenty of books to be bought besides this; why do you love the Bible so much?" The boy replied, "No book has stood my friend so much as the Bible." "Why, what has the Bible done for you?" He answered, "When I was a boy about seven years of age I became a Sunday scholar in London where I learned to read my Bible. This Bible showed me that I was a sinner, and a great one too. It also pointed me to the Savior, and I thank God, I have found mercy at the hands of Christ, and I am not ashamed to confess him before the world." To try the boy still farther, six shillings were offered to him for his Bible. "No," said he, "it has been my support all the way from London. Hungry and weary, often have I sat down to read my Bible, and have found refreshment from it, and I have experienced the comfort David felt, when he said, 'In the multitude of my thoughts within me, thy comforts delight my soul.'" He was then asked, what he would do when he got to Liverpool, should his uncle refuse to take him in? His reply may excite a blush in many other Christians; "My Bible tells me, 'When my father and mother forsake me the Lord will take me up.'" The children had in their pockets tickets, as rewards from the Sunday school to which they belonged, and thankfulness and humility were visible in all their deportment. At night they committed themselves to God in prayer, and the next day pursued their journey to Liverpool.

(*f*) CLASS OF TWENTY CHILDREN.—Rev. Mr. ——, of H——, Mass., in August, 1830, thus wrote: "Since the 1st of February, of the present year, 161 persons have been admitted to this Church, most of whom have generally attended my Bible class instruction, for the last six years, and nearly 60 of them have been members of the Sabbath school. *I have a class of twenty children*, all of whom are members of the Sabbath school, *who are cherishing the hope that they have passed from death unto life*. These children are from *eight* to *fourteen* years of age. The object of bringing them into a class, has reference to their making a profession of religion.

(*g*) THE CLASS OF LARGE SCHOLARS.—In 1833, the superintendent of a school in Massachusetts made an attempt to gather into the school again, some of the youth who had left under the impression that they were too old to be members. At first a class of about 16 females was formed. The next summer [1834] it numbered 40 males and females. Twenty of this class in two years after its formation, made a public profession of religion.

(*h*) SAILOR CONVERTED IN PRISON.—F. O. was a sailor, illiterate and headstrong. Left in early life without a father to guide his youthful steps, he rushed thoughtlessly along in the path of folly and dissipation, regardless of the remonstrances of a widowed mother. His progress was consequently downwards, until he was arrested by the hand of civil justice, for a deed of midnight villainy. He was convicted, and sentenced to the Auburn prison, New York. As he was about to take his leave of home, with the officer who conducted him to the place of confinement, he was entreated by all the force of a mother's love, to think upon his ways, to conform to the laws of the prison, to read his Bible, to repent, and obey God. He mocked at the counsels and tears of maternal tenderness, declaring, with dreadful oaths, that he would "listen to none of her pious entreaties; that he cared not for God or man; and that he intended to give himself to sin while he lived!" During the first two years of his imprisonment, all the bitterness of his hostility against religion continued. A Bible was put into his cell, but he refused to read it, and, to use his own expression, "would rather see the devil than the face of a chaplain." At the end of two years he was persuaded to enter the Sabbath school kept in the prison. Here the "sword of the Spirit" found an avenue to his heart; his enmity was slain; his stubbornness yielded to tenderness; and his hatred was transformed to love. He now spoke of the Savior with a bursting heart. "Oh," said he, "I bless God that I was ever brought to this prison! It was this that saved me from destruction. I should certainly have ruined myself if I had not been arrested." At the mention of his mother's name, I have seen, said the writer of the account, the tear start in his eye, and his frame shake with convulsive emotion. "Ah, my mother! had I listened to her counsels! but I have broken her heart! How many sighs and tears, how many sleepless nights and agonizing prayers I have caused her! When I think of my poor mother, I sometimes feel that I could burst the walls of my cell, that I might go and fall before her, to ask her forgiveness." He was released from prison, and immediately called on a friend, to whom the above confessions were made. After pledging himself to unite with the people of God, a Bible was put into his hands, when, with a bounding heart, he took his leave and set his face towards the mansion of his mother.

(*i*) THE WIDOW AND HER SON.—At the annual meeting of a Sunday School Union, in England, in 1824, the Rev. Jacob Stanley related the following fact respecting a Sunday scholar. Some years ago, there was a widow in Staffordshire, whose son attended the Sunday school, but he did not at first regard the religious instructions he received. He became wild and profligate, enlisted as a soldier, and was several years on the continent. Another young man from the same town, was proceeding to join the regiment to which he belonged, and called on the poor widow to ask her if she had any thing to send to her son. She said she was very poor, she had no money to send, and, if she had, it might do him no good, but that she could send him a Bible; and she added, "Give my love to him, and tell him that it is my earnest wish that he would read this book, and, beginning at Matthew, that he would read one chapter every day." The young man took the Bible, and when he joined the regiment, he found out his townsman, who asked him, "Well have you seen the old woman, and how is she?" "She is well and has sent you this present, a Bible; and she desired me to say that it was her request, and perhaps her last request, that you would read a chapter in it every day." "Well," replied he, "I will comply with her request, on condition that you will join with me in reading this chapter." The engagement was made, and they read to the third chapter of John, with which they were much struck. A pious sergeant explained what they read, and the Holy Spirit applying the truth to their minds, they became the subjects of godly sorrow, and attained that peace which passeth all understanding. Soon after they were called into an engagement, when the son of the widow was wounded, and carried into the rear by his comrade. When the battle was over, he went to look for his wounded comrade, and found him with that Bible open which had been the means of his conversion; it was covered with his blood, and his spirit had fled. He took up the Bible, and on his return waited on the widowed mother, and presented her with it.

(*j*) THE SHIPWRECKED SAILOR.—A young man, about to retire from a school in Scotland, received from the Rev. Dr. Colquhoun, on one occasion that he visited the institution, a Bible, with a suitable inscription, as a reward for good conduct. Many, who were present on that occasion, will long remember with what earnestness that venerable servant of God invoked the blessing of the Almighty on the young man here alluded to, while he stood with the sacred gift in his hand; that he might be protected by God in whatever situation he might be placed, and that the Bible he had that night received might prove a source of consolation to him in the hour of adversity and distress. The subsequent history of this unfortunate youth, showed that these supplications had been abundantly answered; for shortly after he went to sea, and the vessel in which he was on board, as a mariner, was wrecked on the western coast of Scotland, and all hands perished. The corpse of the young sufferer was found stretched on the shore, and his name and birth place came to be known by the inscription on this Bible, which was found in his bosom.

(*k*) A SAILOR'S TESTIMONY.—The following letter, of a sailor, is extracted from the American Sunday School Magazine:—

"I consider a Sunday school, properly conducted, a great blessing to the poor of our land. I am a living witness of its benefits. I was born of poor parents, who could send me to no other school. It was there, in the course of one year, together with my private tuition at home, that I acquired that degree of education which I now possess. I was taught to fear God, obey my parents, reverence the Sabbath, abhor the sins of lying, cheating, stealing, and a catalogue of others: and had it not been for a wicked relation, who inspired me with a notion for the sea, I perhaps never should have sunk to such depths of wickedness as I have done. But being surrounded, while a sailor, with sinful company, I soon forsook the holy counsel given me by my teachers; but I never could plead ignorance in sinning, for the convictions I received at the Sunday school never left me, although I sailed eleven years on the ocean, in daily rebellion against God. Surely I may say that goodness and mercy have followed me.

"During those eleven years, I have frequently sailed from England, my native country, to almost all parts of Europe and Africa, to the East and West Indies, South America, and British North America. And, oh! how many times has the Lord saved me from an untimely death, both in storms and battles! Had I room, I would now record them, and thereby render a public thanksgiving to God my Savior. But I cannot forbear inserting one instance of his goodness. In May, 1812, we were sailing to the East Indies, from London, being near the equinoctial line, two ships in company, with a detachment of soldiers on board of each; it being a fine day, and our ship and her consort not more than three-fourths of a mile apart, the crews and soldiers of both ships obtained leave from their officers to go a swimming. I, then a daring sinner, plunged into the water, in company, perhaps, with one hundred more. A man from the other ship, at the same time, with a bottle of rum in his hand, while swimming, challenged any of us to meet him half-way between the two ships. A soldier who was a better swimmer than I was, agreed with me to meet him; but none of the rest would dare to go. We had scarcely reached him, at the distance of nearly half a mile from our ship, when our mate, who was up in the rigging, saw a shark coming astern of our ship, and called to us to make haste on board. Those who were near the ship, got immediately on board, and a boat was lowered down for the rest; but she could not hold all the soldiers, and I, who was furthermost from the ship, was in consequence left. By this time, some on board had thrown overboard a hook, with an eight-pound piece of pork on it, with the intention of decoying the shark from us; but it seemed to take no notice of it, but steered directly for us. By this time my companion, who outswam me, had reached the head of the ship, and taken hold of a rope that hung from thence, but was so exhausted that he could not climb it. While he was trying to climb the rope I came up to him, and caught him by the leg as he hung about half out of water. My clinching him caused him to slip down, and being more expert than he, I caught hold of the rope above his hands, and placing my knees upon his shoulders, I made an effort to reach the head of the ship! but at that instant the rope broke, and plunged us both in the water alongside of the shark. I then swam round the stern of the ship, and took hold of another rope, and was soon on deck and out of danger. I looked down at the soldier, and saw the shark open his mouth to receive his prey. The men on deck called at the same time to the man to kick with his feet. He did so, and struck the shark on his nose; when he directly turned away from the man, who, at that instant, was caught by a rope with a noose on it, and hauled up into the ship. The shark then took the bait, and we hoisted him in. He measured about sixteen feet; and his jaws, when extended, would admit of a bulk nearly as large as a barrel. It was now that the serious impressions which I received at the Sunday school came fresh to my mind, and reproached me with ingratitude against God. But glory to his holy name, he rescued me from an untimely death, and I trust I shall praise him for the same, in time, and to all eternity. "GEORGE P. HOLMES."

(*l*) THE WELSHMAN'S SABBATH SCHOOL.—"When I stand in the pulpit before my own people on the Sabbath," says the Rev. John Todd, "I see before me an aged man in the gallery, for each Sabbath he is there, and the sight of him brings with it delightful associations.

"In former days he resided in North Wales. There were no Christians in his neighborhood. He wished to commence a Sunday-school, but could find no better place than a back-kitchen. Here he weekly assembled his little flock, and, for eleven years, labored alone, except with the aid of the scholars he had trained. Among his first pupils were two children of impenitent parents. These two girls had a little brother, to whom they were accustomed to teach what they learned in the Sabbath school. They were so interested in the Bible, that, being occupied in braiding straw as a business, they would first braid the length of a straw, then study a verse, then braid, and then study, so that they always came prepared with their Bible lesson.

"Their instructor, a long time ago, emigrated to this country, and this aged parishioner showed me a letter he had received from this scene of his early labors. The Sunday school is still taught there, not as before, in a *back kitchen*, but in a neat *house of God*. The minister of this sanctuary is a devoted man, laboring faithfully and successfully in his Master's vineyard. He is the "little brother" of those "little girls." His sisters are married. One is the mother of nine children, and lost her husband the last year by the falling in of a coal mine; but she had the happiness to know that, only the day before this event, he had renewedly consecrated himself to God. The minister lives contentedly upon forty pounds a year, happy in his home—happy in his people—happy in his Savior—blessed of God, and blessing others. This minister, this church, this flock, all sprang from that *Sunday school;* and, when I look upon my aged parishioner in the gallery, I cannot but reflect what a crown he has for his hoary head."

394. Revivals.

(*a*) HAPPY RESULTS OF ONE SCHOOL.—In a certain school in New England, in 1832, *sixty-one* out of fifteen classes of 160 pupils, under 16 years of age, became hopefully pious. In six classes, embracing 71 young persons over 16 years of age, *sixty* indulged hope that they had passed from death unto life, making in all ONE HUNDRED AND TWENTY-ONE who became hopefully pious, in a school of 231 scholars.

(*b*) REPORT OF 1836.—The Report for 1836, mentions *one hundred and seventy-three* teachers, and *one thousand four hundred and forty-four* scholars, who had united with the church during the year.

(*c*) REVIVALS IN TEN SCHOOLS.—In a County Sabbath school Society, in Mass., embracing ten parishes, and the same number of schools, the Lord smiled upon this institution, in 1834-5, and shed down upon it the influence of his Holy Spirit. Six schools were blessed with powerful revivals of religion. THREE HUNDRED scholars from these ten schools made a profession during the year. It is supposed the whole number that passed from death unto life is over FOUR HUNDRED! "This is the Lord's doing, and it is marvelous in our eyes."

(*d*) ONE HUNDRED SCHOLARS CONVERTED.—In ——, Mass., efforts were made in the early part of the year 1835, to excite a more general and deeper interest in the Sabbath school concert. The influence of these efforts was to increase the number of the school and the fidelity of the teachers. "This general interest," says the pastor, "increased through the summer till September, when more manifest signs appeared—though two or three conversions had before taken place—of the presence of the Holy Spirit. In a few weeks the attention had become general throughout the school. The work of God was very solemn, as well as animating, still and deep. ONE HUNDRED OR MORE MEMBERS OF THE SCHOOL, we hope, HAVE BEEN CONVERTED.

(*e*) WHAT A TEACHER CAN DO.—About the first of September,

1833, a deep and solemn interest upon the subject of religion, began to be visible in the Presbyterian church and congregation of Washingtonville, New-York, and particularly in the Sabbath school. Here commenced that revival flame which subsequently spread through the county, and brought salvation to a multitude of souls.

One *Sabbath school teacher,* feeling deeply the responsibility resting upon her, and the worth of immortal souls, before the school was dismissed on the Lord's day, affectionately requested her class, consisting of little girls about twelve or thirteen years of age, to remain after the rest of the school had retired. She then began, with an aching heart and with flowing tears, to reason and plead with them upon the subject of personal religion. They were deeply affected, and "wept bitterly" in view of their lost condition. They then all knelt together before the Lord, and the teacher prayed for their salvation; and immediately the scholar next to her commenced praying for herself, and then the next, and so on, until the *whole class,* with ardent supplications, begged for the forgiveness of their sins and the salvation of their souls. It would take long to tell the *history* of this class, and relate particular instances of conversions, and the happy changes which took place in the families to which they belonged, and show the family altars which were established. These scholars, with their teacher and their fathers and mothers, brothers and sisters, were ere long seen commemorating a Savior's dying love together. The revival extended itself to other towns, and the great day can alone unfold the astonishing results.

395. Happy Deaths.

(*a*) THE CHILD'S LAST PRAYER.—A pious little boy, who attended the Sabbath school, a few hours before his death broke out into singing, and sung so loud, as to cause his mother to inquire what he was doing. "I am singing my sister's favorite hymn, mother." "But why, my dear, so loud?" "Why," said he, with peculiar emphasis, "because I am so happy." Just before his death, with uplifted hands, he exclaimed, "Father! Father! take me, Father." His father went to lift him up, when, with a smile, he said, "I did not call you, father; but I was calling to my heavenly Father to take me; I shall soon be with him:" and then expired.

(*b*) "I HAVE GIVEN MYSELF TO MY SAVIOR."—I take the liberty (writes the wife of a pastor in Massachusetts) to add a few particulars of the remarkably happy death of a young lady who was nurtured in the Sabbath school, with which she was connected from early childhood until her marriage about two years since.

S. A. E. was constant in her attendance on the Sabbath school, punctual and very correct in her lessons, and amiable in her deportment. But it was not until the age of 16, that the precious treasure of divine truth, stored up in her memory, was made instrumental of awakening her conscience, and leading her to the "Fountain opened for sin." The moment will never be forgotten when, in a circle of weeping associates, who had assembled to inquire of their pastor, "What shall I do to be saved?" S. A. E. arose, and with her characteristic decision exclaimed, "I have given myself to my Savior!" Nor will those who had assembled at that hour to *pray* for their beloved children, forget the thrill of joy which pervaded the room as the pastor announced the fact, that this child of many prayers and tears, had, it was believed, accepted the offers of mercy. Five years she adorned her profession, and the rich fruits of gentleness, meekness, submission under severe trials, and filial piety, hung thickly on this youthful plant.

But, at length, it pleased God to try the strength of her faith in sickness and death. Her illness was of several weeks' continuance, but her mind was calm, collected, and with entire submission patiently waiting the result. The writer, who was formerly her teacher in the Sabbath school, was permitted to enjoy the high privilege of looking upon this young Christian as she lay in the embrace of the king of terrors. But there was no terror there. Her pallid face was radiant with smiles of perfect peace. "I am very low," she remarked, in clear and distinct accents. "Yes, but you may be raised up again." "If it be the will of God, I desire to live; if not, I desire to die. Whatever may be *His* will, is *mine*. I desire nothing but his will. I hope I shall never desire any thing but *His will*." "You are happy in your Savior?" "Oh, yes! Millions of worlds would be nothing in comparison with my hope in Him. His dying blood, how precious! It is all, all to me now."

"You can then resign your dear babe to His care?" "Yes, and I *know* he will take care of it. I have not one doubt of that. It is," she added, "a great thing to die. I have been an unprofitable servant, but Christ and his pardoning blood are my hope." More she would have said, but the day had chiefly been spent in bidding farewell to her numerous friends, and expressing to all the happiness which she felt in her Redeemer. And there she stood amid the billows of death, with her foot firmly fixed on the Rock of Ages. None could look unmoved upon that scene. None could listen to such expressions of confiding trust without exclaiming, "It is well to be a Christian—it is well to die a Christian." Lovely in life, happy in death, and glorious in eternity, is our departed young friend. These precious words she left for the subject of her funeral sermon: "The blood of Jesus Christ his Son, cleanseth us from all sin." 1 John 1 : 7.

(*c*) DEATH FROM HYDROPHOBIA.—A little boy, about eleven years of age, a Sunday scholar in Camberwell, was bitten by a mad dog; the part was cut out, and caustic applied, but the fatal poison could not be arrested in its progress, and nine weeks after the accident, decided symptoms of hydrophobia were manifested. It appears that the poor boy had depended chiefly, if not entirely, on Sunday school teaching for all his religious instruction, and now the great advantage of correct information on scriptural subjects was evinced. He was aware of the nature of his disease, took patiently the medicines recommended to him, and bade farewell to a playmate, saying, he should never see him again. But frightful paroxysms of pain came on; sometimes he was lifted suddenly upright in the bed, while the agony of speaking was so great that he could only utter words at intervals, and then in reply to necessary questions. But in the midst of judgment God remembered mercy,—an interval of comparative composure, a fact almost unprecedented in this disease, was granted the sufferer; and then was felt the sweet influence of that religion which he had been taught, and which gives divine wisdom to the meanest capacity. He knelt on the bed, and prayed—prayed to Jesus, and besought the salvation of his soul. He needed comfort; but he had not, as is too frequently the case, to seek it amid the pains and confusions of a dying hour, and, in the darkness of nature, mistake broken reeds for substantial supports; no, the way of peace and life had again and again been pointed out to him; he believed, and who can doubt that he was saved? He repeated and sung most of the hymns he had been taught; joy beamed on the countenance which had been so lately distorted with agony; he called on those around to attend to the things of religion, and prayed that their hearts might be turned from stone to flesh. How sweet, when sinking with apprehension, to find the means of support so near, with so firm a foundation secured to us! "Come to Jesus, come with me," said the little sufferer, as he quietly passed to glory.

(*d*) CHILDREN'S INFLUENCE ON PARENTS.—I can state, says Mr. Wilderspin, that a man discontinued drunkenness from the simple prattle of his infant. He was in the habit of frequently getting drunk; there were two or three children under seven years of age, and they all slept in the same room, though not in the same bed. The man came home one night drunk; his wife remonstrated with him, when he struck her. The woman cried very much, and continued to cry after she got into bed; but a little creature, two or three years old, got up, and said, "Pray, father, do not beat poor mother;" the father ordered it to get into bed again: the little creature got up again, and knelt down by the side of the bed, and repeated the Lord's prayer, and then concluded in this simple language: "Pray, God, bless dear father and mother, and make father a good father. Amen!" This went to the heart of the drunkard; the man told me he covered his face over with the bed-clothes, and that the first thoughts he awoke with in the morning, were thoughts of regret, that he should stand in need of such a remonstrance from such a young child, and it produced in him self-examination and amendment of life. The family became united to a Methodist chapel in that neighborhood, and I have learned that they are useful and valuable members of that society.

(*e*) LEARNING FROM THE BEST TEACHER.—The Rev. John Griffin, of Portsea, England, gave the following account of the death of one of his Sunday scholars, in the year 1813. His mother at first had opposed his going to the school, but afterwards determined to go and hear what was taught there, and by this means was converted to God. Not long after this, her son, about eleven years of age, was brought to his death-bed, and was visited by his ministers and teachers.

The first time I asked if he expected to go to heaven; "I do," was the reply. I asked him, "Why do you expect to go to heaven? All that die do not go there, do they? and why then do you think you shall go to heaven?" He replied, "I hope I shall go there, because I love the employment of the heavenly. I think I shall be happy in praising God, and serving him without sin; and I think I shall go to heaven, because I delight in the society of heaven; I shall rejoice in the presence of a holy God, and holy angels, and the spirits of just men made perfect." He paused, and I asked if he had any other reason. He replied, "I hope I shall go to heaven, because my heart is already there; and I do not think the Spirit of God would have drawn my heart to him, and made me delight in holiness and his service, if he had not intended to take me to heaven." I asked him if he had always thought in this way. "No, no," said he; "I was once a naughty and wicked boy, but by attending the Sunday school I have learned this: but I hope I have learned it from a better Teacher than our Sunday school teachers. I think I have learned it from the Spirit of God."

BENEFITS OF SABBATH SCHOOLS TO PARENTS, ETC.

396. Moral Benefits.

(*a*) SABBATH SCHOLAR AND THE PRISONERS.—At a Sunday school anniversary, the Rev. Mr. Hoover related the following facts:—

He had been called, in the providence of God, some months before, to preach to the inmates of a prison. On approaching a cell with the keeper, he heard the voice of supplication to God; and when the door was opened, discovered the occupant, an old man, in chains, sitting on a log, with the Bible before him, the open leaves of which were wet with his tears. Into two other adjoining cells was he conducted, each of which was tenanted by men whose demeanor and conversation indicated that they had passed from death unto life. To Mr. H.'s questions of surprise and pleasure, the keeper related, that shortly after the imprisonment of the first mentioned convict, the unhappy man received a letter from his little son, in words to the following effect:—

"Dear Father—Soon after you left us, a kind Sunday school teacher came to our house, and took us with him to the Sunday school. Several of my companions go there too, and we pray for you very much. We have laid up some money for you, and are saving all that we can to try to get you out. Do, dear father, be good, and trust in God."

The artless expression of love manifested in this letter touched the father's heart; and he, who had hitherto resisted the Bible and his own conscience was now bowed to the dust, in the anguish of a smitten soul.

He began to pray, and to read that

neglected word of life, and ceased not, till He who had wounded, showed him that it was his merciful prerogative to heal. The prisoners in the adjoining cell, meanwhile, hearing the language of prayer, at first wondered, but shortly betook themselves to the same throne of mercy. The feeling was communicated to the next cell, and the inmates were constrained to cry out, "What must we do?" The fruits of this awakening were testified, in the judgment of charity, in the conversion of three of these convicts to God.

(*b*) THE PUPIL AND HER MISTRESS.—A girl, who belonged to a Sunday school in Birmingham, obtained a situation as nurse maid in a respectable family. One Sunday evening her mistress was informed that Mary had been to the chapel, and she immediately gave the girl warning to quit her service in a month, saying that she would have no chapel-going servants in her house. In the course of the ensuing week, one of the servants told her mistress that Mary used to pray every night before she went to sleep. The mistress inquired whose prayer-book Mary took to bed with her. She was told that she prayed without a book. The mistress replied, "That cannot be, for no one can pray without a book." The servant asked her mistress to come up stairs and listen, after they were gone to bed, that she might hear Mary pray in the dark without a book. The mistress accordingly went up that night, and heard Mary praying aloud for her master and mistress, and particularly for the little child whom she used to nurse. The mistress was much affected, and informed her husband of it. He went up the next night, and heard Mary's fervent prayer, at which he was so greatly affected that he afterwards told his wife. with tears, that she must not part with Mary. They ascertained that the girl had learned to pray by attending the Sunday school; and on the next Sunday evening the master, the mistress, and Mary, all went to chapel together. Thus Mary was confirmed in her situation, and became the means of bringing her master and mistress to attend a place of worship, which they afterwards did regularly, and became subscribers to the Sunday school.

397. Religious Benefits.

(*a*) AN AFFECTING MEETING.—At the foot of a lofty hill, writes a correspondent of an American periodical, crowned to the summit with the richest verdure, a miserable mud cabin peeped out from among encircling bushwood and straggling elms. A stillness seemed to lie around the spot, and I felt an indescribable sensation creep over me as I drew near the house of mourning. I paused at the entrance. A low murmuring kind of sound stole upon my ear, and again all was hushed. I gently opened the door, and bent myself forward, as if to ascertain, unnoticed, what was passing within. I saw at the first glance that death had been there. The apartment on the threshold of which I now stood, was of the meanest construction; it was without a single piece of furniture that deserved the name. In one corner of it a dead body lay stretched out, very slightly covered with a tattered coat, and a cold kind of horrible feeling ran through my very soul; and it would probably have shrunk away from any further investigation, if I had not been suddenly arrested by a soft sweet voice, mingled with a low groan, somewhat like a death-rattle, that seemed to issue from the same apartment. I turned my head around, and beheld a sight that chained me, as if by magic, to the ground. Oh, it was heart thrilling to behold! On a bundle of straw, a woman, somewhat in years, lay apparently in the agonies of death. Near her head hung, reclining in deep sorrow, a beautiful little half naked child. On one side, a lovely girl, about thirteen years of age knelt; a Bible clasped in her thin slender hands, with which she was endeavoring to comfort her dying mother. I instantly recognized two of my Sabbath school children. The meeting was affecting. They had been without food for some days. The mother died next day, in the triumph of that faith which her little daughter taught her out of the Bible. The girls grew up to be respectable members of society, and one of them has been a teacher in a Sabbath school for several years.

(*b*) THE SKEPTIC AND HIS SON.—A pastor's wife solicited a little boy whose father was dissolute in his habits and skeptical in his sentiments, to attend the Sabbath school. He obtained consent of his parents, came the following Sabbath, and took his place in the class. Books were served out to him among the rest; he carried them home; they were read. This had a tendency to draw his father out to church, to hear preaching, and lectures on the subject of temperance. At one of the lectures, the pastor presented the pledge to him —he signed it with his own hand. Very soon the pastor was sent for to pray and converse with him on the subject of religion. In short, he found the husband and wife both deeply convicted on account of their sins! They were converted, baptized, and added to the church. They both honored their profession. The husband became an active, zealous member of the church. His efforts were untiring, his prayers simple, fervent and effective.

(*c*) MY SON IS MY SPIRITUAL FATHER.—At a Wesleyan class meeting, a man rose and addressed the leader thus:—"I am very thankful to God, and to you, for your Sunday school. My son, who now sits beside me, is my spiritual father. He heard me cursing, while in a state of drunkenness, and said to me, 'O father! my teacher said to-day, at the Sunday school, that neither drunkards nor swearers could enter into heaven.' This so affected my mind, that from that time I was enabled, by the grace of God, to leave off those wicked practices; and both myself and my son are now members of your society." He then laid his hand on his son's head, and repeated, "My son is my spiritual father."

(*d*) "SPELLING REPENTANCE." —In one of the counties in England, celebrated for its valuable mines, there lived a collier, grossly ignorant of divine things; and the doctrines of the gospel were totally unknown to him. From his habits of vice, and aversion to the worship of God, there seemed little hope that any moral change could be effected in him. But that which to man seemed so doubtful, God was pleased to accomplish in a way exceedingly simple, yet truly marvelous. Destitute, as he appears to have been, of concern for his spiritual welfare, he was induced to permit the attendance of his children at a Sunday school, conducted on religious principles; where the children were taught to practise moral duties, and instructed in the essential doctrines of Christianity. It pleased God to visit one of the daughters of this wicked father with mortal sickness; but, before her death, she was instrumental in exciting the attention of her parent to the concerns of his soul. "Father," inquired the dying child, "can you spell repentance?" This artless question, through the blessing of God, was effectual to awaken concern. "Spell repentance!" repeated the astonished father; "why, what is repentance?" Thus he became desirous of knowing, and ultimately was taught its sacred meaning; and discovered that he had been a stranger to it, both in theory and experience. He also discovered that he needed repentance; that he was a guilty condemned sinner, deserving God's wrath and everlasting misery; and repentance unto life was granted to him. He spelled out its divine import; and obtained an acquaintance with that Savior whom God has exalted to give repentance and remission of sins; and, by bringing forth the fruits of righteousness, he, in after life, supported and adorned his Christian profession.

(*e*) A PIOUS BOY'S FIDELITY. —In New-York city a little boy lived, who appeared to take little or no interest in learning, so that he was pronounced by his teachers a very dull scholar. He learned to read but very slowly, and finally neglected the school, thinking he should never succeed. There was a Bible class organized, which he was induced to attend. And here he soon began to manifest an interest in the study of the Scriptures. He learned to read well, which much astonished his father, who was a very wicked man. One Sabbath his father took some nails and a hammer to nail up a fence, when he was reproved by his little son, who spoke about working on the sabbath day, and invited him to attend public worship. The enraged father drove him from his presence, and threatened to punish him, if he ever talked in that way again. The child went away sorrowful. Not long after this, as the little boy returned from public worship, he went and looked over his father's shoulder, and observed that he was reading Hume's History of England. He went into the middle of the room, and said, "Father, where do you expect to go when you die?" Such a question from such a child could not be borne. "Away," said he, "from my presence immediately, or I will whip you." The child retired; but the father was troubled. He went out to walk, but still a load was pressing on his agonizing soul. He thought of attending public worship, for nothing else seemed so likely to soothe his troubled feelings. He entered while the minister was at prayer, and that day was the beginning of better days to him. He sought from God the forgiveness of his sins, and soon obtained the hope of eternal life.

A few years passed away, and the old man was on his dying bed. His son attended him, constantly ministering to his spiritual wants. To a Christian minister the father said, "I am dying, but I am going to heaven; and my son has been the instrument of saving my soul." Soon his spirit was released to be welcomed, as we have no reason to doubt, into the mansions of glory. Happy child! to be the instrument of saving his father from death. Happy parent! to be blessed with such a child.

(*f*) THE SAILOR AND HIS DAUGHTER.—In conversation with a respectable middle-aged seaman, at one of the prayer-meetings of the Liverpool Seamen's Friend Society, a friend asked, what first induced him to attend to religion. After a pause of some moments, he related the following narrative:—

I have been a sailor from a very early age, and never thought about religion, or the concerns of my soul, until my return from my last voyage. My home, where I have resided eighteen years, is at a village near Workington, in a small cottage, the next to a neat chapel; but the people who go to this chapel being called by the neighbors, methodists, I never would venture inside the door, nor suffer my family to do so, if I could prevent it. I usually sail out of Liverpool. During the winter the vessel is laid up. At those times I return home for a few weeks to my family. Having a small family, and the times pressing rather hard upon us, during my absence last summer, my wife, endeavoring to save a little, sent my eldest girl, about six years of age, to the Sunday school established at the chapel. My stay, when at home, being generally of short duration, my wife might suppose it would be no difficult matter to keep me in ignorance of the circumstance.

I came from my last voyage before Christmas, and went home. Being late when I arrived, I had not the opportunity of seeing my eldest girl until the following day. At dinner time, when we had sat down, I began to eat what was before me, without ever thinking of my heavenly Father, who provided my daily bread; but, glancing my eye towards this girl, of whom I was dotingly fond, I observed her to look at me with astonishment. After a moment's pause, she asked me, in a solemn and serious manner, "Father, do you never ask a blessing before eating?" Her mother observed me to look hard at her, and hold my knife and fork motionless (it was not anger—it was a rush of conviction which struck me like lightning); apprehending some reproof from me, and wishing to pass it by in a trifling way, she said, "Do you say grace, Nanny." My eyes were still riveted upon the child, for I felt conscious I had never instructed her to pray, nor even set an example, by praying with my family. The child, seeing me waiting for her to begin, put her hands together, and lifting her eyes up to heaven, breathed the sweetest prayer I ever heard. This was too much for me; the knife and fork dropped from my hands, and I gave vent to my feelings in tears. [Here a pause ensued, and he appeared much affected; on recovering himself, he continued.] I inquired who had thus instructed the child. The mother informed me the good people at the chapel next door; and the child never would go to bed, nor rise in the morning, without kneeling down to pray for herself, and her dear father and mother.

Ah! thought I, and I never prayed for myself or my children. I entered the chapel in the evening, for the first time, and continued to attend the means of grace there. The Lord having wakened me to a sense of my danger through the instrumentality of a dear child, I am now seeking him with all my heart, and truly can I say, I am happy in the thought, that Jesus Christ came into the world to save poor sinners, of whom I am chief.

(*g*) THE GAMBLING FATHER.—Hannah Price, a poor girl, had been instructed in a Sunday school. The serious impressions made upon her mind were soon visible; and she showed that she was converted to God. Her father, though in his earlier years he had received a better education than the most respectable of the poor have usually obtained, had become the companion of the most profligate men in his native village, and, by degrees, the worst of them all. The alehouse, at night, received the earnings of the day; and if any part remained after the guilty revels of the week, it was spent on Sunday in the same haunt of vice. His wife never reproached him, and only endeavored to lure him from such society, and such practices, by the comforts of home. But his home was the scene of his greatest misery; for there he had time to reflect, and there he was surrounded by the wife and children whom he was daily injuring.

One Sunday evening, after drinking and gambling all the day, and having lost all the earnings of the week, he turned from his companions, and scarcely knowing what he did, took the road homewards. One of them called to him to return, entreated him to have one more game, and added,

"Why, you will be sure to win it all back, you know."

He stopped—"Why, if I could get it back," said he to himself.

"Come, come," said his companion, "one more game, only one."

"No," said Price; "I've lost all my money, and so I can't if I would." But at that moment it occurred to him, that all his quarter's rent, except what was to be made up out of his last week's work, had been put in a cupboard, in the kitchen at home; and that if he could get that, he should be sure to win back all he had lost. The money was to be paid the next day, and, hardened as he was, he trembled at what he was going to do, and was terrified lest his wife and children should see him.

He approached the house, then ventured to look in at the window, and perceiving no one, he entered the kitchen, and went hastily up to the cupboard. It was locked, and he felt a momentary relief in the thought that he could not get the money. But again he said to himself, I shall be sure to win; and he hastened softly up stairs to look for the key, thinking he knew where his wife had put it. As he passed the room in which the children slept, he thought he heard a faint noise, and, listening he heard several sobs, and then a voice. It was poor little Hannah, praying that her father might see the error of his ways, that God would change his heart, and make him a comfort to her mother, and to them all. Her sighs and tears seemed almost to impede her utterance; and when he heard her call him her "dear, dear father," and felt how ill he had deserved such a name, he could scarcely forbear groaning aloud, in the anguish of his feelings. He forgot the key, crept to his bed-room, and fell on his knees. He uttered not one word, but the language of the heart is audible in the ears of Mercy; and that evening, for the first time, it might be said of him, "Behold he prayeth."

(*h*) LEAVING ALL FOR CHRIST.—A large family, who resided a few miles from the city of New-York, were accustomed entirely to neglect both the church and the Sabbath school; in fact, the father and mother were very much opposed to religious instruction of any kind. It so happened, however, that a little daughter of these parents became connected with a sabbath school, and was soon very much interested in the instruction she received. When her father heard of her attending the school, he forbade her going again; but the little girl supposing that he was not really in earnest, continued to go. At length, the father, mother, brothers and sisters threatened in decided terms to turn her out of the house, if she should again be seen at the sabbath school. She, however, when Sunday morning came, dressed herself as usual, except putting on her bonnet. When the hour arrived for the school to commence, she went to her father, and taking him by the hand, said, "Father, I love you, but I love Jesus Christ more, so I now bid you farewell!" She then took leave of her mother in the same way, and of her brothers and sisters, and left them for the school. The warmth of regard of their little daughter for religious instruction, touched a tender chord in the bosom of the father, notwithstanding his apparent hard-heartedness: he did not repeat his prohibition, but followed silently after her to the school—went in—and, on witnessing the instructions given to the children, became at once reconciled towards his daughter, and interested in the school. The next sabbath he persuaded his wife to accompany him, and she was pleased also; and, finally, the whole family became not only interested in the sabbath school, but useful and active members of the church. This little girl, in following the dictates of her conscience, little thought that she should be the means of bringing her father, mother, brothers and sisters to the knowledge of the truth. But God in his infinite goodness, saw fit to make her the instrument in bringing about such a blessed result.

398 Connection of Sabbath Schools with the Ministry and Missions.

(*a*) THE BEREAN CLASS.—A writer speaking of a certain Sabbath school in Boston, says: "One of the former teachers in that school, is now settled in the ministry in this vicinity; another is a useful printer in the Sandwich Islands; another is a superintendent of a Sabbath school in this city; and a fourth is studying at Andover, to fit himself for teaching in a day school. One of the former pupils is now studying with reference to the ministry; two others are far advanced in their college course, and one of these will probably become a herald of that Gospel which he loves.

(*b*) VARIOUS INSTANCES.—It is said, that of the missionaries who have gone from Great Britain to the heathen, nineteen twentieths became pious at the Sabbath schools; and that, of the orthodox ministers in England, who are under forty years of age, more than two-thirds became pious at the Sabbath schools.

Henderson and Patterson, who have done such wonders on the continent, in regard to the Bible cause, it is said, received their first impressions at Sabbath schools. The celebrated Dr. Morrison, missionary in the vast empire of China, who has translated the whole Bible into Chinese, a language spoken by the largest associated population on the globe, became pious at a Sabbath school! O! who can tell, how many Brainerds, and Buchanans, and Morrisons, and Martyns, and Harriet Newels God is training in these schools, to become the blessed instruments of renovating the world!!

(*c*) ROBERT MAY AND HIS SCHOOL.—Robert May was the son of a common mariner, in indigent circumstances. He was sent to the Sunday school at Woodbridge (Eng.), where he obtained his education, and greatly improved his privileges.

One Lord's day morning, as the minister was going to the meeting-house, Robert put into his hand a humble petition, requesting that he might be permitted to be a teacher in the Sunday school; an office in which he afterwards appeared to be both happy and useful.

On the eleventh of March, 1806, when he was seventeen years of age, he was admitted a member of the independent chapel at Woodbridge.

Robert now felt an earnest desire to go abroad as a missionary. He often told his minister that he thought there were plenty of teachers at home, and that he should like to go abroad, to teach poor black children to read the Bible, and to learn hymns and catechisms.

After being eminently useful in improving and extending the Sunday school system in the United States, his final destination was Chinsurah, in the neighborhood of Calcutta. Here he spent his time chiefly in instructing the children of the poor benighted heathen in the great principles of Christianity, and in other parts of useful knowledge.

In connexion with his other exertions, he published a small volume of sermons, which he had preached to children, and which have since been reprinted in England.

He had three thousand children under his care, and was about to add two thousand five hundred more to that number, when he was seized by a violent fever, which, in a few days, terminated his valuable life, and brought him to the house appointed for all living.

(*d*) HANDS' TESTIMONY.—At a public meeting, the Rev. W. Hands, a missionary in the East Indies, observed that, "he owed every thing to Sunday schools; for it was there that the heavenly spark had first caught his soul; it was there that he had first lifted up his voice for the purpose of imparting Christian instruction to others. If it had not been for that opportunity, he should probably never have offered himself to the Missionary Society. Therefore, again he said, that he had every reason to bless God that he had begun by being a Sunday school teacher, especially as he believed that it was principally through the labors of Sunday schools, that the Gospel of the Redeemer was extended throughout the world.

(*e*) MUNDY'S TESTIMONY.—On the same occasion, the Rev. George Mundy, missionary at Chinsurah, in the East Indies, states that he might truly say, that if he had never been a Sunday school teacher, he should never have been a missionary.

(*f*) KNILL'S TESTIMONY.—The Rev. Richard Knill wrote from St. Petersburgh, in 1819, as follows: "As an individual, I feel peculiarly indebted to such institutions, and to the glory of God I record it, that all the blessings which have been given to others, through my instrumentality, may be traced up to a Sunday school. It was my privilege to be a teacher in a Sunday school at Bideford: hearing a sermon preached in behalf of the institution led me first to think of being a missionary. Most of my fellow-students at Axminster had been Sunday school teachers; and out of twenty missionaries, who were my colleagues at Gosport, three-fourths of them had been engaged in the same way.

(*g*) PHILIP'S TESTIMONY.—At the annual meeting of the Sunday-School Union, in May, 1829, the Rev. Dr. Philip, missionary from the Cape of Good Hope, stated that he commenced his labors in the church of Christ as a Sunday-school teacher. The first prayer that he offered up in the presence of others, was in a Sunday-school. The first attempt he ever made to speak from the Holy Scriptures was in a Sunday-school. And he was fully persuaded, that had it not been for his humble exercises in the capacity of a Sunday-school teacher, and the advantages he there acquired, he should never have had the confidence to become a minister of the gospel, or a missionary of Jesus Christ. He informed the meeting, further, that when he commenced his ministerial labors in Aberdeen, he felt the importance of promoting Sunday school instruction; and the benefits which had resulted from the schools established in that town were, at the present moment, incalculable. During the period that he labored there, twelve or fourteen young men went out into the field of ministerial labor, many of whom became missionaries. One of them was the lamented Dr. Milne, and the other was the amiable Keith. Several other ministers owed their first religious impressions to the tuition they received in Sunday-schools.

(*h*) FOURTEEN MINISTERS FROM A CLASS.—Mr. Clark, afterwards schoolmaster at Sierra Leone, taught a Sunday school at Edinburgh. His method of giving instruction was, after the pupils had read, or repeated a portion of Scripture, to put such explanatory and practical questions to them as naturally arose out of the passage, and to conclude with a short address and prayer. Of one class, consisting of sixteen boys, fourteen of them at adult age, were brought to the saving knowledge of God, and acknowledged the early instruction he had given them as the means of their conversion. The whole of these were afterwards engaged in preaching the gospel, some of them in Great Britain, and others in foreign lands.

(*i*) REPORT OF BATH UNION.—The Bath Sunday school Union Report, of 1824, gives the pleasing information, that several missionaries, and upwards of twenty other persons, had been called out of its schools, to preach "the glorious gospel of the blessed God."

(*j*) THE ORPHAN HOUSE SUNDAY SCHOOL.—At a meeting of teachers conected with the Newcastle-on-Tyne Sunday School Union, in 1823, an old teacher observed that he had known the Orphan House Methodist Sunday school for twenty-one years; and that, during this period, no less a number than twenty-six preachers had issued from it, either from the scholars or the teachers. Can there be a stronger proof of the utility of Sunday schools?

(*k*) THE CLERGYMAN'S VISIT.—I was, one Sabbath afternoon, says a superintendent, about to close the school in which I was engaged, when a well-dressed genteel person, who presented himself as a visitor, requested me to allow him to speak to the children. This being readily granted, he addressed them nearly to the following effect:

There was once a poor lad, who was noted, even among his sinful companions, for wickedness, but especially for swearing and Sabbath breaking. He, along with others, resolved, one Sabbath, to pelt some steady boys who were going to their school. However, it so happened, that the lads, on being attacked, ran away; this lad followed them to the very doors of the school, which, when opened, as they were then singing, such a sound came from the place as seemed to stun him. He wondered what they could be doing inside; and a teacher at that moment admitted the other boys, and invited him in. A new scene now opened itself upon him; nearly three hundred boys, seated with their teachers. They all appeared so neat and clean, and in such order that he wished he was "one of them." He stood, for some time, a spectacle for the whole school dirty and ragged, and with his wooden clogs on. After some consultation, it was resolved to admit him into the A B C class. Every thing was new to him. The next Sabbath he appeared, his hair was combed, his face washed, and a pair of shoes were given to him. He now found himself so much behind the other boys, that he resolved to strain every nerve to get up to them. This determination was the means of his rising to the very first class; when his conduct being approved of, he was chosen a teacher. He now felt he had something more to do than to teach; he had a soul to be saved or lost. In a little time he was enabled, after much prayer, to believe on the Lord Jesus Christ, and to rejoice in his salvation. The Lord then called him to preach these glad tidings, and happening some time after to officiate within twenty miles of his own much beloved school, he rode hard, after the morning's labors, and reached the place just in time to see the poor lads in his own, very own school;—and here he is now speaking to you.

The scene now became truly affecting; he burst into tears, as did several others around him; at last, he sobbed out, "O, my dear lads, be in right good earnest to make the most of your very great Sabbath school privileges; I have kept you too long!" He then concluded with a most affecting prayer.

399. Miscellaneous.

(*a*) CHIEF JUSTICE MARSHALL AND JUDGE WASHINGTON.—Chief Justice Marshall and the late Judge Washington, of the Supreme Court of the United States, were both active in the Sabbath school cause. At the age of seventy, the chief justice regarded it as his high honor to walk through the city of Richmond at the head of a Sunday school procession.

(*b*) EFFECT OF FAITHFULNESS.—"A class," says the report from F——, Mass., "consisting in all of six scholars, usually numbering three or four on the Sabbath, was left vacant by the removal of its teacher, who might be denominated a good commonplace teacher. Her place was supplied by one who felt the solemn responsibility of her station and the worth of souls. Her influence was soon seen and felt. Numbers flocked to her class. In a short time it increased from six to *fourteen*, and others were necessarily denied admission. A deep interest and general seriousness soon pervaded the whole class. This was evidently the result of direct and personal conversation with them on the subject of their salvation. In a short time this devoted teacher was obliged by ill health to resign her place to another; the class has now lost much of its interest in spiritual things, and has gradually dwindled away to nearly its former number. This instance goes to show that even the thoughtless have a disposition to covet and listen to the instructions of those who deal faithfully with their souls."

(*c*) THE THREE CLASSES AND THE THREE RESOLUTIONS.—In the State of New-York, a pious young lady was once requested by the superintendent to take a class of girls in the Sabbath school. She accepted the invitation and engaged in the work. She was observed to be very earnest, faithful and affectionate with her charge. Soon a change was observed. One after another became thoughtful, serious, anxious and hopefully pious, until, in the judgment of charity, every member of her class was converted to God.

She was at length requested to give up her class, and to take another, none of whom were pious. With some hesitation she at length consented. She had not been in her new class long before similar effects were observed, and ultimately every member of the class cherished a hope in Christ. She was finally induced to give up this class also to be instructed by others, and to take another class, all of whom were unconverted. She had not labored long before precisely the same results followed her labors as before, and every member of this third class became hopefully pious. And now her work was done. Her Master called her to her rest in heaven. She died, but her labors lived.

After her death, her friends, on examining her religious journal, found the following resolutions, viz.—RESOLVED, *that I will pray once each day for each member of my class by name*. On looking farther in the journal, they found the same resolution re-written and re-adopted, with a slight addition, as follows, viz.—RESOLVED, *that I will pray once each day for each member of my class by name, and agonize in prayer*.

Looking on still farther in her journal, the same resolution was again found re-written and re-adopted, with *another* slight addition, as follows, viz.—RESOLVED, *that I will pray once each day for each member of my class by name, and agonize in prayer, and expect a blessing*. Did that teacher do too much and pray too much? What answer would her glorified spirit now give could she speak to us?

(*d*) DYING TEACHER MISTAKEN.—Mr. M. was for many years a pious and indefatigable Sunday school teacher. It pleased God to call him to suffer severe affliction, and to an early death. During his long affliction, though it was painful even to see him walk, he went to his class, nor would he resign as long as he could possibly reach the school. "It was my happiness," says a writer in the 'Teacher's Magazine,' "to visit him during his trying illness; and the calmness of his mind under affliction, and his triumphant departure, I never shall forget. Nor shall I cease to remember another circumstance. Turning to me, and with something like despondency, he said, 'Well, I believe I never was useful as a Sunday school teacher.'

"Some short time after his death, I visited a Sunday school in a small town some distance from that in which Mr. M. had lived. I soon recognized among the teachers one who had been a Sunday scholar; I conversed with him and found that he was a professor of religion, and a member of a Christian church in that town. I congratulated him upon his employment, and inquired by what means he had been led to love the Lord Jesus Christ? He replied, 'The advice which my teacher again and again gave me, led me to reflection and to prayer, and I hope was the means of leading me to Christ.' And who was that teacher? He replied, 'Mr. M.' Yes, that same dear friend, who, upon a dying bed, said, he believed he had never been useful as a Sunday school teacher."

(*e*) PRESIDENT HARRISON A TEACHER. — President Harrison taught, for several years, in a humble Sabbath school on the banks of the Ohio. The Sabbath before he left home for Washington, to assume the duties of chief magistrate of the nation, he met his Bible class as usual. And his last counsel on the subject to his gardener, at Washington, it may be hoped, will never be forgotten by the nation. When advised to keep a *dog* to protect his fruit, he replied—"Rather set a *Sunday school teacher* to take care of the boys."

(*f*) EXAMPLE OF SEVERAL STATESMEN.—A writer in the New-York Journal of Commerce for 1844, says; "The present Chancellor of the University of New-York city, (Mr. Frelinghuysen,) was a Sunday school teacher while he held the office of Attorney General of New Jersey, and afterwards, while a Senator in Congress; and he may still be seen cheerfully associating with the humblest teachers.

The Hon. B. F. Butler was a Sunday-school teacher while holding the office of Attorney General of the United States, and has, at the present time, his Bible class for young men.

And the visitor at Saratoga Springs, who will look into the Sunday school, may there see the Hon. Chancellor of the state of New-York (R. H. Walworth) with other literary gentlemen, animating the young in their Bible investigations.

Hon. Wm. Ellsworth, while governor of the state of Connecticut, instructed a Bible class from Sabbath to Sabbath, in one of the Congregational churches of Hartford. He remarked that when he quitted the gubernatorial chair in the State-house and came before his class to teach them the word of God, he felt that he was not going down, but *going up*."

(*g*) A GOOD RESOLUTION.—At the close of an Agent's address to a meeting in the western part of the state of Massachusetts, in 1828, after alluding to the fact that a neighboring town was laboring to bring all into the Sabbath school, that old and young, in the interval of divine service, should be employed in teaching or studying the Bible, he inquired whether it was not the duty of the people of that place to follow an example so worthy of imitation? Some with locks already white for the grave, said they would become Sabbath-school scholars, and, in accents tremulous with emotion, gave thanks to God that they could now come and enjoy the privileges with which he was blessing their children. The following resolution was then almost unanimously adopted by male and female, viz: *That, in the opinion of this meeting, it is the duty of* EVERY PERSON, *not prevented by the providence of God, to be connected with a Sabbath school. And that we will do all in our power to effect this object.*

(*h*) SCHOOLS IN WALES.—A poor family, in Wales, had acquired, by great industry, he sum of thirty pounds. This, for greater security, as they thought, they placed in the hands of a person reported to be very rich; but he shortly afterwards failed, and they lost their little all. They were nearly broken-hearted; and, from their abject condition, did not like to be seen in a place of worship. After some time, however, their little boy found his way to a Sunday school, was very attentive, and went regularly for a long time. At length he was taken very ill, and requested the teachers to come and pray with him. He gradually got worse, and it became evident to himself and others, that he was soon to leave this world. This little boy then told his parents he felt quite happy in the love of God; and said, that if he had not attended a Sunday school, he should have known nothing of the Lord Jesus Christ. He entreated, as his dying request, that his mother would attend and take his place in the Sunday school; for, in Wales. there are nearly as many adults, or grown people, in the schools, as children. The poor weeping mother consented, and, after her little boy's death, attended where he used to sit; the result of which was, that both she and her husband became truly converted to God.

(*i*) EFFECT OF HAVING ADULT SCHOLARS.—A gentleman, speaking of a certain Sabbath school in Massachusetts, says: The school embraces those of all ages, from 3 to 80. With a few exceptions, the whole congregation attend the school.

A more interesting school I have never seen: all seem desirous of understanding the word of God—and many, I trust, that they may obey it. We think that a deep interest is felt in consequence of all being together. The adults give *character* to the school. The younger members feel the importance of the study in which the older ones are engaged.

The happy effects of the Sabbath school in this town are perceptible in all classes of persons. The aged have opened their eyes upon a new world. The Bible has become the delightful study of many who, till within three years, scarcely ever perused it: those who are past the meridian of life often remark to me that they find subjects of thought and inquiry which never suggested themselves to them till they studied for the purpose of teaching others, or to give answers to questions. Our adult classes are on the plan of mutual instruction—and I think there is quite as much interest manifested among them as among the youth. This has had a very salutary effect on the younger scholars.

400. SATAN, AGENCY OF.

(*a*) A HARD QUESTION. — An islander in the South Seas, once proposed the following query to the missionaries:—"You say God is a holy and a powerful Being; that Satan is the cause of a vast increase of moral evil or wickedness in the world, by exciting or disposing men to sin. If Satan be only a dependent creature, and the cause of so much evil, which is displeasing to God, why does God not kill Satan at once, and thereby prevent all the evil of which he is the author?" In answer he was told, "that the facts of Satan's dependence on, or subjection to the Almighty, and his yet being permitted to tempt men to evil, were undeniable from the declarations of Scripture, and the experience of every one accustomed to observe the operations of his own mind. Such an one, it was observed, would often find himself exposed to an influence that could be attributed only to satanic agency; but that why he was permitted to exert this influence on man, was not made known in the Bible."

(*b*) "THE DEVIL IS WROTH." —"I asked the Rev. Legh Richmond," says one, "how we were to reconcile the increase of religion with the acknowledged growth of crime, as evinced in our courts of justice? He answered, 'Both are true. Bad men are becoming worse, and good men better. The first are ripening for judgment, the latter for glory. The increase of wickedness is, in this respect, a proof of the increase of religion. The devil is wroth, knowing that his time is short.'"

401. SELF-CONTROL.

(*a*) THE MERCHANT AND THE QUAKER.—A merchant in London had a dispute with a quaker respecting the settlement of an account. The merchant was determined to bring the account into court, a proceeding which the quaker earnestly deprecated, using every argument in his power to convince the merchant of his error; but the latter was inflexible. Desirous to make a last effort, the quaker called at his house one morning, and inquired of the servant if his master was at home, the merchant hearing the inquiry, and knowing the voice, called out from the top of the stairs, "Tell that rascal I am not at home." The quaker looking up at him, calmly said, "Well, friend, God put thee in a better mind." The merchant, struck afterwards with the meekness of the reply, and having more deliberately investigated the matter, became convinced that the quaker was right and he was wrong. He requested to see him, and after acknowledging his error, he said, "I have one question to ask you, how were you able, with such patience, on various occasions, to bear my abuse?" "Friend," replied the quaker, "I will tell thee; I was naturally as hot and violent as thou art. I knew that to indulge this temper was sinful; and I found that it was imprudent. I observed that men in a passion always spake aloud; and I thought if I could control my voice, I should repress my passion. I have, therefore, made it a rule, never to let my voice rise above a certain key; and by a careful observance of this rule, I have, by the blessing of God, entirely mastered my natural temper." The quaker reasoned philosophically, and the merchant, as every one else may do, benefitted by his example.

(*b*) MARLBORO' AND HIS SERVANT.—The Duke of Marlborough possessed great command of temper, and never permitted it to be ruffled by little things, in which even the greatest men have been occasionally found unguarded. As he was one day riding with Commissary Marriot, it began to rain, and he called to his servant for his cloak. The servant not bringing it immediately, he called for it again. The servant, being embarrassed with the straps and buckles, did not come up to him. At last, it raining very hard. the duke called to him again, and asked him what he was about, that he did not bring his cloak. "You may stay, sir," grumbled the fellow, "if it rains cats and dogs, till I can get at it." The duke turned round to Marriot, and said, very coolly, "Now I would not be of that fellow's temper for all the world."

(*c*) NEWTON AND HIS DOG.—Sir Isaac Newton's temper, it is said, was so equal and mild, that no accident could disturb it. A remarkable instance of which is related as follows:—

Sir Isaac had a favorite little dog, which he called Diamond. Being one evening called out of his study into the next room, Diamond was left behind. When Sir Isaac returned, having been absent but a few minutes, he had the mortification to find that Diamond had overturned a lighted candle among some papers, the nearly finished labor of many years, which were soon in flames, and almost consumed to ashes. This loss, from Newton's advanced age, was irreparable; but, without at all punishing the dog, he exclaimed, "O, Diamond, Diamond! you little know the mischief you have done!"

(*d*) THE LOGICIAN'S DIGRESSION.—Of Mr. John Henderson, it is observed, that the oldest of his friends never beheld him otherwise than calm and collected; it was a state of mind he retained under all circumstances. During his residence at Oxford, a student of a neighboring college, proud of his logical acquirements, was solicitous of a private disputation with the renowned Henderson; some mutual friends introduced him, and, having chosen his subject, they conversed for some time with equal candor and moderation; but Henderson's antagonist, perceiving his confutation inevitable, (forgetting the character of a gentleman, and with a resentment engendered by his former arrogance,) threw a full glass of wine *in his face.* Henderson, without altering his features or changing his position, gently wiped his face, and then coolly replied, "This, sir, *is a digression; now for the argument.*"

(*e*) THE HARDEST FOE.—Peter the Great made a law in 1722, that if any nobleman beat or ill-treated his slaves, he should be looked upon as insane, and a guardian should be appointed to take care of his person and of his estate. This great monarch once struck his gardener, who, being a man of great sensibility, took to his bed, and died in a few days. Peter hearing of this, exclaimed, with tears in his eyes, "Alas! I have civilized my own subjects; I have conquered other nations; yet I have not been able to civilize or to conquer myself."

(*f*) SELF-CONTROL OF SOCRATES.—Socrates finding himself in great emotion against a slave, said, "I would beat you if I were not angry." Having received a box on the ear, he contented himself by only saying with a smile, "It is a pity we do not know when to put on a helmet." Socrates meeting a gentleman of rank in the streets, saluted him, but the gentleman took no notice of it. His friends in company observing what passed, told the philosopher "they were so exasperated at the man's incivility, that they had a good mind to resent it." But he very calmly made answer, "If you meet any person in the road in a worse habit of body than yourself, would you think you had reason to be enraged at him on that account; pray then, what greater reason can you have for being incensed at a man for a worse habit of mind than any of yourselves?"

His wife, Xantippe, was a woman of a most fantastical and furious spirit. At one time, having vented all the reproaches upon Socrates her fury could suggest, he went out and sat before the door. His calm and unconcerned behavior but irritated her so much the more; and in the excess of her rage, she ran up stairs and emptied a vessel upon his head; at which he only laughed, and said, "that so much thunder must needs produce a shower." Alcibiades, his friend, talking with him about his wife, told him he wondered how he could bear such an everlasting scold in the same house with him: he replied, "I have so accustomed myself to expect it, that it now offends me no more than the noise of carriages in the streets."

(*g*) A GREAT CONQUEST.—Antigonus, king of Syria, during one of his campaigns, one day overheard some of his soldiers reviling him behind his tent. But instead of summoning them to appear and answer for their contumely, and exercising his authority in their punishment, he barely drew aside the curtain of his tent, and said, "*Gentlemen, just remove to a greater distance, for your king hears you.*"

402. SELF-DECEPTION.

(*a*) THE CHURCH MEMBER'S EXCUSE FOR DRUNKENNESS.—In the town of ——, in the State of New-York, there lived a man who occasionally drank to intoxication. He was a professor of religion; and as private admonitions proved ineffectual, he was at length brought before the church. The evidence of his intemperance was clear and unquestionable; but that he might not be condemned without the privilege of defence, he was permitted, before the final vote was taken, to say what he could in vindication of his conduct. He arose and acknowledged his offence, apparently with the deepest contrition, and entreated his brethren (tears all the while falling down his cheeks) that they would not excommunicate him from the church, alleging, as a reason for the helpless state in which he was sometimes found, that "*his constitution required more spirit than his legs would bear up under!*"

(*b*) THE MORALIST CONVERTED.—Mr. B. had received a highly religious education, and from earliest years had been surrounded with pious connections. So great was his respect for religious ordinances, and his conviction of the importance of maintaining its forms, that for years he heartlessly officiated at the family altar. By this means, by regular attendance on the sanctuary, and by his blameless deportment, his friends were led, in the blindness of their charity, to believe him a truly pious man. Hence, without any inquiry into his inward experience, they often urged him to join the church. But some secret misgivings led him to decline; yet, as he has since remarked, that it was his prevailing opinion, that he was better than many professors of religion. Indeed, such was the influence of the opinions of his friends over him, that he gradually fell into the belief, that at some former period he had, *unawares*, passed from death unto life. While in this state of mind a revival commenced in the congregation of which he was a *member*, with great power. Striking instances of painful conviction and joyful conversion passed under his observation. The officiating clergyman appointed an evening lecture, near Mr. B.'s residence. With accustomed hospitality, Mr. B. invited the minister home with him after the lecture. After some general remarks, Mr. B. took occasion to dwell upon the inconsistencies of professors of religion. Little or no reply was made.

At length he began to expose his own views and feelings respecting what he thought *true religion*. But, much to his disappointment, the clergyman waived the subject with some indefinite reply. Mr. B. thought he discovered, in this unexpected silence, that his guest (as was the fact) considered his religion suspicious, which not a little disturbed his quiet. And this incident, slight as it may seem, was the means, apparently, of apprising this man of the complete deception under which he and others had labored, respecting the true state of his heart. He was now constrained to explore its dark recesses; and the more he examined, the more he was convinced, that he had for years been wrapping himself in a delusion; that the foundation of his hope was a lie. He soon became more deeply sensible to his own sins than to the sins of professors of religion, or of any other human being. At length he submitted, as he believes, to the conditions of divine grace; and continued afterwards to rejoice in the God of his salvation. "Oh! I shudder," said he, to a friend, "at the thought of my HAIR-BREADTH ESCAPE. How *easy*, how *easy* to be deceived in the *belief* that we are Christians, *without the least spark of vital piety!*"

(*c*) THE RUM-DRINKER'S CONVERSION.—During the revival at S., says Rev. Mr. Nettleton, I witnessed an instance which, if you please, I will relate. Mr. A. was one of the most respectable men in that village, about thirty years of age, who kept a large boarding-house. His wife was under deep conviction, and soon was rejoicing in hope, and prayed with and for her husband. This was the means of his conviction; though, at the time, it was not known. Report said he was confined to his bed, and dangerously ill. Hints were privately circulating that he was anxious for his soul, and was ashamed to have it known. It was late in the evening, when Brother G. went to his house, and found him in a bedroom, in a remote corner, in the greatest agony. "What is the matter?" said Brother G. "Oh, I am sick! I am in such distress!" "But your pulse is regular. Where is your pain?" He made no reply; but with violence smote upon his breast. He was asked, "Is it there?" "It is," he replied. The next evening I called, and found him still in the same distress. His convictions appeared to be deep. But when I returned, I suggested to Brother G. a suspicion of the smell of ardent spirits. I then related a number of anecdotes of false conversions, connected with this suspicious scent. "Mr. A. is a very moral man," said he, "and far from suspicion on that point." But, for fear, he sent me back to give him a solemn caution. I returned, and with much delicacy, warned him not to taste, lest ——. He seemed startled at my suggestion, and assured me that he was far from that habit. I requested his wife to watch him, and learned from her, that through his distress his strength had greatly failed, and that he had taken a *very little, only,* to prevent his sinking entirely. I returned, and observed to Brother G. that I feared Mr. A. was a ruined man. His concern continued for a few days, when he became exceedingly joyful. His conversion was considered wonderful. But my joy was checked. I could not forget the smell of ardent spirits. I called and found him much elated with joy. But when I cautioned him, he seemed surprised and somewhat offended, and observed—"I think I have been distressed enough to experience religion." "Ah!" said I, "now I doubt more than ever whether your heart has ever been changed. Do you think there is any merit in the distress of an awakened sinner? Suppose you had been to hell, and endured the torments of the damned; what then? It is not distress, but love to God and a change of heart which alone can fit the sinner for heaven." After a little conversation, his heart rose in such opposition, that he relinquished his hope. His distress returned in a moment, and he cried out "What shall I do?" His heart was evidently unrenewed, and still quarreling with the justice of God. From some expressions, I caught a glimpse of his heart; and that if he should ever experience religion, it was his secret purpose never to make a public profession of it. He was evidently unhumbled, *like a bullock unaccustomed to the yoke.* I put into his hands "Edwards on the Justice of God in the Damnation of Sinners." Shortly, he again found relief. He wished to profess religion with others, but prudence led us to wait; and the result was, that in progress of time he became a sot. I know not of a more hopeless being on earth. He does no business; has drunk himself out of his property, and almost out of his reason; and, as Brother G. says, he has become a brute.

403. SELF-DENIAL.

(*a*) TRANSCRIBING FROM DODDRIDGE.—The Southern Religious Telegraph states that Miss T——, of —— county, who was very thoughtless, was induced by a friend to promise that she would read the "Rise and Progress." For many weeks she postponed it; but at length became interested for her soul, and took up the work and read it with care. Her feelings followed those of the writer generally, and with as little opposition as could be expected until she came to the 17th chapter. That is styled the "self-dedication chapter." While transcribing this chapter, according to the author's direction, to make it her own act—consecrating herself to Jehovah's service for time and forever—she hesitated. Her wicked heart arose in opposition. She could not surrender *all* to God. There was a *small portion* of her earthly treasures; a *little shining dust*—used as ornaments of her perishing body which she was unwilling to surrender for that "glittering crown of glory" which Christ promises to all those that love and serve him. In great agony her pen was laid aside, and for several days she refused to finish the dedication chapter. One day, while complaining to a sister (since gone to rest) that she could find no peace, her sister replied, "Perhaps there is something you are unwilling to part with—some *little* thing that you will not give up for the sake of an interest in Christ. Remember, he requires *entire* consecration—*all.*" She soon left her sister—retired to her closet—resolved to part with her jewelry and all things else for an interest in her Redeemer. She was immediately able to finish transcribing her chapter—light began to dawn upon her soul—and her proud spirit was humbled. Peace gradually dawned upon her mind, and as soon as an opportunity presented, she united with the church, and now walks in newness of life.

(*b*) UNPURCHASED, UNSEDUCED.—The Marquis de Bougy, a gallant general in the service of Louis XIV, was greatly esteemed by that monarch, and by his prime minister, Cardinal Mazarin. He would have made a great fortune, if he had been a Roman Catholic; and he received several letters from the queen and from the cardinal, wherein they exhorted him to change his profession, and thereby remove the obstacle which lay in the way of his advancement. They also offered him a marshal's staff, and a considerable government, provided he would become a Roman Catholic. His answer was, that if he could resolve to betray his God for a marshal's staff, he might betray his king for a less advantage; but that he would do neither of them, being contented to see that his services were acceptable, and that his religion was the only reason why he was not rewarded for them.

(*c*) THE EAR-RINGS SACRIFICED.—"A gentleman," says Mr. Knill, missionary at Petersburg, "resident on the shores of the Caspian, who once cared nothing about Christ or his cause, has, within a few years, become a warm-hearted disciple. Knowing his character, I wrote to him to assist me in the distribution of the Holy Scriptures. To my request he joyfully agreed; but he did not think it sufficient to contribute towards it himself, but he tried to enlist others also in the good work. He mentioned it in particular to a pious lady of his acquaintance, who had just before received a present of a hundred roubles, to purchase a pair of ear-rings. Fired with the hope of promoting the eternal happiness of her fellow creatures, she determined to sacrifice her ear-rings to the cause of God, and sent the hundred roubles to me. Perhaps this was the first time that ever her attachment to the Savior had called for a sacrifice; and it must be unspeakably gratifying to her mind, when reviewing the transaction, to feel that she could part with her ornaments for her adorable Redeemer."

(*d*) SELF-DENIAL OF VARIOUS MARTYRS.—[illegible] PALMER, in Queen Mary's days, [illegible] and preferment offered him, if he would recant his faith in Christ. His answer was, that he had resigned his living in two places for the sake of the gospel, and now was ready to yield his life on account of Christ.

WILLIAM HUNTER, when urged by Bonner to recant, replied, he could only be moved by the Scriptures, for he reckoned the things of earth but dross for Christ; and when the sheriff offered him a pardon at the stake, if he would renounce his faith, he firmly rejected it.

ANTONIUS RICETO, a Venetian, was offered his life, and considerable wealth, if he would concede but a little; and when his own son, with weeping entreated him to do so, he answered, that he was resolved to lose both children and estate for Christ.

The PRINCE OF CONDÉ, at the massacre of Paris, when the King assured him that he should die within three days, if he did not renounce his religion, told the monarch that his life and estate were in his hand, and that he would give up both rather than renounce the truth.

(*e*) PATRIOTIC THEOLOGIAN.—Mr. Weed, in one of his letters from Scotland, says:

"While at Liberton, which place is about two miles from the centre of Edinboro', I was informed of an instance of theological patriotism that would have made the old "Cameronian cow-feeder," were he alive, leap for joy. Observing a dozen stone masons actively engaged in putting up the walls of a small edifice, at which as many persons were lookers on, my cabman informed me that they were building a new Kirk for a "non-intrusionist minister," and on further inquiry, I ascertained that this humble temple was designed for an eloquent preacher who, with a devotion worthy of "Reuben Butler," or even of the stoutest Cameronians, who hid themselves in caverns during the "persecuting times," had renounced a living of $3,500 per annum, with a fine parsonage-house and glebe, rather than compromise his principles."

(*f*) THE CEYLONESE CONVERTS.—The simplicity of many of the heathen, when they receive the truth of God in the love of it, is often very admirable. Rev. W. M. Harvard states, in his narrative relative to Ceylon, that when he was once addressing a native congregation in the government school-house at Pantura, from 1 John iii. 8, he endeavored to show that the Kappooa system was one of the works of the devil which the Son of God came to destroy; and urged their immediate renunciation of all confidence in their vain charms, and to commit the keeping of their bodies and their souls to God. Appealing to their understandings and consciences, he inquired, "Which of you will now cast away these works of the devil, and place himself under the protection of the Son of God?" He looked round upon the congregation, as for a reply. Presently a charm was handed up to the pulpit, which had been broken off for that purpose. He held it up, and gave thanks to God, that in that place he had begun to destroy these works of the devil. He then repeated the inquiry, "Who next?" &c., and two or three more abandoned charms were handed up in a similar way. Before the close of the service, a handful of them was in his possession.

(*g*) THE ONLY DRESS.—A missionary in India says, "I rode to Nallamaram, and saw some people of the congregation there, together with the catechist. The clothes of one of the women were rather dirty, and I asked her about it. "Sir," said she, "I am a poor woman, and have only this single dress." "Well, have you always been so poor?" "No, I had some money and jewels, but a year ago the Maravers (thieves) came and robbed me of all. They told me," she said, "*If you will return to heathenism we shall restore you every thing.*" "Well, why did you not follow their advice? Now you are a poor Christian." "O, Sir," she replied, "I would rather be a *poor Christian* than a *rich heathen.*"

404. SERVANTS.

(*a*) THE DESPISED CONGREGATION.—A worldly man began to taunt a celebrated preacher, and, among other things, told him it was true his congregation was large, but it was chiefly made up of servants and low people. "I know it is," said the sagacious divine; "my church is composed of such converts as Jesus Christ and his apostles gained; and, as for servants, I had rather be instrumental in converting them than their employers."

"Why so?" inquired the man.

"Because," observed the minister, "they have the care of all the children.'

(*b*) DIDEROT'S SERVANT.—The Abbé Barruel, in the account he gives of the closing scenes of Diderot's life, tells us, that he had a Christian servant, to whom he had been kind, and who waited upon him in his last illness. This servant took a tender interest in the melancholy situation of his master, who was just about to leave this world, without preparation for another. Though a young man, he ventured one day, when he was engaged about his master's person, to remind him that he had a soul, and to admonish him, in a respectful manner, not to lose the last opportunity of attending to its welfare. Diderot heard him with attention, melted into tears, and thanked him. He even consented to allow the young man to introduce a clergyman, whom he would probably have continued to admit to his chamber, if his infidel friends would have suffered the minister to repeat his visits. Let us be encouraged to attempt good under the most unpromising circumstances, and, in our different stations, to remember we are commanded to labor for the welfare of those with whom we are connected.

(*c*) MELANCTHON'S SERVANT.—Philip Melancthon, who is universally known as one of the reformers, was highly esteemed for his great generosity. Indeed his friends were astonished at his liberality, and wondered how, with his small means, he could afford to give so much in charity. It appears to have been principally owing to the care and good management of an excellent and faithful servant named John, a native of Sweden. The whole duty of provisioning the family was intrusted to this domestic, whose care, assiduity and prudence amply justified the unbounded confidence reposed in him. He made the concerns of the family his own, avoiding all needless expenditure, and watching with a jealous eye his master's property. He was also the first instructor of the children during their infancy. John grew old in his master's service, and expired in his house amidst the affectionate regrets of the whole family. During a service of thirty-four years, how much usefulness was effected by honest John, and by his master through his instrumentality! Melancthon invited the students of the university to attend the funeral of his faithful servant, delivered an oration over his grave, and composed a Latin epitaph for his tombstone, of which the following is a translation:—

"Here, at a distance from his native land,
Came honest John, at Philip's first command;
Companion of his exile, doubly dear,
Who in a servant found a friend sincere;
And more than friend—a man of faith and prayer,
Assiduous soother of his master's care.
Here to the worms his lifeless body's given,
But his immortal soul sees God in heaven.'

(*d*) A LIVING EPISTLE.—"One day, in my travels," says Mr. Jay, "I heard of a servant who had attended a Wesleyan chapel. This offended her master and mistress, who told her that she must discontinue the practice, or leave their service. She received the information with modesty, said she was sorry, but so it must be; she could not sacrifice the convictions of her conscience to keep her place. So they gave her warning; and she was now determined, if possible to be more circumspect and exemplary than ever; determined that, if she suffered for her religion, her religion should not suffer for her. Some time after this, the master said to the mistress, "Why, this is rather a hard measure with regard to our servant; has she not a right to worship God where she pleases as well as ourselves?"

"Oh, yes," said the mistress; "and we never had so good a servant; one who rose so early, and got her work done so well, was so clean, and was so economical, never answering again."

And so they intimated that she might remain. Some time after this the wife said to her husband, "I think Mary's religion does her a great deal more good than our religion seems to do us; I should like to hear her minister." And so she went, and was impressed; and prevailed upon her husband to go, and he was impressed; and now they are all followers of God, and have the worship of God in their house.

405. SIN.

(*a*) FIVE DIRECTIONS.—"Five persons," says Mr. Brooks, "were studying what were the best means to mortify sin; one said, to meditate on death; the second, to meditate on judgment; the third, to meditate on the joys of heaven; the fourth, to meditate on the torments of hell; the fifth, to meditate on the blood and sufferings of Jesus Christ; and certainly the last is the choicest and strongest motive of all. If ever we would cast off our despairing thoughts, we must dwell and muse much upon, and apply this precious blood to our own souls; so shall sorrow and mourning flee away."

(*b*) DEATH PREFERRED TO SIN.—Count Godomar, a foreigner of note, often professed, in the declining part of his years, when death and the eternal world seemed nearer, "That he feared nothing in the world more than *sin;* and whatever liberties he had formerly taken, he would rather now submit to be torn to pieces by wild beasts, than knowingly or willingly commit any sin against God."

(c) USHER'S LAST WORDS.—SINS OF OMISSION. — The last words that Archbishop Usher was heard to express, were, "Lord, forgive my sins, especially my sins of *omission*."

(d) THE INFANT'S ANSWER.—At a missionary station among the Hottentots, the question was proposed, "Do we possess any thing that we have not received of God?" A little girl of five years old immediately answered, "Yes, sir, *sin*.'

(e) "THEY BROKE THE ORDER."—A poor villager in England supplied an answer to the cavil of an unbeliever; he said, "Time was, when I got amongst a set of people who would not believe the Bible, and I heard all their objections, and some of them did me great hurt; for I was not able to answer them, and my belief became almost as bad as theirs. I felt all the time I was wrong, and I could see the folly of some of their objections. They asked me one day, how it could be supposed that God would destroy Ada i and his descendants, only for eating an apple? In my worst state I could see that there was nothing in this often answered and weak objection; it was not that our first parents had only eaten of some kind of fruit; it was that they had disobeyed God; it was sir," said the poor man, "that they broke the order."

(f) NEWTON'S OPINION. — "Many have puzzled themselves," says Mr. Newton, "about the origin of evil; I observe there *is* evil, and that there is a way to escape it, and with this I begin and end."

406. Sin Against the Holy Ghost.

a) THE INFIDEL'S CONFESSION.—Mr. F——, the subject of the following narrative, was a respectable inhabitant of one of the northern towns of Pennsylvania. About seven years previous to his death, Mr. W——, a missionary, visited the town where Mr. F—— resided. Under his faithful labors, a revival of religion commenced, in which numbers were hopefully born into the kingdom of the Reedemer. The attention of Mr. F—— was also arrested. He was led to see his sinfulness and danger, and to inquire, "what he must do to be saved." His convictions of sin were pungent for some time, but, after a few months, his seriousness began to abate. Levity and profaneness succeeded, and, like the unclean spirit who walked through dry places, seeking rest and finding none, Mr. F—— returned to a state of stupidity seven times more dreadful than before. He soon adopted the sentiment of Universalism, and thence, as a natural course, he descended to infidelity; and, at length, boldly denied the inspiration of the Scriptures, and became an avowed Deist. In this situation, he was often asked by those acquainted with his previous seriousness, what he thought of his former convictions. He uniformly imputed them to enthusiasm or the work of the devil. The consequence was, as might have been expected, he became more and more confirmed in his infidel principles, until about four or five months previous to his death. It was at this time that the writer first became acquainted with him, and it was from his own lips, and from his neighbors, that the above account of his life was received. On reading to him the first nine verses of the sixth chapter of the Hebrews, and the last four verses of the second chapter of the Second Epistle of Peter, he was again awakened. The above words were like "a sharp two-edged sword." His infidel principles appeared in a surprising manner to leave him, and to be succeeded by a dreadful sense of the threatenings of the Divine law. The view which he had of his sinfulness was great, and such an awful feeling of danger pervaded his mind, that he trembled with fear. Great pains were taken to instruct him into the way of salvation by Jesus Christ, and prayer was literally made incessantly for him. But all availed nothing, his distress increased every day. After a few weeks he appeared to be verging fast to a state of complete despair. This appeared to be accelerated by a fixed opinion that he had committed the unpardonable sin. For some time he refused to tell the sin which he considered unpardonable. After much importunity, however, he said it consisted in imputing to the devil his previous religious impressions. He was informed that it might have proceeded from an error in judgment, and not from deliberate malice of heart. He decided that this could not be the case, for when he said that his former convictions were enthusiasm and from the devil, he knew they were produced by the Holy Spirit; that the above declaration proceeded directly from enmity, and had sealed his perdition. His distress and horror of mind increased, until they arose to the most alarming degree. At times he appeared to be in as much mental agony as he could possibly endure and live. He often declared he felt the very pains of hell in his bosom, and that if his soul and body were then in everlasting burnings, he could not suffer more. All means used to relieve him appeared only to increase the misery and aggravate the horror of his mind. Often with a countenance distorted with all the features of despair, he would entreat those present never to quench the Spirit, never to deny the work of the Holy Ghost, or embrace the sentiments of infidelity, especially never to impute revivals and awakenings to the devil. His sufferings soon impaired his health; he lost his appetite for food, and sleep entirely forsook his eyes. A fearful earnest of future misery took deeper and stronger hold on his mind, till at length reason reeled from her throne, and he died by his own hand. We suppose this to be a plain instance of the sin against the Holy Ghost.

(*b*) DELIVERANCE FROM A DELUSION.—There are instances of distressing fears on this subject, fears which, as the event shows, were unfounded. The following case is one; and one of the many which might be cited to show the truth of this. Mr. L—— had enjoyed the privilege of sitting under an able and successful ministry. His heart had been touched; and, during a remarkable period, in which he saw many of his friends embracing the hope of salvation, his own convictions increased. Not long after his feelings of impatience became sensitive. His attention was subsequently turned from its own proper object to one more nearly connected with our natural selfishness. He ceased to be an inquirer and became an objector. It is hard to stop here. Opposition succeeded a habit of objecting. An apparent bitterness of prejudice and malevolence of expression, were observable whenever he opened his lips on the subject of religion. Still the past day of conviction was a memorable time to him. Five years afterwards he was again roused to a sense of his danger. And with the alarm came the frightful recollection of his former conduct. Language which he had uttered—and which appeared nearly allied to blasphemy—returned fresh to his memory. He accused himself of having committed the unpardonable sin. All efforts to persuade him to the contrary were unavailing. The impression was daily deepening. His mind lost its elasticity; and a moody temperament succeeded. His friends were alarmed. A suspicion was started among them, that his conclusions might be just. This he marked, and labored to confirm it. He seemed to take a negative satisfaction in stating the desperation of his case; and in watching the fallen countenance of sympathy.

Many months had transpired, during which he was the subject of religious gossip with some, of a kind of superstitious dread with others, and of fervent prayer with a few of the remainder;—when the case was stated to a judicious minister, whom Divine Providence had called into the neighborhood. He waited on Mr. L., who, far from being averse to any conversation relative to his own state, seemed rather to court it. He was fluent in all his details of time and circumstance; and always ended his narrative with a declaration that he had ceased for ever to pray. After a preparatory interchange of remarks, he was asked, "You believe yourself guilty of the unpardonable sin?"

"I am sure of it."

"In what did the crime consist?"

"I opposed the work of God."

"So did Saul."

"I denied Jesus Christ."

"So did a disciple afterwards honored by his master."

"I doubted the power of Jesus Christ after strong evidence in his favor."

"So did Thomas."

"What? are you attempting to prove by such examples that I am a Christian?"

"Not at all: I am only inquiring into the nature of your guilt; and thus far I see no reason for despair."

"I have hated God," rejoined the self-condemned, "and openly avowed my enmity in sight of his Divine operations."

"Thus far your case is lamentable indeed; but not hopeless still. Our hearts are naturally at enmity with God. And I do not see why the open avowal of this, drawn out by the sight of the Law into visible form, must necessarily and always constitute the guilt of which you accuse yourself."

"I *feel* that I am cut off from salvation."

"It is difficult to reason against your feelings."

"But are they no proof on the present subject?"

"Let me inquire whether you desire the pardon of your sins?"

"Assuredly, if it were possible."

"Do you regret the conduct of which you accuse yourself?"

"Certainly."

"Do you sincerely desire repentance?"

"I would give the world if it were mine to be able to do so."

"Then it is not possible that you have been guilty to an unpardonable extent; for these are characteristics of a state of mind faithless, but far from being desperate. And they come within the design of the Gospel invitations."

There was something simple and touching in this mode of ministering to a mind diseased. And it produced an effect which, probably, no other process would have accomplished. Mr. L—— did not long survive this interview. But his living and dying were those of a favored Christian. Alas, that many persons laboring under a like delusion respecting the sin against the Holy Ghost, should not be enlightened by similar instruction! Doubtless not a few who never committed this sin, have lived for years, and then died under the horrible conviction, that they had thus sinned away the day of grace.

407. SLANDER.

(*a*) WAY TO AVOID CALUMNY.—"If any one speaks ill of thee," said Epictetus, "consider whether he has truth on his side; and, if so, reform thyself, that his censures may not affect thee." When Anaximander was told that the very boys laughed at his singing, "Ay," says he "then I must learn to sing better." Plato being told that he had many enemies who spoke ill of him. "It is no matter," said he; "I will live so that none shall believe them." Hearing at another time that an intimate friend of his had spoken detractingly of him, "I am sure he would not do it," said he, "if he had not some reason for it." This is the surest as well as the noblest way of drawing the sting out of a reproach, and the true method of preparing a man for that great and only relief against the pains of calumny—a *good conscience*.

(*b*) BOERHAAVE'S ADVICE.—The celebrated Boerhaave, who had many enemies, used to say that he never thought it necessary to repeat their calumnies. "They are sparks," said he, "which, if you do not blow them, will go out of themselves. The surest method against scandal is to live it down by perseverance in well-doing, and by prayer to God, that he would cure the distempered minds of those who traduce and injure us."

(*c*) XIMENES AND ADRIAN.—Adrian, the coadjutor of Ximenes in the government of Castile, was much disturbed at the libels which flew about against them. Ximenes was perfectly easy "If," said he, "we take the liberty to act, others will take the liberty to talk and write: when they charge us falsely, we may laugh; when truly, we must amend."

(*d*) DR. WAUGH'S REBUKES. —Dr. Waugh, of London, had a great dislike to every thing bordering on slander or defamation. The following is an illustration of his character in this point:—

One of his people had traveled all the way from Newton to his father's house, where he usually resided, to communicate to him an unfavorable report concerning another member of the congregation. Some friends being with him, this person was requested to stay and dine with them. After dinner, he took occasion, in a jocular manner, to ask each person in his turn, how far he had ever known a man travel to tell an evil report of his neighbor; when some gave one reply, and some another. He at last came to this individual, but without waiting for his self-condemning reply, or unnecessarily exposing him, he stated, that he had lately met with a Christian professor, apparently so zealous for the honor of the church, as to walk fourteen miles with no other object than that of making known to his minister the failings of a brother member. He then in a warm and impressive manner enlarged on the praise of that charity which covers a multitude of sins; which "rejoiceth not in iniquity, but rejoiceth in the truth."

The same excellent man being in company with a number of ministers, the bad conduct of a brother in the ministry became the subject of conversation, and every gentleman in the room joined warmly in condemning him. Dr. Waugh sat for a time silent. At last he walked up to his companions, and said, "My dear friends, surely we are not acting in accordance with our profession. The person you speak of is one of ourselves, and we ought not to blow the coal. But do you know that he is as bad a man as he is represented? and if he is, will railing against him do any good? It is cowardly to speak ill of a man behind his back; and I doubt if any of us would have sufficient courage, if our poor friend were to appear among us, to sit down and kindly tell him of his faults. If there be one here who feels himself quite pure, and free from error, let him throw the first stone; but if not, let us be silent; and I confess that I feel that I must not say one word." He resumed his seat, and the company looked at each other, struck silent by this rebuke from one so good and mild.

(*e*) HENRY AND THE BROKEN STORY.—Mr. Philip Henry used to remind those who spoke evil of people behind their backs, of the law,—"Thou shalt not curse the deaf." Those that are absent are deaf, they cannot right themselves, and therefore say no ill of them. A friend of his, inquiring of him concerning a matter which tended to reflect upon some people; he began to give him an account of the story, but immediately broke off, and checked himself with these words,—"But our rule is *to speak evil of no man*, and would proceed no farther in the story. The week before he died, a person requested the loan of a particular book from him. "Truly," said he, "I would lend it to you, but that it takes in the faults of some, which should rather be covered with a mantle of love."

(*f*) EFFECTS OF SLANDER. —The famous Boerhaave was one not easily moved by detraction. He used to say, "The sparks of calumny will be presently extinct of themselves unless you blow them." It was a good remark of another, that "the malice of ill tongues cast upon a good man is only like a mouthful of smoke blown upon a diamond, which, though it clouds its beauty for the present, yet it is easily rubbed off, and the gem restored, with little trouble to its owner."

(*g*) WHY BOERHAAVE BECAME A PHYSICIAN.—The affecting story of *Boerhaave*, so distinguished in the medical profession, is well known. With piety, and learning, and gifts, and an ardent zeal to glorify his divine Master, his heart was fixed upon consecrating his life to the sacred ministry. The preliminary steps had been so far taken, that he had gone to Leyden to obtain his license to preach—when to his utter astonishment he found the way completely hedged up. An insinuation was dispersed through the University that made him suspected of error no less shocking than Atheism itself. It was in vain that his friends pleaded his published sentiments, which contained unanswerable confutations of the very heresies with which he was charged; the torrent of popular prejudice was irresistible; and thus this *pre-eminently* great and good man was utterly frustrated in his pious purpose by the slander of an insignificant person, who had become his enemy from mortified pride. So true it is, as his biographer well observes, that no merit, however exalted, is exempt from being, not only attacked, but wounded by the most contemptible whispers. Those who cannot strike with force, can *poison* their weapons, and weak as they are, give mortal wounds, and bring a hero to the grave.

(*h*) THE MONARCH'S QUESTION.—When any one was speaking ill of another in the presence of Peter the Great, he at first listened to him attentively, and then interrupted him. "Is there not," said he, "a fair side also to the character of the person of whom you are speaking? Come, tell me what good qualities you have remarked about him." One would think this monarch had learned that precept, "Speak not evil one of another."

(*i*) THE WAY TO TREAT A CALUMNIATOR.—A clergyman in New-York state, in early life, had engaged in business which led him to buy a good deal of coal; and after he became a minister of the Gospel, two of his members, who were making a bargain respecting a load of coal, agreed to leave it to their minister to decide how much the load contained. He accordingly acceded to their request, and told them how much it contained, or how to find out the amount it contained, by the law of the state. The member who wished to buy, was well pleased; the one who wished to sell, was quite dissatisfied. After the minister left them, the former came to see him, and stated that the brother who sold the coal had just said—that he did not believe what his minister had stated; that if he *was* a minister, he was not too good to *lie*, &c. The Rev. Mr. S., in the first place, felt deeply wounded, and strongly inclined to go and give the rash and unkind brother a severe rebuke. But on reflecting a moment, he replied to his informant, "I presume Brother —— does not really think so;" and under that conviction he determined to take no notice of it, and treat the brother's offence with silence. The offender came afterwards to see his pastor; and his uneasy and anxious appearance seemed to say—"I wish you would call me to account for my expressions against you;" but the pastor studiously avoided all reference to them. And now, as if to appease his own conscience, the offender, who before had been quite indifferent to his minister, began to load him with his kindnesses, and became one of his warmest friends.

(*j*) PHILIP AND THE ATHENIAN ORATORS.—Philip of Macedon was wont to say "that he was much beholden to the Athenian orators; since by the slanderous and opprobrious manner in which they spoke of him, [*e. g.* that he was a barbarian, an usurper, a cheat; perfidious, perjured, depraved; a companion of rascals, mountebanks, &c.] they were the means of making him a better man, both in word and deed. For," added he, "I, every day, do my best endeavor, as well as my sayings and doings, to prove them liars."

Let Christians be benefited in a similar way, by the reproaches of the world.

(*k*) SLANDER BOOK.—When in the town of ——, I was struck with the above words, says a newspaper writer, written on the back of a small blank account book. I found on examining the contents, that different persons were charged with so much, for one or two slanders as the case might be. The accounts were very neatly and correctly kept, credits entered, &c., with as much precision as the merchant keeps his books. Upon inquiry I was informed, that this plan (of fining people for slander,) originated with M——, the daughter of the man at whose house the book was seen, to prevent evil speaking and its consequences. She, a girl of twelve or thirteen years, perceived the evil of slander; the many interruptions produced by it in families and neighborhoods; obtained a blank book, and determined to fine every person who slandered or spoke evil of another in her presence—the money thus collected to be applied to benevolent purposes. She gave me four dollars, a donation to the Missionary Society of the ——— Conference, a part of her collections only for a few months. It is very desirable and commendable, that every family have such a book, and enter into such a compact; because—

1. The money thus collected is to be appropriated to a most noble purpose.

2. It would make people, and especially the members of every family, more circumspect, and watch with more diligence and care over that little member which no man can tame; and thereby prevent much slander and evil speaking, which is the cause, no doubt, of half of the broils and animosities which occur in families and neighborhoods.

408. SOUL, EXISTENCE AND VALUE OF.

(*a*) A JEW'S REPLY.—A converted Jew, pleading the cause of the society through whose instrumentality he had been brought to a knowledge of Christianity, was opposed by a learned gentleman, who spoke very lightly of the objects of the society, and its efforts, and said, "He did not suppose they would convert more than a hundred all together." "Be it so," replied the Jew; you are a skillful calculator; take your pen now, and calculate the worth of one hundred immortal souls!"

(*b*) DR. SCOTT'S REMARKS.—Dr. Scott, in one of his lectures to young clergymen, says: "I must own that I feel in my best moments, that I had rather be the author of the "Discourse on Repentance," than of Sir Isaac Newton's Principia; for the salvation of one soul gives joy in heaven, but we read not that angels notice philosophical discoveries."

409. SUBMISSION TO GOD'S WILL.

(*a*) THE CHILDREN'S ANSWERS.—A Sabbath school teacher, instructing his class on that petition of the Lord's Prayer, "Thy will be done on earth as it is in heaven," said to them, "You have told me, my dear children, *what* is to be done—*the will of God*: and *where it is to be done*—*on earth*; and *how* it is to be done—*as it is done in heaven*. How do you think the angels and the happy spirits do the will of God in heaven, as they are to be our pattern?" The first child replied, "They do it *immediately*:" the second, "They do it *diligently*:" the third, "They do it *always*:" the fourth, "They do it *with all their hearts*:" the fifth, "They do it *all together*." Here a pause ensued, and no other children appeared to have any answer; but, after some time, a little girl arose, and said, "Why, sir, they do it *without asking any questions*." Happy world! Our Father who art in heaven, whose will is always wise and always good, thy will be thus done on earth as it is done in heaven!

(*b*) GOD'S DEMANDS ANSWERED.—"I see God will have all my heart, and he shall have it," was a fine reflection made by a lady when news was brought of two children drowned, whom she loved very much.

(*c*) THE INFIDEL AND HIS WIFE.—When I was in the United States (says a Christian writer), I heard of the conversion of a complete man of the world; which, as far as means were concerned, owed its existence to the following circumstance:—God laid his hand on a lovely, and, I think, an only daughter; and the affliction terminated in death. When the terrible moment arrived in which the idol of his affections must die, he stood at the head of her bed, almost frantic with grief; and, having no consolation above what nature and education supplied, as is freqently the case, his grief terminated in rage; he was almost ready to curse the God who, as he thought, could be so cruel as to deprive him of so dear a child. His wife, an amiable and sensible woman, at the same time stood at the foot of the bed. Her eyes were suffused with tears, her hands lifted to heaven: and, while every feature spoke the feelings of her soul, she exclaimed, "The will of the Lord be done! The will of the Lord be done! The will of the Lord be done!" These exclamations very naturally called the attention of her frantic husband from their dying daughter to herself; and, as he afterwards confessed, he was on the point of wreaking his vengeance on, what he then considered, an unfeeling wife, and an unnathral hard-hearted mother. After a while, however, the storm of passion gave place to reflection. He was a man of eminence at the bar, a colonel in the army; he prided himself on being a philosopher; and was therefore led to examine how his courage and philosophy had supported him in the day of trial. Here he saw reason to reflect on his conduct with shame; the more so, as he contrasted it with the conduct of his amiable and pious partner. "How is this?" he could not but exclaim: "I am a man and a soldier. I boast of my courage, and pride myself in philosophy, in which I am versed, as being equal to the support of man in every emergency. But in the hour of trial I acted an unworthy part. My wife, a delicate female, and, notwithstanding my suspicions to the contrary, one of the most affectionate of mothers, was alone the magnanimous sufferer on this trying occasion. What, under circumstances so directly opposite, could lead to such contrary results?" "She is a Christian," said a still small voice; "and I am not: surely the secret is here!" This train of thought led to the most pleasing consequences. He concluded that there must be a reality in that religion which he had hitherto despised; and if so, that was the one thing needful. He conferred not with flesh and blood; but immediately began to seek the consolations of true religion, and, ere long, found

"What nothing earthly gives, or can destroy,
The soul's calm sunshine, and the heartfelt joy."

(*d*) DUMB BOYS' EXAMINATION.—A clergyman once paid a visit to a deaf and dumb asylum in London, for the express purpose of examining the children in the knowledge they possessed of Divine truth. A little boy, on this occasion, was asked in writing, "Who made the world?" He took up the chalk, and wrote underneath the question, "in the beginning God created the heaven and the earth." The clergy man then inquired in a similar manner, "Why did Jesus Christ come into the world?" A smile of delight and gratitude rested on the countenance of the little fellow, as he wrote, "This is a faithful saying, and worthy of all acceptation, That Jesus Christ came into the world to save sinners." A third question was then proposed, eminently adapted to call his most powerful feelings into exercise: "Why were you born deaf and dumb, while I can hear and speak?" "Never," said an eyewitness, "shall I forget the look of holy resignation and chastened sorrow which sat on his countenance as he took up the chalk and wrote, 'Even so, Father, for so it seemed good in thy sight.'"

(*e*) NONE BETTER FITTED FOR TROUBLE. — An aged and pious lady, who lost the use of her arm by a fall in winter, said to a friend, smiling, that she had just been considering the circumstances of all her acquaintances, but had not been able to fix upon one who could with less inconvenience sustain such a loss than she could. She, therefore, admired the Divine wisdom and goodness in appointing her to bear that affliction rather than any other person.

(*f*) PICKING STRAWS FOR LIFE.—Mr. Hey, an eminent surgeon, early in the year 1778, received a stroke upon his thigh, which threatened the complete suspension of his professional labors. The remedies applied under his own directions, and those of his medical friends, proved altogether unser viceable; and it appeared in the highest degree probable to himself and them, that he would never regain the power of walking. He was the father of a large family, and was soon to be the parent of the eleventh child. He was in full business, and had the most reasonable prospect of distinction and emolument, as creditable to himself as advantageous to his family. Mr. Hey felt this afflictive dispensation of Divine Providence as every considerate man in similar circumstances would feel it—he was deeply affected by it; but his language and conduct were constantly expressive of the most humble submission, and meek acquiescence in the Divine will. To an intimate friend, who was lamenting the apparent consequences of a disorder which extinguished all his prospects of future usefulness, he replied, "If it be the will of God that I should be confined to my sofa, and he command me to pick straws during the remainder of my life, I hope I should feel no repugnance to his good pleasure."

(*g*) FENELON AND HIS PUPIL.—A most remarkable instance of Christian resignation was discovered on one particular occasion, in the conduct of Archbishop Fenelon. When his illustrious and hopeful pupil, the Duke of Burgundy, lay dead in his coffin, and the nobles of his court, in all the pomp of silent sadness, stood round, the archbishop came into the apartment, and having fixed his eyes for some time on the corpse, broke out at length in words to this effect: "There lies my beloved prince, for whom my affections were equal to the tenderest regard of the tenderest parents. Nor were my affections lost; he loved me in return with all the ardor of a son. There he lies; and all my worldly happiness lies dead with him. But if the turning of a straw would call him back to life, I would not for ten thousand worlds be the turner of that straw in opposition to the will of God."

(*h*) THE WISEST PREFERENCE.—There was a good woman, who, when she was ill, being asked, whether she was willing to live or die, answered, "Which God pleaseth."

"But," said one standing by, "if God should refer it to you, whether would you choose?"

"Truly," said she, "if God should refer it to me, I would even refer it to him again."

(*i*) INSTANCE OF JOHN BROWN.—"No doubt," said the late Mr. Brown of Haddington, "I have met with trials as well as others; yet so kind has God been to me, that, I think, if God were to give me as many years as I have aleady lived in the world, I would not desire one single circumstance in my lot changed, except that I wish I had less sin. It might be written on my coffin, Here lies one of the cares of Providence, who early wanted both father and mother, and yet never missed them."

(*j*) ALL WITH CHRIST, OR IN CHRIST.—"I have had six children," said Mr. Elliot, "and I bless God for his free grace they are all with Christ, or in Christ; and my mind is now at rest concerning them. My desire was, that they should have served Christ on earth; but if God will choose to have them rather serve him in heaven, I have nothing to object to it. His will be done."

(*k*) THE BEREAVED OFFICER—During the siege of Barcelona, in 1705, Captain Carleton witnessed the following affecting fact, which he tells us in his memoirs:—"I saw an old officer, having his only son with him, a fine man about twenty years of age, going into their tent to dine. Whilst they were at dinner, a shot took off the head of the son. The father immediately rose up, and first looking down upon his headless child, and then lifting up his eyes to heaven, while the tears ran down his cheeks, only said, 'Thy will be done.'"

410. Submission, Want of.

(*a*) "HE SHA'N'T DIE."—In a parish in the county of Gloucester, the widow of a gentleman resided with her only son, a lad about twelve years of age. Mrs. —— had unhappily taken great prejudice against the doctrines preached by her pastor, which carried her so far, as not only to induce her to break off all communications with him, but even to absent herself from his ministry. The clergyman adopted every method of lawful conciliation, but in vain; and he was left to regret what he could not remedy. About this period, the boy was taken seriously ill, and the clergyman thinking that the mother's mind might be softened by the affliction, called to inquire after the sufferer, and offer his ministerial services. The lady admitted him to the house, and after he had endeavored to point her to the great Controller of all events, and the object of his fatherly chastisements, he proposed that they should kneel down to prayer. The mother acquiesced in the proposition, but the feeling with which she did so will be seen by the sequel.

The worthy minister prayed that, if it was the Lord's will, the child might be restored; but, if otherwise, that God's will and not theirs might be done. As he uttered the petition, the unhappy mother rose from her knees, and exclaimed in the agony of despair—"He sha'n't die!" All efforts to compose her were unavailing, and the clergyman was compelled to take his departure. But the fearful issue of the narrative yet remains. From that hour the boy began to improve in health, and, in the course of time, he entirely recovered. But, alas! the life of this lad, on which the mother was thus intent, was not a blessing to her or the world; for, thirteen years afterwards, he suffered death for forgery.

411. THEATRES.

(*a*) THE CURATE AND THE TRAGEDY.—When Racine composed the tragedy of Esther, to please Madame Maintenon, she very strongly recommended it at court, and every one was charmed with the performance, except one honest curate, who refused to see it. Being very urgently pressed for his reasons, he told Madame M. that she knew he was in the habit of publicly reprobating the stage from the pulpit, and, that though the tragedy of Esther was far different from the generality of plays, yet it was still known to be a play: adding that were he to yield to the request, his hearers would compare his conduct with his sermons, and, in their practice, would pursue the course most suited to their sinful inclinations.

(*b*) THE WAY TO THE PIT.—A young man, on reaching the door of a theatre, overheard one of the door-keepers calling out, "This is the way to the pit." Having had some instruction in the word of God, in early life, what the man said reminded him that the employments of the theatre led to hell. The thought haunted him, and made him cease frequenting such amusements: he became attentive to the concerns of his soul, and afterwards was a minister of the gospel.

(*c*) PLEASURES OF THE THEATRE.—While traveling, Mr. Hervey met with a lady who largely expatiated on the amusements of the stage, as being, in her opinion, superior to all other pleasures. She remarked that there was the pleasure of thinking on the play before she went, the pleasure she enjoyed while there, and the pleasure of reflecting on it on her bed at night. Mr. Hervey, who had heard her remarks without interruption, now said, with his usual mildness, that there was one pleasure more, which she had forgotten. "What can that be?" she eagerly asked; for she thought she must have included them all. With a grave look, and striking manner, Mr. H. replied, "Madam, the pleasure it will give you on a death-bed." A clap of thunder, or a flash of lightning, could not have more surprised her; the remark went to her heart. She had no reply to make; the rest of the journey was occupied in deep thought; she abandoned the theatre, and heartily pursued those pleasures which can afford satisfaction even on a death-bed.

(*d*) UNHEARD OF PRAYER.—"He that is not satisfied," says Bishop Wilson, "that plays are an unlawful diversion, let him, *if he dare*, offer up this prayer to God *before he goes*, 'Lord, lead me not into temptation, and bless me in what I am now to be employed." There are many other occupations and amusements, in which the same advice is worth attending to.

(*e*) A YOUNG MAN'S CAREER.—A young man, says a correspondent of the Journal of Commerce, of about twenty-two, called on the writer in the fall of 1831, for employment. He was a journeyman printer, was recently from Kentucky, and owing to his want of employment, as he said, was entirely destitute of not only the comforts, but the necessaries of life. I immediately procured him a respectable boarding-house, gave him employment, and rendered his situation as comfortable as my limited means would permit. He had not been with me long before he expressed a wish to go to the theatre. Some great actor was to perform on a certain night; and he was very anxious to see him. I warned him of the consequences—told him my own experience and observation had convinced me that it was a very dangerous place for young men to visit. But my warning did him no good. He neglected his business, and went. I reproved him gently, but retained him in my employment. He continued to go, notwithstanding all my remonstrances to the contrary. At length my business suffered so much from his neglecting to attend to it as he ought, that I was under the necessity of discharging him in self-defence. He got temporary employment in different offices in the city, where the same fault was found with him. Immediately after he accepted a situation of bar-keeper in a porter house or tavern attached to the —— Theatre. His situation he did not long hold—from what cause I know not. He again applied to me for work; but as his habits were not reformed, I did not think it prudent to employ him, although I said or did nothing to injure him in the estimation of others. Disappointed in procuring employment in a business to which he had served a regular apprenticeship,—being penniless, and seeing no bright prospect for the future, he enlisted as a common soldier in the U. States' service. He had not been in his new vocation long before he was called upon, with other troops to defend our citizens from the attacks of the Indians. But when the troops had nearly reached the place of destination, that "invisible scourge," the Asiatic Cholera, made its appearance among them. Desertion was the consequence, and among others who fled, was the subject of this article. He returned to New York—made application, at several different offices, for employment, without success. In a few days the dreadful news came that he had been detected in pilfering goods from the house of his landlord. A warrant was immediately issued for him—he was seized—taken to the police office, convicted, and sentenced to six months' hard labor in the Penitentiary. His name being published in the newspapers, in connection with those of other convicts—was immediately recognized by the officer under whom he had enlisted. This officer proceeds to the city—claims the prisoner—and it is at length agreed that he shall return to the United States service, where he shall, for the first six months, be compelled to roll sand as a punishment for desertion, serve out the five years for which he had enlisted, and then be given up to the City authorities, to suffer for the crime of pilfering.

Night after night has the writer of this attended the theatre; and night after night has he witnessed the attendance of those who were in the want of the common necessaries of life. He has frequently seen, among the theatre-going public, *men* who called themselves *gentlemen*, who were in the habit of associating with the "vilest of the vile," and whose actions, could they but be known to the reflecting part of the community, would cover them with infamy and disgrace. But these facts, to many, will appear like a thrice-told tale. The simple narrative related above may be relied on as correct. Names and dates can be given if required.

(*f*) WORDS OF PLATO.—Plays raise the passions, and pervert the use of them; and of consequence are dangerous to morality.

(*g*) WORDS OF ARISTOTLE.—The seeing of *Comedies* ought to be forbidden to young people; until age and discipline have made them proof against debauchery.

(*h*) WORDS OF TACITUS.—The *German* women are guarded against danger, and preserve their purity by having no play-houses among them.

(*i*) OPINION OF OVID.—Ovid, in a grave work addressed to Augustus, advises the suppression of theatrical amusements as a great source of corruption.

(*j*) OPINION OF ROUSSEAU.—The infidel philosopher ROUSSEAU declared himself to be of the opinion, that *the theatre is in all cases a school of vice.* Though he has himself written for the stage, yet, when it was proposed to establish a theatre in the city of Geneva, he wrote against the project, with zeal and great force, and expressed the opinion, that every friend of pure morals ought to oppose it! Alas! that which infidelity has condemned as a fruitful source of corruption and shame, is publicly advocated and patronized in our midst—yea, more: vindicated and patronized by some professing godliness.

"It is impossible, says Rousseau, "that an establishment [the Theatre at Geneva] so contrary to our ancient manners, can be generally applauded. How many generous citizens will see, with indignation, this monument of *luxury and effeminacy* raise itself upon the ruins of our ancient simplicity! Where would be the imprudent mother who would dare to carry her daughter to this *dangerous* school? And what respectable woman would not think herself dishonored in going there? In all countries the profession of a player is dishonorable, and those who exercise it are every where contemned."

(*k*) DR. RUSH'S OPINION.—Dr. Rush was a great enemy to theatrical amusements. He was once in conversation with a lady, a professor of religion, who was speaking of the pleasure she anticipated at the theatre, in the evening. "What, madam," said he, "do you go to the theatre?" "Yes," was the reply: "and don't you go, doctor?" "No, madam," said he, "I never go to such places." "Why, sir, do you not go? Do you think it sinful?" said she. He replied, "I never will publish to the world that I think Jesus Christ a hard master, and religion an unsatisfying portion, which I should do if I went on to the devil's ground in quest of happiness." This argument was short, but conclusive. The lady determined not to go.

(*l*) THE COMEDIAN'S CONFESSION.—A celebrated comic performer on the English stage, retiring from London for a short time on account of ill-health, and meeting with a pious friend whom he had once intimately known, said, "I have been acting *Sir John Falstaff* so often, that I thought I should have died; and had I died, it would have been in the service of the devil." The testimony of a player against himself.

(*m*) RESOLUTION OF CONGRESS. — The American Congress, soon after the Declaration of Independence, passed the following motion:

"Whereas, true religion and good morals are the only foundation of public liberty and happiness,

Resolved, that it be, and hereby is, earnestly recommended to the several states, to take the most effectual measures for the encouragement thereof, and for the suppression of *theatrical entertainments*, horse-racing, gaming, and such other diversions as are productive of idleness, dissipation, and a general depravity of principles and manners.

(*n*) PRYNNE'S COLLECTION OF TESTIMONY.—William Prynne, a satirical and pungent writer, who suffered many cruelties for his admirable productions in the time of Charles I, has made a catalogue of authorities against the stage, which contains every name of eminence in the heathen and Christian world: it comprehends the united testimony of the Jewish and Christian Churches; the deliberate acts of fifty-four ancient and modern, general, national, and provincial councils and synods, both of the Western and Eastern churches, the condemnatory sentence of seventy-one ancient Fathers, and one hundred and fifty modern popish and Protestant authors; the hostile endeavors of philosophers and even poets; with the legislative enactments of a great number of pagan and Christian states, nations, magistrates, emperors and princes.

(*o*) ADVOCATE OF THEATRES.—There was a poor gentleman in Paris, who used to go powdered and decorated with ruffles and ribbons. He happened to be in a company where were even some of morals so stern that they questioned the utility of the theatres with which Paris abounds. At that time, they had twenty-one in that city, and they were opened every evening, not excepting the Sabbath. This ruffled gentleman, in a long harangue, undertook to show that the theatres were a great public benefit. And he used arguments often urged by advocates of similar public nuisances. There were the thousands of actors, scene-makers, candle-lighters, hack-drivers, footmen, printers, &c. &c., whose mouths were daily supplied with bread by these establishments. He grew warm, and, in a manner, eloquent. He could not deny but thousands had their morals corrupted, their hopes crushed, their property lost, and their hearts broken, in consequence of these sinks of vice. Still, he pleaded in their behalf as if for life. After he had withdrawn, and the company were musing on his arguments and vehemence, a gentleman remarked that their eloquent friend had good reason for his opinions—for he spent all his small pension in going to the play, but staid every night till the play-house was cleared, and then *went round in the ladies' boxes, and picked up pins enough to buy his food till the next play!*"

(*p*) GOOD TEST FOR AMUSEMENTS.—Two professors of religion were standing at the door of a theatre in the city of New-York, when one of them proposed to go in and see the play, and desired his friend to accompany him. The other declined the invitation; and after being repeatedly solicited to enter, gave this excellent reason for his refusal: "If I should go in, and while there be called into eternity, and should be asked at the door of heaven *where I had come from*, I should be ashamed to answer."

This incident furnishes a rule for general observance: *Never go to a place where you would be ashamed to die.*"

(*q*) THEATRES IN THE FRENCH REVOLUTION.—During the progress of the most ferocious revolution which ever shocked the face of heaven, theatres, in Paris alone, multiplied from *six* to *twenty-five*. Now, one of two conclusions follows from this: either the spirit of the times produced the institutions, or the institutions cherished the spirit of the times, and this would certainly go to prove, that they are either the parents of vice, or the offspring of it.

(*r*) THE MUSICIAN'S REPLY.—An accomplished musician, who had been engaged for many years performing at theatres, assemblies, and other places of amusement, on being asked why he relinquished his employment, answered, "Because I cannot look to heaven for a blessing upon it."

412. TOBACCO.

(*a*) REFORMED MAN'S TESTIMONY.—A correspondent of the New-York Evangelist says: "I had chewed this poison more than fifteen years. I had often doubted the utility of this practice before I relinquished it. I found that one argument which I had employed against the use of ardent spirits applied with as much propriety to the use of tobacco. The argument is, that it must be unfriendly to true piety, for the Christian, while in health, to be under the continued influence of poison. This produces a morbid excitement, directly opposed to that excitement which the Holy Spirit is producing. Thus I reasoned in reference to the use of ardent spirits, and was persuaded that the argument applied also to the use of tobacco. In this state of mind I read several articles in the New-York Evangelist, in opposition to this practice. I was in this way brought to the determination that I would suspend the use of tobacco, and see whether I could do without it. I had been moderate in the use of this poison, if there can be any moderation in using it, and supposed that it was exerting very little influence over me. In less than two days after I had commenced this self-discipline, I experienced such a tormenting restlessness, such a prostration of strength, as fully convinced me that tobacco was exerting a very powerful influence upon my system. When I perceived its influence, I was determined to break up this bad habit; and then resolved fully to renounce the use of tobaoco, as a powerful and hurtful stimulus for the human system. For a few days I suffered much from an almost insupportable uneasiness in the whole system, which was calling loudly for its accustomed stimulus. But this only served to strengthen my resolution, and to convince me more and more of the importance of conquering this habit. I have persevered for more than six months, and have enjoyed during this period, much better health than while I used it. It is now hateful to me, and I have no desire again to resume its use. I would, from my own experience, call on my friends, and all others who are in bondage to this hateful weed, to follow my example. I mean to persevere, and am persuaded that I shall."

(*b*) GOOD RULE FOR THE LORD'S STEWARDS.—Says a correspondent of the Ohio Observer:—"When the use of tobacco was fashionable even among the genteel, in walking through a village, I passed a store where I knew there were some very fine cigars. I was immediately seized with the hankering so well known to habitual smokers. The determination arose to lay out a few shillings in purchasing some. As I had been endeavoring to accustom myself to regard my money as the Lord's, and myself as the steward, I tried the rule in that case. I found myself unwilling to charge such an item on my account book. A faithful steward would make no such expenditure, thought I. The money which had been taken out was dropped again into my pocket, and I passed on. I have ever found it difficult to smoke cigars since that time. The cure which I propose is, *to ask the blessing of God on all expenditures, and to try to be faithful stewards of the Lord's money.*"

(*c*) THE MINISTER'S REPENTANCE.—A country minister being invited to preach the weekly lecture to a congregation in the City of New-York, after dismissing the people, took out his tobacco, and began to chew the filthy weed. A member of the church remonstrated with him on the sinfulness of the practice, and stated that he could not expect that impenitent sinners under his instructions, would give up their sins while he indulged in a sin himself. "I know it is wrong," said the minister. "I have often resolved to give up the habit, but I have not resolution enough to persevere."

"Why," said the other, "that is the very excuse the impenitent give for not repenting and forsaking their sins."

"Well, I'll think it over as I go home," observed the minister, "and perhaps I will give it up."

"That will not do," replied the church member, "for we never allow this, if we can help it; we exhort the impenitent to repent *on the spot;* we never tell them to go home and repent, nor do we pray that they may repent when they reach home."

"I see," said the minister, "I cannot get away so—therefore I will try to give up chewing."

"But," remarked the other, "that will not do either. We never urge sinners to try to give up their sins—do you?"

"Why, no; I think it wrong to intimate that they cannot do it at once."

"Will you act then as you preach, or let your conduct give the lie to your preaching?"

"With the help of God," said the minister, "I will leave off the practice *from* this moment."

A member of the church where this conversation took place, who was in the practice of chewing tobacco, was so impressed with what had taken place, that he too solemnly promised to abjure the filthy habit without delay.

(*d*) PRAYING OVER TOBACCO.—A pious sea captain had been in the habit of using tobacco, for upwards of twenty years, and had made many and strenuous efforts to abandon its use, but without success. He was a nervous man, and loved strong tea and coffee as well as tobacco, for the stimulus it afforded him. He loved tobacco, as the drunkard loves alcohol. The force of the habit may be seen in the following circumstance:—

He had given up its use, as he thought, without mental reservation, and congratulated himself on the victory he had obtained, after months of total abstinence. One day, being on charge in the city of N—— (he was a ship mate at the time), and conversing with a brother shipmate, he found tobacco in his mouth without knowing how it came there. He expressed his surprise at the fact to his companion, who answered with a boisterous laugh, "I took out my tobacco box and handed it to you, and you deliberately helped yourself." He had acted under the influence of an old inveterate habit, and was not conscious of having done so, until he had tasted the tobacco. Such was the strength of the habit. Finding at length that it clung to him like a disease, and defied all his efforts, and being persuaded that the conflict of mind to which he was subject, by reason of its use, was actually impairing his usefulness as a man and a Christian, he decided upon making one more effort. He was persuaded that Divine assistance alone could make that effort successful, and acted accordingly. He took the tobacco from his pocket, placed it in a chair, knelt before it, and solemnly pledged himself to God, that he would use it no longer, even as a medicine, though prescribed by a physician. He then implored the Divine blessing upon the attempt, arose from his knees, threw the tobacco into the street, and went about his business. He has not, he states, had a particle of a desire for its use from that time to the time of his narration, a period of more than two years.

(*e*) THE CULPRIT'S RULING PASSION.—The Editor of the Chenango Telegraph, in giving an account of the execution of George Denison, who suffered at Norwich, New-York, says that while standing upon the fatal drop, and during the exhortation of the clergyman, the prisoner asked in a whisper, for the tobacco box of the deputy sheriff, from which he coolly took a quid, deposited it in his mouth, and returned the box. In ten minutes, he was launched into eternity! On the morning of the day that Hamilton, who shot Major Birdsall, was to be executed, the clergy passed two hours in solemn exercises with him. After they left the cell, Hamilton gave some directions about his gallows wardrobe. As the keeper was leaving to execute his commission, he asked Hamilton if he wanted any thing else. He replied, "*You may get me a paper of tobacco.*" After a moment's reflection, he added "*Stop, perhaps I have enough,*"—and rising on his elbow, drew a part of a paper from under the pillow of his pallet, and measuring in his mind the quantity of tobacco by the few hours he had to live, calmly remarked, "*This will last me.*"

(*f*) MONEY FOR MISSIONS.—A minister in England had been pleading with his congregation the claims of the poor heathen on Christian benevolence, and strongly urging on them the duty of contributing to the support of missionary exertions. His friends readily contributed according to their several abilities. The next year, when the missionary collection was about to be made, the minister received a one pound note from a poor laboring man, with a statement to the following effect:—"Sir, when you preached the missionary sermon last year, I was grieved that I had it not in my power to give what I wished. I thought and thought, and consulted my wife whether there was any thing which we could spare without stinting the poor children; but it seemed that we lived as near as possible in every respect, and had nothing but what was absolutely necessary. At last it came into my mind, 'Is that fourpence which goes every week for an ounce of tobacco absolutely necessary?' I had been used to it so long, that I scarcely thought it possible to do without it; however, I resolved to try;

so, instead of spending the fourpence, I dropped it into a box. The first week I felt it sorely; but the second week it was easier; and, in the course of a few weeks, it was little or no sacrifice at all; at least I can say, that the pleasure far outweighed the sacrifice. When my children found what I was doing, they wished to contribute also; and, if ever they got a penny or a half-penny given them for their own pleasure, it was sure to find its way into the box instead of the cake shop. On opening the box, I have the pleasure to find that our collected pence amount to one pound, which I now inclose, and pray that the Lord may give his blessing with it. I am thankful for having thus broken off a dirty and expensive habit, and I have enjoyed more health and cheerfulness since I left off that which I once thought it was impossible for me to do without."

(*g*) BATTLE WITH APPETITE.—A gentleman (he is such now,) who used to be a tremendous rum-drinker, tobacco-chewer and smoker; but for several years past has been a reformed man, writes to a friend in the city of N. York, in the following terms:

"I have seen the time that my desire for tobacco has been vastly stronger than it ever has been for food. Once I was on a lee-shore; the wind blew, the sea was tremendous. The last time I saw the rocky shore, it was three miles to the leeward. It was late in the afternoon; I felt certain we should be on the rocks before morning, if the wind continued. I felt in my pocket for some tobacco, but could find none. I examined every part of the vessel where I thought it possible to find any. I inquired of the crew but there was none on board. At that time I would have given fifty dollars for one quid. The gale ceased, we soon found a harbor, and the first thing I inquired for was tobacco.

I chewed about twenty-one years, and smoked about eighteen. For a long time before I quit the use of tobacco, I believed it was injurious to me, but I felt it was almost impossible to leave it off. Eventually I was awakened, and felt that such practices were sinful. I then thought I would try to leave them off. When I quit smoking, I felt comparatively that I had lost all my friends. I could not eat or sleep as usual; I felt restless, and for some weeks thought it uncertain whether I should be able to conquer a habit that had become so strong. But at last it was overcome. I then thought I would quit chewing—then came the struggle. To quit smoking was but a trifle in comparison. After I had determined to try to quit chewing, I always kept a piece of tobacco in my pocket. I was doubtful whether I should be able to leave it off. Many times, before I was aware of it I found I had had a piece in my mouth a long time. As soon as I perceived it, I would take it out, but often before it was discharged, I would give it one solid grind. There is nothing in the world so exquisitely sweet as tobacco. In a few months the habit was overcome, but it was almost like plucking out my right eye, or cutting off my right arm. When I had entirely ceased from using it—I had a better appetite—my sleep was sweeter, my mind more composed—my nerves were more firm—I grew more fleshy; and now I enjoy perfect health, and can endure double the fatigue that I could for a long time before I quit the use of tobacco."

(*h*) TOBACCO AND PROFANITY.—A pious man moved into a little village where there was much swearing. One of his little boys, two years old, caught the contagion. The father and family labored with their neighbors until a thorough reformation was effected in that part of the town where they lived; except the little prattler, who swore on with increased malignity; often cursing his mother's soul to hell; yet always avoiding his father's presence. From this circumstance, it was concluded that he was conscious of guilt; and, therefore, ought to be whipped. The father, as his manner was, waited until he caught him in the very act of swearing. Then he tried to show the heinousness of the crime, and the disagreeable necessity that he was under to use coercive measures; after which he lynched him well. To convince the child that it was a principle of love that compelled him to use this correction, he said it was better to whip and break him from swearing; for, if he did not quit it, God would cast him into hell, there to burn for ever. And in the vehemence of his desire to awaken conviction, offered up a short prayer to God, to change his wicked heart; and then inquired:

"Why do you swear, my son?"

The child sobbed out, "Father, because I have such a wicked heart."

Father — Well, my son, you must pray to God to give you a good heart."

Child—Father, you must pray.

Father — I do pray, and whatever you see me do, you must do.

The father turned within himself and said, Have I done every thing I ought to do, and been every thing I ought to be, before my children? Conscience awakened, and forced the mind on the BACK TRACK, marking out every deviation from the path of rectitude. Nature had been in the habit, for twenty years, of leaning on the narcotic stimulant of tobacco, while it answered to blunt the conscience a little. The hands, ever faithful to the calls of nature, through nervous sympathy, had already extracted from the deposit, the plug and the knife. Just at this instant a new and pleasing thought shot across the little swearer's mind; that there was one duty he had never complied with; and, by so doing, he would please his father and his God; for, surely, my praying, good father, by this act, is pleasing God. With eyes beaming with joy, through tears that yet trembled on their surface, he determined now to quit the detestable practice of swearing, and take his father's godly example. Enraptured at the thought of having so easy an opportunity of convincing his father of the great change that had taken place in his mind, and with a voice as sweet as infant lips could speak, he said, "Father, give me a chew of tobacco!"

I will not attempt to describe the father's feelings; I will leave that to the reader. But what did the father do? what could he do? Could he contradict himself? Could he convince the child that it was right for the father to do a thing, and wrong for the son? No, no. With a conscience already awakened, by previous light, and having half-heartedly attempted to abandon the evil before—with a conscience now driving lashes inconceivably severe, the tobacco was tossed into the street, with this candid confession:

"My son, I have done wrong; I will now ask God to help me that I may do so no more. Will YOU ask God to help you that you may swear no more?"

The child looked disappointed, and sobbed out, "Well."

The father then took him in his arms, and retired into the garden to pray, a great deal worse whipped than the child.

413. TOLERATION.

(*a*) BURNING A HERETIC.—A popish princess was entreated by some Romish ecclesiastics to concur with them in bringing a supposed heretic to the flames. "Is it not true," asked she, "that heretics burn for ever in hell-fire?" "Without doubt was the reply of the priests. "Then," added she, "it would be too severe to burn them in both worlds. Since they are devoted to endless misery hereafter, it is but justice to let them live unmolested here."

(*b*) REPLY OF A POLISH KING.—When certain persons attempted to persuade Stephen, king of Poland, to constrain some of his subjects, who were of a different religion, to embrace his, he said to them, "I am king of men, and not of consciences. The dominion of consciences belongs exclusively to God."

(*c*) HENRY VIII AND HIS BUFFOON.—Henry VIII king of England, wrote a silly book against Martin Luther, for which the Pope conferred on him the title "*Defender of the Faith.*" As that tyrant appeared to be overjoyed at the acquisition, the Jester of the court asked the reason; and being told that it was because the Pope [illegible] given him that new title, the *shrewd fool* replied—"My good Harry, let thee and me defend each other, and *let the faith alone to defend itself!*" That pretended buffoon must have been the wisest man of his day; for at that period no party had learned the wisdom of leaving truth to support itself by its own vigor.

TRACTS, RELIGIOUS.

HAPPY EFFECTS OF TRACTS.

414. Morality Promoted.

(*a*) THE PROFANE CREW.—The Evangelical Magazine, for 1823, gives an account of a gentleman at Liverpool furnishing the steward of a merchant vessel, which was about to leave that port to trade in the Mediterranean, with a parcel of tracts. The following is the account of the effects they produced:

You recollect, on my taking leave of you, you placed in my hand a small parcel of tracts, and I promised to read them; this I have done. On leaving this port, we had a favorable wind through the Channel; the wind then chopped round direct in our teeth. We had to contend with light contrary winds till we entered the Gut of Gibraltar. During this part of our voyage I had little or no opportunity to read the tracts: I did, on the first Sabbath, turn them over, and put a few in my pocket; and occasionally taking one out, gave it a sneering glance, and then handed it to one of the boys or men with a smile of ridicule. On passing the Gut, we had a tedious though pleasant voyage to Smyrna. Having much time upon my hands, I now and then looked at a tract to pass it away. One evening I was looking over the ship's side, viewing the calm and peaceful close of another day. This brought to my recollection the scenery and calmness of the evening when I took my last farewell of my friends at home. It was at sunset, on a lovely evening in July. Musing thus of home, I just then put my hand in my jacket pocket, and feeling a paper, took it out, and it proved to be a tract, "THE SWEARER'S PRAYER." I read it aloud, in the hearing of the whole crew, and, I suppose, much of my feelings was mixed with my tone of voice. When I had read it, a curious kind of silence ensued; not one of us felt inclined to raise his eyes from what they were fixed on, fearing to meet the look of another, and knowing that, to a man, we were all shockingly guilty of swearing. At length we looked at each other in a sidelong kind of way, and one man said, "Mr. William, I never heard or thought of this before; this kind of reading has made me feel very strange; I'm all over trembling. I don't think I shall like to swear again: shall you, Jack?" turning short to a seaman alongside of him, who looked him full in the face, and burst into tears. The shedding of tears ran like a contagion through the whole of us, even to the boy across the gun. After weeping in silence, with our faces hid with our hands, one man said, "Jack, suppose we hand up a prayer to God for forgiveness. Mr. William, you have had more learning than we, you can make a prayer." Alas! I had never prayed; I could only sigh; I really thought my heart would burst. Oh, how dreadful did sin appear! One of the men then broke the silence of grief; with his arms across his breast, and the tears of penitential sorrow rolling down his face, he cried out, "O God, who made our souls, have mercy, and pardon the miserable and damned crew on this deck." Not a heart but what responded, "Lord, hear this prayer, and forgive." But not to enter too long into detail, a change took place in the whole ship's company. One circumstance I must not forget to mention. The captain, a drunken, swearing character, thought his men bewitched. On the following morning he came on deck, and, as usual, was giving his orders, mixed with fearful oaths, when one of the men, in a most respectful manner, begged he would not swear at them [illegible] they would obey his orders with more comfort to themselves without it. Indeed, the captain remarked to a person on his return, that he was himself obliged to refrain from swearing, it began to appear so singular on board.

(*b*) THE TORN TRACT. — In the summer of 1825 (says a gentleman) I left the tract entitled "*The Swearer's Prayer*," in a place where it would be found by a companion who was notoriously wicked and profane. A few weeks afterwards, I went to the place where I had left it, and found it with a few lines written on the margin with a pencil, of which I do not recollect the precise words; but the amount was as follows: "The writer has erred in thinking that a pack of lies is a proper means of breaking a bad habit; and it would be better for him who has left this here not to repeat such an insult." I wrote at the bottom, "Reprove a wise man, and he will love thee;" and left the tract in the same place. At my next visit I found it torn into a number of small pieces. I was immediately reminded of a fact recorded in ancient history, of a certain king, who, on receiving a petition from a poor person, hastily glanced at it, and returned it unanswered. The petition was presented the next day, and treated in the same manner. The petitioner repeatedly presented it with the same ill success, until, at last, the king being exasperated with her importunity, tore it to atoms. These were carefully gathered up, stitched together, and again presented. The king, struck with her perseverance, read the petition, and immediately returned a favorable answer. This circumstance being brought to my mind, I determined to try a similar experiment. The fragments were put together in their proper order, and replaced in the drawer in which the tract had before been laid. Soon after, the tract disappeared, and I heard nothing more of it until eight months afterwards, when I had a conversation with the person for whom it was intended, and he said, that he had determined, by the grace of God, to leave off the practice of swearing. He had treated "The Swearer's Prayer" with contempt when he first saw it; but, when he found the fragments re-united, he believed that I was in earnest. He took the tract home, read it carefully, and resolved to swear no more. He had determined not to part with the tract as long as he lived. A great reformation in his conduct has taken place, and I cannot but hope that a work of Divine grace has been begun in his heart.

(*c*) BREAD CAST ON THE WATERS.—A sailor, though he had become so wicked that few would employ him, was engaged for an eighteen-months' voyage. Just before sailing, he walked out one evening with a number of his companions, and passing the Bethel Flag, concluded to stop. After sermon, the preacher gave them some tracts, which they took without thinking or caring what they contained. They carried them to the ship, and soon after set sail.

After having been some months at sea, this man, feeling somewhat melancholy, concluded he would look at the tracts which had been given to him. He did so, and conviction seized his mind. He knew not what was the matter. He had never felt so before. He could not rest; and in this state he continued waiting for the end of his voyage, that he might return home and find some one to tell him what he must do to be saved. He broke off his habit of profaneness and open impiety, and thus remained till he arrived at port; soon after which, he trusts, the Lord Jesus Christ took possession of his soul. He has since made one voyage, during which he *established a prayer meeting* on board, and won over a number to attend it, *two of whom hopefully experienced religion;* and all disorder was banished from the ship. Speaking of some seasons he had enjoyed since he experienced a change, he mentioned one in particular which he had during his last voyage, while reading the tract "Memoir of Harriet Newell." He said, it appeared to him *his soul was wrapped up in Christ.*

(*d*) TRACT PICKED UP ON THE WHARF.—The Seventh Report

of the American Tract Society contains the following letter from a mechanic in New-York city:—

"I was at work on the wharf—saw a man pick up a little book, look at it, and then throw it down. I ran and got it. I saw it was called, 'THE WATCHMAKER.' I read it; I shed tears. I read it for five days, and became so deeply distressed for my sins, that I was determined to drink no more. I told my wife, who was once a member of the church, but I had been the cause of her leaving it. We had not for many years ever been inside a church. I used to swear, and curse at religion, and was an awful deist and drunkard. My family was in a destitute condition, and often distressed on my account. But, glory to God! all is changed now. My wife and I went to a prayer-meeting, and it pleased God to bless her also; and so we are both happy now. Our little children are altered. Our house and all are altered. I am laughed at by my shopmates, and those who used to drink with me, and curse and swear at religion. But I don't mind them now. I thank the Lord that he stooped so low as to have mercy on one of the wickedest of sinners. I can never thank him enough."

(*e*) HITTING THE RIGHT NAIL.—At the annual meeting of the Religious Tract Society, in 1832, John Fyson, Esq., of Thetford, stated among others, the following pleasing facts:—

A tract distributer, in passing through a village a few miles from where he lived, met a man, whom he asked if he could read; and, on being answered in the affirmative, he gave him a tract on drunkenness. The man went to a woman who stood at her door, and said, "You have been telling that man I'm a drunkard." The woman of course denied it. The man said, "You know that I am the greatest drunkard in the village, and you told him so, or he would not have given me this book." The woman again said she had not, and added, "But he has hit the right nail on the head."—The tract proved the means of converting this man. As the first fruits of this reformation, he went to his aged father, whom he had frequently beaten, fell on his knees, and begged his pardon. After this he was engaged at harvest, at which, according to custom, the farmer gave a feast. He saw an old companion there; and, calling him out, told him, that unless he left off drunkenness, and became sober, he could not associate with him any more. The man burst into tears, and told him he had left it off, and that, in fact, he had also been reformed, through the instrumentality of a tract. He, Mr. Fyson, had been told, by the master of the man himself, that he was astonished at the change in him, it was so great. A clergyman called upon him, Mr. Fyson, and expressed his great joy at what had taken place in his parish, which had originated from some young men whom he had sent to distribute tracts; the people had become regular in their attendance at the parish church, and the congregation was trebled.

(*f*) THE HUNTER AND THE TRACT.—Mr. H. was one day passing through a small piece of wood, near York, Upper Canada, to a Sunday school. Seeing a hunter about to cross the path, he asked him if he was on the direct road to such a place. The hunter told him he was not; that he must return nearly to York, and take a different road. Mr. H. thanked him kindly, and taking a tract from his pocket, said, "I myself have read this little book with pleasure. If it be as useful to you, as it has been to me, you will never regret it." "What is it?" said the hunter. "It is of the utmost importance to you, my friend," said Mr. H.; "take it: read it, and then read it again, and then read it to your family." The hunter thanked him. Mr. H. went on his way. After the lapse of a few months, Mr. H. attended a prayer meeting in that neighborhood. At the close of the exercises, a man came to him, and, after the usual salutation, told him that he was the hunter to whom he had, some months before, on a Sabbath morning, given a little book; and then added, "That tract brought me to the prayer meeting this morning: I feel thankful to you for it. My mind has been troubled. I have read the Bible. Since you have been so kind to me, I may as well tell you the history of my life. I used to be a mere devil at home, and was not much better abroad. Liquor was my ruin. Whisky, whisky, was my ruin. I have read the little book several times: I have read it to my family, as they were unable to read it themselves. But every time I read it, and my Bible, I feel worse. Sometimes I think there is no mercy for me. My wife told me I had better look for the man who gave it to me." Mr. H. gave him the best instruction in his power, from the Scriptures, and left him. In a few weeks he was in the same neighborhood, and again saw the hunter. The hunter was then indulging a trembling hope in the Lord Jesus. "I have reason," said he, "to bless God for the little book. I have not spent my money in the usual way, nor abused my family, since I received it." "SEARCH THE SCRIPTURES," was the title of the tract.

(*g*) THE TRACT IN THE JUG HANDLE.—A writer in the "Christian Index," Georgia, states that a brother, calling at a blacksmith's shop, discovered a jug containing ardent spirits, and put a tract in the handle. The blacksmith returned, resorted to the jug, commenced reading—dashed the tract upon the ground and trampled on i—conscience awoke—he took it up—read, wept, and read again—and now the despised family is respected; the disconsolate wife is filled with joy; and peace, love, and happiness reign where sorrow made her home. What has done this? A tract that cost one-fourth of a cent.

(*h*) THE LORD'S PRAYER IN A BROTHEL.—A gentleman was requested to distribute tracts among some houses of the worst description in Liverpool. He replied, "I should be willing to go, but it would affect my character to visit those places alone; if any body will accompany me, I will cheerfully go." A pious friend, advanced in life, went with him. They entered a cellar, and the tracts were received with thankfulness by its inmates. They entered another place, in which they found six sailors carousing, in company with six unhappy females. When the distributers entered, one of the sailors said. "Messmates, what are you come about?" "We have something to give you." "That's right, hand it over." "I will read some of it, if you please." The gentleman began to read a tract. The seaman presently said, "Avast there, master I think I can read that myself." He ook it, and read about a page and a hal'; it was the tract "ON THE LORD'S PRAYER;" and then he said, "I tell you what, master, this won't do. God bless you, sir, that ever you should think of us poor creatures." "Come, master," said another, "hand it over to me." He took the tract and went on reading it, but soon burst into tears, and said, "Ah, master, we are all wrong." The gentleman then himself addressed them, and gave each of them a tract. They all thanked him in a grateful manner, and said, "God bless you, sir, that any of us sailors should be thought of." The distributers had not gone far before they were overtaken by one of the young women, who said to one of them, "Sir, I have long seen the error of my ways, and am most completely miserable." The gentleman appointed her to come to his house the following evening. She accordingly came, and he brought her to his wife, and a friend who was then staying with them. The young woman related her tale; it was truly "a tale of woe." At its recital, the gentleman and his wife, and their friend, all wept. But joy was mixed with their sorrow, hoping that the prodigal might be restored to her father's house. Her father was a respectable person, living in London; they wrote to him, and took the young woman under their care. By the return of post they received a letter, which satisfied them that the statement she made was correct. They gave her money sufficient to buy her clothes, and paid for her journey home. A letter of thanks was afterwards received from her father; and also one from the young woman, expressing her gratitude to them as the means of restoring her to the paths of virtue, and the socie y of her friends.

(*i*) SHOEMAKER AND COLPORTEUR.—As I was passing from house to house, on the second week in January, (says one) inviting all to attend public worship, then held every evening, a shoemaker, about middle age, replied, "No; I can't attend. We are on the point of starvation, and it takes me morning, noon and night to get something to live on. I used to go; but I have been a hard character these last nine years, and we now see the consequences of it." Who can tell, thought I, but here is an immortal spirit that may yet be a star in the Redeemer's crown; and does not his providence beckon me here to concentrate humble prayer and efforts? I called the next day, and found he was the son of a Methodist preacher in Ireland. That for about nine years he had frequented the grog-shop, and often reveled in gross intoxication, which led to quarrels, abuse of his family, and want of bread to satisfy their hunger. His Sabbaths were whiled away among intemperate companions; he had become an advocate of infidelity, and for about three years had not entered the sanctuary. After a miserable fight, a few days before I saw him, from which he reached home at three in the morning, no unusual hour, he was about to take the law of his antagonist, when he said to himself; "What a fool I am. I am reduced to poverty and misery; my wife and children are wretched, and it is all from strong drink and my ungodly associates. Henceforward, God helping me, not another drop, and no more of such company."

When I manifested an interest in his moral and spiritual welfare, he grasped me, as if I had been a deliverer sent from heaven. He felt that the resistless temptation lay in his companions, and that he must get *a new train of social influences*, or he was lost. I preached to him "Christ crucified"—sin, and salvation from sin through atoning blood; and as I saw him almost daily, for many weeks, I found, all the way, that his sorrow for sin, discernment of the plan of salvation, love of the Bible and of the people and sanctuary of God, went forward of my anticipations, so that I seemed rather to be watching how the Spirit taught him, than teaching him myself.

His clothes, and his wife's clothes, which had been pawned, were early redeemed, with other aid, that they might go to the house of God; and he was helped to resume his business with more energy and advantage. He early gave his name to the total abstinence pledge; read me letters received in the days of his folly from his father, which rebuked him terribly, especially for abuse of his amiable wife; and again and again he poured out the full sorrows of his heart over his heaven-daring sins. At one time, raising his right hand clenched, "There," said he, "are five bones which have been put out of joint in fighting in my revels. I have been a great sinner, and it is a wonder I have not been cut off and sent to hell. I have been guilty of every sin but murder—yes, and of that, too, a thousand times—I murdered Him who was murdered for me."

Speaking of the anguish caused by his sins, I said, "Yes, but confessing them to God, there's a pleasure in the pain." "Yes," said he seriously, in a meditating mood, "there is—it is so—I know it—I feel it."

Soon he began to see more clearly the sins of his heart, and even when hoping in Christ, declared that the sin and short-coming of every day appeared to him, and were, probably, in the sight of the heart-searching God more heinous than were his outbreaking sins, which were against less light and mercy. All the earth, it would seem, would not shake his purpose to trust evermore wholly and alone in Christ, and join himself irrevocably to his cause and people.

But he did not come alone. His wife would sit in silence, listening to all that was said. I knew she rejoiced in her husband's temperance; but feared that our religious conversation would pall upon her ear. Sometimes I said; "I want you to take each other by the hand, and come together—place your feet on the Rock of Ages, and devote yourselves to the service of Christ; train up your children for him; be a family for God, and nothing will turn you aside." To my surprise I soon found that her heart had sympathized in all she had heard; and she seemed as steadfastly determined to serve the Lord as was her husband; and at length she told me that the last three days had been *the happiest of her life*. The care of her little ones, and a want of clothing which for some time I did not ascertain, had detained her from the house of God; but when, after about ten weeks, her husband proposed to join the church, she felt that she also must claim to eat of "the children's bread." The evidence of their saving conversion was deemed satisfactory, and we, last Sabbath, sat down together at the table of our common Lord.

The bonds that bound them to their old associates are broken, and their friends are the friends of Zion. They cheerfully bear their privations; erected, some weeks since, the family altar; their children were in the Sabbath school; and now the first sound that strikes the ear of the father, as he wakes at peace with God, is often their morning hymn of praise. The Bible and the place of prayer are loved; and not unfrequently he, who once scoffed, points me to passages, especially in Paul's epistles, so rich in the fullness and glory of the gospel and of the cross, that I must believe he will have a harp to strike to his Redeemer's praise for ever and ever.

My own soul has been richly blessed in these interviews. I thank and praise God for them and for what he has done. Give me the joy of such labors, and it is enough, till I join the song of, I trust, these and all redeemed spirits before the throne.

(*k*) THE STRIKING PICTURE.—In a large manufacturing town in the West Riding of Yorkshire, some pious persons were in the habit of leaving tracts at the different dwellings of the poor. This was done every Sunday morning, and the same tract was deposited at each habitation. On one occasion, the tract which came in course for circulation, was the narrative of "WILLIAM KELLY." There was a cut on the frontispiece to this tract representing the subject of the story sneaking bareheaded from the presence of the storming hostess, who had seized his hat as a security for a public-house score. Such a circumstance actually did take place, and proved the turning point in his life who was afterwards appropriately designated "The Happy Christian." The disgrace of the incident induced sober reflection, sober reflection issued in repentance, and repentance in one of the most pleasing specimens of lowly piety that modern days can furnish.

This tract, thus embellished, was left at the house of one of the most profligate drunkards in the place; and to him, strange to say, a circumstance precisely similar to that which arrested Kelly in his career, had occurred the evening before. His hat being detained for debt by the landlady of a neighboring alehouse, he had hastened homeward, bareheaded, incensed and ashamed, and retired to rest raging like a she-bear robbed of her young. Sunday morning found him sullen and perturbed; he hurried down stairs half dressed, and flung himself into a chair which stood beside the breakfast table; when lo! the first object that caught his attention was the frontispiece of the tract which we have been describing, placed we will not say accidentally, full in his view. Glancing at it with an eye of fierceness, he seized it, and striking the table with his fist, at the same time uttering a fearful imprecation, exclaimed, "Those villainous Methodists!—if they haven't got me already painted up to be the laughing-stock of the town; here I am without a hat. I'll be even with them." Thus he raved till the tempest of his anger had somewhat exhausted itself in oaths and menaces; then, prompted by curiosity, he thought he would ascertain what was said concerning him. A near inspection of the object of his wrath immediately corrected his preposterous error; but his curiosity having been excited, he read the little narrative, and the perusal was productive of the happiest effects. He resolved, in the strength of God, that he would reform; he repaired to a place of worship, began to search the Scriptures, and exhibited every symptom of real repentance. From being a disgrace to society, a curse to the neighborhood, and a scourge to his family, he became one of the kindest of neighbors, most faithful of servants, best of fathers, and most sober of men.

The lessons to be gathered from this interesting incident are sufficiently obvious. It needs no comment. There is, however, one particular which deserves to be appended, because it strikingly illustrates the principal inference which ought to be deduced from the fact; even the perfection of that Providence which orders the minutest circumstances in wisdom. I well remember that the venerable author was not a little chagrined, when he first saw the cut with which his production was decorated: he deemed it unfair to give such prominence to the most disgraceful feature in the history of his friend. Yet this very picture, insignificant as it might seem, was destined to conduce to an event which, contemplated in its bearings on eternity, is of a magnitude too mighty for a man to grasp.

415. Suicide Prevented.

(*a*) TRACT IN THE BARBER'S SHOP.—At the annual meeting of the Religious Tract Society, in 1824, the Rev. S. Curwen related, that a poor man was reduced to profligacy, and determined to rush, unbidden, into eternity. He went into a barber's shop, intending to use one of the razors for his horrid purpose. The boy had a broad sheet in his hand, containing, "THE SWEARER'S PRAYER:" it had been left there to be affixed to the wall. It engaged the attention of this wretched man. It struck him to the soul; he forgot his purpose, but he could not forget what he had just read; it brought him eventually to sit at the feet of our Savior, "in his right mind."

(*b*) THE TRACT AND THE HALTER.—The following interesting fact was communicated to the Board of the American Tract Society:

A gentleman of respectable family and genteel appearance, while traveling on Long Island, indulged repeatedly in drinking ardent spirits, contrary, it would seem, to his usual practice; and, before he was aware, he became intoxicated. Deeply mortified at finding himself in this situation, he resolved, in a rash moment, to destroy himself, and for this purpose retired to the woods. After finding a suitable place, he took from his hat the handkerchief with which he intended to execute his dreadful purpose; but, providentially, with the handkerchief he drew out from his hat a little tract, which arrested his attention. It had on the title-page, "A Word in Season." He perused it; it struck conviction to his heart; he instantly fell on his knees, cried to God to have mercy on him, and after continuing some time in earnest prayer, arose, and made his way to a neighboring house, where, happily, a pious Christian dwelt. Here he gave no sleep to his eyes, but spent the whole night, like Jacob, wrestling with God. In the morning he returned to the city, thanking God for the deliverance he had effected, through the instrumentality of the "Word in Season."

(*c*) SUICIDE PREVENTED.—The Rev. Basil Wood once related in a sermon, that a person belonging to his congregation, who had for some time been confined by sickness, derived great benefit from reading a certain tract. While thus confined, he was visited by an acquaintance who appeared to be laboring under great depression of spirits. His sick friend, observing his dejected frame of mind, pointed to the tract lying on the table, and requested him to sit down and read it to him. He assented, and had not proceeded far in his task before his whole attention became absorbed in the contents of the tract. As he read on, his heart became more and more affected, till at length, unable to control his feelings, he burst into tears, and pulling a weapon of destruction from his pocket, threw it upon the floor, exclaiming, "There, with that weapon I was just going to take away my own life, but thought I would first look in to see you once more before I committed the horrid deed. What I have now been reading has saved me."

416. Conversion of the Heathen.

(*a*) FIRST ORIYA CONVERT.—"The conversion," says a quarterly missionary paper, "of *Gunga Dhor*, the first Oriya convert, a Brahmin of high caste, and of great respectability and influence among his own people of every class, was an event of no ordinary importance. It may, in truth, be said, that, when Gunga Dhor threw off his poita, the badge of his divinity, and assumed a Christian profession by public baptism, the temple of Juggernaut received a severe shock. Then, that progress of ruin commenced, which will work till one stone shall not be left upon another, which shall not be thrown down. When he delivered his first Christian address, the Brahmins gnashed their teeth upon him and uttered their curses and imprecations, wishing that he might die.

"The first Christian light, which entered Gunga Dhor's mind, was from a small tract, (written by Rev. Mr. Ward), entitled 'Jugernatha Ruth na chullebar a kottha,' or 'The account of the not proceeding of Juggernaut's car.' The tract induced in his mind a supreme contempt for that idol; then he found other tracts and single Gospels; these led him to the house of the missionary at Cuttack, whom he woke from his bed very early in the morning of January 1, 1826, *begging an explanation* of his books. Mr. Sutton was immediately sent for; and 'great was the day, the joy was great,' when the missionaries met the first Christian inquirer at Orissa. He accompanied Mr. Lacey on a tour to Calcutta; saw Dr. Carey; returned to Orissa; parted with kindred, friends, and every thing for Christ; was baptized, and became a laborious and faithful native Christian evangelist."

(*b*) RENOUNCING MOHAMMEDANISM.—"On a late visit to Soerabaya, Java" says Mr. Medhurst, in 1841, "I was informed of a spirit of inquiry which had broken out among the natives of a village about eight miles from that town, *forty of whom* had resolved to renounce Mohammedan customs, and to adopt the profession of Christianity.

On inquiry, it appeared that one of them formerly obtained a *tract*, at the annual fair held at Soerabaya, from which he learned, that *he was a sinner, and in danger of perdition, while the only Savior to whom he could look for help, was Jesus Christ, the Son of God.* He communicated his views to some of his fellow-villagers, who shared with him in a desire to know more of this new way. They accordingly proceeded further into the interior, to the house of a Dutchman, who was in the habit of instructing his tenants in the outlines of Christianity; and having been taught by him to a certain extent, they were directed to go back to Soerabaya, and inquire further after Christians there. This, they accordingly did, and have continued to this time coming and going weekly for instruction.

They abstain from work on the Sabbath day; when they meet together, they read the New Testament, *sing* the *tracts* for hymns, and offer up such prayers as they find therein contained. They have committed to memory a short catechism, printed in Javanese, and know a great portion of the contents of the tracts by heart.

Their knowledge of Christianity is of course circumscribed, but they stick fast to the great truth of trusting in Jesus Christ alone for salvation. I gave them what instruction I could, during my stay, and put means in operation for having them regularly visited in their own village, for the purpose of maintaining Christian worship among them.

(*c*) WHAT TWO CENTS CAN DO.—The Rev. Dr. Scudder, 1842, says, "A young man belonging to Panditeripo received from Rev. Mr. Poor, the tract, '*Heavenly Way.*' On reading it, he came to converse with me on the subject of the Christian religion; placed himself under the instruction of the sanctuary; dedicated himself to Jesus in a covenant never to be broken; and in due time was received into the communion of the church.

This young man became a valuable helper in making known the Gospel of Christ, and is, so far as I know, at this day devoting his energies to the same momentous work.

His conversion was followed by a younger brother of his being brought under religious instruction. He attended a meeting which I held for candidates for the church, for nearly, or quite, a year, when he was suddenly taken off by the cholera. When near to death, his mother told him that she must make offerings to her god, that he might be induced to restore him. The little boy replied, 'I do not worship idols; I worship Christ the Lord, and if he is pleased to spare me a little longer in this world, it will be well; if not, he will take me to himself.' Not long after, he lifted up his dying voice and uttered, 'I am going to Christ the Lord,' and I trust slept in Jesus.

After the death of the little boy, the hoary-headed *father* came forward and publicly professed his faith in the Lord Jesus.

As the young man after his conversion could not marry a heathen, he chose a young female among his relations, whom he wished to marry, and had her sent to the Oodoovill boarding-school. There she remained a heathen three years; but in the ever to be remembered season, in which God visited the school at that place, in 1833, she, with nearly twenty others, was humbled at the foot of the cross, and publicly professed her faith in Christ. They have long since been united in marriage, and I hope are training up a Christian family in that land of darkness. Such is the history of a tract, which cost about two cents, and how much more good in ages to come it may do, will best be known in that day when the affairs of the world are to come to a close.

(*d*) PERSECUTED HINDOO.—A Hindoo met a missionary in India one day, and had ten minutes' conversation with him. It was a rule with the missionary, not to leave any one without giving him a copy of the Scriptures, or a tract. He gave the man some tracts and a copy of the New Testament, and heard no more of him. He almost forgot him. But the man did not forget the missionary. He read the books, and as he read them, he began to feel that he was a sinner, and needed some better Savior than a dumb idol. Gradually he left off worshiping idols, and no longer paid any thing towards the support of the temple. Soon, he said, "I want to go and see the missionary again." He had several grown up children, and they exclaimed, "No, you shall not go; for you will only receive more tracts, and you will disgrace us among our people." At the same time they brought fetters, and bound him hand and foot, so that the poor man could not stir. No Christian was near to encourage him or to instruct him; but Christ was near, and he prayed for the man, that his faith might not fail. It did not fail. He still resolved that as soon as his fetters were unloosed, he would find his way to the Christian teacher. For thirteen years he was kept in chains! But the Hindoo man had read his New Testament too well to forget it; and had learned too much of his Savior's love to give it up.

How do you think he gained his release at last? A wedding was about to take place in the family, and his children were anxious that he should go to it; so they unchained him. He took good care to put the tracts and the Testament in his cloth under his arm, without the knowledge of his friends. He went to the place where the marriage ceremony was to be performed, and when they were all busy and excited in the festival, he gave them the slip, and made the best of his way to the missionary's house, which was twenty-five miles off. When he arrived there, the missionary did not remember him. He looked at him from head to foot, but could not recall him. No wonder! it was fourteen years since he had seen him, and then only for ten minutes. The man said to him, "I wish to be a Christian." He replied, "What do you know about Christianity?" He said, "Ask me some questions, and I will tell you what I know." The missionary asked him some questions, and he answered them all very correctly. Of course, the missionary was very much surprised, and he inquired of the man, how he had gained his knowledge of Jesus. He replied, "Did you not, when you passed by my village, fourteen years ago, give me some tracts? They taught me that Christ is the only Savior and I was unhappy as long as I was a heathen. I have for some time left off idol worship; and I should have come to you before now to tell you that I believed in Jesus, but I have been chained to my house." He then showed the wounds which the fetters had made on his hands and his feet. The missionary was glad, and after some further conversation with him, in the course of a few weeks, baptized him in the name of the Lord Jesus.

417. Conversion of Infidels.

(*a*) CHANGING BOOKS.—A pastor in ——, related in substance the following fact: An infidel in Western New-York wished him a few years since when residing there, to read one of his books. He consented to do it on one condition, viz., that the infidel would read one of his in turn, which was "*Leslie's Short Method with Deists.*" It was the means, under God, of his hopeful conversion; and of the many whose minds he had before polluted, he was the instrument of bringing back ten or twelve to the knowledge of the truth.

(*b*) DESTROYING ONE'S OWN WORKS.—A young man, says a tract distributer, who has aided me zealously for a week in the distribution of volumes, informs me that a few months ago he was the ringleader of about fifty infidels in ——. He was their *preacher;* and that he might make the Bible ridiculous, he says he has taken it, and in reading it publicly, *put in words and taken out others, to show his hearers that it contradicts itself!* The Tract, "*The Sinner Condemned Already,*" was the means of his conversion, and he entertains a lively feeling of gatitude to the American Tract Society as the means of his salvation. He is now anxious to prepare to preach the Gospel, that he may build up the faith he has labored so hard to destroy. He has assembled his infidel friends, renounced his infidelity, and preached Christ to them, which he intends to do day by day.

(*c*) THE INFIDEL'S PRINCIPLES SHAKEN.—I was requested, writes a Christian minister at Godalming, in Surrey, (England,) to visit a poor man who was ill. Upon inquiring as to his previous character, I found that he had been the leader of a band of infidels, who assembled weekly to contemn the Bible. I went; he confessed what he had been, and expressed a desire for spiritual instruction. The third chapter of John was the one I chose for reading, after which I prayed with him, and left. The following week I heard he was very desirous to see me. I went, found him anxious to know "how he could be born again." He was much worse in body, and too ill to walk across the room; but while I was engaged in prayer, he got out of bed, and knelt by my side. When leaving, I offered him a small donation, when he replied, "I don't want your money, but your instructions and your prayers. Do come again." I visited him many times, and have reason to believe he was a sincere penitent.

A short time before he died he said, "There is one thing which I am anxious to know. Soon after I was afflicted, a person brought me a small packet, but was not to give it to me unless I should engage to ask no questions. I promised, and found a tract and half-a-crown. The tract must have been sent by some one who knew my character and principles, and before I die I should like to know the person." I knew the history, and satisfied him; but asked, "What effect had the tract upon you." He replied, "it shook my principles, and set me thinking." He had forgotten its title, but said it commenced with, "How do you use your reason?" I said, "I regard you now as a dying man, and I ask upon what are you placing your hope of mercy?" He replied, "Only upon Christ." I said, "What! upon Him whom you have openly blasphemed?" "Yes; wretch that I have been!"

Shortly after he died, and, I trust, entered into peace.

418. Converts Distinguished for Usefulness.

(*a*) BECOMING A MAN-OF-WAR'S-MAN.—I know a man, said Rev. Mr. Lord, seaman's chaplain at Boston, who is now a member of the church, and was hopefully converted four years ago by reading "*Little Henry and his Bearer*." He went home; but on reflection, made up his mind to go on board a man-of-war, *for the purpose of doing good*. He shipped at Charlestown, furnishing himself with tracts, Bibles, and the Society's volumes. The crew were so wicked, that at the end of nine months, the chaplain was compelled to leave the ship. But this man and one or two other pious men remained. At last God blessed him. One of the men was sent up to the fore-top-sail as a punishment. He asked this man to lend him a book, which he did. He was a wicked man, and had been accustomed to read Tom Paine and similar works. But now he came down serious, and inquired what he should do to be saved. God opened the windows of heaven, and in three weeks there were between twenty and thirty inquirers, and fifteen or twenty entertaining hope. There was great and continued opposition from the officers. But at the end of three years and a half the vessel arrived, and *eleven men* who had endured this fiery persecution all this time, *sat down to commemorate the dying love of Jesus*.

(*b*) THE PHYSICIAN'S EARLY IMPRESSIONS.—A pious young physician called on a gentleman one day, after friendly salutations and expressions, of Christian affection, said, "Do you know, sir, how much I am indebted to you, for giving me a tract many years ago?" His friend told him he had no knowledge of ever presenting him with one; but recollecting that the father of this young physician formerly kept a turnpike-gate, and that often, when he stopped to pay his toll, he used to give tracts to the children who were playing about the door, it occurred to him a spossible, that he might have given him one on some of these occasions. "When I was a boy," said the physician, "you gave me a tract, as you were riding by my father's house, and the first words that caught my eye were, 'Stop, poor sinner! stop, and think.' I was much affected with the whole hymn beginning with these words, and committed it to memory. Five years ago, while a member of an university, in a time of universal attention to religion, I was present at a meeting for prayer and other devotional exercises, when they commenced singing the hymn, 'Stop, poor sinner! stop, and think.' My early impressions were all instantly revived: I saw that I was ruined by sin; that an eternity of woe was before me; and I found no peace till I looked to the Savior who was crucified for me; and, as I hope, by true repentance and faith in his blood, gave myself to him, to be his for ever." This student became an active, pious, praying physician.

419. Converts becoming Ministers.

(*a*) DR. COKE AND HIS HOSTESS' FAMILY.—In attempting to cross a river in America, Dr. Coke missed the ford, and got into deep water; he and his horse were carried down the stream, and were in considerable danger; he caught hold of a bough, and with some difficulty got upon dry land; his horse was carried down the stream. After drying his clothes in the sun, he set out on foot, and at length met a man, who directed him to the nearest village, telling him to inquire for a Mrs. ——, from whom, he had no doubt, he would receive the kindest treatment. Dr. Coke found the good lady's house, and received all the kindness and attention she could show him; messengers were sent after his horse, which was recovered, and brought back. The next morning he took leave of his kind hostess, and proceeded on his journey. After a lapse of five years, Dr. Coke happened to be in America again. As he was on his way to one of the provincial conferences, in company with about thirty other persons, a young man requested the favor of being allowed to converse with him; he assented with Christian politeness. The young man asked him if he recollected being in such a part of America about five years ago; he replied in the affirmative. "And do you recollect, sir, in attempting to cross the river, being nearly drowned?" "I remember it quite well." "And do you recollect going to the house of a widow lady, in such a village?" "I remember it well," said the doctor; "and never shall I forget the kindness which she showed me." "And do you remember, when you departed, leaving a tract at that lady's house?" "I do not recollect that," said he; "but it is very possible I might do so." "Yes, sir," said the young man, "you did leave there a tract, which that lady read, and the Lord blessed the reading of it to the conversion of her soul; it was also the means of the conversion of several of her children and neighbors; and there is now, in that village, a little flourishing society." The tears of Dr. Coke showed something of the feelings of his heart. The young man resumed, "I have not, sir, quite told you all. I am one of that lady's children, and owe my conversion to God, to the gracious influence with which he accompanied the reading of that tract to my mind, and I am now, Dr. Coke, on my way to conference, to be proposed as a preacher."

(*b*) THE CAPTAIN'S CLERK.—The Rev. J. C. Smith gives the interesting history of a young man who was a friend of the captain of the United States ship Hornet; and had engaged to sail with him, from the Navy Yard, Brooklyn, as clerk on the voyage in which the Hornet was lost—probably in a hurricane in the West Indies. At the hour of sailing Providence prevented his embarking—but he had already, when alone in the cabin, discovered in the sideboard drawer a tract, (Heaven Lost, by Baxter,) having on the title-page a cut, with the words, "If thou art lost say not that thou hast not been faithfully warned." "I was amazed," he says; "I trembled; I opened the book and read its few but powerful pages. The life, the energy, the reality I found in every paragraph are fresh in my memory. I began to pray, I searched the Scriptures. I had received a wound which nothing could heal but atoning blood." It was while in this state of mind that the cruise was abandoned. On his way home to Maryland, he found in a steamboat, and read with profit, another tract—on the authenticity of the Scriptures. The insignia of the navy were laid aside. A desire to make known the love of God to sinners was awakened in his heart; he began to prepare for, and in due time entered the ministry. God has owned his labors and blessed many souls through his instrumentality; and few ministers have a stronger hold on the affections of their people than Rev. A. W——. "the captain's clerk."

(*c*) THE SOCINIAN AND THE TRACT.—At one of the anniversaries in Paris, a clergyman rose, and related the case of a Socinian minister, who had read many books of controversy respecting the Divinity of Christ, and the kindred evangelical doctrines, but still remained a champion of Socinianism, living himself in darkness and sin. While in this frame of mind, he was presented with a little tract, entitled "The Best Friend," which simply told of Jesus. There was not one word of controversy in it. But he felt that this was just the friend he needed. He laid the tract on the table, fell on his knees, and yielded up his heart to Jesus. "And now," says the clergyman, "I am that man." He is now one of the most devoted ministers in France.

(*d*) HOUSE-BREAKER AND THE TRACT.—Hon. Mr. Wilson, agent in Vermont, writes that a respectable clergyman, while residing at the West, became acquainted with a very devoted minister who was converted under the following circumstances.

He was long a most abandoned, dissipated character. One night he was found trying to get into a neighbor's house at a late hour. The family were aroused by the noise, got up, helped him in and made him comfortable till morning, and then put a small tract in the crown of his hat, and sent him home.

When he discovered the tract, he wondered how it should have come there. He read it again and again, still wondering where such a message should have come from. He was finally brought under deep conviction for sin, and fled to the Savior; was drawn to the ministry, and is now a very successful preacher of the gospel.

420. Revivals and Numerous Conversions.

(*a*) THE NORWEGIAN FARMER.—Many years ago, a Norwegian farmer was, at the age of twenty-five, in the habit of making excursions from his father's dwelling, for the purpose of distributing religious tracts, which he had caused to be printed at his own expense, and which he sold or gave away. The effects of his labors were perfectly astonishing; not less than 50,000 peasants dating the period of their conversion to sound and vital Christianity, at the time when they first became known to that remarkable individual. To the sufferings which he had undergone, it is most distressing to advert; he endured eleven several imprisonments, one of which lasted for a period of ten years. There is a passage towards the close of his journal, dated in the year 1814, from which it appears, that a fine of a thousand rix-dollars was imposed upon him, and that all which he possessed on earth was sold for the liquidation of that debt: he might have escaped it, could he have prevailed on himself to petition the king, saying that he was unable to pay the amount; but such was his love of truth, that no consideration under heaven could induce him to declare a falsehood; and, in consequence, he suffered himself to be reduced to the lowest degree of poverty: he allowed every thing which he possessed, down to the meanest utensil, to be sold, rather than declare that which he knew to be false.

(*b*) THE CADET AND GREGORY'S LETTERS.—Bishop M'Ilvaine, in an address delivered at the anniversary of the Naval and Military Bible Society in London, in May, 1830, gave the following pleasing statement:—

I was appointed chaplain to a military academy in my native country. I was forewarned of the rugged soil which I was destined to cultivate; and was recommended to relinquish all idea of making any progress in the work of the Lord, under such circumstances as those by which I was then surrounded. Shortly after my arrival, I received a communication from an officer in the depôt, stating that he should feel himself accessory to a falsehood, did he not distinctly convey to me a faithful account of the position in which I was placed. However I might believe and rejoice in the doctrines which it was my duty to inculcate, there were those among my congregation who believed not a word of them; and he reckoned himself among the number of the unbelievers. He had to state further, that he believed there was not a person in the neighborhood who put the slightest faith in my doctrines. I have reason to believe that the individual from whom I received that communication, professed opinions little different from those of an atheist.

One day, soon after my appointment, a cadet came to my apartments, and told me that his father had recently died, and that he had enjoined him to come and seek my acquaintance. I gave the young man a tract; it might not produce its effect at the moment, but it was like throwing bread upon the waters: there was little doubt that it would be found after many days. In two weeks from that period, a young man, one of the finest in the academy, came to me, attired in his full uniform: his eyes were filled with tears; his utterance was nearly choked with emotion. At first, it appeared to me that he had been the victim of some sad disaster; at length, he articulated the words, "Gregory's Letters!" He stated that he had been brought up without religion; that he had lived unacquainted with God; that his mind was disposed towards skepticism. "Gregory's Letters" had fallen into his hands; and such was the effect which they produced upon his heart and mind, that, when reading them, he could not refrain from laying his hand upon the table, and saying, "This must be true." He told me that he had found a tract in his room, but was ignorant how it came there. I explained to him how that tract had been given away by me;

and how it had found its way to the man by whom it was needed. When the young man to whom I had given the tract was on guard, this officer had put the very tract which he had found into his friend's hand, for the purpose of ascertaining how he felt on the subject of religion. The effect was such, that in a short time both were on their knees; soon after, they came to my apartments, and one of them, throwing his arms round my neck, inquired what he should do to be saved. It soon came to be whispered abroad that many persons were inclined to attend public worship; and it was not long before there were many professing, steady, zealous, practical Christians. Nor was it long before our prayer meetings were joined by the professors of military and civil engineering, the professors of mineralogy and chemistry, and the instructor of artillery, and as many as seventeen cadets.

(*c*) "THE GREAT QUESTION ANSWERED."—It is related by Dr. Henderson, that during his travels in Northern Europe, he was detained for a time in Copenhagen. While there, he states that he employed himself in translating the tract entitled, "The Great Question Answered," and that the circulation of this tract had been traced as the source of all the Bible Societies in Russia, Sweden, and the neighboring countries.

TRAFFIC IN ARDENT SPIRITS.

421. Injurious to Customers, their Friends, and the Community.

(*a*) THE TWO RED CENTS.—A grocer in Clinton County, New-York, sold a drunkard a pint of new rum *according to law*, and made *two red cents clear profit*. The drunkard shot his son-in-law while intoxicated; and his apprehension, confinement in jail, execution, &c., cost the county more than *one thousand dollars*, which temperate men had to earn by the sweat of their brows! What say you, tax-payers, are you willing to pay a thousand dollars to enable the grog-seller to make *two red cents*?

(*b*) THE TWO RED CENTS AGAIN.—About the 1st of July, 1843, an Indian, one of those half-civilized, rum-loving creatures who abound in the West, stepped out of Cataraugus County into the State of Pennsylvania, where, it seems, men are sold indulgences to sin, as well as in the Empire State; and then filled his pocket-bottle with real "red-eye," and the seller of the poison made *two red cents* clear profit. While under its maddening influence, he went into a farmer's house near by, with whom he was totally unacquainted, and murdered a mother and five children—all that comprised the little family, except the husband and father, who was from home. When he returned to his little interesting family what a sight met his eyes! —enough, it would seem, to curdle his blood, and change the man to stone. There lay the mother and her five little ones—from ten years of age down to infancy—stretched upon the floor, swimming in blood, *and all dead!* Oh! what desolation was there!

(*c*) "WHAT HAVE I DONE THAT I SHOULD BE USED SO?"—said a forlorn woman, whose appearance gave every assurance of poverty and suffering, while she covered her eyes, no longer capable of shedding tears. The fountain was dried up.

"Used how?" I asked. "He," pointing to a rum-seller living on Chesnut-street, "he took my husband, as faithful a man as ever wedded woman, got all his money, burnt up his heart, ruined his body, palsied his tongue, and sent him home to inflict on me all the curses which overhung his own guilty head, and on his family, shame, that neither toil nor tears can wipe away; and now that husband is in the grave, with no one to weep for him, or console his wife and children.

My son caught the spirit and followed the example of his father; was enticed by the same rum-seller, and drained of all that he could earn or supply, till he came back upon me, not a son, but a useless carcass, quickened with the spirit of a fiend, and has ended his career, not in death, but crime, at the thought of which I cannot hold up my head; *widowed, childless, and old.* Oh God! what have I done that I should be used so?"

Our heart melted over this picture of wo, as we exclaimed, "God will not allow the cry of the widow to go unheard, or her cause unavenged."

Alas for the man whose business calls him to such responsibility!

122. Injurious to Traffickers and their Families.

(*a*) FARMER TURNING RUM-SELLER.—D. B. was an industrious farmer, and by great prudence and economy, had accumulated a capital of near $5000.—Hitherto, industry and frugality had been the only means of his advancement, but now more ambitious thoughts took possession of his mind. He resolved to live more at ease, and become a merchant in the village of ——. He procured a license for selling liquors to be drank on the premises. Gradually, he became intemperate; at the end of three years, his wife was a widow, his children fatherless! The amount found due the estate rather exceeded the capital he had three years before embarked in the business: but of all these debts, less than $500 could be collected. The remainder passed through the hands of several intemperate customers, and the family is left utterly destitute.

123. Immoral in its Character.

(*a*) THE PETITIONER FOR LICENSE.—Some twenty years ago, a carpenter, who was tired of making an honest living, came to a friend of mine in Philadelphia, with a petition for a tavern license, which he requested him to sign. My friend looked at him, and asked him why he did not stick to his plane and bench? The answer was, "Tavern keeping is a more lucrative trade; I want to get richer." "Well, but do you not think you will be affording additional facilities to drunkards to destroy themselves?" "Perhaps I shall." "Do you not believe that at least five men every year will die drunkards, if you succeed in getting a license?" "Why, I never thought of that before; but I suppose it would be so." "Then if the Lord lets you keep tavern ten years, fifty men will have died through your agency—now what becomes of the drunkard? Does he go to heaven?" "I suppose not." "I am sure he does not, for no drunkard shall inherit the kingdom of heaven; what becomes of him then?" "Why, he must go to hell." "Well, do you not think it will be just if the Lord, at the end of ten years, sends you down to hell too, to look after those fifty drunkards?"—The man threw down his petition, went back to his honest occupation, and was never tempted to desire a license again.

(*b*) A RUMSELLER NO GOOD CITIZEN.—The Rev. John Chambers, of Philadelphia, in a speech before the American Union, said:—

"A dealer in liquor was tried for some crime, convicted, and sentenced by Judge Parsons. The next day a laywer waited upon the judge and told him he could show a defect in the proceedings wherefore the man should be released. 'O,' said the judge, 'that matter's settled.' 'But,' said the lawyer, 'he is a worthy man.' 'A worthy man!' said the judge, 'and make drunkards?' 'But,' said the lawyer, 'he is a good citizen.' 'A good citizen,' said the judge, 'and fill up our jails and almshouses and cause men to commit murder and arson, and every iniquity? That question's settled, sir, and the man must abide by the law. The name of that judge was PARSONS, and may God send us more such *parsons* as these!"

(*c*) THE MYSTERIOUS WOMAN.—At a certain town meeting, the question came up whether any person should be licensed to sell rum. The clergyman, the deacon, and physician, strange as it may now appear, all favored. One man spoke against, because of the mischief it did. The question was about to be put, when all at once there arose from one corner of the room, a miserable female. She was thinly clad, and her appearance indicated the utmost wretchedness, and that her mortal career was almost closed. After a moment of silence, and all eyes being fixed upon her, she stretched her attenuated body to its utmost height, and then her long arms to their greatest length, and raising her voice to a shrill pitch, she called upon all to look upon her. "Yes!" she said, "look upon me, and *then* hear me. All that the last speaker has said relative to temperate drinking, as being the father of drunkenness, is true. All practice, all experience, declares its truth. All drinking of alcoholic poison, as a beverage in health, is *excess*. Look upon *me*. You all know me, or once did. You all know I was once the mistress of the best farm in the town. You all know, too, I had one of the best —the most devoted of husbands. You all know I had fine, noble-hearted, industrious boys. Where are they now? Doctor, where are they now?--You all know. You all know they lie in a row, side by side in yonder church-yard; all —every one of them filling the drunkard's grave! They were all taught to believe that temperate drinking was safe,—*excess* alone ought to be avoided; *and they never acknowledged excess*. They quoted *you*, and *you*, and *you*," pointing with her shred of a finger to the priest, deacon and doctor, as authority. "They thought themselves safe under such tender teachers. But I saw the gradual change coming over my family and prospects, with dismay and horror; I felt we were all to be overwhelmed in one common ruin; I tried to ward off the blow; I tried to break the spell, the delusive spell—in which the idea of the benefits of temperate drinking had involved my husband and sons; I begged, I prayed; but the odds were greatly against me.

"The priest said the poison that was destroying my husband and boys was a good creature of God; the deacon (*who sits under the pulpit there*, and took our farm to pay his rum bills,) sold them the poison; the physician said that a little was good, and *excess* ought to be avoided. My poor husband and my dear boys fell into the snare, and they could not escape, (there were no Washingtonians then,) and one after another was conveyed to the dishonored grave of the drunkard. Now look at me again, you probably see me for the last time—my sand has almost run. I have dragged my exhausted frame from my present abode — *your poor-house* — to warn you *all*—to warn you, deacon!—to warn you, false teacher of God's word;" and with her arms high flung, and her tall form stretched to its utmost, and her voice raised to an unearthly pitch, she exclaimed—"I shall soon stand before the judgment seat of God—I shall meet you there, you false guides, and be a witness against you all." The miserable female vanished—a dead silence pervaded the assembly—the priest, deacon and physician hung their heads—the President of the meeting put the question—Shall we have any more licenses to sell alcoholic poisons, to be sold as beverage? The response was unanimous, No!

(*d*) A RUMSELLER CAUGHT.—One of the speakers at a meeting in Northern Liberties Temperance Hall, related the following striking incident: He had been lecturing at a meeting in Jersey, and dwelling quite plainly on the course of the rumseller, when a man rose and said, "Sir, I am one of the trustees of this church, and you call me a murderer.—You can't have this church to lecture in any more. I appeal to those around me to say if I am a murderer." A woman instantly rose and cried out, "*Yes, you are a murderer, you murdered my husband* by giving him rum." Another woman exclaimed, "Yes, and *you murdered mine also!*" This was plain dealing, and the rumseller and trustee must have felt his casks of liquid fire pressing with heavy weight on his soul about that time.

(*e*) THE PORTUGUESE TRAFFICKERS REFORMED.—Says the Maryland Temperance Herald, a man who was in the habit of selling a considerable quantity of liquor, a Portuguese by birth, who had settled on the eastern shore of Maryland, related the following account of his own experience:

I went to a temperance meeting; the

speaker said a good many things which hurt me very much. I felt angry with him, and would not go any more for some time; but a short time after, while I was absent from home, one of my neighbors sold a man a gallon of rum, he got drunk upon it, went home and killed his wife. When I returned, I said to myself, what if I had sold this man the rum? No, but I did not sell it. But something said, but if you had been at home you might have sold it to him. I said to myself, I will sell off what I have very cheap, and then I will sell no more. But something said, you may sell to some other man, and he may kill somebody,—that won't do. Then I will send it back to Baltimore to the merchant I bought it of; but something said, that won't do. He may sell it to somebody who may get drunk and kill somebody also; that won't do. I heard soon after of a temperance meeting; I went there; I almost ran, I jumped over the heads of the people; I said, put my name down. Somebody said, Mr. ——, what will you do with your liquor? Oh! I said, that is settled. So early the next morning I turned all my liquors out, and pulled out the spigot, and said, from the earth you came and to the earth you must go back.

(*f*) THE ELDER'S TWELVE PRAYERS.—Elder S—— was a distiller, carried on the business largely, and supplied his neighbors with the good creature. At length one and another, and another, became drunkards, squandered away their property, and reduced their families to beggary and wretchedness. Nevertheless, the Elder continued to supply them, "for the public good," and being a sober man, did it very regularly. By and by one of his customers came to settle with him, and on settlement owed him twenty dollars; and yet had nothing to pay, and nothing with which to supply his family with a rag of clothing or a morsel of bread. He and they were literally destitute. And the Elder inquired of himself, "What has made this man a drunkard, and brought his family to poverty and wretchedness?" Conscience answered, "Your whisky." "And who must answer in the day of judgment?" said the Elder. Conscience replied, "You;" and spoke with a voice which the Elder could not but hear. He went away heavy-hearted; and sorely pressed, as conscience continued to echo, "You must answer at the day of judgment for making that man a drunkard." He retired to bed, but not to rest, or to sleep. He got up, kneeled down and prayed, and went again to bed, but obtained no relief. He got up, and kneeled down and prayed again, and retired, and so again and again, till he got up, prayed, confessed his sins, implored mercy, prayed for the man and his family whom he had ruined, and laid down no less than *eleven* times. And his distress grew greater and greater. Not only this man, but one, and another, and another, great numbers whom he had made drunkards, and for whose ruin he must answer at the day of judgment, rose up to his view, and he was well nigh overwhelmed with the conviction of his guilt. He rose and kneeled down the *twelfth* time before God, and not only confessed his sins, but now, for the first time, resolved without delay to forsake them. He promised, before the Lord, that no portion of his time, or property, should ever again be employed in making that which tends to destroy the bodies and souls of men. And he meant what he said. He then laid down and slept till morning Next morning he rose, cleared out his distillery, and said that no whisky should ever be made there again. He made known his determination to his children and his neighbors. One of them thought he had become too superstitious, and offered them for the use of his distillery five hundred dollars a year. But he utterly refused, saying that none of his property should ever again be employed by any body in that way. He held to his resolution till his death, and tried to induce all to follow his example. With his children he was successful, and numbers of them before his death were hopefully made partakers of divine grace and heirs of the kingdom of God. The Elder appeared to live the life and die the death of a penitent, and went to give up his account to the Judge of the quick and dead. There he expected to meet with many whom his business had ruined, but as, during the time of divine forbearance, he trusted that he had confessed his sins, he died, hoping for pardon, through the boundless mercy of God in the Redeemer.

UNIVERSALISM.

424. Moral Tendency of Universalism.

(*a*) END OF THE SQUIRE'S UNIVERSALISM.—Some three or four years since, (says the New-York Evangelist of 1832) the Universalists of B——, Allegany Co., New-York, met for the purpose of forming themselves into a religious society; and certain of them supposing prayer to belong to a transaction of this kind, the inquiry was made for some one of the "brethren" to open the meeting by prayer. But in vain. Not one among them all could be found to open or close the meeting in this appropriate and solemn way! One of them, Mr. H——, a justice, perceiving this, and having an idea that religion was a serious, prayerful concern, "took the hint," and left them! He thought it unsafe to embark his religious and eternal interests with a prayerless, not to say wicked people. Hence the beginning and ending of the squire's Universalism.

(*b*) THE JUDGE AND THE PREACHER.—In one of the Middle States, a Universalist preacher made great efforts to establish a society of his own faith. A few persons, of little character and influence, were deeply anxious that such a society should be formed amongst them, but knew not how to effect their object and build a house. It was finally agreed, that the preacher and one of his followers should wait on a distinguished judge who resided in the village, and solicit his patronage. The judge heard the loquacious preacher with great patience for almost half an hour, when he closed by asking the judge's aid in establishing the society.

"No," says the judge: "I shall not be disposed, sir, to lend you any assistance in forming such a society. For in the the first place, it seems to me that your system of faith is not supported by the holy Scriptures. I confess I am not so thoroughly versed in those writings as I ought to be; yet I should hardly know how to express the eternity of future punishment more clearly than I often see it there described. But this, sir, I do believe, (let the Scriptures say what they may,) that were all clergymen to preach this doctrine which you preach, there would soon be a hell in this world, if not in the next." The judge then added with seriousness, that, if all who profess to preach the gospel were to adopt and inculcate such sentiments, he did not believe it would be possible to hold civil society together. Human laws would be trampled under foot, and their penalties, if not backed by Divine threatenings, would be but a subject of mockery. With these views, he must be excused from making any efforts to establish a Universalist society in that place or any other.

(*c*) I BELIEVE IT, BUT DON'T PREACH IT.—After Mr. Haynes was dismissed from his charge in Rutland, which he had held more than twenty years, he was employed about two years as a stated supply to the Congregational church in Manchester. In this town was a Universalist society, which was supplied with only occasional preaching; but, as in most other cases, its adherents were very fond of discussing their sentiments with other denominations. One of these took frequent occasion to dispute with Mr. Haynes: and though he *generally*, not to say *always*, came off second best, he seemed determined to renew the controversy on every convenient occasion.

At the close of one of these interviews, apparently under the full conviction of his own inferiority, he said: "Mr. Haynes, you are a learned man, and I cannot argue with you; but I expect one of our ministers here before long, and I intend to bring him to see you; he will be able to defend our doctrine." Mr. Haynes replied, in his usual good-natured way: "O, well: bring him along; I shall be pleased to talk with him."

Some weeks afterwards, the Universalist minister arrived; and the parishioner embraced the first leisure hour to take him up to the village to see Mr. Haynes. On their way, they were met by one of the brethren of their own faith, who, after learning whither they were bound, advised them to turn back; "for," said he, "he is an old fox, and you can't get to the windward of him." They, however, persisted in their purpose, and soon arrived at the parsonage.

Mr. Haynes was called from his study, to receive the visitors, without knowing or receiving the least intimation who they were. As he entered the room, the parishioner, after exchanging compliments, said: "Mr. Haynes, this is Mr. ——, my minister, whom I promised to bring to see you." "How d' do, how d' do?" said Mr. Haynes, taking the minister familiarly by the hand; "well, you are the man, then, who preaches that men may swear, and lie, and get drunk, and commit adultery, and all other abominations, and yet go to heaven after all:— ain't you?" "No, no," said the Universalist minister, "I don't preach any such thing." "Well," said Father Haynes, "*you believe so*, don't you?"

This was a blow that completely annihilated all desire for theological discussion, and well nigh took away the power of utterance from both the minister and layman. After a few remarks on the state of the weather, and the pleasant situation of the village, the minister said to his attendant: "Is it not time for us to be going?" and both withdrew, apparently satisfied to dispense with all further intercourse.

(*d*) LEWIS C. TODD'S TESTIMONY.—Mr. Lewis C. Todd, who was once a Universalist editor and preacher, and subsequently a Methodist, in a work of his published since his change, says:

"I became a preacher of universal salvation, and was ordained as such in Fairfield, Herkimer county, New-York, some eight years ago. I believed the doctrine true, and thought that in proportion as it was propagated, mankind would become good and happy. I preached in different parts, far and near, and itinerated over an extensive region of country, suffering the excesses of heat and cold, and the pitiless peltings of stormy skies and muddy roads. No danger or effort did I consider too great that was possible; for I believe, for a number of years, I should often have rejoiced in the martyr's privilege of attesting my faith. Some years since however, I occasionally reflected, that although the doctrine had spread much further than I anticipated, it did not seem to produce the effects I had expected. This gradually cooled my ardor and diminished my zeal, so that for some years I cared but little whether I preached or not. In this state of mind, believing Universalism to be the true sense of the Bible when rightly construed, and being unable to see any considerable good resulting from the system, I was much inclined to doubt Divine revelation. I could not go entirely into infidelity, nor feel much confidence in revelation.

"I had seen the blessed influences of the doctrine spread out often upon paper, but I could not see them any where else! No—God knows I am honest in this assertion. I do not feel to abuse the denomination; but it is true I could not for my life see any good resulting to society from the sentiment. This conviction rolled in upon my mind with tremendous effect. Alas! thought I, have I been spending my 'labor for that which satisfieth not?' Are all my efforts useless, and only tending to make looser the restraints of religion and virtue?

"I know individuals among them of the most amiable dispositions and characters, that would honor any profession But I do not think that their doctrines ever made them so. I candidly aver, in the fear of God, that I do not believe the doctrine ever made a single soul any better than he otherwise would have been, while it has been the means of removing necessary restraints, and giving latitude to thousands whose propensities and passions needed restraint, whereby they have indulged in criminal pursuits and gone to perdition.

"When I learn of a single drunkard, or gambler, or debauchee, or knave, being reformed in consequence of the Universalist doctrine, I shall think better of its influence than I do now; for it is my solemn opinion that such an instance never occurred. And I would gladly hold up this truth to all the friends of the doctrine, and make it speak out in thunder to their consciences; and then ask them if they will still teach this doctrine to their children.—*Millennial Harbinger*, Vol. II., p. 492.

"I am personally acquainted," says the editor of the above-named periodical, "with some four or five Universalian preachers, who have joined the church of Christ of which I am a member, who all say that Mr. Todd speaks their experience, or who all concur with him in opinion."

(*g*) A CHILD'S INFERENCE.—Some time since, a gentleman was at the house of the widow W——, in T——, and in the evening engaged in vindicating the doctrine of Universalism with zeal. The next morning, a child seven or eight years of age, who overheard the conversation the preceding evening, said to her mother, we may now steal, lie, and do other wicked things; for there is no punishment for us when we die.

(*e*) UNIVERSALIST'S ATTEMPTS AT SUICIDE.—The editor of the Western Recorder, published at Utica, N. Y., says:—We recollect to have been present at the examination of a candidate, who during his relation, stated in substance the following details: Educated very young in the orthodox creed, he afterwards lived among the Universalists, fully imbibed their sentiments, and gave himself up to various indulgences, with a view of enjoying a heaven both here and hereafter. In process of time he became tired of his earthly heaven, and thought it advisable to die and try the other. An enormous dose of laudanum taken for this purpose, proved ineffectual; and a little time afterwards, he removed into our section of the country. Once more he thought it advisable to exchange the present heaven for a better one. Not doubting of the issue or fearing death, he settled up his accounts, procured two new pistols, and fitted them with cool deliberation, till he found they would not miss fire. Having next loaded them, and laid them aside for future use, he sent for Mr. —— and Mr. ——, two Universalist preachers, to stand by him, and bear witness to the world, that he died in the full faith of that creed, and with entire self-possession. The preachers, however, advised him to desist. He gave his reasons for dying, and going where he should for ever be free from trouble. But they finally told him, that there was, after all, too much reason to fear that there might be a hell. "Why then do you not preach so and tell us of it?" said he. "It will not do," they replied, "it will make the people crazy." Amid the conversation he stepped into the hall; and, as he believes, with entire self-possession, aimed the two pistols at his head, and snapped them; when, to his great astonishment, they both missed fire, and were afterwards taken from him. The strange results of such efforts led him to salutary reflection. He saw in it the hand of Providence—thought upon his past conduct—began to fear there might be a hell, and that at least there ought to be a place of eternal punishment for one so vile as he had been. He sought forgiveness through the blood of Jesus; determined to yield unconditionally to his disposal, and to serve him whatever might be the result.

(*f*) WHO THAT BELIEVES HIS DOCTRINE COULD BLAME HIM?—A young man by the name of John S——, (whom the editor of this work knew,) a confirmed Universalist, resided in the town of R——, N. Y. For several years he had been subject to a painful disease. One Sabbath while alone, and engaged in shaving himself, he turned his razor's edge to his neck and cut his throat. His friends, hearing, likely, some disturbance, came in, and found him bleeding to death. They rushed up to him endeavoring to stanch the blood, and with agony and horror besought the dying man to tell them why he had committed so horrible an act as self-murder. He was just able to tell them, that he had suffered a great deal from his long illness, that he could not expect to recover, that he was tired of living; and that being a firm believer in the doctrine of Universal Salvation, he had no doubt that all would be well with him, and he had taken this step to rid himself of his miseries and go home to heaven! This was the substance of his explanation. It was found impossible to save his life, and in a few moments he expired. If all men are to be immediately happy at death, why did not John S. act consistently? Probably if those who profess to believe the same doctrine, were as confident of its truth as he was, very many of them would "go and do likewise"—cutting their way to heaven through their own throats, or swinging thither in a halter like Judas Iscariot.

(*g*) THE SWEARER ENCOURAGED.—Some time since, (says the N. Y. Evangelist of 1832,) in the town of ——, in New-York, a number of little boys, from eight to ten years old, were engaged in play together; and during their sport, two boys of a professed Universalist used much profane language, for which they were reproved and reminded of the awful consequences, by a boy whose parents are pious.

One of them promised that he never would swear again, but the other replied, "*I shall go to heaven if I swear as soon as those that don't swear.*"

(*h*) AFFINITY OF UNIVERSALISM FOR INFIDELITY.—Universalism and modern infidelity are twin sisters, They mutually support each other. We ventured the remark, says the Editor of the New-York Evangelist, a short time since, before a large company of infidels, that they had a strong affinity for the Universalists—that they were quite contented with any kind of preaching that denied a future retribution,—and that the fact that the Bible taught this doctrine, was their chief reason for casting it away. We were acquainted with the fact, that the infidels in our neighborhood often frequented and patronized the preaching of Universalist ministers. One of the chief speakers at Tammany Hall being present at the close of our discourse, in personal conversation, remarked, that what we had said of Universalism was all true. He added, "They often find fault with us for being infidels. But why, I tell them, find fault with us? You have no hell to put us in?"

(*i*) THE SUICIDE AND THE DRUNKARD.—Says the editor of the Southern Religious Telegraph, "We have known Universalists from our childhood, but we have never known one who appeared to embrace the creed from an honest conviction that it was the truth as taught by Jesus Christ. One, within the circle of our acquaintance, who was in other respects a man of good moral character, and a respected citizen, and who appeared to be more honest in his religious opinions than his brethren, *committed suicide!* Another of his fraternity, who was so religious as to pray with his family, and was equally distinguished as a profane swearer and a lover of strong drink, *died in a drunken fit*, in the street! His death corresponded with his life.

(*j*) GETTING UP A UNIVERSALIST PRAYER-MEETING.—An interesting and intelligent young man in Canada, gave decisive evidence of a change of heart, and made a profession of religion. The church had strong hopes of his usefulness, and the firmest confidence in his piety; but, for some time they were much tried, in consequence of his leaning to the doctrine of universal salvation. For years the church was without any communion or regular preaching. He wandered away from God and his brethren; and, for a time, even the most sanguine had almost given him up. He had not, however, utterly lost a sense of divine things and his own duty. And the singular proposal which he made to his Universalist friends, and the result, brought him to doubt, more than ever, the practical tendency of their sentiments. As some of them worked in the same shop, he one day asked them, "Why don't you pray—why don't you have a prayer meeting? If I am going to be a Universalist, I am going to have a prayer meeting." They found he was in good earnest. A Universalist prayer meeting! How and by whom should it be conducted? The proposal was not seconded. He did not succeed. Reflection, and the merciful interposition of God, seemed to humble him, and brought him back to the prayer meeting and the communion of the church.

THEORY REDUCED TO PRACTICE.—A young man in A., N. Y., had been visited by a sad misfortune, and life had now but few attractions for him. In this state of mind he paid a visit to a Universalist minister, and concealing his purpose, questioned him very pointedly about his belief respecting the future destiny of different classes of evildoers. "Do you sincerely believe that the drunkard will be saved? Will the robber? Will the murderer? WILL THE SUICIDE?" To all these questions the minister promptly replied in the affirmative; it was his firm conviction that, according to reason and Scripture, all men, in whatever manner they lived or died, would be happy after death. After hearing his views on this subject, the young man went back to the store in which he was clerk, and committed suicide in a manner too shocking to detail. The next morning he was found dead in his room, having literally cut himself to pieces. The facts occurred at A. in 1844, and caused a great excitement at the time.

425. Absurdity and Folly of Universalism.

(*a*) THE REJECTED PILLS.—In a town in the interior of America, the board of selectmen who governed its local affairs was composed of four universalists, (or men who contended for the final happiness of all mankind, whether believers or not,) and a pious physician. They acted through the year in great harmony as to the business of the town, but at their last meeting it was determined to attack the doctor. After they had finished their transactions, one of them said, "Doctor, we have been very happy in being associated with you the year past, and that the business of the town has been conducted in harmony, and to the satisfaction of our constituents. We have found you to be a man of good sense, extensive information, unbending integrity, and of the purest benevolence. It is astonishing to us, that a man of your amiable character should believe the doctrine of future punishment." The doctor replied, "Gentlemen, I should regret very much the forfeiture of the good opinion which your partiality has led you to entertain of me. Will you have the goodness to answer candidly a few questions? Do you believe in a future state?" They replied, "We do." "You believe that death will introduce all men to a state of perfect happiness?" "Of this we have no doubt." "Are you now happy?" "We are not; we are far from it.' "How do men act when they are unhappy, and know that happiness is within their reach?" "They endeavor to attain that happiness." "Do you believe that I understand the nature and operation of medicine?" "We have no doubt, doctor, of your skill in your profession; but what has that to do with the subject?" "In this box," said the doctor, taking a tin box in his hand, "are pills, which, if you swallow each of you one, will, without pain, carry you, within one hour, out of this world of trouble; and, if your doctrine be true, place you in a world of perfect felicity. Will you accept one of them?" "No, sir." "Will *you?*" "No, sir." When they had all refused, the doctor said, "You must excuse me, gentlemen, from embracing your doctrine, until I have better evidence that you believe it yourselves." This closed the debate.

(*b*) NOT NEEDED OR NOT WANTED.—Mr. W., a Universalist, preaching at the village of M——, where a large congregation had come out to hear something new, endeavored to convince his hearers that there is no punishment after death. At the close of his sermon, he informed the people, that if they wished, he would preach there again in four weeks; when Mr. C., a respectable merchant, rose, and replied, "Sir, if your doctrine is true, we do not need you; and if it is false, we do not want you."

(*c*) A UNIVERSALIST BIBLE.—There once lived in England a man who professed to believe in the final salvation of all men. To sustain this doctrine, whenever he came to a passage in the Bible which seemed favorable to his creed he *turned down a leaf*. In this way he converted his Bible into a kind of Universalist Text Book for the indoctrination of his family. He had a son, who imbibed the sentiments of his father. At the death of the father, the son inherited the Bible referred to, and in accordance with paternal example, he used to read where the leaves were turned down, and comfort himself in the belief that the way of sin is not death. After a few years the young man removed to the West. He went to hear a Universalist minister preach. The sermon being rather a lame performance, the man, so far from being confirmed by it, was rather shaken in his confidence. He thought, however, that he could make a stronger argument himself. He went home and sat down to the task. But the Bible with the leaves turned down was away in England, and he had forgotten where to look for the detached portions upon which he rested his faith, and thus was forced to read his Bible in its legitimate connexions and dependencies. So he read on, chapter after chapter, looking all the while for his favorite doctrine. But he did not find it. Nay, he was soon convinced that in order to salvation he must be born again. He sought and soon found peace in believing.

(*d*) THE UNIVERSALIST CONFOUNDED.—Dr. Harris, of Dunbarton, walking out one day in one of the large villages of a neighboring State, he met one of the champions of Universalism. It was Gen. P——, the leader and main supporter of the large Universalist society, which had for many years existed in that place. He was a high-minded man, quite wealthy, and very influential—having a good deal of general information, and considerable skill in argument—which last he did not hesitate to use whenever and wherever opportunities were presented. He and Dr. H. were personally strangers; but knowing something of each other by reputation, they readily introduced themselves. The General very soon lifted up his standard, and began his war of words—not doubting that, though he might fail to convince his opponent, he should at least show him that he was no ordinary combatant: but knew well on what ground he stood and how to wield the sword of sectarian warfare to good advantage. The Doctor heard him through: then calmly turned to him, and said—"General P—— it is of no use for us to contend. We shall probably not convince each other, by arguments ever so protracted. But there is one thing in relation to this matter which deserves consideration. It is this. I can treat your religion just as I please, I can turn from it, as an utter abomination; I can *despise* it; I can *spit* on it, and trample it under my feet—and yet after all I SHALL BE SAVED—*sha'n't I, Gen. P——?*" The General, of course, was obliged to assent, or give up the doctrine. There was no room for evasion. "But," added the Doctor, while the General was writhing at the contempt thus thrown upon his gods, "it will not do for you to treat my religion so. If you do, YOU ARE A LOST MAN!" This was enough—nothing more was said.

(*e*) THE INFIDEL'S CHARGE.—An infidel in the town of C., Allegany Co., N. Y., meeting one day with a Universalist, addressed him in a strain like the following. "You Universalists are the most inconsistent theorists in the world. You say there is no future punishment, and yet you profess to believe the Bible, and, what is more absurd, attempt to prove your doctrine *from* the Bible! You stretch out one passage interminably, and cut another short off; you pull connected sentences apart, and put disconnected sentences together; and you set prophets at war with prophets, apostles at war with apostles, and each one at war with himself. As sure as your Bible is true, so surely there is a hell. For my own part, I do not believe there is a hell any more than yourself; but, more consistent, I throw the doctrine of future punishment out of my creed, by first throwing out the Bible itself. And there is no other way to appear consistent. Get clear of that old book, and then you can easily get rid of the rest."

(g) THE DEVIL ONLY AN EVIL CONSCIENCE.—It happened in a town with which I am somewhat acquainted, says a gentleman in England, that three gentlemen met together in an omnibus, which was going a few miles out of the town. One of these three gentlemen was a grave and venerable divine, the others were Universalists; there were several other persons in the carriage.

First Universalist. (Addressing his friend,) Well, sir, was you at the Hall last evening to hear our friend *Rushey?*

Second Universalist. No, I was not.

F. U. That was a pity, for Rushey did the business most manfully; you know the subject was *whether there is any evidence of the being and personality of the devil.* I assure you he gave the most solid and positive proofs that there is *no devil.* And, indeed, there cannot be found, now-a-days, any man of common sense who believes in the existence of the devil, or who will attempt to prove such a doctrine; I say, (looking our divine full in the face,) I say, no man of common sense can believe in such an absurdity.

Divine. Sir, I lay claim to common sense, without pretending to any thing more, and I believe that there is a devil.

F. U. Ah! do you, sir? do you, indeed? I am astonished! I am astonished! Believe there is a devil! believe there is a devil! after what Mr. Rushey has said, and many others beside, who have with equal clearness proved the contrary? O, no sir, there is no devil; it is only a trick of the priests: there is no devil.

D. I suppose, sir, you believe in the Scriptures.

F. U. O yes, sir, to be sure I do: it was from the Scriptures that Mr. Rushey gathered his proofs.

D. Well, then, do we not read again and again of the devil in the Scriptures?

F. U. Truly, sir, truly! but *devil* means only an *evil conscience!*

D. Ah, indeed! an evil conscience; an evil conscience; let us try it: "Now there was a day when the sons of God came to present themselves before the Lord, and Satan came also among them"—*an evil conscience* came also among them! "and the Lord said unto Satan"—and the Lord said unto *an evil conscience.*

F. U. O, sir, you need not go any farther there—to be sure, it does not mean an *evil conscience* there.

D. Well, sir, we will try it in another case: "Then was Jesus led up of the Spirit into the wilderness, to be tempted of the devil"—to be tempted of *an evil conscience.*

F. U. (A little mortified,) Why, yes, it does not seem to hold good there neither.

D. Let us try it once more: "And there was a good way off an herd of swine feeding. So the devils"—the *evil conscience*—"besought him, saying, If thou cast us out, suffer us to go away into the herd of swine; and he said unto them, Go; and when they"—*the evil conscience*—"were come out, they" —*the evil conscience*—"went into the herd of swine."

I have only to add, that the quotation was arrested here, and that the *evil conscience* of the Universalist was so provoked, that you would have supposed *him* possessed, rather than the swine!

(*h*) "GO WHERE YOU HAVE A MIND TO."—About the year 1823, a celebrated Universalist preached in the court-house at New-Haven, Ct., and at the close of his sermon had some disputation with a clergyman of the city. After hearing the debate awhile, one of the audience took the liberty to ask the following questions:—"Reverend sir, is it our duty to believe in the salvation of all men?" "Yes," answered the preacher. Said the other, "Where shall we go when we die if we do not believe it?" "Go where you have a mind to!" said the preacher. This powerfully affected the risible feelings of the audience, and broke up the meeting.

426. Death of Universalists.

(*a*) A DELUSION EXPLODED. —Some time in the month of November, 1828, Capt. O. T., of N., when lying on his death-bed and a few hours before the close of his life, in the full possession of his reason, became alarmed, and sent for the Rev. Mr. W., of U. On his arrival, Capt. T. stretched out his hand, and thus addressed him: "I am a dying man; I shall soon be in eternity. My views and feelings are essentially altered. For several years past, I have followed Wood and Ballou, Universalist preachers, and believed as they did. But I find it now all a delusion. Such sentiments will do to lull the conscience to sleep while living, but will not stand the test in a dying hour. Tell my old acquaintance and friends not to trust in such refuges of lies, but to repent and be converted."

This is but one instance of a thousand, which might be adduced, of the dying confessions of Universalists, relative to the fallacy and wretchedness of their scheme.

Query. Did you ever know a person on a death-bed become a Universalist, who had previously lived in the belief of orthodox sentiments?

(*b*) RECANTATION AND DESPAIR.—David W. Bell, a zealous defender of the doctrine of Universalism, some of whose writings may be found in the Gospel Advocate, a noted mouthpiece of that pernicious system, was called, in 1827, by the sudden death of his two youngest brothers, to visit his afflicted parents, residing in Windham, Greene Co., N. Y. Here he was seized with the typhus fever, and was soon brought to view the time as not far distant, when he himself must exchange worlds, and appear before his Omniscient Judge. Now it was with him an honest hour, and his presumptuous heart, that could boldly challenge the injustice of God, now yielded to the conviction of truth.

He exclaimed one day to his father, "Father, I find eternal punishment, which I have so long disputed, now to be an awful reality."

At another time he says, "As soon as I am dead, write to brother E., in ʻ.., and to Z. T. and S. T., that the doctrine we have tried to propagate is an awful delusion—that it forsook me on a death-bed."

His conviction of the nature of sin was clear and pungent. Sometimes he would cry aloud to God for mercy—again entreat his Maker to annihilate him; sometimes he would call on others to pray—again would beg them not to pray for him, for he had already sealed his own damnation. "Oh!" said he, "it can alone be for the glory of God and the good of others, for me to be damned! I must be damned! I am damned!—damned to all eternity!! I cannot live in peace—I cannot die in peace, without an assurance that my renunciation of that delusive and dangerous heresy, the doctrine of Universalism, shall be made as public as my defence of it was. Oh, could I speak once to those deluded Universalists!" He died Sept. 29th, 1827.

"The above recantation," says David Bell, his father, "was made by my son when in the full exercise of reason. Of this there are many witnesses. Neither was it extorted from him, or occasioned by a sudden fright, as some may pretend. It was from a deliberate and settled conviction for weeks."

(*c*) DEATH OF A YOUNG LADY.—The subject of this notice was the daughter of Universalist parents, and had herself, together with others of the family, become attached to the doctrine of universal salvation. This furnished a quiet to her fears, whenever her conscience was oppressed with the guilt of living in sin and rejecting the gospel. The village where she lived was blessed with a revival of religion. While many were made subjects of the kingdom of God, by being born again, the delusive dream of Universalism led her to believe that there was no necessity of being born of the Spirit, in the present life. Suddenly, sickness visited her, and recovery was impossible; she must die. But ah! where were her hopes of heaven? The refuge under which she had taken concealment was swept away, and the wrath of God was revealed from heaven against her unrighteousness. She lost forever all hope of being reconciled to God. The offers of mercy she could not appropriate to herself. Her last hour was at hand. A minister of Christ stood by, and prayed for her departing soul. She could not ejaculate, "Lord Jesus! receive my spirit;" but with the giving up of the ghost uttered a shriek that will never cease to ring in the ears of those who heard it.

A death so full of horror, made such an impression on the minds of the parents of the wretched girl, that they abandoned a doctrine so treacherous, and by the converting grace of God, became hopeful subjects of the revival, together with one or two others of the family.

How many parents are there in our country, who by their countenancing a doctrine which they do not themselves more than half believe, occasion their children to adopt it, and thus inevitably, here or hereafter, bring distress and anguish on their souls.

(*d*) THE DIE IS CAST.—Rev. Mr. S., once pastor of the Baptist church in H., Mass., gives the following account of an interview which he had with a Universalist on his death-bed, in 1837. During Mr. L.'s illness Mr. S. had called on the family once before; but when the nurse informed her charge that Mr. S. would like to converse with him, the sick man sent back word: "Tell him when I want to see him I will send for him."

The next and last time Mr. S. called, which was two weeks afterwards, he came at the especial request of Mr. L., who said he could not die until he saw him.

As Mr. S. came to his bed-side, the sick man opened his dying eyes and said with much anxiety to his nurse, "Do you think that man will pray for me?" The preacher approached, and as he took hold of Mr. L.'s hand, the latter turned up his eyes and exclaimed, "It is too late!" In detailing his history, he stated that his mind was susceptible, and his conscience tender; but being led into the snares of Universalism, his feelings of guilt and his tenderness of conscience left him, till he had scarcely any more religious sensibility than a brute. Mr. S. directed him to Christ as an all sufficient Savior. "Ah!" said he, as at first, "it is too late." He knelt by his bed-side, and tried to pray for him. Soon after prayer Mr. S. felt called upon to return. As he took the sick man's cold and motionless hand in his, to bid him adieu, he said, in a loud, full voice, "Do pray for me when you get home. But I don't expect God will hear; it is too late; the die is cast; my damnation is sealed."

He died a few hours after, in awful and utter despair.

(*e*) THE WAY TO GET FREE FROM UNIVERSALISM.—The narrator of this fact called at the house of an intelligent member of the church in the State of New-York, and in the course of conversation learned, to his surprise, that this individual had been formerly a warm advocate of the doctrine of universal, unconditional salvation. His narrative was briefly as follows: "I was first led to embrace the creed of Universalists by hearing a sermon from the Rev. Mr. P——. The argument by which he convinced me, was that he had formerly been a minister of the Baptist persuasion, and had been converted from that to his present faith. I subscribed for a periodical in which these doctrines are advocated, and read nothing else. I looked occasionally into the Bible, but it was only to select the passages commented on by Universalists, with a view of convincing myself of the correctness of the interpretation; and as it was my wish to regard these passages in the light in which they were represented, I became daily more established in the faith which I had embraced. My wife was very much opposed to these sentiments. She manifested her opposition in the most gentle, inoffensive, and Christian manner; it was simply by attending religious meetings, and that frequently, where doctrines opposed to my own were advocated. She was particularly fond of attending prayer meetings. I manifested my disapprobation; I treated her harshly; but she still resisted my efforts to keep her at home, with the same meek, Christian spirit. After awhile, I was subdued by this unwavering forbearance and gentleness, and one day, when my wife had gone to the prayer meeting, I went into my barn, fell down upon my knees, and prayed sincerely if she was right and I was wrong, God would enlighten me and lead me into the right path. I felt willing to be led. I had no desire to cherish prejudices, if I before entertained them, against the truth. After pouring out my soul before God, I returned to the house, opened the Bible, and read it as I never read it before. A flood of light poured in upon me; my mind was open to conviction; I found no difficulty in discovering the truth, because I earnestly sought, and from that day abandoned the destructive sentiments of Universalism.

427. UNITARIANISM.

(*a*) DR. PRIESTLEY'S AVOWAL TO DR. MILLER.—The Rev. Dr. Miller, of Princeton, N. J., in a note to his sermon preached at the ordination of Rev. Mr. Nevins, in Baltimore, speaking of the dreadful and soul-destroying errors of Arius and Socinius, remarks, that in conformity with this view of the subject, the author cannot forbear to notice and record a declaration made to himself by the late *Dr. Priestley*, two or three years before the decease of that distinguished Unitarian. The conversation was a free and amicable one, on some of the fundamental doctrines of religion. In reply to a direct avowal on the part of the author that he was a *Trinitarian* and a *Calvinist*, *Dr. Priestley* said, "I do not wonder that you Calvinists entertain and express a strongly unfavorable opinion of us Unitarians. The truth is, there neither can, nor ought to be, any compromise between us. If *you* are right, WE ARE NOT CHRISTIANS AT ALL; and if *we* are right, YOU ARE GROSS IDOLATERS." These were, as nearly as can be recollected, the words, and, most accurately, the substance of his remark. And nothing certainly can be more just. Between those who believe in the Divinity and Atonement of the Son of God, and those who entirely reject both, "there is a great gulf fixed," which precludes all ecclesiastical intercourse.

(*b*) AFFINITY OF UNITARIANISM FOR INFIDELITY—DR. JEWETT'S TESTIMONY.—Dr. Thomas Jewett, of Rindge, N. H., who was for some time an avowed infidel, was hopefully converted in 1833, and received on the last Sabbath in August, of the same year, into the church. At his request, a communication from his pen was read on that day from the pulpit From this we quote the following significant passage.

"Led astray first by the plausible but fallacious arguments of Elkanah Winchester, I adopted his sentiments fully; and from his doctrine of *temporary* future punishment the transition to Universalism, or the disbelief of *any* future punishment, was very natural and easy. This latter scheme, so perfectly agreeable to the doer of evil, I readily adopted, and warmly advocated for several years.

"At thirty years of age I tried to become an Atheist, but though I never was left to deny or disbelieve the existence of God, yet I adopted the system of Deism; utterly rejecting the Bible, as the work of man and an imposition upon the world. My course of conduct in relation to evangelical ministers and Christians was such as might be expected from one who cherished such sentiments. I have it in painful remembrance that I opposed them, and made them and the cause the subject of ridicule and contempt.

"But the names of Infidel and Universalist, I was aware, were not popular. For a few years past I have assumed the name of *Unitarian*, for two reasons; one was, that it exposed me to less odium; the other, I found that I could be reckoned in that class without any material change in my religious opinions. And here I honestly and soberly declare that these several names were assumed at different times as a mere disguise, as convenience or interest might require. And I now regard these several schemes as essentially the same. I have been intimate with men in all ranks of society belonging to these religious persuasions, and I have found none of them, so far as I could discover, receiving the Bible as decisive authority in religious faith. This, I need not say, is denying its inspiration."

(*c*) A DEIST'S OPINION OF UNIVERSALISTS AND SOCINIANS.—A writer in the Western Intelligencer says: In conversation with one of the most open and virulent Deists I ever saw, after venting his spite against Jesus of Nazareth and his ministers, or "*the supposed Jesus*," as he would have it, and condemning the Bible, he said, "Within fifty years, the religion of Jesus will be banished from the world; and I am determined to do all I can to destroy it." I remarked to him he had undertaken a work of too great magnitude for one man, or any body of men, to accomplish; and that I believed a Universalist or a Socinian, or in other words Unitarian, would make many Deists to his one. To which he replied, "Sir, we consider Universalists and Socinians in the same light in regard to our doctrine, that your people do John the Baptist with regard to yours—THEY ARE MERELY FORERUNNERS!!"

(*d*) THE DEIST'S OPINION.—A friend of ours, says a writer in the Columbian Star, called some days since at the house of an intelligent Deist, who has long been known as a determined and envenomed opposer of the Christian religion, and found him reading Dr. Channing's discourse preached at a dedication in the city of New-York. The conversation turned upon the merits of the sermon, and the distinguished ability of the author, when our friend inquired of the gentleman how he liked the production. "I like it much," said he, with particular animation. "It strikes a broad blow at the Christian system, and will prove a decisive triumph for the Religion of Nature. Dr. Channing differs from me in a very few points, an in five years I am satisfied he will preach the doctrine which I believe."

(*e*) THE SOCINIAN'S JUDGE.—A physician, who had imbibed Socinian principles, made it his chief concern, in matters of religion, to degrade the character and dignity of Christ. Such was his contempt for him, that he seldom spoke of him in conversation under any other name than the carpenter's son. At length he was seized with affliction, which terminated in his death. A while before his departure, the servant who attended him, on entering his room, found him in great agitation. On inquiring the cause, he answered, "I am a dying man, and that which most of all affects me is, that I must be *judged* by THE CARPENTER'S SON!"

428. USEFULNESS, CHRISTIAN.

(*a*) A COLPORTEUR IN NORWAY.—When there was great spiritual darkness on the continent of Europe, and every thing seemed to threaten that the light of the gospel would be completely removed from Norway, God, in his providence, raised up a poor peasant, who lived near Indenckihill, on the confines of Sweden. He had received nothing but a common education, but the Lord made him acquainted with the truth, and filled him with zeal to communicate that truth to his countrymen, who were perishing for lack of knowledge. This good man, with his knapsack on his back, set out on the road, went through the length and breadth of Norway, proclaiming the gospel in that wild and romantic country, to thousands and tens of thousands; and the Lord gave testimony to the word spoken in a most remarkable manner; for hundreds were in a short time, by his instrumentality, made to see and embrace the truth. It may be easily conceived, that he was not allowed to go on in peace: the unenlightened clergy would not endure him; they stirred up the magistrates against him, and he was cast into prison; as soon, however, as he got out, he was again at his work; but, at length, having come to Christiana, the capital, a most bigoted place in regard to religion, he was apprehended, and cast into a dungeon, and kept eleven years, from 1800 to 1811. But he was not idle there; for, like Bunyan, he was writing treatises, and sending them forth into every part of the country; contriving, in the space of a very short time, to have one hundred and twenty-two tracts published at Cassel. The effect of this peasant's labors is, that at this day there are not fewer than ten thousand followers of the Lord Jesus in that country.

(*b*) "I HAVE HANDS, AND I CAN WORK."—A man in W., who depended for support entirely on his own exertions, subscribed five dollars annually in support of the Bombay schools. His friends inquired, "Why he gave so much, and how he could afford it?" He replied, "I have for some time been wishing to do something for Christ's cause, but I cannot preach, neither can I pray in public, to any one's edification, nor can I talk to people, but I have hands, and I can work."

(*c*) THREE ACTIVE YEARS PREFERRED TO SIX IDLE ONES.—Cardinal Gonsalvi was suffering under a chronic disease, and consulted three physicians, who declared on being questioned by the sick man, that this disease would be followed by death in a shorter or longer time, according to the manner in which he lived; but they advised him unanimously to give up his office because, in his situation, mental agitation would be fatal to him. "If," inquired the Cardinal, "I give myself up to repose, how long, gentlemen, will you guarantee my life?" "Six years," answered the doctors. "And if I continue in office?" "Three years at most." "Your servant, gentlemen, replied the Cardinal, "I should prefer living two or three years in doing some good, to living six in idleness."

(*d*) A YOUNG LADY'S DAY'S LABOR.—A young lady commenced a tour of active duty in a street in Boston, with a view to *do something* for the cause of the Redeemer. She devoted a whole day to visiting the poor, and the following statistics show the result of the day's labor. Visited forty families; found fifteen children who did not attend any Sabbath school, and who engaged to go; seven families that would be pleased to receive visits from her minister; and twelve families having no regular place for public worship, who promised to attend. Reader! the field of usefulness in the city and country is extensive; the laborers are few; by active and judicious efforts you can do much to enlighten and save dying sinners; then "go thou and do likewise."

(*e*) THE RESOLUTE SOLICITOR.—A lady in Bristol, (Eng.) deeply impressed with the importance of the Bible Society, determined to make personal application in its behalf to an elderly gentleman of her acquaintance, who possessed great wealth, but never contributed to objects of this nature. She was told by her friends it would be in vain, but this did not shake her resolution. She called and presented the case, exhibiting all the documents calculated to promote her object. They produced no impression. She then reasoned with him, but without effect. At length she asked him the question, "Have you a Bible, sir?" "Yes." "What would induce you to part with it?" "I would not part with it on any consideration." "Sir," said she, "there are thousands in this land who are destitute of that which you profess to prize so highly. A trifling portion of your property would supply a fellow creature with the book which you would not part with on any consideration." This appeal produced the desired effect. The gentleman, however, concealed his feelings, and simply asked, with an air of indifference, "What do you think I ought to give?" Supposing that he was balancing between a small sum and an absolute refusal, she replied, "We receive any sum, sir, however small." He then went to his bureau, took a bag of guineas, and began very deliberately to count them upon the table—one, two, three, four, and so on. After he had proceeded some time in this way, the lady presuming he had forgotten the subject on which she came, and was engaged in his other business, ventured to interrupt him with the remark that her time was precious, and that if he did not intend to give, she begged to be informed, that she might solicit elsewhere. "Have patience for a few minutes," he replied, and proceeded until he had counted 73 guineas. "There, madam," said he, "there is one guinea for every year I have lived; take that for the Bible Society."

(*f*) THE INEBRIATE'S WIFE.—In a publication of the Massachusetts Sabbath School Society, which abounds with excellent sentiments, entitled "A Practical Directory for Young Christian Females," is the following narrative:

The amazing influence of one Christian, who shows in her life the spirit of Christ, is illustrated in a striking manner, in the life of a lady who died not long since, in one of the principal cities of the United States. I am not permitted to give her name, nor all the particulars of her life. But what I relate may be relied upon, not only as *facts*, but as far below the *whole truth*. She had been for a long time afflicted with a drunken husband. At length the sheriff came, and swept off all her property, not excepting her household furniture, to discharge his *grog bills*. At this distressing crisis, she retired to an upper room, laid her babe upon the bare floor, kneeled down over it, and offered up the following petition: "O Lord, if thou wilt *in any way* remove from me this affliction, I will serve thee *upon bread and water*, all the days of my life." The Lord took her at her word. Her besotted husband immediately disappeared, and was never heard of again till after her death. The church would now have maintained her, but she would not consent to become a charge to others. Although in feeble health, and afflicted with the sick headache, she opened a small school, from which she obtained a bare subsistence; though it was often no more than what was contained in the condition of her prayer—literally bread and water. She was a lady of pleasing address, and of a mild and gentle disposition. "In her lips was the law of kindness." Yet she possessed an energy of character and a spirit of perseverance, which the power of faith alone can impart. When she undertook any Christian enterprise, she was discouraged by no obstacles, and appalled by no difficulties. She resided in the most wicked and abandoned part of the city, which afforded a great field of labor. Her benevolent heart was pained at seeing the grogshops open upon the holy Sabbath. She undertook the difficult and almost hopeless task of closing these sinks of moral pollution upon the Lord's day, and succeeded. This was accomplished by the mild influence of persuasion, flowing from the lips of kindness, and clothed with that power which always accompanies the true spirit of the gospel. But she was not satisfied with seeing the front doors and windows of these houses closed. She would, therefore, upon the morning of the Sabbath, pass round, and enter these shops through the dwellings occupied by the families of the keepers, where she often found them engaged secretly in this wickedness. She would then remonstrate with them, until she persuaded them to abandon it, and attend public worship. In this manner, she abolished, almost entirely, the sale of liquors upon the Sabbath, in the worst part of the city.

She also looked after the poor, that the gospel might be preached to them. She carried with her the number of those pews in the church which were unoccupied. And upon Sabbath mornings, she made it her business to go out into the streets and lanes of the city, and persuade the poor to come in and fill up these vacant seats. By her perseverance and energy, she would remove every objection, until she had brought them to the house of God. She was incessant and untiring in every effort for doing good. She would establish a Sabbath school, and superintend it until she saw it flourishing, and then deliver it into the hands of some suitable person, and go and establish another. She collected together a Bible class of apprentices, which she taught herself. Her pastor one day visited it, and found half of them in tears, under deep conviction. She was faithful to the church and to impenitent sinners. It was her habitual practice to reprove sin, and to warn sinners wherever she found them. At the time of her death, she had under her care a number of pious young men preparing for the ministry. These she had looked after, and brought out of obscurity. As soon as their piety had been sufficiently proved, she would bring them to the notice of her Christian friends. She persuaded pious teachers to give them gratuitous instruction, and pious booksellers to supply them with books. In the same way, she procured their board, in the families of wealthy Christians. And she formed little societies of ladies, to supply them with clothing. There was probably no person in the city whose death would have occasioned the shedding of more tears, or called forth more sincere and heartfelt grief. Her memory is still deeply cherished in the heart of her pastor. He has been heard to say, that he should not have felt so severely the loss of six of the most devoted men in his church.

(*g*) THE PIOUS SCHOOL-BOY'S EXERTIONS.—A little lad, in one of the villages of Connecticut was converted to God. He attended school at this time; and he began to study how he might benefit his playmates, and win their hearts to Christ. He was not satisfied with merely living like a Christian before them, watching carefully over his words and actions, and bearing with patience all their persecutions and ridicule on account of his piety; but he determined to use some active means for their salvation. With this in view, he gave notice that there would be a prayer meeting in the school-house during the intermission.

Drawn by curiosity, and to enjoy the sport they wickedly expected, the scholars assembled. But who was to conduct the meeting? Our little friend, strengthened by the Savior, gives out his hymn, sings and prays, and then simply, affectionately, and faithfully, exhorts his companions. Some during the exercises behave with propriety, others jeer, laugh, and attempt to break up the little service.

Unmoved by these persecutions, and his apparent ill success, the little hero continues the meeting on succeeding days.

The master attended, to see if every thing was properly conducted, and was astonished undoubtedly, (for he was an unconverted man,) at the confidence and calmness of the lad. He severely reprimanded those who were only present to disturb the devotions, and saved the young Christian from further persecution. Soon some of the lads became anxious, patient, and were hopefully converted. Their parents witnessing the change, were induced to come with them at their hour of devotion, and ere long several of these were seeking for mercy among the little flock of pious, praying lambs. The ministers of the place, hearing this wonderful intelligence, were aroused, and eventually came in and took charge of the services. Other meetings were appointed, and the result was, that about sixty obtained the salvation of their souls. The whole work, the importance and value of which eternity alone can show, originated, and was in a large sense carried on by this pious, faithful, and courageous little lad! O! how much good young Christians may accomplish!

(*h*) A YOUNG LADY'S EFFORTS.—Rev. Joel H. Linsley, in a letter to Mr. E. C. Delavan, says:

A female member of one of the churches in the vicinity of Marietta, Ohio, (supplied with preaching by one of the professors in college,) took a school in one of our most destitute counties. There was there only occasional Methodist preaching, and the people had barely heard of cold water societies. This single-handed female got up a meeting, presented a constitution, signed it herself, and secured four or five more signers. At a second meeting a few more were added. At a third meeting she got her brother (a farmer), member of the same church with herself, to write and send for an address, which she was obliged to read at the meeting, (as none present could readily read,) and the issue was a large addition of members—if I mistake not about thirty, and that society now numbers one hundred and seventy, or one hundred and eighty members. The reformation was immediately followed by a great revival of religion, where one had never been known before. Three distilleries were shut up, and the whole face of things in that community is changed almost beyond the power of language to describe. I heard this but a few weeks since, with some other striking facts connected with it, and could hardly credit it, but I went out a week since to preach in that little church, and conversed with the lady myself (a very modest, intelligent, and devoted female), and found every fact had been correctly reported to me. O, sir, what cannot the gospel do to gird weakness with strength, and make even the gentleness of a modest, retiring woman resolute to act for God. How such efforts shame timid, time-serving disciples among our own sex.

429. VANITY OF THE WORLD.

(*a*) DYING WORDS OF SEVERUS.—When Severus, Emperor of Rome, found his end approaching, he cried out, "I have been every thing, and every thing is nothing;" then ordering the urn to be brought to him in which his ashes were to be inclosed, on his body being burned, according to the custom of the Romans, he said, "Little urn, thou shalt contain one for whom the world was too little."

(*b*) PITT LYING IN SOLITUDE.—Pitt died at a solitary house on Wimbledon Common. Not far off, by the roadside, stood a small country inn, where the various parties interested in the great statesman's life were accustomed to apply for information, and leave their horses and carriages. On the morning of the 23d of January, 1806, an individual having called at the inn, and not being able to obtain a satisfactory reply to his inquiries, proceeded to the house of Pitt. He knocked, but no servant appeared—he opened the door and entered—he found no one in attendance—he proceeded from room to room, and at length entered the sick chamber, where, on a bed, in silence and in perfect solitude, he found to his unspeakable surprise, the dead body of that great statesman who had so lately wielded the power of England, and influenced, if he did not control, the destinies of the world. We doubt whether any much more awful example of the lot of mortality has ever been witnessed.

(*c*) CONSTANTINE AND THE MISER.—Constantine the Great, in order to reclaim a miser, took a lance and marked out a space of ground of the size of the human body, and told him, "Add heap to heap, accumulate riches upon riches, extend the bounds of your possessions, conquer the whole world, and in a few days such a spot as this will be all you will have."

(*d*) INSTABILITY OF GREATNESS.—Xerxes crowned his footmen in the morning, and beheaded them in the evening of the same day; and Andromachus, the Greek emperor, crowned his admiral in the morning, and then took off his head in the afternoon. Roffensis had a cardinal's hat sent to him, but his head was cut off before it came to hand! Most say of their crowns, as a certain king said of his, "Oh crown, more noble than happy!"

(*e*) DIOGENES' REPLY TO ALEXANDER.—Diogenes was not in the wrong, who, when the great Alexander, finding him in the charnel-house, asked him what he was seeking for, anwered, "I am seeking for your father's bones and those of my slave; but I cannot find them, because there is no difference between them."

(*f*) NEWTON AND MARLBOROUGH.—It is truly humbling to the pride of man to see to what a state of mental and physical ruin he is brought by the lapse of time. Sir Isaac Newton, that wonderful scholar, of whom it is said, that he "surpassed the whole human race in genius," and who, if any one can be properly styled great and illustrious, is surely entitled to these epithets, when in his declining years he was requested to explain some passage on his chief mathematical work, could only, as it is reported, say, that he knew it was true once. A circumstance in some degree similar is related of that celebrated military commander the first Duke of Marlborough, who flourished about the same period. When the history of his own campaigns was read to him, to beguile the tedious hours in the evening of life, we are told, so far were his intellectual faculties impaired, that he was unconscious of what he had done, and asked in admiration, from time to time, "who commanded?" Here, then, not to cite more examples, we have fresh proofs that "all the glory of man," even in what he is most especially apt to value himself, is but "as the flower of grass."

(*g*) LORD CHESTERFIELD'S CONFESSION.—The Earl of Chesterfield was a nobleman for whom nature had done much, and birth and education more. He was in his day universally allowed to be the most elegant and accomplished man in Europe; and he was no less conspicuous in the political than in the fashionable world. No man ever possessed greater advantages for the attainment of and the enjoyment of worldly pleasures; and no man ever drank deeper of the sweet, but poisonous draught. Let us hear him at a time when disease and age hung heavy upon him, and rendered him incapable of further enjoyment. "I have seen," says he, "the silly rounds of business and of pleasure, and have done with them all. I have enjoyed all the pleasures of the world, and consequently know their futility, and do not regret their loss. I appraise them at their real value, which is, in truth, very low. Whereas those that have not experienced, always overrate them. They only see the gay outside, and are dazzled at the glare. But I have been behind the scenes. I have seen all the coarse pullies and dirty ropes which exhibit and move the gaudy machines; and I have seen and smelt the tallow candles which illuminated the whole decoration, to the astonishment of the ignorant audience. When I reflect on what I have seen, what I have heard, and what I have done, I can hardly persuade myself that all that frivolous hurry of bustle and pleasure of the world had any reality; but I look upon all that is past as one of those romantic dreams, which opium commonly occasions; and I do by no means desire to repeat the nauseous dose, for the sake of the fugitive dream. Shall I tell you that I bear this melancholy situation with that meritorious constancy and resignation, which most people boast of? No, for I really cannot help it. I bear it, because I must bear it, whether I will or no! I think of nothing but killing time the best way I can, now that he has become my enemy. It is my resolution to *sleep* in the carriage during the remainder of my journey."

(*h*) DUKE OF ATHOL.—The estate of the present Duke of Athol, Mr. Colton informs us, "is immense, running in one direction more than seventy miles. On his estate there are thirty-six miles of private road for a carriage, and more than sixty miles of well made walks which are being extended every year. These roads and paths being made for pleasure, are laid through the most picturesque and romantic scenery; along the river's bank, up the glen, cut in the steep sides of the mountains and over their tops, and along the margin of the precipitous cliffs—now into the forest gloom, now opening on a boundless prospect, or some sweet vale, now bursting on a waterfall, and next along the side of a murmuring brook. The father of the present duke began in his lifetime, one of the most magnificent palaces in the kingdom. It is said that in the estimate of the cost of the edifice, the single item of raising the walls and putting on the roof, together with the materials, would have been one hundred thousand pounds, about five hundred thousand dollars."

Do you envy the possessor of all this wealth?

For more than thirty years he has been in a lunatic asylum of London

430. VERACITY.

(*a*) MAGNANIMOUS INDIAN.—A pledge is considered very sacred and binding among the North American Indians. The following is an instance. During the Winnebago war of 1827, Dekkerre, a celebrated chief of that nation, with four other Indians of his tribe was taken prisoner at Prairie du Chien. Colonel Snelling, who then commanded that garrison, dispatched a young Indian into the nation with orders to inform the chiefs of Dekkerre's band that unless the Indians who were perpetrators of the horrid murders of some of our citizens were brought to the fort and given up within ten days, Dekkerre and the other four Indians who were retained as hostages, would be shot at the end of that time. The awful sentence was proclaimed in the presence of Dekkerre, who. though proclaiming his own innocence of the outrages that had been committed by others of his nation, exclaimed, that he feared not death, notwithstanding it would be fraught with serious consequences to his large and dependent family of little children; but if necessary, he was willing to die for the honor of his nation. The young Indian had been gone several days, and no intelligence was yet received from the murderers. The dreadful day being near at hand, and Dekkerre being in a bad state of health, asked permission of the Colonel to go to the river and indulge in his long accustomed habit of bathing; in order to improve his health. Upon which Colonel S. told him that, if he would promise, on the honor of a chief, that he would not leave the town, he might have his liberty and enjoy all his privileges until the day of the appointed execution. Accordingly he first gave his hand to the Colonel, thanked him for his friendly offer, then raised both his hands aloft, and in the most solemn adjuration, promised that he would not leave the bounds prescribed, and said, if he had a hundred lives, he would sooner lose them all than forfeit his word, or deduct from his proud nation one particle of its boasted honor. He was then set at liberty. He was advised to fly to the wilderness and make his escape. "But, no," said he, "do you think I prize life above honor; or that I would betray a confidence reposed in me for the sake of saving my life?" Nine days of the ten elapsed and his nation was not heard from, but Dekkerre remained firm, his fidelity unshaken, his countenance unmoved. It so happened that on that day Gen. Atkinson arrived; the order for the execution was countermanded, and the Indians were permitted to repair to their homes.

(*b*) KING JOHN AND HIS HOSTAGE.—John, king of France, left in England two of his sons as hostages for the payment of his ransom. One of them, the Duke of Anjou, tired of his confinement in the tower of London, escaped to France. His father, more generous, proposed instantly to take his place; and, when the principal officers of his court remonstrated against his taking that honorable but dangerous measure, he told them, "Why, I myself was permitted to come out of the same prison in which my son was, in consequence of the treaty of Bretagne, which he has violated by his flight. I hold myself not a free man at present. I fly to my prison. I am engaged to do it by my word; and if honor were banished from all the world, it should have an asylum in the breast of kings." The magnanimous monarch accordingly proceeded to England, and became the second time a prisoner in the tower of London, where he died in 1384.

(*c*) THE HONEST REBEL AND THE KING.—In Calamy's Memoirs, there is an account of a man named Story, who was condemned for being in Monmouth's rebellion, but was reprieved by the interest of a friend with Judge Jeffries, and subsequently removed to Newgate. He was soon afterwards ordered to be brought before the Privy Council, in the same plight in which he then was, which was truly miserable. The keeper advised him, in case the king was present, that the wisest way for him would be to answer the questions put to him in a plain and direct manner, without concealing any thing—advice which he strictly followed.

When he was brought into the Council Chamber, he made so sad and sorrowful a figure, that all present were surprised and frightened; and he had so strong a smell, by being so long confined, that it was very offensive.

When the king first cast his eyes upon him, he cried out, "Is that a man, or what else is it?"

Chancelor Jeffries told his Majesty, that that was the Story of whom he had given his Majesty so distinct an account.

"Oh, Story," says the king, "I remember him. That is a rare fellow indeed!" Then, turning towards him, he talked to him very freely and familiarly. "Pray, Mr. Story," said he, "you were in Monmouth's army in the west, were you not?"

He, according to the advice given him, made answer presently, "Yes, an't please your Majesty."

"And you," said he, "was a commissary there, were you not?"

And he again replied, "Yes, an't please your Majesty."

"And you," said he, "made a speech before great crowds of people, did you not?"

He again very readily answered, "Yes, an't please your Majesty."

"Pray," says the king to him, "if you hav'nt forgot what you said, let us have some taste of your fine florid speech; let us have a specimen of some flowers of your rhetoric, and a few of the main things on which you insisted."

Whereupon, Mr. Story told us that he readily made answer, "I told them, an't please your Majesty, that it was you that fired the city of London."

"A rare rogue, upon my word," said the king. "And pray what else did you tell them?"

"I told them," said he, "an't please your Majesty, that you poisoned your brother."

"Impudence in the utmost height of it," said the king; "pray let us hear something further, if your memory serves you."

"I further told them," said Mr. Story, "that your Majesty appeared to be fully determined to make the nation both Papists and slaves."

By this time, the king seemed to have heard enough of the prisoner's speech; and, therefore, crying out, "A rogue with a witness;" and cutting off short, he said, "to all this, I doubt not but a thousand other villanous things were added. But what would you say, Story, if, after all this, I should grant you your life?"

To which he, without any demur, made answer, that he should pray heartily for his Majesty as long as he lived.

"Why, then," said the king, "I freely pardon the past; and hope you will not, for the future, represent your king as inexorable."

(*d*) DYING PREFERRED TO LYING.—The minister of the seminary at Clermont having been seized at Autun by the populace, the mayor, who wished to save him, advised him not to take the oath, but to allow him to tell the people that he had taken it. "I would myself make known your falsehood to the people," replied the clergyman; "it is not permitted me to ransom my life by a lie. The God who prohibits my taking this oath, will not allow me to make it believed that I have taken it." The mayor was silent, and the minister was martyred.

(*e*) HEGIAGE AND THE PRISONERS.—Hegiage was a celebrated Arabian warrior, but ferocious and cruel. Among a number of prisoners whom he had condemned to death, was one who, having obtained a moment's audience, said, "You ought, sir, to pardon me, because when Abdarrahman was cursing you, I represented to him that he was wrong; and ever since that time I have lost his friendship." Hegiage asked him if he had any witness of his having done this; and the soldier mentioned another prisoner who was likewise about to suffer death. The prisoner was called and interrogated, and having confirmed the fact, Hegiage granted the first his pardon. He then asked the witness, if he had likewise taken his part against Abdarrahman. But he, still respecting truth, answered, that he had not, because he believed it was not his duty to do so. Hegiage, notwithstanding his ferocity, was struck with the prisoner's greatness of spirit. "Well," said he, after a moment's pause, "suppose I were to grant you your life and liberty, should you be still my enemy?" "No," said the prisoner. "That's enough," said Hegiage; "your bare word is sufficient; you have given undoubted proof of your love for truth. Go, preserve the life that is less dear to you than honor and sincerity; your liberty is the just reward of your virtue."

Here we see, that truth serves us best at the very crisis when we are apt to be most afraid that it will injure us. Would it not have been supposed that the truth and integrity of the witness above mentioned would have redoubled the fury of a man so imperious and sanguinary? Yet the fact is, that, instead of irritating, it softened and disarmed the tyrant.

WAR.

431. Battles, Battle-Fields.

(*a*) BATTLE OF SOLDIN.—We take the following account of scenes after the battle of Soldin, from the pen of a clergyman. "At one o'clock the cannonading ceased; and I went out on foot as far as Soldin, to learn to whose advantage the battle had turned. Towards evening, seven hundred Russian fugitives came to Soldin, a most pitiful sight! some holding up their hands, cursing and swearing; others praying, and praising the King of Prussia; without hats, without clothes; some on foot, others, two on a horse, with their heads and arms tied up; some dragging along by the stirrups, and others by the tails of the horses. When the battle was decided in favor of the Prussians, I ventured to the place where the cannonading had been. After walking some way, a Cossack's horse came running full speed towards me. I mounted him; and on my way for seven miles and a half on this side the field of battle, I found the dead and wounded lying on the ground, sadly cut in pieces. The further I advanced, the more these poor creatures lay heaped one upon another. That scene I shall never forget. The Cossacks, as soon as they saw me, cried out, 'Dear sir, water, *water*, WATER!' Righteous God! what a sight! Men, women and children, Russians and Prussians, carriages and horses, oxen, chests and baggage, all lying one upon another to the height of a man! and seven villages around me in flames, and the inhabitants either massacred, or thrown into the fire! Nor were the embers of mutual rage yet extinguished in the hearts of the combatants; for the poor wounded were still firing at each other in the greatest exasperation! The field of battle was a plain two miles and a half long, and so entirely covered with dead and wounded, that there was not even room to set my foot without treading on some of them! Several brooks were so filled up with Russians, that they lay heaped one upon another as high as two men, and appeared like hills to the even ground! I could hardly recover myself from the fright occasioned by the miserable outcries of the wounded. A noble Prussian officer, who had lost both his legs, cried out to me, 'Sir, you are a priest, and preach mercy; pray, show me some compassion, and despatch me at once.'"

(*b*) NUMBERS SLAIN IN DIFFERENT BATTLES.—At Durham, 1346, there fell 15,000; at Halidonhill and Agincourt, 20,000 each; at Bautzen and Lepanto, 25,000 each; at Austerlitz, Jena and Lutzen, 30,000 each; at Eylau, 60,000; at Waterloo and Quatre Bras, one engagement, 70,000; at Borodino, 80,000; at Fontenoy, 100,000; at Yarmouth, 150,000; at Chalons, no less than 300,000 of

Attila's army alone! The Moors in Spain, about the year 800, lost in one battle 70,000; in another, four centuries later, 180,000, besides 50,000 prisoners, and in a third, even 200,000. Still greater was the carnage in ancient times. At Cannæ, 70,000 fell. The Romans alone, in an engagement with the Cimbri and Teutones, lost 80,000. The Carthaginians attacked Hymera in Sicily with an army of 300,000 men, and a fleet of 2000 ships, and 3000 transports; but not a ship nor a transport escaped destruction, and of the troops, only a few in a small boat reached Carthage with the melancholy tidings. Marius slew, in one battle, 140,000 Gauls, and in another, 290,000. In the battle of Issus, between Alexander and Darius, 110,000 were slain, in that of Arbela, 300,000. Julius and Cæsar once annihilated an army of 363,000 Helvetians; in a battle with the Usipetes, he slew 400,000; and on another occasion, he massacred more than 430,000 Germans, who "had crossed the Rhine, with their herds, and flocks, and little ones, in quest of new settlements."

432. Sieges.

(*a*) SIEGE OF GENOA.—In 1800, Genoa, occupied by 24,000 French troops, was besieged at once by a British fleet and a powerful Austrian army. We will not detail the horrors attendant on the sallies and assaults; but let us look at the condition of the soldiers and citizens within. The former, worn down by fatigue, and wasted by famine, had consumed all the horses in the city, and were at length reduced to the necessity of feeding on dogs, cats, and vermin, which were eagerly hunted out in the cellars and common sewers. Soon, however, even these wretched resources failed; and they were brought to the pittance of four or five ounces a day of black bread made of cocoa, rye, and other substances ransacked from the shops of the city.

The inhabitants, also, were a prey to the most unparalleled sufferings. The price of provisions had from the first been extravagantly high, and at length no kind of grain could be had at any cost. Even before the city was reduced to the last extremities, a pound of rice was sold for more than a dollar, and a pound of flour for nearly two dollars. Afterwards beans were sold for two cents each, and a biscuit of three ounces weight, when procurable at all, for upwards of two dollars. A little cheese, and a few vegetables, were the only nourishment given even to the sick and wounded in the hospitals.

The horrors of this prolonged famine in a city containing above 100,000 souls, cannot be adequately described. All day the cries of the miserable victims were heard in the streets, while the neighboring rocks within the walls were covered with a famished crowd seeking in the vilest animals, and the smallest traces of vegetation, the means of assuaging the intolerable pangs of hunger. Men and women, in the last agonies of despair, filled the air with their groans and shrieks; and sometimes, while uttering these dreadful cries, they strove with furious hands to tear out their ravening entrails, and fell dead in the streets! At night the lamentations of the people were still more dreadful; too agitated to sleep, and unable to endure the agonies around them, they prayed aloud for death to relieve them from their sufferings.

Dreadful was the effect of these protracted calamities in hardening the heart, and rendering men insensible to any thing but their own disasters. Children, left by the death of their parents in utter destitution, implored in vain the passing stranger with tears, with mournful gestures, and heart-broken accents, to give them succor and relief. Infants, deserted in the streets by their own parents, and women, who had sunk down from exhaustion on the public thoroughfares, were abandoned to their fate; and, crawling to the sewers, and other receptacles of filth, they sought there, with dying hands, for the means of prolonging their miserable existence for a few hours. In the desperation produced by such long-continued torments, the more ardent and impetuous rushed out of the gates, and threw themselves into the harbor, where they perished without assistance or commiseration. To such straits were they reduced, that not only leather and skins of every kind were devoured, but the horror at human flesh was so much abated, that numbers were supported on the dead bodies of their fellow-citizens!

Still more cruel, horrible beyond all description, was the spectacle presented by the Austrian prisoners of war confined on board certain old vessels in the port; for such was the dire necessity at last, that they were left for some days without nutriment of any kind! They ate their shoes, they devoured the leather of their pouches, and, scowling darkly at each other, their sinister glances betrayed the horrid fear of their being driven to prey upon one another. Their French guards were at length removed, under the apprehension that they might be made a sacrifice to ravening hunger; and so great did their desperation finally become, that they endeavored to scuttle their floating prisons in order to sink them, preferring to perish thus rather than endure any longer the tortures of famine.

Pestilence, as usual, came in the rear of such calamities; and contagious fevers swept off multitudes, whom the strength of the survivors was unable to inter. Death in every form awaited the crowds whom common suffering had blended together in the hospitals; and the multitude of unburied corpses which encumbered the streets, threatened the city with depopulation almost as certainly as the grim hand of famine under which they were melting away. When the evacuation took place, the extent of the suffering which the besieged had undergone appeared painfully conspicuous. "On entering the town," says Thiebault, "all the figures we met bore the appearance of profound grief, or sombre despair; the streets resounded with the most heart-rending cries; on all sides death was reaping its harvest of victims, and the rival furies of famine and pestilence were multiplying their devastations. In a word, both the army and the inhabitants seemed fast approaching their dissolution."

(*b*) BOMBARDMENT OF ST. JEAN D'ACRE.—The bombardment of St. Jean d'Acre, in Syria, English newspapers of the day called "a most brilliant exploit;" but let us see what it was. "At half past four in the morning," says an eye-witness, "all firing ceased, as if by one consent, when—heavens! what a sight!—the whole town seemed to be thrown into the air! We saw nothing but one dense cloud extending thousands of yards into the air on all sides; and then we felt an awful shock, which gave the line-of-battle ships a keel of two degrees. It was the explosion caused by one of our shells bursting in their main magazine of powder, by which, to speak within bounds, two thousand souls, besides beasts of burden of every description, were blown to atoms! The entire loss of the Egyptians is computed at three thousand. At daylight, what a sight was exposed to our view! The stupendous fortification, that only twelve hours before was among the strongest in the world, was so riddled that we could not find a square foot which had not a shot. I went ashore to witness the devastation; the sight beggared all description! The bastions were strewed with the dead, the guns dismounted, and all sorts of havoc. The spot of the explosion was far worse—a space of two acres laid quite bare, and hollowed out as if a quarry had been worked there for years! Heavens! what a sight was there before me! Mangled human bodies, of both sexes, strewed in all directions, women searching for their husbands and other relatives, tearing their hair, beating their breasts, and howling and crying most piteously!" All this was done by England herself in 1840!!

(*c*) SIEGE OF MAGDEBURG.—In the siege of Magdeburg, in 1836, the resistance was long and obstinate; but at length two gates were forced open by the besiegers, and Tilly, marching a part of his infantry into the town, immediately occupied the principal streets, and with pointed cannon drove the citizens into their dwellings, there to await their destiny. Nor were they held long in suspense; a word from Tilly decided the fate of Magdeburg. Even a more humane general would have attempted in vain to restrain such soldiers; but Tilly never once made the attempt. The silence of their general left the soldiers masters of the citizens; and they broke without restraint into the houses to gratify every brutal appetite. The prayers of innocence excited some compassion in the hearts of the Germans, but none in the rude breasts of Pappenheim's Walloons. Scarcely had the massacre commenced, when the other gates were thrown open, and the cavalry, with the fearful hordes of Croats, poured in upon the devoted town.

Now began a scene of massacre and outrage, which history has no language, poetry no pencil to portray. Neither the innocence of childhood, nor the helplessness of old age, neither youth nor sex, neither rank nor beauty, could disarm the fury of the conquerors. Wives were dishonored in the very arms of their husbands, daughters at the feet of their parents, and the defenceless sex exposed to the double loss of virtue and life. No condition, however obscure, or however sacred, could afford protection against the cruelty or rapacity of the enemy. Fifty-three women were found in a single church with their heads cut off! The Croats *amused* themselves with throwing children into the flames, and Pappenheim's Walloons with stabbing infants at their mothers' breasts! Some officers of the League, horror-struck at scenes so dreadful, ventured to remind Tilly, that he had it in his power to stop the carnage. "Return in an hour," was his answer, "and I will see what is to be done; the soldier must have some recompense for his dangers and toils!"

No orders came from the general to check these horrors, which continued without abatement till the smoke and flames at last stopped the course of the plunderers. To increase the confusion, and break the resistance of the inhabitants, the invaders had, in the commencement of the assault, fired the town in several places; and a tempest now arose, and spread the flames with frightful rapidity, till the blaze became universal, and forced the victors to pause awhile in their work of rapine and carnage. The confusion was deepened by the clouds of smoke, the clash of swords, the heaps of dead bodies strewing the ground, the crash of falling ruins, and the streams of blood which ran along the streets. The atmosphere glowed; and the intolerable heat finally compelled even the murderers to take refuge in their camp. In less than twelve hours, this strong, populous, and flourishing city, one of the finest in all Germany, was a heap of ashes, with the exception of only two churches, and a few houses.

Scarcely had the flames abated, when the soldiers returned to satiate anew their rage for plunder, amid the ruins and ashes of the town. Multitudes were suffocated by the smoke; but many found rich booty in the cellars where the citizens had concealed their valuable effects. At length Tilly himself appeared in the town, after the streets had been cleared of ashes and corpses. Horrible and revolting to humanity was the scene that presented itself! the few survivors crawling from under the dead; little children wandering about, with heart-rending cries, in quest of their parents now no more; and infants still sucking the dead bodies of their mothers! More than five thousand bodies were thrown into the Elbe just to clear the streets; a far greater number had been consumed by the flames; the entire amount of the slaughter was estimated at thirty thousand; and in gratitude to the God of peace for such horrid success in the butchery of his children, for this triumph of Christian over Christian in blood, and fire, and rapine, and brutal lust, a solemn mass was performed, and *Te Deum* sung amid the discharge of artillery!!

(*d*) SIEGE OF ZARAGOSSA.—The French fought their way into the entrance of the ill-fated city, by mining and exploding one house after another, while the inhabitants were confined to that quarter of the city still in possession of the Spaniards, who were crowded, men, women and children, into the cellars, to avoid the cannon balls and bombs. Pestilence broke out as a matter of course; and when once begun, it was impossible to check its progress, or confine it to one quarter of the city. It was not long before more than thirty hospitals were established. As soon as one was destroyed by the bombardment, the patients were removed to some other building, which was in a state to afford them temporary shelter, and thus the infection was carried into every part of Zaragossa. The average of daily deaths from this cause was, at this time, not less than three hundred and fifty. Men stretched upon straw, in helpless misery, lay breathing their last, and with their dying breath spreading the mortal taint of their own disease, without medicines, food, or attendance; for the ministers of charity themselves became the victims of the disease. The slightest wound produced gangrene and death in bodies so prepared for dissolution by distress of mind, agitation, and want of proper aliment and of sleep; for there was no respite, either by day or night, for this devoted city. By day, it was involved in a red sulphuric atmosphere of smoke and dust, which hid the face of heaven; by night, the fire of cannon and mortars, and the flames of burning houses, kept it in a state of horrible illumination. The cemeteries could no longer afford room for the dead. Large pits were dug to receive them in the streets, and in the courts of the public buildings, till hands were wanted for the labor; they were laid before the churches, heaped upon one another, and covered with sheets; and not unfrequently these piles of mortality were struck by a shell, and the shattered bodies scattered in all directions. When the French entered the city, *six thousand bodies* were lying in the streets and trenches, or piled up in heaps before the churches.

433. Military Hospitals.

(*a*) HOSPITAL IN PORTUGAL.—The following sketch from a British officer in Portugal will help us further to conceive the horrors of a hospital. "I entered the town of Mirando Cervo about dusk. It had been a black, grim, gloomy sort of day. Huge masses of clouds lay motionless on the sky; and then they would break up suddenly as with a whirlwind, and roll off in the red and bloody distance. I felt myself in a strange sort of excitement; my imagination got the better of all my other faculties; and, while walking out in the principal street, I met a woman, an old haggard-looking wretch, who had in her hollow eyes an unaccountable expression of cruelty, a glance like that of madness; but her deportment was quiet and rational, and, though clad in squallidness, she was evidently of the middle rank in society. Without being questioned, she told me in broken English, I should find comfortable accommodations in an old convent at some distance in a grove of cork-trees, pointing to them with her long, shriveled hand and arm, and giving a sort of hysterical laugh.

"I followed her advice, anticipating no danger or adventure; yet the wild eyes, and the still wilder voice of the old crone so powerfully affected me, that I walked, in a sort of muse, up a pretty long flight of steps, and found myself standing at the entrance to the cloisters of the convent. A strange sight now burst upon my view! Before me lay and sat more than a hundred dead bodies, all of them apparently in the very attitude or posture in which they had died. I gazed at them a minute or more before I knew that they were all corpses; and a desperate courage then enabled me to look steadfastly at the scene before me. The bodies were mostly clothed in mats, and rags, and tattered great coats; some of them were merely wrapt round about with girdles composed of straw; and two or three were perfectly naked. Every face had a different expression, but all painful, horrid, agonized, bloodless. Many glazed eyes were wide open; and perhaps this was the most shocking thing in the whole spectacle—so many eyes that saw not, all seemingly fixed upon different objects; some cast up to heaven, some looking straight forward, and others with the white orbs turned round, and deep sunk in their sockets. It was a sort of hospital; and these wretched beings, nearly all desperately wounded, had been stripped by their comrades, and left there either dead, or to die.

"This ghastly sight I had begun to view with some composure, when I saw, at the remotest part of the hospital, a gigantic figure sitting, all covered with blood, and almost naked, upon a rude bedstead, with his back leaning against the wall, and his eyes fixed directly on mine. I first thought him alive, and shuddered; but he was stone dead! In his last agonies he had bitten his under lip almost entirely off, and his long black beard was drenched in clotted gore, that likewise lay in large blots upon his shaggy bosom. One of his hands had convulsively grasped the wood-work of the bedstead, and crushed it in the grasp. I recognized the corpse. He was a sergeant in a grenadier regiment, and had, during the retreat, been distinguished for acts of savage valor. One day he killed with his own hand Harry Warburton, the right-hand man of my own company, perhaps the most powerful man in the British army. There sat the giant frozen to death. I went up to him, and raised his brawny arm, it fell down again with a hollow sound against the bloody side of the corpse.

"My eyes unconsciously wandered along the walls. They were covered with grotesque figures and caricatures of the English, absolutely drawn in blood! Horrid blasphemies, and the most shocking obscenities in the shape of songs, were in like manner written there. I observed two books lying on the floor, and picked them up. One was full of the most hideous obscenity; the other was the Bible! It is impossible to tell the horror produced in me by this circumstance. The books dropt from my hand, and fell on the breast of one of the bodies—it was a woman's breast! Yes, a *woman* had lived and died in such a place as this! What had been in that now still, death-cold heart, perhaps only a few hours before, I knew not—possibly love strong as death, love, guilty, abandoned, linked by vice unto misery, but still love that perished only with the last throb, and yearned in its last convulsion towards some one of these grim dead bodies.

"Near this corpse lay that of a perfect boy not more than seventeen years of age. Round his neck was suspended, by a chain of hair, a little copper figure of the Virgin Mary, and in his hand was a letter in French. I glanced at it, and read enough to know it was from a mother—*My dear Son*, &c. It was a terrible place to think of mother—of home—of any social, any human ties. What! have these ghastly things parents, brothers, sisters, lovers? Were they once all happy in peaceful homes? Did these convulsed, bloody, mangled bodies, ever lie in undisturbed beds? Did these clutched hands once press in infancy a mother's breast? Now, alas, how loathsome, terrible, ghostlike! Will such creatures, thought I, ever live again? Robbers, ravishers, incendiaries, murderers, suicides—a dragoon there had obviously blown out his own brains—here is a very pandemonium of guilt and horror!"

434. Punishment of Soldiers.

(*a*) THE GAUNTLET.—"One day," says a military man, "I was on parade when preparation was making for a kind of punishment called the *gauntlet*. All the soldiers of the regiment were placed in two ranks facing each other, and about five feet apart. To each soldier was given a stick three feet long, or more. I could not bear to stay and witness the execution; but I was afterwards informed that the culprit, stripped naked to his waist, and his hands tied before him, was marched between the ranks, preceded by a soldier walking backwards with a bayonet at the sufferer's breast, to keep him from going too fast. In this way he was struck once by every soldier, officers going down on the outside of the ranks to see that each man did his duty! and, if any one was merely suspected of not laying on hard enough, he received over his own head a blow from the officer's cane. Sometimes the criminal has to retrace his steps; and, as a regiment consists of six hundred or a thousand men, and some German regiments of two thousand, he must receive from twelve hundred to two or even four thousand blows! The punishment often proves fatal; and to such a pitch of despair were those soldiers carried by their sufferings, that many of them committed suicide; and one poor fellow shot himself near my lodgings."

(b) PUNISHMENT OF A SOLDIER.—"One wintry morn," says an eye-witness, "when the bleak wind whistled along the ranks of a regiment paraded to see corporal punishment inflicted, every eye was turned in pity towards the delinquent"—his offence was drunkenness—"until the commanding officer, with stentorian lungs, cried out, 'Strip, sir.' The morning was so bitterly cold, that a mere exposure of a man's naked body was itself a severe punishment. When the offender was tied, or rather hung, up by the hands, his back, from intense cold and previous flogging, exhibited a complete black-and-blue appearance. On the first lash, the blood spirted out several yards; and, after he had received fifty, his back, from the neck to the waist, was one continued stream of blood. When taken down, he staggered, and fell to the ground. The poor man never looked up again; his prospects as a soldier were utterly destroyed; and so keenly did his degradation prey upon his spirits, that he at length shot himself in the barrack-room."

(c) THE DESERTER'S EXECUTION.—A surgeon, stationed during the war of 1812–14 at Greenbush, N. Y., says, "One morning several prisoners, confined in the provost guard-house, were brought out to hear their sentences. Some wore the marks of long confinement, and upon all had the severity of the prison-house stamped its impression. They looked dejected at this public exposure, and anxious to learn their fate. I had never seen the face of any of them before, and only knew that a single one had been adjudged to death. Soon as their names were called, and their sentences announced, I discerned, by his agony and gestures, the miserable man on whom that sentence was to fall—a man in the bloom of youth, and the fullness of health and vigor.

"Prompted by feelings of sympathy, I called next morning to see him in his prison. There, chained by his leg to the beam of the guard-house, he was reading the Bible, trying to prepare himself, he said, for the fatal hour. I learned from him the circumstances of his case. He was the father of a family, having a wife and three young children, thirty or forty miles distant from the camp. His crime was desertion; and his only object, he declared, was to visit his wife and children. Having seen that all was well with them, it was his intention to return. But, whatever his intention, he was a deserter, and, as such, taken and brought into the camp, manacled. The time between the sentence and its execution was brief; the authority in whom alone was vested the power of reprieve or pardon, distant. Thus he had no hope, and requested only the attendance of a minister of the gospel, and permission to see his wife and children. The first part of the request was granted; but whether he was permitted or not to see his family, I do not now remember.

"Dreading the hour of his execution, I resolved, if possible, to avoid being present at the scene. But the commander sent me an express order to attend, that I might, in my official capacity of surgeon, see the sentence fully executed. The poor fellow was taken from the guard-house, to be escorted to the fatal spot. Before him was his coffin—a box of rough pine boards—borne on the shoulders of two men. The prisoner stood, with his arms pinioned, between two clergymen. A white cotton gown, or winding sheet, reached to his feet. It was trimmed with black, and had attached to it, over his heart, the black image of a heart—the mark at which the executioners were to aim. On his head was a cap of white, also trimmed with black. His countenance was blanched to the hue of his winding sheet, and his frame trembled with agony. Our procession formed, we moved forward with slow and measured steps to the tune of a death march, (Roslin Castle,) played with muffled drums, and mourning fifes. The scene was solemn beyond the power of description; a man in the vigor of life *walking* to his grave—to the tune of his own death march—clothed in his burial robes—surrounded, not by friends assembled to perform the last sad offices of affection, and to weep over him in the last sad hour, but by soldiers with bristling bayonets and loaded muskets, urged by stern command to do the violence of death to a fellow soldier. Amid reflections like these, we arrived at the place of execution, a large open field, in whose centre a heap of earth, freshly thrown up, marked the spot of the deserter's grave. On this field the whole force then at the cantonment was drawn up in the form of a hollow square, with the side beyond the grave vacant. The executioners, eight in number, had been drawn by lot. No soldier would volunteer for such a duty. Their muskets had been charged by the officer of the day, seven of them with ball, the eighth with powder alone. Thus each may believe that *he* has the blank cartridge, and therefore has no hand in the death of his brother soldier—striking indications of the nature of the service.

"The coffin was placed parallel with the grave; and about two feet distant. In the intervening space, the prisoner was directed to stand. He desired permission to say a word to his fellow-soldiers; and thus standing between his coffin and his grave, he warned them against desertion, continuing to speak until the officer on duty, with his watch in his hand, announced to him in a low voice, '*Two o'clock, your last moment is at hand—you must kneel on your coffin.*' This done, the officer drew down the white cap, so as to cover the eyes and most of the face of the prisoner. The kneeling was the signal for the executioners to advance. They had before, to avoid being distinguished by the prisoner, stood intermingled with the soldiers who formed the line. They now came forward, marching abreast, and took their stand a little to the left, about two rods distant from their living mark. The officer raised his sword. At this signal, the executioners took aim. He then gave a blow on a drum which was at hand; the executioners all fired at the same instant. The miserable man, with a horrid scream, leaped from the earth, and fell between his coffin and his grave. The sergeant of the guard, a moment after, shot him through the head, holding the muzzle so near that his cap took fire; and there the body lay upon the face, the head emitting the mingled fumes of burning cotton and burning hair. The whole line then marched by the body, as it lay upon the earth, the head still smoking, that every man might behold for himself the fate of a deserter.

"We then started on our return. The whole band struck up, with uncommon animation, our national air, (Yankee Doodle,) and to its lively measures we were hurried back to our parade ground! Having been dismissed, the commander of the post sent an invitation to all the officers to meet at his quarters, whither we repaired, and were treated to a glass of gin and water!!"

435. Punishment of Marines.

(*a*) STEALING A HANDKERCHIEF.—Mark the severity visited upon the slightest offences. "A midshipman named Gale, a most rascally, unprincipled fellow, found his pocket handkerchief in possession of one of the crew. He charged the man with stealing it. It was in vain that the poor wretch asserted that he found it under his hammock. He was reported as a thief; a court-martial sat upon him, and returned the shamefully disproportionate sentence of three hundred lashes through the fleet, and one year's imprisonment! Nor was that sentence a dead letter; the unhappy man endured it to the letter. Fifty were laid on alongside the Macedonian, in conformity with the common practice of inflicting the most strokes at the first ship, in order that the gory back of the criminal may strike the more terror into the crews of the other ships. This poor tortured man bore two hundred and twenty, and was pronounced by the attending surgeon unfit to receive the rest. Galled, bruised, and agonized as he was, he besought them to suffer the infliction of the remaining eighty, that he might not be called to pass through the degrading scene again; but this prayer was denied! He was brought on board, and when his wounds were healed, the captain, Shylock-like, determined to have the whole pound of flesh, ordered him to receive the remainder!

(b) PUNISHMENT WITH THE COLT.—During the three years' cruise of the Fairfield, says Mr. McNally, I do not believe a single day elapsed that punishment by flogging did not take place. At that time there was a custom in the service, directly contrary to law, whereby any officer of the deck could inflict punishment. This was not with the *cat*, as the law directs, but with what is termed a *colt*, a piece of eighteen-thread ratline, or one-inch rope, which generally has one or two hard twine whippings upon each end. Twelve lashes with this, over a thin frock or shirt, gave greater pain, and bruised the flesh more than the cat would have done; and it was with this instrument that the deck officers of the Fairfield punished the men, and there was no limit to the number of lashes, but just as many as it might please the officer to order—sometimes one dozen, and at other times three. Such punishment frequently brought the blood through the shirt, and often left the flesh black for two or three weeks, and then yellow for as many more, before it healed perfectly.

Never let citizens in the Northern States rail at slavery, or the punishment inflicted on slaves, or say that it is wrong, so long as their own sons, their own flesh and blood, their own seamen, their own free citizens, and the men to whom they look for protection in case of war, are daily subject to the same treatment as the southern slaves. The late John Randolph openly declared in the legislative halls of Congress, that he had witnessed, in a few months, more flogging on board the man-of-war that carried him to Russia, than had taken place during ten years on his plantation, where there were five hundred slaves.

436. War and the Domestic Ties.

(a) HORRORS OF WAR IN CHINA.—The late English war in China furnishes some revolting instances of the domestic desolation consequent on this trade of blood. "In almost every house the children had been madly murdered. The bodies of most of these victims were found lying usually in the chambers of the women, as if each father had assembled his whole family before the massacre; in some instances these poor little sufferers were the next day still breathing and writhing in the agony of a broken spine; the way in which they were usually put to death. In one house were found in a single room the bodies of seven dead and dying persons. It was evidently the abode of a man of some consideration; and the delicate forms and features of the sufferers indicated the high elevation of their rank. On the floor, essaying in vain to put food into the mouths of two young children that were writhing in the agonies of death from dislocated spines, sat a decrepit old man, weeping bitterly at the piteous moans and convulsive breathings of the poor infants. On a bed near these children, lay a beautiful young woman apparently asleep; but she was cold, and had long been dead. One arm clasped her neck, over which a silk scarf was thrown to conceal the gash in her throat which had destroyed life. Near her was the corpse of a woman somewhat older, her features distorted as if she had died by strangulation; not far from her lay a dead child stabbed through the neck; and in a narrow verandah adjoining, were the corpses of two more women suspended by their necks from the rafters. They were both young, one quite a girl; and her features, in spite of their hideous distortion from the mode of her death, still retained traces of their original beauty."

(b) A WIFE AFTER BATTLE.—The battle-field makes terrible havoc of domestic sympathies and hopes. I once read of a devoted wife who left her babes, and walked some forty miles to see her husband in the army. She arrived the night before a battle, and contrived, by a dextrous appeal to the sentinel's heart, to gain admission to her husband's tent. The hours sped swiftly away, and the dawn heard the signal for battle. She hurried from his fond embrace with many a tender kiss for his babes, but lingered near the scene, and watched from a neighboring hill every movement of the two armies, until the combat ceased, and all was quiet once more. The shades of night now hang in gloom over that battle-ground, and forbid all search for the wounded, the dying or the dead. Morn approaches; and with its earliest dawn this faithful wife, with a throbbing heart, wanders over that field of slaughter to see if the father of her babes has fallen. Alas, it is too true! There he is, all covered with gore. She sinks on his bosom in a swoon, and rises no more!

(*c*) THE MOTHER AND HER BABE.—Glance at one scene in the campaign of 1794–5. "We could not," says an eye-witness, "proceed a hundred yards without perceiving the dead bodies of men, women and children. One scene made an impression which time can never efface. Near a cart we saw a stout looking man, and a beautiful young woman with an infant about seven months old at the breast, all three frozen and dead! The mother must have expired in the act of suckling her child, as she lay on the drifted snow with one breast exposed, and the milk apparently drawn in a stream from the nipple by the babe, and instantly congealed. The infant seemed as if its lips had but just been disengaged, and its little head reposed on its mother's bosom with an overflow of milk frozen as it trickled from the mouth."

(*d*) COL. HAYNE AND HIS SON.—Col. Hayne, of South Carolina, a man of high character, endeared to all that knew his worth, and bound fast to life by six small children, and a wife tenderly beloved, was taken prisoner by the British, and sentenced to be hung! His wife, falling a victim to disease and grief combined, did not live to plead for her husband; but great and generous efforts were made for his rescue. A large number, both Americans and Englishmen, interceded in his behalf; the ladies of Charleston signed a petition for his release; and his six motherless children were presented on their knees as humble suitors for the life of their father. It was all in vain; for war has no heart but of iron. His eldest son, a lad about thirteen years old, was permitted, as a special favor to stay with him awhile in prison. On seeing his father loaded with irons, and condemned to die on the gallows, the poor boy was overwhelmed with consternation and grief. The wretched father tried to console him by various considerations, and added, "to-morrow, my son, I set out for immortality; you will follow me to the place of my execution, and, when I am dead, take my body, and bury it by the side of your dear mother." Overcome by this appeal, the boy threw his arms around his father's neck, crying, "O my father, I'll die with you! I *will* die with you, father!" The wretched father, still loaded down with irons, was unable to return his son's embrace, and merely said in reply, "No, my son, never! Live to honor God by a good life; live to serve your country, and to take care of your brother and little sisters."

The next morning, Col. Hayne was led forth to execution. That fond and faithful boy accompanied him; and, when they came in sight of the gallows, the father turned to him, and said, "Now, my son, show yourself a man. That tree is the boundary of my life, and all its sorrows. Beyond that, the wicked cease from troubling, and the weary are forever at rest. Don't, my son, lay our separation too much at heart; it will be short at longest. It was but the other day your dear mother died; to-day I die; and you, my son, though young, must follow us shortly." "Yes, my father," replied the broken-hearted boy, "I *shall* follow you shortly; for I feel indeed that I can't, can't live long." And so it was; for, on seeing his much-loved father first in the hands of the executioner, and then struggling in the halter from the gallows, he stood transfixed with horror. Till then he had all along wept profusely as some relief to his agonized feelings; but that sight!—it dried up the fountain of his tears;—he never wept again. His reason reeled on the spot; he became an incurable maniac; and in his last moments, he called out, and kept calling out for his father in tones that drew tears from the hardest hearts.

(*e*) SCENE NEAR MARSEILLES.—"We were some ten miles from Marseilles," says an officer, "when we saw a small vessel anchored in a narrow bay; and, fierce for prize-money, we manned a boat, and pushed forward till we came within pistol-shot of the craft, without seeing any one except an old woman seated in the door of a cottage at some distance. Just then a musket-shot from behind a rock laid our bowman a corpse, another disabled our marine, a third tore his cravat from the lieutenant's neck, and a fourth crippled the coxswain's arm. Still we saw no one; and, exasperated by these discharges, we gave three cheers, and, pulling for the place whence they seemed to come, saw at length a man and a boy running from us. We interchanged several shots in vain, until the lieutenant, resting his musket on a rock, shot the child while in the act of handing a cartridge to the man. The father instantly threw down his musket, and fell by the side of his son. We seized his musket; but he paid no attention to us. When we bade him follow us, he heeded us not; but, with the child's head in his lap, he kept wiping away the blood that oozed from the wound in his forehead, and neither wept nor spoke, but watched the last chilling shiver of his boy with an eye of inexpressible sadness. Then he jumped from the ground with a frantic air; the marine brought his bayonet to the charge, and the miserable father tried to run upon its point; but the marine, dropping his musket, encircled him in his arms. We desired him to lead us to the cottage. The marine carried the corpse, and the father walked by its side in silence, till we suddenly came upon the rear of the cottage. The old woman was still at her wheel, and, on discovering her son a prisoner, gave a shriek which announced to a lovely female in the hut that something painful had occurred. She rushed to assist her mother—her eye fell first upon her dead son in the arms of an enemy; and, seizing the boy, she tore him from the marine, kissed him more like a maniac than a mother, and, giving one deep, piercing sigh fell at her mother's feet. We could stand it no longer, and hastened away; but that scene I can never blot from my memory."

(*f*) GENERAL WASHINGTON'S CONFESSION.—Perhaps few facts would more forcibly illustrate the views, which even reflecting military men take of the nature of war, than the following:—

Thomas Mullet, Esq., an English gentleman, being in America, called on General Washington, at his residence at Mount Vernon, soon after the close of the contest between that country and Great Britain. Washington asked him, in the course of conversation in his library, if he had met with an individual in that country, who could write the history of the recent contest. Mr. M. replied that he knew of one, and only one, competent to the task. The general eagerly asked, "Who, sir, can he be?" Mr. M. replied, "Sir, Cesar wrote his own Commentaries." The general bowed, and replied, "Cesar could write his Commentaries; but, sir, I know the atrocities committed on both sides have been so great and many, that they cannot be faithfully recorded, and had better be buried in oblivion!"

437. Testimonies against War.

(*a*) CICERO AND SENECA ON WAR.—We could not expect the heathen to denounce a custom so emphatically their own; yet we find the wisest and best of them reprobating it in the strongest terms. CICERO speaks of war, "contention by violence, as belonging to the brutes," and complains bitterly of its effects on liberal arts and peaceful pursuits. "All our noble studies, all our reputation at the bar, all our professional assiduities, are stricken from our hands as soon as the alarm of war is sounded. Wisdom itself, the mistress of affairs, is driven from the field. Force bears sway. The statesman is despised; the grim soldier alone is caressed. Legal proceedings cease. Claims are asserted and prosecuted, not according to law, but by force of arms."

SENECA, the great moralist of antiquity, is still more strong in his condemnation of war. "How are we to treat our fellow-creatures? Shall we not spare the effusion of blood? How small a matter not to hurt him to whom we are bound by every obligation to do all the good in our power!—Some deeds, which are considered as villanous while capable of being prevented, become honorable and glorious when they rise above the control of law. The very things which, if men had done them in their private capacity, they would expiate with their lives, we extol when perpetrated in regimentals at the bidding of a general. We punish murders and massacres committed among private persons; but what do we with wars, the glorious crime of murdering whole nations? Here avarice and cruelty know no bounds; enormities forbidden in private persons, are actually enjoined by legislatures, and every species of barbarity authorized by decrees of the senate, and votes of the people."

(*b*) DECISION OF A PRIMITIVE CHRISTIAN. — Maximilian having been brought before the tribunal to be enrolled as a soldier, Dion, the proconsul, asked him his name. Maximilian, turning to him, replied, "Why wouldst thou know my name? *I am a Christian, and cannot fight.*" Then Dion ordered him to be enrolled, and bade the officer mark him; but Maximilian refused to be marked, still asserting that he was a Christian; upon which Dion instantly replied, "Bear arms, or thou shalt die." To this Maximilian answered, "I cannot fight, if I die; I am not a soldier of this world, but a soldier of God." He refused the expostulations of Dion, and was accordingly executed.

(*c*) EARLY CHRISTIANS AND WAR.—The absolute inconsistency of war with the gospel was the prevalent belief of the early Christians. Justin Martyr, A. D. 140, quoting the prophecy of Isaiah already cited, says, "That these things have come to pass, you may be readily convinced; for we who were once slayers of one another, do not now fight against our enemies." Irenæus, bishop of Lyons, 167, discusses the same prophecy, and proves its relation to our Savior by the fact, that the followers of Jesus had disused the weapons of war, and no longer knew how to fight. Tertullian, 200, indeed alludes to Christians who were engaged in military pursuits, but, on another occasion, informs us, that many soldiers quitted those pursuits in consequence of their conversion to Christianity; and repeatedly expresses his own opinion, that any participation in war is unlawful for believers in Jesus, not only because of the idolatrous practices in the Roman armies, but because Christ has forbidden the use of the sword, and the revenge of injuries. Origen, 230, in his work against Celsus, says, "We no longer take up the sword against any nation, nor do we learn any more to make war. We have become, for the sake of Jesus, *the children of peace*. By our prayers, we fight for our king abundantly, but take no part in his wars, even though he urge us."

(*d*) OPINION OF ERASMUS.—Erasmus, the glory of his age, wrote against war with unrivaled beauty and force. "What infernal being, all-powerful in mischief, fills the bosom of man with such insatiable rage for war! If familiarity with the sight had not destroyed all surprise at it, and custom blunted the sense of its evils, who could believe that those wretched beings are possessed of rational souls, who contend with all the rage of furies? Robbery, blood, butchery, desolation, confound without distinction every thing sacred and profane."

(*e*) WALTER RALEIGH ON WAR.—Sir Walter Raleigh, a scholar, a statesman, and a soldier, declares "there is no profession more unpropitious than that of warriors. Besides the envy and jealousy of men, the spoils, rapes, famine, slaughter of the innocent, devastations and burnings, with a world of miseries laid on the laboring man, they are so hateful to God, as with good reason did Monluc, the marshal of France, confess, 'that, were not the mercies of God infinite, it were in vain for those of his profession to hope for any portion of them, seeing the cruelties by them permitted and perpetrated are also infinite.'"

(*f*) LORD CLARENDON'S OPINION.—Lord Clarendon, illustrious in the annals of England, is very explicit in his denunciations of this custom. "Of all the punishments and judgments which the provoked anger of divine Providence can pour out upon a nation full of transgressions, there is none so terrible and destroying as war. A whole city on fire is a spectacle replete with horror; but a whole kingdom on fire must be a prospect much more terrible. And such is every kingdom in war, where nothing flourishes but rapine, blood, and murder. We cannot make a more lively representation and emblem to ourselves of hell, than by the view of a kingdom in war."

(g) NEVER A GOOD WAR OR A BAD PEACE.—Franklin was a stanch opposer of the war-system. "If statesmen," says he, "were more accustomed to calculation, wars would be much less frequent. Canada might have been purchased from France for a tenth part of the money England spent in the conquest of it; and if, instead of fighting us for the power to tax us, she had kept us in good humor by allowing us to dispose of our own money, and giving us now and then a little of her own by way of donation to colleges or hospitals, for cutting canals, or fortifying ports, she might easily have drawn from us much more by occasional voluntary grants and contributions, than ever she could by taxes. Sensible people will give a bucket or two of water to a dry pump, in order to get from it afterwards all they want."

"After much occasion to consider the folly and mischiefs of a state of warfare, and the little or no advantage obtained even by those nations which have conducted it with the most success, I have been apt to think *there has never been, nor ever will be, any such thing as a good war, or a bad peace.* All wars are follies, very expensive and very mischievous ones. When will mankind be convinced of this, and agree to settle their difficulties by arbitration? Were they to do it even by the cast of a die, it would be better than by fighting and destroying each other. We daily make great improvements in natural philosophy; there is one I wish to see in moral—the discovery of a plan that would induce and oblige nations to settle their disputes without first cutting one another's throats."

(h) WAR MULTIPLIES LOSSES.—Thomas Jefferson both wrote acted with great decision in favor of peace. "I stand in awe," he says in 1798, "at the mighty conflict to which two great nations (France and England) are advancing, and recoil with horror at the ferociousness of man. Will nations never devise a more rational umpire of differences than force? Are there no means of coercing injustice more gratifying to our nature than a waste of the blood of thousands, and of the labor of millions of our fellow-creatures? Wonderful has been the progress of human improvement in other respects. Let us then hope, that the law of nature will in time influence the proceedings of nations as well as of individuals, and that we shall at length be sensible, that *war is an instrument entirely inefficient towards redressing wrong, and multiplies instead of indemnifying losses.* Had the money which has been spent in the present war been employed in making roads, and constructing canals of navigation and irrigation through the country, not a hovel in the Highlands of Scotland, or the mountains of Auvergne, would have been without a boat at its door, a rill of water in every field, and a road to its market-town. Were we to go to war for redress of the wrongs we have suffered, we should only plunge deeper into loss, and disqualify ourselves for half a century more for attaining the same end. These truths are palpable, and must in the progress of time have their influence on the minds and conduct of nations."

(i) WAR MAKES VILLAINS.—Macchiavel himself denounces war as "a profession by which men cannot live honorably; an employment by which the soldier, if he would reap any profit, is *obliged* to be false, and rapacious, and cruel. Nor can any man, who makes war his profession, be otherwise than vicious. Have you not a proverb, that *war makes villains, and peace brings them to the gallows?*"

(j) LOUIS BONAPARTE ON WAR.—"I have been as enthusiastic and joyful as any one after victory;

yet I confess that even then the sight of a field of battle not only struck me with horror, but even turned me sick. And now that I am advanced in life, I cannot understand any more than I could at fifteen years of age, how beings who call themselves reasonable, and who have so much foresight, can employ this short existence, not in loving and aiding each other, and passing through it as quietly as possible, but in striving, on the contrary, to destroy each other, as though time itself did not do this with sufficient rapidity. What I thought at fifteen years of age, I still think, that war, and the pain of death which society draws upon itself, are but organized barbarisms, an inheritance of the savage state."

(*k*) PRINCE EUGENE ON WAR.—"The thirst of renown sometimes insinuates itself into our councils, under the garb of *national honor.* It dwells on imaginary insults; it suggests harsh and abusive language; the people go on from one thing to another, till they put an end to the lives of half a million of men. A military man becomes so sick of bloody scenes in war, that in peace he is averse to re-commence them. I wish that the first minister who is called to decide on peace and war, had only seen actual service. What pains would he not take to seek, in mediation and compromise, the means of avoiding the effusion of so much blood!"

(*l*) LORD BROUGHAM ON WAR.—"My principles—I know not whether they agree with yours: they may be derided, they may be unfashionable; but I hope they are spreading far and wide—my principles are contained in the words which that great man, Lord Faulkland, used to express in secret, and which I now express in public—*Peace*, PEACE, PEACE. I abominate war as unchristian. I hold it the greatest of human crimes. I deem it to include all others—violence, blood, rapine, fraud, every thing which can deform the character, alter the nature, and debase the name of man."

(*m*) COST OF WAR. — What a boundless spendthrift is war! It is estimated that every gun of our navy costs an average of fifteen thousand dollars a year; enough to support twenty or thirty missionaries! Forty millions of dollars wasted in our war with a handful of Indians in Florida! fifty millions a year in our last war with England! hundreds of millions in our old revolutionary war! Still worse do we find it in the old world. England, as stated by one of her ablest and best men, has lavished upon Lord Wellington alone, eleven millions of dollars! As much upon a single warrior as all Christendom has ever given in five years for the support of missionaries among the heathen!! The war operations of England, near the time of the battle at Waterloo, are said to have consumed one million sterling a day; about twice as much *every day* as the whole church of Christ is even now contributing *annually* for the spread of his gospel! It has been estimated, that the late wars of Europe, in little more than twenty years, wasted in one way and another some $40,000,000,000, the bare interest of which would be, at six per cent, $2,400,000,000 a year, and, at only two and a half per cent, no less than $1,000,000,000! the simple interest at this low rate, enough to support, at $500 each, two millions of missionaries, or one to every three hundred souls in all the pagan world!!

438. Miscellaneous.

(*a*) SUFFERINGS OF THE FRENCH.—"The French soldiers," says an eye-witness, "on their retreat from Moscow, would, on halting at night, throng into the houses, throw themselves down on the first dirty straw they could find, and there perish, in large numbers, with hunger and fatigue. From such sufferings, and from the infection of the air in the warmer season by putrefied carcasses of men and horses that strewed the road, there sprang two dreadful diseases, the dysentery and typhus fever, before which they melted away like dew before the sun. At times they were so overwhelmed with whirlwinds of snow, that they could not distinguish the road from the ditches, and often found their grave in the latter.

The roads, league after league, were checkered with dead bodies covered with snow, and forming undulations or hillocks like those in a grave-yard. Many of the survivors scarce retained the human form. Some had lost their hearing, others their speech; and many, by excessive cold and hunger, were reduced to a state of such stupid frenzy, that they roasted the dead bodies of their companions, and even gnawed their own hands and arms. "No grenade or grape," says an eye-witness, "could have so disfigured those victims of the cold. One of them had lost the upper joints of all his ten fingers; and he showed us the stumps. A. other wanted both ears and nose. More horrible still was the look of the third, whose eyes had been frozen; the eyelids hung down rotting, the globes of the eyes were burst, and protruded from their sockets. It was awfully hideous; but a spectacle yet more dreadful was to present itself. Out of the straw in a car that brought them, I now beheld a figure creep painfully, which one could scarcely believe to be a human being, so wild and distorted were the features. The lips were rotted away, the teeth stood exposed; he pulled the cloth from before his mouth, and grinned on us like a death's-head!"

(*b*) EXPENSE OF MILITIA DRILLS.—In a small town of New England, there were formed even in 1842, no less than three military companies with some aid from an adjoining town, and one company of juvenile volunteers. Of the latter, a shrewd, economical man said, "I wish this training fever were over; for it has cost me eight or ten dollars to fit up my boys, and lost me a great deal of their time during the best season of the year." If there were only forty boys in the company, and their equipments cost four dollars each, and their time was worth only twenty-five cents a day, the sum total for these items alone, would have been $340. If we suppose the whole number from that town in the adult companies to have been only one hundred, the time spent through the season, a single week at merely half a dollar a day, their incidental expenses at barely twenty-five cents more, and their equipments of every kind eight dollars each, the aggregate, though most of these estimates are too low by half, would amount to no less than $1250, in all, for boys and men, $1590; and, should we reckon the loss of time and money to the spectators, and the general suspension or derangement of business, the sum total would probably reach $3000 or more. Put it, however, at only $2000 for a population of one thousand; and, even at this rate, you would make our militia drills now (1845) a tax upon the country of some $40,000,000 a year!

(*c*) LADD'S DIALOGUE WITH CHILDREN.—"A distinguished instructor of youth," says the late William Ladd, "told me his sons were so taken up with military notions, that he could not reason with them; and he asked me to talk to them. I took the oldest boy, aged about seven years, between my knees, and something like the following conversation ensued:—'Do you love to see the soldiers?' 'Yes, I love to see the rub-a-dubs.' 'Would you like to be one yourself?' 'O, yes!' 'Well, but do you know what these soldiers are for?' 'No.' 'Why, they are learning to kill people. Those bright guns are made to kill people with, and those bright bayonets to stab them with.' The boy turned pale; such a thought never before entered his head. 'Do you know who killed the little babes in Bethlehem, because a wicked man told them to?' 'No.' 'They were soldiers. Do you know who crucified our Lord, and drove the spikes through his hands and feet?' The boy was silent. 'They were soldiers, and soldiers would burn *your* house, and cut down your fruit-trees, and kill your pa, if they were told to.' Both the boys were astonished; tears stood in their eyes. 'Do you want to be a soldier?' 'No.' 'Do you want to see the rub-a-dubs?' 'No.'" How easy for a mother or teacher to impress such artless, susceptible minds with the horrors of war, and cast their views and feelings in the mould of peace!

(*d*) TEN THOUSAND LIVES FOR A BUCKET.—About seven hundred years ago, there was a country in Europe called Modena, and another country lying beside it called Bologna. Some soldiers belonging to the state of Modena took a *bucket* from a well in the state of Bologna, and carried it away. The old bucket was of no value, and might have been replaced by a few cents; and it is said the soldiers carried it away in mere fun and frolic. But the people of Bologna took it as a great insult. They declared war against Modena, and had a long and bloody conflict about it. More than ten thousand human beings were butchered because of the *old bucket!*

(*e*) THE THIEF'S REPARTEE.—A soldier of Marshal Saxe's army, being discovered in theft, was condemned to be hung. What he had stolen might be worth five shillings. The Marshal meeting him, as he was led to execution, said to him: "What a miserable fool you were to risk your life for five shillings." "General," replied the soldier, "I have risked it every day for five pence." This repartee saved his life.

(*f*) SOLDIERS' BONES FOR MANURE.—In the year 1830, it is estimated that more than a million bushels of "human and inhuman bones" were imported from the continent of Europe into the port of Hull, England. The neighborhood of Leipsic, Austerlitz, Waterloo, &c., where the principal battles were fought some fifteen or twenty years before, were swept alike of the bones of the hero, and the horse which he rode. Thus collected from every quarter, they were shipped to Hull, and thence forwarded to the Yorkshire bone-grinders, who by steam engines and powerful machinery, reduced them to a granulary state. In this condition they were sent chiefly to Doncaster, one of the largest agricultural markets of the country, and were there sold to the farmers to manure their lands. The oily substance gradually evolving as the bone calcines, makes better manure than almost any other substance—particularly human bones. Some of the good farmers of Yorkshire, were thus perhaps indebted to the very bones of their children for their daily bread! What a commentary on war and military glory does such a fact furnish us. The soldiers of England going forth to fight her battles on the Continent, their blood fattening the fields of her allies, and their bones brought back to fatten the soil of their fathers!

(*g*) CONQUEROR GOING TO JUDGMENT.—William the Conqueror, extremely alarmed on his death-bed, entreated the clergy to intercede for him. "Laden with many and grievous sins," he exclaimed, "I tremble; and, being ready to be taken soon into the terrible examination of God, I am ignorant what I should do. I have been brought up in feats of arms from my childhood; I am greatly polluted with the effusion of much blood; I can by no means number the evils I have done these sixty-four years, for which I am now constrained without stay to render an account to the just Judge."

(*h*) THE REWARD OF WAR.—The Duke of Marlborough observing a soldier leaning pensively on the butt-end of his musket, just after victory had declared itself in favor of the British arms at the battle of Blenheim, accosted him thus: "Why so pensive, my friend, after so glorious a victory?" "It may be glorious," replied the brave fellow, "but I am thinking that all the human blood I have spilled this day *has only earned me fourpence.*"

(*i*) SCENE WORTH CONSIDERING.—The New-York Journal of Commerce has the following article, depicting the happiness which the news of peace spread in New-York:—

Years ago, the office of the old Gazette was in Hanover Square, near the corner of Pearl-street. It was a place of resort for news and conversation, especially in the evening. The evening of February 15th, 1815, was cold, and at a late hour only Alderman Cebra and another gentleman were left with father Lang, the genius of the place. The office was about being closed, when a pilot rushed in and stood for a moment so entirely exhausted as to be unable to speak. "He has great news!" exclaimed Mr. Lang. Presently the pilot, gasping for breath, whispered intelligibly, "*Peace! peace!*" The gentlemen lost their breath as fast as the pilot gained his. Directly the pilot was able to say, "An English sloop-of-war is below with the news of a treaty of peace." They say that Mr. Lang exclaimed in greater words than he ever used before or after. All hands rushed into Hanover Square, crying, "Peace! *peace!* PEACE!" The windows flew up, for families lived there then. No sooner were the inmates sure of the sweet sound of peace, than the windows began to glow with brilliant illuminations. The cry of "Peace! *peace!* PEACE!" spread through the city at the top of all voices. No one stopped to inquire about "free trade and sailor's rights." No one inquired whether even the national honor had been preserved. The matters by which politicians had irritated the nation into the war, had lost all their importance. It was enough that the ruinous war was over. An old man in Broadway, attracted by the noise to his door, was seen to pull down a placard, "To let," which had been long posted up. Never was there such joy in the city. A few evenings after, there was a general illumination, and although the snow was a foot deep and soaked with rain, yet the streets were crowded with men and women, eager to see and partake of everything which had in it the sight and taste of peace.

(*j*) CAST THY BREAD UPON THE WATERS.—At a meeting of the Cincinnati Branch of the U. S. Christian Commission, among other speakers was Bishop McIlvaine.

His remarks were designed to show that the life of the soldier was not necessarily inimical to religious influences; that, indeed, most of the circumstances to which the soldier is subjected, render him peculiarly subject to spiritual reflections, and it required only the proper means to be exercised to secure the happiest results. He narrated several incidents to show the opportunities afforded for making good impressions, one of which ran as follows:

After a battle, two men were driving an ambulance over the field, gathering up the wounded. One of them, after examining a poor fellow, passed on, saying "he is too far gone, we can do nothing for him, he will soon die." The unfortunate man cried out, "Oh yes you can, you can pray for me." The driver of the ambulance replied that he could not pray. The dying man begged him to stop and try to pray with him. His appeals were so affecting that the heart of the driver was moved, and sought to comfort him. Suddenly he thought of a little book torn and soiled, that he picked up in the road a few minutes before. Possibly it might be a religious book, and he drew it from his pocket. The first half was gone, and on the first of what remained, he found "a prayer of a dying soldier." With joy he read it to his dying companion, whose spirit took its flight. He preserved the little book, and when afterward he was a prisoner in rebel hands, he made it his daily companion, and became a praying Christian man. That little book was one of the many thousand volumes the Christian Commission has distributed so freely in the army.

(*k*) THE DRUMMER BOY.—I met, the other day, near here, a little drummer boy, who says he loves the Lord Jesus. I love to talk with the boys in the army. I asked the little drummer:

"Was your mother willing that you should come into the army?"

"Yes sir. She said other mothers were giving their boys, and she was willing to give me."

"Perhaps she needed the money you can earn, and that made her give you up."

The poor boy looked up, hurt and indignant, and answered:

"It was not the money, sir. It was something better. She said I could do something for my country, for, as a drummer, I could take the place of a man. I am here for my country, sir."

"You are a noble boy," said I, "and your mother is a noble mother. I hope God will spare her to you, and you to her, and give a country worth saving to both of you to be your happy home."

"If you could hear my mother pray," said he, "you would think we had a God and a country."

(*l*) MUSIC AND LIGHT ON THE BATTLE-FIELD. — A brave and godly captain in one of our regiments told one of us his story, as we were removing him to the hospital. He was shot through both thighs with a rifle bullet—a wound from which he could not recover. While lying on the field, he suffered intense agony from thirst. He supported his head upon his hand, and the rain from heaven was falling around him. In a little while a little pool of water formed under his elbow, and he thought if he could only get to that puddle he might quench his thirst. He tried to get into a position to suck up a mouthful of muddy water, but he was unable to reach within a foot of it. Said he, "I never felt so much the loss of any earthly blessing. By-and-by night fell, and the stars shone out clear and beautiful above the dark field; and I began to think of the great God who had given his Son to die a death of agony for me, and that he was up there—up above the scene of suffering, and above those glorious stars; and I felt that I was going home to meet him; and praise him there; and I felt that I ought to praise God, even wounded and on the battle-field. I could not help singing that beautiful him,

'When I can read my title clear
To mansions in the skies,
I'll bid farewell to every fear,
And wipe my weeping eyes.'

And," said he, "there was a Christian brother in the brush near me. I could not see him, but I could hear him. He took up the strain; and beyond him another and another caught it up all over the terrible battle-field of Shiloh. That night the echo was resounding, and we made the field of battle ring with hymns of praise to God!"

(*m*) "TELL THEM HOW I DIED."—A surgeon in one of our military hospitals, in a private letter related the following incident:

A soldier from the "stern and rock-bound coast" of Maine—a victim of the slaughter at Fredericksburg—lay in this hospital, his life ebbing away by a fatal wound. He had a father, brothers and sisters, a wife, and one little boy, two or three years old, on whom his heart seemed set. Half an hour before he ceased to breathe I stood by his side, holding his hand. He was in the full exercise of his intellectual faculties, and knew he had but a brief time to live. He was asked if he had any message to leave for his dear ones whom he loved so well. "Tell them," said he, "how I died—they know how I lived!"

One might speak of the characteristic New England quality of this uncomplaining, unboastful utterance—the hard-handed hero, dying in his virtue and simplicity for his country—but he is by no means exceptional, and we will make no boast of that for which he took no merit. It is safe to say that he lived as he died, and this fact possesses an intimation of the utmost general importance. If we know how a man lives, we can scarcely err in anticipating the manner of his death; and while the last memorials of a virtuous person's life are, of course, full of interest to those who loved him, they are only so for love's sake, and for the witness they bear to what he was known to be, aforetime, by his acts. It is the man's life that must be his record, rather than his death; sufficient that the latter fitly closes this first part of his existence, and can open the doors to the next unshamed. "They know how I lived," said the soldier, "tell them how I died." With an honest gladness in what his loved ones would feel when they heard of the faithful closing of a life that they knew had not swerved, and would say, "We knew him, and knew that it would be so"—he fell asleep on his arms. If a Christian, it was a closing that could be but an opening into a glorious and eternal manhood! a bright example, that will shine on while He who set it is far out of sight, in the higher tasks of immortality!

(*n*) THE RIGHT PERSUASION.—In terrible agony a soldier lay dying in the hospital. A visitor asked him, "What church are you of?" "Of the church of Christ," he replied. "I mean of what persuasion are you?" then inquired the visitor. "Persuasion!" said the dying man, as his eyes looked heavenward, beaming with love to the Saviour: "I am persuaded that neither death, nor life, nor angels, nor principalities, nor powers, nor things present, nor things to come, nor height, nor depth, nor any other creature, shall be able to separate me from the love of God which is in Christ Jesus."

(*o*) THE DYING SOLDIER.—The wounded were being brought in from the battle-field, and the surgeon was passing around trying to alleviate their sufferings. He paused beside a bed, and after examining the wound of a soldier, said:

"It is useless to do anything here, you must die; we cannot save you."

"What is that, doctor? *Die*, did you say? No, I can't die; I *won't* die. Do anything, give me anything, and I will take it without a murmur."

"It is useless; human skill cannot save you."

"Oh! I *can't*, I *won't* die!"

And the surgeon left him.

Night comes on. The hospital is dimly lighted, and those who are not suffering intense pain, have fallen asleep to dream of their far-off happy homes, and of the happy hours spent by them in sunny childhood.

The wounded soldier still lives, but he tosses restlessly on his bed, vainly endeavoring to sleep. The words of the surgeon ring in his ears, and he feels that they are true. But he dares not pass from earth and stand before his Creator, without a plea for forgiveness. He has neglected his God through life, and openly and wilfully violated His laws, but now that death draws near, he feels the need of a Saviour.

"Oh! how many like him put off seeking their soul's salvation until their dying hour, and then pass from earth with their sins unforgiven! Oh, why do they not heed the injunction of the Lord of Hosts to remember their Creator in the days of their youth? They do not mean to die in their sins, yet they delay. Soldier friend, delays are dangerous. Put off no longer turning to the Lord. "Behold now is the accepted time, behold now is the salvation."

But to return to the wounded soldier. At length he starts up and tries to rouse a companion, saying:

"Wake up, Bill; I believe I am dying. Won't you pray for me?"

"I can't, is the answer; "I don't know how."

"Oh, must I die, and no one to pray for me? Can't you say a short prayer, Bill?"

"No, I never prayed in my life."

"Can't you say the Lord's prayer?"

"No, I learned it once from my mother, when I was a little boy, but I have forgotten it."

"Oh, must I die? *Our Father*—"

That was all he could remember. Again and again he repeated it; and so he died.

Who would wish to witness such a scene? All his life this soldier had lived in disobedience of God's laws, and when too late to remedy it, saw his fatal error.

Dear soldier, are you in his case?

(*p*) "LIGHTS OUT."—It was while we were camped at Suffolk, during Longstreet's siege, in the spring of 1863, if I remember right, that, one night after "lights out" had sounded, my comrade, who lay sick in our tent, and who had been delirious several days, and constantly called for "mother," and his home away up beside the old St. Lawrence, said to me: "Comrade! soon it will be 'lights out' with me for this world. Here is my Bible, which she gave me when I left her for the 'Sunny South.' Take it to her, and tell her, although it is 'lights out' with me here, I hope to go to another land where it is always light."

Comrades, how many of us can say, when it comes to be "lights out."

with us here, we, too, are bound for that beautiful land?

(*q*) "IS THAT MOTHER?"—Among the many brave, uncomplaining fellows who were brought up from the battle of Fredericksburg, was a bright-eyed, intelligent young man, or boy, rather, of sixteen years, who belonged to a Northern regiment. He appeared to be more affectionate and tender than his comrades, and attracted a good deal of attention from the attendants and visitors. Manifestly the pet of some household, he longed for nothing so much as the arrival of his mother, who was expected, for she knew he was mortally wounded and failing fast. Ere she arrived, however, he died. But he thought she had come, for while a kind lady visitor was wiping the death sweat from his brow, as his sight was failing, he rallied a little, like an expiring taper in its socket, looked up longingly and joyfully, and in the tenderest pathos whispered, quite audibly, "is that mother?" in tones that drew tears from every eye. Then, drawing her toward him, with all his feeble power, he nestled his head in her arms like a sleeping infant, and thus died, with the sweet word "mother" on his quivering lips.

(*r*) DIFFICULTIES OF PIOUS SOLDIERS.—A chaplain in the English army says: "The soldier who makes a profession of religion may count upon the enmity and the opposition of the majority of his comrades. We have known cases where such men, on lying down, have covered their faces, that they might be able to pray without attracting attention; they were led to adopt this expedient from the annoyance they had suffered on attempting to pray openly. And yet even among soldiers a sort of rude, imperfect idea of religious toleration is occasionally to be met with. On one occasion a young soldier had knelt down to pray at night; a howl of derision rose from the other inmates of the barrack-room, and several missiles were thrown at him, when a stalwart Yorkshireman, whose word was law to his comrades, stood up and commanded them to desist. 'This,' he said, 'is Liberty Hall; if a man chooses to pray, he may pray; if another chooses to swear, he may swear; but the one had better not interfere with the other, unless he wishes to feel the weight of my arm.'"

(*s*) "SOLDIER, ARE YOU HUNGRY?"—About eighteen months ago a regiment passed through Baltimore, *en route* to Washington, and having occasion to halt for awhile in one of the streets, one of the soldiers was approached by a little fellow, who inquired of him, "Soldier, are you hungry?" The soldier replying in the affirmative, the little fellow invited him to his home near by, and set before him a bountiful repast. A few weeks since the regiment returned through Baltimore *en route* home, their term of enlistment having expired, and the soldier who, for meritorious service in the field, had risen to the rank of captain, not forgetful of the kindness of his little friend, sought him out and presented him with a handsome photographic album, containing the photographs of all the most prominent generals in the Union army. Inscribed upon the back of the album in beautiful gilt letters, were the words, "Soldier, are you hungry?" This little boy is the son of a Lutheran minister of that city.

(*t*) A ROLLING CHAPLAIN.—The son of Dr. Eastman, Secretary of the Tract Society, is a chaplain. His horse plunging during a battle, struck him on the knee-pan. His leg swelled and stiffened until the pain became almost unendurable. When he could no longer stand, he gave his horse up to a servant, and had himself to lie on the ground.

As he lay on his back, suffering and thinking, he heard a voice—"Oh, my God!" He thought, can anybody be swearing in such a place as this? He listened again, and a prayer began. It was a wounded soldier praying. How can I get to him? was his first thought. He tried to draw up his stiffened limb, the while setting his teeth and clenching his hands for the pain. But he could not rise. He then thought, "I can roll." And over and over, in pain, he rolled, in blood, and over dead bodies, until he fell against a dying man, and there he preached Christ, and prayed. At length one of the line officers came up and said: "Where's the chaplain? Where's the chaplain? One of the staff officers is dying."

"Here he is, here he is," cried out the suffering hero.

"Well, such an officer is dying, can't you come and see him?"

"I cannot move. I have just rolled up to this dying man to talk to him."

"If I detail two men to carry you, shall they do it?"

"Yes."

They took him gently up and carried him. And that livelong night, these two men carried him over the battle-field, and laid him down in blood beside bleeding, dying men; and he preached Christ to them, and prayed. He had to look up then, brethren; he could look no other way from that position, not even into the face of the dying; and with God's stars shining down on him, and heaven bending over him, he had to preach Christ and pray.

439. WORSHIP. PUBLIC.

(*a*) MR. DOOLITTLE AND HIS UNEASY HEARER. — The Rev. Thomas Doolittle, at one time, having finished prayer, looked round upon the congregation, and observing a young man, who had just been put into one of the pews, very uneasy in his situation, adopted the following singular expedient to detain him. Turning to one of the members of his church, who sat in the gallery, he asked this question aloud, "Brother, do you repent of coming to Christ?" "No, sir," he replied, "I never was happy till I came; I only repent that I did not come to him sooner." The minister then turned to the opposite gallery, and addressed himself to an aged member in the same manner, "Brother, do you repent of coming to Christ?" "No, sir," said he, "I have known the Lord from my youth upwards." He then looked down upon the young man, whose attention was fully engaged, and, fixing his eyes upon him, said, "Young man, are you willing to come to Christ?" This unexpected address from the pulpit, exciting the observation of all the people, so greatly affected him, that he sat down and concealed his face. The person who sat next to him encouraged him to rise and answer the question. The minister repeated "Young man, are you willing to come to Christ?" With a tremulous voice he replied, "Yes, sir." "But when, sir?" added the minister in a solemn and loud tone. He mildly answered, "Now, sir." "Then stay," said he, "and learn the word of God, which you will find in 2 Cor. vi. 2: 'Behold, now is the accepted time; behold, now is the day of salvation.'" By this sermon he was greatly affected, and came into the vestry, after the service, bathed in tears. The reluctance to stay, which he had discovered, was occasioned by the strict injunctions of his father, who threatened, that if he went to hear such preachers, he would turn him out of doors. Having now heard the gospel, and being unable to conceal the feelings of his mind, he was afraid to meet his father. The minister sat down, and wrote an affectionate letter to him, which had so good an effect, that both father and mother came to hear for themselves. They were both brought to a knowledge of the truth; and, together with their son, were joyfully received into Christian communion.

(*b*) THE EARLY HEARER.—A woman, who always used to attend public worship with great punctuality, and took care to be always in time, was asked how it was she could always come so early. She answered, very wisely, "It is a part of my religion not to disturb the religion of others."

(*c*) THE COUNTESS'S EXAMPLE.—The Countess of Burford, for the last few years of her life, had to ride, almost constantly, on horseback, upwards of sixteen miles, to and from the place where she attended to hear the gospel; yet neither frost, snow, rain, nor bad roads were sufficient to detain her at home, nor to prevent her being there before the worship began.

(*d*) THE DRUNKARD REFORMED.—The Rev. W. Ward, of Serampore, once preached from Eccles. xi. 9: "Rejoice, O young man, in thy youth," &c. A notorious drunkard became, under this sermon, very seriously convinced of the importance of religion; and, with his wife, a short time afterwards made a profession of faith in Christ. Previously to this, his master had used every means he could devise to persuade him to become sober, but in vain. After this change, his employer wished to prevail on him not to attend the chapel; but he replied, "You know, sir, what a drunkard I have been, and how often you have urged me in vain to leave it off; yet by going once to the chapel, I was constrained to do that which none of your remonstrances were able to effect: therefore I wish to go again."

440. WRATH OF MAN PRAISING GOD.

(*a*) DR. KALLEY SELLING THE SCRIPTURES IN PRISON. — Dr. Kalley, who was so long imprisoned at Madeira for distributing the Scriptures, and speaking to the people of the things of the kingdom, sold more copies of the Scriptures weekly during his imprisonment, than he had been able previously to do monthly; and in a few months of the same period, he distributed 30,000 religious tracts, besides receiving regular visits from between two and three hundred natives, to obtain religious instruction—all of whom were more or less under gracious influence, and some of them hopefully converted to God. The government could not have taken a more effectual way to spread what they call heresy, than to imprison this faithful servant of God. So it ever has been, and ever will be. All opposition to the gospel turns out to its furtherance. Were men as wise as they fancy themselves to be, they would let it alone, for measures of violence against the truth never fail to recoil on the heads of their authors. "The righteous flourish like the palm-tree." Their strength and beauty increase in proportion to the weight of oppression laid on them.

441. ZEAL IN DOING GOOD.

(*a*) PAINTING WITH THE MOUTH.—At a public meeting, the Rev. Dr. Henderson related the following anecdote respecting a female in one of the large trading towns of England. She was formerly a most abandoned character—one of the most wicked women, perhaps, that ever trod on the face of the globe. However, by the grace of God, she was brought to a knowledge of the truth, and was sent to a penitentiary, where she gave the most decided evidence of a saving change of heart; but, shortly after being put into that situation, she was deprived of the use both of her hands and her feet. Her heart, however, was full of love to the Savior, and she was at a loss to show forth the praises of that God who had called her out of darkness into his marvelous light. She could not walk about to tell what God had done for her soul; she could not employ her hands, but she learned to write with her mouth, and the letters thus written being sold for small sums, produced something considerable to the funds of the penitentiary. She began to learn the art of painting, and the sale of those paintings, which she accomplished with her mouth, produced last year $75 to the funds of the institution. We would not say, Go and do likewise; but we would say, You have hands and you have feet, and you have a tongue to tell the wonders of Redemption: go and do what you can.

(*b*) LE PELLETIER AND THE MERCHANT. — I was traveling through Orleans, says Diderot, accompanied by an officer. Nothing was talked of in the town but of what had lately happened to an inhabitant of the name of Le Pelletier; a man who showed the deepest commiseration for the poor; so that, after having, by his great liberality, exhausted a considerable fortune, he was reduced to a state of poverty himself. Though he had barely sufficient for his daily wants, he yet persisted in the benevolent labors he had undertaken, and went from door to door, seeking, from the superfluities of others, that assistance for the destitute which it was no longer in his power to bestow.

The poor and well-informed persons had but one opinion of the conduct of this individual; but many rich men, who wasted their substance in riotous feastings and journeys to Paris, looked upon him as a madman, and his near relations treated him as a lunatic who had foolishly spent his wealth.

Whilst refreshing ourselves at the inn, a number of loiterers had assembled round a man who was speaking, a hairdresser, and were earnestly addressing him, "You were present, do tell us how it was."

"Willingly, gentlemen," replied he, and appeared as impatient to relate as they were to hear, the following narrative:—

Monsieur Aubertot, one of my customers, whose house faces the church, was standing at his door, when Mons. le Pelletier accosted him, "Monsieur, can you give me nothing for my friends?" (thus he called the poor.)

"Not to-day, sir."

Mons. le Pelletier added, "Oh! if you but knew for whom I ask your charity! There is a poor woman! a distressed mother! who has not a rag to wrap round her new-born babe!—"

"I cannot to-day!"

"There is a daughter, who, though young, has for a long while maintained her father and her mother; but now she wants work, and starves."

"I cannot, Mons. le Pelletier; I cannot afford it."

"There is a poor working man, who earns his bread by hard labor; he has just broken his leg by a fall from a scaffolding."

"But, sir, I cannot afford it, I assure you."

"Pray, pray, Mons. Aubertot, allow yourself to be moved; oh, have compassion!"

"I cannot afford it, sir; I cannot, indeed, afford it."

"My good, good, merciful Mons. Aubertot—"

"Mons. le Pelletier, I beg you will leave me: when I wish to give, you know I do not need to be entreated."

Saying these words, he turned and passed into his warehouse. Mons. le Pelletier soon followed him to his warehouse, to his back shop, and then into his apartment. Here Mons. Aubertot exasperated by his continued and pressing entreaties, lifted his hand, and struck him! The blow was received. The hero of Christian charity smiled, and with a bright smiling look exclaimed, "Well, that for me; but the poor! what for the poor?"

[At these words all present expressed their admiration by a burst of applause, and the feelings of some produced tears.]

The officer with whom I was, had the presumption to exclaim, "Mons. le Pelletier is but a poltroon, and had I been there, this sabre would soon have obtained satisfaction for him. A blow, indeed! a blow!"

The hairdresser replied, "I perceive, sir, you would not have allowed the insolent offender time to acknowledge his fault."

"No, indeed!"

"Well, sir, Mons. Aubertot, when he saw such a benevolent spirit, burst into tears, fell at the feet of the injured man, offered him his purse, and a thousand times asked his forgiveness."

"But, what of that?" said the officer, his hand upon his sabre, and his countenance inflamed with anger, "I would have cut off the ears of Mons. Aubertot."

I then answered calmly, "You, sir, are a soldier; Mons. le Pelletier is a Christian!"

These few plain words had a wonderful effect. The street resounded with applause; and I said within myself, How much more dignified are we with the gospel in our heart, than when we would maintain, at the point of the sword, that imaginary idol, that vain phantom, which the world calls honor!

(*c*) MELVILLE AND HIS BRETHREN.—Mr. Andrew Melville, professor of divinity at St. Andrews, in the reign of James VI, was a very bold and zealous man for the cause of God and truth. When some of his more moderate brethren blamed him for being too hot and fiery, he was wont to reply, "If you see my fire go downwards, set your foot upon it and put it out; but if it go upward, let it return to its own place."

(*d*) HOWARD'S LABORS.—The great philanthropist, John Howard, after inspecting the receptacles of crime, of poverty, and of misery throughout Great Britain and Ireland, left his native country, relinquished his own ease, to visit the wretched abodes of those who were in want and bound in fetters of iron in other parts of the world. He traveled three times through France, four through Germany, five through Holland, twice through Italy, once through Spain and Portugal, and also through Denmark, Sweden, Russia, and part of Turkey. These excursions occupied (with some short intervals of rest at home) the period of twelve years.

Never before was such a considerable portion of the life of man applied to a more benevolent and laudable purpose. He gave up his own comfort that he might bestow it upon others. He was often immured in prison that others might be set at liberty. He exposed himself to danger that he might free others from it. He visited the gloomy cell that he might inspire a ray of hope and joy in the breasts of the wretched. Yea, he not only lived, but died in the noble cause of benevolence; for in visiting a young lady, who lay dangerously ill of an epidemic fever, in order to administer relief, he caught the distemper, and fell a victim to his humanity, January 20th, 1790.

TOPICAL INDEX.

THE numbers in this Index refer to the regular topics, which may be found in the book at the top of the page; and when letters are joined to the figures they refer to particular anecdotes, which are designated by the same letters where they are placed.

SCRIPTURAL INDEX.

In this Index, the correspondence between texts and anecdotes, though mostly obvious and direct, is not uniformly so. Sometimes only a single clause of the text is illustrated by the anecdote; and sometimes the text refers only to a single paragraph or sentiment of the anecdote and what is merely incidental to the principal subject. Sometimes the text points to an inference to be drawn from the anecdote, or the anecdote to an inference to be drawn from the text. Occasionally the passage of Scripture is illustrated in the way of contrast by the fact referred to, and sometimes they are here joined together, simply because the former is quoted or mentioned in the latter.

The FIGURES in the right hand columns are the numbers used throughout the work to designate the various subjects, which will readily be found by looking for similar figures at the top of the foregoing pages. When LETTERS are joined to the figures, the reader is cited to particular anecdotes under these figures,—anecdotes which are marked by the same letters where they stand in the work.

PSALMS.—Continued.

PROVERBS.

ECCLESIASTES.

SONG OF SOLOMON.

ISAIAH.

LUKE.—Continued.

JOHN.

ACTS.